Encyclopedia of
THE PEOPLES OF ASIA AND OCEANIA

VOLUME II (M TO Z)

Encyclopedia of
THE PEOPLES OF ASIA AND OCEANIA

VOLUME II (M TO Z)

Barbara A. West

Facts On File
An imprint of Infobase Publishing

Encyclopedia of the Peoples of Asia and Oceania

Copyright © 2009 Barbara A. West

Facts On File, Inc.
An imprint of Infobase Publishing
132 West 31st Street
New York NY 10001

Library of Congress Cataloging-in-Publication Data

West, Barbara A., 1967–
Encyclopedia of the peoples of Asia and Oceania :/ Barbara A. West.
p. cm.
Includes bibliographical references and index.
ISBN-13: 978-0-8160-7109-8
ISBN-10: 0-8160-7109-8
1. Ethnology—Asia—Encyclopedias. 2. Ethnology—Oceania—Encyclopedias. I. Title.
GN625.W47 2009
305.80095—dc22   2008003055

Facts On File books are available at special discounts when purchased in bulk quantities for businesses, associations, institutions, or sales promotions. Please call our Special Sales Department in New York at (212) 967-8800 or (800) 322-8755.

You can find Facts On File on the World Wide Web at http://www.factsonfile.com

Text design by James Scotto-Lavino
Cover design by Salvatore Luongo
Illustrations by Jeremy Eagle and Lucidity Information Design

Printed in the United States of America

MV Hermitage 10 9 8 7 6 5 4 3 2 1

This book is printed on acid-free paper and contains 30 percent postconsumer recycled content.

CONTENTS

LIST OF ENTRIES

LIST OF ILLUSTRATIONS, MAPS, AND GRAPHS

LIST OF ILLUSTRATIONS

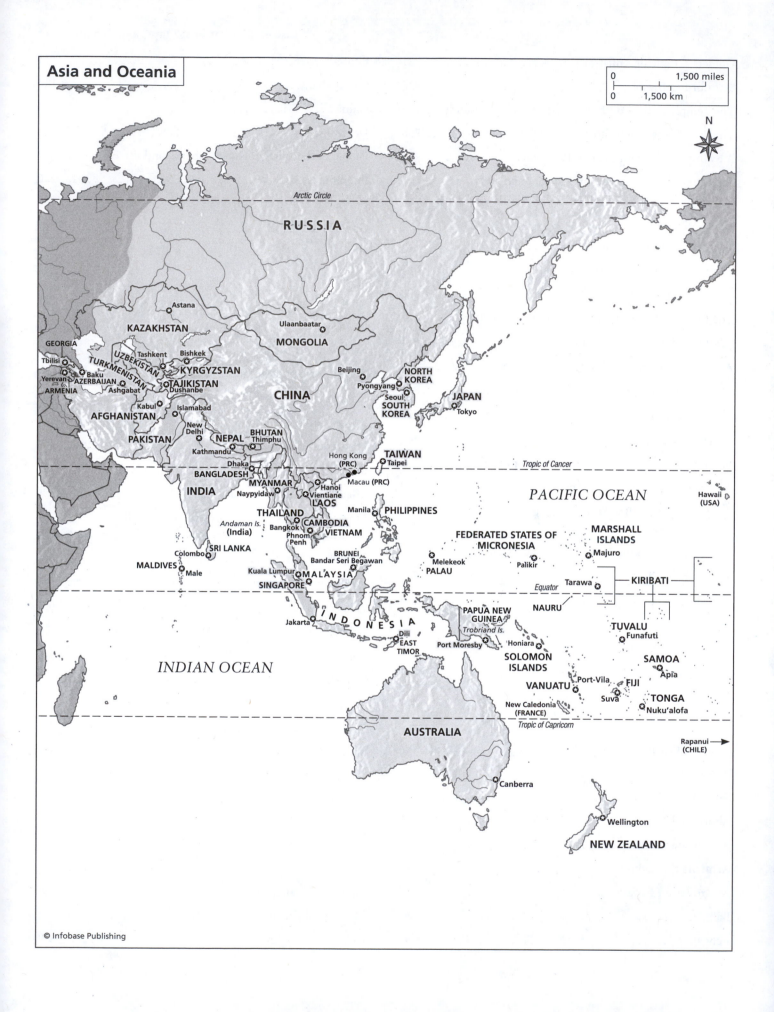

Asia and Oceania

0		1,500 miles
0	1,500 km	

N

Arctic Circle

RUSSIA

Astana

KAZAKHSTAN

Ulaanbaatar

MONGOLIA

GEORGIA
Tbilisi
Baku
Yerevan
ARMENIA
AZERBAIJAN
Ashgabat
TURKMENISTAN
Tashkent
UZBEKISTAN
Bishkek
KYRGYZSTAN
TAJIKISTAN
Dushanbe
Kabul
AFGHANISTAN
Islamabad
PAKISTAN
New Delhi
NEPAL
Kathmandu
BHUTAN
Thimphu
Dhaka
BANGLADESH
INDIA
MYANMAR
Naypyidaw

CHINA

Beijing
NORTH KOREA
Pyongyang
Seoul
SOUTH KOREA
JAPAN
Tokyo

Hong Kong (PRC)
Macau (PRC)
TAIWAN
Taipei

Tropic of Cancer

PACIFIC OCEAN

Hawaii (USA)

Hanoi
Vientiane
LAOS
THAILAND
Andaman Is. (India)
Bangkok
CAMBODIA
Phnom Penh
VIETNAM
Manila
PHILIPPINES

SRI LANKA
Colombo
MALDIVES
Male
Kuala Lumpur
MALAYSIA
SINGAPORE
BRUNEI
Bandar Seri Begawan

FEDERATED STATES OF MICRONESIA
Melekeok
PALAU
Palikir

MARSHALL ISLANDS
Majuro

Equator

Tarawa
NAURU

KIRIBATI

Jakarta
INDONESIA
Dili
EAST TIMOR
PAPUA NEW GUINEA
Trobriand Is.
Port Moresby
Honiara
SOLOMON ISLANDS

TUVALU
Funafuti

SAMOA
Apia

INDIAN OCEAN

VANUATU
Port-Vila
New Caledonia (FRANCE)
Suva
FIJI
TONGA
Nuku'alofa

Tropic of Capricorn

Rapanui (CHILE)

AUSTRALIA

Canberra

Wellington

NEW ZEALAND

© Infobase Publishing

ENTRIES M TO Z

Macanese (people of Macau)

Macanese is currently the term used to refer to the approximately half a million people of the Macau Special Administrative Region of China. In the past, however, the term has referred to many different groups of people, including all citizens of Macau, those who had one Chinese parent and one Portuguese, those of purely Portuguese descent, or Chinese or biracial individuals who had been baptized Roman Catholic and adopted Portuguese names.

The islands and territory around Macau have been inhabited for many thousands of years and were integrated into the Chinese empire as early as the third century B.C.E. The Chinese village of Wangxia, sometimes also called Mongha, is the oldest continuously inhabited settlement in the region and dates from sometime in the Yuan dynasty (1279–1368). Wangxia also contains the region's oldest temple, which is dedicated to Guanyin, the Buddhist goddess of mercy, and an A-ma temple built in the Ming dynasty (1368–1643), used by fishermen praying for safety while at sea. Some people believe the name *Macau,* assigned by the Portuguese after settlement in 1553, comes from the name of this temple.

As the site of both the first and last European colony in China, Macau today retains a special position in the region's history. The colonial era began in 1513 when Portuguese sailors from their colonies in Goa and Malacca landed on Lintin Island and claimed the territory for the Portuguese king; they marked the

site with a stone marker. Four years later a Portuguese fleet arrived at Haojingao, the original Chinese name for Macau, upsetting the Chinese emperor but not remaining long enough to incite violence. The Portuguese were ejected from Guangdong Province in 1521 due to their attempts to land and establish a European presence, but in 1536 Portuguese traders rescued from a shipwreck were finally allowed to remain in Haojingao. Despite these early interactions, the Portuguese themselves count 1553 as the formation date of their Macanese colony since it was in that year that they set up several onshore trading depots.

From their small settlement in the Pearl River estuary, the Portuguese in the region prospered. They traded with the mainland city of Guangzhou as well as with the distant lands of Japan, India, and elsewhere. In addition, merchants from throughout the entire Asian region, including China, India, Japan, and all of mainland and insular Southeast Asia, flocked to the new entrepôt for access to goods from around the world. By 1557 Portuguese control of the small port was a fait accompli, requiring only official payments to the Chinese emperor to make it completely legal and legitimate. A treaty between the two countries was signed in 1557, the same year the Portuguese built their first walled settlement, and payments to Beijing began in 1573; payments were subsequently made to Xiangshan county, starting in 1582. According to the agreement signed by Beijing and Lisbon, China retained sovereignty in the

MACANESE

location:
Macau

time period:
Early 16th century to the present

ancestry:
Chinese, Portuguese, other

language:
Cantonese, Mandarin Chinese, Portuguese; English is extremely common as a second language for use in business and tourism

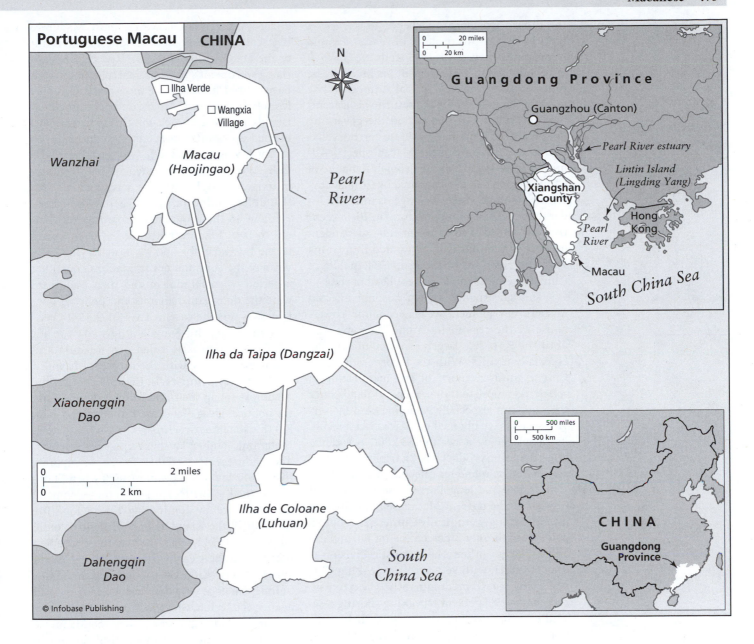

colony, and its people were subject to Chinese laws; however, Portuguese administration made this agreement relatively meaningless. Based on this de facto relationship, Macau became self-governing in 1586, though China did not recognize its existence as a foreign trade port until 1685, at about the same time that Portugal had lost its preeminent position in world trade and Macau had been overshadowed by Hong Kong and other British, French, and Dutch ports in the region.

The 19th and 20th centuries again brought significant change in Macau's status on the world stage and thus its people's position as well. In 1845 Portugal ejected all Chinese administrators and soldiers and charged the local

Chinese population a significant tax to remain on what it considered a free port. Just four years later the Portuguese also annexed the neighboring island of Wanzhai, and within a decade two more islands, Taipa and Coloane, were annexed. Although they lost Wanzhai in 1887, the Portuguese incorporated Ilha Verde in 1890, and through a long process of land reclamation they actually linked the offshore island to the Macanese Peninsula by 1923.

Throughout this entire period the Portuguese signed several treaties recognizing all of these islands as their colonies, but none of them was ever ratified by China. Not until five years after the fall of Portugal's fascist government in 1974 did the two countries even recognize the other's existence and begin to engage in talks about the future status of Macau. Formal negotiations began in 1986 and 1987, which eventually led to an agreement for Macau to be returned to China as a Special Administrative Region; the date set for the return was December 20, 1999. From that period the governing document of the small Chinese territory has been the Basic Law of the Macau Special Administrative Region of the People's Republic of China, which had been adopted by China's governing National People's Congress in 1993. Under that law, Macau retains its own chief executive as the head of government and independent judicial system but is incorporated into China with the president of the People's Republic of China serving as the Macanese head of state.

This governance system has not affected Macau's development as an economic powerhouse in the region. Its strong economy was, until 1999, based largely on manufacturing, especially textiles. With the incorporation into China, however, much of the manufacturing sector has moved to the cheaper mainland. Since then tourism, especially gambling, and the service sector have boomed on Macau. As a result, its people enjoy a healthy $22,000 per capita gross domestic product (GDP), tripling the average on the mainland for calendar year 2006.

Despite the long Portuguese involvement in Macau, the current Macanese population is overwhelmingly ethnically Chinese at about 95 percent, with only 3 percent being Portuguese and 2 percent other. The linguistic division is even stronger, with 96.1 percent speaking Chinese languages, predominantly CANTONESE, and only 1.8 percent speaking Portuguese. While these two languages retain their position as official languages in the region, English is rapidly becoming the most important second language for anyone involved in international business or tourism.

FURTHER READING

Geoffrey C. Gunn. *Encountering Macau: A Portuguese City-State on the Periphery of China, 1557–1999* (Boulder, Colo.: Westview Press, 1996).
Jonathan Porter. *Macau, the Imaginary City: Culture and Society, 1557 to the Present* (Boulder, Colo.: Westview Press, 2000).

Madurese (Orang Madura, Tijang Madura, Wong Madura)

The Madurese were originally the inhabitants of the Indonesian island of Madura, located to the east of Java, and the archipelagoes of Kangean and Sapudi. Today, however, most Madurese live scattered throughout Indonesia, the result of the Dutch colonial regime and the Indonesian government's *transmigrasi* schemes, which have moved hundreds of thousands of people from Java, Bali, and Madura onto less-inhabited islands in the archipelago. The schemes have opened up significant economic opportunities for those who moved but have often angered the indigenous populations who have felt the influx of so many people with languages and cultures that differ significantly from their own.

Due to the geographic proximity of Madura to Java, Madurese history has been linked to the JAVANESE for many centuries. The early years of the common era in Madura constitute a period when Hinduism and then Buddhism were the dominant religious and political doctrines, as was the case in Java. In the 14th century the Majapahit Kingdom, Java's last major Hindu kingdom, also ruled over Madura and disintegrated only with the arrival of Islam in the following centuries. In the 16th century the Madurese set up their own state structure using the political ideas that came to them with Islam, but this state was overrun by the Islamic state of Mataram, another Javanese kingdom, in 1624. The Madurese attained their freedom temporarily in 1672 but lost it again in 1680 when Mataram turned to the Dutch East Indies Company for assistance in dominating the region. The Dutch held the island as part of their colonial empire until 1942, when the JAPANESE occupied it as part of their Pacific strategy during World War II. Many Madurese participated in the war of independence waged by Indonesians in 1945 against the Dutch, who tried to retake their colony at the end of the war. Today the Madurese are one of the most dominant ethnic groups in Indonesia, after the Javanese who dominate in most political and economic spheres.

Although politically the Madurese have been connected to the Javanese for many centuries, economically they have differed significantly due to differences in island geography. Madura is much drier than Java and allows for only a single rice harvest per year, while on Java two and even three harvests are possible in some regions. Prior to their migration to other islands, many Madurese adapted to these dry conditions by focusing their economic activity on cattle, sheep, and to a lesser extent, goats. Much of the resulting meat, milk, and other products was then sold in Java in exchange for grain and other food products. The relatively small size of Madura in conjunction with its

MADURESE

location:
Madura and throughout Indonesia

time period:
Probably 2000 B.C.E. to the present

ancestry:
Austronesian

language:
There are two Madurese dialects, Madura and Kangean, both in the larger Austronesian family.

Many thousands of Madurese refugees have had to turn to Indonesian officials for assistance when protests against them have turned violent. These women and children have been taken to Pontianak, West Kalimantan, to escape four days of violence that claimed the lives of 64 fellow Madurese. *(AP/JH)*

large population also meant that many families had to rely on trade, fishing, and handicrafts instead of farm or pastoral work; working as domestics for wealthy families was also common for Madurese women.

The many hundreds of thousands of Madurese who have moved away from their home island and taken up residence in the Kalimantan region of Borneo and other islands in the archipelago have largely brought with them their traditions of wage labor, petty trade, and a bit of farming and herding where possible. Moving into the lower rungs of the economy in their new homes has often put them at odds with the local tribal populations who themselves are subordinate to the Javanese, BALINESE, and Chinese in their economic enterprises. The situation in Kalimantan has been the most dire for the new Madurese populations; gangs of DAYAKS have murdered hundreds, destroyed property, and looted Madurese neighborhoods in an attempt to drive out their economic rivals.

Madurese culture today reflects the blend of Hinduism, Buddhism, and Islam that is similarly evident in Java. Most Madurese, both on Madura and elsewhere, consider themselves devout Muslims, usually Sunnis of the Shafi school, considered a more conservative branch of Sunni Islam than is the norm in Indonesia. Most individuals pray five times per day, pay their required tithe, fast for Ramadan, and celebrate the other important Islamic holidays. It is a great honor to be able to make the pilgrimage to Mecca, the hajj, and any Madurese who can afford to do so makes the trip if at all possible. Nonetheless, Islam as it is practiced among the Madurese is not of a purely orthodox variety. Shamans and sorcerers still work among the Madurese, and local and familial spirits are believed to be active in most communities. Both male and female children inherit the property of their parents equally, in contradiction to some interpretations of Islamic law. The Madurese are also practitioners of both male and female circumcision, or genital mutilation as it is sometimes called by its critics. This practice is believed by many to be linked to their Islamic faith but may have predated their conversion to the religion in the 15th or 16th century.

Madurese society begins with the creation of kin groupings through the principle of bilateral descent; in other words, children are considered to belong equally to the kin groups of their mother and their father. Both nuclear and extended families are common as the group with which individuals identify most. Beyond the family or household, villages are made up of 10–15 households, often people who are unrelated through blood or marriage but are connected through ownership of a small plot of land. Postmarital residence is ideally neolocal, which means that most couples try to set up their own households as soon as possible, but often matrilocal residence, or living with the bride's parents for a few years, is necessary to be able to afford to build or purchase a new home for the couple. While men are technically allowed to have multiple wives due to Islamic law, very few are financially able to do so outside of village headmen or other leaders. In the past, the Madurese nobility could all afford to take on polygynous families, but with the disappearance of this class of people, the practice has largely died out.

Throughout Indonesia, the Madurese are known for their practice of *carok,* or blood revenge, to avenge instances of adultery, theft, especially of cattle, or public shame or loss of face. *Carok* requires sneaking up on the perpetrator and stabbing him or her with a sickle-shaped knife, usually to the point of death. Instances of *carok* usually result in extended feuds between families or even villages, which can last for generations. To put an end to the blood revenge, individuals can turn to a Muslim specialist called a *kiyai,* who tries to settle the matter on both secular and supernatural levels.

Mae Enga   *See* ENGA.

Magars

The Magars are the most populous of the inhabitants of the midmountainous regions of Nepal, which were forcibly integrated into the kingdom of Nepal in the mid-18th century. It is assumed that the Magar way of life was derived from Tibetan and Southeast Asian hill cultures. Traditionally the Magars were subsistence farmers who grew corn, wheat, and rice, as well as bananas, barley, beans, buckwheat, cabbages, carrots, cauliflower, cucumbers, lentils, mustard, onions, potatoes, pumpkins, radishes, sesame, sugarcane, tobacco, tomatoes, and yams. Many families also kept herds of cattle, which required them to migrate yearly to summer and winter pastures at different elevations. Families with buffalo remained more sedentary as these animals were largely kept in stalls rather than open fields. Pigs, chickens, goats, and horses were also kept by Magar families for trade, subsistence, and ritual purposes. In the present period, Magar people have entered mainstream professions such as medicine, law, civil service, politics, and others.

Magar religious practices vary depending on the location of the particular group. Generally, some form of Buddhism is important to most Magars. In addition, northern Magars practice shamanism, which plays a central role in daily living as life, health, and overall existence are heavily intertwined with the spirit world. In addition to shamanism, the northern Magars also practice animism, which is a belief that animals, plants, and other bodies possess spirits. Those in the south developed a syncretic type of Hinduism, which incorporates some animist and Buddhist beliefs and practices into their practice of Hinduism.

Magar kinship is patrilineal, which means that all people inherit their membership in both their lineage and clan from their father, father's father, and so on. Both lineages and clans, which are made up of groups of lineages, are exogamous groups, requiring people to marry someone from another group. Generally, the Magars prefer matrilateral cross-cousin marriages, in which a male marries his mother's brother's daughter. Like other Nepalese tribes, some Magars engage in fictive kinship ties, where unrelated individuals enter into ritual brotherhoods that serve as a system for mutual aid and social bonding. The ensuing relationships are recognized by the respective families to the extent that incest taboos are adhered to, sometimes for generations to come.

An important event in recent Magar history occurred on January 9, 2004, when Maoist militants declared the Magarat Autonomous Region in Rolpa District. An autonomous regional government was established, placing political power into the hands of a minority group that had otherwise been socioeconomically marginalized in the past. It should be noted that the Magarat Autonomous Region is in fact made up of different caste groups of Hindus, including Dalit, hill Brahmin, and Chhetri, while the tribal Magars make up the majority at 35.7 percent. A key decision that the Magarat regional government made was the building of a road through the difficult terrain of the heart of Rolpa. The road is being built by volunteers: It is a road constructed by the people, for the people, with virtually no mechanized tools, and it is a link to the outside world that has created opportunities for commerce along the route.

Maingtha   *See* ACHANG.

Makassarese (Macassan, Makasarese, Tu Mangkasara)

The Makassarese are speakers of Makassar who originally came from the southwestern corner of Sulawesi, an island in the Indonesian Archipelago; today some Makassarese live away from their original homeland as well, the result of small-scale migrations. Their name comes from the term they use to refer to themselves, Tu Mangkasara, "people who behave openly."

The early history of the Makassarese in all likelihood resembles that of the other AUSTRONESIANS of the Indonesian Archipelago. Their ancestors migrated from southern China into Taiwan, the Philippines, and then down through Borneo into Sulawesi. These early settlers were probably farmers and fishermen who traded with their neighbors and eventually with Indian, Chinese, and Arab traders who came via the Indian Ocean. In the 14th century there were several small Makassarese polities ruled by minor kings and princes. They came together sometime around 1400 to form the Gowa Kingdom, which was based on the same principles as the JAVANESE and BALINESE Hindu kingdoms of the time: A divine king exercised almost total political, economic, and, through his priests, religious control over his people. Starting in about 1530, this kingdom dominated not only the Makassarese population on Sulawesi but also the BUGINESE, their closest neighbors and cultural and linguistic cousins. In 1605 the king converted to Islam, also following the trend in Java, and the Dutch arrived just four years later. In the early 1660s the Buginese king allied his forces with the Dutch and conquered both Makassar itself and other islands in the region; this established about 100 years of Buginese domination in this region of the archipelago and saw the relative demise of the Makassarese. Nonetheless, until 1906, when the Dutch finally killed the last king, Gowa continued to maintain its royal family and was feared for the piracy that ruled along the coasts; there is evidence of the Makassarese landing in Australia's Arnhem Land by the 18th century. Both during the periods of Dutch colonialism and Indonesian independence Makassarese nobles have served in the bureaucracy and in other important government and private-sphere positions.

Fishing and rice cultivation are the two most important economic activities of the Makassarese now that piracy in the Java and Bali Seas and Makassar Strait has been eliminated. Corn, bananas, cassava, and other fruits and vegetables are also important subsistence foods, while coffee is the most important cash crop. Most families in the lowlands have a water buffalo or two to assist in plowing, while goats, cattle, chickens, and dogs are important in all regions.

The Makassarese have been Muslims since the early 17th century, but in some areas, local gods, spirits, and religious practitioners continue to exist side by side with more orthodox Muslim beliefs, practices, and practitioners, especially in rural areas. Another important traditional belief that has continued into the present day concerns the centrality of each person and family's dignity, or *siri*. *Siri* is so important to the Makassarese that they are willing to engage in violence or even commit murder, *ripakasiri,* to protect their own or their family's dignity, for a person without *siri* is no longer considered human; he or she becomes the moral equivalent of an animal. Maintaining *siri* is considered one of the most important activities of each person's life and violent retribution, even many years after an offense, is a core value.

Malayalis (Keralites, Malayalees)

The Malayalis are native speakers of the southern Dravidian Malayalam language who also live in the Indian state of Kerala. Linguistically they are most closely related to the large Tamil population of India and Sri Lanka, from whom they split over the course of about 300 years starting in the ninth century C.E. The first texts with words that distinguish them from their proto-Tamil-Malayalam predecessors were a copperplate issued by the Chera king Rajasekhara, known as the Vazhappalli inscription of about 832, and the Tharissappalli copperplate inscription of about 849, issued by the Venad chief Ayyanadikal Thiruvadikal. Both works deal more with religious affairs than administrative ones and give only a hint of the earliest transformation from Tamil to Malayalam. The 12th century usually marks the period when linguists can distinguish a separate Malayalam language, highly influenced by Sanskrit but still bearing the grammatical hallmarks of its southern Dravidian roots. Today it is the official state language of Kerala, where its speakers make up more than 95 percent of the population.

Kerala became the home state of the Malayali people in the reorganization of India in 1956, which prioritized language over other aspects of identity in the creation of state boundaries. It was created by combining the Malabar coastal district, which had been taken from the state of Madras, with the former state of Travancore-Cochin.

Malayalis are a diverse people in terms of occupation, caste, and religion. About half the population of Kerala today and a slightly higher proportion of Malayalis work in agriculture growing rice, coconuts, cashews, spices, and other subsistence and cash crops. The other half are engaged in a variety of activities, including fishing, handicrafts, and many jobs within the urban service sector of the economy such as banking, insurance, and tourism. Regardless of occupation, however, Keralites generally are better educated and have a higher life expectancy and lower birthrate than the rest of India. This apparent paradox—remarkable social indicators despite relatively low productivity figures—have led many demographers, economists, and others to write and speak of the Kerala Model of development.

The Malayali caste and kinship systems, while highly diverse, in general differ from those of the rest of India. The Malayalis were incorporated into the Hindu caste system later than much of the rest of the subcontinent, and as a result their matrilineal kinship structure survived into the modern era in ways that did not occur elsewhere. The highest caste in Malayali society, the Nayars, is divided into Tharwads or Taravads, matrilineal descent groups that can

---

MALAYALIS

location:
India, especially the state of Kerala and the Lackshadweep Islands; there is also a large Malayali diaspora throughout the world

time period:
About 830 C.E. to the present

ancestry:
Proto-Tamil-Malayalam speakers

language:
Malayalam, a southern Dravidian language

trace their ancestry through a common female ancestor. Instead of moving into their husbands' homes, Nayar wives remained in their natal homes, allowing their husbands to visit at night occasionally. Rather than fathers, mothers' brothers provided the primary socialization for boys, and it was through them that all property and titles were inherited.

There are also differences among Malayalis with regard to religion. A small majority are Hindus, but there are also large Muslim and Christian minorities at about 25 and 20 percent each. There are also much smaller numbers of Cochin Jews, Malayalam Jews whose ancestors migrated to India's southern coast in ancient times, perhaps during the reign of Israel's King Solomon in the 10th century B.C.E.

See also DRAVIDIANS; TAMILS.

Malays

There are several, overlapping usages for the term *Malay*. The first use refers to the Malay language, a Malayo-Polynesian language spoken by about 18 million people in Malaysia, Indonesia, Brunei, Singapore, and southern Thailand. A second use for the term is geographical. The Malay Peninsula is made up of southern Thailand and Myanmar (Burma) plus the 11 peninsular states of Malaysia; the Malay Archipelago, the largest archipelago in the world with more than 20,000 islands, encompasses the countries of Indonesia, the Philippines, Singapore, and Brunei, plus the Malaysian states of Sarawak and Sabah on the island of Borneo. Based on the 18th-century racializing work of Johann Friedrich Blumenbach, who categorized all humans into five separate racial categories—Caucasian, Ethiopian, American, Mongolian, and Malay—the concept of a Malay race is sometimes still drawn upon in the contemporary world to refer to many of the inhabitants of the Malay Archipelago, Malaysia, and even the Philippines. Certainly during the early years of the British colonial era in this region, the term *Malay* was used to refer to all brown-skinned inhabitants of both insular and peninsular Southeast Asia. Today few social or biological scientists have maintained a racial usage for the word *Malay,* and it remains on the margins of our understanding of "Malayness."

The Malay ethnic group is generally defined as speakers of the Malay language who adhere to the tenets of Sunni Islam. These people make up a slim majority of the population of Malaysia plus significant minorities in Indonesia, Brunei, Singapore, and southern Thailand. However, caution must be taken when labeling such a large number of people because there is nothing inherent or inevitable about membership in this community. For example, from the Malaysian side, the Malay ethnic group includes speakers of the Indonesian language as well as Malay since the two languages are mutually intelligible. From the Indonesian side, however, most would not consider themselves Malay but rather Indonesian or some other local identity, such as JAVANESE or BALINESE; many would also consider themselves both Indonesian and their local identity. In addition, however, some individuals and even groups in Indonesia and the southern Philippines move in and out of the Malay category depending on the political, economic, and social utility of being so categorized. For example, Indonesia's MINANGKABAU people are often considered a unique ethnic group based on language and culture; however, for the past decade or more, influential members of this community have been working to define themselves as Malay. In 2000 Malizar Umar, an important Minangkabau politician, established Movements of People Concerned about Malay Culture, a cultural organization that hosts conferences, sponsors events, and otherwise promotes the development of a pan-Malay identity in Indonesia and beyond.

GEOGRAPHY

The Malay world is made up of the Malay Peninsula in the extreme southern part of the Southeast Asian mainland, many of Indonesia's 13,000 islands, plus a small number of islands in the southern Philippines. Some sources count all of the islands of these two countries, which amount to more than 20,000 in total, as part of the Malay Archipelago, but many of these islands are not inhabited by Malay speakers or Muslims, so we do not include them here.

The region is bisected by the equator and thus has a tropical climate. There are two monsoon seasons: the southwest from April to October and the northeast from October to February. The terrain ranges from coastal plains at sea level to high volcanic mountains, the highest being Mount Kinabalu at 13,435 feet. Many of the islands are also very hilly.

ORIGINS

The origins of all the AUSTRONESIANS, including the Malays, are probably south China, from where they sailed in double outrigger dugout

MALAYS

location:
Malaysia, Indonesia, Brunei, Singapore, and Thailand

time period:
1500 B.C.E. to the present

ancestry:
Austronesian

language:
Malay or Bahasa Malay, a Malayo-Polynesian language

canoes to Taiwan, and then later to the Philippines, Indonesia, and eventually as far west as Madagascar and as far east as Rapanui or Easter Island. Linguistically, the oldest forms of Austronesian languages are spoken on Taiwan, and thus many sources cite this island as the origin of the Austronesian people; however, archaeological evidence points to south China as the ultimate homeland. This evidence includes pottery decorated with cord marks; similarities in stone tools including sinkers, points, bark beaters, and adzes; and domesticated plants and animals, including pigs and dogs, and millet, rice, and sugar cane. There is no certainty as to why this population left south China; however, archaeologists have hypothesized that it was a combination of population pressure, increased commerce coming from the Yangtze (Chang) River region of China and moving southward down the river and its tributaries, a growing demand for marine and tropical forest goods, and climate change.

Contemporary Austronesian languages can be subdivided into two distinctive groups that separate the languages of Austronesian Taiwan from those of the remainder of the family, which include all Malay and Oceanic languages. This linguistic division, in addition to several anomalies in the archaeological record, such as a lack of rice in the earliest Austronesian sites in Taiwan, indicates that the origins of the Austronesian people may have been two separate exoduses from southeast China. If this is so, the first exodus was probably from Fujian province in China to Taiwan, which saw the rise of TA-P'EN-K'ENG CULTURE, with its distinctively marked pottery and stone tools, but without archaeological evidence of domesticated rice. The descendants of this first wave would be the contemporary speakers of Taiwan's Austronesian languages, the ABORIGINAL TAIWANESE. The second exodus may have occurred around 3000 B.C.E., taking a second wave of Austronesian speakers from southeastern China to Taiwan and then almost immediately to Luzon in the Philippines around the same period. This second migration pattern continued southward into Borneo, Celebes, and Timor between 2500 and 2000 B.C.E. and then moved north and east into the Bismarck Archipelago and New Guinea around 1600 B.C.E. and eventually west to Madagascar in 500 C.E., north to Hawaii from 300 to 500 C.E., east to Rapanui from 300 to 900 C.E., and finally south to New Zealand around 1000 C.E.

The immediate origins of the Malays are probably the ancient Austronesians who settled

in Borneo by about 1500 B.C.E. and then spread into Sumatra and northward into the Malay Peninsula. A second origin theory posits that the first Malay language was spoken in Riau, currently an Indonesian province that includes eastern Sumatra and approximately 3,000 small and midsized islands. The people of Riau claim that their ancestors were the first speakers of Malay.

HISTORY

Although little is known about the kingdom of Sri Vijaya, perhaps founded in the third century C.E.

Malays time line
B.C.E.
5000–4500 Approximate period of the first Austronesian exodus from southeast China.
3000 Period of the possible second wave of Austronesians to leave China.
2500–2000 Years between which the first Austronesian speakers arrived on Borneo, Celebes, and Timor, forming the backbone of the proto-Malay people.
1500 The earliest period in which we can speak of the Malays.
C.E.
third century Possible period for the formation of Sri Vijaya.
seventh–14th centuries Sri Vijaya encompasses Peninsular Malaysia, Sumatra, western Java, and western Borneo.
10th century Javanese kingdoms begin to challenge Sumatran powers for preeminence in the region.
14th century The Hinduized Javanese kingdom of Majapahit conquers Sumatra, including Sri Vijaya and Jambi; however, Malay continues to be the dominant language in the region.
1402 The Sultanate of Melaka is established on the Malay Peninsula by Parameswara, a prince from Palembang, Sumatra.
1409 Parameswara converts to Islam after marrying a princess from the Islamic kingdom of Pasai, on the northern shore of Sumatra.
1511 Melaka is conquered by the Portuguese.
1786 Britain establishes its first colony in the Malay Archipelago on the island of Penang when the British East India Company leases the island from the sultan of Kedah.
1824 The British acquire Melaka and form the Straits Settlement with Penang and Singapore.
1874 The Pangkor Treaty with Perak sets the scene for the British to extend control throughout the peninsula.
1909 The colony of Malaya is formed when the Straits Settlements and Malay peninsular colonies of the Federated States of Malaya are brought together under one British administrative unit.
2000 Malizar Umar establishes Movements of People Concerned about Malay Culture.

and centered in the southeast of the Indonesian island of Sumatra, it is usually considered the first Malay-speaking kingdom to form in Southeast Asia. Sri Vijaya was a maritime kingdom that by the seventh century controlled the rivers and shorelines of Sumatra, the Malay Peninsula, Borneo, and much of the rest of western Indonesia. Inscriptions carved into stone in the seventh century and found in the 20th century near Palembang, which is thought to have been the Sri Vijayan capital, are written in Old Malay using the Pallava script imported from southern India; it is the same script used in Sri Lanka at the same time. In addition to this writing system, Indian traders visiting Southeast Asia from the second century onward also brought both Hinduism and Buddhism. The former religion with its attendant worldview took hold in Java and on the mainland Southeast Asian kingdoms of the CHAMS and FUNANESE, but in Sri Vijaya it was Buddhism that took hold and replaced the local religion and worldview. By the late seventh century Sri Vijaya was noted in Chinese sources as being an important seat of Buddhist teaching and learning.

The seventh century also saw the emergence of a second coastal and riverine power on Sumatra: Jambi, sometimes called Malaiyur. This kingdom was sometimes incorporated into the larger and stronger Sri Vijaya, sometimes a semi-independent vassal state, and an independent entity for at least a short period. A piece of writing from the TAMILS' Chola kingdom in 1030 clearly states the existence of these two separate Malay-speaking kingdoms. Like Sri Vijaya, Jambi's wealth and power came from its geographic position on the Straits of Malacca. Both kingdoms used a combination of taxation and shipping rights to control the flow of goods and people between eastern and western Asia, primarily China and India, but also the Khmer states of mainland Southeast Asia.

These Sumatran Buddhist kingdoms continued to dominate their region until about the 14th century. Prior to this, as early as the 11th century, Javanese kingdoms began to challenge their power, but it was the Hindu kingdom of Majapahit, located in eastern Java, that finally conquered all of Sumatra and supplanted these kingdoms in the 14th century. However, the dominance of the Malay language continued unabated in the region's seaports and even among diplomatic circles, comparable to the use of English in much of the world today.

At about the same time, Paramesvara, a Sumatran prince from the city of Palembang, fled his homeland under pressure from the invading Javanese and continued his political career in Temasek, contemporary Singapore. There he is said to have killed either a local leader or a Thai prince and thus was chased out by other members of the aristocracy. From there he sailed to Melaka on the Malay Peninsula and again raised himself to the level of local leader. The kingdom he established, later known as the Sultanate of Melaka, is often referred to as the first Malay kingdom because its leaders drew on a court document from Jambi, also known as Melayu, called Sulalat al-Salatin, or the Descent of Kings, to depict themselves as the originators of the political, social, and economic legitimacy of a Malay kingdom on the previously Mon-Khmer lands of Southeast Asia.

Melaka survived for only about 110 years, 1402–1511, before being overrun by the Portuguese, but even today the Malaysian state refers to it as the foundation of Malay dominance in the region. This seems odd at first, given that Sri Vijaya lasted for at least 700 years and probably closer to 1,000 while Melaka was so short-lived, but it makes sense in terms of the geographic and religious orientations of both kingdoms. Sri Vijaya ruled from Sumatra and was Buddhist, while Melaka ruled from the Malay Peninsula and was, from 1409 onward, Muslim. Since today it is the Malaysian state based on the peninsula that is dominated by the Malay-speaking people and not Indonesian Sumatra, Melaka makes more geographic sense as the foundational state for contemporary Malay identity as conceptualized in Malaysia. Similarly, since the two most important cultural features for membership in the Malay ethnic group are use of the Malay language and practicing Islam, Sri Vijaya's Buddhism makes it a problematic ancestor state. Several other Malay-speaking kingdoms emerged in Sumatra and Aceh during the 15th century, including Siak and a Minangkabau state, and tried to legitimate their international power through descent from Sri Vijaya, but none of them was as successful as Melaka in doing so.

The European colonial period in the Malay world, especially in the early stages, did not end the rivalries between local princes and kings for control of trade and commerce in the region. For the approximately 100 years that the Portuguese held Melaka, they were never fully able to take advantage of its vast wealth or lucrative position. In 1641 the Dutch replaced the Portuguese as the dominant colonial power in Melaka after supporting the Malay city-state of

Johor in its rebellion against the Portuguese. The Dutch likewise were unable, or perhaps unwilling, to take advantage of the port's geographic advantages, favoring their colony in Batavia, contemporary Jakarta. During that period the ACEHNESE, BUGINESE, Minankabau, Melakan kings, and others all competed to control both inland trade routes and parts of the coasts as well.

In the late 18th century the British, who were to be the final colonial power in the region, began to take action to secure a port for their ships plying between India and China. They acquired Penang in 1786 from the sultan of Kedah, who ceded it to them in exchange for British support against the THAIS. Initially the port thrived by instituting a tax- and duty-free trading strategy to lure trade away from the Dutch ports. By 1800 this virtually uninhabited island supported a thriving population of 10,000 inhabitants. In 1824 the Anglo-Dutch Treaty was signed in London, dividing the peninsula into Dutch and British spheres of influence. The kingdom of Johor was split into the British administration on the mainland and the Dutch-administered Riau Lingga Islands. Two years later the British Straits Settlement was formed, and the British brought together the Straits Settlements of Melaka, Singapore, Penang, and the mainland province opposite known as Province Wellesley (now known as the mainland part of Penang State).

During this period of British expansion, the population of this region changed significantly, with the Malay speakers going from the dominant majority to less than half of the population. This is largely due to the British policy of importing Indians as workers for the burgeoning rubber and palm plantations, tin mining, and other industries. At the same time, there was also a massive influx of Chinese immigrants, who established agricultural plantations and worked in the tin mines. Under the guise of helping internal Malay dynastic disputes and settling the destabilizing influence of Chinese secret society wars in the tin mines, the British pushed their influence into the interior. Their policy of indirect rule allowed the local leaders the prestige of self-determination while giving the British economic supremacy.

By 1919 every state on the Malay Peninsula was under this kind of British rule. The British established an extensive communication infrastructure to allow efficient transport of tin and rubber to its ports, as well as a colonial legal and administrative system. An ethnic division of labor was established in which elite, British-educated Malays worked in the administrative system while other Malays continued fishing and farming. Chinese immigrants from the coastal areas of Fujian (Hokkein) and Guangdong worked in tin mines and as traders. Indians largely worked in the bureaucracy, the rubber plantations, and as laborers in public works.

The colonial society established by the British continued relatively unabated until the JAPANESE occupation during World War II. This occupation occurred quickly and was devastating for Europeans, Malays, Chinese, and Indians alike. By February 1942 the Japanese had taken all Malaya, Singapore, and even Borneo, with the assistance of some of the Malay population who believed Japanese claims that they were there to liberate them as part of their "Asia for the Asians" campaign. European residents were sent to prison camps and thousands died, but the local population did not fare much better. In response, many sectors of Malayan society rebelled, laying the groundwork for postwar anticolonial activities. The Japanese also captured the rest of the Malay people's territories, from the southern Philippines to Indonesia.

In 1945 the Japanese surrendered, and the fate of the Malay people differed depending on where they lived. Those residing in the former colonies of the Dutch East Indies became citizens of the independent country of Indonesia, where they made up a small minority in a large, multiethnic state dominated by the Javanese. The small number of Malay speakers in the Philippines also achieved independence from the United States in 1946. The largely Malay population of the British colony of Malaya remained under British control until 1963, at which time Singapore remained part of the new country of Malaysia. Singapore withdrew from Malaysia in 1965, giving its small Malay population citizenship in the new country. Brunei was the last country with a significant Malay population to achieve independence when the British relinquished their hold on the small sultanate in 1984.

Although politically the Malay people have had widely varying experiences in the postwar world, generally speaking the rural population of Malays has continued to lead very similar agricultural existences. Rice is the primary subsistence crop grown in the region, and rubber is the dominant cash crop. Islam is at the center of most people's worldview, and this guides the relationships not only between men and women

The Japanese military may be infamous for their Malayan prison camps during World War II, but it was certainly not the first to impose harsh conditions on the local population, nor the last. The 19th-century Pudu Prison shown here was used first by the British, then the Japanese, and most recently the Malaysian government. *(AP/Mike Fiala)*

and different kin groups but also between individuals and the states in which they live.

In the early 21st century, interest in a pan-Malay identity and culture has resurfaced, and this has inspired individuals from the entire Malay-speaking world to come together for conferences and other events. One of these, a series of international meetings called Malay World, Islamic World, has been meeting occasionally since October 2000 to promote Malay culture and trade in the region. The group Movements of People Concerned about Malay Culture has also held both cultural and academic events in 2002 and 2003 to discuss the meaning of Malay identity, promote Malay culture, and inspire academics and others to pursue these questions in other forums.

CULTURE

It is difficult to speak of just one Malay culture given the fact that Malay speakers in the contemporary world live in six different countries spread across insular and mainland Southeast Asia, plus a diaspora throughout the world. Their different political statuses, from domi-

nating the politics of Malaysia to being a small minority in the Philippines, Thailand, Singapore, and Brunei, mean that they have different political, economic, and social experiences.

That said, there are some bases for speaking of a unified Malay world in terms of culture. Prior to the 14th-century conversion to Islam, Malays were heavily influenced by both Hinduism and Buddhism. From Hinduism, Malays inherited a hierarchical political structure, which today means that class differences continue to be important social distinctions. Hierarchy is also evident within individual families where most marriages continue to be arranged by parents and other senior relatives, and sons are favored over daughters in most matters. The surrounding Thais, Javanese, and Sumatrans also contributed features of Malay cultural life, from specific vocabulary words to ritual techniques.

Traditionally Malay villages, *kampongs,* tended to develop along riverbanks, especially at their mouths, and along the region's many beaches. Each village was made up of stilt houses for each individual family set among fruit trees and surrounded by rice fields on the outskirts. Generally these settlements had no public buildings, with the occasional exception of a small mosque; these structures were limited to towns and cities. Markets were also held only in towns and cities, providing ample opportunities for the rural population to mix with people from other regions and to attend to business in mosques, schools, and other seats of power.

Most Malay-speaking farmers focused their energy on subsistence crops, the main one being wet rice, which was introduced in the region in the fifth century. The second-largest occupation among rural Malays was fishing, again, on a small scale for personal consumption and exchange in a local town's market. Since the colonial era, many rural Malays have also participated in the production of coconuts, pineapples, coffee, cattle, and most important, rubber. As a result of this widespread activity, in Malaysia nearly half of the rubber crop is produced by small-scale growers rather than on large plantations. Even with the development of the tin industry in the colonial period, few Malays have engaged in mining, preferring to allow this industry to be dominated by the Indian and Chinese immigrants who flowed into British Malaya in the 19th and 20th centuries. Since the British takeover of the region, there has been a class of well-educated Malays who have participated fully in the region's political and economic life. Since 1971 in Malaysia, it has been state policy to provide special assistance to Malays and other indigenous peoples, collectively called *bumiputras,* or "sons of the soil," to attain educational places, state contracts, and other lucrative positions in an attempt to wrest some of the country's wealth and power away from the wealthier but smaller populations of immigrant Indians and Chinese. These policies have achieved some of their aims, and today Malaysia is dominated by the Malay people (*see* MALAYSIAN CHINESE; MALAYSIAN INDIANS; MALAYSIANS: NATIONALITY).

Across the entire Malay world, kinship is an important marker of belonging, but it is generally of the bilateral type rather than being dominated by large lineage or clan groups. Only the Minankabau and Negri Sembilan, somewhat marginal Malay groups that are often considered separate ethnic groups due to their cultural distinctiveness, are matrilineal and thus trace their lines of descent through women only; no Malay group is patrilineal. Instead, relatives from one's mother's and father's family are considered equal, and each generation is labeled according to gender only. As a result, all women in one's mother's generation in both one's mother's and father's families are called by the same kinship term, which translates generally as mother. The same is true of men, who are all called father. Cousins as the children of both mother's and father's siblings are called by the same term as brothers and sisters, and so on with grandparents, great-grandparents, children, grandchildren, and even more distant relatives. Instead of creating large, historically relevant lines of descent that can be traced far back in time, this form of kinship creates a wide net of contemporary relatives who can be drawn upon for assistance and support.

Marriage is the most important institution in the lives of most Malay individuals, and it is expected that all adults marry at least once in their lifetime. Islamic law allows Malay men to have up to four wives, but very few have the wealth necessary to maintain four households, and most Malay marriages are monogamous. Marriages in many rural regions continue to be arranged by parents and other senior relatives, but the partners' wishes are usually respected, which was not generally the case in the past. Both bride price, gifts of money and other wealth given to a bride's family by the husband's, as well as a dowry—gifts from the bride's family to the new couple but especially the new husband and his family—are exchanged during the course of the marriage ceremony. Generally the new husband and wife move into their own home, a pattern called neolocal residence, but occasionally they start their new life in the larger household of one or the other's parents.

The most important task of each new couple is to have children, and not doing so may lead to divorce, which is relatively easy for Malay men to attain. Child rearing is so central to the Malay worldview that childless couples frequently adopt at least one child from a relative; requests to adopt a child are rarely turned down by those with children of their own because of the duty to assist close relatives. People without children are considered children themselves and are barred from participating in certain village ritual and political events, especially gift exchanges and feasting.

Proper Malay personhood requires not only childbearing and rearing but also *budi bahasa,* the language and character attained through being raised properly. This entails being polite but, more important, recognizing hierarchy through proper speech and manners. Respect is central to the Malay worldview, and ignoring the grammar and behavior of respect brings great shame on oneself as well as one's family. Lacking these sensibilities is a sign of *kurang ajar,* loosely defined as lacking education but closer in meaning to being rough, rude, or uncouth.

Another central feature of Malay culture is adherence to Sunni Islam. Obviously this religion is not exclusive to the Malay people since it is practiced in such diverse places as Saudi Arabia, China, and Indonesia. But it is important to the construction of Malay identity, and those few individuals who speak the language but are not practicing Muslims are often considered outside the Malay world. As in Central Asia, Sufism is important in the Malay world, with its charismatic brotherhoods in existence in many Malay towns and cities. Generally the Malay ritual calendar is dominated by Islamic events such as Ramadan and the yearly hajj, or pilgrimage to Mecca, engaged in by many wealthy and middle-class Malays.

Despite the centrality of Islam in Malay identity, this religion has dominated most people's lives only since about the 17th century, and there remain many features in Malay culture that come from Buddhism, Hinduism, and local animistic religions. For example, the spirits of the pre-Islamic world are generally known as *hantu-hantu* in Malay, and most people try to avoid the ill effects of angering or upsetting these spirits or ghosts. Most households, especially in rural areas, maintain shrines to them and engage in a variety of rituals aimed to propitiate these supernatural beings. Most rural residents are also familiar with ceremonies during which ritual specialists known as *bomoh* or *dukun* try to cure patients of the ailments brought on by these spirits.

Another facet of Malay culture that predates the conversion to Islam is the *wayang kulit,* a shadow puppet theater that generally shows plays from the Hindu epic tradition.

FURTHER READING

Timothy P. Barnard, ed. *Contesting Malayness: Malay Identity across Boundaries* (Singapore: Singapore University Press, 2004).

Raymond Firth. *Malay Fishermen: Their Peasant Economy* (New York: W. Norton & Co., 1975).

Edmund Terence Gomez, ed. *Politics in Malaysia: The Malay Dimension* (New York: Routledge, 2007).

Zawawi Ibrahim. *The Malay Labourer: By the Window of Capitalism* (Singapore: Institute of Southeast Asian Studies, 1998).

Joel S. Kahn. *Other Malays: Nationalism and Cosmopolitanism in the Modern Malay World* (Singapore:

The Wayang shadow puppets of Java have been named by UNESCO as a Masterpiece of the Oral and Intangible Heritage of Humanity. Many of the stories told through this genre are more than 1,000 years old and predate the Islamic period in Indonesia. *(Shutterstock)*

Asian Studies Association of Australia in association with Singapore University Press, 2006).

Suzanne Lauridsen and Sally Heinrich. *Malay Muslim Festivals* (Singapore: Educational Pub. House, 2001).

Henk Maier. *We Are Playing Relatives: A Survey of Malay Writing* (Singapore: Institute of Southeast Asian Studies, 2004).

Patricia Sloane. *Islam, Modernity, and Entrepreneurship among the Malays* (New York: St. Martin's Press, 1999).

Malaysian Chinese

The residents of Malaysia who are of Chinese descent are culturally distinct from their fellow citizens who are either Malay or Malaysian Indian; they are equally distinct from their Chinese ancestors who resided mostly in southern China (*see* MALAYS; MALAYSIAN INDIANS). They are part of a large Chinese diaspora, often referred to as the Overseas Chinese, who have lived and worked in both mainland and island Southeast Asia for many generations.

Chinese traders first began visiting the region prior to the seventh century, when it was not generally considered important to trade. By the 15th century, however, a more significant Chinese community had established itself in Melaka as part of that region's merchant class. The main immigration period came in the 19th century, when large numbers of poor and peasant migrants came from southern China. For the most part the Chinese immigrants of this massive influx were escaping appalling conditions in the coastal areas of Fujian (Hokkein) and Guangdong provinces. These people established agricultural plantations, worked in the tin mines of Malaysia, and were the ancestors of the majority of the Chinese now living in Peninsular Malaysia.

While these migrants left their homes and settled in Peninsular Malaysia voluntarily, in Sabah, Northern Borneo, the Chinese population is largely made up of HAKKA Chinese who were brought in by the British North Borneo Company in the 1880s to plant rubber trees; in the 1890s more Hakka Chinese arrived to work on the railway. Many of these individuals remained and formed the basis of the Chinese business community there. In Sarawak, northwest Borneo, Chinese from Foochow, Teochow, and Hokkein Provinces played an important role in opening up the interior and establishing pepper and rubber plantations along Sungei Rajang (River) in the late 19th century.

Colonial control of British Malaya, as it was known from the 18th century until 1946, was managed through a divide-and-conquer philosophy, and racial divisions among the Malays, Chinese, and Indians formed the basis of these divisions. In northern Borneo the colonizers also had to contend with the many indigenous groups who had lived among the Malay population there for millennia. Hence, postwar Malaysia was a country divided, and this was most evident in the two largest ethnic groups, the Chinese and the native Malays.

The year 1948 saw the Malayan Communist Party (MCP), a largely Chinese organization, begin a guerilla struggle to end British rule; this period is often referred to as "the Malayan Emergency." The communists' actions were particularly effective in their early years under the leadership of the charismatic Chin Peng. However, in 1950 many rural Chinese were relocated, placed under surveillance, and subjected to curfews. As a result, the guerillas found their support withering, and by the end of the Malayan Emergency in 1960 it was not particularly popular. Malays had never been very supportive of the MCP's actions, not because they were opposed to independence but because they feared that a Chinese-dominated independence would leave them just as marginal to economic and political development as they were under the British.

From 1960 onward, the efforts of most Chinese Malaysians, as they came to be known after 1963, were focused on economic advancement and consolidation of political power. Even with the introduction in 1969 of laws that granted special privileges to Malays and the indigenous peoples of Sarawak, Sabah, and Peninsular Malaysia, the Chinese who remain today in Malaysia still make up the majority of the middle- and upper-income classes, despite accounting for only approximately 25 percent of the population. On a political level, the Chinese are also well represented and currently hold about one-quarter of ministerial positions.

CULTURE

Among the earliest settlers, intermarriage between the Chinese immigrants and local Malays was common because male Chinese immigrants rarely brought their women. The Chinese Malay children of these marriages are known as PERANAKANS, the male descendants being Babas and the females Nonyas. Once established, this group developed a distinct cultural identity and generally married other Chinese Malays, a

MALAYSIAN CHINESE

location:
Throughout Malaysia, Peninsular Malaysia, Sarawak, and Sabah—also known as Eastern Malaysia

time period:
Beginning in the 15th century to the present

ancestry:
Chinese

language:
The early Chinese immigrants and their offspring spoke various dialects of Chinese, depending on their origin; the second generation could neither speak nor read much Chinese and over time communicated mainly in Malay. Baba Malay is a dialect of the Malay language that borrows substantially from Hokkein Chinese. It has also been called the Baba language, as although the vocabulary is basically Malay, it differs from Malay in many important aspects and is almost another language. A proportion of the Chinese population also speaks English as a first language, which is a remnant of the British colonial days. These Chinese often do not speak or write Chinese and are derogatorily known as bananas (yellow on the outside and white on the inside).

MALAYSIAN INDIANS

location:
Predominantly Peninsular
Malaysia

time period:
Possibly fourth century to
the present

ancestry:
Mostly southern Indian,
especially Tamil

language:
Mostly Tamil, also Telugu,
Malayalam, and Hindi;
most speak Malay as
well

practice that continues to today. This pattern is largely due to cultural and religious reasons. Malaysian law requires non-Muslims who wish to marry Muslims to convert to Islam, and since most Malaysian Chinese consider that being "Chinese" involves an entire ethnic, cultural, and political identity, conversion to Islam is quite rare; only 1 percent of Chinese Malaysians are Muslim.

When Chinese immigrants arrived en masse in the 19th century to work in the mines, rubber industry, and railway construction, they built shrines dedicated to their gods as well as cemeteries. Buddhist and Taoist monks also came to manage the temples, and as a result today most Chinese Malaysians still consider themselves Buddhists. However, in reality the lines are often blurred, and elements of Buddhism, Taoism, Confucianism, and traditional ancestor worship are still widely practiced. Chinese folk religion in Malaysia also includes beliefs in local guardian spirits, Na Tuk Kong, which originated from traditional animism and mysticism. Other local gods include Tnee Kong, the celestial god; Teh Choo Kong; the earth god; Choy Sun Yeh, the god of fortune and prosperity; Kwan Yin Ma, who originated from Sanskrit Avalokiteśvara and is the goddess of mercy; Matsu, the Taoist goddess of the sea who protects fishermen and sailors; and Di Zhu God, the lord of the land. In addition, about 19 percent of Chinese are Christians, with East Malaysia having a larger proportion of Chinese Christians than other regions.

Another important aspect of Chinese Malaysian cultural identity is the cuisine. Malaysian cuisine generally reflects the multiculturalism of its people, and often individual dishes are adaptations of the various dominant cultures. For example, Nonya cooking, the cuisine of the Peranakan people, is like the people themselves, essentially a blend of Chinese and Malay cooking. Nonya cooks also prepare Indian-style curries that have been watered down and made milder to suit the Chinese Malay palate. In addition, the social etiquette of eating is that of the Malays and not of the Chinese, using fingers only and not chopsticks.

FURTHER READING

J. E. Khoo. *The Straits Chinese: A Cultural History* (Amsterdam: Pepin Press, 1998).

K. H. Lee and C. B. Tan, eds. *The Chinese in Malaysia* (New York: Oxford University Press, 2000).

Craig A. Lockard. *Chinese Immigration and Society in Sarawak, 1868–1917* (Sarawak: Sarawak Chinese Cultural Association, 2003).

Malaysian Indians (Indian Malaysians, Indo-Malaysians)

The Indian population of Malaysia is the smallest of the three main ethnic groups in the country, accounting for about 10 percent of its population. The majority of Malaysian Indians originated in southern India and speak Tamil (*see* TAMILS). Other Indian communities that live mainly in the larger towns of the west coast of Peninular Malaysia speak Telugu (*see* TELUGUS), Malayalam, and HINDI, while middle-class Indians often speak Malay as a first language. The population of PUNJABIS, mostly SIKHS, is more than 83,000. There are also people originating from Pakistan, Bangladesh, and Sri Lanka who are included in the Indian category for statistical purposes.

The earliest history of Indian contact with Southeast Asia remains obscure but probably occurred when Indian traders sailing between the subcontinent and China stopped in what is today Malaysia and Indonesia. It is believed that it was primarily Tamil influence that brought Indian culture to the region in this early period. By the first century C.E., Hindu and Buddhist kingdoms had emerged in Java, Cambodia, and elsewhere in the region, and their influence spread to the Malay Peninsula not long after that. The first evidence of an Indian-influenced kingdom on the peninsula comes from about the fourth century at Kadaram, contemporary Kedah, on the west coast. The earliest relics from this kingdom indicate its largest and possibly state religion was Buddhism, but in the subsequent three or four centuries Hinduism superseded Buddhism among the Indianized Malay population.

Following this early period of Indian colonization of Malaysia, Indian traders continued to trade in and around the peninsula. In the 11th century it was the southern Chola kingdom, another Tamil domain, that was the most powerful and had the greatest influence among the MALAYS. Indian Muslims were also among those who brought this religion to the Malays in the 14th century.

Although these early periods may have brought many Indians into the Malay world, most of today's population of Malaysian Indians need only look back to the 19th-century British colonial period to find their migrating ancestors. The 19th and early 20th centuries brought thousands of Indians, mostly Tamils, into Malaya, as it was called at the time, to work on British sugar and coffee plantations. Later migrants also worked on rubber plantations, in the oil fields, and as construction workers in building railways and roads. A few of these migrants left their homes voluntarily to escape poverty, caste discrimination, or other persecution at home, while many were forced into migration by the British. Sri Lankan Tamils also came to Malaya at that time to work in white-collar positions such as clerical and hospital assistants, while Punjabis from the north joined the army in Malaya, handled the bullock-cart services in the country, and worked in other areas as well. As they did throughout their large empire, the British used their divide-and-conquer policy effectively with the Indian migrants by dividing various castes and language groups into separate work roles, as well as different geographic locations, effectively preventing them from becoming a cohesive, powerful group.

The predominantly Hindu culture that these migrants brought with them to Malaya introduced a rich cultural heritage to Malaysia and is still prominent today, most evident in their beautiful temples, unique cuisine, and colorful clothing. Approximately 87 percent of Malaysian Indians, including most Sri Lankans as well, are Hindus; the rest are mainly Muslims and Christians. The most common form is Shaivite Hinduism, with Murugan, a youthful god of knowledge, and Mariamman, the smallpox goddess, being the most popular deities. On all rubber and oil palm plantations with Indian workers, there is a Hindu temple where the practices from their homeland are followed closely. The larger temples in the towns are usually dedicated to the universal Hindu deities of the Hindu pantheon. These are supported by the wealthier professional and middle classes. Among the best known of these urban temples are the Maha Mariamman Temple and the Lakshmi Narayanan Temple in Kuala Lumpur.

In conjunction with the centrality of the Hindu religion and various Indian languages, another important way that most Malaysian Indians maintain their connection to one another and their past is through a number of festivals. The two most important are Thaipusam and Deepavali (or Diwali). The three-day Thaipusam festival in January or February is dedicated to the Tamil deity Murugun and has been celebrated by immigrant workers from early times. Participants engage in a multitude of activities in order to do penance, including piercing their skin with metal hooks and rods of up to a yard in length. In Kuala Lumpur, Thaipusam is celebrated in a shrine in the Batu Caves. A chariot procession carries the image of the deity to the caves eight miles from the city, where people

The world's tallest Murugan statue was erected at the Sri Maha Mariamman Temple, also known as the Batu Caves, outside Kuala Lumpur, Malaysia, in 2006. More than 30,000 Malaysian Indians witnessed the unveiling. *(OnAsia/Jerry Redfern)*

from all over Malaysia come to see and practice penance. Deepavali is the Hindu festival of lights to celebrate the New Year.

In addition to their language and religion, most Malaysian Indians have maintained their separate identity through continuing to eat primarily Indian foods and to raise their children with a conscious Indian identity. Many women continue to dress in saris rather than western or Malaysian dress, and much of the population is endogamous, marrying within their own ethnic, linguistic, and even caste groups. One exception to this general pattern is the Chitty community in Malacca, which is the result of the integration of Indian immigrants with the local culture. Although they remain Hindu, the Chitties speak Bahasa Malaysia, and the women dress in *sarong kebayas* instead of saris.

Malaysians: nationality (people of Malaysia)

GEOGRAPHY

Located between 2° and 7° north of the equator, peninsular Malaysia is separated from the

MALAYSIANS: NATIONALITY

nation:
Malaysia

derivation of name:
The name *Malaysia* was adopted in 1963 when Singapore, Sabah, and Sarawak formed a 14-state federation. Singapore left Malaysia in 1965 to become an independent country. The name is derived from the name of the dominant ethnic group, the Malays.

government:
Federal constitutional monarchy with a bicameral legislative system. The head of state is the Yang Di-Pertuan Agong, commonly referred to as the king of Malaysia, who is elected for a five-year period. This makes Malaysia one of only two elective monarchies in the world, the other being Vatican City. The head of government is the prime minister.

capital:
Kuala Lumpur

language:
Bahasa Melayu (Malay) is the official language, but English is widely spoken. The ethnic groups also speak various languages and dialects.

religion:
Islam is the official religion and is practiced by 60.4 percent of the population. Other main religions include Buddhism 19.2 percent; Christianity 9.1 percent, mostly in East Malaysia; Hinduism 6.3 percent; Confucianism, Taoism, other Chinese religions 2.6 percent; other, unknown, or none 2.4 percent.

Malaysians: nationality time line

C.E.

seventh–14th centuries Sri Vijaya imperial state encompasses Peninsular Malaysia, Sumatra, western Java, and western Borneo.

1400s Sultanate of Melaka is established by Parameswara, a prince from Palembang, who has fled from the island Temasek (now Singapore).

1511 Melaka is conquered by the Portuguese, and a colony is established.

1570s Hamzah Fansuri is thought to have introduced Syair poetry, a form of sung verse. As well as stories of fantasy, travel, and love, important historical events are recorded in Syair until the end of the 17th century.

1600s *Sejarah Melayu* (The Malay Annals) is written by Malay court official Tun Seri Lanang and is considered an important work about the historical and cultural aspects of Malay society. It portrays the various sultanates of Melaka, Johor, Pahang, Perak, and the sultanates on the Sumatran shores.

1641 With the assistance of the Dutch in Java, Johor ousts the Portuguese.

1786 Britain establishes its first colony in the Malay Peninsula on the island of Penang when the British East India Company leases it from the sultan of Kedah.

1824 The British acquire Melaka and form the Straits Settlement with Penang and Singapore.

1874 The Pangkor Treaty with Perak sets the scene for the British to extend control throughout the peninsula following British intervention to bring a peaceful resolution to civil disturbances caused by Chinese gangsters.

Late 1800s Logging begins in Sabah and later in Sarawak on the island of Borneo. (Malaysia is today the world's largest exporter of hardwood timbers although at a slower pace than in the 1970s and 1980s.)

1941–45 Japanese occupation.

1948 The Federation of Malaya is formed.

1948–60 The Malayan Emergency, when rebels under the leadership of the Communist Party launch guerilla operations designed to force the British out of Malaya.

1957 Independence from the British is declared.

1963 The Federation of Malaya is renamed Malaysia, with Tunku Abdul Rahman elected the first prime minister.

---

states of Sabah and Sarawak by the South China Sea. To the north of Malaysia is Thailand, while its southern neighbor is Singapore. Sabah and Sarawak are situated on the north and western regions of the island of Borneo, respectively, and are bordered by Indonesia to the south and east. Sarawak also shares a border with Brunei.

INCEPTION OF A NATION

The dominant ethnic group in contemporary Malaysia, the MALAYS, probably settled in this region between 500 B.C.E. and 500 C.E. and initiated the development of a settled way of life. There are many stories and legends surrounding several Malay kingdoms existing between the fifth and 14th centuries C.E. but very little tangible evidence to support these stories outside of references in Chinese mariners' guides, Arab sailors' tales, diaries of Buddhist monks en route to India, and the writings of Marco Polo.

In the early 15th century the Sultanate of Melaka was founded by Parameswara, a prince from Palembang who was forced to flee from Temasek (now Singapore) during a JAVANESE attack. This marks the first definite date for the founding of a state in this area. The port was strategically positioned on the Melaka Straits and quickly rose to prominence. Dominant among the many traders were wealthy Indian Muslims who favored Muslim ports. This may have been a contributing factor in the monarch's conversion to Islam and the spread of this religion throughout the archipelago. At its height, the sultanate controlled the areas now

1969	Racial riots between Chinese and Malays.
1971	Tunku Abdul Razak is elected prime minister, and a new economic policy period begins, intended to increase the economic output of the *bumiputras* (indigenous people, which includes the majority of Malays, but not always the indigenous people). Malaysia has since maintained a delicate ethnopolitical balance with a system of government that has attempted to combine overall economic development with political and economic policies that favor *bumiputras*.
1981	Tun Dr. Mahathir bin Mohamad is elected prime minister and adopts the Look East policy. During the period of Dr. Mahathir's prime ministership, Malaysia shifts from an agricultural-based economy to one based on manufacturing and industry in areas such as computers and consumer electronics.
	Pulau Sipidan (Island) becomes a marine reserve. An ancient underwater volcanic crater there plunges to 1,970 feet; French marine explorer Jacques Cousteau proclaims it a rare pearl. It is often considered to be the best diving spot in the world.
1980s	Deforestation is reduced to 560 square miles a year, almost a third slower than the previous rate.
	The government designates 29,200 square miles of land as Permanent Forest Estates. Critics argue that this is inadequate for the forest to recover from the depletion of the 1970s and point out that the 1988 log output was more than 2 million cubic meters higher than the 1986 figure and is in apparent disregard of the National Forestry Policy (NFP).
Late 1990s	Malaysia is shaken by the Asian financial crisis as well as political unrest caused by the sacking of the deputy prime minister, Datuk Seri Anwar Ibrahim.
1998	The Commonwealth Games are held in Kuala Lumpur; Malaysia wins a record 36 medals (10 gold, 14 silver, 12 bronze).
2003	Dr. Mahathir, Malaysia's longest-serving prime minister, retires in favor of his deputy, Abdullah Ahmad Badawi, commonly known as Pak Lah.
2005	The novel *The Harmony Silk Factory* by Tash Aw is published and is long-listed for the 2005 Man Booker Prize; it wins the 2005 Whitbread Book Awards First Novel prize and the 2005 Commonwealth Writers Prize for Best First Novel (Asia Pacific region). It has been translated into 17 languages. Aw is arguably the most successful Malaysian writer of modern times.
2006	Swearing-in of Malaysia's 13th king, or the Yang di-Pertuan Agong, 44-year old Sultan Mizan Zainal Abidin, the youngest king to take the throne.

early inhabitants:
The Orang Asli (first people), a gamut of indigenous tribes, were thought to have migrated to mainland Malaysia about 50,000 years ago from the Philippines, which was then connected by a land bridge to Borneo and Southeast Asia.

demographics:
Malays, more than 50 percent; Chinese, 25 percent; Indians, 10 percent; small numbers of Orang Asli and others

known as Peninsular Malaysia, southern Thailand (Patani), and the eastern coast of Sumatra. It existed for more than a century and was the foremost trading port in Southeast Asia, thus attracting the interest of the Portuguese in the early 16th century.

Beginning in 1511, the Portuguese captured and held Melaka for more than 100 years; however, they were never fully able to take advantage of its vast wealth. In 1641 the Dutch replaced the Portuguese as the dominant colonial power in Melaka after supporting the Malay city-state of Johor in its rebellion against the Portuguese. The Dutch likewise were unable, or perhaps unwilling, to take advantage of the port's geographic advantages, favoring their colony in Batavia, contemporary Jakarta.

In the late 18th century the British, who were to be the final colonial power in the region, began to take action to secure a port for their ships plying the trade between India and China. They acquired Penang in 1786 from the sultan of Kedah, who ceded it to them in exchange for British support against the THAIS. Initially the port thrived because the British instituted a tax-and-duty-free trading policy as a strategy to lure trade away from the Dutch ports. By 1800, this virtually uninhabited island supported a thriving population of 10,000. In 1824 the Anglo-Dutch Treaty was signed in London, dividing the peninsula into Dutch and British spheres of influence. The kingdom of Johor was split into the British administration on the mainland and the Dutch-administered Riau Lingga Islands.

Despite efforts in the 1980s to slow deforestation in Malaysia, the country has lost 140,200 hectares of rain forest per year since 2000, a far worse rate than the 78,500 hectares per year lost during the 1980s. *(AP Photo/Vincent Thian)*

Two years later the British Straits Settlement was formed and the British brought together the Straits Settlements of Melaka, Singapore, Penang, and the mainland province opposite known as Province Wellesley (now known as the mainland part of Penang State).

Meanwhile, there was a massive influx of Chinese immigrants, who established agricultural plantations and worked in the tin mines. Under the guise of helping internal Malay dynastic disputes and settling the destabilizing influence of Chinese secret society wars in the tin mines, the British pushed their authority into the Malay interior. Their policy of indirect rule allowed the local leaders the illusion of self-rule, while giving the British economic supremacy.

By 1919 every state on the Malay Peninsula was under this kind of British rule. The British established an extensive communication infrastructure to allow efficient transport of tin and rubber to ports, as well as a colonial legal and administrative system. An ethnic division of labor was established in which elite, British-educated Malays worked in the administrative system while other Malays continued fishing and farming. Chinese immigrants from the coastal areas of Fujian (Hokkein) and Guangdong worked in tin mines and as traders. Indians were introduced to work in the bureaucracy, the rubber plantations, and in public works (*see* Malaysian Chinese; Malaysian Indians).

The colonial society established by the British continued relatively unabated until the Jap-anese occupation during World War II. This occupation occurred quickly and was devastating for Europeans, Malays, Chinese, and Indians alike. By February 1942 the Japanese had taken all Malaya, Singapore, and even Borneo, with the assistance of some of the Malay population who believed Japanese claims that they were there to liberate them as part of their "Asia for the Asians" campaign. European residents were sent to prison camps and thousands died, but the local population did not fare much better. In response, many sectors of Malayan society rebelled, laying the groundwork for postwar anticolonial activities.

Postwar Malaysia saw a polarization in the ethnic divide between the Chinese and ethnic Malays. The British responded by proposing the Malayan Union, giving Chinese and Indians equal citizenship and transferring the Malayan sultans' sovereignty to the British. Many Malays were outraged at this loss of special status and formed the United Malays National Organisation (UMNO). In 1948 the Malayan Union was revoked and replaced by the Federation of Malaya. This gave the Malays special privileges over the other inhabitants and upheld the power of the sultans. The Federation of Malaya's leaders did not want Singapore to be part of the union, as it would tip the balance from a majority Malay-speaking population to a Chinese one; however, they finally agreed to accept Singapore if Sabah, Sarawak, and Brunei were included. This compromise did not satisfy everyone, and many in the Chinese community continued to agitate for independence; many Malays likewise desired independence from Britain but did not want to see power handed to the Chinese. In 1950 many rural Chinese were relocated and placed under surveillance and subject to curfews. This made it extremely difficult for them to support Chinese communist guerillas, and the Malayan Emergency dissipated. Finally, in 1955 the British agreed that Malaya would gain full independence within two years. Elections saw the Alliance Party, a multicultural alliance, sweep into power.

On August 15, 1957, Britain relinquished its sovereignty over Malaya, and Tunku Abdul Rahman was declared the first prime minister. In 1963 Sabah, Sarawak, and Singapore joined Malaya to become the Federation of Malaysia. However, Brunei decided at the last minute to stay independent as it feared losing its lucrative oil wealth. Singapore also lasted only two years as part of the federation as it refused to extend constitutional privileges to the Malays and was

Malaysia

THAILAND

Gulf of
Thailand

VIETNAM

PHILIPPINES

MALAY PENINSULA

Kelantan

Perlis Kedah
George Town

Penang
Perak
Ipoh

Terengganu

Pahang

Selangor
Kuala Lumpur

Negeri Sembilan
Melaka
Malacca   Johor

Strait of Malacca

Spratly Is.

South China Sea

M A L A Y S I A

BRUNEI

Sabah

Baram R.

Sarawak

Borneo

Rajang R.

Kuching

Natuna Is.
(INDONESIA)

Anambas Is.
(INDONESIA)

SINGAPORE
Riau archipelago

INDONESIA
(Kalimantan)

Equator

Sulu Sea

Turtle Is.
(Philippines)

Pulau
Sipadan

Celebes
Sea

Makassar Strait

Sumatra

Palembang

INDIAN
OCEAN

I N D O N E S I A

Java Sea

Jakarta

Java

| | Federation of Malaya,
1948–1963 |

0   250 miles
0   250 km

N

© Infobase Publishing

therefore forced to leave. The formation of Malaysia was arguably the most successful merger of postcolonial entities in Southeast Asia.

CULTURAL IDENTITY

One theme that looms large in the Malaysian national identity is multiculturalism, although not without significant problems. From its earliest days the mix of aboriginals, Malays, Indians, Chinese, and Europeans have all contrib-

uted to this identity. For example, a prehistoric settlement in the Kedah region became an important landfall for Indian shipping. Although Hinduism died out with the coming of Islam in the 14th century, there is still an important Indian influence in the Malaysian way of life. Vocabulary, wedding traditions, court rituals, vital cooking ingredients, and legendary tales are some of the pervasive Indian influences on modern-day Malaysia. Also, embedded in mod-

MALDIVIANS: NATIONALITY

nation:
Republic of Maldives, the Maldives

derivation of name:
Probably Sanskrit *male-dvipa*, "garland of islands"; referred to by Maldivians as "Dhivehi Raajji," or Island Kingdom

government:
Independent presidential republic

capital:
Malé

language:
Maldivian (Dhivehi), English, and Arabic

religion:
100 percent Sunni Muslim

earlier inhabitants:
Possibly Dravidians and Sinhalese who came from south India and Sri Lanka. Giraavaru people claim to be original inhabitants, descended from earlier settlers from southern India (Tamil), and are referred to as Maldives' aborigines.

demographics:
100 percent Maldivian

ern Malaysia's culture are the early influences of Hinduism, Buddhism, and Sanskrit. Traces of these may be found in political ideas, social structure, rituals, art, and cultural practices.

Despite this obvious mixture of many cultural backgrounds, multiculturalism in Malaysia has never gone unchallenged by the ethnocultural identities of the Malay, Chinese, and Indian communities. In part this trend comes out of the British colonial strategy of privileging some groups over others in terms of education and prestige. In addition, the external networks and resources of the Indian and Chinese communities also contributed to a sense of disadvantage on the part of many Malays, perhaps not without justification. In 1969, only 1.5 percent of business assets were owned by Malays, and the average income per capita of Malays was 50 percent less than that of other citizens.

On the other hand, the positive discrimination benefiting Malays, or *bumiputra* (sons of the soil), in land ownership, business licenses, educational opportunities, and government positions continues to be resented by non-Malays to this day. These policies came out of events in the late 1960s, which saw ethnic rivalries come to a violent peak. In May 1969 the Alliance Party lost its two-thirds parliamentary majority, and the next day riots broke out, killing hundreds of people, mostly ethnic Chinese. The Malay-dominated Malaysian government responded quickly. It created the term *bumiputra* and a host of positive discriminatory regulations to benefit the Malays and the various aboriginal peoples of Sarawak, Sabah, and Peninsular Malaysia. Government guidelines stipulated several rules to ensure the *bumiputra*'s share of the nation's wealth. Many Chinese left the country or withdrew their commercial interests as a result. Malaysian Indians likewise felt the effects of this discrimination, and today they continue to leave the country when opportunities arise to migrate to Australia, the United States, or Britain.

FURTHER READING

Sharon A. Carstens. *Histories, Cultures, Identities: Studies in Malaysian Chinese Worlds* (Singapore: Singapore University Press, 2005).

Khoo Gaik Cheng. *Reclaiming Adat: Contemporary Malaysian Film and Literature* (Vancouver: University of British Columbia Press, 2006).

Ronald McKie. *The Emergence of Malaysia* (Westport, Conn.: Greenwood Press, 1973).

R. S. Milne and Diane K. Mauzy. *Malaysia: Tradition, Modernity, and Islam* (Boulder, Colo.: Westview Press, 1986).

Hussin Mutalib. *Islam and Ethnicity in Malay Politics* (New York: Oxford University Press, 1990).

Barbara Aoki Poisson. *Malaysia* (Philadelphia: Mason Crest, 2006).

Maldivians: nationality (Dhivehin, people of the Maldives)

GEOGRAPHY

The archipelago of the Maldives is made up of about 1190 coral islands grouped into 26 coral atolls, stretched out in a vertical strip across the Indian Ocean, 460 miles southwest of Sri Lanka. The coral atolls that form this archipelago sit upon a volcanic ridge about 600 miles in length. The larger islands, none of which is more than 10 feet above sea level or more than five miles long, are covered with thick bush, mangroves, and coconut trees. Due to their small size, there are no mountains or rivers on any of the islands. The Maldives has a land area of 185 square miles and a sea area of approx 66,797 square miles, which makes the country more than 95 percent water. Approximately 202 islands are inhabited, and 90 islands (considered uninhabited) are tourist resorts. Approximately one-third of the entire population lives in the capital, Malé, which at fewer than 82,000 people is one of the smallest capitals in the world.

INCEPTION AS A NATION

The development of Maldives as a nation can be divided into two stages: before and after the conversion to Islam in 1153. Little is known about the pre-Muslim period, based on archaeological discoveries, which are inconclusive, and mythology. The best estimate about the origins of the Maldives people is that they came to the archipelago before it was converted to Islam, possibly some 2,500 years ago. Although historians have argued that the population is a mix of DRAVIDIANS from southern India and SINHALESE from Sri Lanka, recent evidence suggests that there may well be links with the NAGAS and Yakka people who developed the pre-Buddhist civilization in Sri Lanka. These earliest settlers brought their Buddhist faith with them and established a settled community of farmers and fishermen.

Later history, after the inhabitants converted to Islam in 1153, is much better understood. According to local legend, the Maldives was converted to Islam when a visiting North African Arab, Abu Al Barakaath, believing the

Maldivians: nationality time line

C.E.

second century First reference to the Maldives by Greek geographer Ptolemy, who states that "1,378 little islands" lie west of Taprobane (Sri Lanka).

300 Excavations indicate earliest settlers from this period were of the Buddhist faith, probably from south India and Sri Lanka.

Islands used as a staging post for Arab traders (possibly from Oman and Yemen) who dominate trade in Indian Ocean.

1153 First recorded Buddhist king, Theemugey Maha Kalaminja, converts to Islam and strives to introduce Islamic law throughout all of the islands.

1345 Abdulla Ibn Battuta, an Arab trader, provides earliest account of the Maldive Islands. The people export dried fish, turtleshells, copra, ambergris (a whale product used in perfume making), and coir rope (made from coconut husks) to Sri Lanka, Arabia, India, and China.

1503 The Portuguese first spot the Maldives.

1518 Sultan Kalhu Mohammed enters into a treaty with the Portuguese, who establish a trading post in Malé.

1558 The Portuguese invade, kill the sultan, and plunge the country into a period of economic havoc and religious persecution remarkable mostly for its brutality.

1573 Sultan Muhammad Thakurufaanu frees the country from Portugal and introduces a new judicial system, a defense force, the Thaana script, and the first local coins to replace the cowry shell currency. He fights to regain independence from the Portuguese and is considered a national hero.

1648 Sultan Ibrahim Iskander builds the Malé Friday mosque and minaret.

1759 Malé is attacked and the royal palace burned. Sultan Mohammed Imaduddin III and his courtiers are abducted, and the Maldives comes under Dutch domination.

1887 The Maldives becomes a protectorate under the British, who agree to refrain from interfering in local affairs.

1932 The first written constitution in Maldivian history severely limits the sultan's powers. A legislative body, the *majlis,* is formed, laying the groundwork for a representational form of government.

1953 The first republic, with Mohammad Amin Didi as president, is short-lived, and a constitutional monarchy is established again.

1957 Under Premier Ibrahim Nasir, the British cease to be responsible for the defense of the Maldives, although a British airbase remains in Gan until 1976.

1959 The three southernmost atolls secede from the Maldives and form the United Suvadive Republic. The rebels hold on for more than three years but are defeated and banished to the Seychelles.

1965 The Maldives gain independence from Britain and becomes a member of the United Nations as a fully independent sovereign state.

1968 The sultanate is once again abolished, and a republic is established for a second time with Ibrahim Nasir as president.

1972 The constitution is amended to give the president far greater powers. The country's name changes from Maldive Islands to Republic of Maldives.

Tourism first comes to Maldives, and Nasir is accused of using government cash to set up a hotel and travel agency; he is eventually banished.

1976 Independence Day is to be dated from March 29, 1976, the date of the final withdrawal of the British from Gan.

1978 Maumoon Abdul Gayoom is elected president. He remains in power to this day despite coup attempts in 1980, 1983, and 1988.

(continues)

Maldivians: nationality time line *(continued)*

1998	El Niño causes coral bleaching, which is detrimental to the tourism industry, the mainstay of the economy.
2004	A massive tsunami ravages the country, leaving many islands uninhabitable and resorts badly damaged. More than 100 are killed, 14 islands evacuated, and more than 100,000 Maldivians directly affected.
2005	Tourism is back on track, and the government opens more islands for the development of hotels and resorts.
	The first opposition party, the Maldivian Democratic Party (MDP), is allowed to register officially.
	The population reaches 350,000, with 63,000 living in the capital of Malé.
2006	The United Nations reports that Maldives is violating the human rights of its citizens. Many tsunami survivors are still living in inadequate housing two years after the tragedy.

islanders to be a colony of ignorant idolaters, convinced the king that Islam allowed him to control the terrible ocean *jinni* then afflicting the people. The king subsequently converted to the new faith and ordered the whole country to follow his lead.

The actual conversion of the people of this region was quite different. Arabs arrived on the islands in the early 12th century as traders and missionaries for their faith, and the islands' leaders recognized the economic power of these traders and sought their favor through religious conversion. However, even after this conversion Buddhism remained important to many. A century after the forced conversion of the population, the chiefs of Dambidu Island returned to their Buddhist traditions, as did many individual families who had merely buried their family shrines and other Buddhist relics rather than destroy them. This rebellion was met by violent repression; the chiefs were executed, and the people reconverted to Islam.

In subsequent centuries, the Maldives continued to be an important territory for traders and pirates alike. Indians, Arabs, and Moroccans are among the people who are recorded as playing a role in internal Maldives politics in the years prior to European "discovery." A Moroccan explorer, Ibn Battuta, even served as chief judge in the capital during the 14th century.

The first recorded European presence in the archipelago is a relatively peaceful few years at the beginning of the 16th century, when the Portuguese were granted a trading port at Malé. By mid-century, the Portuguese were not content with their small port and the slow progress in Christianization and began 15 years of colonization by killing the ruling sultan, Ali VI. At that time the Portuguese were able to forcibly convert much of the population of Malé to their faith, if only briefly. The islands prospered economically, but the period is considered disastrous in terms of Maldivian identity and culture.

The brutality of the Portuguese against the local population inspired the independence movement of Mohammed Thakurufaan, who succeeded as ruler in 1573. As part of his new policies, he reinforced the country's Islamic heritage and made reconversion a legal necessity. It was at this time as well that the Arabic-style Thaana script was invented for the DIVEHI language; its use facilitated the introduction of numerous Arabic terms into the country's language and thus reinforced the strengthening connections between the state and Islam. The Portuguese were followed by other European advisers and traders, with the Dutch and British both holding the archipelago as a protectorate during the 17th–19th centuries. Neither country, however, actually colonized the Maldives, and this independence remains extremely important in the identity of many Maldivians today.

The 20th century was one of great change in the Maldives, with the sultanate or ruler's position becoming an elected rather than an inherited position in 1932. In 1948 the country also signed a defense pact with the British, which gave them control of the foreign affairs of the islands but not the right to interfere internally. In return, the British were provided with facilities for their defense forces on Gan. This relationship was to last until 1976, when the British finally pulled out; it is this date that Maldivians recognize as the final attainment of their independence.

Ibrahim Nasir, who was elected president in 1972, encouraged the liberalization of commerce and will be forever remembered as the man who started tourism in the Maldives, the key to the current economy. Maumoon Abdul Gayyoom followed, becoming president in 1978, a position he holds to this day, much to the consternation of some Maldivians. He continued to promote education, health, and industry, particularly tourism. His leadership has survived through at least three coups and has been criticized locally and internationally for being corrupt, with the United Nations along with the Human Rights Commission expressing concerns about continuing human rights abuses. Approximately 15 percent of the population lives below the World Bank's poverty level.

With the ongoing success and growth of tourism and the influence of the outside world, the capital and surrounding islands are rapidly adapting to modernity. Many Maldivians run their own businesses, and there are a growing number of wealthy entrepreneurs in the country. Although inhabitants are not taxed, all tourists pay an $8 bed tax per person, per night, which generates huge foreign currency revenues. Fishing has been the traditional base of the economy and is still a big export earner, but it is declining in relative importance. Although schools and health clinics have been developed on the outer atolls, Malé remains the political, economic, and cultural hub of the widely scattered archipelago. While no one goes without food or shelter, the Maldives remains one of the least developed countries in the world.

CULTURAL IDENTITY

The people of the Maldives are a relatively homogeneous ethnic group, having a unique history, culture, and language, and a unique cultural tradition. Islam is central to the life of all Maldivians, and the law is based on the Muslim code of sharia as interpreted by a judge (*gazi*), who applies the principles of the Quran to society. The Maldivian society traditionally observes a liberal form of Islam similar to India and Indonesia. From the early age of three, children are taught Arabic so that they can recite the Quran.

As mentioned above, in addition to Islam, independence makes up another aspect of Maldivian national identity. Most Maldivians today continue to be proud of their relative independence during the era of European colonialism in Asia, and the current ruler, Maumoon Gayyoom, often mentions independence to jus-

In 2003 Maumoon Abdul Gayyoom announced his candidacy for a sixth term as president and caused fighting to break out on Male Island, as a result of which this Department of Elections building was torched and looted by protesters. *(AP Photo)*

tify his leadership. He has been able to use his country's status as an Islamic state independent of Western influence to win favor with many of the Arab states and Indonesia. At the same time, he has also used the fact that the style of Islam practiced in his country is independent of any fundamentalism to win favor in the West. Those Maldivians who have been struggling to free their country from the grip of Gayyoom also use independence as an important rallying cry, so far with little success.

While the Divehi make up the vast majority of Maldivian citizens, there is one extremely small minority, the Giraavaru people, once considered the most important community in Malé atoll. These people claim to be the original inhabitants of the Maldives. Very little is known about them except that throughout the centuries they kept themselves apart from the rest of society. They are considered to be descendants of TAMILS from southern India; are virtually endogamous; and, unlike the other Maldivians who have the highest divorce rate in the world, see marriage as a permanent state. The Giraavaru women are recognizable by their custom of tying their hair in a bun on the right side of the head, while Divehi women tie theirs on the left. They also wear a special kind of silver embroidery around the tops of their dresses. The women are extremely modest, and it is said that they do not completely undress themselves, even in front of their husbands.

MANCHUS

location:
Northeastern China;
possibly North Korea,
Siberia, and Russia as
well

time period:
1630s to the present

ancestry:
Tungusic

language:
Manchu, a Tungusic
language, and Mandarin
Chinese

Sadly, only about 150 Giraavaru people remain today, and as the young are now marrying outside the group, it is unlikely they will remain an identifiable people for more than a generation.

FURTHER READING

Clarence Maloney. *People of the Maldive Islands* (Bombay: Orient Longman, 1980).

Adrian Neville. *Dhivehi Raajji: A Portrait of Maldives* (Seoul: Samhwa Printers Ltd., 2003).

John M. Ostheimer, ed. *The Politics of the Western Indian Ocean Islands* (New York: Praeger, 1975).

Lars Vilgon. *Maldive Odd History: The Maldive Archipelago, Vols. 1 to 4* (Stockholm: published privately by Lars Vilgon, 1992–93).

Paul A. Webb. *Maldives, People and Environment* (Bangkok: Media Transasia, 1988).

Malgal *See* MOHE.

Manchus (Baqi, Jurchens, Man, Manju, Manzhouren, Manzu, Nuzhen)

ORIGINS

The Manchu people were originally a group of Tungusic clans from Manchuria, in northeast China. Their early ancestors included the Sushen, the Yilou, the Wuji, and the MOHE. In the 12th century, a Mohe tribe named the Heishui became the JURCHENS, the most direct ancestors of the Manchus. In the mid-17th century a leader named Hong Taiji, in an effort to continue his father's consolidation of the clans under one authority, renamed all of his followers Manchus. Many of the Manchus traced their ancestry to the Jurchens, but the new ethnic designation also incorporated ethnic MONGOLS, HAN Chinese, and eventually RUSSIANS who had joined or been absorbed by Manchu martial and administrative groups known as *banners*. Many scholars believe that Hong's decision to name all of his followers Manchus, regardless of ethnic background, indicates that the identity was more accurately a political designation than a cultural category at first. After the Manchus founded the Qing dynasty, the ruling elite devoted more attention to strengthening and validating the cultural and genealogical elements of their identity. For example, *Researches on Manchu Origins,* which aimed to formalize Manchu history and mythology, was completed under the rule of Emperor Qianlong. Over the following centuries, Manchu identity took root, and currently more than 10 million Chinese citizens identify themselves as part of this group, one of the largest in China.

HISTORY

Manchu history is a combination of individual clan histories and the common history of the Qing dynasty. In the 12th century, Jurchen leaders established the Jin dynasty and adopted some Chinese administrative systems, including civil service exams and a legal code similar to that of the Tang dynasty (618–907). The Jin dynasty, which did not incorporate all of the Jurchen tribes, lasted a bit more than 100 years before falling under the sway of the Mongol Yuan dynasty (1279–1368). At its peak, the Jin dynasty controlled what is now northeastern China, in addition to parts of Mongolia and Siberia.

In the early 15th century a group of the eastern Jurchen tribes came together to form another association, the Jianzhou Federation. In the late 16th century the Jianzhou leader Nurhaci began to emphasize his connection with the Jin Jurchens and draw on this legacy to unite and motivate the Jianzhou Jurchen clans under his leadership. This emphasis on continuity across clan divisions was key to his effort to unite the disparate groups under a single authority. Nurhaci also sought to strengthen Jurchen allegiance by gradually replacing the existing clan system with a system of eight banners who performed both martial and administrative tasks in various regions of the country. In the early 17th century, when the Jianzhou armies seized more Chinese territory and began to absorb more Han Chinese into the existing Jurchen banners, ostensibly Han and later Mongol banners were created, although their ethnic composition was still mixed. Nurhaci's successor Hong Taiji used this system in 1636 to officially designate all of his followers as Manchus, regardless of their ethnic origins. Scholars believe that the urgency of the Manchu court to systematize clan origin and draw on a common genealogy indicates the relative weakness of other unifying traits among the people who were now all classified as "Manchu."

These newly designated Manchu armies gradually pushed back the Chinese Ming forces, and in 1644 they established the Qing dynasty, with Beijing as the capital. They solidified Manchu rule by combining military leadership with some elements of the Ming civilian bureaucracy. Over the next few decades, in a further effort to utilize genealogy to reinforce a common identity, the ruling imperial clan, the Aisin Gioro of the Prime Yellow Banner, worked to strengthen Manchu identification with their ancestors as well as with the Changbai Mountains, which the Manchus identified as the ancestral home of the Aisin Gioro.

Some modern scholars argue that conscious distinctions between the Manchu and Han political elite eroded further over the course of the 19th century in the face of foreign and domestic challenges to the Qing dynasty. Others argue that the Taiping Rebellion and the 1911 revolution that finally brought down the dynasty reinforced an already independent Manchu identity. The rhetoric of the Taiping Rebellion and the 1911 revolution identified the Qing dynasty and the Manchus as sources of China's contemporary troubles and weaknesses that contributed to the country's inability to face European colonial advances. For example, Sun Yat-sen, who founded the Chinese Republic in 1911, stated that "in order to restore the Chinese nation, we must drive the barbarian Manchus back." In the early 20th century, many Manchu families became targets of Han anger, and many chose to disassociate themselves from their ethnic heritage and assimilate into largely Han communities.

Today many Manchu have essentially become Han in their linguistic and cultural outlook on life. At the same time, recent censuses have found more than 10 million people continue to identify themselves as Manchu or Man, despite speaking Mandarin or other Chinese dialects.

CULTURE

The Manchu language in the 21st century is in danger of extinction and is spoken only by a few dozen native speakers. Manchu is an agglutinative language and part of the Tungusic language family. Most spoken and written words originate from the Jurchen language, but in tribute to the cultural integration between the Manchus and other ethnic groups, there are also a number of loanwords from Mongolian and Chinese. The written alphabet was commissioned by Manchu leader Nurhaci in 1599 and drew heavily on both Mongolian and Jurchen. The traditional script is written in vertical columns that proceed from left to right, and most of the letters have multiple forms depending on their position in a word and their proximity to vowels. Many Manchu people also speak and write Mandarin Chinese. During the 18th and 19th centuries the Manchu elite initially sought to protect the status of their language, and formal imperial documents were written in both Manchu and Chinese. However, by the late 19th century even the imperial court, which

was predominately Manchu, rarely spoke the language. Thanks largely to the Internet and to Manchus' renewed interest in this link to their ethnic heritage, lessons in the Manchu language are becoming more popular, but there are still

Manchus time line

C.E.

1115 The Jurchen tribes establish the Jin dynasty.

1234 The Jurchen Jin dynasty falls to the Chinese Yuan dynasty.

1583 Gioro clan leader Nurhaci (also spelled Nurhachi or Nurgaci) begins to unify the Jurchen tribes.

1599 Nurhaci commissions what becomes the Manchu alphabet.

1616 Nurhaci establishes the Late Jin dynasty and unifies the Jurchen tribes under a military banner system.

1620s Nurhaci conquers Mukden (Shenyang in modern China) and makes it the capital.

1635–36 Nurhaci's son and heir Hong Taiji reorganizes his followers and formally names them the Manchu; he also changes the name of the dynasty from Late Jin to Qing.

1644 The Qing army captures Beijing and makes it the new capital.

1662–1722 Rule of Emperor Kangxi; as part of their territorial expansion, the Manchus annex Taiwan and invade Tibet.

1668 Manchuria is closed to non-Manchu Chinese to protect the Manchu homeland.

1723–36 Rule of Emperor Yongzheng.

1736–95 Rule of Emperor Qianlong. During his reign, *Researches on Manchu Origins* is completed, Chinese Turkestan (currently Xinjiang) in western China is incorporated into the empire, and the imperial library catalogues 3,450 Chinese works during 20 years while destroying more than 2,000 works that the Manchu elite find offensive or subversive.

1800s The Qing government actively fights the opium trade.

1842 The Qing lose the first of the Opium Wars to the British and sign a treaty transferring control over Hong Kong to the victors.

1850–64 The Taiping Rebellion.

1858 The Treaty of Tientsin (Tianjin) ends the two-year Second Opium War with Britain; China is forced to concede more ports and trade privileges to the Europeans and to allow Christian missionary activity.

1895 Following their defeat by Japan in a short war, the Qing give up Taiwan.

1898 Coup and internment of the Qing emperor.

1900 The ruling Manchus tacitly support the Boxer Rebellion against the foreign presence in China.

1911–12 The Qing dynasty falls, and many Manchus are targeted and killed.

1931 Imperial Japan creates a puppet state in Manchuria called Manchukuo and designates a Manchu emperor named Puyi, although the population is predominately Han Chinese.

1957 Lao She, a leading Chinese writer of the 20th century and an ethnic Manchu, writes his famous play *Teahouse*.

Empress Dowager Cixi

Empress Dowager Cixi of the Manchu Qing dynasty ruled over China for 47 years, from 1861 to 1908, and her overly conservative, anachronistic policies are believed by many to have caused the ultimate downfall of imperial China. Born to Manchu parents in 1835, Cixi spent most of her childhood in Anhui Province before moving to Beijing. In 1851 she was selected by the Kang Ci imperial dowager consort to become a concubine for the new Xianfeng emperor and moved to the emperor's Old Imperial Summer Palace Complex, where she became Noble Lady Yi, a concubine of the second-lowest rank. She moved up in rank to Imperial Consort Yi when she gave birth to the emperor's only male son in 1856, and over time Cixi climbed the ranks to become Noble Consort Yi, second only to Empress Zhen. Upon the emperor's death during the second Opium War, Empress Zhen became Empress Dowager Ci'an and Noble Consort Yi became Empress Dowager Cixi.

Through manipulation and the forging of crucial alliances, Cixi managed to secure political power in court, and soon a formal request was issued to Cixi to "listen to politics behind the curtains," which essentially asked her to rule. While Cixi was open to a limited amount of change, she refused to accept anything that posed a potential threat to her power. In the early 1860s she encouraged westernization among her subjects and invited European teachers into China; however, she was shocked by the liberal thinking of people who studied abroad in the United States and promptly halted her campaign for Western education. When her son, Tongzhi, came of age, he proved to be a licentious and incompetent ruler, and soon after taking the throne, he died of smallpox. Shortly afterward, Cixi's nephew, Zaitian, was crowned Emperor Xuangu, but he also proved unsatisfactory to Cixi, who resumed her reign until her death in 1908.

very few native speakers. The largest group of speakers is an estimated 10,000 XIBE in western China, who are ethnically distinct from the Manchus but who speak a language that is almost identical to classical Manchu.

The Manchu people and their Jurchen ancestors engaged in some agriculture prior to the 17th century, but they were largely hunters, gatherers, and fishers. Since that time the majority in the northeastern provinces of Heilongjiang, Jilin, Liaoning, and Hebei have adopted settled agriculture and begun growing corn, soybeans, sorghum, tobacco, and various fruit crops. Many families also raise pigs, chickens, and a few other animals to supplement their crops for both subsistence and the market. Forestry and the lumber industry also employ a number of Manchu men in this region, while large numbers have migrated into China's northern cities to take up urban occupations in the professions, construction, and civil service.

The clan system that predated the *banner* system was one of the most persistent elements of Manchu identity and was arguably more influential for ordinary Manchus than subsequent Qing imperial prescriptions for Manchu cultural norms. Prior to the *banner* system, clan leaders were responsible for organizing hunting and farming as well as spiritual lives. Many Manchu clans practiced a combination of shamanism and Tibetan Buddhism. Shamans, who could be either male or female, were identified by a series of trials and were officially designated, often as members of the White Banner.

Marriage customs among the Manchu demonstrate, in part, the difficulties in preserving a distinct Manchu identity. Prior to the mid-1600s, Manchu marriage customs included the levirate, whereby male members of a household could marry the widows of their uncles, brothers, or fathers (excepting their birth mothers). However, this custom was later banned as Manchu society adapted to Han Chinese norms. During the Qing dynasty, the Manchu elite sought to balance this cultural adaptation with efforts to keep the Manchu identity distinct from the Han. For example, the Qing rulers limited Manchu marriage to members of the *banner* system and forbade marriage with civilian Han Chinese, except for a brief period between 1648 and 1655.

Manchu dress became another tool for preserving the distinct Manchu culture. Under the Qing dynasty, the Manchu elite introduced and mandated fashions such as a shaved forehead for men accompanied by a short pigtail or queue worn on the left as well as traditional Manchu clothing. While several of these fashions have been incorporated into broader Chinese history, items such as the queue became icons of Manchu rule and were targets of anti-Manchu sentiment in the early 20th century. As most Manchus sought to assimilate with their Han neighbors, traditional dress was replaced with more commonplace Chinese dress and norms. Today most Manchus continue to live in China's northeast, and new scholarship and resources are reviving their interest in renewing their connection to their Manchu identity, traditions, and language.

FURTHER READING

Pamela K. Crossley. *Orphan Warriors: Three Manchu Generations and the End of the Qing World* (Princeton, N.J.: Princeton University Press, 1990).

———. *A Translucent Mirror: History and Identity in Qing Imperial Ideology* (Berkeley and Los Angeles: University of California Press, 1999).

Mark C. Elliot. *The Manchu Way: The Eight Banners and Ethnic Identity in Late Imperial China* (Stanford, Calif.: Stanford University Press, 2001).

Mandayas (Dibabaons, Divavaonons, Magosans, Managosans, Mangrangans, Mangwangas, Mansakas, Pagsupans)

The Mandayas are a subgroup of the larger LU-MAD peoples of the highlands of Mindanao, the Philippines. Their name means "upland people" and refers to their homeland in Davao, Agusan, Surigao del Sur and del Norte, and parts of Cotabato in the highlands of eastern Mindanao. In the 1960s and 1970s many households adopted abaca hemp production and thus settled into permanent hamlets and villages. Prior to that the Mandayas lived in impermanent household settlements and engaged in shifting cultivation of rice, tubers, and tropical fruit. After small fields were cut from the forest, the vegetation was allowed to dry and then was burned away to leave a fine layer of ash as a natural fertilizer. Each year a new plot would need to be cut for rice and vegetables, while many tubers could be grown in a field for a second or third year. After that the fields would be allowed to sit fallow for up to a dozen years before the whole process began again. In addition to these plants, many households had use rights over several banana trees, and others kept a few chickens for food or dogs for use in hunting wild deer, pigs, monkeys, lizards, and birds.

Mandaya social organization traditionally centered on individual households, which could be nuclear families, polygynous families with multiple wives, or extended families of several generations. Regardless of their makeup, these households were fairly isolated from others, with distances of a sixth to a third of a mile between them. Above the level of the household, even prior to the settlement of most Mandayas into hamlets and villages, was the headman, or *bagani*, a man with considerable experience in warfare who had killed at least seven enemies in battle. The headman worked in conjunction with a council of elders in making decisions about warfare and raiding, judicial matters, and other community issues.

There is some disagreement in the literature about the dominant religion of the Mandayas, which is probably indicative of the number of different subgroups within the larger ethnic category. Some sources claim that many Mandayas adopted Christianity from the Spanish before the mid-19th century, while others claim the Mandayas are a non-Christian, non-Islamic people. Even the sources that claim Christianity is dominant among them, however, point to the large number of non-Christian beliefs and practices among them in the late 20th century.

Many still retain and believe in the power of wooden idols, called *manauag* and made from the wood of a *bayog* tree. Each idol is painted with tree sap from the chest upward and ensconced in a special altar within the house; these idols can be either female or male, with the distinguishing marker being a comb that adorns the former.

The Mandaya world is also inhabited by a large number of natural and ancestral spirits, called *anito,* who bring illness, death, and other misfortune to the Mandayas. Female spirit mediums, called *balyan,* communicate with these spirits to find out the cause of their grievances and how the afflicted person or his or her family can make amends and thus get better. Rituals for improved hunting, fishing, and farming are also common, as are life-cycle rituals marking coming of age, marriage, and death. Coming-of-age rituals have attracted the most Western attention because they require the youths to shave their eyebrows and file their teeth for beautification purposes.

Mangyans (Barangans, Buhids, Buids, Buquits, Lactans, Manghianes, Mangianes, Manguianes, Nauhans, Pulas, Tagaydans, Tirons)

Mangyan is a collective term for the eight tribal groups who live in the mountains of Mindoro Island, the Philippines. These eight groups are the Alangan, Bangon, Tau-Buid, Buhid, HANU-NOO, Iraya, Ratagnon, and Tadyayan.

GEOGRAPHY

Mindoro is the seventh-largest island in the Philippines and is located just to the south of Luzon. It is divided into two provinces, Oriental and Occidental, with a large chain of mountains, the Mindoro Mountains, running down the middle north to south and creating a natural boundary for these provinces; the Mangyans live in these mountains. The highest peak on the island is Mount Halcon at 8,482 feet, with Mount Baco a close second at 8,161 feet. Oriental and Occidental Mindoro differ significantly in their climates, with the former having no particular wet or dry season, while the latter is dry from November to April and wet for the remaining months.

ORIGINS

The origins of the Mangyans, like all Austronesian speakers in the Philippines, are probably in

MANDAYAS

location:
Mindanao, the Philippines

time period:
3000 B.C.E. to the present

ancestry:
Austronesian

language:
There are three separate Mandayan languages, all Meso-Philippines languages within the larger Austronesian family.

MANGYANS

location:
Mindoro Island, the Philippines

time period:
3000 B.C.E. to the present, though they may have been in Mindoro only since about 1200 C.E.

ancestry:
Austronesian

language:
There are eight different Mangyan languages. Iraya, Alangan, and Tadyawan are classified as Northern Philippine languages, while Bangon, Tau-Buid, Buhid, Hanunoo, and Ratagnon are Meso-Philippine languages; all are Austronesian languages.

Mangyans time line

B.C.E.

3000 The initial migration of the Austronesians to the Philippines, including the ancestors of the Mangyans.

1000 Approximate period in which the Mangyans adopt and adapt a script from India for writing their own poetry.

C.E.

1225 Chinese merchant Chao Ju-Kua writes about his travels among the Mangyans in *Chu Fan-Chi*.

1572 Spanish captain Juan de Salcedo arrives on Mindoro, beginning more than 300 years of colonial exploitation among the Mangyans.

1899 The Spanish cede the Philippines to the United States, and a local war of independence breaks out.

1902 A civil U.S. administration replaces military rule upon the pacification of the independence fighters.

1908 U.S. Secretary of the Interior Dean Worcester sues the Filipino newspaper *El Renacimiento* for libel because of an editorial by Don Fidel A. Reyes called "Aves de Rapina," about the U.S. administration in Mindoro.

1941 The Japanese occupy the Philippines during World War II.

1944 The United States retakes the Philippines.

1946 The Philippines attain independence from the United States.

1969 The New People's Army is formed as the military arm of the Communist Party of the Philippines.

1986 Corazon Aquino comes to power in the Philippines.

south China, from where they sailed in double-outrigger dugout canoes to Taiwan about 5,000 years ago, and then later to the Philippines and Polynesia. There is no certainty as to why this population left south China; however, archaeologists have hypothesized that it was a combination of population pressure, increased commerce coming from the Yangtze (Chang) River region of China and southward down the river and its tributaries, a growing demand for marine and tropical forest goods, and climate change.

Contemporary Austronesian languages can be subdivided into two distinctive groups that separate the languages of Austronesian Taiwan from those of the remainder of the family, which include all Malay and Oceanic languages. This linguistic division, in addition to several anomalies in the archaeological record, such as a lack of rice in the earliest Austronesian sites in Taiwan, indicates that the origins of the Austronesian people may have been two separate exoduses from southeast China. If these did occur, the first exodus was probably from Fujian Province in China to Taiwan, which saw the rise of the TA-P'EN-K'ENG CULTURE, with its distinctively marked pottery and stone tools, but without archaeological evidence of domesticated rice. The descendants of this first wave would be the contemporary speakers of Taiwan's Austronesian languages, the ABORIGINAL TAIWANESE people. The second exodus may have occurred around 3000 B.C.E., taking a second wave of Austronesian speakers from southeastern China to Taiwan and then almost immediately to Luzon in the Philippines around the same period. This second wave, with its red-slipped pottery, may also have been the ultimate source of the LAPITA CULTURE.

HISTORY

When they arrived in the Philippines about 3000 B.C.E., the Austronesian speakers would probably have met small bands of people who had already been residing on the islands for approximately 20,000 years. The hunting and gathering AETA peoples, as they are now called, probably lived in the most productive areas of the country, the coastlines, valleys, and lower hills, in very small, impermanent settlements. With their ability to grow their own crops, the incoming AUSTRONESIANS were able to maintain significantly higher population densities than the Aeta and thus push the hunter-gatherers into the more marginal highland forests and mountaintops, where they still live today. The numerically and technologically stronger agriculturalists also seem to have lent their language to the Aeta, all of whom today speak Austronesian languages rather than the more ancient languages they would have brought with them in their much earlier migrations.

The various Mangyan peoples are believed to have lived in the coastal and lowland regions of the archipelago, south of Mindoro, until about 1300 C.E. What forced them to migrate north and into the mountains is unclear, but the most accepted hypothesis is that they were confronted with a more aggressive and numerous population in the south and chose migration rather than war. Subsequent actions by the Spanish and United States pushed the Mangyans further into the mountains and away from the coastal populations with whom they traded and interacted upon arriving on Mindoro.

Prior to the arrival of the Spanish in the 16th century, the peoples of Mindoro, including the Mangyans, engaged in trade relations not only with local Austronesian tribes but also with visiting Chinese traders. The Mangyans dealt in cotton, root crops, beeswax, and various medicinal plants and received beads, gongs, plates, and jars in return. Chinese merchant Chao Ju-Kua wrote about his experiences in Mindoro in his text of 1225, *Chu Fan-Chi.*

While the Chinese engaged in relatively peaceful trade expeditions on Mindoro, the Spanish arrived in the 16th century with the purpose of colonization. Rather than trade for local products, especially gold, they subjugated the local population, charged high taxes, and forced the people into mandatory workforces. As a result many people fled into the mountains, temporarily swelling the local Mangyan population beyond its precolonial population density. Flight into the mountains also allowed the Mangyans to escape the attempts of Roman Catholic missionaries to proselytize and prohibit indigenous rituals, dances, and festivals.

In addition to their colonial project in the Philippines, on Mindoro the Spanish were also fighting against their old foe, the Muslims. One of the reasons suggested for the use of excessive Spanish force on Mindoro was the presence of Islamic traders and other peoples. For the Spanish, who had been fighting against the Muslims both at home and in the Middle East for several hundred years, the wars in the Philippines were just a continuation of the fight between Christianity and Islam. The Muslims often fought back with equal ferocity when they found their trade networks had been disrupted by the Spaniards or their access to gold and other resources had been cut off. As a result of more than 300 years of colonialism and Muslim-Christian warfare on Mindoro, the Mangyan population decreased throughout most of the period. Trade with the Chinese was completely cut off, and malaria and other diseases swept through the region occasionally, taking large numbers of people with them.

The end of the Spanish regime in the Philippines in 1899 did not bring an era of peace and prosperity to the Mangyan people. Early in the American colonial period the U.S. secretary of the interior, Dean Worcester, arranged for the sale of a large plot of land on Mindoro to an American sugar company. The perceived passivity and hardworking nature of the Mangyans tagged them as potential laborers on the new estate, and thus began many more decades of colonial exploitation. In the early 20th century an editorial published in a Filipino newspaper, entitled "Aves de Rapina" (birds of prey), denounced the actions of the American government and sugar company, with particular attention paid to Worcester. Not long after, Worcester sued the newspaper, *El Renacimiento,* for libel even though his name and title were never mentioned. Under the American regime the Mangyans were also moved onto reservations, similar to those created for Native Americans.

Filipino independence in 1946 and the creation of successive government administrations run largely by lowlanders in their own interests have left the Mangyans today struggling to maintain their way of life in the highlands of Mindoro. Many lost access to their ancestral lands when large multinational logging and mining companies moved through the area. Others have been displaced by natural disasters, mainly landslides caused by deforestation. The majority have a lower life expectancy, lower literacy rates in Tagalog, English, or Spanish, and lower income levels than the majority of Filipinos, especially the lowlanders. As they have done in the past, the Mangyans have tried to avoid the worst effects of these outside factors by turning their backs on the external world and living according to their own subsistence and cultural ways of life. Their ability to continue this strategy is probably limited to the next generation, but predictions of the end of Mangyan culture have been heard for more than a century and have come to nothing, so they may be able to find a way to move forward without complete assimilation into mainstream Filipino society.

CULTURE

The Austronesian migrants to the Philippines arrived from Taiwan bearing several domesticated plants, including rice, domesticated pigs, dogs, and chickens, and a lifestyle built around the agricultural calendar. Among the Mangyans, swidden, or extensive slash-and-burn agriculture, dominates the landscape, rather than irrigated farms on intensively used fields. Each season new fields must be cut from the mountain forests, allowed to dry, and then burned to provide fertilizer for the crops of upland rice, corn, beans, and sugar; secondary use of these fields results in crops of cassava, sweet potatoes, yams, and taro. The Mangyan form of swidden agriculture, which prohibits the cutting of virgin forest, has been studied extensively by anthropologists in the mid-20th to early 21st centuries and has been found to suit the landscape and climate of Mindoro perfectly so that land degradation and deforestation have not resulted from their subsistence practices.

Mangyan hamlets are generally made up of five to 12 nuclear family houses built above mountain streams and named after the family's oldest member. In addition to people—who are all related to one another through blood or marriage—pigs, chickens, and dogs also reside in and around the village where they can be watched by young children and the elderly. Kinship generally is considered bilateral as it is in the West, with both one's mother's and one's father's families contributing to each individual's kin network. At marriage most Mangyan men move into their wives' households for at least a few years, a pattern known as matrilocal marriage, but over time the new couple will reside in both families' settlements for at least short periods, a pattern sometimes called bilocal residence.

An important aspect of Mangyan traditional culture is the fact that they had their own writing system prior to their interactions with either the Chinese or the Spanish. Their script, called Surat Mangyan and based on an alphabet borrowed from India possibly as far back as 1000 B.C.E., is still used by the Buhid and Hanunoo to write indigenous poetry, known as *ambahan*, and songs.

FURTHER READING

Yasushi Kakuchi. *Mindoro Highlanders: The Life of the Swidden Agriculturalist* (Quezon City: New Day Publishers, 1984).

Violeta Lopez-Gonzaga. *Peasants in the Hills: A Study of the Dynamics of Social Change among the Buhid Swidden Cultivators in the Philippines* (Quezon City: New Day Publishers, 1984).

Severino N. Luna. *Born Primitive in the Philippines* (Carbondale: Southern Illinois University, 1975).

Mani (Forest People, Goy, Hoh, Mos, Negrito, Ngoh, Ngoh Pah, Sakae, Sakai, Seemang, Semang, Senoy, Siamang, Thai Mani, Tonga', Tongko)

MANI

location:
Trang, Phatthalung, and Satun provinces in the far southwest of Thailand, on the Malay Peninsula

time period:
At least 10,000 B.C.E. or earlier to the present

language:
Tonga', an Aslian language within the Mon-Khmer language family of the larger Austro-Asiatic phylum

The Mani are an ancient tribal people of Thailand, very closely related to the SEMANG of Malaysia in physical traits, culture, and language. Both peoples are short of stature, dark-skinned, with hair that resembles that of many black African populations; however, these groups are not Africans but Asians who migrated into their current homes long before the dominant MALAYS and THAIS.

In the mid-1990s there were still three groups of Mani people living a fairly traditional life in the Banthad Mountains of southern Thailand. They had suffered during the 1970s when the Thai government was fighting against communist insurgents in that region, and many relocated from Trang and Phatthalung provinces into a sanctuary in Satun province. But by the 1990s these groups had dispersed into the jungle-covered mountains once again to continue living by hunting and gathering, with only occasional forays into Thai villages to trade.

The heart of Mani social structure is the band, a loose-knit community defined by bilateral kinship and residence and made up of between 15 and 30 people. Within the band each nuclear family has its own hut, and all huts are built in a circle around the communal village center. Bands generally migrate together when lack of food or a birth, death, or illness within the village forces the group to move; they can also split if social discord or population growth requires it. Those who split from an established band may set up their own village and thus begin a new band, or they may move into a relative's band. Bilateral kinship patterns, which recognize all blood relatives equally, means that this move could be toward one's mother's or father's relatives; moving into one's in-laws' band is also an option. Leadership in the band comes from all adults; however, elders, men, and particularly an elected chief have more influence than youngsters, women, or others.

The traditional subsistence system of the Mani is hunting and gathering, or what is sometimes called food collecting. The vast majority of their calories come from the 10 different kinds of wild yams and potatoes available in their territory, which they supplement with other vegetables, fruit, and some meat. Hunting, while a very prestigious occupation, brings in food only every few days. All Mani food must be cooked before eating since they consider raw food to be uncivilized. Traditionally, all food was cooked merely by throwing it into the fire, the process that is still used with most meat. Today, however, using utensils traded or purchased from the Mani's Thai neighbors, boiling, roasting, and frying are additional methods of food preparation.

While bands do not own land, each group has usufruct rights over specific territories for hunting, gathering, and collecting firewood and water. In the past these rights would have been fairly strictly adhered to, but in the present, incursions by outsiders, including loggers, rubber tappers, and others, has meant that it is becoming more difficult for the Mani to maintain their way of life on their own lands. Incursions onto other bands' land does not bring retribution but a recognition that sharing and working together is a necessity in the face of such outside pressure.

As is the case among most small-scale societies, the Mani world is occupied by a large number of benevolent and malevolent spirits in addition to humans, animals, and plants. Evil spirits are believed to live in the jungle, and when a band migrates, ash from the last fire is rubbed onto the face and body of small children so that these spirits do not recognize them as human children and thus take them away. Most Mani groups also cremate their dead inside a specially built hut and then quickly migrate away from that spot, telling the spirit of the dead person not to follow them and bring them harm. The blood shed during birth is also believed to contain evil spirits, and thus as soon as possible after a birth, the band will abandon its place and move to a new one, again telling the spirits not to follow them.

Manobos (Manuvus)

The 15 different Manobo peoples are themselves part of a larger group of tribal peoples of the highlands of Mindanao, the LUMAD. They occupy the southern portion of the highlands region in the provinces of Cotabato and Davao as well as Agusan, Bukidnon, Misamis Oriental, and Surigao Del Sur. They are an ancient population of AUSTRONESIANS, probably having migrated to Mindanao before such groups as the IFUGAO and BONTOC arrived on Luzon. They were also among the first of the Lumad peoples to feel the reach of American colonialism in the 20th century when both Dole and Del Monte began operating banana and pineapple plantations; these industries were followed by sugar plantations and logging and mining companies. The long-standing military actions of the region's Muslim communities and more recent struggles of the New People's Army, the armed wing of the Communist Party of the Philippines, have also had grievous effects on Manobo communities and individuals, such as the creation of government hamlets as part of the struggle against insurgency.

Traditional Manobo life, as for all the Lumad peoples, centered on an agricultural way of life, growing highland dry rice and root crops such as sweet potatoes and cassava; today corn has become extremely important as well. Rather than permanent fields with irrigation systems and external fertilizers, the Manobos generally practiced swidden, or slash-and-burn agriculture, requiring them to move every few seasons as their farmlands became infertile. After a decade or more of the lands lying fallow, communities could return to a particular plot and start the process over again; however, the practice, sometimes called extensive agriculture, required each kin group to have access to a large amount of territory. In addition to using land for farming, kin groups also controlled hunting and fishing grounds, water resources, and the other necessities of life.

The kinship system traditionally at the center of Manobo social organization has been bilateral descent, similar to the system in the West. Both mothers and fathers are considered equally the source of ancestors and networks of contemporaries. This kind of system generally favors networks among closely related individuals such as first and second cousins from both sides, rather than lineage systems that can extend to fifth and sixth cousins on either one's mother's or father's side only, depending on which kind of lineage system is practiced. Generally kinship intersects with residence in the Manobo network system since villages are usually made up of people who are related to one another in some way. Each village would traditionally have had at least one chief, or *datu*, a man who could convince others to follow his lead in hunting, agriculture, or other activities; he also had to be seen as a fair judge for arbitrating disputes in the village. In addition to the chief, settlements would also have at least one religious specialist and healer, a large number of commoners who worked in the fields, and dependent children and the elderly.

Maonan (A-nan)

The Maonan are one of China's recognized 55 national minority groups. They live mostly in the Guangxi Zhuang Autonomous Region of Guangxi Province, a hilly region in southern China. This is not a monoethnic region as communities of HAN, YAO, ZHUANG, and HMONG also live there, which has led to significant cultural syncretism, particularly from the dominant Han. About 80 percent of all Maonan, or A-nan as they call themselves, have the same family name, Tan, and this group believes its origins are in Hunan Province, northeast of Guangxi. The other 20 percent have one of four different family names—Lu, Meng, Wei, and Yan—and believe their origins are in Fujian and Shandong Provinces, to the east of Guangxi. Generally each Moanan village is made up of people with the same family name and from the same clan.

Maonan economic activity centers on agriculture, which is very successful in their

MANOBOS

location:
Mindanao, the Philippines

time period:
3000 B.C.E. to the present

ancestry:
Austronesian

language:
There are 15 separate Manobo languages subdivided into central, north, and south subgroupings; all are Austronesian languages in the Southern Philippine subfamily.

MAONAN

location:
Huanjiang and Hechi Counties, Guangxi Province, China

time period:
Unknown to the present

ancestry:
Dong

language:
Maonan, a Zhuang-Dong language in the larger Sino-Tibetan language phylum

subtropical climate. Their major crop is wet rice, which they irrigate using the region's many streams and rivers; they supplement this crop with corn, wheat, sorghum, tobacco, cotton, sweet potatoes, and soybeans. Many families also keep beef cattle for the markets of Shanghai and Hong Kong. Those communities who live in the Dashi Mountain region struggle more than their lowland cousins due to lack of rain and tend to focus on drought-resistant crops such as corn and wheat rather than rice. Both before 1949 and after the 1980s economic reforms in China, the Maonan gained much of their income from beef cattle and crafts such as carving in stone and wood, bamboo products, weaving, and ironwork.

Maonan social structure is built around kinship. Kinship patterns are patrilineal, in which each person inherits membership in his or her lineage and clan from the father. Lineages are about five generations deep and require exogamy or marriage to somebody from outside this group of kin. However, clans, made up of groups of lineages, are not exogamous, and people with the same family name often marry each other. Before the communist revolution in 1949, marriage tended to be arranged by parents when children were just five or six years old, but the ceremony did not take place until the children were 12 or 13. Young wives remained at home until they gave birth to their first child and then moved into a neolocal residence or independent home with their husbands, except for those who married a youngest son, who was required to stay at home and care for his parents. These patrilocal marriages were more difficult for the young brides because they had to remain subservient to their mothers-in-law for many years, while those in neolocal residences had no one but their husbands to answer to. Regardless of their residence patterns, daughters were expected to return to their parents' home for New Year's Eve, the second day of the year, and several other holidays throughout the year. When they returned, they had to bring gifts such as wine, noodles, and meat to thank their parents for having raised them.

Maonan religion is similar to that of many other Chinese peoples in focusing on both ancestors and natural spirits. It differs from that of many, including the Han, however, in that the ancestors included on a family altar come from both the husband's and wife's family. Buddhist and Taoist beliefs also come into play in village rituals, and ceremonies celebrating the Lord of the Three Worlds along with his wife the Divine Mother are particularly important. Offerings of meat and wine are also given to the spirit of General Meng in order to protect people from illness or to drive the illness away after the fact. Each family holds at least one ceremony per year to protect themselves from misfortune and to thank the gods and spirits for their benevolence. Life-cycle rituals such as those for birth, marriage, and death are also held on an as-needed basis.

Maori (Te Maori)

The Maori are POLYNESIANS who began settling in the islands of today's New Zealand around 1000 C.E. after having sailed southwest from earlier Polynesian settlements in the Pacific. Maori legend describes the settlement process as coming in waves of canoes from Hawaiki, the mythical Polynesian homeland. Like other Polynesians, the Maori brought a number of domesticated plants and animals with them. However, the rich supply of game in the form of several species of flightless birds meant that the earliest phase of Maori settlement relied primarily on hunting. Once these birds, including the moa, were hunted to extinction after about 100 years, the Maori shifted their subsistence focus to the more traditional Polynesian practice of agriculture. In the northern, warmer islands of New Zealand, agriculture was successful and the Maori population flourished. In the south island, the climate was too cold for most traditional Polynesian crops, so a much sparser population survived primarily by fishing, food collecting, and a small amount of hunting. By the time British captain James Cook arrived in New Zealand in 1769, the total Maori population was between 100,000 and 200,000 people.

During the British colonial era, Maori society underwent considerable change. The activities of missionaries disrupted the traditional religious system, which, as with all Polynesians, was largely developed around the themes of ancestor worship, mana—the impersonal force that resides in all people and other beings—and *tapu*, or activities or things forbidden due to their sacredness or impurity. The English word *taboo* is derived from this Polynesian term. Another change came in the form of loss of land. Traditionally, all land was controlled by large kinship groups and tribes, with the fluid boundaries between groups serving as the most common source of frequent Maori warfare. With the arrival of British colonists, the majority of Maori land wound up in the hands of Europeans despite the Native (Maori) Land

MAORI

location:
Aotearoa (New Zealand)

time period:
About 1000 C.E. to the present; the exact date of earliest settlement is under considerable debate, with dates as early as 800 C.E. and as late as 1300 being considered.

ancestry:
Polynesian

language:
Te Reo Māori, often referred to as Te Reo, or the Language, an Eastern Polynesian language closely related to Tahitian

Maori time line

C.E.

ca. 1000–1200 The Maori settle the island group they call Aotearoa.

1642 Abel Tasman is the first European to see the Maori islands of Aotearoa and names them Nieuw Zeeland.

1790s European and American whalers establish permanent settlements on New Zealand, bringing diseases and trade goods that change Maori society forever.

1820s A decade of intertribal warfare brought on by the introduction of Western technology and population pressures caused by European diseases.

1840 The Maori sign the Treaty of Waitangi with Britain, granting that country authority over the islands and their people.

1845–47 The First New Zealand War between the Maori and Britain, in which the British are defeated at first but later come back and claim victory.

1858 The Europeans and their descendants outnumber the Maori in New Zealand for the first time.

1860 The Second New Zealand War breaks out over land disputes and continues off and on for 12 years.

1897 Two Maori parliamentarians from the Young Maori Party, Maui Pomare and Apirana Ngata, are named to cabinet positions.

1918 Maori prophet Tahupotiki Wiremu Ratana forms the Ratana Church with a fusion of Christian and Maori beliefs and practices. It proves to be popular primarily with poor and marginalized Maori.

1939–45 A Maori battalion fights in Europe and the Middle East and becomes a source of pride for many Maori.

1945 The Maori Social and Economic Advancement Act establishes tribal executives and committees that further integrate Maori social and political structures into New Zealand public life.

1961 The Hunn Report highlights the continuing social inequalities between the Maori and *pakeha* (people of European descent) in New Zealand's highly urbanized society.

1970s–80s Maori protests, including 1975's Maori Land March in the North Island, seek to highlight and redress injustices with regard to Maori land rights.

1982 Maori-language preschools are established to revive linguistic and cultural traditions.

1984 The Waitangi Tribunal begins investigating Maori land claims from as far back as 1840.

1985 Paul Reeves becomes New Zealand's first Maori governor general, the Queen's representative in the country.

Court, which was established in 1865 in order to translate Maori collective rights into the individualized system recognized by British law. Today only about 5 percent of land in New Zealand is held by Maori in communal ownership. In conjunction with this transformation, Maori residency patterns changed immensely, so that today the majority of Maori are urban dwellers in the North Island.

Despite these tremendous changes, not every aspect of Maori society has undergone a total transition from precolonial times. Maori kinship continues to follow the generational kinship structure of the HAWAIIANS, which is common throughout Polynesia. Contemporary Maori society consists of four different levels of organization: the extended family, or *whaanau,*

led by an elder; the subtribe, or *hapuu,* led by a chief; the tribe, or *iwi,* led by a junior paramount chief; and the confederation, or *waka,* led by a senior paramount chief. While there is considerable debate about the relative importance of all these levels of structure in the precolonial era, particularly the strength and permanence of the confederation of tribes, there is no doubt that extended families and tribes were at the center of Maori social organization from earliest times.

Another important aspect of Maori culture that has continued into the present and has even been adopted by some *pakeha* New Zealanders, particularly New Zealand's international rugby team, the All-Blacks, is the *haka.* This series of dance, chants, grunts, and slaps is associated with a number of different events in traditional Maori

Paul Reeves

Among his many accomplishments, Paul Reeves is best known for being New Zealand's first governor-general of Maori heritage. Born on December 6, 1932, Paul Alfred Reeves attended Wellington College and Victoria College, University of New Zealand, where he received a bachelor's degree in 1955 and a master's degree in 1956. In 1958 he received a licentiate degree in theology from St. John's College, Auckland, and became an ordained deacon. In 1959 he traveled to England, where he studied at St. Peter's College, Oxford, and was ordained into the priesthood in 1960. He returned to New Zealand in 1964 and taught church history at St. John's College, Auckland, and in 1971 he became bishop of Waiapu. From 1974 to 1976 he served as chair of the Environmental Council, and in 1980 he became archbishop and primate of New Zealand. In 1985 he was knighted by Queen Elizabeth II, who also appointed him that same year as the 16th governor-general of New Zealand, where he remained in office until 1990. After his retirement, he became the Anglican Consultative Council observer at the United Nations in New York, as well as assistant bishop of New York. Between 1991 and 1995 he served as the deputy leader of the Commonwealth Observer Group to South Africa; chair of the Nelson Mandela Trust; and chair of the Fiji Constitution Review Commission, which resulted in Fiji's readmission to the Commonwealth. Today Reeves is chancellor of the Auckland University of Technology.

culture, including psychological preparation for warfare and, on the other end of the spectrum, welcoming strangers. Dancers bulge their eyes, stick out their tongues, jump, slap their chests and thighs, and sometimes even brandish traditional Maori weaponry, all while chanting and grunting as a way of expressing whatever emotion that particular version of the *haka* is dedicated to.

See also NEW ZEALANDERS: NATIONALITY.

Mappilas (Mappillas, Moplahs)

The Mappilas are the indigenous Muslim population of the Malabar coast and Lakshadweep Islands, India. Their origins stretch as far back as the time of the Muslim prophet Muhammad, 570–632, when Arab traders brought their new religion with them to their numerous trading ports on the coast. The Mappilas are believed to have been the first Indian Muslims, about a century earlier than Muhammad Ibn Qasim's conquest of Sindh in 711–15.

Arabs had been visiting Malabar from ancient times and had intermarried with the local population and settled down as early as the fourth century. This trade declined in the sixth century, but by the time of the prophet in the early seventh century it was beginning to pick up again. The peak period of Arab-Indian trade in the region was the ninth through the 11th centuries. Many of these migrating Arab traders and settlers came from the Hadramawt Valley of Yemen, and many contemporary Mappila

families today can trace their ancestry back to traders from this region. As a result, both the Islam religion and the language of the Mappilas are more Arabic than other Indian Muslims, who were converted primarily by Persians.

After many centuries of peaceful Arab-Indian interactions in Malabar, the Portuguese arrived and disrupted the mutually beneficial trade relations that had been established. They first landed in 1498 seeking both souls to convert to Roman Catholicism and economic benefits, especially from the lucrative spice trade. In 1502 Vasco da Gama finally broke the economic power of the Arab and Mappila traders when his men seized two dozen ships, tortured 800 crew members, and burned them to death on their own ships. The Mappilas quickly declined from the wealthiest population in the region to simple peddlers of coconut and cloth. Taxes imposed upon them by Hindu landlords and political leaders reduced most to the edge of existence.

In 1792 the Portuguese were replaced by the British as the rulers of Malabar, and conditions for many Mappilas improved somewhat. They cooperated with the British administrators in the region and even paid for British protection against incursions by their Hindu neighbors. Nonetheless, relations with the British were not peaceful until the end of their rule in 1947. In 1921 Mappila resistance to colonialism burst forth in a violent uprising known by the British as the Moplah Rebellion. Interpretations of this event vary but tend to point to economic exploitation by both Hindu landlords and British colonials, though some commentators at the time of the rebellion also indicated that religious fanaticism was to blame, a discourse that is strikingly similar to many being repeated in the West since September 2001. As is the case today, mosques and other religious institutions provided rebellion leaders with access to people and resources, while religious solidarity provided the communal identity of those who rose up. However, religion itself seems not to have been the cause of the Mappilas' discontent.

As was the case in the early 20th century, Kerala today is heavily populated, probably overpopulated for the amount of food, jobs, and resources the state is able to produce. Unlike in the past, however, today's unemployed tend to be university or trade school educated rather than landless peasants, leading to significant outmigration from the state, especially to the Middle East. As was also the case in the past, agriculture remains the most important

MAPPILAS

location:
Malabar coast and islands, Kerala, India

time period:
Sixth and seventh centuries to the present

ancestry:
Arab and Indian converts to Islam

language:
Malayalam, a Dravidian language

occupation for most people. Cash crops of rubber, pepper, coconuts, cardamom, cashews, coffee, and tea bring in above-average incomes for those who control the land or obtain good rates as tenants. Most farmers also grow rice, sorghum, and a variety of legumes for their own use. For the Laccadive Mappilas, those who reside on the Lakshadweep Islands, coconuts are by far the most important crop, grown both for copra and for coir, the husky fibers used in rope, net, and other industries. Breadfruit, papayas, plantains, corn, yams, and a variety of other vegetables are also important subsistence foods grown in the region.

The Mappila kinship system in the past was dominated by the principle of matrilineal descent, whereby children were seen as members of their mother's line of descent rather than their father's and the central male figure in their life for purposes of inheritance was their mother's brother. This kinship pattern probably came to the Mappilas from the matrilineal Nayar community of Malabar, a Hindu caste group dominated today by professionals. Today most Mappilas on the mainland have adopted patrilineal forms of descent more common in the Islamic world and, indeed, throughout India. However, some wealthy Mappilas and many on the Lakshadeep Islands have maintained their adherence to matrilineality as the basis of their family structure. Whether matrilineal or patrilineal, family for the Mappilas remains the most important unit with which they identify, even when economic conditions have allowed them to move out of large, extended family homesteads and into nuclear family units. Loyalty to and reciprocal assistance with extended kin remain vitally important for identification as a Mappila.

Almost as important as family as a central characteristic of most Mappila communities is adherence to Islam. Most villages have at least one mosque and both formal and informal schools to educate their children in Arabic and the tenets of Islam. However, both modernization and the rise of the Communist Party in Kerala have weakened the power that mullahs have over their communities. Most people continue to observe Ramadan and Islamic birth, marriage, death, and burial rituals, and to avoid pork, but some other aspects of Muslim life are not always evident. Women are relatively free to seek work outside their homes, which has always been the case for poor or lower-caste women, but is also true today for middle-class or wealthy urban professionals. Polygamy, or a man having more than one wife, is not practiced, and many do not stop to pray toward Mecca five times per day.

FURTHER READING

Stephen Frederic Dale. *Islamic Society on the South Asian Frontier: The Mappilas of Malabar, 1498–1922* (New York: Oxford University Press, 1980).

R. H. Hitchcock. *Peasant Revolt in Malabar: A History of the Malabar Rebellion, 1921* (New Delhi: Usha, 1983).

K. N. Panikkar. *Against Lord and State: Religion and Peasant Uprisings in Malabar, 1836–1921* (New York: Oxford University Press, 1989).

Mara (Khongzai, Lakher, Magha, Maring, Shendoo, Shendu, Tlosai, Zao, Zho, Zyu)

The Mara are one of the SCHEDULED TRIBES of India, where they live primarily in the far northeast state of Mizoram; smaller numbers also reside in the nearby state of Meghalaya and in Myanmar (Burma). The British called them "Lakher," but they refer to themselves as Mara, and in Mizoram they were renamed according to this self-identification in the late 1980s. There are six subgroups of Mara who differ slightly from one another in language and culture.

Local legend states that the Mara migrated from the Chin Hills to the east of their current homeland between 300 and 400 years ago, presumably due to population and political pressures in that region. They became one of the largest and most powerful tribes in the hilly area of northeast India and were able to withstand pressure from the British for several decades. The British began their assault on that region in 1888, but it was not until 1924 that they finally subdued the Mara and brought them under colonial administrative control. At that time Christian missionaries also became active among them so that today the majority consider themselves Christian, specifically Protestant.

The economic base upon which Mara culture developed is based on swidden, or slash-and-burn agriculture, known locally as *jhum*. Each season the Mara would cut down a swathe of forest, allow it to dry, and then burn back the foliage to provide fertilizer for crops of corn, millet, dry rice, vegetables, spices, cotton, and tobacco. Most families owned a range of domestic animals, including cattle, pigs, dogs, and fowl, and hunting and fishing supplemented the diet considerably. While elephants, bears, snakes, and rats were hunted by men and consumed by all, dogs and goats could be eaten only by men, and horses, cats, tigers, and leopards could not be eaten at all.

Mara handicrafts include bamboo objects such as mats and baskets; metal farm implements and knives; cloth; jars; and, before the

---

MARA

location:
The states of Meghalaya and Mizoram, India, and Myanmar

time period:
Unknown to the present

ancestry:
Tibeto-Burman

language:
Mara Chin, a Tibeto-Burman language

introduction of modern weapons, bows and arrows. During the British period the Mara were also brought into the local and national economy through the sale of their rice, cotton, and sesame; this has been supplemented in contemporary times by bamboo, flowers, and lumber.

Mara society is divided into six named and hierarchical patrilineal clans into which each individual is born based on his or her father's clan membership. Ideally clans are groups of lineages that can trace their membership to a common male ancestor, but in this case the six clans each bear the name of an ancestor about whom nothing else has been remembered. In the past, clan solidarity was expressed through alliances in war and other intergroup conflicts, but today cohesion is evident only in the celebration of various life-cycle rites such as marriages, funerals, and births. Even strict clan exogamy is no longer the norm among the Mara, although few individuals marry someone from their own clan.

The primary group with which modern Mara identify is not a kin-based one but the village. Villages own considerable amounts of land, held by the village headman and used by residents with his permission. Each family also pays dues to the village for the use of the land, which are used for communal festivals and upkeep, and to maintain the headman or chief. Villages are generally built on hillsides and even in the past were relatively permanent because of the requirement of remaining near one's ancestors' burial ground. When swidden requirements involved using fields far from the village, each family would set up a temporary shelter to be used during intensive agricultural periods.

Maranao (Hiloona, Lanon, Maranaw, Ranao)

The Maranao are the largest subgroup of the FILIPINO MUSLIMS, with a population of nearly 1 million. Their name, which means "lake dweller" or "people of the lake," points to their original homeland around Lake Lanao in Mindanao.

Geography is important not only in the naming of this group but also in its history and social relations. As an inland people, the Maranao were among the last in the southern part of the Philippine archipelago to come into contact with Islam and subsequently to convert to the new religion. This does not mean, however, that their religion is not central to their identity. From the earliest Spanish period until the present day, many have resented the external control of the colonial and Filipino governments over their people and have worked in both peaceful and military organizations for the creation of an autonomous or even independent Muslim state in Bangsamoro, the Muslim homeland in the Sulu Archipelago, Palawan, and Mindanao.

Like most Filipinos, the Maranao are largely agriculturalists, as they have been since the earliest AUSTRONESIANS migrated into the archipelago. They grow dry, upland, and wet paddy strains of rice, corn, sweet potatoes, coffee, citrus fruit, cassava, and peanuts. Fishing in Lake Lanao from elaborate dugout canoes provided most protein in the past, but this has declined as soil erosion and other pollutants have affected fish stocks. Metal- and woodworking have long been male activities that have brought trade goods into the area, while Maranao weaving is famous throughout the country for its elaborate designs and brilliant colors.

Maranao social structure begins with the household, which can contain several families who all participate in food-sharing activities. These families are generally related to one another through bilateral kinship ties, which can come from either the mother's or father's side. Villages are usually thought of as kinship units rather than geographic ones, and they contain households that are all related through the various ties of bilateral kinship. Despite the difficulty of tracing genealogies very far back in history in a bilateral system because the number of individuals involved is so great, most families are able to trace their heritage back through both actual and fictive kinship ties to Sharif Kabunsuan, who brought Islam to the Magindanao and Maranao peoples. The importance of Islam is also visible in the villages, most of which are built around a mosque.

Despite the importance of Islam at many levels of society, the version of Islam practiced by the Maranao has many features that would not be recognized as part of that religion by most individuals outside the Philippines. Most Maranao still believe in a wide array of pre-Islamic nature spirits, especially those that control the agricultural cycle and the weather, and most villages have informal specialists who are able to communicate with these spirits to give thanks and request favors.

Marathi (Maratha, Marathe, Maharashtrian, Mahratti, Mahratta)

There is a certain degree of confusion inherent in studying the Indian ethnolinguistic group called the Marathi. Most but not all members of this group are also members of the caste group called Maratha, so that the two groups should

MARANAO

location:
North-central Mindanao, the Philippines

time period:
3000 B.C.E. to the present

ancestry:
Austronesian

language:
Maranao, a southern Philippine language within the larger Austronesian language family

be studied separately. However, the primarily Marathi-speaking kingdoms that were established in the Deccan region in the 18th century are usually called Maratha because they were dominated by members of this caste group, and this usage is adhered to here. In addition, residents of the Indian state of Maharashtra are also sometimes called Marathi instead of Maharashtrians, and vice versa, because the state was established in 1960 specifically based on linguistic affiliation; however, only about 65 percent of the state are speakers of this language, and so the two categories should remain analytically distinct. As much as possible, this entry focuses on Marathi speakers rather than on these other groups.

HISTORY

Although there is evidence of the Marathi language being spoken in the Deccan region of western India for more than two millennia, these people emerged from obscurity to rule their own kingdoms only in the 17th century. Shivaji Bhonsle's Maratha kingdom centered on the city of Pune, currently located southeast of Mumbai in the state of Maharashtra. From the 1660s, when Shivaji challenged the Mughal rulers in this region, Maratha chiefs were able to free themselves from service to the sultans of Bijapur and other places in the region and worked to consolidate the Marathan state. By 1674 Shivaji was crowned Lord of the Universe and became known as father of the Maratha nation, a title that is still used for him to this day. The Mughal ruler Aurangzeb, or Alamgir I, tried to subdue the Maratha for several decades, but by 1705 he had given up the fight; he died just two years later. The following decades brought more peaceful relations between the two Indian kingdoms, although the Maratha continued to expand to the east, taking much of Orissa and Bengal in the early 18th century, and to the south. By the mid-18th century, when armies of Afghans or PASHTUNS began challenging the Indian kingdoms for sovereignty on the subcontinent, the Mughals and Maratha had become allies against their common external enemy. In 1761 Afghan forces defeated those of the Indians at the battle of Panipat, and the Maratha gave up their dream of uniting the country and expanding their language beyond the Deccan.

Despite this great loss, various smaller Marathi-speaking kingdoms continued to survive in western India until the Third Anglo-Maratha War in 1818. Following Balaji Bajirao's loss to the Afghans, his second son, Madhav Rao, took up the mantle of *peshwa,* or prime minister,

the leading Brahmin position in the Maratha kingdoms from about the mid-18th century onward. Madhav won many important military victories against his rivals from Hyderabad, Mysore, and Nagpur. He also sent an expedition into north India and defeated the Jats, the dominant caste group at Agra and Mathura. Madhav Rao's successor, Narayan Rao, was murdered just one year into his reign, which began a period of chaos when various rivals for the position of *peshwa* plotted against one another and generally encouraged factionalism. This period also coincided with the First Anglo-Maratha War, which was settled only in 1782 with a Maratha victory over the British and their local allies. In 1784 a strong administrator emerged in the person of Nana Phadnis, who united the various chiefs and defeated the British yet again, this time in an isolated battle near Pune.

Fighting between rival chiefs at the turn of the 19th century again brought the British into the fray in the Second Anglo-Maratha War, but this time the British were victorious and gained territory for the British East India Company in

MARATHI

location:
India, primarily in the western state of Maharashtra

time period:
10th century C.E. to the present

ancestry:
Indo-Aryan

language:
Marathi, an Indo-Aryan language

Marathi time line
B.C.E.
1800 The Indo-Aryans begin to enter the Indian subcontinent from their homeland in Central Asia.
C.E.
10th century Marathi is first noted as the lingua franca of the entire region from Bombay to Goa.
1627 Shivaji Bhonsle, often known as the father of the Maratha nation, is born.
1660s Shivaji Bhonsle leads many campaigns against the Mughal Empire, resulting in his coronation as Chhatrapati, Lord of the Universe, in 1674.
1680 Shivaji Bhonsle dies.
1717 The Mughals sign a treaty with the Maratha, acknowledging the latter's dominance and sovereignty in the western Deccan region of India.
1761 Afghan forces under the nationalist Ahmad Shah Durrani defeat the Maratha.
1769 Madhav Rao restores Maratha power and territory in western India.
1775–82 First Anglo-Maratha War.
1803 Second Anglo-Maratha War.
1817–18 The Third Anglo-Maratha War eliminates the Maratha challenge to British power on the subcontinent.
1947 India achieves independence from Great Britain.
1960 The largely Marathi-speaking state of Maharashtra is created in western India.
2001 The Marathi-speaking population of Maharashtra is recorded at 65 percent in the national census.

Gujarat, Orissa, and Delhi. Just 15 years later the British and remaining Maratha chiefs went to war again, with the same result as in the Second Anglo-Maratha War. This time, however, the British dismantled the remaining Maratha territory, eliminated the position of *peshwa,* and brought the entire region under their colonial political and economic control.

During the colonial period in India, the rulers of more than 650 native states continued to dominate their own people in a form of administration that provided maximum profit for the British without their having to expend the forces or energy to engage directly with the entire population. Many Marathi-speaking principalities or states continued to exist throughout the period, which fostered a form of Marathi nationalism based on language, the glorious history of the Maratha kingdoms, and a national homeland. As a result, when India achieved its independence in 1947, the Marathi were among the leaders of the movement pushing for a linguistic basis for the country's divisions into states. In 1960 this dream was achieved with the creation of the predominantly Marathi-speaking state of Maharashtra, in India's western and central region. In 2001 this state was the country's second largest by population, with 96.8 million people, 9.42 percent of the country's total. It is also a much more urban state than the rest of India, with 42.4 percent living in an urban area in Maharashtra and 27.8 percent overall in India.

Contemporary Marathi-language poets continue to be honored throughout India for their prowess with the written word. Here Marathi poet Govind Vinayak Karandikar receives the 2003 Jnanpith Award from Indian president A. P. J. Abdul Kalam and L. M. Sangvi from the Bharatiya Jnanpith, a trust fund dedicated to literary awards. *(AP/ Saurabh Das)*

CULTURE

It is difficult to speak of a single Marathi culture beyond that fostered by the ability to speak its language; read its literature, which was first produced about 1,000 years ago; and watch its films. Devotional poetry and songs from the medieval period, 13th–17th centuries, as well as love poetry and heroic ballads from the 18th century are perennial favorites for the Marathi-reading public. Today the Mumbai film industry, sometimes called Bollywood, produces some Marathi-language films as well, though the heyday for this particular regional cinema in India was the 1960s.

Within the larger language category of Marathi are many caste divisions, including the Maratha and Kunbi, who are largely agriculturalists, and the Deshastha or inland Brahmins, who can be priests, teachers, or professionals. Each of these caste groups lives differently from others because of the ritual prohibitions associated with caste. Most groups are endogamous, meaning that individuals must marry within their own caste, and many have exogamous lineage and clan groupings within the subcaste group, limiting marriage partners even further, since people are required to marry outside these groups.

In general, however, all Marathi speakers are patrilineal: They trace their relatives through the male line only. Daughters inherit membership in their fathers' patrilineages but cannot pass that membership to their children. In fact, in some Marathi-speaking communities daughters lose their own patrilineal membership at marriage when they become subordinate members of their husbands' patrilineages. In Marathi, families are called *kul,* which refers to extended lineage groups rather than simply nuclear families. The next larger kinship group is the *devak,* clan-like groupings that worship a common deity and have a common totemic symbol to represent them; the most common symbols are elephants, cobras, and sword blades. Both *kul* and *devak* communities are exogamous. However, cross-cousins, the children of one's mother's brother or father's sister, are suitable marriage partners because they are outside these family groupings. It is also acceptable and in the past was very common for a man to marry his deceased wife's sister, though widows and divorced women are strictly forbidden from remarrying. Polygyny, the practice of having more than one wife, was also a common pattern among wealthier Marathi speakers in the past. This was the case for the wealthy only because Marathi marriages require men to give gifts of cash or other wealth to their new in-laws to compensate them for the loss of their daughters' domestic labor as a result of their patrilocal residence after marriage; new wives move into the homes of their husbands. Bride wealth also serves to bring legitimacy to any children the couple bears. Nonetheless, because marriage is seen as uniting not just two individuals but two *kuls,* gift exchange after the initial bride wealth is paid tends to go in both directions and is generally much more reciprocal than in the northern, HINDI-speaking regions of India.

Although these marriage and residence patterns are the ideal among most Marathi speakers, extenuating circumstances can sometimes bring about different outcomes. For example, among poor men, matrilocal residence after marriage, in which the man moves in with his wife's family, can sometimes occur so that the man works off his required bride price instead of paying with cash or gifts. This kind of marriage arrangement takes place most often when the wife's family has no sons to inherit the family home and land. In this case, the new son-in-law becomes the family's heir and takes over the farm or other duties upon the death of his father-in-law. Daughters are strictly forbidden to inherit property, so adoption, especially of a daughter's son, or matrilocal marriage are the only options available to a family that does not want its property to be taken over by distant members of the *kul* or *devak.*

Beyond the family and clan, Marathi communities are organized around villages. Most are made up of just one caste, with larger subcastes also sometimes organizing themselves into villages. Villages tend to have tight groupings of houses rather than the more spread-out pattern of many Bengali villages, with fields, orchards, and other agricultural land on the outskirts. The Indian state in which most Marathi reside, Maharashtra, is also India's most urbanized, so a large number of Marathi speakers also live in cities. Within urban areas, many neighborhoods are made up of a single caste or subcaste as well, although this pattern tends to

break down in wealthier urban neighborhoods. Urban residence can also affect where couples live after marriage, with wealthier couples establishing their own homes or apartments, called neolocal residence, rather than moving in with the husband's parents.

The dominant religion among the Marathi is Hinduism, although there are also a number of Marathi Christians, Muslims, and Buddhists. The Hindu majority looks to Siva, his consort Parvati, Maruti the monkey god, and Ganesh as their dominant gods, though Vishnu is also a common god in village shrines. There is also a wide variety of local deities, family spirits, ancestors, and evil spirits that occupy the dominant Marathi pantheon. Most people believe in the evil eye, ghosts, spirits, and other supernatural beings that can bring either harm or increased well-being depending on their mood or desire for a gift. Religious specialists include Brahmin priests, who inherit their positions and deal with major Hindu gods and goddesses and the rituals associated with them; they also conduct birth and purification ceremonies associated with childbirth and death rites. Most Marathi communities also have a number of shamans who are called to their roles through special skills for communicating with the spirit world; they tend to deal with the lesser deities, spirits, and ghosts.

FURTHER READING

Anthony Carter. *Elite Politics in Rural India: Political Stratification and Alliances in Western Maharashtra* (Cambridge: Cambridge University Press, 1974).

Randolf G. S. Cooper. *The Anglo-Maratha Campaigns and the Contest for India: The Struggle for Control of the South Asian Military Economy* (New York: Cambridge University Press, 2003).

J. G. Duff. *History of the Mahrattas* (London: Longman, Rees, Orme, Brown, and Green, 1826).

Mahadav Govind Ranade. *Rise of the Maratha Power* (Bombay: University of Bombay, 1962).

Rao Bahadur Govind Sakharam Sardesai. *New History of the Marathas,* 3 vols. (Berkeley and Los Angeles: University of California Press, 1957).

Mardu (Martu, Mardudjara, Martujarra)

The Mardu are a subgroup of the larger AB-ORIGINAL AUSTRALIANS. They are the traditional inhabitants of territory around Lake Disappointment, the Rudall River, and Percival Lakes in the Western Desert of Western Australia. They have occupied this territory for at least 30,000 years and perhaps as long as twice that time. They were some of the last Aboriginal

MARDU

location:
The Western Desert of Australia

time period:
At least 30,000 B.C.E. to the present

ancestry:
Asian origins but so far in antiquity that their exact ancestry is unknown; they do have some genetic markers that indicate an ancient connection to New Guinea Highlanders

language:
English is the official language of Australia. The Aboriginal language is Martu Wangka, a Western Desert language that is still spoken by many Mardu.

Australian groups to encounter Europeans and their Anglo-Australian descendants when limited contact began in the early 20th century, with some Mardu having this experience for the first time as late as the 1970s. They were largely left alone at the start of the colonial era in Australia because their territory offered nothing the white people wanted, although this did not stop colonizers from building missions, removing children, and otherwise undermining Mardu society. The well-known film *Rabbit Proof Fence* as well as the book on which the film was based documented the experiences of one Mardu family during what became known as the period of the Stolen Generations. In the 1960s, drought and external pressure drove many Mardu into the outstation camps of Jigalong and a number of others, where many remain today. Many camps have a variety of western amenities, including schools, clinics, and stores, but most Mardu continue to prefer camping and hunting-gathering to adapting fully to "white fella" ways.

Mardu social structure emphasizes the importance of kin groupings. Mardu kinship is bilateral in that they recognize and give equal attention to the ancestors of both mothers and fathers. Like all Aboriginal Australians, they practice a form of classificatory kinship, in which mother and her sisters are structurally equivalent to one another but different from father's sisters, while father and his brothers are equivalent to but not the same as mother's brothers. They therefore link parents with some, but not all, people whom westerners would consider aunt and uncle. The preferred marriage partner is a first or second cross-cousin—that is, the children of one's mother's brother or father's sister. Girls are not allowed to marry until after their first menses, while boys must undergo four stages of initiation before being considered marriageable: nose piercing, circumcision, penile subincision, and a final stage of maturation.

As the preferred subsistence method, hunting and gathering remain extremely important, bringing in between one-quarter and one-half of all calories. These activities are even more important during ritual times than on ordinary days. Both women and men among the Mardu participate in hunting; however, they do so in different ways. They both travel to hunting sites by vehicle nowadays, but while women tend to focus their hunting on small animals, utilizing wood or metal digging sticks, men focus on larger animals utilizing rifles. Women also use fire in their hunting, burning off spinifex grass in lines of about three square miles to reveal the burrows and trails of goannas, skinks, pythons, and even feral cats. This kind of burning off has been proved to be an extremely important long-term land-management strategy in the desert regions of Australia, increasing plant diversity and animal populations, as well as a short-term hunting strategy. Combining this hunting with their gathering activities, Mardu women contribute between 60 and 80 percent of the total food collected, most of which is eaten by small family units. Men's activities, on the other hand, hunting kangaroo and emu with small rifles, bring in small amounts of food but of a higher status. The meat of these animals gets shared with the larger community, providing successful hunters with a path to prestige and high status.

See also AUSTRALIANS: NATIONALITY.

FURTHER READING

Robert Tonkinson. *The Mardu Aborigines: Living the Dream in Australia's Desert,* 2nd ed. (Forth Worth: Holt, Rinehart and Winston, 1991).

Marshallese (Marshall Islanders)

The Marshallese are the indigenous people of the independent country of the Marshall Islands, which is located in the North Pacific Ocean between the Northern Marianas and Federated States of Micronesia to the east, the Gilbert Islands of Kiribati to the south, and Hawaii to the northeast. The Marshallese speak a Micronesian language and are the descendants of migrants from the original populations of AUSTRONESIANS who left south China between 5000 and 500 B.C.E. Their immediate ancestors probably hailed from eastern Melanesia and parts of Kiribati. The date of this migration is still uncertain, with estimates ranging from as early as 2000 B.C.E. to as recently as the first years of the common era.

The traditional society of the Marshallese is highly structured and hierarchical with head chiefs (*iroij*), ordinary chiefs (*burak*), magistrates (*leataketak*), and commoners (*kayur*) making up the four immutable ranked positions. Membership in one of these classes is inherited from one's mother in a matrilineal system of descent, as is membership in one's clan, which determines the land one can either own or use for subsistence, depending on one's class. Clan membership also determines marriage partners to some extent because it is forbidden to marry someone in one's own exogamous clan.

MARSHALLESE

location:
Marshall Islands

time period:
Perhaps 2000 B.C.E. to the present

ancestry:
Austronesian

language:
Marshallese; English is also used throughout all the islands and atolls

As is evident, kinship is still the most important social category in defining each individual's relationship to every other Marshallese person. Even within families, kinship relations determine with whom the Marshallese must be formal and reserved and with whom they can joke and speak informally. Brothers and sisters, in addition to parallel cousins (the children of two sisters or two brothers) in traditional Marshallese society are expected to maintain a formal relationship within which joking, especially of a sexual nature, is strictly prohibited; the same is true of the relationship between a man and his wife's brother, which is perhaps the most formal relationship of all. Conversely, cross-cousins of the opposite sex (children of a brother and sister) are expected to maintain extremely informal and joking relationships; these cousins are also the ideal marriage partners. Grandparents and grandchildren can also have informal and joking relationships, while people of adjacent generations, parents and children, must remain formal with one another. A married woman can joke with her husband's brother, and her husband can joke with his wife's sister. While some of these social rules have been bent and broken over the course of the colonial and postcolonial eras, *manit*, or Marshallese custom, remains extremely important for many individuals. Chiefs still hold considerable power in Marshallese society, serving as the first two elected presidents of the republic, and traditional land tenure is still maintained on many islands and atolls.

While *manit* has served to preserve many precolonial aspects of Marshallese society, it has also preserved some features from the colonial era as well. When the first missionaries arrived in the Marshall Islands, they introduced the important dates of the Christian calendar, particularly Christmas and Easter. The indigenous interpretation of Christmas, Kuirijmoj, continues to serve as a central organizing event for much of the Marshallese calendar of traditional events. Kuirijmoj, however, is not Christmas, which is also celebrated by the largely Christian Marshallese, but rather a huge communal party in which individuals, lineages, and clans seek to outdo one another in their sponsorship of feasts and events. The entire event is seen as a competition with the goal of overwhelming one's rival clan or lineage with food and hospitality; there are also competitions in singing, dancing, and other arts and crafts. The event takes at least a third of the year to organize and uses up a third of a community's resources.

See also MARSHALL ISLANDERS: NATIONALITY.

Marshall Islanders: nationality
(Marshallese, people of the Marshall Islands)

GEOGRAPHY

The Republic of the Marshall Islands is made up of two separate archipelagos, the Ratik ("Islands toward the dawn") and Ralik ("Islands toward the sunset") chains, made up of 29 atolls and five islands in the North Pacific Ocean. The Northern Marianas and Federated States of Micronesia lie to the east, the Gilbert Islands of Kiribati to the south, and Hawaii to the northeast. Together the islands and atolls constitute just 75 square miles of land, about the same area as Washington, D.C., within about 375,000 square miles of ocean.

The Marshall Islands were an important site for the U.S. Defense Department. The island of Kwajalein was a major battleground during World War II and is still used as a U.S. missile test range. Bikini and Enewetak atolls are both former U.S nuclear test sites.

INCEPTION AS A NATION

Although the date is uncertain, the first inhabitants of the Marshall Islands probably sailed from eastern Melanesia and the region of Kiribati and landed in their new home in the last years before the start of the common era; some sources argue the origins are much earlier, around 2000 B.C.E. These origins are based on both linguistic and cultural similarities to peoples in those regions. Like many other Pacific societies, the Marshallese lived in a ranked society in which head chiefs and lesser chiefs dominated both political and economic life while commoners engaged in subsistence agriculture and fishing.

The colonial era did not begin suddenly in the Marshalls but rather slowly and stealthily from 1529 onward. In the 16th century Spanish explorers and traders landed on many of the islands and atolls but did not stay longer than needed to trade for food and other resources before sailing away again. More extensive colonizing occurred after 1788, when British sailor John Marshall landed and named the paired archipelagos after himself. He was followed in 1816 by a Russian ship, whose German-Estonian captain, Otto von Kotzebue, stayed in the islands long enough to record the first ethnographic information about the people and their way of life. Real change was introduced in 1857 when Reverend Hiram Bingham, Jr.,

MARSHALL ISLANDERS: NATIONALITY

nation:
Marshall Islands; Republic of the Marshall Islands

derivation of name:
Named for British sailor John Marshall, the first European to land on the islands in 1788

government:
Republic, in free association with the United States since 1986, amended 2004

capital:
Majuro

language:
Marshallese (official) 98.2 percent, other languages 1.8 percent; English is widely spoken as a second language

religion:
Protestant 54.8 percent, Assembly of God 25.8 percent, Roman Catholic 8.4 percent, Bukot nan Jesus 2.8 percent, Mormon 2.1 percent, other Christian 3.6 percent, other 1 percent, none 1.5 percent

earlier inhabitants:
None.

demographics:
Marshallese 98 percent; other Pacific Islanders, Asians, Caucasians, and other 2 percent

Marshall Islanders: nationality time line

B.C.E.

2000–0 The first humans arrive on the Marshall Islands, probably from eastern Melanesia and Kiribati.

C.E.

1526 The islands are claimed for Spain by Alonso de Salazar.

1529 Spanish sailor de Saavedra lands on the islands; he is followed by several other Spanish explorers, who visit many of the islands and engage in trade but do not establish settlements.

1592 Spain lays formal claim to the islands.

1788 The Marshall Islands are named for British captain John Marshall.

1816 Captain Otto von Kotzebue, sailing on a Russian ship, lands in the Marshall Islands and records the first ethnographic information about the inhabitants.

1857 Hawaiian missionaries from the American Board of Commissioners for Foreign Missions begin proselytizing, and within 40 years they have established churches on most inhabited atolls in the region.

1885 After setting up the first trading post in the Marshall Islands, Germany buys the islands from Spain as a protectorate.

1914 Japan takes over from Germany and sets up its own commercial interests.

1922 The Marshall Islands become part of Japan's League of Nations Mandate in the Pacific.

1942 The United States attacks Japan's fortified holdings throughout the Marshall Islands; three years of fighting ensue before the Japanese surrender.

1946–58 The United States tests 67 nuclear and hydrogen bombs on Bikini and Enewetak atolls.

1947 The Marshall Islands become part of the United States Trust Territory of the Pacific Islands, along with the Caroline Islands (current Federated States of Micronesia) and Mariana Islands.

1979 The Marshall Islands become self-governing with the establishment of an independent government.

1982 The name of the Republic of the Marshall Islands is adopted.

1983 The United States pays $183.7 million in damages to the Marshall Islands for harm caused by nuclear testing.

1986 The Republic of the Marshall Islands signs the Compact of Free Association with the United States.

1991 The Marshall Islands join the United Nations.

2000 Kessai Note becomes the first commoner to be elected president; both prior presidents had been chiefs.

2004 The United States and the Marshall Islands sign an Amended Compact of Free Association.

---

atoll and island in the region. As a result, today most MARSHALLESE are Protestants.

Following this successful missionary venture, the Germans established the first trading posts in the region in the 1860s, which led them to purchase the islands from Spain in 1885 and hold them as a protectorate. The Germans were followed in 1914 by the JAPANESE, who occupied the islands during World War I and were then granted rights over them by the League of Nations in 1922. Throughout this period the Marshallese continued to lead relatively traditional lives, at least in terms of subsistence and the centrality of kinship. With the militarization of many of the atolls in the 1930s, however, their lives were disrupted. The Japanese built fortifications on many of the atolls and islands, using local labor and disturbing local land-tenure practices. Even more destruction was wrought between 1942 and 1945 when the United States and Japan fought many land and sea battles in the area of the Marshall Islands. Even today the wreckage of these battles is still evident in and around the lagoons of the area.

The postwar era brought more destruction to these atolls and islands. As part of the U.S. Trust Territory of the Pacific Islands, the Marshall Islands were used 67 times by the United States between 1946 and 1958 to test both nuclear and hydrogen bombs. The atolls of Bikini, from which the local population was evacuated in 1946 to make way for the testing, and Enewetak were both so damaged that nothing much remains of them, and they are unsuitable for human inhabitation. To repay the islanders for the destruction of their homes, the U.S. government paid $183.7 million in damages in 1983; a later settlement also compensated the former inhabitants of Bikini individually.

Throughout the 1970s and 1980s the United States and Marshallese negotiated the conditions of the islanders' independence, and in 1986 they achieved it, within the confines of the Compact of Free Association with the United States, which was amended in 2004. Under the compact, which was arranged jointly by the two governments, the United States must provide at least $57 million per year to the Marshall Islands until 2023. The United States was also made responsible for the security and defense of the Marshall Islands and operates more than 40 different government agencies on the islands, such as the U.S. Postal Service, Federal Aviation Administration, and Federal Emergency Management Agency (FEMA). For their part, the Marshallese use the U.S. dollar as

and missionaries from the American Board of Commissioners for Foreign Missions (ABCFM) set up their first mission on Ebon. They were extremely successful, and by 1900 there were ABCFM missions on almost every inhabited

On July 25, 1946, the United States detonated an underwater atom bomb, code-named Baker, at Bikini Atoll; this followed a prior explosion on July 1 of the same year. The two were part of the same program, Crossroads, and were the first of the more than 65 bombs tested in the Marshall Islands. *(AP/HO)*

their national currency and must allow the U.S. Defense Department to use Kwajalein atoll as a missile test range at least until 2066; also they cannot make further claims for compensation for the nuclear testing that occurred between 1946 and 1958 and must not engage in practices that contradict U.S. security and defense priorities. The agreement was renegotiated and extended in 2004.

CULTURAL IDENTITY

The two most important concepts within Marshallese cultural identity are *manit*, or Marshallese custom, and the centrality of the native land-tenure system. Within *manit*, one of the important features is the prestige and power of the *iroij*, the traditional chiefs. While traditional chiefs continue to serve alongside democratically elected parliamentarians and to play a lead role in local areas, even at the national level they are still the holders of most power. The first two democratically elected presidents of the Marshall Islands were themselves *iroij*. There has been a movement within parliament to limit the ability of the *iroij* to hold such positions, but so far the weight of custom has kept public opinion from supporting the proposal.

Chiefs and the clans they represent are also the owners of all land in the Marshall Islands. When the government renegotiated its Compact of Free Association with the United States in the early years of the 21st century, many people, chiefs and commoners alike, were angered at the administration's signing away the use of Kwajalein Island for another 50 years with-

out ever consulting the actual owners of those lands. The government and foreigners cannot own land in the Marshall Islands because all of it is held in the traditional land-tenure system of matrilineal clans and chiefs. For many Marshallese this overstepping of the government, in addition to numerous other incidents of the breaking of *manit* in the public sphere, is a frightening sign that they are losing their identity as Marshallese.

FURTHER READING

Francis X. Hezel. *The First Taint of Civilization: A History of the Caroline and Marshall Islands in Pre-Colonial Days, 1521–1885* (Honolulu: University of Hawaii Press, 1983).

Laurence Marshall Carucci. *Nuclear Nativity: Rituals of Renewal and Empowerment in the Marshall Islands* (DeKalb: Northern Illinois University Press, 1997).

Alexander Spoehr. *Majuro, A Village in the Marshall Islands* (Chicago: Chicago Natural History Museum, 1949).

Marwats

The Marwats are a subgroup of the PASHTUNS who live primarily in Pakistan's North-West Frontier Province (NWFP). The Marwats are further subdivided into 20 *khels*, or tribal kinship groups who trace their descent through the patriline. Women are members of their father's *khel* but cannot pass that membership to their children, who are automatically members of their father's *khel*. In the district of Lakki Marwat, the Marwats are the political and economic leaders.

MARWATS

location:
District of Lakki Marwat, North-West Frontier Province, Pakistan

time period:
Unknown to the present

ancestry:
Pashtun

language:
Marwat, a dialect of Pashtun

Most Marwats continue to live as subsistence farmers, growing wheat, corn, sugarcane, vegetables, melons, and dates on small plots. Some farmers have access to irrigation water from canals that run from the Baran Dam or Kurram River, but most rely on wells sunk on their property or on rainfall. Rainfall is the least reliable method in a region that is considered arid to semiarid and can be about 100°F most days in June.

In recent decades, with the political instability in nearby Afghanistan and an influx of Taliban members in Pakistan's NWFP, many young men have left the area to seek work in the Middle East and beyond. Many have gained work in Pakistan's civil service or military as well. There is a very limited industrial sector in Lakki Marwat, including a cement factory, two flour mills, seven ice factories, and one each of textile and edible oil mills.

In the 21st century the Marwat community has experienced significant division between those who support the Talibanization of their society and those who oppose the Taliban's draconian policies. In 2007, two music stores in Lakki Marwat were firebombed for selling Western music, and an English-trained obstetrician-gynecologist experienced significant harassment for having opened a clinic for pregnant women and infants; he has been accused of being a Western spy. Individual musicians also experience harassment at the hands of both local and Afghanistani Taliban, and as a result most have either quit or moved away to play in other parts of Pakistan.

Massagetae (Great Saka)

The Massagetae were related to the Saka, a subgroup of the larger SCYTHIANS, nomadic Iranian-speaking people who occupied the steppes of Eurasia between the Tian Shan mountains and the Black Sea. We do not know what they called themselves; "Massagetae" is the Greek ethnonym assigned to them by Herodotus, a fifth-century B.C.E. Greek historian who visited much of the ancient world and wrote about his experiences from a Greek perspective. Almost everything we know about the Massagetae comes from Herodotus's writings, and as he never traveled to Central Asia, he was relying on hearsay for his information about the Massagetae. Although contemporary scholars have associated the Massagetae with various nomadic groups mentioned in Chinese records, and various sites of the period have been exca-

vated in Central Asia and Siberia, none of the archaeological remains can certainly be associated with them.

The Massagetae probably lived in the plains east of the Caspian and north of the Oxus River or Amu Darya, which currently divides Uzbekistan from Kazakhstan, and must have resembled other Scythian tribes in their nomadic way of life. They probably herded horses and cattle and caught fish as a protein source. Herodotus wrote that milk was their primary beverage, possibly in the form of koumiss or fermented mares' milk, which was a common beverage among the steppe nomads. Herodotus also stated that the Massagetae each had one wife but held all their wives in common, a custom that he found strange. Still stranger, according to Herodotus, was their practice of sacrificing old people and eating them. Those who died of disease were considered unlucky; they were not eaten but buried in the ground.

Herodotus claimed that the Massagetae were reputed to be fierce warriors. They no doubt used the same weapons as the other Scythian subgroups—battle-axes, bows and arrows, and spears. The Scythians carried a short compound bow, a technological advance on the longbow known in the civilized centers of the ancient world. This bow was powerful and easy to carry in a *gorytus,* or bow case slung off a rider's belt; it was designed to be convenient for shooting in all directions while on horseback and easily stowed away when not needed. This tactic suited the nomadic style of sudden, swift attack and just-as-sudden disappearance.

The Massagetae, stated Herodotus, had only one god, the sun, to whom they sacrificed horses. They used bronze, not iron, and were very fond of gold. Their weapons, armor, and horse gear were decorated with gold, a taste shared also by the Scythians on the Black Sea steppes, among other nomads, and a practical way for nomads to carry their wealth with them while also dazzling and impressing the enemy.

The Massagetae warrior best known to us was a woman, Queen Tomyris, who led the Massagetae against the invading Persians in the sixth century B.C.E. Cyrus the Great, the Persian ruler, had captured the queen's son in a previous skirmish, after which the disgraced prince committed suicide, and Tomyris vowed to avenge her son's death. Herodotus wrote that the Massagetae fought ferociously against the Persians; each side fired arrows at the enemy, and then everyone rushed forward to engage

---

MASSAGETAE

location:
Central Asia, especially the region northeast of the Caspian Sea and beyond the Amu Darya, the ancient Oxus River. Some sources say that the Massagetae at one time conquered the entire steppes, from Macedonia to the Tian Shan mountains.

time period:
First millennium B.C.E.

ancestry:
Indo-Iranian

language:
A Scythian language that belonged to the northeastern group of Iranian languages

in bloody, hand-to-hand combat, during which Cyrus was killed. Once the Massagetae had secured their victory, Herodotus claimed that Tomyris found Cyrus's body, filled an animal-skin bag with blood, and dipped Cyrus's head in it to avenge the capture of her son.

See also PERSIANS, ACHAEMENIDS.

Medes (Mada, Madai, Mdy, Anshan(?))

The Medes were an Iranian-speaking people whose empire incorporated territory in northern Iran, northern Mesopotamia, Afghanistan, and Armenia in the ninth through sixth centuries B.C.E.

GEOGRAPHY

The Median homeland was in northwestern Iran, centered around the city of Hamadan, which the Medes called Ecbatana, "Place of Assembly." Little archaeological evidence of the Medes has come to light, and because Ecbatana lies beneath the modern city of Hamadan, it has not been excavated. In the seventh century B.C.E. an ambitious Median king, Cyaxares, expanded his territory into Turkey, the Caucasus, and Afghanistan by conquering the Urarteans and other peoples in northern Iran and Armenia and the Assyrians in northern Mesopotamia.

The region around Hamadan experienced long, severe winters, similar to the northern steppe regions that were the home of the Indo-Iranian peoples, with plenty of snow that began as early as September and lasted until May. Summers in this region were significantly cooler than in other areas of Iran due to its relatively high elevation of 5,577 feet.

ORIGINS

The Medes were Indo-Iranians who, along with other Iranian speakers such as the Persians, moved into the region of present-day northwestern Iran possibly around 1500 B.C.E. According to Herodotus, the fifth-century B.C.E. Greek historian, the Medes were made up of six separate tribes: Busae, Paretaceni, Struchates, Arizanti, Budii, and Magi. The name of the last of these tribal groups is also the general term used for Zoroastrian priests, which may indicate that this tribe was of a priestly class or was responsible for sacrifices and other rituals. However, due to a lack of written records, nothing is known with certainty about the Medes until they appear in the Assyrian records in the mid-ninth century B.C.E.

Tomyris ◢◣

Tomyris, made famous in Herodotus's *Histories,* was probably a legendary queen of the Massagetae, an Iranian tribe that resided in the southern steppe regions of modern-day Kazakhstan. According to Herodotus, Tomyris succeeded to the throne after her husband's death in 530 B.C.E. With an obvious wish to absorb her kingdom into his own, the Persian ruler Cyrus the Great sent ambassadors to her court to propose marriage. Tomyris refused to see the ambassadors, and Cyrus marched his army toward Araxes with plans to invade the kingdom and seize it by force. Upon learning that Cyrus was ordering the building of bridges over streams so that his army could safely cross into her land, Tomyris sent a message warning him to be content with his own kingdom and leave her kingdom in peace. Cyrus ignored her advice and pressed forward. Knowing that the pastoral Massagetae people were not familiar with wine, Cyrus and his advisors designed a scheme in which their troops left behind a seemingly abandoned camp full of wine, making the scene look like they had made a hasty retreat. When one-third of the Massagetae army came upon the camp, the men predictably drank themselves into a daze, and the Persians swiftly attacked and slaughtered them, capturing their leader, Tomyris's son Spargapises. When he became sober, Spargapises killed himself. Tomyris sent a message to Cyrus condemning his deceitful tactics and challenging him to an honorable war. When the two armies met, the Persians under Cyrus were defeated, and Cyrus himself was killed. Tomyris ordered the corpse to be beheaded, and she stuffed his head into a wineskin filled with blood.

HISTORY

The written history of the Medes began in approximately 840 B.C.E. when the Assyrian king Shalmaneser III mentioned receiving tribute from them. The Medes were also mentioned in chronicles of later Assyrian kings, who forced them to give tribute, and it is apparent that the Medes were a frequent source of trouble for the Assyrians.

According to Herodotus, the first Median king was Deiokes, a tribal leader who had a reputation for being fair and honest in his dealings with his people. As a result, Medes from all six tribes came to him for his judgment on both civil and criminal complaints. Eventually all the tribal leaders got together and proclaimed Deiokes the king of all six tribes as well as the supreme judge. In exchange, Deiokes requested that a seven-walled citadel be built for his protection; he also asked for the right to conduct all business and court cases in writing rather than in person. The Deiokes saga as described by Herodotus, however, is usually seen as an origin myth told to the Greek author by Persian sources. Alternatively, Herodotus himself may have pieced together various oral histories and legends to create his written text.

Sometime during the second half of the seventh century B.C.E., Phraortes and his son

---

MEDES

location:
Northwestern Iran, with an empire that stretched from the Caucasus, through Turkey and Iran to Afghanistan

time period:
840 to 549 B.C.E.

ancestry:
Indo-Iranian

language:
Median; probably most closely related to Old Persian

Medes time line

B.C.E.

ca. 840 First mention of the Mada people, who occupy the area of present-day northwestern Iran, in an Assyrian text of King Shalmaneser III, who claims to have received tribute from them.

late eighth century The Assyrian king Sargon mentions subjecting the Medes.

700–673 Deiokes, the first great ruler of Media (possibly mythological), begins building a capital at Ecbatana, contemporary Hamadan, Iran. Medes continue to rebel against Assyrian control but pay tribute to Assyria.

647 Deiokes dies and is possibly succeeded by his son Phraortes, who rules from 646 to 625, according to Herodotus.

late seventh century 28 years of domination of the Medes by the Scythians. Medes battle the Mannae, a settled people in Iran, and finally conquer them. Phraortes and his son Cyaxares (rules 623–585) unite all the Median tribes into a single kingdom. Cyaxares the Mede conquers Urartu, a kingdom around Lake Van in present-day Armenia, north of Assyria.

612 Cyaxares allies with Nabopolassar, king of Babylonia, and their armies destroy the Assyrian capital, Nineveh. By 606, Assyria ceases to exist. Medes rule much of Iran, northern Mesopotamia, and Armenia.

590–585 Medes attack the Lydians in Anatolia (Turkey). War ends after the Battle of Halys, or Battle of the Eclipse, when the two kingdoms agree to the Halys River (Turkey) as their common border. The peace is negotiated with the help of the kings of Cilicia and Babylonia.

550 Cyrus the Great vanquishes the Median king Astyages, his own grandfather, and becomes "king of kings" in Persia and Media. Medes remain prominent figures in the Persian Empire.

Cyaxares united all the Median tribes into a kingdom, after a 28-year period of domination by invading SCYTHIANS from the Black Sea steppes. The Medes then conquered the Mannae, a settled people in northwestern Iran, and Cyaxeres invaded the Urartean kingdom around Lake Van in present-day Armenia and added it to his domain. In 612 B.C.E. Cyaxeres allied with Nabopolassar, king of Babylonia, and their two armies destroyed the Assyrian capital of Nineveh, near present-day Mosul in Iraq; by 606 B.C.E., Assyrian power had been vanquished. Cyaxeres invaded Lydia in Asia Minor, but the rulers of Babylonia and Cilicia negotiated a peace settlement after five years of fighting. Media and Lydia agreed that the Halys River would serve as their common border. Their final battle, known as the Battle of Halys or the Battle of the Eclipse, on May 30, 585 B.C.E., is sometimes recorded as the first ancient battle for which we have an exact date.

Soon after reaching the apex of Median power, Astyages, the son of Cyaxares, lost his father's empire to the Persian king Cyrus the Great in 550 B.C.E. Astyages was actually the grandfather of Cyrus, a daughter of Astyages having been given in marriage to a Persian who became Cyrus's father. When the Median king fell into disfavor with his nobles, they captured him and handed him over to Cyrus, who proceeded to form a new empire that included Media and its territories.

As a fellow Iranian people, the Medes seem to have been absorbed by the Persians (*see* PERSIANS, ACHAEMENIDS) with little difficulty. They would have shared a similar language, material culture, and probably religion as well. Medes occupied important military and political positions in the Persian Empire and stood second only to the Persians themselves in status. The Median court rituals were said to have been adopted by the Persians, and the Median capital, Ecbatana, became the summer residence of the Persian kings.

CULTURE

There is little archaeological or textual evidence of Median culture, aside from depictions of Medes in Achaemenid art. From these later sculptures, we can see that the Medes wore rounded felt caps and trousers suitable for riding. According to Herodotus, Median and Persian dress was similar, the Persians having adopted the Median costume. A breed of horse known as Nissaean is mentioned by Herodotus as being bred in Media. These were large, white horses ridden by kings and generals and having an almost religious significance. Persian sculptures show the king's chariot being drawn by two large horses that perhaps represent this famous breed.

It is possible that the Medes had adopted Zoroastrianism, the religion that was later to dominate both the Achaemenid and Sassanid Empires. However, several rock tombs have also been identified by archaeologists as Median, which makes this assignment of their religion somewhat questionable. Zoroastrians do not bury their dead but instead leave them in the open to be devoured by sacred birds and dogs. Therefore the Median beliefs may have represented an early stage of Iranian religion, before Zoroastrianism was completely adopted.

See also PERSIANS, SASSANIDS.

FURTHER READING

Robert Collins. *Medes and Persians: Conquerors and Diplomats* (New York: McGraw Hill, 1972).

Megrelians *See* MINGRELIANS.

Mehrgarh (Mehergarh, Pre-Harappan culture)

The Mehrgarh people were among the first in the world to invent agriculture and settle down in villages, both of which were accomplished by about 7000 B.C.E. Their remains, found in the 1970s by French and Pakistani archaeological teams, are made up of at least four separate mounds of about seven separate layers, each containing building structures, burials, and other remains. Each of the seven layers constitutes a separate development in their technological advancement, beginning before the invention of pottery and ending with complex metalwork at the dawn of the Bronze Age.

GEOGRAPHY

The Mehrgarh site is located in contemporary Baluchistan, Pakistan, on the Kachi plain. The most important geographic features of this region are the Bolan River, which provided water for the settlement's agricultural and personal use, and the Bolan Pass, which allowed movement between the plains of Baluchistan and the high country of Afghanistan. The area today experiences relatively frequent flooding from the Bolan River, which would have been the case in the Mehrgarh period as well.

ORIGINS

The origins of Mehrgarh society were bands of hunter-gatherers who moved throughout the Kachi plain in search of game and wild plants. Sometime before 7000 B.C.E. these people began to experiment with some of the wild cereal crops that grew in the region, such as einkorn and emmer varieties of wheat and barley. Whether due to population pressure, diminishing amounts of game, or a combination of these and perhaps other factors, eventually these experiments led to the domestication of the cereal crops. This process, which probably took at least 1,000 years, was followed by the establishment of settled villages and the domestication of animals such as sheep, goats, and cattle. Once these developments occurred, the people involved began to be known in the archaeological record as Mehrgarh, named for the present-day village near the archaeological site.

HISTORY

Mehrgarh history spans about 5,000 years of technological development and population growth. The earliest phase of this history, from about 9,000 years ago to about 7,500 years ago, was aceramic—that is, the people had not yet learned how to work clay into pottery vessels or other objects. At this time woven reed baskets, sometimes coated with tar or bitumen, served as the primary storage vessels, and bone and stone served as the primary tool-making materials. Seashells and colored stones served as jewels for personal adornment. Some of these objects are not native to this region and were clearly the result of trade with other Neolithic peoples.

Although cereals such as barley and two kinds of wheat had been domesticated by this time, as had goats, this earliest phase of Mehrgarh history also saw a continued reliance on hunting for much of the protein intake. An absence of residential structures in the archaeological record in this period also indicates that the people may have continued their seminomadic pursuit of game animals at the same time as they were storing grain in the village. Another possibility is that they lived in tents or tentlike residences that have not survived but stored their grain in the permanent structures made of air-dried mud brick unearthed by archaeologists.

MEHRGARH

location:
Baluchistan, Pakistan

time period:
About 7000 to 2000 B.C.E.

ancestry:
Uknown, probably indigenous South Asian

language:
Unknown

Mehrgarh time line

B.C.E.

7000–5500 Aceramic Neolithic period of civilization at Mehrgarh, known as Period I. Early stages of agricultural development, basket making, stone and bone tools.

6000 The first signs of crude terra-cotta pottery and figurines begin to appear.

5500–4800 Period II. Technological skills advance.

4800–3500 Period III. Pottery becomes much more complex and finely designed.

4000 Copper is used extensively for the first time.

2600–2000 At some point during this 600-year period, the people at Mehrgarh move on, perhaps into true cities at Harappa and Mohenjo-Daro.

C.E.

1974–86 French and Pakistani archaeological teams excavate the Mehrgarh sites.

1996 French and Pakistani archaeologists resume their excavations at Mehrgarh.

The next phase of technological development, which began about 8,000 years ago but was not perfected until about 1,500 years later, saw the invention of the first pottery, made from an unrefined clay. Later the clay became smoother, and the firing and glazing processes became much more intricate. After about 5000 B.C.E. geometric designs began to be painted onto pottery vessels, which themselves became more elegant and fine-featured. Mud-brick houses also became common in this second period, indicating that domesticated animals had superseded seminomadic hunting as the most important protein source.

In all, archaeologists have discovered between seven and nine separate layers of burials, building, and development at Mehrgarh, each with advances in technological skills. By the time of the abandonment of the 300-hectare village, between 2600 and 2000 B.C.E., the Mehrgarh had domesticated a wide range of plants beyond barley and wheat, including cotton, dates, peas, and sesame, as well as water buffalo, cows, and sheep, along with their earliest domesticated animal, goats. They had learned to tan animal hides and to create a wide variety of human-shaped figurines as well as beads and other objects from lapis lazuli, turquoise, soapstone, copper, and at the end, bronze. Some of these raw materials came from other ancient civilizations in Mesopotamia and Egypt, as well as from nomadic peoples in Afghanistan, the Persian coast, and India. To engage in trade across the sea, boats and a harbor at Lothal on the Arabian Sea were both in use by the end of the Mehrgarh period.

The end of the settlement at Mehrgarh coincides with the expansion of the culture of the HARAPPANS between about 2600 and 2000 B.C.E. Whether this coincidence of time is relevant is yet a matter of debate. It is possible that the residents of Mehrgarh migrated to the larger cities of Harappa or Mohenjo-Daro, but it is also possible that they simply dispersed due to climatic change or other natural causes. Perhaps deciphering Harappan script will provide answers to this earlier history as well.

CULTURE

Like their technological skills, the culture of the Mehrgarh people changed over the course of their 5,000-year history. One of the most obvious changes occurred in the area of burial practices. In the earlier phases of Mehrgarh history, burials were elaborate affairs in which a large variety of goods was included with the body. The usual goods were baskets, tools, and jewelry; some burial sites also included animal sacrifices. Later Mehrgarh burials included far fewer goods, especially for men, who might be sent off with just a few ornaments for the body. Women were buried with more goods but still far fewer than are evident in the burials from earlier Mehrgarh periods. This difference between women and men in the later periods may indicate the relative importance of women in this society, but it may also indicate a greater need among women for objects in the afterlife, while men were seen as able to rely on their personal strengths. At this point it is impossible to do any more than conjecture about the meaning of this difference.

Another aspect of Mehrgarh culture that remains a relative mystery is their religion. While some experts indicate the Mehrgarh may have practiced a form of shamanism, in which religious specialists were able to communicate with the spiritual world and engage the assistance of spirits in healing, controlling nature, or even harming others, other experts do not find enough evidence for this kind of practice. Some people familiar with the archaeological record at Mehrgarh believe that they may have practiced a form of fertility ritual or animal worship, rather than shamanism. Among the remains found in many layers of Mehrgarh history were large numbers of both male and female figurines, as well as those of bulls, all made from clay. Some experts point to the female figures in particular as a sign that these people engaged in fertility rituals and may even have worshiped the figurines as gods. However, other experts are less willing to conjecture about the use these figures may have been put to; they could have been children's toys or just attractive statues used to adorn homes and other spaces.

One thing these figurines do provide is some clue about the dress, hair, and adornment styles favored by the Mehrgarh people in different eras. Many of the female figures show them wearing necklaces and a lacelike material at their waists, with their hair in a braid down their backs or over one shoulder. Male figurines are often depicted in turbans, a hair adornment that remains popular in Pakistan today.

A final interesting aspect of Mehrgarh culture evident in the archaeological remains found in the past 30 years is that as long ago as 9,000 years, these people used flint drills to remove cavities from people's teeth. The teeth that have been found to have been worked on were clearly drilled during the person's lifetime, rather than after death, and showed continued wear and tear after the period of drilling, so that they did not lose the use of the tooth due to the procedure. The archaeologists who have written about this find suggest that perhaps the skills and tool kits needed to create beads from stones, shells, and other materials may have been the basis for the development of this early dentistry. Strangely, this practice lasted only for about 1,500 years before it was discontinued.

FURTHER READING

Mohammad Usman Hassan. *Mehergarh, The Oldest Civilization in South Asia* (Rawalpindi: Pap-Board Printers, 1992).

Melanesians   (people of Melanesia)

The Melanesians are a group of people who are loosely related by geography and culture and who reside in the South Pacific, northwest of Australia. Many aspects of their religious life, subsistence patterns, and exchange systems have common features. The most notable similarity lies in the ceremonial trading systems that are common in the region, such as the ritualized exchange of shell jewelry in the Trobriand Islands and of prestige foods in the New Guinea highlands. The emergence of cargo cults and other millennial movements as a reaction to colonialism also provides a cultural link among these diverse peoples. The origin of this population is ancient, stemming from an original migratory population or populations who left Asia between 40,000 and 60,000 years ago. From these early origins, the population we know today as Melanesian spread to parts of Indonesia and New Guinea, the Solomon Islands, Bismarck Archipelago, Torres Strait Islands, New Caledonia, and much later, Fiji and Vanuatu.

The contemporary Melanesians continue to have some features in common, while there are also some significant differences in social and political structures. Some of these differences, such as those relating to subsistence patterns and social structure, are the result of indigenous developments and local geography and climate. Others are the result of past experiences with both the later settlement by AUSTRONESIANS and with European colonialism.

GEOGRAPHY

The current area of Melanesia, a name coined in 1831 by Jules Dumont d'Urville to refer to the areas of the Pacific inhabited primarily by peoples with black or dark brown skin, is located in an arc of islands in the South Pacific, beginning with New Guinea and stretching southwest to Fiji, encompassing the Bismarck Archipelago, the Torres Strait Islands, the Solomon Islands, Vanuatu, and New Caledonia. Some maps also include the Malaku Islands, Flores, Sumba, Alor, Pantar, and Timor, all located east of this region and within Indonesia, because they are inhabited by Papuan peoples who differ significantly in language and culture from their Austronesian neighbors. Fiji's inclusion in this list is also somewhat misleading because Fiji's original inhabitants were Polynesian settlers who established themselves on the islands around 3,500 years ago. About 1,000 years later a group of Melanesians also settled on Fiji, intermarrying with the local POLYNESIANS and largely adopting their language. Despite having arrived later on Fiji, the fact that Fijians look like other Melanesians and consider themselves as such has caused most sources to categorize them in this way.

While the term *Melanesia* was originally a racial designation, that is somewhat misleading because of the cultural differences it hides, such as Fiji's Polynesian language and the fact that Papuan languages are themselves classified based on their lack of commonality with other languages rather than any similarity among themselves. Furthermore, in the contemporary world the concept of Melanesia has been embraced by a number of states and territories. For example, Vanuatu, the Solomon Islands, Papua New Guinea, and Fiji are all member states of the Melanesian Spearhead Group Preferential Trade Agreement, which the first three countries formed in 1993 to foster economic development and regional cooperation. Fiji joined the group in 1998. Their cultural similarities have also led many contemporary scholars to speak of Melanesians as a common people.

ORIGINS

The history of the Melanesian people begins between 40,000 and 60,000 years ago, when a seafaring population from Asia sailed south. Very little is known about these earliest settlers except the fact that they must have been able to sail for at least 200 miles in open water and thus had intimate knowledge of the water and wind. It is still a mystery whether they came south through the Indian subcontinent or down through mainland Southeast Asia.

At that time what are today the separate islands of mainland Australia, Tasmania, and

MELANESIANS

location:
The South Pacific

time period:
Approximately 50,000 B.C.E. to the present

ancestry:
Unknown, but probably Southeast Asian

language:
About 1,200 different Papuan and Austronesian languages

Melanesians time line

B.C.E.

60,000–40,000 Probable era of Melanesian settlement in New Guinea, possibly in two or three initial waves of Melanesian peoples coming out of Asia.

30,000 Probable era of Melanesian settlement in the Bismarck Archipelago and Solomon Islands.

10,000 New Guinea and Australia become separate territories as sea levels rise with the end of the last Ice Age.

7000 Probable era in which New Guineans transition from food collecting to agriculture as their predominant mode of subsistence, having domesticated sugarcane, taro, yams, a type of banana, and a variety of grasses and vegetables.

2000 Melanesian settlement in Vanuatu.

1500 Lapita-style settlement in the Bismarck Archipelago and New Caledonia.

500 Melanesians settle Fiji, joining a population of Polynesians who had been there for at least 1,000 years.

C.E.

1828 Beginning of the Dutch colonial era in western New Guinea.

1853 France asserts control in New Caledonia and uses it as a penal colony until 1922.

1874 The British colonize Fiji.

1884 The British establish control in southeast New Guinea.

The Germans annex New Britain, New Ireland, Manus, and northeastern New Guinea.

1893 The British take control of the Solomon Islands.

1906 The Australian government takes over from the British in governing southeast New Guinea.

Britain and France agree to joint control over Vanuatu.

1914 Australia captures German New Guinea and joins it to the rest of its colony on the island.

1942 Japanese invasion of New Guinea.

The Battle of Guadalcanal in the Solomon Islands sees an Allied victory over Japan after three difficult months of near-constant land, sea, and air battles.

1962 Indonesia establishes control over West Papua, setting off decades of strife and independence movements on the part of the Papuan peoples.

1970 Fiji achieves independence from the British.

1975 Papua New Guinea gains independence from Australia.

1978 The Solomon Islands establish independence from Britain.

1980 Vanuatu gains its independence.

1987 Melanesians become the dominant majority in Fiji once again after a series of coups sees a large number of Fijians of Indian descent leave the country.

1996 Attempted coup in Vanuatu follows nearly a decade of political instability.

1997 The Solomon Islands begin a downward spiral of political corruption, inept governance, insurrection, and economic collapse.

2001 The Solomon Islands' prime minister, Sir Allan Kemakeza, requests outside assistance, which results in the Regional Assistance Mission for the Solomon Islands (RAMSI), an Australian-led security initiative that brings more than 2,000 police and military personnel from more than 20 countries to establish law and order.

2006 Continued strife in the Solomon Islands, including riots in the capital of Honiara.

New Guinea were all joined as one land mass, called Sahul. However, because of the great length of time in which the ancient populations of these three islands were separated, only a few biological, linguistic, and cultural similarities have been found to link their present-day descendants. The strongest biological relationship has been found between NEW GUINEA HIGHLANDERS and ABORIGINAL AUSTRALIANS, for whom remote genetic and skeletal links have been found. There is also some slight evidence that the languages of the ABORIGINAL TASMANIANS are remotely related to the Papuan languages of New Guinea. With the near destruction of the peoples and languages of Tasmania in the 19th century, however, this hypothesis will probably never be properly tested.

Another hypothesis that may never be properly tested is that the Melanesian population shared remote ancestors with the other black populations of Asia, the so-called Negritos of the Philippines, Andaman Islands, and Malay Peninsula and the Veddoid population of Sri Lanka. While archaeological evidence does exist that these populations were probably the first inhabitants of all of these regions, in the Philippines and Malay Peninsula going back at least 30,000 years, little evidence has been presented to connect them to the Melanesians aside from this ancient heritage and their relatively dark skin color and frizzy hair.

LANGUAGES

The 1,200 or so languages of the Melanesian region, excluding Fiji, constitute between 20 and 25 percent of the world's total number of languages. About one-quarter of these languages are Austronesian in origin, while the other three-quarters fall into what has often been called the Papuan group, or more accurately non-Austronesian, since the only real criterion for being called Papuan is to be outside the Austronesian family. Given this enormous linguistic diversity within a world region that is not as densely populated as some others, it is not surprising to find that each language has a very small number of speakers, fewer than 3,000 on average.

Linguistic experts are uncertain about the exact reasons for this immense diversity, although many hypotheses have been posited. First, this area of the world has been inhabited for much longer than the New World or parts of Europe, leaving ample time for significant differentiation between language groups to occur. However, given the fact that Africa and much of the Asian mainland have been inhabited for much longer, this explanation tends to obscure more than it illuminates. Another possible reason is that the rugged landscape of New Guinea prevented the different groups from interacting with one another consistently enough to bring about linguistic change. This explanation, too, tends to obscure more than it explains, given the fact that many other aspects of Melanesian cultures are quite similar. A third hypothesis, possibly related to the second, is based on the fact that New Guinea and the other areas of Melanesia generally failed to develop any political unit larger than the clan. The development of kingdoms, protostates, and even empires in much of the rest of the world caused speakers of languages of subordinate groups to voluntarily or otherwise adopt the languages of the more powerful groups around them. This did not happen in Melanesia with its small-scale political units. Finally, for some unknown reason, when confronted with speakers of other languages, the people of this region tended to add linguistic elements to their own language in order to increase its complexity and make it even more distinct from their neighbors, causing even languages in the same family to become more and more distinct over time. The end result, regardless of the cause, is enormous linguistic diversity.

HISTORY

The very long period of independent social evolution in Melanesia came to an end in the 19th century when the Dutch began the colonization process from the western end of the region in what is currently Indonesia; the British and French began this same process on the opposite side in Fiji and New Caledonia, respectively. The Germans were also active in the region, taking the Bismarck Archipelago late in the century. The Dutch had been the first Europeans to land in the Bismarck Archipelago (1616) and in Fiji (1643), but like the rest of Melanesia, which had been seen by Portuguese and Spanish explorers in the same period, these areas did not come under European control for another two centuries.

The earliest colonial period in Melanesia was very similar to that in Micronesia and Polynesia under the Europeans: primary products, such as sandalwood, were harvested, missionaries moved in to try to convert the indigenous peoples, and in some areas European diseases took a heavy toll. Not long after this initial period, this region experienced an even more difficult period of blackbirding, in which people from the Solomon Islands, New Caledonia, New Guinea, and Vanuatu were taken as indentured laborers (or slaves, according to some reports) to Fiji and Australia to work on sugar plantations. The methods used to capture people included trickery, kidnapping, and the sale of alcohol and other trade goods in exchange for labor. These practices were extremely detrimental to the societies that experienced them and led to some very stiff opposition to the colonial regimes.

While the practice of blackbirding ended with the start of the 20th century, new colonial regimes and practices emerged to replace them. World War II was particularly difficult for many people in the region as the result of JAPANESE occupation, with its imposition of forced labor and starvation conditions; heavy fighting between Allied and Japanese forces; and the commandeering of local resources to feed, house, and protect the Japanese troops. Guadalcanal in the Solomon Islands and the New Guinea highlands saw particularly heavy fighting, while almost no island chain in the region was entirely spared from the war.

The postwar era has been an era of mixed results for Melanesia. On the positive side, the people of Fiji, the Solomon Islands, Vanuatu, Papua New Guinea (PNG), and the Bismarck Archipelago as part of PNG attained their independence from European and Australian colonization. However, New Caledonia remains on the United Nations' list of Non-Self-Governing Territories in 2008, and the people of West Papua (formerly Irian Jaya) have also struggled for many decades to free themselves from Indonesian rule, some with the thought of joining their neighbors in the independent country of Papua New Guinea, others with the thought of outright independence. Political independence, however, has not brought economic prosperity or even peace to many areas in the region. The Solomon Islands today are considered by many to be a failed state. In late 2006 the Australian government accused the Solomon Islands' government headed by Prime Minister Manasseh Sogavare of harboring a fugitive wanted in Australia for charges relating to child sex crimes; the accused, Julian Moti, was serving as attorney general of the Solomon Islands at the time. Despite being rich in mineral, gas, and timber resources, Papua New Guinea has also struggled in the postindependence era to achieve political and economic prosperity. The highly fragmented nature of PNG society, with more than 700 different tribal groups and a majority of the population that does not recognize the legitimacy of state authority, has stymied all political parties and prevented leaders from achieving their goals of national unity and economic development. An initial coup in Fiji in 1987, which highlighted the lasting divisions between indigenous peoples and Indians who were brought to the islands in the 19th century as indentured servants, has shown that even relative economic prosperity has not led to peace and stability in a region so divided by linguistic, ethnic, religious, tribal, and even clan differences.

Melanesian Kanaks in New Caledonia marching in a tourist event in 2005 that marks the start of the French colonial period in 1853. Marketing their "tribal" heritage through carvings, rituals, and other events staged for tourists has become an important source of cash throughout the Melanesian culture area. *(AP Photo/Rob Griffith)*

CULTURE

Economy and Society

Prior to around 7000 B.C.E., Melanesians were food collectors who gathered wild fruits and vegetables, hunted, and fished. With the indigenous invention of agriculture in New Guinea, this subsistence pattern changed as Melanesians adopted such products as sugar cane, taro, yams, and, beginning between 700 and 450 years ago, sweet potatoes. For the past several thousand years at least, domestic pigs have also been a mainstay of Melanesian subsistence systems. However, research is still ongoing to determine whether pigs were independently domesticated on New Guinea or imported from elsewhere in Asia, as well as the era in which one of these two events occurred.

In general, Melanesian society was different from the ranked, hierarchical societies that developed throughout much of Polynesia. While several Polynesian and even one society of MICRONESIANS, YAP, developed large chiefdoms or kingdoms, the societies of Melanesia tended to remain on a much smaller scale. The largest political units were lineages or clans, which were based on either matrilineal or patrilineal descent, or villages. These kinds of societies, classified by anthropologists as tribes, are acephalous, meaning that they have no authority figure at their head. Rather than a legitimate authority figure who attains his or her position through either ascription (birth) or achievement, tribes grant all men (and occasionally women) the ability to compete with their peers for power and prestige. These competitions might entail the control of resources, people, and even sacred rituals or knowledge. Tribal competition is fierce and constant since once a man has gained the recognition of his people, he has to defend it continually against his rivals. There is no respect for, or inherent power in, the top position in this kind of political system, only a constant need to prove oneself as the most able, generous, and connected person in the clan or village.

Throughout Melanesia men traditionally competed in this way to attain the position of Big Man. This position is not equivalent to a chief or king in any way. Rather, the Big Man is the member of the clan, lineage, or village who is best able to rally others around him in support, and once that support is withdrawn, someone else emerges as the Big Man. He may be the man with the largest number of daughters whom he can marry off to other men, who then become indebted to him. Or he may be the most persuasive man, who can convince others to contribute to his building projects or exchange *patterns.*

Generally in Melanesia there are two kinds of resources that men can control in their quest for power and prestige. In some societies, the most desirable resource is a material item, whether it is pigs in the New Guinea highlands or shell jewelry in the Trobriand Islands. In both cases, the control of resources is never about accumulating material goods for their own sake, as is the case in a market society, but rather for the sake of being able to distribute them to others. For example, the control of pigs in the highlands is for the sake of giving them away in the form of large gifts. If one man gives a gift that another man is unable to repay, then he has won the competition for prestige. While the "loser" winds up with hundreds of pigs plus other prestige items, the "winner" winds up with the power and prestige of having overwhelmed his opponent with his gift. The other kind of resource that some Melanesian societies use as the basis of their competitive political system is ritual knowledge. In these societies the winner is the man who is able to debate best and convince others of his claim to control the use of ancestral names, mythology, and ritual. The strategies and desired outcomes of these two systems are similar despite the apparent difference between controlling material resources and controlling ritual knowledge. In both cases the object for the Big Man is convincing others to work for him and support his claims to represent them to others. As soon as this support is withdrawn and given to a younger, stronger, or more convincing man, the position is lost.

In many of the Melanesian societies for which the control and distribution of material resources is the basis of political power, there developed elaborate ritual exchange systems to control and regulate the movement of these prestige items. Three elaborated and well-known exchange systems in this region are the *tee* exchange of pigs among the ENGA of New Guinea, a similar system involving pigs and other items among the Melpa of New Guinea known as *moka,* and the *kula* ring of the TROBRIAND ISLANDERS. The *kula* is particularly interesting because it involves the exchange of red shell necklaces and white shell armbands, both being prestige items that have no use in Trobriand society other than exchange for the purpose of building networks and developing the reputations of the men who give them as gifts. Conversely, the exchange of pigs among the Enga and Melpa could be seen as part of a wider subsistence system in which pork is the primary source of protein. To view *tee* and *moka* as part of subsistence is, however, inaccurate because pigs in both societies are more important for their exchangeability than their edibility. Marriages cannot take place without the exchange of pigs; births are not legitimate if not accompanied by an exchange of pigs; and men's reputations are made and broken by their ability to convince other men to contribute to their large gifts of pigs, exotic birds, and feathers, and in the 20th and 21st centuries, money, trucks, motorcycles, and other material items.

A final cultural component that features heavily in many Melanesian societies is the men's house, a separate structure in which the adult men of a village or clan eat, sleep, rest, engage in ritual activity, and generally live out their daily lives. The marked separation of the sexes throughout Melanesia is highlighted in this institution, which requires the initiation of boys to cleanse them of their connections to women before being able to enter the house and the strict taboo against women entering at all. As is the case with most male activities in Melanesia, even the building of men's houses is part of the near-constant competition in which men participate to try to elevate their prestige among their peers. The ability to gather workers, name the location for building, and dedicate the house to a particular ancestor or ancestors are all arenas for men in their prime to compete against others. In the contemporary world, men's houses and the rituals that take place within them have also been used by a number of tribes to lure tourists seeking a "primitive" experience to a particular village. In these cases, the taboos against women, at least foreign women, have been lifted in a bid to bring in foreign or domestic currency.

Religion

While most Melanesians today have been at least nominally Christian for many generations, traditionally they were what are known as animists, people who believed in multiple spirits and the power of the dead to affect the living. Most Melanesian societies distinguished between what is often glossed as the newly dead, those whose spirits continue to walk the earth and bring harm to the living, usually to those who are believed to have caused their death; and the truly dead, those ancestors who were settled in the land of the dead or into ritual objects such as drums and able to assist or harm their living relatives. The barrier between the newly and truly dead was breached in many societies through rituals that confirmed the place of that person within the social and cosmological hierarchy, often many years after biological death. For many Melanesian societies the power of the ancestors was the only truly legitimate power available, and those who could claim to have powerful ancestors or ritual objects within which they resided were able to use these family connections to influence others.

Sorcery is also a common feature of many Melanesian religions. Sorcerers are those people who actively seek to bring either harm or favor to others, usually through the use of medicines and ceremonial chants. Because Melanesian societies did not develop political structures that provided legitimate claims to power for one person to use in order to control others, sorcery provided one path to power for those who were able to develop a reputation in this area. This power was not legitimate authority as granted by an election or inherited position but rather a persuasive power with fear of retribution as its primary source.

One interesting feature of Melanesian religion came out of the people's experience of colonization and Christian proselytizing. In Fiji, New Guinea, Vanuatu, and elsewhere in Melanesia, aspects of Christianity, indigenous religions, desire for political change, and commercialism were often brought together in millennial movements by charismatic leaders seeking material and spiritual change in their communities. Dozens of millennial movements have been documented in Melanesia since the late 19th century, most notably the Vailala Madness in New Guinea, the Tuka Movement in Fiji, and the John Frum Movement in what was then the New Hebrides (Vanuatu) (*see* VANUATUANS: NATIONALITY). As a category, millennial movements generally are religious movements that proclaim an imminent end to this world and a reversal of the social order. The roots of these ideas are clearly visible in Christian ideologies of the meek inheriting the earth and the rapture, which were important teachings for the Protestant and Catholic missionaries who worked in Melanesia beginning in the 19th century.

In Melanesia, however, these movements often took on a different tone from their counterparts in other areas of the world. In Melanesia most millennial movements were more accurately cargo cults, movements with a belief that not only was the end of the world and a reversal in the social order imminent, but that this end was to be brought about by ancestors or Jesus returning in either ships or airplanes and delivering western goods (cargo) to indigenous peoples. While the indigenous peoples were to become rich and powerful, their European, Australian, and Japanese colonizers were to experience deprivation and loss. There are many examples of Melanesians burning their houses and crops, razing their villages, slaughtering their pigs, feasting, and building airstrips for the imminent arrival of the ancestors bearing their loads of cargo. As happened elsewhere, when these loads of cargo failed to make their appearance on the designated day, most of these movements disappeared along with the leaders who proclaimed them. However, some movements continued to emerge in different villages or even regions over the course of many years. For example, the most extensive cargo cult that has been documented for Melanesia, the Yali Movement in New Guinea, continues to attract attention into the 21st century despite its founder having died in 1975. James Yali, a son of the movement's founder, Yali Singina, has been governor of Madang since 2003. Upon seizing power, Yali began a process of bulldozing signs of Western development and removing Europeans from Madang, perhaps as a way of continuing the politicoreligious message of his father's movement.

FURTHER READING

Peter Lawrence, and Mervyn John Meggitt, eds. *Gods, Ghosts, and Men in Melanesia: Some Religions of Australian New Guinea and the New Hebrides* (Oxford: Oxford University Press, 1965).

Matthew Spriggs. *The Island Melanesians* (Boston: Blackwell, 1997).

Michael Stevenson. *Wokmani: Work, Money, and Discontent in Melanesia* (Sydney: Oceania Publications, 1986).

Andrew Strathern. *Inequality in New Guinea Highlands Societies* (New York: Cambridge University Press, 1982).

Peter Worsley. *The Trumpet Shall Sound: A Study of "Cargo" Cults in Melanesia* (London : MacGibbon & Kee, 1957).

Melayu Asli (Aboriginal Malay, proto-Malay)

The Melayu Asli are one subgroup of the larger category of ORANG ASLI, or Aboriginal Malaysians, along with the SEMANG and SENOI. All three groups predate the contemporary Malay population in Peninsular Malaysia and seem to have been driven into the highland and forest regions by the arrival of the newer peoples. There is a contested view about whether the three Orang Asli groups had the same origins in HOA BINH CULTURE about 25,000 years ago and developed significant cultural and physical differences in their current locations or whether they are the result of three separate migrations over the course of more than 20,000 years. The latter view is the more accepted, but the former has gained adherents in the past decade.

The Melayu Asli are generally thought to have inhabited the southern areas of Peninsular Malaysia for at least 3,000–4,000 years, although there are few known prehistoric records. They are thought to have migrated from the Indonesian islands, perhaps due to population pressure. Despite being known as proto-MALAYS, these people are not the immediate ancestors of the contemporary Malay population of Malaysia, who probably migrated from Borneo and Sumatra in around 1500 B.C.E.

Generally the Melayu Asli who live in the forests engage in swidden (slash-and-burn) agriculture, growing dry upland rice, vegetables, and other products both for use and trade. Those who reside in the lowland plains have permanent fields and use both artificial fertilizers and irrigation technologies to grow paddy rice and other crops. Both groups differ from the Semang and Senoi due to their extensive trade networks with the Malays, Chinese, and others. For thousands of years they have traded forest products and produce for consumer goods, seafoods, animals, and other items. Those who advocate a common origin for all Orang Asli argue that it is these trade networks and their associated social relations that have made the contemporary Melayu Asli resemble Malays physically while maintaining social relations and languages that are more like those of the Senoi and, to a lesser degree, the Semang. Today, however, most Melayu Asli groups do not intermarry with outsiders, preferring localized kin groupings that tend toward endogamy or marriage within the group.

While a small number of Melayu Asli groups have converted to either Islam or Christianity, most adhere to their traditional beliefs about local spirits and gods. Much of the Melayu Asli music that has been recorded and published throughout the world actually comes from religious rituals and originally accompanied shamans as they went into trances in order to contact the spirit world for healing or other purposes.

Meo   *See* HMONG.

Miao   *See* HMONG.

Micronesians   (people of Micronesia)

The Micronesians are a group of people who are loosely related by geography, language, and culture, residing on nearly 1,000 islands in the western Pacific. They all speak some form of

---

MELAYU ASLI

location:
Peninsular Malaysia

time period:
Probably about 2000 B.C.E. to the present

ancestry:
Possibly the same as other Orang Asli subgroups: Hoa Binh Culture

language:
Southern Aslian languages within the Mon-Khmer family as well as a number of Malay and Senoic languages

MICRONESIANS

location:
The western Pacific Ocean, east of the Philippines, north of New Guinea and Melanesia, west of Polynesia, and south of Hawaii

time period:
2500–1500 B.C.E. to the present

ancestry:
Austronesian

language:
There are 20 separate Micronesian languages within the much larger Central-Eastern-Oceanic language family.

Micronesians time line

B.C.E.

2000–1500 First human habitation in the Mariana Islands.

C.E.

0 The central Micronesian islands of Chuuk, Pohnpei, and Kosrae, as well as the Marshall Islands, are settled by late-Lapita-era peoples.

1000 *Latte* houses begin to be built on Guam and other Mariana Islands.

1521 Portuguese explorer Ferdinand Magellan arrives in the northern Mariana Islands and calls them the Islands of Thieves because of an incident in which the locals take control of one of his ships.

1526 Spanish explorer Toribio Alonso de Salazar discovers the Caroline Islands, naming them the Carolinas after Carlos I, emperor of Spain.

1668 Spanish missionary Padre Diego Luis de Sanvitores establishes a mission on Guam to support the profitable way station for Spanish galleons plying the trade between Manila and Acapulco. He also renames the island group the Marianas after the widow of Spain's King Philip IV.

1850s Protestant missions are set up in Pohnpei and Kosrae, American whalers frequent the islands, and trading posts are established for the export of copra (dried coconut).

1898 The United States takes Guam from the Spanish in the Spanish-American War and also colonizes Wake Island.

1899 Spain sells many of her Spanish East Indies colonies to Germany.

1914 The Japanese military secretly takes control of Micronesia from their large base in Truk Lagoon. Their headquarters are in Dublon Town on the island of Tonoas, Chuuk.

1922–37 Japanese civilian control replaces the military on Chuuk.

1942 The United States defeats Japan at the Battle of Midway.

1944 The United States invades Yap, Palau, and Woleai.

1945 Japanese forces in Truk Lagoon, their largest base in Micronesia, surrender to U.S. forces, and the war ends in the Pacific.

1946 Operation Crossroads, the code name given to one of the series of U.S. nuclear tests on the Marshall Islands, selects the Bikini Atoll as the site for extensive nuclear testing.

1947 The United Nations gives much of Micronesia to the United States as the Trust Territory of the Pacific Islands.

1958 The United States detonates the last of the 66 nuclear tests it conducts in and around the Marshall Islands.

1968 Nauru attains independence from its position as a trustee of Australia, New Zealand, and the United Kingdom.

1979 Kiribati gains independence from Britain after having split from the Ellice Islands (which became independent Tuvalu) one year earlier.

1986 The Federated States of Micronesia attains independence from the United States.

1990 The Marshall Islands is recognized by the United Nations as an independent country.

1994 Palau (Belau) attains independence from the United States.

2006 The Commonwealth of the Northern Mariana Islands gains notoriety in the United States as having the worst labor relations in the country, a fact that comes to light during the investigation of political lobbyist Jack Abramoff, who had previously lobbied against improving workers' conditions in the territory.

Oceanic language. In addition, many aspects of their religious life, origin stories, even subsistence patterns have common roots in their Austronesian heritage. This heritage is ancient, stemming from an original migratory population who left South China between 4,500 and

5,000 years ago. More than 4,000 years ago, the populations we know today as POLYNESIANS and Micronesians began to spread, slowly at first, to parts of Southeast Asia and eventually into the Micronesian islands of the western Pacific.

As is the case with other Oceanic peoples, notably Polynesians and MELANESIANS, the contemporary Micronesians continue to have some features in common, while there are also some significant differences in social and political structures. Some of these differences, such as those relating to subsistence pattern and social structure, are the result of indigenous developments and local geography and climate. Others are the result of past experiences with colonialism.

GEOGRAPHY

The current area of Micronesia, a name coined by Jules Dumont d'Urville in 1831, refers to an area of the western Pacific that contains eight countries and territories: the Federated States of Micronesia, the Marshall Islands, Kiribati, Palau, Nauru, Guam, Wake Island, and the Commonwealth of the Northern Mariana Is-

lands. During colonial times the Federated States of Micronesia were also known as the Caroline Islands and today are made up of four island groups: Yap, Chunk (called Truk until 1990), Pohnpei (called Ponape until 1984), and Kosrae. The Marshall Islands are made up of 29 atolls and five islands, including the capital Majuro and Ebey. Kiribati is made up of one island, Banaba, and three chains of atolls, the Gilbert, Phoenix, and Line Islands, which together total 32 atolls (*see* MICRONESIANS, FEDERATED STATES OF: NATIONALITY; KIRIBATESE: NATIONALITY; MARSHALL ISLANDERS: NATIONALITY; NAURUANS: NATIONALITY; PALAUANS: NATIONALITY; YAP).

ORIGINS

The original settlement of the culturally and linguistically heterogeneous Micronesian Islands is more complex than that of either Polynesia or Melanesia. Rather than just one wave of settlers from one place of origin, Micronesia was probably settled from several directions at different times. The Mariana Islands were probably settled about 4,000 years ago by the earliest

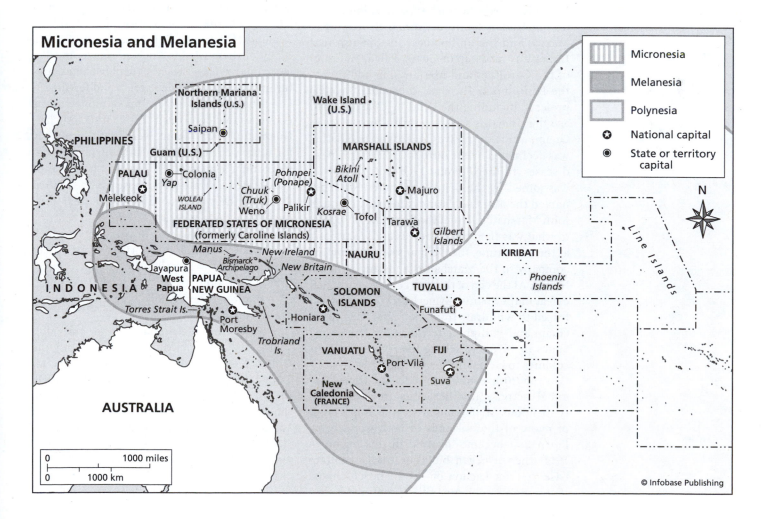

waves of AUSTRONESIANS leaving southeast Asia and Taiwan. The rest of Micronesia, however, was populated by Austronesians who had already settled other Pacific islands. Palau and Yap were probably colonized by people originating in New Guinea, and the Caroline and Marshall Islands and Kiribati were probably settled by people originating in the Bismarck Archipelago and bearing a late Lapita-style cultural complex (*see* LAPITA CULTURE).

HISTORY

The history of Micronesia after its discovery by Spanish explorers in the 16th century is likewise more complex than the histories of both Polynesia and Melanesia due to the number of countries that took part in the colonial process. While Polynesia was largely colonized by France and Great Britain, with just slight German and American involvement in Samoa, Micronesia experienced colonization at the hands of the Spanish, Germans, British, JAPANESE, and Americans over the course of four tumultuous centuries.

The first Europeans to play an active role in Micronesia were Spanish explorers, missionaries, and traders sailing between their colonies in Mexico and the Philippines. The Spanish East Indies was made up of Guam, Palau, and most of the Carolines and Marianas, in addition to the Philippines. The most substantial Spanish projects, including the building of a large palace that remains standing today, took place in Guam, where the native CHAMORRO population was decimated by the introduction of European diseases. In the 18th and 19th centuries, Spain was joined by the British in Micronesia. They named the Marshall Islands after naval captain John Marshall and sent the first wave of settlers to what was then the Gilbert Islands (Kiribati); at the same time, the Germans set up a trading company in the Marshall Islands and annexed Nauru. At the end of the 19th century, with their defeat in the Spanish-American War, Spain was forced to withdraw from the region, ceding its Guam and Philippine territories to the United States in 1898 and selling the remainder of its colonies to Germany one year later.

The 20th century brought continued colonial activity to Micronesia in addition to tremendous strife caused by the importance of many of these islands in both world wars. Japan first became involved in this region in 1914 when it began building a large military base in Truk Lagoon on the island of Chuuk; that same year the Australians captured Nauru from the Germans and were allowed to control the territory and its large phosphate reserves jointly with the United Kingdom and New Zealand. The Japanese continued to involve themselves during World War I when they captured the Marshall Islands from the Germans. The Americans also involved themselves more fully in the region at this time, primarily building up their bases in Guam and Wake Island, a previously uninhabited island on which Pan American Airlines built a village in 1935 to serve as a comfort station for long flights between the United States and China.

The islands of the region of Micronesia experienced extremely heavy fighting and hardship during World War II. The Japanese captured the American bases on Guam and Wake Island in 1941 and the Gilbert Islands and Nauru in 1942, using the indigenous populations of all these islands as a slave labor force in building infrastructure, agriculture, and other war-related employment. Finally, in 1944–45, the United States captured all Japanese-held territory in the Pacific, holding onto some of the territories themselves after the war, such as Guam and Wake Island, and turning others back over to their British, Australian, and New Zealand allies, including Nauru and Kiribati. Many of these islands, such as Nauru and Palau, contained large reserves of phosphates, useful in the making of detergents and fertilizers, and thus provided large sums of money to the countries that controlled them. Others, such as Guam and Wake Island, were useful primarily for strategic reasons, especially during the Korean and Vietnam wars. The Marshall Islands also served a strategic purpose for the United States as the site of 66 different nuclear tests during the middle decades of the 20th century, including the test named Bravo in 1954, which was so powerful that it vaporized several small islands. Many Marshallese residents continue to suffer the aftereffects of having been exposed to radiation at extremely high levels during their youth.

While the Melanesian island and atoll chains that were held by Australia and the United Kingdom after World War II have all gained independence over the years since 1968, the United States continues to hold onto Guam, the Commonwealth of the Northern Mariana Islands, and Wake Island, despite a counterclaim by the Marshall Islands for the latter territory. The residents of Guam gained U.S. citizenship in 1950 while the Commonwealth of the Northern Mariana Islands is in political union with the United States but has a government of its own.

CULTURE

As is the case throughout much of the rest of Oceania, the most important social unit throughout Micronesia is the extended family, with many societies favoring residence based on clan membership rather than on the nuclear family. In the Federated States of Micronesia, this extended family is largely a matrilineal one; descent is traced through one's mother, except on Yap, which is patrilineal and where descent is traced through fathers. And while older research in Micronesia pointed to a kinship system similar to that of the HAWAIIANS, more recent historical and linguistic work has found that most Micronesian societies were probably matrilineal until the decrease in interisland travel and communication during the European colonial era. In Palau and a few other Micronesian islands, there was also a strong tradition of a men's house, in which the men and boys of the community gathered to eat, celebrate, engage in ritual activity, and even sleep. A similar tradition is found in the Sepik region of Papua New Guinea (see NEW GUINEA SEPIK BASIN PEOPLE).

The traditional subsistence bases of most Micronesian societies rest on seafood and a few root crops, such as taro and yams, and tree crops, notably coconuts, breadfruit, and mango, particularly on Palau. Bananas and some citrus varieties have been grown on some lowland Micronesian islands as well. In addition to these food crops, hibiscus was once an important crop that was used for its fibers in making rope, nets, and clothing, and betel nut was central for both exchange and ritual purposes. In Guam and the Northern Marianas, agriculture was of limited importance, and most subsistence came from either the sea or hunting fruit bats and birds.

Like some Polynesian societies, several Micronesian societies also developed a tradition of building enormous structures out of stone. On Guam, the Chamorro built giant stone houses called *latte*, while the people of Yap utilized enormous stone disks, as large as 4,000 pounds each, as a form of indigenous money.

In the years about 1200–1300 C.E., near the island of Pohnpei in what is now the Federated States of Micronesia, the indigenous population built a series of 92 small, artificial islands out of stone and connected them through a series of canals. This complex, Nan Madol, was a ceremonial residence for local nobility and priests as well as the site of death rituals for other Pohnpeians. On Palau, giant standing stones, or *menhirs*, have been found both singly and in groupings, some with faces carved onto them, others that may have served as the foundations of buildings.

FURTHER READING

William Alkire. *An Introduction to the Peoples and Cultures of Micronesia*, 2nd ed. (Menlo Park, Calif.: Cummings Publishing, 1977).

K. R. Howe, Robert Kiste, and Brij V. Lal, eds. *Tides of History: The Pacific Islands in the Twentieth Century* (Honolulu: University of Hawaii Press, 1994).

Robert Johannes. *Words of the Lagoon: Fishing and Marine Lore in the Palau District of Micronesia* (Berkeley and Los Angeles: University of California Press, 1981).

David Labby. *The Demystification of Yap: Dialectics of Culture on a Micronesian Island* (Chicago: University of Chicago Press, 1976).

Micronesians, Federated States of: nationality (people of the Federated States of Micronesia)

GEOGRAPHY

The 607 islands of the Federated States of Micronesia (FSM) are spread across 1,800 miles of the archipelago formerly known as the Caroline Islands. This nation of islands is in the western Pacific Ocean, east of the Philippines, north of New Guinea and Melanesia, west of Polynesia, and south of Hawaii. The four major states of FSM, from west to east, are: Yap, Chuuk (called Truk until 1990), Pohnpei (called Ponape until 1984), and Kosrae. Each of the four states is represented on the national flag with a white star.

The islands that make up the FSM are largely volcanic in origin although a few low-lying atolls are made of coral. Due to these origins only about 6 percent of the territory of the FSM is arable land, on which such products as black pepper, coconuts, tapioca, sweet potatoes, and tropical fruits are grown. The climate is tropical and wet, especially in the east, where occasional typhoons cause significant damage.

INCEPTION AS A NATION

The archipelago in the western Pacific that became the Federated States of Micronesia got its first Western name in 1526 from the Spanish, who called it the Carolinas, after Carlos (Charles) I, king of Spain and Holy Roman Emperor (as Charles V). Commonly referred to as the

FEDERATED STATES OF MICRONESIANS: NATIONALITY

nation:
Federated States of Micronesia (FSM)

derivation of name:
A Frenchman, Jules Dumont D'Urville, coined the term *Micronesia*, or small islands, in 1831.

government:
Federated States of Micronesia; constitutional government in free association with the United States of America

capital:
Palikir, Pohnpei

language:
English is one of seven official languages but is the only one common to all FSM islands. Other official languages are Chuukese, Pohnpeian, Yapese, Kosrean, Ulithian, and Woleaian. Nukuoro and Kapingamarangi are also spoken.

religion:
Roman Catholic 50 percent, Protestant 47 percent, other 3 percent

earlier inhabitants:
Polynesians and Micronesians were the first inhabitants of these islands.

demographics:
There are seven different Micronesian groups and two Polynesian groups, primarily on Nukuoro and the Kapingamarangi atolls of Pohnpei. Total population as of 2006 was 108,004.

Federated States of Micronesians: nationality time line

C.E.

0   The central Micronesian islands of Chuuk, Pohnpei, and Kosrae are settled from the east by late Lapita-era peoples. Yap is settled from the west.

1526 Spanish explorer Toribio Alonso de Salazar discovers the Caroline Islands, naming them the Carolinas after Carlos I, king of Spain.

1850s Protestant missions are set up in Pohnpei and Kosrae, American whalers frequent the islands, and trading posts are established for the export of copra (dried coconut).

1899 Spain sells many of her Spanish East Indies colonies to Germany, including the Carolines.

1914 The Japanese military secretly takes control of Micronesia from their large base in Truk Lagoon. Their headquarters are Dublon Town on the island of Tonoas, Chuuk.

1922–37 Japanese civilian control replaces the military on Chuuk.

1942 The United States defeats Japan at the battle of Midway.

1944 The United States invades Yap, Palau, and Woleai.

1945 Japanese forces in Truk Lagoon, their largest base in Micronesia, surrender to U.S. forces and end the war in the Pacific.

1947 The United Nations gives much of Micronesia to the United States as the Trust Territory of the Pacific Islands.

1960s Micronesians begin to push for independence from the United States.

1979 A constitution setting up the Federated States of Micronesia is ratified by Kosrae, Pohnpei, Chuuk, and Yap.

1986 The Federated States of Micronesia attains independence from the United States.

        The Federated States of Micronesia and the United States sign the Compact of Free Association, in which Washington provides significant economic support in exchange for taking control of FSM defense affairs including the establishment of military bases.

1991 FSM joins the United Nations.

1999 FSM and the United States begin talks on the future of the Compact of Free Association as the existing pact expires in 2001.

2002 Typhoon Chata'an kills dozens of people on the island of Chuuk.

2003 A 20-year compact between the United States and FSM is renegotiated; it provides approximately $1.2 billion in grants and trust funds to FSM.

2004 Typhoon Sudal devastates the island of Yap, destroying almost its entire infrastructure.

Caroline Islands for most of the next four and a half centuries, the region played host to four foreign occupiers up to the late 20th century: Spain, Germany, Japan, and the United States.

Even with the early discovery and naming of the islands, Spain was far less active in the region than the Germans, who dominated the copra and other trade for decades prior to the establishment of a Spanish colonial administration in 1886. In fact, Spain did not attempt to assert legal rights over the area until 1875, when it was placed under the Spanish East Indies along with the Philippines, Guam, Palau, and the Marianas. By 1885, however, Germany had annexed the archipelago and challenged Spain's claim based on an "absence of exercise." In 1885 the matter went for arbitration to Pope Leo XIII, who decided in favor of Spain but gave free trading rights to Germany. Then a mere 14 years later, after having lost the Spanish-American War, the Spanish empire could no longer afford the resources necessary to maintain its presence in the Pacific and sold the Caroline Islands to Germany in 1899.

Indigenous populations were affected to varying degrees by the outsiders' presence. Some more remote populations, especially before 1800, were barely affected and maintained their own governments, laws, and social structures. Others, however—particularly after 1800 with the arrival of European traders and the establishment of a colonial administration—were acutely aware of the threat posed to their way of life and sovereignty by foreign occupiers. Almost immediately on the island of Pohnpei, one of Spain's colonial headquarters, people took up arms against foreign rule. In 1887, in response to the contemptuous attitude toward local culture and mishandling of local workers' wages, the Sokehs and Nett people attacked and killed the governor and several of his men.

German occupiers also faced significant resistance when in 1910 the injustices of foreign occupation sparked what became known as the Sokehs' Rebellion. The rebellion was triggered by a tax imposed on all Pohnpeian men that was to be paid in labor for the construction of a road around the Pohnpeians' own island. Violence flared when the one of the governor's staff manhandled the highest-ranking Sokehs chief and several local workers were flogged. The next day the men showed up at work with weapons and killed the governor and several staff. It took the Germans four months, five warships, and assistance from opposing factions on the island to track down the Sokehs men who had retreated high into the mountains. Many were captured and others eventually surrendered to face either execution or relocation to the island of Palau, which was the fate of 460 of the rebels. Even today the Sokehs people sing the refrain of the brave but doomed warriors who challenged the Germans.

Japan first became involved in the Caroline Islands at the outbreak of World War I in 1914 when they secretly began building a large military base in Truk Lagoon on the island of

In September 1944 the United States landed on Palau to retake the archipelago from the Japanese; these forces are being led by the 81st Wildcat Division and are landing on Angaur Island. *(AP Photo)*

Chuuk. Within a short time the JAPANESE swept through the islands, occupying Germany's former possessions and establishing a new colonial administration. This marked the beginning of Japan's 30-year rule over Micronesia. After the war the League of Nations awarded Japan authority over Micronesia, and Japan's military rule changed to civilian control from 1922 to 1937. In addition to building a thriving trade in copra, phosphate, and fishing, the Japanese used the indigenous population of the islands as a slave-labor force to build infrastructure, agriculture, and other war-related employment. Despite Japan's tremendous economic development of the islands, little was done to encourage political participation.

The Second World War, 1939–45, produced a different outcome for Japan than had the First World War. From 1944 to 1945, the United States captured all Japanese-held territory in the Pacific. In 1947 the United Nations gave much of Micronesia, including what was later to become the Federated States of Micronesia, to the United States as the Trust Territory of the Pacific Islands. In 1951 the U.S. Navy handed the administration of the islands over to the Department of the Interior, which initiated a decade of rebuilding schools and hospitals and laying the foundations for the rapid development of the 1960s and 1970s.

In 1965 the congress of Micronesia was established, with representatives from each of the islands assuming positions of authority under the U.S. policy of "Micronization." Over the next decade the congress negotiated with the United States the status of its political future and the establishment in 1979 of the Federated States of Micronesia, consisting of Kosrae, Pohnpei, Chuuk, and Yap. The first president of the Federated States of Micronesia was Tosiwo Nakayama from Chuuk, who had been a member of the old congress of Micronesia and served as president of the senate for a number of years.

In 1986 the Federated States of Micronesia gained its independence and signed the Compact of Free Association with the United States. The compact, in which Washington provides significant economic support in exchange for taking control of FSM defense affairs, including the establishment of military bases, was renegotiated in 2003 for an additional 20 years.

While FSM is officially independent, its name is somewhat of a misnomer given the depth of its economic dependence on the United States. Compact funding is the primary source of FSM revenue, and as a result the U.S. government has become the key player in its economy. While the islands have the potential to build up a tourist industry, geographic isolation and an underdeveloped infrastructure seriously hinder long-term expansion in this area. Today subsistence farming and fishing are the main economic activities of the people of the FSM.

MINAHASANS

location:
Sulawesi, Indonesia

time period:
1689 to the present

ancestry:
Austronesian

language:
There are 10 different Sangir-Minahasan languages, all Austronesian.

CULTURAL IDENTITY

While the people of the Federated States of Micronesia represent a diverse group of cultures and languages, they are also united as a nation by common economic bonds and traditions of extended family and clan systems dating back hundreds of years.

A shared history of colonial domination with its inevitable interruption of local social, political, and economic power structures created common experiences from which a reactive culture emerged. While interisland trading existed prior to colonial involvement in Micronesia, foreign trade interests and colonial administrations organized the islands into more centralized economic systems. As a result, a common network of industries such as copra processing, fishing, and phosphate mining was established, connecting this otherwise economically disparate group of islands. In addition, in the 21st century a shared experience of civil service has united much of the labor force on all the islands, where two-thirds of all paid workers are government employees.

Another common feature is the existence of kinship and political ties that extend back hundreds of years, if not more. While most Micronesian islanders are matrilineal and thus trace their ancestry from the mother's side, the YAP are a patrilineal exception in tracing their ancestry through the father. Among the nation's many matrilineal peoples, nonlocalized clans play an important role in uniting people from many islands across the archipelago, a factor that has been used to create a common Micronesian identity for some members. Equally important are the political and ritual ties that emanated from Yap to many of the islands of Truk, incorporating most of FSM's inhabitants in traditional bonds of ritual and trade obligations. Like the bonds of matrilineal clanship, these religious and political bonds are frequently referred to today as central to the national identity of the Micronesian people.

FURTHER READING

Asian Development Bank. *Federated States of Micronesia: Towards a Self-Sustainable Economy: 2005 Economic Report* (Manila, Philippines: Asian Development Bank, 2006).

Ward H. Goodenough. *Property, Kin, and Community on Truk* (Hamden, Conn.: Archon Books, 1978).

James G. Peoples. *Island in Trust: Culture Change and Dependence in a Micronesian Economy* (Boulder, Colo.: Westview Press, 1985).

Saul H. Riesenberg. *The Native Polity of Ponape* (Washington, D.C.: Smithsonian Institution Press, 1968).

Mikirs   *See* KARBIS.

Minahasans (Manadonese, Minahasas, Minahasser, Minhasas, Tombalu, Tombula, Toumbulu)

The Minahasans are members of a confederation of ethnic groups, all speaking Sangir-Minahasan languages and residing in the northeastern corner of Indonesia's Sulawesi. Their name comes from *minahasa,* the local term for "united, become one." The reasons for this loose unification vary, depending on the source consulted. Most Western sources claim that the various peoples of this region were unified by the Dutch in the 1660s after expelling the Spanish and Portuguese, who were the first Europeans to land in the area about a century earlier. Local Minahasan sources claim unity occurred a bit earlier, possibly in 1460, in opposition to the neighboring kingdom of Bolaang Mongondow, with whom they fought several wars. Both versions of the story probably contain a degree of truth since the first Dutch reference to the name Minahasa comes very late, in 1789, and even prior to the direct Dutch colonial presence there was some degree of common identity among the nine or more separate linguistic groups in the region.

The treaty of 1689 between this population and the Dutch East Indies Company (Vereenigde Oost-Indisc Compagnie, or VOC) is probably the best founding date for the formation of a separate Minahasan people since it is at that point that the various *walak,* or leaders of the tribes, renounced their ties to the Spanish, which had been created individually starting in the 16th century, and swore allegiance to the VOC. Nonetheless, even at this time Dutch attempts to create a king or even paramount chief of the Minahasans failed due to the endemic rivalries between the various units included within this classification. Instead, VOC officials met with a council of chiefs occasionally to discuss details of trade between the two peoples and to address disputes. Rice was the main commodity provided by the Minahasans, while the Dutch provided external security, trade goods, and the opportunity for many Minahasans to advance in the larger Dutch colonial world.

By the start of the 19th century the VOC had been replaced by a direct Dutch colonial regime, and military capabilities increased. A Minahasan rebellion against Dutch control was crushed in 1809, and in 1822 growing coffee for sale to the Dutch became mandatory in

Minahasan territory. This last event led to the ever-increasing bureaucratization of Minahasan life as central to the colonial project in Sulawesi, which was called Celebes at the time. The other change brought to Minahasan society by the Dutch in the 19th century was Christianity. During the Portuguese and Spanish eras a small number of people in this region converted to Roman Catholicism, but it was under the missionaries of the Dutch Missionary Society (Nederlandsch Zendelingge Gnootschap, or NZG) that the majority of Minahasans converted to Protestantism. Commentary on the great success of these missionaries in Minahasa in comparison with the rest of Indonesia points to the weakness of Islam in the region, the strength and prestige of the Dutch bureaucracy, and the interference with traditional ritual activity caused by mandatory participation in the coffee economy. Other changes that the Dutch introduced include eliminating headhunting and slavery, building both houses and settlements using Dutch patterns rather than local ones, and even a desire on the part of many Minahasans to colonize the rest of Sulawesi.

In 1899 mandatory coffee cultivation came to an end, and this unpopular crop was quickly replaced by coconuts. The coconut economy did fairly well for Minahasa until the Great Depression of the 1930s, but even in that struggling era the Minahasans fared better than most of the rest of the colony due to their strong allegiance to the Dutch. Real struggle came in 1942 when Celebes (Sulawesi) was occupied by the JAPANESE and then in 1949 when Indonesia became independent. The region's former ties to the Dutch and the dominance of Christianity in the region made a few leaders wish to remain part of the Netherlands as a 12th province, while others even looked toward joining the Philippines rather than remaining part of a predominantly Muslim Indonesia. Although many Minahasans welcomed Indonesian independence since one of their own leaders, Sam Ratulangi, was named governor of eastern Indonesia, actions by the central government in the 1950s made many change their minds. Closure of the port at Manado in 1956 due to claims of smuggling convinced many that independence, or at least local autonomy, was preferable to being held within the JAVANESE-dominated Indonesia, and for about five years the government and local forces fought a minor war in the region. The government's superior forces won, and the Minahasans have been semireluctant Indonesian citizens ever since.

Minangkabau (Menangkabau, Minang)

The Minangkabau are a large ethnic group of West Sumatra, Indonesia. They generally live in the highlands of that province, though rarely further than 37 miles from the Indian Ocean.

Archaeological evidence from the Minangkabau region indicates that the ancestors of today's people migrated into the region around 2500 B.C.E., at about the same time that AUSTRONESIANS entered the archipelago from the Philippines. As was the case in Java, Bali, and elsewhere, the first formal political structures in the region were based on the Indian model of kingship where rulers were seen as the link between the gods and other supernatural forces and life on earth. Their paraphernalia and heirlooms were important not only as symbols of their rule but also as justification for their power. Ancient amulets, statues, and, later, letters were shown as proof of the kings' connection to the gods, even after Islam came to the Minangkabau from the ACEHNESE just before the 16th century. Today Buddhist stupas and Hindu memorials are still evident in western Sumatra from this pre-Islamic period and point to the power of these kings. According to Minangkabau mythology, their kings were descended not only from gods but also from Alexander the Great, or Iskandar Zulkarnain, as he is known locally. A more likely line of descent of the Minangkabau kings was from the JAVANESE, whose domination of the eastern region of the archipelago began before the common era and has lasted off and on through the present.

The first European to visit western Sumatra was Tome Pires, a Portuguese sailor who arrived in the 16th century. Like many Europeans who followed him, he arrived in Sumatra because of stories he had heard about vast goldfields on the island and evidence of wealth in black pepper and other spices. The Portuguese were followed in the 17th century by the Dutch, whose domination of the colonial economy began in 1641. Nonetheless, Minangkabau life did not change significantly until the 19th century when the Dutch East India Company (Vereenigde Oost-Indisc Compagnie or VOC) was replaced by the Dutch government as a true colonial power that imposed mandatory delivery of certain spices and food crops such as pepper, coffee, and rice. The Minangkabau rose up against the Dutch several times during the remainder of the colonial period: between 1820 and 1837 in the Paderi Wars, in 1908 in the form of an antitaxation rebellion, and in 1926–27 in a communist

MINANGKABAU

location:
West Sumatra, Indonesia

time period:
About 2500 B.C.E. to the present

ancestry:
Austronesian

language:
Minangkabau, closely related to Malay

revolution. All of these events, even the last one, had both secular and religious overtones: The people were seeking to free themselves from both colonial taxes and Christian laws and ideologies. Indeed, the Paderi Wars began as a conflict between different Islamic groups and only later took on the anticolonial overtones for which the wars are remembered today, both inside and outside Minangkabau territory.

In 1942 the JAPANESE occupied Sumatra as they did all of the Dutch territory in Asia and used their colony for the extraction of resources. Some segments of the local population welcomed the Japanese forces at first, because they claimed to be liberating Asia for the Asians. But people learned all too soon that Japanese occupation was to be no gentler or to provide no more independence than Dutch colonialism. Nonetheless, when the Japanese finally capitulated in 1945, large numbers of Minangkabau had attained significant bureaucratic and other governing experience and quickly moved to declare the country's independence. One of these activists, Mohammad Hatta, who later became the country's vice president under Sukarno, was a Minangkabau who raised the profile of his people among the core elite of the country. However, few Minangkabau have been able to follow Hatta's lead, and the leadership of the country has generally fallen to the Javanese since these early days of independence.

Minangkabau territory varies significantly from region to region, affecting the base subsistence practices in different localities. In the valleys, wet rice in permanent, well-irrigated fields is the norm and has been for hundreds of years or more, while in the highlands dry, upland rice

Mohammad Hatta, an ethnic Minangkabau, studied in the Netherlands, was jailed for his anticolonial activities, and was integral to Indonesia's independence movement against the Dutch. He served as his country's prime minister in 1948–50, as vice president in 1950–56, and he remains today one of Indonesia's greatest heroes.

is the norm. The hills also support a number of important cash crops, from coffee in the Dutch period to cinnamon, fruit, and rubber today. Fishing is important in west Sumatra's coastal waters as well as its rivers and lakes, while the highland forests support important foraging activities for honey, herbs, medicines, firewood, and other products. Most rural Minangkabau still maintain household gardens to produce most of their own vegetables and fruit, while urbanites maintain strong ties to their rural kin and obtain some of their food in this way.

An important part of the Minangkabau economy since recorded history began in the region is the act of *merantau*—temporary migration away from one's village to gain work experience, cash, and an expanded job network. Communities of emigrants continue to send remittances back to their home villages and families from as close as the Sumatran city of Padang and as distant as workplaces in the Middle East. This act of going *merantau* is not only a central economic strategy but also considered an important rite of passage in the community and one of what the Minangkabau consider their defining features as a unique people. Having a large number of Minangkabau young people engage in this activity over the centuries has also meant that these people are known throughout the archipelago for their trade and other economic activities.

The other defining characteristic of Minangkabau culture is its kinship structure. Rather than patrilineal descent and patrilocal residence patterns, the Minangkabau consider the most important line of descent to come through women, who remain in their family home at marriage. Husbands may move into their wives' homes; more commonly, however, they visit sometimes but spend most of their time with their own sisters and their children. The reason men focus their energies on their sisters' children rather than their own is that their own children are not in their kinship group, or *suku*; they are in their mothers' groups. Matrilineal descent means that land use, titles, and any other kind of movable or conceptual property are inherited from one's mother and mother's brother instead of one's father. Membership in a clan and subclan are also inherited from one's mother. This pattern is relatively unique in Indonesia and has generated significant interest in the Minangkabau among anthropologists and others during the past 150 or more years. Many Minangkabau themselves have also written about their unique social structure and point to their unique ability to maintain this traditional pattern even in the context of an Islamic society, which usually favors men and sons over women and daughters.

FURTHER READING

P. E. de Josselin de Jong. *Minangkabau and Negri Sembilan: Socio-Political Structure in Indonesia* (New York: AMS Press, 1980).

Joel S. Kahn. *Minangkabau Social Formations: Indonesian Peasants and the World Economy* (New York: Cambridge University Press, 1980).

Mingrelians (Mengrelians, Megrelians)

The Mingrelians are a subgroup of the GEORGIANS of the central Caucasus. As speakers of a Kartvelian language, the Mingrelian people are descended from the same ancient proto-Kartvelians as Georgians, LAZ, and SVAN. They are most distantly related to the Svan, who broke from the ancient community about 4,000 years ago, and most closely related to the Laz, from whom they were separated by the Turks in the past 500 years. Some sources say the Laz and Mingrelian peoples share the same language, called Zan, but this ignores the fact that the two languages are only partially mutually intelligible. Mingrelians are not officially recognized as separate from the dominant Georgians, so there are no official figures for the contemporary population; the best estimate is that there are about half a million Mingrelians in contemporary Georgia.

The region of Mingrelia, or Samegrelo, has historically been connected to the kingdom of the COLCHIANS, whom many Laz and Mingrelians consider their ancestors, and that of Egrisi (*see* LAZ). They were united into the larger Georgian kingdom in the 11th century and remained there until the 15th century, when they achieved a degree of independence within the larger Ottoman empire. In the early 19th century the RUSSIANS replaced the Ottomans as the dominant power in the province until 1918, when the Democratic Republic of Georgia absorbed it. As a province of Georgia, Samegrelo was part of the Soviet Union until 1991, when Georgia achieved its independence. Due to the period of Russian rule in Samegrelo, there is a greater fluency in Russian among many Mingrelians than among the Georgian population as a whole.

During the Soviet era, the Mingrelians came to be known outside their Caucasian homeland from the 1951–53 "Mingrelian Affair," when Joseph Stalin, himself an ethnic Georgian, pursued one of his rivals for state power, Lavrenti Beria, an ethnic Mingrelian. The purge was nominally about quelling corruption in Georgia but more about consolidating power at the supreme Soviet level. When Stalin died in 1953, the purge ended before achieving its ultimate goal of eliminating Beria.

Mingrelians emerged again on the global scene at the time of the breakup of the Soviet Union in 1991. The first president of independent Georgia was Zviad Gamsakhurdia, an ethnic Mingrelian who had been one of the country's leading dissidents during the Soviet era. Upon taking power, however, Gamsakhurdia became more autocratic than democratic, which inspired an armed uprising against him not long after he took power in 1991. By September that year, the Georgian civil war had seen its first casualties and the declaration of martial law, and in January 1992 Gamsakhurdia fled the country, eventually setting up a government in exile in Chechnya.

Perhaps even more central to the experiences of many Mingrelians in the post-Soviet era, however, were the activities in their neighboring province of Abkhazia. During the Soviet era many Mingrelian-Georgians had been moved into Abkhazia to dilute and neutralize the power of the ABKHAZIANS. After Georgian independence, the Abkhazians took up arms to reclaim their land, language, and culture, making refugees out of about 200,000 Georgians, most of whom were Mingrelians, who now reside in Georgia's capital Tbilisi or other regions of the country.

See also GEORGIANS: NATIONALITY.

MINGRELIANS

location:
Mostly in the Samegrelo or Mingrelia region of western Georgia

time period:
About 1500 to the present

ancestry:
Proto-Kartvelian

language:
Mingrelian or Margaluri, a Kartvelian language with Georgian, Svan, and Laz. Among these four languages, only Georgian is written, and Mingrelian speakers use Georgian as their church and literary languages.

Mizo (Kuki, Lushai, Zomi)

The Mizo, whose name means "people of the highland," are one of the SCHEDULED TRIBES in India who live largely in Mizoram, Manipur, and Tripura; much smaller numbers live in the adjoining countries of Myanmar (Burma) and Bangladesh. The name of the Indian state of Mizoram means "country of the Mizo," which has been their accepted name since the 1950s. Prior to that the British called them Lushai and the BENGALIS called them Kuki.

As speakers of Tibeto-Burman languages, the various subgroups of the Mizo probably have their ancient origins in China. Sometime prior to 1000 C.E. they migrated into Myanmar and then India a few hundred years later. The first written mention of them as Kuki was in 1777 when a chief of a rival tribe in the Chittagong region asked the British for assistance in driving out a

MIZO

location:
India, Myanmar (Burma), and Bangladesh

time period:
Before 1000 C.E. to the present

ancestry:
Tibeto-Burman

language:
Mizo, a Tibeto-Burman language

Kuki incursion. The British entered the region of contemporary Mizoram in about 1844, when they began punitive raids on land held by various Mizo chiefs. When the British pulled out of India in 1947, many tribal peoples in the northeast wanted to revert back to the precolonial status quo when they were free to rule their own peoples in their own way. However, there was a distinct class division between traditional chiefs, who wanted to revert to the precolonial status quo, and the newly emerging educated, urban middle class, who thought that inclusion in the newly formed India would benefit them more. The latter, who were largely represented by the Mizo Commoners Union, or Mizo Union, were extremely organized and ultimately successful in their bid to defeat the traditional chiefs' United Mizo Freedom Organization.

After about a decade of inclusion in India as part of the state of Assam, many Mizo came to regret their decision to support the Mizo Union. The Indian central government reneged on its promise to abolish the position of chief, threatened the continued viability of local languages, gave almost no power to the local district councils, and perhaps most important, did little to counter the terrible effects of the Mautam famine in 1959. This confluence of events allowed the traditional leadership to reemerge in the 1960s with tremendous support from the people, who by that point had united behind a common Mizo identity rather than identifying solely with their local and dialect communities. This new Mizo separatist movement mobilized Mizo at all levels of society and made it almost impossible for the central and state governments not to take their demands seriously. In 1972 Mizoram was upgraded to the status of union territory, and in 1987, after a full armistice with the Mizo National Front, Mizoram became a state.

The traditional subsistence activity of most Mizo was swidden, or slash-and-burn agriculture. Using fire to burn off primary or secondary growth, the Mizo then planted rice, corn, cabbages, and other crops; ginger and cotton have been important cash crops for many decades. A few domesticated animals, such as pigs and poultry, plus some hunting and fishing provide most protein for rural families to supplement their garden produce. Wealthier families have a few head of cattle, and in the past each village maintained a few *gayals*, a cattle relative, which were communally used during festivals and other events, a custom that has since passed out of favor.

Most Mizo live in nuclear family groups, although anybody who lives in the same household and eats with the family is considered family, regardless of blood ties. At marriage most sons move out of their family homes with their wives or, in the past, multiple wives, but youngest sons tend to remain at home, care for their elderly parents, and inherit the house at their parents' deaths. All the rest of the father's property is divided among his sons; if a woman has any property, jewelry, or other items, her daughters usually inherit it.

Since the British colonial period, most Mizo have been adherents of Protestant Christianity, with a variety of denominations represented, including Seventh Day Adventists, Baptists, United Pentecostals, and even the Salvation Army. Nonetheless, most rural villages also have exorcists who engage in healing practices by casting out demons and Satan, which tends to be a syncretic practice involving the Holy Ghost and a variety of local spirits and gods.

M'nong (M.Nông, Mnong Gar, Phii Bree)

The M'nong are one of the many VIETNAMESE ethnic minority groups who reside in the Tay Nguyen, or central highlands region of the country. They are indigenous to that region and over the past two millennia have been pushed into the highlands by the CHAMS, Vietnamese, and then the French colonial regime. During the Vietnam War the M'nong, along with many other DEGA or Montagnard groups, worked with the United States to try to defeat the National Liberation Front (NLF) and the North Vietnamese as part of their thousand-year struggle against Vietnamese domination. As a result many M'nong were relocated to the United States and Australia following the war. Those who have remained are extremely poor and have been persecuted for the past 30 years. The most recent events occurred in 2002, when a number of M'nong asylum seekers were granted entry to the United States from the UN refugee camp in Cambodia where they had been living, afraid for their lives if they were forced to return to Vietnam.

The M'nong economy is dominated by swidden (slash-and-burn) agriculture. Each family uses a garden plot for a year and then allows it to lie fallow for between five and 20 years. The longer the fallow period, the easier it is to clear the land, since a few large trees are easier to remove than secondary-growth bamboo covering a plot of ground; the longer periods also put more nutrients back into the soil and thus allow for a greater yield at harvest time. Larger trees also provide much-needed firewood, charcoal, and building materials, which can be used, exchanged, or sold. Unfortunately, many families do not have access to enough land to allow them to let each plot remain unused for the full 20 years, with 8–10 years being the average.

The staple crop grown on these fields is upland rice, with corn and vegetables also produced. A few M'nong families grow coffee, but the region is not ideal for this crop and it remains marginal. Cotton was once produced as well but was abandoned more than a quarter of a century ago because of the drain on land and human resources it entailed with little reward. Livestock provide both food and products to exchange or sell, with pigs and smaller animals cared for in and around the household and larger animals like cattle and buffalo allowed to graze in the open. If a family produces a surplus of any food product, it is much more likely to be given in exchange with another M'nong family or, more rarely, with a Vietnamese trader, than to be sold. The M'nong engage in almost no cash cropping, and their greatest access to cash comes from selling their own labor to Vietnamese farmers or selling a spare cow, bull, or buffalo. The M'nong also train elephants, both for their own use in clearing fields and for sale, but this is a rare event and cannot be relied upon as a steady source of income.

Some agricultural activities are engaged in by both women and men, but women and daughters work much harder than their husbands, brothers, and sons. Women are responsible for gathering the family's firewood and carrying water, both extremely heavy and arduous tasks, especially if the nearest forest and stream are located many miles from the village. They do all the child care, cooking, other housework, tending of chickens and pigs, and most gardening, although men do participate in clearing the fields and harvesting. Women are also responsible for milling the family's rice, which is usually done in such small amounts that it is impractical and too expensive to have it done commercially. Girls as young as nine or 10 begin to participate fully in these household chores, while boys are left alone much more to play and attend school. The only task that may be assigned to a boy is herding larger animals, and that may be done by elderly relatives if the boy is studying. The position of women has been diminished over time and through interactions with outsiders, especially Vietnamese officials and educators who assume that household heads are men, that decisions about the household economy are always made by men, and that training provided to men will be passed on to women. All of these assumptions have turned out to be inaccurate for most M'nong families, where women almost always control the family finances and serve as household heads in up to 15 percent of families.

Although they bear the greater burden in subsistence and household chores and have had some of their authority within the family unit diminished by outsiders, women among the M'nong continue to have higher status than women generally in Vietnamese society. M'nong kinship is matrilineal: Membership in lineages is handed down from mother to children rather than from father to children. Because of this inheritance pattern, women tend to have much more control over their families' land; decisions about renting or selling a plot, exchanging the use of a plot for some other resource, or other land uses tend to be made jointly. In cases of separation and divorce, the M'nong also grant custody of the children to the mother, who raises them in their matrilineal family, rather than to the father, who belongs to a different matriline than his children. When a couple marries, the husband moves into his wife's family's longhouse, usually into a new segment that has been built for the young couple and is connected to the woman's parents and other married sisters' homes; this pattern is matrilocal residence. The new husband also works her family's land rather than his own.

Outside the family and lineage, the most important social unit among the M'nong is the village. In the village most important decisions about land tenure, conflict resolution, and civil justice have traditionally been made by the village headman or chief, instead of by a council of elders, which is common among many other Dega groups. There is some debate about whether this position has always been of central importance or whether it was enhanced during the colonial period by French bureaucrats who wanted one individual to whom they could turn for administrative purposes. Either way, for much of the 20th century the headman was the key figure in the political life of the village, a position that remains somewhat true today despite the changes brought by the Vietnamese communist state. In addition to a headman, most villages also have a shaman who acts as a healer, diviner, ritual specialist, and general mediator between the material and spiritual worlds. In many cases these shamans are women, indicative of the relatively high status accorded to women among the M'nong.

M'NONG

location:
The central highlands of Vietnam, especially Dak Lak Province, and Cambodia, especially Mondolkiri Province

time period:
Unknown to the present

ancestry:
Proto-Mon-Khmer

language:
M'nong, a Mon-Khmer language in the larger Austro-Asiatic language family

Mohe (Malgal, Mogher, Moho)

The Mohe were a confederation of many Tungusic-speaking tribes who lived between the Changbaishan Mountains of China and the Heilongjiang or Amur River, which currently divides Manchuria from Russia. One of the largest of these tribes was the Heisui, or Black Mohe. They are believed to be the ancestors of the JURCHENS, who formed the Jin dynasty in China in 1115, as well as the later MANCHUS, who formed the Qing dynasty in 1644. There are many references to the Heisui Mohe during the Tang era, 618–907, which point to their golden age as part of the Parhae kingdom. Prior to their being referred to as the Mohe or Malgal during the Tang dynasty, these people are assumed to be the same as the Sushen (249–207 B.C.E.), Yilou (206 B.C.E.–24 C.E.), and Wuji (386–534).

Mohe culture is closely associated with the kingdom of Parhae, or Bolhai, as it is sometimes written, which emerged in the eighth century in Manchuria and the northern Korean Peninsula. Unfortunately, no written records from this kingdom survive today, the archaeological record is unclear about its cultural background, and Chinese sources that do mention its existence are heavily biased against it. Korean records do not mention Parhae at all. What we do know is that after entering Manchuria in about 494 C.E., the Wuji, who soon came to be known as Mohe or Malgal, quickly became a significantly large minority in the Korean kingdom of Koguryo. When that kingdom collapsed at the hands of a joint Chinese and Shilla army in 668, Shilla, a largely Korean kingdom, drove the Tang dynasty out of the region. This action left a vacuum in the north that was soon filled by the emergence of Parhae, dominated by remnants of the northern Koguryo nobles and soldiers. Chinese records indicate that while Parhae was a multiethnic kingdom, the Mohe made up a considerable percentage of the population and may even have been among the earliest rulers; Mohe-style pottery has been found in the grave sites of the first generation of Parhae rulers, and Mohe names appear in many lineages and documents from the first and second generations of rulers. After this period, however, the Mohe names disappear entirely, and cultural artifacts can be found only on the northern margins of the kingdom. Archaeologists and historians believe that some segments of the Mohe people became Sinicized and integrated into Tang Chinese culture, while those among the nobility integrated into the old Koguryo culture and society. By the time Parhae fell to the KHITANS' Liao empire in 926, nothing remained of Mohe; those in the south had become Chinese, while those in the north had developed into the independent Jurchen culture.

The Mohe were not a single tribal group but rather a loose union of peoples, such as the Sumo or Sumuo, Heisui, Yulou, Yuexi, and others. All of them survived primarily on hunting and gathering rather than agriculture in the years before the consolidation of Parhae, and they were known in Chinese documents as good horsemen and archers. Even as early as the Sushen period, leaders from this tribe gave tribute to the Chinese rulers in the form of bows and stone arrowheads. Chinese sources also describe their living arrangements as underground caverns that were entered and exited through a hole that also allowed smoke to draft from their indoor fires. This style was said to protect the Mohe from the cold winds that howl across Manchuria during the autumn and winter seasons. Although these houses have not survived, from about the fifth through the 10th centuries Mohe culture is identifiable in archaeological sites from its double-rimmed pots in the shape of a small urn as well as decorated belt buckles. Mohe culture can be said to have disappeared entirely once these pots had been replaced even in the far north of Manchuria by the standard Jurchen-style pottery, with its pumpkin shape and long neck.

Although the Mohe emerged as hunters and gatherers, Parhae was an agricultural kingdom, which indicates that by this period the Mohe too had probably settled down as farmers, herders, and craftsmen. Metallurgy became more advanced in this period, and hardy strains of wheat, millet, and other crops had been adapted to the relatively short growing season of this northern region. The Chinese even describe Parhae as having its own writing system, although it has never been found, and five separate cities, which points to a division of labor that would have been alien to the Mohe tribes of previous centuries.

See also KOREANS.

Mohenjo-Daro culture   *See* HARAPPANS.

Moken   *See* SEA GYPSIES.

Mol   *See* MUONG.

Mon (Mun, Peguan, Talaing, Taleng, Raman, Rmen)

The Mon are the most ancient population in the region of contemporary Myanmar; they are also known as Talaing in Thailand, where several hundred thousand currently live, either as a result of migrations beginning about 400 years ago or as refugees having fled from the military regime in Myanmar.

GEOGRAPHY

The traditional homeland of the Mon is lower Burma and the northern section of Tenasserim, a lowland delta region, and parts of western Thailand. Today the boundaries of Mon State do not exactly coincide with their historical homeland, which at one point in the 18th century was all of contemporary Myanmar.

Mon lands are characterized by the monsoon climate that brings significant rain from June to October, a cool interlude for a month or two, and then a hot, dry period lasting until the rains return.

ORIGINS

The Mon are the descendants of a wave of migrants who entered Southeast Asia between 2500 and 1500 B.C.E., probably from the area of the Mongolian plateau in north Asia. Linguistically, their closest relatives are the KHMERS, who made a similar migration at about the same time. Their Southeast Asian homeland is the Tenasserim region and along the southern Irrawaddy delta in Myanmar as well as adjoining lands in Thailand. Many Mon nationalists have tried to connect their territory along the Bay of Bengal with the semimythological kingdom of Suwarnabhumi as described in the Indian Edicts of Asoka, but this cannot be taken as necessarily accurate; Thai nationalists have done the same, and according to many historians the real Suwarnabhumi would probably have existed in southern India rather than in Southeast Asia.

HISTORY

While the origins and early history of the Mon remain unclear, historians of the region generally agree that they were one of the first peoples to convert to Buddhism, perhaps in the third century B.C.E. The various Mon kingdoms that flourished in Southeast Asia all sponsored the building of significant Buddhist monasteries, temples, and pagodas as well as Buddhist scholarship. When the Burman king finally conquered the Mon in 1057, the BURMANS carried off not only the Mon king and his family but also large numbers of Buddhist texts and sculptures and had enormous monasteries and other buildings commissioned by Mon architects and builders in their own capital, Pagan.

Although there are many earlier kingdoms and city-states postulated to have been of Mon origins, the first verified Mon kingdoms were Dvaravati, located on the lower reaches of the Chao Phraya River in contemporary Thailand, and Thaton, located in northern Mon State in Myanmar. However, even with these two kingdoms, we cannot be certain as to the extent of their realms since some Chinese and ancient Mon sources speak of the two as one and the same kingdom. Haripunjaya, on the Mae Nam River of northern Thailand and sometimes cited as among the earliest Mon kingdoms, was actually a northern colony of Dvaravati set up in the seventh century; it did later attain its independence.

The wealth of all these Mon kingdoms was based on trade with Indonesia, India, China, and other Southeast Asian regions. The Mon were seafarers who carried camphor, tropical hardwoods, copper, tin, areca nuts, rubies, and other precious stones and traded them for a wide variety of goods. So-called Martaban jars from the inland region of the Mon kingdoms have been found as far away as Turkey in the west and Japan in the east. Politically, like Funan, CHENLA, and Angkor, the early Mon states borrowed their political system from India's mandala system, in which the king of each city-state was acknowledged as divine. Part of the confusion around the names and extent of these kingdoms lies in this decentralized political structure in which local princes and kings could rise and fall quickly, leaving the archaeological record unclear.

Early Mon history is often described as coming to an end in 1057, when the Burman King Anawrahta of Pagan is said to have defeated the Mon. However, this version of history has been interpreted in a very different manner by others, who claim that the Mon actually moved north to colonize Pagan. While the circumstances of the period are unclear, what is a certainty is that in this period the Burman city was transformed by Mon architecture and Buddhism. The Mon king, Manuba, often spelled Manuha as well, and his family lived very well in Pagan, which gives some credence to the colonization story; however, the consolidation of Burman power in the region points the other way. Regardless, Pagan ruled much of the area of central Myanmar for a period of about 200 years, until 1287, when the MONGOLS arrived, sacked the city, and allowed various Mon, Shan, and other small kingdoms to flourish in the area formerly controlled by Pagan.

The most important Mon kingdom to emerge in the post-Mongol era was the Martaban kingdom, founded in 1287 by King Wareru,

MON

location:
Southern Myanmar (Burma), northern Thailand, with very small numbers in both Cambodia and Vietnam

time period:
Possibly 2500–1500 B.C.E. to the present

language:
Mon, an Austro-Asiatic language related to Khmer

Mon time line

B.C.E.

2500–1500 Period of migration; Mon-Khmer peoples move south from the Mongolian plateau to mainland Southeast Asia.

300 Possible founding date for the kingdom of Thaton, though this is more likely many hundreds of years later in the sixth century C.E.

third century Possible period of widespread Mon conversion to Buddhism.

C.E.

573 Hongsavatoi (Pegu) is said to be founded by two Mon princes, Samala and Wimala.

sixth century Dvaravati, an early Mon kingdom, is established along the Chao Phraya River in Thailand. Thaton, a Mon kingdom in what is now southern Myanmar, is probably founded at about the same time.

seventh century Haripunjaya is established as a colony of the Dvaravati kingdom.

1287 The Mongols conquer Pagan, allowing for the emergence of many independent Mon kingdoms. The most important is Martaban, founded in the same year.

1369 The Wareru dynasty moves its capital from Martaban to Pegu.

1385–1423 King Rajadhirij comes to the throne at Pegu, unites all the Mon peoples in a newly formed Ramanyadesa, and expands their territory into upper Burma through constant warfare.

1533 The Mon kingdoms fall to the Burman king Thabinshwehti, who takes over the city of Pegu as his capital.

1740 The Mon take advantage of Burman weakness and reestablish the Hongsavatoi kingdom at Pegu.

1752 Hongsavatoi conquers the Burman capital at Ava and consolidates control over the country.

1757 Hongsavatoi, the last independent Mon kingdom, is overrun by the Burmans who kill thousands of people and destroy many Mon-language texts.

1824 The British take control over the Mon lands; two years later they annex the entire country.

1939 The All Ramanya Mon Association is formed to preserve the Mon language, religion, and culture. It is considered the first modern Mon national organization.

1942 The British are expelled from Burma by the Japanese.

1945 The British retake Burma.

1947 Independence leader Aung San is assassinated, and hopes for a multiethnic leadership in an independent Burma are extinguished.

1948 Burma becomes independent from Britain in January, and the civil war begins.

1958 Mon insurgents agree to lay down their arms and work within Burma's democratic system.

1962 A military junta in Burma leaves the Mon with no choice but to pick up their arms and continue fighting.

1995 The Mon and Burmese government sign a cease-fire agreement, which ends the formal fighting but solves none of the associated problems.

2007 About 45 Mon refugees are arrested in Malaysia for having entered the country illegally or failing to produce legal documentation. Twelve are subsequently released, and two others transported to the Thai-Malaysian border. About 30 are detained in camps.

who ruled from there till 1306. Like the earlier Mon kingdoms, Martaban's economy was based on trade and shipping, especially with the Thai kingdom at Sukhotai. Also like the earlier period, at times Martaban aligned itself with other Mon kingdoms in the region, such as Pegu and Bassein-Myaungmya. These loose alliances in both periods are sometimes called Ramanyadesa, which makes studying their history extremely difficult. However, in the 14th century Martaban tried not only to ally itself with its fellow Mon kingdoms, but to dominate their politics and economies. They were successful only to a small degree and by 1369 these two lesser kingdoms had united to overthrow Martaban. King Bannya U moved his capital to Pegu, relegating Martaban to a small trading city within the larger kingdom.

Bannya U was relatively powerless in the face of competing kings at Martaban and Bassein-Myaungmya, but with the ascendance of King Rajadhirij in 1385 the Mon were once again unified under the loose confederacy of Ramanyadesa in the face of a military attack from the north. This larger Mon kingdom was also able to send military missions to Arakan and Ava to wage war on these territories as well. Despite his success, the Mon kings who followed him were not able to hold onto the territory he gained or to expand their kingdoms beyond lower Burma. They fought several defensive wars against the THAIS of Ayutthaya, who invaded Tenasserim, but never went on the offensive after the death of Rajadhirij. Finally, in 1533 the Burman king Thabinshwehti conquered the Mon and set up his own capital at Pegu.

The various Mon kings and princes who followed did not abandon the hope of one day emerging from under the yolk of their Burman overlords, and in 1740 Burman weakness allowed for the reemergence of the Hongsavatoi kingdom at Pegu. The Mon then went on the offensive and a dozen years later captured the Burman capital at Ava. They held their Burmese territory for only half a decade before finally falling to the Burmans for the last time in 1757. At that time U Aungzeya or King Alaungphaya's invasion of Pegu and other Mon territories was catastrophic. Tens of thousands of Mon were killed, including more than 3,000 Buddhist priests in Pegu alone. Thousands of Mon-language documents and texts, mostly written on palm leaves, were destroyed by the marauding Burmans, leaving us with a largely Burman view of history today, and any official use of Mon in public was forbidden. Some of the Mon population in Thailand today has its roots in the persecution that followed this victory, which drove thousands of priests and laypeople to abandon their homes and land and seek refuge in the Thai kingdom.

The worst excesses against the Mon took place right after the war in 1757, but general persecution, forced labor, language restrictions, and loss of land and homes continued to take place for the following 68 years, until the British consolidated their power over the Mon territories in 1824. Indeed, the British utilized the Mon during the Second Anglo-Burmese War and encouraged their insurrection in their divide-and-conquer strategy generally in the region. This strategy, combined with the relative peace that reigned in the region under the British, allowed for the reemergence of the Mon language and culture and the birth of a modern nationalism among the Mon, which sought autonomy and even independence over what the Mon called the Monlands. At this time a number of Mon communities even left their homes in Thailand and returned to Burma to assist in the dual project of overthrowing the Burmans and forming a modern national community among the Mon, strong and stable enough to work with the British as allies. When the British reneged on a deal they supposedly made with the Mon to grant them relative independence, this national project turned against British colonialism just as it had turned against Burman colonialism seven decades earlier.

During World War II many of Burma's non-Burman minorities worked with the British against the Burmans and JAPANESE, which ultimately backfired when the Japanese took the country in 1942 and then when the Burmans emerged as the dominant force in postwar negotiations with the British for national independence. The Mon, however, did not generally side with the British, despising their European colonizers as much as their Burman ones. On an individual basis, many Mon youth did join Aung San's Burma Independence Army (BIA), which at first assisted the Japanese and then turned against them at the end of the war.

Despite this participation in the BIA, which led to Burmese negotiations with the British when the transition to postcolonialism was on the table from 1945 to 1947, the Mon were not granted a territory of their own at independence in 1948. The All Ramanya Mon Association, which was formed in 1937 but mostly sat quietly during the war, re-emerged, along with the United Mon Association and Mon Freedom League, to lead the push for Mon autonomy in their lower Burmese territory. Their claims were rejected by the government of U Nu, who led Burma after the assassination in 1947 of the more moderate leader Aung San.

In the widespread civil war that erupted soon after independence, the Mon participated largely through the military organization of the Mon People's Front (MPF). They waged war in the south for about a decade until 1958, when they put down their arms and agreed to work for autonomy within the larger, democratic system in Burma. This was short-lived, however, because in 1962 the military took over the government in Burma, and the democratic route to autonomy was closed. The New Mon State Party (NMSP) replaced the MPF in the armed struggle against the national army and continued into 1995. In 1974 the Burmese government gave nominal recognition to some ethnic groups, including the Mon, by creating states that largely coincided with ethnic boundaries, but this concession has done little to appease any of the peoples involved, including the Mon.

In 1995 the government and the Mon signed a historic cease-fire, but this has not conciliated many Mon nationalists who desire greater autonomy, if not outright independence, in Mon State. The government has done very little to stop the persecution and violence committed against Mon civilians by the military. Since 1996 the Mon umbrella organization the Mon Unity League has engaged in nonmilitary actions to combat these atrocities and to reach the Mon goals, but with little success. Over the course of the past decade, the Mon and other ethnic groups fighting against the military government have lost an important ally in the government of Thailand, which has taken up a policy of "constructive engagement" with Myanmar. As a result, thousands of refugees have been repatriated to Myanmar, those who remain have been denied Thai citizenship, and support for the insurgents as anticommunist buffers between Thailand and Myanmar has disappeared. In 2007 Mon refugees in Malaysia were detained, returned home, or released along the border with Thailand, indicating that assistance from any neighboring country is probably not going to be forthcoming in the near future. For the present, the Mon will struggle along with the vast majority of the Burmese people against their illegitimate military government and hope a democratic future will improve their situation, if not provide their ultimate goal of a country to call their own.

CULTURE

Mon culture is built around the pillars of an agricultural and fishing subsistence economy and Theravada Buddhism, adopted prior to the start of the common era. Like the other lowland Southeast Asians, the Mon focus most of their agricultural production on wet rice, which they supplement with yams, sweet potatoes, sugarcane, and pineapples. Fishing at the commercial level has decreased due to Thai competition but remains an important subsistence practice for all coastal and riverine communities. Mon who have lived in rural Thailand for the past four centuries or so have a similar life to their Burmese cousins; however, without the persecution of the past half century, many have fully integrated into Thai society and have become indistinguishable from their neighbors. This is quite different from the more recent Mon migrants who have entered Thailand illegally as refugees from the wars in Burma/Myanmar. These people are often denied any basic rights as citizens or residents and live on the margins of society as sharecroppers or fishermen. In Sangkhlaburi a Mon Culture and Literature Survival Project has emerged to capture the stories of these refugees, to teach their children about Mon history and culture, and to make sure their language does not disappear.

Mon society is considered bilateral with regard to kinship, which means that each individual counts his or her relatives on the mother's and father's sides as equal to each other with regard to ritual obligation and incest taboos. The *kalok,* or ghost dance, which is an elaborate festival dedicated to ancestral spirits that are believed to guard homes, still takes place in Mon communities in both Thailand and Myanmar. In addition to these revered ancestors, the Mon recognize the existence of a number of other spirits from both the natural and human worlds, and each traditional village has its own *bau ju,* or shrine, dedicated to these beings. Offerings are regularly made in order to prevent or heal illness, protect animals and children, and give thanks for a good harvest. Mon shamans, or *don,* act as mediators between the human and spirit worlds, passing messages between them by going into trance or dancing.

Despite the existence of these spirits, the Mon are the most ancient Buddhist people in mainland Southeast Asia and are often described as the conduit of the Theravada school between India and the FUNANESE and Chenla kingdoms. Whether that is true is unknown, but certainly Buddhism in both its formal and lay varieties has been central to Mon life for thousands of years. Mon architecture and learning have until the present time focused on religious works, and all the Mon city-states of the past exhibit spectacular gold and terra cotta buildings to house monks, books, and relics.

FURTHER READING

Brian L. Foster. *Commerce and Ethnic Differences: The Case of the Mons in Thailand* (Athens: Ohio University Center for International Studies, 1982).

Michael Smithies. *The Mons* (Bangkok: Siam Society, 1986).

Ashley South. *Mon Nationalism and Civil War in Burma: The Golden Sheldrake* (New York: Routledge Curzon, 2003).

Monba (Menba, Monpa)

The Monba are one of China's recognized 55 national minority groups; members of this ethnolinguistic community who live in India are known as Monpa, and a small number of this group also reside in Bhutan. The name *Monba* means "people of the Mon Yul" or "land" in Tibetan and points to their dominant economic activities, farming and herding. Within the larger Monba or Monpa category, there are six subgroups distinguishable by their dialect and geographic location: Tawang Monpa, Dirang Monpa, Lish Monpa, Bhut Monpa, Kalaktang Monpa, and Panchen Monpa. The most distinctive of this group of six are the Bhut Monpa, who engaged in hunting and gathering rather than agriculture and combined their Buddhist beliefs and practices with those of animism and a local religion known as Bon.

Monba prehistory remains somewhat uncertain, but there is some archaeological evidence to support local legend that they ruled their own kingdom in the region from about 500 B.C.E. until about 600 C.E. The kingdom, Monyul or Lhomon, may have included territory from Tawang to West Bengal, including sections of contemporary Assam and Sikkim. What is more certain is that the Monba or Monpa are the aboriginal population in the eastern Himalayan territory and were overrun by the migrations of Bhutia and others.

Like the Tibetans, the Monba engage in the rarest form of marriage on earth, polyandry, which technically means that women can have more than one husband. In reality, what polyandry in the context of Himalayan cultures means is that brothers marry just one woman among them, often a cross-cousin or the daughter of their mother's brother or father's sister. This form of marriage limits the birthrate and is an adaptation to the limited land resources of the mountainous region in which they live. Instead of each brother marrying a woman and having his own family, which would require the original family's land holding to be subdivided among all the brothers' new families, the brothers work together on the same piece of family land and thus keep it intact. If a brother decides not to participate in marriage with his brothers, he is not able to inherit any family land but must move away, often relocating to a city or joining a monastery as a monk. As is the case among all societies that allow polyandry, the Monba also allow both monogamous and polygynous marriages. The latter form is a necessity in societies that allow polyandry because otherwise there would be a large number of adult women living alone; while in Western and urban situations that is perfectly fine, rural women in Tibet, India, and Bhutan would find it very difficult to survive without a male head of household.

Most Monba communities focus their agricultural activity on growing corn, rice, wheat, barley, pumpkins, beans, chilies, tobacco, indigo, and cotton. They use a combination of terraced, irrigated plots, which are carved into the mountain sides to prevent erosion, and swidden (slash-and-burn) fields that are used only for a season or two. Their herds are made up of cattle and yak, the wool from which is woven into blankets and sweaters to keep them warm in their cold mountain homes. Many Monba keep pigs, sheep, and chickens as well. Many families supplement their subsistence activities with woodcarving, weaving, carpet and paper making, working with bamboo, and creating *thangka* religious paintings. For centuries the Monba have engaged in both trade and market exchange with their neighbors, which has brought consumer items from many regions into their communities and has seen the dispersion of their crafts throughout China and India.

The central feature of Monba culture is their adherence to Buddhism of the Gelugpa or Yellow Hat sect, the branch ruled by the Dalai Lama. The Monba place great weight on this religion as central to their identity, and both prayer flags and wheels are visible in and around every house. Every day most Monba families engage in private rituals that include offerings of water and lighting butter lamps to facilitate reincarnation as a higher being; many Monba boys spend a period as a monk to prepare for adulthood. Even the youngest Monba children are able to tell strangers about the sixth Dalai Lama, Tsangyang Gyatso (1683–1706), who was a Monba himself.

The Monba are also responsible for Asia's second-largest Buddhist monastery, Tawang Gompa, built in the mid-17th century to protect its monks and larger lay community from attacks by the Bhutanese, who are members of a rival branch of Buddhism. Tawang is located about 10,000 feet above sea level and can accommodate about 300 monks. Its library is world renowned and continues to produce Buddhist scholarship from its own print shop,

MONBA

location:
Tibet; China; Arunachal Pradesh, India; Bhutan

time period:
At least 500 B.C.E. to the present

ancestry:
Unknown

language:
Monpa, a Tibeto-Burman language in the larger Sino-Tibetan phylum

The Tawang Monastery in Arunachal Pradesh, India, with its variety of religious and secular buildings set high in the Himalayas. *(OnAsia/Thierry Falise)*

while the local people look to its religious specialists for both life-cycle and annual rituals. Today Tawang is also important as a secular political center that houses government offices, a military base, markets, and hotels for its many visitors.

The traditional political organization of the Monba recognized the centrality of Buddhism in their lives as the abbot of Tawang, other lamas, and two monks were always members of their six-man ruling council called the Trukdri. The other members would generally be drawn from large land-holding families or other secular elites.

Although perhaps not usually associated with a highly religious community, the Monba are also known for their home-brewed alcohol and joyous approach to life. They are well known in their region for their songs, dancing, and loud belly laughs.

See also BHUTANESE: NATIONALITY.

FURTHER READING

Ashok Biswal. *Mystic Monpas of Tawang Himalaya* (New Delhi: Indus Pub. Co., 2006).

Mongolians: nationality (Mongols, people of Mongolia)

Mongolia is a north Asian country with a history that goes back to the unifying efforts of the great emperor Genghis Khan in the 13th century.

GEOGRAPHY

Mongolia encompasses a variety of different geographic zones, all of which are relatively harsh, including the arid Gobi Desert; the semiarid steppe region; and the cold, high elevations of the Altai Mountains, Yablonovvy Range, and Da Hinggan Mountains. The region where the Gobi meets the steppes at Dariganga is also known throughout the world for its vast volcanic field, hosting more than 200 cones left over from eruptions during the Pleistocene and Holocene eras.

INCEPTION AS A NATION

There are two distinct periods of national development in Mongolia, separated by about 700 years. The first Mongol state was established in 1206 when Genghis Khan united all the Mongol tribes and began his conquest of Asia and eastern Europe. His empire grew even larger under his grandson, Kublai Khan, who reigned from 1260 to 1271 as khan and then until 1294 as emperor of the Yuan dynasty of China. During this period he conquered Korea and invaded Japan, Myanmar (Burma), Vietnam, and Java, all without success. During the 1270s he was supposedly visited by Marco Polo, who wrote of the empire's vast wealth and power. The power of the Yuan empire rapidly diminished after Kublai's death and was finally eliminated in 1368–88. From that period until its declaration of independence

Mongolians: nationality time line

B.C.E.

1000 Desertification and other aspects of climate change result in the development of nomadism in the region of Mongolia as a strategy for survival in the cold, dry climate.

500–400 Evidence of a proto-Mongol culture in the Altai area.

Third century The Chinese begin to build the Great Wall to protect against various nomadic peoples' incursions into their settled territories, including proto-Mongols.

C.E.

100 Buddhism travels from India to Mongolia along the Silk Road.

1167 Temujin, the future Genghis Khan, is born.

1206 Genghis Khan unifies the various Mongol tribes and begins his campaign to conquer the world.

1227 Genghis Khan dies in China's Gansu province.

1260–94 Reign of Kublai Khan, first as khan of the Mongol empire and from 1271 onward as emperor of the Yuan dynasty of China.

1267 The Mongol Empire begins to disintegrate and a century later is expelled from Beijing by Chinese Ming armies.

1388 The Chinese destroy the Mongol capital at Karakorum.

1636 Inner Mongolia is created when the Manchu, or Qing, empire defeats the southern Mongols.

1691 Outer Mongolia is created when the northern Mongols accept a protectorate relationship with the Qing that lasts until 1911.

1727 Russia and China sign the Treaty of Khiakta, creating the border between China and Mongolia, most of which is still recognized today.

1911 Mongolia achieves independence when the Qing dynasty collapses, and both Russia and China recognize their sovereignty over Outer Mongolia. Inner Mongolia remains a Chinese territory.

1919 Chinese armies withdraw their recognition of Mongolia and occupy the country when its Russian supporters are busy at home during the Russian revolution.

1921 With the support of the Soviets, Mongolian armies drive out Chinese forces.

1924 The Mongolian People's Republic is declared by the ruling Mongolian People's Revolutionary Party (MPRP). The Mongolians try to follow Soviet leader Vladimir Lenin's advice to developing countries to take the road to socialism that bypasses capitalism.

1928–39 Consolidation of power by the MPRP leads to purges, murders, religious persecution, and frequent shifts in power.

1935 The Mongolian cinema company, Mongol Kino, produces its first film, the documentary *74th Celebration of the 1st of May*. The following year it releases its first feature.

1939 Mongolian armies, with the assistance of the Soviets, repel a Japanese invasion at the Battle of Nomonhan (Halhyn Gol).

Khorloogiyn Choybalsan, a close follower of Stalin, becomes prime minister and head of government. Previously he had also served as head of state, 1929–30.

1952 Choybalsan dies and is replaced by Yumjaagiyn Tsedenbal, who had been the MPRP's general secretary since 1940. Pro-Soviet in Mongolia's foreign affairs, he is even married to a Russian woman and is a close friend of Leonid Brezhnev, which makes him an enemy of the Chinese.

1955 The Republic of China (Taiwan) blocks Mongolia's entrance to the United Nations on the grounds that Mongolia is actually a Chinese territory.

1961 With the support of the Soviet Union, Mongolia enters the United Nations.

(continues)

MONGOLIANS: NATIONALITY

nation:
Mongolia

derivation of name:
The Mongols are the dominant ethnic group in the country.

government:
Parliamentary democracy with the prime minister as head of government and the president as head of state

capital:
Ulaanbaatar

language:
Mongolian

religion:
Tibetan-style Buddhism 50 percent, none 40 percent, shamanist and Christian 6 percent, Muslim 4 percent

earlier inhabitants:
Many different nomadic peoples, including Eastern and Western Mongols, Turkic peoples, Huns (possibly Xiongnu), Scythians, and others

demographics:
Mongol 94.4 percent (of that, 90 percent Eastern Mongol or Khalkha, 10 percent Oirat, Dariganga, and other Mongol groups); Turkic (mostly Kazakh) 5 percent; other (including Chinese and Russian) 0.1 percent

Mongolians: nationality time line *(continued)*

1964 Mongolia first enters the Olympic Games in Innsbruck, Austria, with an unregistered team of cross-country skiers; the country also competes in the 1964 summer games in Tokyo.

1966 Mongolia secretly allows the Soviet Union to place troops on Mongolian territory.

1983 Mongolia expels about 7,000 Chinese, many of whom had been born in Mongolia to parents who had arrived in the 1950s to contribute to construction projects.

1986 Soviet troops are withdrawn from Mongolia when Mikhail Gorbachev seeks détente with China.

1990 Ardchilsan Kholboo, the first democratic alliance in Mongolia, launches a successful hunger strike that brings down the last president of the Mongolian People's Republic, Jambyn Batmonh.

1992 The Mongolian People's Republic becomes just "Mongolia" under the new constitution; human rights and individual freedom are also codified in the new document. The first democratic elections see the MPRP claim 71 of 76 seats in the new parliament, or great *hural*.

1993 The first direct presidential elections result in a victory for Punsalmaagiyn Ochirbat of the National and Social Democrats. He serves a single four-year term.

1996 The National and Social Democrats win a majority of seats in the great *hural* but are hindered in their efforts to pass legislation by MPRP members who fail to appear to make a quorum.

1997 The MPRP reclaims the presidency when Natsagiyn Bagabandi wins the election; he serves two four-year terms.

2000 The MPRP retakes the great *hural* with 72 of the 76 seats. The opposition parties unite as a new Democratic Party.

2002 The Dalai Lama and Kofi Anan each visit Mongolia. This year is also the 840th anniversary of Genghis Khan's birth, resulting in celebrations throughout the year.

2003 Mongolia sends about 200 peacekeepers to Iraq as part of the Coalition of the Willing, with 100 still remaining in 2007.

2004 Russia cancels all but $300 million of Mongolia's debt.

The Story of the Weeping Camel, a film about a Mongolian family in the Gobi Desert, is nominated for an Academy Award (Oscar) for Best Documentary. It is also Mongolia's entry for best foreign film.

2005 George W. Bush visits the country, the only sitting U.S. president to do so.

in 1911, Mongolia was ruled largely as a protectorate of subsequent Chinese dynasties.

In the 20th century an independent, or at least semi-independent, Mongolia again emerged on the geopolitical map, largely as a client state of the RUSSIANS. In 1911 Mongolia was able to attain independence from China with Russia's assurances of protection against their southern neighbor. When the Russians became distracted during their revolution in the late teens, China again marched into Mongolia and reestablished the territory as a region of China, only to be ousted again in 1921 by a joint Mongolian-Soviet military force. Three years later, the Mongolian People's Revolutionary Party (MPRP) declared the creation of the Mongolian People's Republic and attempted to create a socialist state without first passing through the capitalist phase of economic development. The following decades were a period of consolidation of power during which there were frequent purges of political dissidents on the right and troublesome officials on the left; significant religious persecution of monks, lamas, and other Buddhists; and frequent shifts in power.

The decades after World War II saw less violence and persecution in Mongolia but a continuation of the country's close relationship with the Soviet Union. After an initial failure to enter the United Nations in 1955, having been blocked by China (Taiwan), Mongolia was finally admitted in 1961, when the Soviet Union threatened to veto the applications of all the newly independent states if China did not acquiesce to Mongolia's application. Mongolia also allowed the Soviet Union to secretly place troops in the country in 1966 as part of the two countries' long-lasting friendship; they were withdrawn 20 years later when the Soviet leader Mikhail Gorbachev sought a closer relationship with China.

The period after 1990 and the disintegration of the Soviet Union brought a change in both economic and political structure to Mongolia, with free elections taking place every four years from 1990 onward. In many of these elections the MPRP, the communist party that had led Mongolia from 1924 to 1990, was able to maintain its hold on the 76-seat parliament, called the great *hural,* or on the presidency, or sometimes on both. However, the political and economic platform followed by this new MPRP was in line with both democratic and capitalist ideals rather than with those of a single-party, socialist state. The National and Social Democrats and later the Democratic Party also emerged as powerful political forces at this time.

In the postsocialist world, Mongolia has continued to maintain a close relationship with Russia, with the former canceling most of Mongolia's $11 billion debt in 2004. Mongolia continues to purchase the majority of its energy from Russia, resulting in great trade imbalances with that country. Despite its troubled history, Mongolia also remains close to China, with that country serving as the destination for a large amount of Mongolia's exports in agricultural products and minerals, some legally sold in China, others moved out of the country through the black market. Mongolia has also become much closer to the United States since 1991, even to the point of joining the Coalition of the Willing in the war in Iraq in 2003.

CULTURAL IDENTITY

A great deal of Mongolia's national identity derives from the conquests of the country's great ancestor, Genghis Khan. His having conquered much of the known world in the 13th century continues to be a source of national pride for many Mongolians, and many of their traditional literary works in epic and other forms of poetry, legend, stories, and proverbs come out of this period of history. These cultural forms have been handed down for hundreds of years by *khurchins,* who combine both storytelling and singing in ways that Mongolians feel are unique to their people. The stories they tell and the songs they sing are infused with traits that many Mongolians feel characterize them, as

Images of Genghis Khan are also very important on the Mongolian art scene, as this sand sculpture of the great leader shows. *(Shutterstock/ Martin Green)*

against their Russian and Chinese neighbors: a sense of humor, a love of life, and a bit of craftiness, but always in a good-natured way.

Despite the importance of nomadism in early Mongol history and identity, about half the country's population of just under 3 million today currently resides in the capital city of Ulaanbaatar or in other regional cities. Settled agriculture has also emerged in rural regions as an important source of income. However, despite these changes, the culture of nearly half the population continues to be that of the seminomad who follows his herds across the country's arid expanses and values his freedom to move more than the ability to accumulate consumer goods. Even the Mongolian form of chess, *shatar,* expresses the importance of this way of life, with a dog represented on the piece of the queen and a camel as the bishop.

Another important aspect of Mongolian national culture is the centrality of Tibetan-style Buddhism. Buddhism has a very long history in Mongolia, dating from the fourth-century activities of some Chinese monks. Little is known about the effect of these attempts at conversion except that at least one large monastery was built in Karakorum, the ruins of which served as the foundation of a royal palace built in the mid-13th century. The mid-13th century was also a period of greater Buddhist activity among the MONGOLS after Kublai Khan conquered Tibet and brought several monks home as political hostages. In 1269 one of those monks invented a Mongolian script and began translating Buddhist texts into the language, thus opening the door to greater conversion, at least among the nobility. But even these activities did not solidify Buddhism's hold on the Mongolian people, and the end of the Mongol Yuan dynasty in 1368 saw a reemergence of shamanism and local animistic beliefs and a lessening of Buddhist adherence. The 16th century, however, witnessed the rebirth of Mongolian Buddhism under the tutelage of Altan Khan of the Tumet Mongols. He was visited by the Dalai Lama in 1578, and within 50 years all of the nobility had converted or reconverted to Buddhism; ordinary people were induced to do the same by legal proscriptions against shamanism in addition to other more positive inducements. As they did in medieval Europe, the monasteries of Mongolia became centers of learning, scholarship, and social welfare for the entire community. By the 19th century there were more than 700 monasteries in Outer Mongolia, and one-third of men were Buddhist monks or other clergy.

One important characteristic of Mongolian Buddhism that makes it somewhat unique is the importance of the many independent lamas. Rather than belonging to a particular monastery, many lamas survive by serving as spiritual or even medical consultants, blessing weddings or building projects, or practicing the Mongolian form of acupuncture. They may also have taken only some of the vows to become a full monk, but with their specialized skills they can survive on gifts and handouts from the people they serve.

While this and all other religions were actively persecuted for most of the 20th century, with just one monastery allowed to continue as a sort of living museum, Buddhism has reemerged as a central feature of Mongolian identity in the past generation. Article 12 of the Mongolian constitution of 1992 outlines the various emblems of Mongolian national identity: the state emblem, banner, seal, and flag, all of which draw on symbols from Buddhism and highlight the centrality of this religion to the national culture. In addition, almost 200 monasteries have been rebuilt and resanctified, and

more than 3,000 monks have registered as having taken vows; there may be as many nuns as well, but this number has not been registered. The Mongolian government has also contributed a significant amount of money for these rebuilding projects, again underscoring the importance of Buddhism in the construction of the Mongolian national identity.

FURTHER READING

Benedict Allen. *Edge of Blue Heaven: A Journey through Mongolia* (Parkwest, N.Y.: BBC/Parkwest Publications, 1998).

Tsedendambyn Batbayar. *Modern Mongolia: A Concise History* (Ulaanbaatar: Offset Printing, Mongolian Center for Scientific and Technological Information, 1996).

Uradyn E. Bulag. *Nationalism and Hybridity in Mongolia* (New York: Oxford University Press, 1998).

Frederick Fisher. *Mongolia* (Milwaukee, Wis.: Gareth Stevens Pub., 1999).

George G. S. Murphy. *Soviet Mongolia: A Study of the Oldest Political Satellite* (Berkeley and Los Angeles: University of California Press, 1966).

Ricardo Neupert and Sidney Goldstein. *Urbanization and Population Redistribution in Mongolia* (Honolulu, Hawaii: East-West Center, 1994).

Igor de Rachewiltz, trans. *The Secret History of the Mongols: A Mongolian Epic Chronicle of the Thirteenth Century* (Boston: Brill, 2006).

Mongols (Monggols, Mongghols, Mongolians, Mengwu, Menggu, Moghuls, Mughals, Tatars, Tartars)

Today's Mongolian people are descendants of a number of different nomadic tribes of Mongols who resided in what is today's Mongolia and Siberia. Prior to the beginning of the 13th century, they were a small and relatively unimportant group among a large number of other tribal nomads living in their region. Then in 1206 a tribal leader named Temujin, under the name of Genghis Khan, unified not only the various Mongol tribes, who at the time referred to themselves as Tatars, but also large numbers of other nomadic peoples and established one of the vastest empires ever known. The Mongol Empire spread from the gates of Vienna in the west to Korea in the east, from Siberia in the north to Southeast Asia in the south. For about 100 years the Mongols also ruled China as the Yuan dynasty, moving their imperial capital from Karakorum in the north to the site of present-day Beijing in the south. As a result of these migrations and subsequent power struggles, Mongol peoples currently reside in

MONGOLS

location:
Mongolia, China, Russia, Kazakhstan, Afghanistan

time period:
Third century B.C.E. to the present

ancestry:
Shiwei tribes

language:
Mongolian, an Altaic language with many different subgroups and dialects

Mongols time line

B.C.E.

1000 Desertification and other aspects of climate change result in the development of nomadism in the Eurasian steppes as a strategy for survival in the cold, dry climate.

Third century The Chinese begin the Great Wall against various nomadic peoples' incursions into their settled territories. This is the first recorded history of these northern nomadic peoples, the predecessors of the Mongols.

C.E.

100 Buddhism travels from India to Mongolia along the Silk Road.

Early 11th century The Hamag Mongol Ulus (pan-Mongolian state) is one of the larger tribal units of the steppe region.

1135 Kabul Khan, leader of one branch of the Mongols, begins a series of raids into Jin territory and is recognized as khan by the rulers of the Jin dynasty.

1162 or 67 Temujin, grandson of Kabul Khan and the future Genghis Khan, is born.

1175 Yesugei, Temujin's father and a chief of the Borjigin Mongols, is killed by the Tatars. His immediate family is abandoned by the clan. Revenge for these acts is often cited as one of Temujin/Genghis Khan's motivations for military domination.

1206 Genghis Khan unifies the various Mongol tribes and begins his campaign to conquer the world.

1213 Mongol armies conquer all the territory north of the Great Wall; they capture land to the south, including Beijing, by 1215.

1220 The Mongols expand westward, defeating the Khwarizmian empire, and march into Europe.

1227 Genghis Khan dies in China's Gansu province.

1229 Genghis Khan is replaced by his third son, Ogodei.

1240 Mongols invade Russia, and Mongol rule is established there, where it is called the Golden Horde or Khanate of Kipchak.

1241 Ogodei dies without having secured an heir; after much wrangling by various royal families, Mongke takes the throne in 1252.

The Mongols destroy Lahore but ultimately withdraw from India before establishing themselves fully. Various Mongol tribes repeatedly attack the region until about 1327, even reaching Delhi several times, but never settle for long.

1242 The Mongols withdraw from Hungary in Eastern Europe, perhaps due to Ogodei's death.

1260 The Mongols withdraw from the Middle East, probably due to Mongke's death a year earlier.

1260–94 Reign of Kublai Khan, first as khan of the Mongol Empire and from 1271 onward as the emperor of the Yuan dynasty of China.

1336 Timur Leng (Timur the Lame), or Tamerlane, is born near Samarkand.

1368 Fall of the Yuan dynasty and its expulsion from the winter capital in Beijing.

1370 Timur Leng claims to be the direct descendant of Genghis Khan.

1388 The Chinese destroy the Mongol summer capital at Karakorum.

1405 Timur Leng dies.

1480 Fall of the Golden Horde, or Khanate of Kipchak, in Russia.

1526 Founding of the Mughal Empire in North India by Babur, possible descendant of Timur Leng and of Genghis Khan.

(continues)

Mongols time line *(continued)*

1636 Inner Mongolia is created when the Manchu, or Qing, empire defeats the southern Mongols.

1691 Outer Mongolia is created when the northern Mongols accept a protectorate relationship with the Qing that lasts until 1911.

1857 Fall of the Mughal Empire in India.

1911 The Mongolian state achieves nominal independence.

(*See* MONGOLIANS: NATIONALITY for a continuation of this chronology.)

European Russia under the name Kalmyk; in Asian Russia as BURIATS; in Afghanistan as HAZARAS; in various Chinese provinces and autonomous regions as OIRAT, Khalkha, Buriat, and other subgroups; and in Mongolia as Khalkha, Oirat, DARIGANGA, DURBETS, and others. Innumerable Mongol peoples also intermarried with local populations and have become part of the genetic makeup of most of the Eurasian land mass. Geneticists have recently discovered that a vast Y-chromosome lineage originated in Mongolia or nearby about 1,000 years ago and must be associated with a common forefather who lived around the same time as Genghis Khan. This forefather's direct patrilineal descendants make up about 8 percent of men in Asia, amounting to some 16 million living descendants of one man.

GEOGRAPHY

The original homeland of the Mongols around Lake Baikal was largely arid to semiarid, encompassing the vast steppe lands and tundra of southern Siberia. Various mountain ranges, including the Altai, Da Hinggan, and Yablonovvy, encroached on them and provided the sources of the rivers that fed their lands and animals. From these harsh lands, which are temperate in the summer and extremely cold in the winter, the Mongols spread out to Europe and southern Asia.

The Mongols currently live in European Russia, especially on the lower reaches of the Volga River, which has a climate similar to the Mongolian steppes; in the mountainous regions of central Afghanistan; in China, where sum-

The Mongolian steppe is a barren, harsh location where even today pastoral nomadism remains the only viable economic strategy for many. *(Shutterstock/Pichugin Dmitry)*

mer temperatures can reach 100°F; and in their original Mongolian and Siberian homelands. In each new territory the Mongol people have adapted to the climatic and geographic conditions, taking up agriculture where possible, engaging in trade, and moving to cities in the 20th century. At the same time, a large number of Mongols, especially in Mongolia, China, and Siberia, continue to reside on the steppes and in the desert and to engage in the same nomadic or seminomadic pastoral activities that sustained their ancestors in these climates 1,000 or more years ago.

ORIGINS

The exact origins of the Mongol people are mostly a matter for conjecture due to the large numbers of different clan, chiefdom, tribal, and confederation ties of the various peoples of the steppes. The term *Mongol* itself probably comes from the Mengwu tribe, part of the larger Shiwei people, of the 10th century. It was not generally used by Genghis Khan's people, who referred to themselves as Tatars, but was adopted about 40 years after his death by Kublai Khan. The term had a meaning of "monstrous" or "cannibal" in Chinese and of "silver" in Mongolian itself.

HISTORY

Genghis Khan

Genghis Khan, or Temujin as he was born, came from a noble family of chiefs of the Borjigin Mongols. His great-grandfather, Kabul Khan, had been a fierce chief and warrior, recognized for his power by the Chinese Jin dynasty. His father, Yesukhei, was killed by a rival tribe of Tatars when Temujin was a child, at which time the family was banished from the tribe for a number of years. By 1206, however, Temujin had returned from exile and succeeded in the project begun by his ancestor Qaidu five generations earlier: uniting all the nomadic people of the steppes into a large militaristic state. At this time he also received the title Genghis, or Chinggis, Khan, approximately meaning "universal monarch."

In addition to uniting the various TURKIC PEOPLES and Mongol peoples of the steppes, Genghis Khan's armies also conquered Beijing by 1215 and the KHITANS a year later. In 1218 he sent a mission to the KHWAREZMIANS' capital at Urgench, his closest neighbors to the west, and when it was rebuffed he dispatched an army that by 1221 had captured not only

Genghis Khan ⚔

One of the most ruthless and successful warlords in history, Genghis Khan ruled over the Mongol Empire, the largest contiguous empire in history. He was born Temujin in 1162, and his childhood was fraught with violence and poverty. His father, Yesukhei, was chieftain of the Mongol Borjigin tribe, but upon Yesukhei's death the tribe refused to be led by Temujin, who was only nine years old, and he and his mother and siblings were abandoned. The family managed to survive on wild vegetation and small game, and at age 16 Temujin married Borte of the Konkirat tribe, a union that had been arranged by his father shortly before his death. Temujin found his way back into tribal politics by offering himself as an ally to Toghrul, khan of the Kerait. At this time the central Asian plateau was divided into several competing tribes, the most prominent of which were the Naimans, Merkits, Uighurs, Mongols, Keraits, and Tatars. Though relations between Temujin and Toghrul were initially friendly, they soured when Toghrul suspected Temujin of aiming for a position of authority, and Toghrul allied himself with a close but treacherous friend of Temujin's named Jamuka, with whom he attempted to drive Temujin out of the area. However, many generals and tribesmen were loyal to Temujin, who consequently defeated Toghrul and Jamuka.

With a stronger, larger army at his command, Temujin embarked on a campaign to conquer neighboring tribes, and by 1206 he had succeeded in uniting all of the clans under his leadership. His success is attributed to his openness to alliance, his practice of appointing generals based on merit rather than birth, and his efforts to learn and make use of new military techniques. Between 1213 and 1240, Temujin and his army swept across central and east Asia, conquering China, the Kara Khitai khanate, and the Khwarezmian empire. Little is known regarding his death, other than the fact that he died during his last campaign against the uprising of the Jin and Western Xia dynasties in 1227. After his death, his army, under his son Ogodei's leadership, went on to conquer Georgia and Volga Bulgaria by 1240.

Urgench but also Samarkand and Bukhara. Armies under his youngest son Tolui captured Afghanistan and northern India, while those under the great strategist and Genghis Khan's chief general Sabutai took the Caucasus and Russian lands as far west as the Black Sea. In 1225 some of the steppe-dwelling peoples who had earlier submitted to the Mongol armies' tactics rose up against them, bringing Genghis Khan home from his western victories. The rebels were reconquered by 1227, the same year in which Genghis Khan died.

During his lifetime, Genghis Khan placed great emphasis on codifying both law and succession within his empire. Upon his death his will divided his territories into four segments, each to be ruled by one of his four sons. These were not to be independent units but interdependent segments of a unified empire. He named his third son, Ogodei, as his political heir, thus bypassing the traditional period of chaos and uncertainty that had always followed the death of a tribal leader among the nomadic

Mongol Empires, Thirteenth and Fourteenth Centuries

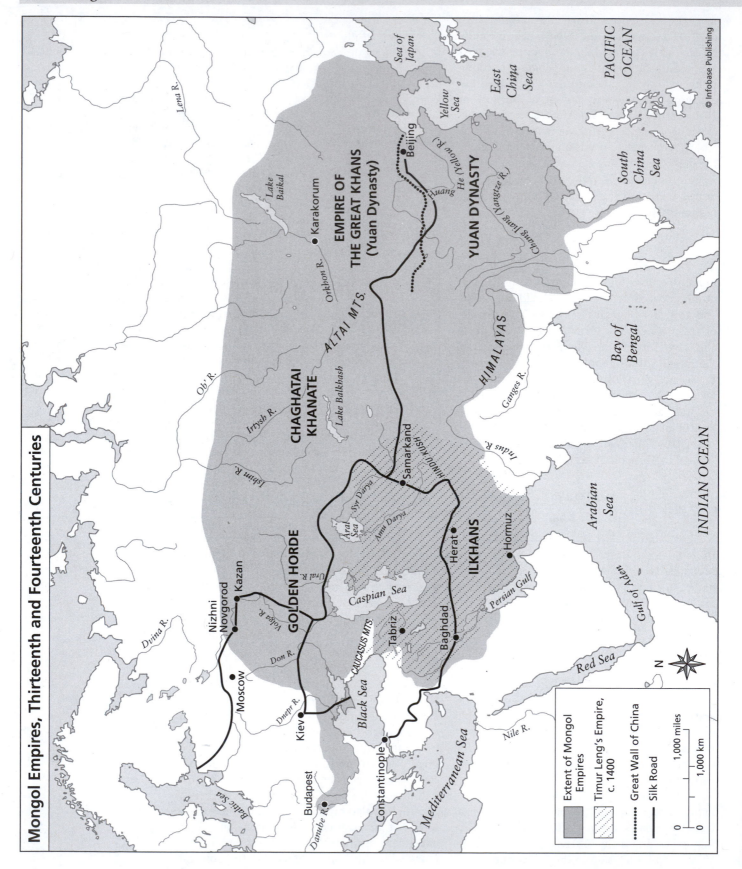

PACIFIC OCEAN

© Infobase Publishing

Lena R.

Lake Baikal

EMPIRE OF THE GREAT KHANS (Yuan Dynasty)

Karakorum

Orkhon R.

Beijing

Huang

Huang He (Yellow R.)

Sea of Japan

Yellow Sea

East China Sea

South China Sea

YUAN DYNASTY

Chang Jiang (Yangtze R.)

ALTAI MTS.

Ob' R.

CHAGHATAI KHANATE

Irtysh R.

Lake Balkhash

Ishim R.

HIMALAYAS

Ganges R.

Indus R.

Bay of Bengal

Samarkand

HINDU KUSH

Syr Darya

Aral Sea

Amu Darya

Hormuz

Arabian Sea

INDIAN OCEAN

GOLDEN HORDE

Kazan

Ural R.

Caspian Sea

ILKHANS

Herat

Nizhni Novgorod

Volga R.

Don R.

CAUCASUS MTS.

Tabriz

Baghdad

Persian Gulf

Gulf of Aden

Moscow

Dnepr R.

Kiev

Black Sea

Red Sea

Dvina R.

Budapest

Danube R.

Constantinople

Mediterranean Sea

Nile R.

Baltic Sea

N

Extent of Mongol Empires

Timur Leng's Empire, c. 1400

Great Wall of China

Silk Road

1,000 miles

1,000 km

steppe people. He codified Mongolian tribal law into a formalized legal document, the *Ikh Zasag*, which proscribed water pollution and protected soil and other natural resources. It also described the roles of men and women, dictating that all men were required to serve during wartime and that wives of soldiers must travel with them in order to carry on the nonmilitary tasks that their husbands could not undertake, including herding their animals.

The military successes of the Mongols arose from sophisticated strategies of warfare developed by Genghis Khan and from the use of fear as a motivation in subduing foreign peoples. When the Mongols destroyed a city, they razed it to the ground, brutally slaughtered many inhabitants, and enslaved others; prized prisoners such as goldsmiths and other craftsmen of luxuries were sent off to live out their lives at the Mongol court. Although not every city in their path was destroyed, conquered lands were forced to pay heavy tribute to the Mongols, and their reputation as ruthless conquerors spread throughout Asia and Europe.

At his father's death, Ogodei inherited an empire that ranged from the western reaches of Central Asia to China. Ogodei's 12 years as khan, or khagan, saw even greater imperial growth when Mongol armies captured all of China as far as the Yangtze (Chang) River, much of Persia, most of Russia and the Caucasus, and central Europe as far west as the gates of Vienna. In addition, like his father, Ogodei contributed greatly to the administrative side of the empire, building a capital city at Karakorum, codifying the conquered territories' taxation schemes, and drawing on Muslim talent in financial management. Unfortunately, Ogodei did not successfully settle the question of succession, and on his death numerous potential heirs began negotiating and struggling to step into the void. At this point the Mongol armies withdrew from Hungary to return home for this internal struggle.

The Mongols' incursion into eastern Europe caused Europeans to fear that they would return, a dire prospect as no European ruler had an army large enough to face them. To deal with the threat, Pope Innocent IV sent a letter to the khan via a mission of Franciscan monks. In the letter the pope asked the Mongols' intentions, exhorted them to stop killing Christians, and tried to get them to convert to Christianity. The mission reached the Mongols in 1246, in time for the friars to witness the enthroning of Ogodei's successor, Guyuk. In his letter of reply Guyuk instructed the pope and other European princes to pay homage to the khan and follow his orders. Guyuk maintained that the Mongol atrocities in Europe had been warranted by the arrogance of the people the Mongols had murdered. His final words were: "From where the sun rises to where it goes down, all the lands belong to us. Were it not for the will of God, how could that have happened?" Despite these words, the Mongols never again tried to conquer Europe, because, according to many scholars, they had found nothing in Europe worth conquering.

Succession finally fell to Mongke—the son of Tolui, Genghis Khan's youngest son—in 1252 after more than 10 years of regency and failed succession in the Ogodei line. The seeds of the empire's later disintegration began to be sown at this point when some lesser khans accepted Mongke's succession only with reluctance.

The Yuan Dynasty

In 1260 Kublai Khan, grandson of Genghis Khan, succeeded his older brother Mongke as the ruler of the Mongol Empire, but only after defeating his younger brother Ariqboka in a civil war of succession. During Mongke's lifetime, Kublai had been the governor of the southern portion of the empire, extending its reach ever further into China. Once he secured the khagan (khan) position at the head of the empire, he turned his focus almost entirely on China, although he also led unsuccessful attempts at taking Japan, Vietnam, Myanmar, and Java before concentrating on his Chinese territory. This focus allowed him to take over as emperor of all of China in 1279 when the Song dynasty fell. His Yuan dynasty, meaning "first" or "beginning," reigned in China and Mongolia until 1368 by adapting to the local Chinese administrative and cultural traditions.

Kublai was an effective ruler who brought many changes to the Chinese state. He favored Mongols first, other ethnic groups second, in the distribution of administrative positions, and pursued a policy of discrimination against the formerly dominant HAN Chinese, especially those from the south as the Song dynasty had been. He reformed the taxation system so that the tax burden was lessened during difficult times, improved agriculture, distributed food to the poor, built public institutions such as hospitals and orphanages, and expanded the capital city, including building the Forbidden City. Other public works included lengthening

The Forbidden City in Beijing was begun during Kublai Khan's reign but was completed under the reign of Yongle in the subsequent Ming dynasty. Both emperors were striving to keep out the world beyond through the use of walls and moats, as seen here. *(Shutterstock/Jonathan Larsen)*

and improving the Grand Canal, developing the country's roads, and building public granaries for food storage.

Kublai Khan's most famous visitor, at least among westerners, was Marco Polo, who is said to have visited the emperor along with his father and uncle. Growing scholarship in the past decades, however, indicates that he may have gathered his information about China secondhand from traders he met through his family's business on the Black Sea. Although thoroughly Venetian in political allegiance and cultural outlook, the Polos were traders who began their lucrative careers in Constantinople. They later moved to the shores of the Black Sea, a region that had been conquered by the Mongol Golden Horde. Marco's father and uncle may first have traveled to Beijing as part of an ambassadorial entourage in 1266, returning in 1271 with young Marco. Marco claims that he immediately stood out for his language abilities and was taken into the employ of Kublai Khan for the next 17 years. Upon his return to Europe he spoke extensively of his travels and experiences with the great khan and wrote a book that sold widely and was translated into many languages; its English title is *The Travels of Marco Polo*. Many European poets and writers have borrowed from Polo's work to create images of the vast wealth and unknown cultures of the East; one of the best known of these in English is Samuel Taylor Coleridge's poem *Kubla Khan*, published in 1816.

Although Kublai Khan's focus was almost entirely on his Chinese territory and legitimating his rule as an authentic Chinese emperor, the Mongol Empire of Genghis Khan remained as a semiunitary political unit. However, large cracks emerged at the time of Kublai's war of succession and continued during his reign, since some of the minor khans refused to recognize him.

Upon Kublai Khan's death in 1294, the Mongol Empire was divided permanently into four separate khanates, representing almost exactly the divisions named by Genghis Khan himself when he assigned a portion of his empire to each of his four sons. One of these successors was the Chinese Yuan dynasty, which incorporated much of the land of present-day Mongolia as well. The others were the Golden Horde of Russia, the Iklhanate of Persia, and the Chagatai Khanate, which incorporated most of Central Asia.

The Golden Horde

During Ogodei's imperial reign (1229–41) his nephew, Batu Khan, along with Genghis Khan's great strategist, Sabutai, conquered much of Russia and eastern Europe. Despite their plans to march into Germany, Italy, Spain, and France, the Mongols withdrew in 1242, just after Ogodei's death, to return home to Karakorum for the next *kurultai,* or council, which would elect Ogodei's imperial heir. When Batu failed to receive this position, he returned to Russia and set up his capital at Sarai, on the lower Volga River, never following through on the earlier plans to conquer all of Europe. What Batu's heirs did succeed in, however, was maintaining the longest-ruling Mongol state in history. The Khanate of Kipchak, as it was sometimes known, or at other times as the Golden Horde for the color of the khan's tent, ruled in both European and Asian Russia, including Siberia, the Caucasus, and the former Khwarezmian territories until 1480, more than 100 years after the fall of the Mongols in China. The Golden Horde utilized a form of indirect rule that allowed local chiefs and leaders to exercise direct power over people and resources in their own area and to collect the heavy tribute owed the Mongols, a strategy that many historians believe was the cause of their longevity. This strategy also contributed to the emergence of the next ruling power in the region, the Muscovites.

While the rulers of the Golden Horde were Mongols and their Turkic allies, and they maintained a loose allegiance with the Mongol capital at Karakorum until its fall in 1388, they also were extremely independent. The religion of state for the Kipchaks was Islam, which brought changes in administrative forms and custom in addition to religion. They also allied themselves with the Mamluk sultanate of Egypt against the Mongol Ilkhanate after the latter sacked and destroyed Baghdad, and with the Byzantines to oppose the Ilkhanate in Azerbaijan. By the end of their rule in the late 15th century, the leaders of the Golden Horde were no longer considered by either themselves or others as a Mongol people. They had largely assimilated to the local Turkic population, the Kipchaks, and adopted Arabic as the language of state. Their power in the region diminished slowly and gradually was swept away by the emerging Russian empire with very little change in the lives of the people.

The Ilkhanate

The Ilkhans, or Lesser Khans, were the inheritors of Mongol territory in Persia conquered by Hulegu, who was Mongke and Kublai Khan's brother, grandson of Genghis Khan. In addition to Iran and Iraq, their lands included much of Afghanistan, Azerbaijan, and parts of Pakistan. These lands largely coincided with the Khwarezmian empire, conquered by Genghis Khan after the mistreatment of his envoys in the 1220s. The name *Ilkhan* refers to Hulegu's initial recognition of the greater Mongol empire and Mongke as his superior; however, during the reign of Kublai Khan this recognition was largely withdrawn, and the Ilkhans maintained their own empire for approximately 80 years, falling to their own Turkic administrators in 1335.

Like the Golden Horde, the official religion of the Ilkhans changed from shamanism to Islam during the course of their reign. They also became completely autonomous from Karakorum and Beijing when Ilkhan Mahmud Ghazan withdrew contact with Kublai Khan sometime between 1295 and 1304. They faced increasingly strong opposition from their relatives in the Golden Horde and Chagatai khanate, the quarter of the empire that was originally given to Genghis Khan's second son, going to war with the former over land in the Caucasus and Russia.

Disintegration

Many factors contributed to the disintegration of the Mongol Empire, from Kublai Khan's single-minded focus on China to the inherent succession problems of a nomadic empire. The Mongols' inability to bring their conquered peoples into the Mongolian social world also meant that they were left either ruling populations of socially and culturally different people or themselves assimilating to those they conquered, which they often did. In fact, this characteristic was so common that many of the successor khanates of the Mongols are seen today as largely Turkic realms rather than Mongol because of their adaptation to Islam, use of Arabic and Turkic languages, and adoption of other Turkic cultural traits.

Also contributing to the demise of most of the Mongol successor states was their war with Timur Leng, or Tamerlane, who himself claimed descent from Genghis Khan. This claim was probably a false one but has been repeated many times. Timur was born in Transoxiana in 1336 and during his lifetime conquered the territory formerly held by the Ilkahanate in Persia as well as that of the Golden Horde, which split into three portions as a result of this warfare. His armies were largely Turkic instead of Mongol but did include large numbers of Turkic-speaking Mongol peoples from these successor khanates. His short-lived empire died soon after him in 1405 and left a power vacuum the Mongol khans could not refill.

Babur's Mughal India

Despite the name *Mughal,* the Persian word for Mongol, the Indian empire established by Babur or Zahir ud-Din Muhammad, was not technically a Mongol one. The title comes from Babur's claim to have descended from Timur Leng on his father's side and from Genghis Khan on his mother's. The truth of these claims remains far from verified, but the name continues to be used to refer to the Muslim empire that ruled northern India from 1526 to 1857.

Post-Empire History

By the time of the fall of the various successor khanates to the larger Mongol Empire, most of the Mongol people in these regions had been assimilated into the populations in which they resided. The Mongol leadership had always constituted a very small part of these khanates to begin with, and after their demise even these former leaders became indistinguishable from the surrounding Turkic, Russian, and other Central Asian peoples. Two regions in which this was not the case were the middle highlands of Afghanistan, where a distinctive Mongol population continues to reside to this day as the Shiite Hazaras, and in Inner and Outer Mongolia.

Right after the fall of the Yuan dynasty in 1368, the succeeding Ming dynasty, dominated by ethnic Han Chinese, rebuilt the Great Wall, which had been begun many hundreds of years earlier to keep the northern nomads out of China proper. Most of this barrier continues to serve as the southern boundary between Inner Mongolia and China's other regions. During the subsequent centuries Mongols tended to continue their independent, nomadic way of life as much as possible. The Qing instigated a series of administrative reforms that tied Mongols to their particular region, thus limiting nomadism to some extent; however, these reforms were difficult to police and many Mongols were able to continue in their former economic activities and social structures. At the same time, a small number of Han Chinese also moved into the region. This population movement increased after the MANCHUS conquered first the Mongol territories and then all of China by 1644. During the later years of that century, even more Han Chinese entered what is now Inner Mongolia, with the greatest years for migration coming at the end of the 19th century, when China became concerned by Russian advances in the region. Chinese settlers took advantage of the construction of a railway line and of their ability to take land away from its nomadic owners; some also purchased land from its Mongol

titleholders, usually chiefs of larger clans and tribes. Under the Manchus or Qing dynasty, Inner and Outer Mongolia were not administered together as a unified region but divided into six different sections, which also included portions of northern China that today lie outside the Inner Mongolian Autonomous Region.

During the destruction of the Qing and establishment of the Republic of China in 1912, Outer Mongolia was able to free itself entirely of Chinese rule. Drawing on the support of the RUSSIANS, the region declared independence in 1911; during the Russian revolution China retook Mongolia only to lose it again, permanently, in 1921. At that time Inner Mongolia remained part of China, although in 1937 it was able to declare itself independent with the assistance of the conquering JAPANESE army, which had declared war on China that year. China retook the region following World War II and created the Inner Mongolia Autonomous Region in 1947 from all the territories with a significant Mongol population. Despite this policy, Han incursions in the region beginning in the 17th century have meant that today the Mongols make up only about 17 percent of the population of their autonomous region; the Han are about 80 percent, with the remaining 3 percent made up of Manchus, HUI, DAUR, EVENKIS, KOREANS, and Russians.

Today Mongolia is a large but sparsely populated democratic state between China and Russia that is dominated by an ethnic Mongol population. A large number of those Mongols are Khalkha Mongols, about 90 percent, with smaller numbers of Oirat, Dariganga, and other Mongol subgroups (see MONGOLIANS: NATIONALITY).

CULTURE

Economics

The traditional economic activity of the Mongol people was nomadic to seminomadic pastoralism, living off the products and proceeds of herds of animals, including horses, goats, sheep, cattle, and camels. In the dry, cold region of the Eurasian steppes, this form of subsistence was the most viable since the animals and people could move as often as was necessary to search for grass and water to survive. Due to the limited growing season and dry conditions, agriculture was not a viable permanent subsistence strategy. However, for hundreds of years some Mongols have planted crops and then returned to their gardens at harvest time. Grains such as barley, millet, and wheat and vegetables such as potatoes, sugar beets, cabbage, and carrots, and fruit trees, especially apples, were commonly grown near the region's many rivers. Both irrigation and dry-farm methods were employed and continue to provide food for many Mongolians today.

In addition to these activities, Mongols were also great hunters, an activity that continues to bring both prestige and resources to men who are successful in this area today. Wild antelope, foxes, wolves, rabbits, and a variety of game birds are all still available to hunters in Mongolia and China's Inner Mongolia region. Residing along the major trade routes between China and Europe also meant that many Mongols engaged in trade. As was the case in the past, much of this trade went on between Mongols and Chinese on the one hand and Mongols and Russians on the other. Mongols offered animal products, hides, and fur in exchange for manufactured goods, grain, tea, silk, and cloth. During *naadam,* a festival in which men competed in wrestling, archery, and horse racing, Mongols also traded, sought out marriage partners, and fostered friendships and alliances, a practice still observed to the present time.

Today many Mongols continue these economic patterns developed by their ancestors many centuries ago, with sheep and goats replacing other animals as the predominant herd animals in Mongolia due to the high prices they fetch for meat and wool. In Mongolia, only about half the population has moved to an urban area to engage in the limited manufacturing and service sectors; others engage in the slightly more extensive mining industry, while the rest of the population continues to live by their herds or crops. During the socialist era in Mongolia, 1924–90, state farms and collectives were established throughout the country, many of which continue to control the production of both fodder and grain. In Inner Mongolia, wheat production occurs along the major river valleys, while pastoralism continues to serve as an important subsistence strategy, with goats and sheep taking precedence over other animals. The region also has large coal and natural gas deposits, which provide jobs for some Mongol men.

Social Structure

As a tribal culture, Mongol social structure was dominated at the bottom by the patrilineal family group and at the top by the tribe and clan. Even during the peak of the Mongol Empire, this social structure provided the backbone for all political and social organization.

Kinship among the Mongols was strongly patrilineal, with inheritance and membership in all kin, clan, and tribal groups being handed down from fathers to their children. The most basic unit of production and consumption was sometimes the nuclear family but more commonly extended family units consisting of several generations of related men along with their wives and children. The next larger unit, at least among nomadic Mongols, was the *ail,* a group of one to 10 families who migrated together and largely shared both household and pastoral duties and resources. Men of the *ail* worked together to tend the horses, cattle, and camels; collect hay; and hunt; while women milked the animals, made butter, cooked meals, and tended children. Both sexes worked with the sheep, especially at shearing time.

The next larger social unit among tribal Mongols was the clan, a group of between 200 and 600 households, all related through patrilineal descent. Clans sometimes acted together to raid neighboring territories or engage in local warfare but did not generally come together during times of peace. Frequent interclan warfare among the fiercely independent Mongols was one contributing factor in the weakening of the Mongol Empire. The largest politicosocial unit was the tribe, which averaged 20,000–30,000 households and was bound by ties of kinship, both real and imagined. Like the clan, the tribe could also serve as a unitary group during times of warfare. Also like the clan, tribal leadership was largely selected by the men of the tribe from the most able and intelligent candidates from the chief's family. The election process was called *tanistry* and made for a difficult period of succession at the death of any clan or tribal leader. Only Genghis Khan was able to name his own heir successfully, while the deaths of all the other emperors and clan and tribal leaders initiated a period of uncertainty and divisiveness, including acts of fratricide and the murder of other close relatives by their rivals for leadership. This method also required all high-level Mongol chiefs and military leaders to return to the capital at the death of an emperor or other leader, which probably saved western Europe from the Mongol onslaught in the 13th century.

When the Manchus conquered China and Mongolia and instigated administrative reforms in both Inner and Outer Mongolia, much of the structure of both the clan and tribe disappeared from Mongol society. These were replaced by more geographically defined political units such as the league, province, and county, which continue to dominate in both Mongolia and the Inner Mongolian Autonomous Region of China today.

Religion

The religion of the steppe-dwelling Mongols was shamanism, in which religious specialists used their ability to communicate with the gods and spirits to read the future, heal the sick and injured, and even play a significant role in politics. This system was combined with a belief in the ultimate control of Tenggeri or Tengri, the universal sky god whose mandate was required for an individual to claim authority over others. The *tanistry* system, in which the political heir to clan and tribal chiefs, and even emperors, was chosen from among the appropriate candidates, was often about deciding which man could most effectively claim the mandate of Tengri. There is also some evidence that the Mongols engaged in the worship of fire. This trait, along with the belief in Tengri and the practice of leaving their dead outside to be eaten by wild animals, and even their words for all levels of tribal leadership, points to an ancient affiliation between the ancestors of the Mongols and those of the Indo-Iranians who had left the steppes thousands of years earlier.

As the rulers of multinational empires and khanates, the Mongols tended to convert to the religions of the people around them. In the Middle East and Central Asia, this religion was Islam. In Mongolia itself, a Tibetan-style Lamaist Buddhism became the religion of state in the 16th century, while the Mongols of the Yuan dynasty relied heavily on the divination skills of Taoist priests. In each of these lands, a degree of religious freedom was allowed as long as it did not interfere with the more important aspects of empire building: taxation, tribute, and trade.

Contemporary Mongols continue to practice this same variety of religions. Afghanistan's Mongol Hazara population is Muslim; the majority of religious people in Mongolia are Buddhists; and the Mongol Buriats in Siberia are Buddhist, shamanist, and even Orthodox Christian.

See also BURIATS; DARIGANGA; DURBETS; HAZARAS; OIRAT.

FURTHER READING

Thomas T. Allsen. *Culture and Conquest in Mongol Eurasia* (New York: Cambridge University Press, 2001).
Christopher P. Atwood. *Encyclopedia of Mongolia and the Mongol Empire* (New York: Facts On File, 2004).
Sechin Jacchid and Paul Hyer. *Mongolia's Culture and Society* (Boulder, Colo.: Westview Press, 1979).
David Nicolle. *The Mongol Warlords: Genghis Khan, Kublai Khan, Hülegü, Tamerlane* (New York: Sterling Pub. Co., 1990).
Igor de Rachewiltz, trans. *The Secret History of the Mongols: A Mongolian Epic Chronicle of the Thirteenth Century* (Boston: Brill, 2006).
Morris Rossabi. *Khubilai Khan: His Life and Times* (Berkeley and Los Angeles: University of California Press, 1988).
Jack Weatherford. *Genghis Khan and the Making of the Modern World* (New York: Crown, 2004).

Monpa   *See* MONBA

Montagnards   *See* DEGA.

Moplahs   *See* MAPPILAS.

Mori

The Mori are AUSTRONESIANS who live in the central highlands region of Sulawesi, Indonesia. There are two separate Mori dialects, Mori Atas and Mori Bawah, which are about 73–86 percent mutually intelligible; a third language group, Padoe, has about 75 percent mutual intelligibility with them both. Despite this classification, some authors argue there is little logical reason for Mori Bawah and Mori Atas to be grouped together. The former population were largely coastal dwellers, including members of the Mori kingdom that ruled from Tinompo, while the latter were highlanders whose culture was more typical of the traits associated with the general category of Mori.

The region in which the majority of today's Mori live, the hilly center of Sulawesi, is home to a wide diversity of peoples. It includes both those indigenous to the region, such as the Mori, and others, such as the JAVANESE, BUGINESE, and GORONTALESE, who have moved to the region in the past generation or two. These moves are largely the result of the Indonesian government's policy of *transmigrasi*, whereby peoples on overpopulated islands are given incentives to move to islands and regions with

MORI

location:
Sulawesi, Indonesia

time period:
2500 B.C.E. to the present

ancestry:
Austronesian

language:
Mori Atas and Mori Bawah, both Austronesian languages

lower population densities. A second important distinction in central Sulawesi is between the majority Muslim population, both indigenous groups and *transmigrasi* ones, and a significant Christian minority. The Mori are part of this minority group that was converted to Protestant Christianity by Dutch missionaries working in the first half of the 20th century. The large church they established with local leadership in 1947, the Gereja Kristen Sulawesi Tengah (GKST), or Christian Church of Central Sulawesi, has separate incorporated churches for each ethnolinguistic group. Nonetheless, Christians have tended to ally with one another against their Muslim neighbors in recent conflicts over political, economic, and social resources. The most extreme events have taken place since 1998, and over the past decade dozens of people on both sides have been killed or injured and thousands of properties damaged or destroyed.

In 1999, a year of relatively peaceful relations, the district in which most Mori lived, Poso, was divided into two smaller divisions, and the majority of the Mori wound up in the new division of Morowali. This was supposed to solve the ethnic and religious problems Poso had been having, but this has not turned out to be the case. The newly created Morowali district contains not only Christian Mori but also Muslim Bungku, and elite members of these two communities have had to compete for the few newly created positions in the local bureaucracy. This has resulted in further violence and conflict since the partition, and there is talk of subdividing Morowali even further to separate these two religious communities.

Although the traditional economic activities for the Mori were swidden agriculture and trade, today many are members of the middle-class, urban elite living in the towns of Poso or Tentena, home of the GKST headquarters or synod. Those who remain in their rural, mountain homelands continue farming rice and vegetables; maintain small numbers of domesticated animals; and do some hunting, fishing, and forest foraging where possible.

Moros   *See* FILIPINO MUSLIMS.

Mosuo   *See* NAXI.

Mountain Jews   *See* TATS AND MOUNTAIN JEWS.

Muhajirs   (Indian migrants, refugees)

The Muhajirs are migrants who entered the new state of Pakistan between 1946 and about 1950, just before, during, and after the partition that separated the newly independent India and Pakistan; today the descendants of these migrants are still classified as Muhajirs by SINDHIS and some other Pakistanis. Many so-called Muhajirs, however, especially elites, do not use the term to refer to themselves or their communities and simply identify as Pakistanis.

The Muhajirs are largely an Urdu-speaking Muslim population; Gujurati is another important language of this community. Their homelands in India were primarily Uttar Pradesh, Bihar, and the western coast of the country, and most were urban residents with some degree of education, wealth, or both. Most settled in the state of Sindh in Pakistan, especially the urban areas, with the highest concentrations in Karachi and Hyderabad. By the late 1940s about 70 percent of the Muhajirs in Sindh were literate, compared with just 10 percent of the local population. The new migrants also brought their wealth and business and entrepreneurial experience with them and quickly came to dominate the local public and private sectors. For example, the first governor-general of Pakistan, Muhammad Ali Jinnah, who is also considered the father of independence in the country, was a Gujurati-speaking Muhajir, and the official language of the country became Urdu, despite the fact that fewer than 10 percent of the population spoke it as their mother tongue.

By the 1970s the overwhelming preponderance of Muhajirs in positions of power in Karachi and throughout the country set off a wave of resentment among the local Sindhis, PUNJABIS, and other groups who had been living there for centuries, if not millennia. In 1973 Muhajirs held 33.5 percent of public-sector jobs and more than half of the senior positions in the private sector; they also held a greatly disproportionate number of positions above brigadier in the Pakistani army: 11 of 48, or 23 percent. In 1971, with the withdrawal of East Pakistan, or Bangladesh, from the country and the election to prime minister of an ethnic Sindhi, Zulfikar Ali Bhutto, many significant political changes meant to curb the power of the Muhajirs were enacted at both provincial and national levels. Sindhi replaced Urdu as the official language in the state of Sindh, and this was followed by a law that made ethnic representation in the civil bureaucracy

MUHAJIRS

location:
Pakistan, especially Sindh Province

time period:
1946 to the present

ancestry:
Indian refugees fleeing the country just before, during, and after partition in 1947

language:
Predominantly Urdu and Gujurati

proportionate to population figures. This change clearly benefited the Sindhi people, who had been vastly underrepresented, and put the minority Muhajirs at a disadvantage.

These changes resulted in rioting in the streets of Karachi, which killed many people in the 1970s and the 1980s. The Muhajir Qaumi Mahaz (MQM), Muhajir National Movement, emerged in this political situation to represent the interests of this once-powerful minority and has continued to do so ever since. Today MQM is once again in a position of power and is allied with the governments of Prime Minister Pervez Musharraf, himself a Muhajir, and the governor of Sindh, who also comes from this ethnic group. In 2007 ethnic violence in Pakistan continued at levels not seen since the worst violence in the mid-1980s; over a two-day period in May, more than 40 people were killed and more than 130 wounded as urban violence rocked Karachi when MQM refused to allow ousted supreme court chief justice Iftikhar Muhammad Chaudhry to speak publicly about the circumstances surrounding his dismissal by Prime Minister Musharraf.

Mulam (MuLampungese, Mulaozu, Jin, Ling, Bendiren, Kyam)

The Mulam, one of 55 national minority groups in China, is a relatively small group with a population of 207,352. The Mulam have lived in Guangxi Zhuang Autonomous Region, China, since the Yuan dynasty (1271–1368) and have a history that may go back as far as the Jin dynasty (265–420). The majority of the Mulam people, about 90 percent, live in Luocheng County; the rest are scattered in the neighboring regions, sharing the land with the HAN and ZHUANG. Their territory is mountainous and contains many mineral resources such as coal, iron, and sulphur. The Wuyang and Longjiang rivers run across their land.

The Mulam language is in the larger Tai-Kadai family. Most Mulam people are multilingual, speaking the languages of Han and Zhuang as well. They are largely literate and use Chinese characters to write in their own language.

The main economic activity of the Mulam is agriculture. Even before the communist victory in 1949, which brought modern agricultural techniques to some areas of the country that lacked them previously, the Mulam had fairly advanced farming technologies and used irrigation and fertilizer to maintain intensively used plots. Glutinous rice, corn, wheat, and sweet potatoes are among their main subsistence products. In addition, cash crops and activities such as growing tea, collecting medicinal herbs, keeping livestock, blacksmithing, and making both pottery and woven cloth have helped to make the Mulam fairly economically stable in recent decades.

The Mulam kinship structure is patrilineal: Descent and property are inherited from fathers, fathers' fathers, and so forth. In the past, only sons inherited property because they remained in the family home and continued to work the property, while daughters left upon the birth of their first child. This patrilocal residence pattern required a new bride to move into her husband's family's home and to work for her new in-laws. In most cases of patrilocal residence, brides must move into their husbands' homes at marriage; the Mulam in the past differed in allowing the young woman to remain in her own family's home until the birth of the couple's first child. Since these marriages tended to have been arranged by parents and go-betweens during childhood, this arrangement allowed the girl a chance to grow up before having to take on the arduous tasks of a new wife. However, once her first child was born a woman often had an extremely difficult time due to the isolation from her own family and the hard work necessary to prove her worth in her new home.

The homes these brides moved into were patriarchal and multigenerational, with at least two generations residing under the same roof, often three, and all controlled by the senior male. The houses offered little privacy to the new couple and were just single-storied, with a few rooms. The center room contained the fire pit for cooking family meals and was the public gathering spot. While some of these rules have relaxed today, especially the arrangement of marriage during childhood, patrilocal residence, patrilineal descent, and an emphasis on sons remain central not only to the Mulam but to many other patriarchal societies as well, both inside and outside China.

There is no single religion that unifies all the Mulam people, but both Buddhism and Taoism are important sources of ritual and belief. Indigenous animism, the belief in the spirits of nature and ancestors, is also important for many. Due to the activities of the communist state in China to limit religious belief and practices, religion among the Mulam has generally decreased in importance. Nonetheless, many festivals that had their origins in the religious calendar or in the belief in the power of nature

MULAM

location:
Primarily Luocheng Mulam Autonomous County, Guangxi Zhuang Autonomous Region, China

time period:
Yuan dynasty (1271–1368) to the present

ancestry:
Possibly Ling and Liao tribes

language:
Mulam, a Tai-Kadai language

continue to be celebrated regularly. Each year the Mulam celebrate the lunar New Year's Day by cooking and eating lavish dinners and visiting their relatives and friends. In addition, married women return to their parents' homes for a gathering on that day. Another traditional holiday is Ox Birthday, which is held on the eighth day of the fourth month, when people let their oxen rest and feed them on glutinous rice; the Ox God is offered wine and meat. A third festival is the Dragon Boat Festival, held on the fifth day of the fifth lunar month, when the Mulam carry their paper boats into fields and chant spells to drive away insects for a good year's harvest. Of all festivals, Yifan Festival is the most important one, dedicated to safeguarding life and good fortune, expelling evil, and celebrating a good harvest. The event is held only every three to five years and includes singing, dancing, sacrificing to the gods and spirits, and carving models of farm animals out of sweet potatoes, to symbolize the good health of these beasts.

Multanis   *See* SERAIKIS.

Mumun culture (prehistoric Koreans, Bronze Age Koreans)

The people of the Mumun period on the Korean peninsula are known for their pottery, megalithic burial sites, and development of agriculture. Though the period in which they lived is often referred to as Korea's Bronze Age, the early phases of the Mumun culture actually predate the onset of the Bronze Age in Korea by about 800 years. The origins of the Mumun culture are probably the Liao River basin in northern China and North Korea in about 1800 B.C.E., with a steady southern migration throughout the subsequent centuries. As they moved south, the bearers of Mumun culture, named for their unmarked pottery, displaced, absorbed, or killed the previous residents of the Korean peninsula, the hunting and gathering people of the Jeulmun or Chulman culture.

The Mumun period is significant in Korean history because it marks the origins of intensive agriculture and political formations beyond the tribe. While their predecessors in the Jeulmun period were primarily hunters and gatherers who also fished and engaged in some low-level gardening, the people of the early Mumun period practiced shifting cultivation—that is, using a garden site for a season or two and then moving to a fresh plot once the soil has been depleted. They also hunted and fished. By the middle Mumun period (850–550 B.C.E.), the Mumun people were engaged in intensive agriculture on large dry fields and wet paddies that were used over and over with the assistance of animal, vegetable, and human fertilizers. Some rice was grown in both the early and middle periods, but millet, barley, wheat, and legumes were more important crops than rice.

Politically the early Mumun peoples probably lived in relatively egalitarian, tribal-based units led by Big Men who were able to influence their people but had no legitimate authority to make others submit to their will. By the middle Mumun period, however, most experts agree that a class system had developed, with some families emerging as wealthier and more powerful than others. Political power probably rested in hereditary chiefs and nobles, and a further division of labor saw the separation of skilled artisans, religious specialists, and landowners from peasants and laborers. The late Mumun period (550–300 B.C.E.) was marked by intensive conflict between these different chiefdoms, perhaps over resources and land, as evident in the large number of fortified settlements found from this era.

The transformation from relatively egalitarian tribal society in the early Mumun period to stratified chiefdoms in the middle or classic Mumun period was accompanied by a change in residential units as well. In the early period, houses were large, rectangular structures partially dug underground and containing many hearths to accommodate several families; whether they were nuclear or extended families is impossible to tell. In the middle Mumun these large structures were replaced by a multitude of smaller square and round houses, probably to accommodate just a single family. These differing shapes and sizes may have indicated differences in status. Other markers of status in this period were the large stone burial sites that, by the end of the middle period, were beginning to contain more and more bronze artifacts such as daggers, jewelry, and other adornments, and some jade pieces as well. By the late Mumun period, residential units were beginning to cluster together for protection; one village has been found inside a 13.7-foot deep, 33-foot wide ditch, presumably dug for protection from enemy villages or chiefdoms. The burials of this period are marked by an increasing number of bronze items, though iron had also started to be used for implements and military matériel.

MUMUN CULTURE

location:
The Korean Peninsula

time period:
1500 to 0 B.C.E.

ancestry:
Probably Altaic

language:
Probably the Altaic predecessor of contemporary Korean

MUNDAS

location:
Eastern India,
Bangladesh, Nepal, and
Bhutan

time period:
Unknown to the present

ancestry:
Austro-Asiatic

language:
There are 22 different
Munda languages divided into north and south
branches. All Munda
languages come from
the larger Austro-Asiatic
language family.

Mundas (Kol, Buno, numerous individual tribes)

Munda is a collective term for about 22 related ethnolinguistic groups residing in northeastern India; a small number of individuals from various subgroups also live in Bangladesh, Nepal, and Bhutan. At the turn of the 21st century they numbered about 9 million in total, and that number is not expected to have changed dramatically in recent years.

HISTORY

Munda origins remain a contentious issue among scholars. On the one hand, the Mundas represent the westernmost boundary of all Austro-Asiatic languages, with the rest of the language family residing in Southeast Asia. Due to this geographic distribution, some experts believe that all Austro-Asiatic groups originated in Southeast Asia and that the Munda migrated to their present home sometime during prehistory. A second hypothesis claims the opposite: that the Mundas are the last remnants of Austro-Asiatic speakers in their original homeland in eastern India and that the peoples of Southeast Asia speaking related languages themselves migrated several thousand years ago. The Mundas themselves speak of origins farther west, in Uttar Pradesh, India, and a steady migration eastward as larger, stronger groups moved into their former homelands. Indeed, most experts, regardless of their belief concerning Munda origins, believe that Munda tribes once inhabited a much larger territory and that over the course of many hundreds of years, they have been pushed farther and farther away from the centers of Indian civilization and into the marginal, forested hills of Bihar, Orissa, Jharkhand, West Bengal, and Madhya Pradesh.

Prior to the coming of the British, most Mundas continued to live in relatively small-scale societies for which kinship and residence provided the only important organizing principles; most states in the region were dominated by others, such as Hindus or Muslims. However, the Chota Nagpur region may have seen the emergence of a kingdom dominated by the Ho, a Munda subgroup, several hundred years ago, and the 18th-century Bhumij state of Barabhum likewise developed complexity beyond that of the rest of the Munda subgroups. Nonetheless, by the time the British began to seek to control the region, the Mundas already had a long history of dealing with larger, more powerful political units. As a result, anti-Hindu and anticolonial sentiments ran strong in the region, and the 19th century saw many Munda subgroups rebelling against outsiders. The most notable of these uprisings were the Ho rebellion of the 1830s, the rebellion of the SANTAL in the 1850s, and the Birsa Munda movement in the last five years of the century. Some of the Mundas who currently reside in Bangladesh also have their origins in the upheavals of the 19th century, having left Bihar in the early decades and gone to Bangladesh to work as laborers digging canals and lakes and in the tea plantations of Duars.

The same local and tribal affiliations that drove some Mundas to fight against the British during the 19th century have led to a strong tribal identification today. Most Mundas are proud of the tribal label and continue to identify with their own ethnolinguistic group, such as Ho, Santal, Mundari, and others; with the larger category of Munda; and with the concept of being part of India's SCHEDULED TRIBES. In part this strong identification is connected to centuries of anti-Hindu activity by many Munda groups and individuals; another part of the identification is the benefit that comes from being a member of a Scheduled Tribe, such as reserved places at universities and in the public employment sector, and even seats in both state and national parliaments. The Jharkhand Party, which had as its raison d'être the establishment of a tribal state, was a largely Santal-dominated political movement based in Ranchi, Bihar, from the late 1940s until it merged with the Indian National Congress in the 1960s. Two generations later, in 2000, the dream of many Santal, other Mundas, and even other tribal groups on the Chota Nagpur plateau was finally achieved when the state of Jharkhand was established out of territory in what had been southern Bihar. The Jharkhand Party's former home of Ranchi has become the new state capital.

CULTURE

Despite the rough terrain in which they live, characterized by thick forests, hills, and rugged plateaus, the Mundas have not been isolated. Their language has both been influenced by and in turn influenced the two dominant literary languages of the subcontinent, Sanskrit and Dravidian. Indeed, the term *Munda* itself is believed to be a Sanskrit word meaning "wealthy"; it later came to mean head or headman and referred to the group's dominance in the tribal belt of eastern India. Some of the many gods worshiped by the different Munda subgroups also resemble various Hindu gods to such a degree that most experts believe that there has been considerable sharing in this aspect of the culture of the two groups as well.

Most of the Munda population in India continues to rely on small-scale agriculture for their livelihood. In the past they depended largely on swidden agriculture, which required them to cut down either virgin or secondary growth forest, let it dry for several months, and then burn it to provide ash for fertilizer. After a season or two this process would have to be repeated on a new plot because the fragile forest soil could not support agriculture for more than a planting or two. This process has been outlawed in contemporary India, and most Mundas have started using permanent, irrigated fields and external fertilizers. Some have also turned to plantation work, mining, and unskilled labor in the urban area around Ranchi. In Bangladesh, many Mundas worked as forest clearers for others, especially on tea and indigo plantations, and when this work dried up in the 20th century, they too turned to subsistence-level agriculture. Most Munda groups also supplemented their garden foods with wild forest products and engaged in hunting and fishing. These activities continue into the present day but at a much lower rate since population growth has limited these resources.

Although the rule among Munda communities is that they generally hold onto their tribal identity and engage in agricultural labor at the subsistence level, there are a few exceptions to this rule. Some Munda groups have taken up a particular occupation, such as the ironworking Asur and basket-making Turi, and have thus joined the Hindu caste system at the lowest level of the hierarchy. Subgroups that have done this are required to maintain group endogamy—that is, they must marry within their own community—and are generally seen as fairly polluting to others in the caste system because of their occupations. Ironically, joining this system at its lowest level did not improve an individual or group's status in the eyes of the dominant Hindu majority. Since India's independence in 1947, being a member of a Scheduled Tribe has actually been more advantageous for ambitious Mundas than has been being part of a caste because of the reserved jobs and other advantages available to them.

As was the case throughout history, the two most important principles of Munda social organization are kinship and residence. All Munda tribes are patrilineal: Children all inherit their membership in their kin group from their fathers, fathers' fathers, and so on. Groups of patrilineages are combined into patriclans that likewise trace their descent from a common male ancestor. Unlike lineages, however, which can trace their origins back to an actual male ancestor, clan founders are often mythological figures: part animal and part human, or entirely animal. All members are required to respect the particular animal connected to their clan by avoiding harming or eating them; however, other clans' totemic animals are not forbidden. These clans, like lineages, are exogamous and require their members to marry individuals from other clans but preferably from the same tribe. Some of the larger clans also have another level of organization between themselves and the tribe, that of the phratry, also a patrilineal group made up of groups of clans that likewise claim mythological founders; phratries are also exogamous.

Although clans are kinship and not residential units of organization, most Munda villages are actually dominated by a single clan, with the exception of the women who have married into the village in patrilocal residence patterns and perhaps a few poor men from different clans who have moved into their in-laws' homes and villages in a matrilocal residence pattern. Like lineages, clans, and phratries, villages are exogamous units that require even nonrelated men and women to marry people from other villages. Villages can also be the primary units of alliance during times of need, such as plowing, harvesting, conflict, and, in the past, warfare. Generally these units are defined by kinship, but the strength of residence often outweighs that of lineage or clanship, especially among clan members who live far from one another and among villagers who have lived in close proximity for many years. Entire villages also participate in individual marriage negotiations, gift giving, and celebrations on the part of their sons and daughters. In many kinship-based societies a lineage or clan serves this purpose, but among the Mundas the village has emerged as the primary unit for these occasions. Even bride price, which is usually money and gifts provided by a new husband's family to compensate the family of a new bride for the loss of her domestic labor, is in the Munda case collected by the man's village and presented to the village leaders of his bride-to-be.

While lineage, clan, and village exogamy are the rules among all Mundas, other marriage rules differ according to the norms of different subgroups. Most prefer people to marry their cross-cousins, but generally not at the first-cousin level. Therefore, a grandmother's brother's child's child or a grandfather's sister's child's child is an ideal partner in many Munda groups. Some subgroups allow young people quite a degree of choice in their marriage partners and even establish a teen dormitory in which both boys and girls reside for a number of years to be trained in Munda history and culture and to find a marriage partner. Other groups allow parents to choose and arrange marriage partners for their children. Generally, most Munda marriages are monogamous; however, some sororal polygyny was the norm in the past—that is, wealthier men were allowed to marry two or more sisters. Divorce has always been allowed, and remarriage for divorced or widowed women and men are both allowed as well. In the past, a man was encouraged to marry the widow of his older brother, but this practice has very low status throughout India and does not occur with great frequency.

At marriage, most women move out of their family home and village and into those of their new husbands. The exception to this is the case of very poor men who have no land or house to offer a new bride. In this case, the man may marry into a family with no sons to inherit the house or land, move into his in-laws' home, and eventually inherit all of their land. Despite the financial advantages of this arrangement, it remains fairly rare because of the low status it brings to both the men and women who engage in it. The households that these women, and occasionally men, move into can be composed of either nuclear or extended families, depending on the family's wealth, phase of life, or other factors.

Munda religious beliefs differ somewhat from tribe to tribe, with some having been more influenced by Hinduism than others. In general, the Mundas believe in a single protector god who acts as a judge of human behavior and is associated with the sun. This god should not be conflated with a creator god, which most tribes also believe in. There are also a wide variety of local spirits and minor gods, ancestor spirits, and other both benevolent and malevolent spirits. This variety of spirits and gods requires the engagement of several kinds of Munda religious specialist. Priests, who inherit their positions from their fathers, participate in community-wide festivals and rites of passage and also in the events that mark the agricultural calendar and refer to fertility, planting, and harvesting, as well as those related to hunting. The other specialists, shamans, engage in communication with the spirit world to discern the causes of illness and other misfortunes and to effect healings. The shaman does not have an inherited position but one that an individual attains by virtue of a special gift for going into trance or otherwise communicating with the spirit world. The most important religious rituals for the Mundas are the rites of passage conducted by priests and associated with birth, marriage, and death.

FURTHER READING

Walter G. Griffiths. *The Kol Tribe of Central India* (New York: AMS Press, 1979).
Sarat Chandra Roy. *The Mundas and Their Country* (New York: Asia Pub. House, 1970).
Ryuji Yamada. *Cultural Formation of the Mundas* (Tokyo: Tokai University Press, 1970).

Muong (Mi, Moai, Moal, Mol)

The Muong are one of the 53 recognized national minorities in Vietnam. Some scholars believe that they branched off from the dominant VIETNAMESE ethnicity in about the 10th century, just as this group was freeing itself from Chinese domination. While the Vietnamese proceeded to expand from the northern lowlands southward toward the Gulf of Thailand, the Muong remained in the mountains and established themselves as a separate ethnicity altogether. Other scholars believe that the Muong of today are made up of remnants of many other ethnicities, including Vietnamese, THAIS, TAY, NUNG, and others who established their independent identity over the past 10 centuries. The archaeological record is still unclear and provides little help in accepting or rejecting either of these hypotheses regarding Muong origins.

The term *Muong* is not originally an ethnonym but a reference to the non-Vietnamese ethnic groups within a certain territory. The Muong self-designation is Mol, Moal, or Moai, depending on which dialect of Muong is being spoken, which all mean "man." They reside in the north of the country, just southwest of Hanoi, in a solid block of Muong territory that stretches for about 185 miles and is sandwiched in by the Thais to the west and the Vietnamese

MUONG

location:
The northern highlands of Vietnam, especially Hoa Binh and Thanh Hoa Provinces

time period:
Possibly 10th century to the present

ancestry:
Possibly ancient Dong Son peoples

language:
Muong, an Austro-Asiatic language closely related to Vietnamese

to the east. This territorial integrity has contributed to continued ethnic identification and cohesion today even in the context of increasing pressure to integrate into the dominant Vietnamese society. Given the relative similarity of the Muong to the Vietnamese, their steadfast insistence on remaining Muong has been highlighted in most reports about them.

The main economic activity of the Muong is farming. They rely primarily on wet rice grown in intensively worked paddies, which they supplement with corn, cassava, sweet potatoes, and pumpkins grown on small, shifting plots that have been cut out of the forest. Gathered produce such as tubers, vegetables, fruit, mushrooms, and bamboo shoots adds variety and important nutrients to the Muong diet. Hunting and fishing remain important components of the Muong subsistence diet as well and are solely male activities usually carried out collectively, especially hunting. Some households keep pigs, chickens, or ducks, and the well-to-do may have a buffalo to assist with farming activities. During the off season, or when supplies are short due to a bad harvest, the Muong turn to breadfruit, from which they make a flour that can be baked into bread to sustain them until the next rice harvest. This is a food of last resort, however, and thus is a symbol of struggle.

In addition to hunting, Muong men are responsible for plowing fields, clearing bushland, threshing, making farm implements, and building and repairing houses. Women participate heavily in agriculture by transplanting seedlings, irrigating, weeding, and harvesting rice. They are also primarily responsible for husking rice and all other food preparation, gathering wild foods and firewood, child care, cleaning, basket making, and weaving both cotton and silk into clothing. This division of labor is fairly strict and maintained from an early age, when girls begin helping their mothers with child care, food gathering, and food preparation and boys herd buffalo and assist their fathers. In general, Muong boys have more free time than girls for play activities, developing extrafamilial relationships, and attending school.

Muong social structure at the family level is patrilineal, so that descent and inheritance flow through male lines. Women marry into these units, usually leaving their own families and villages to reside with their husbands and their families, a pattern known as patrilocal residence. Each patrilineage has a headman chosen from among the eldest males in the group and is strictly exogamous, which means that both men and women marry partners from a different patriline. This pattern allows first cousin marriages between cross-cousins, the children of brothers and sisters, but not between parallel cousins, the children of two brothers or two sisters. Lineages provide mutual aid associations for all members, especially with such expensive events as marriages, funerals, and other rites of passage, and in the event of natural disaster. In addition, all Muong lineages are categorized as either noble or commoner. The nobility are divided into four separate clans, or groups of lineages: Dinh, Quach, Bach, and Hoang. All village headmen come from one of these dominant clans; men from noble lineages are also more likely to have more than one wife and many concubines, luxuries few commoners could afford. Commoner lineages, on the other hand, are not organized into clans per se, but most use the surname Bui to indicate their membership in this lower caste.

Historically, in addition to the bonds, obligations, and rights accorded to the Muong through kinship, residence in a hamlet, *quel*, provided another level of social organization and another set of rights and responsibilities. Each hamlet contained about 50 households, each made up of a nuclear family. Residence in a hamlet provided each family with access to the communal rice fields, hunting lands, and forest, both for gathering foods and firewood and for shifting agriculture. Each hamlet had a hereditary headman who made decisions about access to these communal resources; he also received tribute from each family and organized unpaid labor of commoners. When the head of a commoner family died without leaving a male heir, all access to land and forest reverted back to communal ownership and control of the headman, and the family was forced to rely on the goodwill of others. The next level of social organization was the village, which was made up of a number of hamlets and was ruled by a village headman, followed by a commune with its subordinate chief ruler, and finally a canton, made up of a number of communes and dominated by a chief. All headmen, subordinate chiefs, and chiefs were drawn from noble lineages and had a variety of other nobles who worked with them. During the French colonial period this hierarchy was maintained with French bureaucrats at the apex of the pyramidal structure, but with the Viet Minh victory in 1954, this system collapsed and was replaced by a communist state bureaucracy, which has been maintained in various forms through the present day.

Murut (Baukan, Beaufort Murut, Gana', Kalabakan, Keningau Murut, Nabai, Okolod, Paluan, Serudung, Sulangai, Tagal, Timugon)

The Murut are a conglomeration of tribes who all speak Murutic languages and reside in northern Borneo, where Sabah, Sarawak, Kalimantan, and Brunei come together. Their group name means "hill people" in their language, but most prefer to use their individual tribal names, such as Timugon, Tagal, Nabai, and many others. In addition there is also a significant cultural and linguistic division between the Northern and Southern Murut, a split that is sometimes glossed Sabah Murut and Sarawak Murut, respectively. This is somewhat inaccurate since these geographic boundaries do not coincide exactly with the cultural and linguistic boundaries between Northern and Southern.

AUSTRONESIANS probably arrived on the island of Borneo from Taiwan and ultimately from southern China about 2500 B.C.E.; however, the period in which the Murut became a distinct ethnolinguistic group separate from the many others that occupy the region remains unknown. We do know that they brought domesticated plants and possibly chickens and dogs with them as well as pottery. Today many Murut remain shifting cultivators, growing rubber and cocoa to sell for cash and rice, corn, yams, and cassava for their own subsistence. They also rely heavily on fish for protein as well as animals hunted with a blowpipe. Today some Murut are urban dwellers, well-educated, and hold important government, professional, or business positions.

In the past the most important prestige activity for Murut men was headhunting. A Murut man was not able to marry until he could present a head he had taken to the family of his betrothed. As a result of this cultural rule, the Murut were among the last of the Bornean tribes to abandon the practice of headhunting, sometime during the first half of the 20th century. Some Murut men also utilized their skill in hunting other humans to work as policemen in the force of the North Borneo Chartered Company, 1882–1946.

With the passing of headhunting as a cultural practice, the Murut have replaced human heads with jars, cloth, gold and ivory jewelry, and beads as bride wealth, the gifts a young man's family must present to his new bride's family. The same objects also play a role in the woman's dowry, the gifts given to her and her new husband by her own family. Jars, *sampa* in Murutic languages, are especially important in the Murut material culture, particularly those of Chinese origin. Jars were the traditional containers holding the bodies of the dead, and the age and lineage of each jar were known by all, with older jars that had been exchanged more often having more value than newer jars.

Traditionally the Murut lived in longhouses that were located along the region's many rivers. Each community also had a communal house for ceremonies, meetings, and even play activities. Each communal house contained a *lansaran*, or bamboo trampoline made of planks and pliant logs and used for dances.

Until the beginning of the last century, the Murut tribes were isolated and had little to do with the outside world. With the arrival of Europeans and their missionaries, many Murut abandoned their traditional animist religion, with its belief in spirits of nature and the dead. Today the Murut population is largely Christian, with a small proportion being Muslim. Other changes have come from the logging that took place in vast areas of the region in the 1970s and 1980s, which has irrevocably changed the habitat and forced many out of subsistence agriculture and into the cash-oriented economy.

Mussur See LAHU.

Mutanchi See LEPCHA.

Myanmarese: nationality (Burmese: nationality, Burmese, Myanma, people of Burma, people of Myanmar)

The people of Myanmar inhabit one of the poorest countries in the world due to the mishandling of the economy by the single-party state that took power through a military coup in 1962.

GEOGRAPHY

Myanmar, the largest mainland Southeast Asian country, shares borders with Thailand, China, India, Laos, and Bangladesh; it also has an extensive coastline along the Bay of Bengal. The are two ecological niches in the country: the lowland central plains, which lie between the

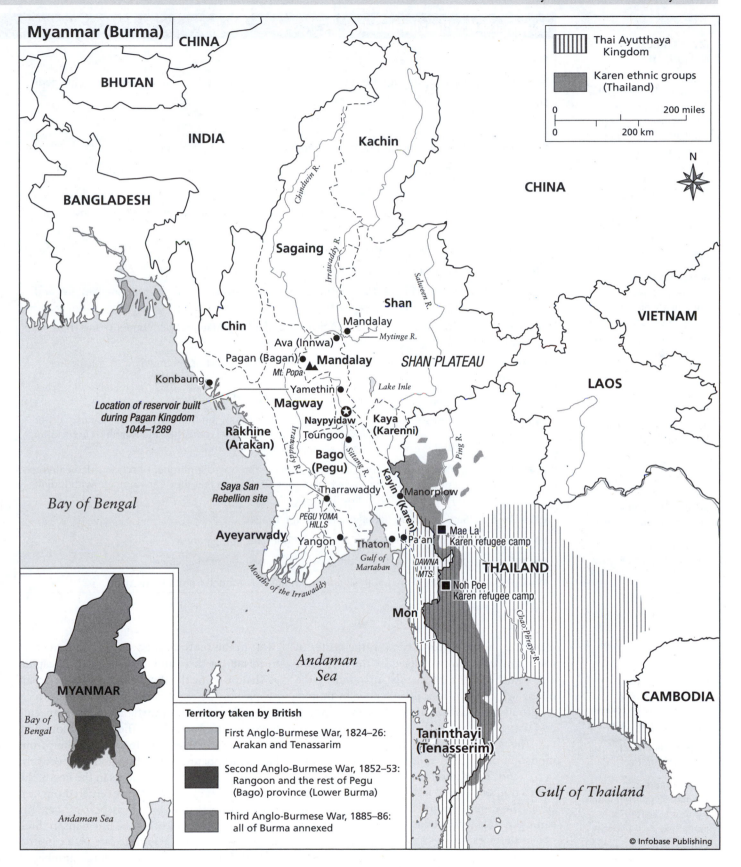

Myanmar (Burma)

CHINA

BHUTAN

INDIA

BANGLADESH

Chindwin R.

Kachin

Sagaing

Irrawaddy R.

Salween R.

Shan

CHINA

Mandalay

Ava (Innwa)

Chin

Mytinge R.

VIETNAM

Pagan (Bagan)

Mandalay

SHAN PLATEAU

Mt. Popa

Konbaung

Yamethin

Lake Inle

LAOS

*Location of reservoir built
during Pagan Kingdom
1044–1289*

Magway

Naypyidaw

Rakhine
(Arakan)

Toungoo

Kaya
(Karenni)

Irrawaddy R.

**Bago
(Pegu)**

Ping R.

Sittang R.

*Saya San
Rebellion site*

Tharrawaddy

Kayin (Karen)

Manorplow

Bay of Bengal

PEGU YOMA
HILLS

Mae La
Karen refugee camp

Ayeyarwady

Yangon

Thaton

DAWNA
MTS.

THAILAND

Mouths of the Irrawaddy

Pa'an

Gulf of
Martaban

Noh Poe
Karen refugee camp

Chao Phraya R.

Mon

*Andaman
Sea*

CAMBODIA

Taninthayi
(Tenasserim)

Gulf of Thailand

Thai Ayutthaya
Kingdom

Karen ethnic groups
(Thailand)

0   200 miles
0   200 km

N

MYANMAR

*Bay of
Bengal*

Andaman Sea

Territory taken by British

First Anglo-Burmese War, 1824–26:
Arakan and Tenasserim

Second Anglo-Burmese War, 1852–53:
Rangoon and the rest of Pegu
(Bago) province (Lower Burma)

Third Anglo-Burmese War, 1885–86:
all of Burma annexed

© Infobase Publishing

MYANMARESE: NATIONALITY

nation:
Union of Myanmar is the name promoted by the current military government, which has not been recognized by many countries as legitimate. Union of Burma or just Burma are the pre-1989 names, which are still recognized by some governments and organizations around the world.

derivation of name:
Burma is derived from the primary ethnic group in the country, the Burman, while *Myanmar* comes from the local name of the country, Myanma Naingngandaw, a 12th-century name that derives from the ancient name for the Burmans: Mranma, or Myanmar.

government:
A military junta, which took power in 1962 and annulled elections to maintain power in 1990

capital:
Yangon, formerly known as Rangoon

language:
Burmese, Shan, Karen, Kachin, Chin, and a wide variety of other languages

religion:
Buddhist 89 percent, Christian 4 percent, Muslim 4 percent, animist 1 percent, other 2 percent

earlier inhabitants:
The Mon and Pyu

demographics:
Burman 68 percent, Shan 9 percent, Karen 7 percent, Rakhine 4 percent, Chinese 3 percent, Indian 2 percent, Mon 2 percent, other 5 percent

---

Myanmarese: nationality time line

B.C.E.

Ninth century Probable date for the entry of the Mon, who migrated to Southeast Asia from the north.

First century The first Pyu city-state, Beikthano, is established.

C.E.

832 The final Pyu city-state, Sri Ksetra, falls to the Nanzhao kingdom of China.

Ninth century Probable date for the initial migrations of the Burmans south from China.

1044 Founding of the Burman kingdom of Pagan.

1056 Buddhism arrives in Pagan from the Mon court of Thaton, and King Anawrahta converts at once.

1057 King Anawrahta of Pagan defeats the Mon.

1287 The Pagan kingdom falls to the Mongols.

1486 King Minkyinyo of Toungoo founds the Second Burmese empire by conquering the Mon and Shan.

1752 Toungoo falls to the rival Konbaung dynasty under King Alaungpaya, founder of the Third Burmese empire.

1824–26 The first Anglo-Burmese War sees the British defeat the Kongbaung dynasty for the first time.

1852–53 The Second Anglo-Burmese war expands the British territory.

1883–85 The Third Anglo-Burmese War sees the final defeat of the Burmans and the annexation of all their territory along with that of neighboring minority groups like the Kachin, Karen, Chin, and Shan. All these territories are ruled as part of British India.

1906 The Young Men's Buddhist Association is formed and opens a number of schools dedicated to raising the cultural and educational levels of Burmans, so that they can compete with Indians for jobs in the colonial government.

1930–31 Saya San's Burmese Rebellion against the British.

1941 The Karen fight with the British against the Burmans and Japanese.

1942 The British are expelled from Burma by the Japanese-Burman alliance.

1945 The British retake Burma with significant military assistance from the Karen.

Irrawaddy and Salween Rivers in the center of the country and are occupied by the dominant BURMANS; and the highlands surrounding the plains, which are primarily inhabited by minority groups such as the SHANS, KACHIN, KAREN, and CHIN.

The lowland plains are dominated by a monsoon climate of rain from June to October, a cool interlude for a month or two, and then a hot, dry period lasting until the rains return. The mountainous regions experience the same general seasonal fluctuations with slightly cooler temperatures.

INCEPTION OF NATION

Myanmar's early history is largely one of the rise and fall of various ethnic kingdoms. The Mon in the south of the territory were the first to formalize their authority from their capital at Thaton, while the Pyu were the earliest urban peoples in the region's central dry zone, which was to become the heartland of Burman culture many centuries later. They were followed by three separate Burman kingdoms, ruling from Pagan, Konbaung, and Toungoo, respectively, and a variety of Shan kingdoms in the north, the most important of which was centered on Ava. The British ruled Myanmar as part of their Indian colony after defeating the Burmans in three successive wars in the mid- to late 19th century; they also imported a relatively large number of Indian bureaucrats to assist in their direct rule over the dominant Burmans. The region's other ethnic groups, who inhabited the hills surround-

1947 Independence leader Aung San is assassinated, and hopes for a multiethnic leadership in an independent Burma are extinguished.

1948 Burma becomes independent from Britain in January, and the dominant Burman population consolidates its hold on state power at the expense of all the other ethnic groups in the country.

1958 The military under Ne Win is invited to take over the government to quell rebellion and set the stage for elections in 1960.

1960 Elections are held, and the military withdraws from governing.

1962 A military coup puts Ne Win back in control of the state.

1970s General Ne Win formulates and puts into action the Four Cuts Policy, which leads to attempts to cut off food, money, recruits, and intelligence to the non-Burman rebels.

1989 Burma under Ne Win is renamed Myanmar; the capital Rangoon becomes Yangon.

1989 Activist Aung San Suu Kyi is put under house arrest for the first time.

1990 The election won by Suu Kyi's National League for Democracy is annulled by the military. In the next couple of years Myanmar becomes one of the 10 poorest countries in the world.

1991 Aung San Suu Kyi wins the Nobel Peace Prize but cannot leave her home to accept it; her son does so on her behalf.

1995 Aung San Suu Kyi is released from house arrest but is told if she leaves the country she will not be allowed to return.

1997 The State Law and Order Restoration Council is renamed the State Peace and Development Council (SPDC); the new name does not decrease the atrocities committed by national forces against its ethnic, student, and prodemocracy enemies.

2000 Aung San Suu Kyi is rearrested and held until May 2002, when she is freed again for one year before being reimprisoned.

2007 In May the military government extends Aung San Suu Kyi's house arrest for another year. In September–October, the largest prodemocracy demonstrations in the country for 20 years are staged and result in the deaths of hundreds of protestors and the disappearance of at least 1,000 people. Many monks are confined to their monasteries, arrested, or killed.

2008 Cyclone Nargis destroys much of the Irrawaddy Delta in central Myanmar, killing tens of thousands and leaving several million homeless.

ing the Burman plains, mostly experienced the British as indirect rulers who used local chiefs and princes in their strategy of dividing and conquering Myanmar (then called Burma) as a whole. In 1937 the British allowed the people of the territory to vote on whether they would remain as part of India or would be ruled as a separate colony. It was a divisive battle that ended with Burma being separated from India for the remaining decade of the colonial era; however, the divisions fostered by the vote were maintained long after independence and continue to plague the country even today.

During World War II the British and their hill tribe allies, especially the Karen and Kachin, were unable to hold off the invading JAPANESE, who had the assistance of many ethnic Burmans. The Japanese occupied the country for three years before the British retook their colony in 1945, again with significant assistance from some highland peoples. Despite this assistance, when the British began negotiating with local leaders for independence, it was the ethnic Burman people, their former enemies, who were seen as the most viable leaders of the new country. This might not have ended badly if Aung San, leader of the Anti-Fascist Organization and chief negotiator, had not been assassinated in 1947, before the constitution he helped draft had taken effect. This constitution gave significant autonomy to the country's many minority groups and allowed for some important power-sharing mechanisms at the federal level.

Aung San Suu Kyi with two of her bodyguards in 1995, the year she was released from six years of house arrest. House arrest was reimposed in 2000. *(AP Photo/Richard Vogel)*

This assassination, along with those of many other members of the constitutional committee, allowed other, more nationalist Burman factions to take control of the government and limit the power of the other minorities. As a result, almost from the moment of independence in January 1948, the country has experienced a state of near-constant civil war. The Shans, Karen, and Kachin all took up arms to press the government for greater autonomy in their home states. In 1962 the situation became so dire that the military under Ne Win dissolved the government and took over the country. Despite allowing elections in 1990, won by the opposition, the military has maintained its grip over the country since that time. Ne Win himself was at the center of the political scene, first as military ruler and then as president, from 1962 until 1988. In that year he was himself the victim of a military coup by Saw Maung in the wake of a period of chaos caused by prodemocracy protests and government crackdowns. The new State Law and Order Restoration Council planned and held elections two years later but has never allowed the National League for Democracy, led by Aung San's daughter, Aung San Suu Kyi, to take over. Today Suu Kyi continues to be held prisoner under house arrest, prodemocracy activists are regularly harassed and jailed, and the state is fighting a multisided battle against student, democracy, and ethnic groups all trying to topple the illegitimate military junta. In late 2007 the situation became even more dire with thousands of monks imprisoned, killed, and disappeared in the wake of the largest prodemocracy events in the country for decades.

CULTURAL IDENTITY

There is no common cultural identity that binds together all the competing factions in the contemporary state of Myanmar. Since the early 20th century, the dominant ethnic Burmans have put Buddhism at the center of their attempt to build a local national identity. In 1906 Burman leaders formed the Young Men's Buddhist Association, and with the assistance of the colonial government they established schools and other educational institutions to help raise the status of local leaders over the Indians and Chinese brought into the country by the British. While this strategy may have worked with the nearly 90 percent of the population that considers itself Buddhist, it has proved extremely difficult to maintain in the face of the Christian, Muslim, and other religious minorities who consider their own religions as central to their own identities. The official language, Burmese, also marginalizes and isolates about a third of the country, which does not speak it.

Perhaps most important in the 21st century, the military government has been unable to create any nationalism or common national identity because it is seen as illegitimate by a majority of the population, including many ethnic Burmans. Student and prodemocracy groups have joined the country's many minorities in their fight against the status quo, and violence is a regular occurrence in the country. In 2007 the government once again clamped down on these movements, and the possibility of a democratic transition seems very far off.

Perhaps the one identity shared by most ordinary citizens of Myanmar is that of poverty. Since the military coup in 1962, the government has aimed to promote "the Burmese way to socialism" through single-party control over the economy. This path clearly failed, and by the early 1990s the country had become one of the world's 10 poorest, despite being rich in natural resources, from teak and other tropical hardwoods to newly discovered gas and oil reserves. During the colonial era, the rich central plains became a world leader in rice production and export, but today the country grows barely enough to feed itself. Today, due to the illegitimacy of the government and its harsh treatment of the opposition, the country receives no aid from or trade with the United States or many other western countries. Its neighbors continue to trade with Myanmar, but this has not been enough to raise the income levels of the approximately 90 percent of the population who live on about $300 per year, or less than $1 per day.

FURTHER READING

Gerry Abbott, ed. *Inroads into Burma: A Travellers' Anthology* (New York: Oxford University Press, 1997).

Stephen Brookes. *Through the Jungle of Death: A Boy's Escape from Wartime Burma* (London: John Murray, 2000).

Peter Carey, ed. *Burma: The Challenge of Change in a Divided Society* (New York: St. Martin's Press, 1997).

Michael Fredholm. *Burma: Ethnicity and Insurgency* (Westport, Conn.: Praeger, 1993).

Monique Skidmore, ed. *Burma at the Turn of the Twenty-First Century* (Honolulu: University of Hawaii Press, 2005).

Nagas

The Nagas are a group of more than 20 different tribal communities living in the border region between India's Brahmaputra Valley in Assam, Nagaland, Manipur, and Arunachal Pradesh and the Sagaing Division of Myanmar (Burma), especially along the Chindwin River. The derivation of *Naga* remains a mystery to this day; there are several possibilities, including *nagna*, the Sanskrit term for "naked," *nag*, the Hindustani word for "mountain," and *naga*, the Assamese word for "naked."

ORIGINS

The exact origins of the Nagas are unknown today, but linguistic evidence points to migration from northern Asia more than 2,000 years ago. The Greek geographer Ptolemy knew of their existence in about 150 C.E. from Indian sources that referred to them as "Naked People."

GEOGRAPHY

The Nagas inhabit highland territory in far-eastern north India and northwestern Myanmar. The state of Nagaland, the 16th created by the Indian state, is a wet and humid area crossed by many important rivers, including the Dhansiri, Dikhu, Doyang, Melak, and Tizu, which rise significantly during the monsoon season, June through September. The highest peak at 12,600 feet is Saramati, while the state's other peaks average more than 3,000 feet. The adjoining Sagaing district in Myanmar has very similar geography and climate.

HISTORY

Prior to the 20th century there was no common identity as "Naga," which is an Indo-Aryan label, as all the possible derivations indicate; rather, each tribe referred to itself using its own tribal name and thought of itself as unique. The largest tribe is the KONYAK; the KACHARIS and Angami have been studied fairly extensively. With the decline of British authority in their highland region and the greater imposition of Indian power, the term *Naga* became more accepted generally among those labeled as such. Several indigenous organizations adopted the name in the 1940s, including the Naga National Council and Naga People's Convention, which contributed to further acceptance of the name. The creation of the Indian state of Nagaland in 1963 solidified the identity, and today in both India and Myanmar the Nagas are firmly established as relatively cohesive tribal communities.

Although their exact history is unknown, from the 13th to 19th centuries the leaders of Assam, the AHOM people, documented extensive trade and political relations with the various tribes that came to be known as Nagas. Sometimes these relations were positive, as when the Nagas traded salt, herbs, cotton, wax, ivory, and adzes for Assamese rice, beads, and cloth. At other times the Ahom raided Naga villages or demanded tribute from the Nagas; however, these relations never devolved into Assamese direct control over the highlands.

The Naga tribes did finally lose their independence in the 19th century when the British

NAGAS

location:
The borderland between far northeastern India's Brahmaputra Valley and northwestern Myanmar (Burma)

time period:
Mid-20th century as Nagas, unknown as individual tribes to the present

ancestry:
Tibeto-Burman

language:
There are more than 20 Naga languages and dialects, all within the Tibeto-Burman family; Naga Pidgin, sometimes called Nagamese, Kachari, or Bodo, is the region's lingua franca.

East India Company annexed their territory after many decades of Naga resistance. The British first tried to annex Nagaland in 1832 but were repelled by extensive guerrilla fighting in the jungles of the highlands. Between 1835 and 1851, 10 more British expeditions tried to pacify and settle Nagaland with some success, but rebellion marked the region long after this period as well, especially in 1878 when the British burned many Naga villages in response to local fighting. This resistance to external power structures continued to mark Naga relations with outsiders well into the period of Indian independence as well.

Under the British the Nagas changed significantly. The people generally continued to think of themselves as members of individual tribes rather than as Nagas but Christianity was introduced in the region by British and American Protestant missionaries and many communities quickly converted. Literacy in both English and some Indian languages by a small Naga elite also contributed to the later development of a common Naga identity and solidarity. The British also maintained a degree of separation between the dominant lowland Indian communities and the hill tribes, which, as the history with the Ahom indicates, had not always been positive for the Nagas; they tried to prevent Indian bureaucrats from administering the highlands, utilizing local or British clerks as necessary.

This degree of separation during the colonial period, combined with the development of a local elite, led to calls in 1947 by the Naga National Council for regional independence. This was a political impossibility given the politics of unification in independent India, and the 1950s were marked by violence between Indian forces and Naga secessionists. In 1956 the latter even created a Federal Government of Nagaland, which went unrecognized throughout the world. In 1963 the Indian government finally recognized the existence of a separate group of Naga peoples through the creation of the state of Nagaland, but fighting continued until mid-1964, when the two sides signed a lasting peace agreement.

Unfortunately the 1970s brought a recurrence of violence in relations between the Naga National Council and the Indian government when a 1972 assassination attempt in Nagaland led to India's banning the council from meeting or organizing. The Shillong Accord in 1975 tried to end the violence but actually recognized very few Naga demands and thus drove those seeking independence to push their agenda even harder. Another peace agreement in 1997, which was extended in 2001, has attempted to

Nagas time line	
C.E.	
150	Ptolemy, a second century C.E. Greek geographer, writes of an Indian tribe whom the locals refer to as "Naked People"; they live in the same region as the contemporary Nagas.
13th century	The Ahom of Assam record significant trade and military relations with the various Naga tribes.
1832	The British try to annex Nagaland but are repelled.
1835–51	The British send 10 different military expeditions into Nagaland to try to pacify and settle the region.
1878	The last significant Naga rebellion against the British sees many Naga villages burned.
1947	Indian independence and the start of the 60-year fight on the part of some Nagas for complete independence.
1956	The Federal Government of Nagaland is created by Naga separatists but is not recognized by any sovereign state.
1963	Nagaland is created, but this does not end the violence.
1964	Indians and Nagas sign a peace agreement that lasts for about eight years.
1972	An assassination attempt in Nagaland leads to further violence between Indian forces and Naga separatists.
1975	The Shillong Accord tries to end the violence but creates several new Naga rebel groups.
1985	Swedish journalist Bertil Lintner travels to Naga territory in Burma and discovers that none of the people he speaks with has ever even heard of Burma much less recognizes it as the country in which he or she lives.
1997	Yet another peace agreement is signed by some Naga factions and the Indian government.
2001	The 1997 agreement is reiterated but fails to bring peace.
2005	The existence of three rival Naga separatist groups means that intra-Naga violence is at least as damaging to lasting peace as discord between Nagas and the Indian government.

settle relations between the Indian government and leaders of several different Naga independence movements, as well as among these various groups, but bombings and other violence in all subsequent years point to the difficulty of creating lasting peace. In 2005 members of the National Socialist Council of Nagaland-Isak Muivah faction (NSCN-IM) stated that reconciliation with two other Naga groups, the Khaplang faction of the NSCN and the Naga National Council, was impossible and that the violence would continue for years to come.

CULTURE

The Nagas are generally small-scale agriculturalists who grow rice, millet, potatoes, beans, cucumbers, spinach, gourds, corn, and taro in swidden-style fields that use fire to create an ash fertilizer. Some cotton, jute, thatch, and bamboo are also grown for local use as well as for sale. A few tribal groups utilize permanent terraced farms that are irrigated and artificially fertilized, but this is not the norm. Wealthier Naga families keep a variety of domestic animals as well, including cows, pigs, dogs, cats, chickens, ducks, bees, goats, and *gayals,* a Southeast Asian breed of bovine. Many tribes and subgroups also engage in hunting with spears and guns and in fishing with poisons to supplement their meat supplies.

While there are significant cultural differences among the 20 or more individual Naga tribes, one of the consistencies across groups is a patrilineal kinship system in which membership in lineages, subclans, and clans is inherited from one's father; the one exception to this rule may be the Kohima, who display some matrilineal tendencies. Lineages and subclans are exogamous units among the Naga, requiring members to marry people from outside their own group. In addition, subclan membership provides individuals with their most important alliances, superseding even the importance of village quarters. Indeed, subclans and clans are so important among the Nagas that it is these units rather than individuals who are held responsible for offenses committed by their members. At the same time, both subclans and clans often splinter to form two or more derivative clans, which shows that, like residence, kinship is not a completely stable system for the creation of networks through time.

Although not the primary source of individual alliances, Naga villages and their subunits, quarters or neighborhoods, are significant in the life of all Nagas who live in them because they control agricultural land. They also tend to overlap with kinship but in different ways among various Naga tribes. Some tribes practice patrilocal marriage, requiring newly married couples to live in the household of the groom, while others require matrilocal marriage, in which the new couple lives with the bride's family for a period before establishing its own, neolocal residence or moving into a patrilocal residence. In patrilocal communities, village quarters tend to include just one or two patrilineal subclans and their in-marrying wives, while matrilocal communities have a wider array of individuals, related to one another through kinship or marriage.

In the past, two of the most commented-on features of the Naga tribes were their practice of headhunting, which was stopped during the British era, and their elaborate tattooing. Headhunting took place in the course of warfare carried out to settle individual or clan disputes, which tended to be the same thing since subclans and clans are held responsible for individual behaviors, as a way to increase individual prestige and status in the community, and as a dedication to the gods. The Nagas sometimes took arms and legs as well as enemy heads, all presented to their gods as part of their request for good weather and a bountiful harvest. Unlike headhunting, which was entirely a male activity, both men and women among the Nagas had tattoos that indicated their village of residence and clan membership. Like headhunting, Protestant missionaries working in Nagaland in the 19th century put a stop to most tattooing, and today it is visible only in some remote villages and as part of tourist shows.

FURTHER READING

V. K. Anand. *Nagaland in Transition* (New Delhi: Associated Publishing House, 1969).

Verrier Elwin, ed. *The Nagas in the Nineteenth Century* (New York: Oxford University Press, 1969).

Milada Ganguli. *A Pilgrimage to the Nagas* (New Delhi: Oxford and IBH Publishing Co., 1984).

M. Horam. *Social and Cultural Life of Nagas* (New Delhi: B. R. Publishing Corp., 1977).

Julian Jacobs with Alan Macfarlane, Sarah Harrison, and Anita Herle. *The Nagas: Hill Peoples of Northeast India, Society, Culture, and the Colonial Encounter* (New York: Thames and Hudson, 1990).

Naiman

The Naiman were a tribe of Mongol speakers who lived primarily in what is today eastern Kazakhstan; *naiman* means "eight" in Mongolian. The MONGOLS, under Genghis Khan, conquered the entire region, including other Mongol tribes, one of which were the Naiman, and integrated them into the Mongol confederation in 1218.

Prior to their incorporation into the Mongol Empire, the Naiman were one of the largest and most powerful rivals to the Mongols in the steppes of Central Asia. Like the Mongols, they were largely nomadic pastoralists whose primary responsibilities were to their families and clans; tribal affiliations were secondary and weak until the 12th century. In addition to raising livestock, the Naiman practiced a little cultivation, returning to garden plots at harvest

---

NAIMAN

location:
The Altai Mountains of eastern Kazakhstan

time period:
Unknown–1218 C.E.

ancestry:
Mongol with some Turkic elements as well

language:
Mongol

time; the tribe also possessed skilled craftsmen in areas such as blacksmithing and carpentry. The Naiman engaged in trading livestock, metals, and furs not only within the tribe but also with outsiders such as other Mongol tribes, the Chinese, and Turkic peoples, among others.

In their intellectual life the Naiman were literate people, utilizing the Uighur script to write their Mongol language; the Uighur script itself was based on the writing of the Sogdians, who had borrowed significant elements of their alphabet from Aramaic. After conquering the Naiman, Genghis Khan adopted the Naiman script to write the Mongol language. Much of the Naiman religious belief system came from outside the tribe; many Naiman converted to Nestorian Christianity (after 431, an eastern branch of the Byzantine Church, which maintained that the divine and the human Jesus were two separate beings), especially after they had become a vassal state within the Kara-Khitai khanate in 1177, while others practiced a form of Tibetan Buddhism. Prior to these conversions all Mongol-speaking people, including the Naiman, practiced shamanistic religions, in which individual religious leaders used trance and other methods to communicate with the spirit world and to facilitate interactions between that world and this one. Even after conversion to Buddhism and Nestorian Christianity, many shamanistic elements remained in the Naiman belief system.

The Naiman were the last of the Mongol tribes to succumb to Genghis Khan. However, Kuchlug, or Kuchluk, one of the sons of the Naiman khan who had been killed in the final battle, refused to acquiesce to Mongol rule and fled west. With his battle-weary troops he took over, in 1211, the khanate of the Kara-Khitai, a confederacy of Uighur, Persian, Chinese, and Turkic tribes who had previously held the Naiman as a vassal state. Before Kuchlug subjugated the Kara-Khitai, Khitai subjects had been free to practice any religion, but after their subjugation Kuchlug refused to recognize the rights of Muslims, even murdering an imam to make his point. As a result, the majority of the Kara-Khitai supported Genghis Khan and even invited him to take over their lands. In 1218, with 20,000 Mongol troops marching west toward the Kara-Khitai, Kuchlug was murdered, probably by his subjects, and the territory was subsumed into the Mongol empire. These events mark not only the end of the Naiman as a separate people but also the first westward movement of the Mongol Empire, which eventually reached the gates of Vienna in Central Europe. Today many Kazakhs count the Naiman among their ancestors, and there is a site called Naiman in Xinjiang, China, but these connections to the 12th-century Naiman are tenuous at best and probably largely legendary.

See also Khitans.

Nanai (Nanay, Nani, Gol'd, Goldi, Fishskin Tatars, Hezhe, Hezhen, Nabei, Nanai, Naniao, Sushen, Wild Nuchen, Yupibu)

The Nanai are a Tungusic-speaking people who reside along the Amur River in far-eastern Siberia, largely in Khabarovsk Kray, Amur Oblast, and the Yakutia Autonomous Republic. A few Nanai also live in Manchuria, China, where they are called Hezhe, or Hezhen.

For most of their history the Nanai did not consider themselves an ethnic group or people. Each settlement existed in relative isolation from all the others along about a 375-mile stretch of the Amur River and another 60 miles of tributaries. Ancient Chinese sources mention a people called Sushen who resided along the Amur in the second and first millennia B.C.E., but little other information is available until the Manchus moved into the region in the 12th century and called it the Land of the Nivkhs, a related people. Russian troops arrived in the mid-17th century but left in 1689 when the Treaty of Nerchinsk gave the region to China. A few Chinese farmers settled beside the Nanai communities along the rivers, but Chinese attempts at taxing the region's native inhabitants were unsuccessful.

The mid-19th century saw the reintroduction of Russian colonization along the left bank of the Amur River; this incursion created much greater disruption to Nanai communities than had the Chinese because the Russians were competing for the most profitable fishing grounds. A few Nanai became rich as merchants and entrepreneurs in fish and fish products, but in general the economy in the area lagged behind other regions because of a lack of processing technology for shipping the fish long distance. Nonetheless, these native-Russian trading relationships set the stage for further Russian encroachment on the local economy in the 1920s, when native peoples were administered by the newly formed Far East Revolutionary Committee, and then later with the beginnings of collectivization in the 1930s. Interestingly, the forced settling imposed by

NANAI

location:
Siberia, northeast China

time period:
Unknown to the present

ancestry:
proto-Tungusic

language:
Nanai, a Manchu-Tungus language with two distinct dialects, Upper and Lower Amur. Most Nanai in Siberia speak Russian as well, often as their first language; Nanai in China, where they are called Hezhe, also often speak Mandarin Chinese.

the Russians, the creation of a written Nanai language, as well as the education of children created the opportunity for the previously scattered Nanai to develop a common ethnic identity for the first time.

The traditional Nanai way of life had been based on fishing for those residing in the Amur River valley and on hunting for those residing along its tributaries. Summer residences were semicircular houses built from birch bark, while winter residences tended to be partially dug underground to maintain warmth and offer protection from the wind. Animal and fish skins served as the material for clothing. Influences from the Chinese Manchus could be seen in the fireplace and chimney systems of many houses, which vented smoke under the sleeping areas and out through a tall chimney next to the house, as well as in women's and men's hairstyles. Nanai metalworking also resembled that of the Manchus, and the Nanai of the Upper Amur began cultivating grain and raising pigs after living among the Chinese.

Nauruans: nationality (people of Nauru)

The Nauruans are the indigenous people of the tiny island nation of Nauru. Once the second-wealthiest people per capita in the world as a result of phosphate mining, today's Nauruans are destitute and struggling to create a post-phosphate economy.

GEOGRAPHY

Nauru is a 13-square-mile island in the Pacific located just 26 miles south of the equator. Its nearest neighbor is the island of Banaba, part of the independent country of Kiribati and one of the two other sources of phosphate in the Pacific; the third is Makatea in French Polynesia. Like Banaba in 1979, Nauru's phosphate reserves have largely been depleted, leaving a once-wealthy country destitute. The small island has no other resources, and the two large-scale phosphate mines have left about four-fifths of the island's land stripped and useless. The other fifth, located in a narrow strip along the coast, is used to grow coconuts, bananas, pineapples, and some vegetables. About 90 percent of the island's food must be imported.

INCEPTION AS A NATION

The origins of the indigenous Nauruans are still unknown today because their language differs so significantly from all the other Oceanic languages. The presumption is that Naururans are the descendants of the original AUSTRONESIANS who left south China between 5000 and 4500 B.C.E. and that they are most closely related to other MICRONESIANS, but their language is divergent enough to have left some question in many experts' minds. Many sources list both Polynesian and Micronesian origins for the Nauruans based on social structure and physical features such as skin color and hair type.

Nauruans first entered world history in 1798 when British sailor John Fearn landed on their island and named it Pleasant Island. At that time 12 tribes inhabited the small island, but little else is known about their social structure or way of life, although it most certainly was dominated by fishing and by harvesting coconuts, pandanus fruit, and other local products. In 1878 the first of several destructive outside forces manifested itself when the introduction of guns and alcohol during the previous decades led to a 10-year war among the tribes. The fighting lowered the population from an estimated high of 1,400 to about 900 in 1888, when the Germans annexed the island as part of their Marshall Island protectorate. They later transferred administration to New Guinea.

The most important date in Nauruan history is 1900, the year phosphate was discovered on the island. Phosphate has been both a blessing and a curse for Nauruans over the past century: Colonialism destroyed their way of life, the Germans and JAPANESE attacked Nauru during World War II, and the mining brought fabulous wealth in the postwar era and ecological destruction and destitution in the 21st century with the resource's depletion. The first period of phosphate extraction, 1900–14, was dominated by the Pacific Phosphate Company, a German-British joint effort. This period ended with World War I and the capture of the island by Australian forces. In this early period the indigenous population began to be incorporated into the market economy and to give up subsistence fishing and gardening in favor of the imported canned and processed foods of the colonizers.

Following the First World War the League of Nations granted Australia, New Zealand, and Britain joint trusteeship over the island, and phosphate mining was resumed by the British Phosphate Company, which was also jointly owned by these three countries. In this period the outside influence on Nauru brought much of the remaining aspects of traditional

NAURUANS: NATIONALITY

nation:
Nauru; Republic of Nauru

derivation of name:
Nauru might come from the local term *anáoero*, "I go to the beach."

government:
Republic with the president serving as head of state and government

capital:
There is no official capital, but all government offices are in the Yaren district.

language:
English is the official language; Nauruan, considered only remotely related to Micronesian languages, is in a family of its own.

religion:
Christian (two-thirds Protestant, one-third Roman Catholic)

earlier inhabitants:
None

demographics:
Indigenous Nauruans 58 percent, other Pacific Islanders 26 percent, Chinese 8 percent, Europeans 8 percent

life to an end. The Spanish influenza pandemic killed dozens of Nauruans, and in 1925 the first case of diabetes was diagnosed, a harbinger of things to come.

As one of the world's richest supplies of phosphate, Nauru became a target during World War II. In 1940 a German raiding ship attacked the little island, and two years later the Japanese occupied it, relocating much of the indigenous population to Chuuk, ostensibly due to the lack of food on the island but also to utilize them as slave laborers. Unlike much of the rest of the Pacific, the U.S. Navy did not attack Nauru; the Japanese surrendered their position to the Australians in 1945. The Australians were subsequently granted rights to Nauru as a UN Trust Territory under their administration, which they held until Nauruan independence in 1968.

As in the first half of the 20th century, Nauruans' lives were once again dominated by phosphate in the latter half. At the time of independence, Nauruans were vastly wealthy, with the second-highest per capita income in the world after Saudi Arabia. Unfortunately, this wealth was not invested wisely, and failed property and other investments have meant that today the country is bankrupt and its people destitute. Easy-to-reach phosphate disappeared in 2000, leaving the Nauruans no way to pay back their substantial debts. In 2001 Australia stepped in again and for a payment of US$70.4 million dollars was able to house a boatload of asylum seekers on Nauru rather than on Australian soil, the so-called Pacific Solution. This funding was not enough to salvage the ailing Nauruan economy, and in 2004 many of the country's property assets in Australia were put into receivership and sold; in 2005 the country's single airplane was repossessed and sold as well.

Today most Nauruans are employed by the civil service and in state-run enterprises. About 90 percent of all food and other goods must be imported and paid for, and water and electricity are both limited. The future for the approximately 13,000 residents is bleak, and many may have to emigrate in the near future.

CULTURAL IDENTITY

Indigenous Nauruan cultural identity is based on membership in matrilineal clans, those that reckon descent only through women, as is the case throughout most of Micronesia. Only Nauruans born of an indigenous Nauruan mother can own land in the country, because the matrilineal clans control all such access, which means that the country's large percentage of nonindigenous peoples and companies all lease the land on which they live and work. This connection between individuals, lineages, clans,

Nauruans: nationality time line

C.E.

1798	John Fearn, a British sailor, is the first European to land on Nauru; he names it Pleasant Island.
1830s	Whaling ships land on Nauru, the first outsiders to visit the island since Fearn, and bring guns and alcohol with them.
1878	Start of a 10-year war among Nauru's 12 native tribes.
1888	Germany annexes Nauru as part of its Marshall Island protectorate, and King Auweyida is recognized as the local leader.
	Christian missionaries arrive from the Gilbert Islands.
1900	Phosphate is discovered, and mining begins six years later.
1914	Australia captures Nauru at the start of World War I.
1919	Australia, New Zealand, and Britain receive a League of Nations mandate to control Nauru and its lucrative phosphate industry.
1920	King Auweyida dies and is replaced by a council of chiefs.
1940	A German raiding ship shells Nauru and damages its phosphate mines.
1942	The Japanese occupy Nauru and relocate most of its inhabitants to Chuuk.
1943	Japanese and Korean laborers build an airfield, which is still in use today by Air Nauru.
1945	The Japanese surrender Nauru on an Australian warship.
1946	Nauru becomes a UN trusteeship controlled by Australia.
	Seven hundred thirty-seven of the 1,200 Nauruan previously deported to Chuuk return; the others have died.
1967	Nauruans take control of their phosphate resources.
1968	Nauru becomes independent, the world's smallest republic, with the second-highest per capita income in the world after Saudi Arabia.
1992	The International Court of Justice rules that Australia must pay compensation for the ecological destruction caused by phosphate mining prior to Nauruan independence. Australia eventually pays US$70.4 million.
1999	Nauru joins the United Nations.
2000	Easy-to-reach phosphate disappears, and the reserves are presumed totally depleted.
2001	Australia sends a ship of mostly Afghanistani asylum seekers to Nauru in what the Australian government calls the Pacific Solution; these people are joined by two other shiploads in subsequent years. Nauru shuts its borders to outsiders so that no monitoring of the refugees' conditions can occur. Most have since been allowed to enter Australia as refugees.
2006	Limited phosphate production begins from the small amount of difficult-to-reach phosphate still available.

NAXI

location:
Southern China, primarily in Yunnan Province, Lijiang county

time period:
Unknown to the present

ancestry:
Qiang people of the Qinghai plateau

language:
Naxi, in the Yi branch of the Tibeto-Burman family

and the land also means that any proposal to resettle the Nauruan population elsewhere, as Australia has offered with Curtis Island several times since the 1950s, will always be refused, for to separate Nauruans from their land would be to take away their identity as Nauruans.

In addition to matrilineal clans, which divide the island into 14 districts, each district has its own chief, all of whom together constitute the council of chiefs. During the colonial period this council was the primary source of governance for the indigenous community, but today the council works alongside the democratically elected parliament and president. The Nauru Protestant and Roman Catholic churches are also active on the island, the legacy of missionaries who came to Nauru along with the German, British, and Australian colonizers.

A final component of Nauruan identity that is important today is a traditional association of fatness with beauty and fertility. Chiefs' families, especially the women, were traditionally supposed to put much of their effort into getting fat and staying that way. The process began with girls at the time of their first menses and continued well into middle age. Some men engaged in fattening rituals as well but did not undergo seclusion, as was the case with girls. They were sequestered in specially built huts, which prevented the sun from darkening their skin since light skin was another marker of beauty. Prior to the colonial era the only foods available for this fattening process were coconuts, pandanus fruit, and fish, but with the introduction of processed foods in the early 20th century the standards of health for Nauruans dropped precipitously. While the fattening rituals themselves stopped in the 1920s, the cultural ideal of a fat body and light skin did not disappear. Today's high rates of obesity (75 percent) and type 2 diabetes (45 percent), the second-highest rate in the world after Native Pima Indians in the southwest United States, is the legacy of this combination of cultural ideal and imported food.

See also POLYNESIANS.

FURTHER READING

Carl N. McDaniel and John M. Gowdy. *Paradise for Sale: A Parable of Nature* (Berkeley and Los Angeles: University of California Press, 2000).

Solange Petit-Skinner. *The Nauruans: Nature and Supernature in an Island of the Central Pacific,* 2nd ed. (San Francisco, Calif.: MacDuff Press, 1995).

Nancy Viviani. *Nauru, Phosphate, and Political Progress* (Canberra: Australian National University Press, 1970).

Naxi (Nakhi, Naqxi, Nashi, Nahi, Na, Moxiayi, Mosha)

There are currently more than 300,000 Naxi living in southern China. The official Chinese ethnic category includes self-identified Naxi and Mosuo, a smaller group who live east of the Naxi. Both groups are thought to have descended from the QIANG and migrated from the Qinghai plateau to their current home in the Lijiang area. Naxi territory spans Himalayan peaks, valleys, and foothills, all features conducive to a mixture of agriculture and hardy livestock.

From the 11th to the 13th centuries, the Naxi were the dominant ethnic group in their region, but they were conscious of their relatively small size. When the MONGOLS invaded in 1253, the Naxi pragmatically agreed to become tributaries of the Yuan dynasty. The Yuan rulers established hereditary chieftains to govern the Naxi, but when the Naxi became formal residents of China in 1723, court officials were sent to replace the local chieftains. Over time, Confucian influences on marriage and kinship structures grew pronounced, and kinship became patrilineal, so that lineage membership was passed directly from fathers to their children. The smaller Mosuo group is an exception to this pattern and maintains a matrilineal structure, in which lineage membership is inherited from one's mother and inheritance is passed from mother's brothers to sister's sons.

Chinese influences also appear in one of two traditional Naxi scripts, known as Geba. Geba combines symbols derived from Chinese characters with new designs and with the second, older Naxi script known as Dongba. *Dongba* is a term that includes the script, the priests who used it to record spells and stories, and a system of religious beliefs. The Dongba script is written in pictograms that range from superficially simple images to complicated symbols representing verbs, particles, homonyms, phonetic clues, and cosmological beliefs. Today very few Naxi learn to read and write Dongba. Economic and educational reasons have led younger generations of Naxi to learn to speak and write Mandarin Chinese, sometimes to the detriment of their Naxi fluency. Dictionaries and oral stories have been compiled in libraries to prevent them from being lost.

The Dongba religion stems from Tibetan Bön shamanism and is not considered indigenous to the Naxi. It is thought to have been introduced 900 years ago, and over time it has coexisted with other foreign religions practiced by Naxi, including Chinese and Tibetan Buddhism and Taoism. Pre-Dongba religious practices are thought to have involved female shamans called *llü-bu*. Dongba priests assumed many of the same functions as the shamans, including exorcism, but they were also responsible for leading souls out of hell, for managing relations between humans and nature, and for appeasing the gods and spirits that could cause natural disasters.

Naxi oral history recounts the split between Shu and human beings, who were brothers. Shu protected wild animals and areas, while humans were given domesticated crops and animals. Dongba priests manage an accord between the two, whereby Shu shares resources and humans offer worship and payment rather than encroaching on, and helping themselves to, Shu's property. These beliefs manifested themselves in careful resource management that included a ban on logging, which has been eroded in recent years by government-driven projects.

Dongba beliefs are also reflected in traditional Naxi music. The priests used music, primarily chants accompanied sparingly by a single instrument for dance segments, to please the spirits, pacify and exorcise ghosts, and keep the people entertained and attentive through long ceremonies. The tempo, volume, and smoothness of these chants varied with the purpose of the event, but influences from the chants can still be heard in other forms of Naxi music today.

Contemporary ideals for Naxi men are similar to those portrayed in Dongba texts and include bravery, hardiness, competitiveness (especially between men), and the ability to woo women. Important status symbols include urban residence, the retention of Naxi cultural attributes, and academic achievement. Female ideals include hard work, thriftiness, and cooperation (especially with other women). In contemporary local economies, this cooperation is sometimes reflected in female credit associations. Naxi women may wear a *qixin yangpi*, a sheepskin cape with stars embroidered on it that are meant to ease and symbolize their long hours of labor. Other distinctive articles of clothing include decorated belts, black turbans, and silver earrings, although younger women may choose modern clothing and forgo these cultural signifiers.

Naxi holidays include the Sanduo Festival, typically held on the eighth day of the second lunar month or early July, and the Torch Festival, held in February. The Sanduo Festival celebrates Sanduo, a protective war god who appeared in the dream of a Naxi leader of the Song Dynasty period (960–1279), Mai Cong. Following this dream, a white-armored warrior would appear every time the Naxi engaged in battle and usher them to victory. The Naxi believe Sanduo was born in the second lunar month and thus celebrate this period with their most important festival.

Some Naxi are concerned that important cultural traditions will be lost as more young people choose to dress in contemporary clothing, learn to speak and write Mandarin Chinese, and are drawn toward the economic lure of urban areas and the tourist industry. From the Yuan dynasty to today, the Naxi have tended to be relatively close to larger, more powerful groups such as the HAN Chinese majority. This closeness has produced various political and economic benefits, such as local leadership positions and access to government resources, but it also causes tension between integration into Han society, which brings these benefits, and assimilation, which would eliminate identification as Naxi altogether. Younger, urban residents have even turned to the Internet, where more than 500 Naxi participate in an online forum to foster identification as Naxi to prevent outright assimilation into the wider Chinese society.

FURTHER READING

Cai Hua. *A Society without Fathers or Husbands: The Na of China,* trans. Asti Hustvedt (New York: Zone Books, 2000).

Joseph Franz Rock. *The Life and Culture of the Na-khi Tribe of the China-Tibet Borderland* (Wiesbaden, Ger.: F. Steiner, 1963).

Nayakas (Jenu-Koyyo-Shola-Nayakas, Jenu Kurumba, Kattu Naikr, Kattu Nayakas, Naickens, Naikens, Naikr, Sola Nayakas)

There are two separate groups of people known as Nayakas in Indian history. The first is a small group of hunter-gatherers who inhabit the Nilgiri Hills of Tamil Nadu and Kerala, southern India, and are the subject of this entry. The second group is a subdivision of the TELEGUS, who emerged as the military rulers of Tamil Nadu in the 16th through 19th centuries; culturally they were primarily Telegu and do not need to be addressed separately.

The Nayakas with whom we are concerned here are a small-scale society who call them-

NAYAKAS

location:
The Nilgiri Hills of southern India

time period:
Unknown to the present

ancestry:
Indigenous to the region

language:
Nama basa, part of the Kannadoid subgroup within the larger Dravidian language family

selves *nama sonta,* which means approximately "our family." It was outsiders, probably MALAYALIS, speakers of Malayalam, who first referred to them as *Nayaka,* and the name stuck through both the colonial and Indian independence eras. The Nayakas' language as a member of the Dravidian family contains many loanwords from Malayalam as well as Tamil and Kannada, and most individuals also speak one or more of these major languages as second and third tongues.

There have been two different theories posited about Nayaka origins. According to the first, all the small-scale communities of the Nilgiri Hills were descended from people who fled from the powerful Chola kingdom when it emerged in Tamil Nadu in about the ninth century. The second theory, more common today, is that the Nayakas were the descendants of the indigenous inhabitants of this region who were gradually pushed into the hills during the rise of various kingdoms and empires in southern India, including the British Empire in the 19th century. Most Nayaka communities remained local, tightly knit groups that had little contact with their linguistic cousins in other localities. However, trade and other relations with their most immediate neighbors have been common for centuries. Trade in forest products, especially honey, firewood, and bamboo for grain, tobacco, and weapons, was always common, and during the British period waged labor became part of many communities' economic strategy. Some Nayakas even worked as security guards for other tribal groups.

Throughout most of their history, the Nayakas have depended largely on wild yams, nuts, berries, fruit, honey, birds, fish, and deer for their subsistence. Since the 1980s, however, their primary foraging grounds in the Nilgiri-Wynaad plateau have seen a large-scale immigration of TAMILS, which has interrupted much of this hunting and gathering activity. Nowadays, waged labor is as common as foraging and the sale of forest products for family and community economic survival; most still do not grow their own food or keep domesticated animals, besides dogs used for hunting. Communities are also less mobile than they were in the past, when they frequently shifted locations to find food or other resources or to escape political problems with outsiders. However, their religious system still recognizes the centrality of their ancestors, the forest, and the other natural features in their world that provided all the resources they needed in the past to survive.

Like all small-scale societies, the Nayakas do not recognize any political leaders; in fact, only two positions occur in their communities, the shaman and the organizer of the primary ritual that honors their ancestors, which takes place every two years. Each family is relatively independent of all others, living and moving together with a few other communities as needed. Kinship is considered bilateral, and new couples can choose to join the band of either partner, or neither if there are opportunities with other relatives.

See also DRAVIDIANS.

Nenets (Nentsy, Yurak-Samoyeds, Yurak, Samoyeds)

The Nenets are one of the indigenous peoples of Siberia, native to northeastern Europe and northwestern Siberia. Prior to the 1917 Russian revolution the Nenets ("human beings" in their language) were called Samoyeds, a term of unknown ancestry; Yurak-Samoyeds and Yuraks were also common. The term *Samoyed* was considered derogatory in Russian and has not been used since the early 20th century to refer to any group. Nonetheless, the term still refers to the linguistic family that includes Nenet, Enet, Selkup, and Nganasan, of which Nenet is the largest and the lingua franca of the western and central far-north regions of Russia, or what is sometimes called the Polar-Ural region.

The Nenets today occupy at least 621 thousand square miles of territory that stretches from the Kanin Peninsula in the west to the Yenisey River delta in the east. Nenets also live on many of the islands in the Arctic Ocean. This land is largely tundra and forest, crossed by many rivers, the most important of which is the River Ob. However, archaeological and linguistic evidence points to the Altai Mountains, where southern Siberia meets Mongolia and Kazakhstan, as the homeland of all Samoyed speakers. From there the Samoyed speakers migrated north, separating from other Finno-Ugrian speakers, the ancestors of today's Finns, Estonians, and Hungarians, between 5,000 and 8,000 years ago. In their migrations the Samoyed speakers interacted with the indigenous populations of the Arctic region, probably the ancestors of the CHUKCHIS and other Paleoasiatic language speakers, and learned some of the skills necessary to survive on the cold, dark tundra. These necessary skills included hunting sea mammals in the frozen sea, making clothing and housing appropriate to the cold temperatures, and recognizing and finding the few edible berries and roots that grow in the Arctic during the summer. The housing they learned to build was very similar to a Native American tepee, conical in shape and made from larch boughs covered with skins in winter and boiled birch-bark cloth in summer.

There is some evidence that the Nenets were already reindeer herders and breeders before their northern migrations. Southern Nenets, sometimes called Forest Nenets, continued to breed and milk reindeer and even ride them with specially made saddles until the modern era. Northern or Tundra Nenets were hunters and neither milked nor rode reindeer, though they did harness them to their sleds. Interestingly, although the Arctic dogs that pull sleds bear the name Samoyed, none of the Samoyed peoples originally used dogs for transportation; this practice was introduced by the RUSSIANS in the 18th century.

As is the case among all indigenous peoples, the primary organizing principle of Nenet society was kinship. Membership in matrilineal clans—that is, those in which membership was handed down from mothers to children—determined appropriate marriage partners, fishing and hunting or grazing grounds, migration patterns, and ties of reciprocity. The Nenets are al-

most unique among Siberian peoples for this female-centric kinship pattern. Perhaps related to this pattern, the Nenets also worshiped a female earth spirit called Ya-nebya, who was thought to cure sickness and help women through childbirth. Other gods, particularly the distant sky god Num, were male. Nonetheless, the Nenets were not a female-dominated society. Among Tundra Nenets, who made up the majority of Nenets, hunters and warriors were far superior to most women in the social structure, and women in all Nenet communities were limited in their movements and activities by strict taboos. They were forbidden to walk around the outside of their tents, to eat the head of a reindeer or any bear meat, to step over ropes, and to touch any hunting equipment. Breaking any of these taboos would bring misfortune to the woman's family and punishment to the transgressor for having brought on the misfortune.

Among the Nenets, both men and women could occupy the all-important position of shaman, the person who was able to travel between the human and spirit worlds to cure sickness, predict the future, and prevent misfortune. The shamans' most important tools, which they tended to receive at separate times during their careers, were the drum and the baton. The drum symbolized reindeer and boats and had

NENETS

location:
Siberia

time period:
Unknown to the present

ancestry:
Proto-Samoyed

language:
Nenet is a Samoyedic language in the Uralic family along with Enet, Selkup, and Nganasan.

Reindeer-drawn sleds are still very important to many Nenets, even those who are employed in the region's industrial sector; this man is waiting with his harnessed animals and sled outside the Val Gamburtseva oilfields. *(AP Photo/Misha Japaridze)*

NEPALESE: NATIONALITY

nation:
Nepal

derivation of name:
Possibly from the Sanskrit term *nipalaya,* meaning "at the foot of the mountains," in reference to Nepal's location in the Himalayas

government:
Parliamentary democracy

capital:
Kathmandu

language:
Nepali 47.8 percent, Maithali 12.1 percent, Bhojpuri 7.4 percent, Tharu 5.8 percent, Tamang 5.1 percent, Newar 3.6 percent, Magar 3.3 percent, Awadhi 2.4 percent, other 10 percent, unspecified 2.5 percent

religion:
Hindu 80.6 percent, Buddhist 10.7 percent, Muslim 4.2 percent, other 4.5 percent

earlier inhabitants:
Many of Nepal's current minorities, including the Magar, Tharu, and Tamang, and others have lived in the region for thousands of years.

demographics:
Chhettri 15.5 percent, Brahman-Hill 12.5 percent, Magar 7 percent, Tharu 6.6 percent, Tamang 5.5 percent, Newar 5.4 percent, Muslim 4.2 percent, Kami 3.9 percent, Yadav 3.9 percent, other 32.7 percent, unspecified 2.8 percent

to be brought alive during an initiation ceremony before it could be used to communicate with the spirit world. The baton symbolized the tool for driving reindeer or the oar of the boat. In addition to these, Nenet shamans also used food to thank spirits who had assisted them; spirits who had not given any help could be punished as well. Similar objects and ideas existed among all the Samoyed speakers as well as among other Siberian indigenous peoples prior to their near-elimination by Russian missionaries and governments.

The Asian Nenets escaped the earliest contact with Russians encountered by those Nenets who live in Europe, who experienced Russian domination as early as 1200; the Asian Nenets escaped contact until the 14th century. Nonetheless, by the early 17th century all Samoyed speakers, including the Nenets, were under indirect Russian control. As was the case among the far-eastern EVENS and EVENKIS, this indirect rule meant having to pay a fur tax to the Russian imperialists and engaging in trade that favored the Russians; as a result, the Nenet population dwindled in size through disease, alcoholism, and violence.

After the start of the Soviet era in the 1920s, the Nenets and all the other Arctic peoples experienced even greater changes through direct rule. In the 1930s the Arctic region was divided into several administrative areas that limited the ability of some Nenets to migrate to their traditional summer or winter lands. The government also established "cultural bases," which they modeled on Russian villages; these contained schools, hospitals, day-care centers, and shops, in an attempt to settle the largely nomadic Siberians. Unfortunately for the Nenets, as for all the other indigenous Siberians, the language of instruction in the schools, for public administration, and for almost everything else was Russian, which meant a severe restriction on the utility of their indigenous languages. Russian culture was also taught as superior to the indigenous cultures, which brought great stress to these populations as communities and as individuals.

World War II and the decades that followed also brought great economic change to the region with the Soviet push for industrialization east of the Ural Mountains. This was originally intended to keep the industries out of the hands of the Germans during World War II, but the process continued after the war when oil and gas were exploited in Siberia. Industrialization brought huge numbers, relatively speaking, of ethnic Russians into territory that had formerly

had just a handful of nonindigenous people. It also brought jobs in construction and mining and work on oil and gas wells to the native peoples, many of whom abandoned traditional subsistence patterns in favor of the cash economy. The end result is a damaged environment, increased morbidity and mortality, and near-destruction of the indigenous way of life.

Although the post-Soviet world has not seen a push for Nenet nationalism and independence, there has been a reawakening of Nenet traditional culture. The language has been revived somewhat, and young people are being taught the mythology and cosmology of their ancestors. This cultural activism has been joined by protests against the industrialization of the North, which has damaged the environment so severely. In addition, the Nenets have united with other indigenous northern peoples in the Russian Association of Indigenous Peoples of the North, Siberia and Far East (RAIPON), in the fight to maintain their linguistic, cultural, and ecological integrity in the face of increasing industrialization in their region.

FURTHER READING

Alla Abramovich-Gomon. *The Nenets' Song: A Microcosm of a Vanishing Culture* (Brookfield, Vt.: Ashgate, 1999).

Andrei V. Golovnev and Gail Osherenko. *Siberian Survival: The Nenets and Their Story* (Ithaca, N.Y.: Cornell University Press, 1999).

Nepalese: nationality (Nepali, people of Nepal)

GEOGRAPHY

Nepal is probably best known by westerners for the world's tallest mountain, Mount Everest, or Sagarmatha as it is known in Nepali; its peak rises to 29,029 feet above sea level. However, while the northern third of Nepal is part of the Himalayas and thus extremely high, the southern borderlands of the Tarai Plain are low, tropical, and humid; the lowest point in the country is Kanchan Kalan at just 230 feet. Between these two extremes is an east-to-west belt of territory made up of foothills and lower mountains; this is where most of the country's cities are located, including the capital, Kathmandu.

INCEPTION AS A NATION

The first unified government in Nepal emerged in the late 18th century when the founder of the Shah dynasty, Prithvi Narayan Shah, conquered two other rival kingdoms and estab-

Nepalese: nationality time line

C.E.

1768 Prithvi Narayan Shah unifies the Nepali kingdom after conquering two rival kings in the region.

1814–16 Anglo-Nepalese or Gurkha War; British victory sets Nepal's southern boundaries with India.

1846 Nepal's Ranas, or hereditary chiefs, become the de facto rulers of the country and largely withdraw it from the global political scene.

1951 The Shah dynasty regains de facto control in Nepal, and anti-Rana rebels create a government.

1953 Tenzing Norgay and Edmund Hillary are the first climbers to reach the top of Mount Everest, the highest mountain in the world.

1959 Nepal adopts a constitution and parliament; the king is retained as a figurehead.

1960 King Mahendra suspends parliament and retakes control of the state after elections bring the Nepali Congress Party and B. P. Koirala to power.

1962 A new constitution is adopted, which creates a series of nonparty councils, or *panchayats,* within the framework of the kingdom.

1972 King Mahendra dies and is succeeded by his son, King Birendra.

1980 Election reform creates a new national assembly, but political parties remain forbidden.

1985 The Nepal Congress Party (NCP) begins agitating for the restoration of party-based politics and democracy. The NCP boycotts nonparty elections held the following year.

1990 More protests lead to arrests, violence on the streets of Kathmandu and other cities, and eventually a democratic constitution.

1991 Nepal holds democratic elections, and the NCP's G. P. Koirala, a relative of the first prime minister, B. P. Koirala, becomes prime minister.

1994 New elections bring in a communist government, which dissolves just one year later. This ushers in a decade with frequent changes of government; there are nine governments by 2000.

1996 Several leftist political organizations begin a "People's War" to liberate Nepal from the royalists.

2001 A member of the royal family kills the king and most of his family during dinner; a related prince, Gyanendra, becomes king.

2003 Peace talks in the People's War break down, which leads to further violence.

2006 Nepal's 10-ten year civil war comes to an end when Prime Minister Koirala and the head of the Maoist Communist Party sign the Comprehensive Peace Agreement.

2007 The United Nations establishes the United Nations Mission in Nepal (UNMIN), a political and peace mission in Nepal.

Elections, originally scheduled for June, are rescheduled twice and may be held by mid-April 2008.

2008 Nepal becomes a republic, with Ram Baran Yadav as president; Maoists withdraw from government in opposition to Yadav.

lished the first kingdom of Nepal. From its violent beginnings, which saw entire populations of men slaughtered while others had their lips and noses removed for having opposed the new king, Nepal has often been the site of widespread violence and unrest. Most recently, in 2006, Nepal ended a decade-long civil war between royalists and Maoist rebels, which saw the deaths of tens of thousands of Nepalese citizens and forced many others to become both internal and external refugees.

Between the years 1768, when Prithvi Narayan Shah unified Nepal, and 2007, when a UN mission arrived to stabilize the recently established peace, Nepal was also the site of a colonial war against the British. The Nepalese lost the Gurkha War of 1814–16; however, Nepal was not incorporated into the large, British south Asian colony of India. Indeed, the British respected the fierceness and fighting capacities of the GURKHAS and used many of their number in a domestic police force in the northern reaches of their Indian colony.

Mount Everest, or Sagarmatha, continues to challenge mountaineers and their porters and guides, despite the more than half-century that has passed since Hillary and Norgay first ascended the peak. *(Shutterstock/Bruce Yeung)*

Following the establishment of Nepal's contemporary borders with the treaty that ended the Gurkha War, the country's people continued to experience more than a century of repression at the hands of both the legitimate Shah kings and the hereditary chiefs or premiers, called Ranas, who were the de facto rulers of Nepal from 1846 to 1951. These authoritarian rulers used their power to impose the hierarchy of the Hindu caste system on the large minority in the country who did not consider themselves Hindus and who did not recognize its ranked caste positions. Nonetheless, most were incorporated into this system as members of the lowest, or untouchable, caste.

While the Nepalese people had a glimpse of democracy in 1990, when a new constitution allowed for limitations on the king's power and relatively free elections, their freedom was short-lived. Within a few years the king had dissolved the parliament, and by 1996 the country had fallen into a full-scale civil war that lasted until the

Comprehensive Peace Agreement was signed by the two sides in 2006. During that period the violence in the country even spread to the royal family: In 2001 the heir to the throne, Dipendra, shot his parents, eight other family members, and himself to death as they sat around the dinner table. It is believed that he was distressed that his choice of a bride had been rejected by his mother.

The years 2006 through 2008 may be a turning point in Nepal's centuries-old pattern of civil strife and violence. In 2006 Prime Minister G. P. Koirala and the head of the Maoist Nepali Communist Party, Prachanda, signed the Comprehensive Peace Agreement, which set out the rights and responsibilities of the two sides in establishing a lasting democratic peace in the country. Since then the United Nations has heeded the request of the Nepalese government for a peace mission, the United Nations Mission in Nepal (UNMIN), which began its work in January 2007 by monitoring the seven cantonment sites and 21 satellite sites of the Maoists. The UNMIN has made sure that the Nepalese army remains in its barracks and the Maoists' weapons remain cached in the cantonment sites. In 2007 the Communists also joined the newly reconvened Nepalese parliament as legitimate members of this legislative body. Yet despite these important steps toward a lasting peace, the country has not become entirely stable. Originally, according to the first post-peace agreement, parliamentary elections were scheduled for June 2007, but these were pushed back to November 22 of the same year in the hope that disarmament and stabilization of the countryside will allow free and fair elections at that point. In November the elections were postponed yet again, but did take place April 2008, with the Communist Party of Nepal (Maoist) winning the most seats in the constituent assembly.

At the same time, several armed rebel groups from the eastern Tarai region of the country, such as Janatantrik Terai Mukti Morcha, the Madheshi National Liberation Front, and Madhesi Rashtriya Mukti Morcha, have continued to struggle for recognition of their culture, way of life, and even complete autonomy from the Nepalese government. In addition, in July 2008 Ram Baran Yadav was elected Nepal's first president, leading the Maoists to withdraw from the government to sit in opposition. Only time will tell whether peace will emerge in this small, mountainous country.

Perhaps due to its poor climate for agriculture, the mainstay of the economy, and perhaps due to the long-standing civil strife in the country, Nepal today is one of the poorest countries

Prithvi Narayan Shah

Prithvi Narayan Shah was the Nepalese king responsible for uniting Nepal in the 18th century. Born in 1723 into the ruling Gorkha house, which had ruled part of Nepal since 1559, Prithvi Narayan Shah succeeded his father, Nara Bhupal Shah, to the throne in 1743. Conscious of the political and economic instability of the Kathmandu Valley kingdoms, Prithvi Narayan Shah saw the necessity for unification to ensure survival of all of the kingdoms. In 1744 his army conquered Nuwakot, which lies between Kathmandu and Gorkha, and then took up strategic positions in the hills surrounding the Kathmandu Valley, cutting off the valley's communications with the outside world. By 1756 the valley could no longer maintain trade with Tibet, and King Prithvi Narayan Shah invaded. In reaction to the invasion, leaders in the valley called on British East India for aid. A contingent of soldiers was sent in 1767, but it was defeated by Prithvi Narayan Shah's army. In 1769 the Kathmandu Valley was conquered, and Kathmandu was made the capital of modern-day Nepal.

in the world. The one sector of the economy that has tremendous growth potential, tourism, has been in decline since the start of the People's War in 1996 and has yet to begin its recovery. The other sector that could be of benefit to some people, hydroelectric power, would simultaneously disrupt the lives of many subsistence farmers living along the country's many rivers and has not yet become a real possibility.

CULTURAL IDENTITY

Nepal is made up of many different ethnic groups who speak a variety of languages and dialects, engage in a variety of cultural and economic pursuits, and practice several different religions. In the past, each of these differences served as an important divider, preventing the creation of a common Nepalese cultural identity. Today's Nepalese government and people are attempting to meet the challenge of creating a pan-Nepalese identity that is both respectful of cultural and ethnic differences and able to unify the people. One important step that was taken in this direction in 2007 was the acceptance of a new national anthem that recognizes Nepal's diversity rather than merely extolling the centrality of the king, which was the theme of the previous anthem that had been used since 1899.

Another movement that seeks unity in Nepal is one that works for the acceptance of the country as a secular rather than a Hindu state. There is still a way to go toward this end since caste divisions remain central to most people's understanding of their cultural identity. However, several movements recognizing the centrality of Buddhism in many people's lives, and even in the history of the country, have helped to mitigate some of the divisive effects of centuries of suppression of any religion or tradition outside Hinduism.

See also NEWAR.

FURTHER READING
Mary M. Cameron. *On the Edge of the Auspicious: Gender and Caste in Nepal* (Urbana: University of Illinois Press, 1998).

Gil Daryn. *Encompassing a Fractal World: The Energetic Female Core in Myth and Everyday Life—A Few Lessons Drawn from the Nepalese Himalaya* (Lanham, Md.: Lexington Books, 2006).

David N. Gellner and Declan Quigley, eds. *Contested Hierarchies: A Collaborative Ethnography of Caste among the Newars of the Kathmandu Valley* (New York: Oxford University Press, 1995).

John Gray. *Domestic Mandala: Architecture of Lifeworlds in Nepal* (Burlington, Vt.: Ashgate, 2006).

Leo E. Rose and John T. Scholz. *Nepal: Profile of a Himalayan Kingdom* (Boulder, Colo.: Westview Press, 1980).

Joanne C. Watkins. *Spirited Women: Gender, Religion, and Cultural Identity in the Nepal Himalaya* (New York: Columbia University Press, 1996).

Newar (Newa, Sahu)

The Newar are an indigenous people of Nepal. Many live in the Kathmandu Valley, while others reside in the towns and cities of Tarai, Nepal's tropical lowlands. Their alternative ethnonym, Sahu, means "shopkeeper" and points to the economic activities of many of these town-dwelling Newar.

The Newar tribes speak a Tibeto-Burman language that has been heavily influenced by Sanskrit and other Indo-Aryan languages. It is also a written language that has used a variety of different scripts, all borrowed from various Indian scripts, such as Devanagari. Indian culture has influenced the Newar well beyond their language as well. Between the ninth and 13th centuries a form of Indian Buddhism was introduced to the Newar, who adopted many rituals from this religious tradition; the centrality of monasteries as seats of higher learning also came from Indian Buddhism. In the 14th century an influx of Hindus into Nepal, who were fleeing from the Muslim conquest of northern India, brought the caste system, the large Hindu pantheon with its accompanying rituals and myths, and other aspects of Indian culture. At that time Newari Buddhism lost the tradition of celibate monks and accepted the hierarchical caste system, so antithetical to Buddhism's ideology of equality. From the mid-19th century until its demise in 2008, the dominant Nepali kingdom, that of the Shah dynasty, sought to unify the region's peoples into a single Nepali ethnic group. For many Newar their own ethnolinguistic identity was strengthened in the face of this kind of external opposition, and today many continue to hold on to their own culture, language, and identity.

Newar society is organized by the overlapping principles of kinship and caste. Above the level of the extended, multigenerational family, each individual is also a member of a patrilineage, a group of relatives who all trace their descent through their fathers, fathers' fathers, and so on, to a common male ancestor about five or six generations back. All of these patrilineages, and their members are also part of larger kin groupings known as clans. Like patrilineages, Newar clans are exogamous groups, requiring everyone to marry outside their clan. Clans can also trace their origins back to a common male ancestor. One difference is that the founding ancestor of most clans is a mythological figure rather than an actual person, while lineage founders are

NEWAR

location:
Nepal, Bhutan, the Indian state of Sikkim

time period:
About 1200 to the present

ancestry:
Uncertain, but possibly Kiratas

language:
Newari, a Tibeto-Burman language with at least four different dialects

always actual ancestors. Beyond these exogamous groups, each Newar also inherits membership in a caste group from his or her parents. Unlike lineages and clans, however, castes are endogamous groups, requiring each individual to marry someone from the same caste. As is the case in India, Newar castes are hierarchical, with some being seen as ritually and socially superior and more pure than others.

Another important social identity held by all Newar comes from their village of residence. For the most part, people marry people from outside their own village, though this is not as necessary as marrying outside the lineage and clan and within the caste. In addition, at marriage women move from their own homes and villages into their new husbands' villages, a pattern known as patrilocal residence. Generally, villages are built on higher ground for protection from attack and are surrounded by rice and other fields. With their two- and three-story buildings and paved lanes and courtyards, many Newar villages actually look like small cities, and some contain more than 1,000 people as well.

New Guinea Highlanders

The people of the New Guinea Highlands are members of hundreds of different linguistic and cultural groups who reside in the mountainous area of the world's second-largest island, New Guinea. The Highlands, and the island in general, are divided roughly in half by a somewhat arbitrary international boundary between Indonesia and the independent country of Papua New Guinea. Although they differ among themselves in language and some aspects of their culture, such as rituals, the Highlanders are often spoken of as a people based on their common history, agricultural practices, religious beliefs, exchange practices, and social structures. With regard to these features they resemble other MELANESIANS somewhat, based on a shared common origin at least 40,000 years ago. They also resemble other New Guinea populations to some degree, especially those who live in the Sepik River basin (*see* NEW GUINEA SEPIK BASIN PEOPLE); however, differences in climate and terrain have led to some important differences between them as well.

GEOGRAPHY

The New Guinea Highlands are one of the most rugged terrains in the world, certainly in Oceania. The highest peak, at 16,023 feet, is Puncak Jaya, sometimes called Mount Carstensz after the Dutchman who first sighted its glaciers. Mount Wilhelm, at 14,793 feet, and Mount Hagen, at 12,434 feet, also present climbers with steep and difficult ascents. Even the swampy valleys in the Highlands are high in elevation, averaging about 4,900 feet above sea level. This harsh terrain has often been seen as the reason for the tremendous linguistic and cultural differentiation on the island, since people living in one valley must undergo long and difficult journeys to interact with people in the adjacent valleys. This is not to say that these interactions did not happen but that the region's geography may have prevented the kind of political unification that often accompanied the development of agriculture elsewhere in the world, such as the Middle East, China, and Central America.

ORIGINS

The origins of the New Guinea Highlanders are extremely ancient, dating to at least 45,000 B.C.E. and possibly as early as 75,000 B.C.E. (For comparison purposes, England's Stonehenge monument was begun in only 3000 B.C.E.; the building boom of the great Egyptian pyramids at Giza was around 2500 B.C.E., when this population had already been in Sahul/New Guinea for a minimum of 42,500 years!) Very little is known about this founding population due to both a lack of research and the great expanse of time that has passed since their arrival. Genetically they bear some slight resemblance to ABORIGINAL AUSTRALIANS, while linguistically they share a classification with a few other Papuan languages in Indonesia. However, these linguistic similarities may have arisen long after the initial settlement of the Highlands.

There are hundreds of languages spoken throughout the New Guinea Highlands, all of them classified as Papuan languages generally and Trans-New Guinea languages more specifically. The Trans-New Guinea phylum also includes languages from other regions of the island so that this category is not specific to the Highlands. The features that lead to this classification are common sound patterns; pronoun use; frequent use of prefixes and suffixes; and verb changes, depending on whether it is an action verb or an existential one, such as the equivalent of the English verb *to be*.

HISTORY

The most important historical event to occur in the Highlands after initial settlement as early as 60,000 years ago is the independent develop-

NEW GUINEA HIGHLANDERS

location:
The Highlands of Papua New Guinea and the Indonesian provinces of Papua and West Irian Jaya. (The division between these provinces and the creation of the latter are currently contested by many Papuans, while more recent migrants from elsewhere in Indonesia tend to support the split.)

time period:
Perhaps as early as 60,000 B.C.E., definitely no later than 45,000 B.C.E. to the present

ancestry:
Asian origins, but so far back in antiquity that their exact ancestry is unknown; they do have some genetic markers that indicate an ancient connection to Aboriginal Australians

language:
Papuan languages, which are classified together solely for their inability to be classified together with other Oceanic languages

New Guinea Highlanders time line

B.C.E.

68,000–56,000 Contested dating of some archaeological sites in New Guinea.

45,000 Date used by more conservative archaeologists to mark the establishment of human cultures in New Guinea/Sahul.

10,000 Australia and New Guinea are separated by rising sea levels.

7000–5000 Independent development of agriculture in the Highlands.

C.E.

1526 Portuguese explorer Jorge de Meneses visits one of New Guinea's largest islands and names it Ilhas dos Papuas, "land of fuzzy-haired people."

1546 Spanish sailor Inigo Ortiz de Retes names the other main island New Guinea because the people remind him of the population of African Guinea.

18th century Introduction of the sweet potato, which transforms Highlands life.

1884 Britain and Germany annex the southeast and northern regions, respectively, of the island.

1906 Australia takes over from Britain in the southeast and renames the region Territory of Papua.

1933 Gold prospectors enter the Highlands and find more than a million people living in areas that had been considered devoid of significant human population.

1942 The Kokoda Track Campaign sees around 1,000 Australian soldiers and their Papuan porters, guides, and assistants defeat a Japanese force at least five times larger during the course of seven months of warfare and extreme hardship in the Highlands.

1954 The first aerial survey shows several Highlands valleys with a joint population of more than 100,000 people; these regions had previously been completely unknown to the colonizers.

1963 The United Nations grants Indonesia control over the western half of New Guinea, today called Papua or West Papua. The United Nations had taken over from the Netherlands one year earlier.

1965 The Free Papua Movement, or Organisasi Papua Merdeka (OPM), is established on the Indonesian half of the island; conflict over this issue continues through the present.

1973 The eastern half of New Guinea achieves self-government as Papua New Guinea.

---

ment of agriculture at least 7,000 years ago. Archaeological excavations in the Kuk Swamp of the Wahgi Valley of New Guinea have shown that taro was domesticated here several thousand years before agricultural AUSTRONESIANS arrived from Southeast Asia. There is also evidence of bananas and sugar cane growing in New Guinea. In addition to domesticating these crops, New Guinea Highlanders also managed their rugged terrain through the use of fire, drainage channels, and the building of mounds to aerate the soil.

There are several possible reasons that this population developed agriculture while their genetically related neighbors to the south in Australia did not. First, the space available in the Highlands is considerably less than that on the mainland of Australia, and lack of land could have led to population pressures for developing greater food-production capacity. Second, much less game could be supported in the Highlands than in many other regions of the world and certainly much less per capita than in most of Australia, making it much more fruitful to put effort into agriculture instead of hunting. Third, there may have been more locally available plants that provided a viable possibility for domestication; even with the coming of Europeans to Australia, the only indigenous Australian plant to have been domesticated for agricultural purposes was the macadamia nut.

The next important date in the historical trajectory of the New Guinea Highlands is the 18th century, when the sweet potato was introduced by European explorers. Prior to this introduction, the primary agricultural products in the Highlands were taro, sago, bananas, and sugar cane. As the main starchy fillers, taro and sago required more work for less output than sweet potatoes and thus did not allow for the production of a significant surplus. New Guinea Highlanders

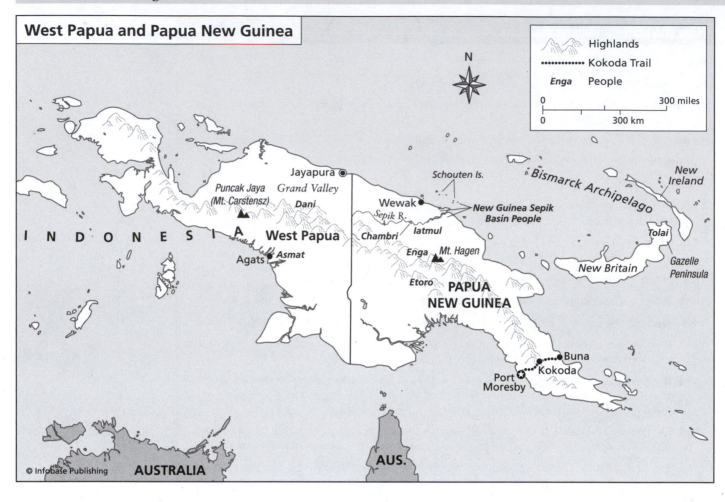

West Papua and Papua New Guinea

had been raising and eating pigs for thousands of years prior to the introduction of the sweet potato, but this new food source created the context in which pigs achieved the extraordinary value that they continue to have today.

Due to their relative isolation, the Highlanders were colonized quite a bit later than most other Pacific peoples, and thus they did not experience the worst aspects of European colonialism, such as blackbirding (slave trading) or large-scale theft of their land. The 1930s saw the first large-scale meetings between New Guinea Highlanders and people of European descent, in this case gold prospectors and missionaries. In one instance the meeting was actually filmed, allowing students today to glimpse what was perhaps the last moment of "first contact" between indigenous people and westerners. These were followed in the 1940s by World War II soldiers when the Australian army, with its Papuan porters, guides, and assistants, routed a much larger Japanese force from the Kokoda Track region. After the war, Australia maintained its position as colonial master in the western half of the region while

the Netherlands dominated in the east, with the western area gaining independence in the 1970s and the eastern being handed over to Indonesia by the United Nations in the early 1960s. In both cases, the change from colonialism to independence did not bring significant alterations to the life of the Highlanders.

As they did in the past, most Highlanders today engage in subsistence agriculture, growing crops and raising pigs for their own use. For some, mining and, in Papua New Guinea (PNG), coffee have also brought cash into this traditional economy; a very small number of people derive income from tourism as well. Due to the importance of sharing and exchange in the Highlands, much of this cash immediately gets disbursed throughout the community for ritual payments or in large-scale competitive exchanges.

CULTURE

Economy and Society

Culturally, nothing is as important as pigs in the Highlands. Today there are an estimated

2.5 million pigs on the entire island, about one pig for every three people; in the Highlands, this ratio is more heavily weighted toward pigs. For a Highland man, having pigs means being able to get married, influence his fellow tribesmen, protect himself from witchcraft and sorcery, and even gain prestige outside his kinship group. For women, contributing to the health and well-being of her husband's pigs through difficult agricultural labor is as important as bearing and raising children. In short, pigs are the standard against which all other wealth and prestige are measured.

While pigs today are at the very heart of all Highlands societies and seem to have been entrenched for a long time, in relation to the estimated 40,000–60,000 years of highland history, the *centrality* of pigs is a fairly new phenomenon. Due to a lack of evidence and research, the origins of pig raising in New Guinea are obscure. Some sources give a date of 9,000–10,000 years ago for the introduction of pigs, while others posit that they arrived with the island's settlement by Austronesians around 5,000 years ago. The next level of debate concerns whether Highlanders began hunting feral pigs and only much later domesticated them, or whether the pigs arrived as domesticates and entered the subsistence economy in that form. Regardless of their origins, based on the number of bones found in various archaeological sites, pigs remained a fairly marginal food and exchange item throughout the Highlands until the introduction of the sweet potato about 250 years ago. Sweet potatoes, unlike taro and sago, are extremely prolific plants and grow well in a variety of soils; they are also a good food source for humans and pigs alike. With the sweet potato came the ability to produce large food surpluses to support large numbers of pigs, not just for food but for use as wealth. Indeed, pork today remains a relatively rare food item for many Highlanders because it is their ability to give pigs away to others that grants men high prestige, rather than the ability to serve up a good roast.

Although husbands and wives agree that pigs are the mainstay of Highlands life, there are actually very few activities that the two sexes engage in together. As is the case throughout Melanesia, the Highlands reveal a high level of sex segregation. Men tend to live with other men and initiated boys in men's houses, while women live with girls, young boys, and pigs. The two sexes come together only occasionally for ritual purposes or when men lower themselves to take care of pigs or children. Traditionally, even sexual relations between women and men have been fraught with fear and anxiety, particularly on the men's side, because of a variety of taboos, ritual protections, and sexual practices.

Like all small-scale societies, the single most important criterion for social membership in the Highlands is kinship, and for many groups this means patrilineal groups. Children inherit membership in both their lineage and their clan through their father. In the past there was also a high incidence of polygyny: Men could have more than one wife. Along with many religious rituals and dances, this aspect of Highlands culture was heavily targeted by missionaries when they entered the region in the first third of the last century.

Religion

Today many people throughout New Guinea have converted to various Christian denominations, including Roman Catholicism, Evangelical Lutheranism, and Seventh-Day Adventist. However, most westerners would not recognize the beliefs or the ways some of these religions are practiced in the more remote regions of the Highlands. For example, due to the sacred nature of pigs throughout the Highlands, the belief that the Virgin Mary was actually a pig (humans cannot give virgin births, after all!) is relatively common.

Traditionally, and in many remote areas of the Highlands even today, religion is largely a matter of making sure that ancestors and other spirits are satisfied and that rituals are done properly. The spiritual side of life is actually of relatively little importance, while the ritual aspects of Highlands life, especially initiations and other rites of passage, are significant. For example, throughout the Highlands, boys can become adult men only through shedding the blood and other symbolic attributes of women. There are also many myths and rituals to memorize. Like so much of life in the Highlands, religion provides yet another arena for adult men to compete with one another for prestige. The man who can convince others of the legitimacy of his clan's version of a common myth or who can rally supporters for a large initiation ritual will go a long way toward convincing others of his status as a Big Man.

See also AUSTRALIANS: NATIONALITY; CHAMBRI; DANI; ENGA; ETORO; PAPUA NEW GUINEANS: NATIONALITY.

FURTHER READING

Douglass Baglin. *The Jimi River Expedition, 1950: Exploration in the New Guinea Highlands* (New York: Oxford University Press, 1988).

Mervyn Meggitt. *Blood Is Their Argument: Warfare among the Mae Enga Tribesmen of the New Guinea Highlands* (Palo Alto, Calif.: Mayfield Publishing Co., 1977).

Paul Sillitoe. *A Place against Time: Land and Environment in the Papua New Guinea Highlands* (New York: Routledge, 1996).

Andrew Strathern and Pamela J. Stewart. *Arrow Talk: Transaction, Transition, and Contradiction in New Guinea Highlands History* (Kent, Ohio: Kent State University Press, 2000).

New Guinea Sepik Basin people

The people of New Guinea's Sepik Basin are members of around 200 different linguistic and cultural groups residing in the north-central region of the world's second-largest island, New Guinea. Although they differ in language and some aspects of their culture, such as subsistence practices, the people of the Sepik Basin are often spoken of as a cultural group, based on their common religious beliefs, exchange practices, and social structures. As early as 1938, American anthropologist Margaret Mead commented on the common practices in this region of trading, selling, and otherwise exchanging ritual knowledge, charms, and even new social structures; it was based on this common exchange of cultural rather than material products that Mead labeled the Sepik Basin a culture area. Mead was by no means the first anthropologist to travel to New Guinea to study the inhabitants, whose isolated existence and the difficulty of travel in the thick jungles, swamps, and Highlands had allowed little contact with distant neighbors on the island, much less with westerners. Other scholars, arriving as early as 1899, included Bronislaw Malinowski; Gregory Bateson; and Michael Rockefeller, son of New York governor Nelson Rockefeller. The young Rockefeller produced two documentaries on New Guinea before disappearing forever off the southwest coast of the island in 1961. Some have speculated that he was captured and eaten by cannibals, others that he fell prey to headhunters, who are not unknown even today.

GEOGRAPHY

The Sepik River itself is very long, running 700 miles from the central Highlands to the Bismarck Sea. The section under discussion here, the Sepik Basin within East Sepik Province, is about a 170×250-mile expanse of land in the north-central region of Papua New Guinea. It incorporates a wide variety of terrains, from the volcanic coastal Schouten Islands to the Prince Alexander, Torricelli, and Bewani Ranges. In the southern part of the region, dry foothills provide yet a third terrain. In this region there are also populations who live on tributary rivers and lakes and in both fresh and brackish swampy regions. In short, almost every kind of geographic feature in New Guinea is represented in this tiny corner of the island.

ORIGINS

The origins of all New Guinea Papuan speakers are extremely ancient, dating to at least 45,000 B.C.E. and possibly as early as 75,000 B.C.E. (For comparison purposes, England's Stonehenge monument was begun in only 3000 B.C.E.; the building boom of the great Egyptian pyramids at Giza was around 2500 B.C.E., when this population had already been in Sahul/New Guinea for a minimum of 42,500 years!) Very little is known about this founding population due to both a lack of research and the great expanse of time that has passed since arrival. Genetically they bear some slight resemblance to ABORIGINAL AUSTRALIANS, while linguistically they share a classification with a few other Papuan languages in Indonesia. However, these linguistic similarities may have arisen long after the initial settlement in New Guinea.

In addition to Papuans, some of the peoples of the Sepik Basin, such as the inhabitants of the Schouten Islands, are Austronesian speakers. These people have a much more recent history in New Guinea, having arrived from Southeast Asia about 3,500 years ago. The arrival of AUSTRONESIANS and their settlement along New Guinea's coast introduced new subsistence, sociopolitical systems, and languages to the region, making it one of the most diverse in the world.

Populations of both Papuans and Austronesians are fairly new to this region of Papua New Guinea due to climatic changes in the past 1,000 years. Prior to this time, the Sepik River delta and Murik Lakes district formed a large, brackish inland lake. During the course of several thousand years, silt from the river filled in the lake and created the landscape we see today, allowing peoples from other areas of the island to establish themselves here.

LANGUAGES

There are approximately 200 languages divided into 40 different families spoken throughout

---

NEW GUINEA SEPIK BASIN PEOPLE

location:
The Sepik River Basin, including most of both East and West Sepik provinces and the Schouten Islands, Papua New Guinea

time period:
Possibly around 1000 C.E. to the present

ancestry:
Melanesian

language:
About 200 different languages are spoken in this region from both the greater Papuan and Austronesian families.

the Sepik Basin. Many of these are classified as Papuan languages generally and Sepik languages more specifically. A few of the peoples in this culture area also speak Austronesian languages. The most important feature of most Sepik languages is that the societies that speak them practice a high degree of esoterogeny, the practice of borrowing linguistic features from other languages in order to make one's own language more complex and thus more unique. As a result, all of the languages in the region display a very high number of features, including words, sounds, and structures, borrowed from other languages; they are also all very complex.

HISTORY

The history of the Sepik Basin is one of constant change. Environmentally, the region is very different today than it was 5,000 or 6,000 years ago, due to the existence of the large, brackish inland lake that then covered most of the region. During that time, NEW GUINEA HIGHLANDERS had much more access to the coast and its peoples and products than they have had in the past few thousand years, when the establishment of the hundreds of Sepik communities formed a barrier between the Highlands and the sea. About a thousand years after this ecological event, the region changed again with the arrival of Austronesian peoples, bringing a totally new language and culture pattern to the region from their ancestral home in Southeast Asia. Perhaps because they form a bridge between the culture areas of the mountains and the offshore islands and their associated economic and social patterns, many Sepik societies themselves are quick to embrace cultural change introduced from the outside, especially linguistic, artistic, and ritual aspects of culture.

In the late 19th and early 20th centuries, the region experienced yet another wave of change from the outside world, this time in the form of German colonization. While German bureaucrats did little to transform the region, German explorers were quick to realize the artistic and commercial value of carvings from the Sepik region. Even today, the Sepik area is best known outside Papua New Guinea for its elaborate woodcarving and prolific artistic output. The other feature of German colonialism that has lasted until contemporary times is the German-based Catholic mission, Society of the Divine Word. First established in the mid-1890s, this mission survived World War I and Germany's loss of New Guinea in that war, in part be-

New Guinea Sepik Basin people time line	
B.C.E.	
68,000–56,000	Contested dating of some archaeological sites in New Guinea.
45,000	Date used by more conservative archaeologists to mark the establishment of human cultures in New Guinea/Sahul.
10,000	Australia and New Guinea are separated by rising sea levels.
4000–3000	The brackish inland sea that makes up the region of today's Sepik Basin is at its largest.
1600	Austronesian speakers settle on New Guinea's north coast and coastal islands.
C.E.	
1000	The inland sea has finally been filled in with alluvial deposits from the Sepik and Ramu Rivers, establishing the coastline and alluvial plains evident today.
1526	Portuguese explorer Jorge de Meneses visits one of New Guinea's largest islands and names it Ilhas dos Papuas, "land of fuzzy-haired people."
1546	Spanish sailor Inigo Ortiz de Retes names the other main island New Guinea because the people remind him of the population of African Guinea.
1884	Germany annexes the northern regions of the island, including the Sepik Basin.
1906	Australia takes over from Britain in the southeast, renames the region Territory of Papua.
1914	Australia takes over from Germany in the northeast and joins it to the Territory of Papua.
1938	Margaret Mead, American anthropologist, describes the Sepik Basin as a culture area because of the similarities among the various tribal groups residing there.
1945	The Japanese surrender to the Allies at Cape Wom in the Sepik region.
1975	Papua New Guinea attains independence from Australia, and Sepik's greatest son, Michael Somare, begins his first of three separate stints as prime minister (1975–80, 1982–85, 2002–present).

cause its first bishop had established a series of farms and coconut plantations, making it fairly independent of the original host country. The other key to the longevity of this organization in the Sepik was the ownership of a steamer ship in the early days, and airplanes since the end of World War II, to reach peoples well beyond mission headquarters. Finally, since 1980 and the formation of the Divine Word Institute, this organization has been linked not just to primary and religious education but to higher education as well; in 1996 the institute became the Divine Word University and is considered by many to be one of the leading providers of tertiary education in Papua New Guinea.

Following the German defeat in World War I, Australia took over the colonial administration of northeastern New Guinea, which the Australians continued to hold until independence in 1975. During World War II, however, the JAPANESE invaded the island and had to be expelled by an Australian force on what is known as the Kokoda Track Campaign. The Sepik region, specifically Cape Wom, was the site of the Japanese surrender, on September 13, 1945. The Sepik region was also the childhood home of Papua New Guinea's three-time prime minister Michael Somare, who continues to speak fondly of the Murik Lakes region.

CULTURE

Economy and Society

Due to the wide variety of ecological zones that run through the Sepik Basin, from dry foothills to coastal mangrove swamps, no one single subsistence pattern characterizes the region. Depending on available resources and terrains, peoples in the area practice a combination of hunting, gathering, gardening, fishing, and even raising pigs in the tradition of the Highlands.

The Sepik region is as diverse in the area of sociopolitical organization as it is in forms of subsistence. The range is from more ranked and hierarchical societies on the coast, dominated by Austronesian populations, through Big Men societies with their temporary, achieved positions of respect and prestige, to fairly small-scale, relatively egalitarian societies where the only significant social differences are those marked by age and gender. In the area of kinship as well, both matrilineal and patrilineal societies are evident, with some societies reckoning descent through women and their children, others through men and theirs.

Despite these vast differences with regard to some of the most basic features of social structure, the Sepik continues to be seen by scholars as a culture area. One of the features that holds the region together is the interconnections between its societies at the level of cultural borrowing and trade. Like other MELANESIANS, the peoples of the Sepik have highly developed exchange networks, but unlike these others, who trade in pigs and/or shells, in the Sepik the primary trade goods are much more esoteric—things like ritual knowledge; mythology; dances; linguistic features; and some ritual objects, such as masks, drums, and flutes.

Throughout the Sepik, men's status is largely connected to their control of this kind of esoteric knowledge, rather than production

Carving and other aspects of the tourist economy, such as selling tickets to staged rituals, are important sources of cash for many Sepik Basin communities. Masks that are carved to be sold are not consecrated or imbued with ancestral spirits and thus lack the power of those that are carved for local use. *(Art Resource)*

or exchange of prestige products. As a result, most Sepik societies have highly elaborated male-initiation ceremonies in which access to the society's ritual knowledge is handed down from fathers and uncles to sons and nephews. Big Men in this region tend to be those with great musical or artistic talent or with the ability to memorize copious amounts of clan knowledge, rather than those who can gather large numbers of resources and people around them. As a result of these features, Sepik societies tend to be less antagonistic than those in the Highlands, both among men in the form of warfare and between men and women in the form of strict separation and ideas about women's pollution. In the Sepik, men certainly compete with one another for status and prestige but use dancing, chanting, and control of ritual knowledge rather than pigs, shells, and people. Men and women in the Sepik are also more equal, and men lack the fear of women's pollution that is evident in such Highlands societies as the ETORO, leading to a much greater emphasis on sex and sexuality than in the Highlands. This is connected to the fact that in the Sepik, men control the resources that contribute to their own prestige—hunted meat, yams, and esoteric knowledge—while in the Highlands, men are dependent on women's labor in raising pigs in order to increase their own status and prestige. In the one Sepik society that does exchange pigs, the Boiken, relations between men and women are much more antagonistic than in the rest of the region.

Religion

The most important sacred figures in most Sepik societies are ancestors, both actual and mythological, and the cult associated with them is often called *tambaran*. As the voices of the ancestors, musical instruments, particularly drums and flutes, are central to most Sepik religious events. Boys must be initiated into men's cults before being able to see or hear the flutes, while women are prohibited from any contact with the flutes at all. Many psychological readings of this cultural trait see a direct connection between flutes and penises, both controlled solely by men. Drums can also be made sacred in the Sepik region if they have been imbued with the spirit of an ancestor; however, they tend to be less restricted in their use since both uninitiated boys and women can see and hear them in use.

See also CHAMBRI; IATMUL; PAPUA NEW GUINEANS: NATIONALITY.

FURTHER READING

Nancy Lutkehaus, Christian Kaufmann et al., eds. *Sepik Heritage: Tradition and Change in Papua New Guinea* (Durham: Carolina Academic Press, 1990).

New Zealanders: nationality (Kiwis, people of New Zealand)

New Zealand is a multicultural society composed of migrants from almost every country in the world as well as the indigenous MAORI population.

GEOGRAPHY

In appearance, New Zealand looks like a slender little curve of islands, dwarfed by its neighbor Australia; however, the two countries actually occupy separate continents that are about the same size. New Zealand's continent, Zealandia, is 93 percent submerged under the Pacific Ocean and so provides significantly less living space than its seemingly larger neighbor. The country of New Zealand is an archipelago consisting of two main islands, named simply the North Island and the South Island, which are separated by a 20-mile-wide strait and several smaller islands. The South Island is the largest landmass and is characterized by its mountainous terrain, while the North Island is less mountainous but volcanically active.

New Zealand is home to many different species of plant life, nearly 90 percent of which can be found only in New Zealand. Indigenous animal life includes a wide range of bird species, such as the now extinct Moa and the endangered Kiwi, which is the country's national symbol. The Haast's eagle, also native to New Zealand, was once the world's largest bird of prey but has gone extinct since European settlement. Sadly, many animal and plant species are in danger of being eradicated due to deforestation and human encroachment; this has ignited efforts to restore the natural wildlife indigenous to New Zealand by eliminating foreign pests and reintroducing rare native plants and animals to offshore islands.

INCEPTION AS A NATION

Many current perceptions of New Zealand tend to focus on European settlement and heritage, which does account for more than 69 percent of the population, but the very first inhabitants of the narrow archipelago were the Maori people, POLYNESIANS who now constitute only 7.9 percent of the population. The primary cause of the imbalance is massive immigration in the early years of New Zealand's colonization in the mid-19th century, at which time boats full of British immigrants were arriving on a weekly basis. The settler population quickly outnumbered the Maori population. Allegedly, a Maori man one day asked a British official whether the whole British tribe was coming to the islands.

The genesis of contemporary New Zealand was the 1840 signing of the Treaty of Waitangi, which ultimately transferred authority over New Zealand from the Maori chiefs to the British Crown. The Maori had previously declared their independence, but French interest in the islands prompted the British to take action. In 1839 Lieutenant Governor William Hobson was dispatched to negotiate the Waitangi Treaty quickly with northern tribes; this treaty would cede power to the Crown. Translations were faulty and inconsistent, and the Maori were led to believe that a British official would preside over the nation as a governor, allowing the Maori to retain their land and cultural habits. The exact phrase used in the Maori text to explain their authority over the land was *tiro rangatiratanga,* which means "absolute chieftainship." The English text, however,

---

NEW ZEALANDERS: NATIONALITY

nation:
New Zealand; Aotearoa

derivation of name:
Originally called Nova Zeelandia after the province of Zeeland (meaning "sea land") in the Netherlands

government:
Parliamentary democracy

capital:
Wellington

language:
Both English and Maori are official languages.

religion:
Anglican 14.9 percent, Roman Catholic 12.4 percent, Presbyterian 10.9 percent, Methodist 2.9 percent, Pentecostal 1.7 percent, Baptist 1.3 percent, Other Christian 9.4 percent, Other 3.3 percent, unspecified 17.2 percent, none 26 percent

earlier inhabitants:
Polynesian Maori

demographics:
European 69.8 percent, Maori 7.9 percent, Asian 5.7 percent, Pacific Islander 4.4 percent, other 0.6 percent, mixed 7.8 percent, unspecified 3.8 percent

New Zealanders: nationality time line

C.E.

1000 The first Polynesian settlers arrive in New Zealand from Hawaii and become the indigenous Maori people. They name the land Aotearoa, "Land of the Long White Cloud," allegedly referring to the long white cloud that the settlers saw when they approached the island for the first time.

1642 Dutch explorer Abel Tasman is the first European to sight New Zealand and names it Staten Landt. He believes that the land he is seeing is an island just off the coast of Chile in South America, which Jacob Le Maire spotted in 1616. Dutch cartographers name the land Nova Zeelandia after the province of Zeeland in the Netherlands. It is called Niuew Zeeland in Dutch. Tasman flees the land after the friendship party he sends ashore is killed and eaten by angry Maori.

1643 Dutch explorer and governor-general of the Dutch East Indies, Hendrik Brouwer, proves that the newly discovered continent is too large to be Le Maire's Staten Landt.

1769 Captain Cook surveys the archipelago and calls it New Zealand.

1807 Northern Maori tribes obtain muskets from European explorers and use them against enemy tribes who have never before seen muskets, sparking the Musket Wars, a series of gruesome battles that eventually grind to a halt when all of the tribes become equally armed and no one has an advantage over another. By the time the wars end, the Maori population is devastated and tribal boundaries are no longer clear.

1835 Appointed British resident to New Zealand by the British Colonial Office, James Busby convinces Maori chiefs to declare independence as the United Tribes of New Zealand. Nevertheless, the Church Missionary Society continues to push for British annexation of the country, which comes to fruition in 1840 due to mounting French interest in the archipelago.

1840 Maori chiefs and representatives of Queen Victoria of Great Britain sign the Treaty of Waitangi, which gives the queen sovereignty over all of New Zealand, officially making New Zealand a British colony. In exchange, the Maori chiefs are allowed to retain and govern their own land. The Maori translation of the treaty is inconsistent with the English version, and conflicts ensue.

1845–72 The New Zealand Land Wars arise from the violent retaliation by the Maori against European settlers attempting to seize Maori land.

1852 Britain grants the New Zealand settlers self-government.

1863 The New Zealand Settlements Act allows for massive confiscation of Maori land by government officials as punishment for Maori rebellions.

1865 Protestant missionary Karl Volkner is brutally murdered by his congregation for reporting Maori antigovernment activity to the governor. In response, British troops terrorize the Maori community until those responsible for Volkner's death surrender. Twenty chiefs surrender and are transported to Auckland, where they are tried. Five are given the death penalty and are hanged the next year.

1891 New Zealand representatives discuss with Australian officials a possible constitution for the proposed federation of the Australasian colonies, but New Zealand later chooses not pursue a federation.

1893 New Zealand becomes the first nation in the world to grant women the right to vote.

1894 New Zealand is the first nation to create a minimum-wage law.

refers to *tiro rangatiratanga* as "self-determination." Furthermore, the Maori were told that the British Crown would act as *kawana*, a term invented by Bible translators to explain the authority of Pontius Pilate over the Jews of Judea.

Ultimately, the land reserved for the Maori was gradually infringed upon as increasing numbers of British settlers arrived on the is- lands and developers attempted to seize Maori land to sell to the new arrivals. A series of gruesome battles ensued, known today as the New Zealand Land Wars, which lasted from 1845 to 1872. During this period the Maori were at a disadvantage for a number of reasons, the first being their much smaller numbers. The Maori were farmers, and thus they could afford to

1901 The Cook Islands are annexed and made a part of New Zealand.

1907 New Zealand becomes an independent dominion by royal proclamation.

1914 New Zealand seizes Western Samoa from the Germans.

1915 Troops from New Zealand and Australia land in Gallipoli, Turkey, in an attack on a stronghold of the Turkish Ottoman Empire, but they suffer one of the bloodiest defeats in World War I. In a single night, 20,000 Australian and New Zealand troops flee Gallipoli unseen by Turkish troops guarding the peninsula.

1916 New Zealand–born author Katherine Mansfield publishes her novel *Prelude*, an account of domestic life in New Zealand and a biting critique of the nature of the family.

1919 Women in New Zealand are granted eligibility to stand for parliament.

1923 Katherine Mansfield dies of tuberculosis.

1939 Britain and France declare war on Germany, and New Zealand promptly joins the Allies, along with Australia. New Zealand troops fight in Greece, Crete, North Africa, Italy, and the Pacific.

1951 New Zealand, Australia, and the United States become allies when they sign the ANZUS treaty.

1962 Western Samoa obtains independence from New Zealand.

1975 The Waitangi Tribunal is established to investigate and settle claims of violations by the British government of the Waitangi Treaty. At this time, however, the tribunal investigates only current violations.

1985 The Waitangi Tribunal begins to investigate claims of treaty violations as early as 1840, including the period of the Land Wars.

New Zealand declares itself a nuclear-free zone. No warships can enter New Zealand ports without first declaring that they are not in possession of nuclear arms. As this declaration goes against U.S. government policy, American warships are no longer allowed entrance to New Zealand ports, and the United States suspends its obligations to New Zealand under the ANZUS treaty.

1986 Maori writer Witi Ihimaera publishes *The Whale Rider*, based on the Maori legend of a man who traveled back to New Zealand on the back of a whale after his canoe capsized. The book is later made into a major motion picture.

1993 New Zealand–born director Jane Campion shoots *The Piano* in New Zealand.

1996 The New Zealand government settles the largest claim ever made by the Maori people and awards the Ngai Tahu tribe NZ$117 million.

1998 The New Zealand government offers the Whakatohea tribe NZ$40 million as compensation for its historical claims of treaty violations, but the offer is refused.

2002 The prime minister apologizes for New Zealand's mismanagement of Western Samoa, which resulted in the death of one-fifth of the Samoan population during the 1918 influenza epidemic.

2006 Maori queen Te Arikinui Dame Te Atairangikoahu dies at 75.

2008 Sir Edmund Hillary dies at 88.

campaign only for a maximum of two or three months. Consequently they had to develop rotating shifts of active warriors and could never have all of their men fighting at once. The settlers were defended by the British troops, which could number as many as 18,000 men, but the Maori could fight them with only a fraction of their own warring unit, which was already minuscule in comparison. The largest war was the Tauranga Campaign, in 1864, which ended in the large-scale confiscation of Maori land. During this time, missionary Karl Volkner was killed by his own Maori congregation for openly reporting their activity to the governor in exchange for information on the movements of the Catholic missionaries. During his last

Katherine Mansfield

Katherine Mansfield was a prominent modernist writer from New Zealand who is considered today to be one of the best writers of her time. She was born Katherine Mansfield Beauchamp on October 14, 1888, to an affluent family in Wellington, New Zealand. In 1902 she moved to London to attend Queen's College, London, where she displayed little interest in literature. She briefly returned to New Zealand in 1906, after finishing her studies, but moved back to London two years later. She began writing short stories around this time but would not see anything published for several years. The same year of her return to London, she met, married, and left her first husband, George Bowden, all within a span of three weeks. Shortly afterward she became pregnant by a family friend, a professional violinist named Garnet Trowell, and her mother sent her to Bavaria, where she suffered a miscarriage.

While in Germany, Mansfield wrote satirical sketches, which were published in *The New Age*. When she returned to London in 1910, she contracted gonorrhea, which crushed her with arthritic pain for the remainder of her life. In 1912 she submitted "The Woman at the Store" to a new magazine, *Rhythm*. Soon after the story's publication in *Rhythm*, Mansfield moved in with the magazine's editor, John Middleton Murry, and married him in 1918, a year after she contracted tuberculosis. While traveling to various health spas throughout Europe, she wrote some of her most critically acclaimed works, such as *Bliss* and *The Garden Party*. By 1922 her health had deteriorated considerably, and sensing that her days were waning, she decided to dedicate more of her time to her spiritual life by moving to Georges Gurdjieff's Institute for the Harmonious Development of Man in Fontainebleu, France. In 1923 she suffered a pulmonary hemorrhage after running up a flight of stairs to prove to her husband that she was well, and she died on January 23. Despite her short period of residence in New Zealand, Mansfield remains among that country's greatest literary figures.

visit to town, the Maori seized Volkner, hung him from a tree, and then decapitated him. When government officials learned of the brutality with which Volkner was killed, a militia of 500 men was dispatched to the region, where it freely pillaged and murdered without scruple. Eventually 20 chiefs surrendered and confessed to their involvement in Volkner's murder. Five were hanged, and much of their land was confiscated as punishment.

Meanwhile, as the Maori were attempting to regain independence from the settlers, the new colony was attempting to obtain independence from the United Kingdom, which was achieved in 1907. The Maori continued to fight for their land, and in 1975 the Waitangi Tribunal was established to help ease race relations. Today the New Zealand government is still compensating the Maori people for land that was unlawfully confiscated and has made further efforts at fostering a more peaceful relationship with the Maori by making Maori an official national language and recognizing New Zealand's original Maori name, Aotearoa.

CULTURAL IDENTITY

As a nation with one of the highest percentages of foreign-born citizens (25 percent), New Zealand is a complex amalgamation of different cultures, the most dominant being English, Irish,

The New Zealand national rugby team, the All Blacks, begin every match by doing the traditional Maori hakka, a warrior dance that uses loud chanting, stomping, and slapping to intimidate opponents; an important aspect of the movement is to protrude the tongue as far as possible, as some of these players are doing. *(AP Photo/NZPA, Pool)*

Scottish, and Maori. Many divide the New Zealand culture into two distinct groups: the Maori, and the *pakeha*, a term used to describe people of European descent. As a Polynesian people, the Maori emphasize respect, family, and tradition, and today they maintain their distinct culture through Maori language schools and even a Maori television station, which broadcasts popular television programs in Maori.

The *pakeha* culture division, or the more mainstream New Zealand culture, is allegedly centered on the "Three R's": Rugby, Racing, and beeR. This "blue collar" common-man cultural image is often paired with the concept of "Kiwi ingenuity" to produce a cultural identity of blunt, hard-working people.

In many ways, the white *pakeha* culture is very similar to the Maori culture. In the 11th century, the Maori people traveled 3,000 miles in narrow oceangoing canoes to New Zealand and had to develop their settlement with ruggedness and ingenuity to avoid exposure, starvation, and injury. Similarly, the European settlers had to brave the unknown to ensure the survival of their new colony. Thus, the two have commingled in a subtle way to produce the New Zealand culture of today.

FURTHER READING

Augie Fleras and Paul Spoonley. *Recalling Aotearoa: Indigenous Politics and Ethnic Relations in New Zealand* (Auckland: Oxford University Press, 1999).

Witi Ihimaera. *The Whale Rider* (Auckland: Reed Publishing, 1987).

Eva Rask Knudsen. *The Circle and the Spiral: A Study of Australian Aboriginal and New Zealand Maori Literature* (New York: Rodopi, 2004).

Graeme Lay. *Pacific New Zealand* (Auckland: David Ling Pub., 1996).

Katherine Mansfield. *Prelude* (London: Hesperus Press, 2005).

Phillipa Mein Smith. *A Concise History of New Zealand* (Melbourne: Cambridge University Press, 2005).

Nicobarese (Nicobar Islanders, Nicobarians)

The Nicobar Islands are an archipelago of 12 inhabited and numerous uninhabited islands located in the Bay of Bengal, south of the Andaman Islands. In addition to recent settlers from India, the islands also have two indigenous groups, the Nicobarese, who live on the coast of all 12 islands, and the Shompen, probably an older population, who reside in the inland jungles of just one island, Great Nicobar. The Nicobarese see themselves as superior to the Shompen and have been more amenable to change from the outside. Both populations are genetically most closely related to mainland Southeast Asian populations such as KHMERS and VIETNAMESE, rather than to AUSTRONESIANS as had been hypothesized early in the 20th century. However, both populations tend to be a bit shorter than their distant mainland relatives, with Nicobarese men averaging about 5 feet 3 3/4 inches and women about 5 feet, and the Shompen about 1 inch shorter.

These two separate populations, the Nicobarese and Shompen, differ in many ways beyond the physical. On the one hand, the Nicobarese are horticulturists who grow coconuts, areca nuts, yams, bananas, and pandanus, in addition to raising large herds of pigs. Pigs are raised primarily as a prestige product to be used for ritual and exchange and as a symbol of life and well-being, rather than for daily protein requirements, which are primarily fulfilled with fish and other seafood. On the other hand, the Shompen are hunters of wild pigs and gatherers of wild forest products. However, the two groups have traditionally coexisted through trade, with the Shompen providing forest products and the Nicobarese fish and seafood. The Shompen also build canoes and rafts for their coastal trading partners.

The two groups also share some cultural features, such as a fondness for chewing betel nut, which stains the teeth a dark color; piercing the ears; and flattening infants' foreheads. Prior to the large-scale conversion of the Nicobarese to Christianity after 1945, divorce in both populations was a fairly simple affair and occurred with regularity. Also prior to 1945, there was a widespread belief in spirits and ancestral powers, both of which could cause illness if not propitiated with gifts and rituals.

Although the Nicobar Islands have been part of written history since first being mentioned by Ptolemy, a Greek geographer of the second century C.E., the first Europeans to visit the islands were Danes in 1754, subsequently joined by a number of Moravian missionaries in 1768. For seven years in the early 19th century, Britain took control of the islands following its defeat of Denmark in a brief war in 1807 over the Danes' willingness to join Napoleon's Continental System, but it gave them back to Denmark at the end of the Napoleonic era in 1814. For another 55 years the Danes attempted both settlement and missionary activities, failing on both fronts and finally ceding the entire archipelago to Britain in 1869. Britain held the islands and administered them from its penal

NICOBARESE

location:
The Nicobar Islands in the Andaman Sea, Bay of Bengal

time period:
Unknown to the present

ancestry:
Unknown, but genetics point to mainland Southeast Asia

language:
There are six Nicobarese languages, all subgroups of the Mon-Khmer language family.

NI-VANUATU

location:
Vanuatu, a South Pacific island between New Caledonia to the south-west and the Solomon Islands to the northwest

time period:
Probably 2000 B.C.E. to the present

ancestry:
Melanesian and proto-Polynesian

language:
Bislama, Vanuatuan pidgin English, is the national language. Bislama, English, and French are official languages, and 113 different indigenous languages are spoken throughout the islands.

colony on the Andaman Islands, Port Blair, until Indian independence in 1947. Since that time the Nicobar Islands, along with the Andamans, have been an offshore Indian territory.

See also ANDAMANESE; SCHEDULED TRIBES.

ni-Vanuatu (Vanuatuans)

The ni-Vanuatu, or the Vanuatuans, are the indigenous people, primarily MELANESIANS, in the independent state of Vanuatu. They are characterized by great diversity in their languages and cultures, which were brought both by the original inhabitants and by the European colonizers in the 19th and 20th centuries.

GEOGRAPHY

Vanuatu's 83 islands are located in a Y-shaped pattern in the South Pacific, between the Solomon Islands and New Caledonia. Two of their islands, Matthew and Hunter, are also claimed by New Caledonia, a French overseas territory, and only 65 of them are inhabited. Together the islands constitute just 8,600 square miles, with only four islands that are larger than 500 square miles: Espiritu Santo, Malakula, Efate, and Erromango.

Most of the islands are volcanic, and there is still an active volcano on the island of Tanna; there are other volcanoes that are currently below the waterline. A few of the islands are made of coral. The highest point on the islands is Mount Tabwemasana at 6,158 feet above sea level, and the lowest point is 0 at the shoreline. Most of the islands rise quickly from the deep seabed so that there are few reefs or other shallow areas in the region, limiting the fish stocks of most species.

ORIGINS

The large number of indigenous languages in Vanuatu, 113 plus many other dialects, points to the diverse origins of the ni-Vanuatu. The different cultural complexes in the north, central, and southern islands also indicate the people's different origins.

Melanesian people from the region of the Solomon Islands and New Guinea were probably the first arrivals, as long as 4,000 years ago. They were followed about 3,000 years ago by the makers of Lapita-style pottery who left behind a cemetery on the island of Efate that is the oldest found in the Pacific so far.

See also LAPILA CULTURE.

LANGUAGES

Most ni-Vanuatu are multilingual, speaking at least one of the 113 indigenous languages spoken on the islands, along with Bislama and English and/or French. Bislama, the indigenous pidgin spoken as the lingua franca on all of Vanuatu's islands, developed from the vocabulary of the bêche-de-mer (sea cucumber) fishermen who traveled the region in the last two centuries. The structure and tone of the language come from English, but its structure is much simpler. For example, the single word *mi* is used for all forms of the first-person pronoun: I, me, mine, and my. Bislama resembles the pidgins used in New Guinea and the Solomon Islands, but it is also unique to Vanuatu, and speakers of these other languages would need assistance in understanding the ni-Vanuatu. In addition to Bislama, the colonial languages of English and French are also officially recognized on Vanuatu and are still the main languages for both primary and secondary education, although Bislama is used more and more for administrative purposes, even in schools.

HISTORY

The first ni-Vanuatu were Melanesians who probably arrived on the islands in dugout canoes, having sailed northeast from the Solomon Islands. They were followed by the ancestors of today's POLYNESIANS, the makers of Lapita-style pottery, who added their own languages and cultures to the already established Melanesian way of life. For thousands of years these two populations intermarried; exchanged material, linguistic, and social traits; and formed a unique blend of many different cultures on the 65 inhabited islands in the archipelago.

In the 18th century this independent social development process came to an end with the beginning of both French and British colonialism in the area. The first Europeans to bring significant change were the sandalwood traders, who were followed by missionaries, blackbirders who kidnapped local men or bribed locals to turn over their enemies to be taken to other islands for work on plantations, and finally the full colonial apparatus of both the British and French empires.

Vanuatu, or the New Hebrides as it was known then, was unique in the Pacific for having been simultaneously colonized by both the French and British. Both countries established schools in their own languages, sent missionaries, and administered sections of the islands. This situation did not divide the islands down some arbitrary line, with the British administering one half and the French the other, but rather it was somewhat haphazardly arranged on a piecemeal basis. Sometimes rival villages made the decision themselves; if their enemy had an English school or hospital, then they might ask the French to build one for them. This unique colonial circumstance was labeled the "condominium" by the British and French to refer to their shared venture; local ni-Vanuatu often used "pandemonium" instead to point to the chaos of the situation.

During World War II the copra and other colonial industries were temporarily interrupted when the United States established naval bases on the islands of Efate and Espiritu Santo. While the colonial economy was disrupted by the war, the U.S. soldiers posted on the islands maintained the same hierarchical social structure established by the French and British, with outsiders at the top. Much of the local population, who had felt cheated of their land and of access to the material possessions of the colonizers since at least the 1930s, turned their frustrations toward all outsiders. On the island of Tanna, many began to join a movement that had begun in 1936: the John Frum movement, which was essentially a cargo cult. Members believed that John Frum was a messianic figure who would return to Tanna, chase away the outsiders, and deliver large amounts of material possessions to the local population. The John Frum movement, like all cargo cults, combines elements from the Christian teachings about the messiah and judgment day, local spirit beliefs, and anticolonial politics. The movement continues to attract members today; February 15 is celebrated every year as the possible return date of John Frum, who will bring significant cargo with him. But in the 1970s Frum supporters were focused at least as much on an anticolonial indigenization movement as on the return of cargo and joined with others in a secessionist group on Espiritu Santo.

Although this secessionist group, Nagriamel, was not at the forefront of the movement for independence in the New Hebrides, independence was nonetheless achieved in 1980. Since that time the ni-Vanuatu population has grown and the tourism and offshore banking industries have developed, but little else has changed. About 65 percent of the population continues to work as small agriculturists, growing enough for subsistence and joining the market economy by selling copra only when school fees, taxes, or some other need for cash arises.

CULTURE

Due to the different peoples who settled Vanuatu in the years before the common era, there are at least two significantly different culture areas on the islands today, and some sources point to three. The northern islands of Vanuatu have an indigenous social structure that resembles those seen throughout Melanesia. Rather than an institutionalized hierarchy, these structures grant temporary prestige and power to individuals who show strong personalities and the ability to convince others to assist them in amassing large numbers of pigs and other indigenous wealth so that they can give it away to others. Ceremonies of feasting on pork, giving away pigs, and other rituals are common in this region and the primary pathway to power and prestige. Despite the importance of the Big Men who achieve prestige in this way, there are no recognized authority figures who can force others to do as they wish based simply on their positions.

The central islands of Vanuatu are culturally different from this characteristic Melanesian model and resemble the societies of Polynesia to a greater extent. The people of the central islands recognize a series of hereditary chiefs who inherit their power and authority over others. Below the chiefs are other royal or noble lineages, and below them in the social hierarchy are commoners. This institutionalized class system does not exclude women, who can inherit very high positions and even achieve the position of chief on the islands of Shepherd and Ambae.

The southern islands, such as Tanna, have a slightly different social system from this classic Polynesian model, one that sits between the relative egalitarianism of the Melanesians and the hierarchical Polynesians. Chiefs are recognized in the south, but their positions are earned or bestowed only on certain men, based on their abilities. Their status gives them access to land and even the labor of other people, and women in this region always hold very low status.

In addition to these cultural differences brought in thousands of years ago by the first settlers, the more recent European influences have introduced even more differences to the ni-Vanuatu. Having had both Francophone and Anglophone schools and administrations on their islands for more than 100 years has led to very different postcolonial experiences and identities. The Francophone ni-Vanuatu are more likely to have been influenced by Roman Catholic missionaries and to have gone to schools taught by French citizens or mixed-race, French-educated teachers. The curriculum taught in these schools would have been

NU

location:
Yunnan Province, China

time period:
At least eighth century to
the present

ancestry:
Luluman and other tribes
of the Gongshan region

language:
Nu, a Tibeto-Burman
language in the larger
Sino-Tibetan phylum

exactly the same as that taught in the schools of France and so would have focused on the development of a unique French linguistic and cultural identification. Conversely, the Anglophone ni-Vanuatu, who made up about 70 percent of the population at independence, are more likely to have been influenced by Presbyterian or Anglican missionaries and to have gone to primary schools taught by locals and secondary schools taught by British or local teachers. The curriculum would have been much less European and intellectual and more focused on creating a literate, religious, and docile local workforce.

Despite these social structural and colonial differences, other aspects of ni-Vanuatu culture are uniform throughout the islands. One of these aspects is the importance of ritual events that include the exchange, killing, and eating of pigs. Every transition in a person's life, birth, coming of age, male circumcision, marriage, and death, is marked by extensive ceremonies. Extended families have come together to celebrate and mark these changes in status for thousands of years, and they continue to be a central feature of ni-Vanuatu culture today. Even now, if an economic crisis or natural disaster precludes a family's accumulating enough pigs to sponsor their son's circumcision, men in their 20s continue to be treated like children until the ceremony can take place. In addition to the exchange of pigs, another important aspect of all rituals is the centrality of storytelling, singing, and dancing. As nonliterate people, the precolonial ni-Vanuatu had to rely on these methods to pass on their genealogies and histories, origin and other myths, taboos, and other cultural features. These forms of communication, along with other art forms, such as carvings, tattooing, and making masks, continue to be important in ni-Vanuatu culture today.

Another ritualized event that is standard throughout the country is the drinking of kava, although the style of preparation and rules about its consumption differ from island to island. On Tanna, for example, only circumcised men can drink kava, which is made there by virginal boys who chew the kava root before it is squeezed through a coconut fiber cloth.

Finally, the subsistence practices throughout the islands are also fairly consistent, with yam, taro, and manioc serving as the primary source of calories everywhere. Breadfruit and coconut are also extremely important, as are the omnipresent pigs. Some fish and seafoods are also important, but the lack of shallow reefs around most islands limit the number and range of species available.

See also VANUATUANS: NATIONALITY.

FURTHER READING

Michael Allen, ed. *Vanuatu: Politics, Economics, and Ritual in Island Melanesia* (Sydney, Aus.: Academic Press, 1981).

Joel Bonnemaison and Kirk Huffman, eds. *Arts of Vanuatu* (Honolulu: University of Hawaii Press, 1996).

Felix Speiser. *Ethnology of Vanuatu: An Early Twentieth Century Study,* trans. D. Q. Stephenson (Honolulu: University of Hawaii Press, 1996).

Nu (Along, Anu, Nusu)

The Nu are one of China's recognized 55 national minority groups. They live in the rough terrain of Yunnan Province, with its high mountains, deep valleys, and numerous rivers, including the Lancang (Mekong), Dulong, and Nujiang.

The first recorded information about the Nu comes from the eighth century C.E., when they were ruled by the expansive Nanzhao kingdom of the DAI. In subsequent centuries, when China was ruled by the Yuan and Ming dynasties, 1279–1644, the Nu came under the jurisdiction of the NAXI, who collected tribute from them and passed it along to the emperor's local representatives. Then, from 1644 until the communist revolution in 1949, the Nu were subjugated by Tibetan and BAI headmen, under whom many were treated like slaves. For a brief period in the mid-19th and early 20th centuries the Nu allied themselves with other local peoples, such as the LISU and TIBETANS, to fight off intrusions by European traders and French missionaries, who had come north from their strongholds in Southeast Asia. Since 1949 the Nu have been citizens of the People's Republic of China, subject to its laws and the vicissitudes of its leaders concerning land reform and economic policy.

Historically, the traditional economic activity of the Nu was farming. In some communities this was done in feudal conditions where the Nu worked largely as tenant farmers or sharecroppers on the landholdings of a few wealthy families, while in others local clans and lineages continued to hold their own land and to assign a parcel to each family. They grew barley, buckwheat, corn, beans, potatoes, and yams. These cereals and vegetables were supplemented by hunting, gathering, and fishing. Many individuals also engaged in various crafts including wood-, bamboo-, and ironworking, as well as weaving and distilling. Items were made for personal use, trade, and sale in local markets.

Nu social structure recognized 10 separate clans who generally lived in their own villages and worked their own lands. Women married into their husbands' clans and moved into their households at marriage. As is usually the case with these kinds of patrilineal and patrilocal systems, women's status was quite low. This meant hard work during a woman's lifetime, and at her death she was buried lying on her side facing her husband, with her arms and legs bent. Men, on the other hand, were always buried on their backs with their arms and legs stretched out to symbolize their relatively high status. Each son was granted a piece of his family's land at marriage and was able to establish his own household. Usually these households were monogamous, but a few wealthy Nu men managed to have more than one wife; usually, additional wives were set up in their own homes within the same family compound.

Nu religion recognized a wide variety of nature spirits, including the sun, moon, various animals, mountains, rivers, trees, and other distinctive features, as well as their dead ancestors. Village shamans went into trances and practiced divination to discern the causes of illnesses and other misfortunes and to learn from the spirits what gifts or sacrifices the victim needed to provide to improve his or her situation. They also presided over both individual life-cycle rituals such as birth, marriage, and funerals as well as large community events to celebrate harvests and other occasions.

Nung (Giang, Khen Lai, Nung An, Nung Chao, Nung Coi, Nung Din, Nung lnh, Phan Sinh, Qui Rin, Thai Nung, Xuong)

The Nung are a Tai-speaking group of northern Vietnam, one of that country's 53 recognized minority groups. Today they number about 700,000, making them one of the larger of these minority groups. They also have higher literacy rates, life expectancies, and health statistics than most other national minority groups, although nowhere near as high as the dominant VIETNAMESE or the Chinese minority, known locally as HOA. They are linguistically and culturally similar to the TAY, with whom they are sometimes grouped as the Nung-Tay, but the Tay arrived in Vietnam in a later wave of mi-gration from southern China. During the war against the French in northern Vietnam, between 1945 and 1954, some Nung communities fled the area and settled in southern Vietnam and Laos; about 100,000 Nung fled to China's Yunnan Province, where they are grouped together with the ZHUANG minority and are called Thai Nung.

Historians estimate that the Vietnamese Nung left their original homeland in Guanxi province, China, around the 12th or 13th century and made their way south toward Vietnam. They settled in the same region as their distant Tay cousins, who, it is said, allotted them the least fertile and desirable farmlands. Like the Tay, the Nung developed a composite swidden economy in which they established intensively worked rice paddies in the valleys and lower elevations, using water wheels for irrigation, and slash-and-burn terraced gardens in the hills and mountains; this same pattern remains today. In their gardens they grow a variety of vegetables, corn, peanuts, and fruit; many also grow tangerines, persimmons, anise and other spices, and bamboo as cash crops.

The Nung social structure is patrilineal, so that children inherit their lineage membership from their father, father's father, and so forth, and strongly patriarchal—that is, male-dominated. Upon marriage, a new wife must move into her husband's family's home, which is called patrilocal residence, and must work very hard to please her husband and in-laws. In wealthy Nung families the husband may have several wives, so that the new wife may have her senior co-wife to please as well. Nung patrilineages are grouped together into clans, which denote the region of China from which the group came. In the past, some Nung men married outside their clan, but women tended to marry endogamously or within their own clan; this trend has diminished today. Clan members no longer live together in the same village, and today village and commune membership, which often see the Nung and Tay mixed together, is probably more important for organizing day-to-day living than lineage or clan membership.

Nung material culture is similar to that of the other northern Vietnamese highlanders in many ways. They live in houses that are built on the ground on higher elevations and on stilts when there is a risk of flooding from nearby rivers; the family shrine is always located in the main room, opposite the entranceway. Unlike those of most others, these houses are built with clay walls and tiled roofs. The Nung, like the

NUNG

location:
Northern Vietnam and southern China

time period:
12th century to the present

ancestry:
Thai

language:
Tay, a Tai-Kadai language

Tay, are known for their iron forging and silver-smithing, as well as weaving, which some Nung women have turned into a cottage industry, making baskets and paper. The Nung are also renowned for their embroidery, which serves to decorate the hems of their clothes; their clothing is otherwise generally indigo and resembles that of the Tay. Neck scarves, shoulder bags, and other cloth items are also decorated with embroidery. Some typical motifs are the sun, flowers, and stars.

Nung religion combines elements from Buddhism, Confucianism, and indigenous beliefs about the power of spirits and ancestors. The most important feature of Nung belief taken from Buddhism is the worship of Quan Am, also known as Quan Yin in Chinese, the goddess of compassion and the embodiment of loving kindness. Confucian elements of hierarchy, the importance of education, and filial piety were all adopted from the dominant Vietnamese society slowly over the course of the past seven or eight centuries. In addition to these two fairly formalized religious systems, the Nung continue to support a village shaman, usually a man who is able to communicate with the spirit world and assist in exorcisms, divinations, curings, and other activities that bring together the material and spiritual worlds, especially birth and death rituals. The shaman also oversees animal sacrifices, usually pigs, ducks, or chickens, when they are necessary to appease or thank the gods and spirits. Ancestor worship is important among the Nung, who continue to feed and care for their lineage ancestors. If the spirits are not properly fed, they become angry, evil spirits who then must be appeased in rituals overseen by shamans. Nature spirits, *phi,* are also an important part of the Nung cosmology and are believed to inhabit certain mountains, rocks, bodies of water, fields, and trees.

Nuristanis (Black Kafirs, Kafirs, Kaffirs, Nuris, Red Kafirs)

The Nuristanis live in an approximately 5,000-square-mile area in northeastern Afghanistan and northwestern Pakistan, especially Nuristan Province of the former country. This region is extremely rugged, with high mountain peaks and thick, old-growth forests preventing most outsiders from venturing in. It is said that the first two-wheel-drive car did not enter the province until 1978, a Volkswagen Beetle. The region is cross-cut by five major valleys running north to south and by 30 smaller east-to-west valleys.

Each valley contains separate populations who refer to themselves either as Nuristanis or as the people of their specific geographic locale; they also speak sometimes mutually unintelligible Nuristani languages, which bear the names of their valleys.

This is an ancient population that has been living in this rugged region for thousands of years. Certainly by the time Alexander the Great invaded Afghanistan in 329–327 B.C.E., the Nuristanis were already there. Some people actually claim the Nuristanis are descendants of some of Alexander's soldiers, but that seems improbable, at least for the entire population, given that his own historian wrote about them. Some Nuristanis themselves claim descent from the Qureish, the prophet Muhammad's tribe. According to the legend, during the conversions of the people of Mecca to Islam, a few individuals decided to maintain their old religion and were exiled from the city. They moved to Central Asia and were the ancestors of the Nuristanis; however, there is no other evidence of these origins. Linguistic evidence points to ancient Indo-Iranian origins for the Nuristanis, with their languages said to make up an independent branch of this family along with Iranian and Indo-Aryan.

The region of contemporary Nuristan remained independent of any colonial power or state structure until 1893–96, when it was finally conquered by King Abdur Rahman, the nationalizing Pashtun leader of Afghanistan. He forcibly converted the population, then known as Kafirs, or infidels in Arabic, to Islam. The name of the region and its people was changed at this time from Kafir and Kafiristan to Nuristan, meaning "Land of Light," or "Enlightenment." While the conversion was not voluntary, contemporary Nuristanis are devout Sunni Muslims who are deeply offended by their prior designation.

The economic life of the Nuristanis even to this day is dominated by cows and land. Some Nuristanis have also achieved powerful positions within the Afghanistani state, especially with the military. Their society is strictly divided along several social divisions. First, the division between upper-class landowners and lower-class craftsmen and artisans, such as woodworkers, weavers, blacksmiths, and potters, is extremely strong. While trade and commerce in these goods are important within the local markets, they do not bring high status to their makers, even those with extremely refined skills. Only land ownership provides a

Nuristani family with access to local power and prestige. Within this upper class of Nuristani society, however, a type of male egalitarianism seems to prevail, or did so in the past. All landowners had the ability to speak at village gatherings, and it was only temporary differences brought about by success in warfare or feast-giving that elevated one man above others in terms of power and influence; differences in authority, or socially legitimated power that is attached to a position like chief or king, traditionally did not emerge. The second important social division is that between women and men. This division is maintained through a strict gendered division of labor and rules of purity and impurity that forbid women to enter sacred areas or handle sacred objects; for example, women must remain within the house and the valleys rather than venturing into the fields and especially the mountaintops.

This gendered division mirrors a further set of dualisms that underlie all of Nuristani life and come from their pre-Islamic religious beliefs. This ancient religion categorized every aspect of nature and human society within the dualistic framework of sacred and profane, pure and impure, male and female. For example, mountaintops, wild animals, the backs of houses, and men were classified as sacred and pure, while valleys, domestic animals, the fronts of houses, and women were the opposite, profane and impure. Rather than merely dismissing the latter grouping as impure and thus bad, however, this ancient belief system recognized the importance of the union between sacred and profane. The procreative union between men and women was seen as the model for all creative energy. All quests for success, wealth, and power necessitated the input of both sides of their strict dualistic worldview, but always within the limits of their place in society. So while women and all other impure aspects of the world were considered necessary for success, they had to be strictly limited and controlled. If a family was suffering from specific misfortunes, such as the death of a child or a goat, purification rites could be performed by religious specialists to strengthen the sacred forces and weaken the profane.

In addition to this important division between the sacred and profane, the pre-Islamic worldview of the Nuristanis included a range of nonhuman characters, usually translated as fairies, who were seen to participate in human life. The fairies, who lived parallel lives to humans with the same family structure and division of labor and could speak and interact with men, lived in the mountains, a sacred space. They were the keepers of wild mountain goats, a favorite animal of Nuristani hunters. They believed that before a hunter could kill a goat, it first must have been eaten by the fairies, who drained the animal of its power and then returned its bones to the skin. When they released the animal, they directed it to a particular Nuristani hunter who would then be able to kill it. While most of the substance of the fairy beliefs disappeared from the Nuristani worldview about 100 years ago with conversion to Islam, fairy stories continue to abound, and fear of being captured by them continues to inform people's behavior at some level.

In Afghanistan's recent, troubled history Nuristani soldiers have been significant participants. Some Nuristani soldiers fought continuously for their region's independence from the time of their inclusion in the Afghan state in 1896 to the Communist takeover in the 1970s. This tradition of rebellion laid the groundwork, both ideologically and materially, for continued struggle against the left-wing coup in 1978 that brought the Communists to power. Nuristanis also raised arms against the Soviet invasion in 1979, led by the resistance movement's second in command after the king, General Issa Nuristani. Most recently, Nuristani soldiers have been most closely associated with the warlord Gulbuddin Hekmatyar's Islamic Party of Afghanistan, the leading insurgency movement in Afghanistan's northern regions, while the Taliban engages in the south; the group's Nuristani leader is Haji Ghafour. A second Nuristani insurgency group, Maulvi Afzal, is also active in the province, while a third group, led by General Dod Mohammad, is connected to the Northern Alliance and is currently not actively fighting. Given the Nuristani history of both regional fighting and rebellion against state structures, this condition may not last long.

See also Afghanistanis: nationality; Pashtuns.

Further Reading

Nicholas Barrington, Joseph T. Kendrick, Reinhard Schlagintweit, and Sandy Gall. *A Passage to Nuristan: Exploring the Mysterious Afghan Hinterland* (London: I. B. Tauris, 2006).

Lennart Edelberg and Schuyler Jones. *Nuristan* (Graz, Austria: Akademische Druck-und Verlagsanstalt, 1979).

Karl Jettmar. *The Religions of the Hindukush: The Religion of the Kafirs: The Pre-Islamic Heritage of Afghan Nuristan* (Oxford: Aris & Phillips, 1986).

NURISTANIS

location:
Afghanistan, especially in Nuristan Province in the country's northeast, and portions of northwest Pakistan

time period:
Prehistory to the present

ancestry:
Indo-Iranian

language:
Nuristani, formerly known as Kafirstani, said to be a separate branch of the Indo-Iranian language group along with Iranian and Indo-Aryan. Nuristani has five separate languages, each with several dialects.

Oirat (Oyrat, Oyirad, Western Mongols, Kalmyks)

OIRAT

location:
Mongolia, China, Russia, and Kazakhstan

time period:
13th century to the present

ancestry:
Mongol

language:
Western Mongolian

Oirat is a collective term that refers to the Western Mongols generally, a group that includes the Zunghars, Durbets, and other smaller tribes in northern Asia. The Kalmyk are an Oirat group who migrated westward and established their own polity in the lower Volga region of European Russia in the early 17th century. In 1711 many of those who fled to Russia returned to the Xinjiang area in northwest China; the name of the small Russian Oirat community, Kalmyk, means "to remain." Today the Oirat who returned to China and Mongolia make up a distinct minority within Mongolia itself, with the Eastern Mongols, or Khalkha, constituting about 90 percent of the country. Descendants of the 13th-century Oirat today also live in Kazakhstan, China, and eastern Russia.

The dating of the Oirat in the 13th century is based on the text of *The Secret History of the Mongols,* which chronicles the lifetime and military campaign of Genghis Khan. This work refers to the Oirat as forest people ruled by their shamanic chief. It is probable that the Oirat existed before this period, but the records are unclear. Initially the Oirat struggled against the military and political hegemony of Genghis Khan's empire but in the end realized that alliance with their powerful cousins was more fruitful than continual warfare they probably could not win. Oirat sections of the armies of Genghis Khan distinguished themselves for their bravery and skill.

After the fall of Kublai Khan's Yuan dynasty in China in 1368, an alliance of separate Oirat tribes, known as the Dorben Oirat, ruled a patch of territory in the Altai Mountains. Over the course of the next 60 years the Oirat gradually began to challenge the Eastern Mongols in their territory, until the latter succumbed to the greater military power. From 1439 to 1454 the Oirat were ruled by Esen Tayisi, who not only unified both Inner and Outer Mongolia under his leadership but also challenged the Chinese Ming dynasty along the boundary at the Great Wall. The alliance of Oirat and Mongol tribes that Tayisi had ruled disintegrated after his death, and the next two centuries were dominated by frequent battles between Western and Eastern Mongol groups. The last emergence of Oirat supremacy occurred during the Zunghar state, from 1634 to 1760, which ruled all the steppes between the Russian and Chinese Empires.

Culturally, the Oirat resemble their Eastern Mongol cousins in their adherence to pastoral subsistence patterns and a nomadic lifestyle. Each extended family raised a variety of different animals, including sheep, goats, cattle, and camels, and followed the availability of grass and water for their herds. They were united into larger clan units that occasionally met for ritual and militaristic purposes. Much of this lifestyle continues today for the Oirat living in Mongolia and China. The Oirat, like many Mongol groups, also converted from their traditional shamanistic belief system to Tibetan Buddhism in the early 17th century. Prior to this conversion, shamans, who could communicate with the spirit world to effect curing and other mystical events, also served as community leaders. After their conversion, Buddhist lamas tended to serve a similar role in their societies, acting as consultants in religious, spiritual, medical, and other matters as needed. In the 1920s–1940s this religion was viciously persecuted in Mongolia and continues to cause tensions in China today.

Okinawans (Amamijins, Loochoo Islanders, Okinawajins, Ryukyu Islanders, Ryukyuans, Ryūkyūjins, Sakishimajins)

The Okinawans are the inhabitants of Okinawa, the largest of the Ryukyu Islands, the southernmost islands in the Japanese Archipelago.

GEOGRAPHY

Okinawa, a Central Ryukyuan island, is located about halfway between Tokyo, Japan, and Southeast Asia, also between Japan's southern island of Kyushu and Taiwan. The Ryukyuan chain of which it is a part is about 250 miles long north to south and about 620 miles wide east to west. It is made up of 160 islands, 48 of which are inhabited. Prior to rises in sea levels globally between 20,000 and 10,000 years ago, these islands were part of a larger landmass that included Japan and southern Asia. Prior to this period of separation, many plants and animals had migrated to the area of the Ryukyus from other areas of what was then the combined landmass of Japan and Southeast Asia and then were stranded by rising sea levels. As a result, the Ryukyus, especially Okinawa, have frequently been referred to as the Galapagos of the East for their many unique species.

The climate on Okinawa is warmer than in the rest of Japan, averaging about 74°F; it is also wet and humid, receiving 80 inches of rain annually and averaging about 76 percent humidity. Rainfall comes on quickly and heavily, as in the tropics, and is influenced by the Kuroshio

OKINAWANS

location:
The Ryukyu Islands of Japan, especially Okinawa

time period:
Possibly 605 C.E. to the present

ancestry:
Possibly Japanese, Malay, and Manchurian

language:
Okinawan is one among the 11 different Ryukyuan languages, which are all subgroups within the larger Japanese language family; the only other language in this larger group is Japanese.

Okinawans time line

B.C.E.

30,000 The first human inhabitation of Okinawa, as evident in archaeological remains found in the 20th century.

20,000–10,000 The Ryukyu Islands are cut off from both Japan and southern Asia by rising sea levels.

C.E.

605 Approximate year of the first written record of Okinawan people, from a Chinese source.

Seventh to ninth centuries Imperial Japan maintains loose connections with all of the Ryukyu Islands.

1372 Okinawan kings first begin to pay tribute to Ming China.

1429 Sho Hashi unites all of Okinawa and rules from Shuri castle.

1609 The Shimazu family leads the Japanese colonial assault on Okinawa.

1846 British missionary-physician Bernard Jean Bettelheim arrives in Okinawa, capital of the Ryukyu kingdom, in order to spread the Protestant faith.

1853 Commodore Matthew C. Perry lands in Naha in his effort to open up Japan to international trade.

1879 Okinawa is annexed by Meiji Japan.

1945 The United States invades Okinawa as part of World War II in the Pacific.

1949 The United States begins building a large air base on Okinawa.

1951–52 The San Francisco Peace Conference gives the United States power over most functions in Okinawa and thus formally separates the island from Japan.

1972 The United States gives Okinawa back to the Japanese but maintains 39 military bases on the island, taking up 20 percent of the island's territory and 40 percent of the arable land.

1995 Three members of the U.S. forces in Okinawa rape a local 12-year-old girl, resulting in massive protests by the Okinawans.

1996 The Okinawa prefecture holds a nonbinding referendum on the removal of U.S. military bases, which passes with 95 percent of the vote.

Current. Okinawa is the northernmost limit for many Southeast Asian species of plants such as the *Ficus retusa* and Indian coral bean.

ORIGINS

There is some evidence of human life in the Central Ryukyu Islands from about 30,000 years ago, including the skeletal remains of a young child. The earliest inhabitants of Okinawa seem to have migrated to the island from three different places. JOMON-era JAPANESE people came south from Kyushu and the other main Japanese islands. MALAYS from Southeast Asia or the Philippines also landed on Okinawa and its closest island neighbors during the prehistoric period, as did Manchurian or Mongol peoples (*see* MONGOLS) from north Asia, probably having come through Korea. Despite this diversity in prehistory, today's population can for all intents and purposes be considered close relatives of the Japanese. The languages of Okinawa and the other Ryukyu Islands are the only close relatives of Japanese and are considered to have broken off from the Kyoto or main Japanese dialect between the sixth and 12th centuries. During this long period of separation, however, the Ryukyu dialects have developed some significant differences from Japanese, mostly through close interactions with the Chinese.

HISTORY

Much of Okinawa's ancient history must be patched together from remote Chinese sources. The first mention of the island and its people comes from about 605 C.E., when the HAN Chinese made contact with the island's people. Some sources indicate that this period initiated about 500 years of Chinese domination on the island, but there is little evidence supporting this claim. Most sources point to close interactions with the Japanese at this time. Probably the truth is that the Okinawans and other Ryukyu Islanders had trade and other relations with both Japan and China and possibly with other seafaring peoples as well.

The first real historical information about the Okinawans comes from the 14th century, when three rival Okinawan rulers from the Hokuzan, Nanzan, and Chuzan kingdoms began vying for a premier relationship with the Ming emperor of China. The first king to initiate this relationship was Satto of the Chuzan kingdom (r. 1350–95), who sent his brother to China in 1372 bearing gifts for the Ming emperor. Chinese diplomacy at the time required

the emperor to reciprocate the gifts he received and to exceed their value by many times. This inspired Satto's two rivals from Hokuzan and Nanzan to send their own gifts to China and initiated a period of more than 200 years of relatively peaceful trade relations between the two realms. In all domestic areas Okinawa remained independent, though nominally its kings were in a vassal relationship with the larger, stronger Chinese empire.

This era of peace came to an end in 1609 when the Shimazu family from Satsuma, Kyushu, the southernmost main island of Japan, invaded Okinawa. For the next 259 years Okinawa remained in a colonial relationship with Satsuma, with the former paying heavy taxes to the latter and providing both resources and manpower for Japanese projects. The sugar cane industry soon came to dominate the local economy, and the period is often called "sugar hell" by the Okinawans. Nonetheless, the royal house of Ryukyu, the Sho dynasty, continued to hold at least nominal control of Okinawa and most of the other Ryukyu Islands. The relationship between imperial Japan and Okinawa was revised only in 1868, to reinforce the Okinawans' subordinate position through the use of Japanese military power. The final Japanese thrust came in 1879 when they annexed the island and formally incorporated it into Japan, thus bringing a close to more than 500 years of Okinawan royal control on the island. The Sho dynasty came to an end, and Okinawa became Japan's 47th district.

The first task of the Meiji regime in the Ryukyus was to incorporate the population fully into the Japanese empire. One of the main tactics toward this end was the expansion of Japanese education in the islands. Even more than administrative changes, this change was successful in creating a population that saw itself as almost completely Japanese. The expansion of Japanese military conscription into the Ryukyus in 1898 likewise created a population of men who held Japanese national identities rather than local ties to the defunct Ryukyu kingdom or Sho dynasty. As a result, at the start of World War II Okinawans saw themselves largely as part of the Japanese war machine and generally worked to support the national effort.

Okinawa's geographic position as the "keystone of the Pacific" placed it directly in the line of attack when U.S. forces began island hopping their way north across the Pacific during World War II. To prepare for the onslaught, Japanese forces arrived in Okinawa in June 1944, and 10

The U.S. invasion of Okinawa is known locally as the "typhoon of steel." The numbers of ships and other war matériel visible in this photo from 1945 give some hint as to what the experience must have been like for the local population. *(AP Photo)*

months later the Americans followed suit. The long and deadly Battle of Okinawa lasted for 11 weeks between April and June 1945, making it one of the longest in the war's history. During that period almost 50,000 American soldiers were killed, injured, or went missing, while the Japanese and Okinawans suffered even greater losses of life: 60,000 Japanese were killed plus about one-third of the Okinawan population, totaling 150,000 people. The event is known locally as the "typhoon of steel," and the most tragic part for many Okinawan families is that their friends and relatives were killed by Japanese soldiers who doubted the loyalty of the Okinawan people.

The immediate postwar years were a mixed blessing for the Okinawan people. Certainly everybody was grateful for the war's end and the resumption of normalcy in education, health care, banking, jurisprudence, and even the delivery of news. However, the building of 39 separate U.S. military bases on the island, starting in 1949, ignited protests over the loss of land that lasted for years. The local agricul-tural economy was destroyed, and the island became almost entirely dedicated to servicing the enormous U.S. military presence, an economic feature that continues today. In addition, the 1951 peace treaty granting the United States administrative control of the former territory of the Ryukyu kingdom was a difficult pill for many Okinawans to swallow. Local feelings were even more disturbed in the 1970s when it was made public that the Japanese emperor Hirohito had voluntarily signed away the island territory, rather than being forced to do so by the Americans. The feeling in Japan at the time was that the Ryukyus were a hotbed of radicalism that would disturb Japan's postwar rebuilding process, and it would be safer and easier for Japan to have the United States dealing with those problems.

In 1972 Okinawa was returned to Japanese control by U.S. president Richard Nixon. At the time most Okinawans supported the move since their dismemberment from Japan had been seen as a shameful loss of control in the early 1950s. However, some islanders have since come to regret the change. The Okinawan economy has suffered since reunification because it had to start competing freely with other regions within Japan, leading to the highest rate of unemployment in the country. As a result several independence movements have emerged in the past generation, including that led by Shima-okoshi, the Island Revival Society, which held its most recent island-reviving seminar in April 2007.

CULTURE

The indigenous economy of Okinawa and the rest of the Ryukyu Islands was based on rice farming first and fishing as a secondary activity. As a result, much of the ritual calendar was built around the Honen harvest festivals, fertility rites, and other agricultural events throughout the year. Ancestor worship was also central to Okinawan religious beliefs, as was the case throughout Japan. Female priests, or *noro,* dominated these events as well as most other religious and supernatural affairs. Women placated Hinukan, the fire or hearth deity, who was responsible for the health and well-being of the household; they also led rituals for larger groups such as clans and villages. *Utaki,* sacred groves of trees in Okinawa, are the sites of rituals dedicated to nature goddesses called *shinjo* in Okinawan. Most traditional shamans, or *yutas,* were women who had been called to the profession through illnesses or other signs of their ability to communicate with the spirit world. These shamans were consulted on an individual basis for reading omens, curing illnesses, or bringing good luck, while leaving more public rituals to the priests.

Despite the importance of women in traditional Okinawan religion, overall Okinawan and Ryukyuan society was male-dominated. Only men could inherit property as members of patrilineal clans, membership in which was inherited from fathers, and a woman had to leave her family home at marriage to take up residence in her husband's family's home, in a pattern called patrilocal residence. Generally villages were endogamous units—that is, most people married within the same village where they grew up. This practice mitigated women's loss of family somewhat, but this was only an expectation and not a formal rule, so some women at marriage had to move out of their villages as well as their homes.

Another aspect of traditional Okinawan culture is the martial art of Karate, or "open hand." The origin myth of this martial art form says that when the Japanese invaded the Ryukyu Islands in 1609, all military arms on the islands were confiscated to keep the islanders from rebelling. But the islanders had a traditional martial art form they had adapted from the kung fu styles of the Chinese, with whom they had had close contacts for centuries; they called this *te,* or hand. In the early 17th century many of the islands' men began training with local monks to toughen their hands, knuckles, and elbows so that they developed enormous calluses. They also developed a series of lethal kicks, for dismounting Japanese cavalrymen. With this training the Okinawans' hands were so tough that they could easily punch through the Japanese armor, made from bamboo and leather, and kill people in hand-to-hand combat. A number of agricultural implements, including rice grinders and sickles, were also utilized as weapons for fighting back against Japanese domination. While these efforts failed at the time, the practice of Karate has continued in Okinawa, Japan, and throughout the world ever since.

FURTHER READING

Tony Barrett and Rick Tanaka. *Okinawa Dreams OK* (Berlin: Die-Gestalten-Verlag, 1997).

Robert Eldridge. *The Origins of the Bilateral Okinawa Problem: Okinawa in Postwar US–Japan Relations, 1945–1952* (New York: Routledge, 2001).

George Kerr. *Okinawa: The History of an Island People* (Rutland, Vt.: Charles Tuttle Company, 1952).

Allan Smith. *Ryukyuan Culture and Society: A Survey* (Honolulu: University of Hawaii Press, 1964).

Old Balinese   *See* BALI AGA.

Orang Asli (Aboriginals, Aboriginal Malaysians, Sakai)

The Orang Asli are considered the aboriginal people of Peninsular Malaysia; their name means "natural peoples" in Malay and was assigned to this group by the Malaysian government in 1966 to replace the more derogative *aborigine.* Other than being so classified by the Malaysian government, the Orang Asli share very little else and can be divided into three distinct groups who probably arrived on Peninsular Malaysia during many different periods: SEMANG, or Negritos; SENOI; and MELAYU ASLI, or proto-MALAYS. Altogether there are approximately 20 different indigenous groups with a combined population of between 100,000 and 148,000 people, or about .5 percent of Malaysia's population.

ORIGINS

The conventional wisdom about the Orang Asli states that the Semang are the oldest population on Peninsular Malaysia and may have lived

---

ORANG ASLI

location:
Peninsular Malaysia

time period:
Possibly 60,000 B.C.E. to the present

ancestry:
Different groups with separate origins: Semang, proto-Malay, and Malay

language:
The Semang, or Negritos, speak the Northern Aslian division of the Mon-Khmer language; the Senoi speak Austro-Asiatic languages of the Mon-Khmer subgroup; the Melayu Asli or proto-Malays speak southern Aslian, Malay, and Senoic languages.

there for about 60,000 years. This date is contested, however, because recent archaeological evidence has also linked them with the Hoa Binh culture of Southeast Asia, which existed between 16,000 and 5,000 B.C.E. Other dates such as 25,000 B.C.E. have also been presented as possible periods for the migration of this population to Peninsular Malaysia. The Senoi are an East Asian people who came to the Malay Peninsula between 8,000 and 6,000 B.C.E. from the north and are descendants of both the Hoabinhians and Neolithic cultivators. The Melayu Asli, or proto-Malays, are thought to have inhabited the southern areas of Peninsular Malaysia for at least 3,000–4,000 years, although there are few known prehistoric records of them. They are thought to have migrated from the Indonesian islands, perhaps due to population pressure. Despite being proto-Malays, these people are not the immediate ancestors of the contemporary Malay population of Malaysia.

Despite the relative certainty of most scholars concerning these different origins and time frames, there is a contested view that all three groups originated from the same population and that all contemporary differences developed in situ. This theory has gained some popularity in recent years but still remains at the level of an interesting hypothesis.

HISTORY

The prehistoric period of the Orang Asli is largely unknown to us due to a lack of written languages and the use of building materials that do not last long enough to provide archaeologists with a complete picture of their societies. From about the fifth century forward, however, many Orang Asli groups have engaged with the outside world through trade, labor, and even tribute. There are records of both Semang and Senoi leaders offering tribute or gifts to the Malay kings who ruled Peninsular Malaysia in the first centuries C.E. through the start of the colonial period in the 19th century. In addition, Orang Asli groups who lived in the tropical forests provided lumber, resin, game, and other products to lowlanders and those residing on the plains, while those on the coast traded in fish and other sea products. The Melayu Asli have long participated in local and extensive trade networks, both with other Orang Asli groups and with Malays and others.

In the 18th and 19th centuries, and probably much earlier as well, some Orang Asli were kidnapped by Malays and others and sold as slaves. Because the Orang Asli were not Mus-

Orang Asli time line	
B.C.E.	
60,000	The ancestors of today's Semang, or Negrito, subgroup of Orang Asli may have arrived in Peninsular Malaysia. This event may actually have occurred significantly later and remains highly contested.
8000	The ancestors of the Senoi may have entered Peninsular Malaysia at this time.
2000	Possible entry period of the Melayu Asli or proto-Malay population, who may have come to Peninsular Malaysia from what is today Indonesia. This too may have occurred significantly earlier.
First century	Establishment of the first Hindu-Buddhist kingdoms on Peninsular Malaysia.
C.E.	
Fifth century	The Orang Asli become important to the economy through trade and commerce, especially in forest products.
18th and 19th centuries	Malay and Batak slave raiders kidnap many Orang Asli, forcing the remainder deeper into the forests, where they seek isolation.
1884	Official abolition of slavery, although it is known to have continued into the 20th century.
1936	H. D. Noone proposes an aboriginal policy protecting the Orang Asli and their lands where they can live according to their traditions and customs. This is not officially accepted by the Malay government; however, it does provide the groundwork for later government policy toward the Orang Asli.
1948–60	The Malay Emergency drives many communist insurgents into Orang Asli territory and pushes the British authorities to acknowledge their presence.
1954	The Aboriginal Peoples' Ordinance of 1954 is established; it is revised in 1974.
2002	Court cases granting land rights to the Orang Asli provide for adequate compensation when land is taken by the government or purchased by private companies.

lims, they were considered to be somewhat outside the purview of regular human interactions, more the equivalent of a jungle animal than a human being. Slave raiders would often attack an entire village, killing the adult men and taking the women and children away as slaves. Officially this practice was ended by the British in 1884, but oral histories in many Orang Asli communities indicate that it continued well into the 20th century.

Another way that the dominant Malay population, as well as other outsiders, interacted with the Orang Asli was through missionary activity. Perhaps the first missionaries to arrive were Roman Catholics who began work among the Temuans, a subgroup of the Melayu Asli, in the mid-19th century. Later Protestants also aimed to attract Orang Asli to their congregations, and since the 1980s Muslims have been hard at work trying to convert the Orang Asli from their indigenous religions. This activity has been part of an overall assimilation policy by the Malaysian government, which has sought to eliminate the Orang Asli entirely from the population. The belief fostered in the 1980s was that as soon as the Orang Asli became Muslims and started speaking Malay as their first language, they would cease to exist as aboriginal peoples. Many Orang Asli groups and individuals have fought against this policy and resisted both proselytizing and language change through the development of local community organizations.

During the mid-20th century the Orang Asli also became caught up in the global political activities affecting the Malay Peninsula at that time. From 1948 through 1960, the region experienced a civil war as the British government tried to eliminate the risk of communist insurgency in their important Southeast Asian colony. The Briggs Plan was implemented in 1950 by the government to clear the rural area of both Chinese and other settlements, in an attempt to cut off supplies and support to the insurgents. Although the Orang Asli were not targeted specifically in the plan, the creation of new villages watched over by special constables and home guards forced many insurgents to flee even further into the jungles and highlands, territory inhabited primarily by the Orang Asli. The British believed the Orang Asli were assisting these runaways with food, shelter, and intelligence and began targeting the Orang Asli for the first time. They established an adviser on aborigines and forced large numbers of Orang Asli into resettlement camps. Many people died in these camps, mostly of depression, which forced the British to change tactics. At this point they tried to win the support of the Orang Asli through the creation of a Department of Aborigines that was to provide education and health care facilities in their regions. In 1954 the Aboriginal Peoples' Ordinance of 1954 (later revised in 1967 and 1974) was published. It was considered an important milestone for the Orang Asli, as the government was seen to have officially acknowledged its responsibility to them as human beings.

Malaysian independence in 1963 did not significantly change the social, political, or economic position of the Orang Asli population. They are classified along with Malays and the indigenous peoples of both Sarawak and Sabah as *bumiputra*, "sons of the soil," and granted extra privileges denied to the large Chinese and Indian populations within Malaysia. However, they do not receive all of the benefits of this *bumiputra* group because they have not converted to Islam and refuse to participate in Malaysian society as Malays. Nonetheless, court cases in the past decade have begun to right the wrongs committed against Orang Asli communities who have tried to defend their land against logging and mining companies, road and dam construction, and other forms of national development. Since 2002 they have had the right to receive complete compensation for their losses and have successfully fought off several large multinational corporations.

Because of these activities the Orang Asli have been considered antidevelopment by the Malaysian government and its corporate allies, but many organizations that speak for these people disagree. The Centre for Orang Asli Concerns (COAC) has presented the argument many times that the people they represent are not antidevelopment, as long as economic development takes place in the context of the integrity of their culture and language. They do not want to lose their languages or ways of life in exchange for more hydropower or tropical hardwoods that ultimately make their way to China or Japan.

CULTURE

It is impossible to speak of a single Orang Asli culture since there are so many distinct subgroups within this artificially created "ethnic group." The only thing they have in common is residence in the peninsula prior to the establishment of the first Hindu-Buddhist kingdom in the region in about the first century B.C.E. Some groups, such as the Orang Laut, earn their living from fishing, boating, and other coastal activities, while many Melayu Asli were until very recently swidden horticulturalists, growing dry upland rice in impermanent fields, prepared using slash-and-burn methods of preparation. Other Melayu Asli groups have taken up intensive agriculture with the use of fertilizers, irrigation, and more technological inputs to grow cocoa, rubber, or palm oil for the market. Until recently a small number of Semang groups even remained nomadic hunter-gatherers, living in the forests and highlands and engaging in trade with more settled communities. At least one enterprising village has even begun to showcase its way of life to a few passing tourists to earn money for use in town on consumer items, which they carefully hide away when the tourists arrive to see their "primitive" way of life. A number of Orang Asli from all three groups have also migrated into Malaysia's cities and towns, where they work as laborers, domestics, and in other areas.

Although their traditional religions differ, the Orang Asli are largely similar in having withstood the pressure to convert to Islam or to some denomination of Christianity. In 1983 the Malaysian government's Department of Orang Asli Affairs, Jabatan Hal Ehwal Orang Asli (JHEOA), stated that it was the government's intention to convert the entire population to Islam. This was part of the larger assimilation project inspired by the *bumiputra* policy of granting privileges to local "sons of the soil." Most Orang Asli, however, have not taken up the new religion. Some of the markers that indicate their refusal are the names they give their children. For many Orang Asli subgroups, there was no formalized institution of giving individuals formal names that would remain the same throughout their lifetimes. They practiced various forms of teknonymy, naming of people after others, so that an infant may be called "son of his father's name" or "daughter of her mother's name," and then receive a new name at puberty, a third at marriage, and so forth. When the British, and then later the Malaysian government, instituted formal naming and registering of infants, many Orang Asli refused to participate in the scheme, until they realized that education, health care, and other benefits came with naming. However, most Orang Asli are very careful not to give their children names that might be mistaken for Muslim ones.

See also MALAYSIAN CHINESE; MALAYSIAN INDIANS; MALAYSIANS: NATIONALITY.

FURTHER READING

Iskandar Carey. *Orang Asli: The Aboriginal Tribes of Peninsular Malaysia* (New York: Oxford University Press, 1977).

Roy Davis Linville Jumper. *Power and Politics: The Story of Malaysia's Orang Asli* (Lanham, Md.: University Press of America, 1997).

John D. Leary. *Violence and the Dream People: The Orang Asli in the Malaysia Emergency, 1948–1960* (Athens: Ohio University Center for International Studies, 1995).

Orang Laut   *See* SEA GYPSIES.

Oraon (Dhangad, Dhangar, Dhanka ["farmworker"], Kisan, Kuda, Kurukh, Kurunkh, Orao, Uraon)

The Oraon are one of the larger tribal groups inhabiting eastern India and Bangladesh, with smaller numbers living in Nepal and Bhutan. Estimates of the total Oraon population in all four countries vary significantly and are difficult to obtain since Bangladesh does not specifically count tribal groups, and members of the SCHEDULED TRIBES in India are undercounted in the national censuses. The figures for all Oraon in the region range from somewhat more than 2 million to almost 4.5 million. They are fairly closely related to the MUNDAS, another tribal group in the region.

Although most Indian Oraon are nominally Hindu, with a few Christians as well, significant aspects of their social order and religious life differ from orthodox Hinduism or from Christianity; their indigenous religion is called Sarna. There are no subcastes among the Oraon that dictate marriage patterns, although laborers (*kudas*) and cultivators (*kisans*) tend to marry within their occupational groups. Instead, clans (*gotra*) with totems from the animal, plant, and mineral kingdoms make up exogamous groups, which require individuals to marry outside their own clan but within the larger, endogamous tribal organization; villages also tend to be exogamous. These exogamous totemic clans are made up of groups of patrilineages that have a common male ancestor, usually a mythological rather than an actual human forefather. Each individual Oraon inherits his or her lineage, clan, and tribal affiliation from the father's side of the family only.

Another aspect of Oraon society that differs from that of orthodox Hinduism is the worship of a large number of gods, such as Chandi, Gaon Deoti, Jai Budhi, and Dharmesh, who are not recognized elsewhere in India. Traditionally, the Oraon are also supposed to have practiced human sacrifices in order to promote the fertility of their fields. Even as late as the 1980s, Indian police records indicate that an occasional orphan or homeless person was sacrificed in an Oraon community. Of course, the practice is illegal and considered homicide, but the distinctive marks on the body—a slit throat and part of a little finger removed, being laid out with other *puja* offerings, and taking place at sowing season—all mark it as sacrifice rather than other forms of murder.

Ideally Oraon households include extended kin within a single patrilineage; however, nuclear family homes, with just a couple and their unmarried children, are almost as common. Each household controls its own agricultural production as well as consumption practices. In the past swidden (slash-and-burn) agriculture was

ORAON

location:
Indian states of Orissa, Bihar, Jharkhand, Chhattisgarh, and West Bengal, Bangladesh, Nepal, and Bhutan

time period:
Unknown to the present

ancestry:
Probably proto-Munda

language:
Kurukh, a Dravidian language; many Oraon also speak Bengali, Hindi, and Nepali, depending on the region in which they live

the norm, but this kind of shifting agriculture requires far more land than is currently available to the Oraon community, and more intensive forms of farming with the use of additional fertilizers and irrigation are currently the norm. Traditionally hunting also provided a significant amount of the Oraon's protein as well, but this has been reduced to ceremonial status. Gathering of wild products, such as leaves, seeds, roots, fruits, and flowers also contributed significantly to the Oraon diet, with 87 different wild foods commonly gathered and eaten; many other wild products were also gathered for medicinal purposes and for religious offerings.

Generally both agricultural and other tasks followed a gendered division of labor among the Oraon, with men engaging in hunting and the heaviest agricultural tasks while women cared for the home and children, gathered wild foods, did all food preparation, and participated in lighter agricultural tasks. However, there were some forms of ceremonial hunting engaged in by women, and even into the late 20th century a women's hunting ritual continued to take place every 12 years. Another important social institution that is not divided by sex or gender is the youth dormitory, or *dhumkuria*. Both boys and girls in their early teen years spend time living in the dormitory, gaining the skills and knowledge needed to succeed in Oraon society as well as mixing with one another in order to find a marriage partner. Residents in the dormitory are also called upon by the community to assist with agricultural labor during busy times for sowing, transplanting, or harvesting rice.

The Oraon people are well known in South Asia for their anticolonial political movements in the 19th and early 20th centuries. The best known of these Oraon movements started in 1914 when Jatra Oraon claimed to receive a message from the Oraon god Dharmesh that their religion should be revised and cleansed of such features as ghost hunts, exorcisms, and animal sacrifice. He also advocated vegetarianism, abstinence from alcohol, and general restraint in people's consumption patterns. After this initial period of religious reform, Jatra and subsequent movement leaders revised their message to one that included land reform and other political issues. The movement advocated "no-rent payment" and stop-work campaigns for those Oraon who worked as sharecroppers or unskilled laborers for Hindus, Muslims, or the British. The color red was avoided by movement members because of its association with the British, as were both colonial and missionary schools.

The belief system that movement leaders used to justify these anticolonial activities was that land was a gift to the Oraon from Dharmesh, and thus nobody had the right to interfere with their use of it, either by charging rent or forcing them to work at other, nonagricultural activities.

Altogether around 26,000 people joined the Jatra Oraon movement, especially in the regions of Ranchi, Palamau, and Hazaribagh on the Chota Nagpur plateau where Oraon exploitation was at its highest; even a few non-Oraon joined from other tribes in the area, especially the Mundas and Kharia. As occurred in the anticolonial religious movements of early 20th-century Melanesia, the Oraon movement also turned toward millenarian revivalism. Jatra preached that his people would be delivered from the "hateful" Hindus, Muslims, and British by a savior in the form of the German Baba or Kaiser who would bring peace and prosperity to the Oraon. The predicted battle between the British and Germans in India would see a German victory and Oraon liberation.

By 1919 Jatra had been arrested and later released, and a number of movement leaders had come and gone in his place at the head of the Tana Bhaghat movement, as it came to be known. The movement also spread to other regions and gained new momentum as its political message gained force. In 1919 the new movement leaders, Sibu and Maya Oraon, changed its outlook somewhat by removing the religious prohibitions on alcohol, meat, and other personal conduct and focusing their message on tribal equality with Hindus and Muslims. Two years later more changes were introduced, which brought the movement into line with Mohandas Gandhi; homespun cloth was the required uniform and vows in Gandhi's name were introduced. Eventually the movement itself disappeared as its members became more aligned with Gandhi and his form of nationalism, and the Congress Party replaced Tana Bhagat as their main political voice.

FURTHER READING

Abhik Ghosh. *History and Culture of the Oraon Tribe: Some Aspects of Their Social Life* (New Delhi: Mohit Pub., 2003).

Oriyas (Odias, Odiyas)

The Oriyas are the native speakers of the Oriya Indo-Aryan language who live in and around the Indian state of Orissa and generally consider themselves Hindus. They are sometimes conflated with a farming caste called Odia,

ORIYAS

location:
Orissa and adjoining
states, India

time period:
Possibly sixth century
B.C.E. to the present

ancestry:
Possibly the Odra
peoples

language:
Oriya, an Indo-Aryan
language and the state
language of Orissa

Puri is also host to a large festival, Jagannath Rath Yatra, which entails a procession of chariots to commemorate a journey taken by Lord Krishna, or Jagannath. *(AP Photo)*

but while the Odia are Oriyas because of their language, residence in Orissa, and religion, all Oriyas are not Odias. This population includes a large number of SCHEDULED TRIBES and SCHEDULED CASTES as well as the dominant members of the state's social order.

Oriya origins date to about the sixth century B.C.E. when various Sanskrit texts, including the *Mahabharata,* identify the territory north of the Mahanadi River as Odra Desa, "country of the Odra." This territory was conquered by many different kingdoms over the course of the past 2,600 years, including the Kalinga, Maurya, Mughal, and Maratha (*see* MARATHI), the last of whom lost this territory to the British in 1803. In the third century B.C.E., Buddhism was introduced during the reign of the Mauryans under Asoka, who conquered the region in 261 B.C.E. For the next few centuries Buddhist monasteries and universities flourished in the region in conjunction with the other two dominant religions, Hinduism and Jainism. After Asoka, who was a Buddhist, the majority of rulers until the mid-16th century were Hindus, and that religion came to dominate the region due to royal patronage. In 1568, however, Islam came to Orissa with its conquest by the Bengali

sultanate, and then 22 years later this new faith was reinforced by the Mughal takeover. The Mughals ruled for about 150 years, generally without persecuting the local religion, until the region came under the control of the Marathas in 1742. The Marathas were Hindus from Maharashtra and encouraged pilgrimage to their new territory in Orissa to see the 12th-century Jagannath Temple at Puri.

The British conquered the coastal sections of Orissa as early as 1759 but did not displace the ruling Marathas entirely until 1803. They quickly found that the region was difficult to control, both because its hilly terrain had always encouraged relative autonomy from any centralized authority figure and because of the power of the landed militia of the region, the Paiks. In 1817 this group rose up against the British in the Paik Rebellion, one of the first armed anticolonial uprisings on the subcontinent. Finally, in 1936 Orissa became a province within Britain's larger Indian colony, and upon independence in 1947 all of the Oriya princely states were incorporated into the newly created state of Orissa.

Since independence Orissa has been one of India's poorer regions, largely due to its poor soils and drought-stricken regions affecting the agricultural economy, which employs about 87 percent of the state. But at the same time population density is lower than the nation's average, and the sex ratio of men to women is better than the national average as well, indicating that women may be somewhat less disadvantaged on the whole.

The traditional economic base of the Oriyas is farming, generally wet or paddy rice. In some suitable regions double and triple cropping is possible, while in others drought in some years limits the harvest of even a single crop. Most farming today is still done on a small scale with human and animal labor rather than as large agribusinesses with mechanized plowing and high capitalization. Sugar cane, jute, coconuts, betel nuts and leaves, rape seeds, and legumes have been grown in addition to rice for generations, mostly as cash crops. More recently bananas, cardamom, cocoa, coffee, and pineapples have also been introduced as successful cash crops in some areas. Chickens, cows, goats, ducks, water buffaloes, pigs, and dogs are also plentiful in many areas, and fish are caught in rivers, coastal swamps, and flooded paddies.

While the majority of Oriyas are members of various agricultural castes, there are also castes of artisans represented throughout the region, including ironworkers, carpenters, potters, weavers, and others. The region has hosted regional markets from at least the sixth century B.C.E., which have allowed these various people to come together to sell and trade their wares.

Oriya social organization at the family level is based on the principle of patrilineal descent, whereby each individual is born into the lineage and clan of his or her father, father's father, and so on. Males also inherit their father's property almost exclusively since daughters move into their husbands' households and clans at marriage. There are three different familial organizations evident among Oriyas, including compounds with separate households for each son, large multigenerational households where all sons and their families live together, and obligatory reciprocal relations among patrilineal kin who do not live together. In the past, families that were not of the highest caste required new husbands and their families to pay a bride price to the families of their wives to compensate them for the loss of the wives' labor and to legitimate any children the couples had. Today, however, this has been replaced by the dowry system of the Brahmins, where the wife's family is obligated to give large gifts to the new

couple and the groom's family. This is sometimes described as the woman's inheritance since she could not make any claims on her natal family's resources after marriage. Since 1956 Indian law has changed and allows daughters and widows to inherit, although this practice still is not common; divorce was also legalized in that year.

Part of the identification as an Oriya is to be a Hindu, and this religion has traditionally been an important unifying feature for most of the community. Two sects, Vaishnava and Jagannatha, are particularly important, although temples for Siva, Viraja, and Shunya Parama Brahma also draw worshipers from all over the state to Bhubaneswar, Jajpur, and Joranda, respectively. Every Oriya village has a Brahman priest who assists with life-cycle rituals and other important communal, familial, and personal events; most villages also have a variety of other ritual specialists glossed in English as magicians, sorcerers, or diviners who conduct their own rituals for healing, fertility, or other purposes. The small number of Oriyas who practice Christianity, Islam, Buddhism, Jainism, or their own tribal religions generally do so in a very syncretic manner, incorporating some of these other beliefs and practices into their daily life as well.

Oroqen (Orochen, Orochon, Oroqin)

The Oroqen are a Tungusic-speaking people whose language is sometimes classified as a subcategory of Evenki, although recent research has indicated that it is more accurate to classify the two separately. They reside almost entirely in China's far-northeastern corner in the Inner Mongolian Autonomous Region, with a few scattered in Heilongjiang Province as well. Some sources also claim that there is a small population of Oroqen in Siberia, which is probable given that their historical homeland was north of the Amur (Heilong) River, the contemporary boundary between Russia and China. They fled that region in the mid-17th century to escape the onslaught of Russian colonialism. Upon their arrival in Manchu-held China, the Oroqen were separated into two units, Horse-Riding and Foot Oroqen, with the former employed as soldiers and the latter as hunters of marten, the fur of which was coveted by the Qing court.

At the time of their entry into China, the Oroqen were made up of seven patrilineal clans whose membership was handed down from father to children, which they called *mokuns*.

OROQEN

location:
China's Heilongjiang Province and Inner Mongolian Autonomous Region; possibly eastern Siberia as well

time period:
Unknown to the present

ancestry:
Proto-Tungusic

language:
Oroqen, a northern Tungusic language related to Evenki

That number gradually increased as these exogamous clans subdivided in order to provide greater choice in marriage partners; the rules of exogamy required people to marry outside their own clans. Each clan was headed by an elder male who was able to claim the respect of, and authority over, his people. Nonetheless, decision making was largely by consensus, with all adults, male and female, participating in major decisions, such as when to migrate in search of game or fish, when to go to war, and when to flee from enemies. Groups of five to seven families from the same clan generally lived in proximity to one another, hunted together, and shared all food and resources. With the introduction of shotguns, iron tools, and agriculture after the 17th century, nuclear families tended to replace these larger groups as the primary unit of production and consumption.

Traditional Oroqen life was dictated by the availability of game and fish, with groups of families migrating throughout the Greater Hinggan Mountains in search of these basic food items. Men and women both participated in hunting activities, although being especially skilled in hunting was more important for men than women. As animists, or people who worshiped spirits of the natural world, hunting was also intimately connected to their religious beliefs. For example, hunters could not make specific plans to go out on a hunt since the animals' spirits were believed to be able to read their minds and escape from them. Hunters were also forbidden from killing more animals than they could eat or from saying the names of bears, tigers, or wolves; in the same way they were forbidden from mentioning their own dead ancestors. They also ritually thanked the spirits of the animals they hunted and gave some of them a ritual burial.

The Chinese began to impose a new way of life on the Oroqen after the fall of the Qing (Manchu) dynasty in 1911. At that time local warlords recruited Oroqen men into their armies while others were settled onto agricultural plots to grow wheat and other hardy crops for the militia. This organization lasted until 1931 and the JAPANESE invasion, which hit the Oroqen even harder than any previous Chinese regime. The Japanese used some Oroqen in medical experiments and forced others to work for them. By 1945 and the Japanese surrender, the Oroqen population had been reduced to fewer than 1,000 people, and it looked as if their language and culture would die out within a generation. This has not happened, and today

their population of about 7,000 ranks them as one of the smallest ethnic groups in China, famous for bravery in fighting forest fires in the Oroqen region and for hunting skills.

See also EVENKIS; MANCHUS; RUSSIANS, ASIAN.

Osing (Jawa Osing, Orang Osing)

The Osing, or Jawa Osing, are a subgroup of the JAVANESE who reside in Banyuwangi Province in east Java. Their language, Ngoko Osing, or Bahasa Osing, is usually considered a mere dialect of Javanese and felt to be old-fashioned by speakers of more orthodox versions of the language. Generally they are culturally very similar to other Javanese populations; however, influences from the MADURESE and BALINESE have added many unique features, including Balinese-style wigs, drums, and dances and Madurese linguistic features. Even the ethnonym *Osing* points to strong connections with the Balinese, for *sing* means "denial" in Balinese and indicates the degree to which this population identifies as different from other Javanese peoples.

The history of the Osing is similar to that of the rest of Java until the early 16th century. At that time the dominant kingdom in Banyuwangi, Blambangan, which had probably reached its zenith in the early 14th century, was a vassal state of the last major Hindu kingdom on the island, Majapahit. When Majapahit was conquered by the sultanate of Demak in about 1500, much of the nobility fled to Hindu-dominated Bali, while the remaining population eventually converted to Islam. In Banyuwangi, however, Blambangan did not immediately fall to Demak or to any of the other dominant Islamic states in the region and continued its vassal relationship with Gelgel, a Balinese Hindu kingdom largely made up of migrants from Majapahit. From 1613 until 1646 the sultan of Mataram, Agung, tried several times to rid the island of the last Hindu stronghold and in so doing devastated much of the region but largely failed to change the political or religious landscape of the region. Finally, in 1767 it was a determined Dutch force that overthrew Blambangan when their Balinese protectors were engaged in their own civil war and thus unable to come to the rescue. The Osing put up a brave fight in the face of the onslaught until 1772, when they were no longer able to hold back the flood of Javanese, Madurese, and other Muslim migrants moved into the region by the Dutch. Most Osing eventually converted to the new

OSING

location:
Banyuwangi Province, Java, Indonesia

time period:
2500 B.C.E. to the present

ancestry:
Austronesian

language:
Ngoko or Bahasa Osing, an Austronesian language closely related to East Javanese

religion, although it took until the mid-19th century for the process to be complete, and even today other Javanese often associate the Osing with sorcery and other black magic because of their relatively recent conversion to Islam.

Like other Javanese, many Osing make their living through farming, mostly paddy or wet rice, raising water buffalo and other animals, and through trade; urban Osing fill the whole gamut of positions, from government and other professional roles to unskilled workers. Both farming and livestock raising are quite lucrative in Banyuwangi because of the plentiful water supply from their location adjacent to Mount Merapi. The city also has a thriving tourist industry as east Java's largest city and the final stopping point for people taking the ferry to Bali, which today takes about an hour. Osing culture itself has also been protected by the Indonesian government due to its importance in the history of Java and Bali more generally, which also brings tourists to see local dances and art and to listen to Osing music.

Ossetians (Ossetes, Ossets, Jas)

The Ossetians are an Iranian-speaking people who reside in two enclaves in the Greater Caucasus Mountains: North Ossetia, which is located in European Russia, and South Ossetia, located in the Republic of Georgia. The latter territory was the scene of fierce fighting between Ossetians and GEORGIANS in the early 1990s, and its legal status is still contested by the two sides. It is the Ossetian population in this southern territory that is the focus of this entry.

GEOGRAPHY

South Ossetia, with its capital at Tskinvali, is a 2,423-square-mile enclave surrounded by the rest of Georgia on its eastern, western, and southern borders, and by Russian North Ossetia on its northern border. The two Ossetias are connected by the Roki Tunnel, which was blasted through the Caucasus Mountains by the Soviets in the 1980s when they ruled the entire region. South Ossetia is a very high region in the southern reaches of the Greater Caucasus Mountains, with most land lying more than 3,300 feet above sea level. The rugged terrain and altitude have meant that less than 10 percent of the land is cultivated in vines, other fruit, and wheat, while animal husbandry dominates most of the rest of the productive areas. Sheep, cattle, and goats are all raised for meat, milk and dairy products, and leather.

OSSETIANS

location:
South Ossetia, in the Republic of Georgia, as well as throughout Georgia. There are also a large number of Ossetians in North Ossetia, Russia (Europe), Turkey, and Azerbaijan.

time period:
Fourth century C.E. to the present

ancestry:
The Iranian-speaking Alans and Sarmatians

language:
Ossetian, a northeastern Iranian language, said by some to be a descendant of the language spoken by the Alans

ORIGINS

Unlike many of the other groups living in the Caucasus, the Ossetians have Iranian roots and speak an Iranian language. They are thought to be the descendants of Iranian-speaking Alans who were themselves descended from the Sarmatians or perhaps even the SCYTHIANS. The Alans migrated westward on the Eurasian steppes in the first century C.E. and moved down into the Caucasus, where they had settled to the north of the Caucasus Mountains by the fourth century. During the invasions of the MONGOLS in the 13th century, some Alans fled into the mountains and established the communities that would later become the Ossetians.

HISTORY

The history of the Ossetians is hotly contested by the Ossetians themselves and by the Georgians, with the political status of the territory of South Ossetia at stake. The one fact that both sides agree on is the Iranian origins of the Ossetian people generally.

The key difference between their views on history is the time in which the Ossetian peoples moved from their home north of the Caucasus into the region of South Ossetia. The Ossetians believe their people have lived beside the Georgians for perhaps as long as 2,000 years. They also believe they have always sided with the Georgians against their common enemies, such as the Mongols, Persians, and Ottomans. They point to the Georgians' Queen Tamara of the 12th century and her Ossetian husband as a symbol of the long-lasting friendship between the two peoples. The Georgians agree that the Ossetians have an ancient nomadic heritage but that their entry into Georgian lands in the southern reaches of the Caucasus was much more recent, occurring only in the past two centuries. They argue that Ossetians tried but failed to occupy the southern Caucasus during the Mongol invasions of the 13th century. Many Georgians believe that the Ossetians finally crossed the border from North Ossetia to work on the lands of Georgians' feudal estates only in the 1860s.

In addition to these differences, the Ossetians and Georgians also view their relationships with Russia in very different ways. The Georgians were involuntarily incorporated into the czar's empire in 1801 and at the first opportunity, in 1918, declared their independence, which included the land and people of South Ossetia. The Ossetians, on the other hand, voluntarily became subjects of the czar in

Ossetians time line

C.E.

0 The Ossetians believe their ancestors migrated into the southern Caucasus at this time.

fourth century Alan tribes migrate to the Caucasus region.

12th century Georgian Queen Tamara marries an Ossetian.

13th century The Mongol invasions. The Ossetians believe that they fought with the Georgians to repel this attack; the Georgians believe the Ossetians tried to invade their territory but failed.

1774 The Ossetians voluntarily become subjects of the Russian czar.

1801 Georgia is incorporated into the czar's empire.

1860s The Georgians believe that the Ossetians crossed the border from Russian North Ossetia into Georgia to work on the farms of Georgian feudal estates.

1918 Georgia declares its independence and takes the lands of South Ossetia.

1920 South Ossetians declare their independence from Georgia and take up arms at what they believe is an illegal division of North and South Ossetia; they are crushed by the Georgian army.

1921 The Soviet Union occupies Georgia.

1922 The South Ossetian Autonomous Oblast is created in Georgian territory, which the Georgians see as an illegal action by the Russians to divide their nation.

1980s The Russians build the Roki Tunnel through the mountains connecting North and South Ossetia to facilitate troop movements.

1988 Typhoid breaks out in South Ossetia, which soon sparks protests against Georgian domination.

1989 Violence erupts in South Ossetia between Ossetians and Georgians. This is made worse when Georgia proposes a language reform program that would strengthen Georgian at the expense of various minority languages, including Ossetian.

1990 The South Ossetian Autonomous Oblast declares its independence from Georgia and seeks recognition from Moscow as the South Ossetian Democratic Soviet Republic.

South Ossetians boycott the Georgian elections, which brings nationalist Zviad Gamsakhurdia to power, and stage their own parliamentary elections.

Georgia moves to abolish the South Ossetian Autonomous Oblast as a legal entity, which sparks the beginning of the civil war.

1991 The newly formed Georgian National Guard enters South Ossetia and wreaks havoc on the night of the Orthodox Christian Christmas, January 5.

1992 A cease-fire is signed on July 14, and the Commonwealth of Independent States begins a peacekeeping mission in South Ossetia.

1996 Ludvig Chibirov is elected president of South Ossetia in elections considered illegal by the Georgians.

2001 Eduard Kokoity, a Russian citizen, is elected president of South Ossetia; he is reelected in November 2006, again without international or Georgian recognition.

2004 A Georgian attempt to regain control in South Ossetia backfires and nearly draws the region into another civil war.

2007 Violence continues in South Ossetia, considered an illegal breakaway region from Georgia. The Georgian state puts millions of dollars into infrastructural development in the sections of South Ossetia it controls in an attempt to incorporate the region into Georgia and create support for this policy.

2008 An escalation of the Ossetian-Georgian conflict leads to a Russian invasion and bombing raids in Georgia.

1774 and claim that the Russian Empire did not divide the lands of North and South Ossetia, so that the split in 1918 was an illegal land-grab by the Georgians. In 1920 the South Ossetians declared their independence from the Democratic Republic of Georgia, only to be crushed militarily by the Georgian army. Russia protested this action, which included the deaths of many Ossetians, but did nothing to stop it.

The occupation of Georgia by the Soviet Union in 1921, followed a year later by the creation of the South Ossetian Autonomous Oblast on Georgian territory, is likewise viewed very differently by Ossetians and Georgians. The Ossetians saw this as a move by their Russian allies to return to the legal status quo of the czar's days: a single Ossetia, a loyal region of the larger Russian empire. The Georgians saw both moves as illegal infringements on their rights as a sovereign state, which they sought to redress when independence came in 1991.

South Ossetia remained quiet throughout most of the Soviet-dominated 20th century, but with the loosening of central control initiated by Mikhail Gorbachev, the nationalities question emerged once again. This began in South Ossetia in 1988 when a typhoid epidemic broke out. At first the Ossetians blamed it on the generally poor state of their infrastructure and society due to Soviet domination but soon shifted blame onto the Georgians, who were seen as keeping them in a state of poverty. A year later violence between South Ossetians and Georgians erupted again on the anniversary of Georgia's brief independence in 1918 and then escalated at midyear when Georgia proposed a language reform program that would strengthen their language at the expense of various minority languages, including Ossetian.

The beginning of the 1990s saw the worst violence between Ossetians and Georgians, beginning in 1990 when the South Ossetian Autonomous Oblast declared its independence from Georgia and sought recognition from Moscow as the South Ossetian Democratic Soviet Republic. This request was rejected by Moscow, but this did not deter the South Ossetians from pursuing their nationalist agenda. They boycotted the Georgian elections later in 1990 and then staged their own in December that same year. By January 1991 the newly formed Georgian National Guard had entered South Ossetia, which they had stripped of the status of autonomous oblast, and committed atrocities while the South Ossetians were fighting for their lives from their capital, Tskinvali.

The next year and a half saw considerable violence in and around this city, with the Georgians withdrawing to the hills, largely cutting off the city, and the Ossetians holding firm in the capital itself.

The civil war ended with a cease-fire in July 1992, but the issues that sparked it in the first place have yet to be resolved. Russia has sent several thousand peacekeeping troops at a time into the breakaway region and violence has erupted several times, as recently as early 2007. The Russian presence is reassuring to many Ossetians, who look to the RUSSIANS as their only hope for maintaining their separate identity, while they are seen by many Georgians as a threat to the sovereignty of their country. The election in 2001 and again in 2006 of a Russian citizen, Eduard Kokoity, as president of South Ossetia has done little to reassure Georgians, despite the total lack of international recognition for the post of president. In addition to maintaining heavy troop numbers in the area, the Georgian government has also tried using infrastructural development and law-and-order tactics to win support from the Ossetian people. So far these efforts have had minimal success.

CULTURE

The Ossetians are linguistically distinct from most of the other citizens of contemporary Georgia, the Georgians, MINGRELIANS, LAZ, and SVAN peoples, who all share membership in the south Caucasian or Kartvelian language family. In contrast, Ossetian is an Iranian language derived from the Iranian-speaking nomads who moved south into the Caucasus from the Eurasian steppes in the centuries before the common era. Russian is a more common second language among Ossetians than is Georgian, even for those who have resided in Georgian South Ossetia for all of their lives. During the Soviet era, Russian was the predominant language in South Ossetian schools and in all areas of public administration, despite Georgian being the official language of the region.

Despite these linguistic differences, Ossetians and Georgians largely share membership in the Orthodox Christian faith, although Georgia's Orthodox Church is autonomous while most Ossetians look to the Russian Orthodox Church as their own. A small minority of Ossetians are also Muslims, having been converted along with others in the Caucasus during occupation by the Ottomans in the 16th century.

Economically, the people of South Ossetia have struggled for most of their existence. The region has also struggled for electricity and other energy sources since the civil war, when Georgia cut off supplies and forced the people to connect to Russia's electricity grid to the north. Subsistence farming on the mere 10 percent of South Ossetian territory that is suitable for agriculture is the major economic activity pursued by most South Ossetians, along with some animal husbandry in the mountains. A few have also turned to the illegal arms or drug trades to provide for their families, while the majority participate in the black market in some form or other. The Georgian government's attempt to win the hearts and minds of the Ossetians in 2004 by shutting down this black market seriously miscalculated the importance of such activities and nearly drove the two sides back to the battlefield. Many foreign economists claim that the South Ossetians' only economic asset is the Roki Tunnel, which connects Russia and Georgia, and from which they benefit greatly through customs duties.

See also GEORGIANS: NATIONALITY.

FURTHER READING

Reuven Enoch. *Two Mirrors: Georgian Events of 1988–89, as Reflected in the Georgian and Central Soviet Mass Media* (Jerusalem: Harry S. Truman Research Institute for the Advancement of Peace, Hebrew University, 1998).

Ostiak   *See* KHANT.

Ostyak   *See* KHANT.

Other Backward Classes (OBC)

Since the colonial era in India, various individuals and organizations have tried to eliminate some of the worst consequences of the hierarchical caste system, as well as inequalities based on economic class and political disenfranchisement. One of the tactics used by the Indian government since independence in 1947 is a policy of positive discrimination in which members of groups classified as SCHEDULES TRIBES and SCHEDULED CASTES, those once considered Untouchables and currently called Dalits, have a certain number of state and national parliamentary seats, university places, and public-sector jobs reserved only for them.

Another group of relatively impoverished and disenfranchised people is made up of those who come from the lowest of the *varna* castes, those considered to have sprung from the body of the first human being, the Shudras. In addition, those Dalits who converted to religions other than Hinduism and some nomadic castes and tribes have received special treatment based on social position. This combination of three groups has been categorized by the Indian constitution of 1949 as Other Backward Classes (OBC). They currently make up about 50 percent of India's population and receive 27 percent of the reserved parliamentary seats, university places, and public-sector jobs. As is the case with this reserve system for the Scheduled Tribes and Castes, urban middle-class members of this special group tend to receive most of the benefits while the poor remain deprived and unrepresented.

There have been a number of attempts in India to define and clarify what the constitution means when it refers to "socially and educationally backward classes." A backward-class commission was first established in 1953 and made its final report in 1955. It created a list of 2,399 backward castes and communities, made a number of suggestions for the criteria for classification, and recommended solutions. However, the commission's report was rejected by the government, and few decisions were made. A second commission established in 1979 submitted its report in 1980. This report estimated that the OBCs made up about 52 percent of the population, although this number has been criticized as being too high, with 32 percent being postulated by the analysts of the National Sample Survey. This report also recommended that the reservation system for parliamentary, university, and public-sector places be set at 27 percent for this group and established the 11 criteria upon which membership in the OBC category should be based. The 11 criteria were further subdivided into social, educational, and economic headings, and a point system was devised in which the total for all criteria added up to 22. Those groups with a backwardness score of 11, or 50 percent of the total, were considered by this commission as included in the OBC. Using this system, the commission found that 3,743 castes and other groups should be so classified.

OTHER BACKWARD CLASSES

location:
India

time period:
Unknown to the present; the category was codified in the 1949 Indian constitution and has been reiterated ever since.

ancestry:
Mixed

language:
Hundreds of different languages

P

Paharis

The Paharis are largely Hindu peasants who live in the Himalayan region of India and Nepal, though there are a few Muslim subgroups as well. The term *Pahari,* meaning "of the mountains" in Hindi, is a collective term for a wide variety of ethnic, regional, and caste groups. Region is more important in India than in Nepal for distinguishing separate subgroups of Paharis, such as Himachal Pradesh's Gaddi and Sirmuri groups and Uttar Pradesh's Jaunsaris and Garhwalis, but in both countries there are significant differences based on caste that remain central to subgroup identities.

The most likely origins of the contemporary Pahari population are migrations of INDO-ARYANS from the Indo-Gangetic Plain and into the mid-elevations of the Himalayas; the higher elevations are inhabited by Tibeto-Burman populations who may have prevented the Paharis from advancing beyond the range of about 7,000 feet above sea level. Linguistic evidence indicates that the first wave of migrations may have occurred as early as 3,000 years ago, and contemporary ethnographic work points to migrations as recent as 300 years ago. This pattern of migration was probably very slow, with small communities and even individual families generally making decisions to migrate based on a variety of factors, including population pressure, famine, plague, natural disasters, and war. The largest number of migrants may have moved from the plains into the mountains between 1000 and 1600, coinciding with the Mus-

lim invasions of territory that is today northern India and Pakistan. In addition to these migrations from lowlands to highlands, the Paharis also frequently moved within the narrow belt of territory, about 50 miles wide, but about 1,000 miles long, which makes up their mountain homeland. Finding new pasturage and escaping from ethnic or other conflicts or from natural disasters necessitated relatively frequent moves of both long and short distances. However, there are language and cultural differences that indicate there was more interaction and migration between central and eastern Pahari populations, including the Nepalese in the east, than between central and western ones.

The Indian Pahari region, although nominally under the control of the Mughal and other northern Indian empires and dynasties, was largely autonomous under a wide variety of princely states and kingdoms until Indian independence in 1947. In Nepal the kingdom of the GURKHAS and later the Nepalese under the Shah dynasty unified much of the territory into a single state that included part of the Pahari belt. The British nominally included the region in the larger Indian colony, collected tribute and taxes, and solidified the border between Nepal and India, but for the most part the Pahari communities continued to live much as they had done for centuries. Since independence the Paharis have been divided into different Indian states, including Kashmir, Himachal Pradesh, and Uttar Pradesh; they have also been divided between India and Nepal.

PAHARIS

location:
The outer Himalayan region of India and Nepal

time period:
Probably about 1000 B.C.E. to the present

ancestry:
Indo-Aryan

language:
A variety of Pahari dialects of Indo-Aryan languages

Pahari culture is in many respects similar to that of its lowland Hindu neighbors, but there are some important differences in terms of social organization, religious practice more generally, and gender roles. Probably the most commented-on difference between Paharis and lowland Hindus is the recognition of just two caste distinctions, high caste and low caste, or SCHEDULED CASTES. The dominant high-caste category, at about 90 percent of the population, generally comes from the Rajputs and Brahmins and makes up the large agricultural class as well as the small priestly and professional one, while those in the Dom, or Scheduled Castes, are primarily artisans, including blacksmiths, weavers, potters, and others. Unlike the rest of India, there are no members of the merchant, or Vaishya, caste or any Shudras, sometimes called "clean" artisans. There are also relatively few ranks internal to the major categories of twice-born and Dom.

Hinduism more generally is also different among the Paharis than in the lowlands of India. For example, regardless of caste membership, there is little difference in religious belief or practice, as opposed to that in the lower elevations, where Brahmins tend to practice a much more textual form of the religion based on the great Sanskrit works while others engage in more folk practices. In addition, few Paharis follow the strict dietary restrictions of orthodox Hinduism; the one exception is the avoidance of beef, but most engage in animal sacrifice, especially of buffalo. Brahmin priests are relatively less important in the completion of many rituals, while diviners, sorcerers, and shamans are relatively more important than elsewhere. Marriage rules are also quite different since, at least in the past, fraternal polyandry, in which a group of brothers marry just one woman, was a common form of marriage to avoid dividing up small family fields and other property. Certain aspects of marriage ceremonies also differ from those requiring strict Sanskritic rituals to be performed. Many other ceremonies, including life-cycle and death rites, are also performed quite differently and in a distinctly Pahari manner, which, according to most Hindu outsiders, is unorthodox at best and illegitimate at worst.

A final set of differences between Pahari society and that of more orthodox Hindu societies further south concerns the place and role of women. Pahari women are generally in a better social position than their lowland linguistic and religious cousins for a number of reasons. First, dowry, the elaborate and expensive gifts a bride's family must present to the groom's upon the marriage of their daughter, is generally not given at all and, where it is, requires more token and reciprocal gift giving than elsewhere. Women are also never secluded but free to participate not only in agricultural life but also in singing, dancing, and other communal festivities that often exclude women in lowland regions. Relations between the sexes also tend to be more informal than in the lowlands, freeing both men and women from the gossip of others.

See also HINDI.

FURTHER READING

Gerald D. Berreman. *Hindus of the Himalayas: Ethnography and Change,* 2nd ed. (New York: Oxford University Press, 1997).

Pakistanis: nationality (people of Pakistan)

Pakistan is a new nation formed from the partition of India as the British pulled out of their crown jewel of a colony in 1947. The two countries have been at war of the hot or cold variety for the past 60 years.

GEOGRAPHY

Bounded by Iran, Afghanistan, China, and India, Pakistan stretches from the Himalayas to the Arabian Sea. Pakistan's capital, Islamabad, rests in the northwestern part of the country, where the climate is desert-like and very warm. Politically, Pakistan is divided into four provinces, a capital territory, and federally administered tribal areas. Additionally, Pakistan exercises de facto jurisdiction over selected western parts of the Kashmir region.

INCEPTION AS NATION

Pakistan developed its first semblance of nationalism from the seventh century C.E.: Islamic rule prevailed in northern India for more than 700 years and divided the Indian population by religion. Islamic rule, instituted by the Muslim Mughal Empire, was brought to an end in 1800 with the beginning of British occupation in India. This left a disaffected and angry Muslim population who feared lack of representation in an increasingly Hindu political environment.

In a measure to help unify the Muslim communities throughout India, Sir Syed Ahmad Khan created the Muhammadan Anglo-Oriental College in 1865. The college was originally

PAKISTANIS: NATIONALITY

nation:
Islamic Republic of Pakistan, Pakistan

derivation of name:
The name *Pakistan,* meaning "land of the pure," is of Urdu origin. First published in the 1933 pamphlet *Now or Never* by Chaudhry Rahmat Ali, *Pakistan* was used as the name for Muslim portions of the subcontinent. More specifically, Pakistan referred to the following regions: Punjab, Afghania, Kashmir, Sindh, and Baluchistan.

government:
Federal republic

capital:
Islamabad

language:
Despite the fact that it is not spoken by the majority, Urdu (8 percent) remains Pakistan's official language. The most widely spoken language is Punjabi (48 percent), followed by six additional unofficial languages: Sindhi 12 percent, Seraiki 10 percent, Pashtu 8 percent, Baluchi 3 percent, Hindko 2 percent, Brahui 1 percent.

religion:
Muslim 97 percent (Sunni 77 percent, Shia 20 percent); Christian, Hindu, and other 3 percent

earlier inhabitants:
Harappans, Indo-Aryans, Persians, Greeks, Scythians, Parthians, Kushans, Pashtuns, Arabs, Turks, and Mughals

(continues)

**PAKISTANIS:
NATIONALITY**
(continued)

demographics:
Punjabis 44.68 percent,
Pashtuns 15.42 percent,
Sindhis 14.1 percent,
Seraikis 10.53 percent,
Muhajirs 7.57 percent,
Baluchi 3.57 percent and
others 4.66 percent

Pakistanis: nationality time line

B.C.E.

2500–1600 Present-day Pakistan is the site of the ancient Indus Valley civilization, which boasts cities such as Mohenjo-Daro and Harappa.

327 Alexander the Great conquers the region, including Pakistan, a satrap of the Persian Empire. Alexander is badly injured in his quest to conquer Pakistan.

C.E.

100–200 North Pakistan is the heartland of the Kushan empire, formed by Yuezhi invaders from Central Asia.

700 First Muslim conquests in Baluchistan and Sindh, followed by increasing Muslim immigration from the west.

1206 The Delhi sultanate is established, stretching from northwest Pakistan and across northern India.

1500 The Sikh religion develops in the area of Punjab.

1500–1600 Lahore serves as the temporary capital of the Mughal Empire, which stretches across the entire northern half of India.

1843–49 The regions of Sindh and Punjab are annexed by the British and incorporated into British India.

1900 Canal irrigation projects in West Punjab and northern India draw immigrants from the east as agriculture and cotton production increase.

1906 The All-India Muslim League is established and led by Mohammed Ali Jinnah.

1933 The name *Pakistan,* meaning "Pure Nation" in Urdu, is invented by Choudhary Rahmat Ali to represent the regions of Punjab, Afghania, Kashmir, Sindh, and Baluchistan. Muslims within British India begin to campaign for secession and the establishment of an independent territory.

1940 India's Muslim League endorses the concept of a separate nation for Muslims in the Lahore Resolution.

1947 Independence from Britain is achieved, and India is partitioned to create present-day Pakistan (formerly East and West Pakistan). Large-scale and violent cross-border migrations of Muslims, Hindus, and Sikhs follow, and a brief border war with India ensues over the disputed region of Kashmir.

1948 Pakistan's first governor-general, Mohammed Ali Jinnah, dies.

1956 Pakistan proclaims itself a republic.

1958 Military rule is imposed by General Ayub Khan.

1965 Border war begins with India over the disputed territory of Kashmir.

1969 Following strikes and riots, power is transferred from Ayub Khan to General Yahya Khan.

1970 General elections produce a clear majority in East Pakistan for the pro-autonomy of the Awami League and in West Pakistan for the Islamic socialist Pakistan People's Party (PPP) led by Zulfikar Ali Bhutto.

1971 Following a civil war, East Pakistan secures independence and is renamed Bangladesh.

1973 Pakistan's third constitution is created, supporting a federal structure in which many powers are reserved for the provinces. However, Bhutto dismisses the constitution, revealing his preference for a powerful center without opposition in the provinces. Baluchi nationalists rebel against central control.

1977 Bhutto is overthrown in a military coup by General Zia ul-Haq following months of civil unrest. Consequently, martial law is imposed.

1978 General Zia becomes president.

1979 Bhutto is executed by hanging for alleged murder. His daughter, Benizir Bhutto, is jailed for nearly five years, most of which she spends in solitary confinement. The Islamic penal code is asserted by Zia's regime.

1980 Three million refugees arrive in the Northwest Frontier Province and Baluchistan as a result of the Soviet invasion of Afghanistan. The United States pledges to protect Pakistan militarily from the Soviets.

1981 Islamization is pushed forward, and General Zia ends the independence of the judiciary.

1985 After several years, martial law is lifted and the Pakistan Muslim League is revived.

1986 Sectarian fighting erupts between Muhajirs and Pashtuns in Karachi, Quetta, and Hyderabad.

Benazir Bhutto leads the PPP in a campaign for fresh elections.

1988 Benazir Bhutto's PPP emerges as the largest party in the general elections. As a result of the elections, Bhutto is sworn in as the country's prime minister, Ghulam Ishaq Khan becomes the president, and Nawaz Sharif forms a government of the Punjab Province.

1989 Tensions with India increase as the result of the outbreak of civil war in Kashmir. Pakistan rejoins the British Commonwealth, which it had originally left in 1972.

1990 Bhutto is dismissed as prime minister by President Ghulam Ishaq Khan on charges of corruption and incompetence. Nawaz Sharif, leader of the conservative Islamic Democratic Alliance (IDA), wins the general elections. As part of Sharif's rule, he launches a privatization and economic deregulation program. Islamic sharia law is made part of Pakistan's legal code.

1993 Khan and Sharif resign, and Benazir Bhutto and the PPP are reelected. Farooq Leghari, a member of the PPP, is elected president.

1994 Sectarian violence increases between Shia and Sunni Muslims; most of the fighting originates in Karachi.

1997 The Pakistan Muslim League and allied parties unanimously elect Nawaz Sharif as the leader of the house in the national assembly; he is sworn in as the prime minister two days later.

1998 Mohammad Rafiq Tarar is elected president. Pakistan conducts nuclear testing as a reaction to India's underground nuclear explosions. Months later, Pakistani radicals hijack a plane and attempt to land in India.

1999 The Lahore Declaration is signed as the result of a meeting between Pakistani and Indian prime ministers. The Lahore Declaration is a commitment on the part of both countries to reduce the risk of accidental or unauthorized use of nuclear weapons. Benazir Bhutto leaves Pakistan and takes up residence in Dubai.

2000 Nawaz Sharif is sentenced to life in prison on charges of terrorism and hijacking. Sharif, in efforts to escape his sentence, leaves for Saudi Arabia. Pakistani police arrest 250 members of the hard-line Sunni Muslim group, Sipah-e-Sahaaba.

2001 Pakistan's new prime minister, Pervez Musharraf, meets Indian prime minister Vajpayee in the first summit between the two neighbors in more than two years. The meeting ends without negotiations due to disagreements over Kashmir.

2002 In efforts to eradicate religious extremism, President Musharraf bans two militant groups: Lashkar-e-Toiba and Jaish-e-Mohammad. Musharraf announces that elections will be held in October 2002 to end military rule, and in a show of support, he wins another five years in office.

2003 Afghanistani authorities seize 330 rockets smuggled into the eastern province of Nangarhar from Pakistan.

Pakistan works with the United States after the September 11 destruction of the World Trade Center and has handed over 443 suspected al-Qaeda members to date.

(continues)

Pakistanis: nationality time line *(continued)*

2004 India and Pakistan commence the process of dialogue in February to resolve all outstanding bilateral issues, including Kashmir. President Musharraf rules out any shift in Pakistan's Kashmir policy, saying both New Delhi and Islamabad must assert flexibility to generate peace in south Asia.

2005 Pakistan and India agree to start a bus service between Muzaffarabad in Pakistan-occupied Kashmir and Srinagar in Jammu and Kashmir. This service is created to allow family members on opposite sides of the territory to visit one another via an entry permit system.

A major earthquake in Kashmir leaves tens of thousands dead, many more homeless.

2006 Pakistan places land mines and a fence along the Pakistan-Afghanistan border as a last resort to stop cross-border movement of terrorists.

2007 Benazir Bhutto returns to Pakistan to begin a power-sharing agreement with Musharraf.

She is assassinated on December 27.

established to provide Muslims with a Western education. To that end, the college focused on the writings of Thomas Paine, John Locke, and John Milton. As products of such teaching, a number of Muslim intellectuals agreed to form a political organization to safeguard and represent their interests in the Hindu-led Indian National Congress (INC). This organization, founded in 1906, would be known as the Muslim League. From the beginning, the Muslim League had a clear ideology, expressed in the *Green Book* written by Maulana Mohammed Ali. The *Green Book* outlined the organization's constitution and goals, most of which expressed the protection of rights for all Indian Muslims.

Within a few years, the Muslim League grew in strength and became the sole representative body for all Indian Muslims. In 1916 Mohammed Ali Jinnah became the organization's president and negotiated the Lucknow Pact with the INC, which officially recognized the principle of separate electorates and weighted representation for the Muslim community. Although the Muslim League experienced success under Jinnah's direction, disillusionment based on increasing Hindu control led to his resignation just four years later. Due to fears of unequal representation, the league's new head, Muhammad Iqbal, proposed the first Muslim request for self-determination and secession from India. The "two nation theory," the idea that Hindu and Muslim interests should be addressed separately, gained popularity among Muslims but failed to be accepted by INC leaders. Leaders of the INC, including the British, favored the idea of a united, secular, and democratic India instead.

In 1935 the Government of India Act proposed to hand over substantial power from British hands to elected Indian provincial legislatures. Consequently, the Indian National Congress assumed power in the majority of Indian provinces, leaving the Muslim League in control of only two areas: Bengal and Punjab. Indian Muslims quickly claimed that representation was unequal due to the high concentration of Muslims in areas outside Bengal and Punjab. Fearing a loss of control and representation, Jinnah returned as the Muslim League's president in 1940 and officially expressed the desire for the creation of Pakistan.

Months after Jinnah's return to the presidency, the league held a conference in Lahore, where a firm commitment for self-determination was established. The Muslim League demanded that the provinces of Sindh, Punjab, the North West Frontier, and Bengal be wholly autonomous and sovereign. The conference, which produced the Lahore Resolution, quickly became the road map for the creation of Pakistan. In the 1940s, Jinnah grew in popularity among the Muslim population and became the official leader of the self-determination movement.

By 1946 the British had neither the desire nor the military power to rule India. Jinnah knew that independence was foreseeable and alleged that he would create widespread instability if self-determination was not granted. The British recognized Jinnah's threat as credible, and political deadlock ensued in the Constituent Assembly. Soon after, Jinnah declared that the Muslim League would resort to violence to achieve the goal of Pakistan and called for a Direct Action Day in Calcutta, which led to riots and massacres throughout India. The riots were carried out by members of the Muslim League in several regions of Bengal, resulting in the ethnic cleansing of 50,000–75,000 in the Noakhali Massacre.

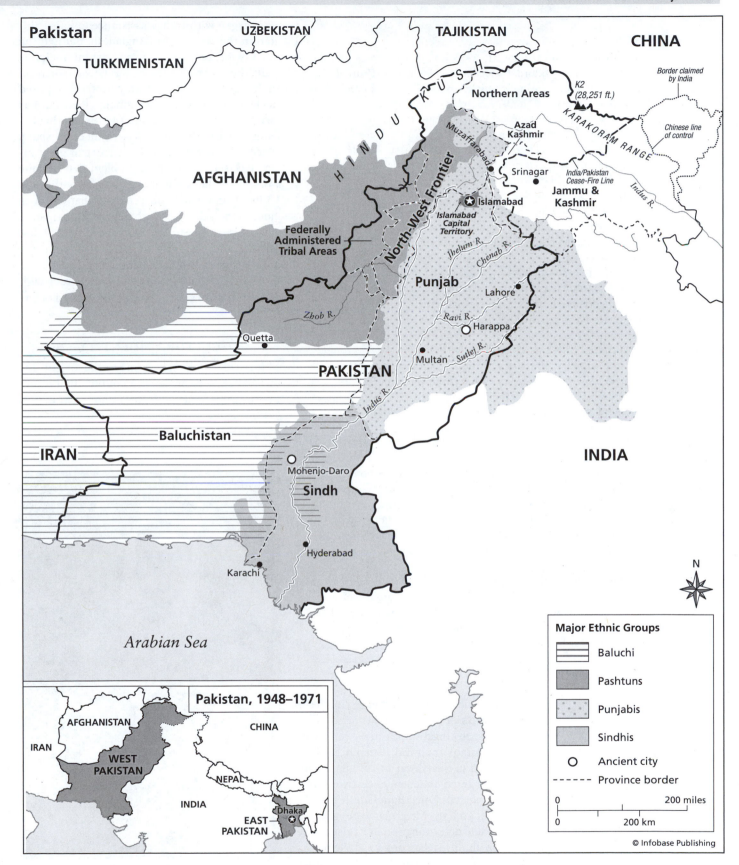

Pakistan

TURKMENISTAN
UZBEKISTAN
TAJIKISTAN
CHINA

AFGHANISTAN

HINDU KUSH

Northern Areas

Border claimed by India

K2 (28,251 ft.)

KARAKORAM RANGE

Chinese line of control

Muzaffarabad

Azad Kashmir

North-West Frontier

Federally Administered Tribal Areas

Srinagar

India/Pakistan Cease-Fire Line

Islamabad

Indus R.

Jammu & Kashmir

Islamabad Capital Territory

Jhelum R.

Chenab R.

Punjab

Zhob R.

Lahore

Ravi R.

Quetta

Harappa

Multan

Sutlej R.

PAKISTAN

Indus R.

INDIA

Baluchistan

IRAN

Mohenjo-Daro

Sindh

Hyderabad

Karachi

Arabian Sea

N

Major Ethnic Groups

Baluchi

Pashtuns

Punjabis

Sindhis

○ Ancient city

– – – Province border

0   200 miles

0   200 km

Pakistan, 1948–1971

AFGHANISTAN
CHINA
IRAN
WEST PAKISTAN
NEPAL
INDIA
EAST PAKISTAN
Dhaka

© Infobase Publishing

In response to the efforts made by both Indian Hindus and Indian Muslims, the British relinquished power on August 15, 1947. In addition to the removal of the Raj, the British partitioned India into two countries: East and West Pakistan and India. The partition not only

Benazir Bhutto

Benazir Bhutto was born on June 21, 1953, in Karachi, Pakistan, and attended Harvard and Oxford Universities. Her father, Zulfikar Ali Bhutto, was elected Pakistani prime minister in 1977 but was deposed in a military coup that same year. In 1979 he was hanged after being found guilty of conspiracy to commit murder. Benazir Bhutto moved to London with her brothers, but after one of them was murdered in 1985, she returned to Pakistan. By this time she had become chair of the Pakistan People's Party (PPP). With frequent arrests for antigovernment activity, she went back and forth between Pakistan and London many times. In 1987 she married Asif Ali Zardari in Karachi.

Bhutto became the first woman and youngest person elected prime minister of a Muslim country in 1988. She was removed from office 20 months later by President Ghulam Ishaz Khan on corruption charges. Both she and her husband were accused of money laundering through Swiss banks, and evidence against them was provided by Switzerland, Poland, and France. Zardari was also implicated in the murder of Bhutto's other brother, who had accused Zardari of corruption, during her second term.

Bhutto was reelected prime minister in 1993, but three years later she was once again removed from office by President Farooq Leghari. In 1997 she lost a reelection bid to Nawaz Sharif, whose government was promptly overthrown by the military. Zardari was imprisoned, and Bhutto left the country, living in Dubai and London with her three children. She returned to Pakistan in October 2007 when the corruption charges were dropped and she was granted amnesty by President Pervez Musharraf. She was met by large crowds of supporters and then immediately attacked by a suicide bomber who did not succeed in harming her. After launching her election bid, she returned to Dubai to visit family. In November President Musharraf declared a state of emergency, and Bhutto was placed under house arrest when she returned to Pakistan. Eventually the house arrest was dropped, and she filed her nomination for candidacy, announcing an intention to address issues of employment, education, energy, environment, and equality. She and Nawaz Sharif, another former prime minister, publicly demanded that President Musharraf withdraw the state of emergency to allow for free and fair elections.

Benazir Bhutto was shot in the head on December 27, 2007, while leaving a rally in Rawalpindi two weeks before the Pakistani election in which she was running as the lead opposition candidate. She had chaired the Pakistan People's Party from 1983 to 2007. Her eldest son, Bilawal, became the PPP's cochair with Zardari after her assassination.

increased sectarian violence but gave rise to the largest migration in history, with more than 17 million people fleeing in both directions. Citing insurmountable cultural differences, East Pakistan waged in a civil war in 1971, and with victory was granted independence from West Pakistan and was renamed Bangladesh.

Although Indian Muslims were granted their right to self-determination in Pakistan, the act of nation building has proven difficult. As a result of the partition, fighting that was once domestic has become international. India and Pakistan have engaged in war three times over the disputed region of Kashmir; one of these

wars began with India's assistance to East Pakistan in the creation of Bangladesh, but fighting quickly spread to the disputed Kashmir region as well. This embattled region has become increasingly dangerous since both countries acquired nuclear capabilities. Additionally, Pakistan has faced government instability, a problem that became worse in the 1990s. As a result of the shaky succession of governments, terrorism grew inside Pakistan's borders, a problem that became worse after the September 11 attacks within the United States. Pakistan, a country that was once close to the Taliban government of Afghanistan, gave up such ties to ally with the United States. To that end, Pakistan arrested al-Qaeda's top aide to Osama Bin Laden and recently deployed more than 80,000 troops along its border with Afghanistan in efforts to curb the growth of terrorism.

CULTURAL IDENTITY

Modern-day Pakistan, home to the ancient Indus Valley civilization, is a country that draws its cultural identity from Hindus, Muslims, Greeks, and South Asians. Most notably, however, Pakistani culture reflects the influence of

Former prime minister Benazir Bhutto in her last moments in Dubai before returning to Pakistan in late 2007; a relative is holding a Quran above her head as a blessing. *(AP Photo/Kamran Jebreili)*

the Islamic Mughal Empire. Islam is the foundation of Pakistan, and as such it enjoys a pervasive position in Pakistani culture. In the arts, Islamic influence is highly visible and can be seen in *qawwali,* the popular devotional style of singing. Islam, responsible for bringing Urdu to modern-day Pakistan, has also heavily influenced poetry. Renowned international poets such as Mirza Ghalib and Allama Iqbal both write their poetry in Urdu, the official language of Pakistan. Pakistani dress also assumes much of its influence from Islam. Both women and men, professional and working class, wear the *salwar kameez.* Although some women from Sindh Province wear the sari, the *salwar kameez* is the national dress of Pakistan.

Aside from the arts, Islam has influenced familial and social organization within Pakistan. Family organization is patriarchal, and most people live in extended families, although nuclear families are becoming more of a trend in cities. Social organization is based on kinship, and men are encouraged to marry the daughters of their father's brother. This practice, known as *beradari,* or parallel-cousin marriage in English, is a testament to the emphasis placed on men in Pakistani society.

Although Islam has contributed to the many unique facets of Pakistani culture, Hindu and British influences also remain. Pakistani wedding ceremonies and dowry practices resemble Indian Hindu traditions, while the national pastime of cricket reflects British tradition. Known for a love of sport, Pakistan won the Cricket World Cup in 1992 and placed second in 1999. In recent years Pakistani culture has changed to reflect an increasingly globalized international order. Although cultural traditions remain intact, new forms of entertainment and economic growth have had an undeniable impact. Increasing economic growth has led to a Pakistani diaspora to the West, and MTV Pakistan has created a healthy appetite for Western rock and rap music.

See also BANGLADESHIS: NATIONALITY; INDIANS: NATIONALITY; MUHAJIRS.

FURTHER READING

Lord Birdwood. *India and Pakistan: A Continent Decides* (New York: Frederick A. Praeger, 1954).
Stephen Philip Cohen. *The Idea of Pakistan* (Washington, D.C.: Brookings Institution Press, 2004).
I. Husain. *Pakistan* (Karachi: Oxford University Press, 1997).
Surendra Nath Kaushik. *Contesting Identities in Pakistan: Region, Religion, and the Nation State* (Jaipur: Pointer, 2006).
Iftikhar H. Malik. *Culture and Customs of Pakistan* (Westport, Conn.: Greenwood Press, 2006).
Jamal Malik. *Colonialization of Islam: Dissolution of Traditional Institutions in Pakistan* (New Delhi: Manohar, 1996).
A. Ramakant, K. Upadhyaya, and S. Upadhyaya. *Contemporary Pakistan: Trends and Issues,* 2 vols. (Delhi: Kalinga, 2001).
Oskar Verkaaik. *Migrants and Militants: Fun and Urban Violence in Pakistan* (Princeton, N.J.: Princeton University Press, 2004).

Palauans (Belauans, Pelewans)

Palau is a north Pacific island chain of 343 islands, divided into 16 separate states spread over at least 500 miles, from the Kayangel atoll to Helen Reef. The islands are located southeast of the Philippines and just to the west of the Federated States of Micronesia (FSM). During the colonial era they were considered part of the islands of the FSM and called the Caroline Islands.

Although the initial settlement of Palau remains somewhat unclear, the best evidence from archaeology and linguistics points to a seafaring people from eastern Indonesia as the initial population. These Malay speakers, who arrived between 4,000 and 3,000 years ago, were then joined by MELANESIANS from the region of New Guinea and POLYNESIANS from throughout the Pacific. Despite their obvious history of being able to navigate hundreds of miles of open seas in their dugout canoes, this initial population remained on Palau rather than continuing to explore the rest of the northern Pacific. The men learned to read the seasonal and migratory patterns of fish and provided food from the sea, while the women produced the bulk of the people's food calories in their taro gardens.

This way of life continued relatively unchanged for several thousand years until European colonizers arrived in the 16th century bearing diseases, firearms, Christianity, and a racial ideology that justified the mistreatment of non-European peoples. The Spanish arrived first in 1526 and named the island chain the Carolinas after Carlos I, king of Spain (and, as Carlos [Charles] V, Holy Roman Emperor). Spain was joined by Germany during the early colonial period, and then the Germans purchased the islands in 1899 and held them until 1914, when Japan invaded and annexed them during World War I. Japan held them until the United States invaded them during World War II. Finally, in 1994 Palau achieved its independence, although within the larger sphere of the U.S. defense pact.

Palauan culture today is an interesting fusion of traditional and modern ideas and

---

PALAUANS

location:
7° north of the equator in the north Pacific Ocean, southeast of the Philippines

time period:
2000–1000 B.C.E. to the present

ancestry:
Descended from Malays of Indonesia, Melanesians of New Guinea, and Polynesians

language:
Palauan, one of the two Western Malayo-Polynesian languages, related to Chamorro

practices. The indigenous culture that had developed in Palau is a complex matrilineal system in which each individual inherits membership in local and regional clans through his or her mother. The most important man in each child's life is not the biological father but the mother's brother, because he controls the wealth and power of the matrilineal clan. In addition to clan membership, all Palauans are also tied to particular villages and parcels of land, which are inherited through specific female ancestors. The last important aspect of this clan system is that it is hierarchical. Some clans are seen as more important than others because of their descent from powerful ancestors, which provides them with access to better farmland or fisheries.

Prior to the colonial system the politics of Palau was dominated by an indigenous system of government in which chiefs from each village, region, and island got together to make decisions about land tenure, justice, and leadership generally. These councils of chiefs were utilized by most of the occupying colonizers to maintain order and to try to legitimate their own domination. Local chiefs also, when possible, used the resources, development projects, and power of these outsiders to bolster their own authority over both their own people and other chiefs. One of the hallmarks of the Palauan political system is its competitive nature, which continues to see individuals, clans, villages, islands, and states competing with one another for political and economic favor within the national and global spheres. The most serious rivalry is that between the chiefs of the north and south, which continues to affect the politics of Palau to this day.

In addition to skilled fishermen and navigators, Palauan men were also excellent builders, constructing 60-foot-long war canoes and large, communal men's houses called *bai*. Without the benefit of metal tools, Palauan men cut down large palm trees, carved plank boards from the trunks, and built large houses by lashing the planks together with rope made from coconut husks.

Although men served as chiefs, this does not mean that Palauan women were without power in their nuclear or extended families. The most important relationship between a Palauan man and woman was not that of husband and wife

This men's house, from 1907, would have been used for male initiations, meetings, and other events. Today the only structures of this sort are built to attract tourists; many lack the symbolic attributes of this one, such as the image of the breadfruit tree bearing fish, which is taken from a local myth. *(Art Resource/Bildarchiv Preussischer Kulturbesitz)*

but of brother and sister because they were at the center of the matrilineal clan system. While brothers can be chiefs, it was sisters who chose the men to serve as chiefs, and traditionally it was women who controlled the clan's money. Obviously, it was also a man's sister's children who were the guarantee of the lineage and clan's future. This centrality of the brother-sister relationship has continued in Palau along with the importance of matrilineal clans more generally.

Years of colonialism and now independence have added many aspects to Palauan culture. Most apparent is the change in the economy from a fish- and taro-based subsistence economy to one in which half the workers in the country are government employees and many others work in the service industry to cater to the islands' foreign tourists. Most men can no longer read the fluctuations in the sea, and when they meet with other men to negotiate clan business, they do so in restaurants rather than in men's *bai*. In addition, these meetings do not have the political weight they once had since traditional authority is often eclipsed by that of elected officials of the state. On the women's side, some older women continue to work in their taro gardens, but most young women prefer government or service-oriented work to spending long hours standing in mud up to their waists to harvest taro. Women have also lost some of the status they had in the past because the traditional bead money they controlled has become limited in its importance to rituals such as marriage, funerary rites, and childbirth ceremonies.

A last cultural feature that colonialism and the postcolonial modern world have brought to Palau is the ability to market their "traditional" way of life to tourists. Instead of building *bai* and canoes for their traditional use for men's business in politics, fishing, and warfare, in the contemporary world these are being built as commodities to show off to tourists in exchange for money. Ritual dances and songs are also being performed as "traditional" spectacles, which tourists pay large sums of money to attend. After these performances, the tourists are then offered "traditional" wood carvings, made not as spiritual offerings or sanctified clan objects but as commodities, comparable to a T-shirt or other tourist items.

See also MICRONESIANS, FEDERATED STATES OF: NATIONALITY; PALAUANS: NATIONALITY.

FURTHER READING

Nancy Barbour. *Palau*, 2nd ed. (San Francisco: Full Court Press, 1995).

George Kate, Karen L. Nero, and Nicholas Thomas. *An Account of the Pelew Islands* (Leicester, U.K.: Leicester University Press, 2001).

Palauans: nationality (Palauans, people of Belau, people of the Black Islands, people of Palau)

GEOGRAPHY

Palau is a north Pacific island chain of 343 islands divided into 16 separate states, spread over at least 500 miles, from the Kayangel atoll to Helen Reef. The islands are located southeast of the Philippines and just to the west of the Federated States of Micronesia (FSM). During the colonial era they were connected to the islands of the FSM as the Caroline Islands. Some of the islands are volcanic, while others, such as the famous Rock Islands, are coral. The 16 states of Palau are Aimeliik, Airai, Angaur, Hatohobei, Kayangel, Koror, Melekeok, Ngaraard, Ngarchelong, Ngardmau, Ngatpang, Ngchesar, Ngeremlengui, Ngiwal, Peleliu, and Sonsorol.

INCEPTION AS A NATION

As inhabitants of the Caroline Island chain, PALAUANS experienced several waves of colonialism, beginning with the naming of the islands by the Spanish in 1526. The Spanish were soon joined by the Germans, who were far more active in pursuing trade and development in the region, although they did not legally achieve domination over the islands until Spain was forced to sell their Pacific properties following their loss in the Spanish-American War in 1899. Germany was then ousted from Palau and the Carolines more generally in 1914 when Japan invaded the island chain at the outset of World War I. The JAPANESE held onto the islands following the war as well, when the League of Nations granted them authority throughout Micronesia. The Japanese established several prosperous industries, from copra and fishing to phosphate mining, but in doing so largely utilized the local population as a slave-labor source. Their mistreatment accelerated after 1937 when Japanese civilian control passed back to the military, from which the civilians had taken over in 1922.

The final phase of the colonial period began in 1944–45 when the United States captured most of Japan's island territories during World War II. This victorious occupation was then supported by the United Nations in 1947, which granted most of Micronesia, including

PALAUANS: NATIONALITY

nation:
Republic of Palau, or Beluu er a Belau (in Palauan)

derivation of name:
From the indigenous name, Belau

government:
Republic, constitutional government in free association with the United States of America

capital:
Melekeok

language:
Palauan, Sonsoral, Tobi, Angaur, Japanese, English, Filipino, Chinese, and Carolinian

religion:
Roman Catholic 41.6 percent, Protestant 23.3 percent, indigenous Palauan Modeknegi 8.8 percent, Seventh-Day Adventists 5.3 percent, other Christian 1.5 percent, other religions 3.1 percent, unspecified or none 16.4 percent

earlier inhabitants:
None

demographics:
Palauan, a blend of Micronesian, Malayan, and Melanesian, 69.9 percent; Filipino 15.3 percent; Chinese 4.9 percent; other Asian 2.4 percent; white 1.9 percent; Carolinian 1.4 percent; other Micronesian 1.1 percent; other or unspecified 3.1 percent

Palauans: nationality time line

B.C.E.

2000–1000 People first arrive on the islands of Palau, probably from eastern Indonesia. They are joined by Melanesians from the New Guinea region as well.

C.E.

1526 Spanish explorer Toribio Alonso de Salazar discovers the Caroline Islands, naming them after Carlos I, emperor of Spain.

1860s German trade interests are established on Palau.

1880s The Yap begin quarrying stone money on Palau.

1891 Capuchin priests (the only representatives of the Spanish government) establish two churches, resulting in the introduction of the Roman alphabet.

1899 After its loss to the United States in the Spanish-American War, Spain sells the Caroline Islands to Germany, which launches a systematic program to exploit the islands' natural resources.

1914 Japan invades Palau and much of Micronesia as part of the Allied forces of World War I.

1919 After Germany's defeat in World War I, the Caroline Islands are awarded to Japan under the Treaty of Versailles. The Japanese establish a market economy and replace communal clan property ownership with individual ownership.

1944–45 The United States takes possession of the Japanese-held Caroline Islands.

1947 Following Japan's loss in World War II, the Caroline Islands become a UN Trust Territory of Pacific Islands (TTPI) administered by the U.S. military, with obligations to build infrastructure in support of eventual self-sufficiency and self-governance.

1950s Administration of TTPI is transferred from the U.S. military to the U.S. Department of the Interior. The Palau congress is chartered, establishing 16 municipalities of Palau.

1960s Two political parties are established, the Progressive Party and the Liberal Party, representing alternative views on Palau's future. English becomes the language of educational institutions.

1975 The Palau Political Status Commission is established to push for separation from Micronesia.

Palau, to the United States, much as the League of Nations had done with Japan in 1920. In a second parallel, the U.S. Navy turned the administration of the Trust Territory of the Pacific Islands over to the civilian Department of the Interior in 1951, again initiating a decade of infrastructural building and economic development. Under the U.S. administration, indigenous Palauans were trained to run their local institutions themselves and to develop a new system of government with a legislature similar to the U.S. system. The Americans also introduced a democratic system in which Palauans voted for leaders of the newly established municipalities that today have become Palau's 16 states. Within this foreign system the indigenous council of chiefs has had to share power with elected officials.

During the 1960s and 1970s the people of Micronesia became involved in Western-style political processes. The first project on the agenda was the establishment of the Federated States of Micronesia (FSM), which was hotly debated throughout the entire region. Rather than join this large federation, the Northern Mariana Islands, Marshall Islands, and Palau decided to opt out and pursue their own agendas, national or otherwise. In 1978 Palauans voted against joining the FSM, and in 1980 the citizens ratified their own constitution as a nuclear-free country. That same year Palau's first democratically elected president, Haruo Remeliik, came to power.

In order to transition out of the status of a trust territory of the United States, Palau was required to vote in favor of a Compact of Free Association in which the United States maintained a nuclear military presence on the islands and was responsible for Palau's defense for 50 years. From 1983 to 1992 the people of Palau voted seven times but could not establish the 75 percent majority required by the constitution on the issue of nuclear material. By 1986 Palau was the only remaining trust territory in Micronesia

1978 Palau votes against a constitution to create a united Federated States of Micronesia.

1980 A new Palau constitution is ratified by 70 percent of voters. Haruo Remeliik is elected president, and Palau's national flag and anthem are selected.

1983 A majority of Palauans—62 percent—vote for a Compact of Free Association with the United States, but the Palau Supreme Court rules this, and six subsequent votes, invalid because they do not meet the 75 percent majority required by the constitution on the issue of nuclear material.

1985 Palau's first president, Harua Remeliik, is assassinated, and Lazarus Salii is elected the country's second president.

1986 The Federated States of Micronesia is established, ending the TTPI. Palau is the only trust territory remaining.

1988 President Salii is found dead by apparent suicide.

1988 The strongly pro-compact Ngiratkel Etpison is elected president.

1992 Palauans pass an amendment to the constitution requiring a simple 51 percent majority on the issue of nuclear material, and the Compact of Free Association passes with 68 percent one year later.

1994 The Compact of Free Association is signed with the United States, and Palau is simultaneously declared independent.

Kuniwo Nakamura is elected president and focuses his presidency on economic development and links with Taiwan, Japan, and the Philippines.

Palau becomes the 185th member of the United Nations and the world's youngest democracy.

2001 Tommy Remengesau is elected president of Palau. He continues to strengthen economic ties with Taiwan and Palau's Micronesian neighbors.

2003 Palau joins the "coalition of the willing" in support of the U.S.-led invasion of Iraq.

2005 Palau has the highest standard of living in the Pacific region, due in part to the $12.8 million provided as aid by the United States this year under the Compact of Free Association.

because it could not attain the 75 percent majority needed to pass the nuclear issue.

Palau's road to independence continued to be fraught when its second president, Lazarus Salii, who had come to power in 1985 after President Remeliik was murdered, was found dead with a gunshot wound to the head in an apparent suicide. Shortly after, pro-compact candidate Ngiratkel Etpison was elected president, and in 1992 Palau's constitution was amended to allow a 51 percent majority vote on the issue of nuclear material, rather than the previously required 75 percent. One year later Palauans voted on the compact with the United States for the eighth time, and this time the vote for the compact passed with 68 percent of the electorate. In 1994 the Compact of Free Association was finally signed with the United States, and Palau declared its independence.

With independence and a new president, Kuniwo Nakamura, a second-generation Palauan of Japanese ancestry, Palau became free to negotiate with other countries and to join international organizations, including the United Nations. Nakamura's presidency focused on economic development and trade and tourism links with Taiwan, Japan, and the Philippines. In 2001 Tommy Remengesau was elected Palau's seventh president, and he has continued to strengthen economic ties with neighbors in the Asia-Pacific region.

CULTURAL IDENTITY

When Palauans decided against joining the Federated States of Micronesia in 1978, they used a number of local features to justify their decision. Since that time some of these same cultural features have been used to try to create a common Paluan national identity out of a number of disparate peoples all resident on the country's 343 islands.

The two most important features that swayed Palauans to remain independent were economic issues and their origin myth, which

PAMIRI

location:
The Pamir Mountains and valleys of the Gorno-Badakhshan region of Tajikistan, Afghanistan, Pakistan, and western China

time period:
At least 2500 B.C.E. to the present

ancestry:
Iranian speakers

language:
The seven Pamiri languages are all Southeastern Iranian languages: Shughni, Sarikoli, Yazgulyam, Munji, Sanglechi-Ishkashimi, Wakhi, and Yidgha.

explains the "unity within diversity" concept that underlies all Palauan nationalism. At the time of the vote in 1978, many Palauans felt that joining the much larger FSM would dilute the effects of any infusions of cash from the United States, since many believed the majority of the money would be spent in the more heavily populated regions of Pohnpei and Chuuk. There was also some feeling that being a small part of a large federation would weaken the islands' ability to attract international tourists.

Perhaps more important, some Palauans also made reference to their origin myth in their refusal to join the FSM. This myth states that long ago Palau was just one island and on that island lived a man named Uab, who grew so large and fat that all the other Palauans starved to keep him fed. In order to keep from starving to death, one day the ancient Palauans set fire to Uab. As the enormous man fell to the ground he gave one last kick, which separated the islands of Peleliu and Angaur. Then Uab's partly submerged body made up the other islands, with each island's characteristic coming from the body part that spawned it. For example, the people of Ngerchelong are believed to be very intelligent because their island formed from Uab's head, while Ngiwal produces the best crops because it formed from Uab's stomach. As this myth explains, the people of Palau believe that despite their physical separation and somewhat different characteristics, they are all unified through the sacrifice of this single man's body.

Palau's traditional religion, Modekngei, has a similar theme of unity within diversity with its core belief of "coming together as one." Some Palauans explain that this religion is a combination of Roman Catholicism, Protestantism, and indigenous Palauan beliefs and thus reinforces the idea that through diversity can come unity.

See also MICRONESIANS; MICRONESIANS, FEDERATED STATES OF: NATIONALITY; MARSHALL ISLANDERS: NATIONALITY.

FURTHER READING

Bob Aldredge and Ched Meyers. *Resisting the Serpent: Palau's Struggle for Self-Determination* (Baltimore, Md.: Fortkamp Publishing Company, 1990).

Bank of Hawaii. *Republic of Palau Economic Report* (Honolulu: Bank of Hawaii, 2000).

David Hanlon. *Remaking Micronesia: Discourses over Development in a Pacific Territory, 1944–1982* (Honolulu: University of Hawaii Press, 1998).

R. E. Johannes. *Words of the Lagoon: Fishing and Marine Lore in the Palau District of Micronesia* (Berkeley and Los Angeles: University of California Press, 1992).

Pamiri (Badakhshani, Badakhshoni, Mountain Tajiks, Pamirian Tajiks, Pamirtsy)

The Pamiri are an Eastern Iranian people who live in the Pamir Mountains of Tajikistan, Afghanistan, Pakistan, and western China. The Chinese Pamiri are referred to as TAJIKS in China. There are seven small ethnolinguistic groups that make up the larger Pamiri family: the Shughni and Yazgulyam who live primarily in Tajikistan, the Sarikoli who live primarily in China, the Munji and Sanglechi-Ishkashimi who live primarily in Afghanistan, and the Wakhi and Yidgha who live primarily in Pakistan. Most are members of the Muslim Ismaili sect, and most are rural herders whose way of life is still very traditional.

Throughout history many different outside forces have tried to centralize authority over the Pamiri, who have never had a state of their own. Persians, Arabs, TURKIC PEOPLES, PASHTUNS, RUSSIANS, and the British all tried to subdue the region and bring its people under their control. In the 18th and 19th centuries it was rulers of the Afghans and UZBEKS who fought each other in order to control the region; the British and Russians also wrangled in the region in what has come to be known as the Great Game. Most Pamiri, who reside in Tajikistan, came under Russian control by 1904 and remained there until 1991, when Tajikistan achieved its independence from the USSR. In the civil war that followed almost immediately, the Pamiri played a major role. The Pamiri political party, Laali-Badakhshan, which advocates more autonomy for the Pamiri people in the Badakhshan region, was aligned with other oppositional groups in the almost decade-long period of chaos and violence.

The Pamiri are largely agriculturalists and herders, tending herds of sheep, goats, and yaks and growing cold-resistant crops of wheat, peas, barley, and vegetables. During the Soviet era many Tajikistani Pamiri were moved out of their mountain homes and into the small agricultural region of the republic to produce cotton for the USSR. Today there are only about 120,000 Pamiri left, and their languages are all considered endangered.

Pamiri society displays greater gender equality than those of most of their neighbors. Women engage in much of the same labor as men, although they do not shear goats or work as shepherds. Men do not shear sheep and tend to leave all the milking to women. Women among the Pamiri are also much less restricted than Tajik or Pashtun women and can participate in public gatherings, work outside the home, and are not expected to cover themselves with a burka or veil. Both women and men are bound by the ties of kinship, however, and tend to live in large households containing several extended families. Marriages often take place between first or second cousins, and it is usually the woman who leaves her natal home and moves in with her husband's extended kin in patrilocal residence.

One of the centerpieces of Pamiri identity is their membership in the Ismaili faith, a form of Islam that branched off from Shiism in the eighth century. Like Shiis, Ismailis believe that Ali was the only legitimate successor to Mohammed following the death of the latter in 632 C.E. Ismailism is an esoteric form of Islam, which means that followers read the Quran for its hidden meanings and in the present tense, as if they themselves were receiving the original message from Allah. Another difference is the importance among Ismailis of educating girls and women in addition to boys and men; the third Aga Khan, the spiritual leader of the sect, even advocated that daughters should be educated first in families that cannot afford to educate sons and daughters equally. Finally, Ismailis do not meet in mosques but in informal houses of prayer; there are no mosques in the Pamiri region of Tajikistan. According to the Pamiri themselves, their ancestors converted to Ismailism when they were visited by Nasir Khusraw, a famous Persian philosopher and poet, in the 11th century. This may be an apocryphal legend connecting the Pamiri to a famous figure, as is often the case among the Turkic peoples of Central Asia and the leading Sufi mystics of the Middle Ages.

In addition to their Islamic beliefs, Pamiri also engage in a wide variety of pre-Muslim rituals and practices, many of which have had Islamic symbolism and meanings fused to them over the past 10 centuries. The most important of these practices for most Pamiri is the building of their houses, or *chids*, in the traditional way. Pamiri *chids* of today resemble those of the Zoroastrian Pamiri of 2,500 years ago and also serve as a symbol of the universe, as they have for the past 25 centuries. These houses are built of stone and plaster with a flat roof. Inside there are three separate living areas: a floor, a raised dais, and a third-floor level, which symbolize the three kingdoms of nature—animal, mineral, and vegetable. Every house also contains five supporting pillars, which today symbolize the five Zoroastrian gods and goddesses, the five members of Ali's family, and the five principles of Islam. In addition to many Zoroastrian symbols that are carved into

This Pamiri boy is standing between two of the most important features of a traditional *chid,* the twin pillars of Hassan and Hussain that serve as a gate to the main room of the house. *(OnAsia/ Agustinus Wibowo)*

these pillars and their crossbeams, the colors red and white are also displayed throughout the house; red symbolizes the Sun, blood, and fire, while white symbolizes light and milk. Other pre-Islamic rituals that continue today with Islamic features fused to them include a number of practices relating to farming, including when and how watering is done and a purifying ritual for wheat that involves the image of an ancient god. The making of bread, which was formerly the most important food eaten by the Pamiri, also required numerous rituals and prayers, especially bread made with the first batch of wheat from a harvest.

See also TAJIKISTANIS: NATIONALITY.

Pampangueños   *See* KAPAMPANGANS.

Pangan   *See* SEMANG.

Pangasinans   (Pangasinense)
The Pangasinans, or "salt makers," are the eighth-largest ethnolinguistic group in the Philippines, with more than 1.5 million people as of the year 2000. They live mostly in Pangasinan Province in the western region of central

PANGASINANS

location:
Pangasinan Province, Luzon, the Philippines

time period:
3000 B.C.E. to the present

language:
Pangasinan, a northern Philippines language in the Austronesian family

Pangasinans time line

B.C.E.

3000 The initial migration of Austronesian speakers to the Philippines, including the ancestors of the Pangasinans.

C.E.

1571 Martin de Goiti is the first Spaniard to visit the Pangasinans and begins the colonization process.

1574 After failing to take Manila, Chinese pirate Limahong tries to conquer Lingayen. He is driven out by the Spanish after six months but leaves behind the Limahong Channel, a human-made waterway that facilitates his escape.

1660 Andres Malong unites the entire western side of Luzon from Ilocos to Pampanga, including Pangasinan, in a revolt against the Spanish.

1762–63 The British occupy the city of Manila, and the Pangasinan leader Juan de la Cruz Palaris rises up against the Spanish over the issue of tribute.

1855 The Spanish complete a port at Sual, Pangasinan, using large amounts of local labor.

1891 A railway line between Pangasinan and Manila is completed.

1899 The Spanish cede the Philippines to the United States, and a local war of independence breaks out.

1901 Emilio Aguinaldo transforms the revolutionary army into a guerrilla force to fight the Americans. The guerrillas are defeated, and the Americans establish a civil government in Pangasinan in the same year.

1902 A civil U.S. administration replaces military rule upon the pacification of the independence fighters in the north.

1941 The Japanese occupy all of the Philippines; they begin on Luzon in Pangasinan.

1944 The United States retakes the Philippines; they also begin on Luzon in Pangasinan.

1945 The Philippines attains independence from the United States.

1969 The New People's Army is formed as the military arm of the Communist Party of the Philippines. In reaction to this and other threats, President Ferdinand Marcos declares martial law in 1971.

1983 Marcos has his political rival, Benigno Aquino, assassinated upon his return to the Philippines after a period of self-imposed exile.

1986 Ferdinand Marcos is deposed, and Aquino's widow Corazon Aquino comes to power.

Luzon, the northernmost large island of the Philippines, where they share many traditions with the ILOCANOS, with whom they have intermarried for many generations.

GEOGRAPHY

Pangasinan Province runs east-west and extends in a peninsula that resembles a backward Cape Cod into the China Sea on Luzon's west coast; the Cordillera Mountains are to the east of the province. The land is largely coastal plains and islands with just two seasons per year: a drier, cooler one from November to April and a warmer, wetter one from May to October. August is the wettest month, but May is the warmest. The province has a very long coastline with many small offshore islands and inlets, promontories, and beaches as well as considerable forest cover on the mainland. Tall, craggy cliffs also mark some of this region's coast, making fishing and other seafaring activities more difficult in those parts. Perhaps the most important geographic feature, besides the region's long coastline, is its location along the Manila Trench, which causes significant deep-focused earthquakes in the province along with its neighbor, La Union.

During the colonial era the region took on the name *Pangasinan*, referring to the salt-making practice of the coastal dwellers. Prior to that, however, only the coastal region bore that name, while the inland regions were called Caboloan, referring to a kind of bamboo that grew wild in the area. It was a lighter, more flexible species of bamboo than we know today and is now nearly extinct due to excessive cutting.

ORIGINS

The origins of the Pangasinans, like most AUSTRONESIANS in the Philippines, are probably in south China, from where they sailed in double-outrigger dugout canoes about 5,000 years ago to Taiwan, and then later to the Philippines and Polynesia. There is no certainty as to why this population left south China; however, archaeologists have hypothesized that it was a combination of population pressure, increased commerce coming from the Yangtze (Chang) River region of China and moving southward down the river and its tributaries, a growing demand for marine and tropical forest goods, and climate change.

Contemporary Austronesian languages can be subdivided into two distinctive groups that separate the languages of Austronesian Taiwan from those of the remainder of the family, which include all Malay and Oceanic languages. This linguistic division, in addition to several anomalies in the archaeological record, such as a lack of rice in the earliest Austronesian sites in Taiwan, indicates that the origins of the Austronesian people may have been two separate exoduses from southeast China. If these did occur, the first exodus was probably from Fujian province in China to Taiwan, which saw the rise of TA-P'EN-K'ENG CULTURE, with its distinctively marked pottery and stone tools, but without archaeological evidence of domesticated rice. The descendants of this first wave would be the contemporary speakers of Taiwan's Austronesian languages, the ABORIGINAL TAIWANESE people. The second exodus may have occurred around 3000 B.C.E., taking a second wave of Austronesian speakers from southeastern China to Taiwan and then almost immediately to Luzon in the Philippines around the same period. This second wave, with its its red-slipped pottery, may also have been the ultimate source of the LAPITA CULTURE.

HISTORY

When they arrived in the Philippines about 3000 B.C.E., the Austronesian speakers would probably have met small bands of people who had already been residing on the islands for approximately 20,000 years. The hunting-and-gathering AETA peoples, as they are now called, probably lived in the most productive areas of the country—the coastlines, valleys, and lower hills—in very small, impermanent settlements. With their ability to grow their own crops, the incoming Austronesians were able to maintain significantly higher population densities than the Aeta and thus to push the hunter-gatherers into the more marginal highland forests and mountaintops, where they still live today. The numerically and technologically stronger agriculturalists also seem to have lent their language to the Aeta, all of whom today speak Austronesian languages rather than the more ancient languages they would have brought with them in their much earlier migrations.

Pangasinan history as we know it began in 1571 with the arrival of the Spanish colonizers and missionaries. Prior to that year the people of the region had extensive trade contact with the Chinese, who called the region Feng-Shia-Shih tan, and with the JAPANESE, as well as with the Aeta and other highlanders on Luzon. Most scholars believe the Pangasinans lived similarly to most other peoples on the island, engaging in shifting agriculture and trade and practicing an animistic religion with beliefs in spirits and ghosts.

Martin de Goiti, who arrived in the archipelago with Juan de Salcedo and Legazpi, was the first of the three Spanish conquistadores to travel to Pangasinan, which he did in 1571 via his conquered lands in Pampanga. Although the colonization process began at that time, it took another 40 years for the region to be declared a province of the Spanish colony; the territory it encompassed then was considerably larger than it is today since it also included parts of the land that was later carved out as the separate provinces of Zambales, La Union, and Tarlac. Lingayen was the provincial capital and housed the Spanish government and its local collaborators. This city was not only of interest to the Spanish, however, because in 1574 it was attacked by the Chinese pirate Limahong, who held it for about six months before escaping through the Limahong Channel, a human-made waterway that had been cut out using local forced labor.

In addition to the Chinese, the Spanish also had to contend with a local population who often fought back against the excesses of the tribute system, forced labor, and lack of liberty associated with the colonial regime. In 1660 a movement by Andres Malong that was to unite the entire western side of Luzon from Ilocos to Pampanga had to be forcibly put down by Spanish soldiers. Juan de la Cruz Palaris again rose up against the Spaniards in 1762 over the issue of tribute; for two years his revolt forced the Spanish to engage militarily in Pangasinan, Pampanga, and other provinces of northwestern Luzon.

The region continued to be central to the plans of a variety of external rulers for the next 200 years. The Spanish opened the region to considerable agricultural development throughout the 19th century, encouraging migrants from Ilocos Norte and Sur with the completion of a port at Sual in 1855 and a railway line to Manila in 1891. As a result, the province was one of the top rice-producing regions of Luzon. When the Filipinos rose up against their Spanish masters in the last days of the 19th and the early days of the 20th centuries, Pangasinan was once again very important to both sides. It was also there that Emilio Aguinaldo transformed the regular revolutionary army of the Philippines into guerrilla units to carry on the fight against the American forces who entered the archipelago in 1901. After their air raid of Clark Air Base in Pampanga Province, the Japanese assault on Luzon began in the Lingayen Gulf; they landed on White Beach in December 1941. Four years later, the Americans also attacked Luzon from the Lingayen Gulf, choosing San Fabian as the landing point from which they began the reconquest of the island and the entire archipelago.

CULTURE

At the start of the colonial period the Pangasinans were agriculturalists who grew wet rice in well-irrigated fields, fished along the coast, hunted, and traded with local tribes and overseas merchants. Their most important trade good was salt, which was made in salt beds along the shore that used solar evaporation. Today rice agriculture continues to be extremely important, as do shrimp and fish farming in human-made ponds in the wetlands along the Lingayen Gulf. The people are known for their craftsmanship in making hats, bricks, and other pottery objects, and in metalworking. Due to the Pangasinans' long history of trade with the Chinese, there is a large Chinese-Mestizo population in the region, much of whom has worked in trade for many centuries.

At the start of the Spanish colonial period, most lowland Filipinos converted to Roman Catholicism within about a century, and the Pangasinans were no exception. While many regions of the country took particularly to the cult of Jesus and his wounds and today hold elaborate reenactments of the crucifixion and other moments in Jesus' life, the Pangasinans are known for their devotion to Mary. The best-known church in the province is Manaoag, dedicated to the Virgin Mary, with a shrine that continues to attract busloads of pilgrims daily. One hypothesis for this local adaptation is its connection to local myths and legends about a female folk hero, Princess Urduja, who ruled this group in prehistoric times. When the Spanish missionaries learned of this folk heroine, they connected her to their stories of Mary as a way of attracting local converts, and thus devotion to Mary became inevitable.

In addition to this particular form of Catholicism, the Pangasinans also engage in a variety of pre-Christian practices. The most important of these is Pista'y Dayat, which takes place each May in the towns along the Lingayen Gulf; it is a way of giving thanks to the sea for its yearly bounty. Parades, dances, music, and other performances plus boat painting and sand sculpture contests all continue into the present as a way of showing the spirits of the sea that people do not take their livelihoods for granted.

FURTHER READING

Rosario Mendoza Cortes. *Pangasinan, 1572–1800* (Quezon City: University of the Philippines Press, 1974).

———. *Pangasinan, 1801–1900: The Beginnings of Modernization* (Detroit: The Cellar Bookshop, 1991).

———. *Pangasinan, 1901–1986: A Political, Socioeconomic, and Cultural History* (Detroit: The Cellar Bookshop, 1991).

Papua New Guineans: nationality
(New Guineans, Papuans, people of Papua New Guinea)

The people of Papua New Guinea come from more than 800 different ethnolinguistic groups and generally identify with these local cultural and linguistic groups much more than with the larger national community.

GEOGRAPHY

Papua New Guinea (PNG) is located on the eastern half of the island of New Guinea, the second-largest noncontinental island in the world after Greenland; the other half is made up of the Indonesian province of West Papua. Along the shoreline of PNG there are also many other smaller islands and atolls, such as New Britain, New Ireland, and Bougainville, which are governed from the country's capital at Port Moresby in the southeast.

New Guinea is an extremely rugged island with a range of mountains down the middle known as the Highlands. The peaks and valleys of this area are forested and extremely difficult to traverse, which has made the island the most diverse cultural and linguistic place in the world. Even today, after many decades of colonial and postcolonial centralization, PNG still maintains at least 820 different language groups from many different, unrelated language families.

The climate is tropical, with the lowlands and coast getting extremely hot in summer, while temperatures on the highest mountains remain temperate throughout the year. Rains can fall at any time throughout the year, but

On important Christian holidays, Our Lady of Manaoag church attracts worshippers and pilgrims by the thousands, as is the case with this Easter procession in 1997. *(OnAsia/Ben Davies)*

Papua New Guineans: nationality time line

B.C.E.

68,000–56,000 Contested dating of some archaeological sites in New Guinea.

45,000 Date used by more conservative archaeologists to mark the establishment of human cultures in New Guinea/Sahul.

10,000 New Guinea and Australia are separated by rising sea levels.

7000 For some Papuans, agriculture first begins to replace foraging.

1600 Austronesian speakers settle New Guinea's north coast and coastal islands.

C.E.

1526 Jorge de Meneses, a Portuguese sailor, accidentally comes upon the main island. He names it after the texture of the inhabitants' hair: *Papua* means "land of fuzzy-haired people."

1546 Spaniard Inigo Ortiz de Retes names the other main island New Guinea because he perceives a resemblance to the people from the Guinea coast of Africa.

1873 The capital city of Port Moresby is named after English explorer Captain John Moresby, who maps the southeast coastline in the 1870s.

1884 The island is divided as Britain establishes control over the southeast and Germany annexes the northeast part of New Guinea; the Dutch control the western half of the island.

1906 The southern, British half of the island is transferred to Australian control.

1914 Australia captures German New Guinea, which it occupies in the aftermath of World War I.

1921 The League of Nations grants a mandate to Australia to govern the former German territory in New Guinea; it remains separate from the Australian southern territory on the island.

1933 Gold prospectors enter the New Guinea Highlands and find more than a million people living in areas that had been considered devoid of significant human population.

1942 During the Kokoda Track Campaign, around 1,000 Australian soldiers and their Papuan porters, guides, and assistants defeat a Japanese force at least five times larger during the course of seven months of extreme hardship in the Highlands.

1949 Australia joins its two colonial territories on New Guinea into one colony called the Territory of Papua New Guinea.

1954 The first aerial survey shows several Highlands valleys with a joint population of more than 100,000 people; these regions had previously been completely unknown to the colonizers.

1975 Papua New Guinea attains independence from Australia.

1988 A secessionist civil war erupts on the island of Bougainville, during the course of which at least 20,000 people die.

1997 The secessionist war is ended in favor of Papua New Guinea.

PAPUA NEW GUINEANS: NATIONALITY

nation:
Independent state of Papua New Guinea (PNG)

derivation of name:
The name *Papua* was given to the island by Portuguese sailor Jorge de Meneses in 1526; it means "land of fuzzy-haired people." Twenty years later, Spanish explorer Inigo Ortiz de Retes gave it the name *New Guinea*, based on his perception that the island's black inhabitants resembled those of Guinea in West Africa.

government:
Constitutional monarchy with parliamentary democracy; Queen Elizabeth II is the head of state, while the government is headed by a prime minister.

capital:
Port Moresby

language:
Official languages are English, Tok Pisin or Melanesian Pidgin, and Motu. Also, there are more than 820 native languages.

religion:
Christianity, mainly Roman Catholic and Lutheran, plus about 35 percent of the population who continue to practice their indigenous religions

earlier inhabitants:
Papuans were the earliest inhabitants of the island; they were followed by Austronesian speakers.

demographics:
Speakers of Papuan, Micronesian, and Polynesian languages all live in PNG; the Papuan speakers are often classified as Melanesians. There are more than 1,000 different ethnic groups.

December to March is the wettest period. While the difficult terrain makes large-scale agriculture difficult, subsistence agriculture has been a way of life for most peoples here since between 7000 and 5000 B.C.E., making the Papuans one of the earliest peoples to have developed agriculture independently.

INCEPTION AS A NATION

Although New Guinea has been inhabited for approximately 60,000 years, there was no form of centralized political authority on the island until the colonial period in the late 19th century. In 1828 the Dutch were the first to establish any kind of European presence on New Guinea, but they were not able to establish their first permanent colonial post on the western side of the island until 1898. On the eastern side the British surveyed the southern coast in the 1870s, and within a decade coconut plantations had been established on the islands of New Britain and New Ireland. In 1884 Germany and Britain divided the eastern half of the island into two separate colonial spheres, with the German-administered sector experiencing greater colonial activity, especially the development of plantations around Madang and the northern coastal islands.

In 1906 Britain turned its New Guinea colony over to the newly federated state of Australia to administer, but economic development remained relatively slow. With the beginning of hostilities in World War I, Australia occupied the German territories, a move that was legitimated by the League of Nations in 1921 when it granted the territory to Australia as a mandate. Despite Australia's possession of both the northern and southern portions of eastern New Guinea, however, these territories were not joined together until after World War II. During the interwar years the northern colony continued to outpace the south in terms of economic development, based both on the discovery of gold in the northern Highlands and on the poor economic policy of the Papuan lieutenant governor, Sir Hubert Murray.

During World War II the JAPANESE occupied most sections of the island until they were finally pushed out by a joint Australian-Papuan force in 1942. Following the war Australia finally brought its two New Guinea colonies together under one administration. The colonial economy also improved somewhat with the development of small landholdings in cocoa and coffee, while the capital at Port Moresby expanded exponentially with an influx of laborers from the Highlands and other coastal regions.

Following the trend in the rest of the colonial world, Papua New Guinea achieved independence from Australia gradually, with self-government coming in 1973 and complete independence two years later. Immediately there were attempts at secession in Bougainville and the former southern colonial region of Papua; both of these were quelled through the creation of relatively strong provincial governments. However, agitation for secession recurred in Bougainville in the late 1980s, and in 1990 this island declared itself fully independent. No other country recognized this independence, and after a nearly 10-year civil war, the country was once again unified in 1998. Bougainville has retained much of the autonomy it won during the war and even elected its own president in 1999 but continues to remain within the sphere of the government of PNG.

The economy of PNG remains almost as weak and decentralized as it was during the long and chaotic colonial period, and Australia continues to provide about 20 percent of the national budget in aid. Furthermore, about 85 percent of the country's 5.8 million people still practice subsistence agriculture, growing just enough food to feed their families and to participate in regional exchange networks for purposes of developing prestige. The country is rich in natural resources, including timber and minerals, but most of the wealth flows onto the global market immediately as unprocessed raw materials rather than as value-added manufactured products. Coffee and cocoa, which are still grown primarily on small individual or clan-owned plots of land, also contribute to the national economy. Nonetheless, most people continue to live on about $580 per year.

CULTURAL IDENTITY

Most commentary on the contemporary state of PNG points to the woeful lack of national cultural identity to unify the entire country. Like many other postcolonial countries, PNG emerged in a context in which a unified nation state was entirely foreign to most of its new citizens. At independence a core group of Papuan elites, who had been educated in mission or state schools and had worked for the Australian colonial apparatus or the military, understood the concept of centralized political authority, bureaucratic norms, and other modern political processes. For the majority, however, who lived in small, rural communities and actively competed with one another for the nonbinding position of local Big Man, an impartial bureaucracy and centralized authority were anathema. Over the past 30 years of independence PNG's national governments

Most coffee grown in PNG is processed by small growers and cooperatives, such as this one in Goroka in the Eastern Highlands. *(OnAsia/Tom Greenwood)*

have tried to create pan-PNG institutions, beliefs, festivals, rituals, and identity, but generally they have failed. The most obvious symbol of this failure was the nine-year civil war on Bougainville in the 1980s and 1990s, but there are many other signs of lack of national identity as well. One of these is the failure of most political candidates to bother campaigning outside their own locality since local support is the only path to success in the "first past the post" voting system adopted by the newly independent PNG in the 1970s.

FURTHER READING

Robert J. Foster. *Materializing the Nation: Commodities, Consumption, and Media in Papua New Guinea* (Bloomington: Indiana University Press, 2002).

Donald Craigie Gordon. *The Australian Frontier in New Guinea, 1870–1885* (New York: Columbia University Press, 1951).

R. J. May. *The Changing Role of the Military in Papua New Guinea* (Canberra: Australian National University, 1993).

Naomi M. McPherson, ed. *In Colonial New Guinea: Anthropological Perspectives* (Pittsburgh: University of Pittsburgh Press, 2001).

Otto I. M. S. Nekitel. *Voices of Yesterday, Today, & Tomorrow: Language, Culture, and Identity* (New Delhi: UBS Publishers' Distributors Ltd., 1998).

Andrew Strathern and Pamela J. Stewart, eds. *Kuk Heritage: Issues and Debates in Papua New Guinea* (Townsville, Australia: James Cook University, 1998).

Parni   *See* PARTHIANS.

Parsees   (Parsis, Zoroastrians)

The Parsees are immigrants from Persia who left their homeland after 651 C.E., when the last Zoroastrian king, Yazdagird III, was overthrown by the Muslim Arabs. At that time numerous Zoroastrian communities fled their homeland rather than submit to conversion to Islam. Many took the Silk Road into China, where they continued to live as traders and Zoroastrians until about the 10th century, while others eventually made their way into India. The exact date of their arrival remains contested but is often posited as 716; some sources date this entry as late as 936.

The early Parsees worked largely as agriculturalists, mostly as tenants on Hindu-owned lands or on marginal land given to them by their Hindu hosts. During the height of the British colonial period in the 18th and 19th centuries, many Parsees began to move into professions that were closed to Hindus due to religious and caste prohibitions. By 1750 much of the rural Parsee population in Gujurat had moved into Bombay, today's Mumbai, to work in a wide variety of professions. The first Indian surgeons, lawyers, pilots, and even members of the British Parliament were Gujurati Parsees. Others opened shops and factories or worked in international trade, finance, and the civil service. As a result, three of the largest industrial families in India—the Wadias, Tatas, and Petits—were Parsees, and much of the rest of the community was also relatively well off by the mid-20th century and the time of Indian independence. Since then, however, the community has experienced much out-migration to Britain, the United States, and Canada, providing less entrepreneurial capital and fewer opportunities for economic growth. The Parsee death rate has also been far higher than the birth rate, leading to a significant decline in the community's numbers since independence. Today a few families remain large landowners in Mumbai and other cities, but in general the community does not dominate the upper echelons of the Indian economy as it once did.

Despite living in India for more than 1,000 years, the Parsees have not adopted any aspects of the Hindu religion or the related caste system, and most remain in their endogamous community, marrying other Parsees and living in Parsee estates. Nuclear families are the dominant household style, although in the past lineages and clans were important social units created through the principle of patrilineal descent. Membership in these large, kin-based units was determined by one's father's line of descent; clans were also ranked hierarchically, with priestly clans being superior to all others, much like the Brahmins in the Hindu system, and it was forbidden for individuals from these priestly families to marry individuals from outside their priestly caste. Aside from this prohibition, which is no longer in force today, there were very few other restrictions to marriage, perhaps due to the small size of the community. Both parallel and cross first cousins were allowed to marry, so that a woman could marry a son of either her mother's brothers and sisters or her father's brothers and sisters. This is almost unheard-of in most patrilineal systems, where the father's brother's children would be strictly prohibited marriage partners as members of the same lineage. There was also no specific prohibition of marriage between the generations, so that an uncle could marry his niece or an aunt her nephew; this was an extremely rare form of marriage but not unheard-of.

PARSEES

location:
Mumbai and other large cities of India and Pakistan, plus a diaspora throughout the world; the small number of Zoroastrians in Iran today are not considered Parsees

time period:
Possibly 716 C.E. to the present

ancestry:
Persian

language:
A Gujurati dialect and English

Bombay's Tower of Silence in the 19th century, shown, was much less grand than that which stands in postcolonial Mumbai today; however, the ever-present vultures remain. *(Art Resource/Anonymous)*

PARTHIANS

location:
Homeland in what is now Iran, with an empire that spread from Armenia to Pakistan

time period:
247 B.C.E.–224 C.E.

ancestry:
Indo-Iranian

language:
Greek and, later, Latin were the official languages of the empire, while Parthian, a northwestern Iranian language, was the language of daily living. It was written in the Aramaic alphabet and contained many loanwords from this language.

The defining feature of the Parsees is their adherence to Zoroastrianism, the religion of the ancient Persians of both the Achaemenid and Sassanian empires. Like these ancient societies, contemporary Parsees continue to use the ancient liturgical language, Avestan, although some Zoroastrian literature is also written in Pahlavi or Middle Persian. They believe in the creator god Ahura Mazda and follow the prophet Zoroaster, who may have lived sometime between the 13th and seventh centuries B.C.E. The underlying principle of their religion is the belief that the world is dominated by the competing principles of good and evil, represented as Spenta Mainyu the good spirit and Angra Mainyu the hostile one, both the offspring of Ahura Mazda, and that this dualism is part of all world history. There are also a number of other supernatural beings, *yazatas*, which came out of the early Indo-Iranian religions from Central Asia and are concerned with the material world. One of the most important symbols of Zoroastrianism is fire; providing offerings of frankincense and sandalwood to a temple's sacred fire is the main role of the religion's priests; Parsee homes also contain sacred fires. Another important aspect of the religion is the unusual method of dealing with the dead. Rather than burial or cremation, Parsees leave their dead in an open air Tower of Silence to be devoured by vultures or other sacred birds.

See also PERSIANS, ACHAEMENIDS; PERSIANS, SASSANIANS.

FURTHER READING

John R. Hinnells. *The Zoroastrian Diaspora: Religion and Migration* (New York: Oxford University Press, 2005).

Jesse S. Palsetia. *The Parsis of India: Preservation of Identity in Bombay City* (Boston: Brill Academic Publishers, 2001).

Parsiwan   *See* FARSIWAN.

Parthians   (Anxi, Arsacids, Pahlavis)

The Parthians were an Iranian-speaking people who rose to prominence in the area of the Seleucid Greek Empire in the third century B.C.E. Eventually, their own empire spanned much of the Middle East and western Central Asia.

GEOGRAPHY

The Parthian Empire was centered around the area of present-day Iran and encompassed all of that region as well as territory in what are now the countries of Iraq, Turkey, Armenia, Azerbaijan, Turkmenistan, Afghanistan, and Pakistan. For the first two centuries, its capital was the city of Hecatompylus, which today is Shahr-e Qumis near Damghan, Iran. Its original Iranian name has been lost, and the ancient city is always referred to by its Greek name. By the first century C.E. the Parthian capital had been moved to Ctesiphon, a city on the Tigris River just outside contemporary Baghdad, Iraq.

ORIGINS

Most of the written records of the Parthian Empire have never been discovered. Therefore most of what we know about them has been pieced together from the writings of others, especially Greek and Roman sources, the plethora of coins that have been found, and the archaeological remains of several towns and cities.

The Parthian origins are twofold. On the one hand, there was a region of the Persian Empire known as Parthava, in northeastern Iran today, whose inhabitants, the Parthians, were historically and culturally connected to the Persian founders of the Achaemenid Empire. However, while this group gave its name to the later Parthian Empire, they were not its founders. The ancestors of the empire-building Parthians were members of the Parni tribe, an Eastern Iranian-speaking nomadic group who belonged to a loose confederacy of nomads known as Dahae, or Daha. Culturally the Dahae resembled their more famous nomadic neighbors the SCYTHIANS rather than the settled Iranian populations they conquered in Persia. Sometime between 300 and 250 B.C.E., the Parni entered Persian territory, specifically Parthava, from their homeland east of the Caspian Sea, killed the ruling Seleucid satrap (governor) Andragora, and more or less settled in this region. From this group emerged, in about 250 B.C.E., two brothers, Arsaces and Tiridates, who used their military strength to gain a degree of independence for their satrapy of Parthava within the larger Seleucid empire. Arsaces took the title of king, and though he and his three successors all pledged loyalty to the Seleucids, he is considered the founder of the Arsacid dynasty of the Parthian Empire.

HISTORY

While Arsaces and his immediate successors were satisfied with reigning in their own region and continuing to pay both respect and tribute to their superiors within the Seleucid Empire, by 171 B.C.E. the Arsacids had emerged as powerful enough to overthrow the Seleucids. Mithradates I, who ruled from 171 to 138 B.C.E., must be counted as the actual founder of the Parthian Empire for it was under his command that Parthian forces conquered Bactria in contemporary Afghanistan and all of the western regions of the Seleucid Empire, including Media, Assyria, and Babylonia in the Middle East. He was succeeded on the throne by his very young son, Phraates II, whose mother served as

Parthians time line

B.C.E.

300 (approximately)	The Parni tribe moves south from the lower reaches of the Oxus River into the Persian region of Parthava, in today's northeastern Iran.
247	Parni brothers Arsaces and Tiridates take over the Parthava satrap within the Greek Seleucid Empire, but recognize the Seleucids as their kings.
171	Mithradates I comes to power.
155	Mithradates I defeats the Medes after six years of fighting, which opens the door to the Middle East.
141	Mithradates I gains access to the Seleucids' capital, Seleucia, and is crowned king, thus replacing the Greek empire with an Iranian one.
138	Mithradates I dies.
123	Mithradates II comes to power.
88	Mithradates II dies and the Parthian Dark Ages, for which we have very little information, begin.
57	The three-year Parthian civil war between two rival claimants to the throne begins.
54	Orodes defeats the Roman general Crassus and sets up a longterm rivalry between the two empires.
36	The Parthians defeat Marc Antony.

C.E.

21	Gondophares establishes the Parthian kingdom in the former territories of the Scythian tribes in parts of Afghanistan, Pakistan, and India.
135	Pakores loses the last vestiges of the Parthian kingdom in Afghanistan.
216	Manes, the father of Manichaeanism (a dualistic Persian religious sect stressing asceticism to release the soul from the body), is born.
224	Artabanus IV is overthrown by Ardashir I, a Parthian who establishes the Sassanid empire.

regent until he came of age. His reign, as well as that of his uncle and successor, Artabanus I, seems to have been largely concerned with fighting off incursions by the Scythians into the empire's eastern regions. No coins bearing the name of Phraates II have been found in the western portion of the empire, and under Artabanus I Babylonia was lost entirely.

The next great Parthian king was Mithradates II, who also took the name Epiphanes, meaning "God Manifest." Ruling from 123 to 88 B.C.E., he expanded the empire beyond its boundaries in both the east and west, eliminating all challenges by the Seleucids, taking land in greater Armenia, and moving eastward into India. After the death of Mithradates II came the so-called Parthian Dark Ages, which lasted until 57 B.C.E., when Orodes II and Mithradates III began their three-year civil war for control of the empire. In 54 B.C.E. a general loyal to Orodes II, Suren, defeated and murdered Mithradates III in the western city of Seleucia, allowing Orodes II to come to power unchallenged.

Almost immediately following these internal struggles, Orodes II faced his next great confrontation, war with the Romans at Carrhae or Harran in northern Mesopotamia. The significantly larger Roman army, probably as many as 35,000 soldiers, was defeated by a Parthian force less than one-third its size. Later commentary on the battle points to a panic mentality in the mind of Roman general Crassus, who lined his men in military formation without allowing them to rest or make camp after a long march through the Middle Eastern desert. After near-defeat in this first battle, many Roman soldiers fled to the city of Carrhae, only to leave it again on the advice of a Parthian spy who led them, ultimately, to their deaths. At this time, only about 5,000 Roman soldiers escaped; 20,000 were killed and another 10,000 were captured and then relocated to Sogdiana in contemporary Tajikistan.

While this is the most notable of the battles fought between Parthians and Romans, it certainly was not the only one, because Rome was seeking to expand its Near Eastern domains, at least to the Euphrates River. The two rival empires faced off many more times on the Romans' eastern borderlands, the Parthians' western ones. In 36 B.C.E. the Parthians defeated Marc Antony (Marcus Antonius), the Roman orator and general famous both for his association with Julius Caesar and ultimately for his suicide with Cleopatra. Indeed, it is notable that the Parthians never lost a major battle with the Romans and were defeated only by one of their own, a Parthian soldier who broke free in 226 C.E., defeated Artabanus IV, and established his own empire, the Sassanids, under the name Ardashir I.

While the Parthians were militarily extremely strong when facing external threats to their sovereignty, as the above example of Ardashir I illustrates, they were less able to control the aspirations of their own soldiers and nobles because they never emphasized setting up a strong central government with a standing army to police their realm. In the eastern portion of the empire, roughly equivalent to southern Afghanistan, northern Pakistan, and portions of northeastern India, a new and rival dynasty developed in the first century C.E. that eventually was able to free itself from the Parthian rulers of the Arsacid line. The first leader of this so-called Indo-Parthian kingdom was Gondophares, who took over the territory that had been consolidated under Vonones and the rest of the Indo-Scythian kings and ruled by them until 12 C.E. Indeed, the Indo-Parthian kingdom itself is sometimes confused with or seen as an extension of the Indo-Scythian kingdom, perhaps because both groups shared the same military culture from their common nomadic steppe heritage. Gondophares ruled from Kabul for at least 26 years, starting in about 21 C.E. He had begun his campaign for independence by defeating the KUSHANS in their Indian territory of Gandhara in 47 C.E. and then moving west until he was able to conquer Parthian territory in Sakastan and Turan, land that today lies in Afghanistan, Uzbekistan, Kazakhstan, and Turkmenistan. The Indian territories claimed by the Indo-Parthians were held until only 75, when they were retaken by the Kushans; the heartland of the kingdom in Sakastan and Turan was lost in 135 during the rule of Pakores.

CULTURE

The material culture of the early Parni tribe resembled that of other steppe nomads to whom the Parni are thought to be related, including the Scythians. They were extremely skilled horsemen who are known even today for having invented the "Parthian shot," in which a rider first galloped away to suggest that he was fleeing, to encourage the enemy to pursue him, and then turned completely around in his saddle and fired his arrows at those behind him. Due to their military might and frequent raids on their settled, agricultural neighbors, the Parni were part of a larger confederation of tribes called Dahae, meaning "robbers" in the Persian language of these settled Iranian farmers. Materially, the Parthians are also known for their woven floor mats, or *gelim,* still famous today in Iran, which both began and thrived under their rule, and for their elaborate use of makeup and jewelry.

During the almost five centuries of Parthian rule over an area ranging from Armenia to India, many different religions were practiced and even condoned by the Arsacid leadership. The original Parthians, those who had been resident in Parthava for centuries, were devoted Zoroastrians when they were invaded and taken over by the Parni, who were probably already familiar with these beliefs and practices when they arrived. However, many Parthian rulers were also believers in the old Iranian religions that worshiped the sun, moon, earth, and other elements; the god Mithra was extremely important. The name *Mithradates,* which was taken by four Parthian kings, comes from the Iranian term *Mithra-Datt,* meaning "given by Mithra." Mithra was an ancient Iranian sun god who was reformed by the Zoroastrians to be the protector of *asha,* the order of the universe, and of truth and friendship, and to be the source of cosmic light. It is unclear if this Iranian and Zoroastrian Mithra is related to the cult of Mithras that emerged in Rome between the first century B.C.E. and first century C.E., itself a syncretic practice incorporating elements from many traditions. Other important influences on Parthian religion were the Greek gods; indeed, the Parthians are often described as Hellenized Zoroastrians who practiced a syncretic religion that combined belief in Ahura Mazda as the highest god with belief in and sacrifice to the important Greek gods as well. In addition, Jews and later Christians also lived under Parthian rule without experiencing significant discrimination or attempts at conversion.

In the areas of art and architecture, the Parthians exhibited a similar ability to borrow features from others and then disseminate them beyond their original homelands. Rather than a royal or imperial style, art under the Parthians has been described as popular, reflecting the many peoples and places conquered by Parthian armies. Some art historians even challenge the existence of something that we can label Parthian art at all since most styles, themes, and even patrons were entirely local rather than empire-wide. However, one important theme can be seen: Parthian artists tended to favor both sculpture and paintings that depicted motion, specifically the flying gallop, as might be expected of a previously nomadic, horse-centered people. In their building styles, the Parthians seem to have borrowed both domed vaults and arched porticoes from the peoples they conquered in Mesopotamia and then introduced them throughout the empire. Their baggy trousers were also adopted by peoples all over the empire, as evident in both sculptures and paintings from the entire region.

As was the case with art, politics too tended to be more decentralized under the Parthians than during the reign of other Middle Eastern and Central Asian empires. In this way the Parthians resembled the Greek Seleucids more than their fellow Iranians in either the Achaemenid or Sassanid Empires. Especially in Mesopotamia, the Parthians ruled indirectly,

This Parthian limestone relief is typical of the art of the period in depicting action on the part of horse and rider. *(Art Resource/Erich Lessing)*

allowing local leaders a great degree of sovereignty, even permitting them to mint their own coins, a key symbol of fealty at that time. Their style of rule no doubt added to the political turmoil that plagued the Parthians; rather than a standing army, they relied on vassals to raise troops when needed, which made it difficult to maintain order in the realm. Nevertheless, the Parthians did develop two impressive types of cavalry: lightly armed mounted bowmen who skirmished with the enemy, and heavily armored cataphracts carrying bows and weighty spears, whose horses were also armored; these last were "shock troops" who battled enemy infantry. These were the main fighting forces of the Parthians, whose battle strategy was based on cavalry and who consistently proved themselves against armies who were used to fighting against infantry. Interestingly, the Parthians never besieged cities and did not use siege machines even when they happened to fall into their hands, but depended on the form of combat that was native to them.

See also GREEKS; PERSIANS, ACHAEMENIDS; PERSIANS, SASSANIDS.

FURTHER READING

Malcolm A. R. Colledge. *Parthian Art* (Ithaca, N.Y.: Cornell University Press, 1977).

Vesta Sarkhosh Curtis, Robert Hillenbrand, and J. M. Rogers, eds. *The Art and Archaeology of Ancient Persia: New Light on the Parthian and Sasanian Empires* (London: I. B. Tauris, 1998).

PASHAI

location:
Eastern Afghanistan

time period:
Unknown to the present

ancestry:
Indo-Iranian

language:
Pashai, an Iranian language in the Dardic family, with at least four separate dialects; most in Afghanistan also speak Pashto

Pashai (Kohistani, PaSai, Pashayi, Pashi, Safi)

The first reference to the Pashai appears in the 13th-century writings of Venetian explorer Marco Polo, who traveled through a land he called Pashai Province, probably southeast of Badakhshan in northeastern Afghanistan and Tajikistan. Polo said of the area that it was extremely hot and that it was inhabited by brown-skinned idolaters who spoke a strange language. He also said they practiced sorcery and other diabolical arts and that the men wore earrings and brooches adorned with gemstones. Their main food sources were rice and meat.

Like the people encountered by Polo, contemporary Pashai still live in the northeastern region of Afghanistan. Those in the lower elevations grow rice as their primary crop, while those living in higher regions rely more on herding goats, sheep, and cattle plus growing wheat and corn. As would have been the case in the 13th century, contemporary Pashai are also Sunni Muslims who take their religion very seriously. Like the PASHTUNS, the dominant group in Afghanistan, the Pashai also see honor as their most important attribute. Feuding and revenge are central activities for many men, most of whom carry a knife or gun at all times.

There are about half a million Pashai alive today, mostly in eastern Afghanistan, with others throughout the country and in Pakistan. A very large proportion of the Pashai are illiterate in any language, with some sources saying the literacy rate for women may be only 2 percent. Many are also bilingual in Pashto. Their language has been spoken for more than 2,000 years but written only since 2003, when Serving Emergency Relief and Vocational Enterprise (SERVE), an interdenominational Christian charity working largely in the Dara-i-Noor region of Afghanistan, created a written form of Pashai. This organization is also starting to teach people to read in both Pashto and their first language.

Many Pashai men have been significant participants during the most recent violence in Afghanistan. A Pashai, Hazrat Ali, is a leading member of the Northern Alliance, the group backed by the U.S.-led coalition in the struggle against the Taliban. In 2002 he was favored by the United States over two rival Pashtun leaders to take over the city of Jalalabad, despite being considered a *shurrhi*, or "ignorant mountain man," by the region's dominant Pashtuns. He had previously proven his loyalty and military skills in the 2001 battle at Tora Bora, in which a coalition of Northern Alliance and U.S. troops fought against al-Qaeda. In the years after 2002, the UN Assistance Mission in Afghanistan has received a large number of reports that Pashai people have participated in land grabbing, house occupation, extortion, and other crimes in the Qarghayi and Nangahar districts, all with the tacit support of Ali.

See also AFGHANISTANIS: NATIONALITY.

Pashtuns (Afghans, Pakhtoons, Pakhtuns, Pathans, Pukhtuns, Pushtoons, Pushtuns)

The Pashtun people are a population of about 40 million who reside primarily in Pakistan (around 25.5 million) and Afghanistan (around 12.5 million). According to the loosest definition of this group, anyone who speaks Pashto, a Southeastern Iranian language, is a Pashtun. However, this linguistic definition is not accepted by most Pashtuns themselves, who also add the two cultural traits: following Pashtunwali, the feudal code of honor and pre-Islamic belief system of the Pashtun people; and being Muslim, usually of the Sunni variety.

GEOGRAPHY

The majority of Pashtuns live in the mountainous region of western Pakistan, especially the North-West Frontier Province and the Federally Administered Tribal Areas, and in central Afghanistan, including the cities of Peshawar and Kabul in the north and Quetta and Kandahar in the south. There are also pockets of Pashtuns throughout both countries as well as in Iran and India.

The Pashtun homeland is largely dominated by the Hindu Kush Mountains, with rugged peaks that average almost 15,000 feet. This high elevation produces long, rugged winters and short growing seasons. The crop that seems to do best here is the heroin poppy, which, along with the poverty and insecurity of other economic activities in post-Taliban Afghanistan, has contributed to that country's producing about 90 percent of the world's crop since 2003.

ORIGINS

The exact origins of the Pashtun people are largely a matter for conjecture. The fifth-century B.C.E. Greek historian Herodotus wrote briefly of a people he called Pactyan who lived within the boundaries of the Persian sphere of influence in the first millennium B.C.E. A few

Pashtuns time line

C.E.

500 (approximately) Groups of Iranian speakers come together to form the Pashtun ethnic group.

982 First reference to Afghans, in the *Hudud-al-Alam (The Regions of the World),* a Persian geographical text.

ca. 1525 Sheikh Mali writes the first Pashto text, *Daftar-e-Shaikh Mali,* which explains the division of land in Swat.

1613 Khushal Khan Khattak is born to the chief of the Khattak tribe near Peshawar. He becomes a warrior poet who urges his fellow Pashtuns to unite against their common enemy at the time, the Indian Mughals.

1690 Khushal Khan Khattak dies.

1709 Ghilzai Pashtuns briefly take power from the Persian Safavid dynasty that rules Iran and Afghanistan.

1731 The Ghilzai Pashtuns are defeated by Nadir Shah, Persian king, and pushed back into Afghanistan.

1747 Durrani Pashtuns consolidate the Afghan state under what is sometimes called the Durrani empire.

1839 First British invasion of Pashtun territory; they are successfully repelled.

1849 The British establish their colonial regime in Peshawar, contemporary Pakistan.

1878 Second British invasion of Pashtun territory; they are successfully repelled again.

1893 The Durand Line becomes the boundary between the Kingdom of Afghanistan and British India, dividing the Pashtun community in two. Afghanistan never recognizes its legitimacy.

1919 The Pashtun-dominated Kingdom of Afghanistan gains its complete independence from Britain in the Treaty of Rawalpindi.

1920s Ahmad Jan and others contribute to a renaissance of Pashtun culture in such magazines as *Sarhad* and *Afghan.*

1947 Pakistan's independence reestablishes the boundary created by the Durand Line, which is still not recognized by Afghanistan.

1973 The final Durrani king, Zahir Shah, is overthrown, and Afghanistan is made a republic under the leadership of General Mohammed Daoud.

1978 In a coup by Hafizulla Amin, power is transferred from the Durrani to the Ghilzai, a separate Pashtun tribe who make up the leaders of the secular Communist Party of the Democratic Republic of Afghanistan (DRA). President Mohammed Daoud Khan is killed on April 28.

1979 The Soviet Union invades Afghanistan to remove Amin and establish its own puppet state, setting off almost 30 years of near-constant warfare and driving many thousands of refugees, many of them Pashtuns, into Pakistan and Iran. They are opposed by U.S.-backed Islamic mujahideen forces.

1989 The Soviet Union pulls out of Afghanistan.

1992 Fall of the Najibullah Communist regime at the hands of the mujahideen. They install a Tajik as president, ending 245 years of Pashtun hegemony in the Afghan state. Fighting continues between the largely Pashtun Taliban and government forces.

1996 The Taliban seize Kabul and initiate strict sharia (Islamic) law. After two years of civil war, the Taliban take control of about 90 percent of the country. They are recognized only by Pakistan and Saudi Arabia as the legitimate government of the country.

2001 The U.S.-led coalition invades Afghanistan in retaliation for its support of al-Qaeda following the attacks in the United States on September 11. The Taliban fall almost immediately, but the violence continues.

Hamid Karzai, a Pashtun, is made chairman of the transitional administration in December.

(continues)

PASHTUNS

location:
Afghanistan and Pakistan, with smaller communities in Iran and India

time period:
Possibly 500 C.E. to the present

ancestry:
Iranian

language:
Pashto, a southeastern Iranian language, with several distinctive dialects, including Western, Eastern, and Southern Pashto. Since the late 16th century, Pashto has used a modified Persian script, which itself is based on a modified Arabic script. Many Pashtuns also speak Dari.

Pashtuns time line *(continued)*

2002	Karzai becomes interim president.
2004	After relatively free elections, Karzai becomes president. His presence in the largely non-Pashtun government reassures some Pashtuns, and some refugees return from Pakistan.
2008	The violence in Afghanistan continues as Taliban and other forces continue their struggle for land and influence.

scholars have considered this a reference to the Pashtuns, though others reject the idea. The same is true for a reference in the Rig Veda, an Indian religious text written between 1700 and 1100 B.C.E., which speaks of the Paktha people in the region of contemporary Afghanistan and Pakistan. There are also some Pashtuns who claim descent from a tribe of ancient Israelites, Jeremiah the son of Saul, but all linguistic and cultural evidence points to Iranian origins rather than Semitic ones.

Aside from these ancient references, many Pashtun specialists believe that a unique ethnic group emerged in their homeland around 500 C.E. from the remnants of other groups of Iranian speakers, including the speakers of Bactrian and Scythian, as well as HEPHTHA-LITES, KUSHANS, and Gujjars. The first written reference to this group comes from a Persian geographical text of 982, which mentions the existence of the Afghans. Still other specialists ignore the Persian reference and claim that a unique Pashtun identity did not emerge until the years 1200–1500.

HISTORY

Pashtun written history probably began in the early 16th century with an account by Sheikh Mali, *Daftar-e-Shaikh Mali,* about the distribution of land in the newly conquered region of Swat, in contemporary Pakistan. The Yusufzai tribe of Pashtuns began settling in Swat in the last quarter of the 15th century, and by the first quarter of the 16th century the region was almost entirely Pashtun. At that time the tribal chief, Malik Ahmed, assigned Sheikh Mali to produce a suitable division of land among the various Yusufzai clans, as well as the few others who lived in the Swat territories. This division, called *wesh* in Pashto, while not terribly useful as far as taking advantage of fertile lands, was agreeable to all concerned and remained in effect until the 20th century. Although no actual copies of the *Daftar* exist, despite British attempts in the 19th century to find a copy, the national poet of the Afghans, Khushal Khan Khattak, confirmed its existence in his 18th-century work, *Swat Nama.*

After this 15th–16th-century influx of Pashtun tribal members from Afghanistan into land that is today Pakistan, the next crucial period of Pashtun history comes in 1747, when Ahmad Khan Abdali was elected king of a united Pashtun kingdom. Upon his election Ahmad took the title Durr-i-Durran (Pearl of Pearls) and became known as Ahmad Shah Durrani. His own tribal group, the Abdali, likewise took the name DURRANIS, which they continue to use to the present day.

Coinciding at this point with Afghanistan's national history, which was constructed largely around Pashtun tribal identities, this election marks the emergence of the Pashtuns into the modern political world. Until that point, the Pashtuns had been tribal subjects of the Persian kings, but with the assassination of the Persian king Nadir Shah in 1747, Abdali was able to consolidate the many Pashtun tribes and clans into a single corporate body. His rule was legitimated at a large tribal *jirgah,* the same kind of egalitarian council that adjudicates disagreements at all levels of Pashtun society today, as well as by the *ulama,* or religious scholars. The territory he ruled was much larger than con-

Ahmad Khan Abdali

Ahmad Khan Abdali, also known as Ahmad Shah Durrani and Ahmad Shah Abdali, was born in 1723 and chosen by jirgah to rule over the Duranni tribes after Nader Shah's assassination in 1747. He founded the Durrani Empire in 1747 and is sometimes called the *baba,* or father, of Afghanistan. Using a nickname given him by Nader Shah, he dubbed himself Durr-i-Durrani, or "Pearl of Pearls." After taking power, he led a military land grab, expanding the territory of his new empire. The pinnacle of his early victories lay at the Third Battle of Panipat in 1761; however, he soon met serious resistance amongst the Sikh rebellions in India, leading to eventual defeat in 1766 outside of Lahore. He then returned to Kabul and died of cancer in 1773. He was succeeded by his son, but the empire soon crumbled without his leadership. Today Abdali's clan, the Durranis, continue to be one of the largest and strongest Pashtun subgroups in Afghanistan.

temporary Afghanistan, stretching from Mashad on the western border to Kashmir and Delhi on the eastern one; the Amu Darya River made up the northern border, while the southern one was the Arabian Sea.

Durrani died in 1773, and after several years of infighting, power shifted away from his section of the tribe and toward the Mohammadzai lineage. This group maintained its control of Afghanistan almost continuously from 1826 to 1978, during the most difficult colonial years of the 19th century and through almost 50 years of independence.

At the beginning of the 19th century, the entire Pashtun region was contained within the Kingdom of Afghanistan. However, after an unsuccessful invasion of Pashtun territory in 1839, just 10 years later the British East India Company established itself in Peshawar, which had been the winter capital of the Afghan kings. The British made another attempt at conquering the Pashtuns in 1878 and again failed. Finally, after almost 50 years of constant military tension between the British and Pashtuns, in 1893 the British created an almost 750-mile boundary between their own territory of British India and the Kingdom of Afghanistan, the Durand Line, which divided the Pashtun community in two. The consequences of this action continue to be felt today since Afghanistan never recognized the legitimacy of this border and rejected the right of Pakistan to inherit the British boundary upon achieving independence in 1947. Even today, the Pakistani Pashtun territories are only loosely administered from the capital, Islamabad, and are primarily ruled according to tribal laws and customs.

Despite the drawing of this boundary, the British never really consolidated their power in the Pashtun territories. Their indirect rule in Afghanistan, established as a buffer zone between British India and imperial Russia, granted only foreign affairs to the British and left the tribal chiefs largely to themselves to deal with internal matters. This situation lasted until 1919, when an Afghan invasion of British India set the stage for complete Afghan independence as established by the Treaty of Rawalpindi, signed on August 19, 1919. Meanwhile, in the Pashtun Indian territories, a frontier mentality continued to dominate throughout the entire colonial period, symbolized by the British creation of the North-West Frontier Province within the Indian territory. This province, which still exists today, was a de facto part of the British colony, but its leaders were granted almost complete autonomy to control their own affairs along tribal lines. It continues to have the same kind of relationship with Pakistan that it had with British India.

It was during the colonial era that the greatest developments in Pashtun identity occurred. These were based not only on opposition to British hegemony but also on internal developments in Pashto literature. At that time the British needed educated Pashtuns to serve as translators and language teachers, and one young man who served in this capacity was Ahmad Jan, the son of an educated member of the Afghan court. With his familiarity with both languages and cultures, Jan began writing in Pashto in the mid-1920s in two Pashto-language magazines, *Sarhad* and *Afghan,* both of which were dedicated to reforming Pashtun culture. Jan dealt with such topics as Pashtun education, blood feuds, and the effects of Pashtunwali in the modern world, in his attempt to remake Pashtun identity and culture. The British themselves also contributed to this renaissance in Pashtun culture and identity by identifying the Pashtuns as a martial race with strong leadership abilities and in some ways the equals of the British themselves. Later commentaries in British texts argue that this characterization was used as justification for the inability of British soldiers to subjugate the Pashtuns as they had done with all other colonized peoples. Regardless of British intentions, the Pashtuns themselves identified with the descriptions and began to reproduce them in their own texts.

The Pashtuns continued to be the dominant force in the government of Afghanistan throughout most of the 20th century. In 1978 President Mohammed Daoud Khan, the last Mohammedzai Pashtun leader, was deposed by the Communist Party, which itself was dominated by a different Pashtun tribe, the Ghilzai. At this point the name of the country was changed to the Democratic Republic of Afghanistan. The invasion of the Soviet Union in 1979 and then Soviet withdrawal in 1989 after failing to secure Afghanistan as a puppet state, much as the British had done 100 years earlier, did nothing to disturb Pashtun dominance in the country. In 1992, however, the multiethnic mujahideen, who had formed the backbone of fighters against Soviet domination and had been funded by the United States, finally succeeded in defeating the country's Communist leadership. Many generations of Pashtun dominance came to an end when Dr. Mohammad

Najibullah was deposed and replaced by a Tajik president.

As might be expected in a land of blood feuds and revenge, many Pashtuns did not accept the legitimacy of this new government. Many fled the country to join the thousands of other Afghan refugees who had been in Iran and Pakistan since the Soviet invasion in 1979. Others joined the Taliban, a largely Pashtun military organization determined to win back the state through violent struggle. By 1996 the Taliban had succeeded in retaking Kabul and instituting the strictest Islamic laws in the world, which were heavily influenced by their tribal code of law as well. Within two years the Taliban had taken control of most of the rest of the country and continued to punish the non-Pashtun government forces. Though recognized globally only by Pakistan and Saudi Arabia, the Taliban remained the de facto head of the Afghanistani government until 2001, when a U.S.-led coalition invaded the country as part of its war on terrorism. In December that year, a Pashtun, Hamid Karzai, was made chair of the transitional administration, in part to reassure Pashtuns that the largely non-Pashtun administration would welcome them. Karzai retained leadership of the country in 2002 when he became interim president and then in 2004 when he won the first post-1979 election. Unfortunately, despite these elections, by early 2008 the Taliban had not yet been fully routed, and today hundreds of both Pashtuns and foreign soldiers continue to suffer injuries and death in the struggle to secure the leadership of this unstable country.

Prime Minister Hamid Karzai just after being selected to head the interim government in 2001. One year later, Karzai became head of state as Afghanistan's president, a position to which he was re-elected in 2004. *(AP/Amir Shah)*

CULTURE

Economics

Prior to the Soviet invasion of Afghanistan in 1979, the dominant economic activities for all Pashtuns who were not serving in the military, either Pakistani or Afghanistani, were subsistence agriculture, pastoralism, and a bit of trade. This remains largely the case today in Pakistan, but in Afghanistan the damage wrought to fields and orchards by the past 28 years of warfare has meant that most Pashtuns have faced great poverty. In 2006 the average wage earner in the country supported five people on less than $35 per day. Many people have turned to heroin poppy cultivation, smuggling, and other forms of banditry to survive. There are also between 1 and 2 million nomadic pastoralists living in contemporary Afghanistan, the majority of whom are Pashtuns (however, most Pashtuns are not pastoralists). They specialize primarily in sheep, though a few also tend goats, and provide nearly 30 percent of Afghanistan's export revenue in wool and mutton. They also tend herds of camels, horses, and donkeys, primarily used for transportation and hauling. Since they make up about 42 percent of the population of Afghanistan and prior to 1992 made up much of the traditional ruling class, there are also many urban Afghanistani Pashtuns, including the current president, Hamid Karzai, who participate in commerce, politics, and education. The current Afghan army is also about 42 percent Pashtun.

The Pashtun minority in Pakistan tends to be poorer, less educated, and more alienated from the state structure than the rest of the Pakistani population. Indeed, residents of the Pashtun-dominated Federally Administered Tribal Areas were allowed to vote only in 1997, though they are represented in both the lower and upper houses of the Pakistani government. The one area in which Pashtuns in Pakistan are strongly represented, however, is the army, where they are estimated to make up almost 20 percent of officers and nearly 25 percent of enlisted soldiers. Since the military in Pakistan is seen as the most powerful and organized institution in the country, some Pashtuns have been able to use their connections to influence both military and civilian policy throughout the country.

Pashtunwali

One of the most important cultural features that defines the Pashtun people is their adherence to Pashtunwali, the way of the Pashtuns.

Even with the fall of the Taliban in 2001, many Pashtun women continue to don the burqa in public, as they are doing here in February 2002—whether by choice or the dictates of their husbands and fathers is difficult to tell from a photograph. *(OnAsia/Alberto Buzzola)*

This is the ancient honor code that delineates almost all human interactions, especially public behavior, but also the relationships among family members, between men and women, and between Pashtuns and strangers. The most important concept within the sphere of Pashtunwali is honor. In addition, Pashtunwali also defines for those who adhere to its precepts the boundaries of independence, justice, hospitality, love, forgiveness, tolerance, and revenge.

Honor is the key to understanding not only Pashtun society but also Pashtun history, especially the violence inherent in both. Protecting his own honor, or that of his family, clan, or tribe, is the foremost duty of all Pashtun men. One aspect of this emphasis on honor is the need for revenge. Individuals sacrifice everything they have, from their money to their lives, to avenge even the slightest breach, usually with interest. A common Pashtun proverb states, "He is not a Pashtun who does not give a blow for a pinch." This aspect of honor means that long-standing feuds both among and between families are common since each vengeful action must be repaid with interest. The triumvirate of *zar, zan,* and *zamin*—wealth, women, and property—is the most common source of feuding, but there are many others as well.

In addition to avenging all slights and injuries, another important focus of a man's honor is the control of his women, including wives, daughters, and sisters. A man's honor is threatened by the behavior of his women, and thus their rules for seclusion are extremely strict. As much as is economically possible, Pashtun women are kept secluded in their household compounds or courtyards, with seclusion being an important marker of family status. Women are generally forbidden from entering markets, stores, or even other households, or participating in any public events. This limits their ability to gain an education or to participate in subsistence activities such as agriculture. Certainly choosing their own marriage and sexual partners is also entirely out of the question for many Pashtun women. Whenever they do enter the public realm, they are required to wear a burka, the long blue or black robe that covers a woman's entire body and that became internationally recognized as a symbol of the Taliban's oppression of women generally. Pashtun men are not only concerned about making sure that their own women do not dishonor them through their actions, sexual or otherwise, but also that other men do not dishonor them through their women. For the Pashtuns, honor is seen as a limited good so that diminishing one man's honor, for example, by seducing his wife, daughter, or sister simultaneously increases his own.

In addition to seeking revenge and protecting their women, Pashtun men are also required to provide hospitality and protection to strangers as part of maintaining their honor. While outsiders may not be trusted or generally welcome, if they appear on a man's land they cannot be turned away. The honorable Pashtun must provide them with food, drink, and protection for the time they are on his land, for if harm comes to the stranger, it is his Pashtun host who will suffer a loss of honor.

While honor is the central feature of Pashtunwali, equality between men is likewise very important. It is this aspect of Pashtun society that has made it so difficult to govern for the past 300 years, and perhaps far longer as well. A man is fully responsible not only for his own honor and reputation but also for defining his own rights and status. Political autonomy is inherent in this egalitarian system, which recognizes no higher authority than each individual man. The one political structure that has emerged in this context of male egalitarianism is the *jirgah,* a council of elders that is able to adjudicate decisions at all levels of community life, from the village to the tribe. Decisions tend to be made based on both sharia, or Islamic, law and Pashtun traditions as interpreted by the *jirgah* members. All adult males can speak equally in front of the *jirgah,* making it the one institution able to regulate a society in which each individual male is seen as both independent of and in opposition to all other men.

Social Structure

The social world of every individual Pashtun is made up of larger and larger groups of affiliation. The most basic and probably most important social units for both production and consumption are the household and family. Households tend to be made up of nuclear families; however, a relatively large number of Pashtun households also contain a couple as well as their sons along with the sons' wives and children. Few Pashtuns practice polygyny (marrying multiple wives), but the few who do maintain them in a single household. These extended family households tend to break up eventually, with each brother going his own way to establish his own extended household by the time his children are in their teens. Establishing a family requires a man to pay bride wealth to his new in-laws, both to provide legitimacy to his children and to help his in-laws make up for the loss of their daughter's household labor. This loss comes about as the result of her patrilocal marriage residency, since a bride must move into her husband's household.

Within households, age, sex, and position in the family all affect not only status but responsibilities as well. Daughters and wives are responsible for cooking, cleaning, and maintaining their families' honor by not breaking any of the rules for seclusion, with relative age determining the position among women. Young daughters and new wives occupy the lowest positions within the family hierarchy and thus are responsible for the most arduous labor, while a mother of married sons can achieve a degree of power over these younger women. Men are responsible for earning money, exacting revenge, and protecting their family, lineage, clan, and tribal honor. Among men, the rules governing equality tend to even out differences in status more than among women, but at the same time the opinions of elders carry more weight than those of younger men.

Beyond the household and family, all Pashtuns are also members of a web of relationships defined by kinship. The most immediate relations outside the household are those within a patrilineal group, *zai* in Pashto, a group of families related through a common male ancestor. Pashtuns make up the largest society organized by patrilineage in the contemporary world. All Pashtuns inherit their lineage membership from their fathers and can trace their patrilineage back many generations. In addition, almost all Pashtuns believe they are descended from one of the three sons of Imraul Qais, the possibly legendary first Pashtun to make the hajj pilgrimage to Mecca: Sarban, Baitan, and Ghourghusht. Some sources also mention a fourth son, Karlan. Membership in their lineage group situates them within the larger Pashtun world, defining rights, obligations, responsibilities, and marriage partners. Land, for example, is always inherited patrilineally, from fathers to sons and, in the absence of sons, to brothers' sons. Marriage, too, usually occurs within the lineage, with most Pashtuns preferring to marry relatively close cousins rather than more distant relatives or, even more rarely, people from outside the lineage.

Beyond the immediate lineage, Pashtuns are also members of clans, *aziiz* in Pashto, which are made up of groups of lineages that claim to have a common ancestor, often one who is mythological or legendary rather than actual. There are about 60 different clan groupings among the Pashtuns, some of which are large and divided into subclans while others are smaller; these clans are also ranked in importance. Each clan occupies a territorial range, and traveling outside one's own clan's land can be dangerous business for Pashtun men; the same is also true of lineages. The levels of social organization beyond the clan are tribes, *khel* in Pashto, which are made up of a number of clans, all of whom see themselves as culturally distinct from other tribal groups.

Kinship-based social organization, even at the tribal level, is very different from the kind of social connections created in a national community. Nations rely on abstract and objective bureaucracies to organize the relationships between people; they also allow people to join them through migration and naturalization. Kinship-based societies, on the other hand, like ethnic groups, are based entirely on birth. Unlike ethnic groups, however, each individual within a kinship system is socially defined by his or her membership in a family, lineage, clan, and tribe; for each individual these memberships also define his or her relationship with all others within the system.

While kinship is the primary organizing principle in Pashtun society, individuals also exist in a geographic reality that creates other kinds of rights and responsibilities. As mentioned above, households, while primarily family organizations, are equally important due to their shared activities: making a living, eating, reproducing, providing hospitality. Wealthier households may also include laborers and others who are not family members, reinforcing the extra-kinship ties created by household membership.

Beyond the household, most Pashtuns also live in villages that are made up of a group of households, usually those from the same patrilineage but with residency providing a further set of rights and responsibilities. In addition to households, villages also include common areas, cultivated lands, and water sources, all of which must be shared among the village's households. For Pashtuns who are either urban or pastoral, these village residencies are not relevant. Nonetheless, urban Pashtuns do tend to situate themselves in neighborhoods or sectors that are primarily Pashtun. Pastoral Pashtuns are connected to others in their camps, with separate residences in the cooler high elevations for summer, and in the warmer valleys for winter. These camps are connected by transport routes that are used each year by the same households, which make their yearly moves from mountain to valley and back again. Like households and villages, pastoral camps are also occupied by lineage members rather than groups of strangers.

The dominant image that comes to mind when picturing the social world of the Pashtun is a series of concentric circles, beginning on the one hand with family being encompassed by lineage, which in turn is encompassed by clan, and then tribe. On the other hand, households are similarly encompassed by villages, crop lands, and orchards. In terms of action, these social organizations combine with the rules of revenge and honor as defined by Pashtunwali to create a situation depicted in another Pashtun proverb: "I against my brothers; my brothers and I against my cousins; my brothers, my cousins, and I against the world." This is one reason that the various invasions of Afghanistan that have occurred over the past 200 years have always resulted in fierce fighting against the common enemy and then chaos and lack of unity once victory has been achieved: Without a common enemy, the Pashtuns revert to seeking revenge and other forms of violence against each other. Another apt Pashtun proverb explains this mentality well: "We are only at peace when we are at war."

Religion

As mentioned above, the founding ancestor for most Pashtun tribes and clans is Imraul Qais, whom they believe was sent to Arabia by his tribe when they heard about the prophet Muhammed and Islam. During his travels he met the prophet himself, who gave him the name Abdur Rashid, and also met Khalid ibn al-Walid, the Arab general responsible for many victories in Central Asia in the early seventh century. Upon returning to his homeland in southern Afghanistan, Qais is believed to have converted his people to Islam, even before the Arab conquest of the area between 634 and 644.

As this origin myth shows, being Muslim is central to the identity of most Pashtuns, and the Islam practiced by most is Sunni rather than Shiite. The differences between these branches of Islam lie in the realm of leadership as well as some interpretations of sharia or holy law. All Muslims, both Sunni and Shiite, believe in Allah as the one god, Muhammad as his final prophet, the ultimate resurrection of all human beings, and the Quran as the word of Allah as spoken by Muhammad. They also agree that prayers; fasting; pilgrimage to Mecca; avoiding sins such as drinking alcohol, adultery, and theft; and paying religious tax are all necessary acts in a Muslim's life. Where they differ is in the recognition of the proper succession to Muhammad's authority. Sunnis recognize

Abu Bakr as the first caliph, or leader, following the death of Muhammad in 632, followed by Umar, Uthman, and Ali. Shiites believe that Ali should have been first because of his kin relationship to the prophet. The term *Shia* comes from the Arabic phrase *shiat Ali,* "partisans of Ali." In the contemporary world, Sunnis outnumber Shiites about nine to one, but in both Iran and Iraq, Shiites make up the majority.

While Islam is extremely important to the Pashtuns, it is important not to conflate their religious beliefs with Pashtunwali, which is even more central to their self-definition and behavior. The Taliban, as a Pashtun-dominated organization, is often viewed only through the lens of Islam. The Taliban's policies toward women, outsiders, and even the non-Islamic heritage of Afghanistan (as evident in their destruction of Bamiyan Buddhist sculptures in 2001) must all be understood in light of the Pashtuns' specific interpretation of Islam as guided by Pashtunwali rather than as Islamic alone.

See also AFGHANISTANIS; NATIONALITY, AFRIDI; BACTRIANS; SCYTHIANS.

FURTHER READING

Akbar S. Ahmed. *Pukhtun Economy and Society: Traditional Structure and Economic Development in a Tribal Society* (Boston: Routledge & Kegan Paul, 1980).

Fredrik Barth. *Features of Person and Society in Swat: Collected Essays on Pathans* (Boston: Routledge & Kegan Paul, 1981).

———. *Political Leadership among Swat Pathans* (New York: Humanities Press, 1965).

Olaf Caroe. *The Pathans, 550 BC–AD 1957* (New York: Oxford University Press, 1976).

Imran Khan. *Warrior Race: A Journey through the Land of the Tribal Pathans* (London: Chatto & Windus, 1993).

Latifa, with the collaboration of Chekeha Hachemi. *My Forbidden Face: Growing Up under the Taliban: A Young Woman's Story,* trans. Lisa Appignanesi. (London: Virago, 2002).

Charles Lindholm. *Generosity and Jealousy: The Swat Pukhtun of Northern Pakistan* (New York: Columbia University Press, 1982).

James W. Spain. *Pathans of the Latter Day* (New York: Oxford University Press, 1995).

Pathans   *See* PASHTUNS.

Peiligang-Cishan culture

Peiligang-Cishan is the name given to two related Neolithic cultures from the area that is today taken up by China's Henan and Hebei Provinces; Peiligang is most closely associated with the Yellow (Huang) River valley. The first discovery of a site from this era was made in 1962, but it took many decades for the full extent of the cultural complex to become known outside China. The name *Peiligang* was assigned in 1977 after an archaeological site deemed to be characteristic of the entire period. Of the two separate cultural complexes, Peiligang was the older and longer-lasting of the two, from about 7000 to 5000 B.C.E., while Cishan can positively be dated only from 6000 to 5500 B.C.E. Due to their similarities, however, the two are often labeled and discussed together as one.

To date, more than 70 archaeological sites have been found to contain artifacts that identify them as Peiligang or Cishan; the site at Jiahu has some of the oldest items found so far. The most important of these artifacts are early agricultural tools such as stone sickles and grinders; evidence of millet and rice farming; remains of domesticated animals such as pigs, dogs, and chickens; red or brown pottery; and even musical instruments. These artifacts attest to the importance of settled agriculture among these communities, with millet and pork forming the backbone of their diet. The best estimates are that millet was domesticated at Peiligang between 7800 and 7200 B.C.E. No date has so far been given for the domestication of pigs in this area, but chickens are believed to have been domesticated at Cishan in 7400 B.C.E. However, like the PENGTOUSHAN CULTURE, which existed at approximately the same time further south in China and is the earliest site of domesticated rice in the world, the people of Peiligang and Cishan could not subsist entirely on domesticated foods. Fishing, hunting, and even gathering of wild grains and other foodstuffs remained important for thousands of years beyond the initial development of agriculture in this region. The people of this culture also developed the ability to ferment rice, honey, and hawthorn into a form of alcohol, the evidence of which has been found in several pottery jars from the period. Whether the alcohol was used for social or ceremonial purposes, or perhaps both, remains unknown at this time.

Little is known about Peiligang and Cishan social structures, but based on the similarities among all grave sites, which contain objects such as pottery, tortoiseshells, and flutes, archaeologists have posited that the culture tended toward relative egalitarianism. The development of agriculture in most societies throughout the world has usually been accompanied by the development of a class structure based on differences in

---

PEILIGANG-CISHAN CULTURE

location:
Henan and Hebei Provinces, China

time period:
7000–5000 B.C.E.

ancestry:
Neolithic Chinese

language:
Unknown

wealth and a complex political system with a full-time bureaucratic apparatus. That this has so far not been identified for Peiligang or Cishan does not mean it did not occur, just that the physical evidence for class differentiation and political complexity have not yet been found. Some of the other things that have been noted about these societies are that their residential settlements were often protected by a moat rather than by a walled enclosure and that they must have housed relatively large settlements. Millet granaries that could hold up to 2,200 pounds of grain have been discovered at one Cishan site.

Among the most exciting discoveries made among the Peiligang and Cishan artifacts are tonal flutes made from the wing bones of Red Crowned cranes. Six complete flutes have been found at the site at Jiahu along with pieces from about 30 more; all of these items have been carbon dated between 7,000 and 9,000 years old. All the flutes have between five and eight holes, and the notes are strikingly similar to the modern Western musical note system that begins do, re, mi. The best-preserved seven-hole flute has been played and its sound analyzed by music scholars in China, and it was found to be completely appropriate for playing a classic Chinese folk tune. This discovery is believed to be the first example found of a Neolithic people who were capable of creating instruments that could play more than just a single note, making music rather than simply sound possible.

A second exciting possibility raised by the findings from Jiahu is that the people of Peiligang may also have been on the verge of inventing writing. Inscriptions carved into tortoiseshells and bones are believed by many archaeologists to be examples of proto-writing.

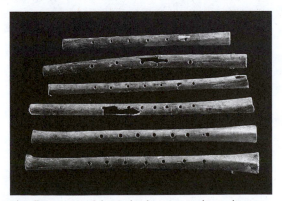

The flute second from the bottom is the only one, of the six complete ones shown, to have been played in modern times; the others are cracked or otherwise flawed. (AP/Institute of Cultural Relics and Archaeology of Henan Province)

Some of these inscriptions are reminiscent of the Chinese writing system that was believed not to have been invented until at least 1750 B.C.E. Two symbols in particular are very similar to the characters for *eye* and *sun*.

Penan (Pennan, Poenan, Poonan, Pounan, Punan)

The Penan are a nomadic people who once resided throughout the island of Borneo; the majority today live in the Malaysian province of Sarawak on the northern coast, while a small minority live in the Kalimantan region of Indonesia. Today most Penan have been forcibly settled due to logging, the creation of a national park, Gunung Mulu, and other activities in Sarawak, but identification as a member of this ethnic group continues despite the changes the group has experienced since the 1980s.

Although there are indications of their being the remnants of an ancient population of nomadic hunter-gatherers, the Penan are believed to be the descendants of individuals and communities of settled peoples who fled into the forest in the 19th century to escape the ravages of IBAN and other headhunters. Rather than trying to continue using slash-and-burn techniques to farm in the rainforest, these communities took up hunting, fishing, and gathering in the rich environment in which they lived. These origins explain the linguistic diversity among Penan groups as well as their vocabulary and other language features shared with many of the settled groups around them.

The hunting-gathering subsistence practices of the Penan centered on gathering wild fruit and sago, a starchy pulp from the sago palm, and hunting bearded pigs and deer; fish were also an important part of their diet. Generally, small bands of Penan would use the resources of a region of forest for anywhere from a few days to a few weeks and then move on before all food and animal resources had been exhausted, so that regeneration was a relatively quick process. The material culture of the traditional Penan reflected this small-scale way of life and consisted of loincloths made from local materials; feather headdresses; blowguns for hunting; and woven bags for carrying children, gathered foods, and other objects. They decorated themselves by piercing their ears and tattooing themselves, all of which made them appear dramatically different from their settled neighbors and distant relatives. The Penan social order also reflected the small scale of their

PENAN

location:
Sarawak; Malaysia; and Kalimantan, Indonesia

time period:
19th century to the present

ancestry:
Austronesian

language:
Eastern and Western Penan, Austronesian languages

Here a Penan man has dressed largely as his father and grandfather would have and is demonstrating the proper use of a blowgun; he has, however, substituted the traditional loincloth for a pair of gym shorts. *(Shutterstock/TAOLMOR)*

society in that no ascribed class or other hierarchies were recognized. They were and in some sense remain a relatively egalitarian society where the only differences were based on age and gender. Each traveling community or band would have a headman who could influence his people's movements but had no actual authority over them. The most important value of the Penan was reciprocity and sharing; the worst crime anyone could commit would be to withhold food or other resources from others.

This traditional way of life began to be encroached upon by the modern world in the 1970s and 1980s, when the logging industry had exhausted much of Malaysia's other rainforest regions and moved into the rich forests of Sarawak. Several groups of Penan and other indigenous peoples fought back against these incursions in 1987 by blocking logging roads for about eight months. The Malaysian government retaliated by arresting community leaders, restricting media access to the region, and making it a federal crime to block roads. In the following years, however, the protests continued, as did the logging and harassment of local peoples by logging company officials in conjunction with the state government.

Further damage to the Penan homelands was brought to bear by the Bakun dam project, which had been begun in the 1980s and is slated to begin creating electricity in 2009. About 70,000 hectares of land claimed by the Penan and other groups was inundated by the project, which was designed to produce hydroelectric power both for Sarawak and for the energy-hungry regions of Peninsular Malaysia.

As a result of these activities, as well as the desire of many Penan parents that their children go to school, the Penan today are a settled community who live in small villages along Sarawak's many rivers. Nonetheless, they still consider themselves people of the forest and make many forays into the forest of Gunung Mulu National Park and other regions to obtain medicinal herbs, other food products, feathers, and fish. Hunting is generally forbidden in the park, and most animals have disappeared from logged regions, but an occasional squirrel or other animal is taken by the Penan as a reminder of life just 30 years ago.

FURTHER READING

Wade Davis, Ian MacKenzie, and Shane Kennedy. *Nomads of the Dawn: The Penan of the Borneo Rain Forest* (Beverly Hills, Calif.: Pomegranate Press, 1995).

Pengtoushan culture

Pengtoushan was a Neolithic culture of the central Chang (formerly the Yangtze) River area of China, particularly northwest Hunan Province. It is important in both Chinese and world history as displaying the first evidence of rice agriculture, dated to about 7000 B.C.E., or 9,000 years ago. One particular Pengtoushan site found in China, in Lixian county, Hunan Province, is also the oldest permanently settled Chinese village excavated so far. Most of the work on Pengtoushan sites was done in the 1990s, so new finds and interpretations are regularly changing our understanding of Chinese prehistory.

Agriculture as it was practiced during the Pengtoushan period was of the swidden, or slash-and-burn, variety. This is an inefficient form of agriculture because it requires that fields be used just once after the primary forest or grass has been burned away to provide fertilizer. Each season these primitive farmers would have had to cut a new field from the virgin land, let the vegetative material dry out, and burn it back before planting could take place. These burnt remains were the only fertilizer, and no irrigation or other form of watering mechanism would have been in use. The grains of rice found from this early period resemble wild varieties but with larger seeds from selective use during the domestication process.

PENGTOUSHAN CULTURE

location:
The central Chang (Yangtze) River area of China

time period:
7500–5500 B.C.E., though some sources mark the end of this era in 6100 B.C.E.

ancestry:
Neolithic Chinese

language:
Unknown

These early farmers would not have been able to grow all the food they required, and hunting, fishing, and gathering remained important subsistence strategies for thousands of years after the first domestication of rice took place. In addition, there is also evidence of the domestication of a few animals in this period, including water buffalo, dogs, pigs, and chickens, which would have provided food and, in the case of the first two, carting labor and protection, respectively.

Despite the domestication of plants and animals in this period, Pengtoushan is still considered a Neolithic or New Stone Age culture because all the tools found so far are made from stone, unlike bronze and iron implements found later. These tools are of three varieties: large flaked, small flaked, and ground. The largest flaked or ground tools were used for chopping, pounding, and perhaps scraping animal hides as well. Smaller tools were also used for scraping as well as slicing and paring. Double-bladed axes or knives of about three inches in length and almost two inches in width are commonly found in Pengtoushan sites, as are blades with holes drilled in them from both sides. Along with stone tools and ornaments, the other implements that appear in many Pengtoushan sites are bits of pottery made from rough, sandy clay and decorated with cord markings. Potsherds, or pieces of pottery, are found both in burial sites and in other domestic sites, indicating their use as practical items and as objects marking status in death.

Pengtoushan culture is also important for the development of walled residential enclosures in China. Near the end of the Pengtoushan era, at least one such settlement emerged, at Bashidang, near Wufu in Hunan Province. Bashidang, dated from about 5540 to 5100 B.C.E. and divided into early, middle, and late periods, is interesting to archaeologists because the site had both walls and moats for protection. These structures enclosed an area about 656 feet long north to south and 525 feet wide east to west. Within this area both semi-subterranean and surface buildings have been excavated, along with numerous fences, platforms, a stone stairwell leading to the Chang River, and hundreds of postholes.

Peranakans (Babas, Babars, Nyonyas, Nonyas, Peranakan Chinese, Straits-born Chinese, Straits Chinese)

The Peranakan community in Singapore, Malaysia, and Indonesia is made up of the descendants of Chinese men who came to Southeast Asia and married local women; the term *peranakan* means "descendants" in Malay. There are also a few Peranakans of Indian descent as well. The separate terms *Baba* or *Babar* and *Nyonya* or *Nonya* refer to the men and women, respectively, in this community. Many experts believe that these terms derive from Portuguese words and point to the earliest European colonizers' attempts to classify the local population by race.

The first Chinese immigrants to settle in the Malay Archipelago arrived from Guangdong and Fujian Provinces in the 10th century C.E. They were joined by much larger numbers of Chinese in the 15th through 17th centuries, following on the heels of the Ming emperor's reopening of Chinese-Malay trade relations in the 15th century. Many came as seamen and traders, married locally, and never returned to their homes in southern China. The 19th century brought another wave of Chinese immigration to the Malay world, largely encouraged by the British administration in the Straits, which needed laborers and traders. Many of the locally born men, after the prohibition on Chinese women leaving their country was lifted in the latter half of the 19th century, imported Chinese wives who infused more contemporary Chinese customs, language, and beliefs into the local Peranakan community.

Generally speaking, Peranakan communities differ from pure Chinese ones in a number of cultural aspects. Most importantly, most speak a form of Malay with many Chinese loanwords, rather than Chinese, Cantonese, or some other Chinese language. Traditionally, Babas wore Chinese clothing while Nyonyas tended to dress in local Malay sarongs. Peranakan cuisine, music, and other material culture also tended to be more influenced by local Malay traditions, with just a small infusion from Chinese elements. Nonetheless, most Peranakans were reluctant to convert to Islam, and most continued to practice traditional Chinese religions, the most important of which focused on ancestor worship. These distinctions have diminished over time, and today, due to significant intermarriage, Chinese and Peranakan differences have become much less important. However, both identities remain important on both individual and community levels and will probably continue to do so well into the 21st century.

The different countries of Southeast Asia have assigned differing statuses to their local Peranakan communities. In Singapore,

PERANAKANS

location:
Singapore, Malaysia, Indonesia

time period:
10th century to the present

ancestry:
Hokkien Chinese, Cantonese, Malay, and to a much lesser degree, Indian

language:
Malay, Bahasa Indonesia, Cantonese, and other Chinese languages. English is a common second language for those engaged in international trade.

PERSIANS, ACHAEMENIDS

location:
Homeland in the area of present-day Iran, with an empire that spread from Macedonia to India

time period:
558–329 B.C.E.

ancestry:
Iranian

language:
Old Persian, Parsi, or Farsi, an Iranian language

Peranakans are considered more beautiful than the Chinese because of the infusion of Malay traits. In addition, while intermarriage is common today in Singapore, for the older Peranakan community the newer Chinese immigrants are derided as foreigners who have yet to prove themselves locally. In Indonesia, however, the derision goes in the opposite direction, with newer Chinese migrants looking down on the Peranakan community as lower-class.

Persians, Achaemenids (Parsargadae)

The Achaemenid period of Persian history is the time of the first Persian empire to emerge in Iran and Central Asia, from the sixth to the fourth centuries B.C.E.

GEOGRAPHY

The Achaemenid Empire at the height of its power in the fifth century B.C.E. stretched from Macedonia and Egypt in the west, through Turkey, the Middle East, and Central Asia to just east of Gandhara in India in the east. The Achaemenid royal sites—Susa (the administrative capital) and Persepolis (the treasury), Ecbatana (summer royal residence and former Median city), and Pasargadae (the city of Cyrus the Great)—were located in what is now Iran, the homeland of the Persian people. There were other royal constructions of the Persians throughout their empire, and additions were made to existing architecture, for instance, in Babylon, after Cyrus the Great captured it. The royal heirs Cambyses and Xerxes lived in Babylon before they succeeded to the throne, perhaps a reflection of the importance of this part of the empire. Other capital cities of the lands conquered by the Persians became the seats of the satraps who ruled locally.

ORIGINS

Until the sixth century B.C.E. the history of the Persian people is somewhat uncertain. The Persians encompassed several tribes speaking Iranian languages. By the early first millennium B.C.E. they were living in present-day Iran, south of the MEDES, and had come into conflict with the Assyrians, who were then the major power in the area. The rise to power of the royal clan, the Achaemenids, seemed to be rapid; from rulers of a small area in southern Iran, they became kings of the largest empire the world had known, conquering lands from the Mediterranean into India and even including part of Egypt.

In the fifth century B.C.E. the Greek historian Herodotus wrote that there were 10 Persian tribes, including the Achaemenid royal clan. Some were settled agriculturalists, and others were nomadic.

HISTORY

The founding of the Achaemenid Empire actually began with events in the Median Empire when Cyrus, the grandson of the ruler of the latter, Astyages, overthrew his grandfather with assistance from some of the empire's discontented nobility. Following that conquest, Cyrus conquered the empire of the Lydians in modern-day Turkey in 546 B.C.E. He then absorbed the city of Babylon and southern Mesopotamia in 539 B.C.E. and allowed the Jewish population who had been conquered by Babylonian king Nebuchadnezzar to return to their homeland if they so wished. Cyrus also permitted the Jews to restore the temple in Jerusalem, and he gave back to the Jews the utensils from the temple that Nebuchadnezzar had taken. For this, and for his tolerant style of rule, Cyrus was praised in the biblical books of Isaiah and Ezra. By the time of Cyrus's death in 529 B.C.E., his empire extended as far east as the Hindu Kush in Bactria or contemporary Afghanistan and

Persians, Achaemenids time line	
B.C.E.	
834	An Assyrian text mentions the rebellious people of Parsuash in Iran, the first written record of the Persians.
700	Time of Achaemenes, the possibly legendary leader of one of the Persian tribes and founder of the royal clan of Cyrus the Great. This tribe rules in southern Iran.
ca. 650–sixth century	Practice of Zoroastrianism becomes widespread.
550	Cyrus the Great defeats the Medes and begins his expansion of the Achaemenid Empire.
529	Cyrus dies, possibly at the hands of Tomyris, queen of the Massagetae.
514	Darius, the Persian king, invades and attempts to conquer the Scythians, who retreat before the Persians but do not submit.
513	Darius conquers the Indus Valley.
	Darius divides his empire into administrative provinces, or satrapies.
486	Height of the Persian Empire, the largest empire ever known; it stretches from Macedonia to India.
	Darius dies.
330–327	Macedonian invasion of Alexander the Great. Alexander defeats the forces of his Persian rival for world domination, Darius III, bringing an end to the Achaemenid Empire.

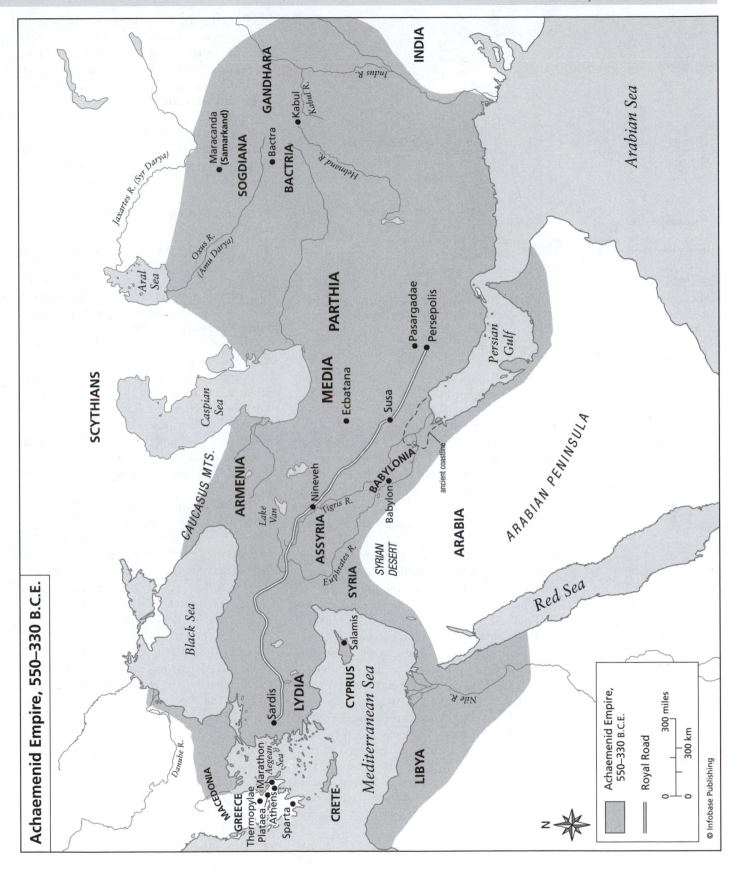

Achaemenid Empire, 550–330 B.C.E.

After conquering lands in what are today Turkey, Iran, and Iraq, Cyrus the Great was entombed in this 36-foot-tall mausoleum in his capital of Pasargadae, Iran. *(Art Resource/Alinari)*

west into Turkey. Cyrus's son Cambyses added Egypt to the empire.

Many sources point to Cyrus the Great as the first ruler for whom the concept of conquering the entire world became a conscious goal. It is not certain that Cyrus was a devout Zoroastrian, but he did introduce the idea of respecting the religions and beliefs of the various regions that he conquered, a sensible move to win the acceptance of the people he ruled. Darius, the successor of Cyrus, was clearly devoted to Zoroastrianism. In Zoroastrian cosmology, the world is locked in battle between two opposing gods: Ahura Mazda, the god of light and goodness, and Ahriman, the god of darkness and evil. At the end of time, Ahura Mazda will finally conquer his rival and goodness will prevail. Until that time all of creation, including humans, gods, and even nature, participates in this great struggle between light and dark, good and evil. Unlike Christianity, a later eschatological religion that focuses on the end of time, Zoroastrians did not see it as their duty to proselytize or convert others because they believed that all religions were equal and that good people of all faiths go to heaven. Therefore the Persian Empire was fairly tolerant with regard to the conquered populations' religious beliefs and practices.

Cyrus's son, Cambyses II, died during his Egyptian campaign and was succeeded by Darius I, an ambitious man who became king by trickery. Bringing together a vast army and navy to add Greece to the empire, Darius sent heralds to the Greek city-states asking for earth and water, symbols of surrender, and many cities submitted rather than face the Persians. Sparta and Athens, however, murdered the heralds and prepared to fight. The Persians had a huge army, with contingents from throughout the empire; a navy of Phoenician ships; and the king's guard, known in Greek sources as the Immortals. This force was 10,000 in number and when one died, he was immediately replaced so that their size remained constant. Nevertheless, the Persians were defeated at the famous Battle of Marathon (for which the race is named) and elsewhere in fierce battles. Darius returned to Persian domains, overcome by the difficulties of fighting an overseas war and the loss of important officers and ships. He did, however, add part of India to the empire in 513 B.C.E. and consolidated Persian rule in the Middle East and Central Asia.

The inclusion of parts of India in the Persian Empire changed that area considerably. For one thing, the idea of coinage was introduced and later was adopted in India. Indian traders were able to accumulate vast amounts of wealth by extending their business contacts across the empire. Some Indians also became fluent in the lingua franca of the empire, Aramaic, and adopted this language's script to write other languages as well.

The immediate successor of Darius, his son Xerxes, tried to succeed where his father had failed in Greece. Xerxes defeated the Spartans at Thermopylae in 480 B.C.E. but suffered great losses at Salamis and Plataea, and he, too, after pillaging Athens and carrying off many Greek objects, was forced to return to Persia. Dynastic discord troubled later rulers, but the Persians managed to maintain their vast domain until Alexander the Great appeared on the scene. He and his Macedonian forces defeated the Persians in several battles and by 329 B.C.E. had brought an end to the Persian Empire. The last Persian ruler, Darius III, was ultimately murdered by one of his own noblemen before Alexander had the opportunity to kill him himself, although Alexander pursued the remaining Persian generals into Bactria to destroy the empire's last remnants.

Darius the Great, who was obviously a skilled administrator, introduced many bureaucratic innovations to consolidate the empire, including a common set of weights and measures; coinage; and the notion of dividing the empire into satrapies, each ruled by a satrap, or governor, who allowed the local inhabitants to follow their traditional customs. Darius understood that different peoples within his multicultural empire lived by different cultural norms and legal requirements and so did not require a centralized or uniform legal system. Instead, he had his local leaders codify the laws for their own regions.

Darius also had Old Persian put into a written script, although he himself was illiterate. He established an extensive road and postal system, the 1,550-mile Royal Road running from Sardis, the capital of Lydia in Turkey, to the Persian capital of Susa. In a journey that took 90 days, messengers could safely facilitate communications in the entire empire; post stations along the road allowed messengers to exchange horses. As a result of Darius's innovations, the empire amassed enormous wealth in the form of tribute regularly given by the various satrapies and stored in the treasury at Persepolis. According to a list of tribute by Herodotus, the Indian lands contributed by far the largest amount in the form of gold dust, but other satrapies donated large quantities of silver. In the words of Darius, "What was said to them [the satraps] by me both night and day that was done."

CULTURE

According to Herodotus, few peoples in the ancient world were as willing as the Achaemenid Persians to adopt cultural features from other peoples. They adopted Median clothing after having conquered the Medes in their Iranian homeland and Egyptian armor for their soldiers. Even the languages of the empire were largely borrowed from other peoples. The official language, Old Persian, acquired its cuneiform script from Babylonian and Elamite. The lingua franca of the empire, which was used in most situations aside from official inscriptions in Babylonian, Elamite, and Old Persian, was Aramaic, an alphabetic Semitic language related to Hebrew and other Cannanite languages and borrowed from the Assyrians, who themselves had adopted it from the Aramaeans.

Herodotus also wrote that the Persians valued sons highly. Such was their value that boy children spent their first five years out of their own father's sight because if a father was to lose a son after seeing him, the loss would be too much to bear. Indeed, in addition to military prowess, having many sons was the primary sign of manliness, and men with the most sons gained great praise from their peers. This focus on boys and men also contributed to a decrease in the status of women throughout many of the lands conquered by the Achaemenids so that they were no longer allowed to own property or appear in court, as they had been able to do in some parts of the empire. However, the mother of the heir apparent had great prestige and power, and her advice to the king was much respected.

Herodotus also claimed that the Persians were polygynous, allowing men to take more than one wife. Achaemenid kings also had large harems of concubines, as many as 250 or more young women. From these wives and concubines, Persian kings had many offspring: sons who served the court in the military and in civil administration, daughters who were given as wives to satraps and other important officials to cement ties to the court.

What is less clear about Persian kinship is the meaning behind Persian texts that state that next-of-kin marriages were not only allowed but actively pursued. Some scholars have read this as meaning that actual mother-son, father-daughter, and brother-sister marriages were allowed, while others believe that only classificatory relatives were allowed (female relatives in mother's generation classified as mother, relatives in one's own generation classified as siblings, and so on). This aspect of Persian kinship has been commented upon in Greek, Roman, and Christian sources, as well as later Iranian sources, but without enough context for us to settle on one or the other possibility.

The power of the Persian king was enormous; Darius and succeeding kings made it clear that Ahura Mazda had given them the throne. With this divine approval, the king of kings could do no wrong, and whatever he did, he did better than anyone else. When he sat on his throne, dressed in royal robes and covered with gold jewelry, he was elevated above the height of visitors who appeared before him and was separated from them by a veil so that no one could gaze directly on the king. Servants who stood behind the throne wore coverings over their mouths so that their breath would not touch the king. When the king walked in the palace, special rugs, used only for him, were thrown on the floors, and when he traveled, silver cans of boiled water from the river at Susa were carried with him in mule-drawn carts. A golden stool was placed beside his chariot to allow the king to step in, and those who came before the king had to bend low before him. The king dined off gold plates and drank from golden goblets. According to Greek sources, when Alexander captured the family of Darius III after the battle of Issus, three or four tons of gold cups were taken as part of the royal dining set.

As mentioned above, the religion of the Achaemenid Empire was Zoroastrianism. The priests of this religion, who sacrificed all varieties of animals, except dogs, with their bare hands, as well as kept the sacred fires going at the temples, were called Magi. (The Three Wise Men who brought gold, frankincense, and myrrh to the baby Jesus, as written in the New Testament, were Magi.) Sacrifices were made to the Sun and Moon as well as to the four elements of earth, wind, water, and most important, fire. While the kinship system of the Persians generally is a bit unclear about brother-sister marriages, the sources are explicit in stating that Magi were allowed to marry and have children with their closest relatives. The other aspect of Zoroastrianism that has attracted the interests of scholars from Herodotus forward was their belief that the bodies of the dead should be neither buried nor cremated but rather left in the open to be devoured by sacred dogs and birds of prey. This practice particularly disgusted the forces of Alexander the Great when they conquered the lands of the Achaemenid Empire and caused them to be particularly brutal with their Persian subjects.

See also BACTRIANS; PERSIANS; SASSANIDS; SCYTHIANS; SOGDIANS.

FURTHER READING

Margaret Cool Root. *The King and Kingship in Achaemenid Art* (Leiden, the Netherlands: E. J. Brill, 1979).

Muhammad A. Dandamaev and Vladimir G. Lukonin. *The Culture and Social Institutions of Ancient Iran* (New York: Cambridge University Press, 1989).

Ilya Gershevitch, ed. *The Cambridge History of Iran, Vol. 2: The Median and Achaemenian Periods* (Cambridge: Cambridge University Press, 1985).

Persians, Sassanids (Sassanians)

The Sassanid Persians emerged in the third century as the most powerful empire in Iran and then later throughout most of the Middle East and Central Asia. They saw themselves as the inheritors of the Achaemenid Empire (*see* PERSIANS, ACHAEMENIDS), which had collapsed hundreds of years earlier.

GEOGRAPHY

The Sassanid homeland is the Fars district of contemporary Iran, located in the southwestern region of the country. This is a varied terrain that includes the Zagros Mountains, giving the central region a relatively cool climate, in addition to Lake Parishan and the lower, hotter regions in the south. From this region, the Persians began to build their second empire, the Achaemenid being the first; at its largest point in the seventh century the Sassanid Empire included territory in contemporary Turkmenistan, Uzbekistan, Afghanistan, Yemen, Oman, Syria, Jordan, Turkey, Georgia, Armenia, Azerbaijan, and parts of Kazakhstan, Pakistan, India, Russia, Saudi Arabia, Egypt, Libya, Kyrgyzstan, and Tajikistan.

ORIGINS

The origins of the ancient Iranian speakers remain shrouded in mystery. They seem to have constituted a disparate group of tribes from the steppes of Central Asia, speaking an Iranian language. Some tribal groups were settled agriculturalists, while others retained a nomadic lifestyle into the early centuries of the common era. The Iranians who settled in Fars eventually became known as Persians and emerged as the most powerful group in the region. From 554 to 331 B.C.E. the Persians were able to expand their homeland into an empire, the Achaemenid, which included territory from the Caucasus to India. About 500 years later, the Sassanids reemerged as a dominant force in the area with the claim of being the second Persian Empire.

The term *Sassanid,* or *Sassanian,* comes from the name of a Zoroastrian priest, Sassan, who was supposedly a distant ancestor of Ardashir I, the founding king of the dynasty and empire; Sassan was also said to be a descendant of the Achaemenids, thus giving the Sassanids legitimate connections with their predecessors. In the mid-220s C.E., Ardashir conquered the last king of the PARTHIANS, Artabanus V, and established his own capital in the former Parthian capital of Ctesiphon. Later Sassanid kings expanded the empire to encompass all the former Achaemenid lands and beyond.

HISTORY

The primary historical narrative of the Sassanid Empire, like the Parthians before them, was one of struggle. For their entire era the Persians struggled to take territory from their neighbors, largely in the belief that they were the only legitimate heirs of the Achaemenid Empire, and then to hold onto the territory they had taken. These struggles put the Persians at almost constant odds with the Romans, KUSHANS, HEP-

---

PERSIANS, SASSANIDS

location:
Homeland in Fars, Persia, in the area of modern-day southwestern Iran, with an empire that spread from Armenia to India, Russia to Yemen

time period:
224–642 C.E.

ancestry:
Iranian

language:
Middle Persian or Pahlavi, an Iranian language

HTHALITES, ARMENIANS, and other local and regional powers. To succeed in this constant warfare, the Sassanids developed well-trained and organized armies, with impressive armor covering most of the soldiers' bodies, and heavy weaponry. Even their horses were armored.

The history of the Persian-Roman struggle is particularly important for understanding the history of the Sassanids, despite having begun during the Parthian era about 300 years before the emergence of the Sassanids themselves. The more than 600 years of conflict between them remain today the longest period of recorded war between two parties.

The first battle between Sassanids and Romans took place less than a decade after the founding of the Sassanid Empire in 224. In 232 the Roman emperor Severus Alexander sent a legion to Hatra, in present-day Iraq, to stop the westward movement of Sassanid armies after their initial success in Mesopotamia. Thus began an almost constant state of battle between the two empires throughout the entire third century, over territory in Mesopotamia and its borderlands. The fourth century, especially during the reign of the Sassanid king Shapur II, saw similar struggles, with the Sassanids taking the offensive during the middle decades of the century but achieving few lasting results. The fifth century was a rare time of stability with just a few small skirmishes in the years 420–422 before full-scale war reemerged in the sixth century, lasting until 591. This year marks an unusual alliance between the Sassanid leader Khosrow II and the Byzantine (Eastern Roman) emperor Maurice. When Khosrow II was deposed by other Persian nobles, Maurice served as his protector and benefactor, helping him to regain his throne in exchange for territory in northern Mesopotamia. After Maurice's death, however, Khosrow II retook that territory as well as lands in Syria, Palestine, Egypt, and present-day Turkey; by 615 the Persians were on Europe's doorstep just outside Constantinople, present-day Istanbul, before retreating again throughout the early seventh century. The decisive battle, which finally tipped the scales toward the Byzantines, was the Battle of Nineveh in 627, just before the Arab invasions supplanted the victorious Byzantines as well.

While most of the struggle between Sassanids and Romans took place in the Middle East, the Sassanids' sovereignty in Central Asia, India, and the Caucasus likewise came as a result of the success of their armies. Until the end of

Persians, Sassanids time line

C.E.

208 Ardashir I becomes shah, or king, of the Istakhr district in Persia. From there he begins to consolidate power and overthrow other local leaders.

224 Ardashir I overthrows the Parthian king, Artabanus V, and establishes his empire, named for his distant ancestor, Sassan, a descendant of the Achaemenids.

229–232 The holiest Zoroastrian book, the Avesta, is compiled from earlier sources. The most ancient portion, the Gathas, is believed to have been written by Zarathustra himself at least 3,000 years ago.

242 Coronation of Shapur I, son of Ardashir I, who expands the empire's boundaries well beyond Persia, makes Zoroastrianism the state religion, and centralizes state rule.

260 Sassanid armies defeat a Roman legion, take 70,000 Romans prisoner, and capture Emperor Valerian I.

272 Death of Shapur I.

ca. 400 The last animal sacrifices take place in the Zoroastrian kingdom.

483 Tolerance of Christians and Christianity becomes official policy with the Edict of Toleration. This is soon ignored, and the persecution continues.

533 Treaty of Endless Peace signed with Roman emperor Justinian I; broken in 540 by Khosrau I when he invades Syria.

557 Persians join forces with nomads to defeat the Hephthalites.

614 Sassanids capture Damascus and Jerusalem.

627 Byzantine emperor Heraclius defeats a Sassanid army at Nineveh; the final battle between these old enemies.

637 Capital city of Ctesiphon falls to Arab armies.

642 Last remnants of the Sassanid army destroyed at Nehavend.

651 The last Sassanid emperor, Yazdegerd III, is killed outside the Central Asian city of Merv, contemporary Mary.

the third century, the Kushans were the most organized enemy of the Sassanids on their eastern border. The Kushan empire had occupied territory in contemporary Afghanistan, Pakistan, and India during the Parthian era but lost it early in the Sassanid period when Ardashir I and later Shapur I began their quest to reclaim all former Achaemenid lands. The Sassanids, or Indo-Sassanians as they are often called when referring to the eastern portions of their empire, held onto their Indian and Bactrian territory until 410, when the Hephthalites invaded and secured Bactria (in contemporary Afghanistan) and Gandhara (in North-Central India). The Hephthalites subsequently lost these lands in 565 when the Sassanids joined with a nomadic army from the Central Asian steppes to take it back. The Hephthalites and TURKIC PEOPLES allied with each other a generation later and then again in 619, in the First and Second Turkish-Hephthalite Wars, to push the Sassanids back toward their Persian homeland.

The fifth century also saw conflict develop between the Persians and Armenians in Greater Armenia. The year 451 saw the greatest battle between these two very different peoples, the Christian Armenians and Zoroastrian Sassanids, the Battle of Avarayr in Armenia. In that year Armenian rebels rose up against the persecution of their religion and fought a bloody, losing battle against a Persian army that vastly outnumbered them. Despite the Armenians' military loss, the strength of their rebellion forced the Sassanid king, Yazdegerd II, to revise his opposition to Christianity in that province and to allow the building of new churches.

Internally, as well, the Sassanids struggled to quell the voices of their diverse populations. Religious, linguistic, and cultural diversity was tolerated on the whim of each individual ruler, with some being more open than others. The empire's Christian minority experienced quite a bit of persecution, especially after the fourth century when it became the official religion of the Sassanids' greatest enemy: the Romans. Being a Christian after this time was treason. Even sects that differed significantly from Christianity as it was practiced in Rome suffered greatly. Manes, a third-century Persian religious figure, believed that he was the final prophet of God; he was a presence in the court of King Ardashir I but angered the priests (Magi) and eventually was crucified in 276 for his beliefs. His religion, Manichaeanism, combines elements from many religions, including Zoroastrianism, Christianity, Buddhism, and other religions from the Middle East. The primary features of Manichaeanism are the dualism of good and evil and the belief in the release of the spirit from the body through asceticism. While dualism is a feature of Zoroastrianism, the Sassanid state religion, the refusal to recognize Ahura Mazda as divine caused significant persecution of this religion during several periods of the Sassanid era.

The final battles between Sassanids and rivals for their territorial ambitions were fought with Arab invaders in the 630s. The first battle between these forces was the Battle of Chains, which took place after the Arab leader Khalid al-Waleed had exhausted his Persian foes by moving his highly mobile forces around Iraq on camel and horseback. The less mobile Persians were exhausted from marching in the desert for weeks prior to the battle and eventually lost to the Arabian horsemen. After probably at least three more years of Persian-Arab fighting throughout the Middle East, the decisive Arab victory finally came at the Battle of al-Qadisiyyah, an event that has developed into a battle of mythological proportions. Most scholars do agree that it actually happened, but even the date, sometime between 630 and 634, has been obscured by the victorious Arab tales that developed around the event.

CULTURE

The structure of Persian society during the Sassanid period was similar to other centralized kingdoms, with rich noble families who occupied inherited positions and castles fully integrated into the state structure. Priests, warriors, peasants, government officials, and merchants made up the official class groupings of society at that time. Unlike in some of their rival lands, such as Sogdiana, merchants were at the bottom of this hierarchy. Indeed, often this activity was left to Jews, Romans, or Armenians due to the low rank it was accorded in the Persian worldview. On the other hand, priests of the state religion, Zoroastrianism, known as Magi, Magha, or Mobed at various times, enjoyed great privileges during the Sassanid period due to their connection with the founding ancestor Sassan, himself a priest. They participated in all coronation ceremonies and in the conferring of the title Shahanshah, "King of Kings," which all Sassanid rulers held. Priests also served as judges and tax collectors at various times in addition to their role as religious specialists, which in the early days of the empire included sacrificing animals to the sun and moon, earth, wind, water, and especially fire.

The Sassanid era is sometimes seen as the transitional period between ancient and medieval times in the Middle East. One of the criteria used is the fact that Ardashir I not only practiced Zoroastrianism himself but declared that religion to be the official state religion for his entire empire, as Rome did in the following century with Christianity. Zoroastrianism by the third century was already an ancient Persian religion, which had developed out of an even older tradition of Mazdaism. Both religions, Zoroastrianism and Mazdaism, place Ahura Mazda at their center as the greatest god. In addition, Zoroastrianism, like Manichaeanism, was a dualistic religion in which the forces of light and good were constantly battling against those of darkness and evil. Zoroastrians believed (and PARSEES and other Zoroastrians continue to believe) that at the end of time the forces of Ahura Mazda, who struggle on the side of good, will vanquish the forces of Ahriman and all the other gods, people, and forces of nature that fight on the side of evil.

In addition to a centralized state religion, the Sassanid Empire is also noted for its centralized political power. Unlike the Parthians before them, who had utilized indirect rule in most of their lands, the Sassanids installed Persian rulers in most of the lands they conquered; these rulers controlled taxation, the raising of armies for both offensive and defensive purposes, and infrastructural development. Only in their marginal borderlands did the Sassanids allow local leaders to continue in their positions, as long as they performed the duties of loyal vassals, including paying tribute and maintaining their borders against the incursions of enemies.

The artistic developments of the Sassanids reflect the transition from ancient to medieval history. The art of the era was largely royal rather than popular, with the images of kings and nobles dominating most works, a trend that became more evident over time. This "court art," as it is called, used images of actual royal figures to depict the gods. Sassanid kings were also often shown single-handedly fighting off the enemy in heroic battle scenes of mythological proportions.

The Sassanid period is also well known as the period in which such games as backgammon, chess, and polo were either invented or disseminated beyond the halls and fields of a few noblemen. The earliest textual references to these games were written in the language of the empire, Middle Persian. It was also a time of great innovation in terms of military gear. The short coat of mail, waist belt, and hip belt for the sword and quiver utilized early in the era were later abandoned in favor of a much longer coat of chain mail, a helmet that provided protection for a soldier's face, and separate belts for bows and quivers on the one hand and a sword and dagger on the other. The use of a lance or ax and a shield that could be put over the shoulder on a strap while a cavalryman rode his horse also emerged as popular armaments during the Sassanid period.

See also BACTRIANS; SOGDIANS.

FURTHER READING

Vesta Sarkhosh Curtis, Robert Hillenbrand, and J. M. Rogers, eds. *The Art and Archaeology of Ancient Persia: New Light on the Parthian and Sasanian Empires* (London: I. B. Tauris, 1998).

Phnong (Pnong)

The Phnong are a population of about 30,000 residing in Cambodia's eastern Mondulkiri Province. They speak a Mon-Khmer language that is rapidly disappearing as the people attain literacy and familiarity with Cambodia's dominant Khmer language; several linguists predict the language will be extinct by 2050.

Traditional Phnong life was seminomadic and entailed moving between villages and farms as the season dictated. In addition, every few years entire villages moved as well. Each year the people would clear a small section of forest, burn off the vegetation to provide fertilizer, and grow rice, corn, beans, squash, and other vegetables. When all the land around a village had been used, the entire village would pack up and move to a new region, either virgin forest or land that had been left fallow for at least 12 years to regenerate its productive capacity. In addition to farming, the Phnong also kept chickens, buffaloes, and elephants for food and domestic use and gathered a wide variety of forest products, from honey and resin to wood, for sale. In recent memory their shifting agricultural techniques have not provided enough food for each family, so cash-generating opportunities have become important. Unfortunately, some of these opportunities have come at the expense of a household's long-term sustainability, especially the sale of elephants, the traditional Phnong sign of wealth, which limits the household's ability to clear forest land for farming.

Phnong society was organized along the twin principles of kinship and residence. Their kinship system was determined by matrilineal descent, in which an individual inherited his or her lineage membership from the mother, mother's mother, and so on. Each matrilineal group also occupied a separate area of each village, which entailed a matrilocal residence pattern of husbands moving into their wives' homes at the time of marriage. This traditional pattern was institutionalized after the People's Republic of Kampuchea was installed following the demise of the Khmer Rouge in 1979 and has been retained today. Women among the Phnong were important decision makers at the household level; nonetheless, men retained the most valued positions in each village.

Today the Phnong are experiencing extensive changes to their way of life due to an influx of tourists, logging companies, and other outsiders coming to Mondulkiri Province. In the 1990s and early 2000s, several Phnong villages invested in coffee production, but by 2003 the low price of

---

PHNONG

location:
Mondulkiri Province, Cambodia

time period:
Unknown to the present

ancestry:
Mon-Khmer

language:
Phnong, probably the same language as Southern-Central Mnong, a Mon-Khmer language of Vietnam

PITJANTJATJARA

location:
Central Australian desert

time period:
Perhaps as early as 60,000 B.C.E. and definitely 45,000 B.C.E. to the present

ancestry:
Aboriginal Australian

language:
Pitjantjatjara

this commodity meant failure; a few have turned to cashew production, while others have returned to subsistence agriculture supplemented by gathering forest products. The Cambodian Family Development Services has also offered microcredits to Phnong women to begin a weaving cooperative to produce scarves and bags to sell. These kinds of projects are vitally important to the Phnong, who are extremely reluctant to engage in waged labor because of the traditional stigma attached to this practice; in the past, the very poorest Phnong individuals would work for wealthier families to clear forestland or to fulfill their communal obligations.

See also CAMBODIANS: NATIONALITY.

Pitjantjatjara (Anangu, Indigenous or Aboriginal Australians)

The name *Pitjantjatjara* refers to both the language and an aboriginal people of the Central Australian desert. Traditionally referring to themselves as Anangu ("people"), they are closely related in language and custom to the Yankunytjatjara and Ngaanyatjarra of the western desert language group. Pitjantjatjara country extends from the northwestern corner of South Australia into both the Northern Territory and Western Australia.

Traditionally a nomadic hunting and gathering people, the Pitjantjatjara survived in harsh arid conditions for thousands of years by moving between temporary water supplies in the rainy seasons and permanent water catchments in the dry seasons. Such mobility shaped a social structure that maximized survival by strategic marriage alliances and an intimate familial connection to the land.

Though a remote desert people, the Pitjantjatjara did not escape the often fatal consequences of early European settlement. In response to the devastating impact of contacts with dingo hunters and settlers, 45,360 square miles of land were set aside in 1921 for their use in the northwest of South Australia. However, ongoing abuses against them prompted the Presbyterian Church to establish the Ernabella Mission in 1938 as a safe haven. Ahead of its time, largely due to the efforts of Dr. Charles Duguid, the mission respected Pitjantjatjara culture and taught in the native language, highly uncommon practices at other missions. In 1948 Ernabella Arts Inc. was established; it is thought to be the longest continually running aboriginal art center in Australia.

In the 1950s the remote desert location at Maralinga, home to the southern Pitjantjatjara

people, Maralinga Tjarutja, became the testing ground for British nuclear bombs. Prior to the tests many were forced to leave their land, but not all inhabitants were accounted for. As a result, large numbers of people were contaminated, and many have subsequently died from the nuclear fallout. Initial cleanup attempts in 1967 proved to be inadequate, with unacceptable levels of radioactive materials still present. A more successful effort was completed in 2000, but debate continues over the safety of the site.

In response to a history of environmental and cultural devastation, the Pitjantjatjara began to assert their rightful ownership of the land in the last quarter of the 20th century. In 1981 the Pitjantjatjara Land Rights Act was passed, granting freehold title over 64,000 square miles of land in northwestern South Australia. In 1984 the Maralinga Tjarutja Land Rights Act passed, granting freehold title over 50,184 square miles of land, and in 2004 the Unnamed Conservation Park in South Australia was transferred to the Maralinga Tjarutja.

Today there are approximately 4,000 Pitjantjatjara living in small communities throughout their traditional lands, including the sacred sites of Uluru and Kata Tjuta, the traditional names of Ayres Rock and the Olgas, respectfully. This is an extremely significant spiritual and ceremonial area with almost 50 identified sacred sites and more than 10 Tjurkurpa (dreaming) tracks. Several of these tracks are said to lead as far as the sea in all directions. Because Uluru is also a significant tourist site, the Australian government, under Prime Minister Bob Hawke, was not prepared to grant land rights to the Pitjantjatjara people without an agreement on a leaseback plan for a joint-management system. An initial 10-point plan was agreed on, but the government reneged on two significant points. The first was that the Australian government would have a 99-year lease on the park instead of the 55 years originally agreed, and the second was that tourists could climb Uluru, a site sacred to its aboriginal owners.

See ABORIGINAL AUSTRALIANS; AUSTRALIANS: NATIONALITY.

Polynesians (Polynésiens, people of Polynesia)

The Polynesians are a group of people loosely related by language, geography, and culture who reside on more than 1,000 islands in the South Pacific. They all speak some form of Malayo-Polynesian language and come originally

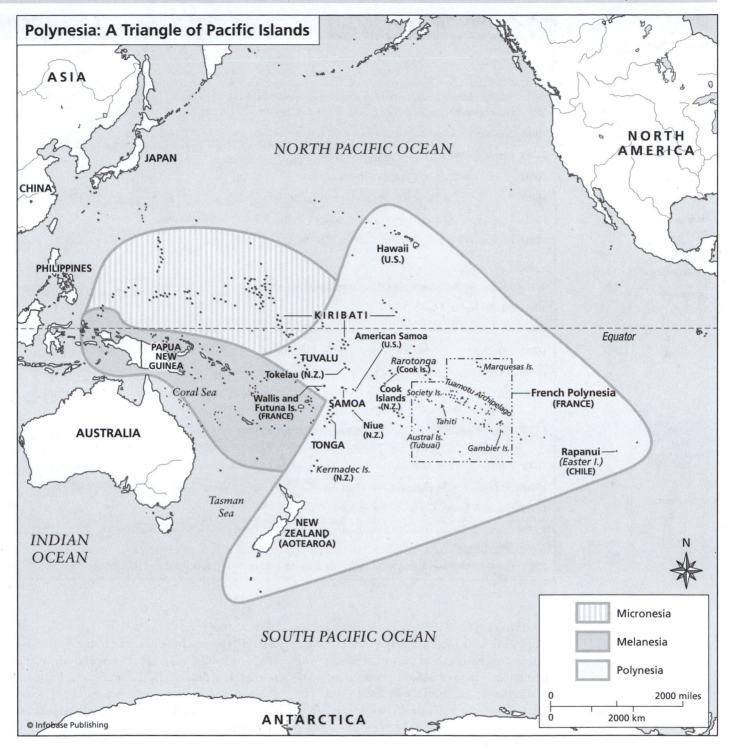

Polynesia: A Triangle of Pacific Islands

ASIA

NORTH PACIFIC OCEAN

NORTH AMERICA

JAPAN

CHINA

PHILIPPINES

Hawaii
(U.S.)

KIRIBATI

Equator

American Samoa
(U.S.)

PAPUA NEW GUINEA

TUVALU

Rarotonga
(Cook Is.)

Marquesas Is.

Tokelau (N.Z.)

Cook Islands
(N.Z.)

Society Is.

Tuamotu Archipelago

French Polynesia
(FRANCE)

Coral Sea

Wallis and
Futuna Is.
(FRANCE)

SAMOA

AUSTRALIA

Niue
(N.Z.)

Tahiti

Austral Is.
(Tubuai)

Gambier Is.

Rapanui
(Easter I.)
(CHILE)

TONGA

Kermadec Is.
(N.Z.)

Tasman
Sea

INDIAN
OCEAN

NEW
ZEALAND
(AOTEAROA)

N

SOUTH PACIFIC OCEAN

ANTARCTICA

© Infobase Publishing

	Micronesia
	Melanesia
	Polynesia

0 — 2000 miles
0 — 2000 km

from one of the many islands within the triangle formed by Hawaii, Rapanui (Easter Island), and New Zealand. In addition, many aspects of their religious life, origin stories, and even subsistence patterns have common roots in their traditional Polynesian heritage. This heritage is ancient, stemming from an original migratory population who left south China 6,500–7,000 years ago. From these early origins, the population we know today as Polynesian spread, slowly at first, to Taiwan, parts of Indonesia and the Philippines, and then eventually to most of the inhabitable islands as far east as Rapanui.

The contemporary Polynesians continue to have some features in common, while there are also some significant differences in social and political structures. Some of these differences, such as those relating to subsistence pattern and

POLYNESIANS

location:
Central and South Pacific Ocean, triangle of islands between Hawaii in the north, New Zealand in the south, and Rapanui (Easter Island) in the east, not including Kiribati and the Line Islands

time period:
1350 B.C.E. to the present

ancestry:
Austronesian

language:
Malayo-Polynesian

Polynesians time line

B.C.E.

5000–4500 First possible departure of Austronesians from south China to Taiwan. They establish the Ta-p'en-k'eng culture there, including domesticated pigs, chickens, and dogs; taro, yams, and sweet potatoes; stone tools; and distinctive pottery.

3000 This cultural package arrives in the Philippines.

2500 Arrival on Celebes and Timor in Indonesia.

2000 Arrival on Java and Sumatra in Indonesia.

1600 Arrival on the New Guinea coast and outlying islands.

1350 Emergence of Lapita (decorated) pottery in the Solomons, Bismarcks.

1200 Arrival in New Caledonia, Samoa, Fiji, Tonga.

C.E.

0 Arrival in the Marquesas, Rarotonga (Cook Islands).

300–500 Arrival in Hawaii.

300–900 Inhabitation of Rapanui (Easter Island).

1000 Maori arrive on New Zealand; Pitcairn inhabited.

1000–1600 *Moai* and *ahu* (giant stone statues and their stone platforms) building frenzy on Rapanui.

1300 Group of Maori depart New Zealand to colonize the Chathams, become Moriori; Tahitians arrive in Hawaii and eliminate original Polynesian settlers.

1595 Spanish explorer Álvaro de Mendaña de Neira is the first European to discover one of the Polynesian island groups when he sees the Marquesas.

1642 Dutch explorer Abel Tasman sights New Zealand islands; four crew members are killed by Maori.

1768 French captain Bougainville visits Tahiti and makes it famous in his *Voyage autour du monde*.

1769 Captain James Cook arrives in New Zealand.

1778 Captain Cook arrives in Hawaii and names them the Sandwich Islands after one of his patrons.

1791 Captain William Broughton sights Chathams and names it for the ship HMS *Chatham*.

social structure, are the result of indigenous developments and local geography and climate. Others are the result of past experiences with colonialism. Today's Maori experienced colonization at the hands of the British in 18th- and 19th-century New Zealand, while the Tahitians experienced it at the hands of the French, and the Hawaiians at the hands of the United States. The Samoans have even more varied experiences, having had colonial interactions with the Germans and New Zealanders in the western islands and the Americans in the eastern islands. Other major Polynesian peoples include Marquesans, Rapanui (Easter Islanders), Tokelauans, Tongans, and Tuamotuans.

GEOGRAPHY

The current area of Polynesia, a name coined by Charles de Brosses in 1756 to refer to all Pacific islands and revised in 1831 by Jules Dumont d'Urville to its contemporary usage, is the triangle of Pacific islands between Hawaii in the north, New Zealand in the south, and Rapanui (Easter Island) in the east, not including Kiribati and the Line Islands, which are populated by Micronesians. This triangular area encompasses French Polynesia, including Tahiti and the other Society Islands, the Tuamotu Archipelago, the Marquesas, and the Gambier and Austral Islands. It also includes the French overseas territory of Wallis and Futuna Islands; New Zealand, which the Maori call Aotearoa; Rarotonga (the Cook Islands) and Niue, which are both independent but in free association with New Zealand; the New Zealand territories of Tokelau and the Kermadec Islands; the U.S. state of Hawaii and territory of American Samoa; the Chilean territory on Rapanui (Easter

1820 Maori chief visits London, receives gifts of muskets that exacerbate Maori internal warfare; this results in the Maori's 1835 destruction of Moriori society on Chathams.

1830s English missionaries settle in Samoa.

1840s New Zealand becomes a British colony with the signing of the Treaty of Waitangi.

1845 Tonga is united into a Polynesian kingdom by Tu'i Kanokupolu, later baptized as King George.

1897 Hawaii is annexed by the United States.

1900–05 Samoa is split in two, establishing American and Western Samoa (today's Samoa).

1916 British protectorates Gilbert and Ellice Islands are incorporated into a single colony.

1943 Tuvalu is selected as an allied air base in the war against Japan.

1959 Hawaii becomes the 50th state of the United States.

1962 Western Samoa is the first Pacific island to gain independence, from New Zealand, which took over from Germany at the end of World War I. It is recognized by the United Nations as Samoa in 1976 and officially changes the name to Samoa in 1997.

1965 Cook Islands become a self-governing territory in free association with New Zealand, joined by Niue in 1974.

1966 France begins nuclear testing on the French Polynesian atoll of Moruroa.

1970 Tongan independence from Britain.

1974 Polynesians on Ellice Islands (Tuvalu) vote to separate from the Micronesian Gilbert Islands (which became Kiribati) due to ethnic differences.

1978 Tuvalu gains independence from Britain.

1996 France conducts its final nuclear test in French Polynesia before agreeing to abide by the Comprehensive Test Ban Treaty.

2003 French Polynesia becomes an overseas collectivity of France, designating a greater degree of autonomy than it had as an overseas territory from 1946 to 2003.

2004 Small number of Tongan soldiers are deployed to Iraq as part of the Coalition of the Willing.

2008 Tonga's King Tupou V promises a democratically elected parliament will rule in the country by 2010.

Island); and the independent states of Samoa, Tonga, and Tuvalu.

While located in the Polynesian triangle and once inhabited by Polynesian people, Pitcairn Island is not currently classified as Polynesian because its sole inhabitants are descendants of the HMS *Bounty* mutineers who settled there in 1789, along with their Tahitian shipmates. Rather than speaking a Polynesian language, their language is an 18th-century English creole with some Tahitian words. At the same time, a few people who speak one of the 36 Polynesian languages, primarily in the Ellicean language group, live outside this triangle in French New Caledonia, New Guinea (*see* NEW GUINEA HIGHLANDERS; NEW GUINEA SEPAK BASIN PEOPLE), Vanuatu (*see* VANAUTUANS: NATIONALITY), the Federated States of Micronesia (*see* MICRONESIANS, FEDERATED STATES OF: NATIONALITY), and the Solomon Islands.

ORIGINS

The history of the Polynesian people begins between 7,000 and 6,500 years ago, when some AUSTRONESIANS left southern China. In the first leg of their journey, constituting the first several thousand years of Polynesian history, they came across populations of hunters and gatherers in Taiwan, Indonesia, and the Philippines who had left Asia tens of thousands of years earlier. In every instance, the proto-Polynesians supplanted the earlier peoples they encountered, probably because their domesticated plants and animals allowed them to live at higher population densities and to dedicate more resources to warfare and technological development. The archaeological evidence of the domesticated root crops taro, yams, and sweet potatoes; the tree crops bananas, bread-fruit, and coconuts; chickens, dogs, and pigs; and polished stone tools and pottery allow us to date the appearance of these proto-Polynesians with relative accuracy.

The first leg of the Polynesians' extensive colonization of the Pacific was thus Taiwan, where their most distant relatives, ABORIGINAL TAIWANESE, continue to speak languages that are part of the greater Austronesian language family. From Taiwan these ancient seafarers used dugout canoes to explore and colonize the Philippines in about 3000 B.C.E. and the Indonesian islands of Celebes, Timor, and North Borneo in about 2500 B.C.E.

Around 1200 B.C.E. what has become known as the heartland of Polynesian culture was established in Samoa and Tonga, as well as in Fiji and the islands of New Caledonia, which were later also occupied by MELANESIANS. During this period Polynesian culture changed in character somewhat, taking on the traits of what has become known as LAPITA CULTURE, with its distinctively decorated pottery. From this heartland of Polynesian culture, other Polynesian groups established themselves further east in the Marquesas, Societies, Hawaiian, and Pitcairn Islands; south in New Zealand and the Chathams, and even as far west as Madagascar off the coast of Africa. For reasons that have yet to be determined, however, most of these islands do not show any evidence of Lapita-style pottery.

LANGUAGES

The Polynesian languages are members of one of the subgroups in the Central-Eastern Malayo-Polynesian family, the other being Micronesian. Within the Polynesian family, two further subdivisions are made between the Tongic languages of Tonga and Niue (and sometimes Niuafo'ou) and the nuclear Polynesian languages of the rest of the region. This nuclear group can also be further subdivided into two branches. The first group consists of the Samoic languages of Samoa, Tokelau, and Pukapuka (from the Cook Islands), as well as the Uvean, Ellicean, and Futunic groups of languages. The second grouping of 13 Eastern Polynesian languages is divided among two branches: the Rapanui, spoken only on the island of the same name; and the branch comprising the Central East Polynesian languages of Rapa; the Marquesan languages of Hawaiian, Marquesan, Pukapukan (French Polynesia), and Mangarevan; and the Tahitic languages of Austral, Maori, Moriori, Tuamotuan, Penrhyn, Rarotongan, Rakahanga-Manahiki, and Tahitian.

With these close linguistic connections, the Polynesian languages that continue to be spoken today share many words, grammatical

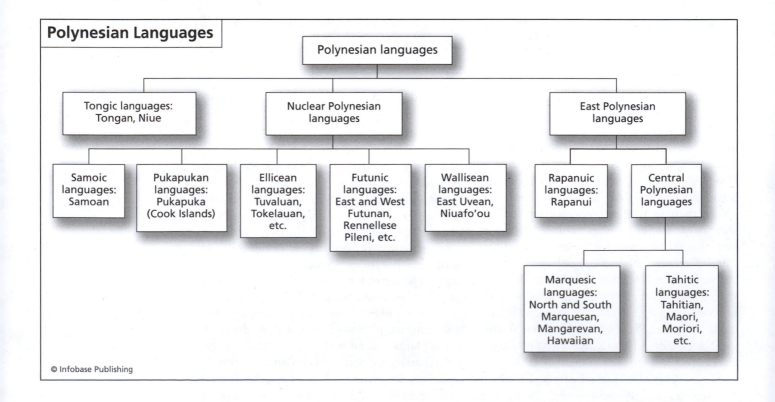

Polynesian Languages

Polynesian languages
- Tongic languages: Tongan, Niue
  - Samoic languages: Samoan
  - Pukapukan languages: Pukapuka (Cook Islands)
- Nuclear Polynesian languages
  - Ellicean languages: Tuvaluan, Tokelauan, etc.
  - Futunic languages: East and West Futunan, Rennellese Pileni, etc.
  - Wallisean languages: East Uvean, Niuafo'ou
- East Polynesian languages
  - Rapanuic languages: Rapanui
  - Central Polynesian languages
    - Marquesic languages: North and South Marquesan, Mangarevan, Hawaiian
    - Tahitic languages: Tahitian, Maori, Moriori, etc.

structures, and phonetic features. For example, the well-known Hawaiian greeting *aloha* corresponds to the Maori term *aroha,* meaning "love." The words for *sky* and *house,* among many others, have common roots, and the rules for forming plural nouns are also shared. Grammatically, all Polynesian languages distinguish between possessives that are temporary (or what grammarians call alienable) and those that are permanent, or are attributes of the possessor. In other words, Polynesian languages distinguish between "my book," which I own, and "my book," which has been written about me by somebody else. Other common traits can be found in pronouns, which come in singular ("I"), plural ("we," two people), and multiple plural ("we," three or more people). Many Polynesian languages also share the heavy use of a glottal stop as a common consonant, written as an apostrophe or other diacritical mark, and a distinction in meaning between long and short vowel sounds. These attributes have been lost in some languages because many missionaries did not realize their significance and wrote Polynesian-language Bibles without them.

HISTORY

Despite the early Polynesians' ability to sail for long periods, sometime after the inhabitation of most of the Polynesian islands significant contact between eastern and western Polynesians ended, leaving many Polynesian societies to develop fairly independently of their remote neighbors.

The independent development of political, social, and economic structures on the various Polynesian islands ended with the large-scale colonization of the area in the 18th and 19th centuries. France and Britain were most active in the region, with the former colonizing Wallis and Futuna Islands and French Polynesia, including the Marquesas and Society Islands and its most famous individual island, Tahiti, and the latter taking New Zealand, the Cook Islands, Tonga, Tuvalu, and a number of smaller islands. Germany, the United States, and even Chile and later Australia and New Zealand were also active participants in the colonization of Polynesia. The colonial relationships that emerged left most societies largely dependent on outside trade and assistance for survival, with only a few island nations and territories able to retain their viable local structures.

In addition to political and economic change, colonization also brought tremendous social change to most Polynesian islands. One of the leading factors in this change was the extensive work of Christian missionaries in the region, including those from various Protestant denominations, Roman Catholicism, and even the Latter Day Saints (Mormons). The usual pattern was that missionaries spent a period learning the local language and customs and only then did they attempt to convert the local population, usually focusing first on Big Men, chiefs, or kings. For example, in 1812 King Pomare II of Tahiti converted to Christianity after a number of years of work by missionaries from the London Missionary Society (LMS); within a few years, the entire island had converted as well. In addition to proselytizing, or spreading the Christian message, many missionaries also devised a written form of many Polynesian languages in order to create local-language Bibles and attempted to eliminate what they thought of as sinful aspects of the local cultures, such as dancing and rituals. Some male missionaries raised families with local women.

Due to their remoteness in the Pacific, most of Polynesia, with the exception of Hawaii, came through World War II without seeing any significant military action. Real change did not reach most areas (outside Hawaii and New Zealand) until after the 1960s and 1970s, when Samoa, Tonga, and Tuvalu were able to establish themselves as independent states. The remaining Polynesian islands continue today to be held as states and dependencies of other countries.

CULTURE

Economy and Society

The various cultures that are considered part of the Polynesian world exhibited a vast array of social, political, and economic traits prior to colonization by Europeans and others. For example, the Moriori of the Chathams were a small, relatively egalitarian society that practiced hunting and gathering, while the much larger societies on Tonga and the Hawaiian Islands engaged in intensive agriculture and were among the most hierarchical societies in the world. One common theory for these great differences is that the geography and climate of the different islands played the deciding role in determining a society's social, political, and economic structures. The Chathams are too cold to support the kinds of domesticated plants that the Polynesian colonizers brought with them, forcing the population to revert to more ancient forms of subsistence and to keep their population density very low (five people per square mile). Conversely, the volcanic soils and fresh-water supply on Hawaii allowed traditional Polynesian agriculture to thrive, thus allowing for the development of a food surplus and a division of labor that supported the creation of a class of royal families who could control that surplus. On Hawaii, Tonga, and Tahiti, this hierarchical structure, with chiefly and commoner families separated by a caste-like social division, led to the independent development of political structures resembling the monarchical states of feudal Europe. If European colonization had not interrupted this process, the whole of the Pacific might have become tributaries to one or the other of these large protostates.

Other very visible facets of the development of hierarchy on some Polynesian islands are the great stone building projects throughout much of east Polynesia. These projects were of two different sorts. The first were *marae,* or large, rectangular meeting spaces enclosed by a wall of stone, often paved with stone or coral and containing a shrine at one end. The Maori always built *marae* in front of their communal meeting houses. The second kind of building project is exemplified by the large stone statues for which Easter Island (Rapanui) is famous. These enormous and difficult building projects indicate that a few members of these societies wielded a great deal of power over others: they were able to control the labor of thousands of individuals in the carving and transport of hundreds of tons of stone, all for the glorification of the most high-ranking ancestors.

The Hawaiian Islands also provide physical evidence of the early development of social hierarchy. Instead of stone building projects, the leaders on the islands of Kauai, Oahu, and Molokai used vast amounts of labor to construct massive irrigation projects, which in turn provided the greatest crop yields for taro in the entire Polynesian world and one of the highest population densities at 300 people per square mile. Hawaiians also used corvée labor, a mandatory period of service that commoners had to provide to chiefs and their families, to construct fishponds and raise pigs for ceremonial purposes.

While the original Austronesian colonizers left south China after the domestication of pigs, dogs, and chickens and the cultivation of taros, yams, sweet potatoes, coconuts, breadfruit, and bananas, not every Polynesian society wound up with this entire subsistence package. For example, New Zealand lacked pigs and chickens, while Rapanui and Tikopia lacked dogs and pigs. The cold climate of the Chathams and the southernmost portion of New Zealand's South Island required the abandonment of agriculture altogether since the traditional Polynesian crops had been domesticated in tropical climates. In both cases, hunting and gathering quickly replaced agriculture as the only reliable subsistence pattern. Many other Polynesian societies also relied heavily on the hunting and gathering of fish, mollusks, and seabirds, though Rapanui, Pitcairn, and the Marquesas are poor in most of these resources due to their absence of coral reefs and lagoons. On Rapanui, the development of intensive chicken farming made up for this lack of local protein sources.

Another shared linguistic and cultural attribute throughout much of Polynesia, indeed much of the Pacific more generally, is the use of *kava,* or *awa,* as it is known in Hawaii. Kava comes from the root or stump of the *Piper methysticum* shrub, a relative of black pepper. The normal preparation in the Pacific is to create an herbal tea from dried kava root, which is drunk at religious, political, and social events. Some of the effects of drinking kava are numbness in the mouth, slight increase in social and even euphoric behavior, and a sense of calmness and well-being. Kava is nonaddictive and seems to elicit no unpleasant aftereffects the next day. It has been linked with liver toxicity in some European and North American tests of the product, but this is probably due to the use of the entire plant rather than just the root, since this effect is not known in its traditional usage.

Religion

While most Polynesians today have been Christians for many generations, traditionally they were known as polytheists, people who believed in multiple gods, spirits, and the power of the ancestors here on Earth. The most important of these many gods had a name similar to the Tahitian god Taaroa, the creator (Tangaroa, the god of the sea, in Maori). Many Polynesians also shared an origin myth detailing the marriage of Sky and Earth, which resulted in the birth of this world and all things in it. There are common stories about the creation of islands, which were pulled up from the sea or thrown down from heaven; about long sea voyages; and about the culture hero Māui, who is sometimes a god, sometimes human, and sometimes something in between. Supplementing these common Polynesian themes, all local communities also had their own myths, gods, spirits, rituals, and even sacred geographic features, which were often believed to be the physical remains of gods and ancestors.

The two most important aspects of all Polynesian religions are the concepts of mana, or sacred power, and tabu, or sacred prohibitions (the origin of the English word "taboo"). All Polynesian languages had words and concepts that encompassed these meanings, ritual practices that brought the concepts to life, and a set of origin myths that explained and contextualized the concepts. These intertwined concepts served to organize much of Polynesian societies generally, including the social relationships between women and men, among different clans and lineages, and among different classes, as well as planting of crops, fishing, and building of both homes and ritual sites. These two concepts are so central to Polynesian life that it was their existence in certain island societies that led Jules Dumont d'Urville in 1831 to categorize them as Polynesian, while those that lacked the concept of tabu were classified as Micronesian.

The names of the Polynesians' gods, the mythology surrounding them, rituals, rules of tabu, and all other aspects of the Polynesian religion were handed down orally from one generation to the next in elaborate storytelling. Considerable human labor and material resources were expended in complex religious rituals, often held in the stone *marae* structures by the *tahu'a,* or priests, for honoring the gods through sacrifice, ceremony, and feasting. In the most hierarchical Polynesian societies on Hawaii, Tonga, and Tahiti, these rituals were often dedicated to preserving the political hierarchy, with the ancestors and mythology of the chief's lineage having the most prominent place in the religious sphere as well.

Throughout Polynesia another aspect of the religious sphere is the practice of tattooing, from the Tahitian word *tatau,* which means "to hit repeatedly," the method of marking the skin with indelible inks. Tattooing, which was believed to be a gift to humans from the gods and was controlled entirely by practiced tattoo masters, was used to indicate social status in the ranked societies of Polynesia, to present one's personality to the world, and even as a protection against evil spirits. It was an important part of both male and female rites of passage, when young Polynesians were recognized as adults. In the Marquesas, 12-year-old girls had to get their right hands tattooed before they were allowed to prepare meals for consumption by others, and throughout Polynesia 12-year-old boys had to show their tattoos in order to be recognized as clan members and welcomed to the world of men. While the art of tattooing almost disappeared in the Pacific during the colonial era due to the activities of missionaries who prohibited tattooing as a heathen practice, since the 1980s it has flourished. Contemporary designs are largely based on the drawings of Polynesian tattooing made by some of those same 18th- and 19th-century missionaries who had banned them.

Navigation

The Polynesians' ability to explore and inhabit a vast area of the Pacific Ocean before the invention of modern navigational techniques has led to considerable speculation, research, and debate about how they did it. Captain Cook assumed that Polynesian sailors had been blown off course and had accidentally colonized the Pacific. Later views of Polynesian navigation, which lasted until well into the 20th century, created a much more heroic image of Polynesian seamen who purposefully sailed from one island to the next until they had covered most of the South Pacific. Norwegian archaeologist Thor Heyerdahl's largely rejected theory that Polynesians originated in South America and colonized the Pacific from the west, which he first published in 1941, fits into this category of romantic theorizing. A more likely scenario was presented by New Zealand amateur historian Andrew Sharp, who argued in the 1950s and later that the Polynesian expansion was probably due to a combination of oceanic drift, able seamanship, and sheer luck.

In addition to academic arguments about the abilities of Polynesian sailors and their boats, a large number of individuals and organizations have attempted to recreate the technology and conditions of the past to test their theories. Heyerdahl's Kon-Tiki expedition in the 1940s, in which he and his crew sailed 4,300 miles from South America to Tuamotu on a raft, was one of the first of these attempts to illustrate the ways and means of Polynesian sailing. He was followed into the water by members of the Polynesian Voyaging Society, who began building Polynesian-style canoes and using them in the regions around New Zealand, Tahiti, and Hawaii in the 1960s. Today the society, located in Hawaii, continues to research, build, and sail traditional Polynesian watercraft.

See also SAMOANS: NATIONALITY; TA-P'ENK'ENG CULTURE; TONGANS: NATIONALITY.

PUMI

location:
Yunnan and Sichuan
Provinces, China

time period:
1960 to the present

ancestry:
Qiang

language:
Pumi, a Tibeto-Burman
language in the larger
Sino-Tibetan phylum

FURTHER READING
Donald Denoon et al., eds. *The Cambridge History of the Pacific Islanders* (London: Cambridge University Press, 2004).
Jared Diamond. *Guns, Germs, and Steel* (New York: W. W. Norton & Co., 1999).
Raymond Firth. *We, the Tikopia* (Stanford, Calif.: Stanford University Press, 1983).
Antony Hooper and Judith Huntsman. *Transformations of Polynesian Culture* (Auckland, N.Z.: Polynesian Society, 1985).
Marshall David Sahlins. *Social Stratification in Polynesia* (Seattle: University of Washington Press, 1958).
Andrew Sharp. *Ancient Voyagers in Polynesia* (Berkeley and Los Angeles: University of California Press, 1964).

Pre-Harappan culture   *See* MEHRGARH.

Pumi   (Pei Er Mi, Peimi, Primi, Qiang, Xifan)

The Pumi are one of China's recognized 55 national minority groups. They live in northwestern Yunnan Province as well as in Sichuan Province directly to the north of Yunnan. They have been called Pumi only since 1960, when they were classified as their own national minority group; prior to that they called themselves QIANG and were called Xifan by the Chinese, a derogatory term meaning "Western barbarian."

Pumi legend states that they were once nomads who traveled throughout the Qinghai-Tibetan Plateau with their herds of animals but that many centuries ago they settled in their current mountainous homeland and began planting crops. Their most important subsistence food is corn, which they supplement with rice, wheat, barley, buckwheat, oats, and a variety of vegetables including beans, cabbage, carrots, and eggplants. Perhaps dating from their days as pastoralists, many Pumi families also keep cattle, sheep, chickens, and pigs. Prior to the start of the Communist era in 1949, a few wealthy Pumi families owned most land in their region while the majority worked as tenant farmers or sharecroppers on this land or that of other ethnic groups, especially the NAXI. Slavery was also a common practice, with very poor families giving away one or more of their children to forgive debts. In addition, the Pumi also engaged in a variety of handicrafts both for their own use and for trade or sale. Most common were weaving and knitting, wood and bamboo working, distilling liquor, making charcoal, and finding and preparing herbal medicines. Prior to the 1950s most agriculture was of the slash-and-burn, or swidden, variety on temporary plots that had to be abandoned after just a season or two. Today artificial fertilizers and irrigation mean that the Pumi engage in more intensive agriculture with higher yields and the ability to feed a larger population.

Pumi social structure is patrilineal, and each individual inherits membership in his or her lineage and clan from the father. Clans are important social units; in the past some owned land that they distributed among their members, and clan leaders served as judge and jury in disputes between members. Eating with one's clan members was also common, and interment of one's ashes in the clan cave was a necessity for creating a proper relationship between clan ancestors and the living. Today clan guidelines continue to dictate marriage practice, for it is a requirement that individuals marry outside their own exogamous clan, preferably to their cross-cousins. Thus the preference is for a Pumi man to marry his father's sister's daughter or, somewhat less preferred, his mother's brother's daughter.

Upon marriage the woman generally went to live in her new husband's home, called patrilocal residence, although in some villages this move did not occur until after the birth of her first child. In those cases the woman's bride price, money given to her family by her husband and his family to compensate them for the loss of her labor and offspring, would also be delayed until pregnancy or birth occurred.

The Pumi are nominally Buddhists and practice a form similar to the Tibetan form of that religion, but many aspects of their indigenous beliefs and practices have survived conversion to this religion. Prior to the clampdown on religion by the Chinese Communist state starting in the 1950s, many Pumi believed in the power of both nature and ancestral spirits. They sacrificed animals to the God of the Kitchen and celebrated a wide variety of personal and communal events with feasting, music, and other forms of worship.

See also TIBETANS.

Punjabis   (Panjabis)

The Punjabis are speakers of both eastern and western Punjabi who inhabit the Punjab, a region that is divided between India and Pakistan; sometimes the term is also used to refer to the SIKHS because Punjabi is the religious language of this faith. The ethnonym is derived from the Persian words *panj*, meaning "five," and *ab*, meaning "river." The five rivers are the

Beas, Chenab, Jhelum, Ravi, and Sutlej. In addition, the Indus and the now-vanished Ghaggar were also part of the Punjabi culture region.

GEOGRAPHY

The Punjab is a large territory that today straddles the border between India and Pakistan, with about four-fifths located in Pakistan and only one-fifth in India. The culture region also includes territory in Pakistan's North-West Frontier Province and in Jammu and Kashmir, Rajasthan, and Himachal Pradesh in India. This is largely a plains region bordered to the east by the Himalayas, and it is crossed by the five major rivers that gave the region its name, all of which run into the Indus. These rivers not only provide the region with water to irrigate crops and water for humans, industry, and animals alike but also make the region extremely fertile. The warm climate is conducive to agriculture and has contributed to its great success in both countries, where harvests take place twice per year, in April–May and September–October. Between the Punjab's five rivers are separate cultural units known as *doabs*, where slightly different dialects and cultural traditions are practiced.

HISTORY

The Punjab has been a center of Indian civilization for as long as there is a historical record. The ancient city-state of Harappa is located on one of Punjab's five rivers, and Mohenjo-Daro is just outside the region. Since that early period it has seen many migrations and been invaded by some of the major empires and important groups of Asia, including the MONGOLS, Persians, Arabs, PASHTUNS, SCYTHIANS, and even GREEKS. Probably the most important event, however, was the migration of the INDO-ARYANS, who brought their language, from which Punjabi has descended.

The first of the three most important historical periods for the creation of the contemporary Punjabi people was the 10th century, when Sultan Mahmud of Ghazni established the first Muslim base in the Punjab. Certainly Islam was not taken up by the majority of the population following the sultan's victories, but by 1320 the Punjab was ruled by a Muslim governor, Ghyasuddin Tughlaq, who began his own dynasty that ruled over much of what is today northern India and Pakistan until 1413. In the 17th century Lahore became one of the most important cities in the Muslim Mughal Empire, by which time a large proportion of the population had converted to Islam. There remains to this day, however, a great deal of controversy surrounding the circumstances of this conversion, with some scholars claiming it was done at the point of a sword while others argue that Buddhists and low-caste Hindus voluntarily converted to escape the discrimination inherent in the Hindu caste system.

The second most important historical period in Punjabi history was the 15th century, when Guru Nanak founded the Sikh religion. The basic tenets preached by Guru Nanak and his followers come from his early statement: "There is no Hindu, no Muslim," which indicates the equality of all in the eyes of god. Guru Nanak mixed with low-caste Hindus and poor people and shared his food and resources with all in need. These basic concepts remain essential to Sikhism today, along with a wide variety of other beliefs, practices, and prohibitions. In the 18th century Sikhs had acquired so much power in their region that they essentially ruled the Punjab; however, they were themselves divided into 12 different principalities rather than a single Sikh kingdom. This situation changed in 1799 when Maharaja Ranjit Singh conquered Lahore and created a unified kingdom, which he held until his death in 1839. The kingdom survived only a single decade after his death before the British conquered it in 1849 and attached the Punjab to its larger, Indian colony.

PUNJABIS

location:
The Indian state of Punjab and the Pakistani region of the same name; smaller numbers in other regions of both countries and in Afghanistan and Bangladesh

time period:
About 2500 B.C.E. to the present

ancestry:
Indo-Aryan

language:
Eastern and western Punjabi or Panjabi, spoken in India and Pakistan, respectively; both are Indo-Aryan languages with a number of dialects

---

Punjabis time line

B.C.E.

2500	About the time that Indo-Aryan speakers entered India.

C.E.

1024	The sultan of Ghazni conquers much of the Punjab.
1320	Ghyasuddin Tughlaq, governor of Punjab, initiates his own Muslim dynasty, which rules over much of contemporary Punjab until 1413.
1799	Ranjit Singh conquers Lahore and begins his 40-year rule over a unified Sikh kingdom in Punjab.
1839	Ranjit Singh dies, and 10 years later the Sikh kingdom passes into the hands of the British.
1940	The All India Muslim League, meeting in Lahore, passes a resolution calling for the creation of Pakistan.
1947	India and Pakistan achieve independence from the British and immediately engage in the first of three wars fought between the two countries in the 20th century.
1965	The start of the Green Revolution, which radically transforms agricultural production throughout the Punjab.
2004	Sunni-Shia violence rocks Pakistani Punjab, where 70 people die in mosque bombings.

Portrait of Maharaja Ranjit Singh during the height of his power in the early 19th century. (Art Resource/HIP)

Perhaps the last important period for the construction of modern Punjabi identity began in 1940 with the resolution for creating an independent Pakistan as put forth by the All India Muslim League, and ended in 1947 when India achieved independence from Britain and immediately divided into the two states of India and Pakistan. At that time millions of Muslim Punjabis migrated into the larger, Pakistani Punjab as part of the chaos that ensued in both countries at partition, while millions of Sikhs fled Pakistan for India. Hundreds of Sikh temples, or *gurdwaras*, were desecrated in the new Pakistan as some elements of the population declared a holy war against Hindu and Sikh residents, while Muslim property in India did not fare any better. The best estimates for the period indicate that about 1 million Punjabis of all three religions were murdered in the immediate aftermath of partition, 10 million more were injured, and property loss was inestimable.

CULTURE

Economic Base

The basis of Punjabi culture is its long agricultural history. Since independence in both India and Pakistan the Punjab region has contributed significantly to both countries' food supplies. Wheat is grown extensively in both countries, while in India rice is the second most important crop; in Pakistan it is cotton. In addition, most farmers grow much of their own food items and then sell the surplus; the most important crops are mustard greens, okra, potatoes, squash, corn, lentils, and chickpeas. The high yields harvested in both countries are accomplished through heavy investment in irrigation technology, external fertilizers, new seed varieties, and both multicropping and high crop densities. The Punjab is also known as an important grazing region where oxen, buffalo, and camels are raised along with traditional cattle.

Since the 1980s India's Punjab has transformed from a largely agricultural state to one where the services, trade, and transport sectors of the economy have outstripped the agricultural sector. The former constituted 43.6 percent of the state's economy in 2005–06, while the latter contributed just 33 percent. The secondary sector, which includes construction, food processing, and other industry, saw only a marginal increase from 1999 to 2006 but remains an important employer throughout the state. Pakistan's Punjab is a similar center for growth in the service sector, making up 63 percent of the country's income in this area. Agriculture has remained important there as well, with a recent emphasis on dairy production so that Punjab contributes 50 percent of all milk produced in the country. In both countries, agroprocessing, transportation, textiles, clothing, bicycles, and other manufacturing have in many instances been transformed from small-scale cooperatives and private enterprises to much larger operations with connections and partnerships throughout the world.

Social Structure

Punjabi social structure recognizes a variety of different categories of people, some of whom are related through kinship; others are fictive kin for whom residence is the primary unifying factor. In order of importance these social units are caste, clan, village, division, and family. In addition, while village and division membership may have less significance for some urban Punjabis, many continue to consider themselves members of their traditional villages for purposes of networks and alliances.

Although caste, or *jati*, is one of the most important kinship groups in the Punjab, it is for most Punjabis a social distinction rather than a religious one since both Islam and Sikhism reject the concept of caste discrimination. Nonetheless, endogamous castes, which require individuals to marry someone from the same group, remain one of the most important social identifiers throughout the region. Castes are defined as groups of related families who live in a circumscribed region and share a traditional occupation. They are organized into higher and lower castes, which differ according to local customs and traditions but generally include Brahmans, skilled artisans, and landowners at the top of the hierarchy and butchers, sweepers, and leatherworkers at the bottom. Carpenters, masons, barbers, weavers, and a large number of others constitute the middle levels of the caste hierarchy. Despite the occupational names of these groups, not all individuals necessarily partake in these activities; for example, many individuals in the lower groups are agricultural workers, while traditional landowners today are not all rural landowners but urban professionals.

Within each caste group are a number of patrilineal clans, or *gots*; larger castes can have hundreds or more clans, while smaller ones have just a few dozen. Clans in the case of the Punjabis are made up of people who consider themselves descended through the male line from a common male ancestor, although the apical male may be a mythological or even unknown figure in the group. Clans are also exogamous, requiring their members to marry someone from a different clan than their own as well as from the clans of all four of their grandparents; nonetheless, the rules of caste endogamy continue to apply.

Although they are residential or even quasi-residential units in the case of many urban Punjabis, villages, or *pind*, are also fictive kinship units with all members, regardless of caste or clan, using kin terms to refer to one another. Older women will be called aunty, while younger men will be called son; peers use the terms for brother and sister. Like clans, villages are also exogamous, so even members of the same caste but different clan cannot marry each other if they were born in the same village or claim village residence through one of their parents. The average number of residents in Punjabi villages at the start of the 21st century was about 1,000, although many were a bit smaller than this. Regardless of size, each village is also divided into smaller units called divisions, or *patti*, which are made up of actually related families from the same caste or even clan. These units tend to provide assistance and alliances for all their members when necessary

and also serve as important sources of social control; the threat of being disgraced or even ostracized from one's *patti* is usually enough to keep people within the boundaries of accepted behavior throughout the Punjab.

At the levels of both the division and the village, there is a tendency for competition and cooperation to dominate social relations. People at these levels of the social structure are extremely familiar with one another's circumstances, and different factions are always available to take advantage of a household's or division's weaknesses, while seeming to offer assistance. Conflicts between them are frequent and sometimes long-lasting, with the most common sources coming from control over land, water, and women. The first two concern limited resources necessary for everybody to survive and thus require an intricate dance of cooperation and competition, while the latter concerns the preservation of the family's and division's honor as it is bound up in its women's purity and chastity. This is particularly important among Muslims but is certainly a concern throughout the entire Punjabi population.

At the lowest level of the social structure, the patrilocal family, or *parivar,* makes up the most important unit for both production and consumption; at marriage, women move into the households of their husbands. Families are often extended units rather than simple nuclear families and include two or more generations of men and women working together in complementary roles to accomplish all necessary productive and reproductive tasks. The household head is usually the senior male, who is at least nominally responsible for the land, shop, or job that maintains the household. This man's wife is the senior female of the household and is responsible for the family's budget, food supplies, and labor of the other women and girls within the household to make sure that all food preparation, child care, and servants, if relevant, are taken care of. At all economic levels women are also able to work outside the home, in agricultural work, as professionals, and in everything in between. This occurs more in India than in Pakistan and among Sikh and Hindu Punjabis more than Muslims, but Punjabi women are generally not as restricted in their movements and labor as many other Muslim women in Pakistan.

Religion

The religious life in Pakistani Punjab is overwhelmingly dominated by Islam, with about 97 percent of the province claiming this faith; only about 90 percent of the province are Punjabi speakers, so the percentage of Muslims among ethnic Punjabis may actually be even higher. Despite this apparent uniformity, Muslims in Pakistani Punjab are increasingly divided by sect. The majority are adherents of Sunni Islam, but a significant minority of between 15 and 20 percent are Shiite. These two groups have always maintained separate mosques and religious communities more generally, but in the past decade they have begun to view one another with greater enmity. The worst violence so far took place in October 2004 when a total of 70 people died in two separate mosque bombings, the first in a Shia mosque in Sialkot and then a week later in a retaliatory strike against a Sunni mosque in Multan. In early 2007 the schism began to be felt at the University of the Punjab, where students from the two sects started to pray separately for the first time since its founding in 1882.

In India the religious picture is even more complex; about 60 percent are Sikhs, 35 percent are Hindus, and the rest are Muslims, JAINS, Christians, Buddhists, or other. Each religious group makes up its own endogamous community and thus affects marriage patterns as much as caste and clan do. Sikhism was founded in the Punjab, outside contemporary Lahore, Pakistan, in the 15th century, and today the city of Amritsar is considered one of this religion's holiest sites. The Punjabi language is also the religious language of Sikhs not only from Punjab but throughout India and the rest of the world as well, and thus it is considered sacred, in the same way that Arabic is treated by Muslims. Each religious community in Indian Punjab maintains its own structures, specialists, rituals, and guidelines for marriage, funeral, and other life-cycle rites. Regardless of religion, however, the agricultural ritual calendar is important at harvest, sowing, and other times; praying for rain and a plentiful wheat crop are common to all Punjabis.

FURTHER READING

Zekiye Eglar. A *Punjabi Village in Pakistan* (New York: Columbia University Press, 1960).
Paul Hershman. *Punjabi Kinship and Marriage* (Delhi: Hindustan Pub. Corp., 1981).
Tom G. Kessinger. *Vilayatpur, 1848–1968: Social and Economic Change in a North Indian Village* (Berkeley and Los Angeles: University of California Press, 1974).
Murray J. Leaf. *Song of Hope: The Green Revolution in a Panjab Village* (New Brunswick, N.J.: Rutgers University Press, 1984).
Holly Sims. *Political Regimes, Public Policy, and Economic Development: Agricultural Performance and Rural Change in the Two Punjabs* (New Delhi: Sage Publications, 1988).
Gurharpal Singh. *Ethnic Conflict in India: A Case-Study of Punjab* (Basingstoke, U.K.: Macmillan, 2000).

Pyu

The Pyu were one of the first inhabitants of territory that is today Myanmar and Thailand; the center of their homeland was the dry zone of central Myanmar along the major rivers and their tributaries, but they also claimed sovereignty over kingdoms in the south and east.

Without irrigation, crops in Myanmar's dry zone fail two-thirds of the time, and thus the Pyu developed extensive weirs, canals, and storage tanks to water 500–3,000 hectares of wet rice at a time. These massive waterworks required the labor of thousands of people to dig and maintain, but they allowed for the development of many urban areas fed by the agricultural surplus grown in the countryside.

The first Pyu city, Beikthano, probably arose in the first century B.C.E. in what is today the Magway Division, central Myanmar; it reached its peak in the first century C.E. and diminished in the fifth century, when the walls and gates protecting the city and palace were burned to the ground, the result of enemy attack. Despite these generally accepted dates, however, charcoal from the site has been carbon dated to about 1950 B.C.E., leaving some doubt as to the initial settlement of both the Pyu generally and this site specifically. In addition, although much of the city was burned down in the fifth century, Chinese documents from the seventh century, which describe the city's green glazed bricks, dozen gates and pagodas, and 100 monasteries, indicate that it was rebuilt later. Archaeological work done on the site from 1959 to 1963 confirmed many of these descriptions and showed that most of the region's inhabitants did not live within the city walls but in the surrounding agricultural areas.

The second Pyu city, Halingyi, in the Shwebo district of central Myanmar, was somewhat smaller than its predecessor and emerged two centuries later, in the first or second century C.E. Like Beikthano, Halingyi's population lived outside the city's walls and grew rice, fruit, and vegetables to feed themselves and the small urban population, made up of the royal family, its retainers, servants, and the court, plus a few artisans. Archaeological work began at Halingyi in 1904, was continued in 1929–30, and then undertaken again for a five-year period in the mid-1960s.

The largest and most important Pyu city-state, Sri Ksetra or Tharay-khit-taya, which is currently called Hmawzar, was built in the third or fourth century C.E. by King Dutta-baung and served as the center of Pyu life until 832, when it was sacked by the Nanzhao kingdom. Texts from the time detail 65 major and minor gates in the city's extensive wall system, but only nine of them have been found in archaeological work that goes back as far as 1904 and extended into the 1990s. Unlike Beikthano and Halingyi, Sri Ksetra was built to the south of the dry zone, closer to the coast where interactions and trade with Indian, Chinese, and other traders contributed greatly to Pyu society and culture. Like these urban forebearers, however, Sri Ksetra's wealth and power came from control over vast agricultural lands and irrigation canals and storage tanks.

In addition to these three major urban settlements, the Pyu also established many minor ones throughout the dry zone of central Myanmar and reaching toward the southern coastal region. Some of the sites that have been excavated include Allakapa, Beinnaka, Hmaingmaw, Mongamo, Pyaubwe, and Wadi I and II. All of these settlements took advantage of a trade route between China and south Asia, which took travelers down the Irrawaddy River and into the Bay of Bengal, where they could sail to India and Indonesia.

Although much of what we know about Pyu society comes from Chinese texts that document the humane system of Pyu governance and the architecture, costumes, and other aspects of daily life, the inspiration and source for much of this material and cognitive culture was India rather than China. The Pyu writing system, which was later adopted by the Mon people, was written in an Indian script. The religion after about the first or second century C.E. was a form of Buddhism adopted from India, and much of the Pyu art and architecture reflect Indian influences.

There are still several mysteries surrounding the culture of the Pyu people, the most important being the details surrounding their religious beliefs and practices. Certainly there is no doubt that some form of Buddhism was important to at least part of the population, as shown in the vast numbers of monasteries, stupas, and other buildings found in all Pyu cities as well as the mention in Chinese texts of a Buddhist population. However, certain questions have been raised by archaeologists and historians interested in Beikthano and Halingyi because no Buddhist artifacts have been found in either city. One hypothesis for this surprising lack is that the form of Buddhism practiced in the city is known as Andran because of its origin in the Indian region of Andhra Pradesh. Andran Buddhism is aniconic and thus presents researchers with no Buddhist images to study.

While Buddhist imagery is lacking in most Pyu sites, many other material remains are available. From them we know that the Pyu were prolific potters, using ceramic containers for everything from carrying water and cooking to burying the ashes of their dead. They also worked in a variety of metals, including iron, gold, silver, lead, and zinc; and in marble, from which they made enormous figures representing the guardian spirits of their cities. Finally, the Pyu economy was monetized since coins have been found in the Pyu cities. While most money would have been controlled by the few residents within the city walls, there is no doubt that the large rural population also had access to coins and used them occasionally instead of barter or other forms of exchange.

FURTHER READING

Janice Stargardt. *The Ancient Pyu of Burma* (Cambridge, U.K.: Pacsea, 1990).

PYU

location:
Contemporary Myanmar (Burma) and Thailand

time period:
Possibly 400 B.C.E. to 12th century C.E., although contested carbon dating data point to the possibility of 1950 B.C.E. as the founding date of an early Pyu religious site.

ancestry:
Tibeto-Burman

language:
Pyu, an extinct Tibeto-Burman language

Qaraqalpag *See* KARAKALPAK.

Qiang (Di, Manzi, Rma, Rong, Stone Tower Culture)

The Qiang are currently one of China's 55 recognized national minorities; most live in the Maowen Qiang Autonomous Prefecture of Sichuan Province, while others are spread throughout the adjoining regions. They call themselves Rma.

The Qiang are an ancient people who are first documented in the Shang dynasty, the first period in which the Chinese had a writing system. This ancient population is believed by many to be the ancestors not only of the contemporary Qiang but also the YI and a number of other contemporary national minorities, although this hypothesis is contested by many other scholars. The name Qiang has also been used throughout Chinese history to refer to many tribal groups who had matrilineal descent, engaged the Chinese in warfare, exhibited no centralized government, and generally lived along China's western frontier. Today Qiang remains a collective term and includes many people who speak languages in the Qiang category; the PUMI were one such group who were finally recognized by the Chinese government in 1960 as their own nationality. The Baima, Ersu, Jiarong, Muya, Muyami, and Namuyi people are still considered subgroups of the Qiang, without the numbers or significant cultural differences to be accorded nationality status of their own.

The first mention of the Qiang can be found in the earliest written Chinese sources, oracle bones from the second millennium B.C.E. Shang dynasty (approximately 1750–1040 B.C.E.). The Qiang were depicted as shepherds with flocks of sheep so that at that early period the majority of Qiang would have made their living as nomadic herders, probably in the region of contemporary Gansu and Qinghai provinces. These early Qiang also revered the tiger, which they used as their most important totem. The Shang dynasty was followed in China by the Zhou, a people who came from the west and considered the Qiang close allies; Zhou records indicate that the two groups frequently intermarried. After this period little is written about the Qiang until about the fourth century C.E., when they were among the non-HAN "barbarian" groups who constantly invaded China from the north. These invasions eventuated in a division into northern and southern Chinese kingdoms and coincided with a rise among the Chinese of the foreign religion Buddhism, in part because its large monasteries provided protection and work, and its many rituals provided comfort during difficult times.

During the Sui and Tang dynasties, 580–618 and 618–907, respectively, the Qiang were systematically pushed out of their original homeland in Gansu and Qinghai and into their present home along the Min River in Sichuan Province. There are records in the fifth and sixth centuries of several semi-independent Qiang kingdoms, but they were destroyed in the eighth century by TIBETANS who invaded the territory. At this time the region also began experiencing loss of forestland to the axes of the invaders, who were opening up grazing lands for their flocks. By about 1400 C.E. this clearing was beginning to outstrip the ability of the trees to regenerate naturally. By the last quarter of the 20th century, the region was so denuded that the Chinese government began a program called "Grain for Green," which paid local farmers—including the Qiang, who had long since settled into an agricultural way of life—to plant trees instead of crops.

Qiang culture prior to the Communist era starting in 1949 was maintained through a combination of highland agriculture, animal husbandry, and hunting and gathering. Some Qiang farmers carved terraced farms along their steep mountainous fields, while others simply used a hoe and spade to plant on the steep mountainsides. Some permanent fields were utilized, which were fertilized with animal manure, while the most marginal land was planted using slash-and-burn, or swidden, techniques. Barley, buckwheat, potatoes, and beans—rather than rice—were the most important subsistence food items. Today corn has replaced barley, at least at lower elevations, and apple and pear orchards are flourishing in land reclaimed as part of the Grain for Green program. Apples, pears, walnuts, and pepper are the most important cash crops as a result of this program, though rapeseed for use in making canola oil is also important. Medicinal herbs and firewood are also important sources of income, having replaced dependence on opium as a cash crop earlier in the 20th century.

Until the past few decades, Qiang social structure was significantly different from the dominant Han society. Descent was handed down from women to their children in a matrilineal pattern instead of a patrilineal one, and it was men who were formally integrated into their wives' lineage at their deaths, when their ashes were interred with those of their wives' families. Marriage was usually not formalized through a ritual or ceremony but was a gradual process of incorporating the man into his new family. It would begin when he traveled to his wife's family and worked on their land for a period of bride service. This might continue even after the birth of several children to the new couple. Eventually the man usually moved into his wife's home, but he continued to retain rights to land and produce from his own family of origin as well. Finally, at the man's death, his ashes were interred with those of his new family, and the incorporation period was complete. Today most Qiang have abandoned this pattern and have adopted the patrilineal kinship system, patrilocal residence, and marriage system of the Han.

Despite the centrality of women in the social structure, Qiang society was neither matriarchal nor even egalitarian. Women were primarily responsible for domestic and agricultural work, while men engaged in construction, transport, and plowing. They also held all important political positions within the village and most important religious positions, although there is some evidence that women were shamans in the distant past. The inequality exhibited in Qiang society, however, was not as great as that among the Han, and men did occasionally assist with cooking, cleaning, and child rearing.

As the importance of the tiger totem among the ancient Qiang indicates, this people's indigenous religion exhibited traits from both animism and shamanism. All beings and even many natural features from the landscape were believed to have a spirit that could be contacted by shamans to discover the source of misfortune or illness. In some areas, white stones were seen as sacred and were placed on altars and roofs. Today some features from Buddhism, especially from Tibet, and from Taoism have been incorporated into the native belief system, and in some areas nearly 10 percent of men have taken some training to become a priest.

FURTHER READING

David Graham. *The Customs and Religion of the Ch'iang* (Washington, D.C.: Smithsonian Miscellaneous Collections, 1957).

R

Rajasthanis

RAJASTHANIS

location:
India and Pakistan

time period:
About 1000 C.E. to the present

language:
There are 18 Rajasthani languages categorized into two groups, Marwari and unclassified; all are Indo-Aryan languages.

The Rajasthanis are speakers of Rajasthani, an Indo-Aryan language that separated from Hindi and others in about 1000 C.E.; nonetheless, there remains some debate about whether it constitutes a separate language with about eight major dialects and many more minor ones or is itself a dialect of Hindi. The term *Rajasthani* is sometimes also used to refer to residents of the state of Rajasthan regardless of their language group, but as this includes a wide variety of tribal peoples as well as ethnic Rajasthanis, this entry is limited to the latter. As is the case throughout India, it is difficult to characterize the great diversity of the Rajasthani people in general terms. Their language affiliation points to the gradual incorporation of the Indo-Aryan tongues on the subcontinent after about 1800 B.C.E., but the wide variety of caste and even religious communities in the state all contribute to differing histories and present-day ways of life.

The Rajputs are the state's dominant caste community, although they make up a relatively small percentage of the population. They are members of the Kshatriya varna, who are considered twice-born, and are usually thought of as great warriors with a long martial tradition, but they are also often linked with the highest varna, the priestly Brahmins. In the past they fought against invasions of Arabs, PASHTUNS, and others, and during the long Mughal period rose up against their Muslim rulers sev-

eral times. However, the reason for their uprisings in the 17th century remains contested to this day: Whether they were Hindus fighting against Muslim overlords or a clan-based society with local political and economic interests fighting against the centralizing power of an expansionist empire remains unknown. Probably the truth includes a bit of both theses and individual motivations varied.

In addition to the Rajputs, Hindu, Jain, and Muslim communities are also important subdivisions of the Rajasthanis. The majority of Rajasthanis are Hindus who worship such gods as Siva, Vishnu, Brahma, Shakti, and a host of others. Muslims make up just under 10 percent of the population of Rajasthan. The majority are the descendants of converts to this religion when it was new to the subcontinent in the 12th century; others converted during Mughal rule in the 16th–19th centuries. The Rajasthani town of Ajmer is the site of an important Muslim shrine, the burial place of the Sufi saint Khwaja Moinuddin Christi, and has been revered by Indian Muslims generally since the time of Akbar, the greatest Mughal prince; some even consider it a second Mecca. There is also a small but influential community of JAINS among the Rajasthanis who tend to be wealthier than their Hindu and Muslim neighbors due to their international and regional business ties. Dhulev, Karera, Mahavirji, and Ranakpur are the most important Jain pilgrimage sites in the state.

See also INDO-ARYANS.

Rakhines (Arakanese, Buddhist Rakhines)

The Rakhine people are the majority of the population of Rakhine, or Arakan, State in southwestern Myanmar. Their Tibeto-Burman language and Buddhist religion make them similar to the country's dominant Burmans, but history and geography have served to differentiate them in important ways.

Historically, the Arakanese established an independent kingdom in that region, which according to their mythology goes back to 3325 B.C.E. The founder of this kingdom, King Marayu of the first Danyawady dynasty, is said to have come from northern India, conquered the local inhabitants, and established a beautiful city. While this early founding date is probably legendary rather than actual, there is evidence for the existence of an independent kingdom in the region of Arakan throughout most of the common era.

The final local dynasty, the Mrauk-U, fell to the Burmese in 1784, when King Boe daw Maung Wyne invaded and annexed the territory. This action set off hundreds of years of struggle on the part of the local population, both Buddhist and Muslim or ROHINGYA, against their Burman, British, JAPANESE, and Burmese overlords. In fact, it was Arakanese rebellions against the Burmans in the early 19th century that caused the Burmans to turn against the British colonies in India since they mistook Arakanese rebellion for British interference in their territory.

During the period of Japanese occupation, 1942–45, the region's Muslim and Buddhist populations turned against one another, and the violence resulted in a displacement of the two populations. When the war ended, most Buddhist Rakhines found themselves living in the southern portion of the territory and most Muslim Rohingya in the north. The antipathy from that period has continued and even worsened in the intervening 60 years, when policies of the Burmese government stripped the Muslim population of citizenship, land, jobs, and homes and drove many out of the country as refugees. The Rakhines, who make up about two-thirds of the state's population, moved in and replaced Muslim civil servants and landowners and occupied their homes and farms. Today there is considerable debate within the Rakhine community about who their true enemy is, the Burmans who annexed their territory in the 18th century when their Muslim neighbors fought by their sides to retain it, or the Muslims, who tried to dismember Arakan in 1947 in order to join the newly independent Pakistan.

See also INDO-ARYANS.

Rapanui (Easter Islanders)

The Rapanui are POLYNESIANS who settled the island that bears their name, also known as Easter Island, after having sailed east from the Marquesas. Like other Polynesians the Rapanui brought a number of domesticated plants and animals with them, including bananas, taro, and chickens, and relied on these foods for their subsistence. For several hundred years the Rapanui flourished on their island home, developing a hierarchical social structure that resulted in a spate of competitive statue building. Easter Island's distinctive statues, called *moai* in the local language, have fascinated outsiders since their initial sighting by Dutch explorer Jacob Roggeveen on Easter Sunday, 1722.

The date of Easter Island's original settlement is somewhat contentious, with some experts using glottochronological calculations, which analyze linguistic changes across groups of people who all speak related languages, and others relying on carbon dating of artifacts. The range of dates of settlement is 300–1200 C.E., with the best estimate according to many contemporary sources being just before 900 C.E.

From about 900 to the time of European discovery in the 18th century, the Rapanui underwent significant changes in terms of social structure and both economic and artistic activity. Like many Polynesian societies, especially eastern Polynesians, the Rapanui developed a highly hierarchical society that supported a number of chiefs, royal clans, and lineages, and a large base of commoners, who also divided themselves into clans and lineages. It is this hierarchy, which allowed chiefs to control the labor of large numbers of commoners, that created the circumstances for the production of *moai* and that later may have led to the destruction of the Rapanui social and economic system.

Prior to the period of European colonization, the main economic activities on the island consisted of agriculture and raising chickens. Due to Easter Island's distance from the equator, some Polynesian staples, such as coconuts, did not grow well; residents were forced to focus greater attention on the crops they could

RAKHINES

location:
Rakhine State, Myanmar (Burma), Bangladesh, and India

time period:
Possibly 3325 B.C.E. to the present

ancestry:
Tibeto-Burman, though their mythological founding ancestor was Indo-Aryan and Mongol ancestors also inhabit their founding myths

language:
Arakanese, a Tibeto-Burman language related to Burmese but with many vocabulary and pronunciation differences making them only partially mutually intelligible

RAPANUI

location:
Easter Island, or Rapa Nui, in the native language, Isla de Pascua in Spanish, an island in the Pacific currently owned by Chile

time period:
Probably between 800 and 900 C.E. to the present

ancestry:
Polynesian

language:
Rapanui, an Eastern Polynesian language

Only one of these *moai* still has its red scoria headpiece balanced on top, while the others have fallen off, have been looted, or were never completed in the first place. *(Shutterstock)*

grow, such as taro. The island also lacked many of the fish and other seafoods of more tropical Pacific islands, which contributed to a great reliance on chicken for protein. The evidence of the importance of chicken remains today in the form of 1,233 large stone chicken houses. It is interesting to note that chickens lived in solid stone structures while the Rapanui themselves relied on wood or thatch for their own homes, using stone only for the foundations.

Sometime before the arrival of Europeans on Easter Island, the Rapanui experienced a tremendous upheaval in their social system brought about by a change in their island's ecology. Two different theories have been presented to explain this change. The first is that the Rapanui themselves denuded their once-tree-covered island in order to use the wood for construction and to roll their giant stone *moai* from the quarry to their final resting places. The competing theory is that palm rats, brought to Easter Island on the original settlers' boats, ate the palm seeds and destroyed the trees' root systems, leaving the island relatively bare. Regardless of the reason for deforestation, there is no doubt that it happened and caused tremendous soil erosion on the windy island. As a result, the

Rapanui experienced a rapid decrease in population, the destruction of their social system, the abandonment of their stone-building projects, and possibly even the advent of cannibalism to make up for lost food sources. By the time of European arrival in 1722, the island's population had dropped to 2,000–3,000 from a high of approximately 15,000 just a century earlier.

The *moai*, the enormous stone structures for which the Rapanui remain famous today, averaged 13 feet tall and about 20,000 pounds in weight, though one as tall as 32 feet has been found and another of 87 tons in weight. These giant heads, as they appear, were representations of powerful ancestors and were used by competing clans to represent their strength and importance relative to other clans. The statues themselves sat on flat stone platforms, called *ahu*, which themselves would have taken enormous effort and resources to build since some of them contain 20 times as much stone as the *moai* themselves. In addition, many later *moai* also had another feature, a cylinder of red scoria (a kind of stone used today to make decorative gravel), that sat atop the *moai's* flat head and increased its size by up to eight feet and weight by up to 12 tons.

In all, 887 *moai* have been found to date, most having been carved between the years 1000 and 1600 C.E., though almost half were never transported away from the tuff stone quarry of Rano Raraku. The archaeological evidence seems to indicate that the *moai* and *ahu* of earlier Rapanui were quite a bit smaller than those carved at a later date; indeed, some of the largest ones remain in the quarry from which the islanders were unable to transport them after the deforestation mentioned earlier.

In addition to these enormous and distinctive statues, the Rapanui were also unique in their development of an indigenous written script, possibly before the arrival of European explorers and missionaries. Some linguists claim that there are actually three scripts that have been found on Easter Island thus far—Rongorongo, *ta'u*, and Mama—while others claim that the latter two are just varieties of Rongorongo. Regardless, all three are read from bottom to top, rather than left to right as is the case with English, and all three remain largely undeciphered. To date, the only point of agreement is that one of the few examples of the script seems to be marking the lunar calendar. Because they are largely undeciphered and unique in Polynesia, the Rapanui scripts have attracted a great deal of attention. Claims have been made based on the shape of the hieroglyphs that the origin of the script was the Indus Valley, a rather farfetched claim at best given the geographic separation of these regions. A more likely claim, according to others, is that the script originated in South America, or that it was invented by the Rapanui after having seen Spanish written in the 18th century. Given that only 34 examples of the script have been found and that they were written on wooden tablets that disintegrate easily, making it unlikely that any others will ever be found, it is possible that the mystery of Rongorongo will never be solved.

Rhade (E-de, Ede, Rade)

The Rhade are one of the many ethnic groups that reside in the mountains of central Vietnam, sometimes called as a group Montagnards or DEGA. They speak an Austronesian language related to that of the CHAMS and may have moved to the highlands from the coast during the VIETNAMESE migrations south after the 10th century.

The primary economic activity for most Rhade in the past was simple slash- and-burn horticulture. In their mountainous terrain they produced rice and a few other staples, to which have been added in the past century corn, peppers, cashews, and even some cotton. During the French colonial period in the 19th and 20th centuries, both coffee and rubber were introduced to the highlands as well. While some Rhade families did take up coffee growing, they are well known in Vietnamese history for having refused to work on the large rubber plantations that the Michelin company tried to establish in the early 20th century. Their resistance, along with that of other Dega groups, forced most of the large landholders to abandon their plans for rubber in the highlands. Today some Rhade also keep chickens, ducks, goats, and other livestock for personal use or exchange with other families, and where possible, hunting and gathering also add variety to the daily diet.

The social structure of the Rhade resembles other Dega groups in being matrilineal—that is, children bear their mother's surname and inherit from their mother and maternal uncle. The Rhade are also matrilocal so that when a young couple marries it is the husband who moves into his wife's family home and begins to work on her family's land. Rhade longhouses are a unique adaptation to this residential pattern. Only 13 feet wide on average, some of these houses can be as long as 100 feet. Every time a daughter in the family marries, the house length is extended by another 12 feet or more to accommodate the new couple's kitchen and sleeping areas. Each section has its own outside door, making the whole structure resemble a multicarriage train elevated five feet in the air on stilts. Underneath the structure wood, food, animals, and other family property are kept safe and dry. Each village contains many of these long family homes and is surrounded by a wide clearing, to protect the village from wild animals generally, but especially tigers.

In addition to economic changes, the 19th and 20th centuries also brought Christianity to Vietnam's central highlands. French Roman Catholic missionaries and their American Protestant counterparts from the Christian and Missionary Alliance often failed in their mission to convert the Rhade to their religions in the 19th and 20th centuries, at least prior to the Vietnam War. However, since the end of the Vietnam War in 1975 and the unification of North and South Vietnam the following year, large numbers of Rhade have converted to evangelical Protestant faiths. Rather than through direct proselytizing, forbidden by the

RHADE

location:
The central highlands of Vietnam, *Tay Nguyen* in Vietnamese

time period:
Unknown to the present

ancestry:
Austronesian

language:
Rade, a Chamic language within the larger Austronesian language family

Communist government of Vietnam, they have come to Christianity via radio broadcasts in their language, transmitted from the Philippines by the Far Eastern Broadcasting Company. Due to the persecution of Christianity, there are no churches for the Rhade to attend; instead, services are held in people's homes. In September 2002 religious persecution became even more active as many of the 440 or more "congregations" throughout the highlands were shut down by state officials.

Prior to their Protestant conversions, the Rhade were animists who worshiped a variety of nature spirits. They buried their dead in shallow graves to allow the person's spirit to escape to the heavens and then surrounded the gravesite with wooden carvings to protect it from other spirits. Trees with creepers, birds' nests, or bees in them were believed to contain spirits and thus were unacceptable for use in building the *k'pal*, a long wooden bench on which only the elderly, musicians or other honored guests may sit and on which no woman may sleep. Among the gods of the traditional Rhade pantheon were those who controlled fire, earth, and water; rice was also believed to be protected and nourished by a special god.

The Rhade have spent much of the past 10 centuries trying to maintain their identity and culture in the face of a much larger and economically stronger ethnically Vietnamese population. In the 20th century this effort combined well with the efforts of first the French to maintain their colonial presence in Vietnam and then the Americans to prevent the spread of Communism throughout all of Asia. During the war between France and the Viet Minh between 1946 and 1954, some Rhade fought on both sides since both promised a degree of autonomy to the Rhade and other highlander groups should they emerge from the war victorious. However, during the subsequent period of hostilities, 1955–75, between the Army of the Republic of Vietnam (ARVN) with their U.S. allies and the National Liberation Front (NLF), sometimes derogatorily called the Viet Cong, with their North Vietnamese and Chinese allies, most Rhade sided with ARVN and the United States. From about 1961 onward the United States sponsored and trained a corps of Rhade fighters known as the Civilian Irregular Defense Group, because U.S. forces were unable to defend the highlands from the NLF. As a result of this alliance, the Rhade make up the second-largest Vietnamese ethnic group living in the United States, after the ethnic Vietnamese community itself.

For those Rhade who remained in Vietnam after the war ended in 1975, the struggle to maintain their independence has not diminished over time. By 1989 only about one-third of the prewar Rhade population remained living in traditional homes and villages and engaging in traditional slash-and-burn agriculture. The Communist government has continued to put pressure on both communities and individual families to move into Vietnamese villages or adapt their way of life to that of the dominant majority. In the 21st century the pressure has intensified and resulted in protests in both 2001 and 2004, mostly over land tenure and religious freedom, which resulted in prison terms for some protestors and even the deaths of at least eight others.

See also AUSTRONESIANS.

FURTHER READING

Barry Petersen. *Tiger Men: A Young Australian among the Rhade Montagnard of Vietnam,* 3rd ed. (Bangkok: Orchid Press, 1994).

Rohingya (Muslim Rakhines)

The Rohingya are a Muslim minority living in Rakhine State, Myanmar. Their ancestors may have settled in this region as early as the seventh century C.E., although this date is heavily contested. On the one hand, the Burman authorities in Myanmar claim that the Rohingya are fairly recent migrants from Bangladesh and on that basis have suppressed their language, persecuted their religion, and most seriously, in 1962, stripped them of citizenship in Myanmar, leaving most entirely stateless. On the other hand, the Rohingya themselves claim their ancestors were Arab traders who worked along the coast more than 1,000 years ago and joined with a local population they converted to Islam. Perhaps the truth is between these two dates since there is strong evidence in the form of mosques and other architectural ruins that the Rohingya have lived in the region of Myanmar for at least the past 500 years.

Regardless of the historic facts, today's Rohingya are a persecuted minority in Myanmar; in addition, about one-third of their 1.5–2 million-strong population live as refugees in Bangladesh, Pakistan, Saudi Arabia, Malaysia, and Thailand. While the Muslims and Buddhists in Arakan or Rakhine State have always been culturally and linguistically different, violence between the two peoples erupted on a large scale after 1947, when a small Rohingya army approached the leaders of newly independent

---

ROHINGYA

location:
Northern Rakhine State, Myanmar (Burma), mostly in the three towns of Maungdaw, Buthidaung, and Rathedaung

time period:
Possibly seventh century to the present

ancestry:
Mixture of Bengali, other Indian, and Arab

language:
Rohingya, a dialect of Bengali within the larger Indo-Aryan language family, with many words borrowed from Arab, Urdu, Hindi, Persian, Burmese, and English; most men understand the related Chittagonian language, while most women do not.

Pakistan and requested annexation of Arakan into East Pakistan, which is today's Bangladesh. Despite this early affront to the Burmese state, the largest number of Rohingya fled their homes only in 1972, right after Bangladesh achieved independence from Pakistan. Another large exodus of more than a quarter million left in 1991–92, just after the Myanmar government annulled the elections and took over the country. As of 2003 there were at least 100,000 illegal Rohingya refugees in Bangladesh alone, plus the nearly 22,000 legal refugees housed in UN High Commissioner for Refugees (UNHCR) camps in Cox's Bazaar. Many of these people have not been back to their homes for nearly 30 years and see no end to their exile while the military junta continues to rule in Myanmar. Nonetheless, since 1994 nearly a quarter of a million Rohingya refugees have been repatriated into Myanmar from Bangladesh as part of a UNHCR scheme; whether these moves have been voluntary continues to be a problematic issue and one that has yet to be verified beyond any doubt. They are not welcome in Myanmar, where they are considered foreigners based on their exclusion by the 1982 Burmese government and the citizenship law, which named the 135 recognized national races.

The most important aspect of Rohingya culture is their Islamic faith, which most distinguishes them from their Buddhist and Christian neighbors in Myanmar. Every Rohingya neighborhood and village has a mosque and religious school, or *madrassah,* and men visit the mosque regularly for communal prayer. Separation of the sexes is very important, so women tend to pray at home, alone or with other women; most also wear the *hijab,* the head and body covering worn by many Muslim women as a religious obligation based on the hadith of Sahih Bukhari, a collection of Mohammad's teachings compiled a couple of centuries after his death in 632 C.E. As Muslims, the Rohingya do not eat pork, pray five times daily, and participate in the village Samaj, a kind of Muslim charity organization that gives food and aid to the poor, assists widows and children, and organizes marriage and funeral rituals.

Like many other peoples in Burma, the Rohingya are an agricultural people who grow the national staple, rice. Over the past decades high taxes and land confiscation by the Buddhist majority have left many Rohingya landless and having to work as tenants or sharecroppers, or to leave the land to work as unskilled laborers, artisans, blacksmiths, fishermen, or carpenters. Prohibitions against Rohingya working in busi-

ness or trade have limited the options of the few who previously engaged in those activities; they are also forbidden from traveling either inside or outside Myanmar, from working in the civil services, and from serving in the military, the most lucrative activity for all men in Myanmar today.

See also BURMANS; INDO-ARYANS; MYANMARESE: NATIONALITY; RAKHINES.

Rong pa   *See* LEPCHA.

Rouran   (Djudjani, Geougen, Jeu-jen, Jorjan, Jou-jen, Juan-juan, Jujan, Jwenjwen, Ruanruan, Rui Rui, Ruru)

The Rouran were a nomadic people of the steppe region north of China, mostly in contemporary Mongolia. Their origins remain somewhat clouded but have been connected with Southern XIONGNU and the DONGHU, Eastern Hu nomads who also were the predecessors of the XIANBEI. Given the large numbers of different ethnic and tribal groups residing in the steppes north of China in the second to fifth centuries and the degree of intermingling that occurred, it is possible that both hypotheses are correct.

A second question about Rouran origins emerges with regard to their language. Some sources state that they were proto-MONGOLS who spoke an early form of the Mongol language, while others ascribe Turkic origins to them. More likely, the Turkic-speaking people who finally overthrew the Rouran in the sixth century borrowed many words from them, such as *khan* and the plural forms of their nouns.

In addition to these difficulties in tracing Rouran origins, there is also considerable debate about what happened to them after their final defeat at the hands of the Gokturks in the 550s. Many scholars believe that they migrated westward and, as the Avars, established themselves as the rulers in the region of Hungary in eastern Europe. This argument is based on Avar origin stories that tell of a defeat and of being driven westward at about the same time as the Rouran defeat. However, this is contested by many scholars who point out that the Rouran probably never lived as far west as the site at which the Avar are said to have been defeated.

Prior to their emergence as a dominant power in Central Asia, the Rouran were a subordinate group within the sphere of Xianbei influence. Yujiulu Mugulu, the grandfather of Yujiulu Shelun, who was the first to unite the various Rouran clans, is believed to have been a slave of the Xianbei, and many Rouran women

ROURAN

location:
From Manchuria to Turkistan, with their administrative center at Karakorum

time period:
End of the fourth century to middle of the sixth century C.E.

ancestry:
Donghu, meaning Eastern Hu nomads, or Southern Xiongnu. Chinese sources claim they have Hunnic ancestors as well.

language:
A Mongol language

Rouran time line

C.E.

402 Yujiulu Shelun is the first chief to unite the Rouran into a single people and to adopt the title of Qagan (khagan, or khan). He also subjugates the Gaoche and Xiongnu to Rouran power.

414 The Northern Wei dynasty (Xianbei) tries to establish peaceful relations with the Rouran but is largely unsuccessful.

415 The Rouran khan, Yujiulu Datan, invades the Wei and is driven out, but the troops that pursue them back into their territory are decimated by the cold.

423 The Northern Wei build portions of the Great Wall to keep the Rouran out of China.

429 The Rouran are defeated by the Northern Wei/Xianbei.

460s The Rouran control much of the Silk Road, charging taxes and tribute to all who pass between Central Asia and China.

470 The Rouran are defeated by the Northern Wei/Xianbei again.

543 More sections of the Great Wall are erected against the Rouran's incursions.

552 The Rouran are defeated by the Gokturk Qagan, Tumen II. This defeat scatters the surviving Rouran people and brings an end to their kingdom. By 555 all the surviving Rouran have been driven west or murdered by Turkic peoples who fear their ability to regroup and challenge their authority.

RROMA

location:
Central or northwestern India

time period:
Unknown to about 1000 C.E.

ancestry:
Indo-Aryan

language:
An Indo-Aryan language possibly called *dom*, which became *Rom* when they entered Greece sometime after 1000

---

were taken by Xianbei as wives and concubines. The name *Rouran* also stems from the derogatory term used by the Xianbei to refer to them, *ruranrua* or *ru ru*, meaning "worms."

Despite these humble beginnings the Rouran began to make a name for themselves as fierce warriors as early as 300, with some sources even ascribing dominance to them for the entire fourth century. Other sources, however, state that the Rouran remained fragmented and thus unable to dominate other tribal groups for more than a few years at a time until 402, when Shelun was able to gain the support of all the chieftains of the Rouran people. During the fifth century, the Rouran consolidated their power in the steppes until they were able to control the lucrative Silk Road trade sometime around 460. Chinese sources also state that they employed TURKIC PEOPLES as slaves and other laborers in the iron mines of the Altai Mountains.

During these decades the Xianbei-ruled Northern Wei dynasty of China attempted several times to crush the Rouran, or at least to fortify the boundary between them. In 423 they built 621 miles of the Great Wall to try to keep the Rouran and other nomads out of the settled agricultural land of northern China; in 543 the East-

ern Wei built another 47 miles in Shanxi County, across the main pass used by northern nomads to invade China. These power struggles between Rouran and Northern Wei continued almost without a break until 534, when the Northern Qi and Northern Zhou wrested the Northern Wei's divided empire from them. From that point, the Rouran took advantage of the transition in northern China, raiding almost at will.

This period lasted just a generation, however, for in 552 the emerging Turkic peoples, who had been one of the Rouran's chief rivals for power in the north, conquered the Rouran. In 554 one section of the Rouran sought refuge from Turkic attack with the Northern Qi, but nothing else is known about this section. What we do know is that these Turkic-speaking peoples, knowing of the ability of the Rouran to regroup and reestablish themselves after defeat, went on a campaign to murder or scatter the entire Rouran population, which they accomplished by about 555.

The culture of the Rouran was very similar to the other nomadic peoples who resided north and west of China's boundaries in the early centuries of the common era. Their economic life depended on a combination of pastoral herding, taxes from the caravan trade along the Silk Road, and tribute taken from subjugated peoples. They lived in yurts, or *ger,* felt tents that were easily broken down, transported, and rebuilt as they followed the pasturelands necessary for their herds of goats, sheep, and cattle. They also used a Mongol writing system to record major events onto wooden tablets. Their society was largely kinship-based, with patrilineal clans, in which membership was inherited from one's father, dominating the political sphere. Extended families remained more important than these larger family units for the purposes of daily production and consumption.

FURTHER READING

Sechin Jagchid and Van Jay Symons. *Peace, War, and Trade along the Great Wall: Nomadic-Chinese Interaction through Two Millennia* (Bloomington: Indiana University Press, 1989).

Rroma (Gypsies, Rom, Romanies, Romany)

Today's Rroma or Romany population—still occasionally called Gypsies—of Europe, the Americas, and elsewhere originated on the Indian subcontinent about 1,000 years ago. Nobody is certain why this population moved away from its homeland although one popular theory is that it coincided with the influx of Muslims into north India. The location of the Rom-Indian homeland is also contentious; some theories posit central India, others the northwestern region of the Punjab. There are also competing theories about whether they constituted a single ethnic, caste, or language group at the time of their migration or whether they became an identifiable group upon entering Persia, their first homeland after leaving the subcontinent. Evidence for the latter theory abounds in the great diversity of dialects of Romany spoken today as well as in the number of words and grammar structures in these dialects that come from at least four different Indian languages. What is certain is that from India, Rroma peoples moved into Iran and Armenia and then in the 14th century traveled from southwest Asia into Europe. Later migrations brought large numbers of Rroma people into North and South America as well as Australia.

Until the late 18th century the ultimate origins of the Rroma remained a mystery, but finally in 1783 a German researcher noticed the similarities between several Indo-Aryan languages and Romany; a British linguist working at about the same time also wrote about this phenomenon. Prior to this period, Europeans ascribed Egyptian origins to this population, thus the derogatory ethnonym *gypsy*.

See also INDO-ARYANS.

Russians, Asian

The Russians are the dominant ethnic group in the Russian Federation as well as the most substantial minority in most of the countries of Central Asia; they also make up one of the 55 recognized national minority groups in China.

GEOGRAPHY

The Asian portion of Russia makes up about three-quarters of the Russian Federation, the largest country on earth. The boundary between Europe and Asia is arbitrary and marked differently on many maps; the most common boundary is at about 60° east, which runs through the Ural Mountains.

The territory of Asian Russia is extremely varied. The Far North is mostly tundra, a treeless plain with black, muddy topsoil above a layer of permafrost or permanently frozen soil, vegetation of mosses, lichens, and dwarf shrubs, and extremely cold temperatures. To the south of the tundra is the enormous taiga belt defined by coniferous forests and vast snowfalls. To the

south of the taiga belt are the Eurasian steppes, prairie-like plains with little rainfall, little tree growth, and temperatures that can be extremely hot in summer, cold in winter. The southeasternmost portion of Asian Russia, bordering on China to the west and surrounded by the Sea of Japan, experiences a subtropical climate and is at a latitude near to that of Rome, Italy, or Boston, Massachusetts.

In addition to the world's largest forest, Asian Russia also has vast quantities of other natural resources, including oil, coal, gold, diamonds, and other important minerals. Russia has been taking advantage of these resources since the mid-20th century, and in some cases even earlier; unfortunately, however, the rapid industrialization of the region has contributed to significant ecological problems, including chemical pollution that has diminished fish stocks and nuclear fallout from the testing of missiles and other weapons. The indigenous populations of Asian Russia have suffered significant losses of population and culture, with many local languages being in danger of being lost forever.

ORIGINS

The Russians are an ethnic group with roots in the Slavic tribes of eastern Europe long before their expansion into Asia in the 16th and 17th centuries. In Asia they established a form of local colonialism parallel to the European colonial project, which saw the British, French, and Germans spread their colonies throughout the world. Rather than send missionaries, government officials, and political prisoners to Africa, Oceania, or the New World, Russia sent them east of the Ural Mountains and south of the Caucasus Mountains, into lands adjacent to their own territories. This colonial expansion was sometimes driven by the same impetus as that of these other European powers, desire for resources such as furs, gold, and, later, oil, but also a desire to push the MONGOLS out of the Asian-European borderlands. As a result of these activities in the 16th–20th centuries, Russians today live throughout Siberia as far northeast as the Chukchi Peninsula, and they exist as ethnic minorities throughout all of the newly independent countries of Central Asia and the Caucasus and in China. While the Sibiriaki, or Russians living in Siberia, those in the Russian Far East, and those in the Russian diaspora in Central Asia and the independent countries of the Caucasus maintain their "Russian" identity, many also have ties to their local regional culture that are distinct from those of European Russians.

ASIAN RUSSIANS

location:
Russia, Central Asia, China

time period:
16th century to the present

ancestry:
European Russian, Slavic

language:
Russian, an Eastern Slavic language

Asian Russians time line

(*See* RUSSIANS: NATIONALITY, for Russian history prior to the expansion into Asia and the Caucasus.)

C.E.

Mid-16th century Russia begins to move into the Caucasus region, which had previously been dominated by the standoff between the Persian and Ottoman empires.

1581 The Stroganoff family and a hired Cossack, Yermak, lead an expedition into Siberia and conquer the area; they claim western Siberia (west of the Ob and Irtysh Rivers) for Moscow.

1604 Tomsk is founded as a trading outpost in Siberia.

1600–1700s Russians start to migrate into Siberia and Asian Russia. The migrants are usually peasants escaping serfdom, fugitive convicts, and after the 1667 reforms of the Orthodox Church, "Old Believers."

1623 The Russians conquer the Tungus (Evenkis), an ethnic group indigenous to Siberia that had resisted Russian expansion.

1639 Russians reach the Sea of Okhotsk and the mouth of the Ulya River.

1648 The Cossack Semyon Dezhnev discovers the Bering Strait and sails through it.

1649–50 Russian forces occupy the Amur (Heilongjiang) River banks.

1667 The Russian Orthodox Church institutes a number of reforms in the church, causing a schism between the church and those who refuse to accept the reforms. These people are known as "Old Believers" and are widely persecuted.

1686 Irkutsk, located near Lake Baikal, becomes a city, having previously been an outpost used to collect taxes in the form of furs from indigenous populations.

1689 After a brief skirmish with the Chinese, Russia signs a peace treaty relinquishing control of the Amur River valley but establishing Russian control of the area east of Lake Baikal and a trade route to Beijing.

1801 Russia annexes Georgia.

1813 Russia captures most of Azerbaijan.

1825 The Decembrists lead a revolt against Czar Nicolas I, demanding the abolition of serfdom, introduction of representative government, and increased freedoms. The revolt is crushed by Nicolas, and the participants are exiled to Siberia as punishment.

1828 Russia takes control of Armenia.

1855 The Great Siberian Expedition begins, lasting until 1863.

1861 Serfdom is formally abolished in central Russia.

1880 The first university in Siberia is opened in Tomsk.

1891 Construction starts on the Trans-Siberia Railroad.

1893 Novosibirsk (originally called Novonikolayevsk) is founded as the site for the bridge over the Ob River for the Trans-Siberian Railroad.

1904–05 Russo-Japanese War. Russia and Japan fight over control of greater Manchuria, Korea, and several islands in the area. The conflict leads to the embarrassing defeat of the Russian navy and the loss of these territories to the Japanese, including the only warm water port on the Pacific that had been in Russia's possession.

HISTORY

Russians began to expand into the southern Caucasus, Siberia, the Far East, and Central Asia in the 16th and 17th centuries, after the Muscovites took control of European Russia. In the case of the Caucasus, Russia's consolidation of power was a very slow process of defeating the already entrenched Persian and Ottoman empires and incorporating the local administrative and other elites into the Russian hierarchy. It took almost 300 years for Russia to be able to claim the Caucasian regions of contem-

1906–11 Czar Nicolas II sponsors a program to encourage central Russians to resettle in Siberia, offering peasants free or cheap land and distributing flyers exalting the quality of life in Siberia. As a result of these programs, about 3 million people resettle to Siberia.

1916 Construction finishes on the Tran-Siberian Railroad.

February 1917 The February Revolution, in which the Duma (Parliament), fueled by popular revolt against the czar, assumes power over the country. The czar abdicates.

1918–20 During the Russian civil war between the Red Army (Bolsheviks) and the White Army (nationalists), most of Asian Russia is a stronghold for the Whites. Aleksandr Kolchak, a former admiral in the czarist army and the leader of the White forces, establishes his capital in Omsk. His government is toppled in 1920, and Asian Russia and Central Asia fall to the Bolsheviks.

1920–24 Siberian agriculture declines, and numerous anti-Soviet riots occur in rural areas where peasants make no efforts to conceal their dislike of the Soviet regime.

1930s Peasants are forced to give up their private farmlands and work on government farms along with other peasants from the area during this period of collectivization. Peasants who resist are exiled to the north.

Stalin's purges create a large number of political prisoners who are exiled to Siberian labor camps called gulags.

1941 Germany invades the USSR, pulling it into World War II. Thousands of people are evacuated from European Russia to the east. Upon arrival, the evacuees set up workshops and enterprises to help with the war effort. These enterprises provide an economic boost to Siberia at the same time as they displace the indigenous population and degrade the fragile ecology.

1945 The Novosibirsk Opera and Theatre holds its first performance. The theater is the largest in Russia.

World War II ends. German and Japanese prisoners of war are sent to Siberian gulags.

1950s Akademgorod (Academy Town) is established in Novosibirsk by the Russian Academy of Sciences. This settlement of scientists becomes the leader in Russian scientific research.

1953 Stalin dies, ending the worst period of political repression in the Soviet Union.

1969 The Soviet Union is involved in major border clashes with China.

1978–82 The Soviet Union invades Afghanistan and installs a puppet Communist regime.

1985–91 Period of glasnost (opening up) and perestroika (restructuring), instituted by General Secretary Mikhail Gorbachev in an attempt to revitalize the Soviet economy.

1991 The Soviet Union disintegrates, and the 14 republics of the Soviet Union become independent nations. Siberia becomes an important source of raw materials, especially oil.

1993–95 Russia becomes involved in a humiliating war with Chechnya, a breakaway republic in the Northern Caucasus Mountains.

1999–2000 Russia becomes involved in a second war in Chechnya, this time crushing the breakaway groups.

2006 Diplomatic problems between Russia and Georgia cause Russia to deport large numbers of ethnic Georgians living both legally and illegally in Russia.

2008 Russia invades Georgia and initiates bombing raids over several Georgian cities in support of the South Ossetians.

porary Georgia, Azerbaijan, and Armenia as part of its empire. Conversely, the Russian conquests of Siberia and the Far East were among the fastest in world history, taking just 68 years to accomplish between 1581 and 1649. Unlike in the Caucasus, the native peoples of Russia's Far North and East had no history of centralized government, imperial control, or even unification beyond the tribal level, so there was little opposition beyond their simply moving out of the way of the Russian administrators and missionaries. The one potential for real opposition was Qing-dominated China, which also sought access and control over parts of the Far East; however, the Treaty of Nerchinsk in 1689 ended this potentiality by demarcating the boundaries between the two empires. Russian domination of Central Asia is more difficult to characterize since it involved both the conquest of other states and the incorporation of largely tribal peoples into the Russian Empire.

The Russian process for conquering their northern and eastern territories included military action, building fortifications and communities, settling farming families on "virgin" territory, annexing "empty" land, and, where possible, incorporating local chiefs into the Russian administrative model for indirect rule. At first this process followed the courses of the region's major rivers, including, from west to east, the Ob, Irtysh, Yenisey, Lena, and Amur. After these river valleys were settled, the few government and Cossack forces in the region were able to demand tribute from even the most remote areas, when disease, warfare, and constantly moving out of the way of these forces had weakened most of the indigenous people to such a degree that they could no longer hold out against Russian power.

By the 19th century Siberia and the Far East were totally under Moscow's control, though few Russians had settled in the region and it was still considered the frontier in relation to "civilized" European areas of the empire. In the 1840s and 1850s the Russian Geographical Society undertook the Great Siberian Expedition, in which patriotic geographers and other scientists sought to study Russia's new territories and peoples for the purpose of incorporating them more fully into the motherland. At about the same time, 1857, the governor of eastern Siberia began the long process of questioning, studying, and financing that went into the development of the 4,660-mile Trans-Siberian Railway. Finally, in the late 1880s the Russian government under Czar Alexander III got involved in the project, and building began in 1891 in the far-eastern city of Vladivostok. Between 1891 and 1916, thousands of Russians were brought from the country's center to Siberia to work on the rail lines; most went home afterward, but some remained to live, work, and raise families on the newly opened Russian frontier. During and after World War II, when Russia had moved much of its industrial production east, out of the way of the Germans, the railway facilitated the movement of millions more Russians into Asia.

The process of Russification in the Caucasus was very different from that in Siberia and

The Siberian landscape changed drastically with the coming of the industrial revolution to the region in the 20th century. Here a metallurgical plant in Novokuznetsk City contributes to the tremendous pollution affecting plant, animal, and human life in Russia's Far North. *(Shutterstock/VK)*

the Far East and took far longer to accomplish. This is largely due to the fact that while the peoples of Siberia and the Far East lived in decentralized tribal units prior to the coming of the Russians, those of the Caucasus had thousands of years of history of unification under national churches and large kingdoms. In addition, while Russians were not competing with other states or empires in Siberia, in the Caucasus in the 16th century the Persians and Ottomans already had long histories of domination and control over some regions and peoples.

The Russian strategy in the region began with seeking alliances with local leaders of the GEORGIANS, ARMENIANS, and AZERIS to fight off the entrenched Persians and Ottomans. After defeating these other empires in the 18th and 19th centuries, the Russians then had to contend with local populations that were no more interested in incorporation into Russia than they had been into Persia or the Ottoman Empire. In order to deal with these issues, the Russians used a strategy of divide and conquer, creating hostilities between local principalities and ethnic groups in order to justify their own military presence and imperializing tactics. At the time this strategy seemed to have worked to maintain Russian power in the Caucasus and to have allowed thousands of Russians to move south into these regions; however, with the disintegration of Russian-Soviet power in the late 1980s and 1990s, the region has suffered enormously because of it. The wars that rocked Georgia, Armenia, Azerbaijan, and the northern Caucasus regions between 1917 and 1921, when the Russians retook the region, as well as those that have occurred since 1989 predominantly have their origins in these 18th- and 19th-century Russian policies.

The Russian Empire's conquest of Central Asia also began in the mid-16th century. Rather than seeking warm-water ports or resources, the primary motivation in the Russification of this region was to prevent the British from establishing themselves as the dominant colonial power there. Similar to their experience in Siberia and the Far East, the Russians conquered the Central Asian steppes with a relatively small military force that established forts and communities that drew the local nomadic and seminomadic populations to them in order to pay taxes and tribute to their new rulers. However, the region also had a few centralized states in the form of Kazakh khanates, most of which were either conquered or indirectly incorporated into the empire by the end of the 19th century. A few Russian peasants followed these military conquests into Central Asia and established farming communities and cities, pushing the pastoral local peoples into more marginal desert or mountain lands where they and their herds could eke out a living with minimal Russian interference. This situation changed during the Soviet era in the 20th century, when Russians began to move en masse to Central Asia to farm cotton and wheat for the ever-hungry Soviet Union. The collectivization process further disrupted the lives of the local populations and saw the deaths of millions over the first decades of Soviet expansion. As a result, in 1991 when the Soviet Union collapsed, all of the newly independent countries of Central Asia had large Russian minorities living there, especially Kazakhstan, with a Russian population of more than 30 percent.

While most Asian Russians reside in Siberia, the Caucasus, and Central Asia, there is also a small Russian population in China, recognized as one of that country's 55 national minority groups. Most of these people live in the towns and cities of Ili, Tacheng, Altay, and Urumqi in the Xinjiang Autonomous Region; a few others live in Inner Mongolia in China's far northeast. The ancestors of today's Chinese Russians—most of whom continue to speak, read, and write only in Russian, practice Orthodox Christianity, and generally live as Russians—entered China as refugees from czarist Russia in the 18th and 19th centuries. A few also fled Russia during the Russian Revolution in 1917; these people were referred to as the "Guihua people" until 1949, when they were renamed Russians. Although small in number at approximately 13,000 people, Russians participate actively in the Chinese government at the local and national levels.

CULTURE

Two of the most important aspects of Russian identity, especially in these outposts of Russian culture, are Russian Orthodox Christianity and the Russian language. While Russians living in all of these Russian frontier areas adapted many aspects of their material culture to suit the economic, ecological, and social conditions in which they were living, Orthodox Christianity and the Russian language remain central to these peoples' definition of themselves as Russians.

Prior to the Soviet era and its attempts to eliminate any belief system other than communism, Russians moving into these outposts were always accompanied by priests, missionaries, and the entire administrative apparatus of the Orthodox Church. In places like Georgia and Armenia, where Christianity had been the state religion for nearly 1700 years, the intrusion of the Russian patriarchate was simply subsumed under an already-existing Christian structure. However, the animistic religions of Siberia and the Far East and the syncretic mix of animism and Islam in Azerbaijan and Central Asia required full-scale conversion, which generally did not happen. Many indigenous peoples nominally accepted conversion for the resources it gave them, but most also continued to believe in and practice the rituals handed down to them from their ancestors. Since the collapse of the Soviet Union, the Russians who live in these regions have often turned back to their religion as one of the most important markers of identity separating them from their neighbors, who likewise have been able to renew their faith in their local religious traditions.

While the Soviets were unable to turn to religion as part of their process of Russifying their subjugated peoples, the Russian language remained central to both Russian identity and the Russification process continued throughout the 20th century. Russian became mandatory in all schools beyond the primary level in the USSR and the only legitimate administrative language in every region. This process served both to reinforce the Russian identity of ethnic Russians residing outside the core areas of the Russian heartland in Europe and to create a sense of national identity in other ethnolinguistic populations. Prior to the 20th century there was little sense of KYRGYZ, Uzbek, or Evenki identity, to give just three examples; most people in Central Asia and Siberia were members of kin groups, villages, and tribes rather than nations or ethnic groups.

In addition to religion and language, many Russians living in these frontier regions also have a shared culture of empire and European heritage that they bring with them into Asia. As it did in the 16th–19th centuries, Russian culture today sees Russian access to the mineral, forest, and petroleum wealth of Siberia, the Far East, the Caucasus, and Central Asia as necessary for the further development of Russian society and people. Colonialism, now in the form of economic rather than political and social subjugation, continues to serve as an important model for how Russians live in these other places.

See also ARMENIANS: NATIONALITY; AZERBAIJANIS: NATIONALITY; CHINESE: NATIONALITY; EVENKIS; GEORGIANS: NATIONALITY; KAZAKHS; KAZAKHSTANIS: NATIONALITY; KYRGYZSTANIS: NATIONALITY; RUSSIANS: NATIONALITY; TURKMEN; TURKMENISTANIS: NATIONALITY; UZBEKS; UZBEKISTANIS: NATIONALITY.

FURTHER READING

David G. Anderson. *Identity and Ecology in Arctic Siberia: The Number One Reindeer Brigade* (New York: Oxford University Press, 2000).

James Forsyth. *A History of the Peoples of Siberia: Russia's North Asian Colony, 1581–1990* (New York: Cambridge University Press, 1992).

Milan Hauner. *What Is Asia to Us? Russia's Asian Heartland Yesterday and Today* (Boston: Unwin Hyman, 1990).

Esther Hautzig. *The Endless Steppe: Growing Up in Siberia* (New York: T. Y. Crowell Co., 1968).

Andreas Kappeler, *The Russian Empire: A Multiethnic History,* trans. Alfred Clayton (Harlow, U.K.: Longman, 2001).

Stephen Kotkin and David Wolff. *Rediscovering Russia in Asia: Siberia and the Russian Far East* (Armonk, N.Y.: M. E. Sharpe, 1995).

Steven G. Marks. *Road to Power: The Trans-Siberian Railroad and the Colonization of Asian Russia, 1850–1917* (Ithaca, N.Y.: Cornell University Press, 1991).

Russians: nationality (people of Russia)

Russia is the largest country in the world, with a landmass that spans two continents. This entry focuses as much as possible on Asian Russia and leaves European Russia to other volumes.

GEOGRAPHY

Russia's enormous territory spans 11 time zones and nearly half the world, averaging about 2,500 miles from north to south. The Ural Mountains divide European and Asian Russia, with about three-quarters of Russian territory located in Asia, although only about 25 percent of the population live in the Asian part of the country. Siberia, which is often used to describe all of Asian Russia, technically refers only to the central part of Asian Russia and excludes the coastal areas.

The west Siberian plain, between the Urals and the Yenisey River, is lower than 1,640 feet in elevation in most places and contains some of the world's largest swamps and floodplains. East of the west Siberian plain is the central Siberian plateau, between the Yenisey and the Lena Rivers. South of the central Siberian plateau are the Baikal Mountains and Lake Baikal, the largest freshwater lake in the world. East of Lake Baikal is a mountainous region, marked

Russians: nationality time line

C.E.

before 600 While the origins of the Slavs are not known, many philologists and archaeologists believe that the Slavs first settled in the area of what is now Belarus. By 600 C.E. the Slavic tribes had split into southern, eastern, and western tribes, and the eastern Slavs, of which Russians are a subgroup, had settled along the Volga River valley (east of present-day Moscow) and along the Dnieper River in present-day Ukraine. The Slavs were not the only ethnic group in the area, but by 600 C.E. they were the dominant ethnic group in eastern Europe.

860 A Varangian (Scandinavian warrior), Rurik, establishes himself as ruler of Novgorod.

880 Oleg, another Varangian, founds Kievan Rus after moving south from Novgorod, subduing the Slavic tribes and expelling the Mongol tribes who had been demanding tribute from the Slavs.

888 The monks Cyril and Methodius develop the Cyrillic alphabet for writing Slavic languages; it is based on the Greek alphabet.

907 Oleg leads a campaign against Constantinople.

911 Oleg signs a treaty with the Byzantine Empire establishing Kievan Rus as equal trading partners with the empire.

988 Vladimir I, the ruler of Kievan Rus, adopts Eastern Orthodox Christianity and begins spreading Christianity among his subjects.

1100s Kiev declines as the economic, religious, and cultural center, a downturn affected by the decline of Constantinople, changing trade routes, and competition from other regional centers and princes.

1150 Sancta Sophia Cathedral is built in Novgorod, an early example of the onion-shaped domes typical of Russian architecture.

1169 Prince Andrei Bogolyubinski of Vladimir-Suzdal invades Kiev and conquers the city, establishing himself as the new ruler of Rus and moving the capital city to Vladimir, near Moscow, but leaving his brother to rule as prince in Kiev.

1237–40 The Mongols, under Batu Khan, invade Kievan Rus and deal the final blow to already weakening Kiev in 1240 when they sack the city.

1271 The capital is moved to Moscow.

1299 The Metropolitan of the Orthodox Church moves to Vladimir, establishing the city as the religious center.

1380 Russian forces defeat the Mongol army at Kulikovo, but the Mongols remain in control of much of Russian territory and continue to demand tribute.

1480 Russian forces expel the Mongols from Russian territory under Ivan III (the Great). Ivan expands the territory controlled by Moscow and is the first ruler to use the title Czar and "Ruler of all Rus."

1552 Ivan IV (the Terrible) defeats the Kazan khanate on the middle Volga River and later the Astrakhan khanate where the Volga River meets the Caspian Sea. This expansion gives Russia access to all of the Volga River and the Caspian Sea, as well as a route to Central Asia.

1555 Ivan the Terrible has St. Basil's Cathedral built on Red Square; the painted onion-shaped dome becomes the symbol of Russian architecture.

1581 The wealthy Stroganoff family and a hired Cossack, Yermak, lead an expedition into Siberia, conquer the area, and claim western Siberia (west of the Ob and Irtysh Rivers) for Moscow.

1604 Tomsk is founded as a trading outpost in Siberia.

1605 Shortly after the death of Ivan the Terrible, who is followed by his mentally challenged son, a series of uprisings occur as various aristocrats compete for the throne; two men, with the support of Russia's enemies Sweden and Poland, each claim to be Ivan's other son, Dimitri, who had died some 15 years previously. This time of chaos is known as the "Time of Troubles."

(continues)

RUSSIANS: NATIONALITY

nation:
Russian Federation; Russia

derivation of name:
From Kievan Rus, the state that marked the beginning of the "Russian" nationality

government:
Federation with a parliament and president

capital:
Moscow

language:
Russian is the official language. Due to the Russification policies of the Soviet Union, Russian is spoken nearly universally, and few other languages remain in widespread use.

religion:
Russian Orthodox 15–20 percent, Islam 10–15 percent, Judaism less than 0.5 percent, and Buddhism less than 0.5 percent (percentage of active followers; most ethnic Russians are nominally Russian Orthodox). In addition, about 2 percent of the population belongs to other Christian religions, and some indigenous peoples in Asian Russia still practice animist religions.

earlier inhabitants:
Indigenous peoples of Siberia and the Russian Far East (Asian Russia). These indigenous people included Asian Eskimos, Turkic and Mongol tribes, and East Asians (Korean, Chinese and similar groups).

(continues)

RUSSIANS: NATIONALITY
(continued)

demographics:
Ethnic Russians 80 percent, Tatars 4 percent, Ukrainians 2 percent, Bashkir 1 percent, Chuvash 1 percent, other or unspecified 12 percent. There are more than 100 recognized ethnic groups in Russia with varying population sizes, but none making up a significant portion of the population.

Russians: nationality time line *(continued)*

1613 Mikhail Romanov, an aristocrat, is proclaimed czar, beginning the 300-year-long reign of the Romanovs.

1600–1700s Russians start exploring in Siberia and Asian Russia. They are soon followed by migrants, usually peasants escaping serfdom, fugitive convicts, and after the 1667 reforms of the Orthodox Church, "Old Believers."

1623 The Russians subdue the Tungus (Evenkis), an indigenous ethnic group in Siberia who had resisted Russian expansion.

1639 Russians reach the Sea of Okhotsk and the mouth of the Ulya River.

1648 The Cossack Semyon Dezhnev discovers the Bering Strait and sails through it.

1649–50 Russian forces occupy the Amur River banks.

1667 The Russian Orthodox Church institutes a number of reforms in the church, causing a break between the church and those who refused to accept the reforms. These people are known as "Old Believers" and are widely persecuted.

1686 Irkutsk, located near Lake Baikal, becomes a city, having previously been an outpost used to collect taxes in the form of furs from indigenous populations.

1689 After a brief skirmish with the Chinese, Russia signs a peace treaty relinquishing control of the Amur River valley but establishing Russian control of the area east of Lake Baikal and a trade route to Beijing.

1703 The city of St. Petersburg is founded by Peter the Great; he institutes many reforms that westernize and modernize Russia.

Peter the Great establishes Russia's first newspaper.

1715 Construction begins on the Peterhof Palace, outside St. Petersburg, designed in the same style as Versailles.

1726 The Russian Academy of Sciences is established in St. Petersburg.

1735–39 The Arctic Ocean coast is explored and charted for the first time by scientists Dimitri Ovtsyn, Fyodor Minin, Vasili Pronchishchev, Pyotr Lasinius, and Dmitry Laptev.

1755 Moscow State University is established.

1799–1837 Lifetime of Aleksandr Pushkin, the famed romantic poet, who writes many much-loved works, including *Eugene Onegin,* 1823–31; *The Bronze Horseman,* 1833; and *Boris Godunov,* 1831. He is killed in a duel.

early 1800s Imperial Russia expands into Alaska.

1825 The Decembrists lead a revolt against Czar Nicolas I, demanding the abolition of serfdom, a representative government, and greater freedoms. The revolt is crushed by Nicolas, and the participants are exiled to Siberia.

1861 Serfdom is formally abolished in central Russia.

1867 Russia sells Alaska to the United States.

1880 The first university in Siberia is opened in Tomsk.

1881 Construction starts on the Trans-Siberia Railroad.

1893 Novosibirsk (originally called Novonikolayevsk) is founded as the site for the bridge over the Ob River for the Trans-Siberian Railroad.

1904–05 Russo-Japanese War. Russia and Japan fight over control of greater Manchuria, Korea, and other islands in the area. The conflict leads to the embarrassing defeat of the Russian navy and the loss of these territories to the Japanese, including the only warm-water port on the Pacific that had been in Russia's possession.

1906–11 Czar Nicolas II sponsors a program to encourage central Russians to resettle in Siberia, offering peasants free or cheap land and distributing flyers exalting the quality of life in Siberia. As a result of these programs, about 3 million people resettle in Siberia.

1914–17 Russians suffer tremendous losses in World War I, which is one of the reasons for the revolution in 1917. Most of the fighting occurs in European Russia, sparing most of central and eastern Russia.

1916 Construction finishes on the Tran-Siberian Railroad.

February 1917 The February Revolution, in which the Duma (parliament), fueled by a popular revolution against the czar, assumes power in the country. The czar abdicates.

October 1917 The Bolsheviks, led by Vladimir Lenin, overthrow the government in St. Petersburg and declare the creation of a socialist country. They immediately negotiate a withdrawal from World War I, ceding large amounts of European Russia to Germany.

1918 Czar Nicolas II and his family are assassinated near Ekaterinburg.

1918–20 During the Russian civil war between the Red Army (the Bolsheviks) and the White Army (the republicans), most of Asian Russia is a stronghold for the Whites. Alaksandr Kolchak, an admiral in the czarist army and the leader of the White forces, establishes his capital in Omsk. His government is toppled in 1920, and Asian Russia and Central Asia fall to the Bolsheviks.

1920–24 Siberian agriculture declines, and numerous anti-Soviet riots occur in rural areas where peasants make no efforts to conceal their dislike of the Soviet regime.

1930s Peasants are forced to give up their private farmlands and work on government farms along with other peasants from the area during the period of collectivization. Peasants who resist are exiled to the north.

Stalin's purges create a large number of political prisoners who are sent to Siberian labor camps called gulags. Prisoners may be given "show trials" and forced to confess before being imprisoned or killed; others simply disappear, never to be seen again.

1941 Germany invades Russia, pulling Russia into World War II. Thousands of people are evacuated from European Russian to the east. Upon arrival, the evacuees set up workshops and establish enterprises to help with the war effort. These enterprises provide an economic boost to Siberia at the same time that they displace the indigenous population and degrade the fragile ecology.

1945 The Novosibirsk Opera and Theatre holds its first performance. The theater is the largest in Russia.

World War II ends. German and Japanese prisoners of war are sent to Siberian gulags. The Soviet Union occupies Eastern Europe, and the cold war begins.

1949 The Soviet Union explodes its first nuclear bomb.

1950s Akademgorod (Academy Town) is established in Novosibirsk by the Russian Academy of Sciences. This settlement of scientists becomes the leader in Russian scientific research.

1953 Soviet leader Joseph Stalin dies, ending the period of the worst political repression in the Soviet Union.

1958 Boris Pasternak wins the Nobel Prize for his novel *Doctor Zhivago,* but he is forced to refuse the prize.

1961 The Soviet Union launches its first manned space flight.

1969 The Soviet Union is involved in major border clashes with China.

1978–82 The Soviet Union invades and tries to subdue Afghanistan.

1985–91 Period of glasnost (opening up) and perestroika (restructuring), instituted by General Secretary Mikhail Gorbachev's attempt to revitalize the Soviet economy.

1991 The Soviet Union disintegrates, and the 14 republics of the Soviet Union become independent nations. Siberia becomes an important source of raw materials, especially oil.

1993–95 Russia becomes involved in a humiliating war with Chechnya, a breakaway republic in the northern Caucasus Mountains.

1998 The Russian currency, the ruble, is devalued overnight, annihilating the savings of the population throughout the country.

(continues)

Russians: nationality time line *(continued)*
1999–2000 Russia becomes involved in a second war in Chechnya, this time crushing the breakaway groups.
2000 Vladimir Putin becomes president of Russia.
2004 Vladimir Putin is elected for a second term as president.
2006 Diplomatic problems between Russia and Georgia cause Russia to deport large numbers of ethnic Georgians living both legally and illegally in Russia.
2008 Russia invades Georgia and initiates bombing raids over several Georgian cities in support of the South Ossetians.

by peaks and valleys that continue to the Pacific Coast. The northeast part of Russia is especially mountainous, and the Kamchatka Peninsula, extending southward from the northeastern part of Russia, has numerous volcanic peaks, many of which are still active. This volcanic activity continues down through the Kuril Islands (claimed by both Russia and Japan) and is a part of the Pacific "ring of fire," the nearly 25,000-mile-long rim at the Pacific Plate named for its frequent volcanoes and earthquakes.

INCEPTION AS A NATION

Areas of Asian Russia have been inhabited by humans since very early in human prehistory, and there have been numerous archaeological finds in Asian Russia dating back 150,000 or more years. For millennia tribes have existed in various political stages, sometimes in small tribal groups and other times as part of larger Chinese, Mongol, or Turkic empires. The Russians in Asian Russia are relatively recent arrivals from eastern Europe, and their national identity is closely tied with that of European Russians, with whom they continue to share a nation.

The ancestors of the Russians, the Slavs, inhabited the areas of modern-day Belarus, western Russia, and Ukraine and lived in varying states of independence and conquest, frequently paying tribute to Turkic empires to the south and east. While the Slavs were not indigenous to the region, by 600 C.E. they had become the dominant ethnic group. However, there are no indications that these Slavic tribes had any sense of identity as a common group as opposed to separate tribes.

The first evidence of a Russian national identity comes from the city-state of Novgorod, founded in 860, and more important from Kievan Rus, founded in 880. Both were founded by Scandinavian warriors who conquered the Slavic tribes of the area and made them their subjects, establishing a hereditary kingdom in both cities. Around the same time, in 888 an alphabet, known as Cyrillic, was developed by two Greek Orthodox monks, Sts. Cyril and Methodius, especially for writing the Slavic language. Today this language is known as Old Church Slavonic and is used in the Russian Orthodox Church liturgy.

In 988 Vladimir I, the prince of Kiev, decided to introduce a state religion in hopes of increasing his subjects' allegiance to the state. Popular legend has it that he considered Islam and Orthodox Christianity and decided on the latter because of the splendor of the Orthodox liturgy. The introduction of Orthodox Christianity increased the ties between Kievan Rus and the Byzantine Empire, exemplified by the adoption of Byzantine architecture and art for the construction and decoration of early churches.

Built originally in 1150, Sancta Sophia in Novgorod, also called the Wisdom of God, provides a classic example of a Russian or onion-domed church. *(Shutterstock/Sergey Khachatryan)*

After the steady decline of the Kievan Rus state and the establishment of numerous cities throughout the Kievan state, which included most of European Russia, the Russians faced their first serious threat in the 13th century, when the MONGOLS conquered all of Kievan Rus and established control over the area. Although the Mongols ruled until 1480, the Russians refused to be assimilated, maintaining their language, Orthodox religion, and most cultural customs. As the Russians emerged from Mongol rule in the late 15th century, it became clear that they had a clear conception of themselves as a people unified by language, religion, and traditions.

Russia began to expand into Siberia and Asian Russia in the 17th century, with those regions being ideal for people fleeing from the czarist authorities as escaped serfs, criminals, or Old Believers. Siberia, isolated both from other countries and from Russian society, also was the ideal place for authorities to send political prisoners. While these prisoners' common heritage with the rest of Russia remained important, the Siberians were aware that the rest of the country regarded them as unimportant. Political dissidents and other new arrivals, voluntary or otherwise, were usually welcomed by the local Russian population rather than shunned as authorities would have preferred.

In the early 1900s, after the fall of the czar and during the civil war, Asian Russia was a stronghold for the Whites (nationalists). At the same time, in a number of areas the Russian population had united with the indigenous population to seek independence. Siberia and Asian Russia remained a place of exile during the time of the Soviet Union but eventually began to gain Russian cultural and academic standing as places like the Akademgorod (Academy Town) in Novosibirsk became the center of scientific research in numerous fields.

Today Asian Russians continue to feel ignored and left behind by the economic growth in Moscow and St. Petersburg and continue to be poorer than European Russians. Economic development has been mostly based on the oil industry, leaving a very few people extremely wealthy and the rest with environmental problems. As a result, there has been significant migration out of Asian Russia to cities, especially Moscow and St. Petersburg, sometimes leaving industries without enough workers.

CULTURAL IDENTITY

Russian cultural heritage is rooted in both European and Asian traditions, having been influenced by the adoption of Christianity and by ties to the Byzantine Empire, but also having been occupied by the Mongols and subsequently isolated from Europe for hundreds of years. Russians often consider themselves a bridge between the East and the West and pride themselves on understanding both Western European and East Asian jokes. This role as a bridge is even more important for Russians in the Asian part of the country, who are physically closer to Eastern cultures and have more contact with other Asian peoples who live in Asian Russia.

Russian attitudes toward individualism and authority reflect this mediating role between the East and West. Individualism is not fully embraced; instead, people are encouraged to think first of the communal good, a concept that was not invented by the Communists, only exploited by them. It is considered bad manners to talk about oneself. This role as a "bridge" may also be the reason for Russians' paradoxical attitude about government: they tend to believe that the government is not to be trusted but have the fatalistic attitude that Russia needs a strong, powerful leader.

Asian Russians, or Siberians, are known in the country for their independence and self-reliance. Since the beginning of Russian settlement and expansion into Asia, the area has been isolated from and often more or less ignored by the government and the rest of society. Most of the first settlers in the area were escaped serfs and criminals who had little respect for czarist or any other authority. Asian Russia, especially Siberia, remained a place to send criminals and prisoners of war until the fall of the Soviet Union. The mistrust of laws and government that is a common thread throughout Russian culture is exaggerated in Siberia, where more people have suffered as a result of laws than have benefited from them. Siberians take pride in this exile heritage, and the homes of famous exiles are often turned into museums.

Aside from the exiles and escaped serfs, the other group to settle Siberia were the "Old Believers." Old Believers, who refused to accept reforms to the Russian Orthodox Church in the 17th century, have a deep-seated fear of government due to centuries of persecution. They have largely held onto old traditions, often including using only outdated technology and living their lives in isolation and governed by religion. While they were an important part of the settling of Siberia, today they do not make up a significant portion of the Russian population in Siberia.

Russification programs for minority groups, starting in the 19th century, have successfully assimilated many of them, often at the expense of their native languages, religions, and traditions. Until recently, ethnicity did not matter (with the notable exception of Jews), and any person who wished to identify himself or herself as Russian would be readily accepted. However, populations that did not Russify are often looked down upon, discriminated against, and mistrusted.

FURTHER READING

Marjorie Mandelstam Balzer, ed. *Russian Traditional Culture: Religion, Gender, and Customary Law* (Armonk, N.Y.: M. E. Sharpe, 1992).

James H. Billington. *The Face of Russia: Anguish, Aspiration, and Achievement in Russian Culture* (New York: TV Books, 1999).

Linda Edmondson, ed. *Gender in Russian History and Culture* (Houndsmill, N.Y.: Palgrave in association with Centre for Russian and East European Studies, University of Birmingham, U.K., 2001).

Monika Greenleaf. *Russian Subjects: Empire, Nation, and the Culture of the Golden Age* (Evanston, Ill.: Northwestern University Press, 1998).

Robert Service. *A History of Twentieth Century Russia* (Cambridge, Mass.: Harvard University Press, 1998).

Ivar Spector. *An Introduction to Russian History and Culture* (Princeton, N.J.: Van Nostrand, 1961).

Eva-Maria Stoberg. *The Siberian Saga: A History of Russia's Wild East* (New York: P. Lang, 2005).

Arthur Voyce. *Moscow and the Roots of Russian Culture* (Norman: University of Oklahoma Press, 1964).

Alan Wood. *The History of Siberia: From Russian Conquest to Revolution* (New York: Routledge, 1991).

Ryukyu Islanders   *See* OKINAWANS.

Sahu *See* NEWAR.

Sai *See* SCYTHIANS.

Saka *See* SCYTHIANS.

Salar (Qaluer, Sala, Salacu, Salahui, Salar'er)

The Salar people are probably the descendants of TURKMEN tribes who left the Samarkand region of Central Asia more than 700 years ago, starting in 1271. Upon their arrival in China, they settled in the semiarid mountainous region of Xunhua county, Qinghai Province. The Yellow (Huang) River provided access to water for those residing nearby, but the region generally suffered from lack of rain, which made agriculture difficult in some years. Today extensive canals and irrigation systems have served to limit the difficulties posed by the region's dry landscape.

Salar social structure before their migration to China was probably based on patrilineal clans and tribal affiliations, as was the case with other Central Asian TURKIC PEOPLES at the time. Under the Chinese one Salar headman was given the title of hereditary chief for the entire minority group, a position that was maintained in the subsequent Ming dynasty (1368–1644) as well. Under these chiefs the Chinese created a bureaucracy that paralleled their own and consisted of positions pertaining to military affairs, taxes, and justice. During the Qing dynasty (1644–1911) the Salar were divided into two separate administrative regions or *gongs*, which were themselves made up of groups of villages.

In addition to new administrative forms, the 17th and 18th centuries also saw the widespread adoption of Islam among the Salar population. Soon the imams joined the chiefs' families as well as those of the village headmen as members of the local aristocracy. This aristocracy held most of the region's agricultural land where the commoners grew their wheat, barley, buckwheat, potatoes, and vegetables, and raised cattle, sheep, and chickens. The introduction of Islam brought a building boom to the region as each village built a mosque. A new language was also introduced, as some Salar men learned Arabic in order to read and study the Qur'an. Polygyny, the practice of having more than one wife, also spread among the landowning class, which could afford to maintain two or more separate families; this last practice has since been outlawed by the Chinese state.

Despite the addition of a Chinese-created bureaucracy and nobility, the Salar did not abandon their own kinship or housing systems. Exogamous patrilineal clans, those in which membership passes from fathers to children and within which marriage is forbidden, continue to be important identity markers among the Salar. Individual households are often made up of extended families of three generations from the same patrilineage into which wives must marry and move, leaving their own families behind. In the past these marriages were often arranged by a matchmaker who saw his or her job as uniting

SALAR

location:
Most live in Xunhua county in Qinghai Province, others in Gansu and Xinjiang Provinces, China.

time period:
13th century to the present

ancestry:
Turkic

language:
Salar, a Turkic language closely related to Uighur and Uzbek; most Salars also speak and read Mandarin Chinese

two families and lineages rather than two individuals. If the two families agreed to the union, the man's family paid a bride price to the woman's in horses, cloth, sugar, and other wealth; this payment served both to compensate the woman's household for the loss of her domestic labor and to legitimate any children that resulted from the union. The woman then moved from her own household into that of her new husband, a pattern called patrilocal residence. Family houses are generally two-story structures built around a courtyard containing fruit trees such as apricots and apples, a common arrangement in the Samarkand region of Uzbekistan as well.

Beyond the household, which is the primary unit of both production and consumption among the Salar, villages serve as the largest units in Salar society, with mosques being the focal point of village activities. While the Chinese state removed all Islamic clergy in 1958, since 1980 there has been a revival of religious activities among the Salar and throughout China so that mosques have once again become the centers of social activity in many villages.

Samals (Muslim Samalan, Sama, Samal Moro)

The Samals are a subgroup of the FILIPINO MUSLIMS. They are probably the first Austronesian speakers to have settled in the Sulu Archipelago after the migration of AUSTRONESIANS, who are more generally from Taiwan and ultimately from southern China. Today they make up the second-largest group in Sulu after the dominant TAUSUG, who moved into the region in the 10th and 11th centuries.

The Samals are a maritime people who occupy the lower-lying coral islands of the Sulu Archipelago, leaving the higher, volcanic islands to the more agricultural Tausug. Boat building and fishing occupy most of the time for men living along the coasts. Cassava and coconuts are also grown, mostly for household consumption, although some small-scale copra production for the market is engaged in by some families. Chickens and ducks provide eggs and meat for Samals regardless of location, while inland groups often keep goats and a cow or two for their meat, usually eaten for special occasions such as weddings and other ceremonies. Sadly today, much of this subsistence agriculture and fishing has been replaced by processed rice, canned goods, and vegetables purchased in Tawittawi and Sitangkai, the largest towns in the Samal region. These processed foods provide fewer nutrients and are expensive in relation to the people's low incomes

from coconuts, fish, and some black-market trading along the coasts.

Samal households vary significantly, from simple nuclear families made up of a married couple and their unmarried children to large four-generation households of about 20 people. In these large, extended households nuclear families are still differentiated from one another by sleeping unit and for subsistence purposes. Beyond the household, groups of related households are connected by bilateral kinship ties that make up a neighborhood or work team. Two or more neighborhoods generally make up a village, the smallest unit containing its own mosque and political leadership, in the form of a village headman.

Samoans: nationality (people of Samoa)

Samoa is a Polynesian society that experienced colonization by Britain, Germany, the United States, and New Zealand before becoming the first Pacific nation to achieve independence, in 1962.

GEOGRAPHY

Situated approximately 2,500 miles southwest of Hawaii and roughly 1,800 miles northeast of New Zealand, Samoa sits comfortably in the center of the Pacific islands. Consisting of 10 landmasses, the largest of which (and most heavily populated) are Savaii and Upolu, Samoa's total area is 1,823 square miles. American Samoa lies 40 miles eastward, consisting of the main island of Tutuila and the group of islands known as Manua, in total an area of 124 square miles. The islands are volcanic, but only Savaii is active, the last eruption having occurred in 1911 when lava engulfed and destroyed the village of Saleaula. Vegetation flourishes in the warm tropical climate, and the rich soil of Samoa is home to lush rainforests; swamps and lagoons are also present in the island country. Indigenous wildlife includes several bird species, lizards, and snakes, as well as the endangered flying fox.

INCEPTION AS A NATION

Before European powers began to pursue control over Samoa, the islands had a king but not a centralized government. Individual villages were ruled by chiefs, and they united occasionally for religious rituals and war. In the late 19th century, Samoa became the object of desire of clashing powers for its use as a coal refueling station for ships; previously, the nearest refueling station had been Honolulu, which was 2,500 miles away. Britain, Germany, and the United States all laid

---

SAMALS

location:
Sulu Archipelago, Mindanao, the Philippines

time period:
3000 B.C.E. to the present

ancestry:
Austronesian

language:
Samalan, a Sulu-Borneo language within the larger Austronesian family

Samoans: nationality time line

B.C.E.

5000–4500 Settlement in the Pacific begins with the Austronesian departure from south China into Taiwan, Indonesia, and the Philippines.

1200 Probable date of Austronesian expansion to Samoa.

1000 The city of Mulifanua on the island of Upolu is the oldest known site of human habitation in Samoa.

C.E.

1722 Dutch explorer Jacob Roggeveen is sent to find Terra Australis, an imagined landmass of enormous proportions, and is the first European to discover the Samoan Islands.

1768 French explorer Louis-Antoine de Bougainville calls the Samoan Islands "The Navigator Islands," for the inhabitants' deft use of canoes.

1797 French painter Nicholas Ozanne paints *The Massacre of MM. de Langle, Lamanon, and Ten Others in Two Boats from La Perouse,* a visual account of the Samoan attack on the shore crew of the French ship *La Perouse* in 1787, which results in the deaths of 12 people.

1830 Christian missionaries John Williams and Charles Barf of the London Missionary Society introduce the Samoan people to Christianity, which is largely adopted and leads to the abandonment of the native Samoan religion.

1857 J. C. Godeffroy and Son, a trade and shipping firm from Germany, establishes its depot in Apia.

1878 Britain, Germany, and the United States all have interests in the Samoan Islands for their use as a coal-refueling station for ships, and they agree to share power.

1889 The power sharing proves futile, and the three nations sign the Treaty of Berlin, which ensures Samoa's independence.

1890 Robert Louis Stevenson, author of *Treasure Island* and *The Strange Case of Dr. Jekyll and Mr. Hyde,* moves his family to Samoa and is given the name Tusitala, meaning "Teller of Tales." His death in 1894 is acknowledged with the ceremonial burial given to royalty.

1898 Samoa's king Malietoa Laupepa dies, and his rival takes the throne. The nation erupts in violence as Samoans fight over the new ruler and Samoa is left vulnerable to foreign takeover.

1899 The Berlin Treaty is annulled, dividing Samoa into two parts. Eastern Samoa becomes American Samoa and Western Samoa becomes German Samoa. The British give up claims to the islands in exchange for Fiji.

1914 New Zealand troops arrive in Upolu and seize control from the Germans.

1918–19 One-fifth of the Western Samoan population dies from the influenza epidemic due to the negligence of the New Zealand administrators. American Samoa closes itself off from outside contact and remains untouched.

1920 The Samoans develop the Mau, which translates to "strongly held opinion," a nonviolent campaign against foreign rule.

1929 A Mau demonstration in downtown Apia turns violent when the New Zealand police open fire on the protestors, killing 11 (including the Mau leader, Chief Tupua Tamasese Lealofi III) and injuring 50 others. December 29 is henceforth known as Black Saturday.

1962 Western Samoa is the first Polynesian nation to obtain independence.

1970 Samoa is accepted as a member of the British Commonwealth.

1979 Albert Wendt publishes *Leaves of the Banyan Tree,* an epic saga depicting Western Samoan life both before and after independence from New Zealand.

1997 Samoa officially changes its name from Western Samoa to the Independent State of Samoa, also known simply as Samoa.

SAMOANS: NATIONALITY.

nation:
The Independent State of Samoa; Samoa; formerly Western Samoa

derivation of name:
Native word meaning "place of the *moa*," the *moa* being a large bird now extinct

government:
Mix of parliamentary democracy and constitutional monarchy

capital:
Apia

language:
Samoan and English; Samoan is the national language and English is the official business language.

religion:
Predominantly Christian: Congregationalist (the London Missionary Society Church) 34.8 percent, Roman Catholic 19.6 percent, Methodist 15 percent, Latter-Day Saints 12.7 percent, Assembly of God 6.6 percent, Seventh Day Adventist 3.5 percent, other Christian 4.5 percent, Worship Centre 1.3 percent, other 1.7 percent, unspecified 0.1 percent

earlier inhabitants:
There were no pre-Polynesian inhabitants of the Samoan islands.

demographics:
Samoan 92.6 percent, Euronesian 7 percent (persons of European and Polynesian descent), European 0.4 percent

claim to the little chain of islands and found the opportunity to seize power in 1898 when the Samoan king Malietoa Laupepa died and the country erupted in civil war. In 1899 Samoa was divided between Germany and the United States (Britain backed away in favor of Fiji). Western Samoa, the larger of the two portions, went to Germany, and eastern Samoa was claimed by the United States, becoming American Samoa.

In 1914, at the beginning of World War I, Western Samoa was seized by New Zealand troops. A number of clashes took place between the Samoan people and the New Zealand administrators, who claimed such rights as dispossessing chiefs of their titles, which infringed on Samoan custom. In 1918 the Spanish influenza epidemic spread through ports all over the world, and due to the negligence of the New Zealand administrators, no quarantine was established for Western Samoa and the nation was devastated by the disease. One-fifth of the population died, while nearby American Samoa was quarantined and remained without a single case. Outraged over the administrators' carelessness and mismanagement of Samoa, the Samoan people began the Mau ("strongly held opinion") movement to protest foreign rule. The campaign was originally led by Olaf Nelson, who was half Samoan and half Swedish, but New Zealand officials claimed that "part-Europeans" were misleading the Samoan people, and the movement was banned.

On December 28, 1929, the newly elected leader of the Mau, Chief Tupua Tamasese Lealofi III, led a nonviolent demonstration in Apia. A confrontation between police and one of the leaders of the protest led to officers firing into the crowd, killing Chief Lealofi as well as 10 others; 50 more people suffered gunshot wounds and injuries from police batons.

Relations between Samoans and New Zealand administrators improved later when New Zealand's first Labour government came to power and acknowledged the Mau as a legal organization in 1935. Nevertheless, the Mau pushed for national independence, which was finally obtained in 1962, making Samoa the first Polynesian nation to liberate itself from foreign rule. In 1970 Samoa became an official member of the British Commonwealth, and in 1997 the Samoan constitution was amended to change its name from Western Samoa to the Independent State of Samoa.

CULTURAL IDENTITY

Following the 18th-century European "discovery" of Samoa, there occurred a number of violent confrontations between the Samoan people and European explorers who came to the islands; these led to the European image of the typical Samoan as a bloodthirsty savage. The Samoans were also known to engage in "headhunting," a ritual of war in which a warrior took the head of his slain opponent to give to his leader, thus proving his bravery. This unsettling tradition probably fortified the European belief that Samoans were brutal and animalistic, while the reality of Samoan culture is one of love and respect for family, community, and God.

The Samoan people identify themselves most significantly by their emphasis on respect, which is visible within the distinct and intricate social hierarchy system in which they function. At the top of the hierarchical social structure is the *matai*, or chief, a title that is given by a family or community to an individual who is either the head of a family or who has done a great service to the village. The *matai* governs his or her *aiga*, the extended family network, and enforces rules of propriety while punishing those who misbehave. He or she serves as a living connection to cultural heritage, as it is the *matai's* responsibility to remember Samoan folklore and family genealogies. The *matai* also acts as a family representative and speaks on behalf of the family at the village council.

The *matai* system is part of Fa'a Samoa (the Samoan Way), a complex set of rules and proprieties that regulate Samoan daily life. Fa'a Samoa is governed by respect and provides rules of etiquette for displaying respect, such as how and when to sit amid elders, or how to eat and drink in a village. Fa'a Samoa is very rigid and specific, and a breech of regulation not only suggests disrespect but is taken as an offense against the people as a whole. This aspect of Samoan identity makes it easy to see why the Samoans were so offended by the liberties taken by the New Zealand administrators. In a society in which every individual has a specific station within the hierarchy and must behave accordingly, foreign rule introduced a disruption to the cultural harmony, particularly in the administrators' removal of specific *matai*. Such a weighty decision had previously been one only the *aiga* could make, so the New Zealand administrators' assumption of the position of supreme authority represented the possibility of cultural obliteration.

It is also little wonder that the Samoan people adapted so readily to Christian organized religion, with its emphasis on the observance of rules and rituals. The Samoans identify themselves as deeply devout Christians, and Sundays are reserved for church in the morning and relaxation with family for the rest of the day. Even to-day, despite heavy tourism, many shops in Samoa close on Sundays. On weekdays a prayer curfew is enforced between 6 and 7 P.M., at which time tourists or visitors may not enter a village until the curfew is over. Guards are usually stationed at crossroads and village entrances to make sure no one enters. True to the tradition of the Samoan Way, disregard for religious custom is viewed as disrespectful and an offense to the village.

Conflicts have recently arisen between Fa'a Samoa and the newest generation as the younger Samoans are more educated than many of their elders and are forced to balance their modern knowledge with the observance of the Samoan Way. This clash between modern understanding and extreme conservatism has led to one of the highest suicide rates in the world: 26 per year within a population of 200,000. As Samoa has been an independent nation only for the last 50 years, those concerned for its future remain hopeful that the Samoan people will one day find a balance between their cultural identity and the changes introduced by the colonial and post-colonial worlds.

See also POLYNESIANS.

FURTHER READING

Joseph W. Ellison. *Tusitala of the South Seas: The Story of Robert Louis Stevenson's Life in the South Pacific* (New York: Hastings House, 1953).

Peggy Fairbairn-Dunlop. *Tamaitai Samoa: Their Stories* (Suva, Fiji: Institute of Pacific Studies, 1996).

Derek Freeman. *The Fateful Hoaxing of Margaret Mead: A Historical Analysis of her Samoan Research* (Boulder, Colo.: Westview Press, 1999).

Lowell D. Holmes. *Quest for the Real Samoa: the Mead/Freeman Controversy and Beyond* (South Hadley, Mass: Bergin and Garvey Publishers, 1987).

Margaret Mead. *Coming of Age in Samoa: A Psychological Study of Primitive Youth for Western Civilization* (New York: Harper Perennial Modern Classics, 2001).

George Turner. *Samoa: A Hundred Years Ago and Long Before* (Boston: Adamant Media Corporation, 2005).

Albert Wendt. *Leaves of the Banyan Tree* (Honolulu: University of Hawaii Press, 1994).

Samoyeds   *See* NENETS.

San Chay   (Caolan, Cao Lan, Hon Ban, Man Cao Lan, San Chi, Sán-Chi, San Ti, San Tu)

The San Chay people have existed as such only since the designation of this group by the government of Vietnam in 1979. The classification combined two groups of people, the Cao Lan and the San Chi, who resembled each other culturally but spoke different languages. The Cao Lan speak a language of the same name, a Central Tai language very similar to those spoken by the TAY and the NUNG, while the San Chi speak a language very similar to the Chinese of the HAN. Some have disagreed about their joint classification, but generally ethnologists have agreed that it is reasonable to combine them due to their great cultural similarities as well as their relatively small numbers; together, the two groups number between only 100,000 and 150,000 people.

The San Chay live in north-central Vietnam, primarily in Tuyen Quang, Bac Thai, and Ha Bac Provinces, as well as in Yunnan Province, China. Both the Cao Lan and San Chi may have originated in China's Guangdong Province and moved away in the early 17th century due to political strife in the region at that time; however, some sources claim that the San Chay people are the descendants of the original migrants who left China for Vietnam thousands of years ago.

In their mountainous homes their subsistence way of life did not change drastically until the French colonial period when Catholic missionaries and French bureaucrats entered the region and tried to impose their way of life on the people. These efforts were largely rebuffed, but colonial land tenure systems left many San Chay, who were still known as Cao Lan and San Chi at the time, as landless tenants working on French- and VIETNAMESE-owned plantations and farms. Even more change was introduced following the Viet Minh's victory over the French in 1954, when the Communist state of North Vietnam began collectivizing all land and attempting to erase class and caste distinctions.

Today many San Chay continue to live in small villages of 20–30 families residing in houses elevated on stilts, although some more contemporary buildings have started to be built on the ground. Each village has a headman who bears responsibility for maintaining social order internally and representing the village externally. In the past, headmen were important community leaders who came from high-ranking families and bore significant responsibility in collecting tribute, distributing food, adjudicating disputes, and external representation. Today most of these tasks have been taken over by the state bureaucracy, leaving the village headman as more of an exalted figurehead than a true authority figure.

SAN CHAY

location:
Northern Vietnam and Yunnan Province, China

time period:
1979 to the present

ancestry:
Cao Lan and San Chi peoples

language:
Cao Lan, a Tai-Kadai language

Most San Chay continue to engage primarily in the agricultural sector of the economy, producing rice in irrigated fields as well as corn, sweet potatoes and other vegetables, peanuts, sesame, and other products in small gardens cut out of the forest and shifted yearly to allow for long fallow periods between plantings. In addition hunting, fishing, and gathering mushrooms, bamboo, and rattan all contribute to the San Chay diet and economy. Some families keep pigs, poultry, and cattle as well.

The San Chay social structure is patrilineal, meaning that inheritance and descent are handed down from fathers, fathers' fathers, and so on. Residential patterns are also patrilocal, which means that a wife lives with her husband and his family in their household. Unlike many patrilocal systems, however, the new wife does not leave her natal home at marriage but only with the birth of her first child. This pattern was established in the past when marriages between children were arranged by their parents. Today women and men are able to choose their own partners in adulthood, but they still tend to require parental consent to have their marriages recognized by the wider community.

San Chay religion is largely a set of indigenous beliefs and practices that incorporate ancestor worship, spirit veneration, and a variety of gods. Buddhism, Taoism, and Confucianism have also contributed to the local belief system, and most villages have temples and shrines from at least two different traditions, if not more. Even the family home is incorporated into the indigenous religious system, with the house structure said to be symbolic of the "buffalo genie." The four pillars holding the house up symbolize the legs, the lathes symbolize the animal's ribs, and the roof symbolizes the backbone. Inside each house is an altar dedicated to the man's lineage ancestors, and at the entrance is placed a basket containing bran and incense sticks in honor of the god who protects cattle. The religion also includes many myths or stories that explain the particular San Chay worldview and the place of humans, animals, genies, spirits, plants, and other natural phenomena within it. Familiar to many Westerners, the San Chay tell of a great flood that destroyed most life on earth with the exception of one couple who went on to repopulate the planet.

In addition to myths and other storytelling, the San Chay entertain themselves with a variety of musical instruments and singing styles. They play various percussion instruments, including castanets, bells, cymbals, and drums, plus a number of different woodwind instruments, including trumpets and flutes; many of these instruments are also used during religious rituals and festivals. The most important song style is the *sinh ca*, or popular song, which has four different varieties: daily songs, nocturnal songs, nuptial songs, and initiation songs. Daily songs are sung by both males and females and are made up of series of questions and answers that are sung in four verses of seven words apiece. Nocturnal songs are obviously sung only at night and are part of a ritual cycle of up to 1,000 different songs performed over a five- to seven-night period. The last two categories are also songs performed only at the appropriate ritual event, marriage and male initiations, respectively.

San Chi   *See* SAN CHAY.

Santal   (Santhal, Saontas, Saonthals, Sauntas)

The Santal are India's largest tribal population and live in the country's northwestern states; there are also smaller migrant populations in Bangladesh, Bhutan, and Nepal.

GEOGRAPHY

The Santal heartland, sometimes called Santal Pargana, is located on the Chota Nagpur Plateau in Jharkhand, Orissa, Bihar, and West Bengal and is bounded by the Ganges, Sone, and Mahanadi Rivers. Even today the region contains significant deciduous forest coverage and lies at elevations ranging from about 600 to more than 3,300 feet above sea level. It is one of the few areas of India where tigers and elephants still remain in the wild. The tree cover and elevation provide the region with a fairly comfortable climate of between 60°F and 70°F in winter and 80°F and 90°F in summer.

ORIGINS

Santal origins, as is the case for all Mundari language speakers, remain a contentious issue among linguists, geneticists, archaeologists, and others interested in Indian and Southeast Asian prehistory. While some scholars believe that Mundari speakers along with the entire Austro-Asiatic language phylum originated in Southeast Asia and only later migrated to India, more recent genetic testing has shown that Mundari speakers probably originated in India and entered Southeast Asia about 8,000 years

SANTAL

location:
The Indian states of Assam, Bihar, Jharkhand, Mizoram, Orissa, Tripura, and West Bengal; also Bangladesh, Bhutan, and Nepal

time period:
Possibly 65,000 B.C.E. to the present

ancestry:
Mundari, probably the most ancient Indian population still in existence

language:
Santali, a Munda language in the Austro-Asiatic phylum

ago. Genetic markers found in about 99 percent of Mundari populations, including the Santal, indicate migration from Africa into India around 65,000 years ago.

Santal mythology states that these people created a kingdom of their own in Santal Pargana, but very little is known about it, if it existed at all. Norwegian missionaries working among the Santal in the 19th century brought a number of medieval weapons back with them to Oslo, which may indicate the development of an advanced state in the region in the distant past. (These remain in Oslo museums.) A number of hill forts from the same period have also been found in the Santal heartland, which may verify the existence of a centralized state, but both forms of evidence are very weak and much more work needs to be done to confirm or disprove the veracity of these myths.

HISTORY

The most important verifiable dates in Santal history all occur after the British came to the region in the late 18th century. For example, in 1784 Baba Tilka Majhi and a small band of men took up arms against the foreign intruders and held them at bay in the Tilapore forest for several weeks. Eventually Majhi was caught, dragged behind a horse to the regional center at Bhgalpur, and then hanged. Less than a century later a second Santal rebellion also broke out and lasted for several years; it ended only with the death of about 20,000 Santal, according to the British chronicler who wrote about it in *The Annals of Rural Bengal*. In addition to exploitation at the hands of the British, the events of 1854–56, sometimes called Santal Hul, or Freedom, was also directed at Hindu moneylenders, landlords, and others who had moved into the region following the British. Many Santal in the interwar years had become unskilled laborers and were charged interest ranging from 50 to 500 percent on advances given on their meager plantation salaries. In reaction, four brothers— Sidhu, Kahnu, Chand, and Bhairay—led thousands of fellow Santal against all the nontribal peoples and organizations in their region.

Since independence most Santal subgroups have been classified as SCHEDULED TRIBES, through which they have access to certain preferential positions in government, education, and civil service. However, only a very small number of Scheduled Tribes people are actually able to take up these posts, and most have remained relatively marginal to the Indian economy. There are also a small number who

---

Santal time line

B.C.E.

unknown time The Santal and their fellow Austro-Asiatic speakers migrate into India.

C.E.

1765 Santal territory in contemporary Jharkhand is captured by the British.

1784 Baba Tilka Majhi leads a resistance against the British but is captured and killed.

1855–57 The Santal Hul, or Freedom, movement is one of the largest uprisings against the British, similar to the Sepoy Mutiny of the same period.

1947 Indian independence and the creation of Pakistan and East Pakistan, the latter with a population of Santal.

1960–75 The communist Naxalite movement is at the height of its power and attracts many Santal into its ranks.

2001 Jharkhand, a largely tribal state with a large Santal population, is carved from southern Bihar.

2005 The All India Santal Welfare and Cultural Society organizes numerous events to commemorate the 150th anniversary of Santal Hul.

---

have migrated into Bangladesh to work on the tea and other plantations there.

As they did during the colonial period, some Santal have been active participants in the rebellions that have marked Indian postindependence history. Some Santal were part of the Jharkhand tribalist movement that ended in 2001 with the creation of the largely tribal state of Jharkhand out of territory from southern Bihar. The new state contains significant coal and other mineral wealth, and the Jharkhand tribalists hoped that by separating from Bihar they and their people would have greater access to the wealth generated by these resources. Santal have also been instrumental in the communist Naxalite rebellions that began in the 1950s but were labeled as Naxalite only in the 1960s and 1970s. Their participation was generated through a discourse that depicted these Maoist rebels as the inheritors of the war in the 1850s. As was the case in the earlier period, Santal and other tribal peoples in the later half of the 20th century were exploited by moneylenders and landowners, and thus many were willing to go to war to change the regional and national economic system.

CULTURE

For most of their very long history the Santal were probably hunter-gatherers who turned to swidden, or slash-and-burn, and more intensive forms of agriculture only in the past two centuries. Anthropologists working among them have discovered more than 80 different kinds of traps and an extensive knowledge of local plants. Interestingly, Santali does not classify nouns in terms of gender—masculine, feminine, or neuter—but rather in terms of whether the object has a soul or not. All animals are classified as having a soul, all minerals and plants as not, with the exception of just one kind of mushroom, the *putka*. Scholars of the life of the Buddha believe that this mushroom was served to him at his last meal, based on the belief of the Hindu blacksmith who served it that it would extend his life. The Santal must have had extensive interactions with the Hindu world of the fifth century B.C.E. because they have preserved some aspect of this belief in their linguistic system long after all other Indian languages have lost it.

Today the Santal economy is largely subsistence-based with crops of wet rice agriculture, millet, legumes, fruits, mustard, cotton, tobacco, and peanuts in some locations forming its backbone. Many families keep cows, goats, ducks, and chickens, and both fishing and sport hunting remain important activities for some. In general, families produce what they need, but trade with other Santal and other communities has been common for centuries, probably for millennia. Since the colonial era many Santal have also worked in the plantations, mines, and factories that are now common in their region. A smaller number of educated Santal work in various professions; among women of this class, nursing is a common career choice.

Santal social organization is largely kinship-based and is organized around nine recognized patrilineal clans and 164 subclans; Santal tradition claims that there should be 12 clans, but several 20th-century ethnographers were unable to find more than nine. This may be because some clans have adopted Hinduism and have become classified as SCHEDULED CASTES rather than tribes and generally do not identify as Santal any more. Santal clans are strictly exogamous groups, requiring that every person marry someone from outside his or her own clan, but within the Santal community more generally. These clans were also ranked with kings and priests—*kisku* and *murmu*, respectively—at the top of the hierarchy and others below. In the past, village assemblies held considerable power over hunting and land rights, justice, and social control. Today political leaders are the most important local authority figures, as seen in their ability to mediate and settle most types of disputes. The *pargana*, or "chief of 12 villages," is one of the highest traditional positions that has been retained into the present, although the person who holds this position no longer operates as a petty king.

Marriage among the Santal is a much less structured institution than among many other Indian ethnicities and can be patrilocal, where the new couple resides with the man's family, or matrilocal, where the pair resides with the woman's. In the case of the former, the groom's family has generally paid a bride price to the bride's family to compensate them for her labor and to legitimate any resulting children. In the latter case, the man tends to be poorer and to engage in bride service, where he works for the bride's family for a period of years in order to legitimate his children and make them part of his clan. Even before the Indian constitution legalized the practice, divorce was relatively easy to obtain, especially before any children were born, and widows could remarry; even the families of unmarried mothers were usually able to purchase husbands for their daughters.

Previously, most traditional Santal households were made up of extended, multigenerational families. The ideal was for sons to remain in the family home with their own wives and children, but of course many poor men found themselves living in their wives' family homes for most if not all of their adult lives. In order to maintain these large households, widows often married a younger brother of their dead husbands and remained in the same home; widowers could do the same with the sister of their dead wives. While not common, nuclear families also existed and have now become more common among urban professional Santal families. The households of the wealthy also include servants, one of the most important markers of wealth in this society.

Prior to the introduction of state or missionary education services to the Santal, the most important time in a Santal child's life was his or her initiation into adulthood, often handled by the child's grandmother. Boys were initiated between ages eight and 10 when their forearms were branded with five tribal marks indicating clan and other status positions. Girls received a tattoo from a Hindu or Muslim specialist following the celebration of their first menses, usually around age 14. Once these two events had occurred, a Santal girl was considered sexually mature and ready for marriage, although the age of marriage has increased greatly in the past few decades.

Traditional Santal religion included many spirits, gods, and other supernatural beings, including witches, some associated with kin groupings, others with residential units. Today, villages all have a sacred grove of trees where many deities are believed to live and where rituals are held. Generally these spirits and gods are seen as benevolent, but forest *bongas,* witches, and the souls of people who died unnaturally are malevolent and can cause illness and other misfortune. A number of Hindu gods and goddesses are part of the Santal pantheon as well. There are two categories of male religious specialists: priests, or *naeke,* and diviner/healers, or *ojha.* In general, priests officiate at large festivals and ceremonies, while diviners are more personal, determining causes of illness, curing, protecting against evil spirits, and the like. While these two specialists are usually men, witches were usually women.

In the 19th century a number of Norwegian missionaries were active in various Santal communities and brought Christianity to a few. Today more families and even entire communities have converted, in part to gain access to education, which is often provided within Christian communities, and in part to escape from the hierarchies of the Hindu caste system, which categorizes tribal peoples in very low positions. Nonetheless, a number of Santal have also adopted the Hindu lifestyle dominant in the country and ceased to associate as Santal entirely.

FURTHER READING

W. G. Archer. *Tribal Law and Justice: A Report on the Santal* (New Delhi: Concept Publishing Company, 1984).

Martin Orans. *The Santal: A Tribe in Search of a Great Tradition* (Detroit: Wayne State University, 1965).

Sarikoli   *See* PAMIRI.

Sarta   *See* DONGXIANG.

Sarts   *See* UZBEKS.

Sasaks (Lombok Islanders)

The Sasaks are the dominant ethnic group on the Indonesian island of Lombok, located to the southeast of Bali. They are speakers of an Austronesian language, which indicates that their ancestors probably migrated into the region from southern China via Taiwan, the Philippines, and Indonesia's larger islands. This first wave of migration arrived in Indonesia about 4,000 years ago, displacing any prior population of hunter-gatherers who may have lived there. Chronicles from Java indicate that the Sasaks are descendants of people from east Java who arrived on bamboo rafts, called *sesek.* Today most Sasaks live in the fertile plains in the center of their island, where settled agriculture is most successful, but smaller groups also live in the hills of the north and the drier southeast.

The first organized polities on Lombok were similar to those throughout Java and the other large islands in the archipelago in following the Hindu pattern of *devaraja,* or god-kings. No Sasak king was able to unify the entire island, and the period from the start of the common era to the mid-14th century was marked by frequent warfare among these rival monarchs. In the 14th century the Sasaks came under the control of the powerful JAVANESE Majapahit kingdom, the last of the major Hindu-Buddhist kingdoms of Indonesia. In the 17th century the BALINESE conquered the western region of Lombok, while the MAKASSARESE conquered the east. The rulers of the latter kingdom brought their religion, Islam, with them and relatively soon after the elite members of the Sasak community had adopted the new religion. Today the Sasaks are largely Muslim, while their Balinese neighbors are the sole people in Indonesia who remained essentially Hindu after the initial Islamic conquest around 1500.

Sasak society was traditionally divided into two subgroups that are often described as similar to castes in that their members were barred from marrying each other and could not move from one group to the other. These subgroups—Wetu, or Waktu Telu, and Waktu Lima—differed in that the former were more traditional, incorporated more pre-Islamic beliefs and practices into their lives, and were primarily subsistence farmers. The latter were more orthodox in their practice of Islam and more cosmopolitan in their occupations and mobility. Since about 1965 this division has all but evaporated, with the members of the more traditional community refusing to be categorized as such. This kind of hierarchical structure may have predated the Balinese conquest of the Sasaks, but certainly this event further divided Lombok into the politically superior Balinese and their Sasak inferiors, positions that were reinforced through elaborate linguistic rituals and etiquette rules.

European colonization arrived on Lombok in 1894 in the form of the Dutch. They legitimated their activities in the eyes of some Sasaks by claiming to be liberating them from the Balinese, but many Sasaks allied themselves with the local authorities to try to fight off Dutch incur-

SASAKS

location:
Lombok Island, Indonesia

time period:
About 2000 B.C.E. to the present

ancestry:
Austronesian

language:
Sasak, an Austronesian language

SCHEDULED CASTES

location:
India

time period:
Unknown to the present;
the category Scheduled
Castes first appears in
the 1935 Government of
India Act.

ancestry:
Mixed

language:
Hundreds of different
languages

sions. They were unsuccessful, and by 1895 the island had been conquered and added to the larger Dutch East Indies colony. In reaction to their defeat, the Balinese royal family committed ritual suicide, *puputan.* The deaths of the Balinese royals, however, did not mitigate the effects of the caste-like hierarchy they had enforced on the island. The Dutch favored the more progressive, Muslim Waktu Lima population over the Wetu Telus, which led to rivalry and even conflict between the two groups that disappeared only in the 1970s with the virtual disappearance of the Wetu Telu classification. Before then, the Dutch were followed on Lombok by the occupying JAPANESE forces, who took Lombok as part of their Pacific strategy during World War II. The Dutch returned in 1945, only to be met by fierce resistance and desire for Indonesian independence, which was finally granted in 1949.

The traditional economic activity of most Sasaks was farming wet rice, both for subsistence and for sale. The small island of Lombok is crossed by nearly 30 rivers, which have been diverted and transformed into vast irrigation works managed by local irrigation societies. In the resulting fertile plains the Sasaks produce not only rice but also soybeans, corn, sweet potatoes, peanuts, onions, coffee, tobacco, and coconuts for sale and private use. While the Sasak ideal is to farm one's own land, population growth and the centralization of land wealth in the hands of a few have meant that many Sasaks today are actually landless and forced to work as farm laborers or in other industries.

Sasak society in the past was dominated by the caste-like divisions between Wetu Telu and Waktu Lima. Despite their bilateral descent system, which acknowledges both parents in the creation of larger kinship groups, there is a bit more emphasis given to people's patrilateral kin, or relatives on one's father's side, than on one's matrilateral kin. The resulting kinship groups of cousins, aunts, uncles, and so on provide assistance in labor, financial matters, and rituals. This ideal has largely been carried on in the contemporary world, but today assistance may be in the form of school or university fees, small loans for setting up a business, or career advancement.

In addition to identifying as members of a kinship group and village, the Sasaks also claim to be ardent Muslims. All villages have their own mosques, and quite a few also have religious schools, either informal ones called *pesantren* or the more formal *madrassahs.* A small number of rural Sasaks also combine their Islamic faith with a syncretic blend of beliefs and practices often called Wetu Telu, like the former caste position of the people who held those beliefs. This system combines beliefs in local spirits, including the rice mother, ancestors, and traditional agricultural and life-cycle rites, with more orthodox Muslim beliefs. Specialists in Wetu Telu rituals are called *pemangku,* though few continue to work outside the most isolated rural settings on Lombok.

See also AUSTRONESIANS.

Sassanians   *See* PERSIANS, SASSANIDS.

Scheduled Castes   (Dalits, Harijans, Outcastes, SC, Untouchables)

Scheduled Castes is the official name in India for more than 450 of the lower caste groups that live in that country; they have also been called Untouchables. Mohandas Gandhi referred to them as Harijans, or Children of God, a name that is considered patronizing today, and the contemporary term preferred by many members of this group is Dalit. The term *Scheduled Castes* was first used during the colonial period and replaced a prior colonial term, *Depressed Classes.* Since 1949, *Scheduled Castes* has had the official legitimacy of being the term used in the Indian constitution and throughout the legal system, despite the vagueness surrounding the specific criteria for inclusion. This vagueness, which parallels that for inclusion in the category SCHEDULED TRIBES, as well as the numerous political, economic, and educational benefits accorded to individuals from scheduled groups, means that being listed is a highly political act.

The original list, or "schedule," of included castes was drawn up in 1950 and has been revised regularly since then. In general, the Scheduled Castes are those that were considered outside the four-part Hindu *varna* system of Brahmins, Kshatriyas, Vaishyas, and Shudras, which is based on the belief elucidated in the Rig Veda that these four different kinds of people sprang from different parts of the first human created by the god Brahma: mouth, arms, thighs, and feet, respectively. Those who did work that was ritually polluting, such as tanning or dealing with death and human waste, were considered outside this system, as were many tribal groups that were later incorporated into the caste system and were placed in the Outcaste, Untouchable, or Dalit category. Even in contemporary India, most workers in these sectors of the economy come from the Scheduled Castes, and they continue to suffer discrimination because of it.

Here some Scheduled Caste members from Bihar work in the dirtiest jobs in the region: emptying latrines by hand and carrying the waste in leaky buckets on their heads. *(AP Photo/James Nachtwey)*

According to India's 2001 national census, members of Scheduled Castes (SC) make up about 16.2 percent of the country's population, with about 166.6 million people. The state of Uttar Pradesh in the northeast of the country has the largest number of SC members at 35 million; West Bengal, also in the northeast, has the second highest number with 18.5 million. However, the states with the largest proportions of SC members are Punjab with 28.9 percent and Himachal Pradesh with 24.7 percent. The primarily tribal states of Mizoram, Meghalaya, and Arunachal Pradesh have extremely low numbers of SC members, while Nagaland, Andaman and Nicobar Islands, and Lakshadweep have none at all. In all states and territories that record having SC members, they are a primarily rural population, with only about 20 percent living in urban areas. In addition, of the nearly 20 million SC members living in urban areas, about 22 percent live in slums, making up about 17.4 percent of the total slum population. Sixteen Indian cities have SC members constituting more than 20 percent of their slum population, with Pimpri Chinchwad the highest at 40.8 percent.

The history of untouchability in the Indian caste system is nearly as old as the system itself, dating from at least 3,000 years ago, and a few scholars and intellectuals through the ages have attempted to rid the country of it. During the British colonial era, however, both the colonial administration and the people from within this community began to bring wider attention to the discrimination suffered by these people and the social and economic barriers to ending the discrimination. The Morley-Minto Reform Act of 1909, which first allowed Indians to vote for other Indians to represent them on various governing councils, provided the first step toward recognizing minority groups as in need of reserved representation. This reservation system as well as a number of other kinds of positive discrimination for SC members was carried over into the 1949 Indian constitution and remains in place to this day. At present, 79 seats, or about 14 percent of the country's lower house of Parliament, are reserved for SC members, as well as about 15 percent of university places and government jobs; at the state level each parliament reserves an amount roughly proportional to the SC population of the state. Unfortunately, some of the university and employment places so set aside go unclaimed because there are no qualified candidates for them, while others are able to take up these places without the proper credentials. This has resulted in a degree of resentment among higher caste members who must compete for a smaller number of posts and places, as well as a degree of ethnocentrism among some SC members because of their special status within

Bhimrao Ramji Ambedkar

Bhimrao Ramji Ambedkar is remembered today for his unflagging efforts to abolish the Hindu caste system in India and establish equal rights for "Untouchables," today's Scheduled Castes, and women. Ambedkar was born in 1891 in the Central Provinces, or what is now Madhya Pradesh, as the last of 14 children in an Untouchable family. Untouchables, in Hindu belief, were the lowest caste of human beings, isolated from the divine universal self and thus pollutants to human society. Though Untouchable children were not permitted to attend school, Ambedkar's father managed to enroll his children, and Ambedkar suffered debilitating discrimination as he was not only ignored by his teachers and segregated from the other students, but sometimes even denied water. Nevertheless, he excelled in school and became the first Untouchable to be admitted to a university in India. In 1913 he won a scholarship to attend Columbia University in New York, and he earned his Ph.D. in Political Science in 1916.

In 1920 Ambedkar began circulating the weekly publication *Leader of the Silent,* in which he vehemently denounced caste discrimination and the orthodox Hindu politicians who passively allowed the persecution to continue. In 1926 he became a member of the Bombay Legislative Council, and in 1927 he decided to catalyze public movements against Untouchability. He led marches petitioning for the sharing of public water fountains as well as the right to enter Hindu temples. He also became openly critical of the Indian National Congress and its leader, Mohandas Gandhi, whom he accused of exploiting the Untouchables for emotional impact. He was particularly critical of Gandhi's reference to the Untouchables as Harijans, "Children of God," which Ambedkar considered condescending and alienating. Rather, Ambedkar urged the Untouchables to educate themselves and push for integration. In 1947 India achieved independence and Ambedkar was appointed the nation's first law minister, drafting a new constitution that granted civil liberties, freedom of religion, and the abolition of Untouchability. He died in his sleep in 1956.

the country. The most unfortunate aspect of this system, however, is that while the social and economic position of SC members generally has improved since the early 20th century, their position relative to higher castes in India has not changed significantly at all. In addition, the dream espoused by Gandhi and the framers of the Indian constitution, such as the Dalit jurist and scholar Bhimrao Ramji Ambedkar—that legal action could eliminate discrimination and negative personal feelings toward these people—has also failed to be realized.

From the period prior to independence until the 1980s, the Indian Congress Party, which led the way to independence and has been the dominant political voice in the country ever since, was the primary political voice for all nondominant Indians, including Scheduled Castes, Scheduled Tribes, and OTHER BACKWARD CLASSES, as they are called. In 1984, however, SC leader Kanshi Ram established a new political party, Bahujan Samaj Party (BSP), which has been fairly successful in luring voters from these communities away from the Congress Party. The BSP currently holds 19 seats in the Indian lower parliamentary house and is part of the ruling United Progressive Alliance with the Congress Party and other left-leaning parties.

FURTHER READING

S. K. Gupta. *The Scheduled Castes in Modern Indian Politics: Their Emergence as a Political Power* (New Delhi: Munshiram Manoharlal Publishers, 1985).

Peter Robb, ed. *Dalit Movements and the Meanings of Labour in India* (Delhi: Oxford University Press, 1993).

Scheduled Tribes (aboriginal tribes, Adivasi, Atavika, Girijan, hill and forest tribes, ST, Tribals, Vanvasi)

Scheduled Tribes is the official name in India for more than 400 of the tribal groups that live in the country. The term was first used during the colonial period, although at that time it was interspersed with "hill and forest tribes" and "aboriginal tribes." Since 1949 *Scheduled Tribes* has had the official legitimacy of being the term used in the Indian constitution and throughout the legal system, despite the vagueness surrounding the specific criteria for inclusion. These criteria are loosely spelled out in the derogatory concepts of primitive traits and backwardness, along with isolation and withdrawal from further contact with the dominant society. This vagueness, which parallels that for inclusion in the category SCHEDULED CASTES, as well as the numerous political, economic, and educational benefits accorded to individuals from scheduled groups, means that being listed is a highly political act. While most of the tribal groups in India are so recognized, there are some that are not. In addition, the distinction between Scheduled Tribes and Scheduled Castes in the Indian context is also problematic in that many caste groups are former tribes that have been incorporated into the Hindu caste system over the course of history, and many current tribes are in the process of becoming castes, albeit low ones. Finally, lack of means testing implies that wealthy tribal individuals can receive preferential treatment in education and politics, while extremely poor Hindi speakers from non-Scheduled Castes do not.

Despite the problems of definition, categorization, and politics, the widespread acceptance in India of the concept of Scheduled Tribes means that it has become an important social category. As of the 2001 census there were 84,326,240 Scheduled Tribal individuals, constituting 8.2 percent of India's total population. The largest number, about 12.2 million, live in the state of Madhya Pradesh while the small state of Mizoram and territory of Lakshadweep are predominantly tribal and have the largest proportion of Scheduled Tribal individuals at 94.5 percent. Since 1950 this group has been given access to reserved places in government and education, and members have even received jobs in the lucrative state banking and productive sectors. Unfortunately, in Bihar and probably throughout India, many of these positions have gone to the very small number of urban, middle-class, elite members of tribal communities, while the vast majority remain extremely poor and without access to many services. Among Scheduled Tribes, for example, 56.2 percent of children are underweight, according to a World Bank survey in the early 21st century, and only about 47 percent are literate; the vast majority, 97.6 percent, are also rural where they make up 10.4 percent of the total population.

The large number of different Scheduled Tribes—more than 400, with a comparable number of different histories, languages, and cultures—means that it is very difficult to generalize about them on these bases. However, the Scheduled Tribes were probably communities that resided on the Indian subcontinent prior to the movement of INDO-ARYANS from the north into India between 1800 and 1500 B.C.E. We do not know what kind of relations existed between these tribes and the Dravidian population (see DRAVIDIANS), which may have been pushed southward by the entrance of the Indo-Aryans. Several tribal groups today, including the ORAON and India's largest Scheduled Tribe, the GOND, speak Dravidian languages. Many others speak Mon-Khmer and other Austro-Asiatic languages, Austronesian languages, and Tibeto-Burman languages more closely related to tribal groups in Southeast Asia and the Pacific than to one another. Today many of these languages are disappearing as individuals and entire communities adopt local pidgins or their dominant local language, but Bhili, Gondi, Ho, Meitei, Mundari, Oraon, and a few others all have more than a million speakers each and are currently at no risk.

Traditionally these tribal groups all followed their own religions, mostly a combination of ancestor and nature worship that can largely be classified as animistic. However, during the colonial period and later half of the 20th century, some people from this group converted to Christianity, with its message of salvation for all and escape from suffering. In addition, because Hinduism is not an exclusive religion and can easily accept and adapt to local gods and goddesses, spirits, and demons, there has been considerable blending of Hindu religious ideas among India's tribes, as well as aspects of tribal religious beliefs and practices among Hindus. Especially in its folk variant as practiced by most rural Hindus and those outside the Brahmin caste, the differences between Hinduism and these tribal religions are sometimes negligible. The integration of certain tribes into the caste system certainly points to the ability of this system to incorporate new people and ideas into its core worldview.

Scheduled Tribes, like all tribal communities, use kinship as their primary organizing principle. Many in India are patrilineal, reckoning descent only through the male line so that both sons and daughters inherit membership into their father's lineage, but only sons pass it on to their children. In India's northwest tribal region, matrilineal descent was primary at one time: mothers passed their lineage membership to their children, and mothers' brothers provided the senior male leadership for the lineal group. However, many in this region today have adopted the dominant patrilineal or bilateral pattern, in which both parents are seen as equal sources of relatives and distant ancestors are of less importance. In addition to providing ancestors, kinship systems also set the rules for exogamy, or who an individual is allowed to marry; provide guidelines for establishing cooperative groups for agricultural, hunting, forestry, or other communal tasks; and give individuals their primary associations, rights, and responsibilities toward others.

FURTHER READING

G. S. Ghurye. *The Scheduled Tribes*, 3rd ed. (Bombay: Popular Prakashan, 1963).
A. V. Yadappanavar. *Tribal Education in India* (New Delhi: Discovery Publishing House, 2003).

Scythians (Sacaraucae, Sacas, Sai, Sakas, Shakas, Indo-Scythians)

The name Scythian is derived from Skythoi, the Greek name for the Scythians, whom the Greeks knew on the Pontic steppes north of the Black Sea. The same ethnonym has been used by scholars for centuries to refer to many different Indo-Iranian-speaking nomads of the Eurasian steppes, usually considered subgroups of

SCHEDULED TRIBES

location:
India

time period:
Unknown to the present. The category Scheduled Tribes was listed only since the 1935 Government of India Act.

ancestry:
Mixed

language:
Hundreds of different languages

SCYTHIANS

location:
The steppes from Siberia to Central Asia, west into Ukraine and south into India

time period:
10th century B.C.E. to 12 B.C.E.

ancestry:
Indo-Iranian; Indo-European more generally

language:
Northeastern Iranian

Scythians time line

B.C.E.

about 800 The Greek poet Hesiod writes of the Scythians as mare-milking nomads; Homer writes of mare-milkers in the Iliad, dated between 1000 and 800 B.C.E.

700 Mention of Scythians as allies of the Assyrians in their battles with the Cimmerians.

653–25 Madyes the Scythian invades and dominates Media.

514 Darius, the Persian king, unsuccessfully attempts to conquer the Pontic Scythians, who merely retreat at the Persian onslaught.

sixth to fifth centuries Several Scythian tribes are mentioned in Persian texts and depicted in Persian relief sculpture.

450 Herodotus journeys onto the Pontic steppes and writes of Scythians as well as of women warriors whom he names Amazons.

329–327 Alexander the Great leads the Macedonian army in his conquest of Asia. In Central Asia his policies disturb the symbiotic relationship between the Scythians and their settled neighbors, the Sogdians and Bactrians.

145 Scythians burn the Greek city of Alexandria on the Oxus in Bactria, or contemporary Afghanistan.

For several decades Scythian invasions bring disquiet to the settled peoples in Bactria, today parts of Afghanistan and northern Pakistan.

100 The Parthian king Mithridates II finally defeats the Scythians in Central Asia.

about 80 Vonones and his brother Spalahores found the first so-called Indo-Scythian or Indo-Saka kingdom in parts of southern Pakistan. They are followed soon after by the foundation of a second Indo-Scythian kingdom to the south, founded by Maues or Moga.

60 Indo-Scythians establish their kingdom in north-central India, near Mathura.

58 Azes I takes the throne of Maues's kingdom and soon after unites it with the kingdom founded by Vonones and Spalahores.

12 The Indo-Scythian kingdom in northwestern India is lost to the Kushans, then the Parthians, and then the Kushans once again.

C.E.

527 Dionysius Exiguus, a monk of European Scythian origin, begins the custom of using Anno Domini, A.D., to refer to times after the birth of Jesus Christ.

---

similar pastoral society with a strong emphasis on militarism and mobility. As much as is possible within the context of scholarship in this area, this entry focuses only on the Scythians who lived in Central Asia and India, leaving the European and Middle Eastern Scythians for other volumes.

GEOGRAPHY

Significant numbers of tombs of people whom archaeologists have identified as Scythians have been found in the Altai region where Siberia, Mongolia, and China all come together; in Kazakhstan and elsewhere in Central Asia; and in Ukraine and the northern Caucasus, reflecting the areas in which the various tribes ranged. In addition, so-called Indo-Scythians, or Saka, conquered parts of northern India and Pakistan. The contemporary Afghan region of Sakastan also points to a Saka presence, but it is unclear whether a Saka tribe once lived in this region or whether Saka had been driven south out of Bactria in 100 B.C.E. and only then established themselves in Sakastan.

The Greek historian Herodotus mentioned many mythical stories about the realms of the nomads, reflecting in part the fact that Greek peoples had little firsthand knowledge of the steppe regions and of its geography, and in part the fact that GREEKS considered the barbarians (the Greek term for those who did not speak Greek) strange, not quite human. Even the weather was considered unusual in Herodotus's writings, with hard winters that might last eight months and extreme cold so that everything was frozen and never thawed. The steppes, according to Herodotus, were also home to bizarre inhabitants, such as a tribe in the Pontic region who turned into wolves one night a year. Herodotus thought the Scythians the best of this population, but he looked down on them as well.

ORIGINS

Although their origins are as yet unknown, most scholars agree the Scythians probably originated in Siberia or the Altai Mountains near the Chinese border in the early first millennium B.C.E. What caused the Scythians to separate from related tribes of Indo-Iranian-speakers and move westward along the steppes, if indeed this was the case, is unknown; some scholars have speculated that a group of young men went off as part of an initiation into manhood to seek an area they could dominate. On the other hand, archaeological remains of

---

the larger Scythian people. Two such examples are the Saka, the name used by the Persians for these Iranian-speaking nomads, and the Sai, the Chinese name for similar peoples. Archaeological work done in these steppe regions has not yet clarified on the exact demarcations between these subgroups, and without a written language of their own to provide contemporary scholars with documents to analyze, we must rely on the writings of Greek, Persian, and Chinese scholars who all describe a people with a

pastoral people in Ukraine predate the Scythian period, so the Scythians in that region, or some part of them, might have emerged from this local culture. Indeed, aside from the Pontic Scythians, who are fairly well known, the many Scythian subtribes mentioned in texts cannot be connected with certainty with archaeological remains that were contemporary with the nomads, such as the Pointed-hat Saka, the Haoma-drinking Saka, the MASSAGETAE, the Sarmatians, the Sauromatians, and the Dahae confederation, founders of the Parthian Empire and the group from which the Parni came (*see* PARTHIANS). Similarities in material culture and way of life mean that we may never determine the exact origins of any of these subgroups or of the larger Scythian population.

HISTORY

The first written records of the Scythians come from Assyrian chronicles of 674 B.C.E. that mention a Scythian ruler, Partutua, who asked King Esarhaddon to give him one of his daughters as a bride. Whether an Assyrian princess was actually sent to the Scythian ruler is not known, but the king's son and heir, Assurbanipal, is shown in his relief sculptures riding to the hunt on horseback, the first Assyrian ruler to do so. Before this time, riding astride a horse had been considered undignified, not proper behavior for important people in ancient Mesopotamia; the Scythians apparently demonstrated the advantages of horseback riding to this part of the world.

At this time both Scythians and Assyrians were fighting a people called the Cimmerians, a group that the Scythians had driven into the Middle East and Europe from the steppes. During the course of the seventh century B.C.E. the Scythians and Assyrians joined forces again to fight the MEDES in what is today Iran, but by the end of the century the Scythians were driven back by a rejuvenated Median state.

Herodotus devoted much space in his writing to the Scythians, and he had probably actually met Scythians in a Greek city-state on the Black Sea. He described at length the Persian invasion of the Pontic steppes by Darius the Great in 514 B.C.E. According to Herodotus, Darius could not understand why the Scythians led him all over the countryside but never met him in battle in the accustomed manner. The Scythians would appear to be ready to fight face to face but would suddenly stop to pursue a rabbit. Darius, frustrated and baffled by these tactics, sent a message to the Scythians, demanding that they either fight in the accustomed fashion or offer the Persians earth and water, symbols of surrender. The Scythian ruler replied, "In return for calling yourself my lord, I say to you, 'Go howl!'" Darius reversed his army and left the steppes.

There must have been other, more successful Persian incursions into the Scythians in Central Asia, about which we have no records because Scythian tribes were included among those who brought tribute to the Persian kings. During Alexander the Great's campaign against the Persian Empire, Greek accounts refer to Scythian contingents fighting with the Persians in approximately 327 B.C.E.; therefore, these tribes must have been associated with the Persians in this way as well. For his part, Alexander had no intention of allowing his most remote borders to be crossed freely by independent nomads, with their flocks coming into his territory, nor did he want his own subjugated, tax-paying people leaving his realm. His attempts to close the borders and contain his people, as well as attempts by the Greek Seleucid leaders who took over the region a generation later, led the Scythians to join with the settled BACTRIANS and SOGDIANS in their almost continual fight against Greek rule.

We know that Scythians remained militarily active in Central Asia for another 200 years. In 145 B.C.E., the Greek city of Alexandria on the Oxus (probably today's Afghan city of Ai Khanoum) in Bactria was burned by Scythians. It was only in 100 B.C.E. that Scythian forces were finally driven out of Central Asia for good by the Persian Parthians. However, this was not the end of Scythian history, because during the first century B.C.E. other Scythian leaders, usually referred to as Saka or Indo-Scythians, conquered areas in today's India and Pakistan. The first Indo-Scythian kingdom was founded by two brothers, Vonones and Spalahores, in approximately 80 B.C.E. in the mountainous region of northern Pakistan and southern Afghanistan. They were followed a few decades later by a second Indo-Scythian kingdom further to the south, that of Maues. About a generation later, Azes I combined these territories into one large kingdom that encompassed territory in the Punjab and around Mathura, which lies in the north-central region between contemporary Delhi and Agra. This larger kingdom was held by the Indo-Scythians until almost the beginning of the common era, when they were finally defeated and driven out by the Parthians. While this is the end of documented Scythian history in Asia, Scythians and other nomadic groups continued to be an important force further west in the northern Caucasus and Ukraine; the OSSETIANS may even be contemporary descendants of these ancient nomads. European origin myths from such disparate countries as England and Hungary also look back to ancient Scythian ones.

CULTURE

Most of what we know about Scythian culture comes from grave sites and from records of the various people who came in contact with them, including the Assyrians, Persians, Chinese, and Greeks. The most extensive description is that of Herodotus, who cannot always be taken literally. Some of his information, however, has been confirmed by archaeological discoveries—for instance, his claim that the Scythians inhaled the smoke of hemp seeds. Discoveries in nomadic graves in the Altai have shown that the nomadic rulers buried there indeed inhaled the smoke of hemp; braziers for burning the seeds and felt tents just large enough to cover a person's head were found.

From the lavish kurgans, or burial mounds, left by the Scythians and other steppe nomads, we can see the importance of the rulers in these tribal societies. The bodies of dead kings were buried along with a wife or concubine, servants, horses, and the belongings the king would need in the afterlife. These burial sites were mounded with earth to create high hills, with greater height seeming to indicate greater status. The entire tribe contributed their efforts to building the huge mound and celebrated the funeral with a feast accompanied by plenty of wine, to judge from the remains of animal bones and clay wine vessels discovered around Royal Scythian burial mounds. As was the case in life, one of the most important features of the items buried with kings was that they were made of gold, with such adornments being an easy way to transport one's wealth. Another feature is the centrality of animal images in nomadic art. Stags or reindeer and griffins, creatures with the bodies of lions and head and wings of eagles, were particularly important images, though large felines, birds of prey, and animal parts were also common; the reindeer may have been an important symbol to these nomads. On the Pontic steppes, much of the lavish material culture seems to have been made by Greeks; farther east the objects found in tombs must have been locally made and showed great skill in carving wood and embroidering designs on

felt. Locally made objects in the eastern steppe burials were often mixed with foreign objects, including Chinese silk and Persian carpets in the frozen graves of the Altai, exemplifying the wider world with which these nomads were in contact through trading and raiding.

Herodotus mentioned that seven different languages were spoken by the many steppe tribes east of the Scythians and that the Pontic Scythians understood them, which gave them a great deal of power in commanding the east-west trade route at its western end. Even the Scythians, however, lacked a complete knowledge of the steppes, for they informed Herodotus that at the farthest point east the inhabitants were one-eyed men and griffins who guarded the gold—a reference, no doubt, to the rich deposits of the Altai Mountains.

The Scythians were excellent horsemen who could strike fear into the hearts of the settled people whom they raided. Their military tactics were suited to their taste for swift attack and equally swift retreat. They could appear suddenly out of nowhere, shoot a barrage of arrows, and just as quickly disappear, tactics that could confuse armies of civilized peoples who were accustomed to confronting warriors in face-to-face combat. Their material culture facilitated this form of warfare as well: They wore trousers and their powerful compound bows, carried in special cases with their arrows, with short swords hanging off their belts. Due to this particular military culture, however, when they had to conform to the proper group behavior for formal warfare, Scythian troops, such as those fighting with the Persians against Alexander the Great, were often unreliable and easily thrown into disarray.

The daily life of Scythian men was probably spent tending flocks, hunting, and fishing, although the Scythians seem to have had slaves, probably captives, who did manual labor. Women probably reared children and made felt for clothing and hut coverings. Horses tended to be the primary source of milk for both drinking and cheese making, and the nomads probably had developed koumiss (fermented mares' milk). Chiefs among the Scythians were polygynous, taking several wives, often from neighboring peoples, to cement alliances with nearby powers.

These cultural features refer mainly to the nomadic, early years of Scythian history in Central Asia. Later both Western Scythians, who had entered Europe, and those who ruled in India took up agriculture and began to adapt to the settled life of the people they ruled.

See also PERSIANS, ACHAEMENIDS.

FURTHER READING

Karl Jettmar. *Art of the Steppes* (New York: Crown, 1964).

Tamara Talbot Rice. *The Scythians* (New York: F. A. Praeger, 1957).

Renate Rolle. *Die Welt der Skythen. The World of the Scythians* trans. Gayna Walls (London: B. T. Batsford, 1989).

Sea Gypsies (Bajau, Celates, Chalome, Chao Ley, Chao Nam [*offensive*], Lanun, Longchong, Longcong, Mawken, Moken, Morgan, Orang Laut, Orang Selat, Orang Suku Laut, Salone, Selung, Thai Mai, Urak Lawoi)

The term *Sea Gypsy* can be misleading because it combines three (sometimes four) separate ethnolinguistic groups in Southeast Asia into one ethnic category. These groups are the Bajau, Moken, and Orang Laut. Sometimes the Urak Lawoi peoples (located primarily in the Adang Archipelago) are also considered a fourth separate group. The common characteristic that links all these groups is their similar traditional nomadic or seminomadic lifestyle on the water. In addition, all Sea Gypsies speak Austronesian languages, a characteristic they share with millions of others throughout the world. Approximately 35,000 Sea Gypsies are estimated to be alive today, yet many if not most of these people no longer live traditional nomadic lifestyles.

GEOGRAPHY

The Sea Gypsies live along the coasts and islands of the Philippines, Malaysia, Myanmar, Thailand, and Indonesia.

The Bajau live in coastal Malaysia, Indonesia, the Philippines, and in various states on the island of Borneo. There is also a large settlement of Filipino Bajau just off the Sabah coast in Pulau Gaya. Regardless of geography, all Bajau speak Austronesian Malayo-Polynesian languages. Sometimes speakers of Makassar and Bugis are also considered Bajau. The term *Bajau* refers to a collection of smaller indigenous groups. The three major subgroups vary widely in terms of culture and language but are united through the Shafii school of Sunni Islam. Linguistically, the Bajau are significantly different from the Moken or Orang Laut.

The Moken are an Austronesian ethnic group that occupy the west coast of Thailand on the Andaman Sea. They also occupy the Mergui Archipelago off Myanmar's coast. The Thai government has attempted to settle the Moken permanently in the Mu Ko Surin National Park on Phuket Island and on the Phi Phi islands. Myanmar is suspected of having enacted similar forced relocations of the Moken. The term *Moken* is used for all the tribes in the region that speak the Malayic language. This language is distinct from the Malayan languages in the area. The Urak Lawoi are sometimes grouped with the Moken but can also be seen as a separate group because of their greater ethnolinguistic proximity to Malayan (as opposed to Malayic) peoples. The Moken are estimated to have 2,000–3,000 members still living nomadic or seminomadic lifestyles.

The Orang Laut are a Malay people who inhabit coastal Indonesia and Malaysia surrounding the Strait of Malacca. They speak an Austronesian Malayan language and are often grouped loosely with the Moken. They are a very small group, although a precise population count is difficult, and not much information about them is widely available.

ORIGINS

There is much debate about the origins of the various groups of Sea Gypsies. No written records exist of their migration into the area, but they are generally regarded as one of the first postaboriginal waves of people to come into Southeast Asia. The people may not have always lived nomadically on the sea, however, and much debate exists about when and why these people adopted their "traditional" nomadic lifestyle. Some claim the Proto-Malay Moken were one of the first waves of people to migrate down the Mekong River to the Malay Peninsula. Others claim that the Moken identity was not formed as separate from other indigenous Malay Peninsula groups until they fled Malay

---

SEA GYPSIES

location:
Coastal Malaysia, Philippines, Myanmar, Thailand, and Indonesia

time period:
Indigenous population who probably moved into the area around 2500 B.C.E. and remain into the present

ancestry:
Debated; however, the Proto-Malay population is generally considered to be one of the first waves of people reaching the Malay Peninsula.

language:
(Multiple) Austronesian family, Malayan, Malayic, and Malayo-Polynesian branches

---

Sea Gypsies time line

B.C.E.

2500 Immigration of first nonaboriginal Proto-Malay peoples into Southeast Asia.

C.E.

1300s Islam spreads through Southeast Asia.

1700s The trepang (sea cucumber) trade causes the expansion of the Bajau.

1990s Moken relocation in Thailand and Myanmar.

2004 Tsunami kills and displaces many Sea Gypsies throughout Southeast Asia.

colonies in Myanmar (Burma) to escape the spread of Islam. A third theory claims they are descended from the Indian Vedas.

The origin of the Bajau is also unknown, although many suspect that they may have come from Johor or from the Philippine coasts. The Bajau believe that they are descended from the royal guard of the sultan of Johor. Whatever the case of their origin, it is generally agreed that their migration out to sea and expansion were due to their pursuit of trade, particularly in sea cucumbers.

LANGUAGES

Language is an important marker of a people's history and origins. The diversity of languages among the Sea Gypsies underscores the difficulties in viewing them as one unified community. The fact that Sea Gypsy languages are not merely different languages within one branch but rather fall within a variety of branches in the Austronesian family highlights the differences in the histories and origins of these diverse peoples.

The Moken language is relatively standard for all Moken people. It is classified under the Austronesian family and Malayo-Polynesian, Malayic, and Moklen branches. The Urak Lawoi language, despite being frequently grouped with Moken, is distinct and somewhat closer to the language of the Orang Laut, being found in the Malayan and Para-Malay branches.

The Bajau speak a variety of languages, which largely fall within the Austronesian family and Malayo-Polynesian, Sama-Bajaw, and Sulu-Borneo branches. The language tree branches out from there into Borneo Coast Bajaw, Southern Sama, Balangingi, Mapun, and Papar.

The Orang Laut speak Loncong from the Austronesian family, Malayo-Polynesian, Malayic, Malayan, and Local Malay branches.

HISTORY

The history of the Sea Gypsies is largely unknown and much debated. Without written records, the origins of the people can be drawn linguistically and ethnically, but the people's transition to a nomadic life on the sea is more difficult to understand. Because of their nomadic lifestyle and lack of nation-state identity, Sea Gypsies are often written out of histories of Southeast Asian states.

The spread of Islam in Southeast Asia in the 13th century was a significant period for the Sea Gypsies, but scholars debate the precise nature of that importance. Some see the introduction of Islam among the Sea Gypsies as a major break with traditional spirituality, while others see it as the cause of the Sea Gypsies' abandonment of a settled life for their "traditional" nomadic lifestyle.

Often international trade and trade law have been the most important outside influences on Sea Gypsies' lives. The role of, and response to, piracy off the shores of Southeast Asia had a large impact on the Sea Gypsies engaged in that practice, particularly the Orang Laut who were well known as pirates of the Straits of Malacca. Piracy was simultaneously punished, rewarded, and manipulated by various rulers in the region, drawing the Moken into national and local disputes. Parameswara, a Palembang prince and eventual founder of the Sultanate of Malacca, survived other encroaching nations in the early 15th century only through the loyalty of the Orang Laut. In other areas, the trade in sea cucumbers was central to the expansion of the Baujau people, and the interests of the Thai and Myanmar governments in offshore drilling had profound effects on the populations of Moken. Many government-driven efforts to settle the Moken in villages, particularly in national parks, occurred through the 1990s.

The close relationship with nature and the sea makes Sea Gypsies particularly vulnerable to the elements but also acutely attuned to nature's moods. Despite faring far better than many other populations in Southeast Asia during the 2004 tsunami, recovery has still been a long process, particularly in more settled communities who have lost much of their traditional knowledge. The attention and aid that Sea Gypsies have received after the tsunami have in many ways been as destructive as they have been helpful, altering their dietary patterns and traditional practices. Sea Gypsies in general maintain a strong insider/outsider mentality, often being described as extremely shy of strangers. In the face of so much international attention, many Sea Gypsies have voiced a preference for simply being left alone.

CULTURE

The common denominator among the many different peoples classed as Sea Gypsies is their traditional lifestyle; however, as countries exercise permanent settlement practices and as globalization and poverty affect the Sea Gypsies, that lifestyle is rapidly changing.

The Sea Gypsies traditionally lived aboard boats made from natural materials and powered with a sail. These boats included living areas, kitchens, and sleeping space. The Sea Gypsies lived from the sea and the resources that could be gathered on the coasts, although notably among the Sea Gypsies, the Moken avoided catching fish, preferring shellfish and other sea life. Knowledge passed down through the generations allowed them to maintain their subsistence lifestyle using only nets and spears to fish and hunt. Sea Gypsies were (and are) physiologically remarkable because excessive time spent diving for food enhanced their ability to see underwater. Any extra food was dried and traded on the mainland for other necessities. Traditionally, the Sea Gypsies came ashore only during monsoon season, when they built raised huts on the beach, buried their dead, and made new boats. Sea Gypsy children were always born aboard boats, and a strict ideological division existed between the dualistic concepts of sea and life, land and death. Aging family members occasionally asked to be left on an island to die, and healing was generally done on land.

In contemporary times not all Sea Gypsies maintain a fully nomadic lifestyle. Many have settled permanently, either voluntarily or not, while others have adopted a seminomadic lifestyle on the edges of society, residing in villages on stilts over the water and still spending much of their time aboard a boat. It is becoming more difficult for Sea Gypsies to support themselves with their traditional subsistence lifestyle. In many cases national interests in offshore drilling have driven governments to attempt to control and settle local populations of Sea Gypsies, generally encouraging them to become active in the tourism industry. The Malaysian state of Sabah on the island of Borneo boasts one of the largest populations of voluntarily settled Bajau. Many others live just off the coast and come ashore each day to seek manual labor.

Nonetheless, local history and knowledge continue to tie many Sea Gypsies to the water. For example, many Sea Gypsies anticipated the 2004 Southeast Asia tsunami because of their intimate knowledge of the sea. A much smaller percentage of Sea Gypsies were injured than any other demographic, although some of the settled villages were severely damaged. The attention that the Sea Gypsies received after the tsunami was arguably much more damaging. That attention, as well as the efforts of their host states to settle them, has resulted in some loss of traditional knowledge and the adoption of mass-produced goods. Many Sea Gypsies who

This Sea Gypsy village had been built on Koh Panyi, or Panyi Island, a place where locals continue to fish. It also serves tourists who travel to the village to restock provisions, eat, and stay just outside Ao Phangnga National Park, Thailand. *(Shutterstock/Khoroshunova Olga)*

SEDANG

location:
The western highlands of Vietnam, eastern Laos

time period:
Unknown to the present

ancestry:
Mon-Khmer

language:
Sedang, a Mon-Khmer language within the larger Austro-Asiatic language family

permanently settle on land become farmers and cattle herders and have been described as the "Cowboys of the East."

Religion and Expressive Culture

Religion is one of the areas in which there is great difference among the cultures of the Bajau, Moken, and Orang Laut. The Moken are animists who believe in the power of nature and of their ancestors, which are embodied in *lobong* poles. Moken shamans communicate with the spirit world and provide healing. The Bajau, however, generally adhere to the Shafii school of Sunni Islam. Descendants of the prophet Muhammad are greatly respected, and despite their nomadic lifestyle and distrust of outsiders, many Bajau seek mosques outside their communities in which to worship. Yet they also retain many of their traditional religious ways. Spirit mediums perform rituals, exorcisms, and other such functions, and a sea god, Omboh Dilaut, is worshiped. Like the Moken, the Orang Laut are often characterized as skeptical of Islam, yet some members of this group do practice a syncretic mixture of Islam and traditional animistic spirituality.

As is typical in peoples with no written history, the Sea Gypsies have a rich tradition of storytelling, folklore, and music. Efforts have been made in recent years to write down many of the stories of the Sea Gypsies and make recordings of their music. They are also known for a number of festivals across Southeast Asia. There have been some reports of governments forcing Sea Gypsies to participate in festivals and perform traditional dances to entertain tourists.

See also AUSTRONESIANS; MALAYS; THAIS.

FURTHER READING

Robert Harrison Bornes. *Sea Hunters of Indonesia: Fishers and Weavers of Lamalera* (Oxford: Oxford University Press, 1996).

Cynthia Chou. *Indonesian Sea Nomads: Money, Magic, and Fear of the Orang Suku Laut* (London: RoutledgeCurzon, 2003).

A. H. Arlo Nimmo. *The Sea People of Sulu: A Study of Social Change in the Philippines* (London: Chandler Publishing Co., 1972).

Michael J. G. Parnwell and Raymond C. Bryant, eds. *Environmental Change in South-East Asia: People, Politics, and Sustainable Development* (New York: Routledge, 1996).

David E. Sopher. *The Sea Nomads* (Singapore: Singapore National Museum, 1965).

Walter Grainge White. *The Sea Gypsies of Malaya* (Philadelphia: J. B. Lippincott Co., 1922).

Sedang (Bri la, Con lan, Cadong, Hadang, Ha-lang, Ha[rh] ndea[ng], Hdang, Hotea, Hoteang, Ka rang, Kmrang, Mo-nam, Rotea, Roteang, Tang, Ta-tri, To-dra, Xa Dang, Xodang)

The Sedang, which is the French name for this group, reside in the western highlands of Vietnam and eastern Laos. They call themselves Ha(rh)ndea(ng), and the VIETNAMESE usually refer to them as Xodang. Like many other DEGA groups, the Sedang live in multigenerational stilt houses located along the region's many rivers, with a men's house serving as the center of most villages. Although extended family living is still common among the Sedang, it is also not unheard of for a young couple to move away from both spouses' families and establish their own nuclear family household. Each village has a chief who manages village affairs and represents the villagers in wider, regional gatherings.

Sedang villagers generally work in slash-and-burn horticulture, growing millet, sweet potatoes, and rice. They also fish, hunt, gather wild plants and roots, and raise cattle and poultry. Some Sedang subgroups are famous for their blacksmithing, others for their finely woven baskets. The Sedang are also known as the makers and users of a kind of transport tool sometimes referred to as a "papoose," which resembles a bamboo and woven rattan backpack. Sedang men use it to transport farm implements, rice, sweet potatoes, and other objects between their home and fields; Sedang women use the same papoose to carry cigarettes, areca, and betel nuts to village and regional festivals.

The Sedang differ from many other Dega groups in that their kinship pattern is neither strictly matrilineal, as are the CHAMS, RHADE, and others, nor patrilineal like the dominant Vietnamese. There are no Sedang clans or other larger kinship structures either. Instead, the Sedang practice a kind of bilateral kinship, like westerners, recognizing both parents' families as related groups. Each individual Sedang does not have a family surname but instead has a given name plus a prefix indicating his or her sex: Y- for women, A- for men. Sedang residence patterns also differ from other Dega in having no prescribed rule of matri- or patrilocality. Rather than always moving in with the wife's or husband's family, a new couple may alternate between the two families, start their own household or neolocal residence, or choose matrilocal or patrilocal residence.

This kind of equality and choice is evident in other aspects of Sedang society as well. Chiefs are chosen from all adult members of the village, and as a result some sources describe them as a fully equal society. This is not strictly true because elders and men have more prestige and value in Sedang society than young people and women; however, some women do act as chiefs. In the past, Sedang villages were often at war with each other and it was only men who could achieve prestige and honor through warfare and headhunting.

During the French colonial period the Sedang were used as laborers to construct a highway from Kon Tum to Danang. As a result of the harsh conditions they experienced under the French and the number of their young men who died, many Sedang sided with the Viet Minh in their war against the French from 1945 to 1954. During the subsequent Vietnam War there were Sedang units that fought with the communists and others that fought with the South Vietnamese and Americans. This kind of disunity had been common prior to the colonial era as well, with each Sedang village being separate from all others. As a result, at least 17 different Sedang dialects have been found to exist in a fairly small region of Vietnam and Laos. Each of these separate Sedang villages not only engaged in warfare with other Sedang but also with Bahnar and other Dega villages as well, using their skills on the battlefield to capture their neighbors and sell them into slavery in Laos and Thailand, prior to the pacification of the region by the French.

The other phenomenon to emerge during the colonial period was the so-called Kingdom of Sedang, which was established in 1888 by French explorer Charles-Marie David de Mayrena. Mayrena was elected king by Sedang, Bahnar, and Rengao tribespeople in June 1888 and took his position as king of Sedang extremely seriously. He traveled to Vietnam, Hong Kong, Britain, and the European continent to recruit fellow adventurers to join him in his new kingdom. He also issued medals and knighthoods to various other Europeans, but Sedang was most famous for its stamps. In 1890, on his return to Sedang, King Marie I died in Malaya without leaving an heir or naming a successor. For more than 100 years the Kingdom of Sedang ceased to exist, but in 1995 at the Assembly for the Restoration of the Sedang Nobility, held in Montreal, Canada, the process of reestablishing a ceremonial nobility for Sedang emerged. Colonel Derwin J. K.W. Mak was elected prince regent of Sedang and became the first reigning king since Mayrena; he was succeeded by Comtesse Capucine Plourde de Kasara in 1997 after Colonel Mak's resignation. In 1999, four grandchildren of King Marie I were found to be alive in France, but none of them has thus far chosen to take up the position of captain regent that was offered to them. If any subsequent relative of King Marie I does step up, he or she will automatically be recognized as the legitimate heir and leader of the reborn Sedang regency.

In 1998 a new Sedang constitution renamed the monarch's position "captain regent." Despite these titles, a ceremonial army and navy, and a royal postal service that has been issuing stamps since 1996, the regency does not seek independence or sovereignty over Sedang territory and fully recognizes the legitimacy of the state of Vietnam.

FURTHER READING

Gerald Cannon Hickey. *Kingdom in the Morning Mist: Mayréna in the Highlands of Vietnam* (Philadelphia: University of Pennsylvania Press, 1988).

Seleucids   *See* GREEKS.

Semang (Negritos, Pangan)

The Semang are a subgroup of Malaysia's ORANG ASLI population along with the SENOI and MELAYU ASLI. The Semang themselves are divided into six subgroups—Batek, Jahai, Kensiu, Kintak, Lanoh and Mendrik—and are the earliest settlers still remaining on Peninsular Malaysia. In the east, Semang are sometimes called Pangan.

There have been many theories concerning the ultimate origins of the Semang peoples because their physical traits seem to link them more to Africans, the ANDAMANESE, or ABORIGINAL AUSTRALIANS than to any other Asians. The conventional wisdom about the Semang states that they are the oldest population on Peninsular Malaysia and may have lived there for about 60,000 years. This date is contested, however, because recent archaeological evidence has also linked them with the HOA BINH CULTURE of Southeast Asia, which existed between 16,000 and 5,000 B.C.E. The people of this ancient culture of mainland Southeast Asia were also small and dark-skinned and lived as hunter-gatherers; even after the arrival of agriculture on the Malay Peninsula about 4,000 years ago, many Semang groups continued to pursue this subsistence strategy as well. Others took up small-scale

---

SEMANG

location:
Peninsular Malaysia and Thailand

time period:
Possibly 60,000 B.C.E. to the present

ancestry:
Probably Hoa Binh culture

language:
Aslian languages in the Mon-Khmer group

farming using slash-and-burn techniques. Both of these patterns are still evident among various Semang subgroups, especially in the mountains of Terengganu, Kelantan, and the northern regions of Perak. Even today a few small Semang communities continue to hunt with their traditional blowguns, fish, and gather wild roots and fruit. At the same time, many groups have also turned to temporary wage labor, small-scale farming, and even performing for tourists to earn some cash.

There is no evidence today of the language spoken by the Hoabinhian people, and the languages of the Semang are of little assistance in discovering it. At least 7,000 years ago the Mon-Khmer people moved into the area of the Malay Peninsula, and for some reason the Semang adopted their language. About 3,000 years after that, a new population arrived in the region, today's dominant MALAYS, but for the most part this arrival did not change the Semang linguistic affiliation very much. Even today, despite the social and cultural pressures to adopt Malay, most groups have retained their own languages with just a small degree of borrowing in terms of vocabulary, syntax, and structure.

Semang social structure is usually described as being of the band variety, where small groups of related people live, work, and move together when necessary. There are no inherited or earned positions of authority; instead, all adults are able to contribute to decision making on a relatively equal basis, though differences based on age, gender, and experience are important when taking each adult's opinion into consideration. Generally these bands are between 15 and 50 people in size, and they live in caves, rock overhangs, or temporary lean-tos or huts made from bamboo, rattan, or other forest materials.

Like that of many indigenous people, the Semang religion is deeply rooted in animism, with strong ties and practices that connect them to the earth and its spirits. They have a large number of myths and legends that explain the presence and power of each spirit and god as well as the nature of human existence. Ritual specialists engage with the spirit world through their dreams or by going into trances, and they are able to cure certain diseases, discover the sources of misfortune, and sometimes even turn into superhuman beings themselves. They also supervise the all-important blood sacrifice that most groups use to thank the spirits for their beneficence. These are not full-time religious specialists but shamans who

also continue to participate in the mundane aspects of subsistence, child care, and daily life more generally.

Today the Semang are seriously threatened by cultural extinction through the destruction of their rainforest environment, population pressures from their neighbors, and increasingly aggressive cultural influences from the outside world. Since 1983 the Malaysian government has had a policy of almost forced conversion to Islam for all Orang Asli groups, including the Semang, which has pressured many to turn away from state-provided services such as health care and education. Nowadays most Semang are permanently settled in regroupment villages established by the Malaysian government, although a few groups of Kensiu, Jahai, and Batek still retain a nomadic existence. Nonetheless, they are not benefiting from the general wealth of Malaysian society and are in fact becoming poorer relative to the rest of the nation by being settled and relying more and more on the cash economy. The few groups that remain outside this economy are generally healthier and cannot be considered poor since their subsistence way of life provides most of what they need to survive.

See also MALAYSIANS: NATIONALITY.

Senoi (Mah, Mai, Orang Bukit, Orang Darat, Orang Seraq, Orang Seroq, Orang Ulu, Sakai, Sengoi, Senoi Temiar, Smaq)

The Senoi are the largest of the ORANG ASLI subgroups in western Malaysia and account for about 54 percent of this group with a population of approximately 40,000. The West Senoi have been incorporated into the dominant Malay way of life to a greater extent than the nearly untouched East Senoi.

The prehistoric period of Senoi history is largely incomplete due to a lack of written languages and the use of building materials that do not last long enough to provide archaeologists with a complete picture of their societies. From about the fifth century C.E. forward, however, many groups have engaged with the outside world through trade, labor, and even tribute. There are records of Senoi leaders offering tribute or gifts to the Malay kings who ruled Peninsular Malaysia in the first centuries C.E. through the start of the colonial period in the 19th century. In addition, groups who lived in the tropical forests provided lumber, resin, game, and other products to lowlanders and those residing on the plains, while those on the coast traded in fish and other sea products.

SENOI

location:
Northwest Pahang and Southern Perak, Selangor, Negri Sembilan, central mountain area, Peninsular Malaysia

time period:
Possibly 8000 B.C.E. to the present

ancestry:
The Senoi are an East Asian people from the north and are descendants of both the Hoabinhians and Neolithic cultivators.

language:
Semai, a Mon-Khmer language in the Senoic subbranch with about 12 different dialects; significant bilingualism in Malay

In the 18th and 19th centuries slave raiders, mainly MALAYS and BATAKS, kidnapped many Senoi as well as other Orang Asli peoples and sold them into slavery. As they were not Muslims, the slavers considered the Senoi to be kafirs, or nonhumans, savages, or even jungle beasts. The kidnapers usually attacked a village and killed all of the adult men and took away the women and children, who were easier to manage and less likely to run away. Officially slavery was abolished in 1884; however, it is known to have continued into the 20th century. A derogatory term, *Sakai*, meaning "slave" or "dependent," was commonly used until the middle of the 20th century and is detested by all Orang Asli groups, including the Senoi.

The Malay civil war of 1948–60 between the British colonial government and communist insurgents brought the colonial regime into the heart of Senoi society. First, many communities were moved into camps that were patrolled and controlled by the British and then by the Department of Aborigines, which was to provide basic education and health care. Malaysian independence in 1963 did not significantly change the social, political, or economic position of the Senoi. They are classified along with Malays and the indigenous peoples of both Sarawak and Sabah as *bumiputra,* sons of the soil, and granted extra privileges denied to the large Chinese and Indian populations within Malaysia. However, they do not receive all of the benefits of this group because they have not converted to Islam and refuse to participate in Malaysian society as Malays.

In the 1980s the Malaysian government built a highway into the interior Senoi region that has transformed the whole of the interior by bringing in large companies to exploit the land and resources. Many Senoi and other forest dwellers have been forced out and have forsaken their traditional lifestyle so that today it is thought that only a few hundred truly nomadic tribal people remain, and even these have been significantly affected by the outside world.

Traditionally, the Senoi were hunter-gatherers, fishermen, and swidden (slash-and-burn) or shifting cultivators who grew a wide variety of tubers, vegetables, and fruit. Even today the majority of the Senoi still depend on the forests for their livelihood in varying degrees, and in addition, they now cultivate rubber, fruit, and cocoa as cash crops.

The center of Senoi consciousness is their worldview that recognizes that everything, from rocks and rivers to trees and humans, has a spirit or soul that must be appeased through ritual in order for life to be smooth and free of misfortune. Some of these rituals come from the Hindu influences on the Senoi, from the earliest kingdoms in Peninsular Malaysia about 2,000 years ago, while others were developed from indigenous ideas about nature. Many westerners are also familiar with the Senoi because of the books and articles that have been written about their ability to control and use their dreams as a therapeutic tool. This particular aspect of their dream life has been discredited as wishful thinking on the part of early Western observers, but all subsequent ethnographers have noted the importance of dreams and trance in healing and other rituals. Some commentators are also willing to posit that perhaps dream therapy, as it was called in the 1930s, was a part of Senoi life prior to the work of Christian missionaries, colonial officers, the Malaysian government, and more recently, Muslim missionaries among the Senoi.

See also MALAYSIAN CHINESE; MALAYSIAN INDIANS; MALAYSIANS: NATIONALITY; SEMANG.

Seraikis (Kandharis, Multanis, Saraikis, Siraikis)

The Seraikis are a large ethnic group in the Punjab, Sindh, and North-West Frontier provinces of Pakistan. Members of the same ethnic group who live in India are called Multanis, while those in Afghanistan are called Kandharis, which is also the basis for the name of the city of Kandahar. They are all speakers of the same Indo-Aryan language, related to that of both the PUNJABIS and SINDHIS and sometimes considered a dialect of one or the other of these languages.

The heart of Seraiki territory, sometimes called Seraikistan, is the southern Punjab of Pakistan. This area is more fertile than much of the rest of the country and has access to water from the Indus River, making it an important region for the production of both wheat and cotton. As a result of the wealth potential of these crops, many Seraikis have been pushing for a province of their own, separate from the Punjab, since the 1960s. They claim that historically their region was not attached to the Punjab; prior to the Mughal era it was independent, and during that time the region was its own province. It was only in the British era in the 19th century and beyond that the area has been subsumed into the larger Punjabi category. The Seraikis also claim that culturally and linguistically they differ enough from their neighbors that they should be allotted a territory of their own within Pakistan's larger

SERAIKIS

location:
Pakistan, India, and Afghanistan

time period:
Probably about 1800 B.C.E. to the present

ancestry:
Indo-Aryan

language:
Seraiki, an Indo-Aryan language that is sometimes considered a dialect of Punjabi or Sindhi

federal system. They feel that they face significant discrimination and even persecution at the hands of northern and central Punjabis under the current political arrangement.

In 1973 Seraiki Suba Mahaz was formed as a political party advocating for a Seraiki province; it has since been joined by the Jag Seraik Party, Pakistan Seraiki Party, Pasban People's Seraiki Party, Seraiki Qaumi Inqalabi Party, Seraiki Qomi Tehrik, Seraikistan National Front, Seraiki Mazdoor Mahaz, Seraiki Inqalabi Council, Seraikistan National Mahaz, Seraiki Qomi Movement, Seraiki Democratic Party, Seraiki Qomi Ittehad, Seraiki Awami Sangat, Seraiki Lok Sanjh, Seraiki National Party, and Seraikistan Qomi Movement. The Seraiki Qaumi Movement (SQM) was formed in May 1989 and reiterated the call of these other parties for a Seraiki province to be created from Multan, Bahawalpur, Dera Ghazi Khan, Dera Ismail Khan, and Jang divisions of southern Punjab. In February 2007 the SQM merged with Mutthaida Qaumi Movement, formerly known as the Muhajir Qaumi Movement (MQM), which fought for the political, social, and economic representation of the Muhajirs of Pakistan. The two parties felt that combining their efforts would bring greater success to them both in their emphasis on ethnic rights.

Culturally, the Seraikis resemble most other Pakistanis in their adherence to Islam; however, there are also Hindu Seraikis who live in Pakistan, India, and Afghanistan. Most Seraikis are farmers, growing wheat and cotton in Pakistan's richest cotton-growing area. Their families are extremely important to them and descent is reckoned through the male line only, which means that their kinship system is patrilineal. However, clans and other corporate kin groups are not generally recognized.

See also INDO-ARYANS; PAKISTANIS: NATIONALITY.

Sgaw   *See* KAREN.

Shang   (Yellow River civilization, Yin)

Shang culture or civilization was one of the Bronze Age cultures that emerged along the Huang (Yellow) River in northern China in the centuries before the common era; the associated Shang dynasty was its best-known accomplishment. The Shang were the cultural inheritors of both the very early YANGSHAO CULTURE and the later LONGSHAN CULTURE, which almost immediately preceded the Shang. Like these earlier cultures, the Shang were agriculturalists who grew millet, rice, and some wheat. They were also skilled potters, and like the Late Longshan, they had bronze, class divisions, a rudimentary writing system, and walled cities. In addition, the Shang also had wheeled vehicles; their writing was more elaborate than that of these earlier cultures, and other aspects of their society were more complex as well. Many archaeologists believe the Shang were connected through trade and other relations with other northern populations from Central Asia, Mongolia, and Siberia, although which remains are indicative of internal innovations and which show cultural borrowing over time remains highly contentious.

According to Chinese history, the Shang dynasty was preceded by the Xia, or Hsia, dynasty, usually dated to 2200–1750 B.C.E., although actual archaeological evidence for the Xia remains inconsistent, and most academic sources today consider it mythological. Interestingly, until the 20th century the same thing had been thought about the Shang, but in the 1920s archaeologists traced "dragon bones" that had been used by herbalists and healers since the 1890s to the last Shang capital of Anyang. The so-called dragon bones were actually examples of Shang writing inscribed onto oracle bones and used by Shang diviners to read fortunes and diagnose illnesses.

Excavations at Anyang in the north of Henan Province began in 1928 and revealed rectangular houses, numerous bronze items, pottery, and a ruler's palace in the center of the walled town. In the 1950s an earlier Shang capital, Ao, was found at Ehr-li-kang near the city of Zhengzhou, the capital of Henan, with the same kind of material remains including millet, wheat, pottery, bronze, and oracle bones. Chinese traditional history of the Shang, most of which was written down during the HAN dynasty (206 B.C.E.–220 C.E.), states that altogether 30 different kings from the Tzu clan ruled over the Shang civilization and that they did so from seven different capitals. In addition, prior to the formal political development of a kingdom, 14 Tzu clan leaders had ruled over smaller segments of the population from eight different capitals. The first king may have been a man named Tang who overthrew a spoiled and ineffective final Xia leader and set up his kingdom from Po, associated with remains at Her-li-tou near Yen-shih; the last, Chou, was similarly overthrown by the founders of China's third dynasty, the Zhou.

SHANG

location:
Along the Huang (Yellow) River basin, China

time period:
About 1750 to 1040 B.C.E.

ancestry:
Probably Longshan culture

language:
An ancient form of Chinese

Shans (Burmese Shans, Chinese Shans, Dai, Hkamti Shans, Ngiaw, Ngio, Pai-I, Tai Khe, Tai Khun, Tai Long, Tai Lu, Tai Mao, Tai Nu, Thai Yai)

The Shans are a Tai-speaking people of eastern Myanmar and northern Thailand. Along with other Tai-speaking populations, most Shans migrated away from Yunnan Province, China, beginning about 1000 C.E. and continuing into the colonial era. Their self-reference is with the name *Tai*, while *Shan* is the Burmese term for these people, which was largely adopted by the British in the 18th and 19th centuries. Linguistically, they are closely related to China's DAI people, but after many centuries of residing in Myanmar (Burma) and Thailand, culturally they have come to differ from the Dai in some important ways.

The Shan migrants into eastern Myanmar established many small chiefdoms and kingdoms in their mountain valley homes, most of which paid tribute and pledged loyalty to the larger Burman, Thai, or Chinese empires that ruled the surrounding lowlands. By 1826 and the British takeover of Burma, there were 18 princely Shan states and 25 smaller realms dominated by local Shan chiefs. During the colonial era the nominal boundaries between Burma and Thailand were relatively loose and allowed the Shans to move fluidly back and forth to find new forested areas to clear for farming, to visit family, and to seek alliances among the various states and chiefdoms. At Burma's independence in 1948, this migration pattern was severely disrupted and the two peoples became administratively and eventually culturally somewhat distinct. The Shans in Burma, which became Myanmar in 1989, have struggled for almost 60 years to gain a degree of autonomy for themselves in the Shan State while those in Thailand have lived relatively peacefully with the other HILL TRIBES OF THAILAND in the country's northeast region. The exception to this characterization of Thailand was in the 1970s, when government anticommunist activities disrupted the lives of many Hill Tribe members, including some Shans.

As was the case in the past, most Shans live as rice farmers; they also grow a wide variety of other products, including soybeans, peanuts, sunflowers, chilies, coconut, and betel nut, for both personal consumption and sale. The preferred farming method is irrigated paddy farming on permanent fields, but some marginal communities and those in higher elevations also turn to swidden (slash-and-burn) methods, especially for vegetables and herbs. This method has largely been eliminated in Thailand, where stopping land degradation and deforestation have been on the royal agenda for about a decade, but it continues in Myanmar, where farming is not mechanized and the military government cannot support or enforce programs for better land-use systems.

While wholesale goods are generally moved in and out of Shan territory by men, local subsistence and market trade are the purview of women, as has always been the case. Today much of this trade takes place in markets located in strategic places along major transportation routes rather than in small, roadside stalls or via one-to-one relationships between women, as in the past, but it still constitutes an important aspect of women's daily activities. In addition, women are responsible for child and elder care; domestic work; transplanting rice seedlings into paddies; and tending domestic animals such as chickens, pigs, and dogs. They are often assisted by young boys and girls of all ages. Men plow and harrow rice fields, hunt, and work in construction and other activities. In Thailand, some Shan men leave their villages to work in towns and cities during the dry season or other slow periods in the agricultural calendar.

While highly structured at the level of the chiefdom or state, with inherent hierarchies based on age, gender, and class, Shan society at the lowest level is much more fluid. Kinship is considered bilateral, with both mother's and father's relatives contributing to one's important familial ties, but kinship generally is not an important organizing principle in Shan society. Large groups of relatives do not ally with one another for either religious or political events, and each individual generally has a large network of neighbors, friends, and other connections to whom he or she owes more loyalty than to extended kin. Even in choosing marriage partners, kinship is relatively unimportant; the only restrictions are against marrying siblings or first cousins.

Unlike kinship, residence is important in creating lasting bonds between Shan individuals. Generally, after marriage a new couple will live with the wife's parents in matrilocal residence for a few years until they are able to establish their own household; the choice of village is important for creating lasting alliances. In Myanmar the Shans are still actively engaged in a military dispute with the Burmese state over independence, and fighting units are often drawn from villages; in addition, there is also some intervillage conflict, which sees

SHANS

location:
Myanmar (Burma)

time period:
1000 C.E. to the present

ancestry:
Dai

language:
Shan, a Tai-Kadai language related to Thai and Lao

different Shan subgroups and villages fighting each other. Village spirits in both countries also require the ritual activity of all members to make sure that humans, animals, and crops remain healthy and productive.

Most Shans identify as Buddhists, similar to the other lowland Southeast Asian peoples, including the BURMANS, THAIS, KHMERS, LAO, and VIETNAMESE. Even where their own beliefs and practices differ significantly from these other, more orthodox Buddhist peoples, the Shans prefer classification along these lines because it distinguishes them from the "tribal" highlanders of Myanmar, Thailand, and the rest of Southeast Asia, who generally practice local, animistic religions, Christianity, or a syncretic mix of both. One important difference between the Shan version of Buddhism and that of the Burmans, Thais, and others is the Shan focus on hierarchy and the ability of powerful beings to protect others from malevolent spirits, government agents, and other evil beings. The entire world is ranked in the Shan mind based on power, with Buddha statues and Buddhist monks having the greatest power, normal human beings being about average, and some spirits having less power than humans; of course, some spirits, especially village spirits, also have more power than human beings.

Sharchops (Bhotia Eastern, Central Monba, Cona Monba, Cuona Monba, Eastern Bhutanese, Memba, Mompa, Monba, Sangla, Sarchapkkha, Schachop, Sharchagpakha, Southern Moonba, Tsangla, Tshalingpa)

The Sharchops are a Tibeto-Burman group living in eastern Bhutan, a thickly forested, dry region; their name means "easterner" and points to their current homeland. Some sources say that they are numerically the largest group in Bhutan, making up between 30 and 45 percent of the entire population, but politically and economically they have been subordinate to the dominant BHUTIA for as long as the two groups have lived in the country. Their language, religion, and culture more generally are similar to the Bhutia or Ngalop people so that the two groups are often categorized together as Drukpas. However, their language is distinctive enough that communication with the Bhutia requires a common language of English or Nepalese, or a translator.

Like the Bhutia, the Sharchops migrated to Bhutan sometime between the ninth and 17th centuries from Tibet and possibly Myanmar (Burma) and Yunnan, China. This population probably intermarried with people of Indian descent to form the Sharchop ethnic group. Today there are even more interactions between Sharchops and Indians, especially Assamese and Hindi speakers, because of the roads and other infrastructure connecting the two territories. Increasing numbers of Sharchops are learning these two Indian languages and looking to India for development assistance and trade relations.

The traditional economic activity of the Sharchops was subsistence agriculture utilizing a swidden, or slash-and-burn, method of fertilization. After cutting down a swathe of forest and letting it dry, they would burn off the dried vegetation and then use the field for dry rice crops. After three or four years the soil in that field would be exhausted and was allowed to revert back to grasses and then forest while other fields were prepared in the same way. This shifting form of agriculture requires rather extensive amounts of land for a small population and is unsustainable in most of the world today, including Bhutan. Today some groups have settled more permanently in larger forest clearings and have turned to artificial fertilizers. In addition to gardening, most Sharchops raise pigs and goats, which are used for animal sacrifices in their indigenous religion, as well as for food; cattle are also used for this purpose and as an important medium of exchange since they are a sign of wealth.

In addition to their indigenous belief system, with its many local spirits and gods, most Sharchops are Buddhists, practicing a form of the religion similar to the TIBETANS and Bhutia. Prayer flags and wheels grace most Sharchop homes, and many larger villages have a monastery to receive the many Sharchop sons who become monks. In the past each family ideally sent at least one son to the monastery for an education; most remained as monks for the remainder of their lives. Today public secular education is available in Bhutan and thus fewer boys are turning to the monastic life, but Buddhism remains central to most people's lives at such events as marriage, birth and death ceremonies, and other auspicious festival days.

She (Dongliao, Dongman, Shanda, Shanha, Shemin)

The She are one of China's recognized 55 minority groups. They mainly live in the mountainous region of southeastern China in Fujian and

SHARCHOPS

location:
Bhutan, Tibet

time period:
Unknown to the present

ancestry:
Tibetan

language:
Tshangla, a Tibeto-Burman language, with three separate dialects

Zhejiang Provinces and the three surrounding provinces of Jiangxi, Guangdong, and Anhui. The region receives plentiful rain and has a warm climate conducive to agriculture. Paddy rice and potatoes are two of the most important subsistence crops, while the She are also famous for their mushrooms and specific variety of tea known as Huiming. In the past, She communities supplemented their agricultural produce with hunting, but today this is not a viable subsistence activity, and only a few She men engage in hunting for sport.

The first definitive appearance of the She in Chinese history comes in the 12th century when records from the Southern Song dynasty mention the existence of the Shemin, or (approximately) "hut people." Other Chinese records refer to them in more derogatory terms such as Dongliao, meaning "cave Liao," and Dongman, meaning "cave barbarians." The She names for themselves, Shanda and Shanha, mean "mountain guests" and refer to their original valley homeland. It was probably in the seventh century c.e. when the She people moved from their indigenous home in Guangdong Province into the higher elevations of Fujian and Zhejiang Provinces; however, other Chinese sources indicate that the She originated in Hunan Province as early as the second century c.e.

Regardless of their beginnings, by the 14th century the She were fully ensconced in their current home and were interacting with the Han on a regular basis through trade, tribute relations, and other political and economic connections. By 1368 and the start of the Ming dynasty, the loyalty of the She was not in question, and they were allowed a great deal of autonomy within the larger Chinese empire. In the following Qing dynasty, which began in 1644, the She lost much of that autonomy and faced military occupation and forced assimilation into the dominant culture. The mid-19th century brought even more changes as their coastal location meant that the She were among the first Chinese peoples to have regular contact with Christian missionaries and European traders; they also fought against the Japanese occupation during World War II. As is the case throughout China, the Communist era has brought its own changes in land tenure, politics, social structure, and every other facet of She daily life.

She culture emerged in the context of slash-and-burn horticulture, and only in the later decades of the 20th century were more permanent agricultural patterns introduced. Today rice, wheat, sweet potatoes, rape seeds for canola oil, peanuts, and teas are all grown for both subsistence and commercial gain. The hillsides have been carved with extensive terraces to allow for permanent irrigation, and artificial fertilizers have been introduced to improve yields and soil quality. Lumber, peaches, pears, and other forest products are also lucrative for some communities.

She social structure is fairly small-scale, with just four lineages corresponding to the only four family names among them: Pan, Lan, Lei, and Zhong. Lineages observe patrilineal descent, which means individuals inherit their name and lineage from their father, and they tend to be exogamous so that people are required to marry someone with a different surname from themselves. In the past, clans and lineages served as the most important political units in villages and other settlements, and even today each village tends to be dominated by a single lineage. Usually women move into the home and village of their new husbands in patrilocal residence; however, poor She men may move into their wives' family home, in matrilocal residence, and then inherit their wives' family property if there is no son to inherit.

In the past, She religion recognized the existence of a variety of local and nature gods and spirits plus village ancestors. Each lineage branch had its own temple for lighting incense to its own ancestors, with each family within the temple having its own incense burner. The She also engaged in many Han ritual practices adopted from outside their community from the Ming period forward. From 1950 to the 1980s most religious activity was banned, but since that time the Chinese government has relaxed this rule, and ancestor worship has become a vibrant part of She community life.

Sherpas (Shar pas)

The Sherpas occupy primarily the mountainous Solu-Khumbu region of northeast Nepal, although pockets of Sherpa culture exist across other areas of Nepal. The 2001 Nepalese census counted 154,622 Sherpas. Smaller populations also reside in Bhutan, China, and the Darjeeling area of India. Sherpas originally occupied eastern Tibet but moved westward starting in about 1480, probably to areas that were previously seasonal pasturage and hunting grounds. Most communities had settled in the Khumbu area of Nepal by 1533. Sherpas share many linguistic, ethnic, and religious roots with Tibetans and

SHE

location:
Fujian and Zhejiang Provinces, China, with scattered others in Jiangxi, Guangdong, and Anhui Provinces

time period:
12th century c.e. to the present

ancestry:
Dong

language:
She, a Hmong language

SHERPAS

location:
Northeast Nepal, Bhutan,
India, China

time period:
1400s to the present

ancestry:
Tibetan

language:
Sherpa, a southern
Tibetan language in the
larger Tibeto-Burman
family of the Sino-Tibetan
phylum

have traditionally maintained strong trade connections with Tibet; however, Chinese policy has made this difficult since the early 1950s.

The word *Sherpa* means "easterner" in Tibetan and is taken from the days prior to the 15th century when Sherpas occupied the eastern sections of Tibet. The misleading term *sherpa*, written with a lower case *s*, is often used to describe a Himalayan guide or porter, but it does not necessarily indicate Sherpa ethnicity.

Sherpa society is composed of exogamous patrilineal clans, membership in which is inherited from one's father. Traditionally, clan groups held communal possession of land, but when Nepalese land-rights policy changed in the mid-20th century, these clans lost community ownership. This shift in policy has allowed private holdings to be sold off to non-Sherpas; many Sherpas have left the region to find work elsewhere. Sherpas were traditionally traders and farmers, cultivating high-altitude crops. Potatoes, introduced in the 1800s, have become a staple food. Yaks are used for milk, butter, and cheese, in addition to wool, leather, fuel, and fertilizer. Trade bazaars are important events, particularly as trade between Tibet and the Sherpa is allowed to flow.

Traditional Sherpa religion was a mix of Yellow Hat or Gelugpa Buddhism, the same sect as that of the Dalai Lama, animism, and shamanism, but during the 20th century religion underwent some interesting changes. Most Sherpas identify primarily as Buddhist, with small minorities is also identifying as Hindu, Christian, and Bon. While traditional religious taboos against setting foot on Chomolungma, or Mount Everest, have been relaxed, modern expeditions still begin with a Puja ceremony, leaving offerings for the gods. Prior to the early 20th century there was a minimal emphasis on celibate monasteries and nunneries among the Sherpa, unlike their Tibetan cousins, but starting in the first decades of last century, a coalition of Sherpas from all levels of the social hierarchy worked together to form two celibate monasteries and a celibate nunnery, and to convert a noncelibate monastery into a celibate one. These four institutions, but especially Tyengboche Monastery, built in 1923 and rebuilt after a fire in 1989, are now at the center of many Sherpas' relationship with Buddhist life and ritual, replacing older, noncelibate institutions so thoroughly that today they seem to be ancient features of Sherpa life. The Mani Rimdu festival that is held at Tyengboche, a masked dance ceremony depicting the vanquishing of a variety of demons and the introduction of Buddhism to

Known more for their mountaineering than their religion, Sherpas are primarily devout Gelugpa, or Yellow Hat Buddhists, whose monks dress similarly to these Tibetan Gelugpas who reside in exile in India, along with their spiritual leader, the Dalai Lama. *(OnAsia/Pascal della Zuana)*

Tibet, has even become a major tourist attraction in Nepal. A second important change that occurred in Sherpa religion in the 20th century and accompanied the rise of these institutions was the decreased reliance on shamans as healers; by the 1960s most Sherpas who wanted to turn to this kind of healer had to look outside the Sherpa ethnic group entirely. The reason for this decline was not modernization and improved access to Western or scientific hospitals and doctors but rather the religious community of lamas, monks, and nuns who had begun a campaign against shamanistic practice in the mid-20th century. While the two different traditions had been rivals among Tibetans since the introduction of Buddhism in the eighth century, neither one had previously been so successful in shutting down the activities and practitioners of the other.

Although it is a mistake to conflate all Sherpas with the Himalayan sherpa porters, today the Sherpas are known primarily for leading and assisting mountaineers in the Himalayas. A culturally welcoming people who are required by tradition to provide hospitality and assistance to strangers in their high-elevation homes, they have adapted to modern life by embracing the tourism and trekking industries, guiding hikers and climbers up mountains they once considered too sacred to ascend. Despite the new predominance of the tourism industry, few Sherpas see real profit in serving as porters or guides, and many Sherpa youth are drawn away from their people and into Kathmandu seeking employment.

John Hunt's 1952 Everest expedition was a turning point for the local population because it introduced Edmund Hillary, a New Zealander, to the Sherpa people. In May 1953 Hillary and Tenzing Norgay, a Sherpa mountaineer, made the first recorded successful ascent of Mount Everest, or Chomolungma in the Sherpa language, meaning "mother goddess of the land." Later, Hillary devoted his life to helping the Sherpa people, building many schools and hospitals throughout rural Himalayan areas; his death in early 2008 was noted with sadness both in his home country of New Zealand and among the Sherpa people of Nepal.

Sherpas are a competitive people, often racing for increasingly fast ascents or engaging in more casual competitive games with each other. In 2003, on the 50th anniversary of the original ascent of Mount Everest, several Sherpas vied to break a variety of records. Women, or Sherpani, have traditionally been less involved in mountaineering; however, in recent years many women have begun to participate in making the dangerous ascents. Lhakpa Sherpa became the first woman to reach the summit of Mount Everest for the third time, after becoming the second woman to scale the mountain at all in 2000, and the first to return from that trip alive. Her 15-year-old sister Mingma Kipa Sherpa became the youngest person to climb Everest on that same ascent. In the same year the previous speed record was broken twice in three days by Pemba Dorji Sherpa and Lhakpa Gelu Sherpa. Pemba Dorji Sherpa returned the following year once again to break the record. In 2007 Appa Sherpa made his unprecedented 17th ascent of Everest.

Further Reading

James F. Fisher. *Sherpas: Reflections on Change in Himalayan Nepal* (Berkeley and Los Angeles: University of California Press, 1990).

Sherry B. Ortner. *High Religion: A Cultural and Political History of Sherpa Buddhism* (Princeton, N.J.: Princeton University Press, 1989).

———. *The Sherpas through Their Rituals* (New York: Cambridge University Press, 1978).

Tenzing Norgay

Tenzing Norgay (1914–86) was a mountaineer and a Sherpa, famous for making the first successful ascent of Mount Everest with Sir Edmund Hillary's British Expedition in 1953. From the time of his birth as Namgyal Wangdi, while his mother was on religious pilgrimage to eastern Nepal, the young boy was destined for great things. When Namgyal was still a youngster, a monk saw his destiny and renamed him Tenzing Norgay, *Norgay* meaning "fortunate." In 1935 a newly married Norgay made his first attempt at ascending Everest with British explorer Eric Shipton. This trek was followed by others with the British Everest Expeditions in 1936 and 1938, with solitary climber Earl Denman in 1947, and two 1952 Swiss expeditions with Raymond Lambert. On these earlier treks, Norgay often came very close to the summit, within 778 feet with Lambert, but never quite achieved his goal. During World War II, when Everest expeditions ceased, Norgay continued to hone his mountaineering skills on expeditions to Nanda Devi and Garwhal in India, Tirich Mir and Nanga Parbat in what is today Pakistan, and the Langtang region of Nepal. In the postwar world, climbs to Everest began again in earnest, with several countries vying for the chance to be the first to ascend the world's tallest mountain. With his extensive experience of nearly 20 years as well as a bit of luck, Norgay's expedition with Edmund Hillary succeeded at 11:30 A.M. on May 29, 1953, just three days after the first climbing duo from the same British expedition failed.

Following this success, Tenzing became a household name throughout the world and a symbol of anticolonialism in Asia. He was honored with the British Empire Medal and the George Medal from the British government for his achievement and was visited in his Darjeeling, India home by the current and two future Indian prime ministers: Jawaharlal Nehru, his daughter Indira Gandhi, and her son Rajiv. Later in life Tenzing became the director for field training for the Himalayan Mountaineering Institute, which he held for 22 years. In 1978 he founded his own trekking company, which is now run by his son, Jamling Tenzing Norgay, who ascended Everest himself in 1996.

Tashi and Judy Tenzing. *Tenzing Norgay and the Sherpas of Everest* (New York: Ragged Mountain Press, 2003).

Shompen   *See* Nicobarese.

Shui

The Shui are one of China's recognized 55 national minority groups; a small number also reside in Vietnam but they are not listed as one of that country's 54 nationalities. The largest number of Shui live on the upper reaches of the Long and Duliu Rivers in the south of Guizhou Province, while smaller communities live in Guangxi and Yunnan Provinces.

The ancestors of today's Shui were not native to the Guizhou region and migrated there prior to the beginning of the Han dynasty in 202 b.c.e. However, where they came from remains a mystery, with some sources indicating

SHUI

location:
Guizhou, Guanxi, and Yunnan Provinces in China and Vietnam

time period:
Possibly before 202 B.C.E. to the present

ancestry:
Possibly Luoyue or Baiyue

language:
Sui, a Zhuang-Dong language in the larger Sino-Tibetan phylum

SIKHS

location:
India, primarily the Punjab

time period:
1499 to the present

ancestry:
Indian

language:
Punjabi

they descend from the BAIYUE of southeastern China and others positing indeterminate ancestors from northwestern China. Regardless of these ancient origins, the Shui took their name, meaning "water," during the Ming dynasty (1368–1644). This period also marked the relative sinicization of Shui culture, when Han culture patterns began to be evident throughout Shui society. One clear example of this change is in Shui agricultural practice. Prior to the Ming period, the Shui were largely swidden horticulturalists who used slash-and-burn techniques to provide fertilizer to impermanent fields; they also focused their grain production on wheat. During the Ming dynasty many Shui adopted Han wet-rice agriculture in permanent paddies and used animal and human fertilizers to maintain crop viability. Even today many Shui are agriculturalists who grow rice, wheat, rape seeds, citrus fruit, corn, barley, and sweet potatoes. Fish are also very important to the Shui as both a subsistence and a ritual food.

By the turn of the last century, many other aspects of Shui society had also been transformed through interaction with the dominant Han society. For example, marriage prior to the 19th century usually entailed relatively free choice for both men and women and a period of courtship preceded marriage. By the 20th century, Shui marriages resembled those of the Han, which were arranged by parents and often entailed marrying girls off to older men. Some aspects of the local tradition did survive, however, such as divorce, widow remarriage, and delayed patrilocality, when the woman waited until the birth of her first child to move into her husband's family.

In the past the Shui also had their own indigenous writing system, called Shuishu, which used a system of hieroglyphics to depict meaning, not entirely unlike the way Chinese characters do. Today this system of about 400 characters is used only by a few old religious specialists in their work of divination or communication with the spirit world. Other works in this script provide an encyclopedia of Shui knowledge about the world, but these are generally collectors' items rather than in daily use since most literate Shui read Mandarin rather than Shuishu. There is a concern today both among the Shui and among scholars in China that the 20,000 or so known manuscripts in this language are at risk of decay because they are generally printed on cotton-based paper that requires specific conditions of heat, light, and humidity to be preserved. Since most manuscripts are still held by private collectors and private owners, these conditions are generally not being met.

Sikhs (Punjabis)

The Sikhs are a religious community in India that can be considered their own group because they differ from the majority of their fellow citizens in their belief in the equality of all people, in their monotheism, and in a variety of other social and historical ways.

The Sikh religion was founded in 1499 when Guru Nanak achieved enlightenment and began to accumulate followers. The basic tenets of the religion come from the guru's early statement "There is no Hindu, no Muslim," which indicates the equality of all in the eyes of god. During the course of his travels throughout the Punjab, the guru mixed with low-caste Hindus and poor people, and he shared his food and resources with all in need. These basic concepts remain essential to Sikhism today, along with a wide variety of other beliefs, practices, and prohibitions. For example, based on a proclamation by the last of the religion's 10 gurus, Gobind Singh, all Sikh men wear "the five Ks" as symbols of their faith. These five items are: uncut hair, or *kesh;* or *kanga,* a comb, to keep it neat; a bangle, or *kara;* a dagger, or *kirpan;* and specially made cotton underwear, or *kaccha.* The last two are to remind Sikhs of their warrior past, particularly the 19th century when Maharaja Ranjit Singh conquered Lahore and created a unified kingdom, which he held until his death in 1839. Another custom common to Sikhs is the practice of giving most girls the last name Kaur, meaning "prince," and boys the last name Singh, as evident in the names of the first and last of the 10 gurus. This is a common custom but not a necessity, and some Sikh families choose to use a family or surname with Kaur and Singh as middle names to indicate the sex of the child; Sikh given names are gender neutral and are used for both boys and girls.

Unlike India's majority Hindu population, Sikhs are monotheists; they believe in just one god. Their god is also a truly abstract figure; there is no body or image that can be depicted in paintings, statues, or other representations. Despite this, Sikhs pray to their god as to a friend or other helpful person. One of the rules of the Sikh religion is that members should rise early in the morning, bathe, and then spend several hours in prayer. There are specific morning and evening prayers they are to say, which can be

The Golden Temple of Amritsar sits in the midst of a lake, which served as a devotional place for Hindus and Buddhists for many thousands of years prior to the building of this temple in the late 16th and early 17th centuries under the fifth guru, Arjan. *(Shutterstock/Holger Mette)*

done alone or in groups. Sikh temples, called *gurdwara*s, are places for members to come together for communal prayer, which they believe pleases God. The most important *gurdwara* is the Golden Temple of Amritsar, the most holy city for Sikhs, built by the fourth and fifth Sikh gurus, Ramdas and Arjan Dev, respectively. Worship held in these *gurdwaras* is not led by a priest or other specialist but by any community member who is able to do so, male or female. The language of prayer among all Sikhs, regardless of where they live, is the religion's sacred language of its first guru, Punjabi.

Sikkimese

The Sikkimese are not a separate ethnic group but a group defined by politics and history as residents of the Indian state of Sikkim; their ethnic background is mixed and includes Nepalese, LEPCHA, LIMBU, and BHUTIA. The Sikkimese language is sometimes referred to as Bhutia or Dzongkha and shares most features with this Tibeto-Burman language that entered the region with the Bhutia possibly as early as the 15th century. At the same time, today the Sikkimese population is actually made up of a majority of Nepalis at around 70 percent of the population, most of whom migrated into the area at the encouragement of the British between 1890 and 1947; the Lepcha are about 20 percent, and the last 10 percent is made up of Bhutia, Indians, and Limbu. It was the last group that gave Sikkim its name; the Limbu term *su him* means "new house" and refers to the migration of the Bhutia.

In the 17th century, when recorded Sikkimese history began, it was the Bhutia who founded the first kingdom under Chogyal, or King, Phuntsog Namgyal. The indigenous Lepcha population was largely pushed into the forests and river valleys at lower elevations, while the dominant Bhutia established themselves in the region's mountains. The new kingdom fought in several wars with the kingdoms of Bhutan and Nepal starting in the mid-18th century, which eventually brought the British into the Himalayan region. While the British defeated the aggressive Nepalese and their army of GURKHAS in 1816, Sikkim was able to sign a treaty with the British a year later, which recognized the autonomy and territorial integrity of Sikkim; the Sikkimese also regained territory taken by the Nepalese in previous decades. However, relations with the British did not remain harmonious. In the 19th century the British agreed to pay the ruler of Sikkim for territory in Darjeeling that they wanted as an easy access point to Tibet; the high elevation also gave it a pleasant climate for Europeans. After a period of a few years the British failed to pay their annual rent for the territory, leading the two into a brief war, which was won by the British. The Anglo-Sikkimese Treaty of 1861 made the former kingdom a princely state within the British realm, but the king's British adviser, Claude White, became the de facto ruler of the small state.

When India attained independence from Britain in 1947, the new government tried to exert claims over all the princely states of the region that had been under the thumb of the British, but the Sikkimese court refused to go along with that position and declared independence at the same time. The newly independent kingdom occupied the most strategic position of all India's borderlands because of its historical location as the primary trade and communications route between Tibet and India. In 1950, after three years of negotiations, the king of Sikkim, Tashi Namgyal, finally agreed to Indian demands and signed a treaty that made his country an Indian protectorate. India was

SIKKIMESE

location:
Sikkim, India

time period:
15th century to the present

ancestry:
Southern Tibetan

language:
Sikkimese, a Tibeto-Burman language almost identical to Dzongkha of Bhutan and very similar to Tibetan

able to control the kingdom's foreign relations, defense, and communications while internal matters remained in the hands of the king. Internally, however, there was no consensus in Sikkim on remaining a relatively independent monarchy, and the state congress was heavily in favor of democracy and joining India. After a referendum in which about 97 percent of Sikkim's population voted in favor of joining India, this came into effect on May 15, 1975.

One of the reasons for the great discrepancy between the wishes of the king and royal family and those of the vast majority of the Sikkimese people between 1947 and 1975 was that the king came from one of the smallest ethnic groups in the country, the Bhutia. Under the Sikkimese absolute monarchy, the majority Nepali and Lepcha were denied the power of their numbers. The majority of the Nepali population is also Hindu, and the Lepcha follow their own religion, while the Bhutia and their king came from the Red Hat Buddhists, who had been driven from Tibet originally by the ruling Yellow Hats, or Gelugpas. The king's connections to this religion meant that considerable state funds were funneled into the country's many monasteries, serving only about a quarter of the population.

Sikkim's mountainous terrain is extremely rugged and allows for only about 8.5 percent to be utilized as crop land; in contrast, almost 14.5 percent is permanently covered in ice and snow. Despite this fact, agriculture has long been at the center of the Sikkimese economy. Rice is the most important crop for subsistence, while corn, potatoes, cardamom, citrus fruit, apples, and pineapples are important cash crops. Most agricultural families also keep sheep, goats, yaks, mules, or cattle and graze them on pastures high in the Himalayas, moving them up and down the mountains seasonally in search of grass and water. These animals provide milk, skins, and wool that are all sold or traded for other necessary commodities. In addition, the state is known for its forest products and minerals as well, which provide local jobs. In recent decades tourism has also become an important source of local jobs and state development funds.

The biggest problem facing the further development of Sikkim's economy is inadequate sources of energy, and toward that end numerous national and international studies have advocated using the state's many Himalayan rivers to create hydroelectric power. Unfortunately, as is often the case, this kind of construction project has numerous side effects for the local population. For example, in mid-2007 the Lepcha of Dzongu, northern Sikkim, burst onto the global scene because several of their leaders were engaged in an indefinite hunger strike in protest over the planned hydroelectric dam project on the Teesta River. A number of leaders of Affected Citizens of Teesta (ACT), Concerned Lepchas of Sikkim (CLOS), and the Buddhist Sangha of Dzongu began their strike in June 2007 to bring attention to the thousands of people who will be displaced from homes, villages, and farmland if the dam projects are allowed to go through. It remains to be seen whether the 22 separate projects slated for the Teesta River, which drains the Himalayas and runs into the Brahmaputra River in Bangladesh, will commence or not.

See also NEPALESE: NATIONALITY.

Sindhis

The Sindhis, speakers of an Indo-Aryan language, live primarily in Sindh Province, Pakistan, although more than 1 million Hindu Sindhis migrated to India at partition in 1947. The early history of the Sindhi people remains uncertain; their language points to migration from Central Asia starting in about 1800 B.C.E., but some sources indicate more ancient origins, claiming that contemporary Sindhis are the descendants of the HARAPPANS of about 3000–1500 B.C.E.

Starting in about 520 B.C.E., Sindhi history becomes clearer, for in that period Darius the Great, king of the Achaemenid Empire (*see* PERSIANS, ACHAEMENIDS) conquered their territory, which remained part of that empire for the next century and a quarter. Alexander the Great also came through the region of Sindh in 326 B.C.E. and was injured during fighting in Multan. Soon after that the Mauryan empire conquered the region, and Buddhism became the state religion under the leadership of Asoka, the empire's greatest ruler. The third to the sixth centuries C.E. brought the Persians back into the region, so that the Persian language continued to be used by the ruling elite until the 19th century. The other invasion that transformed the Sindhi people at a fundamental level was that of the Arabs in 711 C.E. They brought Islam to the region as well as their own literary and poetic traditions, all of which have contributed to contemporary Sindh culture today. Following the fall of the Arabs in 1026, a number of regional and local rulers emerged, the most important of whom were the Soomras, 1026–1350, the Sammas, 1351–1521, and the Mughals, 1608–1701.

SINDHIS

location:
Sindh Province, Pakistan and India

time period:
Probably about 1800 B.C.E. to the present

ancestry:
Probably Indo-Aryan, although some sources claim Harappan origins

language:
Sindh, an Indo-Aryan language

The British arrived in Sindh in the mid-19th century and made it part of the Bombay Presidency (province) in 1847. Under the British, Sindhi replaced Persian as the region's official language of state, and a final version of the language's script based on Arabic, called *naskh,* was put into general use. Until 1870 a second Sindh script, *khudawadi,* was also legal to accommodate the large Hindu Sindhi population, but even prior to that year most Hindus had abandoned it in favor of *naskh* because learning its alternative got in the way of taking civil-service examinations and thus winning positions in the lucrative government sector. By 1936 Sindhi activism had convinced the British to separate Sindh from the larger Bombay Presidency, which set the stage for Sindh nationalism that has dominated the region since Pakistani independence in 1947.

In addition to independence from the British, the other important event in 1947 was the partition of the former Indian colony into India and Pakistan, including both East and West Pakistan, which became Bangladesh and Pakistan, respectively, in 1971. The partition of India into predominantly Hindu and predominantly Muslim countries forced many Sindhis to make a choice, and more than a million Hindu Sindhis left the new Pakistan over the course of about four years and moved to India. Hindu Sindhis had dominated the merchant, trade, banking, and other entrepreneurial sectors of the urban Sindh economy prior to 1947 because of the Islamic prohibitions against taking interest. As a result, the population that left in 1947 was wealthier, better educated, and more connected to the world market than either the population they left behind or the population they joined. Like the Jews in Europe, they have often served as scapegoats in times of economic and social disruption, and today many *Sind-workis,* overseas merchants, live and work outside south Asia in the United Kingdom, the United States, and other parts of Asia. Their flight from Pakistan also opened up Sindh's major cities, especially Karachi, to migration from the MUHAJIRS, Urdu-speaking Muslims who fled India at partition, and today rivalry between the two populations in Sindh province continues to lead to violence on a regular basis.

The first important clash between Sindhis and others living in Sindh province occurred in 1957–58 when the Sindhi-Urdu Controversy rocked the University of Karachi. During that academic year Urdu became the only language that could be used in university exams, and Sindhi became relegated to a minor language, despite the fact that a majority of the province's people spoke it as their first and only language. Previously the University of Sind had also been forced out of Karachi entirely and moved to Hyderabad, a considerably smaller and less cosmopolitan city. Following these events among the elite, university-educated members of the community, the language issue spread throughout the population of the province, and in November 1962 Sindh province celebrated the first Sindhi Day to promote the equality of Sindhi with Urdu in the province. These kinds of nonviolent protests led to riots in early 1971 and mid-1972 over the issues of language, culture, and autonomy.

When Zulfikar Ali Bhutto was elected Pakistan's 10th prime minister in 1971, one of his first acts was to fulfill a campaign promise to make Sindhi equal to Urdu in official documents in Sindh Province. At that time the work of the Sindhi Adabi Board, formed in 1951 to promote the language, became central in the publication and creation of new Sindhi language materials. This was joined in 1990 by the Sindhi Language Authority, which likewise publishes and promotes the language but also acts like the Academie Francaise in France to keep the language up-to-date by creating and standardizing new words and spellings.

Although language and culture have been central to much of the Sindhi political movement over the past 60 years, there are also issues of economic equality and land. Sindh Province today is the richest in Pakistan, but most of that wealth is concentrated in the hands of the urban elite in Karachi, Hyderabad, and a few other cities, and much of the population of these cities is not Sindhi but Muhajir. The province's rural population, which is overwhelmingly Sindhi, is very poor. Movements calling for a separate Sindh country, which became particularly violent in the 1980s, especially 1983, continue to emerge occasionally in both rural and urban areas.

Singaporean Chinese

The earliest Chinese immigrants to settle in the Malay Archipelago arrived from Guangdong and Fujian provinces in the 10th century C.E. They were joined by much larger numbers of Chinese in the 15th–17th centuries, following on the heels of the Ming emperor's reopening of Chinese-Malay trade relations in the 15th century. Many came as seamen and traders, married locally, and never returned to their homes

SINGAPOREAN CHINESE

location:
Singapore

time period:
19th century to the present

ancestry:
Teochew, Hokkien, Cantonese, Hakka, Han, and other Chinese groups

language:
Teochew, Hokkien, Cantonese, Mandarin, English

in southern China; the descendants of this group are known as PERANAKANS and differ culturally from those who have arrived more recently or who maintained their Chinese identity. The 19th century brought another wave of Chinese immigration to the Malay world, largely encouraged by the British administration in the Straits, which needed laborers and traders. By 1849, 17 years after Singapore became the capital of the British Straits Settlements, the Chinese community made up about 50 percent of Singapore's population.

In the later half of the 19th century, the prohibition on Chinese women leaving their country was lifted, and thus began a much more dynamic and China-focused Chinese community in the Malay world. In Singapore this community now makes up about 75 percent of the entire population and dominates its political life and thriving commerce and business. Today this community tends to identify as Singaporean rather than Chinese, despite sharing with the Chinese a strong Confucian culture with an emphasis on hierarchy, authoritarianism, and patriarchy. Many Singaporean Chinese are Buddhists, Taoists, or Christians, which differentiates them from the vast majority of mainland Chinese, who have been subject to the official antireligious policies of the Chinese Communist Party since 1949.

See also MALAYS; SINGAPOREANS: NATIONALITY.

Singaporean Indians (Indian Singaporeans, local Indians)

The first large-scale migration of Indians to Singapore began after the 1819 treaty between Sir Thomas Stamford Raffles, representing the British East India Company, and the sultan of Johor, granting Singapore to the East India Company as a trading colony. The region's tiny population at the time was about 1,000 people, primarily of Malay descent. The British quickly set about transforming the island, and one of their methods was to bring Indians as workers for plantations, mines, and the colonial apparatus. At that time the national boundaries that today divide India, Pakistan, Bangladesh, and Sri Lanka did not exist within the British Indian colony, and all peoples were considered Indian. This categorization has continued in Singapore, where three "racial" groups are currently recognized: Chinese, Malay, and Indian. The Indian group is the smallest today, with about 320,000 people; however, this number includes only citizens

and permanent residents of Indian descent. The inclusion of Indians who live in Singapore on other visas and permits easily pushes the population over 400,000 people, or about 9.5 percent of the population as a whole.

The Indian population in Singapore prior to the 1990s was highly stratified according to economic class. There were a large number of very wealthy Indians who were active in the small nation's political, educational, and legal sectors and a large number of very poor Indians; very few Indians occupied the middle- and working-class strata. Since the 1990s the wealthier Indian community has gained even greater visibility with an influx of Indian professionals newly arrived from India's booming information technology and business sectors. As a result, since the turn of the millennium, Indians have surpassed the Chinese in Singapore in average monthly income and percentage with a university or graduate degree. This dramatic rise has made the income disparities within the Indian community even greater and has served to make the problems of poor Indians relatively invisible within Singapore.

In addition to class, Singapore's Indian population is highly heterogeneous in many other ways. Linguistically, the community speaks dozens of different South Asian languages. Although the large community of TAMILS makes up nearly 60 percent of all Indians, MALAYALIS, PUNJABIS, HINDI, GUJARATIS, and SINHALESE are also well represented in Singapore. While "Indian" cuisine in the country tends to come from the large Tamil community, there is a heavy influence from northern India's diverse cuisines as well. Religion also divides the community, with just over half of all Indians in Singapore identifying themselves as Hindus and another quarter identifying as Muslim. The other quarter is made up of Christians, SIKHS, Buddhists, a number of other religious groups from south Asia, and those professing no religious beliefs at all.

See also MALAYS; SINGAPOREANS: NATIONALITY.

Singaporeans: nationality (people of Singapore)

Singapore is a multicultural society heavily influenced by its largely Chinese and Malay populations but also by the formation of the modern nation during the period of British colonialism.

GEOGRAPHY

The city-state of Singapore includes one main island and more than 50 smaller islets, for a

---

SINGAPOREAN INDIANS

location:
Singapore

time period:
1819 to the present

ancestry:
Indian, Pakistani, Bangladeshi, or Sri Lankan

language:
Tamil, Malayalam, Punjabi, other South Asian languages, English

Singaporeans: nationality timeline

C.E.

13th century The Sumatran Srivijaya empire, encompassing much of modern-day Malaysia and Indonesia, founds an outpost port on the island named Temasek.

1330s Chinese sailor Wang Dayuan, who travels as far as eastern Africa, visits Temasek and writes *Dao Yi Zhi Lue* (Island savages). One of the first written accounts of the island, *Dao Yi Zhi Lue* notes the presence of a Chinese-Malay village.

1414 Temasek is absorbed into the Sultanate of Malacca, formed by a Srivijayan prince who fled to the island several decades earlier.

1511 The Portuguese defeat the Sultanate of Malacca, and Temasek is absorbed into the Sultante of Johor.

1613 The Portuguese burn Singapore during the Malay-Portugal Wars.

1819 Singapore is founded as a British trading colony by Sir Thomas Stamford Raffles of the British East India Company. Raffles signs a treaty with the sultan and the head of state of Johor. The population at the time is about 1,000.

1822 The Jackson Plan separates Singapore into four subdivisions, one each for Europeans, ethnic Chinese, and ethnic Indians, and a fourth division for Muslims, ethnic Malays, and Arabs.

1823 The Raffles Institution is founded. This boys' school has consistently been ranked one of the best secondary schools in Singapore.

1824 The Dutch withdraw objections to British occupation after the two European powers sign the Anglo-Dutch Treaty (or Treaty of London), effectively dividing between them the Malay territories that would become Malaysia and Indonesia, with Singapore in the middle.

1826 The British East India Company establishes and is given rule of the Straits Settlements, which include Singapore, Malacca, and Penang.

1832 Singapore becomes capital of the Straits Settlements.

1859 The Singapore Botanic Gardens, initially an experimental garden established by Raffles, is founded by the Agri-Horticultural Society. The first director will later identify the orchid hybrid that becomes Singapore's national flower.

1867 The Straits Settlements are made a crown colony of Britain.

1869 The Suez Canal opens, and Singapore becomes a major port.

1877 The Straits Settlements establish a Chinese protectorate to look after the well-being of the ethnic Chinese residents, especially those employed as unskilled laborers and domestic servants. Headed by William Pickering, one of the first European officials to speak Chinese dialects such as Mandarin and Hokkien fluently, the protectorate seeks to weaken the influence of secret societies on the island by encouraging the Chinese to bring their complaints to colonial administrators.

1879 The Raffles Girls' School separates from the boys' Raffles Institution; enrollment rises from 11 to 72.

1906 Chinese revolutionary Sun Yat-sen, sometimes called the father of modern China, founds the Southeast Asian headquarters of the Tongmenghui, or United Allegiance Society, in Singapore.

1915 The Singapore Mutiny occurs; several dozen Britons are killed before the mutineers are rounded up.

1942 On February 15 Japan invades in the Battle of Singapore and renames the island Shonan, meaning "Light of the South."

1944 Lim Bo Seng, a Chinese resistance fighter who had studied at the Raffles Institution before the war, is captured by the Japanese army and dies while imprisoned.

1945 British forces return to Singapore, and the Straits Settlement become a military administration.

(continues)

SINGAPOREANS: NATIONALITY

nation:
Republic of Singapore, Singapore

derivation of name:
Malay terms *singa,* meaning "lion," and *pura,* meaning "city"; in Tamil the terms *singam* and *puram* refer to "lion" and "city," respectively.

capital:
Singapore

languages:
Malay is the national language and one of four official languages along with English, Mandarin Chinese, and Tamil, but 23 percent of the population speak other languages, including Hokkien, Cantonese, and Teochiu. Local slang is known as Singlish.

religion:
No state religion; Buddhist 42.5 percent, Muslim 14.9 percent, Taoist 8.5 percent, Catholic 4.8 percent, Hindu 4 percent, other Christian 9.8 percent, none 14.8 percent

earlier inhabitants:
Malays

demographics:
Chinese 76.8 percent, Malay 13.9 percent, Indian 7.9 percent, other 1.4 percent

Singaporeans: nationality timeline *(continued)*

1946 Singapore becomes a separate crown colony following the dissolution of the Straits Settlements.

1948 Britain declares a state of emergency in Singapore and Malaya following communist attacks on rubber plantations and tin mines.

1950 A court decision to grant custody of teenager Maria Hertogh to her biological Dutch Catholic parents rather than to her Muslim primary caregiver of eight years prompts two days of rioting. Nearly 20 people are killed, 173 are injured, and authorities impose two weeks of curfew.

1955 Singapore is granted limited internal self-government, but Britain retains control of defense and foreign affairs. Leading parties Labour Front and People's Action Party (PAP) call for independence and a merger with Malaya.

1956 David Marshall, the first chief minister of Singapore, resigns when his appeal to Britain for full self-government fails.

1959 Full self-government is instituted, and Malay is designated the official language. Singapore's first prime minister, Lee Kuan Yew (1959–90), and the victorious PAP work to curb unemployment, implement a large-scale public housing program, and reduce the threat of racial tension. Encik Zubir Said composes the national anthem "Mujaluh Singpura" (Onward Singapore).

1962 A referendum is held to join with Malaysia.

1963 In August, Lee and the PAP declare independence from Britain, and in September Singapore joins the Malaysia Federation as a state with autonomous powers.

1964 Race riots in July and September between Chinese and Malay groups result in almost 40 deaths and more than 500 injuries. The more severe July riots are partially attributed to strained political relations between the PAP and the United Malays National Organization (UMNO). By contrast, the October riots are attributed in part to Indonesian provocateurs as part of *konfrontasi,* the Malaysian-Indonesian confrontation over the island of Borneo. Authorities use the Internal Security Act, a successor to British emergency regulations targeted at a communist uprising, to make numerous arrests, including hundreds of secret society members. The act remains in effect in Singapore today.

1965 Singapore separates from the Malaysia Federation on August 9 after an ideological conflict between the state and federal governments. In short order, Singapore is admitted to the United Nations and the British Commonwealth.

1967 Parliament passes the National Service bill that establishes compulsory conscription for male citizens and second-generation permanent residents. The system is designed to provide a sustainable and indigenous defense capability and to promote multiracialism; it continues in effect today.

1967 Singapore becomes a founding member of the Association of South-East Asian Nations (ASEAN).

total land area of roughly 435 square miles. Land-reclamation projects are slowly increasing this surface area. Singapore is the second most densely populated independent country in the world and is located 137 miles north of the equator between Malaysia and Indonesia.

INCEPTION AS A NATION

Singapore's strategic location on the Straits of Malacca has made it a historically attractive location to traders since most sea trade between Europe, India, and the Middle East and East Asia passes through the adjacent straits. Even today, Singapore is a center for international trade, and its citizens enjoy a high standard of living.

The Malay people, who also occupied peninsular Malaya and the Indonesian Archipelago, are Singapore's indigenous inhabitants; they are acknowledged as such and given special status in the constitution. When the British East India Company arrived in the early 19th century and negotiated custody of the island from the Sultanate of Johor, fewer than 1,000

1970	The presidential council, renamed the presidential council for minority rights in 1973, is established. The council examines parliamentary bills and works to prevent discrimination against race, religions, or communities.
1971	The last British military forces withdraw.
1973	The first Chingay parade is held in Singapore to ensure that Chinese New Year celebrations do not suffer from the 1972 ban on firecrackers. In 1977 Malay and India groups join the highly celebrated annual performance.
1979	A national Courtesy Campaign begins and for its first year targets the public and the government with the slogan "Courtesy is our way of life. Make courtesy our way of life." The campaign continues until 2001, when it is wrapped into the Singapore Kindness Movement.
1984	Two opposition members are elected to Parliament for the first time, and the election of three women ends 16 years of all-male representation.
1990	Goh Chok Tong becomes the country's second prime minister (1990–2004).
1991	The constitution is amended to create a popularly elected president with limited veto powers, and the Parliamentary Elections Act is modified to enable plurality-based elections.
1993	Ong Teng Cheong becomes the first directly elected president.
1994	American teenager Michael Fay is convicted of vandalizing a car, and after intense media coverage and a failed appeal, President Ong Teng Cheong commutes his caning from six to four lashes.
1997	The Asian financial crisis hits; Singapore's economy is less affected and recovers more quickly than neighboring economies.
1998	The national football team wins the Tiger Cup, its first international tournament.
1999	Sellapan Ramanthan (also known as S. R. Nathan) assumes the presidency without election after being declared the only candidate eligible to run. He continues to serve as president to the present day.
2000	The government establishes an official speakers' corner in Hong Lim Park where citizens who have registered with the police are allowed to speak, provided they do so in one of the four official languages and do not discuss religious issues.
2001	An antigovernment rally is the first legal demonstration outside election campaigns. Hundreds gather to support veteran opposition leader J. B. Jeyaretnam, who faces bankruptcy and thus expulsion from Parliament.
2004	Former prime minister Lee's eldest son, Lee Hsien Loong, becomes the nation's third prime minister.
2005	High-level appeals for clemency fail to halt the execution of an Australian man convicted of drug smuggling.

MALAYS lived on the island, primarily in small fishing villages.

By 1827 the Malays had been surpassed as the island's dominant ethnic group by the Chinese, and the difference increased further after the British annexation of Hong Kong in 1842. Most Chinese and Indian immigrants were attracted by economic opportunity, but some Indians were forcibly relocated to Singapore as convict laborers. By 1867 the total population on the island was more than 86,000. Primarily single and male, Chinese immigrants were essential to the economic success of colonial Singapore, but they also fed the growth of secret societies. Colonial administrators concerned by the growing influence of these societies began a dual process of limited outreach to the ethnic communities and to new arrivals, combined with enhanced internal security measures. To a large degree, Singaporean national identity has been consciously built from the top down and reflects the legacy of these two policies.

Regular influxes of new residents and explicit colonial policies of ethnic division, which

Standing amid the important city-state he helped to create, Stamford Raffles cuts an imposing figure, though certainly not as imposing as he would have seemed to the tiny Malay population of the region prior to the colonial era he initiated in 1819. *(Shutterstock)*

extended to separate neighborhoods, prevented Singaporeans from developing a conception of themselves as Singaporeans. In the early 20th century, Chinese communities were more likely to have an interest in the nationalist movements in mainland China than in any similar efforts on Singapore. Likewise, when the Malayan Communist Party operated on the island, it focused more on organization of labor than on national unity. As occurred in many European colonies in Asia and Africa, World War II and JAPANESE occupation accelerated interest in achieving self-government in Singapore.

Colonial authorities were concerned, however, that the population's external loyalties might lead to a spread of communism, and they opted for a slow transfer of power. In 1963, once the full transition to self-government had been completed, a combination of these same concerns, economic self-interest, and the lack of any strong Singaporean identity prompted the island to join Malaya, Sabah, and Sarawak to form the Federation of Malaysia. However, ethnic tensions between the Chinese majority

in Singapore and the consciously crafted non-Chinese majority in the other territories forced a parting of ways in 1965. Since then, the ruling People's Action Party has made conscious and explicit efforts to build a national identity that fosters internal unity, enhances party legitimacy, and weakens external attachments to Communist China and elsewhere. For example, under a policy of bilingualism, children are taught both English and their "mother tongue" (Mandarin Chinese, Malay, or Tamil) in an attempt to promote "multiracialism" while preserving links to the traditions and values of each ethnic group. The government has also used housing policies to foster ethnic integration in buildings and neighborhoods. Although interethnic relations are largely peaceful, some observers and Singaporeans continue to challenge the notion of a transcendent Singaporean identity.

CULTURAL IDENTITY

The conscious and top-down nature of national identity formation in Singapore means that government efforts to promote multiculturalism, multiracialism, multireligionism, and multilingualism have had a strong impact on Singaporean values. In particular, Singaporeans tend to value meritocracy and hard work, and these values are often cited as contributing factors to Singapore's postindependence economic success and political stability. Singapore is also known as one of the most prosperous and safest countries in the world, attributes that make most citizens very proud. However, these values and attributes are bounded by the importance of succeeding within established norms. This pressure has elicited a degree of ambivalence reflected in emigration rates, disparagement of emigrants, and the criticism voiced in movies such as *I Not Stupid,* a high-grossing 2002 film that highlights flaws in a system that restricts and undervalues alternative avenues to success.

Other key elements of Singaporean cultural identity are respect for authority and the importance of group membership (in extended and nuclear families, ethnic groups, and so on). Family is very important, but a preference for smaller families has contributed to a low birthrate that is driving demographic changes. Beginning in 1996, the Maintenance of Parents Act permits elderly residents whose financial resources are inadequate for basic amenities to apply for required support from their children. This suggests political concern that demographic shifts are eroding traditional filial ties.

Additionally, fear of interethnic tensions in the colonial and postcolonial periods have resulted in a legacy of tight government control. The strict penal system occasionally attracts attention when other countries' citizens are convicted, but the control is also reflected in annual government courtesy campaigns to build a more "gracious society." The perception that Singapore's authoritarian political system reflects a cultural preference is increasingly challenged as prosperity and technology prompt some Singaporeans to contest the primacy and viability of ideals promoted by the government. The issue of what it means to be Singaporean has never been fully settled and continues to be the subject of internal discussion and debate.

See also MALAYSIANS: NATIONALITY; SINGAPOREAN CHINESE; SINGAPOREAN INDIANS; TAMILS.

FURTHER READING

Lai Ah Eng. *Meanings of Multiethnicity: A Case-Study of Ethnicity and Ethnic Relations in Singapore* (New York: Oxford University Press, 1995).

Michael Hill and Lian Kwen Fee. *The Politics of Nation Building and Citizenship in Singapore* (London: Routledge, 1995).

William Peterson. *Theater and the Politics of Culture in Contemporary Singapore* (Middletown, Conn.: Wesleyan University Press, 2001).

H. E. Wilson. *Social Engineering in Singapore: Educational Policies and Social Change, 1819–1972* (Athens: Ohio University Press, 1979).

Singpo   *See* KACHIN.

Sinhalese (Cingalese, Hela, Singhalese, Sinhala, Sinhela)

The Sinhalese are the dominant ethnolinguistic group in Sri Lanka, with about 74 percent of the country's population. They speak an Indo-Aryan language and are predominantly Buddhist.

GEOGRAPHY

Sri Lanka is a small tropical island southeast of India, straddling the Bay of Bengal and Indian Ocean. It is a mere 219 miles long and 114 miles at its widest point but houses nearly 20 million people. The Sinhalese dominate most of the island, except the northernmost coast and a bit of the northeast region, which are largely Tamil.

Despite its small size, Sri Lanka has two distinct ecological zones: the wet zone in the southwest and the dry zone everywhere else. The wet zone produces about 95 percent of the country's agricultural exports in the form of tea, rubber, and coconuts, as well as smaller quantities of cinnamon, citronella, cardamom, and areca nuts. The dry zone receives rain only from November to January and allows subsistence farming just where streams or rivers provide water for irrigation.

ORIGINS

The Sinhalese probably migrated to Sri Lanka in the sixth or fifth century B.C.E., traveling by sea from India. According to Sinhalese origin myths, this first wave of migration was made up of King Vijaya, the offspring of a Hindu princess and a lion, and his 500–700 followers, who arrived on the island at the exact moment of the Buddha's death. The myth is unclear about whether Vijaya and his followers came from northeast or northwest India, but it is certain about their northern origins. Considerable nationalist effort on the part of some Sinhalese has gone into connecting themselves with northern India and not the south, home of the rival TAMILS. However, modern genetic testing has shown that most contemporary Sinhalese are more closely related to the Tamils and Keralites of southern India, as well as high-caste groups in Bengal, than to people in Gujarat or the Punjab. The importance of the lion ancestor to contemporary Sinhalese is evident on the national flag of Sri Lanka, which depicts a lion holding a sword.

HISTORY

The first Sinhalese inscriptions on Sri Lanka can be positively dated from the third century B.C.E. These cave writings indicate that by this period the ancestors of the Sinhalese inhabited the entire island and thus point to an original settlement date that roughly coincides with the Vijaya myth. From this period onward an almost continuous written mythohistory of the Sinhalese can be pieced together from various sources, including the *Dipayamsa*, *Mahavamsa*, and *Chulavamsa*, all historical poems written in Pali, a liturgical Indian language associated with Theravada Buddhism, that trace Sinhalese history from Vijaya onward. The *Dipayamsa* is the oldest written record on Sri Lanka and was probably compiled in the fourth century from monks' records dating back to about the third century B.C.E., the start of the Buddhist era on Sri Lanka. The *Mahavamsa* is a more extensive work covering the same years: 543 B.C.E., when Vijaya is believed to have landed, until 361 C.E., the end of King Mahasena's rule; it was probably compiled in the fifth century C.E. from the same

---

SINHALESE

location:
Sri Lanka

time period:
fifth century B.C.E. to the present

ancestry:
Indo-Aryan

language:
Sinhala, an Indo-Aryan language distantly related to Hindi

Sinhalese time line

B.C.E.

fifth or sixth century The Sinhalese probably migrate to Sri Lanka from India in these centuries.

543 The date that the possibly legendary King Vijaya first lands in Sri Lanka with his 500–700 followers.

fourth century Pandukhabhaya makes Anuradhapura his capital and initiates almost 1,500 years of the Anuradhapura period.

third century Sinhalese inscriptions in caves throughout Sri Lanka can be positively dated to this period.

Buddhism arrives in Sri Lanka, perhaps with a monk named Arihath Mahinda Thero.

C.E.

fourth century The Buddha's Tooth Relic arrives in Sri Lanka.

fifth century The *Mahavamsa,* a historical poem tracing Sinhalese royal history from the time of Vijaya until 361, is compiled from the writings of Buddhist monks. It is later supplemented by the *Chulavamsa,* which covers the rest of this history up to 1815 and the start of the British colonial period.

10th–11th centuries The Tamil-speaking Chola kingdom of southern India invades northern Sri Lanka.

1070 King Vijayabahu I repels the Cholas and reunites the Sinhalese country from his new capital at Polonnaruva.

1200 The Sinhalese centralized kingdom collapses, and much of the population moves to the island's southwest.

1247 Parakramabahu II repels a Javanese attack; his son, Vijayabahu of Dambadeniya, repeats this feat a few years later.

1505 The Portuguese arrive in what they call Ceylon and find two separate Sinhalese kingdoms, the Kandyan ruling the central highlands and a low country kingdom at Kotte. They soon defeat the forces of the kingdom at Kotte.

1656 The Dutch expel the Portuguese as well as the coastal Sinhalese who had converted to Roman Catholicism during the previous century and a half.

1796 The British take control of Ceylon and continue to expand the plantation agricultural economy begun by the Dutch.

1815 The British finally conquer the Kandyan kingdom and unite the island as their crown colony.

1932 Universal suffrage for all adults and self-rule over internal matters is granted by the British.

1948 Ceylon achieves full independence from the British.

1956 A nationalist Sinhalese government is elected and begins changes in educational, religious, and economic policies that alienate the large Tamil minority.

1983 A civil war erupts between Tamil separatists and Sinhalese nationalists.

2002 A cease-fire is finally signed, signaling an end to the war, which has killed at least 60,000 by this time.

2006 Renewed violence threatens the peace process, but both sides claim to want to abide by the 2002 peace documents.

2008 Heavy fighting throughout the previous year pushes the government of Sri Lanka to withdraw from the 2002 cease-fire agreement; roadside bombings kill several dozen people including D. M. Dassanayake, a government minister.

sources as the *Dipavamsa.* The *Chulavamsa* is a more contemporary work, also written by monks in Pali, and covers Sinhalese royal history from the fourth century until 1815, when Sri Lanka—or Ceylon, as it was then known—became part of the British colonial empire.

Upon their arrival, Vijaya and his followers are believed to have established the first royal capital city on Sri Lanka, Anuradhapura in North-Central Province, along the Malwatu Oya River. There are at least three different origin myths for the city, but the most accepted by historians is that one of Vijaya's retainers, Anuradha, developed the first village on the site, and thus the city that developed there later was named after him. The first king to make his capital there, Pandukhabhaya, restructured the village into a proper city in the fourth century B.C.E. and improved infrastructure such as reservoirs, roads, and irrigation works. There were several smaller kingdoms on the island during this period as well, at Mahagama in the south; Gokanna, or contemporary Trincomalee, in the east; Kalyani, or contemporary Kelaniya, in the west; and Nagadipa, or contemporary Jaffna, in the north. The kings who ruled from Anuradhapura, however, were the most powerful on the island and recognized as supreme even by these minor kingdoms. They ruled Sri Lanka for about 1,500 years, a period known as the Anuradhapura after the city from which they dominated island politics.

Another important Sinhalese event that took place in Anuradhapura was the widespread adoption of Buddhism in the third century B.C.E. Buddhism is said to have arrived on Sri Lanka several hundred years after Vijaya, with the cleric Arihath Mahinda Thero and seven other monks. They went first to Anuradhapura and met with King Devenampiyathissa while the latter was on a hunting trip. The king converted to the new religion and began the process of converting his people as well. Prior to this period they had probably practiced an animistic religion that recognized various spirits from the natural world, ancestors, and gods. The monk Arihath Mahinda Thero was followed a few years later by his sister, Sanghamittha Thero, who carried with her a branch of the Bo tree under which the Buddha had gained enlightenment. The branch was planted in Anuradhapura, and the king was called upon to be its rightful caretaker, a task handed down to subsequent kings for many generations.

In the fourth century, Sinhalese Buddhism became important in the wider Buddhist world as the home of one of the most important relics in the religion, a tooth from the Buddha himself. From the fourth to the 10th century the tooth was kept in Anuradhapura and protected by both royal and religious powers. A Chinese monk who lived and worked in Sri Lanka in the fifth century described elaborate processions and other rituals that honored the tooth and those who were responsible for its safety. Possession of the Tooth Relic also led to the invasion of the Sinhalese kingdoms by the JAVANESE as well as to extended trade relations with Burma, contemporary Myanmar, in later centuries.

In addition to Buddhism, this early Sinhalese civilization is widely known for its system of irrigation. Initially, agriculture on Sri Lanka had been largely of the swidden, or slash-and-burn, type that used simple tools and nonsustainable fertilizer from burnt vegetation and relied on rainwater. This was replaced by wet cultivation with the arrival of the Sinhalese, who brought irrigation technology, iron plows, and wet rice with them; they also used cattle to pull the plows and to provide fertilizer. Many water tanks have been discovered in and around Anuradhapura, pointing both to the centrality of agriculture and to the technological prowess of these early farmers. Unlike in their homeland in northern India, agriculture soon became one of the most highly respected tasks in early Sinhalese society, and both politics and the economy were dominated by those who controlled the land and its agricultural products. Over time the Sinhalese also moved from Sri Lanka's wet zone to the dry, where forests were easier to clear and the land was flatter and easier to work with. In addition to rice they grew beans, sugar cane, sesame, fruit, spices, and coconuts, all of which are still grown to this day.

In the 10th and 11th centuries the kings at Anuradhapura and the Sinhalese generally experienced a transformation in their society with the conquest of the northern section of the island by southern India's Chola kingdom. This invasion forms the basis for about half of the contemporary Tamil population in Sri Lanka: The Tamil-speaking Chola established themselves as the dominant ethnolinguistic group in the island's northeast, with smaller communities further south down the east coast and in the northwest as well.

In 1070 King Vijayabahu I repelled the Chola and reunited the Sinhalese country from his capital at Polonnaruva. Within a few years of this move, the Buddha's sacred tooth was likewise brought to the city, and soon a specially built sanctuary was erected for it and its caretaker monks. The greatest king to rule from this city was Vijayabahu's grandson, Parakramabahu I, who not only ended a civil war on the island but also sent military forces to India and Myanmar, expanded irrigation, and both expanded and decorated his capital city to suit his grandiose tastes.

He is said to have built 165 dams, 3,000 canals, and more than 2,500 water tanks. He also built a new palace for himself, Vejayanta Pasada, the ruins of which are still beautiful to this day. He ruled from 1153 to 1186, but his kingdom disintegrated due to civil war and Chola pressure only 14 years after his death.

The rapid demise of the Sinhalese kingdoms after 1200 remains a bit of a mystery even to this day. Both civil war and external pressure have been blamed, but malaria and ecological damage have also been explored, with no single reason able to answer all the questions posed by contemporary scholars. What we do know is that after this time the Sinhalese population experienced large-scale migration into the southwest of the island due to the 14th-century invasions by both the Tamil Pandya kingdom and Kalinga Magha, from eastern India. A large number of weakened Sinhalese kings continued to rule from various cities, including Kotmale in the central hills and Yapahuva in the north. In addition, Javanese rulers twice tried to secure positions on the island during this period and twice were repelled by Sinhalese kings, the first by Parakramabahu II in about 1247 and the second by Vijayabahu of Dambadeniya, Parakramabahu's son, a few years later.

The movements of many Sinhalese in the 14th century sparked the creation of two separate Sinhalese kingdoms, one in Kandy in the central highlands and the other on the coast near Colombo. From these two kingdoms have emerged two Sinhalese communities that to this day remain economically, socially, and ethnically somewhat distinct from each other. The Kandyans, who reside in the central mountainous region almost entirely in the island's dry zone, are believed to be more conservative and traditional than their low-country counterparts, who live in the coastal wet zone. The Kandyans refused to submit to European colonialism and finally had to be conquered by the British in 1815, while the low-country Sinhalese had early dealings with the Portuguese when they arrived in 1505, with many even converting to Roman Catholicism at that time. They served as traders, bureaucrats, and middlemen during all three Sri Lankan colonial regimes: Portuguese from 1505 to 1656, Dutch from 1656 to 1796, and British from 1796 to 1948. Due to these experiences and the education and wealth that accompanied them, low-country Sinhalese see themselves as more urban and progressive than their up-country linguistic cousins; they are also both numerically and economically more powerful. Until recently, mutual distrust between these two groups of Sinhalese speakers resulted in almost entirely endogamous marriages—that is, very few Kandyans married low-country Sinhalese and vice versa. Government-sponsored migration programs since 1945, however, have brought many low-country Sinhalese into the mountainous dry zone and have eroded some of these distinctions, but they often remain salient when the two groups mix.

The three separate colonial periods in Sri Lankan history each affected the two Sinhalese communities somewhat differently. The Portuguese were able to overthrow the low-country kingdom with its capital at Kotte early in the 16th century, and many members of the fishing castes converted to Catholicism in the aftermath. Even today, many low-country Sinhalese have Portuguese surnames dating from this period, with de Silva, Fernando, and de Fonseca among the most common. Portuguese colonialism was largely dependent on the marriages of Portuguese men to local women, and from this period there developed a significant Eurasian population who worked in the middle ranks of the colonial economy and bureaucracy. For the most part, the Kandyan kingdom remained separate and independent throughout this era, able to repel the few attempts made by the Europeans to conquer it.

With the arrival of the Dutch in the mid-17th century, little changed for the Kandyans, but the low-country Sinhalese experienced significant disruptions. In the first years of Dutch rule, 1656–58, most of the Catholic converts among the Sinhalese were either expelled from the colony or abandoned the former occupier's religion. The Dutch also implemented their own legal system on the coast and began the plantation agricultural system that remains in place to this day, including crops of coffee, cotton, and tobacco. The social category that had emerged in the Portuguese period with European fathers and local mothers also gained in numbers and importance during the Dutch period; these people were labeled BURGHERS, the Dutch term for "citizen." Though few Sinhalese converted to the Protestant Dutch Reformed Church, many Burghers were members of this religion, which is still the case to this day.

Finally, in 1796 Ceylon was ceded to the British, who created a Crown colony on the island in 1802 and united the entire island with the defeat of the Kandyans in 1815. Like the Dutch, the British supported the growth of the plantation economy, with particular emphasis on tea and coffee in the newly conquered central highlands. As was the case under the previous regimes, however, it was the low-country Sinhalese and Burghers who learned the colonizer's language and held most of the trusted positions in trading, industry, and agriculture. Rather than relying on the newly conquered Kandyans to work in the plantations, the British also imported thousands of Indian Tamils as indentured servants. The contemporary division between Jaffna, or Sri Lankan Tamils who had been living on the island for at least 1,000 years, and these Indian, or Estate, Tamils has its source in the British colonial period and the reluctance of the Kandyans to work for the colonizers and of the colonizers to trust them.

Sri Lankan independence came about due to a gradual process of decolonization. In 1932 all adult Sri Lankans were granted suffrage, and a degree of internal self-rule was implemented. Full independence was granted by the British in 1948. For eight years the country was relatively calm, and ethnic divisions were less important than nation building for all. Then in 1956 a Sinhalese-dominated government came to power and began implementing policies that favored themselves over the Tamils and Muslims, sometimes called Moors in Sri Lanka. Sinhala became the only official language of government, and Buddhism was enshrined as the only state-protected religion, despite the large Tamil-speaking Hindu minority. Riots took place in 1958, 1977, and 1981, and by 1983 a full-scale Tamil-Sinhalese civil war had driven most Sinhalese out of the country's north and northeast regions. Altogether at least 60,000 Sri Lankans were killed during the 20-year civil war, which was briefly brought under control by a 2002 cease-fire agreement, but fighting in 2006, 2007, and early 2008 has killed hundreds more people and quashed the hopes of millions. Sinhalese nationalists refuse to acquiesce to the demands of the Tamil Tigers, considered a terrorist organization in much of the world, while Tamils refuse to remain second-class citizens within the largely Sinhalese country.

CULTURE

From the earliest period Sinhalese culture has been characterized by its Indo-Aryan language, Buddhist religion, and agriculture. Due to the long period of separation between the Sinhalese and their linguistic homeland, Sinhala is very different from Hindi and the other Indo-Aryan languages spoken in northern India. It has also been heavily influenced by Pali, a liturgical language that has always been associated with Theravada Buddhist writings.

Nearly three-quarters of all Sinhalese are believers in Theravada Buddhism; however, few Sinhalese men take on the role of monk, or *bhikku*, on a full-time basis. In the early 21st century there were only about 20,000 monks estimated to live in a Sinhalese population of nearly 15.5 million. There are three separate sects of Buddhist monks in residence in Sri Lanka, the first two divided by the caste affiliation of their members. The relatively large and wealthy Siyam Nikaya limits its membership to those of the high-caste Goyigamas and is the inheritor of the Kandyan kingdom's political order. The Amapura Nikaya is smaller and made up of Karava, Salagama, and Duraya castes, which were largely coastal in the precolonial and colonial periods. Finally, the smallest Buddhist sect is the Ramanya Nikaya, a reform movement not associated with any particular caste. For ordinary villagers without access to these small and exclusive religious institutions, Buddhist priests, called *kapuralas*, perform many local ceremonies and generally meet the religious needs of the people.

Despite the long-standing association between the Sinhalese and Buddhism, as evident in the importance of the Tooth Relic in Sinhalese politics, this religion in Sri Lanka has been infused with many elements from Hinduism, especially among low-country Sinhalese. For example, many of the gods and goddesses who inhabit the religious cosmology of Hindus but not Buddhists are also worshiped by these Sinhalese. Furthermore, many Sinhalese believe in the power of demons to affect their lives and think that they must be exorcised by ritual specialists. Other aspects of pre-Buddhist animism, such as the belief in the power of many nature spirits, are also evident among Sri Lanka's rural Sinhalese communities.

As is evident in the formation of the three separate Buddhist sects in Sri Lanka, another important feature imported from Hinduism is the centrality of caste in Sinhalese life. Castes are endogamous, ranked social categories based on occupation, but membership is inherited from one's parents rather than at adulthood; people must marry someone from the same caste as themselves. Therefore, societies that recognize the caste system tended in the past to limit social mobility since, for example, the farming, fishing, and priestly caste members all had to take up farming, fishing, and serving as a priest, respectively. Among the Sinhalese the largest caste is that of the cultivators, or *goyigama,* while on the coast the fishing castes are also well-represented. Because Buddhism teaches that all people are equal and can be either reborn as a higher being through good works or cease being reborn altogether and achieve nirvana by giving up all worldly attachments in this life, some of the strictest and most debilitating hierarchical rules of Indian caste are not in practice among the Sinhalese. Nonetheless, rules about ritual purity and endogamy, marrying within one's own caste, continue to inform most people's daily lives, especially in rural areas.

With about half the population considering themselves *goyigamas,* or members of the caste of cultivators, it is not surprising that agriculture remains as important in Sinhalese culture today as it was in the distant past, when the newcomers first imported wet-rice technology to the island. In addition to rice, which is grown by more than 90 percent of all farmers, tomatoes, potatoes, onions, manioc, coconuts, spices, and even marijuana are grown by some for both personal use and for sale. Even today most farmwork is done by hand using only the most rudimentary tools, though cattle and water buffalo may be utilized in plowing. Many farming families also own sheep, goats, pigs, or chickens. As a general rule, the Sinhalese of the Kandyan or highlands region tend to engage in more subsistence-level agriculture, utilize simpler tools, and depend on water-storage systems to keep their crops alive during the long dry season than do their low-country cousins. They are also more likely to engage in shifting or extensive agriculture, moving fields from year to year to allow long fallow periods. Millet is the primary crop grown in this manner, but it can be supplemented with sesame and mustard for cash. Among low-country Sinhalese, work on the tea, coconut, and rubber plantations as well as in processing these products provides access to the cash economy, as does participation in paid work as teachers and bureaucrats.

For most rural residents, who make up about 80 percent of all Sinhalese in Sri Lanka, life is circumscribed by residence in the village and membership in a particular caste. Households tend to be made up of nuclear families, although some extended families live together, and in the past wealthy Sinhalese men could be polygynous and thus have more than one wife. These units are the basic units of production and consumption, producing most of their own food and other needs. Villages are made up of a handful to several hundred of these households in addition to their gardens, fruit trees, and perhaps space for animals, plus religious shrines, reservoirs, and rice paddies. Generally, villages are made up of just one subcaste, called *variga* in Sinhala, but up to five different *varigas* can be represented in the largest villages. In these multicaste villages, those in lower castes tend to reside outside the village proper in their own hamlets beyond the village walls.

Although most social life takes place in the village, in the past caste obligations for certain rituals, marriages, funerals, and other religious events brought individuals together from many villages. With the coming of the British, however, and the relative weakening of these ritual obligations, villages in the 19th and 20th centuries became more isolated than in the past. Nonetheless, caste was not abolished by the British and continues to inform daily life in important ways, such as in choosing potential marriage partners, participating in public religious events, showing respect to superiors, and preventing pollution through contact with lower caste individuals. Caste is less important in Sri Lankan cities but has not disappeared there either and is still evident in advertisements by those seeking suitable marriage partners.

Kinship among the Sinhalese is generally bilateral like most westerners, with both mother's and father's relatives being considered equal contributors to an individual's kin group. However, some aristocratic families maintain a separate connection to the male lines of descent that prove their relatedness to Sinhalese royalty; this is a status marker only. The largest kin grouping is a microcaste, or *pavula,* which is made up of several families' bilateral relatives. These groups are endogamous and thus strongly prefer their members to marry within them with a preference for cross-cousin marriages; that is, males are to marry their father's sister's daughter or mother's brother's daughter. They also share rice fields, cooperate in agricultural, trade, and political tasks, and usually live together in a single hamlet or village segment.

In the past, a few Kandyan families practiced fraternal polyandry, in which a set of brothers married just one woman to keep small family landholdings from being divided among the brothers, but this practice, like polygyny, has essentially disappeared. Residence after marriage depends on the wealth of the families involved. Wealthier men who own some land generally have their wives join them in patrilocal marriages, while poorer men with no land may practice matrilocal marriage, in which they move in with and work for their new in-laws. Dowries—money and gifts given by the wife's family to the husband's—are paid only in rare occasions in which women marry men of a higher subcaste; this occurs among low-country Sinhalese more than among Kandyans.

Unlike among many patriarchal communities, the Sinhalese require that inheritable property be divided equally among all children, sons and daughters alike, although a daughter's inheritance may be in the form of a dowry. Nonetheless, Sinhalese society is strongly patriarchal, and there is a relatively strong preference for sons over daughters. In childhood sons tend to receive better food and medical care, and the infant mortality rate for girls is quite a bit higher than for boys. Girls are also expected to begin working in the household before boys, who are generally allowed to continue longer in school. In adulthood, the gendered division of labor is still largely maintained, with women being responsible for the household and child care while men provide food, housing, and all other necessities. Women are thought to be polluting with the onset of their menses; childbirth and menstruation regularly put them into a state of ritual impurity. Generally, rural Sinhalese men and women lead very separate lives, coming together solely to meet their familial obligations to each other. This is very different from urban Sinhalese, who have entered the mixed-sex workforce and lead lives similar to urban residents everywhere.

See also INDO-ARYANS; SRI LANKANS: NATIONALITY.

FURTHER READING

Victoria J. Baker. *A Sinhalese Village in Sri Lanka: Coping with Uncertainty* (Fort Worth, Tex.: Harcourt Brace College Publishers, 1998).

K. N. O. Dharmadasa. *Language, Religion, and Ethnic Assertiveness: The Growth of Sinhalese Nationalism in Sri Lanka* (Ann Arbor: University of Michigan Press, 1992).

Richard F. Gombrich. *Precept and Practice: Traditional Buddhism in the Highlands of Ceylon* (Oxford: Clarendon Press, 1971).

Tamara Gunasekera. *Hierarchy and Egalitarianism: Caste, Class, and Power in Sinhalese Peasant Society* (Atlantic Highlands, N.J.: Athlone Press, 1994).

Gananath Obeyesekere. *Medusa's Hair: An Essay on Personal Symbols and Religious Experience* (Chicago: University of Chicago Press, 1984).

Michael Roberts. *Caste Conflict and Elite Formation: The Rise of a Karava Elite in Sri Lanka, 1500–1931* (New York: Cambridge University Press, 1982).

Nur Yalman. *Under the Bo Tree: Studies in Caste, Kinship, and Marriage in the Interior of Ceylon* (Berkeley and Los Angeles: University of California Press, 1967).

Sino-Vietnamese   *See* HOA.

Sogdians

The Sogdians were the ancient Indo-Iranian inhabitants of the territory that today makes up Uzbekistan and Tajikistan. Their language and script influenced the conquering Gokturks, who used literate Sogdians as scribes and translators, especially early in their history before the Gokturks had developed a written language of their own.

GEOGRAPHY

The land occupied by the original Sogdians, before their migrations further east as far as China, is today within the countries of Tajikistan and Uzbekistan. Sogdiana is a semiarid country, with two deserts, the Kara Kum and Kyzyl Kum, and the Pamir Mountains, which reach as high as 25,000 feet in some places. The region is crossed by several rivers, including the Zarafshan, Jaxartes (Syr Darya), and Oxus (Amu Darya), to name the largest. These rivers provided the opportunity for irrigation agriculture to develop in what was ultimately an oasis culture. These water sources also fed the various urban areas that developed in the region, including the capital Samarkand, also sometimes called Marakanda or Afrasiab; Bukhara; and Pendzhikent (ancient Panjikent).

ORIGINS

There is archaeological evidence of human inhabitation in the Sogdian region as early as the Middle Paleolithic period, at least 40,000 years ago, and pottery from at least 4000 B.C.E. Bronze Age cultures also flourished in the region around 2000 B.C.E. However, none of the people who left these artifacts behind can be definitively connected to the Iranian-speaking Sogdians. The eighth and seventh centuries B.C.E. encompassed a period of urban expansion in the region, with cities developing around Samarkand and Bukhara; areas around both these cities had extensive irrigation canals, up to 60 miles in length.

HISTORY

The first written records of the Sogdians belong to the period of Persian Achaemenid dominance

---

SOGDIANS

location:
The Zaravshan and Kashka Darya river valleys of Transoxiana, between the Oxus (today's Amu Darya) and Jaxartes (today's Syr Darya) rivers; alternatively known as Western Turkestan. Today this region lies in part of Tajikistan and Uzbekistan.

time period:
sixth century B.C.E. to 13th century C.E.

ancestry:
Indo-Iranian

language:
Sogdian, a Northeastern Iranian language that has been largely extinct since the 11th century. The main script of Sogdiana was Aramaic, but the many Sogdian migrants in Central and East Asia used different scripts depending on the religion of the writer: Manichean script, Christian script, Buddhist script.

Sogdians time line

B.C.E.

sixth century Mention of Sogdians at the court of the Achaemenid rulers Darius and Xerxes provides the first evidence of the existence of these people.

329–327 Alexander the Great of Macedonia invades the region and combines Sogdiana and Bactria into one political unit, or satrapy.

Destruction of the city of Maracanda (Samarkand).

323 Alexander the Great dies at Babylon, and Bactria and Sogdiana are taken over by the Seleucid Empire, with its base in Antioch in today's Syria.

235 The Greco-Bactrian kingdom is established in the former Greek satrapy of Bactria, which includes Sogdiana, by descendants of Alexander the Great's soldiers. Diodotus II is the first Greco-Bactrian king, though his father had started the decades-long process of breaking free of Seleucid rule.

230 Euthydemus I deposes Diodotus II.

Sogdiana regains its independence or is invaded by nomads from the north. The history is unclear as to why the Sogdians are no longer ruled by the Greco-Bactrian kingdom.

C.E.

first century Sogdiana is enveloped in the powerful Kushan empire.

260 Sogdiana is ruled by a royal governor of the Persian Sassanids, but little evidence of the period exists.

early fourth century The Ancient Sogdian Letters, a series of letters in this language discovered in western Gansu Province 1907 by archaeologist Aurel Stein and probably written in the early fourth century C.E., point to a string of Sogdian colonies on the Silk Road, including in China.

509 Sogdians conquered by the Hephthalites, or White Huns.

565 Sogdians recapture their lands with the assistance of the Gokturks, who protect Sogdian trade and commerce and employ Sogdians as diplomats.

650 Sogdiana reestablishes its de facto independence, although nominally under a Chinese Tang dynasty protectorate; its capital, Samarkand, expands rapidly.

715 The Arabs under the Omayid dynasty begin their assault on Sogdiana, with no Chinese opposition.

722 Devashtich, who rules from the Sogdian city of Panjikent, is captured and killed by Arabs at his castle on Mount Mugh.

750 on Considerable Sogdian migration away from their central Asian home begins because the Arab Abbasid dynasty forces Islamicization.

13th century Final disintegration of any remnant of Sogdian culture during the Mongol invasion.

strong mercantile culture, which eventually saw them as the dominant merchants of the entire Silk Road, from Byzantium to China; their language and culture spread well beyond the boundaries of their small homeland in Central Asia. Sogdian texts have been discovered as far west as Belgium and as far east as Japan, carried by Sogdian merchants and migrants working along the ancient trade routes between East and West.

In 329 B.C.E. Alexander the Great marched into Central Asia and conquered the area of the Sogdians, administering them along with their Bactrian neighbors in one satrapy, or province. One of Alexander's first goals was to cut off the border between his own newly won territory and the nomadic Scythians to the north. This, along with the suppression of their religion, angered both the Sogdians and the Scythians and quickly set off wave after wave of armed rebellion, reaching the stage of a full-fledged war in Sogdiana. No one claimed to be the ultimate ruler of all Sogdiana, but small bands of men under a commander, or *hyparch* in Greek, attacked Greek forces and then quickly disappeared into the countryside. The main warlord was a Sogdian named Spitamenes, who began his rebellion by attacking the capital city of Samarkand. During the course of several years the warlords all lost or gave up trying to fight Alexander's forces; when Spitamenes was killed, his head was delivered to Alexander as proof of the victory. Alexander went on to marry the daughter of one of these warlords—Roxanne, daughter of Oxyartes—and thus became forever linked to this furthest outpost of his kingdom. One of Alexander's generals, Seleucus, founder of the Seleucid kingdom, also married a Sogdian, Apame, daughter of Spitamenes; she is often called the mother of the Seleucid dynasty.

Eventually, under Alexander's forces, the later Greek kingdoms of the Seleucids and Greco-Bactrians, and under later conquerors such as the KUSHANS, the Sogdians settled into the routines they had developed under the Persians. About half the population engaged in agriculture while the other half engaged in crafts and trade. Both the rural and urban Sogdians, however, were forced to reckon almost constantly with their nomadic neighbors to the north and east. These steppe-dwelling nomads both raided the settled population's resources and brought their herds across the river to graze on Sogdiana's fertile land.

By the fourth century C.E. the Sogdians had spread far beyond their Central Asian homeland. Colonies of Sogdian traders are often

of the region. In the sixth century B.C.E. Sogdiana, like its southern neighbor Bactria, was held by the Persians in a loose relationship that allowed the Sogdians to interact freely with their nomadic neighbors to the north, the SCYTHIANS. Under Persian rule the Sogdians developed a

mentioned in Chinese writings, and their own language became the lingua franca of the entire Silk Road. The Turkic *khagan*s who conquered the region in the sixth century supported these trading efforts and provided security from nomadic marauders; the Chinese did the same on the eastern branches of the trade route. Finally, however, the Sogdians were overrun in the seventh century by a force that was not willing to let them continue to practice their own religions, speak their own language, or dominate the trade routes between Asia and Europe: the Arabs. The Arab empires of the Omayids and Abbasids combined the Iranian-speaking Sogdians with their Persian neighbors into one administrative unit, and the Persians, with their superior numbers and ancient literary traditions, gradually subsumed the Sogdians. Enforced Islamicization also contributed to the loss of many Sogdian cultural traits, which were connected to their dominant religion, Zoroastrianism.

For a number of centuries, colonies of Sogdians continued to thrive further east, and as a result a significant amount of written material in the Sogdian language exists today. However, without a linguistic or cultural homeland to continue to replenish their numbers, eventually all traces of a live Sogdian culture disappeared with the Mongol invasions of the 12th century. The sole exception is in the Yaghnob Valley, a remote area of Tajikistan inhabited by the Yaghnobi people who continue to speak a Sogdian language today.

CULTURE

The combination of archaeological and textual sources on early Sogdian culture is a bit unclear regarding the structure of their society. Sogdian society has been likened in the literature both to European feudalism and Greek city-states, but neither comparison quite fits. The warlord culture that Alexander encountered points to something neither as centralized nor as stable as either feudal society or city-states. There is also evidence that at least a few rulers in Samarkand were chosen by the people rather than enjoying inherited positions; sadly, there is no explanation of how these leaders were chosen. This kind of sociopolitical structure is quite different from the Persian Iranians to the southwest, who very early were organized into centralized kingdoms and states. This decentralization made the region vulnerable to the many different empires that marched through and conquered Sogdiana, but it also made it very difficult for most of those empires to solidify their rule, since the local leaders had no tradition of relinquishing their power to a central figure.

While the political structure of Sogdian society remains a bit of a mystery, we do know that it was quite an urbanized society in which rural peoples paid in both goods and services to the urban owners of the land they worked on; smaller communities also paid tribute to larger towns and cities, but the records are silent on the amounts or kinds of payments made. We also know that the society was divided into semiseparate classes of aristocrats, merchants, and workers. There may also have been a slave class since the word used for workers also meant "free, nonslave," which indicates that other workers may have been enslaved. These classes were probably not rigidly defined; the remains of a great number of both aristocratic and merchant houses have been found, built in similar architectural styles and with similar decoration. There was an especially rich tradition of painting houses with murals. This indicates that merchants were probably able to move up the social ladder once they obtained the resources to emulate the symbolic attributes of the aristocrats.

The main activities of rural Sogdians were producing grain, largely wheat and rice, horses, and sheep. After the Greek invasion, Sogdians were vintners who helped in the dissemination of both grape vines and a wine culture in the East. For urban people, trade was the most important route to wealth and nobility. Craftsmen worked in metal, cloth, and ceramics and were famous for their silk products.

The Sogdians were primarily known throughout history as merchants and middlemen on the trade routes between China and Central Asia; they have been called the most important players on the Silk Road. As cosmopolitans living and working in such a multicultural business, the Sogdians were open to influences from both East and West. Their own religion, Zoroastrianism, remained the dominant religious force in the Sogdian homelands. However, from their trade with China and India, there also exist a great number of texts and murals depicting scenes from Buddhism, which remained an important religion among some Sogdians until the seventh century. A number of Sogdian gods and goddesses resembled their Hindu counterparts, with the main three male deities, Zrvan, Adbag, and Vesparkar, similar to the Hindu deities Brahma, Indra, and

SOLOMON ISLANDERS

location:
Solomon Islands

time period:
Possibly 30,000 B.C.E. to
the present

ancestry:
Melanesian

language:
About 120 indigenous
languages (85 percent
Melanesian, 9 percent
Papuan, 4 percent
Polynesian) plus Solomon
Island pidgin. English is
the official language but
is spoken by less than 3
percent of the population.

Mahadeva, respectively. Texts also show that a number of emigrant Sogdian communities had taken up Nestorian Christianity sometime after the fifth century, while after the third century still others practiced Manichaeanism, an Iranian religion with no omnipotent god at its center.

See also BACTRIANS; GREEKS; INDO-ARY-ANS; MONGOLS; PERSIANS, ACHAEMENIDS; PERSIANS, SASSANIDS.

FURTHER READING

Guitty Azarpay. *Sogdian Painting: The Pictorial Epic in Oriental Art* (Berkeley and Los Angeles: University of California Press, 1981).
Boris Marshak. *Legends, Tales, and Fables in the Art of Sogdiana* (New York: Bibliotheca Persica Press, 2002).

Solomon Islanders

About 85 percent of Solomon Islanders live in rural areas and continue to practice subsistence farming and fishing. Sweet potatoes, taro, and cassava (tapioca) are the main subsistence crops, and both plantains and breadfruit are also important tree crops that provide starch in the diet. Leafy vegetables, beans, and other imported vegetable plants are also grown and along with fish provide a fairly nutritionally balanced diet if pests, typhoons, or other disasters do not interrupt the local production of food. Most Solomon Islanders supplement their subsistence foods with cereals and processed foods purchased with the proceeds of cash-cropping coconuts, cocoa, and a few other products, other forms of labor, or remittances from urban relatives.

As is the case throughout the Pacific, kinship remains the most important social category recognized on the islands. The great diversity in the country, with more than 100 different languages spoken, means that there is a diversity of kinship systems as well. Patrilineal, matrilineal, and ambilineal kinship systems are all in evidence throughout the islands. In patrilineal systems, individuals trace their membership in their lineage and clan through their father, paternal grandfather, and so forth; matrilineal systems create lineages and clans with descent traced through mothers, maternal grandmothers, and so forth. Ambilineal systems are more complex in that each individual is allowed to choose whether to join his or her mother's or father's lineage; once the choice is made, the structure works the same as one of the unilineal systems described above. Regardless of the specific kinship system, kinship itself is vitally important to all Solomon Islanders for determining friends and enemies, marriage partners, ties of obligation and reciprocity, and access to land and resources. Kinship continues to be far more important than regional or national ties for almost all Solomon Islanders today.

Another important feature of Solomon Island culture today is the relative lack of hierarchy in social relations. Traditionally, MELANESIANS in general did not have centralized authority figures who could exert their power over others, such as the chiefs who ruled over most POLYNESIANS. Instead, most Melanesian societies, including those throughout the Solomon Islands, were competitive ones in which all men had an equal opportunity to become a local Big Man. Big Men earned their position by giving away pigs, shell money, or other prestige items and thus creating bonds of mutual obligation with large numbers of other men. These ties gave the Big Man a certain degree of influence over others but no authority to sanction others for not following him. This aspect of Solomon Island society has made it extremely difficult for a centralized national government to control its people, leading to much localization, chaos, and even violence at times during the past decade.

Although these precolonial social structures remain central to most Solomon Islanders' lives, many changes were also introduced during the past two centuries of colonial and postcolonial history. Perhaps the most important for average Solomon Islanders was the introduction of Christianity in the 19th and 20th centuries. While many pre-Christian beliefs and taboos remain important, especially ancestor worship and ideas about spirits, Christianity also plays a central role in most people's lives. Almost every village in the country has at least one Christian church, usually the Church of Melanesia, an Anglican offshoot, or Roman Catholic and services are commonly held at least once a day.

See also SOLOMON ISLANDERS: NATIONALITY.

Solomon Islanders: nationality
(people of the Solomon Islands)

The Solomon Islanders are the citizens of the independent country of the Solomon Islands.

GEOGRAPHY

The Solomon Islands, a 900-mile-long chain of South Pacific islands that stretch from Papua New Guinea to Vanuatu, is the second-largest country in Melanesia after Papua New Guinea and is made up of six major islands (Choiseul, New Georgia, Santa Isabel, Guadalcanal, Malaita, and Makira) and almost 1,000 small islands and atolls. Altogether they cover about 17,113 square miles of land. While the larger islands are characterized by rugged mountains and contain significant untapped reserves in lead, zinc, nickel, and gold, the smaller islands and atolls are low-lying and mostly made of coral.

INCEPTION AS A NATION

The initial settlement of the Solomon Islands began around 30,000 years ago when MELANESIANS who had migrated from New Britain and New Ireland in New Guinea inhabited the northern islands. After this initial settlement, it is probable that another 15,000 years passed before further contact between these island communities was made. It also took another 9,000 years or so for the southern islands, or at least Guadalcanal, to be inhabited by these early explorers, perhaps around 6,000 years ago. Before the arrival of the Lapita pottery makers and speakers of Austronesian languages from Southeast Asia about 3,000 years ago, these early Melanesians were breeding domesticated pigs and engaging in the cultivation of various tree crops. When the bearers of LAPITA CULTURE arrived, they brought their distinctive pottery, chickens, and other domesticated plants, such as taro and sugar cane; these and other features blended with the local Melanesian culture to form the distinct island culture of the Solomons.

The SOLOMON ISLANDERS' first encounter with Europeans came in 1568 when Álvaro de Mendana de Neira, a Spaniard, visited the region in his quest to find the gold and other treasure of the biblical King Solomon. He claimed to have found the king's lands, but later Spanish explorers were unable to support his claims. Few European visitors followed the Spanish until the British began charting the islands two centuries later; more explorers and traders followed, especially after the settlement of Sydney, Australia, in 1788. Early attempts at bringing Christianity to the islands brought mixed results; Roman Catholics failed to set up a mission in the 1840s, but Anglicans began taking Solomon Islanders to New Zealand in the 1850s to train them as missionaries. Foreign and domestic Anglican missions started working in the islands in the 1870s, while Catholics finally set up their first mission in 1898. Much of this early proselytizing was unsuccessful, however, because of the devastating effects of blackbirding on local societies. Between 1870 and 1910, about 30,000 people were taken from the Solomon Islands as forced laborers from the plantations of Fiji, Queensland, Australia, and elsewhere in the Pacific. Very few of these laborers ever returned home.

Outright colonization of the Solomon Islands occurred in the 1890s when Britain declared the chain a protectorate and then later set up a complete colonial administration. The British also received all of Germany's prior holdings in the region in exchange for recognition of German interests in Western Samoa. Despite the trade, the colony was not a lucrative one for Britain. The region's many mineral resources went undetected, and the coconut plantations that were established in the early 20th century failed to make much money. Blackbirding came to an end in 1910, which opened the doors for the missionaries to work more successfully, but Christianity in the Solomons has always been a highly syncretic form, blending Christian and indigenous beliefs into a new religious tradition.

World War II brought significant changes to the Solomons in the form of many devastating battles between the United States and Japan. Between August 1942 and December 1943 these two countries engaged in almost constant warfare in the Solomons, including the six-month-long Battle of Guadalcanal, often pointed to as a turning point in the war in the Pacific. Solomon Islanders were more than just victims and bystanders in these events; many served as scouts, laborers, and guides during the war, and many others were killed. During the war some local Solomon Islanders began to agitate for a change in their subordinate position as well. Their movement, called Marching Law or, in pidgin, Martin Lo, was a blend of anticolonialism, cargo cult, and millenarianism, or a belief in the end of the world. Members refused to work for the Europeans and Americans and believed the Americans would return to the Solomons with a Liberty Ship full of cargo brought just for them. Some members also believed the Americans would fight off the British, who were seen as much more stingy with their goods than the generous Americans, and would drive them back into the ocean. Despite these negative aspects from the British point of view, Britain did not outlaw the movement initially because of the positive elements they saw in it: unification and political organization

SOLOMON ISLANDERS: NATIONALITY

nation:
Solomon Islands

derivation of name:
Named after King Solomon when the Spanish explorer Álvaro de Mendaña de Neira claimed to have found the king's famous treasure there

government:
Constitutional monarchy with the prime minister as head of government and British monarch as head of state

capital:
Honiara

language:
About 120 indigenous languages (85 percent Melanesian, 9 percent Papuan, 4 percent Polynesian) plus Solomon Islander pidgin; English is the official language but is spoken by less than 3 percent of the population.

religion:
Church of Melanesia 32.8 percent, Roman Catholic 19 percent, South Seas Evangelical 17 percent, Seventh-Day Adventist 11.2 percent, United Church 10.3 percent, Christian Fellowship Church 2.4 percent, other Christian 4.4 percent, other 2.4 percent, unspecified 0.3 percent, none 0.2 percent

earlier inhabitants:
None

demographics:
Melanesian 94.5 percent, Polynesian 3 percent, Micronesian 1.2 percent, other 1.1 percent, unspecified 0.2 percent

Solomon Islanders: nationality time line

B.C.E.

30,000 Probable era of Melanesian settlement on the Solomon Islands after spreading out from northern Sahul, contemporary New Guinea.

1,5000 Further Melanesian expansion from New Guinea.

6000 Melanesian settlement on Guadalcanal and the other southern islands in the chain.

1000 Lapita culture arrives in the Solomons with its distinctive pottery.

C.E.

1568 The Solomon Islands are visited by Spanish explorer Álvaro de Mendaña de Neira, who names them after the biblical King Solomon. He also names Guadalcanal and Malaita, two of the biggest islands in the chain.

1767 British captain Philip Carteret begins to chart the Solomon Islands.

1840s Roman Catholic missionaries fail in their attempt to establish a mission in the islands.

1850s Anglican missionaries begin taking people from the Solomons to New Zealand for religious training; they establish a mission there 20 years later, the foundation for today's Church of Melanesia.

1870s Blackbirding begins, taking about 30,000 islanders as forced laborers to Fiji, Australia, and elsewhere in the Pacific over the next 40 years.

1886 Britain and Germany divide the islands in the chain between them.

1893 The British declare the Solomon Islands a protectorate with full-scale colonization established three years later.

1898 Roman Catholic missionaries finally succeed in setting up a mission.

1899 Germany transfers ownership of its Solomon Islands holdings to Britain in exchange for Western Samoa.

Early 20th century British and Australian companies begin setting up coconut plantations throughout the islands, with little economic gain for either colonized or colonizer.

---

of the previously anarchic Melanesians, a push for education and health care, and caring for the elderly. By the late 1940s, however, the British colonial administration, which had returned after the war, was trying to put a stop to the marches, rallies, and "mass hysteria" they saw in Marching Law. After some of the leaders were imprisoned, the movement finally dissipated in 1953, when the British installed local councils and allowed the Solomon Islanders to vote for their own leadership.

This action in the 1950s set the stage for the decolonization of the entire political process in the Solomons. In 1960 legislative and executive councils were created, and these bodies were granted more and more authority as time progressed. In 1974 a new constitution established a full parliamentary democracy in the islands, and two years later self-rule was instituted, followed by complete independence in 1978.

Unfortunately, independence did not bring peace and prosperity to the Solomon Islands.

A mass movement of people just after the war from the island of Malaita to the new capital, Honiara, on Guadalcanal, contributed to several generations of competition, unrest, and sometimes violence. The year 1998 brought this issue to a head when the Isatabu Freedom Movement started forcing the Malaitans off the island and the rival Malaitan Eagle Force began to fight back. This latter group staged a coup in 2000 because of the 20,000 Malaitans who had been pushed out of their homes and the 100 or so who had died during the years of unrest. Peace was brokered by Australia within the year but was never really established outside the room in which the deal was signed. A 15-country regional peacekeeping mission, Regional Assistance Mission to Solomon Islands (RAMSI), was deployed in 2003 to deal with the lawlessness and remains in the country today at the request of the government of the Solomon Islands. In April 2006 rioting in the capital after a parliamentary election set

1942 The U.S. Navy lands on Guadalcanal, beginning about a year and a half of hard fighting between the United States and Japan in the Solomons. Thousands of Americans, Japanese, and Solomon Islanders are killed, and the coconut plantations are destroyed.

1944 The Marching Law movement begins.

1945 British colonial rule returns and moves the capital to Honiara, which had been a large U.S. Navy base.

1953 The Marching Law movement finally disbands permanently.

1960 The Solomon Islanders are given a degree of autonomy in legislative and executive councils.

1974 A new constitution establishes parliamentary democracy.

1976 The first elected government achieves self-rule in the Solomons.

1978 The Solomon Islands win independence from Britain.

Mid-1990s Japanese, Korean, and Malaysian loggers cut down tropical hardwoods in the Solomon Islands at a rate three times that which is sustainable. This is slowed by the economic crisis in Asia in 1997.

1998 Ethnic unrest in the capital leads to the formation of two rival militia groups.

2000 A coup deposes Prime Minister Ulufa'alu.

2003 The prime minister, Sir Allen Kemakeza, requests Australian help in restoring law and order.

2006 Elections bring widespread change to Parliament: 50 percent of MPs lose their seats; a new prime minister, Manasseh Sogavare, is elected; and renewed ethnic violence and rioting occur as a result.

2007 A series of earthquakes and tsunamis destroy several villages and islands, leaving hundreds dead and many others displaced.

Prime Minister Michael Sogavare loses a vote of confidence in Parliament and steps down.

back some of the reconstruction of both political and economic infrastructure that had occurred in 2003, and the country's future continues to look bleak.

CULTURAL IDENTITY

With more than 100 different linguistic and cultural groups represented in the country, successive governments of the Solomon Islands have never been able to unify their people into a cohesive national community. Regional, ethnic, and linguistic differences, combined with traditional cultures that do not recognize outside authority figures, have led to years of strife and even violence. During the colonial era the British tried to create chiefs who would act as mediators between colonized and colonizer as they had done successfully in many other regions of the world. In Melanesia, however, no such position had ever existed, and all men could compete for the position of Big Man, a role of prestige and temporary power but no legitimate authority. This lack of any tradition of central authority is clearly evident today in the continued importance of ethnolinguistic and regional ties over national ones, even for populations that have lived in the capital and other urban areas for several generations.

Two concepts that do have a somewhat mollifying effect on the decentralization inherent in Solomon Island politics are religion and *kastom*. About 95 percent of Solomon Islanders today consider themselves Christian and attend some form of Christian church regularly. Beside their Christian beliefs, however, is an undercurrent of traditional ideas about ancestors, spirits, taboos, and other pre-Christian elements. These syncretic religious beliefs provide one common identity shared by most Solomon Islanders. The other feature shared by most Solomon Islanders is the centrality of *kastom* in their lives. *Kastom* is the pidgin term for "custom" and points to the importance of indigenous kinship, subsistence foods, art forms,

SRI LANKAN MOORS.

location:
Sri Lanka

time period:
Possibly sixth century to
the present

ancestry:
Arab, Malay, Sinhalese,
and Tamil

language:
Tamil, Sinhala, and a
Malay creole; all three
languages have sig-
nificant borrowings from
Arabic.

beliefs and rituals, and the whole panoply of features of traditional culture. Most political movements and parties draw on the idea of *kastom* to legitimate their platforms, and the few individuals who think of their identity in terms of a unit larger than kinship identify *kastom* as the central feature of this identity.

See also AUSTRONESIANS.

FURTHER READING

Michael Kwa'ioloa. *Living Tradition: A Changing Life in Solomon Islands* (Honolulu: University of Hawaii Press, 1997).

I. Q. Lasaqa. *Melanesians' Choice: Tadhimboko Participation in the Solomon Islands Cash Economy* (Portland, Oreg.: International Scholarly Book Services, 1972).

Geoffrey M. White, David Gegeo, Karen Ann Watson-Gegeo, and David Akin, eds. *Bikfala Faet: Olketa Solomon Aelanda Rimembarem Wol Wo Tu / The Big Death: Solomon Islanders Remember World War II* (Suva, Fiji: Institute of Pacific Studies, 1988).

South Moluccans   *See* AMBONESE.

Sri Lankan Moors (Muslims)

The Moors of Sri Lanka are the island's Muslim population. They come from different backgrounds, including Arab, Malay, Muslim Indian, as well as local SINHALESE and Tamil converts to Islam. In 2001 they made up slightly more than 7 percent of Sri Lanka's population.

The Moors of Arab descent are the most ancient residents of this group, having arrived more than 1,000 years ago. Arab traders and explorers from the Middle East may have landed on Sri Lanka as far back as the sixth century C.E., during the life of the prophet Mohammed. Certainly by the 10th century Sri Lanka had its own Arab community living in the southwest, mostly engaged in long-distance trade but also dealing with the local population. The Sinhalese kings who ruled the country in this period generally employed Arab merchants and traders and even retained Arabs in their royal courts to deal with the kingdoms' commercial affairs. Over time some Arab men married local women, especially TAMILS, and adopted that language for use both at home and in the marketplace. Today Arab Moors make up about 93 percent of the country's entire Muslim population and continue to play a large role in trade and commercial interests in contemporary Sri Lanka.

In addition to the Arab Moors, Sri Lanka also has a small population of Muslims who originally came from India during the colonial period. Some of these Indian Muslims arrived during the 16th and 17th centuries, when the Portuguese dominated politics and economy on what they called Ceylon. They came largely as merchants and traders interested in benefiting from the opportunities that a stable European population on the island afforded them for making money. Others, especially Tamil speakers who are today part of the Estate Tamil minority, came to British-dominated Ceylon in the 19th and early 20th centuries to work on the tea plantations that thrived on the island.

The third group of Muslim migrants were the MALAYS who came to the island during the Dutch colonial period, 1656–1796, from the Dutch East Indies, contemporary Indonesia. Many of these Malay migrants served as soldiers in the Dutch colonial army and then decided to settle permanently on Sri Lanka and marry local women. Still other Malays arrived on Sri Lanka with their entire families, having been deported there either as convicts or as Indonesian nobility exiled by the Dutch administration. Unlike the other Sri Lankan Moors, they retain some Malay words and customs even today and reside almost exclusively in Colombo. They make up only about 5 percent of the island's present-day Moor population.

In contemporary Sri Lanka there are also communities of both Sri Lankan Tamils and Sinhalese who have converted to Islam. While religion divides them from the rest of their ethnolinguistic communities, for Muslim Tamils there is a much greater political division that arises from their lack of support for a separate Tamil state of Tamil Eelam. Most Muslim Tamils reside in the country's southeast, outside the historic Tamil regions in the north and northeast. Many are concerned that if a separate Tamil state comes into existence, their own lives in Sinhalese-dominated Sri Lanka will become much more difficult, and thus they have largely supported the Sinhalese state against the Tamil rebels. Since 2001 groups of Muslim and Hindu Tamils have occasionally turned violent, which confounded the simple conception of a two-party struggle that has dominated most discussions of the Sri Lankan civil war.

See also SRI LANKANS: NATIONALITY.

Sri Lankans: nationality (Lankans, people of Sri Lanka)

Sri Lanka is an island nation made up of two separate ethnic groups, the dominant SINHALESE and the minority TAMILS, who have been at war with the Sinhalese state since 1983.

Sri Lankans: nationality time line

B.C.E.

1400 Sri Lanka begins exporting cinnamon to Egypt.

504 Conquered by Indian prince Vijaya, who names Sri Lanka "Sinhala" after his patrimonial name.

fourth century Sri Lanka is the first country in the world to establish a dedicated hospital, Mihintale.

47–42 First female ruler of any Asian nation, Queen Anula.

C.E.

third–12th centuries Sri Lanka is dominated by Tamil kings and various invaders from India.

sixth century Buddhist monks start recording Sri Lankan history in *The Mahavansa* and continue to do so until 1815. *The Mahavansa* is seen as both a historical chronicle and a work of literature.

1408–38 The Chinese occupy Sri Lanka and partition it into a number of small kingdoms.

1505 The first Portuguese arrive as colonial missionaries.

1517 The Portuguese establish friendly relations with Sri Lankan monarchs and found Colombo as a trading port. By the end of the century they control most of the island.

1638 The Dutch attack Portuguese rule and are supported by many locals.

1658 The Dutch gain control over Sri Lanka, except for the province of Kandy.

1796 The British East India Company declares control of the island and changes the name to Ceylon.

1802 Treaty of Amiens formally cedes Sri Lanka to Britain. Kandy still resists foreign rule.

1815 Kandy is occupied and annexed to Britain, thus putting the whole island under British rule. *The Mahavansa* ceases to be written.

1817–48 Several unsuccessful rebellions against British rule. There are also violent struggles between the Buddhist peasants and Muslim moneylenders.

1870s The British introduce their own tea and rubber plantations, expanding the plantation economy begun by the Dutch and dominating Sri Lanka's economy until the 1970s. Local Sinhalese are unwilling to work cheaply for the British on the plantations, so the British import indentured workers from Tamil Nadu, India. This not only changes the economic structure of Sri Lanka but is also the beginning of tensions between the Tamils and Sinhalese, which continue into the 21st century.

1931 Sri Lanka wins right to limited self-government; universal adult franchise is introduced.

1948 Sri Lanka gains independence from Britain with dominion status in the Commonwealth of Nations. D. S. Senanayake, leader of the United National Party (UNP), becomes prime minister. The ancient Sinhalese flag, which bears a lion, is adopted.

1955 Sri Lanka is admitted to the United Nations.

1956 General election is won by S. W. R. D. Bandaranaike, leader of the Sri Lanka Freedom Party (SLFP). Despite independence from Britain, English is still the national language. To rectify this, Sinhalese is declared the official and only national language. This alienates the sizable Tamil-speaking community and adds tension to already existing friction between the Tamils and Sinhalese.

1959 Bandaranaike is assassinated by a Buddhist monk.

1960 General election is won by Bandaranaike's widow, Sirimavo Bandaranaike. She becomes the first female prime minister in the world.

1970 Sinhalese is declared the only national language, causing discontent among the Tamil population.

(continues)

SRI LANKANS: NATIONALITY

nation:
Sri Lanka; the Democratic Socialist Republic of Sri Lanka

derivation of name:
Sri means "venerable" in Sanskrit, and *Lanka* is the name used to refer to Sri Lanka in the ancient Hindu epics, the *Mahabharata* and the *Ramayana*. When the Indian prince Vijaya became ruler in 540 B.C.E., he named the region Sinhala, meaning "of the lion people"; thus the lion appears on the Sri Lankan flag. The Turks called it Serendip, because they thought it a fortunate discovery. The Portuguese called it Ceilao, which changed to Ceylon under British rule from 1802 on. In 1972 it was officially changed back to Sri Lanka, although Ceylon is still often used in product marketing such as Ceylon tea.

government:
Social Democratic Republic; since 1948 Sri Lanka has adopted a republican constitution.

capital:
Sri Jayawardenapura is the administrative capital; Colombo is the commercial capital and largest city (pop. 750,000).

language:
Sinhala (official and national language) 74 percent, Tamil (national language) 18 percent, other 8 percent. English is spoken competently by about 10 percent of the population and is commonly used in government and commerce.

(continues)

**SRI LANKANS:
NATIONALITY**
(continued)

religion:
Buddhist 69.1 percent,
Muslim 7.6 percent,
Hindu 7.1 percent,
Christian 6.2 percent,
unspecified 10 percent

earlier inhabitants:
Earliest inhabitants were
the Veddhas, also known
as Wanniyala-Aetto peo-
ple and currently recog-
nized as the indigenous
people of Sri Lanka; their
population is only about
3,000.

demographics:
Sinhalese 74 percent,
Tamils 18 percent; the
rest of the population
is made up of Burghers
(European descent),
Moors, Malays, and
Veddhas.

Sri Lankans: nationality time line *(continued)*

1971	The National Film Corporation of Sri Lanka established.
1972	Name officially changes from Ceylon to the Republic of Sri Lanka, with independence from Britain.
1975	The world's first elephant orphanage, at Pinnawela, is established.
1977	General election won by J. R. Jayewardene. He takes a number of steps to restore economic and political stability, including giving the Tamil language the status of national language in Tamil-dominated areas; however, clashes between Tamils and Sinhalese continue.
1981	Sinhalese singer and composer Sunil Santha dies. He has had a significant impact on defining modern Sri Lankan music.
1983	Start of civil war between Sinhalese-dominated government and the Liberation Tigers of Tamil Eelam (LTTE), also known as the Tamil Tigers. As a result of the fighting, more than 50,000 citizens end up in Sri Lankan refugee camps, and more than 100,000 Tamils flee to India. Sri Lanka's economy is severely affected as many businesses are destroyed and tourists are afraid to visit the country.
1987	Indian troops (IPKF) are stationed in northern Sri Lanka, attempting to enforce peace.
1993	Assassination of two leading politicians, including President Ranasinghe Premadasa, allegedly by the LTTE. Government military base in Pooneryn seized by LTTE.
1997	Government offensive Operation Jaya Sikuru (Sure Victory) is launched against the LTTE.
1998	Sri Lanka's most holy Buddhist shrine at Kandy is attacked by a suicide bomber, and 11 visitors are killed. The LTTE are outlawed by government.
	Ambalavaner Sivandan wins the Commonwealth Writers Prize in the Asia-Oceania region for his book *When Memory Dies*.
1999	General election called 11 months early. Kumaratunga is reelected president.
2000	Kumaratunga's People's Alliance wins general election.
2001	United National Party wins majority; Ranil Wickramasinghe becomes prime minister. LTTE announces cease-fire, a move that is reciprocated by the new government.
2002	Permanent cease-fire agreement signed between LTTE and government, and decommissioning of weapons started.
2004	In December, an Indian Ocean earthquake creates powerful tsunamis that devastate the southeast coast of Sri Lanka, killing more than 40,000 people and displacing many more. The rebuilding and recovery process has been slow.
2006	The Sri Lankan army stages an attack to free a waterway leading to the port of Trincomalee; this is just one of many skirmishes during 2005–06 that claim the lives of an unconfirmed 3,000 people, according to government sources.
2008	Heavy fighting throughout the previous year pushes the government of Sri Lanka to withdraw from the 2002 cease-fire agreement; roadside bombings kill several dozen people including D. M. Dassanayake, a government minister.

GEOGRAPHY

Sri Lanka is a small tropical island south of India, straddling the Bay of Bengal and the Indian Ocean. It is a mere 219 miles long and 114 miles at its widest point, with a population of 20,000,000 living in nine separate provinces. About 75 percent of the island's population live in the rural areas.

Sri Lanka's famous tea plantations are located in the high mountainous areas in the central southern region of the island. As the island stretches to the north it becomes flatter and drier. The highest mountain is Piduratalagala, at 8,281 feet; however, Adam's Peak (7,135 feet) is better known and regarded as the island's holiest mountain.

Sri Lanka still has a significant number of untouched rainforests teeming with birds and wild mammals, including the endangered sloth bears, leopards, and elephants. At the beginning of the 20th century, 70 percent of Sri Lanka was covered with untouched rainforest, which by 1981 had shrunk to 20 percent. The aggressive development of a plantation economy has taken its toll on Sri Lanka's rainforests.

INCEPTION AS A NATION

Ancient Sri Lanka, known as Sinhala, was, for centuries, ruled by a succession of Tamil invaders from southern India. In 504 B.C.E. Prince Vijaya conquered the island, married a native princess, and named his realm after his patrimonial name, Sinhala, meaning "of the lion people." This conquest coincided with the Buddha's enlightenment, and the Sinhalese people adopted Buddhism as their religion instead of Hinduism brought by the Indians. Although the Indians also brought the caste system to Sri Lanka, it was only loosely adopted by the Sinhala people because the Buddha abhorred the system.

Sri Lanka has long been an important trading post, invaded and ruled by other nations including the Dutch, the Portuguese, and the British. With each change of rule Sri Lanka's status as an autonomous nation was threatened. British rule in the 19th–20th centuries had a significant impact, not only because it brought a strong Western influence but also because it solidified the economic structure introduced by the Dutch by focusing entirely on a plantation economy, primarily in tea and rubber. Furthermore, because the Sinhalese refused to work on the British-owned plantations, the British imported itinerant workers from India's state of Tamil Nadu. This was the beginning of tensions between the Tamils and Sinhalese.

Nevertheless, Sri Lankans collectively wanted their independence from foreign rule, but their independence was hard won. There were a few unsuccessful rebellions against the British between 1817 and 1848. The struggle against European rule then continued, although in a dormant state. In 1931 the struggle became active when the Youth League, led by a core of left-wing intellectuals, opposed the ministers' memorandum that petitioned the government to increase the power of ministers who did not truly represent the people. The Youth League succeeded in its opposition, and this led to universal franchise for all adult citizens of Sri Lanka. The pressure for independence grew, and in 1948 Sri Lanka was granted independence as the Commonwealth of Ceylon.

In 1972 Sri Lanka became a democratic republic within the British Commonwealth and reclaimed its ancient name of Sri Lanka, discarding the British name of Ceylon. However, it now had to deal with increasing hostilities from the Tamils, who felt marginalized and discriminated against by the Sinhalese-dominated government. Conflict surfaced in the 1970s when Sinhalese was officially made the only national language in Sri Lanka. By 1983, tensions had erupted into a civil war between the Sinhalese state and Tamil separatists, the Liberation Tigers of Tamil Eelam (LTTE), known as Tamil Tigers, who wanted an autonomous Tamil state. The violence of the civil war shattered the long-standing peace and stability of the island, which is predominately Buddhist and adheres to the Buddhist precepts of nonviolence. Since then, thousands of people have been killed and hundreds of thousands displaced. In 2002 the government and the LTTE signed a cease-fire, but the political situation was uneasy and the status between the two parties was one of neither war nor peace. In 2006 hostilities escalated again, and the violence has continued into

---

Sirimavo Bandaranaike

Sirimavo Bandaranaike is famous for becoming the world's first female prime minister when she was elected in Sri Lanka in 1960. Born on April 17, 1916, she married Solomon Bandaranaike, who in 1951 founded the Sri Lanka Freedom Party (SLFP), a nonrevolutionary socialist organization that took power in 1956 when Solomon Bandaranaike was elected prime minister. Solomon was assassinated in 1959, at which point Sirimavo assumed his post as leader of the SLFP. In 1960 she was elected prime minister, and she continued her husband's socialist policies, such as the nationalization of banking and insurance, as well as a policy of nonalignment. Shortly after her election, she implemented the exclusion of English as an official language and ordered all business transactions to be conducted in Sinhala, the language of the majority Sinhalese. These policies enraged the minority Tamil population, which accused Bandaranaike of trying to exclude Tamils from Sri Lankan business and government. She went on to order a state takeover of foreign businesses, which resulted in an aid embargo being imposed on Sri Lanka by the United States and the United Kingdom. Her term ended in 1965, but she was reelected in 1970, at which point a new constitution was created and Sri Lanka was made a republic.

In 1973 an oil crisis crippled the Sri Lankan economy, which was already weakened by Bandaranaike's socialist policies, and rationing was enforced. Around this time she also called for the state takeover of the country's largest newspaper group, *Lake House,* and silenced her critics by quashing a large independent news group. Several uprisings and coup attempts were made during her time in office, but they were always defeated by the Sri Lankan military. In 1977 she was stripped of her civic rights due to her abuse of power. In 1994, however, she was reelected as prime minister, but wielded little power as her daughter, Chandrika Bandaranaike, had been elected president. She died on October 10, 2000.

2008, prompting the government to scrap the 2002 cease-fire agreement.

CULTURAL IDENTITY

Religion plays a significant part in Sri Lanka's cultural identity. The nation's population is 70 percent Buddhist, and many other Buddhist countries look to Sri Lanka as their spiritual home. Many Buddhist temples, *dagobas* (shrines), and larger-than-life statues of Buddha dominate the country's landscape. The holiest and best known of these is the Temple of the Tooth in Kandy, which houses the Buddha's sacred tooth. Despite the dominance of Buddhism, other religions such as Hinduism, Christianity, and Islam are practiced, and many colorful religious festivals are celebrated at various times of the year. These festivals also provide the opportunity for other aspects of Sri Lanka's culture to be displayed, such as traditional theater and dance, *kolam;* singing, *baila;* and of course an abundance of traditional foods, including spicy curries, sweet rice cooked in coconut milk, and hoppers, a thin, cup-shaped pancake made from a fermented rice-flour batter.

Sri Lanka is still predominately an agrarian society, with 75 percent of the population living in villages. Villagers also make traditional crafts such as batik fabrics and wooden masks for the theater. Village fishermen practice a rare and unique form of fishing called stilt fishing, where they climb up on stilts and wait for the tide to bring in the fish. However, Sri Lanka is not an isolated land cut off from globalization. Along with economic growth and the need to compete globally, Western culture is influencing the traditional way of life. This is most evident in the large urban centers such as Colombo and Jaffna, where more people wear Western-style clothes than traditional garb. English is becoming more frequently used in commerce and is being taught in most of Sri Lanka's schools, all of which are free, including the universities. Since Sri Lanka grows the world's best teas, it is no wonder that drinking tea has also become something of a national pastime. Another important Western influence, introduced by the British in the 19th century, is cricket, which has become a national sport. In a Test match between Sri Lanka and England held at Kandy in 2007, Muttiah Muralitharan became the leading Test wicket-taker of all time. As a Tamil, he believes that cricket can be a unifying influence on the island.

FURTHER READING

Roloff Beny and John Lindsay Opie. *Island: Ceylon* (Toronto: McLelland & Stewart Ltd., 1971).

The Temple of the Tooth in Dalada Maligawa, Kandy, holds what many Buddhists believe is a tooth from the Buddha himself. While the complex has been the target of several Tamil Tiger bomb attacks, the tooth has remained unharmed. *(OnAsia/Jerry Redfern)*

E. Valentine Daniel. *Charred Lullabies: Chapters in an Anthropography of Violence* (Princeton, N.J.: Princeton University Press, 1996).

Mohan Ram. *Sri Lanka: The Fractured Island* (New Delhi: Penguin Books, 1989).

Carla Risseeuw. *Gender Transformation, Power, and Resistance among Women in Sri Lanka: The Fish Don't Talk about the Water* (New Delhi: Manohar Publications, 1991).

Suluk   See TAUSUG.

Sundanese (Orang Sunda, Urang Prijangan, Urang Sunda)

The Sundanese are Indonesia's second-largest ethnic group with about 33 million members, or 14 percent of Indonesia's total. The vast majority live in Sunda or West Java, with only about 1 million spread out in Indonesia's other islands and provinces. Although west Java contains two extremely large cities, Bandung and the nation's capital of Jakarta, most Sundanese live in rural areas and make their living in agricultural pursuits.

The earliest history of the Sundanese remains a mystery, even to locals for whom there is no origin myth to explain their founding as a community. The Sundanese speak a Malayo-Polynesian language within the larger Austronesian phylum; we know that their language came to the Indonesian Archipelago between 2500 and 2000 B.C.E., and perhaps the ancestors of the Sundanese arrived at that time as well. The first written record of Sundanese life comes to us from the fifth century C.E. during the reign of King Purnavarman of the Tarumanagara dynasty. Seven short lines of text carved in stone have been found near contemporary Jakarta, which provide the name of this king and his dynasty; a description of his capital city, probably located along the Citarum River; and enough information to discern that this was a Hindu kingdom. There are no earlier records to indicate just how or when Indian civilization was introduced to island Southeast Asia, but it most likely is that traders from south India brought their religion and concepts of kingship with them; why the local population adopted them remains a mystery. This scenario is also somewhat challenged by the location of the most important Hindu kingdoms on Java, not on the coastline but inland. Regardless of the circumstances, western Java was Hindu for more than 1,000 years before the introduction of Islam around 1500.

Tarumanagara was a large and important enough trading center in the archipelago to attract the attention of the Chinese, who sent an envoy in about 413, but it probably did not survive there for more than two or three centuries. The kingdom's exact end date is unknown, but it was probably a victim of the expansion of the central JAVANESE Hindu kingdoms or the Srivijaya kingdom from Sumatra. In west Java several smaller states emerged, but none was able to consolidate the region until the Pajajaran kingdom with its capital near Bogor did so in 1333. Pajajaran existed during the final period of the Hindu states in Indonesia and sometimes paid tribute to Majapahit, the largest and most successful of these states in Java. Pajajaran, however, was known for its independence and in the end outlived its larger and more powerful neighbor by more than three-quarters of a century before finally falling to the Muslim kingdom of Banten in 1579.

From this period until the present day, Islam has been one of the most important cultural traits of people who identify themselves as Sundanese. Through 350 years of Dutch colonialism and efforts by missionaries to convert the population to Christianity, the Sundanese have steadfastly maintained their religion. Their anticolonial uprising in 1880 under the Qadiriyya religious order and the Darul Islam rebellion from 1948 till 1962 were both framed in terms of a holy war, the former against the Christian infidels and the latter against the secular Indonesian state.

The first Europeans to exert influence over at least a portion of the Sundanese were the Portuguese, who in 1522 came to the assistance of Banten when it was being attacked by the central Javanese kingdom of Demak. Two years later, however, the Bantenese ruler converted to Islam, abandoned his former allies of Pajajaran and Portugal, and joined forces with the sultan of Demak. From that period the Portuguese focused their efforts in the archipelago on other islands, such as Ambon, Aceh, and Timor, and Banten was able to expand into the entire region. In 1596 the Portuguese were joined in the East Indies by the Dutch, and one of the first places where they made contact was in Banten, west Java. In 1601 the Dutch conquered a fleet of Portuguese ships in Banten's harbor and began the long Dutch colonial era in west Java; they established a colonial capital at Jayakerta or Jakarta in 1611 to consolidate their lucrative colonial prize. Their hold over the city and its surrounding countryside was tenuous at best in the

SUNDANESE

location:
West Java, Indonesia

time period:
Possibly 2500 B.C.E. to the present

ancestry:
Austronesian

language:
Sunda, an Austronesian language, as well as Bahasa Indonesia, the national language

The Sundanese are particularly adept with these elaborate leather puppets used by the *dalang,* or master, to tell stories from the Hindu *Ramayana.* *(OnAsia/Erick Danzer)*

first years, but by 1619 they were secure enough to rename their capital city Batavia, the name by which it was known until World War II.

Like Islam, which has been central to Sundanese identity for more than four centuries, the backbone of the Sundanese economy has remained the same for hundreds of years. Wet-rice agriculture with a small amount of swidden (slash-and-burn) horticulture in the southwest underpins most people's productive life. Due to the region's climate and rainfall, many years bring in three harvests of rice plus other subsistence crops, such as chilies, peanuts, and vegetables. Corn, cassava, chilies, and tobacco are common cash crops in the region; fishing and fish farming along the coast are also quite lucrative. Despite the economic importance of these crops and activities, rice is the most important food item among the Sundanese, and a meal without rice is not considered eating at all. Simple boiled rice is served three times a day with accompanying side dishes made from meats such as beef, goat, water buffalo, poultry, and fish, or vegetables.

Most landholdings are very small and privately owned by a single farmer or farming family. However, most villages also have some communal lands that are worked by administrators in lieu of a salary or are set aside for use by villagers in general. These villages are fairly large by Indonesian standards: They house between 1,000 and 7,000 people and are surrounded by the villagers' small farming plots and paddies.

In addition to village residence, the Sundanese also organize their society around large bilateral kin groupings in which descent is traced through each individual's mother and father. In principle, each individual must recognize his or her extended family as containing all individuals within a seven-generation span, but this principle is only rarely possible today. In reality, nuclear families are the most important units of production and consumption, with more extended kin, such as grandparents, occasionally being included. Marriages in the past were arranged by parents using a traditional nine-step ritual method but today are most frequently the purview of the young couples themselves.

Outside Sunda or West Java, the Sundanese are most often noted for their performance of elaborate puppet theater pieces based on the *Ramayana* and other Hindu mythology. The music that accompanies these spectacles has been performed in concerts all over the globe, and while few people understand the history of these events, millions have enjoyed them over the past few decades.

See also Austronesians.

Svan   (Misimianelian, Mshan)

The Svan are a subgroup of the GEORGIANS of the central Caucasus. They are first mentioned by the Greek geographer Strabo, who wrote that they lived at the top of the Caucasus, above Sukhumi, the main city of the ABKHAZIANS today. The Greek myth of Jason, who sailed off to find the Golden Fleece with the Argonauts, was probably set in the lands of the central Caucasus; even today the Svan people lay sheepskins on river beds to extract tiny flecks of gold from them. Menander, a Byzantine historian of the sixth century, confirmed Strabo's reference to the Svan. Unfortunately, neither author provided any information about the origins of these people or why they split from the other Kartvelian speakers.

Although they once lived throughout the Caucasus, by the 19th century the Svan had become isolated within Svaneti, a high mountainous region of northwestern Georgia. The area is divided into two separate sections, lower Svaneti along the Tskheniskali Gorge and upper Svaneti along the Enguri Gorge. The Caucasus Mountains rise higher than 13,000 feet in some regions of Svaneti, and Europe's highest permanent settlement, Ushguli, at 7,874 feet above sea level, is located there. The region's capital city is Mestia, which was connected to the rest of Georgia by road only in the 1920s. The difficulty in building a road through the rugged terrain was captured in a Soviet-era docudrama by Mikhail Kalatozov called *Salt for Svanetia*. Svaneti is also known for its unique medieval watchtowers that dot the landscape and provided the Svan with lookout points for both enemies and fire.

The Svan differ from the Georgians in a number of important ways in addition to language. Although they have been members of the Georgian Orthodox Church since at least the ninth century, many Svan continue to practice some pre-Christian rituals as well. They worship gods who protect animals and grant fertility, as well as a goddess of the hearth, women, and cows named Lamaria. (The Christian reference to Maria, or Mary, in the goddess's name is obviously of more recent origin than the concept of a domestic goddess of this sort.) The Svan also revere spirits of the soul and the patron god of fire.

Despite their linguistic and cultural differences from the Georgians, for many centuries the Svan have considered themselves a constituent part of the Georgian people. In fact, they consider their own language to be an ancient and pure version of Georgian. They have also been connected to Georgians through their membership in the Georgian Orthodox Church. The Svan language has no written version, and so learning Georgian as both a spoken and written language has been necessary for church participation for more than 1,000 years. The Svan have also had extensive economic ties to other Georgians for many centuries. Their own mountain homeland does not provide enough food or other resources to maintain the entire population, and for centuries Svan men have migrated, either seasonally or permanently, to the lowlands of Georgia for work. The Svan have also traded salt, wine, and animal products for the lowlanders' grain and vegetables.

In recent decades the outmigration of Svan individuals and families has put the entire ethnolinguistic group at risk because fewer and fewer young people are being taught to speak Svan. It is not taught in any Georgian schools, and as families migrate into other regions of Georgia, the utility of teaching children the language is diminishing. The best estimate in the late 1990s was that only about 30,000 Svan speakers remained, and of that number very few were children.

In the contemporary world the most famous Svan is Emzar Kvitsiani, a former regional governor who has accused the Georgian

The clothing worn by this Svan peasant from the late 19th century shows the care with which these people had to prepare themselves against the cold in their high mountainous home. *(Library of Congress)*

SVAN

location:
Svaneti, northwest Georgia

time period:
At least 0 C.E. to the present

ancestry:
proto-Kartvelian; the Svan divided from the other Kartvelian speakers about 5,000 years ago.

language:
Svan, a South Caucasian or Kartvelian language, related to but mutually unintelligible with Georgian, Laz, and Megrelian

government of starving the Svan people of the upper Kodori River area. He and a group of followers have taken up arms and formed the Monadire, or Hunter, militia. In July 2006 Kvitsiani was charged with treason in Georgia because of his refusal to disarm, and later that month a woman was killed in a fight between the militia and Georgian security forces. At that time some militia members were captured and others surrendered, but Kvitsiani and at least 60 followers remained at large. Georgia takes these actions very seriously because the Kodori River divides Georgia from the breakaway province of Abkhazia, where an armed conflict took place in 1992–93.

See also GEORGIANS: NATIONALITY.

Tagalog

The Tagalog are the largest lowland ethnic group in the Philippines, with more than 28 percent of the country's population in 2007. Their original homeland was along the coasts and in the river valleys of Luzon, but today members of this ethnolinguistic group can be found everywhere in the archipelago as well as in a diaspora throughout the world. Their name is derived from the local phrase *taga ilog,* "inhabitants of the river."

GEOGRAPHY

The original homeland of the Tagalog-speaking people is the Manila Bay region of southwestern Luzon, including the contemporary provinces of Bataan, Batangas, Bulacan, Cavite, Laguna, Quezon, and Rizal, plus sections of Camarines Norte, Marinduque, Nueva Ecija, and Polillio. There were also populations on Mindoro, Palawan, and many of the region's smaller islands. This region is extremely diverse and includes mountains, river valleys, rainforest, swamps, and coastal plains. Most have a monsoon season of at least two months, and typhoons, volcanoes, flooding, earthquakes, landslides, and other natural disasters are not uncommon. In the present time, some coastal areas and low-lying islands are also at risk of being destroyed by rising sea levels due to global warming.

The geographic conditions in which Tagalog society emerged are not entirely bad. The warm tropical climate and plentiful rainfall allowed the region to thrive on an agricultural economy and to host a population explosion that led to the adoption of a form of Tagalog as the official national language in 1937. The region's forests and seas also provided significant resources, from lumber and honey to fish and crustaceans.

ORIGINS

The origins of the Tagalog, like most AUSTRONESIANS in the Philippines, are probably in south China, from where they sailed in double-outrigger dugout canoes about 5,000 years ago to Taiwan, and then later to the Philippines and Polynesia. There is no certainty as to why this population left south China; however, archaeologists have hypothesized that it was a combination of population pressure, increased commerce coming from the Chang (Yangtze) River region of China and moving southward down the river and its tributaries, a growing demand for marine and tropical forest goods, and climate change.

Contemporary Austronesian languages can be subdivided into two distinctive groups that separate the languages of Austronesian Taiwan from those of the remainder of the family, which include all Malay and Oceanic languages. This linguistic division, in addition to several anomalies in the archaeological record, such as a lack of rice in the earliest Austronesian sites in Taiwan, indicates that the origins of the Austronesian people may have been

Tagalog time line

B.C.E.

3000 The initial migration of the Austronesians to the Philippines, including the ancestors of the Tagalog.

C.E.

1565 The Spanish arrive on Luzon and begin the long colonial process among the Tagalog people.

1593 The first Tagalog-language book, *Doctrina Cristiana,* is published.

1660 Andres Malong unites the entire western side of Luzon from Ilocos to Pampanga in a revolt against the Spanish.

1762–63 The British occupy the city of Manila, and many local leaders in Luzon rise up against the Spanish.

1899 The Spanish cede the Philippines to the United States, and a local war of independence breaks out.

1901 Emilio Aguinaldo transforms the revolutionary army into a guerrilla force to fight the Americans. They are defeated, and the Americans establish a civil government in the same year.

1902 A civil U.S. administration replaces military rule upon the pacification of the independence fighters in the north.

1935 Manuel Quezon, a Tagalog, is elected president; he is the country's second president and first president of the Commonwealth of the Philippines.

1937 Tagalog becomes the country's national language even though Cebuano is spoken by more people.

1941 The Japanese occupy all of the Philippines and Quezon leaves the country, eventually going to live in the United States as president of the Commonwealth Government-in-Exile.

1942 The Bataan Death March, on which American and Filipino prisoners of war are walked across the province by their Japanese captors.

1944 The United States retakes the Philippines.

Manuel Quezon dies of tuberculosis in Saranac Lake, New York.

1945 The Philippines attains independence from the United States.

1952 Huk (communist) insurgents in Luzon are finally defeated.

1969 The New People's Army is formed as the military arm of the Communist Party of the Philippines. In reaction to this and other threats, President Ferdinand Marcos declares martial law in 1971.

1983 Marcos has political rival Benigno Aquino assassinated upon his return to the Philippines after a period of self-imposed exile.

1986 Ferdinand Marcos is deposed and Aquino's widow, Corazon Aquino, comes to power.

1998 Joseph Estrada, a Tagalog actor and film director, is elected president of the Republic of the Philippines.

2000 Estrada is impeached over corruption charges, the first Filipino president to be impeached. In January 2001 the supreme court deems the presidency to be empty and makes the sitting vice president Gloria Arroyo president.

two separate exoduses from southeast China. If these did occur, the first exodus was probably from Fujian province in China to Taiwan, which saw the rise of TA-P'EN-K'ENG CULTURE, with its distinctively marked pottery and stone tools, but without archaeological evidence of domesticated rice. The descendants of this first wave would be the contemporary speakers of Taiwan's Austronesian languages, the ABORIGINAL TAIWANESE people. The second exodus may have occurred around 3000 B.C.E., taking a second wave of Austronesian speakers from southeastern China to Taiwan and then almost immediately to Luzon in the Philippines around the same period. This second wave, with its red-slipped pottery, may also have been the ultimate source of the LAPITA CULTURE.

HISTORY

When they arrived in the Philippines about 3000 B.C.E., the Austronesian speakers would probably have met small bands of people who had already been residing on the islands for approximately 20,000 years. The hunting and gathering AETA peoples, as they are now called, probably lived in the most productive areas of the country—the coastlines, valleys, and lower hills—in very small, impermanent settlements. With their ability to grow their own crops, the incoming Austronesians were able to maintain significantly higher population densities than the Aeta and thus to push the hunter-gatherers into the more marginal highland forests and mountaintops, where they still live today. The numerically and technologically stronger agriculturalists also seem to have lent their language to the Aeta, all of whom today speak Austronesian languages rather than the more ancient languages they would have brought with them in their much earlier migrations.

Tagalog history as we know it began in 1565 with the arrival of the Spanish colonizers and missionaries. Prior to that year the people of the region had extensive trade contact with China, Japan, India, and the Malay kingdoms of Southeast Asia, as well as with the Aeta and other highlanders on Luzon. Muslim leaders from the south of the archipelago arrived in Manila prior to the Spanish and began the process of converting the local population to Islam, but this process was interrupted by the Spanish, who drove out the Muslims and quickly began the process of conversion to Christianity.

Despite these extensive international connections, many scholars believe the Tagalog lived much like most other peoples on the island, engaging in shifting agriculture and trade and practicing an animistic religion with beliefs in spirits and ghosts. The arrival of the Spanish changed this way of life considerably when lowlanders like the Tagalog, ILOCANOS, KAPAMPANGANS, and PANGASINANS quickly adopted Christianity and the entire way of life it engendered, while the IGOROT and many other highland tribes continued to withdraw into the interior or to fight the onslaught of colonial society. The two groups, lowlanders and highlanders, began to differ culturally and became enemies in ways they had never been before.

One of the ways that the Spanish were able to convert the lowlanders quickly was to proselytize in native languages. The first book published in Tagalog came out in 1593 and was a book on the Christian faith, *Doctrina Cristiana*. Another way was to connect Christian mythology and historical events to local mythological and historical events. Many local spirits have an equivalent Catholic saint, and the two supernatural figures are usually celebrated or propitiated together in the same ritual or ceremony.

Although conversion and colonialism came relatively easily in the Tagalog region of the country, by the 19th century these people were using their wealth, influence, and education to stage rebellions consistently against Spanish rule. Three of the key figures in the Filipino revolution against the Spanish were Tagalog: José Rizal, Emilio Aguinaldo, and Andres Bonifacio. They began their rebellions in the 1890s and continued until the civilian American takeover in 1902. The first Filipino republic established by these revolutionaries was brought into being at a Catholic church in Malolos, Bulacan, the heart of the Tagalog homeland less than 50 miles northwest of Manila. After the official defeat of the revolutionary army, guerrilla action continued in the Tagalog region for many months until the final defeat and the installation of an American civil administration in 1902.

As they had under the Spanish, the Tagalog people under the Americans held important political, economic, and social positions in the colony. Perhaps in recognition of this importance, in 1937 the Tagalog language became the official language of the colony, along with English. This is astounding considering that there were nearly 200 different languages spoken in the archipelago and Tagalog was not the most common; Cebuano was. Nonetheless, the president of the country at the time, Manuel Quezon, was a Tagalog, as were many of his advisers and the people closest to him and his government.

Quezon himself served as president until 1941 and the occupation of Manila by the JAPANESE; for the remaining three years of his life he was president of the commonwealth government in exile, living and working in the United States until his death of tuberculosis in the small town of Saranac Lake, New York. After independence, it took until the late 1990s for another Tagalog to be elected president. Joseph Estrada was born in Manila and worked as an actor and director in the film industry before entering politics and being elected president in 1998; he served until 2001.

Both Japanese occupation and the fight against communist insurgents made life in the Tagalog provinces of Luzon very difficult in the 1940s and 1950s. One of the most famous incidents of Japanese war crimes during World War II took place just south of Manila: the Bataan Death March, when tens of thousands of U.S. and Filipino soldiers, many of them injured or sick with malaria, were forced to walk 82 miles to a prison camp without provisions. Following the American reconquest of the Philippines and then independence after the war, the Tagalog region could not settle down to rebuild until 1952, because Hukbalahap, sometimes called Huk insurgents, from the Filipino Communist Party continued to wage war against the new republic's governing structure. Many Tagalog people were killed, kidnapped, or raped or lost property during the seven-year fight against these antigovernment insurgents; many also participated in the war on both sides and wound up losing their lives that way.

CULTURE

Agriculture, fishing, and trade have been at the heart of the Tagalog economy for many hundreds of years, going back to before the onset of the Spanish colonial era. The northern Tagalog provinces are located in the island's "rice bowl," while in the south dry upland rice, sugar cane, coconuts, and a variety of tropical fruits have been grown for centuries. As river dwellers, the Tagalog also placed great importance on fishing, both for subsistence and commercial purposes.

Settlements in Tagalog areas tend to be organized around bilateral kinship groups who depend on one another for mutual assistance and, in the past, for defense. Location near waterways, roads, and later railroads and highways was always part of the Tagalog settlement pattern to assist in the movement of trade goods and people throughout the region. During the Spanish period, the development of church communities and plazas meant that only a portion of the settlement would be located on the thoroughfare, while other areas faced the plaza and its church.

As is the case among some other Austronesian peoples, such as the MAORI and HAWAIIANS, sibling groups are the most basic social units in the community, with all siblings inheriting their parents' property equally. Brothers and sisters remain extremely close throughout their lifetimes and can turn to each other in times of need, even after marriage. Kinship generally remains extremely important: Even strangers and non-Tagalog living in Tagalog regions can be unofficially adopted into kin groups for the purposes of association, assistance, and familiarity. These groups are maintained through reciprocal gift giving and feasting, especially at weddings, funerals, and other life-cycle rituals, but also at Christmas and other important times in the Christian calendar.

As is the case throughout the Philippines, the predominantly Roman Catholic Tagalog also engage in a wide variety of pre-Christian practices and hold a set of beliefs that include nature and ancestral spirits, demons, and other non-Christian supernatural beings. Most rural regions and urban neighborhoods have a number of religious practitioners outside the traditional Catholic hierarchy, including spirit mediums and faith healers. In addition, among Tagalog the Protestant Iglesia ni Cristo, or Church of Christ, and the national Aglipayan Church are also quite popular.

See also FILIPINOS: NATIONALITY.

FURTHER READING

Santiago V. Alvarez. *The Katipunan and the Revolution: Memoirs of a General, with the Original Tagalog text,* trans. Paula Caroline S. Malay (Manila: Ateneo de Manila University Press, 1992).

Carl H. Lande. *Southern Tagalog Voting, 1946–1963: Political Behavior in a Philippine Region* (Dekalb: Northern Illinois University Center for Southeast Asian Studies, 1973).

Vicente L. Rafael. *Contracting Colonialism: Translation and Christian Conversion in Tagalog Society under Early Spanish Rule* (Ithaca, N.Y.: Cornell University Press, 1988).

Tai   *See* DAI.

Taiwanese: nationality (people of Taiwan)

Taiwan as a separate, independent country is recognized by only 24 other countries in the world; it has de facto political, trade, and other economic relations with almost the entire globe. The long-standing problem of Taiwan's political status rests on China's unwillingness to recognize Taiwan as separate from the People's Republic of China and much of the rest of the world's unwillingness to challenge China on this issue when de facto recognition of Taiwan is more politically and economically expedient. International sporting events with Taiwanese participants often refer to their country as Chinese Taipei.

GEOGRAPHY

Located about 95 miles off the coast of China, Taiwan is approximately 244 miles long and 89 miles wide and borders the South China Sea, East China Sea, Philippine Sea, and the Pacific Ocean. As an archipelago, Taiwan also includes the smaller islands of Lanyu (Orchid) and the Pescadores, as well as the islets of Green Island and Liuchiu.

Ninety percent of Taiwan's population live on the western side of the island, where there are more flatlands and plains. The other two-thirds of the island is mountainous terrain in which some ABORIGINAL TAIWANESE communities still live. About 55 percent of the island is forest and 25 percent is arable land.

River pollution has become a persistent problem in Taiwan. In 2000, tanker workers were seen dumping tons of dimethyl benzene into the Kaoping River, and this source of water to Kaohsiung was cut off. It was later revealed that river pollution was a direct result of the fact that Taiwan was able to process only 40 percent of its toxic waste.

INCEPTION AS A NATION

Before the Portuguese and Dutch introduced Taiwan to the western world, the island was populated by various Austronesian tribes who are believed to have settled on the island 8,000 years before the Dutch began its colonization. The Dutch East India Company saw the value in Taiwan's key position for trade with China and Japan as well as agricultural prospects and began the process of colonization in 1623. Fort Zeelandia was built in 1624 on the southwestern coast of Taiwan, and missionaries and soldiers applied themselves to the duty of cultivating the rich land and converting the natives to Christianity. They also divided the aboriginal people's land into seven districts, each headed by an aboriginal elder as elected by his own district. Through this elder, the Dutch officials were able to communicate orders to the aboriginal population. Agricultural developments improved production as villages were organized into farm groups headed by a single leader, who answered to an elected captain, who reported back to the governor in charge of keeping peace and order.

During this period the MANCHUS invaded and conquered China and work prospects in Taiwan became an appealing option for many impoverished Chinese. Between 1624 and 1644, approximately 100,000 Chinese immigrated to Taiwan. Most of the Chinese immigrants were young HAN and HAKKA men who were encouraged to go back to China after a period of work, but many married into the aboriginal population and fused the two cultures. While this arrangement helped the Dutch domesticate the island, as they now had a new population willing to navigate jungles and clear vegetation, tensions mounted between the Dutch and the Chinese when the Dutch refused to allow the Chinese to purchase land and then imposed a poll tax on all Chinese individuals over the age of six. Rioting ensued in 1652, and 6,000 Chinese peasants were killed in the Dutch officials' efforts at suppression.

Dutch rule came to an end in 1662 after 38 years of colonial control when Ming supporter Cheng Cheng-kung ousted the Dutch to establish an anti-Manchu base on the island. Though he died shortly afterward, Cheng succeeded in infusing Chinese culture into the population through the establishment of schools and the implementation of Chinese laws and customs. The Cheng family continued to rule for another 23 years but were eventually overthrown by the Manchus, who attacked in 1683. Taiwan subsequently came under Chinese rule, and the next 200 years were riddled with uprisings and rebellions, particularly among the Aboriginal Taiwanese who reacted violently to being forced off their land.

In 1887 Taiwan became China's 22nd province, and Liu Ming-chu'an was appointed Taiwan's first governor. Liu made significant improvements to the island, particularly where the modernization of outdated systems was needed. Under Liu, Taiwan developed a postal system, railroad, telegraph lines, submarine lines, and plans for an irrigation system to make agricultural production more efficient. However, in 1894 China went to war with Japan and lost, ceding Taiwan to Japan as part of the settlement.

The first 20 years of JAPANESE rule were largely devoted to suppressing uprisings and asserting authoritarian control. However, this time was also used to conduct a land survey, standardize measurements, and collect census data. From 1918 to 1937 Taiwan's assimilation into Japanese culture was the primary focus, and Japanese-language education was mandated for the Taiwanese people. The years 1937–45 saw the heaviest push for cultural assimilation. Naturalization as Japanese residents

---

TAIWANESE: NATIONALITY

nation:
Taiwan

derivation of name:
Today *Taiwan* means "terraced bay," referring to terraced rice fields, but the name may have also come from an aboriginal tribe that Dutch explorers came across called the Teyowan.

government:
Multiparty democracy

capital:
Taipei

language:
Mandarin Chinese is the official language; Taiwanese and Hakka dialects are also spoken.

religion:
93 percent practice a mixture of Buddhism, Confucianism, and Taoism; Christian 4.5 percent, other 2.5 percent

earlier inhabitants:
Austronesian Aborigines

demographics:
Taiwanese 84 percent, mainland Chinese 14 percent, aboriginal 2 percent

Taiwanese: nationality time line

B.C.E.

30,000 A community with unknown origins settles in Taiwan, then connected to the Chinese mainland.

15,000 Taiwan is separated from the mainland by rising sea levels.

6000 Austronesians take up residence in Taiwan, which they call Pakan. This date is contested and may be 1,500–1,000 years more recent.

C.E.

1100 The Han Chinese begin migrating to and settling in the Pescadores, an archipelago off the western coast of Taiwan.

1544 Portuguese explorers discover Taiwan and call it Ilha Formosa, meaning "Beautiful Island."

1582 Portuguese sailors are shipwrecked off the coast of Taiwan, where they face attacks from Aboriginal Taiwanese and bouts of malaria. After 10 weeks, they float to Macau on a raft.

1622 The Dutch East India Company establishes a trading base in the Pescadores but is driven out by the Chinese.

1623 The Dutch move their base to Taiwan to facilitate trade with Japan and the coastal regions of China.

1624 The Dutch begin building Fort Zeelandia in the town of Anping, on the southwestern coast of Taiwan.

1626 The Spanish build Fort San Salvador on the northwest coast of Taiwan.

1629 The Spanish move into Tamsui and name it Castillo. There, they build Fort San Domingo and make preparations for colonization.

1636 In response to an aboriginal attack on a shipwrecked crew off Lamay Island, the Dutch deport the entire population. Three hundred twenty-seven people are trapped in a cave and suffocated with smoke; men are sold into slavery in Batavia, and women and children become servants for Dutch officers.

1642 An uprising in the Spanish-occupied Philippines requires the help of the Spanish troops in Taiwan, leaving the territory vulnerable. The Dutch invade Castillo and take control of the region.

1650 The Dutch build Fort Provintia, which becomes the colony's new capital. The Chinese come to refer to it as "edifice of the red-haired barbarians."

1652 Resentful Chinese farmers rebel against the Dutch administrators after a poll tax is instituted; 6,000 Chinese peasants are brutally killed in the suppression.

1661 Seventeen years after Manchu forces overpower the Ming dynasty and take control of China, Ming-loyalist Cheng Cheng-kung leads naval forces in an attack on the Dutch to establish a resistance base in Taiwan.

1662 After 38 years of administration, the Dutch are driven out of Taiwan. Cheng Cheng-kung introduces Chinese ways of life to the island and constructs a Confucian temple.

1683 China attacks Taiwan and the Cheng family surrenders to the Manchu Qing dynasty.

Taiwan consequently becomes a part of China's Fujian province.

1874 The Japanese attack the Taiwanese Aboriginal people in Mutan She; 30 Aboriginal people and 543 Japanese die (12 in battle and 531 from illness).

1875 Taiwan is divided into a north prefecture and a south prefecture.

1887 Taiwan is granted the status of being its own Chinese province, and Liu Ming-chu'an is appointed governor.

1894 Japan and China go to war in the first Sino-Japanese War.

1895 Upon losing the war, China cedes Taiwan and the Pescadores to Japan.

1899 Japanese administrators establish the Bank of Taiwan.

1905 Taiwan has electricity generated by hydropower from Sun-Moon Lake. The island is also self-sufficient and able to function without subsidies from the Japanese government.

1930 Anger among the Aboriginal Atayal people flares over their mistreatment by the Japanese administrators in the Wushe Uprising, which results in the killing and beheading of 150 Japanese officials. Subsequently, 2,000–3,000 Japanese troops are brought in to crush the uprising, the last aboriginal rebellion.

1935 The governor-general of Taiwan holds an Exposition to Commemorate the 40th Anniversary of the Beginning of Administration in Taiwan. Worldwide attention is drawn to Taiwan's dramatic development and modernization in its 40 years under Japanese rule.

1937 Japan goes to war with China. Taiwan produces war matériel, and 126,750 Taiwanese residents join the Japanese military.

1937–45 The Taiwanese are naturalized as Japanese citizens.

1942 As the United States goes to war with Japan, the Chinese government renounces all treaties made with Japan and seeks to reclaim Taiwan as a Chinese territory.

1945 Japan cedes Taiwan to China, and the Republic of China declares October 25 Taiwan Retrocession Day.

1947 The 228 Incident, which takes place on February 28, results in the death of 10,000–20,000 Taiwanese citizens.

1949 In reaction to the 228 Incident, martial law is enacted. During the period of the White Terror, 140,000 Taiwanese citizens are imprisoned or executed for their proven or imagined opposition to the Kuomintang government.

Chinese Communists take over China and establish the People's Republic of China. Two million refugees from the previous government and business sectors flee to Taiwan. The United Nations and many Western nations refuse to recognize the People's Republic and see the Republic of China as the legitimate ruler of Taiwan and all of China.

1952 Japan signs the San Francisco Peace Treaty, officially relinquishing all rights or claims to Taiwan.

1953 U.S. president Dwight D. Eisenhower announces that he will pull the Seventh Fleet out of Taiwan to allow the Nationalists to attack the Communist mainland.

1969 U.S. senator Edward Kennedy urges the United States to close its bases in Taiwan.

1970 The RCA Corporation opens Taiwan's first semiconductor factory, but its northern facilities are declared a toxic site and shut down in 1991. It is later revealed that 1,000 former plant workers had developed cancer and 200 had died.

1971 The United Nations officially recognizes the People's Republic of China as China, replacing the seat held by the Republic of China (Taiwan).

1978 President Jimmy Carter announces that he will recognize the People's Republic of China and forgo ties with the Republic of China.

1979 U.S. officials create the Taiwan Relations Act, which specifies that diplomatic relations with the People's Republic of China hinge upon China's peaceful treatment of Taiwan.

1986 The Democratic Progressive Party is established and pushes for Taiwanese independence from China.

1987 President Chiang Ching-kuo ends 37 years of martial law in Taiwan.

1988 Lee Teng-hui becomes the first Taiwan-born head of state.

1993 The Taiwanese film *The Wedding Banquet* is released.

1994 Former Kuomintang (KMT) or Nationalist officials oppose the separatist Democratic Progressive Party and form the New Party.

(continues)

Taiwanese: nationality time line *(continued)*

1996 U.S. secretary of state Warren Christopher announces that U.S. warships will move closer to Taiwan due to China's provocations toward the island.

Lee Teng-hui wins Taiwan's first free presidential elections.

1997 The ruling party and the pro-independence party join to support a plan to change the constitution and eliminate the provincial government.

The Democratic Progressive Party wins 12 of 23 mayoral and county seats, receiving more votes than the Nationalist Party for the first time.

1998 China and Taiwan hold their first talks in five years in an effort to work toward reunification.

1999 China renounces relations with Macedonia after the nation officially recognizes Taiwan.

2000 The U.S. House of Representatives votes to strengthen military ties with Taiwan in the Taiwan Security Enhancement Act. At the same time, China warns Taiwan that a refusal to negotiate will result in an attack.

Democratic Progressive Party member Chen Shui-bian wins the presidential election, ending 51 years of Nationalist Party rule. Lee Teng-hui resigns as Nationalist Party leader.

2001 President George W. Bush announces that the U.S. policy of selling arms to Taiwan, effective since 1982, will be discontinued, but also warns China that any aggression toward Taiwan will be met with a U.S. attack.

Taiwan ends a 50-year ban on trade with China as well as a 50-year ban on Chinese citizens entering Taiwan, which was originally intended to ward off mainland spies. Chinese citizens living abroad are now allowed to visit Taiwan as tourists.

The Nationalist Party loses 42 seats and its majority in the legislature in the parliamentary elections.

2002 Taiwanese president Chen Shui-bian proclaims in a speech that Taiwan is not a Chinese province, but rather a country independent of China. The comment incites outrage from Chinese mainlanders. Days later, Taiwan announces that it may pursue a referendum on formal independence from China but will not hold a vote unless forced to do so.

required the adoption of Japanese names, food, clothing, and religious beliefs. The Japanese administration also developed Taiwan into an efficient source of food and goods for Japan. Food production increased fourfold, and a health-care system eliminated most infectious diseases. By the end of the Japanese rule in 1945, the average Taiwanese life span was 60 years.

In 1942 the United States went to war with Japan. The Kuomintang (KMT) government declared that all treaties made with Japan were nullified and demanded the return of Taiwan to Chinese control. In 1945 Japan officially surrendered control of Taiwan, and October 25 became known as Taiwan Retrocession Day. Chinese rule proved to be ineffective compared to the former Japanese administration, and the Taiwanese people revolted after only two years. An argument between an antismuggling officer and a female cigarette vendor resulted in the officer's injuring the woman and killing a passerby. As tension between the Chinese administrators and the Taiwanese citizens was already rising, this incident ignited an uproar. Between 10,000 and 20,000 Taiwanese were killed in the suppression, and the massacre became known as the 228 Incident because it took place on February 28. This event ultimately catalyzed the White Terror, in which the KMT government killed thousands of Taiwanese for what it perceived to be opposition to the mainland rule.

In 1949, shortly after martial law was enforced in Taiwan, the Chinese Communists overthrew the KMT government, and the Republic of China became the People's Republic of China. The KMT government fled to Taiwan and established a Republic of China base on the island. Since that time, disputes have persisted over the state of Taiwan as a Chinese province.

2003 The SARS (severe acute respiratory syndrome) epidemic claims 812 lives worldwide. Taiwan struggles more than any other country to control the disease and reports 483 probable cases for the year.

Thousands storm the capital to demand that the island's formal name be changed from the Republic of China to Taiwan. At the same time, Taiwan loses yet another diplomatic ally to China, limiting its official recognition to a few small, developing countries in Africa and South America.

2004 Some 1.2 million people form a human chain spanning the length of the island in response to President Chen Shui-bian's call for the people of Taiwan to create a "Great Wall of Taiwan's Democracy," in opposition to China's military threats. One month later, President Chen Shui-bian and his vice president are wounded in an assassination attempt while riding in an open car during an election campaign.

China offers President Roosevelt Skerrit of Dominica $122 million dollars in return for renouncing his country's recognition of Taiwan.

At least 100,000 people in Taiwan protest the recent presidential election, in which Chen Shui-bian was the victor by a slight lead.

The United States reestablishes an embassy in Taiwan for the first time since 1979.

2005 China and Taiwan agree to allow direct air flights for the first time since 1949.

China announces a law that would authorize an attack if Taiwan pushes for official independence. Approximately 1 million activists march through the capital to protest the new law. Taiwan later announces that it has recently test-fired a cruise missile capable of attacking southeastern China.

Taiwan fails for the 13th time to obtain a seat in the United Nations, an endeavor that is consistently blocked by China.

The Nationalist Party wins the majority in municipal elections. Among its agendas is Taiwan's reunification with China.

2006 Taiwanese president Chen Shui-bian fires the governmental committee responsible for plans to reunite Taiwan with China. The move is met with wide criticism.

Protestors march in the capital to demand President Chen Shui-bian's resignation as rumors of insider trading implicate immediate family members.

In 1952 the Japanese signed the San Francisco Peace Treaty renouncing all rights to Taiwan, without specifying a receiving country. This has allowed pro-independence activists to argue against the legitimacy of China's claim to Taiwan.

Up until the early 1970s, the United Nations refused to recognize the People's Republic of China. However, in 1971 the United Nations recognized Beijing as China's official seat in the United Nations. The Republic of China was therefore replaced by the People's Republic of China, and in 1979 U.S. president Jimmy Carter announced that the United States would recognize the People's Republic of China and abandon all ties with the Republic of China (Taiwan).

In 1987 martial law was lifted in Taiwan, and the 2000 Taiwanese presidential elections marked the end of the KMT rule. Though Taiwan and China have made efforts to mend their tense relations, the possibility of independence for Taiwan remains a divisive issue as China has threatened to take military action if Taiwan ever pursues this course.

CULTURAL IDENTITY

The Taiwanese culture is an intricate blend of various groups, including the Han Chinese, aboriginal peoples, Japanese, and Europeans. Nonetheless, the largest influx of immigrants came from China in different periods; therefore, the core of Taiwanese culture is largely rooted in a fusion of the Chinese and indigenous cultures. Confucian values of hierarchy, obedience, and order are extremely important in Taiwan, and religious practices are a mixture of Buddhism, Taoism, Chinese folk religion, and ancestor worship. However, efforts to distance Taiwan from China have also resulted in attempts to isolate a Taiwanese cultural identity apart from the mainland culture. One great difference between Taiwan and China is the great importance of convenience on fast-paced Taiwan, especially in the cities. Taiwan may have the world's largest number of 24-hour convenience stores (such as 7-Eleven) per capita in the world, with these stores serving a wide variety of functions, even accepting payment for parking tickets, for the always-in-a-hurry Taiwanese.

Many of the Aboriginal Taiwanese were assimilated into the immigrant-Chinese culture, which has resulted in the extinction of 10 of the 26 known Aboriginal Taiwanese languages. Five more are considered moribund, as they are no longer spoken by newer generations, and will therefore die out with the last of the native speakers. This is particularly disconcerting as many consider Taiwan to be the origin of the Austronesian language family. For those who remain part of aboriginal communities today, unemployment rates and inadequate education are prevalent, and efforts are being made to curb those trends. In 1996 the Council of Indigenous Peoples was elevated to a ministry-level rank within the executive Yuan (or the executive branch of government in Taiwan).

See also AMI; AUSTRONESIANS; BUNUN.

FURTHER READING

Melissa Brown. *Is Taiwan Chinese?: The Impact of Culture, Power, and Migration on Changing Identities* (Berkeley and Los Angeles: University of California Press, 2004).

Ted Galen Carpenter. *America's Coming War with China: A Collision Course Over Taiwan* (New York: Palgrave Macmillan, 2005).

Bruce Herschensohn. *Taiwan: The Threatened Democracy* (Torrance, Calif.: World Ahead Publishing, 2007).

Jonathan Manthorpe. *Forbidden Nation: A History of Taiwan* (New York: Palgrave Macmillan, 2005).

Denny Roy. *Taiwan: A Political History* (New York: Cornell University Press, 2003).

John J. Tkacik, Jr. *Reshaping the Taiwan Strait* (Westminster, U.K.: Heritage Books, 2007).

Taiwanese Aboriginal People *See* ABORIGINAL TAIWANESE.

Tajikistanis: nationality (Tajiks, people of Tajikistan)

The Tajikistanis are among the poorest of the former Soviet citizens; this condition has been exacerbated by a five-year civil war in the mid-1990s and by drought. Today the Tajikistanis are peaceful, but prosperity is still a long way off for most.

GEOGRAPHY

Tajikistan is a relatively small, landlocked Central Asian country located between Afghanistan in the south, China in the east, Kyrgyzstan in the north, and Uzbekistan in the west. The 54,000-square-mile country is dominated by the Pamir and Alay Mountains, including the 24,590-foot-high Ismail Samani Peak, the highest in the country. During the Soviet era this mountain, called Communism Mountain or Mount Stalin, was the tallest in the Union of Soviet Socialist Republics (USSR). Because of the mountainous terrain, which makes up 90 percent of the country, only 6 percent of the country is available for agriculture, most of which is used for cotton.

INCEPTION AS A NATION

The Tajiks are probably the oldest group in Central Asia, descending from the Eastern Iranian BACTRIANS and SOGDIANS. In the seventh century, the Sassanids (*see* PERSIANS, SASSANIDS) were conquered by the invading Arabs, and many Western Iranian–speaking, or Persian-speaking peoples fled to Central Asia and mixed with the older Eastern and Western Iranian-speaking populations. Most experts consider this blend of ancient Iranians with the flood of Western Iranian refugees to be the foundations of the contemporary Tajik people. In the ninth century, the Persian Samanid dynasty emerged as the ruling power in Iran and throughout portions of Central Asia. This golden era of Persian culture is considered foundational for many Tajik intellectuals in the formation of their own national identity.

Following these foundational events, the entire Iranian population of Central Asia was conquered by the MONGOLS in the 13th century and subsequently dominated by the majority TURKIC PEOPLES residing in Central Asia from the 14th century onward. The region of Tajikistan was part of the Uzbek khanate of Bukhara in the 16th century, and in the 19th century it was swallowed by the expansionist Russian empire, beginning with the northern region in 1860. As was the case throughout Central Asia, the incorporation of Tajikistan into the USSR did not occur without a fight. In 1917–18 the Tajiks rose up against the RUSSIANS, who could not control the region until 1921. Even at that point the Tajiks were not seen as ready to rule their own lands and were incorporated into the

TAJIKISTANIS: NATIONALITY.

nation:
Tajikistan; Republic of Tajikistan

derivation of name:
Land of the Tajiks

government:
Republic with prime minister as head of government, president as head of state

capital:
Dushanbe

language:
Tajik, an Iranian language similar to Persian and Dari; Russian is also widely used in government and business.

religion:
Sunni Muslim 85 percent, Shia Muslim 5 percent, other 10 percent

earlier inhabitants:
Bactrians, Sogdians

demographics:
Tajik 79.9 percent, including the Pamiri and Yaghnobi minorities who speak Iranian languages other than Tajik but are often classified as Tajiks; Uzbek 15.3 percent; Russian 1.1 percent; Kyrgyz 1.1 percent; other 2.6 percent

larger Uzbek Soviet Socialist Republic in 1924. It was only at decade's end, in 1929, that the Tajiks were granted equal status to the UZBEKS and other constituent peoples of Central Asia and given their own republic. This is the earliest history of Tajik nationhood and begins the process of creating a common national identity, a process that is still very much a work in progress.

Tajiks have been the majority population within their republic since the 1920s, when it was formed, but it is only in the past few years that they have been more than about 65 percent of the population. The country has always had a very large Turkic Uzbek minority and, until 1992, a very large Russian one as well. This ethnic mix has not always lived together peacefully. In 1978 the large Russian population was the target of ethnic violence in riots that took place throughout the republic.

Perhaps even more important than these ethnic divisions in the formation of Tajikistan is the role played by geography. Prior to the region's incorporation into the USSR in 1921, more than 1.1 million Tajiks lived in Central Asia, but with the creation of the Tajik autonomous region within Uzbekistan in 1924 and the separate Tajik republic in 1929, fewer than one-third of these Tajiks wound up in their own republic. In addition, the ancient cultural capitals of Samarkand and Bukhara had been largely ethnically Tajik, but both cities became part of Uzbekistan. This was largely for the prestige these cities would bring to that republic, which Russia saw as the region's capital. Finally, the territory that Tajikistan was granted in the 1920s was dominated by mountains that separated the four separate valleys and their respective population centers. As a result of these geographic factors, in addition to the political program of the Soviet-era Tajik leadership, local ties have always taken precedence over nationalism in Tajikistan.

When Tajikistan achieved its independence from the USSR, the situation quickly devolved into civil war. In part the war was about the peoples in regions other than the capital, Dushanbe, trying to reclaim power that had been denied them for the previous 80 years. These groups were regional, but they also included Islamic segments, democratic ones, and the ethnic PAMIRI peoples. The situation was exacerbated by the support that Uzbekistan and Russia provided to the former Soviet-era leaders from the capital, first under former Communist Party chief Rakhmon Nabiyev and then, after 1992, under President Imomali

Tajikistanis: nationality time line

B.C.E.

sixth century Bactrians and Sogdians are part of the Persian Achaemenid Empire.

fourth century The region is conquered by Alexander the Great and later the Greek Seleucid Empire.

C.E.

first century The region is conquered by the Kushans.

260 The Persian Sassanid empire brings Western Iranian speakers again to Central Asia.

seventh century The first wave of Sassanids is joined by refugees from the Arab invasions. They combine with the indigenous Eastern Iranians of Sogdiana and Bactria, as well as Western Iranians who entered the region with the Achaemenids, to form the Tajik people.

874 The Persian Samanid dynasty gains control of Iran and later rules parts of Central Asia.

1005 The fall of the Samanid dynasty.

13th century The Mongols conquer the region, beginning the many waves of Turkic-speaking peoples migrating into Central Asia.

14th century Timur Leng conquers the region and incorporates it into his empire.

16th century Tajiks are held within the Uzbek khanate of Bukhara.

1860 Russia colonizes the northern portion of Tajikistan; the south is retained by Bukhara.

1917–18 The Tajiks rise up against Soviet rule.

1921 The Soviet army finally pacifies the Tajiks.

1924 Tajikistan is made an autonomous republic within the Uzbek Soviet Socialist Republic.

1929 Tajikistan is separated from Uzbekistan and is made a constituent republic within the Soviet Union.

1930s Collectivization and irrigation projects bring cotton farming to the region; this is the predominant economic activity through the present.

1978 Anti-Soviet riots rock the urban areas of Tajikistan.

1990 The Tajikistan parliament declares its sovereignty, and the Republic of Tajikistan is created a year later.

1991 Former Communist Party chief Rakhmon Nabiyev is elected president.

1992 Nabiyev is deposed; a five-year civil war begins between Russian-backed government forces and pro-Islamic forces, mostly working out of Afghanistan.

1997 The two sides sign a peace agreement, but sporadic violence continues.

1999 A referendum extends the president's term to seven years and allows the formation of Islamic political parties.

2000 Peace returns to Tajikistan.

2005–06 Elections in these years, for Parliament and president respectively, are denounced by the opposition parties and deemed neither free nor fair by outside observers.

Rakhmonov. In 1996 Uzbek forces acting on their own seized towns in the southern region of the country, adding yet another divisive force in a war that was already pulling the country apart.

In the chaos and fighting that took place throughout the 1990s, nearly 100,000 people were estimated to have died, and thousands of refugees were driven into Afghanistan, Russia, and elsewhere. The ethnic Russians who had made up nearly one-quarter of the population prior to 1991 left en masse so that today they constitute a very small urban minority. Ethnic Uzbeks also fled the country, although not quite to the same degree. Most of the country's limited infrastructure was damaged or destroyed, and today the country continues to rely on Russian aid for almost everything, from security to energy.

The Tajikistanis also remain divided by region, ethnicity, language, and class. Elections in 2005 and 2006 delivered victories for the ruling party, the People's Democratic Party, but were denounced by the internal opposition and outside observers as rigged. The creation of a common national identity from these disparate oppositional groups remains a huge task for future governments to undertake, with very few resources at hand to help them succeed.

CULTURAL IDENTITY

There is almost no cultural identity that is common to all the citizens of contemporary Tajikistan. The small Tajik intelligentsia sees the Tajik language as central to the development of a common identity. They classify the Pamiri and Yaghnobi minorities within Tajikistan, who speak Iranian languages other than Tajik, as Tajiks because of this centrality of Iranian linguistic heritage in their construction of a common identity. Uzbeks, Russians, and others are clearly outside this construction of identity, and they tend to look largely to the capitals of Uzbekistan and Russia for national affiliation. Many Tajik Tajikistanis also look back to the historic Samanid dynasty (874–1005), the first Persian kingdom to emerge in Iran and Central Asia after the conquest of the region by the Arabs, as the ancestors of their own nation.

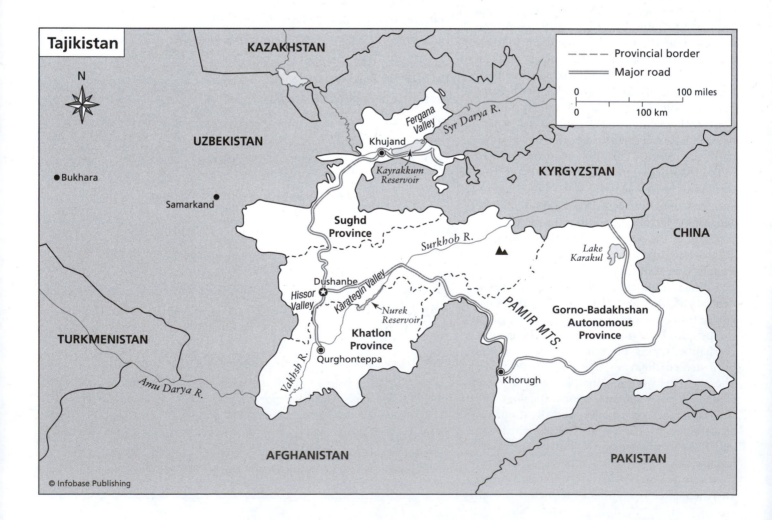

The leadership in each of Tajikistan's four valley-bound population centers, the Fergana Valley's Leninobod Province, the Karategin and Hissor Valleys' central government region, the Khatlon Valley's Kulob Province, and the Pamir Mountains' Gorno-Badakhshan Autonomous Province, fosters its own local identity and economy over those of the nation as a whole. This tactic makes good sense in that the other three regions are cut off from the central one by lack of roads and rail tracks and the debilitating winter weather for at least half the year. However, it also means that local clan ties, which tend to pertain to people connected by geography rather than strictly kinship in contemporary Tajikistan, remain more important to most people than any overarching Tajikistani identity.

The one thing that many Tajikistanis have in common is their rural residence and poverty. By 2003 less than one-quarter of the population was urban and 80 percent lived below the UN poverty line. In rural areas, Tajikistanis grow cotton on collectivized fields irrigated from the Amu Darya and Syr Darya, a legacy of the Soviet era, along with wheat, potatoes, onions, tomatoes, grapes, and apples. They also keep cattle, sheep, and silkworms. They live in small villages of nuclear family households and continue to dress and act in traditional ways.

See also PERSIANS, ACHAEMENIDS; RUSSIANS, ASIAN.

FURTHER READING

Muriel Atkin. *The Subtlest Battle: Islam in Soviet Tajikistan* (Philadelphia: Foreign Policy Research Institute, 1989).

Suchandana Chatterjee. *Politics and Society in Tajikistan: In the Aftermath of the Civil War* (Gurgaon, Haryana: Maulana Abul Kalam Azad Institute of Asian Studies, Kolkata [by] Hope India Publications/Greenwich Millennium, 2002).

Mohammad-Reza Djalili, Frederic Grare, and Shirin Akiner, eds. *Tajikistan: The Trials of Independence* (Richmond, U.K.: Curzon, 1998).

Jane Falkingham. *Women and Gender Relations in Tajikistan* (Manila: Asian Development Bank, 2000).

Colette Harris. *Control and Subversion: Gender Relations in Tajikistan* (Sterling, Va.: Pluto Press, 2004).

Gafur Khaidarov and M. Inomov. *Tajikistan, Tragedy and Anguish of a Nation* (Saint Petersburg, Russia: Linko, 1993).

Julien Thöni. *The Tajik Conflict: The Dialectic between Internal Fragmentation and External Vulnerability, 1991–1994* (Geneva, Switzerland: Programme for Strategic and International Security Studies, 1994).

Tajiks (Tadzhiks, Tadjiks, Tojiks, Tajeks, Farsi, Parsiwan, Dihgan)

The Tajiks are the dominant ethnic group in the independent Central Asian country of Tajikistan and the oldest group of people in Central Asia; they are believed to be the descendants of the original Indo-Iranian people who migrated across the steppes and into the Middle East thousands of years ago. Today more Tajiks actually live outside their own country than within it; for instance, Tajiks are the largest minority community in Afghanistan. There are also Tajik communities in all of the other Central Asian republics and in western China as well, although the Chinese Tajiks differ significantly from these others in both language and culture.

GEOGRAPHY

Tajikistan is a relatively small, landlocked Central Asian country, located between Afghanistan in the south, China in the east, Kyrgyzstan in the north, and Uzbekistan in the west. The 54,000-square-mile country is dominated by the Pamir and Alay Mountains, including the 24,590-feet Ismail Samani Peak, the highest in the country. During the Soviet era this mountain, called Communism Mountain, or alternatively Mount Stalin, was the tallest in the USSR. Because of the mountainous terrain, which makes up 90 percent of the country, only 6 percent of the country is available for agriculture, most of which is used for cotton.

Chinese Tajiks live in the Pamir Mountains in western China. Like most of their fellow Tajiks in Tajikistan, they are a rural population; they endure long winters and a harsh, cold climate in their mountain home. Some of the nearly 3.5 million Tajiks in Afghanistan are also rural mountain dwellers in the northeast part of the country, but the majority are urban and live in Kabul and the towns and cities of the country's northeast; a few also live in the west.

ORIGINS

The Tajiks are probably the oldest group in Central Asia, descending from the Eastern Iranian BACTRIANS and SOGDIANS who ruled the region in the seven centuries before the common era. In the seventh century C.E., the Sassanids (*see* PERSIANS, SASSANIDS) were conquered by the Arabs, and many Western Iranian–speaking, or Persian-speaking peoples fled to Central Asia and mixed with the older Eastern and Western Iranian–speaking populations. Most

TAJIKS

location:
Tajikistan, Afghanistan, Uzbekistan, Kyrgyzstan, Kazakhstan, Turkmenistan, Pakistan, and western China

time period:
Seventh century to the present

ancestry:
Indo-Iranian

language:
Tajik, a Western Iranian language closely related to Persian and Dari. Chinese and Pamiri Tajiks speak different Iranian languages that are only remotely related to Tajik.

Tajiks time line

B.C.E.

sixth century Bactrians and Sogdians are part of the Persian Achaemenid, Empire.

fourth century The region of Tajikistan is conquered by Alexander the Great and later the Greek Seleucid Empire.

C.E.

first century The region is conquered by the Kushans.

260 The Persian Sassanid Empire again brings Western Iranian speakers to Central Asia.

seventh century The first wave of Sassanids is joined by refugees from the Arab invasions. They combine with the indigenous Eastern Iranians of Sogdiana and Bactria to form the Tajik people.

874 The Persian Samanid dynasty gains control of Iran and later rules parts of Central Asia.

1005 The fall of the Samanid dynasty.

13th century The Mongols conquer the region, starting the many waves of Turkic-speaking peoples migrating into Central Asia.

16th century Tajiks are held within the Uzbek khanate of Bukhara.

1860 Russia colonizes the region, beginning in the north, leading to 130 years of Russian and then Soviet domination.

1928 Tajik peasant Bacha-I Saqao ("son of the water carrier") overthrows King Amunullah of Afghanistan and rules the country for nine months as Amir Habibullah II.

1979 Tajiks in Afghanistan lead the fight in that country to remove the Communists.

1991 Tajikistan gains its independence from the USSR and almost immediately becomes involved in a lengthy and destructive civil war.

1992 Tajik military leader Ahmed Shah Massoud leads the first mujahideen forces into Kabul to defeat the Afghan Communists and is rewarded with the presidency of Afghanistan.

1996 Massoud is overthrown by the Taliban, and Tajiks in Afghanistan lead the fight to remove the Taliban from office. Many flee to Pakistan as refugees.

1997 The civil war in Tajikistan comes to an end when President Imomali Rakhmonov's government and the United Tajik Opposition sign a series of peace accords in Moscow. Sporadic violence continues.

2001 In Afghanistan the Tajik-led Northern Alliance and its U.S. allies defeat the Taliban. Massoud is reinstated as president for a short period before being replaced by Hamid Karzai.

2000 Peace returns to Tajikistan, but the country remains divided and extremely poor.

2006 President Rakhmonov wins a third term in office in elections that are boycotted by the opposition.

experts consider this blend of ancient Iranians and the flood of Western Iranian refugees to be the foundations of the contemporary Tajik people. In the ninth century the Persian Samanid dynasty emerged as the ruling power in Iran and throughout portions of Central Asia. This Golden Era of Persian culture is considered foundational for many Tajik intellectuals in the formation of their own national identity.

HISTORY
Tajikistan's Tajiks

Following these foundational events, the entire Iranian population of Central Asia was conquered by the MONGOLS in the 13th century and subsequently dominated by the majority TURKIC PEOPLES living in Central Asia from the 14th century onward. The region of Tajikistan was part of the UZBEKS' khanate of Bukhara in the 16th century, and in the 19th century it was swallowed by the expansionist RUSSIANS, beginning with the northern region in 1860. As was the case throughout Central Asia, the incorporation of Tajikistan into the Union of Soviet Socialist Republics (USSR) occurred in 1921 after a period of civil and military unrest. At that point the Tajiks were not considered a separate nationality and were incorporated into the Uzbek Soviet Socialist Republic, but in 1929 they were granted nationality status and attained their own SSR.

Tajiks were the majority within their republic at that time, but it is only in the past few years that they have been more than about 65 percent of the population. The country has always had a very large Turkic Uzbek minority and, until 1992, a very large Russian one as well. This ethnic mix has not always lived together peacefully. In 1978 the large Russian population was the target of violence in riots that took place throughout the republic. After independence, Tajikistan also experienced five years of civil war, in part dividing the country into ethnic groups but also dividing people by region and political ideology as well. The situation was exacerbated by the support that Uzbekistan and Russia provided to the former Soviet-era leaders from the capital, first under former Communist Party chief Rakhmon Nabiyev and after 1992 under President Emomali Rakhmonov. In 1996 Uzbek forces went out on their own and seized towns in the southern region of the country, adding yet another divisive force in a war that was already pulling the country apart.

In the chaos and fighting that took place throughout the 1990s, nearly 100,000 people were estimated to have died, and thousands of refugees were driven into Afghanistan, Russia, and elsewhere. Ethnic Russians and Uzbeks fled the country, making Tajikistan one of the more ethnically homogeneous states in the region, but also one of the poorest, with 80 percent living below the UN poverty line, and with 76 percent living in rural areas. Most of these rural dwellers are ethnic Tajiks, although the PAMIRI are also a rural people.

Afghanistan's Tajiks

The Tajiks of Afghanistan have a very different recent history from those who reside within Tajikistan. They are the second-largest ethnic group in the country after the dominant PASHTUNS, constituting about one-quarter of the population, and have occasionally put pressure on the government of Afghanistan to recognize their numeric strength with greater political and economic representation. They dominate much of the country's intelligentsia and have been active participants in all the violence and upheaval that has plagued the country since the Soviet invasion in 1979. Their language, Dari, a form of Persian, is the dominant language in Afghan intellectual circles because of the influence of the Tajik minority. Because of their numeric, economic, and social strength within Afghanistan, the Tajiks in that country tend to have a much greater awareness of their identity as Tajiks than do those within Tajikistan, who are divided by region and clan. They even ruled the country for nine months in 1928 when Bacha-I Saqao ("son of the water carrier") overthrew King Amunullah and reigned as Amir Habibullah II; he was overthrown himself by an army of Pashtuns who had tacit British support to restore the previous king's lineage to power.

Tajiks in Afghanistan in the 1990s and early part of the 21st century achieved much greater power than they had ever held in that country before, even during that brief interlude in 1928. This power came from the efforts of Tajik warlords and other participants in the fight against the Soviets between 1979 and 1989 and then in the civil war that followed. Ahmed Shah Massoud was one of the central Tajik personages at that time, leading 10,000 troops against the Soviets in the north of the country and then consolidating his political power under the Supervisory Council of the North. His heroics earned him the nicknames the Lion of Panjshir (the district in which he was born) and National Hero; he was also close to the U.S. Central Intelligence Agency, a fact that may have got him killed by a suicide bomber two days before the 9/11 attacks in the United States in 2001.

Another Tajik who distinguished himself during this time of upheaval in Afghanistan was Burhanuddin Rabbani. Rabbani was the head of one of the many Islamic groups that opposed the Soviet invasion, Jamiat-e Islami of Afghanistan, and the group who first entered Kabul in 1992 to defeat the Communists. For his efforts, Rabbani became president of the country, a position he held from 1992 to 1996, when the Taliban expelled him. With the rise of the Taliban in 1996, Tajiks again became key to the official opposition in the country, leading the United Islamic Front for the Salvation of Afghanistan, or what the Western media usually called the Northern Alliance. This group, as the mujahideen had earlier, had the support of the United States in the civil war that followed and was part of the coalition led by the United States that overthrew the Taliban in 2001. At that time Rabbani briefly became president again before being replaced by Hamid Karzai, an ethnic Pashtun who had nevertheless opposed the Pashtun-dominated Taliban regime. During this period of fighting, many Tajiks also fled Afghanistan to live as refugees in Pakistan.

Tajiks in Afghanistan have remained loyal to the national government since the overthrow of the Taliban in 2001. Many individual Tajiks serve in the Karzai government and at all levels of the bureaucracy, but they do so largely as individuals rather than as representatives of their ethnic group due to election laws instituted for the national elections in 2005. The Jamiat-e Islami party also continues to be an important political force representing Tajiks. This party, as

Afghanistan's Tajik president Burhanuddin Rabbani, left, with fellow mujahideen fighter Gulbuddin Hekmatyar, when the two agreed to set aside their ethnic and political differences and share power in 1996; their joint regime fell apart only months later when the Taliban came to power and drove them both from Kabul. *(AP Photo/Abdullah)*

well as other ethnic Tajik organizations, continues to struggle against the dominant Pashtuns to gain the resources and power it feels its people deserve. The segments of society that are most clearly dominated by Tajiks are the police force and the national army, which could potentially encourage the emergence of further ethnic divisions in the fragile country but so far have not.

China's Tajiks

China's Tajik population is very ancient. A burial plot bearing Eastern Iranian artifacts and dating to 1000 B.C.E. has been found in the Taxkorgan Tajik Autonomous County. These Eastern Iranian speakers, who differ linguistically from the Tajiks residing in Tajikistan and Afghanistan, and who speak a Western Iranian language, came to be known as Tajik after the 11th century because the nomadic Turkic speakers who surged into Central Asia from the northeastern steppe area used the term *Tajik* to refer to all Iranian-language speakers.

During various times in Chinese history, the dominant HAN people have tried to sinicize the entire population of their country. They have used various techniques that include moving Chinese families into minority regions, outlawing other languages and cultures, and neglecting minority rights and customs. Through each of these strategies the Chinese Tajiks have remained consistent in their culture and language, if not in an overarching Tajik identity. Today, living in a largely UIGHUR region of the country, many Chinese Tajiks also speak Uighur, but very few have any knowledge of Han Chinese or other languages.

CULTURE

In Tajikistan

Tajiks in Tajikistan are a predominantly rural population, many of whom are extremely poor. They grow cotton on collectivized fields irrigated from the Amu Darya and Syr Darya, a legacy of the Soviet era, plus wheat, potatoes, onions, tomatoes, grapes, and apples. They also keep cattle, sheep, and silkworms. They live in small villages of nuclear family households and continue to dress and act in traditional ways.

While their urban intelligentsia looks back to the Samanid dynasty, the Persians' first indigenous kingdom after the conquest of Iran and Central Asia by the Arabs, and thinks of the Tajik language as the primary national marker, most rural Tajiks are much more closely affiliated to their region than to the nation as a whole.

Tajikistan's mountainous terrain, with most of its population centers in valleys bordering on the country's central region, leaves much of the rural populace cut off during the long winter months. As a result of this geography and the political motivations of regional leaders who have favored local autonomy over national integration for the past century, much of the rural Tajik population is bound by the ties of lineage and clan rather than nation or state.

In Afghanistan

Tajik culture in Afghanistan has two distinct strains. The first is the culture of the plains-dwelling Tajiks in the west and the urban populations of Kabul and many other Afghan cities. The second is the culture of the poor, rural Tajiks who live in the northeast of the country.

Members of the urban Tajik culture in Afghanistan see themselves as the inheritors of the long literary and cultural history created by the Achaemenid, Sassanid, Samanid, and other Persian regimes throughout history. Its members are soldiers in the national army, police officers, government ministers, public servants, teachers, and entrepreneurs. They constitute the economic and intellectual elite of the country and are culturally more similar to other Western Asian elites than to their rural fellow Tajiks in Afghanistan. There are also plains-dwelling Tajiks in the towns of western Afghanistan, especially in Parwan Province and along the Iranian border. Some of these people are artisans; others farm. Like their urban cousins, most of these Tajiks have ceased to follow many Tajik tribal customs, and their town or region affiliation is generally stronger than ties of extended kinship. A few Tajiks in this region practice a form of Shia Islam, as is the case across the Iranian border, rather than the Sunni Islam that dominates among most ethnic groups in Afghanistan.

The northeastern mountains of Afghanistan contain a large number of poor, rural Tajiks who make their living by herding yaks and in agriculture. They are culturally quite different from their urban and plains-dwelling cousins in that the ties of patrilineal kinship and local clans continue to be of great importance in dictating social life. Clanship among this population is generally more a marker of locality than of actual kinship, but the bonds it creates, to avenge honor and provide assistance, remain just as strong. Most of these rural Tajiks work as migrant farmers or herdsmen, although some also own their own land on which they grow barley and wheat.

In China

China's so-called Tajik population is linguistically and culturally quite distinct from these other Tajik people. They speak a number of Southeastern Iranian Pamir languages, including Sarikoli, but not the Western Iranian Tajik language. They are primarily seminomadic shepherds rather than farmers, leading herds of cows, yaks, sheep, camels, and mules to lush valleys in the winter and to rugged mountainsides in summer. Some Chinese Tajiks also grow a few crops, mostly highland barley, peas, and wheat, but most of their subsistence economy is centered on animal husbandry. This population also differs from the Tajik majority in following the Ismaili sect of Islam, a form of Shiism, while most Tajiks are Sunni Muslims. Nonetheless, several people who have traveled into the Tajik region of China note the lack of mosques or muezzins' calls to prayer and thus claim that their Muslim identity is worn very lightly and with a heavy layer of pre-Islamic beliefs and practices.

These people live primarily in the Taxkorgan Tajik Autonomous County and a few other places in Xinjiang Province, in China's far northwest corner. The region is dominated by the Pamir Mountains with Mount Qogir, the world's second-highest mountain, in the south and Mount Muztagata, "the father of ice peaks," in the north. Almost two dozen other mountains in the region are always snow-capped, indicative of the cold, rugged landscape to which the Chinese Tajiks have adapted.

See also Afghanistanis: nationality; Persians, Achaemenids; Russians, Asian; Tajikistanis: nationality.

Further Reading

Sadriddin Aini et al. *At the Foot of Blue Mountains: Stories by Tajik Authors,* trans. Shavkat Niyari (Moscow: Raduga Publishers, 1984).

Frank Bliss. *Social and Economic Change in the Pamirs: Gorno-Badakhshan, Tajikistan,* trans. Nicola Pacult and Sonia Guss (New York: Routledge, 2005).

Robert W. Craig. *Storm and Sorrow in the High Pamirs* (New York: Simon and Schuster, 1980).

Jane Falkingham. *Women and Gender Relations in Tajikistan* (Manila: Asian Development Bank, 2000).

Colette Harris. *Control and Subversion: Gender Relations in Tajikistan* (Sterling, Va.: Pluto Press, 2004).

Ajay Patnaik. *Ethnicity and State-Building in Tajikistan* (Calcutta: Maulana Abul Kalam Azad Institute of Asian Studies, 2000).

Talaing   *See* Mon.

Tamang   (Dhamang, Murmi)

The Tamang are a Nepalese ethnic group who live primarily in the regions around the Kathmandu Valley, especially in the north and east. Until about 250 years ago the Tamang lived in autonomous tribal groups that looked to village and clan elders as the dominant social and political members of society. Starting in the mid-18th century the Tamang, like many other tribal peoples in the region, were incorporated into the local kingdoms and then the larger Shah family dynasty, which consolidated power in Nepal in 1769. During the colonial period many Tamang men were active as Gurkhas, indigenous members of the British and later Indian armies; even today serving in the Indian and Nepalese armies remains a high-status activity for many Tamang men.

In addition to military service, the dominant economic activity for most Tamang is agriculture. Some families also keep small herds of sheep, goats, or other animals, grazing them at altitudes so high that agriculture is impossible. Working as porters for Himalayan climbers and day laborers on other people's land are also common activities for many Tamang men. When their husbands are away engaging in these activities, Tamang women are able to run their own households, even hiring day laborers themselves to assist with agricultural duties such as plowing and harvesting.

Tamang society is organized according to both kinship and relative degrees of "purity" of Tamang descent. The kinship system is patrilineal, with both lineages and clans organizing people and families into large corporate groups. Both lineages, which are made up of people related through their fathers to a common male ancestor, and clans, which are made up of groups of lineages with a common male, usually mythological, ancestor, are exogamous groups, which means that people must not marry or have sexual relations with a member of their own group. In addition to dictating marriage partners, clans also control commonly owned lands, which they subdivide among lineages and families for agricultural use; villages are usually divided into hamlets or neighborhoods based on lineage membership as well. Beyond the level of the clan, the Tamang also classify their lineages and clans according to their practice of intermarrying with other ethnic groups. Those that are made up of Tamang and Sherpas only are considered more pure than those who have

TAMANG

location:
Midwestern Nepal

time period:
Unknown to the present

ancestry:
Tibetan, with migration into their current Himalayan home sometime in the distant past

language:
Tamang, a Tibeto-Burman language with many dialects

intermarried with MAGAR, GURUNG, or NEWAR people. Marriage between Tamang and members of these three groups is generally looked down upon but not specifically forbidden.

The dominant religion in Nepal is Hinduism, which was brought to the region by migrating Hindus prior to and during the 18th century. The Tamang, like many tribal peoples, have adopted many Hindu gods and incorporated many Hindu festivals and ritual practices into their worldview. However, most villages also have a resident shaman who presides over indigenous rituals and festivals honoring ancestors and other spirits and communicates with the spirit world more generally for the purposes of curing the sick and increasing farm yields. Some Tamang villages, especially larger or wealthier ones, also have a local Buddhist monastery or temple with resident monks or lamas who preside over other rituals, especially those relating to marriage, death, and birth.

Tamils (Tamilars, Tamilans, Tamilians, Dravidas)

The Tamils are a large ethnolinguistic group of southern India and Sri Lanka, with significant numbers also residing in Malaysia, Fiji, Great Britain, and the United States. They are an ancient people whose early kingdoms traded with Greece and Rome.

TAMILS

location:
Southern India; Sri Lanka; and a diaspora in Malaysia, Fiji, and the United Kingdom, among other places

time period:
Possibly 1000 B.C.E. to the present

ancestry:
The ancient civilizations of Harrappa and Mohenjo-Daro were possibly inhabited by the ancestors of contemporary Tamils.

language:
Tamil, the most ancient Dravidian language and the one spoken by the most people

GEOGRAPHY

The two most important homelands for contemporary Tamils are the Indian state of Tamil Nadu, or Tamil Land—created as a Tamil homeland following India's independence from Britain in 1947 when the country was divided into states according to language—and northern Sri Lanka. Tamil Nadu is in southeastern India, extending from Pulicat Lake, just north of Chennai (formerly Madras) in the north to the southern tip of the country; it is divided from Kerala in the west by the Western Ghat Mountains. With the exception of the mountainous towns of Ootacamund and Kodaikanal, the entire state is tropical, with a hot and sunny climate. Monsoon rains start in October and then again in June, but the 30 inches of rain per year are not enough to keep the state from being considered semiarid. The Kaveri River in the center of the state cannot provide enough water to make up for this rain shortfall and the high evaporation rate means that there is currently not enough water for the present population or for the expected population growth over the coming century.

Sri Lanka is a small tropical island southeast of India, straddling the Bay of Bengal and Indian Ocean. It is a mere 219 miles long and 114 miles at its widest point but houses nearly 20 million people, about 18 percent of whom are Tamils. The Tamil-speaking regions of Sri Lanka incorporate the entire north coast of the island and a strip of territory down the east coast as well. Traditionally, Tamils also considered about half the west coast as theirs, but today very few Tamil speakers remain in that area; some have moved to a pocket of territory around Badulla in the island's inland region. The Tamil areas can be subdivided into five regions that share similar cultures and economies: the Batticaloa, Trincomalee, Vanni, Jaffna, and Mannar regions.

ORIGINS

There are many theories explaining the origins of the Tamil people. The most fantastic is that the aboriginal Tamils inhabited the ancient continent of Lemuria, which has since been destroyed by a great flood. Lemuria was supposedly located off the southern coast of India and was named after the lemurs of Madagascar, the only modern survivors of that animal species. Due to the discovery of fossilized lemurs in both Madagascar and India, but not in Africa or the Middle East, 19th-century scientists postulated that the two areas must once have been connected by a now-submerged land, which they called Lemuria. Approximately the same area is said in Tamil legends to be the lost land of Kumari Kandam.

A second origin myth makes the claim that the Tamils, rather than being indigenous to South India, were actually migrants from the western Asian regions of Afghanistan, Iran, and Asia Minor. Linguistic similarities between the Lycians of Asia Minor, who called themselves Trimmlai, and Tamils, in addition to the worship of snakes in both Persepolis, a capital of the Achaemenid Empire (*see* PERSIANS, ACHAEMENIDS), and South India are commonly used to support this theory. Similarities between the archaeological findings at Adichanallur in Tamil Nadu, India, and those in Cyprus and Palestine are also pointed to as evidence for the connections between the ancient populations of these regions. However, a countervailing theory states that Tamils originated in South India and then migrated west toward these regions, rather than the other way around. Neither account has gained scientific primacy, and both await more archaeological and linguistic evidence.

A fourth origin myth, which comes from Tamil sources of the ninth century, states that

Tamils time line

B.C.E.

1000–800 Early Tamils bury their dead in urns, some of which may have an ancient form of Tamil writing on them. Several burial sites have been excavated at Adichanallur in Tamil Nadu, India.

25 Greek geographer Strabo mentions seeing 120 ships leaving Hormuz in Persia for India.

200 Estimated start of the Sangam period of classical Tamil culture.

C.E.

0–15th century The Kalabhras ruled southern India between the Sangam and second Pandyan Eras.

20–50 Extensive trade between Tamils and the Greeks and Romans.

200 Estimated end of the Sangam period of classical Tamil culture.

361 Roman emperor Julian receives visitors from the Pandya Tamil kingdom.

second and fifth centuries Two long Tamil verse romance-epics are written: *Cilappatikaram* (The jeweled anklet) by Ilanko Atikal and its sequel *Manimekalai* (The girdle of gems), a Buddhist work by Cattanar.

sixth century After a period of decline and loss of power, the Pandyans emerge in Madurai again.

590–620 Reign of the Pandyan king Kadungon.

670–700 Reign of the Pandyan king Arikesar Maravarman.

800 The second Chera kingdom is established under Kulasekhara Alvar.

815–862 Reign of the Pandyan king Srimara Srivallabha.

ninth–15th centuries Pallavas dominate Telugu and northern Tamil regions.

950 The second phase of Pandyan sovereignty comes to an end with the emerging Chola kingdom defeating Pandyan king Rajasimha II.

985–1042 The former Sangan kingdom of Chola reemerges and becomes the most powerful state in southern India under Rajaraja and his successor, Rajendra I.

985–1279 The Chola period increases both the numbers and stature of Tamils in the region of present-day Sri Lanka.

1090–1102 Years that the last Chera king, Rama Varma Kulasekhara, sits on his throne.

1190 The Pandyans reemerge for a third time and reclaim their powerful position over the entire Tamil region.

1279 The Chola dynasty comes to an end due to weak leadership and perhaps overextension of the empire.

1310–11 The Northern Delhi sultanate invades the Pandyan kingdom.

16th–17th century Most Tamils are ruled by the Telegu Vijayanagar empire.

1639 The British begin their southern Indian colonization process in Madras by building a trading center at Fort Saint George.

16th–19th centuries British colonials bring new groups of Tamils (Estate Tamils) to Sri Lanka, then called Ceylon, to work on tea and coffee plantations in the central highlands.

1801 The British consolidate control in the Tamil lands in India and hold them until Indian independence in 1947.

1940s The decolonization process causes the Estate Tamils and Sinhalese in Sri Lanka to see each other as long-standing enemies.

20th–21st centuries Tamil Nadu increasingly highlights cultural differences from North India, and Tamil identity surfaces as an important factor in local and state politics.

1950 Half the Sri Lankan Tamil population loses the right to vote in the country.

(continues)

Tamils time line *(continued)*

1960s Sinhala is made the only national language of Sri Lanka and Buddhism is given a central place, both of which marginalize the wealthier, better-educated Tamils.

1960s 600,000 Tamils are deported (or migrate, depending on the source) to India, while another 375,000 are granted Sri Lankan citizenship.

1976 The Tamil United Liberation Front (TULF) is formed to begin the process of Tamil secession from Sri Lanka and attempts to form a separate state of Tamil Eelam.

1983 More than 20 years of civil war begins in Sri Lanka between Sinhalese nationalists and the successors of TULF, the Liberation Tigers of Tamil Eelam (LTTE), or Tamil Tigers.

1990s Frequent suicide bombings in Colombo. Altogether at least 60,000 Sri Lankans are killed during the 20-year civil war.

2002 A cease-fire agreement is signed by the Tamils and Sinhalese, bringing hope to all Sri Lankans.

2003 The remaining 168,141 Estate Tamils are granted Sri Lankan citizenship.

2006 Renewed fighting kills hundreds of people and quashes hopes for a peaceful Sri Lanka in the immediate future.

there were three Tamil academies, or *sangams,* for the creation of poetry and scholarship spanning nearly 10,000 years of Tamil history. The first *sangam,* which was established in southern Madurai and then was swallowed up by the sea, lasted for 4,440 years; the second, at Kapatapuram, which was likewise submerged, lasted for 3,700 years. The third *sangam* is believed to have been convened in the contemporary city of Madurai and lasted for 1,850 years. While the first two *sangams* are probably entirely mythological and the third largely so, the legend is based on the historical fact of a Tamil *sangam* having existed between about 200 B.C.E. and 200 C.E. Like the Lemuria theory, the *sangam* theory posits that the sites of the first two *sangams* were destroyed by floods and now lie submerged under the sea.

A more likely possibility for the origins of the Tamils, although one that is still contested by some experts, is that the ancient HARAPPANS of the Indus Valley were the ancestors of contemporary Dravidian language speakers, the largest and most ancient group being Tamils. This society reached its peak in the years 2300–1900 B.C.E., and then in about 1500 B.C.E. its cities and towns were mysteriously abandoned. Both climate change and an influx of INDO-ARYANS have been blamed for this disintegration, but definitive answers have yet to be uncovered by archaeologists working in the area.

HISTORY

India

The first scientific evidence for a Tamil-speaking people comes from between 1000 and 800 B.C.E. Archeological excavations from Adichanallur in Tamil Nadu, India, have revealed urn burials in which entire bodies have been placed in giant pottery vessels and then buried. These and other practices evident in the sites are described in early Tamil literature as specific to this group, which has led many experts to assign Tamil origins to the remains. The first evidence of Tamil writing, dated to about the second century B.C.E., are simple inscriptions located in Buddhist and Jainist caves and written in a script called Tamil Brahmi.

While these early centuries of Tamil history remain somewhat unclear in terms of their political and social structures, Tamil history finally becomes clearer in the first years of the common era. At this time the Tamil lands as described in the literature of the period stretched from Tirupati northwest of Madras to Kanyakumari, known as Cape Comorin during the colonial era, at the very southern tip of the Indian subcontinent. And while the earlier *sangams* were legendary, there clearly was a *sangam* operating in the Tamil lands by the early common era as a significant amount of poetry has been found from that time forward. The most important collections are *Ettuttogai,* made up of eight separate anthologies, and *Pattuppattu,* the Ten Idylls. This was a period of extensive sea travel and trade between the Tamil kingdoms and other world empires. There are comments made in both Greek and Roman works about the Pandyan kings, who were Tamil speakers, and significant numbers of Roman coins have been found in India in levels dating from this period. Roman pottery found in Arikamedu, on India's southeastern coast, has also been definitively dated to 20–50 C.E. and points to extensive trade between the Tamil kingdom and Rome. In 25 B.C.E. the Greek geographer Strabo mentioned seeing about 120 ships leaving Hormuz in Persia for India; he also spoke of dignitaries from the Pandyan kingdom in residence at the court of the Roman emperor Augustus.

In this age of classical Tamil culture, there were three separate Tamil kingdoms in southern India: Pandya in the far south, Chola in the east, and Chera in the west. Although these dynastic names, some of the rulers' individual names, and a few other features of these kingdoms are known, there is great confusion about many of the details. There is not even an accepted chronology for when each of these emerged, flourished, declined, and reemerged. In addition, at times a number of other dynasties also challenged the Pandya, Chola, and Chera between the start of the common era and the Middle Ages. One of these was the Kalabhras, who ruled southern India between the Sangam and second Pandyan eras; another is the Pallavas, who dominated the TELUGUS and the northern Tamil regions from the ninth to 15th centuries.

Pandya, the oldest of these Tamil kingdoms, with a name that means "big" or "strong" in Tamil, is usually designated as having three distinct periods of power over the Tamil lands around Madurai; however, what the exact dates of these three periods were varies in many of the available sources. Without doubt, the first Pandyan period was associated with the so-called third *sangam* and had its capital at Madurai. The Sangam period of Pandyan history is largely known to us through Tamil literary sources and thus remains extremely vague in terms of social and economic structure, but we do know that the Roman emperor Julian had visitors from Pandya in 361 and that the Chinese knew of the kingdom's existence as well. It probably came into being around the turn of the common era, although some sources claim much more ancient origins, and it lasted for four or five centuries. After a period of decline and loss of power, the Pandyans emerged in Madurai again in the sixth century; some sources claim 550 was the appropriate date, others 590.

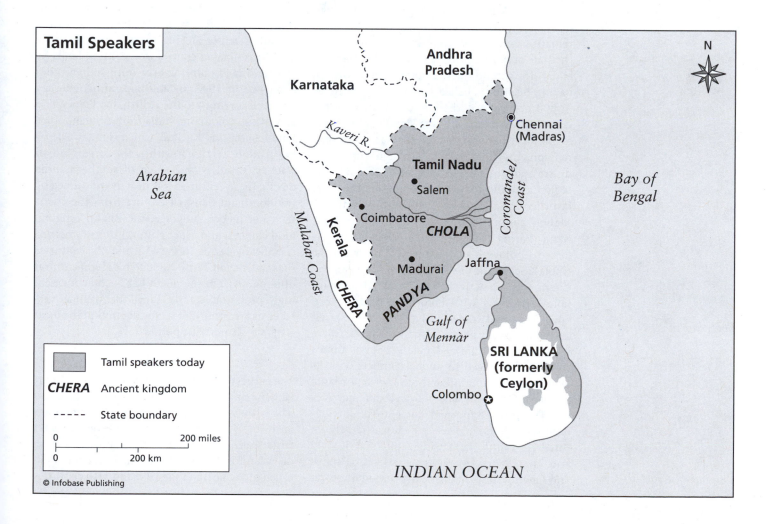

Tamil Speakers

Legend:
- Tamil speakers today
- **CHERA** Ancient kingdom
- State boundary
- 0 — 200 miles
- 0 — 200 km

© Infobase Publishing

The name of Kadungon is usually associated with this period of Pandyan history as the ruler from 590 to 620; other important rulers were Arikesar Maravarman, who ruled from 670 to 700, and Srimara Srivallabha, whose rule lasted from 815 to 862. In around 950, this phase of Pandyan sovereignty came to an end when the emerging Chola kingdom defeated the Pandyan king Rajasimha II. In approximately 1190, however, the Pandyans reemerged and reclaimed their powerful position over the entire Tamil region, holding it until 1310–11, when the Tamil area was invaded by armies from the northern Delhi sultanate. However, local Pandyan nobles continued to hold power in various localities around southeastern India.

Like the Pandyans, Chera, which ruled over much of the territory that is today encompassed by Kerala and Tamil Nadu, can be divided into several ruling periods with several interregnums in the intervals. The most ancient of these periods is associated with the Sangam period, and many poems have been written about the Tamil rulers of that time. The founder of the Chera dynasty was Perumchottu Utiyan Cheralatan, although it was his son who began expanding his father's kingdom and enriching it through military action. The exact dates of these events remain vague but are probably associated with the start of the common era in the Christian calendar. The second Chera empire is better known, having been established by Kulasekhara Alvar in 800 C.E. He was the first of 12 rulers of the Alvar dynasty who all gave significant support to the development of south India's devotional religion, the Bhakti cult, although both Buddhism and Jainism had been introduced into the region and allowed to exist alongside the royal favorite. The capital of Chera at this time was Mahodyapuram, although the last Chera king, Rama Varma Kulasekhara (r. 1090–1102), was forced to move his capital to Quilon when the Cholas sacked the previous capital. Like Pandya, Chera was an active trading state that maintained relations with Rome, the Middle East, and China and traded in ivory, timber, spices, and other luxury goods. Also like Pandya, Chera was a heavily militarized society that was almost constantly engaged in armed conflicts with its neighbors, both Tamil and otherwise, for land, people, trade goods, and political supremacy.

The third important ancient Tamil kingdom was Chola, or Cola, which was largely located in Tamil Nadu with capitals at Kanchi and Thanjavur. As was the case with Pandya and Chera, Chola had an early period of power that is known to us only through the Sangam literature. Then, unlike these other two, nothing much was heard from the Cholas again until 985 when Rajaraja I brought the sleeping giant back to the political stage of southern India. Under Rajaraja and his successor, Rajendra I, Chola became the most powerful state in all of southern India for a short period, until 1042. The Cholas even extended their kingdom to incorporate northern Sri Lanka; invaded Bengal; and occupied sections of Myanmar (Burma), Malaya, and the island of Sumatra. They spread their Hindu culture far and wide and for 300 years were among the most powerful states of Asia. However, by the mid-13th century the Cholas had begun to decline due to weak leadership and perhaps overextension of their empire, and the entire dynasty came to an end in 1279.

Following the fall of these three kingdoms, other rulers stepped in to take their places. The Pallavas were among the most successful, ruling the Tamil people until about the 15th century, though they seem not to have been Tamils themselves. From the 16th century until the arrival of the British in the 17th century, most Tamils were ruled by the Telugu Vijayanagar empire.

The British began their southern Indian colonization process in Madras by building a trading center at Fort Saint George in 1639; they consolidated control in the Tamil lands by 1801 and held onto the area until Indian independence in 1947. In addition, although they lost their territory to the British, the French had also begun colonizing India from contemporary Pondicherry and Karikal, which is today a separate Union Territory within the larger Indian state of Tamil Nadu. Much of southern India during these centuries was heavily influenced by the dominant Sanskrit culture from the country's north, but language, the Bhakti religion, food choices, and other cultural traits remained specifically Tamil. In the 20th and 21st centuries the tendency in Tamil Nadu to highlight cultural differences from the north has become increasingly pronounced, and Tamil identity has surfaced as an important factor not only at the local level but also in state politics.

Sri Lanka

The earliest history of the Tamil presence in Sri Lanka remains a highly politicized subject on which there is little consensus. Contemporary SINHALESE nationalists claim that there was no large-scale Tamil community or power base on the island until the Chola kingdom conquered much of the north in the 10th and 11th centuries and that the country's large, indigenous Tamil community arrived in that period. On the other side of this debate, contemporary Tamil nationalists in Sri Lanka claim their ancestors have been resident on the island for at least 2,000 years. At this point there is not enough evidence for either side to claim an intellectual victory. What is clear is that the Chola period certainly increased both the numbers and stature of Hindu Tamils on the island, whose south is inhabited largely by the Buddhist Sinhalese. At that time the Tamils established themselves as the dominant ethnolinguistic group in the island's northeast, with smaller communities further south down the east coast and in the northwest as well.

During the British colonial period a new group of Tamil speakers was brought to Sri Lanka, then called Ceylon, largely to work on the tea and later coffee plantations of the country's central highland region. This group has been called Indian Tamils, Hill Country Tamils, or Estate Tamils, to refer to their confinement to the estates of the British colonials. Nonetheless, British policy created resentments among the majority Sinhalese people who believed the Tamils generally were receiving preferential treatment. When the island began the decolonization process in the 1940s, the two communities began to see each other as long-standing enemies. In 1950 about half the Sri Lankan Tamil population, who had been brought as Estate Tamils, lost the right to vote in the country, and in the 1960s about 600,000 of them were deported (or migrated, depending on the source) to India, while another 375,000 were granted Sri Lankan citizenship; in 2003 the final 168,141 Estate Tamils who had been without a state for more than half a century were granted Sri Lankan citizenship. In the 1960s Sinhala was made the only national language of Sri Lanka and Buddhism was given a central place, both of which marginalized even wealthier, better-educated Tamils.

In 1976 the Tamil United Liberation Front formed to begin the process of Tamil secession from Sri Lanka and the formation of a separate state of Tamil Eelam. By the early 1980s a more than 20-year-long civil war between Sinhalese nationalists and the successors of TULF, the Liberation Tigers of Tamil Eelam (LTTE), or just Tamil Tigers, was underway. The nationalist Tamils were pushing for self-rule and a state of their own in the country's northeast region, where most Tamils currently live. Most of the fighting took place in this traditional Tamil region in the north, but in the 1990s suicide bomb-

These flip-flop-wearing soldiers, only some of whom are armed, are recruits to the Tamil Tigers in late 1995, when suicide bombings became an important strategy in the group's long-term civil war against the Sinhalese-dominated government of Sri Lanka. (AP Photo/Sherwin Crasto)

ings were not infrequent even in Colombo. Altogether at least 60,000 Sri Lankans were killed during the 20-year civil war prior to a cease-fire agreement that was signed by the two sides in 2002. This event brought hope to the shattered country, but fighting in 2006 killed hundreds more people, and in early 2008 the Sri Lankan government withdrew from the peace process entirely, quashing the hopes of millions.

CULTURE

In India

The most important cultural feature that unites all Tamils is their common linguistic heritage. Tamil, one of two classic languages of India along with Sanskrit, is the most ancient Dravidian tongue and has been a written language for more than 2,000 years. Along with poetry, the ancient *sangam,* or Tamil academy, also produced a book of Tamil grammar called *Tolkappiyar* and other literature. Although the dates for this period of cultural blossoming are contested, the most common period cited is about 200 B.C.E.–200 C.E.

In addition to language, many Tamils share similar household and village structures and agricultural subsistence practices. Households tend to be made up of extended nuclear families rather than large, extended kin groups. Around five or six people live in three-generation houses, but it is also common for older people to live separately from their married children. Wealthier Tamil families tend to have at least one servant living with them as well. Tamil villages are usually between 2,000 and 5,000 people in size and in the past were spatially divided into separate regions for different caste groups; this practice has not disappeared but may not be as strict as it was before caste was made illegal in the late 1940s. Villages provide not only housing but also temples for different deities, wells, land for cremations or burials, a common area for threshing rice, and a reservoir for irrigating land. Many villages had an informal council that controlled local political and judicial matters, but since Indian independence, when formalized, elected councils were supposed to replace these informal ones, the entire village-level political structure has remained relatively neglected in favor of state-level politics.

As this village infrastructure indicates, the predominant economic activity of Tamils has always been agriculture. There is evidence of irrigation having developed in the area of Tamil Nadu in at least the second century B.C.E., and even today irrigated wet rice is the main crop. Other crops include millet, sorghum, beans, oil seeds, coconuts, vegetables, mangoes, tamarind, and bananas; some Tamils have found sugarcane, cotton, and peanuts to be lucrative cash crops as well.

The traditional division of labor in Tamil society dictated that men plowed both wet-rice fields and dry farmland and harvested rice, while women transplanted rice seedlings and weeded; women were also responsible for child care, housework, and milking cows. Women were not allowed to handle men's tools, such as carts, pottery wheels, or fishing nets, and today this has meant a taboo against women driving taxis. These prohibitions, however, have not stopped women from becoming teachers, nurses, and white-collar workers. In the past, oxen provided most of the horsepower on Tamil farms and were used for plowing, turning presses to extract oil from seeds, and other heavy activity; many small, rural areas continue this pattern today. Cows have provided milk, and many villagers continue to keep them as well as chickens, goats, sheep, and donkeys. On Tamil Nadu's coastline as well as in Sri Lanka, there are castes of traditional fishermen who continue to make their living through that activity. The various artisan castes in Tamil society make products from clay, leather, brass, reeds, wood, and cotton.

Like the ownership of these activities, there are also agricultural castes within Tamil society. The dominant Vellalars are the predominant landowners in Tamil villages and pose an interesting problem for understanding Tamil society in relation to the rest of India. Throughout India the concept of caste can be organized along the lines of the four *varnas,* or overarching classifications based on the relative purity of the group. Brahmins are at the top of the hierarchy and are considered the most ritually pure, followed by Kshatriyas, Vaishyas, and Shudras. As agricultural workers, Vellalars should be classified as a subcaste of Shudras, the servant class, and thus ritually relatively impure and low in status. In Tamil society, however, Vellalars are considered just below Brahmins and are often the most politically and economically powerful group in a region. Certain landless subcastes that in northern India may have relatively high status as part of the Vaishya *varna,* pertaining to mercantilism, are considered very low status among Tamils. Both anthropologists and historians of Tamil society have spent considerable time and effort exploring these differences between Tamil and northern Indian notions of caste and subcaste without coming to any clear-cut conclusions about the sources of the differences or the meaning of the similarities; for example, both the very top-status Brahmins and the very bottom-status Dalits remain essentially the same throughout northern and southern India. Also common to both Tamil and northern Indian social organization is that many of the larger subcastes have traditionally had councils to enforce caste rules and norms.

Besides language, agriculture, and their own unique version of the caste system, there are few other institutions that link all Tamils together. For example, while Hinduism is the most common religion among both Indian and Sri Lankan Tamils at about 80 percent, a significant number of Tamils in both countries are Sunni Muslims, and there are increasing numbers of Christian Tamils in both countries; Buddhism and Jainism are also represented among Tamils but only in small numbers. Kinship structures also vary among Tamils. Most are patrilineal and trace their lineage membership only through their father's line of descent, but lineage membership is not as important as in northern India and is usually counted only for three generations. However, in Sri Lanka matrilineal descent among Tamils, the tracing of lineage membership through the mother's line, is common among the supporters of Tamil

Eelam, even among Muslim Tamils. In addition, all Tamils see their matrilateral relatives, those on their mothers' side, as more important than in most patrilineal societies. A few Tamil groups have created wider kinship groupings called *gotras,* which are fictitious exogamous clans out of which all members must marry, but most others do not have these clanlike structures. Most Tamils are also patrilocal, requiring new brides to move in with their new husbands and their families, but this general principle is not always followed, and women are generally expected to return to their own families' homes for childbirth, especially for their first child, and to remain there for several months.

For the 80 percent of Tamils who practice Hinduism, there is a heavy emphasis on village-level religion, with a large pantheon of gods and goddesses representing each local caste and subcaste group, rather than the more textual and formal version of Hinduism and its well-known deities like Siva, Brahman, and Ganesh. Goddesses are more common than gods in Tamil village religion and are called upon to assist in healing, fertility, and other issues of life and death; gods are more commonly associated with the land and nature generally. Within each village the birthday celebrations of the local deities usually make up the most important public events, and for individuals pilgrimages to important sites in Madurai and Palani are important supravillage events. Over the past millennia many Tamil deities have been linked to those in the Sanskrit pantheon, a process called Sanskritization, similar to the incorporation of Tamil castes and subcastes into the more familiar Sanskrit *varna* system.

In Sri Lanka

Some of the cultural features of Tamil life in India are similar to those in Sri Lanka. The Tamil language in both countries is very similar, as are the caste, kinship, and religious systems. However, there are also important distinctions based on the history of the two groups as well as different economic activities. For example, the Tamils in Sri Lanka are divided not only by caste, religion, and kinship but also by history. The more ancient Tamil residents of the island, whether that past goes back 1,000 or 2,000 years, are believed by both Estate Tamils and Sinhalese to be wealthy, caste-conscious, privileged, crafty, and miserly; these Tamils tend not to classify Estate Tamils along with themselves, unless in juxtaposition to the island's Sinhalese majority or in aiming to gain Indian assistance

for their nationalist cause. Estate Tamils, as servants and landless laborers brought to Sri Lanka by the British, tended to be from lower caste and class groups and today are seen by outsiders as the poorest and least-educated Sri Lankans, best suited to being docile servants. Neither group, Tamils long resident in Sri Lanka or Estate Tamils, fully inhabits either of these identities, but the stereotypical images have tended to keep the two groups at least somewhat separate, despite their commonalities.

Since the mid-1970s one of the things that has linked many Tamils in Sri Lanka is a desire for a separate Tamil state on the island, Tamil Eelam. The movement began with wealthier Tamils from the northern peninsula of Jaffna who had recently lost access to many lucrative civil service jobs with the implementation of a Sinhala-language policy at the national level. They were soon joined by poorer Tamils from other regions who had long experienced discriminatory economic policies that brought development to other regions of the country but rarely to them. The disenfranchised Estate Tamils, who lost the vote in 1950, have been keen supporters of Tamil Eelam throughout the years, although their numbers dwindled during the second half of the 20th century with deportation and outmigration to India and elsewhere.

See also DRAVIDIANS.

FURTHER READING

M. Srinivasa Aiyangar. *Tamil Studies: Essays on the History of the Tamil People, Language, Religion, and Literature* (New Delhi: Asian Educational Services, 1982).
E. Valentine Daniel. *Fluid Signs: Being a Person the Tamil Way* (Berkeley and Los Angeles: University of California Press, 1987).
Isabelle Nabokov. *Religion against the Self: An Ethnography of Tamil Rituals* (New York: Oxford University Press, 2000).
K. K. Pillay. *A Social History of the Tamils* (Madras: University of Madras, 1975).
Thomas R. Trautmann. *Dravidian Kinship* (Cambridge: Cambridge University Press, 1981).
Margaret Trawick. *Notes on Love in a Tamil Family* (Berkeley and Los Angeles: University of California Press, 1990).
Susan Wadley, ed. *The Powers of Tamil Women* (Syracuse, N.Y.: Syracuse University, 1980).

Tampuan (Tampuon, Tompuan)

The Tampuan are a Mon-Khmer ethnic group who resides primarily in Cambodia's Ratanakiri Province, in the northeast of the country.

TAMPUAN

location:
Ratanakiri Province,
northeastern Cambodia

time period:
Unknown to the present

ancestry:
Mon-Khmer

language:
Tampuan, a Central
Bahnaric language of the
Mon-Khmer language
family

Traditionally they were swidden, or slash-and-burn, agriculturalists who maintained two houses for each family, one in the village and the other at their field where they grew rice, corn, beans, squash, and other vegetables. Every couple of years, after the soil in these plots had been depleted, families would relocate their gardens either to patches of virgin forest or to plots that had sat fallow for up to 20 years. Men generally did the work of clearing the land and burning off the vegetation, while women did most of the planting, weeding, and harvesting.

The Tampuan matrilocal residences, into which husbands move to live with their wives and their families, consist of longhouses with a main area for cooking and eating off of which there are separate sleeping quarters for each couple. When a daughter marries and her husband joins her, the family extends their longhouse by another 10–12 feet to create new sleeping quarters for the young couple. Each village has 50 or more of these longhouses, usually containing families that are related to one another by way of matrilineal kinship ties—that is, bonds created through descent passed down through lines of women, or through in-law relations. The Danish ethnographic film *Anger of the Spirits,* filmed in 2001–02 in the Tampuan community around Yeak Laom Lake, depicts the life of five individuals representing various generations of Tampuan and their community life.

The Tampuan region around Yeak Laom Lake has attracted the attention of international agencies as well after Ratanakiri Province declared it a protected area in May 1995. The 5,000-hectare zone, which encompasses five Tampuan villages containing about 300 separate families, has hosted projects from the United Nations and Canada's International Development Research Center. These agencies have been cooperating with local leaders to promote economic development as well as natural-resource management. A Cultural and Environmental Center was established after 1996; a handicraft-production project has inserted much-needed cash into the local economy, and an environmentally sustainable tourist project has brought in outsiders to hike, swim, ride elephants, and tour the area. From August 1998 onward, Yeak Laom Commune, an entirely Tampuan organization, was granted a 25-year lease to manage the area and thus receives all proceeds from admittance, parking, sales, and any other activities.

Another international aid organization–sponsored project has helped to bring literacy to a number of Tampuan individuals. Tampuan itself was a preliterate language, but with the assistance of professional linguists the Khmer alphabet has been adapted to some of the unfamiliar sounds in Tampuan. With this alphabet some Tampuan have begun reading and writing in their own language and receiving training in how to teach these skills to their fellow villagers. The governmental and international organizations involved in the project hope that literacy will allow the Tampuan to integrate more fully into Cambodian society as well as to capture aspects of their own cultural tradition, especially mythology and history, which in the past was passed on only orally.

Tamu *See* Gurung.

Tanguts *See* Dangxiang.

Ta-p'en-k'eng culture (Dapenkeng culture)

Ta-p'en-k'eng is not the name that a group of people would have used to refer to themselves but rather a reference to an ancient group of Austronesian-language speakers who established themselves on today's Taiwan after having left the southeastern Chinese provinces of Fujian and Guangdong nearly 6,000 years ago. The name comes from an archaeological site in northern Taiwan near the mouth of the Tanshui River.

Like the Micronesians and Polynesians who established themselves on the islands of the Pacific, the Austronesians who established Ta-p'en-k'eng culture traveled in dugout canoes that could be sailed and probably already had access to a range of domesticated plants and animals, some of which make up the traditional Oceanic subsistence package: dogs and pigs, rice and taro. The archaeological record is still very incomplete, however, and remains of these domesticates have yet to be found alongside the more distinctive aspect of Ta-p'en-k'eng culture, their pottery, which is decorated with cord marks, incisions, and imprints of mollusk shells.

Tatars (Dadas Sibtatars, Tartars)

The term *Tatar* or *Tartar* has been used throughout history in a number of different ways. The Russians applied the term to anybody of Turkic descent or Muslim religion beginning in the 14th century or so; in czarist Russia, *Tartary* was the name given to Siberia. Outside Rus-

TA-P'EN-K'ENG CULTURE

location:
Taiwan

time period:
4500 to 1500 b.c.e.

ancestry:
South Chinese

language:
Proto-Austronesian

sia as well, *Tatar* has often been used to refer to eastern European Turkic-speaking peoples. In addition, the term has often been misused to refer to the MONGOLS who invaded Central Asia and Europe in the 13th century; British and Americans also used the term incorrectly to refer to the MANCHUS of China and on that basis named the body of water that lies between Siberia and Sakhalin Island the Tatar Strait.

The original Tatars were a group of tribes who seem to have come from the region of northeastern Mongolia in about the fifth century, the period of the emergence of TURKIC PEOPLES more generally. Today the term should be used to refer only to those people who speak a form of the larger Tatar language, itself a Western Turkic language group. The largest contemporary group of Tatars resides in European Russia and the Crimea, part of Ukraine. During the Soviet era almost half a million European Tatars were deported from the region and resettled throughout Central Asia and Siberia as well. Since 1989, however, many of them have returned home, only to find that they are as unwelcome there as in their forced homes in the east for much of the 20th century; the Crimea had largely been slavicized by a large influx of Russians and Ukrainians.

In addition to these European Tatars, some of whom resemble their blonde-haired, blue-eyed Slavic neighbors instead of their Turkic and Mongol ancestors, there are also several branches of the larger Tatar ethnic group who reside in Central Asia and Siberia and resemble their ancestors. The largest of these groups is the Siberian Tatars, or Sibtatars, who are indigenous Turkic-speaking peoples from three different dialect groups, as well as a large number of Crimean, Volga, and other European Tatar groups who were exiled to Siberia during the 20th century; this entry will not cover them because of their European background. Tatars are also one of the 55 recognized minority groups in China, residing mostly in the towns of Yining, Tacheng, and Urumqi in Xinjiang Province.

The indigenous Siberian Tatar groups are sometimes divided into separate dialectical or geographical units called Baraba, Chulym, Abakan, and Northern Altai. They all speak dialects of Siberian Tatar, itself considered a subgroup of Tatar more generally. The origins of these people are extremely varied, with Ugric, Samoyed, Mongol, and Turkic, especially Kipchak, tribes contributing to their makeup. They live primarily in three different regions: the land between Tobolsk and Tomsk, the Altai, and the South Yenisey River region. They were originally nomadic pastoralists who relied primarily on their horses for transport, milk, and meat, but depending on their geography many Asian Tatar groups also turned to hunting or agriculture. Today they are largely agricultural and pastoral, activities that were collectivized during the Soviet era but that have once again come under private ownership and the control of small groups of related men. In the Altai, hunting remains extremely important to supplement the few cereals and vegetables they are able to grow in the difficult climate. While most Tatars, including most Siberian Tatars, are Muslims, today there are a small number of Orthodox Christian Tatars in Siberia, especially among the Abakan Tatars; most groups also continue to practice some form of shamanism and to believe in the powers of various spirits from the natural world.

Historically, the Siberian Tatars are the descendants of both the original Gokturk and Oghuz Turkic peoples as well as the Turkicized subjects of the 13th century khanate of Sibir, a khanate established in the far north by Shayban, a grandson of Genghis Khan. For 20 years before the khanate of Sibir fell to the Russians in 1582, the khan, Kuchum, tried to impose Islam on his people as well as collect a tax payable only in native fur; this practice was soon adopted by the colonizing Russians in the region. Another Tatar practice that was widely adopted by the Russians was the distillation of spirits from grain, which the Russians called vodka, or "dear little water." Once Islam had been introduced, it took another 200 years or more for most of the Tatar population to adopt it, and many indigenous beliefs and practices have been maintained alongside Islam ever since.

Chinese Tatars have been residing in their present homeland since the Tang dynasty (618–907), when they fled from the Gokturk and Oghuz Turkic empires during times of strife. Their territory in northern China was overrun by the Mongols in the 12th century, and in many regions these Mongol armies came to be called Tatar, despite their different linguistic and cultural backgrounds. Other Tatars arrived in China only in the 20th century after fleeing from Soviet political repression in Siberia. As a result, as is the case in Siberia, beyond their adherence to Sunni Islam and their various Tatar dialects, there are few common cultural features that unite all 5,000 or so Chinese Tatars.

TATARS

location:
Siberia, all of Central Asia (Uzbekistan, Kazakhstan, Tajikistan, Kyrgyzstan, Turkmenistan), and Xinjiang Province of northwest China. There is also a large population of Tatars in European Russia and Ukraine.

time period:
Fifth century C.E. to the present

ancestry:
Turkic with mixtures of Mongol, Samoyed, Ugric, among others

language:
Tatar, a language group made up of many dialects all within the larger Turkic family

TATS AND MOUNTAIN JEWS

location:
Azerbaijan and Russian Dagestan

time period:
fifth or sixth century to the present

ancestry:
Persian and Jewish or Khazar

language:
Tati, a Persian language or dialect (linguists do not agree) written with the Azeri script. Jewish Tats speak Judeo-Tat, sometimes called Juhuri or Juwri, which is very similar to Tat, with some additional Hebrew words and inflections.

TAUSUG

location:
Sulu Archipelago, Mindanao, the Philippines; and Sabah, Malaysia

time period:
3000 B.C.E. to the present

ancestry:
Austronesian

language:
Tausug, a Meso-Philippine language within the larger Austronesian language family

---

FURTHER READING

Guzel Amalrik. *Memories of a Tatar Childhood*, trans. Marc E. Heine (London: Hutchinson, 1979).

Charles J. Halperin. *The Tatar Yoke* (Columbus, Ohio: Slavica Publishers, 1986).

Boris S. Izhboldin. *Essays on Tatar History* (New Delhi: New Book Society of India, 1963).

Tats and Mountain Jews (Dagchufut, Juhuro [Jewish only], Tatians)

The degree of connection between the Tats and Mountain Jews, sometimes called Jewish Tats, is a matter of great debate. Some sources state that Muslim and Jewish Tats constitute a single ethnic group, based on their common Persian-based language; however, their different cultural patterns, arising from their religious differences, have led others to categorize them separately. The tradition of grouping them together actually emerged less than 100 years ago, during the Soviet era. Soviet ethnographers combined the two populations because they saw in all Tat-speaking communities a common language and "primitive, Asian" beliefs and practices that had to be eliminated in the quest for a modern socialist society. Prior to this Soviet-era ethnic invention, the category of Mountain Jew itself was a czarist bureaucratic invention of the 1820s. This population was seen as very different from the European Ashkenazi Jews of the Russian Pale, and so despite their Jewish faith they were labeled differently. Prior to this bureaucratic labeling, Jewish Tats had been called *Dzhukhur,* meaning "another faith," referring to their difference from the local Muslim population. It is unclear the degree to which the Dzhukhur were considered a subgroup or an entirely separate people.

The Tats are believed to be a Persian community who have been in the southern Caucasus since the fifth or sixth century, when Sassanid (*see* PERSIANS, SASSANIDS) leaders sent them there to protect the northern borders of the empire. The origins of the Mountain Jews are more unclear. According to some theories, they are descendants of the Jews who were captured by the Assyrians in Israel in 721 B.C.E., and then by the Babylonians in Judah in 589 B.C.E., and moved to Media, from where they fled to the Caucasus to escape persecution in the fifth century. Another theory has them descended from Jewish Khazars, who ruled portions of the southern Caucasus from the mid-seventh to the end of the 10th century.

In addition to their Persian-based languages and probable migration from Media in the fifth

or sixth century, these two Tat communities also share some other cultural traits, or at least they did prior to the end of the Soviet era, when many Jewish Tat families left for Israel or the United States. Both preferred extended family households rather than nuclear family residences and were endogamous as much as possible—that is, marrying within their own ethnic group. New husbands and their families also paid a bride price, in which money and gifts were given to the family of a new bride to compensate for the loss of her household labor and to legitimate any children the couple might have. There are some reports that both Jewish and Muslim Tat communities allowed polygyny, or multiple wives, as well, but not all sources support this idea. The concept of family and individual honor is also extremely important, with both Jewish and Muslim Tat–speaking families engaging in blood feuds and vendettas to maintain their honor.

Another similarity is in the realm of economic activity. While Jews in Europe and Central Asia were largely forbidden from owning land, Mountain Jews and Muslim Tats alike were farmers at the beginning of the 20th century. Both experienced collectivization under the Soviets and continued to work the land under those conditions. Grain crops, especially rice, were common, along with vegetables and fruit. Unlike their Muslim neighbors, the Mountain Jews also grew tobacco and made wine, as did their Christian Armenian neighbors.

See also MEDES.

Tausug (Joloano, Jolo Moro, Sulu, Suluk, Sulu Moro, Taw Sug)

The Tausug are a subgroup of the FILIPINO MUSLIMS and the dominant ethnic group in the Sulu Archipelago. Their homeland is Jolo Island, while large numbers also live on Pata, Tapul, throughout the rest of the archipelago, and even on Mindanao. Smaller numbers of Tausug live in the Malaysian state of Sabah as well, but there they are known as the Suluk people.

As AUSTRONESIANS, the Tausug would have migrated to the Philippines about 5,000 years ago from Taiwan and ultimately southern China. Their original homeland in the archipelago seems to have been Mindanao, where they lived until the early years of Chinese trade with the island between 960 and 1279. Linguistic evidence points to the 10th and 11th centuries as the period in which the original Tausug migrants arrived on Jolo. By the end of the 13th century the Tausug had become the dominant group in this region, where they converted to Islam, which further strengthened their position in relation to the neighboring SAMALS. In contemporary times the Tausug continue to dominate the politics of their region; they made up large numbers of the Moro National Liberation Front, the first Muslim insurgency group to negotiate a peace treaty successfully with the Filipino government in 1996.

Despite their name, which means "people of the sea current," the Tausug occupy the highlands of Sulu's larger islands and other domains, while the seafaring Samals tend to live on the smaller coral islands. Their predominant economic activity is intensive agriculture, utilizing irrigated fields on which they grow rice, corn, cassava, and to a lesser extent, millet, sorghum, and sesame. Some subsistence swidden (slash-and-burn) gardens are also used at higher elevations to grow beans, eggplants, onions, peanuts, tomatoes, and yams. For the market, the Tausug grow abaca, which is a kind of hemp; coconuts; coffee; and a wide variety of tropical fruit, including bananas, durians, jackfruit, mangoes, and oranges. Fishing; raising cattle, chickens, and ducks; and trade are also common sources of both subsistence foods and cash.

Tausug society is organized along the dual principles of residence and kinship. Most agricultural Tausug households are located near the family's fields and constitute the smallest geographic unit; sometimes a group of relatives will locate their households near to each other and together make up a settlement cluster. Hamlets are made up of a handful of households, and communities, *kauman,* are groups of hamlets with their own headman, mosque, and rules for endogamy or intermarriage within the group. Generally these geographic political units are crosscut by ties of bilateral kinship so that the members of a hamlet and larger community tend to be related to one another through either blood or marriage. Rights to use particular crop lands are inherited by individual men rather than larger kin groups, but waterholes, pastures, and beaches cannot be held by individuals and instead are available to all members of a community; even strangers can make use of these resources, though it is always safer to request permission from a local headman before doing so.

Tay (Ngan, Pa Di, Phen, Tai Tho, Tho [derogatory], Thu, Thu Lao, T'o)

The Tay are the largest hill tribe in Vietnam, with almost 1.4 million people residing in the northern highlands of the country. Most live in the northeast corner of Vietnam between the Red River and the coastal plain, while a smaller community lives in the northwest province of Hoa Binh. They are linguistically related to the THAIS, sharing about 70 percent of their vocabulary, but may have migrated south from central and southern China later than the ancestral Thai. Some sources state that today's Tay came together as late as the 1700s and were originally members of various other Thai-speaking groups; their original name was Tho, "soil," which is not used today because it is considered derogatory. The Tay are also linguistically related to another Thai group, the NUNG, with whom they have shared a writing system since it was created in 1961. To a greater extent than the Thai and Nung, however, the Tay are integrated into the VIETNAMESE way of life, having adopted many aspects of Confucianism and many religious rituals from this dominant majority. The Tay participate in the state bureaucratic structure and the state education system more than other hill tribes and have contributed a number of high-ranking members to the military as well. They have a higher standard of living, a higher literacy rate, and a longer life expectancy than any other hill tribe in Vietnam, third only to the Vietnamese and HOA, or ethnic Chinese.

This integration of the Tay into wider Vietnamese national society is not a new phenomenon. During the colonial period, especially in the 20th century, the Tay frequently joined with the Vietnamese to resist the French, unlike many of the other hill tribes that sided with the French and later the Americans against the Vietnamese state. Prior to World War II, Chu Van Tan, an ethnic Nung who became a Tay chief, established a Nung-Tay militia unit to assist the Vietnamese against the French. In the mid-1940s his 3,000-soldier Vietnam National Salvation Army had scored several victories over the French in the Red River valley; they eventually became part of the Communist Viet Minh that defeated the French at Dien Bien Phu in 1954. During the Vietnam War the Tay continued to support the Vietnamese state in the north and their National Liberation Front (NLF) allies in South Vietnam against the Army of the Republic of Vietnam (South Vietnam) and its American allies.

Most Tay today engage in composite swidden (slash-and-burn) agriculture for both subsistence and cash crops; that is, they maintain both intensively worked paddies for growing rice in the lower elevations and shifting slash-and-burn fields for vegetables, millet, and other products

TAY

location:
Northern highlands of Vietnam, especially in the northeast

time period:
Possibly 0 to the present

ancestry:
Thai

language:
Tay, a Tai-Kadai language, which has shared a writing system with Nung since 1961

TELUGUS

location:
Southern India

time period:
Sixth century C.E. to the present

ancestry:
Dravidian

language:
Telugu, a Dravidian language related to Tamil, Kannada, and Malayalam

in the higher elevations. Most Tay families also have a family garden and keep cattle and/or buffalo. Tree crops like plums, apricots, and cinnamon, in addition to anise, tobacco, and soy, are common cash crops among the Tay; some Tay families sell trees for lumber or wood chips as well. Hunting and gathering in the mountains also provide occasional ritual foods and specialties that contribute to their varied diet.

Kinship among the Tay seems to be patrilineal, so that descent is traced through one's father, father's father, and so forth. This is similar to the Nung but differs from the Thais, who are largely bilateral, tracing descent equally through mothers and fathers. This difference may be the result of the Tay and Nung integration into Vietnamese society and culture, which favors patrilineal descent. The Tay also tend to live in houses built on the ground, as do most Vietnamese, rather than on stilts as is common among Vietnamese hill tribes.

Among the Tay, Confucianism, Buddhism, and Taoism, all of which were adopted from the dominant Vietnamese, are part of the religious landscape. In addition, indigenous beliefs in genies, gods, and spirits continue to inform people's worldview and ritual practices. Many Tay villages still have a local sorcerer, *thay tao*, or sometimes *vo tao*, who engages in the spirit world to enact curing rituals, divinations, or, most important, burial rites. The sorcerer determines whether deaths occur at an auspicious time for burial or whether the funeral must be delayed until a more auspicious time. The sorcerer assists in lowering the body into its coffin and chants to allow the soul of the dead to enter the body, replacing the soul of the living. He then uses his sword to exorcise the body and places a bowl of glutinous rice with a boiled egg on the coffin lid. Only when this bowl has been placed on the coffin, to provide the departing soul with a meal for its journey, are people permitted to cry and grieve out loud for their deceased relative.

Another ritual supervised by the village sorcerer is the Long Tong Festival, or Going to the Field Festival, dedicated to the god of agriculture, provider of good harvests. The sorcerer engages in a sort of sympathetic magic, in which he scatters rice on the ground and splashes water toward the sky to request that the god of agriculture provide plenty of rain and rice. He also prays for prosperity, peace, and a happy life for all the residents of his village.

Taze *See* UZBEKS.

Tchambuli *See* CHAMBRI.

Telugus (Andhra)

Although the language may have been spoken for centuries beforehand, the first inscriptions proving the existence of Telugu speakers appear in the sixth century C.E.; they were created between 573 and 576 under the patronage of Chola kings. After that time the use of Telugu expanded exponentially in the Telugu lands as other kings began using the local language instead of Sanskrit or the various Prakrits to create their inscriptions. Nonetheless, it took about five more centuries for the creation of other forms of Telugu writing, such as poetry and prose, which began to appear in the 11th century.

Today most Telugu speakers live in the Indian states of Andhra Pradesh, Karnataka, Maharashtra, and Tamil Nadu, with small numbers in the country's largest cities; during the British period in India, large numbers of Telugus also migrated to Fiji, Guyana, Malaysia, Singapore, South Africa, and many other British colonies as well. Prior to the British colonial period, Muslim sultans from Golkanda ruled over the predominantly Hindu Telugu population; today just under 10 percent of Telugus are Muslim from conversions dating from that period.

Modern Telugu identity is connected not only to language but also to kinship ties that link Telugu lineages, subclans, and clans together; membership in all of these units is based on the principle of patrilineal descent so that membership is inherited from fathers only. While all of these kinship units are exogamous, requiring people to marry outside them, Telugus also have their own version of the caste system, which is endogamous and requires each individual to marry within his or her own caste. There are two different kinds of caste among the Telugus, those like Brahmin, Reddy, Kamma, Velama, and others that are based on tribal and religious differences in background and those based on occupations such as potters, smiths, and barbers. With the exception of Brahmins and just a few others, all the rest are unique to Andhra Pradesh and the Telugus and do not coincide with groupings in other parts of India.

The basic unit of Telugu society is the nuclear family created when a woman moves into her husband's home in patrilocal residence after marriage; neolocal marriage, when the couple forms a household, is the ideal and usually occurs after several years. Telugu wives have a great responsibility to maintain the health and well-being of their husbands and children, even to the degree that widows are believed by many traditional families to be at fault because their husbands died before them.

The economic activity at the base of Telugu society for more than 1,000 years has been agriculture, and the most important and valued crop even today is rice. This product grows particularly well along the coast, especially in the Krishna and Godavari deltas, and along the region's many streams and man-made reservoirs. On nonirrigated land, Telugus grow supplementary crops such as beans, peas, sesame, and peanuts. Tomatoes, eggplant, garlic, gourds, onions, coconuts, bananas, limes, cashews, turmeric, mustard, fenugreek, coriander, and a wide variety of other fruits, vegetables, herbs, and spices are also grown both for home use and the market. Fish, chickens, ducks, turkeys, goats, sheep, and pigs provide meat, and in some regions hunting for sport still provides some households with a percentage of their protein intake.

Tenggerese (Tengerese)

The Tenggerese people are a small ethnic group that reside in the Tengger Mountains of East Java, Indonesia. Their name is said to come from the last syllables of the surnames of their two potentially mythological founders, Roro Anteng and Jaka Seger, a princess of the Majapahit kingdom in Java and her Brahmin husband, respectively. A second possibility is that the ethnonym derives from the phrase *tenggering budi luhur,* "eternal peace and high morality."

In 1478 the last large Indianized kingdom in the Malay-speaking world, the Majapahit, finally collapsed after many decades of pressure from the sultanate of Demak as well as from internal strife, caused initially by a war of succession in 1401. In the last years of the kingdom's existence, these centrifugal forces also led many people to flee from the kingdom's center and the influence of the emerging Muslim sultanates that replaced it. The contemporary Tenggerese people are believed to be the descendants of these refugees who fled to the rugged Tengger Mountains. The Tenggerese origin myth describes the marriage of the daughter of Majapahit king Brawijaya, Roro Anteng, to a Brahmin man, Jaka Seger. These two were among those who fled from the disintegrating kingdom sometime before 1500 and became the leaders of the new community. The story continues to detail their childlessness and a promise they made to the god of Mount Bromo: If they were allowed to have children, they would sacrifice the youngest by throwing him or her into the volcano. Their youngest of 25

children, a son named Kesuma, was sacrificed in that manner on the 14th day of Kasada, which coincides roughly with February, and to this day the Tenggerese people continue to celebrate the Kasada festival when they throw offerings into the volcano as a form of commemoration to their ancestors.

The Tenggerese have been participants in commercial agriculture and animal husbandry since about the middle of the 19th century, when they first began selling to the Dutch. Despite this monetization of their world, most families remained small peasant landowners, and the introduction of such social divisions as rich and poor did not bring widespread change in the social order. Most Tenggerese did not look to the values and consumption patterns of either the colonizers or the lowland JAVANESE as role models but continued to engage in the most important prestige-building activity of their own people: redistributive rituals whereby richer members of the community were forced to share some of their wealth with poorer members. The mid-1960s, however, began to bring more significant changes to the rugged Tengger Mountains. On the one hand, many Tenggerese people were killed by lowland Javanese militias on suspicion of either being communists themselves or harboring communist rebels in their mountain homes. On the other hand, the Green Revolution also arrived in the mountains at that time and finally created lasting class divisions among the peasant population. The nouveau riche began to orient their value system and consumption patterns to those of the outside world, with particular emphasis on education and mobility, while the poor no longer looked to the elite members of their own communities as role models and sources of redistributed wealth. As a result, while the Tenggerese were a unified ethnic community in the early 1960s, today they are becoming almost indistinguishable from the lowland majority with the possible exception of their religion. While lowland Javanese have been Muslim for many centuries, the Tenggerese have tended to maintain the syncretic Buddhist-Hindu religion of their Majapahit forebearers, which recognized many natural spirits and gods—Siva, Brahman, Vishnu, and the Buddha, among many others.

Tetun (Tetum, Tettum)

The Tetun are an important ethnolinguistic group on the island of Timor. Their traditional homeland in the alluvial plains of the south-central coast straddles the border between

TENGGERESE

location:
The Tengger Mountains of Java, Indonesia

time period:
About 1478 to the present

ancestry:
Refugees from the Majapahit kingdom

language:
Tengger, an archaic Javanese language from the Majapahit kingdom; most today speak Javanese.

TETUN

location:
The island of Timor, the western half of which is a province of Indonesia, the eastern half the independent country of East Timor

time period:
Possibly 3000 B.C.E. to the present

ancestry:
Austronesian

language:
Tetun, or Tetum, an Austronesian language with four separate dialects, which has been adopted by the new state of East Timor as one of the two official languages of state; the other is Portuguese

West Timor, a province of Indonesia, and the independent state of East Timor. Prior to the European colonial era the Tetun expanded from this small region and came to dominate significant territories in what is now both West and East Timor. As a result of this early expansion, today there are at least four recognized dialects of Tetun. The form spoken on the south-central coast retains much of the original complexity of the language, including different forms of speech depending on the status of the people communicating. A modified version of the language was adopted by the Portuguese as the language of trade and commerce during their more than 400 years of colonialism in East Timor; this dialect, heavily influenced by Portuguese, is often called Dili Tetun because it emerged in the country's capital. This form of Tetun has also been adopted by East Timor as one of its two recognized state languages and is spoken at least as a second language well beyond the capital.

In addition to linguistic differences between the Tetun of the south-central coast and those of the highlands regions of East Timor, there are other significant cultural differences. Perhaps the most important of these is that the Tetun of the south-central coast region, called Wehali, have a matrilineal descent system whereby children inherit membership in their mother's clan rather than their father's. All other Tetun groups have patrilineal descent systems, in which clan membership is inherited from fathers. This kinship pattern also affects residence patterns. Residence in Wehali is matrilocal with husbands moving into their wives' homes, while all other Tetun practice patrilocal residence, where wives move in with their new husbands' families.

Tetun is an Austronesian language, which points to Tetun residence on Timor for about 5,000 years. The earliest AUSTRONESIANS arrived on Timor and the rest of the Lesser Sunda Islands bearing agriculture, which allowed them to displace or subsume the local population of hunter-gatherers. Even today many Tetun continue to engage in subsistence agriculture, growing rice; corn, which was introduced in the 17th century by the Dutch; mung beans; sorghum; cassava; and palm products. Most of this agriculture is done in the highlands of East Timor on shifting plots prepared for planting using swidden, or slash-and-burn, techniques, in which a small field is cut out of the jungle and the cut trees allowed to dry and then burned to provide fertilizer. This method requires new fields to be cut each year and thus is extremely problematic for the long-term viability of subsistence on the island.

Before the dawn of the European colonial era on Timor, which began in the early 16th century with the arrival of the Portuguese, the island was dotted with small indigenous kingdoms and principalities, as noted by Chinese sailors who came to the island seeking sandalwood. The Tetun kingdom of Liurai, with its 46 separate principalities, constituted one of the most powerful of these small groups. In 1756 the newly arrived Dutch colonizers, who eventually pushed the Portuguese off the western half of the island, sent an envoy with a treaty for all of the local kings and princes to sign. One of the most important signatories of this treaty was Hiacijntoe Corea, the Tetun king of Wehali in the south-central coast region, who represented not only his own kingdom but also that of 27 other dependent principalities. Despite the apparent amity between the Tetun ruler and the Dutch, it took until 1904 for another Dutch colonial administrator to be able to meet with a Tetun king, and this meeting required the Dutch to send an armed force to accompany the administrator into Wehali.

While the Portuguese use of Tetun as a trading language in East Timor supported the continued viability of a Tetun community there, in West Timor the Tetun people were eventually subsumed by the more powerful ATONI. In the 16th and 17th centuries, due to their interactions with the Portuguese and then Dutch colonizers, the Atoni emerged in West Timor as the dominant local kingdom. From the Portuguese the Atoni received muskets and iron tools, which put them at a distinct advantage over their local rivals for political power. From the Dutch they received corn, a crop that allowed their population to expand at a faster rate than their rivals. With these advantages the Atoni emerged from under the rule of the previously larger and stronger Tetun kingdom and then subjugated or assimilated most of the other ethnolinguistic groups in their region.

As is true throughout East Timor, most Tetun are members of the Roman Catholic Church. This development, while a legacy of Portuguese colonialism, did not actually occur during the Portuguese period. Prior to the 1974 withdrawal of the Portuguese from East Timor the Catholic Church was active in the promotion of Christianity, both through churches and Catholic schools. However, the majority of the population in 1974 had not yet given up their local animistic beliefs and rituals to convert to Catholicism. This occurred during the Indonesian period, 1974–98, when the Indonesian state actively promoted the practice of world religions in all of its territories as a sign of modernization. Since the Catholic Church had the deepest roots in East Timor, it was to Roman Catholicism that the majority of the population turned. A further impetus for the Tetun to join this organization was the choice by local church leaders to utilize Dili Tetun as the local liturgical language rather than Portuguese or another indigenous language.

Thailanders: nationality (people of Thailand)

Thailand is the only Southeast Asian nation not to have experienced any direct form of colonialism during the 19th and early 20th centuries. This independence remains central to the Thailanders' conception of national identity.

GEOGRAPHY

Thailand is comparable in size to Spain, somewhat larger than the state of California, and about twice the size of Great Britain. It shares

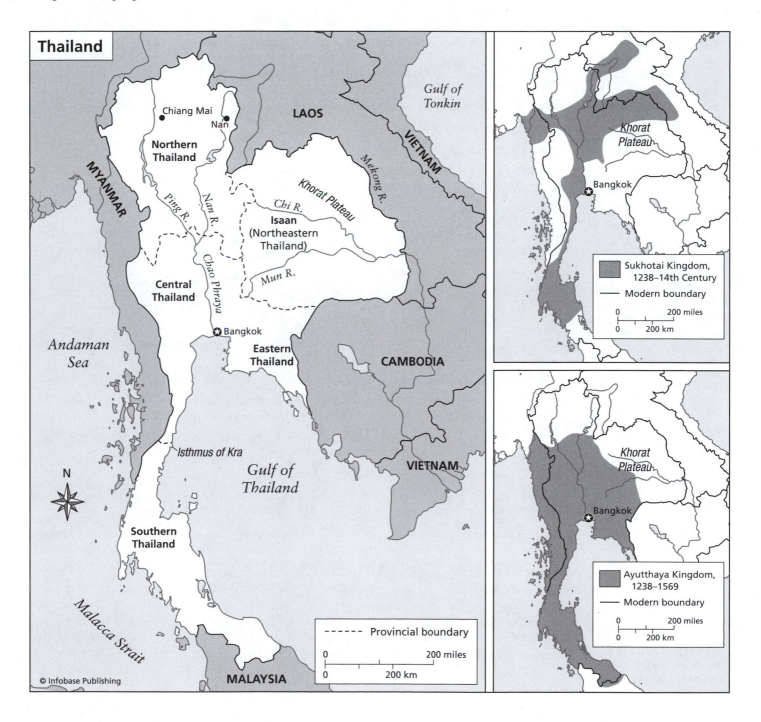

THAILANDERS: NATIONALITY

nation:
Kingdom of Thailand

derivation of name:
Land of the free

government:
Constitutional monarchy, with parliamentary system; the king has a strong unifying and stabilizing role

capital:
Bangkok (to Thais: Krungthep). The official name of the city is the longest name in the world: Krungthep mahanakorn bowon ratanakosin mahintara Ayutthaya mahadilok poprropparat ratchathani burirom udomratchanwiwet mahasathan amonpiman avatansathit sakkathatitya witsanukamprasit.

language:
Thai (central) is the official language. Regional dialects: Isaan, northern Thai, and southern Thai; English is the secondary language of the elite.

religion:
Buddhist 94.6 percent (state religion); Muslim 4.6 percent; Christian 0.7 percent; other 0.1 percent

earlier inhabitants:
Khmer and Mon (Dvaravati) peoples

demographics:
Central Thai 33.7 percent, Isaan (Northeastern Thai or Lao) 34.2 percent, northern Thai 18.8 percent, southern Thai 13.3 percent. As many as 14 percent of Thais are of significant Chinese heritage, but the Sino-Thai community is highly integrated. Malay-speaking Muslims of the

Thailanders: nationality time line

C.E.

seventh century The Nanchao kingdom is established in southwest China.

ninth–13th centuries Tai or Dai peoples gradually migrate south from China to Thailand, Burma, and Laos.

1238 The Kingdom of Sukhothai is established under Intaradit.

1296 Lanna kingdom is founded at Chaing Mai. Mangrai controls much of northern Thailand and Laos.

1280–1318 King Ramkhamhaeng reigns in Sukhothai; the period is called Thailand's golden age.

1283 The Thai writing system is invented by King Ramkhamhaeng.

1317–47 Lo Thai reigns at Suhkothai, and the slow decline of Suhkothai begins.

1350 The city of Ayutthaya is founded. Ramathibodi I becomes king.

1390 Ramesuen captures Chiang Mai.

1393 Ramesuen captures Angkor in Cambodia.

1549 War with Mon kingdom of Pegu (Burma).

1569 The Burmese capture and destroy Ayutthaya.

1590 Naresuen becomes king and frees his people from Burmese rule.

1605–10 King Ekatotsarot begins significant economic ties with European traders.

1610–28 King Songtham. The British arrive and obtain land for a trading factory.

1628–55 King Prasit Thong. Regular trade with China and Europe is established.

1656–88 King Narai. Reputation of Ayutthaya spreads in Europe. A strong French presence begins in the country.

1688 Narai dies. French and other foreigners are evicted.

1767 Burmese king Alaungpaya sacks Ayutthaya. Four months later General Phaya Taksin expels the Burmese and establishes Thonburi on the banks of the Chao Phraya River (opposite the site of present-day Bangkok) as the capital.

1779 General Chao Phya Chakri and his brother expel the Burmese from Chiang Mai and add most of the Lao and Khmer kingdoms to the Thai kingdom.

1782 General Chao Phya Chakri is crowned as Rama I, the first king in the current Chakri dynasty. The capital is moved across the river to Bangkok.

1809–24 Reign of Rama II. Relations with the West are reopened.

1851 Rama IV is crowned. He is the first king to understand the value of Western culture, science, and technology to his kingdom.

1855 Bowring Treaty signed between Siam and Great Britain.

1868 King Chulalongkorn is crowned. The king has been educated by Anna Leonowens, whose story is later immortalized in *The King and I*. He abolishes slavery, modernizes the government and military, and establishes postal and rail systems and coeducational schooling.

borders with Malaysia, Myanmar (Burma), Laos, and Cambodia. The country is divided into four regions based on geography and ethnic differences. Northern Thailand is mountainous with good rainfall and is best known for the diverse cultures of its numerous hill tribe minorities. Northeastern Thailand, known as Isaan, sits on the much drier elevated Khorat Plateau and is the poorest region of Thailand. Central Thailand is largely composed of the fertile Chao Phraya River valley, which runs into the Gulf of Thailand. Southern Thailand consists of the narrow Kra Isthmus and the northern part of the Malay Peninsula. The Thai economy is built on agriculture, particularly rice farming. Tourism is a major industry today.

south make up another significant minority group (2.3 percent). Hill tribe minorities make up a tiny fraction of the population.

————◆————

1910–25 Rama VI. He is educated at Oxford and is thoroughly Westernized.

1932 A constitutional monarchy is established after a bloodless revolution ends the absolute monarchy.

1938 General Phibun Songkhram gains power and becomes prime minister.

1939 Rama VIII is crowned. Prime Minister Phibun instigates forced cultural change, including the Twelve Cultural Mandates, and changes the country's name from Siam to Thailand.

1942 The Japanese invasion (World War II).

1945 Japan surrenders. Thailand's continued independence from Britain and France is negotiated.

1946 King Bhumibol Adulyadej is crowned (current king; Rama IX).

1952 Thailand competes in the Olympics for the first time, the Summer Games in Helsinki.

1964 The onset of the Indochina War brings an influx of westerners and Western culture.

1972 Thailand hosts the Asian Cup (soccer) and places third, the only Asian Cup competition in which they have placed in the top four.

1973 Student demonstrations lead to the establishment of a civilian government.

1976 The government is overthrown by the military in one of the bloodiest coups in Thai history. The next 15 years see much instability and frequent coups deposing civilian governments.

1992 A bloody military coup results in a popular uprising, with hundreds of demonstrators killed in the streets. The coup ends with clashing military and civilian leaders kneeling in contrition before the king. Military political power is reduced, and a new constitution is developed.

1995 Thailand hosts the XVIII South East Asia (SEA) Games.

1996 King Bhumibol Adulyadej's golden jubilee; he celebrates 50 years on the throne, the longest reigning monarch in the world.

1996 Thailand wins its first-ever Olympic gold medal, after 44 years of competing: Kamsing Somluck wins the featherweight boxing gold in Atlanta.

1997 Thai economic crash due to collapses in the financial sector, the result of overinvestment in the property market.

1998 Thailand hosts the 13th Asian Games. The government adopts the economic guidelines given by the International Monetary Fund (IMF).

1999 King Bhumibol Adulyadej celebrates his Sixth cycle birthday (72nd birthday).

2000 The first democratic election of senators for the upper house.

2001 Telecommunications tycoon Thaksin Shinawatra is elected prime minister; his Thai Rak Thai party of national unity wins office with the largest majority in Thai history.

2002 Thailand competes in its first Winter Olympics, in cross-country skiing.

2004 At the Athens Olympics, Thailand wins three gold medals and eight medals altogether, the best-ever performance of Thai athletes at any Olympic Games.

2006 A military coup deposes Prime Minister Thaksin Shinawatr and suspends the constitution; an interim prime minister, cabinet, and national assembly are appointed.

2007 December elections bring the People's Power Party, a pro-Thaksin organization, to power.

Bangkok, in central Thailand, is by far the country's largest city and growing fast. Bangkok's official population is around 7 million, although this figure omits the large group of migrant workers from other provinces who are registered in their home district rather than Bangkok. Including this group, Bangkok's population is probably more like 13 million. Due to its size and level of development, Bangkok is very different from the rest of the country. In the words of a common saying, there are two Thailands: Bangkok and the rest of the country.

INCEPTION AS A NATION

Exactly where the THAIS originated is a matter of some debate. The majority of scholars support

Ayutthaya, with its numerous temples, such as this one, was a center of Thai political and religious activity for more than 200 years. *(Shutterstock/faberfoto)*

the theory that their Tai or DAI ancestors came from the Nanchao kingdom, which was founded during the seventh century C.E. in present-day Yunnan Province of southwest China.

It is generally thought that the defeat of Nanchao by the MONGOLS drove a major migration of the Tai southward into the area of present-day Southeast Asia. The modern-day Siamese (or central Thais) developed chiefly from the blending of Tai, the MON Dvaravati (*Thawarawadi* in Thai), and Khom (ancient KHMERS) cultures, around the time of the Sukhothai period (approximately the 13th and 14th centuries). The Mon and Khom both used Indianized forms of writing, and they were also the conduit for large-scale conversion to Buddhism among some Thai groups.

Thailand has been an independent nation since 1238 C.E. (traditional founding date), and while at times defeated in war, it claims the honor of being the only country in Southeast Asia never to have been colonized by a foreign power.

The golden age, the Sukhothai period, was the reign of King Ramkhamhaeng (1279–98), which is remembered for its ideas and its art. King Ramkhamhaeng is said to have invented the central Thai written script using a combination of Mon and Khom scripts. Most texts date this invention to 1283. Sri Lankan Buddhism (Theravada Buddhism) came to central Thailand during King Ramkhamhaeng's reign, via a Tai *mueang* (principality) in Nakhon Sri Thammarat.

As Sukhothai's power declined, other groups within the region again began to contest for rule of the Siamese. By the mid-14th century the Thai Ayutthaya kingdom was formed, south of Sukhothai, and quickly incorporated its former rival into the larger, stronger Ayutthaya, taking the name Kingdom of Siam. The cosmopolitan flavor of Sukhothai was intensified in the new kingdom, with a great increase in foreign trade and numbers of foreigners living within Siam. About one-third of the population of Siam was foreign. The first significant contact with the West began during this era.

A sudden and unforeseen assault on Ayutthaya by the BURMANS in the mid-18th century had catastrophic consequences: Ayutthaya was completely destroyed in April 1767. However, the conquering armies left quickly, and by October 1767 General Phaya Taksin had moved the people to a new capital in Thonburi, opposite modern Bangkok. The capital was moved to Bangkok by Rama I, the first king in the current dynasty, in 1782.

Siam at that time had a rigidly hierarchical society. Western colonial powers that lay in wait on the doorstep of the Thai kingdom in the 1800s pressed for greater freedom of trade and the removal of many of the royal monopolies. People of varied religious and linguistic backgrounds attended the king. Many foreigners relocated to Bangkok, including immigrants from both the East and the West, to take advantage of the trade and other opportunities that the stable kingdom offered.

Early in the reign of Rama III (1824–51), the British sent envoys to negotiate a treaty with the Siamese. They had hoped to have trade monopolies eased, which finally occurred in 1855 when the Bowring Treaty between Siam's King Mongkut, Rama IV, and Britain abolished many trade monopolies and allowed British subjects the right to both purchase and dwell on land within Siam. At that time the borders between Siam and neighboring British territories were also defined, and foreign advisers were appointed to the court, including translators, military experts, and others who served in port- and police-administration roles. Some Thais adopted Western dress at this time as well.

For the first time Thai princes and princesses were given access to a Western education within the palace. Anna Leonowens was appointed to this task in 1862, primarily by the heir to the throne, Prince Chulalongkorn. When the prince became king in 1868, he introduced Western-style bureaucratic government as well as postal and rail systems and coeducational schools. He also united the country into its present form as a geographic and political entity.

Around the beginning of the 20th century (during the reign of Rama V), many elite young Thais began traveling to Britain and Europe to study, bringing many new ideas back to Siam. One such student was Rama VI, who was crowned in 1910. He promoted the idea of a nation united under the banner of country, religion, and monarch. Despite the modernizing of Siam under his immediate predecessors, Rama VII (1925–35) was forced to capitulate during a bloodless nationalist coup in 1932, which ended the absolute monarchy and propelled Thailand toward a constitutional democracy.

In the years immediately following the coup, Siam was ruled by a succession of army generals. Perhaps the most infamous of these was Prime Minister Phibun Songkhram (1938–44 and 1948–57), due to his program of forced cultural change. Phibun felt the need to demonstrate to Western colonial powers that Thailand could manage its own modernization agenda without foreign assistance. For example, Phibun instigated the Twelve Cultural Mandates, which demanded saluting the flag, knowing the national anthem, and using the national language; in addition, the chewing of betel nut was banned, and Western clothing and shoes were mandated for public servants. In 1939 he changed the name of the country from Siam to Thailand, known in Thai as Pratet Thai.

During World War II, Thailand was conquered briefly by the JAPANESE. However, after the British liberated the country, the Thais regained their sovereignty through careful negotiations with the British and French. Thailand became an ally of the United States at this time.

The Vietnam War brought another new wave of westerners, along with their popular culture, into a country that had not experienced the rapid changes of a prior colonial era. In return for being allowed to bring their military into the country, Western powers, especially the United States, invested heavily in infrastructure and the development of a democracy. Student demonstrations in 1973 led to the establishment of a civilian government. However, this was overthrown by the military in October 1976, in one of the bloodiest coups in Thai history. A succession of military coups ensued, culminating in the coup of 1992. Once again, students and the military clashed in the streets. Hundreds were shot dead and many more disappeared before the king intervened and restored peace. This coup led to a vast decrease in the amount of political power held by military generals. A new constitution was drafted, which lasted until 2006.

In 2001, billionaire telecommunications tycoon Thaksin Shinawatra was elected prime minister, and his Thai Rak Thai party won office with the largest majority in Thai history. He was popular with the rural masses for his development policies, such as a 30-baht medical scheme, which allowed many of the poor to visit a hospital for the first time. He brought about change in many institutions and developed much-needed infrastructure, primarily by using his power to act without consultation. This was perceived by the urban middle class as an abuse of power and led to a decline in his popularity in Bangkok. His controversial war on drugs led to the extrajudicial killings of hundreds of people, and he adopted a hard-line stance toward the Muslim separatists in the southern provinces, where he deployed large numbers of troops to deal with them. This was instrumental in increasing the resolve of the separatists, and violence is currently a common part of life in this region.

During 2005 and early 2006, several major scandals plagued Thaksin. A bloodless military coup on September 19, 2006, removed him, and he lived in self-imposed exile abroad for 17 months before returning to Bangkok in February 2008. The military suspended the constitution and Parliament and appointed an interim national assembly. They installed Interim Prime Minister Surayut Chulanon. General elections took place on December 23, 2007. In that election the populist policies of former prime minister Thaksin were repudiated in the polls when the successor to Thai Rak Thai, the People's Power Party, won a slim majority. Nonetheless, this repudiation did not save Thaksin from facing a number of charges of corruption in Thai courts in 2008. In September 2008 his brother-in-law Somchai Wongsawat was elected prime minister.

CULTURAL IDENTITY

Central to Thai cultural identity is the concept of being "Thai," or *free*. Fiercely independent, Thais are extremely proud of their nation's heritage as the only southern and Southeast Asian nation never colonized by Western colonial powers. The people have been described as having a strong maverick streak and a sense of pragmatism, both of which have created a determination to chart its own course. Thailand boasts the lowest unemployment rate in the world (1.8 percent in 2006, according to the government), largely because so many Thais prefer to work for themselves rather than for an authoritarian boss. Thailand also has the highest rate of sole trader businesses in the world. Thais place great value on life being *sanuk* (fun) and *sabai* (comfortable).

Thai culture is strongly status-oriented. In Thai culture no two people have the same status, which determines everything. It shapes the way in which people interact and communicate, the level of respect accorded a person, and the degree to which people have a voice in family and community. It also affects the opportunities they may or may not receive. A high priority in life, therefore, is to increase one's status. Age is one means of gaining higher status. Status is also affected by being born into the right family, gaining a higher level of education, and possessing more wealth. In folk Buddhism, people of high status are seen to have good karma, and good karma (being a good person) will result in increased status. Thus, one who is poor or has a low level of education has low status because of bad karma. Paying appropriate respect to people of status—for example, parents, teachers, religious leaders, and royalty—is very important. Equally important is not doing or saying anything that may result in a person feeling that his or her status has been challenged. This is behind the Thai concept known as *krieng jai,* not causing others to lose face.

In order for one's implicit status to have any effect on social standing, there need to be cues for others to see the status; therefore, status must be displayed. Thais achieve this by being "presentational"—that is, the way that people present themselves outwardly is the way they are perceived to *be*. People who wish to be seen as modern or developed conduct themselves in a modern and developed manner. Western cultural elements are usually perceived as being more modern and developed, so that at least outwardly these forms are often adopted wholesale.

The central Thai and Sino-Thai people control political and commercial power, respectively. Northeastern, northern, and southern Thais have largely been absorbed into central Thai culture through education and bans on other written scripts. King Rama VI (1910–25) tried to unite the people under the banner of loyalty to nation, religion, and monarch. All schooling and official communication use the central dialect, and the written form of the Isaan (northeastern Thai) dialect has been completely lost through bans on the written script during communist crackdowns during the 1950s, 1960s, and 1970s. While the Isaan or Lao are the largest ethnic group in the country (one-third of the population), they are generally the poorer people. Many of the million Muslim Thais in the south align their identity more with Malaysia than with Thailand, and at times they have accused the government of biased policies. In the present period, much of the anti-Thailand activity by this large minority has been interpreted through the lens of the international "war on terror," rather than as a problem of lack of national integration. In addition, an estimated half a million poor hill tribesmen have arrived over the last century and have settled in villages in the northern mountains; they are likewise often seen as foreigners in their own country and are only beginning to integrate into Thai national culture.

In addition to these diverse ethnic communities that challenge the notion of a Thai identity for all Thailanders or citizens of Thailand, the country has also had to contend with problems caused by HIV/AIDS and the interrelated problem of the sex tourism industry, particularly the child sex trade. In the 1980s Thailand was one of the most severely affected countries in Asia, with more than 40 percent of all sex workers and intravenous drug users testing positive for HIV/AIDS; projections estimated that more than 6 percent of the adult population would be infected by 2000. In reaction, the Thai government launched one of the most successful education and prevention campaigns in the world; the country's rate of infection was estimated in 2003 to be just 1.5 percent. Nonetheless, the sex tourism industry, driven by poverty, continues to destroy the lives of thousands of Thai girls, boys, and women every year. Many of these individuals are sold into the sex trade by family members or others who have been convinced by unscrupulous pimps that their child will receive an education and job in one of the country's large cities. Instead, they end up working in go-go bars, brothels, and other legal and illegal venues that sell sex to the millions of foreign tourists who arrive each year from North America, Europe, and Japan.

FURTHER READING

Chris Baker and Pasuk Phongpaichit. *A History of Thailand* (London: Cambridge University Press, 2005).
Scot Barmé. *Luang Wichit Wathakan and the Creation of a Thai Identity* (Singapore: Institute of Southeast Asian Studies, 1993).

Charles F. Keyes. *Thailand, Buddhist Kingdom as Modern Nation-State* (Boulder, Colo.: Westview Press, 1987).

Frank J. Moore. *Thailand: Its People, Its Society, Its Culture* (New Haven, Conn.: HRAF Press, 1974).

Niels Mulder. *Inside Thai Society* (Chiang Mai, Thailand: Silkworm Books, 2000).

Walter F. Vella. *Chaiyo! King Vajiravudh and the Development of Thai Nationalism* (Honolulu: University Press of Hawaii, 1978).

David K Wyatt. *Thailand: A Short History* (Chiang Mai, Thailand: Silkworm Books, 1984).

Thai Lao   *See* LAO.

Thai Nung   *See* NUNG.

Thais (Central Thais, Khon Thais, Siamese, Siamese Tais, Syams, Tais, T'ais)

The Thais are the dominant ethnic group in Thailand.

GEOGRAPHY

The Thai homeland of Thailand is a country about the size of Spain, located in mainland Southeast Asia. The country borders Myanmar (Burma) to the north and west, Cambodia to the east, Laos to the northeast, and Malaysia to the south. It is divided into seven administrative regions, including the capital, Bangkok Metropolitan Region. The central plains, which are the richest agricultural lands and are known as the Thai Rice Bowl, are primarily Thai, while regions in the north, east, and south house many of the country's minority groups.

The climate is tropical, with the lowest monthly average temperature being 86°F in December and January; the highest temperature occurs in April at more than 95°F. The southwest monsoon, which arrives in June, brings some relief to these high temperatures, but the rainy season brings on even higher levels of humidity. November to February are the most comfortable months when the wind comes from the northeast, diminishing the heat and humidity somewhat. The highlands in the northern regions of the country are quite a bit cooler than the lowland plains around Bangkok and night-time temperatures in winter can drop to as low as 40°F.

ORIGINS

There is considerable debate about the origins of the contemporary Thai people. Theories range from Southeast Asian origins and migrations into southern and even northern China during prehistory to northern Chinese origins and migrations into Southeast Asia. These migrations may have occurred as recently as 700 years ago or as long as 5,000 years ago. The archaeological, genetic, and textual evidence that various sources draw upon are often contradictory and allow various groups to make claims that suit their own contemporary political agendas.

According to one of the most repeated versions of the Thai origin story, Thai ancestors migrated out of Yunnan Province, China, just before 1300, having been driven out of the established DAI kingdoms by invading MONGOLS. This version has been contested by significant archaeological evidence that peoples living in the area of Thailand thousands of years prior to 1300 share significant genetic and physical traits with the contemporary Thai. A resolution of the debate awaits further evidence.

HISTORY

By the middle of the 13th century two Thai kingdoms, Sukhothai and Lan-na, had emerged in the area of southern and northern Thailand, respectively. The former had been part of a large Khmer kingdom prior to being taken over by King Inthrathit in 1238, the first Thai king to gain full sovereignty over his territory; previous Thai kings and princes had ruled in vassal positions in relation to the Khmer kingdoms centered at Angkor. Lan-na, in the area of contemporary Chiang Mai, was established two decades later by King Mengrai the Great.

For their entire existence these two rival kingdoms threatened each other, and in 1321 Lan-na was able to annex some territory from its weaker southern neighbor. This event foreshadowed later circumstances when a third Thai kingdom, Ayutthaya, which was established in 1350, was able to wrest control away from Sukhothai entirely in 1376. This left a powerful Ayutthaya in the south and Lan-na in the north, which once again made inroads into the southern kingdom in 1463, when it sacked the Ayutthaya city of Phitsanulok. In response, Borom Trai-Lokkanot transferred the capital of Ayutthaya to the fallen city to serve as a bulwark against further encroachment by Lan-na. This fierce rivalry came to an end only in 1776 when King Thaksin, having liberated Ayutthaya from a Burman occupation, then turned his attention to his northern rival and captured Chiang Mai. This created Thailand's modern boundaries in a kingdom that was called Siam until an official name change in 1939.

THAIS

location:
Thailand

time period:
Unknown, but possibly 13th century C.E. to the present

ancestry:
Probably Dai

language:
Thai, a Tai-Kadai language

Thais time line

B.C.E.

3000 Some significant archaeological evidence points to a population living in Southeast Asia, which physically and genetically resembles the contemporary Thai people. This theory remains contested by mainstream historians who claim relatively recent immigration of the contemporary Thais.

C.E.

644 Theravada Buddhism arrives in the region of Thailand.

1238 Accepted date for the formation of the first Thai kingdom at Sukhothai from what had formerly been Khmer territory.

1259 Formation of the Thai kingdom of Lan-na in the north, near contemporary Chiang Mai.

1278 King Ramkhamhaeng, Sukhothai's greatest king, takes the throne and five years later invents the first Thai alphabet.

1321 Lan-na takes territory from the Sukhothai kingdom.

1350 A Thai kingdom with a court modeled on Angkor is founded at Ayutthaya (Ayudhya, or Siam), near modern-day Bangkok, under King Uthong or Ramathibodi I.

1376 Ayutthaya takes over the former Sukhothai kingdom.

1463 Lan-na attacks the Ayutthaya city of Phitsanulok, which the king then makes his capital in a bid to strengthen its position against the rival kingdom.

1511 The Portuguese are the first Europeans to make contact with a Thai kingdom.

1569 After many years of warfare between the two peoples, Ayutthaya is conquered by the Burmese.

1584 Phra Naresuan restores Ayutthaya to the Thais and ascends to the throne in 1590.

1592 Ayutthaya signs a trade agreement with the Dutch.

1639 The trade agreement with the Dutch falls apart when the Dutch threaten to go to war.

1685 Catholic missionaries establish themselves in Thailand (Siam).

Following Thaksin's death in 1782, today's ruling Chakri dynasty came to power in the united Siam, making it one of the longest-ruling royal families in the world today. In addition to conquering additional lands for the Thais in what is today Laos, the Chakri kings also continued the process of opening Siam up to European influence. This process had begun in 1511 when the Portuguese arrived in Ayutthaya and continued with an agreement between the latter and the Dutch for the export of rice. In 1826 Siam signed a trade agreement with Britain as a response to the latter's demands five years earlier for opening up the king's territory to European advances. Rather than dealing with the French, who were making incursions on Thai territory in Indochina, the Thai kings preferred to deal with the British as a way of protecting themselves from further advances on their sovereignty. This strategy worked, and Siam was able to retain its autonomy through-out the entire colonial period in Southeast Asia, while its neighbors succumbed to the British in Myanmar (Burma) and to the French in Laos and Cambodia.

The 20th century brought significant change to the Thai people, who had been ruled by absolute monarchs since the formation of the first Thai kingdom in the 13th century. In 1932 a bloodless coup led by a coalition of civil servants and the military toppled the government established by King Prajadhipok but left the position of king relatively unscathed. The coup leaders all claimed to be nationalists who viewed the monarchy as an antiquated form of government for a modern nation-state; nonetheless, as nationalists, they saw the value of maintaining a Thai king as the head of state in a country with a significant number of other nationalities and minority groups. This first coup began a tradition in Thailand of the military playing a role in state governance and set the

1767	Ayutthaya is conquered by the Burmese but is quickly liberated by King Thaksin, who moves his capital to Thonburi; he later attacks the Khmer kingdom as well.
1776	Thaksin conquers Chiang Mai and unites the two Thai kingdoms into one state.
1782	Thaksin dies, and the current Chakri dynasty comes to power in Thailand (Siam) under Rama I; the capital is moved to Bangkok.
1792	Rama I conquers most of Laos and incorporates it into his Thai kingdom.
1826	The modernizing Siam signs a trade agreement with Britain in response to demands for opening up its borders.
1887	Rama V establishes a cabinet, audit office, and department of education in a bid to modernize his kingdom.
1916	Siam's first university, Chulalongkorn, is created.
1917	Siam joins the allies against Germany in World War I.
1932	The absolute rule of the Thai kings is ended by a coup in June.
1937	Direct elections for a national assembly are held for the first time.
1939	Siam changes its name to Thailand, "Land of the Free."
1941	Southern Thailand is occupied by the Japanese, prompting the government to form an alliance with the occupiers.
1944	The Allies bomb Bangkok.
1961	The pro-American prime minister Sarit Thamarat allows the United States to build air bases in Thailand for the war in Vietnam.
1976	The first of several military coups over the next 15 years.
1991	Free elections bring Chatichai Choonhavan to power, but General Suchinda Kraprayoon soon topples the government and makes Panyarachun Anand prime minister.
1992	Suchinda Kraprayoon is elected prime minister, but riots in the street prevent him from governing and he is succeeded by Panyarachun Anand again.
2003	Thailand initiates a "war on drugs," and between 2,000 and 10,000 people are killed.

stage for further military coups throughout the 20th century and into the 21st; the most recent coup took place in 2006.

CULTURE

The backbone of Thai culture is the production of wet rice and has been since the 13th-century establishment of the Sukhothai kingdom. In that period the low plains of central Thailand began to be criss-crossed by irrigation canals and paddy fields, all utilizing water from the Chao Phraya River and delta. In this region, unlike in the hilly north of the country, agribusiness rather than subsistence farming has come to dominate the landscape and people's lives. As a result, ethnic Thais make up a relatively small percentage of the 49 percent of Thailand's population who work in the agricultural sector, while Thais make up the vast majority in the manufacturing and other industrial sectors, including agribusiness.

Prior to this development in the past 30 years, Thai society was notable for the relative lack of a gendered division of agricultural and other labor. Women and men participated in both plowing and harrowing as well as fishing, cooking, cleaning, washing clothes, and tending babies. Certainly women engaged in more domestic tasks than men, but unlike many other patriarchal societies, it was not shameful for Thai men to work in the home. Likewise, women were not constrained by taboos against participating in the most valuable activities related to rice farming. With the transformation of Thai society from subsistence farming to large agribusinesses and a highly developed industrial sector, this aspect of the Thai division of labor has also changed. Outside companies have tended to favor men over women as investors, and in employment the same kind of gender assumptions that guide hiring practices in much of the rest of the world have also taken root in Thailand. Women make up the majority in low-income manufacturing and low-level service industries and civil-service jobs.

Other aspects of Thai gender relations have also changed over time. Prior to the 19th century, Thai society allowed men to have more than one wife, a practice called polygyny, but this was limited to wealthy and royal elite families who could afford the practice. While polygyny was limited in much of the colonized world by laws enacted by the British, French, and other outside powers, Thailand remained independent and was able to control its own marriage policies. One result of this is that polygyny became democratized somewhat, and more men were able to engage in it throughout the 19th and early 20th centuries. Today polygyny is not a legal practice; however, many men, especially the wealthy but some men with average incomes as well, continue to maintain a "little home" or "minor wife" in addition to their legal, primary marriages. The practice is viewed with contempt by most Thai women who are not "minor" wives and may be the cause of a woman's suing for divorce, but it does continue to attract women and married men in both rural and urban areas.

For the majority of legal marriages among Thai partners, the ideal postmarital residence is neolocal, or an independent household for the new couple; sometimes a short period of matrilocal residence, when the couple lives with the new wife's family, also occurs. Regardless of the makeup of the household, nuclear, extended, or blended family, the household itself is considered the primary unit of production and consumption in Thai society. In the past, this meant that it was the household that owned or worked a plot of land, grew its own rice, and produced most of its other consumables. Today all employed members of the household tend to pool their resources and paychecks to pay rent or mortgages and purchase food and all other necessities. The oldest male is often the household head, but it is usually his wife who controls the finances and other resources.

Beyond the household, Thai society does not place great emphasis on the ties of extended kinship. Descent is bilateral, meaning that each individual is equally related to his or her mother's and father's kin, and thus there are no large corporate lineages or clan groups providing alliances and obligations at the kin level. However, in the past, multihousehold compounds, hamlets, and villages have all been connected by ties of bilateral kinship and marriage. These multihousehold units tended to provide recip-rocal assistance in agricultural and other work and possibly in financial matters as well. Since marriage with second cousins is allowed in Thai society, marriages within these interconnected kin-residential units was also extremely common and even preferred.

Beyond the hamlet, Thai villages can be small, with just 300 people, or they can be 10 times that size. They can be clusters of homes and hamlets built in a circular pattern or a strip of buildings constructed along a road, river, or canal; both of these styles are surrounded by individually owned or worked rice fields, orchards, and coconut palms. Some villages are more dispersed than either of these patterns, with homes, fields, orchards, and other village structures spread over an expanse of several hectares or more. Nearly all villages have their own Buddhist temple, school, and shops, and larger villages also house a Buddhist monastery.

As this characteristic of villages indicates, Theravada Buddhism is of central importance in Thai culture; there are more than 31,000 temples spread throughout the country. While 95 percent of Thailand's population proclaim adherence to Buddhism, with regard to ethnic Thais the number is probably very close to 100 percent. Theravada Buddhism first arrived in the region of Thailand in approximately 644 C.E., having been adopted from the MON who lived in the region of contemporary lower Burma and western Thailand. By the end of the 13th century the Sukhothai kings had made this their official religion of state, and thus began the long period of intense building and Buddhist learning that continues relatively unabated in Thailand today. For example, most Thai men undertake at least some Buddhist training in a monastery, and nearly 85 percent are ordained as monks, though far fewer than that actually work in this field. The religion continues to serve as a central organizing principle in hamlets and villages and indeed in Thai society more generally. The Buddhist ritual calendar dominates the Thai year, with the country's main holidays being New Year's celebration in April; Buddha's birth, enlightenment, and death a month later; Buddhist lent, or Phansa, from July to October; and November's Festival of Lights. In addition, each village, monastery, and temple host their own important religious events that require the joint participation of both the monks and laity. In a Thai household, funerals are the most important rite of passage, more important than birth or marriage rituals, because they are the opportunity for the person's community to mark their passage into their next existence. They are presided over by Buddhist priests and monks, with the funeral of an older person requiring the participation of greater numbers of ritual specialists.

Although Theravada Buddhism is their dominant religion, this has not prevented many Thais from incorporating many other religious beliefs and practices from the Hindu kingdoms that reigned in Southeast Asia in the past and from indigenous beliefs. Exorcists, diviners, and faith healers are all very common in Thai communities, providing mediation between the living and spirit worlds. Some illnesses and forms of misfortune are believed to be caused by spirit possession and can be cured only through communication with the offending spirit and then exorcism. Even urban professionals may consult a diviner when planning a wedding, moving house, or other big event to make sure that they are not putting the event at risk of spirit intervention.

Another aspect of Thai society that does not necessarily go hand in hand with their overwhelming adherence to Buddhism is the emphasis on and respect for hierarchy. In principle, Buddhism is a democratic religion that allows anybody to rise from the ranks of poverty, sin, or other misfortune to attain nirvana. In Thai society, however, respect for hierarchy is extremely important, and superior people in terms of age, rank, or position are treated very differently from the young or those of lower rank or position. While monks are the highest-ranked people in Thai society more generally, with senior monks the highest of all outside of the king, the kind of respect that laypeople grant to monks is replicated at all levels of society. The young must grant respect to their elders to such an extent that if two people appear close in age they will discuss their ages to determine who is younger and thus must use the respectful form of speech with the other, who uses a less respectful form of speech in return. This same dynamic emerges between rich and poor as well as between commoners and both politicians and military officers. The respect that superior people receive, however, does come at a price, for they are also expected to provide support and resources to the people below them. Even in urban workplaces, managers who dine with their staff are expected to pay the entire bill.

FURTHER READING

Charles F. Keyes. *Thailand, Buddhist Kingdom as Modern Nation-State* (Boulder, Colo.: Westview Press, 1987.

Arne Kislenko. *Culture and Customs of Thailand* (Westport, Conn.: Greenwood Press, 2004).

Elliott Kulick and Dick Wilson. *Thailand's Turn: Profile of a New Dragon* (New York: St. Martin's Press, 1992).

Anna Harriette Leonowens. *The English Governess at the Siamese Court: Recollections of Six Years in the Royal Palace at Bangkok* (London: Folio Society, 1980).

Lauriston Sharp and Lucien M. Hanks. *Bang Chan: Social History of a Rural Community in Thailand* (Ithaca, N.Y.: Cornell University Press, 1978).

Penny Van Esterik. *Materializing Thailand* (Oxford: Berg, 2000).

Tharu

The Tharu are an Indo-Aryan tribal community of the Tarai region of Nepal and India, notable for its low elevation, about 985–2,625 feet above sea level, and tropical, humid weather conditions. The vast majority of the Tharu, about 720,000 at the end of the 20th century, live in Nepal, with another 10,000 in India. Regardless of their country of origin, the Tharu are primarily wet-rice farmers who live in permanent villages, which are probably a change from shifting agricultural and residential patterns in the past. Their kinship system is patrilineal: All children inherit membership in their lineages and clans through their fathers.

In the past it would have been difficult to speak of a single Tharu ethnic group, at least from the point of view of members of this community, because internal status divisions were far more important than cultural or linguistic similarities. Even to this day the two distinct status groups, called *kuri*, do not intermarry with each other. The high-status *kuri* is an endogamous unit, requiring every individual to marry within this status group, while the low-status *kuri* is made up of several distinct endogamous groups. This structure is similar to the Hindu caste system but is outside of it; Nepali and Indian Hindus classify all Tharu as outside the *varna* system, or as what used to be called Untouchables. Indian Tharu are members of the SCHEDULED TRIBES, but many Tharus on both sides of the border prefer to think of themselves in caste-like terms rather than tribal or ethnic terms.

The Tharu have become well-known in the world since 2000, when a group of them began protesting and even taking legal action against the long-standing *kamaiya* system of bonded labor in Nepal. In this labor relationship, a *kamaiya*, usually from the Tharu ethnic group, bound himself and his family to a landowner,

THARU

location:
Nepal and the Indian states of Bihar and Uttar Pradesh

time period:
Perhaps about 1800 B.C.E. to the present

ancestry:
Indo-Aryan

language:
Tharu, an Indo-Aryan language with many subdivisions

worked the owner's land, and received a small annual payment. Theoretically this was a voluntary relationship; however, most Tharu within this system were not voluntary laborers but indentured servants who had inherited both debt and a position of servitude from their fathers. Another aspect of the system dictated that laborers could be bought and sold by these large landowners. This brought it to the attention of the Anti-Slavery Society in London and the *Times* of London, which exposed the system to the world in 1997. The *New York Times* published a similar story in 2004, this time focusing on a woman who was considering selling herself back into servitude after her husband had been taken away as a revolutionary for having participated in the Maoist People's Liberation Army. The *kamaiya* system was outlawed in Nepal in 2002, and a small amount of land was redistributed to some landless Tharu, but many activists are skeptical, believing that the government was trying to cut off support for the revolutionaries rather than improving the lives of the people involved.

See also INDO-ARYANS.

Tibetans (Bhotia, Bodpa)

The Tibetans are a Central Asian people known for their unique form of Buddhism and their contemporary struggle against Chinese domination.

GEOGRAPHY

The Tibetan plateau, often called the "roof of the world" for its high average elevation at about 16,400 feet above sea level, is surrounded by the political units of Xinjiang and Qinghai Provinces in the north; Sichuan and Yunnan Provinces in the east; Bhutan, India, Myanmar (Burma), and Nepal in the south; and India in the west. It is mostly taken up by China's Xizang Province, or Tibet, with just the margins in India, Nepal, and Bhutan. The plateau's surrounding natural features include some of the most rugged terrain on earth: the Himalayan, Karakoram, and Pamir Mountain ranges in the south and west; the deserts of the Tarim, Taklamakan, and Qaidam Basins in the north; and the Tangkula Mountains in the east. The average temperature is only about 34°F, and rainfall is low to insignificant in some regions. However, the many high mountains are also the source of some of Asia's most important rivers, including the Brahmaputra, Indus, Ganges, Salween, Mekong, Chang (Yangtze), and Huang (Yellow).

TIBETANS

location:
Tibet and other provinces of China, plus Nepal, India, and Bhutan

time period:
Possibly 127 B.C.E. to the present

ancestry:
Tibeto-Burman

language:
Central and Western Tibetan, or Bodish, two of 53 Tibetan languages spoken in the region

ORIGINS

Although many Tibetans themselves believe they came from India, based on stories from the late Vedic period, many contemporary historians and anthropologists believe that Tibetans have the same origins as most other Chinese populations and speakers of Sino-Tibetan languages. They are believed to be the descendants of migrants into the Tibetan Plateau from both the northeast and southeast at the time of the Yellow River civilization, or the SHANG, about 3000–4000 years ago.

HISTORY

Although many legends and myths speak of the history of a Tibetan state as early as the centuries before the common era, very little historical material is available prior to the seventh century C.E. It is possible that a Tibetan kingdom called Yarlung, or Tubo, came into existence in 127 B.C.E., but this remains speculative and contested today; another possible founding date of the first Tibetan kingdom is about 400 C.E.

The first historical period of Tibetan history begins in 627, when Srong-brtsan-sgam-po inherited his position as head of the Yarlung kingdom and began to unite all of the smaller kingdoms and principalities on the Tibetan plateau, including the non-Tibetan Zhang-zhung kingdom in western Tibet. In addition to using his military skill to conquer land in what is today Nepal, Bhutan, India, and China, Srong-brtsan-sgam-po also used marriage to consolidate his power in the region. He had at least three Tibetan wives; a Nepali wife; and a Chinese wife named Wencheng, who was a princess of the Tang dynasty. Tibetan legend states that the Nepali and Chinese queens were instrumental in bringing Buddhism to their husband and thus to Tibet. However, in these early years Buddhism did not immediately win over the entire population, and the pre-Buddhist Bon religion retained many adherents, even within the royal family, until the death of the final Yarlung king, Langdharma, in 842. Indeed, it was Langdharma's antipathy toward Buddhism that led to his death at the hands of monks from this tradition.

This first definitively identified Tibetan king, Srong-brtsan-sgam-po, was extremely powerful and led an army that in 763 was able to defeat the army of the Tang dynasty and occupy the capital at Xian, or Chang-an. Many decades later, in 821–22, the Tang rulers were ready to acknowledge relative equality with the Tibetan kings through the signing of a peace treaty. The two sides recognized their friendship, accepted

Tibetan time line

B.C.E.

127 Possibly the founding date of the Yarlung, or Tubo, kingdom, which eventually unites Tibet under a single ruler.

C.E.

400 Another possible date for the foundation of the first Tibetan kingdom.

627 Srong-brtsan-sgam-po, 33rd Yarlung king, ascends to the throne. Over the next 22 years he expands the empire into China, Nepal, and India. His period is often considered the start of historical Tibet.

641 Buddhism comes to Tibet, an act often attributed to the Nepali and Chinese wives of Srong-brtsan-sgam-po.

649 Srong-brtsan-sgam-po dies.

670 Tibet and Tang China go to war over influence in Central Asia and the trade routes into and out of China.

763 Tibetan armies conquer the Chinese capital at Xian.

767 First evidence of Tibetan writing, indicating the presence of settled kingdoms.

821–22 China and Tibet sign a peace treaty recognizing their common border.

842 Demise of the Tibetan empire when its anti-Buddhist leader and 42nd Yarlung king, Wudum Tsen or Langdharma, is killed by Buddhist monks.

1207 Tibet acknowledges Genghis Khan as its ruler.

1247 Kublai Khan makes the Sakya lamas the rulers of Tibet under the auspices of the larger Yuan empire.

1350s The last of 20 Sakya lamas is deposed, and a series of semisecular dynasties rules Tibet for several hundred years.

1357 Tsongkhapa, founder of the Gelugpa, or Yellow Hat, sect of Buddhism, is born in Amdo, eastern Tibet.

1416 The Drepung monastery is founded.

1578 The abbot of the Drepung monastery is named the third Dalai Lama by the head of the Mongol empire; the first two are named posthumously at this time as well.

1642 Lobsang Gyatso, fifth Dalai Lama, is made the ruler of Tibet by the ruling Mongol khan, Gushri.

1904 Britain invades Tibet, and the 13th Dalai Lama flees to Mongolia.

1910 China invades Lhasa, and the 13th Dalai Lama flees to India.

1935 The infant who becomes the 14th Dalai Lama is born; he is installed as Dalai Lama five years later.

1950 Mao Zedong's army enters Tibet, and the Dalai Lama takes control of his country as a 16-year-old.

1959 Uprisings in Lhasa and throughout Tibet bring Chinese military occupation of the country; the Dalai Lama takes up exile in India.

1960–65 The United Nations passes three separate resolutions on Tibet's independence from China.

1989 The Dalai Lama wins the Nobel Peace Prize.

2007 The Dalai Lama wins the Congressional Gold Medal in the United States, angering the government of the People's Republic of China.

2008 Tibet is rocked by riots and other protests for independence in March and is closed to foreigners until late June.

The Drepung Monastery once housed more than 10,000 Gelugpa, or Yellow Hat Buddhist monks, including most of the Dalai Lamas who have served as the religious and political head of the Tibetan state. *(Shutterstock/Pichugn Dmitry)*

their present borders, and agreed not to "raise any dust" toward each other. In other words, neither would send an army in the direction of the other. Today the text of this treaty is still visible on a column located in Lhasa; a second and third were apparently placed at what was the Chinese-Tibetan border at Mount Gugu Meru and in Xian, respectively, but so far they have not been found.

After Langdharma's death in 842, no other Tibetan principality was able to unite the peoples of the region until the conquest of the region by the MONGOLS, led by Genghis Khan. For the most part, each region of the country was ruled by a local chieftain or feudal lord. Most people remained pastoralists, living off their herds of animals and small gardens. Buddhism also began to expand its hold in the region, with many different sects emerging over the course of about 400 years.

In 1207 Tibet was unified by Genghis Khan's armies and joined with China and much of Central Asia in the Mongol Empire. At first the Mongols sacked many monasteries and destroyed much ancient art and literature, but by 1247 Kublai Khan, ruler of a united Tibet and China under the Yuan dynasty, had reconciled with the Sakya branch of Buddhism and made their lama the head of the Tibetan government.

A series of 20 Sakya lamas ruled in Tibet for about 100 years until they were overthrown in the 1350s by the follower of a rival Buddhist order, Changchub Gyaltsen. He had been a district ruler during the last Sakya period but raised a large army and conquered the other districts in about 1358. His Phagmodrupa lineage held the balance of power in Tibet until about 1435, when this dynasty was overthrown by a rival lineage, which itself ruled until 1565.

The last secular regime in independent Tibet, the Tsangpa kings, ruled until 1641, when the Yellow Hat, or Gelugpa, sect of Buddhism emerged as the most powerful religious and secular institution in the country through the support of the ruling Mongol khans. The Gelugpas were formed in the late 14th century by Tsongkhapa, who focused his followers' thinking on reason as the pathway to enlightenment. He established the first Tibetan university at Ganden, and near the end of his life, when he had tired of traveling, he built a large monastery. One of Tsongkhapa's students was Gyelwa Gendun-drub, who in 1578, long after his death in 1474, was posthumously named the first Dalai Lama. A feature of Gelugpa as well as other forms of Tibetan Buddhism, which distinguishes it from that in other countries and regions, is the focus on the hereditary reincarnation of the lama position. This transformation is believed by some scholars to have been a strategy introduced to diminish the power of feuding sons, cousins, and others in the direct family of the ruling lamas. The focus was turned away from the individual and toward the sacred office of the lama.

For about 300 years the Gelugpas, or Yellow Hats, ruled Tibet with their unique blend of political and religious authority that kept Tibet largely feudal, isolated, and poor. At first their rule was supported by the Mongol khans who had installed them in the first place; significant political power was held by the regent of the khans. But in 1720 it was a Chinese army that installed the seventh Dalai Lama and made him the official ruler of Tibet. His official standing, however, was in stark contrast to his actual position in relation to the Chinese special representative, or *amban,* who held de facto power based on the strength of his resident army. The eighth Dalai Lama, however, was completely disinterested in politics and his period, 1708–57, initiated about a century and a half of Tibetan isolation and rule by a regent. This was a time of great unrest in China, Central Asia, and India as the Qing dynasty tried to withstand pressure from both inside factions and Europeans who wanted access to trade and ports; Britain sought greater influence in Tibet as a strategic midpoint between Russia, China, and India. The ninth, 10th, 11th, and 12th Dalai Lamas all died quite young; some have assumed that they were murdered in the chaos of the period.

Finally, the 13th Dalai Lama, 1876–1933, only the second in history to attain the title of "Great," was able to bring some stability to the remote, isolated mountain state. He began introducing such amenities as roads, paper money, electricity, and a postal service to smooth the secular side of life in Tibetan society. He also experienced multiple invasions of his country, first from the British in 1904 and then from the Chinese while he was in exile in Mongolia following the British attack. He returned to Lhasa, only to flee again to India in the face of an increasingly hostile Chinese army. Most people believe Tibet was spared from Chinese colonialism in the early 20th century by the 1911 revolution in China that deposed the Qing dynasty and established the Republic of China. At that time the Chinese army withdrew almost entirely from Tibet, and its influence dwindled to nothing. Numerous commentaries on the rule of Thupten Gyatso, the 13th Dalai Lama, indicate that he was fully intent on opening and modernizing

Tsongkhapa

Tsongkhapa is revered today as a Tibetan holy man and the founder of the Gelugpa order of Tibetan Buddhism. Tsongkhapa was born in 1357 in the Amdo province of Tibet and received the layman ordination at the age of three. By the age of seven he was able to recite many sutras and reportedly received the empowerments of the three foremost Buddhist deities, Heruka Chakrasamvara, Hevajra, and Yamantaka. He became a prominent student of Buddhism, and at the age of 24 he was ordained a full monk in the Sakya tradition. His studies of Buddhism ranged across various disciplines, and he studied under 100 different teachers. He is also said to have been able to communicate directly with Manjushri, the patron bodhisattva of the Gelugpas, among others, to clarify scripture. As he began teaching Tibetan Buddhism, his wisdom and compassion gained him a reputation as a second Buddha. Over time he developed the Gelugpa order in works such as *The Great Exposition of the Stages of the Path, The Great Exposition of Tantras, The Essence of Eloquence on the Interpretive and Definitive Teachings, The Praise of Relativity, The Clear Exposition of the Five Stages of Guhyasamaja,* and *The Golden Rosary.* He established the first Gelugpa monastery in Ganden in 1409, and the head of the order is the Dalai Lama. Tsongkhapa died in 1419 at the age of 60.

his country in the face of these external threats and that he managed a significant amount of change despite the extremely conservative religious orders that maintained their control over most land and other resources in the country.

Two years after the death of the 13th Dalai Lama, Tenzin Gyatso was born in a small village in northeast Tibet, and two years later his holiness was recognized by monks engaged in the search to find the reincarnated lama; he was installed at the age of five. The remainder of his childhood was spent in a monastery with his older brother, learning how to fulfill his later political and religious roles. He took over the leadership position as head of state and government in Tibet at age 16 following the invasion of Tibet by the Chinese Red Army. He subsequently met with Mao Zedong, Chou En-Lai, and Deng Xiaoping to negotiate for Tibet's position. These and later negotiations failed, and in 1959 the Chinese military occupied Lhasa, forcing the Dalai Lama and his government into exile, in India. Since 1960 Dharamsala, India, has been the seat of the Tibetan government-in-exile, while the Dalai Lama himself has traveled the world to seek justice and autonomy for his people. In 1989 he was awarded the Nobel Peace Prize for his efforts, and in 2007 he received the U.S. Congressional Gold Medal. More than 100,000 Tibetans continue to reside in India, Nepal, and elsewhere, waiting for China to give up control over their mountain homeland, an event that in mid-2008 did not look likely in the near or even distant future.

The elaborate headgear worn by Gelugpa monks has given them their nickname, Yellow Hat Buddhists; they ruled Tibet from 1642 until the 14th and reigning Dalai Lama was driven from Tibet by the Chinese in 1959. *(AP Photo/ Vincent Yu)*

CULTURE

For many centuries the subsistence base of Tibetan culture has been high-altitude barley, wheat, buckwheat, and a few hardy vegetables that can survive the short growing season and low moisture, such as radishes, peas, and potatoes. Many Tibetans were also nomadic herders prior to the Chinese takeover in 1950, moving seasonally with their herds of yaks, cattle, and goats. Large rural markets brought these herders together a few times each year to exchange animal products for other consumer goods, to socialize, and to marry. However, the economy, even for settled agriculturalists, remained essentially exchange based, despite the introduction of paper currency during the 13th Dalai Lama's reign. Villagers worked together on communal irrigation and other projects since very few families had enough resources to hire others to do this work for them. They owed both labor and produce to their landholders, whether they were a monastery or aristocratic family, and were relatively limited in their movement by these feudal ties to the land.

While the lives of most average Tibetans in 1949 were similar to what they had been in 1649, when the Gelugpas first dominated Tibet, the few aristocratic families in Lhasa lived a very different life. They were able to hire laborers to work their land; purchase consumer products from China, India, and the rest of the world; and participate in the day-to-day political life of the country. They differed from their peasant cousins in almost every way, from dress to speech. They were even able to hire poor Tibetans to participate for them in the many mandatory Buddhist ceremonies, rituals, and other events that dominated the lives of both monks and laypeople alike. Certainly, the most important and prestigious events attracted both rich and poor. All of this changed in 1950, however, when the Chinese occupation introduced all of the land reform, political reform, and other changes brought to China by the Communist revolution. Most aristocratic Tibetans fled the country at that time and set up a parallel society in India, while the peasants remained behind to continue working the land and herding their animals.

Before 1950, rich and poor shared their focus on the extended family as the most important kin group. Households were usually made up of at least two generations of married sons and their children. Generally women moved into their husbands' households in patrilocal residence, but the wide variety of marriages that were allowed in Tibetan society sometimes produced a variation on this theme. The most common form of marriage was simple monogamy, with two unrelated families uniting in the marriage of their son and daughter. Perhaps the most unusual forms of marriage evident in Tibet were fraternal and father-son polyandry, which allowed a group of brothers or a father and son to marry one woman. This was done most often in families who owned a small amount of land or a herd of animals; having all the sons marry a single woman and live in the same household meant that the land or herd did not have to be divided between them. It also lowered the birthrate since three, four, or more men could father only the number of children that one woman was capable of bearing during her reproductive years. Other forms of marriage that were also legal and relatively common were sororal polygyny, where a group of sisters married a single man; mother-daughter polygyny, where a mother and daughter married a single man; and both polyandry and polygyny with unrelated men and women.

Regardless of the kind of marriage, one of the most important factors in marriage generally was class endogamy. For the most part, it was impossible for people to marry outside their own class. For serfs, it was sometimes impossible even to marry outside their own lord's land since they were required to seek permission from him to marry at all. And indeed, not all Tibetans did marry, since the country's large monasteries and convents provided an alternative to married life for those who chose other options; prior to 1950 about a quarter of the population may have resided in these institutions. Choosing the cloistered life of a monk or nun meant that the person was unable to inherit any land, animals, or other property, but it also brought great prestige to the person's family. Wealthier families might donate a parcel of land or other item of wealth to a monastery or convent in place of individual inheritance.

As has been presented throughout this entry, Tibetans are generally devout Buddhists, although there is a very small Muslim minority. Buddhism as it is practiced in Tibet, Mongolia, and much of the Himalayan region is a fairly syncretic religion that combines elements from Indian Buddhism, local spirituality, and Tantrism. Monasteries from a variety of different sects or orders, including the ruling Gelugpa or its rivals, such as Kagyupa and others, provided the bulk of all education in Tibet, and it was generally monks who practiced medicine, taught other monks, and even worked in the country's bureaucracy. The class background of a monk when he entered his monastery generally dictated what his training would be once he entered, with aristocrats' sons entering the highest echelons while peasants' sons trained for less prestigious roles within the monastery. They could be priests, craftsmen, mediums, and even exorcists.

FURTHER READING

Barbara Aziz. *Tibetan Frontier Families* (Durham, N.C.: Carolina Academic Press, 1978).
Ashild Kolas and Monika P. Thowsen. *On the Margins of Tibet: Cultural Survival on the Sino-Tibetan Frontier* (Seattle: University of Washington Press, 2005).
Dalai Lama. *My Land and My People* (New York: Potala Corporation, 1962).
Thubten Jigme Norbu and Colin M. Turnbull. *Tibet, Its History, Religion, and People* (Harmondsworth, U.K.: Penguin, 1972).
Barry Sautman and June Teufel Dreyer, eds. *Contemporary Tibet: Politics, Development, and Society in a Disputed Region* (Armonk, N.Y.: M. E. Sharpe, Inc., 2006).
David Snellgrove and Hugh Richardson. A *Cultural History of Tibet* (Boulder, Colo.: Prahna Press, 1980).

Tiele (Chile, Tura)

There is considerable confusion in the Chinese and other sources on the Tiele. They are sometimes conflated with the DINGLING, Gaoche, and Chile tribes as if these names all referred to the same people in the same period. Other sources claim the Gaoche were the predecessors of the Tiele, who were the ancestors of the UIGHUR people. Yet other sources say Tiele and Chile are the same name in Chinese and just written differently in English, while others claim the Tiele descended from the Chile. To add to the confusion, still other sources add another name to the mix and claim the Tiele were the descendants of the XIONGNU, or Asian Huns.

Most sources, however, agree that the Tiele, sometimes written Tura, were a confederation of many tribes rather than just one tribal community. They resided in the northern reaches of western China, parts of Mongolia, and Siberia. By the years 580–618, which coincides with the Sui dynasty in China, the Tiele were subjects of the Turks, to whom they were probably related. Several of the possible derivations of the name *Tiele* point to Turkic ancestry as well. The name may come from *tirāk,* "supporter" in Turkic languages, or it may be a mispronunciation of the plural for Turk, *Turkler.* Still another possible derivation comes from Zoroastrian religious writing, in which *Tura* means "Turkic."

One of the first references to the Tiele appears in 542, when the Turkic-speaking Bumin, or Tuman, assisted the ROURAN in putting down a Tiele uprising. A few years later the Bumin incorporated the Tiele into the burgeoning Gokturk empire. This incorporation was never fully accepted by the Tiele, despite their linguistic and cultural similarities to their Turkic overlords, and in the seventh century they rebelled several times, especially in the early portion of the century. In 627 several Tiele tribes, including the Xueyantuo, the largest tribe, staged a rebellion against their Turkic overlords, and a year later Turkic khan Tuli requested assistance from Chinese Tang emperor Taizong in putting it down. In 629 the Xueyantuo declared themselves independent and requested an alliance with the Tang; they were followed by other Tiele tribes such as the Bayegu, Tongluo, and Pugu. Probably during this same period of unrest, the Turks invited the major chiefs of the Xueyantuo to a gathering and killed them all. Members of the Bayegu tribe were also responsible for the murder of the leader of the Eastern Gokturks, Khan Muchuo. Despite these small

TIELE

location:
The Altai region

time period:
Probably sixth to seventh centuries

ancestry:
Uncertain, probably Turkic or Altaic

language:
Uncertain, probably Turkic or Altaic

successes over the Turks, the Tiele were not their equals but rather their vassals, with their chiefs bearing the title of governor within the larger Gokturk empire.

Chinese sources indicate that the Tiele did not differ significantly from the Gokturks in their customs and beliefs except in a few important areas. For example, the Tiele practiced a matrilocal marriage pattern so that a man moved into his wife's household after marriage and she could not return home until after the birth of their first child, while the Gokturks were patrilocal.

See also TURKIC PEOPLES.

T'in (Chao Dol, H'tin, Katin, Kha Che, Kha Pai, Kha Phai, Kha T'in, Lawa, Lua, Lwa, Mai, Mal, Pai, P'ai, Phai, Praj, Pral, P'u Pai, Thin, Tie, Tin)

The T'in are one of the smaller HILL TRIBES OF THAILAND; they also live in Laos, west of the Mekong River. Some experts believe that they lived in China's Yunnan Province until about 150 years ago, when population and political pressures drove them into the highlands of Thailand and Laos, while others believe they have been in the region of contemporary Laos for many centuries. Certainly migrations into Thailand are more recent and coincide with the estimated migration date of 150 years ago. In general, the T'in have received much less attention from outsiders than other highland groups, like the LAHU, LISU, and HMONG, because they do not wear bright, colorful clothing or unique head coverings.

The period since the mid-1960s has been very difficult for the T'in due to the war and the aerial bombing of Laos and anticommunist government activity in Thailand. In Thailand especially, many have adopted Thai language and culture, including Buddhism, and no longer speak T'in or practice their indigenous, animistic religion. Trade with lowland THAIS and LAO communities has further encouraged enculturation into these dominant societies, which may explain why American Protestant missionaries have had less success with the T'in than with some other Hill Tribes.

Those T'in who have not adopted lowland, wet-rice agriculture generally grow glutinous or sticky rice, corn, millet, gourds, peppers, cucumbers, eggplants, and chilies in swidden (slash-and-burn) fields. The forest is cleared in January and February, allowed to dry for a few months, and then burned away in April or May. Planting takes place in May or June before the monsoon rains, which allows the plants to germinate. At this time entire families are kept busy around the clock protecting the seeds and seedlings from birds and animals. Rice is harvested in October and November, while other plants ripen as early as August. Generally a field can be used for rice just once, but in the following year some vegetables or condiments can be grown before it must lie fallow for several seasons to allow the regrowth of wild ground cover. In addition to rice and these vegetable foods, T'in also keep pigs and chickens for food, and a few wealthy households have a water buffalo to sell, trade, or use for sacrifice. Dogs, cattle, pigs, and chickens can also be used in sacrifice and then eaten afterward. The T'in also hunt wild game, fish with nets or poison, and gather a wide variety of wild forest products, including honey, berries, roots, and herbs.

Residence rather than kinship is the backbone of T'in social structure, and there is no overarching T'in political organization that holds their many villages together. In general, T'in men and women marry within their own villages and spend their whole lives there as well. Each village is an autonomous unit with a village council that makes all judicial and other decisions. In theory, all adults have the ability to participate in these council meetings, but in practice it is male household heads who are the real decision makers in most villages. Villages do not control the land that surrounds them, and households from various villages may work fields adjacent to one another. Land is not owned by these households either, for there is no concept of private ownership of land. Instead, each household is allowed to use the land it has cleared, or to rent it to others. Only rice is allowed to be owned by those who have sown it, while other crops, including all vegetables, condiments, betel nuts, or other such products, can be taken by anybody in need.

Although kinship is not the backbone of the social order, bilateral ties through one's mother and father are important for determining appropriate marriage partners, for marriage with a close kinsperson is considered incestuous. After marriage, most couples spend at least a few years in matrilocal residence, living with the wife's family and working in their gardens. After the new couple have a child or two, they often move to a new home of their own, built on stilts out of bamboo and thatch.

T'IN

location:
Laos, west of the Mekong River, and Thailand

time period:
Unknown to the present

ancestry:
Mon-Khmer

language:
Mal, a Mon-Khmer language of the larger Austro-Asiatic phylum

Tirurays (Tedurays)

The Tirurays are a subgroup of the LUMAD, 18 tribal communities living in the highlands of Mindanao, speaking Austronesian languages, and traditionally practicing swidden (slash-and-burn) agriculture and indigenous religions. As a group they resisted the onslaught of four different colonizing forces: the Arabs in the 15th century, the Spanish from the 16th to the 20th centuries, and the Americans and JAPANESE in the 20th century. Since Filipino independence in 1945, many communities have continued to struggle for independence and recognition of ancestral domain on their lands, generally with little success when faced with the power of the government of the Philippines and large multinational corporations like Weyerhauser and Del Monte.

Historically, relations between the Tirurays and their Muslim neighbors were usually marked by peaceful trade and coexistence, a pattern that has continued into the present, although some Tirurays have joined the armed militias seeking independence from the Philippines. The coming of the Spanish and Americans, however, disrupted Tiruray lives much more than the earlier Arab colonial period. The Americans especially reached into the highlands of Mindanao with their schools, religion, and corporations and changed the lives of the Tirurays forever. The first American school in Tiruray territory was established in 1916; this was followed 10 years later by an Episcopalian mission. The worst policy decision for the Tirurays was put into action in the mid-1920s, when the Cotabato and other highlands regions were opened up to immigration by Christians from the Filipino lowlands. These migrants brought not only their religion but also languages and way of life very different from the tribal Tirurays specifically, and Lumad more generally. They were also much more familiar with both bureaucracy and private land ownership and were able to take advantage of colonial land registration schemes that saw the widespread annexation of Lumad ancestral territory. Those Tirurays and other Lumad who did not convert to these new lifeways often moved even further into the highlands, where they could continue their own cultural customs under the leadership of indigenous chiefs and other leaders, but they rapidly ran out of places to go after a few decades.

Although most Tirurays have had to give up their swidden agricultural way of life and turn to more intensive farming, the local religious system has been more difficult for outsiders to displace. Even the nominal Christians among the Tirurays believe in the female creator deity Minaden and her brother Tulus, who have remained central to their belief system. Tulus is believed to control the world's good spirits and thus is the patron of all gifts and favors that are granted to the Tirurays, such as healthy children, plentiful crops, and good weather. The Tiruray cosmology is also inhabited by bad spirits, *busaw*, who live in caves and devour the souls of some unfortunate people. A wide variety of charms, amulets, rituals, and medicines are used by even the most urbanized Tirurays to protect themselves from these *busaw*; they also engage the skills of a *beliyan*, or religious leader, who can communicate with the good spirits to maintain their good will and protection. Both agriculture and hunting also require the actions of a *beliyan* to ensure proper balance in the world and positive outcomes in these activities.

See also AUSTRONESIANS.

Tiwi

The Tiwi Islands include the islands of Melville and Bathurst off the northern coast of Australia, approximately 37 miles north of the city of Darwin, capital of Australia's Northern Territory. The islands were separated from mainland Australia at the end of the Holocene sea level rise in approximately 10,000 B.C.E. It is likely that the resulting long period of isolation contributed to the development of distinctive cultural features that differentiate Tiwi Islanders from mainland ABORIGINAL AUSTRALIANS. Such features include the language, which shares only general similarities with mainland aboriginal languages, and the prominence of matrilineal clans, which trace descent through women. Additionally, unlike many other Aboriginal Australians, the Tiwi never incorporated circumcision or subincision into their initiation ceremonies, preferring instead that the initiates display poetic creativity. Singing, carving, painting, and dance were used to distinguish the initiates from one another and from outsiders. Skill in the performing arts has always been a pathway to prestige and leadership among the Tiwi.

After the islands' separation from each other and the mainland, voyages to the mainland appear to have occurred only sporadically. The first consistent contact with outsiders is likely to have been with the annual visiting

TOALA

location:
Southwest Sulawesi,
Indonesia

time period:
Possibly 2000 B.C.E. to the
present

ancestry:
Indochinese
Austronesian

language:
Toala', one of the Toraja-
Sa'dan Austronesian
languages

MAKASSARESE (early Indonesian fishers of *trepang*, or sea cucumber) during the 18th century. As for European contact, historical evidence points to the Dutch East India Company as being the first, in 1705; however, some historians suggest that Portuguese slavers may have made contact earlier.

The Tiwi have never been completely cut off from outside contact, and the results of those contacts occasionally worked their way into their songs, rituals, and dances. Such contact, however, was transient enough to pose little threat to the traditional structures that defined Tiwi society. Even the British attempt to establish a military/trade outpost in 1824 at Punata on Melville Island was short-lived, lasting only four years. Colonial retreat is highly unusual, if not unique, in the context of European settlement of Australia and provides yet another distinction between the Tiwi and mainland aboriginal peoples.

The establishment of the first mission in 1911 on Bathurst Island by Father Gsell, an Alsatian Catholic priest, marked the beginning of fundamental changes to the Tiwi way of life. The introduction of a capitalist economy and schooling inhibited traditional activity in ways that had never been experienced before. Historically the Tiwi relied on hunting, gathering, and fishing for subsistence, but the arrival of the mission meant the introduction of Western consumer goods. The people became more sedentary and ritual ceremonies were scaled back. Even the *pukumani* burial ceremony, the most important event in traditional Tiwi ceremonial life, has been reduced to a one-day affair and on some occasions incorporates the burial of more than one deceased person at a time. The Tiwi had also been polygynous, so that men were allowed to take more than one wife, a practice that was quickly ended by the Catholic missionaries.

Today the Tiwi know that all decisions about the islands can be made only by the approximately 2,400 indigenous inhabitants in accordance with aboriginal law. They gained this right in 1976 through the Northern Territory's Aboriginal Land Rights Act, which returned ownership of the Tiwi Islands to the Tiwi people and made the islands inalienable.

FURTHER READING

C. W. M. Hart, Arnold R. Pilling, and Jane C. Goodale. *The Tiwi of North Australia*, 3rd ed. (New York: Holt, Rinehart & Winston, 1988).

Toala (East Toraja, Luwu, Sada, Telu Limpoe, To Ale)

The Toala are a subgroup of the TORAJA, a people of the highlands of southern Sulawesi. Like the other Toraja subgroups, the Toala are mostly farmers who grow rice on terraced paddies. In slash-and-burn, or swidden, gardens they also grow corn, beans, potatoes, yams, and chilies for personal consumption and coffee and cloves for the market. When the local ecology allows it, some groups gather wild foods and fish for eels, snails, and fish. Water buffalo are used for plowing and transport, while pigs and chickens are kept for food, especially for sacrifices at funerals and other ritual events. The region in which the Toala live also has many copra plantations that provide employment for a few individuals.

Like other Toraja subgroups, the Toala are well known throughout the world for their material arts, especially carvings and effigies of the dead; their houses and rice barns are decorated with carved beams and other decorations. However, unlike many other Toraja communities, who converted to Christianity in the 20th century, most Toala have either maintained their local religious traditions or converted to Islam, the majority religion throughout Indonesia.

The Toala social structure is divided by class, as is the case among the Toraja generally, with aristocrats, commoners, and slaves making up the dominant groups; today only aristocrats and commoners are recognized. As a subgroup of the Toraja, the Toala are also subdivided into three major kinship groups or subtribes, each of which has its own chief who previously had inherited his position from either his mother's or his father's family. Today chiefs act as village headmen who mediate between local populations and the state bureaucracy, and they are elected to the position rather than inheriting it. Other changes in the social structure include the elimination of the threat posed by their lowland neighbors, the BUGINESE and MAKASSARESE, of kidnapping and theft. Headhunting as a way of avenging deaths and aristocratic polygyny, where aristocratic men were able to have more than one wife, have also ceased as central cultural practices.

Tocharians (possibly Arsi, Kuci, Tocharoi, Toxri, Tushara, Twghry—all of these may be misnomers for this group)

In the late 19th century, Western explorers began discovering documents in abandoned Buddhist monasteries in Xinjiang, Tarim Basin, China, that had been written in Tibetan, Chinese, and other languages, as well as two unknown but closely related languages, or two dialects of the same language. With the help of bilingual texts among these writings, scholars were able to translate the documents, whose contents included Buddhist works and materials concerned with monastery affairs, dated mostly to the seventh and eighth centuries C.E. The translators found that the unknown language was Indo-European, but a form of Indo-European that could not be classified as belonging to any known branch of the Indo-European language family. In 1907 German scholar F. W. K. Müller gave the name *Tocharian* to this hitherto unknown Indo-European language because the ancient Greek geographer Strabo had mentioned a tribe called *Tocharoi*. The two dialects were subsequently named Tocharian A and Tocharian B; generally, texts in Tocharian A were associated with the eastern Tarim Basin and those in Tocharian B with the western region.

The linguistic remains of the Tocharians point to an Indo-European past with origins far to the west of the Tarim Basin and with influences from both Iranian and Sanskrit, perhaps through Buddhist missionaries who converted the tribe. There is also some evidence of contact between these Tocharian dialects and the Altaic and Uralic languages, spoken originally in and around Mongolia, in the form of agglutination, the creation of complex words from basic roots and many prefixes and suffixes. These texts also show them to be an odd member of the Indo-European language family, although some scholars dispute this categorization. Tocharian is considered a "centum" Indo-European language because the Tocharian word for 100 contained the root *cent*. All the other "centum" languages were/are western European languages, including Latin, Greek, Germanic, and Celtic languages. The eastern European and Asian Indo-European languages—including Albanian, Armenian, Slavic, Iranian, and Indic languages—are considered "satem" languages because their word for 100 resembles that term. As residents of Central Asia and Chinese Turkestan, their language should logically have been a "satem" language, but it was not.

On the basis of these linguistic findings, researchers have deduced that the Tocharians probably originated somewhere on the Eurasian steppe, perhaps in the region of southern Russia today. At some point after the domestication of the horse by the Proto-Indo-European tribes, they began to migrate eastward, where they settled in the Tarim Basin of northwestern China. The reason for the Tocharian migration eastward or the exact dates are a matter for speculation at this point but may have occurred as early as 2000–1800 B.C.E. as a result of climate change or population pressure. The Swedish explorer Sven Hedin (1865–1952), who first discovered evidence of the Tocharian Indo-Europeans buried in the sands of Turkestan, postulated a much later date for this migration to the region, about 157 B.C.E. Regardless of when they arrived in the Tarim Basin, the bulk of the texts found so far in their language date from 500–700 C.E., and further archaeological evidence places them in Central Asia until about 1000. After that period it is unknown whether they assimilated into the growing communities of TURKIC PEOPLES in the region or were wiped out by those same Turkic speakers.

The clearest aspect of the Tocharian culture that comes out of the evidence we have so far is that in the sixth century they were Buddhists; we do not know when this conversion occurred. Most of the Tocharian texts, dating to the sixth through eighth centuries, are translations of Buddhist texts originally written in other languages. There are also a few letters and passes for caravans among the textual evidence but very little else. All of these secular materials were written in Tocharian dialect B, which has led some scholars to speculate that perhaps Tocharian A was already a dead language by the seventh century, used only for ritual purposes.

A large number of mummies of blonde and red-haired individuals with round-shaped eyes have also been found in Chinese Turkestan. Although they are about 1,000 years older than the Tocharian texts, many scholars have assumed that the mummies are the remains of the early Tocharian speakers. The mummies were often clothed in a kind of tartan cloth that resembles that of the Celtic peoples of Ireland and Scotland, which provided evidence for their Indo-European heritage. However, we cannot definitely link the two populations, because no texts have ever been found with the European-looking mummies that would clearly identify them as Tocharian. Nor can we assume that ancient Chinese sources that spoke of green-eyed military and political figures referred either to the relatives of these mummies or to the readers and writers of the Tocharian texts, although

TOCHARIANS

location:
Northwestern China

time period:
Possibly 2000 B.C.E. to 1000 C.E.

ancestry:
Indo-European

language:
Tocharian, an extinct Indo-European language, with two distinct dialects, Tocharian A and B

many sources do make this claim based on circumstantial evidence.

FURTHER READING

Douglas Q. Adams. *Tocharian Historical Phonology and Morphology* (New Haven, Conn.: American Oriental Society, 1988).

J. P. Mallory and Victor H. Mair. *The Tarim Mummies* (London: Thames & Hudson, 2000).

Toda (O.l, Todava, Ton, Tutavar)

The Toda are one of the SCHEDULED TRIBES of India; they live in very small communities in the Nilgiri Mountains or Blue Mountains of Tamil Nadu in the southern part of the country.

The ancient history of the Toda remains purely speculative due to a lack of written records, but many unlikely scenarios have been proposed since 1603 when the first Europeans, Jesuit missionaries, came upon them. The oddest of these theories states that the Toda are the lost ancestors of the ancient Israelites, a theory that was first posited in the 1840s. This is most certainly not the case since the Dravidian language of the Toda places them in South India from as far back as the third century B.C.E., when their language broke away from Tamil and Malayalam. They probably lived somewhere to the west of their current homeland at that time because archaeological evidence places them outside the Nilgiri Mountains until about the start of the common era. The first written record, however, comes from 1117, when a stone inscription was created in Kannada to record the military defeat of the Toda.

Prior to the formal inclusion of the Nilgiri region in the British Indian colony in 1819, the Toda were integrated into the regional social order with its wide variety of castes and tribes. They traded their animals and milk products with, and possibly paid tribute to, the agricultural Badaga tribe; they also traded with the Kota, who worked with clay, iron, and leather, and with such forest-dwelling peoples as the Kurumba and Irula. Due to their isolation in the highest elevations of the Nilgiris, about 7,500 feet above sea level, the Toda largely chose when and where they interacted with their neighbors and could determine the extent of their interdependence. This relative autonomy ended with the arrival of the British, who brought a significant immigrant population into the highlands and a cash economy based on plantation agriculture, which needed the unskilled labor of most of the peoples of the region. The primarily Indian migrants to the region brought their dominant religion with them, which, with its concepts of social hierarchy, purity, and exclusivity, even further eroded the local culture of interdependence. The Toda and others were incorporated into the Hindu caste system at the bottom of the hierarchy, which further eroded the possibility of their participating in the newly emerging national life as political, social, or economic equals. Today they constitute a very small minority in Andhra Pradesh but receive the benefits of preferential treatment in education and government positions as members of a Scheduled Tribe.

Prior to the onset of the plantation economy in the 19th century, the Toda were largely pastoralists who herded mountain goats and water buffalo. As vegetarians they did not eat these animals themselves but drank the milk and made butter, ghee, cheese, and other dairy products. Male calves were traded both to the Badaga for grain and to their other trading partners for food and other needs. Today many families still keep several buffalo or cattle for home use and sell the surplus milk through local cooperatives or shops; however, the most important economic activity today is agriculture. They do not grow their own rice but rather purchase it to accompany their own cabbage, carrots, and potatoes. This change from pastoralism to agriculture has also engendered a distinct change in the domestic division of labor, for in the past men were responsible only for dealing with their herds while women were largely responsible for domestic affairs. Today both men and women work in the fields, which has led to a greater value being placed on the lives of women and girls and an elimination of female infanticide.

Toda kinship groups and marriage patterns are extremely rare and have attracted the attention of many anthropologists. Their kinship is of the double-unilineal variety, which means that each Toda is a member of both a matrilineal and a patrilineal clan that is exogamous and can delineate its ancestors back for 10 generations or more. Lineal societies are usually either matrilineal, in which case everybody inherits his or her lineage and clan membership from the mother, or patrilineal, in which case membership descends from men only. Western societies are not lineal at all but rather lateral, which means that each individual is seen as an equal relative of his or her mother and father but that generations generally do not get counted beyond five or six at the most. There are no large, corporate groupings of kin in most

TODA

location:
Tamil Nadu, India

time period:
Possibly third century B.C.E. to the present

ancestry:
Dravidian

language:
Toda, a Dravidian language in the Tamil-Malayalam subdivision

bilateral societies; each individual family maintains as few or as many ties to relatives as desired. The Toda are one of the few societies in the world in which individuals are seen as full-fledged members of both their mothers' lineage and their fathers'. They must marry outside both of these lineages, maintain alliance and ritual ties to both corporate groups, and can trace their ancestry back for 10 or more generations on both sides.

Marriage among the Toda is a complex affair of finding someone who is outside both exogamous lineages, no easy feat with a population that has hovered around 1,000 people for the past generation. Many different forms of marriage were allowed in the past, including monogamy between one man and one woman, polygyny between a man and several women, and polyandry, especially fraternal polyandry, between a group of brothers and one woman. The latter marriage form was used to maintain small herds of animals within a single family, rather than having to divide them up at the death of the father. It also helped to keep the birthrate low since a group of brothers could have only as many children as it was possible for a single woman to bear, rather than each brother having his own family. This form of marriage has fallen out of favor and has not been seen among the Toda for at least two generations.

The traditional Toda religion recognized two separate worlds, that of the living and that of the dead, each ruled by a separate god. Besides activities concerned with these two divine figures, the most important sacred events for the Toda concerned the care and milking of their buffalo, building dairy buildings, and making butter and ghee from their milk. Rituals accompanied all aspects of a dairy family's activities and differed depending on the ritual grade of the person, buffalo, and equipment. In addition, the Toda also worshiped a variety of Hindu gods, goddesses, and other divine spirits. While most of these ritual activities have continued within most Toda communities, especially those considered "traditionalist," there are a small number of Christian Toda communities where all of these activities have become anathema.

See also DRAVIDIANS; KANNADIGAS; MALAYALIS; TAMILS.

Tolai (Gunantuna)

The Tolai are one of the largest indigenous groups in Papua New Guinea as well as one of the most economically successful, with many Tolai having entered white-collar professions and, since independence in 1975, politics. Unlike many other languages in New Guinea, the Tolai language, or Kuanua, is not at all under threat from Tok Pisin, the pidgin language common throughout the entire island. In part this success can be attributed to the fact that the Tolai were one of the first groups to have sustained contact with Europeans, colonials having arrived in 1872 and stayed as part of the German New Guinea Company's efforts to make and sell copra, dried coconut meat. Another factor in contemporary Tolai economic and political success is that their own culture provided an almost perfect background for the mindset and practices necessary to succeed in the capitalist world: The Tolai were one of the few tribal societies that developed the concept of currency exchange or money.

The indigenous money of the Tolai is called *tambu* and is made up of strings of shells that have been cut apart to create flat disks with a hole bored in the middle; this allows the disks to be strung together, and many of the resulting strings measure thousands of feet in length. Prior to the arrival of European colonizers, this money was used in all aspects of Tolai society, from buying basic food items to performing proper mortuary rituals. Marriages, male initiation rites, and other important events in Tolai society could not take place without strings of *tambu* changing hands or, in the case of death rituals, being broken apart. When the Germans first arrived in New Britain, they had to adopt *tambu* as a legitimate currency, since getting the Tolai to work on their coconut plantations meant paying them in their own currency. Even today tourists in the markets in and around the Tolai territory in New Britain, including the large city of Rabaul, may see locals using either the national currency, the Papua New Guinea kina, or *tambu* to purchase food and other items.

While *tambu* serves the same function for the Tolai as money does in all market economies, this is not all that it does. The word *tambu* refers both to shell money and to all things that are in some way sacred or prohibited. In this way it is comparable to the Polynesian word *tabu* or *tapu*, from which we get the English word *taboo*. As a result of this relationship, *tambu* means more to the Tolai than mere currency. It is a symbolic representation of all that is sacred to them, including ancestors, land, and kinship. It is only through possession of large amounts of *tambu* that a Tolai can enter the afterlife, a

TOLAI

location:
Gazelle Peninsula of New Britain, an island in the Bismarck Archipelago off the northeast coast of New Guinea

time period:
Unknown to the present

ancestry:
Melanesian and Austronesian

language:
The majority speak Kuanua, with small numbers speaking Minigir and Bilur; all three are Oceanic languages within the larger Austronesian language family.

heavenlike place of ease and comfort. As a result, individual Tolai try to be as careful with their *tambu* as possible, with the most successful saving far more strings than they spend to ensure themselves a place in the afterlife. Previously this belief in particular set the stage for later Tolai success in the capitalist world.

When the German colonizers first arrived in New Britain in the 19th century, they found a society that seemed largely anarchic. The Tolai had no word to refer to themselves as a people, nor did they have a word for their language. They lived in scattered villages or hamlets that traded with one another, intermarried, and fought but lacked any overarching political unity. It was not until the 1930s that they developed any sense of being a unique community or people group. Structurally their society was based largely on matrilineal kinship with patrilocal residence after marriage. They were also interconnected, with related societies throughout the Duke of York Islands and New Ireland having two exogamous marriage moieties into which every individual Tolai was born. Some individual Tolai men were able to rise to the position of Big Man based on strength of personality and size of personal and kin networks, but this position was merely one of high status and prestige rather than political strength.

The first colonizers came to New Britain, which they called Neu Pommern or New Pomerania, to establish coconut plantations for the making of copra (dried coconut meat, which yields coconut oil). Their arrival created great inequalities between coastal communities whose inhabitants worked on the plantations both for *tambu* and for European trade goods such as guns, ammunition, tobacco, and steel tools, and inland communities that did not have access to this wealth. This situation quickly resulted in more frequent warfare between indigenous villages, which the Germans eventually halted. While the Tolai increased in wealth, education, and European sophistication throughout the late 19th and early 20th centuries, they also suffered heavy losses from a 1937 volcanic eruption. During World War II they experienced several years of JAPANESE occupation, which resulted in thousands of Tolai starving or being worked to death. Because of Allied air attacks, they also lost most of their well-established coconut plantations. In the postwar period the Australian administration reestablished itself and assisted in the setup of cocoa plantations and processing plants to supplement the established copra industry. In 1994

another volcanic eruption caused immense destruction in the heartland of Tolai society and culture, the city of Rabaul, and resulted in thousands becoming internally displaced persons.

In addition to their relative wealth, the Tolai are also known throughout northern Papua New Guinea as being extremely powerful sorcerers. For most of their fellow citizens, it is the strength of their magic that explains their economic and political success. They are also known in the West as carvers of beautiful masks. Prior to the coming of the art and tourist trades, Tolai masks were used solely as part of the Duk Duk mask ceremony, the initiation of men into adulthood. Today masks are produced without ancestral power to be sold to tourists in addition to those imbued with ancestral power, which are used in initiations.

See also AUSTRONESIANS; MELANESIANS; NEW GUINEANS: NATIONALITY.

FURTHER READING
A. L. Epstein. *Matupit: Land, Politics, and Chang among the Tolai of New Britain* (Berkeley and Los Angeles: University of California Press, 1970).
Klaus Neumann. *Not the Way It Really Was: Constructing the Tolai Past* (Honolulu: Honolulu University Press, 1992).

Tongans

The Tongans are the indigenous people of the independent country of Tonga, which is located in the Pacific Ocean between Fiji to the west, Wallis and Futuna and Samoa to the north, and Niue to the west; New Zealand's Kermadec Islands are Tonga's closest neighbors to the south. The Tongans speak a western Polynesian language and are thought to be the descendants of migrants from the original AUSTRONESIANS who left south China between 5000 and 4500 B.C.E.

Tongans were the only POLYNESIANS who maintained their traditional monarchical political system until 2008, when King Tupou V promised to relinquish power. The Kingdom of Tonga was ruled by a hereditary king; all other Tongans continue to be ranked by patrilineal kin groupings according to their royal or commoner status. Related to this political stability, the *anga fakatonga,* or Tongan way, continues to be important in many spheres of social life, including rank, gender relations, and to a lesser degree child rearing, despite the extreme transnationalism of the Tongan people; about 50 percent more Tongans live outside Tonga in a widespread diaspora than live within the country.

TONGANS

location:
Tonga

time period:
1200 B.C.E. to the present

ancestry:
Polynesian

language:
Tongan, a West Polynesian language, and English

Nowhere is the struggle between tradition and modernity more evident than in most Tongans' attitudes toward the monarchy. The funeral of King Taufa'ahau Tupou IV in 2006 was an opportunity for traditional mourning and monarchical rituals as well as calls for more civilian accountability in government. *(AP Photo/Ross Setford)*

Rank in Tonga is a matter of kinship: Each individual is born into a patrilineal group in which descent is reckoned through his or her father's lineage and which ranks everyone in relation to all other Tongan individuals. On another level, rank is linked to the connection between brothers and sisters, seen as the fundamental building block of all traditional Tongan society. The relationship between chiefs and commoners, for example, is usually viewed as parallel to the relationship between sisters and brothers. Unexpectedly for many westerners, it is the sister in the brother-sister dyad that is seen as superior, and thus chiefs are related to sisters, commoners to brothers. This is not to say that women in general are seen as superior in Tonga; chiefs, after all, are men. But the position of women in western Polynesia generally is quite high in relation to other parts of the world because they are considered primarily in their role as sisters rather than as wives or mothers.

Another interesting feature about Tonga's gender system is that rather than just two genders, men and women, there is a third recognized gendered category: *fakafefine, fakaleiti,* or, as they refer to themselves, just simply *leiti.* These terms, meaning "like a woman," "like a lady," and "lady," respectively, refer to biological males who cross-dress, do women's work, and sometimes partner with other nontransgendered males. In traditional Tongan society almost every extended family would have had at least one *fakaleiti* in its midst, and it was not the cause for alarm that it might be in the West; one of the sons of the late king Taufa'ahau Tupou IV (d. 2006) has lived as a *fakaleiti* since adolescence. However, globalization and increasing westernization have produced changes in this society, including the unquestioned acceptance of these individuals. Even King Taufa'ahau Tupou was worried about what would happen to his son after his death. To date, the changed attitudes have yet to take on the negative associations of transgenderism in the West, and many *fakaleiti* are still held in high regard for their creativity and hard work; however, mainstream Tongans also often try to expose them as men or use humor or other methods to shame them into conformity.

Shame generally is an important feature of social control in Tonga and can be used in a wide variety of contexts. For example, Tongan men of low social status who speak in English in public or spend much time with westerners are often shamed into ceasing their status-enhancing behavior by being called a *fakaleiti*, even if they display no feminine traits. Women are not sanctioned as much for speaking in English and thus tend to speak more English than men. Other behaviors that can bring shame, or *ma*, on Tongan adults are displaying anger or other negative emotions in public, ignoring rank and status, or disrespecting Tongan culture generally. Children are considered outside the purview of shame because they are *vale*, ignorant, and must be taught how to be proper Tongans, who are *poto*, knowledgeable about social boundaries and rules. Toward this end, corporal punishment is often used to help children internalize the rules of their culture; this has caused many problems for Tongans living in societies where this behavior is considered child abuse.

See also TONGANS: NATIONALITY.

Tongans: nationality (people of Tonga)

Tonga is a Polynesian island nation in the South Pacific.

GEOGRAPHY

The Tongan islands consist of 169 islands strewn across over 140,000 square miles of Pacific Ocean. Ninety-six of the islands are inhabited and are grouped into three main clusters: Vava'u, Ha'apai, and Tongatapu. Tongatapu is the largest island, with a landmass covering 99 square miles; it is also home to the nation's capital, Nuku'alofa.

The eastern islands (including Tongatapu) are coral formations and have a limestone base, but the western islands have volcanic bases, some of which are still active. In 1853 an eruption on the island of Niuafo'ou destroyed the village of 'Ahau, killing 25 people. In 1946 a particularly fierce eruption forced the nearly 1,200 inhabitants of Niuafo'ou to evacuate the island and prevented their return until 1958.

The soil of the Tongan islands is fertile because of volcanic ash and supports a rich array of vegetation, including forests and swamps. Indigenous animal life is sparse but includes the flying fox. Domestic livestock such as horses, cattle, chickens, and pigs have been introduced to the islands from overseas.

Threats to the islands' natural stability include cyclones, which can be particularly devastating, deforestation due to efforts to clear land for agriculture and habitation, and over-active hunting and fishing, which are depleting the wildlife and marine life.

INCEPTION AS A NATION

Tonga had enjoyed the exclusivity of being the only surviving monarchy in Polynesia, and much of Tonga's success in retaining its indigenous culture can be attributed to the decision made by King George Tupou I in 1875 to restrict land ownership to Tongan-born citizens. To this day, no foreigner can own land in Tonga; however, for tourism purposes, many companies and organizations can lease land. This decision spared Tonga from the fate of foreign takeover that other Polynesian nations experienced. Thus, the Tonga that exists today was established with the coronation of King George Tupou I.

Tonga's national time line can be divided into Christian and pre-Christian, as the arrival of the Wesleyan missionaries in 1822 ultimately led to the unification of Tonga in 1845. King George I was heavily influenced by the missionaries and was subsequently inspired to convert to Christianity, leading him to cross paths with missionary Shirley Waldemar Baker sometime in the 1860s. Baker, who was the head of the Wesleyan mission in Tonga, was so trusted by King George I that he was designated Tonga's official prime minister; his newfound political power led to the rapid growth of the Wesleyan Methodist church in Tonga. With the assistance of Baker, King George I united the Tongan islands for the first time in history and dedicated Tonga to the Christian god. The unification of Tonga was a gradual process as many rival chiefs refused to recognize King George's authority. Between 1845 and 1852, his growing political strength forced many chiefs to renounce claims to power and acknowledge King George's authority. When the last independent chief finally stepped down, King George I officially became the sole ruler of Tonga. Tonga became an official kingdom in November 1875 with the establishment of the constitution.

The political upheaval was monumental as King George I instituted completely foreign social systems, such as a new form of land tenure in which every Tongan male, at the age of 16, was entitled to rent an 8.25-acre plot of bushland and three-eighths of an acre of village land. King George made even more changes to the Tongan islands by adopting the British system of government, and in June 1864 he opened the first Tongan parliament and abolished serfdom completely.

TONGANS: NATIONALITY

Nation:
Tonga; The Kingdom of Tonga; formerly The Friendly Islands

derivation of name:
Polynesian word for *south,* referring to its location south of Samoa.

government:
Constitutional monarchy

capital:
Nuku'alofa

language:
Tongan is the official language, but most literature is published in English.

religion:
Free Wesleyan Church of Tonga 41 percent, Roman Catholic 16 percent, Church of Jesus Christ of Latter-Day Saints 14 percent, Free Church of Tonga 12 percent, other 17 percent. Both the Catholic Church and the Mormon Church claim that their faith is the chosen religion of 30–40 percent of Tongan citizens, which creates some uncertainty.

earlier inhabitants:
There were no pre-Polynesian inhabitants of the Tongan islands.

demographics:
Tongan 98 percent, other (Chinese, European, or Euronesian) 2 percent

Tongans: nationality time line

B.C.E.

1200 Austronesians from South China arrive in Tonga.

C.E.

1200 The Tongan monarchy is at its peak, with political power reaching as far as the Samoan Islands, parts of Fiji, and the Cook Islands.

1300 A Tongan king delegates his secular power to his brother while retaining spiritual power, a structure that is repeated years later, thereby establishing the tradition of three ruling powers within the monarchy: the Tu'i Tonga, who hold divine authority; the Tu'i Ha'atakalaua; and the Tu'i Kanokupolu, who hold secular power and oversee daily matters of the kingdom.

1616 Dutch explorers Willem Schouten and Jacob Le Maire sight the Tongan islands while trying to find a new route to the Spice Islands in an effort to avoid the trade restrictions of the Dutch East India Company.

1643 Abel Tasman is the first European to visit Tonga.

1747 The first missionaries from the London Missionary Society arrive in Tonga.

1773 Captain James Cook visits Tonga and names the archipelago "The Friendly Islands" for the hospitable reception he is given. According to British writer William Mariner, the Tongan chieftains were actually planning to kill Captain Cook but could not decide on a way to do it.

1789 The infamous mutiny on the HMS *Bounty,* in which Fletcher Christian and some of the crew take over the ship and set the captain adrift in the ship's launch, takes place in Tongan waters.

1806 The British ship *Port Au Prince* anchors off the coast of the Tongan island Lifuka and is attacked by Tongan warriors at the command of King Fangupo. Most of the crew are killed, but a young William Mariner is spared and lives in Tonga for four years under the tutelage of Fangupo. Upon his return to England, he writes an account of his years in Tonga as well as a Tongan dictionary and thesaurus.

1822 Missionaries from the Wesleyan Missionary Society based in Sydney, Australia, arrive, led by Walter Lawry.

1845 Taufa'ahau of the Tu'i Kanokupolu kingship line unites the Tongan islands for the first time and takes the name Siaosi, which means "George," in honor of King George III of England. He is later baptized King George Tupou I.

1865–75 King George Tupou I adopts the British royal style of rule and establishes Tonga's first constitution, first written law code, and parliamentary government. He also makes land ownership available only to Tongan citizens, abolishes serfdom, and allows for freedom of the press.

1893 King George Tupou I dies at the age of 100 and is succeeded by his great-grandson, King George Tupou II.

1900 An internal struggle between rival chiefs trying to remove the new king convinces King George Tupou II to conclude a Treaty of Friendship with the United Kingdom that puts Tonga under British protection. Tonga remains an independent nation while the United Kingdom manages its foreign affairs and protects it from attack. Under this treaty Tonga becomes a part of the British Western Pacific Territories.

1939–45 World War II erupts, and Tonga develops the Tonga Defence Force. The New Zealand Armed Forces help train the 2,000 troops, and they are deployed to fight in the Solomon Islands while U.S. and New Zealand troops are stationed in Tongatapu.

1958 A New Treaty of Friendship is made between Tonga and the United Kingdom in which the governor of Fiji is the British chief commissioner for Tonga. The bill is ratified a year later.

1967 The Tongan Trilithon is discovered. Similar in structure to the British Stonehenge, the Trilithon consists of three 40-ton stones, at the top of which is carved the name Ha'amonga 'a Maui, which translates as "The Burden of Maui," the mythical Polynesian god who dredged up the Pacific islands from the sea. Markings in the stones are in precise alignment with the rising of the sun on the summer and winter solstices.

Tongans: nationality time line *(continued)*	
1970	On June 4, Tonga obtains full independence from the United Kingdom, making the nation responsible for its own foreign affairs. The king declares the event Tonga's "re-entry into the community of nations."
	Tonga joins the British Commonwealth as an autochthonous monarchy.
1999	Tonga becomes a member of the United Nations.
2008	King Tupou declares his intention to hand power over to a democratically elected parliament, ending Polynesia's only reigning monarchy.

In 1893 King George Tupou I died at the age of 100, having outlived all of his children, and was succeeded by his great-grandson, who took the name King George Tupou II. But the death of the first king left the new king vulnerable as political rivals attempted to dethrone him. In reaction, King George Tupou II signed a Treaty of Friendship with the United Kingdom, which made Tonga a British protected state. Tonga would still retain its autonomy as a self-governing nation, but the United Kingdom would protect it from foreign attack in exchange for the ability to use Tonga as a refuelling station.

In 1970 Queen Salote Tupou III made arrangements just prior to her death that ended Tonga's protectorate status, and Tonga re-emerged into full independence once more.

CULTURAL IDENTITY

Tongan culture, despite its heavy emphasis on adherence to the Tongan way, is one that continually makes accommodations for changing times and modern innovations. Because many Tongans now live overseas and send money home to support their families, the Tongans recognize two distinct codes of behavior: *anga fakatonga,* which translates as "the Tongan way," and *anga fakapalangi,* or "the Western way." The two are often dramatically different, particularly in regard to gender roles and social structure. In traditional Tongan culture, women often hold a higher social status than men due to their roles as nurturers of future generations, and they are thus seen as critical to the survival of the Tongan people. A woman often outranks her brother socially, even if he is older. Traditionally, the opposite has held true in western culture. Though the two codes of behavior are often mutually exclusive, as in this case, many Tongans recognize the necessity of both and adapt accordingly.

The Tongan struggle between retaining traditional customs and accommodating modern western culture is particularly visible in the recent conflict that has arisen between the monarchy and a prodemocracy movement that stresses better representation of nonelite Tongan citizens and accountability in state matters. In recent years a series of unsuccessful money-making schemes proposed by Tongan royalty resulted in the disappearance of millions of dollars, sparking outrage among Tongan citizens and concern in neighboring countries. Nevertheless, many Tongans continue to support the monarchy fervently, especially since the announcement in July 2008 that a fully democratic government will take control in 2010.

One feature that remains markedly present in Tongan society despite the ever-changing cultural rules is religious devotion. The constitution declares Sunday a sacred day of Sabbath, and no trade may take place unless approved by the minister of police, under penalty of fine or imprisonment. Since the nationwide Christian conversion in the reign of King George Tupou I, Tongan religious devotion has remained resolute. Even when Shirley Baker broke from the Wesleyan Methodist church and founded the Free Church of Tonga, most Tongans refused to leave their chosen faith. Today church and religion have become deeply ingrained social institutions that not only provide Tongan citizens with a stable belief system but give the community a sense of support and solidarity. Church is a social gathering and a time to reconnect with friends and neighbors, a custom that likely keeps the Tongan people in touch with their cultural roots.

Like other Polynesian nations, Tonga struggles to maintain its indigenous culture in a world that is becoming increasingly globalized. Up until very recently, it was strictly taboo in Tongan culture for an adult brother and sister to be alone in a room together, but the introduction of television has gradually eroded that cultural belief. Nonetheless, Tongans maintain strong ties to friends and family and place heavy emphasis on social reconnection to keep their culture alive and thriving.

See also POLYNESIANS.

FURTHER READING

David Hatcher Childress. *Ancient Tonga and the Lost City of Mu'a: Including Samoa, Fiji, and Rarotonga* (Kempton, Ill.: Adventures Unlimited Press, 1996).

Stephen L. Donald. *In Some Sense the Work of an Individual: Alfred Willis and the Tongan Anglican Mission, 1902–1920* (Red Beach, N.Z.: ColCom Press, 1994).

Christine Ward Gailey. *Kinship to Kingship: Gender Hierarchy and State Formation in the Tongan Islands* (Austin: University of Texas Press, 1987).

Paul van der Grijp. *Identity and Development: Tongan Culture, Agriculture, and the Perenniality of the Gift* (Leiden, Netherlands: KITLV Press, 2004).

———. *Islanders of the South: Production, Kinship, and Ideology in the Polynesian Kingdom of Tonga,* trans. Peter Mason (Leiden, Netherlands: KITLV Press, 1993).

J. S. Neill. *Ten Years in Tonga* (London: Hutchinson, 1955).

Toraja (Sa'dan Toraja, South Toraja, Tae' Toraja, Toraa, Toradja, Toraya)

The Toraja are a minority group in Sulawesi, formerly Celebes, an island in the Indonesian Archipelago. Their name is an externally derived ethnonym from a BUGINESE term meaning "upstream people" and was adopted by the people themselves only in the 20th century.

Prior to the arrival of the Dutch colonizers in 1906, the Toraja interacted with their Muslim neighbors, the Buginese and MAKASSARESE, through trade and as the targets of these kingdoms' slave raids and other forms of exploitation. The Toraja themselves were not unified into a single polity; rather, they organized their society along the dual principles of locality and kinship. Each locality and kin group had its own leaders whose reach could not extend beyond their village or clan. About 10 years after the onset of Dutch colonialism in 1906, Dutch Reformed Church missionaries arrived in the highlands of Sulawesi, bringing their form of Calvinist worship. At first few Toraja were interested in conversion to the new faith, but by the 1960s the majority of them had become Christian through the efforts of Christian schools and churches in the highlands. These two facts, lack of indigenous political centralization and Christianity, make them distinctly different from their lowland Muslim neighbors in Sulawesi.

Although the Toraja did not have a unified political structure prior to 1906, they did have a complex social structure that recognized the existence of three separate social classes: slaves, commoners, and aristocracy. Every individual was born into one of these classes based on the class of his or her parents and generally remained in that class for life; however, there was some degree of social mobility based on personal traits and success or failure in economic pursuits. Within each class, Toraja society was further subdivided into a hierarchical structure based on age, wealth, and occupation. Today much of this indigenous social structure has been transformed: Slavery is illegal in Indonesia, and far more families claim aristocratic origins because wealth from their participation in the global market economy has allowed them to purchase all the symbolic attributes of this social class. Anthropologists who have studied this phenomenon among the Toraja state that members of the old elite are often disgruntled with the large numbers of commoner and even former slave families who today claim to be aristocratic; they are referred to as "false nobles."

Prior to the incorporation of the Toraja in the Indonesian economy, which began in earnest in the 1950s and 1960s, the Toraja were largely swidden (slash-and-burn) farmers who also maintained some wet-rice paddies in lower elevations. They lived in settlements that perched atop southern Sulawesi's higher mountains and stayed connected with other Toraja

These *tau taus* are funeral effigies, carved to accompany the dead on their journey from funeral house to burial. Once ensconced there, the *tau taus* keep an eye on the spirits of the dead and the living. *(OnAsia/Michael Bierman)*

TORAJA

location:
Southwest Sulawesi, Indonesia

time period:
Possibly 2000 B.C.E. to the present

ancestry:
Austronesian speakers

language:
There are six separate Toraja-Sa'dan languages spoken in Sulawesi, all Austronesian languages.

settlements through ritual exchanges of food and other items. Their native religion, Aluk to Dolo, or "ways of the ancestors," entailed making sacrifices of animals and other foods to their ancestors to guarantee good fortune in farming and other pursuits; misfortune was blamed on the spirit world and elaborate rituals were held to determine the cause and to end the suffering. The most important rituals, however, were funerals, which were costly affairs but necessary for the dead person's soul to enter Puya, the afterworld, and become a divine ancestor. Those whose relatives were unable or unwilling to hold this ceremony were destined to wander the earth, causing problems for the living.

Torres Strait Islanders (Indigenous people of the Torres Strait Islands)

The Torres Strait Islanders take their name from the cluster of islands in the strait that separates the northernmost tip of the Australian mainland from the south coast of Papua New Guinea. While the islands are Australian territory scattered across an area of around 30,000 square miles, the indigenous inhabitants are MELANESIANS related to the Papuans.

At its narrowest point the strait is a mere 93 miles wide and constitutes the only border that Australia shares with another country. Of the 274 islands, 17 are inhabited by about 8,000 people; many more islanders live outside the region, mostly in coastal towns of Australia's mainland state of Queensland. The main administrative center is Thursday Island.

The Torres Strait was once a land bridge that connected the Australian continent with New Guinea, forming a single landmass known as Sahul. With the sea-level rise at the end of the last ice age about 10,000 years ago, the land bridge was submerged. Many of the peaks of the land bridge were not completely submerged, leaving what are now called the Torres Strait Islands.

The first known European navigation of the strait was by Luis Vaez de Torres, a Portuguese seaman on a Spanish expedition from Peru to the South Pacific in 1606. In 1770, when Captain James Cook annexed the whole of eastern Australia, the Torres Strait Islands were not yet included. In 1871 the London Missionary Society arrived, setting in motion momentous upheaval in the traditions that had sustained island life for centuries. Additionally, the Cambridge Anthropological Expedition to the Torres Strait Islands in 1888 resulted in a radical reduction of indigenous cultural artifacts. The pathway to officially becoming part of the Australian territory began in 1879 when Queensland annexed the islands, which were eventually incorporated into the new federation of Australia in 1901.

From the 1860s to the 1970s the Torres Strait had an important pearling industry, and at its peak in the 1890s it supplied more than half of the world's pearl shells. While the industry brought economic opportunities to the islands, it also brought exploitation of local divers and required significant resources to sustain it, taking a drastic toll on the island's food, timber, and water supplies. As a result, by 1990 the islands' population had declined to 50 percent below the pre-pearling levels.

In 1992 Eddie Mabo and four other Torres Strait Islanders won a 10-year court battle for recognition of land ownership prior to the annexation by Queensland. This ruling overturned the legal doctrine of *terra nullius* (no-one's land) and had far reaching consequences for land claims by both Torres Strait Islanders and ABORIGINAL AUSTRALIANS.

The culture of Torres Strait Islanders is imbued with the sea. Traditionally a subsistence-based society, the seafaring islanders traveled long distances to hunt for turtle and dugong and to maintain important trade and political networks. Thousands of years of marine-based trade and interactions with Australian aboriginal people to the south and Melanesians (Papuans) to the north have created a cultural whirlpool among the three groups. Though influenced by their neighbors, the islanders are a culturally distinct group with rich customs and ceremonies. One such custom is the festive "tomb opening" ceremony, which over the years has grown in prominence because of its ability to draw kin home from the mainland. As such this event is a powerful symbol of ethnic identity and home island ties. The ceremony concludes a long period of mourning and is the key to the spirit's journey to the afterworld without which it will remain among the living to cause havoc. The tomb is not actually opened, but an elaborate headstone wrapped in colorful cloth, commissioned on the mainland, is presented by the in-laws to the deceased's family.

Trobriand Islanders (Trobrianders, people of the Trobriands)

The Trobriand Islanders are an Austronesian-speaking people who inhabit a chain of islands off the southeast corner of Papua New Guinea.

TORRES STRAIT ISLANDERS

location:
Between the tip of Cape York in Queensland, Australia, and the south coast of Papua New Guinea. This strait connects the Arafura and Coral Seas.

time period:
Perhaps as early as 60,000 B.C.E. and definitely 45,000 B.C.E. to the present

ancestry:
Melanesian

language:
There are two indigenous languages spoken on the islands: Kala Lagaw Ya and Meriam Mir, as well as a Torres Strait Creole.

Their social organization exhibits some traits that are fairly typical of POLYNESIANS, such as chiefs, as well as some that are more familiar among MELANESIANS, such as ritual exchange. The Trobrianders also look more like their Melanesian neighbors than their closer linguistic relatives the Polynesians, with dark brown-to-black skin and frizzy hair. Like other peoples in the region, Trobrianders produce taro, yams, sweet potatoes, bananas, and other tropical tree fruits in intensively worked gardens. They also raise pigs and eat a variety of fish and seafood.

The contemporary Trobrianders present a number of traits that make their origins a mystery. Melanesian populations are known to have settled the larger islands of the region as early as 30,000 B.C.E.; however, the Trobrianders speak an Austronesian language, which was introduced into the region only around 3000 B.C.E. They also share many genetic traits that link them to the AUSTRONESIANS, such as Samoans and other Polynesians, despite the appearance of being fully Melanesian. Therefore, it is unknown whether an early population of Melanesians was invaded by Austronesian speakers who intermarried with the original population and forced the adoption of their language, or whether the Trobriands were originally settled by Austronesians who then intermarried with Melanesians from the surrounding area, as happened in Fiji.

While very little archaeological work has been done on the origins and early history of the Trobrianders, considerable work was done throughout the 20th century on many aspects of their culture, including their politics, kinship, religion, and exchange systems. With respect to their political system, the Trobrianders differ significantly from other Melanesians in recognizing the ascribed (birthright) position of some subclans as superior to others. In addition, while the Big Man tribal complex of most Melanesians allows for constant competition among men for attainment of a leadership position, the Trobriand system recognizes the right of only select individuals to inhabit the position of chief, one man per subclan per generation. This is clearly a ranked, hierarchical system that recognizes the authority of some people over others, not just the power of persuasion or possession to determine the most important person at any given moment.

Significant work has also been done on the Trobrianders' kinship system, which resembles many others in Polynesia and Micronesia in being matrilineal. This means that clans and subclans, the two primary political divisions in the society, are organized around the lines of descent through women rather than through both parents or through men. In kinship systems like these, a boy's most important relationship with an adult man is not with his father, who is a member of a different matriline, but with his mother's brother, from whom he inherits his position in society as the senior male in his mother's line of descent. A second important aspect of Trobriand kinship is that there is no recognition of relatives as we know of that concept in English. Instead, Trobriand kinship terminology recognizes people who are restricted from eating the same kinds of foods as another person and those who participate in different kinds of exchange with another person. Thus the terms for *husband* and *wife* actually refer not to the marriage per se but to the fact that husbands agree to exchange raw products with women, who in turn agree to exchange cooked foods. In neither case, for food prohibitions or exchange, is there any recognition in this kinship system of people's sharing any bodily substance. Indeed, Trobrianders explicitly deny that people can share substances, which led Bronislaw Malinowski and other anthropologists to comment on the lack of recognition among Trobrianders that sexual intercourse leads to pregnancy and birth.

The Trobrianders' religion combined a belief in spirits with a strong emphasis on ritual or magic that aimed to control the natural world. With regard to the spirit world, the Trobrianders believed that all beings had a spirit, from humans who continue to be reincarnated, to plants, animals, and geographic features that continually interact with the human world and cause a variety of both positive and negative outcomes. Ritual or magic was then used to try to convince these spirits to act in ways that would benefit humans, such as bringing rain or making watercraft safe. It is important to note that this magic did not replace empirical thinking; Trobrianders turned to it only when their scientific or technological knowledge failed.

Finally, the aspect of Trobriand culture that most solidly links them to others within the umbrella of Melanesian people is the *kula* ring. The *kula* is a ritualized exchange system that sees Trobriand men, as well as those from many other cultures in the Milne Bay area, traveling up to several hundred miles in their dugout canoes to one of the other 18 islands that participate in the system in order to exchange red shell necklaces and white shell

TROBRIAND ISLANDERS

location:
The Trobriand Islands are a small chain just to the southeast of Papua New Guinea.

time period:
Unknown to the present

ancestry:
Melanesian and Austronesian

language:
Kilivila, also known as Kiriwina, an Austronesian language

armbands. Two aspects of this exchange have fascinated outsiders for generations. First, these items have no value outside of their use in this exchange system. They are not equivalent to money and cannot be exchanged for food, labor, or other items, although other items usually are exchanged during overseas trips. Unlike other items of wealth, these artifacts gain value only through the act of being exchanged over and over again. The second interesting feature of this system is the fact that the necklaces always travel around the islands in a clockwise direction, while the armbands always travel counterclockwise. Therefore, if an exchange partner brings someone a necklace, that person will always repay him with an armband, and vice versa. This system serves to link many island cultures together, providing a source of power and prestige among men, and even includes women, who supply the other trade goods that are exchanged during *kula* trips.

FURTHER READING

Bronislaw Malinowski. *Argonauts of the Western Pacific* (Prospect Heights, Ill.: Waveland Press, 1984).
———. *Coral Gardens and Their Magic*, vols. 1–2 (Bloomington: University of Indiana Press, 1965).
Annette Weiner. *Women of Value, Men of Renown: New Perspectives in Trobriand Exchange* (Austin: University of Texas Press, 1983).

Tu (Chahan Mongguer, Guanting, Huoer, Huzhu, Mongguer, White Mongols)

The Tu people are one of the 55 recognized national minority groups in China. They live in northwestern China, where they interact with many other minority groups. Some Tu people, as well as some scholars who have written about them, claim that they are descendants of the MONGOLS, perhaps the offspring of Genghis Khan's soldiers who married local women. While the Tu do speak a language that is related to Mongolian, most Western sources claim they are the descendants of many different groups that include the Mongols as well as the TUYUHUN, an ancient group of nomads who were probably related to the XIANBEI.

Like the Mongols and Tuyuhun, the Tu were traditionally pastoralists who lived off the products and proceeds of their herds of goats, sheep, and to a lesser extent, cattle. They moved seasonally to take advantage of the lush grass that grew in the mountains and valleys of their region and remained fairly independent of one another. In the period of the Ming dynasty (1368–1644), which is the era in which a specific Tu ethnic group came to exist, some of these former pastoralists began to settle down to the life of agriculturalism, growing wheat, barley, potatoes, and other dry-field crops. The Ming period also initiated a new political system among the Tu when the Chinese emperor granted 16 clan headmen the right to titles and territory that would be inherited by their lineages only. Most Tu families came to work on the land of these headmen, paying taxes to them and serving in local militias and workgroups. These feudal relations continued through the first half of the 20th century, although from 1931 to 1949 the county and township system of the Nationalist, or Kuomintang (KMT), government replaced the headman system. Many of the former headmen became district or county heads, and thus for most people life continued much as it had for centuries.

In 1949 the Communist Chinese revolution brought this era to an abrupt end when land reform, political change, and both educational and infrastructural development began to reach the Tu's western homeland. As was the case throughout China, the Tu suffered under the Great Leap Forward of 1958–69, when the economy was badly mishandled and millions died of starvation, and during the Cultural Revolution of 1967–77, when many more were imprisoned and killed in the clampdown against any anticommunist ideas and behaviors. The traditional religions of the Tu—animism and Yellow Hat, or Tibetan Buddhism—were both seen as antithetical to a communist people and were severely persecuted until about 1980, but they have since had a revival among the people. Ancestral shrines as well as those to the kitchen god, door god, and god of wealth are visible in most households and villages, and some Tu men are once again becoming monks.

In general, the Tu live in communities of extended patrilineal kin—who are all related through a common male ancestor—along with their wives, who move into their husbands' homesteads at marriage. In addition to this patrilocal marriage, a few Tu women in the past were "married to Heaven" rather than to a specific man. In this case, at the age of 15 the woman was married to heaven, remained living with her own family, and subsequently was able to take lovers from outside her own patrilineal group. The resulting children were considered members of their mothers' patrilineages rather than their fathers' and thus had their mothers' surnames. This form of marriage was relatively rare and took place in cases where a family had no male heir to which to leave their property or to take care of their ancestral shrines.

TU

location:
Qinghai and Gansu provinces, China

time period:
About 14th century to the present

ancestry:
Contested; probably a mixture of Tuyuhun, Mongolian, and others

language:
Tu, a Mongolian language similar to those of the Bonan and Donxiang peoples.

Tuhun   *See* Tuyuhun.

Tujang Djawi   *See* Javanese.

Tujia (Bizika, Tuchia, Tudja)

The Tujia are the eighth largest of China's 55 national minorities, with more than 7 million people living in the region where the borders of Hubei, Hunan, Sichuan, and Guizhou Provinces come together. Despite their large numbers, they were not recognized as their own group until 1956. They call themselves Bizika, meaning "native dwellers," but are probably not indigenous to this region. Their origins have not yet been definitively located, but contesting claims abound. The most common theory states that they are the descendants of the ancient Ba people of eastern and central Sichuan, but other theories state that they descend from the Wuman of Guizhou or some unknown group in Jiangxi Province. At the start of the Five Dynasties period, which followed the fall of the Tang dynasty in 907 C.E., the Tujia emerged from their legendary origins and became a recognized people of the western Hunan region.

Han migrants entered the Tujia homeland in the early 12th century and brought their advanced material culture with them, including agricultural, metal, and craft technologies. Prior to this period the Tujia had engaged in a combination of hunting, fishing, and swidden horticulture, but afterward they began to adopt the Han's intensive farming methods, including irrigation. During the Ming dynasty (1368–1644), many Tujia soldiers were transported, along with those of a variety of other non-Han peoples, to the coast in order to protect the empire from Japanese and other pirates.

The principal area inhabited by the Tujia is fairly high in elevation, from 1,300 to 5,000 feet above sea level, but its mild climate and many rivers mean that agriculture has been a viable subsistence strategy for more than a millennium. The Tujia take advantage of the rich valleys and terraces cut into the hillsides to grow wet rice, corn, wheat, sweet potatoes, plus a large number of cash crops including tung oil, sugar beets, cotton, ramie, and tea. Forest products such as giant salamanders; lumber from pine, fir, and cypress trees; and medicinal herbs are also harvested for profit, and pigs and chickens are raised both for personal use and for sale. Hunting and fishing are also important for sport and as an added source of protein.

Traditional Tujia villages range from just a few households to about 300, and in the past they were generally built at the base of a mountain or along a river in the lower hills. They were originally founded by members of a single patrilineage and thus contained only agnates and their wives, but significant migration and social reorganization over the past few centuries have meant that every village today contains many different patrilineages, and the pressure to marry outside one's village has diminished. Patrilocal residence, where a newly married woman moves into the household of her new husband, continues to be the norm, but neolocal residence, where the couple move into their own home, is also accepted. Prior to the last century many Tujia men married their maternal cross-cousins—that is, the daughter of their mother's brother—but today the custom has fallen away, although the maternal uncle's blessing over the new bride is still a common ritual feature of marriages.

Other important changes to Tujia society during the past 100 years or so include the gradual disappearance of their languages in favor of Mandarin and Hmong, or Miao, as it is sometimes derogatorily referred to in Chinese sources. Linguists in China estimate that the population of native and monolingual Tujia speakers has diminished to about only 70,000 people, mostly northern Tujia speakers, in remote areas, and almost exclusively women and children. Today even parents encourage their children to learn Mandarin in school and to use this language as their primary form of communication because of the advantages it gives its speakers in getting jobs as adults.

The Tujia today practice a syncretic religion with aspects from Taoism, ancestor worship, shamanism, and animism. Taoist priests are often turned to for exorcisms or life-cycle rituals, while local shamans also deal with the spirit world where ancestors, demons, gods, and nature spirits reside. Both kinds of ritual specialists can engage in healing practices, and often a Tujia family tries many different healing strategies, including Western and Chinese medicine, shamanism, and Taoist exorcisms, to deal with the most difficult ailments or misfortunes. One of the most important spirits in the Tujia pantheon is the white tiger because legend has it that the soul of a preeminent ancestor, Bawuxiang, turned into a white tiger upon his death. This is very similar to the legends that abound about the first king of the Ba people, Lin Jun, and provide at least nominal support for Ba origins. Today a statue of a white tiger continues to grace the home of every Tujia family who can afford it. Prior to the onset of the Cultural Revolution in 1966, the efforts of Roman Catholic missionaries earlier in the century had taken

TUJIA

location:
Hubei, Hunan, Sichuan, and Guizhou Provinces, China

time period:
910 C.E. to the present

ancestry:
Perhaps Ba or Wuman

language:
Tujia, a Tibeto-Burman language with two dialects, northern and southern, which are sometimes considered languages rather than dialects. Most Tujia today, however, speak Mandarin Chinese instead.

hold, and some families considered themselves Catholic; since the late 1960s, however, this religion has all but disappeared in the region.

Tujue   *See* TURKIC PEOPLES.

Tu-kiu   *See* TURKIC PEOPLES.

Tu Mangkasara   *See* MAKASSARESE.

Tungus   *See* EVENKIS; EVENS.

Tura   *See* TIELE.

Turkic peoples   (Tourkhs, Tr'wks, Tuchueh, Tujue, Tu-Kiu, Turks, Turuks)

The Turkic peoples today are the approximately 150 million speakers of the 40 different forms of Turkic languages still in existence; a number of others are now extinct. This contemporary Turkic population includes modern Turkish speakers in Turkey and the surrounding countries, as well as speakers of languages of the ALTAI, AZERIS, KARAKALPAK, KAZAKHS,

---

TURKIC PEOPLES

location:
Originally between Lake Balkash and Lake Baikal, but now spread from Europe to far-eastern Siberia with a disapora all over the world

time period:
Sixth century C.E. to the present

ancestry:
Possibly the Xiongnu, but this is highly contested

language:
Various Turkic languages from the Altaic language family

Turkic peoples time line

B.C.E.

2000 A Mesopotamian cuneiform tablet refers to a people called Turukku, possibly ancient ancestors of the Turkic peoples.

1328 Chinese records refer to the Tu-Kiu, possibly ancient ancestors of the Turkic peoples.

1000 Desertification and other aspects of climate change, and possibly other factors, result in the development of nomadism on the Eurasian steppes as a strategy for survival in the cold, dry climate.

300 The Turkic language divides into two branches, the Eastern Oguz and Western Ogur, or Kipchak.

third century The Chinese begin the Great Wall as a barrier against the incursions of various nomadic peoples into their settled territories.

C.E.

546–53 Turkic peoples under the leadership of Bumin rebel against their Rouran overlords in the iron mines of the Altai Mountains and emerge as one of the most powerful groups on the Eurasian steppes, the Gokturk khanate.

565 The Turkic people defeat the Hephthalites and bring an end to that empire.

sixth to seventh centuries Other Turkic people, living north of Transoxiana, begin to unite loosely as the Oghuz Turks.

571 Bumin's brother Istemi conquers territory in Transoxiana and Azerbaijan.

582 The Gokturk empire is split into two khanates, eastern and western, after a civil war.

585 First definite written mention of the Turkic peoples in Chinese. A letter to Ishbara refers to him as "the Great Turk Khan," though at the time he is accepting Tang protection.

630 Both Gokturk khanates are subjugated by the Chinese Tang dynasty.

682 The Gokturks overthrow their Tang rulers and reestablish their empire in the east.

716 The Gokturk territory west of the Altai is taken by the Oghuz, never to return to Gokturk hands.

730 The earliest dating of Turkic writing, in the Orkhon script.

744 The last Eastern Gokturk khan, Baimei, is killed, and the empire disintegrates within the year at the hands of Uighur, Karluk, and other Turkic tribes.

920 The Gokturks disappear from history until their script is deciphered more than 900 years later.

950 (approximately) Bey Seljuq, founder of the lineage that creates the Seljuk Empire, moves to Khwarezm and converts to Islam.

Kyrgyz, Tatars, Turkmen, Tuvans, Uighur, Uzbeks, and Yakuts in Asia, plus many others residing in Europe. The adjective *Turkish* today is usually reserved for the people and language of the country of Turkey; the same is true for the noun form *Turk*, except when referring to ancient populations. None of these people are actually descendants of the ancient Central Asian people who first used the ethnonym *Turk* to refer to themselves; they disappeared in the 10th century. Most Turkic-language–speaking people today are the descendants of groups who were either conquered by Turkic speakers or chose to adopt their language for other reasons. For example, contemporary Turks are primarily genetically related to Greeks and other groups from Asia Minor who adopted Turkic languages after the 10th century.

There probably has not been a time in history when all Turkic peoples were united under one ruler. The Gokturks, the first to use the name *Turk* for their empire, beginning in the sixth century, probably came closest to this feat, but even at that early date the Yakuts had already split from other Turkic peoples and moved to the northeast, away from the Gokturk

962	Founding of the Turkic Ghaznavid empire in Afghanistan and northern India.
1037	Toghril Beg I, founder of the Seljuk empire, is born.
1055	The armies of the Seljuk empire enter Baghdad, an important center of the Islamic world at the time.
1063	Toghril Beg dies and is replaced by Alp Arslan, who expands the empire into Armenia and Georgia the next year.
1071	Battle of Manzikert, at which the Seljuks capture Anatolia (Turkey) from the armies of the Byzantine emperor Romanos IV Diogenes.
1072	Malikshah succeeds Alp Arslan as the sultan of the Seljuks; it is under his rule that the empire is at its strongest and culturally most influential.
1087	The Abbasid caliph calls Malikshah "the Sultan of East and West," to indicate his vast realm.
1092	Malikshah's death sees the weakening of the Seljuks during quarrels over succession between his brother and four sons.
1095	The First Crusade takes advantage of the Seljuk weakness and captures Jerusalem from the Turks. This Crusade lasts until 1099.
1145–48	The Second Crusade is defeated by the Seljuks.
1157	Sultan Sanjar, last Seljuk ruler, dies amid the fragmentation of his empire at the hands of Turkmen, Kwarezm, and other Central Asian tribes.
1187	Fall of the Ghaznavids in the Punjab.
1281	Osman inherits his father's realm in western Anatolia and begins his military campaign in the region.
1501	The Safavid dynasty takes Azerbaijan and within the year conquers all of Iran.
1510	The Safavids conquer portions of Turkmenistan, near the city of Merv (Mary).
1549	The Ottomans conquer Georgia and other portions of the Caucasus.
1578–90	The Ottomans and Safavids go to war in the Caucasus.
1615	The Safavids kill and displace thousands of Georgians in their Caucasian campaigns.
1623–40	Ottoman sultan Murad IV is victorious in Armenia.
1796	Agha Mohammad Khan, of Qajar descent, takes over the throne of Persia and establishes his own dynasty.
1877–78	The Ottomans lose to the Russians in the Caucasus. The Qajars had been expelled from the region earlier in the century in a series of battles with the Russian Empire.
1896	The Turkic Orkhon script is deciphered.

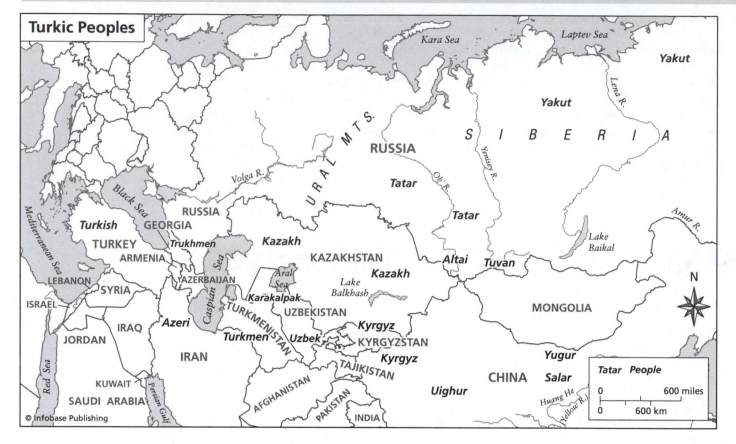

Turkic Peoples

© Infobase Publishing

political center in the Orkhon Valley in Mongolia. Other Turkic speakers simply chose not to join with the Gokturks and later united more loosely as the Oghuz. The Turkic ancestors of the Uighur also remained outside this early alliance of Turkic speakers.

GEOGRAPHY

The original Turkic peoples seem to have emerged in the steppe region between Lake Balkash in Kazakhstan and Lake Baikal in Siberia, which also encompasses territory in contemporary Mongolia and China. The northern reaches of this area are traversed by many rivers, but the Altai Mountains leave the southern reaches semiarid and inhospitable to intensive agriculture. Sometime before 400 C.E., the seminomadic Turkic peoples began migrating from this homeland, mostly to the south and west, but with some groups, like the Yakuts, moving north. In 552, with the founding of the Gokturk khanate, or empire, many Turkic speakers moved from the Altai Mountains to the new capital in the Orkhon Valley of Mongolia. Over the next 10 centuries, some Turkic speakers continued to migrate throughout the Asian landmass and to assimilate others into their language and culture, while others were them-

selves assimilated into Persian, Greek, Arabic, and other languages and cultures along their migratory paths so that today the descendants of Turkic speakers reside in most countries of the world.

ORIGINS

The Turkic peoples composed just one of many seminomadic groups living on the steppes northwest of China prior to the sixth century. Probably the only trait that distinguished them from the XIONGNU, XIANBEI, MONGOLS, and other steppe dwellers was their language. Like these others, they would have relied primarily on their herds for subsistence, resided in felt tents, and moved about as the need for grass and water necessitated. They practiced a shamanistic religion and placed great value on their horses.

In the middle of the sixth century, the ancient Turks emerged from this obscurity as a group of subjugated ironworkers in the Altai Mountains who rose up against their ROURAN overlords, an event that marked the beginning of Turkic history. There were other, earlier mentions in both Chinese and Mesopotamian texts of a people who may have been related to these Turkic speakers, but it has yet to be proven that these ancient references are to Turks. Chinese texts from 585 mentioning Ishbara as "the Great Turk Khan" are the oldest confirmed reference to a people known to themselves and others as Turks.

HISTORY

The history of the Turkic people begins in ancient times and extends to the present with the lives of the contemporary Turkic peoples—Azeris, Uighur, Uzbeks, Kyrgyz, Tatars, Tuvans, and Kazakhs, covered in separate entries—among others. This history section looks at both the oldest of the Turkic federations to come out of the steppe region, the Gokturks, and some of their successor khnanates. It also looks at the most important Turkic federation for the development of the majority of Turkic speakers today, the Oghuz, and some of their successor states, including the two most important: the Seljuks and Ottomans.

Gokturk or Kok Turk

The first people to use the ethnonym *Turk* to refer to themselves were the Turuk peoples of the Gokturk khanate in the mid-sixth century. In Chinese texts they are referred to as Tujue or Tu-Kiu. These were the people who rose up against the Rouran and established themselves as the dominant political unit of the Eurasian steppes, from Mongolia to the Black Sea. The name Gok or Gog Turk means Blue Turk or perhaps Celestial Turk, since the prefix *Gok* could refer to either term; there is also some conjecture that "blue" referred to their origins in the east and that Eastern Turk may also be a suitable translation.

Prior to the development of the Gokturk empire, the Turuk people were known as skilled ironworkers. Many were also seminomadic pastoralists, living off their herds of animals. They practiced a form of shamanism and, like the Mongols centuries later, worshiped the god Tengri. Taspar, the fourth khan of the Gokturks, converted to Buddhism and abandoned his native religion, but others did not follow his lead.

The original Turkic language was unwritten, but with the introduction of Sogdian as the language of state there was a push to develop a Turkic script. With the assistance of literate SOGDIANS, especially merchants and advisers, a runic script, known today as the Orkhon script because of the locality in which it was found in the 19th century, was created in the eighth century to record the deeds of various Gokturk rulers. Monuments to Tonyukuk, Kul Tegin, and Bilge Khan, in addition to various other inscriptions, have all been found in the Orkhon Valley and were deciphered at the end of the 19th century. Although unrelated to the runic scripts of the ancient Germanic populations, it is considered runic because it appears similar, with many straight lines and sharp angles, probably due to the difficulty of creating round or looped figures when carving into wood or stone with straight-edged tools.

The founder of the Gokturk kingdom was Bumin, or Tuman, Khan, a member of the Ashina tribe of Turkic speakers. Prior to defeating the Rouran and establishing the Gokturks in 552, which was also the year of his death, Bumin was in the employ of his Rouran overlords. In 542 he helped them put down an uprising among the TIELE, an act for which Bumin expected to be able to marry a Rouran princess. When this was refused, Bumin approached and was accepted at the court of the Northern Wei state, marrying into the noble family and securing a political alliance by 545. This alliance gave Bumin the political and military clout necessary to unite many groups of Turkic peoples and defeat the Rouran. He named his empire the Gokturk khanate and took the title khan, or khagan, "great king."

Following Bumin's death, his brother and son were the real builders of the expansive Gokturk empire. His brother, Istemi, destroyed the HEPHTHALITES in the west with his Sassanid allies (*see* PERSIANS, SASSANIDS) and joined with the Persians against the Byzantine Empire as well, pushing the Gokturk boundary as far west as the Caspian Sea and the Caucasus. Bumin's son Muhan pushed the Gokturk boundaries to the west and north during his reign as khan, defeating the KHITANS, Tiele, and Kyrgyz people. He also allied himself with the Chinese Zhou kingdom through his daughter's marriage alliance. During his reign the empire adopted the Sogdian language and alphabet as the only available written script in the Gokturk realm; Sogdian merchants and advisers became significant in the development of the empire's overall worldview because of their literacy.

Although the Gokturks occupied one of the largest empires in the world at that time, size led not to internal cohesiveness or strength but to the exact opposite. Before the end of the sixth century, in 582, the khanate split in two over the right of succession, with the eastern section retaining the name Gokturk and accepting a protectorate status from the Chinese Sui and later Tang dynasties, while the independent western section took the name Onoq, or Western Turkic khaganate. Many of the subjugated peoples within the empire also attempted to free themselves from their Turkic rulers. The Tiele revolted in 627 and again two years later, and the Kyrgyz rebelled in 710 but were quickly put down; the Khitans soon followed in 734. In 630 the Tang took advantage of Gokturk weakness to take control of the Silk Road, with its lucrative taxation and trade opportunities, but they were pushed out soon after.

Due to these weaknesses, the Gokturk empire disintegrated in the eighth century. The last strong leader was Bilge Khan, but upon his death in 734 succession problems and stronger Chinese opposition quickly saw the demise of the Gokturks in favor of another Turkic-speaking people, the Uighur. Nonetheless, the Gokturk name lived on. The rise of the Oghuz, Ottoman, and Turkmen empires all guaranteed that the name *Turk* would continue even after the demise of the original holders of the name. These later Turkic people were linguistically related to the original Gokturks; however, genetically and culturally they were almost entirely different from them. The later Seljuk and Ottoman empires both sprang from remnants of the Oghuz Turks, who may have been rivals and even enemies of the Gokturks, rather than from this original Turkic empire.

After the fall of the Gokturks, a number of minor Turkic dynasties emerged to fill the vacuum their disintegration had left behind. From the Western Turks, the Turgesh Turkic people emerged in 706 as a powerful alliance in the Yili Valley region of western China, even gaining recognition from the Chinese as an independent khanate; however, they were defeated by the Arabs in 737 and disappeared from history by the end of the century. The Chigil and Jagma were two other Turkic confederations that emerged at this time, with the former of these becoming quite wealthy due to the large number of cattle kept in the mountainous region south of Lake Issik-Kul in contemporary Kyrgyzstan. While the Chigil formed part of the backbone of the Karakhanid dynasty along with the Karluks, neither the Chigil nor the Jagma emerged from the wider mass of Turkic peoples to dominate much territory or many people for very long. They have disappeared into obscurity along with the Turgesh, Arsu, and many others.

Oghuz Turk

The name *Oghuz,* sometimes Ghuzz or Ouzz, designates a number of Turkic tribes that united during the sixth and seventh centuries, perhaps in opposition to the Gokturks, in the area north of Transoxiana. In the ninth and 10th centuries many Oghuz tribes moved south into Transoxiana and beyond. The name comes from the Turkic word *ok,* meaning either "arrow" or "tribe." It does not refer to any specific ethnic group but merely designates people who spoke Turkic languages and migrated west after the fall of the Gokturk khanate. In the 10th century a number of Oghuz tribes emerged as the most powerful groups north and west of the Aral Sea, absorbing the local Iranian, Kipchak, and Karluk groups.

Oghuz tribes continued to push westward, reaching the Ural Mountains and the Volga River, but never centralizing their control over large amounts of territory. Instead, individual chieftains and minor kings acted autonomously in their region, rarely seeking the company or assistance of their peers. This remained the case until the late 10th century when Seljuk, a tribal leader, unified large numbers of Turkic speakers in what is today Turkmenistan and Iran and established an empire that bears his name.

Culturally and linguistically the Oghuz were described in Muslim works of the 11th century as different from other Turkic tribes and confederations. They were said to have been made up of 22 (or sometimes 24) clans and tribal segments, many of which are counted today as the original ancestors of the Turkmen people. Later, 12th-century Oghuz descendants recorded much of their oral history in *The Book of Dede Korkut,* or "grandfather Korkut," which was awarded a literary prize from UNESCO in 2000 to mark its 1300th-year anniversary. The tales or legends recorded in the book describe the Oghuz as sixth-century tent-dwelling herders who had to fight continually to maintain their freedom. Battle scenes, probably between Oghuz and Turkic Kipchaks and Pechenegs in European Russia, are described in detail, while other tales parallel those of the Greek bard Homer. While these were written down by Muslim Oghuz people and the heroes are described as good Muslims, there are also many references to shamanism, magic, and other pre-Islamic beliefs and practices.

The Oghuz began to convert to Islam in the seventh century, after the Arabs conquered the Sogdian lands of Transoxiana. Sunni Islam began to take hold among the Oghuz when they served as mercenaries in the armies of the Arab Abbasids. By the 10th century the term *Turkmen* was used to designate this population of Muslim Oghuz, particularly those who migrated south from Transoxiana and gave up their nomadic, pastoral way of life.

The Oghuz, like the Gokturks before them, disappeared as a named group in the 10th and 11th centuries, having been replaced by the names Turkmen, Seljuk, and later, Ottoman Turk. However, it is the Oghuz Turkic language that formed the basis for many of the contemporary Turkic languages, including Turkish, Azeri, and Turkoman, since both the Seljuks and the Ottomans had been members of the Oghuz confederations of the seventh to 10th centuries.

Seljuk Turk

The Seljuk line emerged from the Oghuz federation as a unifying force among some Turkic peoples in approximately 950 when Bey Seljuq distinguished himself as a particularly able clan leader and moved his people into the Khwarezmian lands of modern Uzbekistan. His descendants, first led by Toghril Beg I, conquered most of Iran, Iraq, Syria, Anatolia, Transoxiana, and the former Khwarezmian lands in Central Asia. By 1055 the Seljuks occupied most of the Islamic heartland, including the city of Baghdad. The Seljuks established their own capital in Isfahan, contemporary Iran, over which they flew their distinctive flag with its image of an archer shooting his arrow.

Upon Toghril Beg's death, he was succeeded by his son Alp Arslan, who expanded the empire even further into Armenia, Georgia, and Azerbaijan, leaving his Turkic language and customs behind, especially in Azerbaijan. The true test of Seljuk power came in 1071 when the Seljuks defeated the Byzantine Empire in the decisive Battle of Manzikert in eastern Anatolia. This set up the 20-year period of the Seljuk golden era under Malikshah. One of the great accomplishments of this era was the revision of the calendar to the Jalali calendar, which is still used in both Iran and Afghanistan and is based on the true observation of the vernal equinox in Tehran and Kabul, making it more accurate than such rule-based calendars as the Gregorian, in use in the West.

The death of Malikshah in 1092 brought a fatal weakening to the empire when the succession to his throne was contested by his brother and four sons. Three years into their divisive quarreling, the launch of the First Crusade brought thousands of mercenary soldiers, nobles, and peasants from Western Europe into the Middle East. The crusaders captured Jerusalem in 1099, the only Crusade to do so, and established the Kingdom of Jerusalem and the Crusader states. Upon the fall of one of these states in 1145, the Europeans launched the Second Crusade, with Louis VII of France and Conrad III of Germany at its head. This was much less successful than the First Crusade and was repelled from both Jerusalem and Damascus, setting up subsequent Crusades to be dealt with by the successor states of the Seljuks in the Middle East.

Despite their victories over the crusaders in 1148, the Seljuks were on borrowed time by the middle of the 12th century. More than half a century of warfare on several fronts combined with the internal divisions created by the lack of a coherent succession in 1092 led to the final disintegration in 1157 at the hands of Turkmen, Khwarezmian, and other Central Asian tribal warriors. Unlike the previous Turkic empires, however, the Seljuks did not disappear from history upon the destruction of their empire. Following the conquests of the Mongols in the 13th century, smaller Seljuk empires emerged in various places across Anatolia and Central Asia. One of these obscure principalities, headed by Osman, son of Ertugrul, was later to become the Ottoman Empire, which stretched from Morocco to Iran, Yemen to Crimea.

Like the Mongols, Gokturks, and other tribally organized states, the Seljuk empire was organized as a family kingdom, with brothers, cousins, and other more distant relatives all vying for leadership positions at the death of the sultan. Under this system, the ultimate leader, or sultan, could assign different family members to rule in his name in semiautonomous sectors, or appanages. This organization is strong when the sultan is able to inspire the loyalty and trust of his relatives but inherently weak over time, as the rapid disintegration of this kind of state attests. For example, Turkmen tribesmen were loyal forces within the larger Seljuk military for most of the empire's history, but upon its weakening over succession problems, they were able to emerge as even more powerful than their Seljuk overlords in the area of present-day Turkmenistan.

Despite their Turkic beginnings as descendants of the Oghuz, much of the administration of the Seljuk empire was in the Persian language. Following the migration into Iran in the 10th century, many Seljuk nobles adopted the Persian language and culture as a symbol of their advanced civilization. For many in these positions, Turkic languages bespoke of their nomadic, pre-Islamic, and thus uncivilized past, while the Persian language symbolized more than 1,000 years of urban, literate culture. The other important feature of Seljuk society adopted after this migration was its adherence to Islam. Large numbers of mosques were built throughout the Seljuk lands, especially in Anatolia, and the founder of the Sufi sect of whirling dervishes, Jelaleddin Rumi, flourished in the religious environment. Nevertheless, Seljuk rule was also fairly tolerant of religious differences, with both Christian and Jewish populations able to continue worshiping in their own ways throughout the empire.

Other Turkic Empires

In the 13th century a tribal leader named Osman emerged from the other Turkic-speaking peoples to become head of the last great Turkic empire in history, the Ottomans. In 1281 Osman inherited from his father a small territory in northwestern Anatolia, which he expanded to about 10,000 square miles. Osman's son Orhan then expanded even further westward, entering Europe in 1362. Most of the Ottoman Empire is located outside the purview of this volume in Europe and the Middle East; however, from the middle of the 16th century until the last quarter of the 19th century, the Ottomans were one of the key players in the subjugation of the Caucasus, along with Russia and the Iranians, first the Safavid dynasty and later the Qajars. The Ottomans were finally expelled from the region in 1878 after the Russians defeated them in a two-year war over supremacy in the Caucasus.

Although usually thought of as a Persian dynasty since they adopted this language and ruled their Persian lands from Tehran, the Qajars were originally a tribe of Oghuz Turkic speakers. During the Seljuk period they served in the Turkic armies that conquered Azerbaijan, but in 1501 the Qajars joined the Safavid federation and became Persianized. They were subordinate governors and military rulers during the Safavid period, frequently engaging in battle for them in the 17th and 18th centuries. It was only in 1796 that Agha Mohammad Khan, of Qajar descent, took over the throne of Persia and established his own dynasty. He was assassinated just one year later but not before he had united most of the Caucasus under his rule. Like the Ottomans, however, the Qajars also lost their Caucasian territory to the Russians in the 19th century, specifically in 1813 and 1828.

Like the Qajars, the Persian Safavids were also founded by a Turkic speaker. Ismail I was of mixed descent, including Azeri Turk, Kurd, and Greek, but he spoke and wrote Azeri Turkic as his first language. Ismail's lineage descended from a Sufi saint, Safi Al-Din (1252–1334), who lived in Ardabil, Iran, very near the border with Azerbaijan. Ismail was a Shia, as most Azeris are to this day, and was instrumental in the spread of this denomination of Islam throughout his empire; he was the first to make Shiism a state religion. He declared the Safavid Shia state first in Azerbaijan in 1501, and within the following year he had defeated a minor Turkic dynasty, the Ak Koyunlu or White Sheep Turkmen, and spread his religious and political system to all of Iran. Within the decade, Ismail had defeated the Uzbeks in Central Asia as well, turning their leader's skull into a jeweled trophy for himself. The spread of Ismail's Shiite religion beyond the Iranian and Iraqi borders was halted in 1514 when the Ottoman sultan Selim I and his Sunni army defeated the Safavids and drove them back to Iran, taking Ismail's favorite wife hostage as the Safavids retreated from the capital of Tabriz.

Ismail died in 1524 and left behind an empire that had never fully reconciled the linguistic and cultural differences between the two dominant peoples it contained: the militaristic Turkmen tribes, sometimes referred to as Qizilbash for their distinctive red headgear, and the literate, urban Persians. Even during Ismail's lifetime this difference had caused many problems; for instance, Turkmen soldiers sometimes refused to fight under Persian leaders and deserted from their armies. These differences were not worked out until the last decade of the 16th century and early decades of the 17th century, when Abbas I realigned the military to take power from the Turkmen and in many ways Persianized the Safavid state. Abbas was also active in the Persian Caucasus, killing and displacing large numbers of Georgians in battle in 1615 and at the same time remaining fairly tolerant of the Christian institutions and individuals who dominated his Armenian territories.

A third empire that was founded by a Turkic speaker but is rarely thought of as Turkic itself was that of the Indian Mughals founded by Babur, or Zahiruddin Muhammad, in 1526. Babur himself spoke Chaghatai, a now-extinct Turkic language that he wrote of as Torki, as well as Persian, and he practiced Sunni Islam. His own military included significant numbers of Persians, Arabs, and Turkic-speaking peoples from both the Shiite Qizilbash and other, Sunni tribes, though the majority of people the Mughals ruled were Indian Hindus. The

Mughals dominated northern India until 1857, when they were displaced by the British.

The Ghaznavid empire, which ruled parts of Afghanistan from 962 to 1039 and then parts of the Punjab until 1187, was another empire founded by Turkic-speaking soldiers who were originally in the employ of other states. In this case, Turkic-speaking slaves in the Samanid Persian empire broke free and established their own state from the capital of Ghazna during a succession problem among the ruling Samanids. Alp Tigin emerged from the Turkic soldiers to rule the new state, which he handed on to his son in 975. This dynasty ruled an area known as Greater Khorasan in Afghanistan until 1039, when it lost its western territory to the Seljuks at the Battle of Dandanaqan. For the next 150 years the dynasty ruled from Lahore and controlled territory in the Punjab until losing that to the Tajik Ghurids in 1187. Although not as expansive or long-lasting as the Seljuks or Ottomans, the Ghaznavids were important as one of the first dynasties to introduce Islam to the Indian subcontinent, a project that was continued three and a half centuries later under the Mughals.

CULTURE

It is almost impossible to write of a Turkic culture given the large expanses of time and space covered by Turkic history. Turkic culture incorporates everything from the nomadism of the original Turkic-speaking tribes in their homeland between Lakes Balkash and Baikal, living in portable felt tents, subsisting largely on milk products and meat, and practicing a form of shamanism, to the urban life of contemporary Turks, Turkmen, Azeris, and many others.

Besides language, there is, however, one feature that unifies most Turkic peoples today: their adherence to Sunni Islam. This is not a monolithic similarity, because a few Turkic peoples who migrated north and west rather than south and east from their original homeland continue to adhere to their ancient form of shamanism, and the Azeris of both Iran and Azerbaijan are largely Shia; many people in eastern Turkey are also Alevis, a form of Shiism. Nonetheless, the eighth-century conversion of most Turkic peoples to Sunni Islam remains today a unifying force over and above their linguistic similarities.

Sunni is the form of Islam that is practiced by about 90 percent of all Muslims in the world, while Shia makes up just 10 percent. The differences between these two branches of Islam lie in the realm of leadership as well as in some interpretations of sharia, or holy law. All Muslims, both Sunni and Shia, believe in Allah as the one god, Muhammad as his final prophet, the ultimate resurrection of all human beings, and the Quran as the word of God as spoken by Muhammad. They also agree that prayers; fasting; pilgrimage to Mecca; avoiding sins such as drinking alcohol, adultery, and theft; and paying a religious tax are all necessary acts in a Muslim's life. Where they differ is in the recognition of the proper succession to Muhammad's authority. Sunnis recognize Abu Bakr as the first caliph, or leader, following the death of Muhammad in 632, followed by Umar, Uthman, and Ali. Shiites believe that Ali should have been first because of his kinship with the prophet. The term *Shia* comes from the Arabic phrase *Shiat Ali,* "partisans of Ali." Following from this disagreement about the first post-Prophet leader, Sunnis and Shiites today continue to disagree about the nature of leadership in their two respective denominations. Sunnis believe that a caliph can be selected by a previous caliph, elected by all Muslims or by a committee, or can even take power in a coup, while Shiites say their imams are appointed by Allah and are made known to humanity by declarations by the Prophet or the previous imam. In addition to these questions of succession, the leader's character requirements also differ in the two forms of Islam. Shiites believe that their imams must be without sin and possess knowledge, bravery, wisdom, piety, love of Allah, and justice. Sunnis, on the other hand, do not see being without sin as a requirement for leadership, nor do they require all of the above-listed positive character traits. It is enough to be selected.

In addition to these differences with regard to leadership, Sunnis and Shiites also differ in their interpretations of certain Quranic sections. For example, some texts speak of the legs, arms, eyes, and other body parts of Allah, or God. For many Sunnis these lines are to be taken literally, while for Shiites they are symbolic rather than actual, physical body parts. Following from this difference, Sunni scholars believe that Allah can be seen, at least theoretically, while for Shiites Allah is not visible because he has no body. Yet another difference concerns the very nature of good and evil in the world. For Sunnis, good things are good because Allah allows them and evil things are evil because they are forbidden, but if Allah were to change his mind and allow a formerly forbidden thing, it would become good. For Shiites, good and evil characteristics exist, and that is why Allah has seen fit to allow the good things and forbid the evil ones. For example, Sunnis believe that drinking alcohol is evil because Allah forbids it, while Shiites believe that Allah forbids drinking alcohol because it is evil.

While to a non-Muslim these differences may appear inconsequential, to some Sunnis and Shiites they mean the difference between being a Muslim or not. As part of their religious identity, most Turkic peoples today adhere strongly to the tenets of Sunni Islam and see this as an important distinction between themselves and most Iranians and some Iraqis, who are Shiite.

See also Tajiks.

FURTHER READING

Robert L. Canfield. *Turko-Persia in Historical Perspective* (Cambridge: Cambridge University Press, 1991).

Ergun Cagatay and Dogan Kuban, eds. *The Turkic Speaking Peoples: 1,500 Years of Art and Culture from Inner Asia to the Balkans* (New York: Prestel Publishing, 2006).

Carter Vaughn Findley. *The Turks in World History* (New York: Oxford University Press, 2005).

Peter Golden. *An Introduction to the History of the Turkic Peoples: Ethnogenesis and State Formation in Medieval and Early Modern Eurasia and the Middle East* (Wiesbaden, Ger.: Otto Harrassowitz).

Lawrence Krader. *Social Organization of the Mongol-Turkic Pastoral Nomads* (New York: Routledge-Curzon, 1997).

John R. Krueger. *The Turkic Peoples* (Bloomington: University of Indiana Press, 1963).

Hugh Pope. *Sons of the Conquerors: The Rise of the Turkic World* (New York: Overlook Press, 2005).

Turkmen (Trukhmen, Turcoman, Turkomen)

The Turkmen are a Turkic-speaking people who reside in the independent country of Turkmenistan as well as in Iran, Iraq, Afghanistan, Kazakhstan, Kyrgyzstan, Tajikistan, and Uzbekistan. They are descendants of the Oghuz Turks who migrated to Central Asia in the seventh to ninth centuries C.E., making them a much older Turkic population than most of the rest of the Central Asian Turkic speakers. There may be approximately 9.5 million Turkmen in the world, with about 4.3 million of them in Turkmenistan itself. About 2 million more reside in Iran, and it has been estimated that about 2–3 million may live in Iraq, with a few hundred thousand in Afghanistan and other

smaller populations throughout Central Asia and the northern Caucasus. These Turkmen of the northern or European Caucasus are sometimes called Trukhmen but can be considered to have descended from the same source population as the Turkmen.

GEOGRAPHY

Turkmenistan, where the majority of Turkmen live today, is located in Central Asia and is bordered by the Caspian Sea to the east, Uzbekistan and Kazakhstan to the north, Uzbekistan and Afghanistan to the west, and Iran and Afghanistan to the south. About 90 percent of the country is taken up with the Kara-Kum, or Black Sand desert. It also contains the historic city of Merv, contemporary Mary, in the western region on the Murgab River. In addition to the Murgab, Turkmenistan has access to water from the Amu Darya, which serves as part of the border with Uzbekistan, and the Atrek, Hari Rud, and Kushk Rivers. Beginning in 1954, the region was also watered by the Kara-Kum Canal, an 870-mile-long artificial waterway irrigating the desert, which runs from the Amu Darya to the Caspian Sea. Although generally a low-elevation region at about 1,640 feet above sea level or less, with the Akdzhkaya Depression in the north lying at 360 feet below sea level, the Kopetdag Mountains in the south can rise to almost 10,000 feet. These are geologically very unstable and prone to severe earthquakes, such as the one that completely demolished the capital of Ashgabat in 1948.

ORIGINS

The Turkic peoples comprised just one of many seminomadic groups living on the steppes northwest of China prior to the sixth century. Probably the only trait that distinguished them from the Xiongnu, Xianbei, Mongols, and other steppe dwellers was their language. Like these others, they would have relied primarily on their herds for subsistence, resided in felt tents, and moved when the need for grass and water for their animals necessitated it. They practiced a shamanistic religion and placed great value on their horses.

The Turkmen, as part of the Oghuz Turkic people, probably entered Central Asia from their homeland further north and east after 700 C.E. However, they remained culturally and linguistically almost indistinguishable from other Oghuz tribes in the region. In addition, in later centuries a great deal of intermixing between the various Turkic and Mongol tribes

---

TURKMEN

location:
Turkmenistan, Iran, Iraq, Afghanistan, Kazakhstan, Kyrgyzstan, Tajikistan, and Uzbekistan

time period:
10th century to the present

ancestry:
Turkic, Mongolian, and Persian

language:
Turkmen, a southern Oghuz Turkic language written with a revised Latin script based on Turkish

contributed to the development of all contemporary Central Asian Turkic peoples: UZBEKS, KAZAKHS, KYRGYZ, and Turkmen. Finally, the peoples who had been living in the region of Turkmenistan before the arrival of the Turkic people were largely Iranian speakers, the descendants of the waves of Indo-Iranians who had moved off the steppes in the millennia before the common era. They had established the long-lasting caravan settlements such as Merv, Samarkand, Ferghana, and Bukhara during the periods of the SOGDIANS and BACTRIANS. With the coming of the Turkic peoples, some Iranians fled, though others intermarried with the Turkic peoples and contributed to the development of the contemporary Turkmen population.

HISTORY

As one of the named tribal affiliations of the Oghuz Turks, the Turkmen have a considerably longer history than do their fellow Central Asian Turkic peoples: Kazakhs, Kyrgyz, and Uzbeks. While there was no self-identification among those groups until after the Mongol invasion, some Turkmen began to identify themselves as such as early as the end of the 10th century, upon their conversion to Islam.

The first political structure that can be closely affiliated with the Turkmen was the Seljuk empire, established in 1040, with its capital in Merv. It was the Seljuks residing north of the Kopetdag Mountains who took the Turkmen name. In addition to Merv, which grew wealthy as a caravan stopover point on the silk-and-spice trade routes, the second important Turkmen city in the 11th and 12th centuries was Khiva, now located in Uzbekistan, which dominated the towns and large estates in the Amu Darya valley. Both cities became centers of Muslim culture, art, and architecture under the Seljuks and flourished even after the Seljuk empire collapsed in the region in 1157. In 1221, however, the area suffered the onslaughts of the Mongols, and Merv was pillaged and burned, while its Turkmen inhabitants were murdered or fled north or east.

Upon Genghis Khan's death in 1227, his large empire was nominally divided in four, one section for each of his four sons. While Genghis Khan had decreed that these four subsections were not to be ruled as separate kingdoms, over time they did become separate. The region of Turkmenistan came largely under the purview of the Golden Horde, which had also conquered much of Transoxiana to the north. A second wave of Mongol empire building occurred in

Turkmen time line

C.E.

eighth to ninth centuries Approximate time in which the Oghuz Turkic forebearers of the Turkmen enter Central Asia for the first time.

end of 10th century The Oghuz convert to Islam, and some tribes come to be known as Turkmen.

11th century Some Turkmen tribes migrate into the Caucasus, Mesopotamia, and Asia Minor. Others remain in Transoxiana as the ancestors of the contemporary Turkmen people.

1040 Founding of the Seljuk empire, which includes many Turkmen people and territory in contemporary Turkmenistan.

1157 Collapse of the Seljuk empire.

1221 The Mongols under Genghis Khan conquer the region of present-day Turkmenistan.

1227 Genghis Khan dies, and his empire is divided into four parts. The two sons of his son Jochi, Batu and Orda, split the western section, which includes land that becomes Turkmenistan. Batu's Golden Horde eventually emerges as the most powerful Mongol khanate in the region.

14th–17th centuries Decline of the Turkmen in Turkmenistan during the Safavid-Uzbek military rivalry period.

1378 Founding of the Black Sheep Turkmen, or the Kara Koyunlu state in the southern Caucasus region.

1387 Founding of the White Sheep Turkmen, or the Ak Koyunlu state to rival the Black Sheep in the southern Caucasus.

1469 The White Sheep conquer the Black Sheep Turkmen.

1502 The Black Sheep state is conquered by the Safavids.

1716 The first representative of the Russian czar sent to the Turkmen is killed, delaying the onset of the Russian conquest for another century.

1860s The Russians send troops to assist the Turkmen in their rebellions against the Uzbeks and Persians.

1869 The Russians found the port city of Krasnovodsk on the Caspian Sea, present-day Turkmenbashi, and begin their conquest of Turkmenistan.

1881 The Russians conquer the Dengil Tepe fortress near Ashgabat, which secures all Turkmen territory for them.

1925 The Turkmen Soviet Socialist Republic is incorporated into the larger USSR.

(For a continuation of this time line, see TURKMENISTANIS: NATIONALITY.)

the southern portions of Turkmenistan under Timur Leng, or Tamerlane, who established himself in the last decades of the 14th century. Following the collapse of the Timurids in 1469, the Turkmen were once again relatively autonomous as nomadic herders in the desert steppes of Turkmenistan, nominally under the Uzbek khanates that ruled from Bukhara and Khiva. At the same time, the Safavid Persian rulers in Iran were constantly pushing northward, threatening the khanates in Turkmen territory.

The 14th–17th centuries were a period of great instability in the region, with some Turkmen converting to Shiism in the 16th century and supporting the Safavids, while others supported the Uzbeks. The majority, however, moved into the remote deserts to escape the chaos and economic decline brought on by almost constant military turmoil.

The 18th century finally saw a revival of Turkmen unity and cultural reawakening after several centuries of political domination by outsiders, frequent warfare, and population dispersal in the desert. The military strategist Keimir-Ker staged a rebellion against the Safavids, who had come to dominate most Turkmen territory, while the first literary Turkmen language was developed by Magtymguly Pyragy, a poet and Sufi who is considered the father of modern Turkmen culture. The early 18th century also saw Russian attempts to enter the region of Turkmenistan, but when the czar's first representative was killed near Khiva in 1716, the RUSSIANS withdrew for another full century.

The 19th century was a period of incorporation into the larger geopolitical sphere for the Turkmen. Many gave up their nomadic lifestyle to participate in agriculture or trade, which expanded in this period, especially with the Russians. By 1802 several important Turkmen clan leaders had taken out Russian citizenship; others requested Russian assistance against both the Uzbek khans and the Persian shahs, who continued their struggle for domination in the region. The Russians, seeing an opportunity to gain access to the land and resources of Turkmenistan, provided supplies to Turkmen rebels at several points early in the century. They began sending their own military into the region in the 1860s at the same time that they defeated and annexed the territories of the Uzbek khanates in Bukhara and Khiva. At this point some Turkmen, especially in the west, were grateful for the Russian presence and willingly became subjects of the czar. In the east and south of Turkmenistan, however, the Russians met aggressive resistance. In 1879 a large force of Tekke Turkmen, the same tribe who had repelled the Safavids under Keimir-Ker, defeated the Russians near Ashgabat, the modern capital, and it took the Russians another two years before they pushed back and conquered the region.

By the last decade of the 19th century, the Russians had conquered or annexed all of Turkmenistan, even pushing the country's borders into land that had been held by the Persians and PASHTUNS. They built the Transcaspian Railroad, starting at their port at Krasnovodsk (Turkmenbashi) and running through Ashgabat and Merv in Turkmenistan and then linking to Samarkand, Fergana, Tashkent, and Andijan in Uzbekistan. Under Russian domination, however, Turkmenistan was defined as the Transcaspian region, and the Turkmen themselves had a lower status than the other Central Asian peoples. This left the region less economically developed but better able to maintain its own culture, language, and (for some) the nomadic economic system. Despite this fact, the czar's attempt at forced conscription throughout Central Asia in 1916 did affect the Turkmen, sparking a rebellion.

The Russian Revolution in 1917 changed the political landscape of Turkmenistan once again. For a brief period, in 1918–19, the Social Revolutionary Transcaspian Republic was established with British support but was soon conquered by the Red Army in April 1919. The Turkmen Soviet Socialist Republic was incorporated into the USSR in 1925 and existed as a satellite republic until independence in 1991.

Other Turkmen

In the 14th century two empires were established by the descendants of Turkmen tribesmen who had migrated in the 11th century into the southern Caucasus region of contemporary Armenia and Azerbaijan. The Black Sheep Turkmen, or Kara Koyunlu, established their state in 1378 and were able to maintain their position in the Caucasus and northwestern Iran until 1469, while the White Sheep Turkmen, or Ak Koyunlu, were established in 1387, conquered the Black Sheep in 1469, and were themselves conquered by the Safavids in 1502. The Black Sheep centers were in Van, central Armenia, and Tabriz, Iran, from which they raided the lands of southern Armenia with great regularity. They also conquered Baghdad temporarily in 1410, when they ended the rule of the Timurids' western empire. The White Sheep ruled from their capital in Diyarbakir, in contemporary Turkey, and often allied with the Timurids against the Black Sheep.

Both Turkmen empires demanded heavy tribute from the people they ruled but allowed their conquered populations to continue practicing their own religions and ways of life. Under them, 15th-century Armenia saw the rebuilding of several Christian churches. Eventually the Turkmen of both of these empires began to assimilate to the Persian and Armenian groups whom they dominated. They gave up nomadic pastoralism in favor of settled agriculture, and after the defeat of their empires even the Turkmen ethnic identity was lost in the region.

CULTURE

Contemporary Turkmen use three criteria to establish Turkmen identity: membership in the large Turkmen descent group called the *taypa*, speaking Turkmen as one's mother tongue, and being a Sunni Muslim. Although Turkmen see themselves as members of one large descent group, within that group there are seven major tribal descent groups: Yomut, Tekke, Goklan, Salor, Saryk, Ersari, and Chaudor, all of whom are descended from the grandsons of the common Turkmen ancestor, Oghuz Khan. As is evident from the centrality of these descent groups, kinship remains one of the most important organizing principles for the daily lives of even contemporary Turkmen.

Traditionally, Turkmen made a distinction between two different kinds of assistance that they would grant to others: political, which entailed primarily coming to an individual's or group's aid in a fight or war; and social, where kinship determined what, if any, assistance an individual or group would give to another. The only groups that received both social and political assistance were those with close patrilineal ties—that is, connections through common male ancestors in the father's, grandfather's, or at the furthest, great-grandfather's generation. More distant patrilineal ties required Turkmen to provide political but not social assistance, while close matrilateral relatives—that is, those connected through mothers and grandmothers—and close in-laws could ask for and receive social but not political assistance. More distant matrilateral relatives and in-laws received neither political nor social assistance and were essentially treated like strangers in that these relatives could engage in blood feuds and go to war with one another over slights to family and individual honor.

Unlike some other Central Asian Turkic peoples, such as the Kazakhs, the Turkmen did not see their kin groups as hierarchical. There were no inherited positions within the larger Turkmen descent group, although slaves and those who were not so-called pure Turkmen were decidedly inferior in Turkmen society. No lineage or clan could claim a position superior to any other and leaders were chosen by the consensus of tribal male elders. Outsiders who interacted with the Turkmen in the 19th century often described them as providing a model of liberty, equality, and fraternity far superior to that the so-called democratic states of Europe.

Within the economic structure of Turkmen society there were two separate occupational categories, known at least among Yomut Turkmen as *chomur* and *charwa*. The *chomur* were agricultural people who grew cotton and, among Iranian Turkmen, wheat and barley as well; they also kept small numbers of sheep and goats. The *charwa* were pastoral people who lived primarily off the products and sale of their sheep and goats, moving seasonally when necessary to find grass, water, and shelter. This distinction between settled agriculturalists and nomadic or seminomadic pastoralists is common throughout not only Central Asia but the Middle East and any place where pastoralism remains a viable economic alternative. Among the Turkmen, however, this distinction is somewhat blurred because even many of the agriculturalists, at least in Iran until the mid-20th century, maintained a seminomadic existence. They wintered near their agricultural lands for plowing and planting but with the coming of spring tended to move away from these low-lying plains areas with their infestations of mosquitoes and flies, coming back only in late spring for the harvest and then retreating to higher, drier territory until autumn. In Turkmenistan proper, most Turkmen were more or less settled prior to 1917 because only a few river valleys and oases provided enough water for crops and animals throughout the year.

Despite being settled, the Turkmen of Turkmenistan began the 20th century without any tradition of national unity or state development and continued to think of themselves primarily as a kinship group. This made the transition to the Soviet state difficult, both for the Russians who were trying to incorporate them and for the Turkmen themselves. On the Turkmen side, Russian alliances and resources were often used during the 1920s and 1930s to fight long-standing kin-based feuds and battles. Turkmen learned very quickly that denouncing their tribal enemies as class enemies brought quick reprisals from the Russians at the same time that using the language of class struggle increased their own material resources. On the Russian side, the lack of any national consciousness on the part of the Turkmen meant having to create it, along with modern political structures, land collectivization, and industrialization.

Of these goals, the first three were relatively successful so that today Turkmen think of themselves as both lineage members and citizens of the state, and much of the land continues to be held by large, state-run collectives. However, the last goal, industrialization, was much more difficult to attain. Despite the presence of large cotton fields and a great deal of oil and gas, Turkmenistan remained a producer of primary resources throughout the entire 20th century, exporting raw materials to other socialist republics for value-added processing. Turkmenistan today is still a very poor country. It also has a very low population density at 24 people per square mile, the least populated of all five of the Central Asian republics. Most people continue to live along the country's rivers or the Kara-Kum Canal, eking out a living from producing cotton on the irrigated desert plains, herding sheep and goats, or working in the gas- and oil-sector of the economy. The large numbers of Turkmen in Iran, Iraq, and Afghanistan are also largely rural herders and agriculturalists. They brought karakul sheep to Afghanistan and are known for the finely woven tribal carpets they make from the wool they produce.

As a traditional Sunni Muslim people, many Turkmen continue to engage in arranged marriages, especially in rural areas. Women are symbolically marked as married or not by their hair and head-covering practices: two braids and a small scarf indicate an unmarried woman, while one braid and a large scarf symbolize marriage. This use of a head scarf is as far as most Turkmen women go toward covering themselves for modesty; veiling or wearing the more encompassing *burqa* is extremely rare among Turkmen women. Like other Central Asian Turkic peoples with a recent history of nomadism, women, while seen as inferior to men and not eligible for tribal leadership, are not entirely segregated from men and are not relegated to work inside their own houses or courtyards.

Another cultural feature the Turkmen share with their Turkic neighbors is a history of traveling singers, *bagshy,* who recite epic poetry, sing, and perform. The most famous epic poem cycle among the Turkmen is the Gorogly cycle, which includes the famous segment known as The Tale of Crazy Harman. Gorogly is a Turkic hero about whom more than 40 branches of the

The long scarf that drapes over the left shoulder of this Turkmen woman indicates that she is married. *(OnAsia/Jean Chung)*

poem have been produced, most written down for the first time in the first third of the 20th century. Like most works in this genre among the Turkic peoples, Gorogly is performed as both prose, which is spoken, and verse, which is sung.

FURTHER READING

Carole Blackwell. *Tradition and Society in Turkmenistan: Gender, Oral Culture, and Song* (Baltimore: Curzon Press, 2001).

Alexander G. Park. *Bolshevism in Turkestan* (New York: Columbia University Press, 1957).

Mehmet Saray. *The Turkmens in the Age of Imperialism: A Study of the Turkmen People and Their Incorporation into the Russian Empire* (Ankara: Turkish Historical Society Printing House, 1989).

Turkmenistanis: nationality (people of Turkmenistan)

GEOGRAPHY

Turkmenistan is dominated by a flat, desert landscape that makes up about 80 percent of the country's area. The Kara-Kum Desert stretches through central Turkmenistan from the northern to the southern border. Mountainous areas lie on Turkmenistan's borders, with the Kopetdag Range along the border with Iran and the Pamir-Altai range in far-eastern Turkmenistan.

TURKMENISTANIS: NATIONALITY

nation:
Turkmenistan

derivation of name:
Scholars believed for many centuries that the name derived from *Turk* and the Iranian word

Turkmenistanis: nationality time line

748   Abu Muslim, the Arab ruler of Merv, declares a new Abbasid dynasty and sets out to invade Iran and Iraq and to establish the capital in Baghdad. In a famous story, the goldsmith of Merv challenges Abu Muslim to do the right thing and not make war on fellow Muslims; the goldsmith is subsequently put to death.

775–785   The Oghuz tribes migrate from the Altai Mountain area to Central Asia, first to the steppes in western Kazakhstan and Kyrgyzstan and by the end of the eighth century spreading through Turkmenistan and Central Asia.

813–833   The name Oghuz starts to appear in Islamic history texts.

874   Arab rule in the territory of present-day Turkmenistan ends.

900s   The name Turkmen starts to appear, referring to Oghuz Turks who have converted to Islam.

1040   The Selijuk Turks, an Oghuz tribe, found the Persian Selijuk dynasty and take control of Merv and Herat, establishing their capital at Merv.

1000s–1100s   The Turkmen cultural centers are Khiva in the north and Merv in the south, with the latter prospering as a commercial center for trade in silk and spices. A growing class of wealthy merchants and landowners begins to challenge Selijuk rule by the end of the 1100s.

1157   The Selijuk dynasty collapses during a revolt of powerful landowners, and a group of wealthy landowners from Khiva takes control of Turkmenistan.

1221   Turkmenistan is invaded by the Mongols under Genghis Khan, who conquers Khiva and burns Merv to the ground, orders all of Merv's inhabitants massacred and the farms and irrigation systems destroyed. The surviving Turkmen flee to the plains of Kazakhstan or eastward to the shores of the Caspian Sea.

1227   Genghis Khan dies, and the Mongols lose control of Turkmenistan.

1227–1370   Turkmenistan is ruled by small independent states under the control of local wealthy landowners.

1370   The small independent states of Turkmenistan are invaded by Tamerlane (Timur Leng, or the Lame), who establishes the Timurid dynasty.

1405   Tamerlane dies and his Timurid dynasty disintegrates; Turkmenistan returns to small independent states.

1500s–1800s   Turkmenistan is divided and ruled by Uzbek khans centered in Bukhara and Khiva (the Bukhara and Khiva khanates). Rivalry between these two khanates as well as their rivalry with Persia cause numerous wars throughout this period, most of which are fought on Turkmen territory. The period is marked by isolation, poverty, and conflict for the Turkmen, who largely migrate to remote deserts to escape fighting.

1700s   (unknown date) Keimir-Ker, a Turkmen, leads a rebellion against Persia. His deeds continue to be a popular subject of folk legends and ballads.

1716   Peter the Great, czar of Russia, sends emissaries to Turkmenistan in search of a trade route between Russia and Central Asia; these emissaries are murdered by Turkmen clansmen.

1733–83   The lifetime of Magtymguly Pyragy, a Turkmen spiritual leader and poet who works to promote freedom for Turkmen.

1770–1840   The lifetime of Mametveli Kemine, a Turkmen satirical poet who frequently criticizes clergy and landowners.

1800s   Russia slowly begins to conquer Turkmenistan and wrest control from the Uzbek khanates, using a base on the Caspian Sea (Krasnovodsk, modern Turkmenbashi) to launch its attacks.

1879   The Transcaspian Railroad opens, connecting the Caspian shores with the Afghan border and providing rapid transportation for the Russian military.

1881   Russians win the Battle of Gokdepe, eliminating the last serious resistance in Turkmenistan and massacring thousands of Turkmen.

(continues)

---

manand and meant "resembling a Turk." Modern scholars have proposed that the suffix *man* actually is meant as an intensifier and that *Turkmen* really means "pure Turk" or "the most Turk-like of all of the Turks."

government:
Republic under authoritarian presidential rule

capital:
Ashgabat

language:
Turkmen is the official language; Russian is spoken as a first language by 12 percent, Uzbek by 9 percent of the population, and another 7 percent of the population speak other languages as a first languages. Most of the population speak Russian as a second language.

religion:
Muslim 89 percent, Russian Orthodox 9 percent, other 2 percent

earlier inhabitants:
While some archaeological finds suggest that Turkmenistan was home to Neanderthals and may have been the site of advanced Bronze and Iron Age civilizations, the first undisputed inhabitants of Turkmenistan were Persian horse breeders and nomads, although the desert areas remained more or less uninhabited until the arrival of the Oghuz, the ancestors of the Turkmen.

demographics:
Turkmen account for 85 percent of the population, followed by Uzbeks 5 percent, Russians 4 percent, and other ethnic groups 6 percent.

Turkmenistanis: nationality time line *(continued)*

1884 Russia takes control of the entire territory of Turkmenistan.

1897 The Transcaspian Railroad is extended to Tashkent.

1898 Turkmenistan is formally called Turkestan and begins being governed from Tashkent, having previously been governed from Tbilisi and been part of Transcaucasia.

1906 The Transcaspian Railroad is connected to the European Russian rail system through a connection from Orenburg to Tashkent.

1916 Russia becomes involved in the First World War, prompting a widespread anticonscription movement in all of Central Asia, including Turkmenistan.

1916 The Turkmen, under Dzhunaid Khan, defeat the Russians at Khiva and set up a national government that holds until 1918.

1920s Turkmen join in large numbers with other Central Asia groups to resist rule by the Soviet Union.

1923 The Turkmen language is changed from being written in Arabic letters first to Latin letters and then to Cyrillic in 1940.

1924 The Turkmen Soviet Socialist Republic is formed.

1927 The Soviet Union loses control of the Turkmen Republic to the Turkmen Freedom Movement.

1932 Stalin regains control of Turkmenistan and institutes brutal policies of collectivization and oppression of nationalism.

1930s Soviet policies and collectivization force the Turkmen to abandon their nomadic lifestyle.

1940s–50s The Soviet Union begins building factories in Turkmenistan, and large numbers of Ukrainians and Russians arrive to take advantage of the new jobs.

1991 Turkmenistan declares its independence from the Soviet Union on October 27. The former Soviet leader, Sapamurat Niyazov, is declared president. President Niyazov becomes famous for his dictatorial and oppressive rule as well as for his cult of personality.

1993 Turkmenistan changes the alphabetic script from Cyrillic back to Latin.

1999 Sapamurat Niyazov declares himself president for life

2005 Sapamurat Niyazov closes all hospitals outside Ashgabat as well as all rural libraries.

2006 On December 21 Sapamurat Niyazov dies unexpectedly without leaving a clear successor. A former deputy prime minister believed to be Niyazov's illegitimate son, Gurbanguly Berdimuhammedow, takes power.

2007 On February 11 Berdimuhammedow wins a presidential election with 89 percent of the votes; the election is deemed unfair by outside observers.

The Amu Darya, in the northeast, is the most important river. Turkmenistan's coastline on the Caspian Sea dominates the landscape of the western part of the country, where elevation is often at or below sea level up to 93 miles inland.

INCEPTION AS A NATION

From ancient times Turkmenistan was conquered by waves of invaders, often on the way to other, more fertile regions. These frequent waves of newcomers blurred geographic and ethnic distinctions, and many important developments for the TURKMEN occurred in territory outside present-day Turkmenistan.

Until the eighth century, Turkmenistan was inhabited primarily by Iranian (Persian) peoples, many of whom were settled and practiced sericulture (breeding of silkworms) and horse breeding. However, the direct ancestors of the Turkmen are considered to be the Oghuz Turks, seminomadic tribes that emigrated south from the steppes in the eighth century. Arriving originally in present-day Kyrgyzstan and Kazakhstan, they gradually moved into the territory of Turkmenistan and assimilated the Iranian peoples in the area. When the Oghuz converted to Islam in the 10th century, they began to be identified as Turkmen and to distinguish themselves from other TURKIC PEOPLES.

The Oghuz tribes, despite having considerable political power throughout most of Central Asia, did not act as a single unit but as separate tribal groups with separate political agendas. In 1040 the Seljuk tribe, one of the Oghuz tribes, founded the Seljuk empire, encompassing much of present-day Turkmenistan and Iran. During the Seljuk empire, Oghuz living in the Seljuk empire, further south than the rest of the Oghuz domain, began to be known as Turkmen, the first major political entity to be identified that way.

In spite of the Seljuk empire's success, the Turkmen identified themselves as such only on an ethnic basis and not as part of a national identity. When the Seljuk empire fell apart in the 12th century, it was largely due to revolts by Turkmen themselves, and the region was subsequently governed by independent tribal groups until the arrival of Genghis Khan and his armies and then Timur Leng (Tamerlane). After the Timurids disintegrated in 1405, northern Turkmenistan fell under the rule of Uzbek khanates and southern Turkmenistan came under Persian rule. Turkmenistan became the front line for conflicts between the Persians and Uzbeks and most Turkmen retreated to remote desert areas to escape the war and turmoil engulfing the territory.

Finally, in the 18th century the Turkmen began to develop a national identity. Keimir-Ker, a Turkmen from the Tekke clan, led a rebellion against the Persians that was celebrated by all Turkmen and remains a popular theme for Turkmen poetry and folk songs. Magtumguly Pyragy, a Turkmen poet of the 18th century, was one of the first to call for unity, brotherhood, and peace among Turkmen tribes. Prior to these developments, most individual Turkmen identified primarily with their clans and tribal groups and did not see the Turkmen as a unified nation. During this time, Turkmenistan was dominated by Uzbek and Persian rulers.

Despite these efforts among urban and intellectual Turkmen, in general this people lacked any significant national identity until the institution of the Soviet policy of demarcating national groups through the creation of the Union of Soviet Socialist Republics (USSR) in 1924. Ironically, although the USSR sought complete domination over the constituent SSRs, the policy that created them actually reinforced and even developed national identity that did not exist prior to the 1920s. Generally, the Turkmen of Turkmenistan began the 20th century without any tradition of national unity or state development and continued to think of themselves primarily as a kinship group. This made the transition to the Soviet state difficult, both for the RUSSIANS who were trying to incorporate the Turkmen and for the Turkmen themselves. On the Turkmen side, Russian alliances and resources were often used during the 1920s and 1930s to fight long-standing kin-based feuds and battles. Turkmen learned very quickly that denouncing their tribal enemies as class enemies brought quick reprisals from the Russians at the same time that using the language of class struggle increased their own material resources. On the Russian side, the lack of any national consciousness on the part of the Turkmen meant having to create such an identity, along with modern political structures, land collectivization, and industrialization.

Of these goals, the first three were relatively successful so that today Turkmen think of themselves as both lineage members and citizens of the state, and much of the land continues to be held by large, state-run collectives. However, the last goal, industrialization, was much more difficult to attain. Despite the presence of large cotton fields and a great deal of oil and gas, Turkmenistan remained a producer of primary resources throughout the entire 20th century, exporting raw materials to other socialist republics for value-added processing. As such, Turkmenistan today is still a very poor country. It also has a very low population density at 24 people per square mile, the least populated of all five of the Central Asian republics. Most people today continue to live along the country's rivers or the Kara-Kum Canal, eking out a living from producing cotton on the irrigated desert plains, herding sheep and goats, or working in the gas- and oil-producing sector of the economy.

CULTURAL IDENTITY

Contemporary Turkmen use three criteria to establish Turkmen identity: membership in the large Turkmen descent group called the *taypa*, using Turkmen as the mother tongue, and being a Sunni Muslim. Although Turkmen see themselves as members of one large descent group, within that group there are seven major tribal descent groups: Yomut, Tekke, Goklan, Salor, Saryk, Ersari, and Chaudor, all of which are descended from the grandsons of the common Turkmen ancestor, Oghuz Khan. As is evident from the centrality of these descent groups, kinship remains one of the most important organizing principles for the daily lives of even contemporary Turkmen.

The Turkmen language has been central to national identity since the start of the Soviet era, when one of the first tasks was to change the script used to write the language from Arabic to Latin. This was later revised in 1940 when Cyrillic, the alphabet used by the Russians, was adopted. With independence in the early 1990s, language again took center stage and the alphabet was changed yet again, back to Latin, as a marker of modernization and Europeanization. Further revisions were made throughout the 1990s and again in 2000 to facilitate Turkmen use of the Internet.

In addition to kinship, language, and religion, modern Turkmenistan has also created a form of patriotism based on allegiance to the country's territory and president. An oath devised in the post-Soviet era speaks to this form of cultural identity directly:

> Turkmenistan, my beloved motherland,
>   my homeland,
> You are always with me, in my thoughts
>   and in my heart.
> For the slightest evil against you, let my
>   hand be paralyzed,
> For the slightest slander against you, let
>   my tongue be lost,
> At the moment of my betrayal of the
>   motherland, its president, or its sacred
>   banner, let my breath be stopped.

See also RUSSIANS, ASIAN.

FURTHER READING

Carole Blackwell. *Tradition and Society in Turkmenistan: Gender, Oral Culture, and Song* (Baltimore: Curzon Press, 2001).
Sir Duncan Cumming. *The Country of the Turkomans: An Anthology of Exploration from the Royal Geographical Society* (London: Oguz Press, 1977).
Adrienne Lynn Edgar. *Tribal Nation: The Making of Soviet Turkmenistan* (Princeton, N.J.: Princeton University Press, 2004).
Saparmurat Niyazov. *Independence, Democracy, Prosperity* (New York: Noy Publications, 1994).

Tuvaluans (Elliceans)

The Tuvaluans are the primarily Polynesian indigenous people of the independent country of Tuvalu; one island, Nui, is primarily Micronesian. The Tuvaluans live on nine very small atolls in the South Pacific and are facing a difficult future due to lack of freshwater, erosion, and rising sea levels. As a result of these problems, especially the rising sea levels, the entire country may have to be evacuated to Australia or New Zealand sometime in this or the next century.

Linguistic evidence points to the original inhabitation of Tuvalu in the first years of the common era. These original settlers probably came from Samoa or Tokelau, both of which lie to Tuvalu's southwest. Others may have come from Tonga and Uvea, also known as Wallis Island, to the southwest and south of Tuvalu, respectively. All of these peoples were speakers of Polynesian languages and descendants of the original AUSTRONESIANS who settled much of the Pacific after having left south China between 5000 and 4500 B.C.E. The original settlers on Nui in Tuvalu's central region were Micronesian speakers who came from Kiribati prior to the 16th century.

There are two dialects of the Tuvaluans' Polynesian language. The inhabitants of the northern islands of Nanumea, Niutao, and Nanumaga speak one of these dialects, while those of the central and southern islands of Nukufetau, Funafuti, Vaitupu, and Nukulaelae speak the other. These dialects are mutually intelligible and constitute core Polynesian languages, related most closely to Samoan. The residents of Nui are linguistically distinct from their Polynesian neighbors in speaking a Micronesian language very closely related to Kiribatese.

Some aspects of contemporary Tuvaluan life are very similar to the traditional Polynesian life established on the islands 2,000 years ago. Subsistence fishing and farming still constitute the main economic activities for most people. The greatest source of calories for most Tuvaluans is taro, while yams, bananas, breadfruit, and other tropical fruits are also grown for local consumption. Many families keep a pig or two and some chickens, both animals that had been domesticated by the proto-POLYNESIANS and transported throughout the Pacific thousands of years ago. Government revenues tend to come from outside sources, such as the sale of stamps, coins, and, in 2000, the lease of the "dot tv" Internet domain name, and thus affect local Tuvaluans very little. Additionally, only about 1,000 tourists visit the islands each year; consequently, less infrastructure has developed to accommodate them and less change has come from that route than in many other Pacific island communities.

Politics among the Tuvaluans today is also similar to what it would have been hundreds, if not thousands, of years ago. Each of Tuvalu's inhabited islands contains one central village

---

TUVALUANS

location:
Tuvalu

time period:
Probably 2000 B.C.E. to the present

ancestry:
Polynesian and Micronesian

language:
Tuvaluan, a Polynesian language that has two distinct but mutually intelligible dialects, and Kiribatese, a Micronesian language spoken on Nui. English is also widely used on all islands.

Cement blocks serve as a walkway to keep people's feet dry as rising sea levels carry the ocean into David Losia's family compound. *(AP/Richard Vogel)*

with its own chief, kin groups, myths, and taboos. The council of chiefs continues to make important decisions and to work alongside the democratically elected parliament of Tuvalu. In 2000 these local, island-based political structures were granted even more power to make development decisions independent of the national government.

While much in Tuvalu has not changed for generations, many other things have been transformed during the colonial and postcolonial eras. For example, in addition to their subsistence farming and fishing, many Tuvaluans participate in the cash economy by producing copra and other coconut products for the world market. The levels of production vary greatly, from 700 tons of copra in 1984 to less than 50 tons in 2001, but the Tuvalu Coconut Traders' Cooperative receives significant subsidies to continue production and maintain the flow of cash to small producers.

One of the most important changes to Tuvaluan society was the introduction of Christianity in the 1860s. Today more than 97 percent of the Tuvaluan people are members of the Church of Tuvalu, or Ekalesia o Tuvalu, a Calvinist and Congregationalist denomination that is their national church. This centralizing institution was introduced by missionaries and ministers from the Samoan branch of the Lon-

don Missionary Society in the first half of the 1860s. Since that time, this church has formed the backbone of many local and national social, political, cultural, educational, and religious institutions. The church also brought change to other aspects of Tuvaluan society, especially in self-expression through song, dance, and the arts. The indigenous dance *fakanau* was believed by missionaries to be sexually stimulating because it required dancers to sway their hips; as a result, they slowly replaced it with a more sedate version of the dance known as *fatele*. Nonetheless, neither the national church nor the other nonindigenous religions that are practiced in Tuvalu, such as Bahaism and Seventh Day Adventism, have been able to eradicate other indigenous beliefs and practices. For example, according to the Tuvaluan origin myth, the sky, night and day, their islands, and the ocean were all created by an eel and a flounder. These two creatures remain taboo to this day and are not eaten, especially the eel, because of their mythical centrality to Tuvaluan existence.

Contemporary Tuvaluans' greatest concern is the continued existence of their islands in the face of rising sea levels: Their total land area has shrunk in the past few years from 18.6 square miles to 16 square miles. A number of different tactics have been taken by the government to find a solution to the problem, including exhorting other nations to support the Kyoto Treaty on climate change. The least desirable solution would be complete migration of the Tuvaluan population to Australia and/or New Zealand, which was proposed by the Tuvaluan government in 2000. A more active approach has been engaged in by almost the entire population and is called the Tuvalu Buoy Project. The islands' 12,000 or so residents have almost all participated in creating buoys out of disused oil barrels, with large blue cloths to hold them together and ropes to attach the buoys to the shore. The theory behind the project is that if the islands can be lifted from the rising seas on these buoys and anchored to the sea floor with giant chains then their way of life can continue on a series of floating islands.

See also MICRONESIANS; TUVALUANS: NATIONALITY.

FURTHER READING

Gerd Koch. *The Material Culture of Tuvalu* (Suva, Fiji: University of the South Pacific, 1983).

A. Pulekai Sogivalu. *A Brief History of Niutao* (Suva, Fiji: Institute of Pacific Studies, 1992).

Tuvaluans: nationality (Tuvaluans, people of Tuvalu)

Tuvalu is a Polynesian state located in the South Pacific between Kiribati and Wallis and Futuna, just to the west of the International Date Line.

GEOGRAPHY

Tuvalu consists of nine coral atolls that together make up just 16 square miles of land. None of the islands has a river or stream, and most groundwater is saline; as a result, water is the primary problem for this tiny nation. Catchments gather rainwater, and the JAPANESE government has built a desalination plant to assist the TUVALUANS in this area. Erosion and rising sea levels also constitute potentially grave issues for the country, and in 2000 the government approached both Australia and New Zealand about taking in Tuvaluan refugees if climate change forces evacuation of their homes.

INCEPTION AS A NATION

The ancestors of today's Tuvaluans probably left Samoa, Tokelau, Tonga, and/or Uvea (Wallis Island) in dugout canoes about 2,000 years ago. Whether they accidentally reached the shores of Tuvalu's islands or had deliberately left their homes to search for another place to live is impossible to tell. What is certain is that they es-

tablished an agriculture-based society, growing taro, pandanus fruit, bananas, coconuts, and papayas. They also thrived on the many fish species that lived in their lagoon environments.

The residents of these islands saw their first European, Spanish explorer Álvaro de Mendaña de Neira, in 1568, but it was another 261 years before American sailor Arent de Peyster named the islands Ellice's Group after the British owner of his ship's cargo. Many other American ships participated in the whaling industry in this region of the Pacific in the 19th century, with some sailors visiting the islands and some Ellicean men joining the crews of these whalers. By mid-century, Australian, German, and American firms had also begun exporting coconut products, such as oil and copra, from the tiny atolls, and in the 1860s several hundred Elliceans lost their liberty and probably their lives as slaves in Peru, Fiji, Samoa, and Hawaii. Many others died from the many diseases brought by the European and American sailors.

The 1860s also introduced Christianity to the people of the Ellice Islands when, in 1861, the first London Missionary Society (LMS) adherents from the Cook Islands arrived on Nukulaelae. They were followed in 1865 by a minister from the Samoan branch of the LMS who established Samoan pastors on many of the nine atolls. Most Tuvaluans today continue to worship in the Ekalesia o Tuvalu (Church of Tuvalu), which was established by the LMS 140 years ago.

The formal colonial period on the Ellice Islands began in 1877 when the British raised their flag on the islands to prevent Germany or the United States from claiming them. They were incorporated as part of the British Protectorate of the Gilbert and Ellice Islands in 1892 and formally colonized in 1915. Fortunately for the inhabitants of the islands, their small atolls provided very few products the British needed, so their colonization was not as onerous as it was for some other Pacific peoples. Coconut oil and copra were the only real exportable products, although in 1856 the United States had claimed several of the southern islands for their guano supplies, used in making fertilizer. Despite the British presence, the United States maintained this claim until Tuvaluan independence in the late 1970s.

The mid-20th century brought more change as World War II battles in the Pacific saw Japan and the United States fighting from island to island, especially in nearby Micronesia. The Japanese occupied the nearby Gilbert Islands,

---

TUVALUANS: NATIONALITY

nation:
Tuvalu

derivation of name:
Tuvalu means "group of eight" and refers to the country's eight inhabited islands.

government:
Constitutional monarchy and parliamentary democracy, with the prime minister as head of government and the British queen Elizabeth II as head of state

capital:
Vaiaku on Fongafale islet, part of Funafuti Atoll. Funafuti alone is often listed as the capital.

language:
Tuvaluan, English, Samoan, Kiribati (on the island of Nui)

religion:
Ekalesia o Tuvalu (Church of Tuvalu) up to 97 percent, Seventh-Day Adventist 1.4 percent, Baha'i 1 percent, other 0.6 percent

earlier inhabitants:
None

demographics:
Polynesian 96 percent, Micronesian 4 percent

but it was the Americans who reached the Ellice Islands first in 1942, when they established a large airfield on Funafuti. Due to the lack of local fighting or bombing, the inhabitants of the Ellice Islands fared much better during the war than their fellow colonized people in the Gilberts. However, the significant postwar rebuilding projects necessary to reestablish Tarawa as the capital of the joint colony lured many residents of the Ellice Islands north. This led to some fierce rivalries between the local Gilbertese population and the visiting Elliceans, enmity that lasted until the mid-1970s, when Britain began to withdraw from the islands.

The division between the Gilbert Islands, which became the independent country of Kiribati, and the Ellice Islands occurred after a referendum in the Ellice group in 1974. An overwhelming 92 percent of eligible voters voted in favor of secession, despite losing access to the profitable phosphate industry in Kiribati. The separation took place in 1975, with Tuvaluan independence as special members of the British Commonwealth following in 1978. Tuvalu achieved full status as a member of the commonwealth in 2000, the same year the country joined the United Nations as that organization's 189th member state. In that year Tuvalu also leased the Internet domain name "dot tv."

CULTURAL IDENTITY

The most important aspect of Tuvaluan cultural identity is the connection to the other POLYNE-SIANS of the Pacific. This ethnic, linguistic, and cultural difference from the people of Kiribati (formerly the Gilbert Islands) is the most often cited reason for having separated from them in the mid-1970s, despite the loss of revenue this entailed. The Polynesian heritage is also pointed to in order to explain why local chiefs, rather than national political parties, continue to dominate the political sphere in Tuvalu. Each island is occupied by a single village with its own chief and both noble and commoner lineage groups. The country's small numbers, estimated at just under 12,000 in 2006, mean that these local kin groups have continued to play the same central role in people's lives at both the national and local levels as they would have done in the largest Polynesian protostates of Hawaii and Tonga prior to the colonial era.

A second important cultural feature of the Tuvaluan nation is the centrality of the national church, the Ekalesia o Tuvalu, or Church of Tuvalu, in which up to 97 percent of the population claims membership. The church runs a school in

Tuvaluans: nationality time line	
C.E.	
0	Approximate period of first settlement on the nine islands of Tuvalu. This first wave of Polynesian settlement is followed sometime during the next 1,500 years by the settlement of Nui by Micronesian speakers.
1568	Spanish explorer Álvaro de Mendaña de Neira is the first European to see the Tuvaluan island of Nui.
1819	American sailor Arent de Peyster names the islands Ellice's Group.
1856	The United States claims several of the Ellice Islands as its own because of their rich guano supplies.
1860s	Blackbirders kidnap hundreds of Elliceans who never return from their forced labor in Peru, Fiji, Samoa, and Hawaii.
	London Missionary Society missionaries establish the church that is now the national church, Ekalesia o Tuvalu.
1877	The British claim the Gilbert and Ellice Islands as their own.
1892	The British Protectorate of the Gilbert and Ellice Islands is established.
1915	The protectorate becomes a full-fledged colony.
1942	The United States establish an air base in the Ellice Islands.
1974	The inhabitants of the Ellice Islands vote overwhelmingly to secede from the Gilbert Islands.
1978	Tuvalu, the former Ellice Islands, achieves independence from Britain.
1979	The United States and Tuvalu sign a Treaty of Friendship in which the United States relinquishes its claims to Funafuti, Nukufetau, Nukulaelae, and Niulakita.
1997	Tuvalu becomes the poster child for the Kyoto Agreement, with the claim that its low-lying islands are sinking into a rising sea.
2000	Tuvalu joins the British Commonwealth as a full member and becomes the 189th member of the United Nations.
	Tuvalu leases its "dot tv" domain name for $50 million over the next 12 years.

the national capital and organizes social, political, cultural, and aid institutions, in addition to religious ones throughout the country. The ideology underlying the church is Calvinism, with its beliefs in predestination and equality, and the organizational structure is Congregationalism, in which each local congregation is independent. This structure mirrors the Tuvaluan chiefly political system, and in many cases the leaders in the political arena are the same individuals as those in the religious one.

Since 1997, when His Excellency the Right Honorable Bikenibeu Paeniu, prime ministerial special envoy on climate change from Tuvalu, spoke to the United Nations Framework Convention on Climate Change, another important identity maintained by Tuvaluans is as a small island nation suffering the effects of climate change because of the actions of the developed world. Whether or not Tuvalu will actually sink into a rising Pacific is a hotly contested political and scientific debate that has been going on for the past 10 years. But in Tuvalu, it matters little what the skeptics think. The Tuvaluan government is concerned enough about the issue to have made a request of the Australian and New Zealand governments in 2000 to take as many environmental refugees from Tuvalu as they can, using as an argument the responsibility of these developed countries to deal with the environmental disaster their burning of fossil fuels has caused.

See also KIRIBATESE: NATIONALITY; I-KIRIBATI.

FURTHER READING

Keith Chambers and Anne Chambers. *Unity of Heart: Culture and Change in a Polynesian Atoll Society* (Prospect Heights, Ill.: Waveland Press, 2001).

W. H. Geddes. *Atoll Economy: Social Change in Kiribati and Tuvalu: Tabiteuea North* (Canberra: Australian National University Press, 1983).

Hugh Laracy, ed. *Tuvalu: A History* (Suva, Fiji: University of the South Pacific and Government of Tuvalu, 1983).

Tuvans (Soyot, Tannu-tuvan, Tiva, Tuvinians, Tyvans, Uriankhai)

The Tuvans are a Turkic-speaking people who reside in the Republic of Tuva, a semiautonomous region within the Russian Federation, and Mongolia. Their territory is largely mountainous and covered with taiga forest, and their climate is extremely cold and dry in the winter, cool to hot in the summer, depending on elevation. Their history is largely defined by having been conquered by other TURKIC PEOPLES, MONGOLS, MANCHUS, and most recently, RUSSIANS.

Although there had been populations of herders living in the cold, dry region of Tuva for millennia, Tuvan history began in the sixth century C.E. when Turkic peoples from the Gokturk khanate entered the region. Tuva was part of the eastern khanate from the time that the Gokturks' civil war divided their territory into eastern and western halves in 582 until they were conquered by UIGHUR armies in 744. The Uighur were followed by KYRGYZ armies from the Yenisey River region of Siberia in the ninth century, who loosely held the territory until Genghis Khan's Mongols took it in the 13th century. The last Mongol peoples to hold the territory were those of the OIRAT state, who themselves were defeated by the ZUNGHARS until the latter lost all of their land with

the expansion of the Manchu Chinese state in the 1750s. China was able to hold Tuva in its sphere of influence for around 150 years before the small country attained nominal independence in 1912. Unfortunately, before Tuva had the time to establish most of the administrative and judicial trappings of an independent state the Russian empire's expansionism swallowed up the small, mountainous country in 1914.

Tuva became a Russian protectorate in 1914, but following the Russian Revolution it did achieve a degree of independence again, from 1921 to 1944. During that 23-year period, Tuvan authorities alternatively looked to Russia and Mongolia for leadership and to socialism and capitalism for a model for development. A new capital was built at Kyzyl, and the country tried to remain as independent as possible within a global political sphere in which its existence mattered little to anyone outside the region. With the disintegration of the USSR in 1991, there might have been a chance for Tuva to follow in the footsteps of the Baltic and Central Asian republics in attaining complete independence from Russia, but it did not. The most recent constitution, which came into effect in 1993, states that the Republic of Tuva is a democratic state within the Russian Federation, a status that can be amended by public referendum at any time. With only 305,510 people (according to the 2002 census), almost half of whom reside in rural areas and engage in subsistence agriculture, the chances of the small republic's attaining economic independence are slim, regardless of what the people's political choices are in the future.

The Tuvan economy is largely based on the same traditional agricultural activities that have sustained people in this region for thousands of years. The most important of these activities is animal husbandry, especially raising cattle, sheep, yaks, reindeer, and camels. A few crops are also grown in Tuva, particularly strains of wheat, barley, and other grains that can mature in the region's short, dry growing season. During the Soviet era the children of the herding families were removed from their homes for most of the year to attend boarding schools, leaving them without solid connections to their families or their way of life, language, or culture. The end result is that today there are many unemployed urban residents who are disconnected from the people and land around them. Families that adapted to agriculture or moved to urban areas suffered in other ways but at least did not experience the generational divisions of the herders.

The Tuvans, like all Turkic peoples, originally practiced a shamanistic religion in which spiritual leaders communicated with, and even moved back and forth between, this world and that of the spirits. Nature worship was important for these people, and cults of fire, water, trees, and the taiga flourished for many generations until they were forced underground by the Soviets. Tuvans always made sure not to take more resources, whether tree, animal, or water, than they needed and thanked the spirits for the gifts they did take. The connection between humans and nature was seen as so important that Tuvans wore heelless shoes with turned-up toes to prevent trampling to death even the tiniest insects. During the period of Chinese domination, the 18th to early 20th centuries, many Tuvans adopted Yellow Hat Buddhism, the form of Tibetan Buddhism headed by the Dalai Lama. Today both Buddhism and shamanism continue to exist side by side in most people's hearts and minds.

Although Tuvan history is not well known outside the region, the Tuvans themselves are famous worldwide for their music, particularly the ability of some singers to sing two or three different notes at one time and to maintain these notes for as long as 30 seconds without stopping to breathe. This throat singing, or overtone singing as it is also called, can be heard throughout Siberia but is particularly well-developed among Tuvan singers, who created six different pitches that they can combine to form unique vocal compositions. Some of the sounds produced seem to outsiders like a drone or other monotonous, low-pitched tone; others are like bird calls or whistles; all are unfamiliar to westerners who are trained to listen to music based on the do-re-mi note scale.

FURTHER READING

Otto Mänchen-Helfen. *Journey to Tuva,* trans. Alan Leighton (Los Angeles: Ethnographics Press, University of Southern California, 1992).

Kira Van Deusen. *Singing Story, Healing Drum: Shamans and Storytellers of Turkic Siberia* (Seattle: University of Washington Press, 2004).

Tuyuhun (Tuguhun)

The Tuyuhun were a nomadic tribe who lived in what is today Qinghai and Gansu Provinces in northwestern China from before the fourth century C.E. and until about 950. They are believed to be related to the XIANBEI, and one origin myth claims that the Tuyuhun lineage was founded by Murong Tuyuhun, an illegitimate son of a Xianbei king.

Over the course of the fourth through the seventh centuries, a succession of Tuyuhun tribal rulers were able to exploit their locality between various larger and stronger polities, such as the Xianbei's Northern Wei, TIBETANS, ROURAN, and Gaoche. Records of their interactions are evident as far away as the southern kingdom of Nanzhao, founded by a branch of the DAI people in 700. Tuyuhun officials served as envoys, messengers, and traders, and some people even acted as mercenary soldiers in the armies of these larger kingdoms. As a buffer between larger polities, the Tuyuhun were largely left alone by them. Most people were nomadic pastoralists breeding horses, sheep, goats, and some cattle and living in tents or yurts similar to other pastoralists of the steppe. Buddhist influences were felt as large numbers of traders and missionaries from this faith crossed the Tuyuhun lands, but it never emerged as the dominant religion of the people.

In the sixth century one Tuyuhun ruler, Murong Kualu, overextended his power by taking the title of khan, or khagan, and thus establishing the first Tuyuhun kingdom. With his new title, Kualu thought that he had the strength to challenge the Chinese armies of the Sui dynasty (580–618). For a short period the Tuyuhun armies were successful, largely due to the relative disintegration of the Sui dynasty, but by the early Tang dynasty (618–907) the Chinese were installing their own khagans as tribal lords over the subservient Tuyuhun tribal people. In about 663 much of the Tuyuhun territory was overrun by the Tibetans' Tubo kingdom, and the Tang overlords allowed them to escape to the north. Some sources continue the story of the Tuyuhun under the name Tuhun during the period of China's history known as the Five Dynasties (907–960), which followed the fall of the Tang; these sources report that they disappeared as a separate group between 947 and 950 when attacked by Liu Zhiyuan, a HAN ruler of the fifth of the Five Dynasties.

TUYUHUN

location:
Today's Qinghai and Gansu Provinces, China

time period:
Fourth century to 950 C.E.

ancestry:
Possibly Xianbei

language:
Perhaps a Tungusic language related to Xianbei

U

Uighur (Eastern Turk, Ouigour, Uighuir, Uiguir, Uigur, Uygur, Weiwuer)

The Turkic-speaking Uighur are today one of the largest of China's 55 national minorities at about 8.5 million people, mostly residing in the Xinjiang Uighur Autonomous Region; about another million Uighur live in other Chinese regions and in the largest Chinese cities, as well as in Kazakhstan, Kyrgyzstan, and Tajikistan. Most Uighur today are Muslim, but they have a long and varied religious tradition, ranging from shamanism through Manichaeanism, Nestorian Christianity, and Buddhism before final conversion to Islam in the 15th century. When referring to ancient times, *Uighur* is often used to distinguish the Turkic speakers of Central Asia who settled around oases to farm and establish cities from those of the Gokturk and Oguz federations, who remained largely nomadic.

GEOGRAPHY

The Xinjiang Uighur Autonomous Region of China, the present-day home of most Uighur and about one-sixth of the Chinese landmass, is a 1-million-square-mile region in northwestern China that borders on Tibet, Qinghai, and Gansu within China, and on Russia, Mongolia, Kazakhstan, Tajikistan, and Pakistan. The region has been known by many different names throughout the course of history, including Turkestan, East Turkestan, Chinese Turkestan, Uighurstan, Inner Asia, and Xinjiang Province.

Xinjiang encompasses many diverse climate zones, including the lowest point in China, the Turfan Depression at 509 feet below sea level; the two low-elevation basins, the Dzungarian in the north and the Tarim in the south; and many mountains, including the Kunlun, Tian Shan, Bagda, and Altai. The highest peak, K2, or Godwin-Austen, in the region's southern borderland with Pakistan, is the world's second-highest mountain at 28,250 feet above sea level. On average, the region is extremely hot and dry in the summer and extremely cold in the winter, but with a long enough growing season to produce a significant amount of fruit, cotton, wheat, and sheep. The region is also an important supplier of minerals and oil to China's developing industrial economy.

ORIGINS

The Uighur are a branch of the Eastern TURKIC PEOPLES, who, along with the western Turkic peoples, were two of many seminomadic groups living on the steppes northwest of China prior to the sixth century. Probably the only trait that distinguished them from the XIONGNU, XIANBEI, MONGOLS, and other steppe dwellers was their language. Like these others, they would have relied primarily on their herds for subsistence, resided in felt tents, and moved about as they needed grass and water. They practiced a shamanistic religion and placed great value on their horses.

Uighur as an ethnonym was first referred to by the Chinese during the HAN dynasty (206

UIGHUR

location:
Xinjiang Uighur Autonomous Region, northwestern China; previously in Gansu Province and Mongolia as well

time period:
Possibly 300 B.C.E. to the present

ancestry:
Turkic, with contributions made by the Gaoche, Tiele, and possibly Yuezhi, as well as many other nomadic and settled peoples in the steppes.

language:
Uighur, a Turkic language of the Karluk group

B.C.E.–220 C.E.). Chronicles produced by the Northern Wei in the third century C.E., Tang (618–907), and Sung (907–960) also refer to the Uighur. By the seventh century, the Tang reference was definitely to the ancestors of today's Uighur; however, there is still some debate over the Han and Northern Wei references, as well as Greek and Iranian ones from before the common era.

According to legend, the Uighur are the offspring of a mystical union between a Hun princess and a wolf.

HISTORY

Uighur history is extremely complex, and many sources divide it into three, four, five, or even six distinct periods. Unfortunately, none of these sources seem to agree on what the best demarcation lines between periods should be, or why. Here we divide Uighur history into three phases, the first two ending in the years 840 and 1759, respectively, and the third continuing up to the present. These dates were chosen to coincide with the fall of the Uighur khanate in 840 and the final disintegration in 1759 of the various Uighur kingdoms that followed this first khanate. The last period incorporates the domination of the Uighur at the hands of the MANCHUS and their incorporation into the larger Chinese state; it also brings Uighur history up to the present day.

Prehistory–840 C.E.

The ancient history of the Uighur remains a contentious issue since the various sources, from Greek, Iranian, and Chinese texts to archaeological evidence from Central Asia and northwestern China, often do not agree. Ancient mentions of a Uighur people may or may not refer to the same ethnic group residing in China today, and the archaeological evidence found on the steppes often makes it very difficult to differentiate between ethnolinguistic groups.

The first solid evidence for the direct predecessors of today's Uighur comes from the early seventh century, when the tribal leader Erkin Tegin sought an alliance with China. In subsequent years the Uighur federation expanded through alliances with other tribal groups until in the 630s it was strong enough to challenge the ruling Gokturks, with the assistance of the Chinese Tang dynasty. By the mid-seventh century, the first Uighur statelet came into being on the Selenga River in the Orkhon Valley of Mongolia under the leadership of Tumitu Il Teber, who was given a Chinese title due to his service

to the Tang. However, Uighur sovereignty did not last long in this case due to the overpowering strength of the Chinese. Tumitu's successor, Pojuan Il Teber, was a realist and rather than fighting this Chinese power, in 648 he pledged his loyalty to it instead. This alliance saw Uighur fighting as mercenaries with the Chinese armies against their common enemy, the Gokturks, who were defeated in 657.

About a century later, in 744–45, the Uighur were once again instrumental in the defeat of a segment of the Gokturk khanate, and this time the victors were able to establish their own state in the Orkhon region of northern Mongolia. They made Ordubalik, near the city of Karabalghasun and located on the upper reaches of the Orkhon River, their capital. Upon the weakening of the Chinese in 751, when they were defeated by an alliance of Arab and Karluk armies (see KARLUKS), the Uighur also claimed most of the Tarim Basin between the Tien Shan and Kunlun Mountains. The Chinese were forced to pay tribute to the Uighur at this time in the form of many thousands of rolls of silk.

During the peak of this first Uighur khanate, the ruling class was strongly influenced by the many SOGDIANS who entered their territory as traders, advisers, and bureaucrats after traveling east along the Silk Road. The Uighur language was put into writing using a form of the Sogdian script, and a new religion brought from the Sogdian lands began to replace the traditional shamanistic practices. This new religion, Manichaeanism, was adopted as the state religion in 762. Manichaeanism was based on the writings of Manes, a third-century Persian who saw himself as the last in the line of many prophets, including Zoroaster, the Buddha, and Jesus. Manichaeanism posited a dualistic world in which the forces of good or light were constantly at war with the forces of evil or darkness. In the human realm, bodily life on earth was seen as part of the realm of darkness, while salvation was available only through the spiritual realm, or world of light. Like Christianity and other religions of salvation, Manichaeanism had a priestly class of religious experts who read and wrote in and about the tradition; it also had lay believers who engaged in the beliefs and practices at a lower level. While most of the six original texts of Manes, written in Syriac, have been lost over time, much of what we know about the ancient form of this religion comes from Uighur texts written in Sogdian script and found in the Turfan region of Xinjiang in the early 20th century.

Uighur time line

B.C.E.

1000 Indo-European people appear in northwestern China; their mummies have European features and light hair. Some Uighur today have red hair and light eyes.

300 Greek, Iranian, and Chinese sources place the Uighur north of China as early as 300 B.C.E.

C.E.

600 Erkin Tegin, leader of the Uighur tribe, seeks contact with China. One year later these two groups sign an alliance in which the Uighur are described as living in the Tola Valley (Hindu Kush Mountains of Afghanistan) in 10,000 yurts.

603 Through an alliance with three other tribes, the Uighur expand to 30,000 yurts under Erkin Tegin.

627–30s Eastern Turkic armies working with the Tang defeat the Gokturks.

646 Tumitu Il Teber declares the first Uighur state at Otuken.

648 Tumitu's successor, Pojuan Il Teber, pledges his loyalty to China and many Uighur become mercenaries working for the Chinese to pacify the western reaches of their empire.

657 Some Uighur support the Chinese in their pursuit of the Gokturk khan as far as Tashkent, where he is captured and his empire divided.

663 Uighur power declines with the death of Pojuan.

715–17 Orkhun inscriptions from the Gokturk khanate mention Uighur as participants in uprisings in these years.

744–45 The last Eastern Gokturk khan, Baimei, is killed and the empire disintegrates within the year at the hands of Uighur, Karluk, and other Turkic tribes. The Uighur found their own state, or khanate, in northern Mongolia after defeating their former allies.

751 The Battle of Talas is fought between the Chinese and the Arabs, along with their Karluk allies. As a result of the Chinese defeat, the Uighur claim most of the land in the Tarim Basin as well as Chinese tribute in the form of rolls of silk.

762 The Uighur kingdom adopts Manichaeanism upon the conversion of the king.

840 Many Uighur people enter northwestern China's Xinjiang region upon the collapse of their own khanate in the Orkhon Valley of Mongolia at the hands of the Kyrgyz. Many others move to the west.

In addition to adopting Manichaeanism, the Uighur at this time also largely gave up their nomadic existence and settled down as agriculturalists, craftsmen, and traders. They developed advanced irrigation techniques to move water considerable distances in canals they called *kariz*, which enabled the development of crops of wheat, corn, millet, potatoes, sugar beets, peanuts, sesame, peaches, grapes, melons, and most lucratively, cotton. Wool, especially when manufactured into carpets in the cities of Hoten, Kashgar, and Turfan, was another valuable product for the Uighur. Living along the Silk Road also gave the settled Uighur the chance to trade their agricultural and manufactured goods to the west as far as the Black Sea as well as further east into China.

About a century after its founding this Uighur state was defeated by the nomadic KYRGYZ who drove many Uighur out of their capital in the Orkhon Valley. Many Uighur went south into Xinjiang, with some settling in the western region around Kashgar and others in the east around Turfan. Still others settled in China's Gansu region. These migrations set the stage for the development of the second stage of Uighur history, the period from 840 to 1759.

840–1759

Following their migration to the western reaches of the Xinjiang region, the largest segment of the refugee Uighur formed an alliance with other Turkic tribes in the region, such as the Karluks and Turgish, to form the Karakhanid kingdom, with its political and economic center at Kashgar. The founding date of this kingdom is under considerable debate, with

846	Founding date of the Karakhoja Uighur kingdom in the Turfan Basin of China's Xinjiang region. This Buddhist kingdom is sometimes referred to as the Kingdom of Kocho, or Gaochang.
850	Founding date of the Kanchou (Ganzhou) Uighur kingdom, a minor state in China's Gansu province.
ninth–10th centuries	Creation of the Karakhanid kingdom, a state established by Uighur, Karluk, Turgish, and other Turkic tribes. Kashgar in the far west of the Xinjiang region is the capital.
934	Many Karakhanid Uighur convert to Islam in the reign of Satuk Bughra Khan, the first Turkic khan in Central Asia to convert.
1124	The two Xinjiang Uighur kingdoms are forced to pay tribute to the Kara-Khitai empire.
1218	The Buddhist Uighur kingdom of Karakhoja voluntarily submits to the Mongols, to unite against their common enemy, the Kara-Khitai.
1228	Disappearance of the Buddhist Kanchou Uighur kingdom.
1284	Complete submission of the Karakhoja Uighur kingdom to the Mongols; it falls under the Chagatai section upon Genghis Khan's division of his empire into four parts, one for each of his sons.
1397	The Muslim Uighur invade and take over their Buddhist cousins, establishing an independent Muslim Uighur kingdom in Xinjiang.
1759	The Manchus conquer the Uighur kingdom but never assimilate them into China; the Uighur rebel more than 40 times over the next 100 years.
1863	The Uighur finally succeed in overthrowing the Qing in Xinjiang and establish an independent kingdom.
1876	The Chinese invade the Uighur kingdom with funding from the British.
1884	Xinjiang is annexed by China.
1933	The Uighur declare their independence from China and establish their own state in Xinjiang, only to have China retake the territory with assistance from the Soviet Union.
1944	The Uighur again declare their independence in the Eastern Turkestan Republic. They are brought back under Chinese rule five years later when the Communists take over.
1955	Xinjiang Province in northwestern China is renamed the Xinjiang Uighur Autonomous Region in 1955. Today about half the population of 17–20 million is Uighur.

scholars positing dates as early as 840, right after the fall of the Uighur khanate, and as late as 999. This variation seems to be the result of the extensive period of migration, struggle, and alliance building that went into the state's formation. There is also some confusion today about which Turkic group dominated the alliance, with Uighur-centered sources saying it was largely a Uighur state that incorporated others, while Karluk-centered sources say it was largely a Karluk state that included refugee Uighur. The truth is very difficult to tease out, especially given the linguistic affinities between these two Turkic peoples.

The most important cultural transformation that took place under the Karakhanids was the conversion to Islam under Satuk Bughra Khan in 934. Satuk Bughra was the first Turkic leader in Central Asia to embrace the new religion that was to become one of the most important characteristics used by Uighur and indeed almost all Turkic peoples to characterize themselves. It is also extremely important today as the Islamic faith is central to contemporary Chinese Uighur identity.

The second Uighur successor state, the Karakhoja, was set up by the segment of Uighur migrants who fled to the Turfan region of Xinjiang, China. While the founding of the Karakhanids is still somewhat unclear, the consensus about the founding of the second Uighur successor kingdom, the Karakhoja, is that it occurred in 846, although the Chinese did not recognize the state's independence or send an ambassador until 981. Like the Karakhanids, the Karakhoja Uighur continued to rely largely on agriculture and trade for their primary economic activities and to use the Turkic Uighur language. However, unlike the Karakhanids, the Karakhojas did not convert to Islam. Instead, because they had moved further into the Buddhist-dominated Chinese territories, many of these Uighur converted to Mahayana Buddhism. Literate Uighur adapted Chinese Buddhist texts for use by the people and even wrote a confession sutra for Uighur laypeople that differed somewhat from those of the Chinese. Mahayana Buddhism generally differs from its Theravadan cousin in being focused more on the beliefs and practices of laypeople and on alleviating suffering for all rather than just for each individual practitioner.

The third Uighur successor state to develop after the fall of the Uighur khanate in 840 was the Kanchou, or Ganzhou, Uighur kingdom, a much smaller kingdom that emerged on the west banks of the Huang He (Yellow River) in China's Gansu Province in about 850. Although the people embraced Buddhism after their migration into China, they differed from the Karakhojas in their adherence to the Yellow sect of Tibetan Buddhism. Their independent kingdom disappeared in 1228 when they were absorbed by the Tangut, or DANGXIANG, state of Western Hsia, but their descendants are alive today and make up China's YUGUR ethnic minority, or Yellow Uighur.

The 12th and 13th centuries saw the absorption of the two Xinjiang Uighur kingdoms into larger and more powerful empires as well. By 1130 they had both come under the thumb of the emerging Kara-Khitai, to whom they paid tribute for almost a century. The Buddhist Karakhojas had succumbed to this vassal position with little resistance, but the Muslim Karakhanids joined with the Turkic Seljuks to attempt to keep the Kara-Khitai out of their territory, with their joint army losing a major battle outside Samarkand in 1130. In 1218 the Buddhist Karakhoja Uighur kingdom of eastern Xinjiang allied itself in a subordinate position to Genghis Khan's Mongols to rid itself of Kara-Khitai rule, and by 1284 the Karakhoja kingdom had disappeared into the Chagatai section of the Mongol Empire. Meanwhile, in 1211 the surviving Karakhanid lands were conquered by the KHWAREZMIANS, who were overrun by the Mongols a few years later.

Following the Mongol victory in Xinjiang, both Uighur kingdoms were absorbed by the Chagatai segment of the empire, which demanded tribute and military participation from its vassals but paid little attention to internal political affairs. This left the Uighur kingdoms subordinate but largely intact. This situation changed in 1397 when the Muslim Uighur under Khizir Khoja invaded the territory of the Buddhist Uighur, and the two Uighur populations in Xinjiang were united into an Islamic Uighur kingdom that was able to maintain its independence as an Islamic state until 1759.

1759 to the Present

In 1759 the Manchus, who had by then established themselves as the ruling Qing dynasty in China, conquered the Uighur kingdom and incorporated it into the larger Chinese state for the first time. The Muslim Uighur never assimilated comfortably into the wider Chinese society, unsuccessfully rebelling more than 40 times over the course of the next 100 years. A popular Uighur nationalist legend from the period tells the story of Iparhan, a Uighur Muslim princess who was kidnapped by the Manchu emperor Qianlong and held as his concubine; she was known as the Fragrant Concubine because of her bewitching scent. In Uighur versions of the tale, Iparhan consistently resisted Manchu domination and plotted to take Qianlong's life until his mother finally had her murdered. Chinese versions of the story are more romantic and focus on her beauty and scent rather than her political activism.

Finally, in 1863 the last rebellion of Uighur against the Qing was successful, and the people were able to establish an independent kingdom in the following year. Unfortunately, the global political sphere interfered with this independence, when the British funded a Qing invasion of Uighur territory in 1876. The British feared the expansion of the Russian empire into what was then called Eastern Turkestan and preferred to see the Chinese retake the territory. The Chinese invasion under Zho Zhung Tang succeeded, and it is at this time that the region was renamed Xinjiang, meaning "new dominion." By 1884 the Chinese had annexed Xinjiang and consolidated their military victory with a political one. Brief periods of Uighur independence in 1933 and 1944 also ended with the Chinese retaking their territory, in both cases with the assistance of the Soviet Union.

Under Chinese Communist rule, which was established in 1949, the Uighur have continued to press for independence, experiencing more than 20 antiseparatist onslaughts by the central government in Beijing since the mid-20th century. In the post-2001 climate of global fear toward many Muslim organizations, Uighur, who make up China's largest Muslim minority group, have once again experienced pressure, harassment, and repression at the hands of the Chinese government. Now, however, rather than being seen as heavy-handed by many outsiders, who used to heed the Uighur claims as those of an oppressed minority group desiring independence from a colonizing state, the Chinese are being praised for their antiterrorist work against the Uighur, whose independence claims are being framed in the language of Muslim terror.

CULTURE

The Uighur adherence to the tenets of Sunni Islam is a central characteristic of their identity in the contemporary world. This religious belief system has contributed to the foods the Uighur eat; they eschew pork in favor of lamb in most meat dishes. Religion has also affected their folktales, music, and dance. The form of Islam practiced by most Uighur is fairly liberal by world standards, with few women covering themselves with a veil, although women and men do avoid physical contact outside the home.

Certainly one of the most important aspects of Uighur culture in the contemporary world is the desire for independence, with linguistic, historical, religious, and other differences between Uighur and Han Chinese and other, more sinicized minorities continuing to be at the forefront of Uighur identity. Unfortunately for these nationalists, efforts at pursuing their independence agenda have been thwarted by a number of factors. First, one of the factors that unites Uighur communities, language, does so only with great difficulty since Uighur in different states and regions use different scripts, including Arabic, Cyrillic, and Latin, to write their language, making cross-state communication difficult. Second, differing agendas among pan-Turkists, Uighur nationalists, and secular and Islamic Uighur all hinder the advancement of a single Uighur cause. In addition, the geopolitical reality of an emerging and extremely powerful China has made all the newly independent Turkic republics of Central Asia reluctant to support nascent independence movements that include any of China's minorities for fear of disrupting lucrative trade deals or political patronage at the United Nations. The post-2001 fear of Muslim movements more generally in the world has also blocked some Uighur movements, especially those that focus on their religion as the center of Uighur identity. Finally, the Uighur movement, while rich in historical and legendary figures, has lacked a charismatic contemporary leader who might be able to bridge these differences and win support for a common agenda and strategy.

Although the original Uighur people were steppe-dwelling nomads, the Uighur have a very long urban history, being among the first Turkic peoples to settle down in the oasis towns and cities of Central Asia. Today the architecture of Turfan, Kashgar, and the regional capital of Urumqi shows the long history of both Islamic and pre-Islamic urbanization. Mosques, minarets, bazaars, and tombs dot the urban and rural landscapes of Xinjiang and remind visitors and locals alike of the long history of Uighur residence. Uighur urbanization over 1,000 years ago was accompanied by a long literary tradition, with the earliest Uighur khanate adopting the script of the literate Sogdians in order to produce texts of their own. Throughout history most Uighur literature has been on religious subjects, from the periods of their conversions to Manichaeanism, Nestorian Christianity, Buddhism, and finally, Islam. But other subjects, such as folktales, Uighur legends, and historical treatises, have also come down from Uighur scholars over the past 1,000 years or more.

This long history of urbanization could have been supported only by a subsistence system that was able to produce a large enough food surplus to allow the majority of the population to work in crafts, trade, and both the religious and secular bureaucracies. As was the case throughout history, the Uighur today live in a region with fertile, sandy soils that are irrigated by the rain and snow that fall in the mountains surrounding their region and by the desert oases around which they established their towns and cities. Wheat, rice, corn, watermelons, mulberries, pears, figs, pomegranates, walnuts, and especially grapes and cotton do very well in the Xinjiang climate. Another tradition handed down from the Uighur past is the practice of carpet weaving. Both Kashgar and Turfan are considered centers of rug production, utilizing the fine wool of Uighur sheep.

FURTHER READING

Basil Davidson. *Turkestan Alive* (London: Cape, 1957).

Hodong Kim. *Holy War in China: The Muslim Rebellion and State in Chinese Central Asia, 1864–1877* (Palo Alto, Calif.: Stanford University Press, 2004).

Colin Mackerras. *The Uighur Empire (744–840); According to the T'ang Dynastic Histories* (Canberra: Australian National University, 1968).

Svat Soucek. *A History of Inner Asia* (New York: Cambridge University Press, 2000).

Christian Tyler. *Wild West China: The Taming of Xinjiang* (New Brunswick, N.J.: Rutgers University Press, 2004).

Cuiyi Wei and Karl W. Luckert. *Uighur Stories from along the Silk Road* (Lanham, Md.: University Press of America, 1998).

Uzbekistanis: nationality (people of Uzbekistan)

The Uzbekistani nationality is made up of a majority of ethnic UZBEKS and minorities of RUSSIANS, KAZAKHS, and other Central Asians.

GEOGRAPHY

Uzbekistan is one of the five formerly Soviet Central Asian republics. It is also only one of two countries in the world, along with Liechtenstein, that is doubly landlocked, which means that it has no ocean coastline and is bordered only by countries that also have no ocean coastline. Uzbekistan is bordered by Afghanistan, Kazakhstan, Kyrgyzstan, Tajikistan, and Turkmenistan; it also has a 261-mile shoreline on the Aral Sea. Politically the country is composed of 12 administrative provinces and one autonomous republic, Qoraqalpog'iston Respublikasi; and one independent city, the capital, Tashkent.

The majority of the country's terrain is made up of plains and deserts, mostly uninhabited; most Uzbeks live in the Ferghana Valley in the east and the Zarafshan Valley in the center of the country. There are two major rivers, the Syr Darya and the Amu Darya, both of which drain into the Aral Sea. Only about 11 percent of Uzbekistan is composed of intensively cultivated valleys, and the dry climate necessitates extensive irrigation systems from these rivers. Due to over-irrigation, from the 1960s onward the Aral Sea has shrunk by about 80 percent of its original volume. Since 1991 Kazakhstan has been proactive in helping to restore the northern Aral Sea, but Uzbekistan, with its cotton-based economy, has been less able to address the twin problems of desertification and salinization.

Uzbekistan has a continental climate with warm summers and short but cold winters. The mountainous regions are much cooler in summer and get very cold in winter, with temperatures as low as -36°F.

INCEPTION AS A NATION

Between the second and first millennia B.C.E., Indo-Iranians entered what is now called Uzbekistan. These nomadic northeastern Iranian peoples eventually settled and created the complex culture of the SOGDIANS on the basis of their irrigated agricultural system. The famous Silk Road ran through this region and connected the West with China and the East. As the Silk Road emerged as an important trade route, many cities of present-day Uzbekistan became centers for trade and culture, including Bukhara and Samarkand. Peoples from India, China, Arabia, and Egypt in the east and Rome, Greece, and Byzantium in the west passed through Bukhara and Samarkand and left behind numerous architectural and other remains. By 328 B.C.E. Alexander the Great had conquered the region in his campaign for Central Asia; he also fell in love with and married Roxana of Amu Darya, a princess of the BACTRIANS.

The Uzbeks probably entered Central Asia from their homeland further north and east after 1000 C.E.; however, at that time they were culturally and linguistically indistinguishable from other TURKIC PEOPLES in the region. In addition, a great deal of intermixing between the various Turkic speakers and MONGOLS contributed to the development of all contemporary Central Asian Turkic peoples: Uzbeks, Kazakhs, KYRGYZ, and TURKMEN. With the coming of the Turkic peoples, some of the earlier Iranian population fled while others intermarried with the Turkic newcomers and contributed to the development of the contemporary Uzbek population.

In the early 13th century the Mongols invaded and conquered the region under their leader, Genghis Khan. With the death of Genghis Khan in 1227, the empire he created was nominally divided into four sections, one for each of his sons. The section granted to his son Jochi and later unified under Tokhtamysh as the Golden Horde included the region of contemporary Uzbekistan. In the meantime, one of the Mongol khans of Jochi's section, Khan Uzbek, converted to Islam in 1282. His section of the Shaybanid horde, within the larger Golden Horde, followed his conversion and came to be known as Uzbeks. However, at this time there was no separate Uzbek ethnic group; this identity emerged in the 15th century when a number of Turkic tribes split from the main Golden Horde and moved south under the leadership of Abul Khayr (1413–69). This new Uzbek people separated from the other Turkic speakers out of

UZBEKISTANIS: NATIONALITY

nation:
Republic of Uzbekistan; Uzbekistan

derivation of name:
Ozbek was the name of a 14th-century khan who surprisingly did not rule over Uzbekistan. There are debates over the name's meaning, including Turkish *uz*, meaning "free," and *bek*, meaning "completely"; or *oz*, meaning "self," and *bek*, meaning "a noble title of leadership."

government:
Republic; authoritarian presidential rule, prime minister, cabinet of ministers, and a two-house legislature called the supreme assembly

capital:
Tashkent

language:
Uzbek (the official language) 80 percent, Russian 5.5 percent, Tajik 5 percent, Kazakh 3 percent, Karakalpak 2.5 percent, Tatar 1.5 percent, other 2.5 percent

religion:
No state religion; Muslim 88 percent (mostly Sunni), Eastern Orthodox 9 percent, other 3 percent

earlier inhabitants:
Indo-Iranians

demographics:
Uzbeks descended from Turkic tribes, Mongols, Persians, and other 71 percent; Russian 8 percent; Tajiks 5 percent; Kazakhs 4 percent; Tatars 2.5 percent; Karakalpaks 2 percent

Uzbekistanis: nationality time line

B.C.E.

Second millennium Indo-Iranians migrate to Uzbekistan, which historically is known as Turkestan.

300 After the campaigns of Alexander the Great, this area emerges as a trade center with increased trade along the Silk Road.

C.E.

600 Arabs enter, and Islam replaces Buddhism as the dominant religion. The area becomes one of the centers of the Muslim world.

800 Bukhara becomes a center of Islamic culture as the Persian Samanid dynasty becomes dominant.

1200 Genghis Khan leads a Mongolian invasion of Turkestan and causes a great deal of destruction.

1282 Khan Uzbek converts to Islam.

15th century Creation of a separate Uzbek identity with the settlement of some sections of the Turkic tribes.

1860–70s Russians conquer the Islamic khanates and establish a colonial relationship with Uzbekistan. At this time cotton becomes the chief crop, and Tashkent becomes the capital of Turkestan.

1917 Following the Bolshevik revolution the Tashkent Soviet is established.

1921 Uzbekistan becomes a part of the Turkestan Autonomous Soviet Socialist Republic.

1924 Formally known as Turkestan, Uzbekistan is officially declared under the control of the Soviet Union.

1930 The Uzbek capital moves from Samarkand to Tashkent.

1944 Joseph Stalin deports 160,000 Meskhetian Turks from Georgia to Uzbekistan.

1980 Mikhail Gorbachev establishes glasnost, which allows for increased Islamic acceptance.

1989 Islam Karimov becomes the leader of the Uzbek Communist Party.

1990 Soviet control is beginning to wane in Uzbekistan as Uzbek laws are declared superior to Soviet laws.

1991 December: Uzbekistan joins the other Central Asian Republics in the Commonwealth of Independent States, and the Soviet Union is officially dismantled. Uzbekistan becomes independent, and Islam Karimov becomes the directly elected president. There is little opposition to Karimov's party, and what little there is is quickly suppressed.

1992 A new constitution is adopted.

2001 The United States sets up air bases in Uzbekistan for use against Afghanistan.

2002 President Karimov wins support for extending the presidential term from five to seven years.

A long-standing border dispute between Uzbekistan and Kazakhstan is resolved.

2003 Prime Minister Otkir Sultanov is removed from office due to the worst cotton harvest in the country's history.

2005 Several killings occur in the eastern city of Andijan, which spark civil unrest.

2007 The International Islamic Educational, Scientific, and Cultural Organization names Tashkent a world capital of Islamic culture.

a desire to abandon nomadic pastoralism and settle down to an agricultural life on the prosperous trade route of Central Asia. For many generations Russian sources distinguished between settled agricultural peoples in the region of Uzbekistan, calling them Sarts, and more nomadic peoples who remained in the north. It was only after 1924 that the name Sart was abandoned in favor of that preferred by the people themselves, Uzbek.

The tomb of Isma'il Ibn Ahmad, a Samanid ruler who extended the dynasty's reign throughout Transoxiana and was buried in Bukhara upon his death in 907 C.E. *(Art Resource/Bridgeman-Giraudon)*

The empire established by Khayr's descendants, known as the Uzbek khanate or Shaybanid dynasty, continued to rule the region until the end of the 16th century. During the zenith of Uzbek power under Abdullah Khan, many of the Iranian-speaking inhabitants of the region began to use the Uzbek language and to consider themselves Uzbeks rather than Persians or Iranians. Despite the creation of these new Uzbeks, the Uzbek khanate was unable to maintain its political hold on Transoxiana beyond the death of Abdul Mumin in 1655 when various Persian and Turkic peoples each rose to prominence and then rapidly fell away again.

Three other statelike structures established by Uzbeks in various regions of Central Asia are the Bukhara, Khiva, and Kokand khanates, which developed largely from the splintering of the previous Uzbek khanate. All three khanates were eventually conquered and absorbed by the Russian Empire during its period of eastern expansion in the 19th century; Bukhara fell in 1868, Khiva in 1873, and Kokand in 1876. Following the Russian Revolution in 1917, Uzbekistan was incorporated into the Turkestan Autonomous Soviet Socialist Republic in 1918. However, the Russians' early experience with trying to incorporate their Turkic subjects into the larger Soviet state caused them to rethink their initial unification process. Pan-Islamic and pan-Turkic sentiments led to a number of uprisings, the most famous being the Basmachi Revolts in Kazakhstan (1916–31). As a result, in 1924 Uzbekistan and the other Central Asian republics were created to coincide as much as possible with the ethnic divisions in greater Turkestan.

While under Soviet control, Uzbekistan became largely a cotton exporter based on monocropping techniques in the country's plains, using developed irrigation systems, chemical fertilizers, and pesticides. These methods had extremely destructive consequences for the water systems and the environment. Since Uzbekistan's independence in 1991, much effort has been focused on relaxing the pressures on the environment and eliminating dependence on cotton, but in a poor country these efforts have not been taken far enough.

Uzbekistan declared its independence from Soviet control on September 1, 1991, after a failed coup against Soviet leader Mikhail Gorbachev; President Islam Karimov became the country's first independent leader. Karimov had been a representative of the Communist Party as its first secretary of Uzbekistan; however, under his presidency communism has not become a central theme of Uzbek nationhood. Instead, the government is often referred to in academic and political circles outside the country as a kleptocracy, government by corruption and theft. Sixty percent of the population continues to live and work on the large, state-run farms begun during the period of collectivization in the 1920s, and while the government claims to support private ownership and production, individual Uzbek citizens who have attempted to pursue this course have been murdered, jailed, and beaten up. Freedom of speech, the press, and religion have also been denied, with library books still having pages ripped out of them by official censors and Islamic groups being persecuted by government agencies afraid of fundamentalism. This latter abuse has won favor for Uzbekistan's autocratic president among top U.S. government officials and agencies but not with many Uzbek citizens, some of whom rioted in reaction to their government's jailing of leading Islamic and business leaders in Andijan in the Ferghana Valley in 2005. Several outside human rights groups estimate that at least 6,000 Uzbeks are currently in prison for political or religious offenses; another 6,000 or so are living as refugees in nearby Kyrgyzstan.

CULTURAL IDENTITY

As is the case throughout the former Soviet countries of Eastern Europe and Central Asia, the new government of Uzbekistan has emphasized trying to create a national identity to accompany the country's status as an independent state. Three of the most important areas focused on have been the standardization and cleansing of the Uzbek language, the creation of "traditional" neighborhoods and holidays, and rewriting Uzbek history to highlight periods of local and national independence. For example, even during the Soviet era the most important community to which each family and individual owed allegiance was the *malhalla,* or neighborhood. The postsocialist government has continued to highlight this important social unit and has created festivals to celebrate these ties created by geographic space. It has been particularly important for the large Tajik minority that territory has become so important to Uzbekistani identity because the Tajiks speak an Iranian language rather than a Turkic one, and they might otherwise have been seen as alien to the newly forming nation.

In addition to this importance of neighborhood communities, the Uzbek language is also vitally important to the new state's cultural identity, largely in opposition to the Russian language. During the 70 years of Soviet domination in Uzbekistan, large numbers of Russian immigrants moved into the republic to take advantage of the booming cotton economy; most did not learn the local language or lose their identification as Russians. In the post-Soviet world the mandatory teaching of Russian in schools has been replaced by the mandatory use of Uzbek, and those who refuse to learn the language are at a clear disadvantage in terms of education and employment. This is the case with regard to Uzbek history as well; of 850 possible history questions posed to Uzbek university students, only one concerns the entire 70-year Soviet period.

This focus on Uzbek language and culture at the national level is accompanied at the local level with many traditional Islamic and Uzbek customs that have remained central to the lives of numerous people. Traditional clothing, in the form of long robes and boots, is often worn by men; for women, traditional clothing includes brightly colored silk dresses and scarves. Many traditions and customs for preparing, serving, and eating Uzbek meals also remain. Important mealtime guests are always seated away from the main entrance, usually at a low sitting table or on the floor. Men sit with their legs crossed and women with their legs to the side. The table should be covered by a *dusterhorn,* or tablecloth, and unclean items may not be placed on or passed over it. Meals may consist of flat, round bread; nuts; dried or fresh fruits; salads; and various meat dishes, including mutton. As Muslims, the majority of Uzbeks do not eat pork.

See also Russians, Asians; Kazakhstanis: nationality.

FURTHER READING

Edward A. Allworth. *The Modern Uzbeks: From the Fourteenth Century to the Present: A Cultural History* (Stanford, Calif.: Hoover Institution Press, 1990).

Zahir al-Din Babur, *Baburnama: Memoirs of Babur,* ed. and trans. Wheeler M. Thackston (New York: Oxford University Press, 1996).

Tom Bissell. *Chasing the Sea: Being a Narrative of a Journey through Uzbekistan, Including Descriptions of Life Therein, Culminating with an Arrival at the Aral Sea, the World's Worst Man-Made Ecological Catastrophe, in One Volume* (New York: Pantheon Books, 2003).

Mary Masayo Doi. *Gesture, Gender, Nation: Dance and Social Change in Uzbekistan* (Westport, Conn.: Greenwood Press, 2002).

Johannes Kalter and Margareta Pavaloi, eds. *Uzbekistan: Heirs to the Silk Road* (New York: Thames and Hudson, 1997).

Neil Melvin. *Uzbekistan: Transition to Authoritarianism on the Silk Road* (Amsterdam: Harwood Academic Publishers, 2000).

Uzbeks (Ozbegs, Ozbeks, Sarts, Taze)

The Uzbeks are a Turkic-speaking people who reside in the independent country of Uzbekistan as well as in Afghanistan, China, and all the other Central Asian Republics. They are the largest group of Turkic-speaking people in the world after the Turks of Turkey as well as the first of the Central Asian Turkic peoples to have settled down after their nomadic past.

GEOGRAPHY

The country of Uzbekistan is located in Central Asia and is bounded by Kazakhstan in the north and west, Kyrgyzstan and Tajikistan in the east, and Afghanistan and Turkmenistan in the south. The geography of Uzbekistan ranges from the high peaks of the Tien Shan range in the east to the low elevations of the Ust Urt Plateau and Aral Sea region in the west. The country's central region is largely desert, known as the Qizil Qum or Red Sand region. Irrigation is used throughout this arid

UZBEKS

location:
Uzbekistan, the Xinjiang Province of China, Afghanistan, Tajikstan, Kyrgyzstan, Turkmenistan, Kazakhstan, and Russia

time period:
15th century to the present

ancestry:
Turkic, Mongolian, and Persian

language:
Uzbek, a Turkic language from the Karluk or Chagatai branch, most closely related to Uighur

Uzbeks time line

C.E.

1000 Approximate date that the Turkic forebearers of the Uzbeks entered Central Asia for the first time.

early 13th century The Mongols under Genghis Khan conquer the region of contemporary Uzbekistan and its Iranian-speaking inhabitants.

1227 Genghis Khan dies, and his empire is divided into four parts. The two sons of his son Jochi, Batu and Orda, split the western section, which includes land that becomes Uzbekistan.

1282 Khan Uzbek converts to Islam.

mid-15th century The Uzbeks begin to split from other Turkic speakers under Abul Khayr.

1598 The Uzbek khanate's strongest leader, Abdullah Khan, dies, weakening the khanate permanently.

16th century Establishment of the khanates of Bukhara, Khiva, and Kokand by Uzbek emirs and khans fleeing the Uzbek khanate.

1655 The Uzbek khanate disintegrates permanently.

1868 The Bukhara khanate becomes a semi-independent vassal of Russia.

1873 The Khiva khanate becomes a semi-independent vassal of Russia.

1876 The Kokand khanate becomes a semi-independent vassal of Russia.

1917 All three Uzbek khanates, Bukhara, Khiva, and Kokand, lose their independence completely during the Russian Revolution.

1920s Thousands of Uzbeks flee their country in reaction to Soviet collectivization policies; most go south to Afghanistan to join an already-flourishing Uzbek agricultural community in the north of the country.

(For a continuation of this time line, *see* UZBEKISTANIS: NATIONALITY.)

region, but the most productive areas of the country are the Ferghana and Zarafshan Valleys, in the far east and center of the country, respectively.

Two major rivers run east-to-west through Uzbekistan: the Syr Darya, which was known as the Jaxartes in ancient times, and the Amu Darya, known as the Oxus. Both rivers drain into the Aral Sea, which is shared by Uzbekistan and Kazakhstan. Due to over-irrigation, from the 1960s onward the Aral has shrunk by about 80 percent of its original volume. Since 1991 Kazakhstan has been quite proactive in helping to restore the northern Aral Sea, but Uzbekistan, with its cotton-based economy, has been less able to address the twin problems of desertification and salinization.

Uzbekistan has a continental climate with warm summers and short but cold winters. The mountainous regions are much cooler in summer and very cold in winter, with temperatures as low as -36°F.

ORIGINS

The TURKIC PEOPLES were just one of many seminomadic groups living on the steppes northwest of China prior to the sixth century. Probably the only trait that distinguished them from the XIONGNU, XIANBEI, MONGOLS, and other steppe dwellers was their language. Like these others, they would have relied primarily on their herds for subsistence, resided in felt tents, and moved about as they needed grass and water. They practiced a shamanistic religion and placed great value on their horses.

The Uzbeks probably entered Central Asia from their homeland further north and east after 1000 C.E. However, they remained culturally and linguistically almost indistinguishable from other Turkic tribes in the region. In addition, a great deal of intermixing between the various Turkic and Mongol tribes contributed to the development of all contemporary Central Asian Turkic peoples: Uzbeks, KAZAKHS, KYRGYZ, and TURKMEN. Finally, the peoples who had been living in the region of Uzbekistan before the arrival of the Turkic peoples were largely Iranian speakers, the descendants of the waves of Indo-Iranians who had moved off the steppe in the millennia before the common era. They had established the long-lasting caravan settlements of Samarkand, Ferghana, Bukhara, among others, during the period of the SOGDIANS. With the coming of the Turkic peoples, some Iranians fled while others intermarried with the Turkic peoples and contributed to the development of the contemporary Uzbek population.

HISTORY

The Turkic history of Central Asia in general, and the Uzbek people more specifically, begins with the incorporation of the region into the Mongol Empire of Genghis Khan in the 13th century. The Mongol armies actually contained large numbers of other steppe dwellers in addition to Mongols, especially Turkic speakers who were linguistically and culturally related to the Mongols. It was at this time that the Iranians began to flee or be incorporated into the more powerful Mongol political structures.

With the death of Genghis Khan in 1227, the empire he created was nominally divided into four sections, one for each of his sons. The section granted to his son Jochi and later unified under Tokhtamysh as the Golden Horde included the region of contemporary Uzbekistan. In the meantime, one of the Mongol khans of Jochi's section, Khan Uzbek, converted to Islam in 1282. His section of the Shaybanid horde, within the larger Golden Horde, followed his conversion and came to be known as Uzbeks. However, at this time there was no separate Uzbek ethnic group; this identity emerged in the 15th century when a number of Turkic tribes split from the main Golden Horde and moved south under the leadership of Abul Khayr (1413–69). This new Uzbek people separated from the other Turkic speakers out of a desire to abandon nomadic pastoralism and settle down to an agricultural life on the prosperous trade routes of Central Asia. For many generations Russian sources distinguished between settled agricultural peoples in the region of Uzbekistan, calling them Sarts, and more nomadic peoples who remained in the north. It was only after 1924 when the name Sart was abandoned in favor of that preferred by the people themselves, Uzbek.

Under Abul Khayr's son Muhammad Shaybani Khan (1451–1510), the Uzbeks captured the region of Samarkand, which had previously been part of the empire of Timur Leng (Tamerlane). They also repelled Babur, founder of the Indian Mughal Empire, and subjugated all of the territory known as Transoxiana, north of the Oxus River or Amu Darya. The empire established by Khayr's descendants, known either as the Uzbek khanate or Shaybanid dynasty, continued to rule the region until the end of the 16th century. During the zenith of Uzbek power under Abdullah Khan, many of the Iranian-speaking inhabitants of the region began to use the Uzbek language and to consider themselves Uzbeks rather than Persians or Iranians. Despite the creation of these new Uzbeks, the Uzbek khanate was not able to maintain its political hold on Transoxiana beyond the death of Abdul Mumin in 1655, when various Persian and Turkic peoples each rose to prominence and then fell away again very rapidly.

Three other statelike structures established by Uzbeks in various regions of Central Asia were the Bukhara, Khiva, and Kokand khanates, which developed largely from the splintering of the previous Uzbek khanate. Bukhara, established as an Uzbek khanate in the 16th century, was probably the most famous of the three khanates because of the vast wealth of its rulers, compared to the destitution of its people, and the strength of the Muslim clergy, who imposed a very strict interpretation of sharia law on the people. The death penalty was enforced by throwing condemned prisoners from the minaret of the Kalian Mosque, the tallest

building in the city. The leading citizens' wealth was derived largely from renting land to peasants, from trade, and from denying public salaries to all civil servants, who received money for services rendered from the poor peasants and traders they served. This poverty was exacerbated by drought caused by Russian irrigation using the Zarafshan River. Like Samarkand before it, Bukhara succumbed to superior Russian military and political strength and was incorporated into the czar's empire as a semi-independent vassal in 1868.

Khiva was also established in the 16th century as an Uzbek Islamic khanate in the territory of the former Khwarezmian state, currently divided between Uzbekistan and Turkmenistan. Khiva was largely an agricultural society with an economy based on irrigated agriculture, animal husbandry, and a bit of trade. Like Bukhara, the city of Khiva is known for its architecture, displaying ornate examples of late feudal Muslim architecture in its madrassas or Islamic schools and other public buildings. Khiva was taken over by the Russians in 1873.

The khanate of Kokand was the third Uzbek state established in Central Asia from a breakaway portion of the earlier Uzbek khanate. In 1709 Shahrukh, an emir in the Shaybanid line, and others from the Minglar tribe of Uzbeks set up their own independent emirate in the Ferghana Valley of eastern Uzbekistan. At the height of the Kokand khanate it also incorporated territory in Kazakhstan, Tajikistan, and Kyrgyzstan. Like Bukhara and Khiva, Kokand was absorbed by the Russians as a semi-independent vassal in 1876 and was dismantled completely during the Russian Revolution of 1917.

In conjunction with the other regions of Turkic Russia, Uzbekistan was incorporated into the Turkestan Autonomous Soviet Socialist Republic in 1918; Bukhara and Khiva became separate people's republics two years later. The Russians' early experience with incorporating their Turkic subjects into the larger Soviet state, however, caused them to rethink their initial unification process. Pan-Islamic and pan-Turkic sentiments led to a number of uprisings, the most famous being the Basmachi Revolts in Kazakhstan. As a result, in 1924 Uzbekistan and all the other Central Asian republics were created to coincide as much as possible with the ethnic divisions in greater Turkestan. During the ensuing chaos and movement of people, at least half a million Uzbeks migrated to Afghanistan to escape sovietization, joining Uzbeks who had been there since the 16th century and forming the backbone of the large Uzbek population in that country today. They were later joined by a few Uzbeks who fled the USSR during the upheavals caused by World War II.

The history of the Uzbeks under the Soviet Union resembles that of the other Central Asian peoples. The predominantly Russian leadership of the USSR tried to eliminate local languages, customs, religions, and ways of life in favor of the Russian language, collectivized farming, and urban industrialism. In Uzbekistan, the Soviets were fairly successful in the second of these goals but much less so in their language and industrialization policies. By the 1980s Uzbeks were among the least urbanized people in the USSR, with only about 25 percent of the population living in cities and of those a great majority were non-Uzbeks and russified Uzbeks who had given up their own language and culture. The Uzbeks also emerged as the largest Central Asian population and the third-largest nationality group in the USSR behind Russians and Ukrainians, due mostly to their high fertility rate and the lack of mobility outside the Uzbek SSR caused by lack of education.

Since the end of the Soviet era, Uzbeks in their own country have experienced few significant changes. The economy is still driven by a central command structure that continually overestimates production and hides the truth in everything, from gross domestic product (GDP) and interest rates to unemployment and population growth, or more accurately, reduction. The government is often referred to in academic and political circles outside the country as a kleptocracy, government by corruption and theft. Sixty percent of the population continues to live and work on the large, state-run farms begun during the period of collectivization in the 1920s, and while the government claims to support private ownership and production, individual Uzbeks who have attempted to pursue this course have been murdered, jailed, and beaten up. Freedom of speech, the press, and religion are persecuted by government agencies afraid of fundamentalism; library books still have pages ripped out of them, and many Islamic groups have been harassed or persecuted. This latter abuse has won favor for Uzbekistan's autocratic president, Islam Karimov, among top U.S. government officials and agencies, but not with many Uzbek citizens, some of whom rioted in reaction to their government's jailing of leading Islamic and business leaders in Andijan in the Ferghana

Valley in 2005. Several outside human rights groups estimate that at least 6,000 Uzbeks are currently in prison for political or religious offenses, and as many as another 6,000 are living as refugees in nearby Kyrgyzstan.

Outside Uzbekistan

The Afghanistani Uzbeks make up about 9 percent of that country's diverse population and reside primarily in the agricultural belt in the country's north. Segments of the population have been there for more than 500 years, having migrated with other Turkic speakers in the 16th century, while others entered Afghanistan from the USSR in the 1920s. Due to the strength of their agricultural- and textile-based economy, Afghanistani Uzbeks had political advantages that other minorities in the country were denied. They served beside the dominant PASHTUNS in the government and were less harshly treated during the nationalization push of Abdur Rahman in the late 19th century.

During the 20th century these Uzbeks have also been spared some of the turmoil experienced by most of the rest of the country. This was the case because they have been able to unify and remain relatively cohesive behind just one political party, the National Islamic Front. In addition, for most of the past 30 years this party has been ruled by just one person, General Abdul Rashid Dostam. Under Dostam, the Uzbeks supported the country's Communist leadership from 1979 to 1992. Upon withdrawing his support in 1992, Dostam briefly allied the Uzbeks with the country's Tajik president, Burhanuddin Rabbani, but soon withdrew to run the northern Uzbek region essentially on his own. He again lined up behind Rabbani in 1995 when the Taliban threatened his autocratic but relatively peaceful rule in the country's north but did not suffer for it upon the Taliban's victory. In 2003 Dostam again served in the country's central government as part of the armed forces' chief of staff, which he continues to do to this day. Uzbeks have tried to pressure the government to give them a greater say and to grant their language equal rights with the dominant Pashto and Dari languages, but they have not engaged in any antigovernment protests since the fall of the Taliban. There has been some violence between Uzbeks and TAJIKS and Uzbeks and Pashtuns.

Uzbeks also constitute one of China's recognized 55 national minorities, where a small number reside in city of Yining and the other cities of Xinjiang Province. Many entered the country in the 17th century as travelers and traders on the Silk Road. Today they remain a largely urban population who work as craftsmen, especially with silk; they are also teachers and other professionals. As Muslims they are culturally associated with China's large UIGHUR population, a language many Chinese Uzbeks speak; many also speak HAN Chinese.

CULTURE

Uzbek culture resembles that of the Iranian-speaking Tajiks more than that of the other Turkic Central Asian peoples because of the large number of urban Iranians who lived in Transoxiana prior to the incorporation of the region into the Mongol and Turkic empires. Uzbeks physically look more like Tajiks than other Turkic Central Asians and share their settled way of life. In addition to this indigenous Iranian component of Uzbek society, there were also social and cultural features added by the Turkic peoples who entered with the Mongols in the 13th century and the Shaybanid Uzbeks of the Uzbek khanate, who came south in the mid-15th century. The creation of a common Uzbek identity out of these disparate communities, in addition to the blending of the long-standing residents whom the Russians labeled as Sarts and those who remained nomadic longer, whom the Russians called Taze or pure Uzbeks, is really a phenomenon of the past century and a half. Nonetheless, some Uzbeks can still name their family's tribal affiliation from the past.

Economy and Society

The Uzbek economy has been dominated by agricultural products since the settling of the Uzbeks in the mid-15th century, and the most important of these products by far is cotton. In addition, grapes, melons, rice, tea, and some wheat are also grown; silk is harvested; and some Uzbek families continue to include animal husbandry as part of their farming activities. From the mid-15th century until the period of Soviet collectivization in the 1920s, much of this farming was done by peasants working the land of wealthy Uzbek families. Peasants lived in villages, which served as their primary form of association outside the extended family, because unlike many Kazakhs and Kyrgyz, the Uzbeks did not maintain most of their tribal, clan, or even lineage ties beyond the 16th or 17th century.

The major push for collectivization in Uzbekistan took place in the early 1930s when more than 40,000 rich Uzbeks lost their land-holdings. By 1937 a full 99 percent of the land had been collectivized into large agribusinesses controlled by the state and worked by the large rural population. This change in economic structure caused a number of corresponding social changes, with the importance of noble birth diminishing and the ability to work long hours on both collectivized farms and individually held garden plots increasing. Villages also lost their central social feature as families turned against each other to compete for the few economic and social resources provided by the state. At the same time, many Uzbeks' lives improved under Soviet domination since the large, successful cotton collectives paid relatively well and household garden plots provided both luxury food items and an extra income unavailable to many in the USSR, especially in cities.

Despite the lack of primacy in Uzbek kinship ties throughout the 20th century, remnants of this important organizing principle did survive and were even strengthened by collectivization. For example, many of the collective farms that worked in Uzbekistan were organized by different *elats,* or clan subdivisions, and run by the same council of elders that would have dominated these clan structures in the past. In the 20th century some rural Uzbeks also allowed their parents to assist them in finding a suitable marriage partner from an appropriate clan or tribe.

Despite the relative lack of importance of lineage, clan, and tribal affiliations among the Uzbeks, the patriarchal extended family remained the center of most people's lives prior to the 20th century, at least outside the cities. Each household was headed by the oldest male, who delegated work and responsibility to all the sons, nephews, grandsons, and even employees who resided in the house. Women lived much more secluded lives than their nomadic counterparts among the other Turkic Central Asians, being relegated to the house and courtyard most of the time and wearing a veil when leaving this private space. Polygyny, having more than one wife, was also much more common among the sedentary Uzbeks than the nomadic Turkic peoples, even surviving into the later half of the 20th century despite being illegal within the USSR.

Most Uzbeks even today remain rural dwellers; about 63 percent of Uzbekistan's population is rural. Uzbekistan also contains most of the oldest and historically significant urban settlements in Central Asia. The cities of Samarkand and Bukhara, which were important

This Mazar, or tomb, is located on the mountain in Shakh-i Zindeh, near Samarkand, and has attracted sufis and other Muslim worshippers for many hundreds of years. *(LOC/Sergei Mikhailovich Prokudin-Gorskii Collection)*

as long ago as the first Persian Empire in the sixth century B.C.E., are located in Uzbekistan, as are Khiva, Kokond, and Urgench. Many famous people from Central Asian history were also born in the region of contemporary Uzbekistan, including Babur and Timur Leng (Tamerlane), giving contemporary Uzbeks cause to claim them as their ancestors. These historic connections in addition to the strength of their educational institutions, both secular and Islamic, led many Central Asians to look to the Uzbeks as the leaders of all of Turkic Central Asia for much of the 20th century.

Religion

The Uzbeks are overwhelmingly Sunni Muslims and have been for much longer than most other Turkic speakers in Central Asia: They converted in 1282. Some Uzbeks see themselves as superior to the Kazakhs and Kyrgyz because of their long Muslim history and their strength of belief in the religion. They practice a much more orthodox version of Islam, with fewer pre-Islamic or folk elements than their Kazakh and Kyrgyz neighbors, though this is not to say that there are no such elements in their religion. Divination, the reading of information from tea leaves or animal entrails, and the use of blessed amulets to ward off the evil eye continued among Uzbeks well into the 20th century. Another important aspect of Uzbek Islam is the centrality of Sufism. Two important Sufi brotherhoods were founded in the cities of what is today Uzbekistan: Kubrawiya, founded in Khiva by Najmuddin al-Kubra in the 12th century, and Naqshbandiya, founded in Bukhara by Bahauddin Naqshband in the 14th century. Having access to the teaching and religious rites performed by Sufis has meant that even today *mazars,* or shrines associated with saints and holy men, are maintained by Sufis throughout the country and visited by Uzbeks seeking religious guidance.

During the Soviet era, religion in Uzbekistan diminished somewhat under the strain of official atheism and religious persecution at the state level. However, three central religious rites of passage continued to be undertaken by even Communist Party members: circumcision of young boys and Muslim-officiated weddings and funerals. Many also continued to celebrate Eid al-Fatr, the party and feast that follow the end of the fasting month of Ramadan, even though few actually engaged in the fasting itself. Since Uzbekistan's independence in 1991, participation in Islamic events and weekly services has increased somewhat, but there is little support for fundamentalism.

See also AFGHANISTANIS: NATIONALITY; MANCHUS; RUSSIANS, ASIAN; RUSSIANS: NATIONALITY; UZBEKISTANIS: NATIONALITY.

FURTHER READING

Edward A. Allworth. *The Modern Uzbeks: From the 14th Century to the Present: A Cultural History* (Palo Alto, Calif.: Hoover Institution Press, 1990).

Johannes Kalter and Margareta Pavaloi, eds. *Uzbekistan: Heirs to the Silk Road* (New York: Thames and Hudson, 1997).

Islam Karimov. *Uzbekistan on the Threshold of the Twenty-First Century: Challenges to Stability and Progress* (New York: St. Martin's Press, 1998).

Bakhtiyar A. Nazarov and Denis Sinor, eds. *Essays on Uzbek History, Culture, and Language* (Bloomington: Indiana University, Research Institute for Inner Asian Studies, 1993).

V

Va (A va, Benren, Da ka va, Ka va, La, Le va, Pa rauk, Vang, Vo, Vu, Wa, Xiao ka va)
The Va are one of China's 55 recognized national minority groups. They live in the country's southwest region as well as across the border in northern Myanmar. The Va, or Wa as they are called in Myanmar, do not have official recognition in Myanmar through the creation of a state of their own akin to the SHANS or KAREN; however, the United Wa State Army (UWSA) does sometimes cooperate with the government's army in crackdowns against Shan and other antigovernment forces. At other times, however, the UWSA has not allowed government soldiers onto its land, and the two have engaged militarily. Both armies have been linked with opium production and trafficking in recent decades, despite promises to the United Nations by UWSA leaders that these activities would cease by 2005.

The traditional Va homeland on both sides of the China-Myanmar border is called A Wa Shan and refers to the region's mountains; their names for themselves—Va, Pa rauk, and A va— all mean "people of the mountain." The highest peak in the region reaches about 9,200 feet above sea level and sits between the Lancang and Salween Rivers. The first reference to this region as A Wa Shan was in about 109 B.C.E., during the HAN dynasty when it was inhabited by speakers of a language from which both Wa and DE'ANG descended. By the seventh century C.E. and the Tang dynasty, the Va had become a distinct ethnolinguistic group but subordinate to the

Nanzhao kingdom of the DAI. At this time the Va remained essentially hunters and gatherers, but between the 13th and 18th centuries they adopted settled agriculture, established permanent villages, and became more politically unified. In 1933 the Va came together to repel the British, who had entered Yunnan Province as part of their overall strategy to colonize China and control its import and export markets, in an event known as the Banhong Incident.

Today the Va continue to work largely as agriculturalists. They maintain a few rice paddies in the lower elevations on the edges of their homeland where they grow rice for sale in both family- and village-owned fields. In the higher elevations they use a combination of swidden, or slash-and-burn, and more permanent agriculture to grow subsistence crops such as wheat, sweet potatoes, and vegetables. Many families also keep an ox, water buffalo, chickens, or other animals. These animals live underneath the families' bamboo houses, which are elevated by four to six feet.

Va villages tend to exist in the higher elevations in their region and are between 100 and 400 families in size. Each village contains individuals from many patrilineal clans, who must marry outside their own groups and, prior to 1949, recognized the authority of their own chiefs. Today clan chiefs continue to exist for ritual purposes but in some regions clan chiefs are also state bureaucrats who legitimate their position through both traditional kinship and modern Communist Party methods. Clan members participate in a variety of ancestral and agricultural rituals each year, banned during the 1960s and 1970s but reintroduced in the 1980s and thriving today. They also support one another through paying debts and other financial assistance, forming political and economic networks, and maintaining clan honor. Through a system of teknonymy, where each man's name contains segments of his father's, father's father's, and so on, clans can trace their heritage back more than 30 generations.

Vanuatuans: nationality (ni-Vanuatu, people of Vanuatu)

Vanuatu is a Melanesian state in the South Pacific. Known as the New Hebrides prior to independence in 1980, Vanuatu had the unique historic experience of being colonized by Britain and France at the same time, a situation known as the Condominium, or locally as Pandemonium, for the chaos it caused.

GEOGRAPHY

Vanuatu's 83 islands are located in a Y-shaped pattern in the South Pacific, between the Solomon Islands and New Caledonia. Two of the islands, Matthew and Hunter, are also claimed by New Caledonia, a French overseas department, and only 65 of them are inhabited. Together the islands constitute just 8,600 square miles, with only four islands that are larger than 500 square miles: Espiritu Santo, Malakula, Efate, and Erromango.

Most of the islands are volcanic, and there is still an active volcano on the island of Tanna; there are other volcanoes that are currently below the waterline. A few of the islands are also made of coral. The highest point on the islands is Mount Tabwemasana, at 6,158 feet above sea level, and the lowest is at sea level at the shoreline. Most of the islands rise quickly from the deep seabed so that there are few reefs or other shallow areas in the region, limiting the fish stocks of most species.

Vanuatuans: nationality time line

B.C.E.

2000 Approximate date on which the first Melanesians settled in Vanuatu, having sailed from the Solomon Islands.

C.E.

1606 Portuguese sailor Pedro Fernández de Quirós is the first European to see the islands.

1768 The French explorer Louis Antoine de Bougainville arrives on the islands but does not name them.

1774 Captain James Cook names the islands the New Hebrides, and European colonization begins.

1887 Britain and France agree to a joint naval commission of the New Hebrides.

1906 Britain and France create the "Condominium," a unique form of colonialism in which both countries maintain an official administration and institutions on the islands.

1936 The John Frum movement begins on the island of Tanna.

1942 The U.S. Navy builds bases on Efate and Espiritu Santo as part of the war in the Pacific during World War II.

1975 First elections in the New Hebrides, for municipal government seats.

1979 Elections bring Walter Lini's pro-independence Vanuaaku Pati to power.

1980 Papua New Guinea sends peacekeeping forces to Espiritu Santo, Vanuatu's largest island, to quell a revolt by Jimmy Stevens's Nagriamel movement.

Vanuatu achieves independence from British and French colonizers.

1991 Jimmy Stevens is released from prison after serving 11 years of his 15-year sentence.

2005 One hundred people from a village on the island of Tegua must be evacuated as a result of rising sea levels. Some scientists point to this incident as the first evacuation to result from global warming.

In 1995 the John Frum movement was still going strong; these members on Tanna Island were celebrating the possibility of their savior's arrival with traditional dancing and other events. *(ONASIA/Thierry Falise)*

INCEPTION AS A NATION

Vanuatu was first visited by the Portuguese at the beginning of the 17th century and then by the French in 1768 but was not named or colonized until Captain James Cook arrived in 1774; he called the islands the New Hebrides. For the next 206 years, Britain and France joined forces to create the unique colonial situation called the Condominium, in which both countries maintained administrative control, educational, health, and missionary institutions and economic interests in the islands. The first period of colonialism was the most difficult for the local population, many of whom were moved off the islands as forced labor in a process known as blackbirding. Later the New Hebrides themselves provided the colonizers with copra and other coconut products.

The 1940s brought still more change to the New Hebrides when the United States set up two naval bases on the islands of Espiritu Santo and Efate to aid in the war effort in the Pacific. At about the same time, an anticolonial religious movement, the John Frum cargo cult, emerged on the island of Tanna. The name may come from the words of many U.S. soldiers who introduced themselves as "John from America." John Frum followers believe that the godlike figure of John Frum is coming to Vanuatu on February 15 of an undesignated year and bringing them all the material wealth that has been denied to them by the colonizers, Americans, and other outsiders. In 1941 John Frum believers got rid of all their money and belongings, quit their associations with schools, plantations, and other colonial infrastructure, and moved inland to celebrate and to await the arrival of John Frum with their cargo. His failure to arrive did not deter Frum believers, who established their own army in 1957 and then their own political party, and they continue to celebrate his possible return every February.

In the 1970s Frum believers participated in the political movements that rocked the rest of the New Hebrides as local politicians and the British and French prepared for national independence. Frum believers opposed the creation of an independent Vanuatu as a nation-state because they feared it would enforce westernization and Christianity over local beliefs and culture. They allied themselves with Nagriamel, another antimodernist movement on primarily Francophone Espiritu Santo but led by Anglophone Jimmy Stevens. Nagriamel was pushing for native land rights; a few years later the group took on more pro-French overtones. Both of these nativist movements were opposed by the church-based Anglophone Vanuaaku Pati (VP),

Jimmy Stevens

Jimmy Stevens was a nationalist and politician in Vanuatu, formerly known as the New Hebrides. Prior to European settlement, the Vanuatu archipelago was inhabited by Melanesian people, but by the late 1800s, England and France had both laid claim to the nation. In 1906 the two countries agreed to a shared management of Vanuatu, which they named the New Hebrides.

Born between 1910 and 1920, Jimmy Stevens, who was of European, Polynesian, and Melanesian descent, protested the colonization of his own home island of Espiritu Santo, and in 1980 he personally declared the island's independence, renaming it the State of Vemerana and giving himself the title of prime minister. The Republic of Vanuatu was granted independence the following month, and Prime Minister Walter Lini dispatched Papua New Guinean troops to Espiritu Santo to suppress the uprising. An American libertarian group known as the Phoenix Foundation offered Stevens and the Nagriamel movement that he headed $250,000 in support. Jimmy Stevens died on February 28, 1994, leaving behind approximately 50 children whom he had fathered with 23 wives.

Our Land Party, fronted by Father Walter Lini, which was pushing for westernization and political independence. Despite the obvious overlaps in their goals, Nagriamel and the VP regarded each other with suspicion and with their sights set primarily on their differences.

In November 1979 the New Hebrides held elections for the representative assembly, and Lini's VP took 62 percent of the vote and 26 of the 39 seats. Very soon after the election the pro-independence assembly voted to set July 30, 1980, as the date for complete independence. This proposal was immediately accepted by the British, but the French, who had been opposing independence for at least a decade, refused to move on it until May. At about the same time, Nagriamel's supporters took to the streets of Luganville on Espiritu Santo, attacking the British compound and declaring Jimmy Stevens president of the newly formed, secessionist "Republic of Vemerana." No French property was touched during the uprising, and neither Britain nor France showed any sign of intervening to assist the democratically elected government. At Lini's behest, the uprising was finally put down with the assistance of troops from Papua New Guinea, the only country in the region willing to assist the almost-independent Vanuatu. Stevens was sentenced to a 15-year prison term; he served 11 years and then was released in 1991 upon the payment of 20 pigs.

Vanuatu did achieve its independence on the scheduled date of July 30, 1980, joining the United Nations a year later and the nonaligned movement in 1983. Since that date the country has seen a growth in population and in both tourism and banking revenues. In addition, at least according to some scientists, the country's low-lying islands also stand to be the first to disappear with the rising seas predicted by global warming, with one village on the island of Tegua having already been evacuated to escape rising sea levels.

CULTURAL IDENTITY

The most important concept utilized by all political parties in independent Vanuatu to construct a unified national identity is *kastom,* or custom, which refers to a variety of indigenous beliefs and practices, especially the centrality of pigs, drinking kava, and exchanging yams. During the first decade of independence, Prime Minister Lini and the VP pursued a form of Melanesian socialism justified and explained in terms of *kastom.* Nagriamel had likewise sought legitimacy through *kastom,* as have the Union of Moderate Parties (UMP) and most other political parties that have emerged since 1980. As a result of this focus, pig tusks appear on the national flag, the official emblem, the local currency, and even in the country's international airport. The national beer also brings the importance of pigs to mind: It is called Tuskers.

In addition to utilizing pig symbolism, all governments since 1980 have highlighted the way that *kastom* can unify the country's diverse language and cultural groups and overcome the divisions of colonialism. Particularly important are the many national arts festivals that seek to revive and even invent *kastom* songs, dances, crafts, and rituals. Almost all elected officials in Vanuatu have participated in at least one *kastom* ritual in which they have clubbed a pig to death while wearing "traditional" clothing; avoiding such a spectacle would allow political rivals to paint the official as anti-*kastom* and thus anti-Vanuatu. The hotly contested election of 1991 even captured the attention of the *Economist* magazine because of the decline it caused in the Vanuatuan pig population: All candidates and even minor political actors used pig-killing rituals and feasts as a way of attracting votes. The winner of that election, Maxime Carlot, a procapitalist secular leader from the VP's main rival the UMP, almost immediately adopted the same pro-*kastom* stance as his VP predecessors. He took a *kastom* name, accumulated a large number of chiefly titles, and participated in as many pig-clubbing rituals as he could.

Despite attempts to create a national identity using the idea of *kastom,* most commentary on Vanuatuan nationalism points to the very weak identity this practice has engendered. Few national institutions exist to back up the state structure, and Vanuatuan citizenship entails almost no sense of shared identity. Local linguistic and cultural ties trump those of the nation on almost every front while the religious, linguistic, and cultural differences created during the colonial era continue to divide the country today.

See also MELANESIANS; NI-VANUATU.

FURTHER READING

William F. S. Miles. *Bridging Mental Boundaries in a Postcolonial Microcosm: Identity and Development in Vanuatu* (Honolulu: University of Hawaii Press, 1998).

Margaret C. Rodman. *Masters of Tradition: Consequences of Customary Land Tenure in Longana, Vanuatu* (Vancouver: University of British Columbia Press, 1987).

Veddhas *See* WANNIYALA-AETTO.

Vedic civilization *See* INDO-ARYANS.

Vietnamese (Kinh, Jing)

The Vietnamese, or Kinh, are the dominant ethnic group in the state of Vietnam and one of the 55 recognized minority groups in China, where they are known as the Jing. Large Vietnamese populations also live in the United States, France, Australia, and other countries, largely as a result of the Southeast Asian wars that began in 1945 and lasted until 1976.

GEOGRAPHY

Vietnam is a 128,000-square-mile country that covers the eastern coast of the Indochinese Peninsula in an elongated S shape. It sits between China to the north, the South China Sea to the east and south, and Cambodia and Laos to the west. Vietnam's geography is dominated by two major rivers and their delta areas, the Red River in the northern part of the country and the Mekong River in the southern part. The northern and central regions are hilly to mountainous, with Fan Si Pan the highest peak at 10,312 feet, while the southern region is low and densely forested. With 2,140 miles of coastline, Vietnam has beautiful beaches and is even beginning to develop a very small surfing culture at some of the best wave beaches in the country.

All of Vietnam is located in the region of the tropics, which makes the climate mostly hot and wet; however, the mountainous north can be chilly and humid from November to April. Both regions receive ample rainfall during the May–October monsoon season; even with the deforestation of the 1960s and early 1970s the country has achieved tremendous growth in agriculture and reforestation.

ORIGINS

The origins of the Vietnamese people have confounded historians and linguists for generations, but recent genetic, archaeological, and linguistic evidence is beginning to present a more balanced picture than has been available until now. Genetic evidence points to strong similarities among the Vietnamese, THAIS, and some Chinese communities, which suggests that Vietnamese origins lie in territory currently held by China. This evidence also supports Chinese theories that all contemporary Vietnamese people descend from Chinese migrants in the centuries prior to the common era. However, the Vietnamese language provides a very different picture of Vietnamese origins and points to migration from insular Southeast Asia and specifically from some of the islands of Indonesia. The archaeological evidence tends to support the second of these theories since stone tools found in Vietnam are similar to those found in Java, Malaysia, Thailand, and Myanmar.

Between 12,000 and 10,000 years ago the Neolithic people of the HOA BINH CULTURE settled along the Red River. They are believed to have been short, dark-skinned people who resembled the contemporary AETA of the Philippines. The Hoabinians were hunters and fishermen who may have cultivated certain plants for their fruits or roots; they lived in caves and rock shelters, where their remains have been examined by archaeologists for the past few decades. Around 7000 B.C.E. the people of the Hoa Binh era further developed their technological repertoire, adding baskets, simple pottery, and double-edged stone tools; they are often called the people of the Bac Son culture. The remains of yet another population from the same period have been found at Quynh-van; these people buried their dead in the same seated position as the early populations of Indonesia and the Philippines and seem to have lived primarily on fish. They may have been related to the ancient ancestors of the MALAYS who migrated north from Indonesia.

In addition to these specific groups, several other Neolithic populations also resided in Southeast Asia and added their own genetic, linguistic, and material traits to the mix of the contemporary Vietnamese people. Such traits as tattooing, chewing betel nut, animistic and

VIETNAMESE

location:
Vietnam and China, with a diaspora throughout the world

time period:
Approximately 1000 B.C.E. to the present

ancestry:
Austronesian, Chinese, and others from Southeast Asia

language:
Three separate dialects of Vietnamese—northern, central, and southern—all Viet-Muong languages within the Mon-Khmer branch of the larger Austro-Asiatic language family. Significant Tai and Chinese elements were added throughout the centuries.

Vietnamese time line

B.C.E.

12,000–10,000 The Hoa Binh culture is established along the Red River and in the Tonkin Delta.

7000 The people of the Bac Son culture establish themselves in northeast Vietnam.

1000–800 Emergence of Dong Son culture, often associated with the formation of the Vietnamese nation.

258 The kingdom of Au Lac is formed by combining various smaller kingdoms in northern Vietnam.

208 Chinese general Trieu Da conquers Au Lac and heads his own kingdom of Nam Viet. From this period forward thousands of people fleeing war in China settle in the territory of Vietnam and bring their own languages, cultures, and customs. For this reason, many Chinese sources claim that the entire basis of Vietnamese culture is Chinese culture.

111 The Han Chinese colonize Vietnam, which they hold for about 1,000 years.

C.E.

First century The Funanese are established as the dominant people in southern Vietnam.

40 The Trung sisters successfully repel the Chinese ruler To Dinh from the prefecture of Giao Chi (Chinese-dominated northern Vietnam).

43 The Trung sisters are defeated and commit suicide.

248 Trieu Au leads her own rebellion against both Chinese rule and customs, which limit the lives of women much more severely than do traditional Vietnamese customs.

542 Former Chinese administrator Ly Bon overthrows the Chinese and forms his own kingdom, which is reconquered by the Chinese in 546.

613 The kingdom of Chenla overthrows Funan, whose territory incorporates the southern portion of Vietnam.

679 The ruler of the newly formed Tang dynasty renames Vietnam "Annam," meaning "pacified south."

939 The Vietnamese under Ngo Quyen finally succeed in expelling the Chinese from their territory.

939–967 Ngo dynasty.

967–980 Dinh dynasty.

980–1009 Early Le dynasty.

1009–1225 Ly dynasty; Buddhism emerges as the state religion of Vietnam.

1225–1400 Tran dynasty, most notable for victories over the Mongols in 1258, 1286, and 1287. This period also sees the height of Nam-ti'n, the Vietnamese expansion to the south.

totemistic religious practices, and both marriage and seasonal rituals among the Vietnamese resemble those of people throughout the region and probably originate in these ancient populations.

The Vietnamese themselves tell an origin myth that begins with the marriage of a male dragon with a female fairy. This couple had 100 sons before deciding that the water-oriented dragon and the mountain-oriented fairy could not remain together. When they split up, the father took 50 of the sons to the coast, where they became the Lac people, including the founder of the Hung dynasty of the country of Van Lang, "land of the tattooed men." The sons who went with their mother to the mountains became all of the various mountain tribes that continue to inhabit Southeast Asia today. This legend ends in 258 B.C.E., when the last of 18 Hung kings is said to have been overthrown and his territory combined with others to form the kingdom of Au Lac.

HISTORY

The North: Prehistory to the Tenth Century

The first culture to be identified by some historians as truly Vietnamese is that of the Bronze Age DONG SON CULTURE, which emerged between 1000 and 800 B.C.E. in the Red River Valley. However, one should be cautious about as-

1400–07 Ho dynasty.

1407–28 Short period of Chinese domination, marked by an attempt by the Ming Chinese rulers to impose Chinese ways of life on the Vietnamese people.

1418–28 Le Loi's rebellion against the Chinese, which begins just after Tet, the New Year, and utilizes guerrilla-fighting tactics to avoid engaging the much larger Chinese armies directly.

1428–1524 Le So dynasty.

1524–92 Mac dynasty.

1592–1788 Late Le dynasty. Sometimes the Le So and Mac dynasties are considered merely subsets of this long dynasty.

1739 All farmland in northern Vietnam is owned by large estate holders, leaving thousands of peasants hungry and having to scavenge for food.

1771–1802 The Tay-Son Uprising overthrows the power of the Nguyen, Trinh, and Le families.

1788 Qing forces from China invade Vietnam and try to roust the Tay-Son Uprising. In response Nguyen Hue is named Emperor Quang Trung and goes on to defeat the Chinese.

1802–1940 Nguyen dynasty and French colonial period, ended by the Japanese occupation of the country during World War II.

1945 The Viet Minh declare Vietnam an independent country, and France reacts by sending troops to reclaim its former colony.

1954 The French finally concede to the Vietnamese after a disastrous loss at Dien Bien Phu; by this time the United States is paying for about 80 percent of France's costs as part of the global strategy to contain Communism.

1955–64 The early years of the Vietnam War, as it is called in the United States, between forces of the National Liberation Front (NLF), supported by North Vietnam and others, and the Army of the Republic of Vietnam (ARVN), supported by the United States, Australia, and others.

1964–75 The intensive period of the war, which spreads beyond South Vietnam into North Vietnam, Cambodia, and Laos when the United States begins bombing these adjoining countries to cut NLF supply lines.

1975 The United States pulls out of South Vietnam, and Saigon falls to the NLF and North Vietnamese troops.

1976 North and South Vietnam are reunified.

1986 *Doi moi,* or economic restructuring, begins to open Vietnam's command economy to capitalist and foreign investment.

2006 The country continues to experience strong economic growth at 7.8 percent but politically remains in the hands of the Communist Party.

signing this people Vietnamese ethnicity because their culture spread well beyond the confines of contemporary Vietnam and encompassed all of Southeast Asia and the Indo-Malaya Archipelago. Some of the important traits of Dong Son culture are the use of intensive agriculture to grow rice and domesticated buffalo for transport and other heavy work; these people also had domesticated pigs. They used long dugout canoes for fishing and traveling throughout the region for trade. Their fine bronzework, typified in the so-called Dong Son drums, may have originated in a skill imported from China or from the region of contemporary Thailand. Dong Son artwork shows houses that were built on stilts to prevent flood damage, as well as a large number of animal images, especially frogs and sea birds, which are believed to have been important religious symbols. The sun and water in the form of rain, rivers, and oceans were also very important to the religion, which seems to have been a form of nature worship. Based on the wealthy and elaborate tombs of some Dong Son people and the modest burials of others, most specialists believe that this society had probably developed into a hierarchical one with a king at the apex by the time of its incorporation into the newly emerging Sino-Vietnamese culture around 1 B.C.E.

Large Dong Son–era bronze drums such as this one have been found throughout island and mainland Southeast Asia, indicating the extensive reach of this culture area. *(Art Resource/Erich Lessing)*

The myth of Vietnam's founding is not entirely legendary because the country of Van Lang with its 18 Hung rulers is associated with the Dong Son period of prehistory; the Hung dynastic line is sometimes called Lac. The subsequent formation of Au Lac, which was ruled by the Thuc dynasty from its capital at Phuc An, near present-day Co Loa west of Hanoi, was also part of the Dong Son era. While quite a bit is known about the material culture of these kingdoms from archaeological evidence, their political structure, rulers' names, and other details remain partly legendary and partly historical because the people of Dong Son did not have writing. The region of Vietnam entered written history about 208 B.C.E. when Chinese general Trieu Da conquered the Au Lac kingdom and formed his own writing system, which he called Nam Viet.

In turn, Nam Viet and what was left of Au Lac were largely overrun by the HAN in 111 B.C.E., and they tried to impose their own culture and way of life on the indigenous Vietnamese. In the first few hundred years of their 1,000 years of colonization, the Chinese were able to make their presence felt predominantly in the coastal trading ports, while village life, especially in the mountains, remained largely untouched. Two Chinese prefectures, Giao Chi and Cuu Chan, were established in 100 B.C.E. in the Tonkin Delta with the assistance of the local Au Lac nobility. These two provinces, however, eventually became seven prefectures with the expansion of the Chinese and Chinese-

Vietnamese population through migration as well as the intermarriage of local women and Chinese men. Chinese education, technology, bureaucracy, and other cultural traits began to infiltrate all levels of society, creating the syncretic Vietnamese culture of today.

The 1,000 years of Chinese occupation in Vietnam were challenged at many points during the period. One of the most important as far as Vietnamese nationalism is concerned is the rebellion of the Trung sisters from 40 to 43 C.E. Trung Trac and Trung Nhi lived in the Chinese prefecture of Giao Chi, whose leader, To Dinh, had angered the local people with his corruption, heavy taxes, and disregard for their way of life. The sisters spent many years studying the art of war and eventually led an army of about 30,000–80,000 soldiers against the Chinese; many of their generals were women, including their own mother. Their forces were initially victorious and drove the Chinese from Giao Chi in 40 C.E. Trung Trac then became queen and liberated the peasantry from the onerous taxes levied by the Chinese. However, the queen and her armies spent the next three years fighting against the Chinese until they were finally defeated in 43. Both sisters committed suicide rather than face defeat and the wrath of the vengeful Chinese. Much of the story of the Trung sisters is probably mythological rather than actual historical fact; however, since the 13th century the story has been an important focus for Vietnamese nationalists in their fight against domination by the Chinese, French, and Americans.

In 248 another Vietnamese woman led a rebellion against the Chinese, this time in central Vietnam. Trieu Au was less successful than the Trung sisters but did make her mark in having fought not only Chinese political and economic domination but also social mores that limited the roles of women. Ancient Vietnamese society seems to have included many powerful women figures, but as Chinese-influenced Confucian values became more and more central to life in Vietnam, women found their life options severely limited to two: wife or concubine.

The fifth and early sixth centuries also saw frequent skirmishes between various factions. For example, Ly Bon, a leader of mixed Chinese and Vietnamese descent, overthrew the local Han ruler in northern Vietnam. Ly Bon ruled his own little kingdom for four years, until 546, when he was overthrown; his followers continued to fight against Chinese hegemony until 603, when the newly formed Chinese Sui dynasty eradicated all opposition in both China and Vietnam.

The seventh century also brought change to northern Vietnam in the form of the new Chinese Tang dynasty, which came to power in 618. This new Chinese leadership set about leading the region much more actively than their predecessors had done, for they had often let local governors and warlords administer their southern colony. The Tang Chinese renamed northern Vietnam "Annam," or "pacified south," in 679 to symbolize that Vietnam was to be fully incorporated into southern China rather than being merely a Chinese colony. These actions led to Vietnamese uprisings in 687 and again in 722, when Mai Thuc Loan tried to make himself emperor of Vietnam. With the help of his southern neighbors the KHMERS and CHAMS, he even took the capital at Hanoi for a few years. Further rebellions also broke out in the years between 767 and 791, then again in 819–20, and in 939. This last rebellion was by far the most successful; Ngo Quyen ruled from his capital at Co Loa, present-day Hanoi, and established about 900 years of Vietnamese independence for his people.

The South: Prehistory to the Tenth Century

At about the same time that the earliest kingdoms were being formed in the Dong Son era in the territory of northern Vietnam, in the south the proto-Malay–speaking FUNANESE were forming their own city-states and even unified kingdoms. While more closely associated with the history of Cambodia and the Khmers, Funan's kingdoms also incorporated much of the Mekong Delta region of southern Vietnam. Their culture was a bit of a hybrid with linguistic traits from their proto-Malay background in insular Southeast Asia; religion and artwork from Hindu India; and trade relations with China, India, and even Rome. In 613 Funan was overthrown by the CHENLA people, whose territory then stretched from Thailand, through Cambodia, and into southern Vietnam.

In the fourth century C.E. another kingdom emerged in central Vietnam, that of the Chams. Like the Funanese, the Chams were heavily influenced by India, as is evident in the stone artwork and many temples archaeologists have found in both Vietnam and Cambodia. Also similar to the Funanese, the Chams were speakers of an Austronesian language similar to those spoken by the MALAYS and POLYNESIANS. The Chams were agriculturalists who grew rice in intensively worked paddies and fished in the region's rivers and coastal regions. During the years in which China dominated the politics and society in the northern section of Vietnam, the Chams sometimes formed an alliance with

---

Trung Trac and Trung Nhi ᴀ▰ᴀ

The Trung sisters, individually known as Trung Trac and Trung Nhi, were two rural Vietnamese women who ignited an uprising against the Chinese overlords in the first century C.E. The exact details of their story are mired in patriotic propaganda, and there are conflicting reports of the uprising's cause and finale between the Vietnamese and the Chinese accounts. The Vietnamese account asserts that the Trung sisters were born in a rural Vietnamese village as the daughters of a prefect of Me Linh, and they were well-versed in the art of warfare. They were also aware of the oppression of the Vietnamese people under the Chinese overlords, and when Trung Trac's husband, Thi Sach, rebelled, he was executed as an example of the Chinese response to disobedience. Enraged, Trung Trac and her younger sister, Trung Nhi, amassed an army in 39 C.E., which successfully drove a Chinese unit out of their village. Their army is said to have been made up almost entirely of women, and by 40 C.E. they managed to reclaim 65 citadels from the Chinese, and Trung Trac proclaimed herself queen of Nam Viet. They were able to repel Chinese invasion for two years, but in 43 C.E. the Chinese invaded again, only this time the male warriors are reported to have charged into battle completely naked, thereby shocking the female Vietnamese warriors. When they realized that they had been defeated, the Trung sisters are said to have drowned themselves in the Hat River, as did many of their warriors. The Chinese account, however, makes no mention of Vietnamese oppression or the sanctioned execution of Thi Sach. Nor does it suggest that the Trung sisters committed suicide.

---

their powerful neighbor and sometimes fought against the Chinese push for domination.

Independent Vietnam

The first 70 years of independence following Ngo Quyen's overthrow of the Chinese in 939 saw the emergence and decline of three separate ruling families. Ngo Quyen himself ruled northern Vietnam for 28 years from his kingdom of Co Loa, which had been the Au Lac capital as well about 1,000 years earlier. This move did not bolster his legitimacy with all the people in the region, however, and he was forced to spend most of his period as emperor fighting other feudal lords. When Ngo Quyen died in 967, his heir could not maintain the kingdom, which disintegrated into 12 separate statelets.

The strongest of the feudal rulers of this period was Dinh Bo Linh, who reunified the country, gave it the name Dai Co Viet, and negotiated a treaty with Song China in which Vietnam was forced to pay tribute every three years. Within the country he also created indigenous justice and education systems, a regular army, and an internal security force. His 22-year reign, though marred by violence at the start, is known today as an era of *thai binh,* or peace. The peace was short-lived, however, because in 980 one of his bodyguards assassinated Dinh Tien Hoang, the imperial name taken by Dinh Bo Linh. Dinh's six-year-old son was

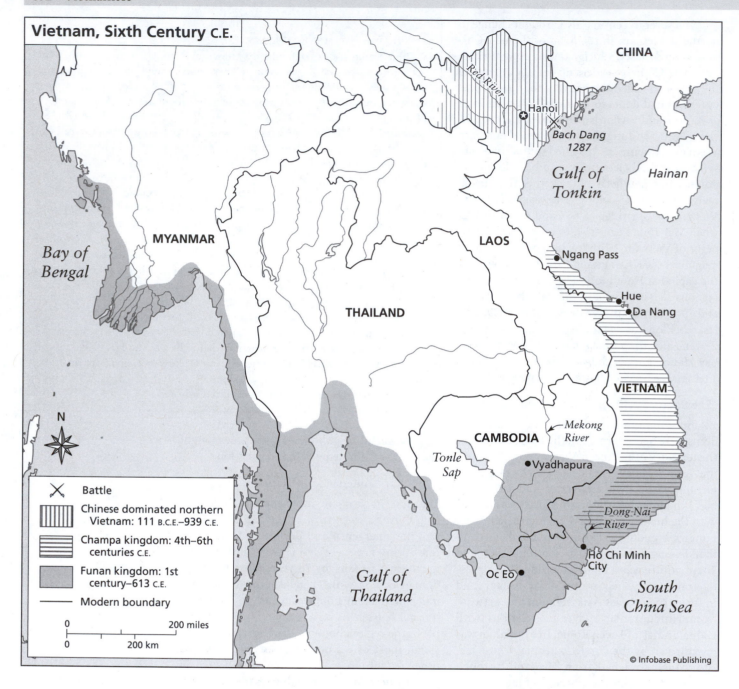

Vietnam, Sixth Century C.E.

CHINA

Red River

Hanoi

Bach Dang 1287

Gulf of Tonkin

Hainan

Bay of Bengal

MYANMAR

LAOS

Ngang Pass

Hue

Da Nang

THAILAND

VIETNAM

Mekong River

CAMBODIA

Vyadhapura

Tonle Sap

Dong-Nai River

N

Ho Chi Minh City

Gulf of Thailand

Oc Eo

South China Sea

✕ Battle

▯▯▯ Chinese dominated northern Vietnam: 111 B.C.E.–939 C.E.

≡ Champa kingdom: 4th–6th centuries C.E.

▓ Funan kingdom: 1st century–613 C.E.

— Modern boundary

0   200 miles
0   200 km

© Infobase Publishing

much too young to take over from his father, and his mother gave the kingdom to Le Dai Hahn, a powerful military figure who founded the Early Le dynasty. Le Dai Hahn continued to pay tribute to China to keep Vietnam's northern border secure and then turned his energies to the south, where he invaded Indrapura, contemporary Quang Nam, the capital of the Cham kingdom; this effort marked the first step toward unifying the entire region that today makes up the country of Vietnam. He also created roads and other administrative tools to help consolidate his large kingdom, but to little avail. After Le's death in 1005, his heir was able

to rule for just four more years before the entire Early Le dynasty was swept away.

The subsequent two dynasties, the Ly and Tran, were much more successful in holding onto power than these prior three. The Ly dynasty, 1009–1225, was started by Ly Cong Uan, a disciple of Buddhist monk Van Hanh. As this event indicates, this period of Vietnamese history marks the emergence of Buddhism as one of the key ideologies unifying the people and bringing order to the chaos of the previous centuries. Buddhism became the official state religion in this period, and monks and other Buddhist masters were always among the emperors' most important advisers. Nonetheless, Confucianism was not abandoned, and administrators throughout the kingdom used guidelines adopted from that philosophy to establish tax and judiciary systems, a professional army, and a centralized, monarchical government with a professional class of bureaucrats. Civil-engineering projects to manage water and agriculture were also implemented during the period, and in 1070 a national college was established to train this bureaucracy. In addition to these impressive accomplishments, in 1054 Emperor Ly Thanh Ton renamed his kingdom Dai Viet, with its capital at Thang Long.

The Ly dynasty came to an end in 1225 when a commoner named Tran Canh married into the royal family and then outmaneuvered the dynasty's legitimate heirs to take power; he and his descendants ruled Dai Viet until 1400. The Tran dynasty is most famous for the Vietnamese victories against Kublai Khan's MONGOLS in 1258, 1286, and 1287. This last victory at the battle of Bach Dang River took place in the same region in which Ngo Quyen had defeated the Chinese in 939, making it one of the most important national sites in the country. In 1307 the king's sister married the Cham king and thus extended Dai Viet's territorial integrity south to Hue without having to pick up arms. During the Tran period the examination system for promoting bureaucrats continued from the Ly period, but Buddhism was weakened in relation to Confucianism and Taoism.

As was the case for the formation of the Tran dynasty, a fortuitous marriage also initiated its demise at the hands of Le Qui Ly, a minister in the Tran government. Le's aunt was married to the emperor, which gave him access to the inner court and its machinations, and he was able to name himself Emperor Ho in 1400. His usurpation of power gave the Ming Chinese an excuse to march into Vietnam and conquer it in 1407. The next 21 years were disastrous for the Vietnamese people as the Chinese tried to eliminate any trace of a unique Vietnamese identity or culture. Vietnamese literature was burned and replaced by Chinese works, Chinese clothing and hair styles became mandatory in public, and wealthy families lost their wealth as many portable goods were taken away to China. The peasants also suffered under high taxes and the violence of the period as the Vietnamese and Chinese fought almost continuously.

In 1418 on the day after Tet, or the Vietnamese New Year, one of the leaders of these resistance movements, Le Loi, began to make his move against the Chinese. His initial goal was to restore the Tran dynasty, but his military prowess soon put him at the forefront of his movement ahead of the Tran figurehead. He took the name Binh Dinh Vuong, the pacifying king, and initially fought a largely guerilla war in his home province of Thanh Hoa. Finally, in 1428 his armies were successful, and he formed the Le So dynasty. His first task was to reconstruct the country after the devastation wrought by 21 years of Chinese persecution and warfare, using about four-fifths of his quarter-million soldier army to work on food production and reconstruction in the countryside.

The 37-year reign of Le Thanh Tong from 1460 to 1497 was probably the high point of the Le So period. In 1471 his armies conquered a fading Champa kingdom, and the soldiers he left in the conquered territories successfully absorbed them into the larger kingdom. Many Cham refugees fled the country in light of Vietnamese persecution of their religion and language, with most moving to what is today Cambodia; just a small number of Cham people remain in central Vietnam today. Le Than Tong was also a historian who founded the Tao Dan Academy and wrote a history of Vietnam. In addition, he was interested in revising agricultural practice and the country's financial policies, as well as placing national emphasis on specifically Vietnamese customs and moral principles.

Following this powerful leader's death in 1497, the Le So dynasty became increasingly weak. Two noble families, the Nguyen and Trinh, emerged to challenge the ruling family from the one side, while Mac Dang Dung emerged on the other. These two factions engaged in a civil war in the early years of the 16th century until 1524, when the emperor Le Chieu Tong was assassinated by Mac's retainers. For a short period Mac Dang Dung ruled Vietnam, but the Nguyen and Trinh families were not satisfied with the situation, and with the support of the remnants of the Le dynasty they engaged in nearly half a century of civil war. The last Mac emperor was finally eliminated in 1592, but still the Vietnamese people did not experience a period of peaceful growth and development under a unified government. The Nguyen and Trinh families, while both nominally supporting the Le dynasty emperors, entrenched their separate power bases in southern and northern Vietnam, respectively, and spent another three-quarters of a century fighting each other for control of the whole country. Finally, in 1672 the two war-weary sides, neither of whom had the strength to eliminate the other, agreed to a division of the country at the Gianh River, with each controlling the land and people in one section. The Le emperors continued to serve as figurehead rulers for a united Vietnam, but in reality theirs was no more than a ceremonial position until the late 18th century.

During the 17th and 18th centuries the lives of Vietnamese peasants became increasingly difficult, with both ruling families raising taxes to pay for their wars against each other, and with most farmland falling into the hands of a few large landowners. By 1739 there was literally no land left in northern Vietnam for peasants because it was all incorporated into these large estates. At the same time that the peasants were leaving their homes to find food and having to scavenge rats, snakes, and other vermin to eat, the Nguyen and Trinh families were accumulating enormous fortunes; one Nguyen man was said to have 146 children by his dozens of concubines. In the Red River Delta alone, this period saw the eruption of four different peasant rebellions, all of which were effectively quelled by forces loyal to the Trinh family. In 1771, however, the Tay Son Uprising finally began to break the hold over the country maintained by the Nguyen and Trinh families for generations.

The Tay Son Uprising was led by three brothers: Nguyen Nhac, Nguyen Lu, and Nguyen Hue, commoners from the village of Tay Son in south-central Vietnam and no relation to the ruling Nguyen family. During the course of about 30 years of fighting and reform, these three overthrew both the Nguyen and Trinh families and the long-lasting Le dynasty. In 1788 a surviving Le heir escaped to China and gained the support of Qing forces against the uprising and in response Nguyen Hue took the title of Emperor Quang Trung and united the country's forces against the Chinese invaders. Although he himself died in 1792, few political or economic changes occurred in this period, and the wealthy Nguyen family defeated the uprising in 1802. The Tay Son Uprising is still seen as an important era of Vietnamese history for ending the division at the Giang River and unifying the Vietnamese people. It is often pointed to as the first event in the modern state of Vietnam.

Modern Vietnam

The most successful soldier of the wealthy Nguyen family, Nguyen Anh, is notable in Vietnam for two reasons. First, in 1802 he defeated the Tay Son, seized Hanoi, and named himself Gia Long, emperor of Vietnam, the first in a line of 13 Nguyen emperors. Second, and perhaps more important, Nguyen Anh also invited the French into Vietnamese politics when he requested assistance from a French missionary and bishop of Adran and gained French military aid in exchange for trading rights and territorial concessions. The French did not follow through on this deal, but the bishop himself raised money and troops for Nguyen, which tied the two countries even beyond the bishop's death in 1799.

The first actions of the new emperor were to undo the few reforms that had been put into effect by the Tay Son leaders. Bureaucrats were reempowered in their districts, women lost the rights they had been granted, and taxes were raised to their previous level. The Confucian moral system, which elevates hierarchy and obedience above most other values, was reinscribed as national doctrine, with the absolute power of the emperor at its center. In addition, the capital, which had been in Hanoi for hundreds of years, was moved to Hue because the traditional power base of the Nguyens had been the south. For the Vietnamese peasantry the new dynasty meant a return to the system against which they had spent more than 100 years rebelling, and they had the same reaction the second time as well. The Nguyen emperors spent their years in power being challenged both by their own people, especially in the north, and by the French, who by the early 19th century were starting to make their trading and missionary presence felt in many Vietnamese cities.

The last Nguyen emperor to have any real power in Vietnam was Tu Duc. It was during his reign, in 1859, that the French finally invaded southern Vietnam, where much of their indigenous support from Vietnamese Catholics was located. Tu Duc, with peasants rebelling in the north and the French occupying the south, was forced to sign away most of his power as sovereign, and upon his death in 1883 the French usurped the remainder. However, the French were not alone in their desire to incorporate Vietnam into their empire, and in addition to having to fight against Vietnamese resistance groups and peasants, especially in the north and central regions, the French forces also had to expel the Chinese, who tried to annex the country in 1883. This period of consolidation for French colonialism in Vietnam and the rest of Indochina ended in 1897 when the governor-general turned his efforts toward modernization of the country's infrastructure and centralization of colonial power, the better to make a profit from Vietnamese natural resources. French missionaries also worked hard to convert the country to

Catholicism and to bring French civilization to Vietnam, a project that had mixed results generally but certainly succeeded to a greater extent in the south than the north.

Under these conditions the Vietnamese people had little choice but to collaborate with the French or continue to work as low-paid, unskilled laborers. Generally, Catholic converts were deemed more trustworthy by the French officials and had an easier time gaining positions in the bureaucracy or civil service. However, the early 20th century did see an indigenous education system, called the Free School Movement, emerge to teach a Vietnamese version of national history, Vietnamese literature, and even a Latin alphabet for writing the Vietnamese language. The French quickly quelled the movement after just two years, but the minor rebellions continued, involving mostly those who had been educated in the French system and had even traveled to France for further education. The best known of these activists was Ho Chi Minh, who went to China, France, Russia, and other European countries, and even presented a plea for Vietnamese independence at the Paris Peace Conference that ended World War I.

Ho returned to Asia in the 1930s but could not go home without risking arrest and so spent his time in China just north of the border, working with other well-educated Indochinese individuals to form the Indochinese Communist Party. He finally returned home in 1941, during the JAPANESE occupation of Vietnam, and started the Vietnamese Communist Party, popularly called the Viet Minh. Although nominally communist, most of Ho's ideology was actually more oriented toward national liberation and patriotism than toward Marxist-Leninist doctrine, despite having been influenced by such ideas during his time in Europe. A number of contemporary historians have conjectured that if Ho had been able to secure Vietnamese independence from France with the economic and political blessings of the United States at the end of World War I or World War II, he would gladly have accepted entry into the U.S. sphere of influence. However, we will never know what might have happened because in both periods the global community chose to side with French economic interests rather than Vietnamese nationalist ones.

At the end of World War II, the Viet Minh negotiated a deal with the retreating Japanese armies; in exchange for the Japanese being able to return home unscathed, the Vietnamese would receive all of their weaponry. In August 1945 the Viet Minh turned these weapons against the returning French forces as well as those of the nominal Nguyen emperor Bao Dai, who abdicated his position on August 25. On September 2, 1945, the Viet Minh declared Vietnam an independent country and received the royal sword and seal, the traditional symbols of legitimate power in the country.

France was not ready to abandon its Indochinese colony and the wealth it created and went to war against the nationalist-communist forces of the Viet Minh in early 1946. The Viet Minh could not maintain their hold over the southern regions of the country, and in September Ho returned Cochin China in the south to the French. Fighting in the remainder of the country continued unabated for almost eight years, with the Viet Minh receiving assistance from the Communist government in China after 1949 as well as from the USSR, while the United States contributed more and more toward the French side of the war. By 1954 and the French defeat at the decisive battle of Dien Bien Phu, the United States was paying for about 80 percent of the entire French endeavor in an attempt to block the spread of communism south from Russia and China.

The Geneva Conference of 1954, which brought an end to the active hostilities of the Korean War, likewise settled the matter of the former French colonies in Indochina. Cambodia and Laos were granted independence, and Vietnam was divided at approximately the 17th parallel into North Vietnam, controlled by the Viet Minh, and South Vietnam, ruled by the returned emperor Bao Dai, the so-called playboy emperor, until he was deposed in 1955. The subsequent presidents—Ngo Dinh Diem, who ruled until 1963, when he was killed in a coup tacitly allowed by the U.S. Central Intelligence Agency, and Nguyen Van Thieu, who ruled until the defeat of South Vietnam by North Vietnam in 1975—were both essentially puppets of the Americans in their quest to "contain" communism. Both rulers had the support of some South Vietnamese people during their combined 20 years in power, but substantial numbers also opposed them, either as supporters of unification with North Vietnam or as Buddhists who experienced tremendous persecution at the hands of both regimes, but especially that of Diem.

Those 20 years between 1955 and 1975 were marked by the violence of guerrilla warfare that tore apart the countryside, especially in South Vietnam; killed millions of Vietnamese civilians and combatants alike; and pulled the United States, Australia, South Korea, and

Ho Chi Minh ᷋᷋᷋

Ho Chi Minh was a Vietnamese revolutionary who became president of the Democratic Republic of Vietnam, or North Vietnam, in 1955. He was born Nguyen Sinh Cung in the Hoang Tru Village in 1890, and as the son of a preeminent Confucian scholar and teacher, he was raised with strong Confucian values. Between 1911 and 1941, Ho traveled to France, the United States, England, China, and Thailand. By the time he returned to Vietnam in 1941, he had studied Western politics intensively and had firm communist leanings. His return saw him dedicate himself to the task of leading the Viet Minh independence movement to drive France out of Vietnam. After the August Revolution in 1945, he convinced Emperor Bao Dai to abdicate, and Ho became chair of the provisional government. That same year the Viet Minh killed off members of rival groups and purged numerous members of the Communist Party who did not have the same vision for the country. By 1946 all competing political parties had been banned, 25,000 noncommunists had been arrested, and thousands more fled to South Vietnam.

In 1955 Ho became president of the Democratic Republic of Vietnam, and though the Geneva Accords required that an election be held to unite all of Vietnam under one government, South Vietnam, as led by Ngo Dinh Diem, refused to participate. The Geneva Accords also required a 300-day period to allow people to move freely between North and South Vietnam, during which approximately 1 million North Vietnamese moved to the South. Some, however, were reportedly forced to stay in North Vietnam against their will by government officials. During this time Ho had also implemented a communist land reform modeled after China and Russia in which hundreds of thousands of people accused of being landlords were tortured and executed. In 1959 Ho's government became openly supportive of the National Liberation Front of South Vietnam, a communist insurgent organization.

Ho Chi Minh died of heart failure in 1969 at the age of 72. Today the remains of Bac Ho, or Uncle Ho as he is known in Vietnam, are viewed by hundreds of thousands of people per year who line up to pass by his mausoleum in Hanoi.

---

other countries into a Vietnamese civil war with the goal of containing communism. Although often confusedly seen as a war between North and South Vietnam, the war was actually more complex than that. The main combatants were the National Liberation Front (NLF), which had the support of North Vietnam, China, and the Soviet Union; and the Army of the Republic of Vietnam (ARVN), which was almost entirely funded by the United States and supported in combat by the United States, Australia, New Zealand, and South Korea. The better known name for the NLF in the United States is the Viet Cong, a derogatory shortening of the Vietnamese phrase *Viet Nam cong san,* meaning "Vietnamese communist."

The end of the 1950s and early 1960s did not bring overt warfare into most Vietnamese lives. At this time both the NLF and the Republic of Vietnam were trying to bolster their support in the cities and countryside alike in order to secure their positions. The United States was sending money, arms, and military advisers to the ARVN and President Diem but was not actively engaged in fighting. Diem, as a Catholic, also engaged in active persecution of not only communists in South Vietnam but also Buddhists and others who might have come to the regime's support had he not alienated them with his family's consolidation of power. For their part, the NLF accepted arms, training, and support from North Vietnam and saw national reunification as an eventual goal, one shared by many Vietnamese regardless of political ideology or religion.

As the fighting increased, at this point only on South Vietnamese territory, foreign troops entered the fray in increasing numbers. Finally, in 1964, sometimes considered in the United States as the start of the Vietnam War, under the pretense of reaction to the apparent bombing of an American ship in the Gulf of Tonkin, President Lyndon Johnson ordered the bombing of North Vietnam and an increase in U.S. troop numbers on the ground. Later evidence has shown that nothing actually happened in the gulf and the entire episode was manufactured to gain public support for an increased U.S. presence in Vietnam. At that time, when about 200,000 U.S. forces were in Vietnam, the war machine on both sides grew tremendously. By 1968 the United States had more than half a million soldiers in Vietnam, and the South Vietnamese people experienced constant harassment and recruitment attempts from both sides. As a village would fall to one side or the other, anybody who had been seen supporting the previous occupier would be persecuted or killed, even if the support had come only at gunpoint.

The turning point in the war came as early as 1968's Tet Offensive, when a heavy push by the NLF on the Vietnamese New Year saw them take significant ground, including much of Saigon and the U.S. embassy. The offensive was almost immediately reversed by the ARVN and their allied forces, but the damage done to the war's public-relations machine in the United States was more permanent. Protests against the war increased in the United States at the same time that bombing throughout Southeast Asia increased, including dropping thousands of tons of the defoliant Agent Orange to denude the countryside of jungle growth. Finally, after negotiations held in Paris in 1973, to which the South Vietnamese were not even invited, both sides agreed to lay down their arms. Neither side did lay down weapons, however, and it was two more years before the last U.S. Marines pulled out of Saigon in 1975. Shortly thereafter, Saigon was captured by the NLF and their North Vietnamese allies, and the country reunified in July 1976.

While the Vietnam War has played an enormous role in U.S. politics since that loss in 1975, Vietnam seems to have shrugged off the victory and moved forward. Even today, former U.S. soldiers are welcomed back to the country, and the largest war memorials in Vietnam are dedicated to the war against France in the 1940s and 1950s. The war with the French is seen by many as much more central to the creation of an independent Vietnam because it ended more than 100 years of colonialism. At the same time, many former South Vietnamese citizens suffered under the communist takeover, including Catholics, former members of the political and military elite, and the large Chinese minority. Most refugees who fled Vietnam in the 1970s and 1980s came from these communities, while many Vietnamese peasants welcomed the reforms that gave them land to work, education, health care, and the possibility to rebuild their destroyed country.

The state-controlled economy, however, could not maintain acceptable standards of living beyond the rebuilding years and during Vietnam's war with Cambodia in the late 1970s. Finally, in the mid-1980s, economic renovation, or *doi moi* in Vietnamese, became state policy and laid the groundwork for increasing foreign investment, privatization, and economic growth. The Vietnam of 2006 experienced a 7.8 percent growth rate and greater economic prosperity for most people. The government, however, is still in the hands of the Communist Party, which, like China's Communist Party, refuses to reform its political ideology to accompany the opening of their economic policy.

CULTURE

Most Vietnamese people throughout the ages have been rural agriculturalists who live in villages, cultivate wet rice, and practice a syncretic religion that has combined elements from animism, ancestor worship, and Buddhism. Confucianism has also played a key role in organizing society due to its focus on hierarchy and obedience, with the father-child relationship serving as a model for all levels of society, including emperor-subject. Children were taught to obey their parents unconditionally, including accepting the marriage partner who had been chosen for them and continuing to support their parents through the burning of incense and other rituals even after the parents' deaths. Ancestor worship was a vital part of their folk religious tradition and remains important today in the

Throughout the Vietnam War some villages were relocated several times as both sides tried to limit the potential for rural collaboration with their enemy. In this case, Ben Suc village is being evacuated by order of the U.S. Battalion of the 1st Infantry Division in January 1967. *(AP/Horst Faas)*

respect Vietnamese people grant to their elders and their history more generally.

While this culture developed during Vietnamese prehistory, Chinese domination, and then about 900 years of Vietnamese independence within China's larger sphere of influence, the brief period of French colonialism and postwar independence brought tremendous changes to Vietnamese culture. The French introduced Catholicism, which even today is practiced by almost 7 percent of the population; individualist values; Western clothing, education, and foods; and other traits. These values and practices expanded much more so in the South than in Viet Minh–controlled North Vietnam after 1954, and much more in cities than the countryside, but they play a role in Vietnamese culture today.

After about 1980, more and more Vietnamese people moved from the rural areas to take up work in the rapidly expanding cities of Ho Chi Minh City (formerly Saigon), Danang, Hue, and Hanoi. By 2005, 26.7 percent of the Vietnamese population resided in urban areas and fewer than 7 percent of adults were illiterate. Economic changes instituted by *doi moi* in the 1980s have increased the ability of many Vietnamese to purchase cars or at least bicycles, televisions, and radios. Individual spending has increased the trend toward individualist values; nonetheless, Vietnamese young people continue to honor and respect their parents and ancestors, attend Buddhist ceremonies, and work for the betterment of their families, not just themselves. At heart, Confucianism remains central to Vietnamese cultural identity. A second concept, *nam-tin*, southward expansion, is also extremely important. Like the idea of manifest destiny in the United States, *nam-tin* in Vietnam points to the Vietnamese people's belief in the superiority of their own culture and the legitimacy of their political supremacy in their country.

See also AUSTRONESIANS; KOREANS.

FURTHER READING

George Dutton. *The Tay Son Uprising, Society, and Rebellion in Eighteenth-Century Vietnam* (Honolulu: University of Hawaii Press, 2006).

Frances Fitzgerald. *Fire in the Lake: The Vietnamese and the Americans in Vietnam* (Boston: Little, Brown and Co., 1972).

Gerald Cannon Hickey. *Village in Vietnam* (New Haven, Conn.: Yale University Press, 1964).

Duncan McCargo, ed. *Rethinking Vietnam* (New York: RoutledgeCurzon, 2004).

Shawn Frederick McHale. *Print and Power: Confucianism, Communism, and Buddhism in the Making of Modern Vietnam* (Honolulu: University of Hawaii Press, 2003).

Mark W. McLeod and Nguyen Thi Dieu. *Culture and Customs of Vietnam* (Westport, Conn.: Greenwood Press, 2001).

Nguyen Hoai Nhan. *The Early Civilizations of Vietnam and Southeast Asia* (Sarthe, France: Nguyen Hoai Nhan, 1976).

Helle Rydstróm. *Embodying Morality: Growing Up in Rural Northern Vietnam.* (Honolulu: University of Hawaii Press, 2003).

François Sully, ed., *We the Vietnamese; Voices from Vietnam* (New York: Praeger, 1971).

Keith Weller Taylor. *The Birth of Vietnam* (Berkeley and Los Angeles: University of California Press, 1983).

Philip Taylor, ed. *Social Inequality in Vietnam and the Challenges to Reform* (Singapore: Institute of Southeast Asian Studies, 2004).

Vietnamese: nationality (people of the Socialist Republic of Vietnam)

Vietnam is a multiethnic state in Southeast Asia. It is dominated by the ethnic VIETNAMESE and has 53 other minority groups.

GEOGRAPHY

With its distinct S shape, the country of Vietnam is approximately 1,025 miles long but a mere 31 miles wide at its narrowest point. It borders China, Laos, and Cambodia, as well as the Gulf of Tonkin, the Gulf of Thailand, and the South China Sea. The terrain consists of towering, jagged hills and mountain ranges; highlands; rich, marshy flatlands; and mangrove swamps on the Ca Mau peninsula. The tropical monsoon climate leaves Vietnam vulnerable to torrential rains, powerful winds, and extreme humidity. The summer actually sees the most rainfall as the heat of the northern Gobi Desert brings moisture inland from the sea. The winter months are comparatively dry.

INCEPTION AS A NATION

Vietnam's history is characterized by varying short-lived dynasties, numerous name changes, and foreign occupations. By the 19th century the nation had finally settled on its current name, and the Nguyen dynasty was fiercely resisting Westernization. Christianity was suppressed, and trade with the West was severely limited. The Nguyen aversion to Westernization ultimately damaged the nation's modernization, and in the late 19th century France invaded on the orders of Napoleon III. The Nguyen dynasty became a puppet government, and rulers who disagreed with French policy were exiled to Africa. Various resistance movements were launched in retaliation against the French occupation, most notably by Phan Boi Chau, who pioneered the Go

Vietnamese: nationality time line

B.C.E.

1200 The Dong Son people emerge in the areas of the Ma River and Red River Plains.

300 The Au Viet people emigrate from southern China and settle in the Red River delta, where they blend with the native Van Lang people.

258 The Au Lac kingdom develops as the Au Viet and Lac Viet people unite. The last prince of China's Shu dynasty, Thuc Phan, ambitiously declares himself king.

208 Chinese general Trieu Da conquers Au Lac and leads his own kingdom of Nam Viet (in Chinese, Nan Yue).

111 Chinese troops invade Nam Viet and claim it for the Chinese Empire. Northern Vietnam comes to be known as Giao Chi.

C.E.

40 The Han governor's oppressive policies drive two Viet women, the Trung sisters, to lead an uprising that captures 65 towns. The sisters declare themselves Trung queens.

42 Han emperor Guangwu dispatches troops to crush the uprising, and the Trung sisters commit suicide in 43. The Viet feudal lords are stripped of their power and forced to adopt Chinese culture and politics.

166 An envoy from Rome travels to China through Giao Chi, which has become a trading outpost. The area soon welcomes new merchants.

541–44 Giao Chi's regional magistrate, Ly Bon, resigns from his post in disgust with the government's corruption and aggression toward the local people. Calling together the local population, he leads an insurrection that drives the Chinese administration out of Giao Chi and renames the region Van Xuan (Land of ten thousand springs).

603 After 60 years of independence, during which China makes numerous attempts to invade the region, Chinese troops finally recapture Van Xuan.

900 China becomes politically destabilized, and Giao Chi attains autonomy and self-rule, though none of the rulers ever assumes the title of king or emperor.

938 The kingdom of Southern Han dispatches troops to invade and conquer Giao Chi, but the Vietnamese prefect, Ngo Quyen, defeats the Chinese troops a year later and proclaims himself king.

945–67 Ngo Quyen dies and his relatives vie for power. Rebellions and struggles for control between the Ngo family and various warlords last for more than 20 years and are today known as the Upheavals of the Twelve Warlords.

965 The Ngo dynasty is overthrown, and the country is fragmented into 12 territories, each of which is ruled by its own warlord.

968 Din Bo Linh, lord of the region of Bo Hai Khau, crushes the 11 other warlords and succeeds in taking control of the country, which he renames Dai Co Viet.

979–81 Dinh Bo Linh and Crown Prince Dinh Lien are assassinated; Dinh Bo Linh's six-year-old son, Dinh Toan, assumes the throne. In an effort to exploit the country's moment of vulnerability, the Chinese Song dynasty invades Dai Co Viet. Le Hoan, commander of Dai Co Viet's Ten Armies, assumes the throne to fend off the advancing forces. Knowing that he cannot meet the power of the Chinese army, Le Hoan tricks them into moving into the Chi Lang Pass, where his troops ambush them and slay their commander.

1005 Emperor Le Hoan dies and his son, Le Long Dinh, assumes the throne. Today he is remembered for being one of the cruelest tyrants in Vietnam's history.

1009 Le Long Dinh dies, and palace guard commander Ly Cong Uan is nominated to take the throne. Ly Cong Uan founds the Ly dynasty and changes the country's name to Dai Viet, meaning "Great Viet." The Ly dynasty goes down in history as being the point of origin for Vietnam's Golden Age.

(continues)

VIETNAMESE: NATIONALITY

nation:
Vietnam; Socialist Republic of Vietnam

derivation of name:
Translates to "South Yue," referring to the Yue people of ancient southeast China

government:
Communist state

capital:
Hanoi

language:
Vietnamese, English, French, Chinese, Khmer, and mountain-area languages (Mon-Khmer and Malayo-Polynesian)

religion:
None 80.8 percent, Buddhist 9.3 percent, Catholic 6.7 percent, Hoa Hao 1.5 percent, Cao Dai 1.1 percent, Protestant 0.5 percent, Muslim 0.1 percent

earlier inhabitants:
Hoabinhians, Dong Son peoples, Cham, and many others

demographics:
Kihn (Viet) 86.2 percent, Tay 1.9 percent, Thai 1.7 percent, Muong 1.5 percent, Khome 1.4 percent, Hoa 1.1 percent, Nun 1.1 percent, Hmong 1 percent, other 4.1 percent

Vietnamese: nationality time line *(continued)*

1225 Court minister Tran Thu Do ushers in the Tran dynasty by forcing King Ly Hue Tong to become a monk and pass his throne to his seven-year-old daughter, Ly Chieu Hoang. Tran Thu Do arranges a marriage between the young Ly queen and his own eight-year-old nephew, Tran Canh, and then forces Ly Chieu Hoang to abdicate the throne to her husband, thereby transferring the throne to the Canh family. With his new power, Tran Thu Do sets into action an all-encompassing purge of the Ly family. Many Ly individuals escape to Korea.

1257–88 The Tran dynasty wards off three attempts at invasion by the Mongol Yuan dynasty.

1400 The Tran dynasty collapses when five-year-old King Thieu De is forced to abdicate his throne in favor of his maternal grandfather, Ho Quy Ly, who renames the country Dai Ngu.

1407 The Ho dynasty is overthrown after only seven years in power when Chinese Ming troops invade and capture Ho Quy Ly and his son Ho Han Thuong under the guise of wishing to reestablish the Tran dynasty. Claiming that they are unable to find a Tran heir to rule Dai Ngu, the Ming dynasty annexes Dai Ngu into the Chinese empire.

1418 After several failed rebellions by Tran loyalists, wealthy farmer Le Loi wages a guerilla war against the occupying Chinese forces. With increasing support from the locals, Le Loi's troops march to Hanoi, the capital of the Ming administration, where the Ming commander Lieu Thang is killed. Ming troops promptly surrender.

1428 Le Loi is named emperor, and he returns to the country its original name, Dai Viet.

The Le dynasty continues in the progressive philosophy of the Ly and Tran dynasties; it is the last dynasty in the country's Golden Age.

1471 Le troops invade neighboring Champa and colonize it in what is now central Vietnam.

1527 The Le dynasty collapses when the last Le king is killed by his own general, Mac Dang Dung, who proclaims himself king and establishes the Mac dynasty. However, a remaining member of the Le family is restored to power in the south with the help of Nguyen Kim, a former court official, and civil war erupts between northern and southern Dai Viet.

1545 Nguyen Kim is assassinated and his son-in-law, Trinh Tung, continues his military command. Fearing that Nguyen Kim's son, Nguyen Hoang, may try to have him killed, Trinh Tung leaves the southern portion of Dai Viet to be ruled by the Nguyen line, while Trinh continues his efforts to conquer the north.

1592 The southern army conquers Hanoi and the civil war between the Mac and Le dynasties ends. The Le dynasty is figuratively restored to power, but Nguyen Kim's descendants are the true rulers.

1600 Feuding occurs between the Trinh and the Nguyen families when Nguyen Hoang declares himself lord and ceases to make payments to the southern armies under Trinh control. He nevertheless continues to honor the Le kings.

1613 Nguyen Hoang dies and is succeeded by his son, Nguyen Phuc Nguyen, who similarly refuses to recognize Trinh power.

1623 Trinh Tung dies and his son, Trinh Trang, succeeds him and issues a demand to Nguyen Phuc Nguyen to honor his authority. Nguyen refuses.

1627 Trinh Trang sends his armies south to conquer the territory of Nguyen Phuc Nguyen.

1627–72 The Trinh-Nguyen war finally ends in a truce, and the country is segmented into two separate domains.

1771 The Tay-Son Rebellion erupts in the Binh Dinh province, which is under Nguyen control. The rebellion is led by three brothers named Nguyen Nhac, Nguyen Lu, and Nguyen Hue, though they are not related to the Nguyen lords.

1786 The Tay-Son army marches north to wage war against the Trinh lord, Trinh Khai, but the Trinh army refuses to fight the Tay-Son army. Trinh Khai commits suicide, and the last Le emperor flees to China. The Tay-Son army seizes the capital, and Nguyen Hue declares himself Emperor Quang Trung.

1792 Emperor Quang Trung is poisoned and dies at the age of 40. Dai Viet is destabilized as Emperor Quang Trung's surviving brothers fight for more political control.

1802 Dethroned prince Nguyen Anh returns to Dai Viet with an army; seizes Hanoi; executes the late emperor's son, Nguyen Quang Toan; and proclaims himself Emperor Gia Long.

During Gia Long's reign, the country is reunified and the Chinese emperor recognizes Dai Viet as Vietnam.

1858 French gunships attack the port of Danang with little effect but further south are able to sack Gia Dinh (Saigon).

1859–67 France takes control of all six provinces in the Mekong Delta and establishes a French colony called Cochin China.

1873 French troops seize Hanoi; this is repeated in 1882.

1887 China cedes Vietnam to France after the Franco-Chinese War. The Nguyen dynasty continues to rule by all appearances, but a French governor makes the political decisions.

1905 The Dong Du ("Go East") movement is founded by Vietnamese nationalist Phan Boi Chau.

1930 The Vietnamese Communist Party is established, but the French administrators suppress its growth by killing some of its top members.

1940 Japan invades Indochina and seizes control of Vietnam but keeps the French administrators in place.

1941 Ho Chi Minh forms the Viet Minh Front, a movement dedicated to Vietnam's independence, but he is overseen by the Communist Party.

1945 A famine cripples northern Vietnam. Two million people starve to death, and the Japanese later surrender to the Allies. In an effort to seize control, the Viet Minh initiate the August Revolution and set out to fill government offices; Emperor Bao Dai abdicates, ending the Nguyen dynasty.

Ho Chi Minh declares Vietnam independent and changes the country's name to the Democratic Republic of Vietnam.

1947 War breaks out between Vietnam and France, during which France allows Vietnam to become a semi-independent state within the French Union, with Bao Dai as the head of the state. Vietnamese forces resist.

The Vietnamese Communist Party launches a violent land-reform campaign to eliminate bourgeois and feudal elements from the arts and literature. Many dedicated Vietnamese revolutionaries are arrested and executed, and the United States openly opposes Ho Chi Minh, choosing instead to recognize the authority of Bao Dai.

1954 The Viet Minh launch an attack against the French strongholds in Dien Bien Phu, and the French army surrenders. Two million northern Vietnamese immigrate south to avoid the new Communist government.

Ngo Dinh Diem is designated the premier of the State of Vietnam.

1955 Ngo Dinh Diem deposes Bao Dai and declares himself president of the Republic of Vietnam (southern Vietnam). Fearing spies and internal threats, Diem eliminates private militias, suppresses revolutionary parties, and attempts to weed out all remaining communist supporters in the south.

1960 Le Duan, a communist from the south, moves north and speaks at the Third Party Congress of the Vietnamese Communist Party, proposing the use of revolutionary warfare to remove President Ngo Dinh Diem from power and to unite northern and southern Vietnam.

1963 Fearing that Ngo Dinh Diem's policies are compromising U.S. efforts to undermine communism in Southeast Asia, the U.S. government, under the Kennedy administration, secretly allows Diem's overthrow.

(continues)

Vietnamese: nationality time line *(continued)*

1965 As southern Vietnam becomes increasingly unstable, the United States, under Lyndon Johnson, sends troops to Vietnam, bombing northern Vietnam in the belief that if southern Vietnam falls under communist rule, then other Southeast Asian countries will be sure to follow.

1967 Lieutenant General Nguyen Van Thieu is elected president of South Vietnam.

1968 The communist-run National Front for the Liberation of South Vietnam (NLF) launches a surprise attack on South Vietnam on Tet, the Vietnamese New Year, bombing all major cities and capturing the city of Hue. The NLF is eventually driven out of these cities, but the violent attack puts the U.S. troops on guard.

A U.S. unit attacks and massacres the small village of My Lai under the belief that it is harboring NLF guerillas.

1969 Ho Chi Minh dies, and despite requests to be cremated, his body is embalmed and displayed in the Ho Chi Minh mausoleum.

1970 As more Americans are beginning to lose hope of any positive outcome of the war, President Richard Nixon reduces the amount of American troop involvement in the fighting but continues to support the South Vietnamese troops with funding and supplies.

1975 The NLF launches an attack on the province of Buon Me Thuot.

President Nguyen Van Thieu resigns and is succeeded by Duong Van Minh, the leader of the coup against Diem.

1975 Concerned more with negotiation and communication than fighting, Duong Van Minh orders a surrender in Saigon, signaling the defeat of South Vietnam and the United States.

1976 Vietnam is officially reunified and called the Socialist Republic of Vietnam.

1978 Vietnamese troops invade Cambodia and overthrow Pol Pot, ending the Khmer Rouge genocide. Vietnam eventually leaves the Cambodian administration to the United Nations.

1986 A period of reforms, *doi moi,* is initiated in response to Mikhail Gorbachev's introduction of the policies of glasnost and perestroika in the Soviet Union.

1989–91 With the collapse of the Soviet Union, the Vietnamese government begins to loosen its grip somewhat on its citizens. Limited freedom is granted to private businesses, and overseas Vietnamese are allowed reentry to visit.

1994 Due to Vietnamese efforts at mending relations with the United States, the latter officially ends the embargo that had been placed on Vietnam in 1974.

1995 Vietnam joins the Association of South-East Asian Nations.

2000 Vietnam opens a stock exchange and allows for a limited amount of political discussion and even open disagreement with the government, although those who vocally dissent are often harassed by police or placed under surveillance.

2006 Vietnam becomes a member of the World Trade Organization.

East movement that sent students abroad to Japan to learn modern skills that would strengthen the Vietnamese people and enable them to fight the technologically advanced French.

In 1940 Japan invaded Vietnam, but most French administrators remained in place. Five years later, colonial exploitation by both the JAPANESE and the French combined with natural disasters led to a famine that killed 2 million people. In 1945 Japan surrendered to the Allies, and the Viet Minh, Vietnam's Communist Party, seized as many government offices as possible. France managed to regain a limited amount of power,

however, and a full-scale war broke out between the Viet Minh and the French. In an attempt to compromise, France granted Vietnam an amount of autonomy by making it a semi-independent state within the French Union. However, as the Viet Minh grew in strength with Chinese support, the French were finally driven out of Vietnam after losing the battle of Dien Bien Phu.

The peace accords that ended the Vietnamese war of independence against France in 1954 divided the country in two. Ngo Dinh Diem was appointed president of South Vietnam, while the Viet Minh took North Vietnam. In 1960 the

Vietnamese Communist Party made the decision to wage war on South Vietnam to overthrow Diem and unite the nation under one Communist government. The movement was named the National Front for the Liberation of South Vietnam (NLF) and received support from China. In the South, Ngo Dinh Diem's regime was becoming problematic for its harsh treatment of its own citizens, especially Buddhists. When the United States became fearful that Diem's regime was jeopardizing its efforts to fight communism in Southeast Asia, the Kennedy administration allowed for the overthrow of Ngo Dinh Diem by South Vietnamese generals.

As the NLF grew stronger, the United States, under President Lyndon Johnson, sent troops to South Vietnam in the belief that if South Vietnam came under communist rule, then other Southeast Asian countries would surely follow, a belief called the domino effect. In 1968 the NLF launched an attack on most of the major cities in South Vietnam on Tet, the day of the Vietnamese New Year. Although the NLF was successfully driven out, the attack shook many Americans, who began to lose faith in the war. By the early 1970s many American people were pushing for withdrawal from the Vietnamese quagmire and for an end to the carpet bombing and other military activities throughout Southeast Asia. Finally, the United States and North and South Vietnam signed the Paris Peace Treaty of 1973. Within Vietnam, however, fighting continued for two more years. Finally, in April 1975 South Vietnamese president Nguyen Phan Thieu resigned, and Saigon fell to the Communists. Duong Van Minh took office and surrendered almost immediately.

In 1976 Vietnam was renamed the Socialist Republic of Vietnam, and heavy industry and agricultural collectivization were emphasized. Private enterprises were seized by the government, and business owners were sent to the New Economic Zone, where they were made to clear land. Agricultural land and implements were likewise seized by the government, and farmers were forced into state-controlled cooperatives. The South Vietnamese economy was devastated, and the South itself faced famine. Tight censorship, reeducation camps, and economic ruin resulted in the mass emigration of more than 1 million people. Many, especially ethnic Chinese who had been heavily involved in private enterprise, fled by boat and were later referred to as "the boat people."

By the 1980s the implementation of glasnost and perestroika in the Soviet Union prompted the Vietnamese government to ease its grip on the Vietnamese people and to experiment with market enterprises; the local movement was called *doi moi*. By the early 1990s a "market economy with a socialist orientation" had been introduced, and the eased controls on art and expression led to a renaissance in Vietnamese art and literature. In 1994 the United States ended the embargo that it had placed on Vietnam in 1975 and re-established trade relations in 1995. The Vietnamese economy consequently began to flourish and in 2000 the Vietnamese government allowed a certain amount of political discussion. In 2006 Vietnam became a member of the World Trade Organization.

CULTURAL IDENTITY

As the Vietnamese people have lived under a number of different rulers and foreign occupations, the Vietnamese culture has been seasoned with a wide range of different influences.

Early Vietnamese culture is believed to have derived primarily from the DONG SON CULTURE, which emerged in the Red River plains around 1200 B.C.E. Early Chinese immigrants who merged with the indigenous peoples also played a foundational role in establishing the Vietnamese culture. As the nation expanded southward throughout the centuries, new communities and cultures were absorbed into mainstream Vietnamese culture and society.

About 1,000 years of Chinese domination have left some of the most profound effects on Vietnamese national identity, not least of which is an adamant national pride that the nation is separate from its larger, northern neighbor. In addition, Confucian principles are predominant at both the household and national levels, with the same principles of leadership, hierarchy, and responsibility being played out in both spheres. Ho Chi Minh is often referred to in Vietnam as Bac Ho, Uncle Ho, to emphasize this connection between the family and the state. For the 74 percent of Vietnamese citizens who continue to reside in rural areas, local values and traditions that come from this Confucianist past are still widely embraced. The clan is heavily emphasized, and whole clans are often composed of a single family name with all members being related.

In addition to these and many other Chinese influences, Vietnamese national identity has likewise been influenced by the long struggle against French colonialism, invasions by the Japanese and Chinese, and the war against the United States. In the past decade or so, many Vietnamese commentators on national life have said that the struggle for national identity has not yet been completed. Capitalist reforms have brought new foreign influences to the country as well as created wide variations in wealth that have not occurred in the past. Both of these features will somehow have to be incorporated into the contemporary understanding of what it means to be a member of the Vietnamese nation in the 21st century.

The other important feature of the Vietnamese nation that the state will have to deal with in the creation of a common cultural identity is its multiethnic character. The dominant Vietnamese make up about 86 percent of the country, while the other 14 percent come from 53 minority groups with vastly different historical, cultural, and linguistic backgrounds. Many of these groups have been fighting the dominant Vietnamese for more than 1,000 years and will continue to do so until they gain recognition of their differences at the state level.

FURTHER READING

Mark A. Ashwill and Thai Ngoc Diep. *Vietnam Today: A Guide to a Nation at a Crossroads* (Yarmouth, Maine: Intercultural Press, Inc., 2005).

Neil L. Jamieson. *Understanding Vietnam* (Berkeley and Los Angeles: University of California Press, 1995).

Stanley Karnow. *Vietnam: A History* (New York: Penguin Books, 1984).

Nguyen Khac Vien. *Vietnam: A Long History* (Hanoi: The Gioi Publishers, 1999).

David Lamb. *Vietnam, Now: A Reporter Returns* (New York: PublicAffairs, 2002).

D. R. SarDesai. *Vietnam: The Struggle for National Identity,* 2nd ed. (Boulder, Colo.: Westview, 1992).

James Sullivan. *National Geographic Traveler: Vietnam* (Washington, D.C.: National Geographic, 2006).

Robert Templer. *Shadows and Wind: A View of Modern Vietnam* (New York: Penguin Books, 1999).

Marilyn Young. *Vietnam Wars, 1945–1990* (New York: HarperCollins, 1991).

Visayans (Bisayas, Bisayans, Pintados)

The Visayans are the largest ethnic group in the Philippines and occupy the central region of the archipelago on the islands of Cebu, Negros, Bohol, Samar, and many others. There are three subcategories of Visayans: CEBUANOS; Samaran, also known as Waray-Waray; and HILI-GAYNON, also known as Ilonggo.

GEOGRAPHY

The Visayas are a group of seven major islands in the central region of the Philippines: Panay, Negros, Cebu, Bohol, Leyte, Masbate, and Samar; there are also numerous smaller islands in the archipelago with Visayan populations on them. The eastern Visayas, including Samar and Leyte, experience the greatest damage due to tropical storms and typhoons because of their location facing the Pacific Ocean, while Masbate, Biliran, and northern Samar are the three regions in the Visayas under the greatest threat from climate disasters in general during the 21st century.

While much of the Philippines is mountainous, with spectacular volcanic cones on both Luzon and Mindanao, the Visayas are comparatively low in elevation and contain far fewer mountains. The highest, Mount Kanlaon at 8,085 feet above sea level and located on the island of Negros, is only 19th in elevation in the country. However, several of the region's mountains are tourist attractions because of their virgin forests and spectacular views, including Mount Madjaas on Panay Island and Mount Cuernos de Negros on Negros Island. Cebu and several other Visayan islands have no mountains at all because rather than being volcanic in origin they are coral; this makes them safer during earthquakes and other seismic activity but at greater risk of flooding due to rising sea levels.

ORIGINS

The origins of the Visayans, like all AUSTRONESIANS in the Philippines, are probably in south China, from where they sailed in double-outrigger dugout canoes about 5,000 years ago to Taiwan, and then later to the Philippines and Polynesia. There is no certainty as to why this population left south China; however, archaeologists have hypothesized that it was a combination of population pressure, increased commerce coming from the Chang (Yangtze) River region of China and moving southward down the river and its tributaries, a growing demand for marine and tropical forest goods, and climate change.

Contemporary Austronesian languages can be subdivided into two distinctive groups that separate the languages of Austronesian Taiwan from those of the remainder of the family, which include all Malay and Oceanic languages. This linguistic division, in addition to several anomalies in the archaeological record, such as a lack of rice in the earliest Austronesian sites on Taiwan, indicates that the origins of the Austronesian people may have been two separate exoduses from southeast China. If these did occur, the first exodus was probably from Fujian province in China to Taiwan, which saw the rise of TA-P'EN-K'ENG CULTURE, with its distinctively marked pottery and stone

VISAYANS

location:
The Visayan Islands, the Philippines

time period:
3000 B.C.E. to the present

ancestry:
Austronesian

language:
There are 21 different Visayan languages, all Central Philippine languages within the larger Austronesian family; Cebuano is the largest with almost 20 million speakers.

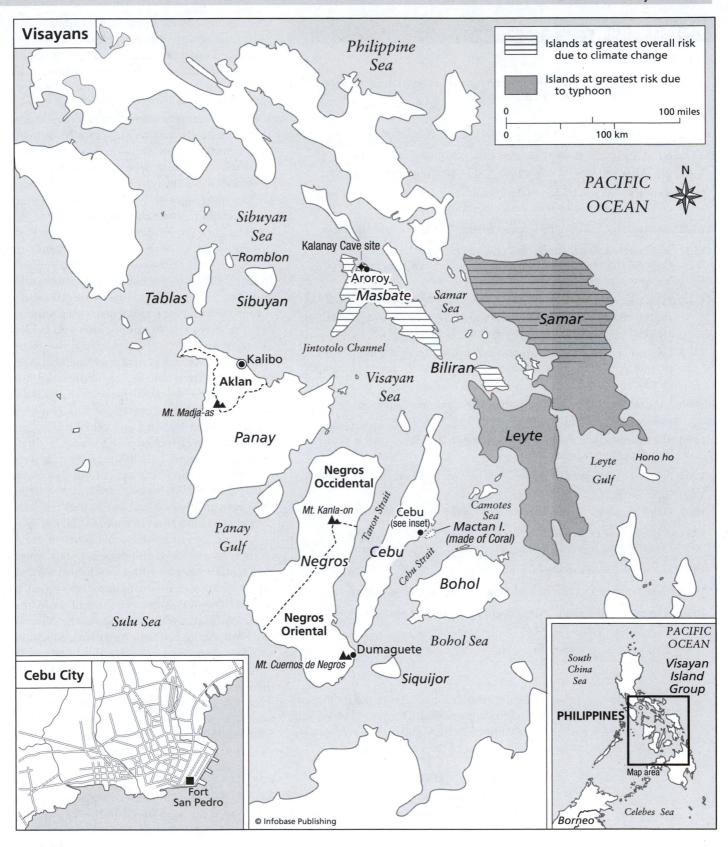

Visayans

Philippine Sea

PACIFIC OCEAN

Islands at greatest overall risk due to climate change

Islands at greatest risk due to typhoon

0   100 miles

0   100 km

Sibuyan Sea

Romblon

Kalanay Cave site

Tablas

Sibuyan

Aroroy

Masbate

Samar Sea

Jintotolo Channel

Samar

Kalibo

Visayan Sea

Aklan

Biliran

Mt. Madja-as

Panay

Leyte

Leyte Gulf

Hono ho

Negros Occidental

Mt. Kanla-on

Cebu (see inset)

Camotes Sea

Panay Gulf

Tanon Strait

Mactan I. (made of Coral)

Cebu

Negros

Cebu Strait

Bohol

Sulu Sea

Negros Oriental

Bohol Sea

Mt. Cuernos de Negros

Dumaguete

Siquijor

© Infobase Publishing

Cebu City

Fort San Pedro

PACIFIC OCEAN

South China Sea

Visayan Island Group

PHILIPPINES

Map area

Borneo

Celebes Sea

tools, but without archaeological evidence of domesticated rice. The descendants of this first wave would be the contemporary speakers of Taiwan's Austronesian languages, the Aboriginal Taiwanese people. The second exodus may have occurred around 3000 B.C.E., taking a second wave of Austronesian speakers from southeastern China to Taiwan and then

Visayans time line

B.C.E.

3000 The initial migration of the Austronesian speakers to the Philippines, including the ancestors of the Visayans.

C.E.

third century Possible date of the initiation of the Kalanay pottery complex on Masbate and other Visayan islands, which displays similarities to the Dong Son culture in Vietnam and other groups in Laos.

fourth century Chinese traders make contact with the Cebuanos and begin centuries of trade between the two peoples.

1400 Arab traders arrive in the Visayan Islands, bringing Islam with them.

1521 Ferdinand Magellan lands on Cebu and converts the local ruler to Catholicism. He is killed a few days later in a battle on the nearby Visayan island of Mactan.

1565 Don Miguel López de Legazpi and Fray Andrés de Urdaneta are successful in their Christianization project in the Visayas. They also build Fort San Pedro, the oldest Spanish fort in the archipelago.

1575 Legazpi and others establish the first Spanish settlement in the archipelago, Villa del Santisimo Nombre de Jesus, on the site of contemporary Cebu City.

1898 General León Kilat leads a band of Cebuanos against the Spanish at Fort San Pedro; he is murdered after five days of battle.

1899 The Spanish cede the Philippines to the United States, and a local war of independence breaks out.

1902 A U.S. civil administration replaces military rule upon the pacification of the independence fighters.

1907 Pedro Alcantara Monteclaro compiles and names the Maragtas legends.

1941 The Japanese occupy the Philippines during World War II and use Cebu as their headquarters.

1944 The United States retakes the Philippines.

1945 The Philippines attains independence from the United States.

1950s The people of Kalibo, Aklan, begin acting out the Maragtas during their feast of the Santo Niño.

1986 Corazon Aquino comes to power in the Philippines.

almost immediately to Luzon in the Philippines around the same period. This second wave, with its red-slipped pottery, may also have been the ultimate source of the LAPITA CULTURE.

HISTORY

When they arrived in the Philippines about 3000 B.C.E., the Austronesian speakers would probably have met small bands of people who had already been residing on the islands for approximately 20,000 years. The hunting and gathering AETA peoples, as they are now called, probably lived in the most productive areas of the country—the coastlines, valleys, and lower hills—in very small, impermanent settlements. With their ability to grow their own crops, the incoming Austronesians were able to maintain significantly higher population densities than the Aeta and thus to push the hunter-gatherers into the more marginal highland forests and mountaintops, where they still live today. The numerically and technologically stronger agriculturalists also seem to have lent their language to the Aeta, all of whom today speak Austronesian languages rather than the more ancient languages they would have brought with them in their much earlier migrations.

One version of pre-Hispanic history in the Philippines, the Maragtas, are legends or myths that tell of the earliest interactions between these two populations, Austronesians and Aeta. According to the Maragtas, Datu (Chief) Makatunaw fled Borneo with a number of his relatives and 10 minor chiefs and landed on the island of Panay. Upon arrival the group was met by Marikudo, leader of the local Aeta population, from whom they purchased the lowlands of the islands; the price was a solid gold hat. For many generations this founding myth has been repeated and celebrated by the Visayans, who all looked back to those 11 chiefs as their ancestors. In 1907 these stories were compiled by Pedro Alcantara Monteclaro, who called them the Maragtas, and since the 1950s they have also been acted out as part the feast days of the Santo Niño in Kalibo, Aklan.

While there may be some basis in truth to these stories, it is impossible to tell where that truth ends and where myth begins. One aspect of ancient Austronesian history that is not mythological is the existence of trade and other cultural relations between the Visayas and both southern China and mainland Southeast Asia at least as early as the third and fourth centuries C.E. The Kalanay pottery complex of the Visayas, named for the cave site on Masbate where the greatest amount of artifacts has been found, is notable for its red and brown pottery with scalloped edges and designs. It is very similar to pottery from the DONG SON CULTURE of Vietnam as well as other early civilizations in Laos. While Dong Son is most noted for its bronze drums and other metalwork, which have not so far been found in the Visayas, the pottery of the two cultures is very similar. Artifacts from both cultures are also most plentiful in caves; although cave dwelling is not unique among prehistoric peoples, its existence in both regions does serve as a possible sign of communication between them.

The Spanish colonial era in the Philippines began in the Visayas, specifically on the island of Cebu, where Magellan first landed in 1521. After his murder on the neighboring island of Mactan, no further Spanish expeditions arrived in the region for 44 years, but when the next ships arrived, they too landed first in the Visayas. It was this second expedition, in 1565, that saw the widespread introduction of Christianity in the archipelago as well as the first colonial battles for control of land, resources, and souls. The Visayans on Cebu continually harassed the Spanish during the first decades of the colonial period, which saw the establishment of both the first fort, Fort San Pedro, and the first city, Cebu City, seven years prior to the founding of Manila.

Eventually Roman Catholic proselytizing did engender widespread cultural change, and the majority of the Visayans converted to the colonizers' religion. Many also learned to speak Spanish and began to work in the sugar estates of Negros or on the coconut plantations located on many other islands. When the Spanish were replaced by the Americans at the beginning of the 20th century, the Visayas were again an important site of both rebellion and colonial control, a pattern that was repeated in 1942 when the Japanese occupied the Philippines and made Cebu their headquarters. The Visayans again emerged as central to the political origins of the new country, with Sergio Osmeña, the first vice president of the Commonwealth of the Philippines, who was the second president, being a Cebuano of mixed Mestizo and Chinese descent.

CULTURE

The Austronesian migrants to the Philippines arrived from Taiwan bearing several domesticated plants, including rice; domesticated pigs, dogs, and chickens; and a lifestyle built around the agricultural calendar. For those Visayans who continue to work in agriculture, rice and corn today make up the most important food crops, while sugar cane and coconuts are important cash crops. Fishing is also an important traditional and present-day source of food and trade goods. Today the region is relatively industrialized; for example, Cebu City is the home of the Timex factory that produced most Timex watches in the late 20th century.

Since the 17th century the vast majority of Visayans have considered themselves Roman Catholic, with only small numbers of Muslims and believers in indigenous animistic religions. Nonetheless, numerous indigenous beliefs and practices have survived more than 400 years of colonialism and modern statehood. One of the most striking is the belief in witchcraft and especially sorcery. These belief systems were particularly important during the transition from traditional to modern ideologies and ways of life as they were experienced at different times on the various islands. When traditional beliefs and practices were still dominant in a community's way of life—which usually included belief in the Catholic trinity, saints, mass, and transubstantiation; subsistence agriculture and fishing; and the centrality of kinship in most people's lives—accusations of sorcery and witchcraft were fairly uncommon. At that time local indigenous or Catholic social control methods were still able to maintain the status quo. However, when a community began to be affected by immigration and emigration, new economic patterns, public schooling, other trappings of modern life, and rival (usually Protestant) religions, but before they became fully entrenched, sorcery and witchcraft accusations became extremely common in the Visayas. Most anthropologists believe that these accusations became a form of local social control to replace kinship and religion before the entrenchment of bureaucratic or governmental controls were able to do so. In the poor barrios around Cebu City and other urban areas in the Visayas, these accusations remain an important way for elders and others with local power to control their populations and maintain at least some of the social status quo.

FURTHER READING

Richard Arens. *Folk Practices and Beliefs of Leyte and Samar* (Tacloban, the Philippines: Divine Word University, 1971).

Jean-Paul Dumont. *Visayan Vignettes: Ethnographic Traces of a Philippine Island* (Chicago: University of Chicago Press, 1992).

Wa *See* VA.

Wakhi *See* PAMIRI.

Wanniyala-Aetto (Vedda, Veddah, Veddha, Wanniya-laeto)

The Wanniyala-Aetto are the indigenous people of Sri Lanka; their name means "forest dweller" in their own language. They are often referred to by the derogatory SINHALESE term *Veddha*, which means "hunter" and refers to a primitive way of life. Today only between 2,000 and 2,500 Wanniyala-Aetto survive.

The Wanniyala-Aetto are believed to be the descendants of Sri Lanka's original Neolithic community, which moved onto the island by at least 16,000 B.C.E. and possibly as early as 30,000 B.C.E. The people survived 2,500 years of colonization by the Sinhalese, TAMILS, Portuguese, Dutch, and British, as well as the formation of the independent state of Sri Lanka in 1948, largely by moving deeper and deeper into the island's dry-zone forest. They lived by hunting boar, deer, birds, and other animals; gathering honey, fruit, roots, and nuts; and in recent centuries by practicing some shifting swidden, or slash-and-burn, horticulture. Each year a family would cut down a small parcel of forest, let the vegetation dry, and then burn it away, leaving a natural ash fertilizer. On the plot they planted grain and vegetables to supplement their gathered foods and meat. This practice has probably been adopted since the colonial period because

the first European to record the locals' existence, Englishman Robert Knox, wrote in the 17th century that they did not till any ground.

Wanniyala-Aetto social structure is similar to the vast majority of small-scale societies in being dominated by kin-based social groupings. There are two conflicting patterns exhibited in their basic kinship system. On the one hand, descent is traced bilaterally, so that both parents are considered equal contributors to a child's kindred. On the other hand, however, each individual Wanniyala-Aetto is also a member of a matrilineal exogamous clan that he or she is born into, based on the mother's clan group. In contemporary terms, Wanniyala-Aetto bear the family name of their mother rather than their father. This is considered a logical practice in that the identity of one's mother can never be in question while fathers are less certain; men also tend to die younger due to hunting accidents and upon a mother's remarriage children need not change their name or clan membership. Despite these patterns, the Wanniyala-Aetto are also patrilocal so that at her marriage a woman must move into her husband's home.

Religion among the Wanniyala-Aetto was traditionally animistic and recognized a variety of nature spirits, ancestors, and gods. The forest was the most important sacred being in their cosmology, and it was inhabited by a large number of ancestors and spirits whom each individual was bound to protect. In recent decades most Wanniyala-Aetto have adopted either

---

WANNIYALA-AETTO

location:
Sri Lanka

time period:
Possibly 30,000 B.C.E. to the present

ancestry:
Unknown

language:
Sinhalese, Tamil, and their own language, commonly called Veddah

Buddhism or Hinduism, depending on which region of the country they live in, with those in Sinhalese areas adopting the former, those in Tamil regions the latter. However, these conversions are largely nominal rather than actual. There are several Wanniyala-Aetto villages in the Anuradhapura region, however, where the inhabitants are not only practicing Buddhists but also agriculturalists very much like their Sinhalese neighbors. Nonetheless, men in these communities still consider themselves "hunters," and the majority identify themselves as people of the forest.

The worst dislocations suffered by these people have occurred since 1955. In that year the construction of the World Bank–funded Gal Oya Dam was begun, flooding much of the remaining Wanniyala-Aetto hunting grounds, caves, and honey sites. At that time most people were moved into "rehabilitation villages" and forced to adopt Sinhalese agricultural practices, language, and other cultural traits. However, a few families followed tribal leader Uru Warige Tissahamy further into the forest and escaped the pressures to assimilate into Sri Lankan society. This group experienced the same dislocation again after 1977 when the World Bank funded yet another hydro project, this time the Mahaweli Ganga hydroelectric project. More than 11,000 hectares of Wanniyala-Aetto forest lands were clear-cut, and thousands of internal migrants, both Sinhalese and Tamil, moved into the area. The last refuge for about 900 Wanniyala-Aetto families was finally taken from them in November 1983 when the Sri Lankan government turned their homeland into the Maduru Oya National Park. Ironically, the park had widespread international support, from the United Nations Environment Program to the World Wide Fund for Nature.

Since 1983 these remaining families, estimated to be between 2,000 and 5,000 people at that time, have been again resettled in villages outside their sacred forest. The least fortunate were moved to the Pollonaruwa district, one of the sites of the worst fighting of the Sri Lankan civil war between Sinhalese nationalists and Tamil rebels. Curfews meant an inability to visit families and friends outside their region, and war led to the destruction of fields and property, and even death. Even those who were moved elsewhere, however, suffered from the sudden change in diet and subsistence pattern and loss of culture. Many live on state welfare, and depression, alcoholism, and obesity and its related diseases are common problems. Few older Wanniyala-Aetto speak Sinhalese or Tamil well enough to understand the state's bureaucracy or to work as anything other than unskilled laborers, and younger people tend not to do as well in school as children from these other ethnic groups.

In 1990 the Sri Lankan government did try to address the grievances of a group of Wanniyala-Aetto, represented by Tissahamy, who is sometimes referred to as a chief of the Wanniyala-Aetto. Sri Lankan president Ranasinghe Premadasa and his minister for lands, irrigation, and Mahaweli development set aside 1,500 acres that had been designated Maduru Oya National Park lands for Wanniyala-Aetto traditional subsistence activities and established a government agency to deal with cultural questions concerning this population. Unfortunately, this small amount of land is insufficient for more than a handful of individuals, and all traditional subsistence activities, from honey gathering to swidden agriculture, are forbidden in the national park. Therefore, occasionally over the years, small groups of Wanniyala-Aetta have tried to reenter their forest home either for short periods to engage in traditional subsistence practices or to live. In the early 21st century several were shot by park rangers aiming to protect the Maduru Oya National Park from the land's traditional owners.

FURTHER READING

James Brow. *Vedda Villages of Anuradhapura: The Historical Anthropology of a Community in Sri Lanka* (Seattle: University of Washington Press, 1978).

Warlpiri (Ilpirra, Wailpiri, Walbiri, Walpiri)

The Warlpiri are a subgroup of the ABORIGINAL AUSTRALIANS that live in the Tanami Desert of the Northern Territory, outside Alice Springs. This group first came into contact with European explorers during the 1860s, but in the first decades of the 20th century the development of large cattle stations in the region brought sustained interactions between the two communities. The greatest impact on the Warlpiri in this period followed the 1928 killing at Coniston Station of a station hand; afterward, 31 Warlpiri were officially reported as being killed by local police, though this number is generally regarded to be underestimated. The Warlpiri people scattered to various cattle stations in the area seeking protection, and many Warlpiri men became stockmen while the women did domestic work in the station homesteads. In

---

WARLPIRI

location:
Northwest of Alice Springs in the Tanami Desert, east of the Northern Territory–West Australia border, Australia

time period:
possibly 60,000 B.C.E. to the present

ancestry:
Aboriginal Australian

language:
Warlpiri, a member of the Ngumpin-Yapa subgroup of Pama-Nyungan languages, closely related to Warlmanpa

1946 the seminomadic existence of the Warlpiri generally came to an end when the remaining hunter-gatherers were almost entirely relocated to the new government settlement of Yuendumu, 180 miles northwest of Alice Springs.

Anthropologists working with the Warlpiri not long after settlement believed that prior to settlement there were four separate subgroups: Yalpari, Waneiga, Walmalla, and Ngalia, the members of which referred to one another as "countrymen." Notes on the early settlement of Yuendumu state that residences there continued to follow the lines from the past, so that "countrymen" of the same subgroups tended to live in closer proximity to one another than to others. More contemporary anthropologists, however, have found that today's residents of Yuendumu tend not to use membership in a particular country as the basis for decisions to move, a common occurrence; instead, these decisions come about as the result of a wide variety of other social, economic, and political choices.

Changes in aboriginal policies in Australia generally in the 1960s and 1970s once again changed the dynamics of life in and around Yuendumu and the other, smaller Warlpiri settlements in the Central Desert. For example, the introduction of equal pay for aboriginal and nonaboriginal workers in the cattle industry in 1968 resulted in most Warlpiri being laid off. Consequently, many Warlpiri even today remain unemployed and live by federally subsidized transfer payments; Yuendumu in the early 21st century had a 90 percent unemployment rate. Further change occurred in 1976 when the Northern Territory passed its Aboriginal Land Rights Act; this ultimately returned about 62,000 square miles of Warlpiri land to its native owners, territory that included Yuendumu. A year later the creation of the Community Development Employment Projects (CDEP) provided meaningful employment for tens of thousands of remote and rural indigenous Australians, including many Warlpiri. In the 21st century, however, under a Liberal (conservative) Australian government, these last two gains were rolled back in favor of government leases to aboriginal communities and the abolishment of not only the CDEP but also the Aboriginal and Torres Strait Islander Commission (ATSIC), the political unit representing many remote, rural, and urban aboriginal peoples in Australia. It remains to be seen what the Labor government elected in late November 2007 will do with regard to these inherited policies.

Although many changes have occurred in Warlpiri society in the past century, some aspects of traditional culture remain central to Warlpiri identity as individuals and as members of communities. While the Warlpiri follow the principle of patrilineal descent with regard to land rights, their kinship system is actually more complex than a simple unilineal system; instead, each individual recognizes all four grandparents' lines of descent. These lines of descent are further divided into patrilateral, matrilateral, and generational moieties, semimoieties, and subsections, resulting in eight named categories that distinguish between male and female members of each group. This intricate system serves to define who can and cannot marry, responsibilities during grieving and other rituals, and most other aspects of Warlpiri social organization.

Even today religion for the Warlpiri is focused on a central concept of *jukurrpa,* or "the dreaming," referring to the time that the world was created, long before the arrival of Europeans. Ancestral heroes from this period of time shaped the land into what it is today. These ancestral figures, along with *gugu,* or semimalevolent figures designed to encourage proper behavior, and *mungamunga,* or female ancestral spirits, are central to Warlpiri religion. While some adults are regarded as especially knowledgeable, there are no religious leaders in the Warlpiri tradition. The ceremonies and songs that formed out of these traditions have shaped the various dances for which the Warlpiri are known today.

FURTHER READING

Mervyn J. Meggitt. *Desert People: A Study of the Walbiri Aborigines of Central Australia* (Sydney, Austral.: Angus and Robertson, 1962).

White Huns *See* HEPHTHALITES.

Wong Djawa *See* JAVANESE.

X

Xianbei (Hsien-p(e)i, Syanbiy, Xianbi)

HISTORY

The Xianbei were a formerly nomadic people from northeast of China who established the most powerful and longest surviving of the Northern Dynasties during a period of relative unrest in China in the first half millennium of the common era. They were descendants of the proto-Tungusic DONGHU people and until they were thoroughly sinicized spoke the Tungusic Xianbei language. Genetically, they have been most closely linked to China's OROQEN people, Mongolians and EVENKIS.

The Xianbei themselves believed that their ancestors emerged from a sacred cave in what is today Inner Mongolia. In 1980 archaeologists working in the region of the Gaxian Cave site in Inner Mongolia discovered an inscription and a variety of material finds indicating that this probably was the region from which the Xianbei migrated toward China in the first century of the common era.

The Xianbei were made up of a variety of different clans. The most powerful was the Toba, or Tuoba, who formed the backbone of the Northern Wei dynasty that ruled this northern region from 386 to 534. Other clans include the Tufa, who also established a short-lived state in the early fifth century; the Murong, who exerted extensive control over the other northern peoples for shorter periods in the third and fourth centuries; and the Qifu,

who established the Western Qin dynasty in Shaanxi, 385–431.

The Northern Wei state was formed by Tuoba Gui in 386 after he had been held as a hostage by the ruling Qin dynasty for a number of years; many of the Xianbei people had also been transported to Shandong Province and settled as agriculturalists rather than nomadic pastoralists by the anxious Qin. Tuoba Gui was able to consolidate his power over rival chiefs and nomadic peoples and establish his capital at Pingcheng, which is today Datong in Shaanxi Province, by 398. He ruled most of contemporary Xinjiang Province as well as territory stretching north to the Gobi Desert.

The history of the Northern Wei dynasty is one of open struggle against the influx of other northern nomadic groups coming south to raid Chinese territory and establish themselves as politically dominant. The ROURAN were the largest of these nomadic groups, but many others also fought the Wei along their northern borders, inspiring them to rebuild portions of the Great Wall in 423 and then again in 543. In 429 the Northern Wei began a 10-year military campaign against these northern nomads, who repeatedly came south from Outer Mongolia to raid the settled farms and villages of northern China. This campaign was successful for a time, but the rebuilding of the wall in 543 indicates that the strategy was not a permanent solution.

The other dominant thread in Northern Wei history is the sinicization process of abandoning Xianbei cultural traits in favor of HAN

XIANBEI

location:
Originally from Inner Mongolia, migrated southward and ruled much of the region north of the Yangtze (Chang) River

time period:
First century C.E. to 589

ancestry:
Donghu, a proto-Tungus group

language:
The Xianbei language, which was probably Tungusic and was largely replaced by Han Chinese in the fifth and sixth centuries

Xianbei time line

C.E.

early first century Probably the era in which the Xianbei first migrate south from their original homeland in Inner Mongolia. This marks the transition from Donghu to Xianbei and Wuhuan peoples.

156 Tanshikui, a Xianbei chief, creates a Xianbei alliance with thousands of Huns. It disintegrates upon his death in 181.

258 The first Xianbei federation is formed from the various Xianbei clans.

270s Tuoba Yituo becomes the first Xianbei to earn a military rank in a Chinese dynasty when he comes to the assistance of the Western Jin dynasty.

317 All of northern China has been subsumed by nomadic groups, including the Xianbei from the north.

338–76 The Tuoba Xianbei form the short-lived Dai state in the region of Shanxi.

386 Formation of the State of Wei by Tuoba Gui; within a dozen years he controls most of northern China from his capital at Pingcheng or contemporary Datong in Shaanxi Province.

397–414 The Tufa Xianbei establish the Southern Liang state as part of the larger Jin dynasty.

415 The Rouran khan, Yujiulu Datan, invades the Wei and is driven out, but the troops that pursue them back into their territory are decimated by the cold.

423 The Northern Wei build portions of the Great Wall to keep the Rouran and other nomads out of China.

429 The Rouran and other nomadic groups from the north are defeated by the Northern Wei.

443 The legendary cave of Xianbei origin myths is found in Inner Mongolia, known today as the Gaxian Cave site.

446–52 Emperor Dai Wudi changes the religion of state for the Wei from Buddhism to Taoism and tries to eliminate Buddhist clergy, monasteries, art, and literature from the state. Buddhism returns to its central place at the Wei court upon his death in 452.

470 The Rouran are again defeated by the Northern Wei.

496 Emperor Xiaowen, who believes himself a Confucian scholar, orders all Xianbei family names to be replaced with those of the Han in conjunction with his overall plan to sinicize his people; Xianbei clothing and language also come under fire in his attempt to assimilate the people to the Han.

524 A military uprising occurs in protest over what is felt to be excessive sinicization and Buddhist patronage by the Wei royal court.

534 After a period of civil war the empire is divided into Eastern and Western Wei dynasties.

589 The Sui dynasty supplants the two Wei dynasties and brings an end to Xianbei power. By this time many Xianbei had been thoroughly sinicized, and it is difficult to speak of Xianbei people any more.

1980 The inscription for the Gaxian Cave site is found, verifying the stories from 443.

Chinese ones. Often this process was voluntary. The numbers of Xianbei burial sites that have been found with Chinese-style statues of animals and humans indicate how widespread this process was. However, when voluntary sinicization was not forthcoming from the Xianbei people, their rulers were not averse to using coercion. Many Xianbei rulers forced their assimilating agenda onto a reluctant populace because they saw assimilating to Han culture as both legitimating their rule in the north of the country and as a way of pleasing the emperors in the south. For example, in the last years of the fifth and early sixth centuries, Emperor Xiaowen began a period of intensive sinicization by outlawing Xianbei surnames and clothing in favor of Han ones; he also attempted to replace the Xianbei language entirely with

Mandarin Chinese. After the division of the Northern Wei into eastern and western sections in 534, the ruler of the Western Wei attempted to reverse the name policy but with little success. The author of the state-sponsored history of the Northern Wei Dynasty, Wei Shou, writing between 551 and 554, consistently utilized the shorter Han names throughout his volume, *The Book of Wei*, even for historical periods before this overt act of sinicization, and he thus solidified the usage in later periods as well.

Another long-term aspect of this sinicization process was the adoption of Buddhism as the state religion of the Northern Wei. Large amounts of money and land were given to Buddhist monasteries and convents as well as for the production of Buddhist art and literature. This extravagant support continued throughout most of the period of Northern Wei dominance, except for the years 446–452, when Taoism temporarily supplanted Buddhism as the religion of state. At that time anything Buddhist came under fire from the emperor Dai Wudi. In the decade following this short lull, Emperor Wencheng revived Buddhism, and to atone for his grandfather's acts of desecration, he commissioned the carving of more than 50,000 Buddhist statues within more than 50 caves at Yungang. Many of these statues have survived and are still visible today.

While sinicization may have been a useful strategy for gaining the support of China's southern emperors as well as the large numbers of Chinese who lived within the territory of the Northern Dynasties, it was not always accepted by ordinary Xianbei without a struggle. Indeed, it was these struggles rather than any outside force that eventually led to the dismantling of the Northern Wei. In 524 Xianbei who were frustrated with their leaders' overt favoritism toward anything Chinese as well as the great amounts of state wealth given over to Buddhist organizations rose up against these leaders. This was soon followed by a full-scale civil war a few years later, leading to the division of the empire into Eastern and Western Wei in 534. These two separate dynasties survived only about 50 more years before being replaced by the Sui dynasty, which finally reunified northern and southern China for the first time in several hundred years.

CULTURE

In the early years of their existence, the Xianbei resembled many of the other nomadic peoples who resided in the frontier region north of China.

These are just two of the tens of thousands of statues that were carved in the Yungang caves during the period after 452 C.E. *(Shutterstock/Buddhadl)*

They fought with bows and arrows while at full gallop on horseback and survived largely as nomadic pastoralists and on tribute taken from vanquished enemies. Unlike many other nomadic groups, however, the Xianbei did not have hereditary rulers but temporary military leaders who were chosen based on skill and bravery.

Once they began to rule their portion of the north of China in 386, the Xianbei came to resemble their settled neighbors in many ways. Rather than pastoralism they engaged in agriculture, growing cereal crops, vegetables, and fruit as well as raising a few animals for personal use, which required them to live in villages rather than practicing nomadism. They also engaged in the active trade between China and Central Asia that marked the era, which brought Indian, Persian, Hellenistic, and even Roman goods to their region, including pottery, glass, and metal objects. These wide-reaching trade relationships also significantly influenced their own art, literature, and architecture. Burial sites in and around the Northern Wei capital of Pincheng were especially rich in luxury goods from these far-off places.

See also MONGOLIANS: NATIONALITY; CHINESE: NATIONALITY.

FURTHER READING

Jennifer Holmgren. *Annals of Tai: Early T'o-pa History According to the First Chapter of the Wei-shu* (Canberra: Faculty of Asian Studies in association with Australian National University Press, 1982).

Luo Zongzhen. *Nationalities in Division and Merger: The Wei and Jin Period as Well as the Northern and Southern Dynasties* (Hong Kong: The Commercial Press Limited, 2001).

Xibe (Shive, Sibe, Xibo)

The Xibe are one of China's recognized 55 national minority groups; they live in two different provinces, Liaoning and Xinjing, separated by more than 1,000 miles. The Xibe consider their ancestors to be the ancient XIANBEI people, a Tungusic people of Inner Mongolia, but there is no genetic or archaeological evidence to support this origin myth. Their language is very closely related to that of the MANCHUS and may indicate common ancestry with the MOHE or other ancient peoples of Manchuria.

The Xibe first came to the attention of Chinese chroniclers during the reign of the MONGOLS in the 12th century, when the Xibe were living largely as hunter-gatherers; they also relied heavily on fish for protein. They were forced to pay tribute to the Mongol rulers but did not significantly change their way of life. More drastic changes emerged in the 16th century when Manchu rulers settled the nomadic Xibe into agricultural villages. While the Manchus recognized that the Xibe were culturally and linguistically related to them, the nomadic, warrior way of life of the Xibe was a threat to Manchu hegemony. When settlement failed to assimilate the Xibe fully to Manchu society, at the end of the 17th century large numbers of Xibe soldiers and their dependents were dispatched throughout the empire, particularly to remote Xinjiang. This dispersal process continued for about 100 years and resulted in the split population of Xibe today in China's northeast and northwest regions.

Today's Xibe are both pastoralists who manage herds of sheep, goats, cattle, and other animals and farmers who grow wheat, rice, cotton, and a variety of other subsistence and cash crops. Rice was part of the cultural package the Xibe adopted from their HAN neighbors after dispersal in the 16th–18th centuries and, as with many other Chinese traits, is much more common among Liaoning Xibe than among those in Xinjiang. Other differences between these distant communities include village size; religion; language, where those in the northeast are more likely to speak Chinese or to infuse their language with Chinese vocabulary; and even identification as Xibe.

Xibe villages in Xinjiang are walled enclosures containing 100–200 houses and fewer than 1,000 people, while those in Liaoning are considerably larger and reflect the housing and settlement patterns of the surrounding Han. The religion of the Xinjiang Xibe is also more traditional than that in Liaoning and features numerous gods, spirits, and other supernatural beings. Central to these is the earth spirit, Dragon, and insect kings Xilimama, who is a domestic god overseeing tranquility in the household, and Hairkan, who overseas livestock. Xibe shamans commune with these and other spirits and pass messages back and forth between the human realm and that of the spirits in order to heal the sick and to give thanks. Most religious activity in China was strongly persecuted until the early 1980s, when they ceased, but today a few activities have revived in Xinjiang.

Like their neighbors in both the northeast and northwest, the Xibe are patrilineal and trace descent through the male line only. Above the level of the family and lineage, there are also larger kinship groups of *mokon,* which are essentially clans in that they link together groups of lineages based on a common male ancestor; and *hala,* or phratries, made up of people with the same patrilineal surname. These groupings, as with so much of traditional Xibe culture, are more salient among Xinjiang Xibe, while those in Liaoning are more likely to associate and identify with residential units called *gashan,* people who come together to engage in common labor. In Liaoning this is usually farm or irrigation work; those *gashan* that exist in Xinjiang are as likely to be for hunting as for farmwork.

Xiongnu (Asian Huns, Asiatic Huns, Hongnu, Hsiung-nu, Hunnu, Huns of Asia, Qun, Xwn)

The Xiongnu were a nomadic pastoralist confederation originating in the plains of northern China and Mongolia. They rose to prominence in the fourth and third centuries B.C.E. through their raids on the settled, agricultural Chinese communities to their south. Over the next few centuries the Xiongnu incorporated many other nomadic peoples into their confederation and drove the Yuezhi west, where they are better known as the KUSHANS, before eventually disintegrating in the face of a stronger Chinese force.

GEOGRAPHY

The Xiongnu originated on the steppes of northern China and Mongolia, eventually spreading out toward Central Asia and deeper into China. This region experienced a change in climate about 3,500 years ago, which allowed for the development of a vast, grassy plain, more suitable for nomadic pastoralism than for the agricultural societies that had developed there prior to this change. Numerous nomadic groups faced the challenge of the centralized Chinese state to the south and the other nomadic groups with whom they shared the plains. Only the names and cultures of the most successful of these groups have come down to us today, including the Xiongnu, MONGOLS, and TURKIC PEOPLES. During the initial height of Xiongnu power in the years between 208 and 175 B.C.E., their territory stretched from Lake Baikal in the north to the Ordos Plateau in the south. A century and a half later, when their power in the east had diminished in the face of Chinese might, their influence extended into the Ural foothills and the Volga region of European Russia.

ORIGINS

Many theories about the origins of the Xiongnu have emerged in the past 200 years, but none of them has been proven to be incontrovertibly true. The two most common claims are that they were a Siberian branch of the Mongols or that they had Turkic origins. Due to their lack of writing and their cultural similarities to both groups, this matter may never be fully resolved.

HISTORY

The first commentary on the Xiongnu comes from Chinese sources of the fourth and third centuries B.C.E., which mention the increasing success of Xiongnu raids on Chinese communities at that time. In the third century the incursions from the north became so troublesome to his people that the Qin leader, Qin Shi Huangdi, decided to build a giant defensive wall to keep them out. A large number of independent fortifications had been built about two centuries earlier to protect China's northern border, but it was the Xiongnu who pushed Qin to connect many of these structures into a 1,400-mile-long defensive barrier, the Great Wall of China.

The first known leader of the Xiongnu was Touman, or Batur Tengriqut, who united all of the nomadic peoples of the northern steppes and ruled them from 220 to 209 B.C.E. During his reign, nomadic raids on China increased, and the Xiongnu prospered due to the extensive pasture land they captured from their enemies. According to legend, Touman feared for the succession of his oldest son to his throne and gave his younger son, Maodun or Motun, to the

Xiongnu time line

B.C.E.

220–209 Touman rules the Xiongnu and unites many of the nomadic tribes living in the region of Mongolia to invade northern China.

214 The Great Wall of China begins as defense against the Xiongnu and other nomadic groups from the north.

209–175 Maodun expands the Xiongnu empire to its greatest extent.

203 The Xiongnu conquer the Yuezhi.

160 Beginning of the decline of the Xiongnu empire with the death of Laoshang.

127–117 The Han take control of the Tarim Basin region away from the Xiongnu.

58 The Xiongnu empire breaks up into eastern and western sections when Huhanye accepts Han protection for the east and Zhizhi Chanyu declares his independence in the west.

36 The western empire in Transoxiana is conquered by the Han.

18 The eastern empire regains its independence.

C.E.

48 Eastern Xiongnu break up into Northern and Southern Xiongnu.

156 The Xianbei subjugate the Northern Xiongnu.

216 The Han conquer the Southern Xiongnu.

Fourth century Individuals fleeing the disintegration of the Xiongnu empire migrate westward from Turkestan.

rival Yuezhi tribes as a political slave. Maodun eventually escaped this bondage by killing the Yuezhi chief and returning to his own people, where his father, impressed by his son's skills, made him a high-ranking military leader. Not long after, in 209 B.C.E., Maodun killed his father and possibly his older brother as well in what is sometimes labeled a hunting accident. He then was able to take the title of Chanyu, probably meaning something like "The Magnificent" or "The Great" in the Xiongnu language. This story, like those that ascribe great power to Maodun because of the mystical jade ornaments he stole from the graves of other nomadic kings, is probably a legend that developed around his military might, but without any written Xiongnu texts we will probably never know.

The Xiongnu achieved their greatest military triumphs and glory during Maodun's reign, 208–175 B.C.E. Rather than focus his armies' energies on China, Maodun looked east and west for sources of slaves and tribute. In 208 B.C.E. the Xiongnu defeated the DONGHU, another nomadic steppe people, who split into two separate groups, XIANBEI and Wuhuan.

XIONGNU

location:
Northern China and Mongolia, with an empire that stretched from Lake Baikal in the north to the Ordos plateau in the south

time period:
Third century B.C.E. to fourth century C.E.

ancestry:
Uncertain, possibly Mongol or Turkic

language:
Uncertain, possibly Mongol or Turkic

The fortification known as the Great Wall that was begun more than 2,200 years ago to deter the marauding Xiongnu; it stretches approximately 4,160 miles (6,700 km). *(Shutterstock/ Goydenko Tatiana)*

Maodun also defeated a number of Turkic peoples, including the DINGLING, and in 203 B.C.E. he conquered the people who had held him captive in his youth, the Yuezhi, initiating their migration westward into Bactria.

With these victories the Xiongnu achieved even greater prosperity and military strength, which gave Maodun the ability to challenge China once again. He discovered that the Great Wall did not pose a difficult challenge to breach, and by the end of his reign he had forced the Chinese ruler Gaodi into paying tribute to him. In fact, by the time of his death his dominion stretched from Korea in the east to Lake Balkash in the west, from Lake Baikal in the north to Tibet in the south. Rather than rule these areas directly, as they did with their fellow nomads, the Xiongnu simply extorted tribute from the settled populations and made occasional forays into their territories to take supplies, animals, and slaves. To date, Maodun's gravesite has not been found, and the cause of his death remains unknown.

The next key period in Xiongnu history comes two generations later when, between 130 and 121 B.C.E., the Chinese finally expelled the Xiongnu and forced them back across the Great Wall as far north as central Mongolia. In 58 B.C.E. the strength of the HAN was so great that the leader of one portion of the Xiongnu empire, Huhanye, accepted the position of protectorate of the Chinese state, thus reversing the positions between the two empires, at least temporarily. In response, Luanti Hutuwusi declared his independence from his brother Huhanye and took the title Zhizhi Chanyu, thus splitting the Xiongnu empire into a Han protectorate in the east and an independent Western section. This independent section then turned its forces westward, reaching as far as Afghanistan, Turkmenistan, and even the Volga River by 44 B.C.E. A revitalized Han army, however, also marched west and in 36 B.C.E. attached Zhizhi's capital in the Talas Valley of contemporary Kyrgyzstan and killed him, destroying the last remains of the Western Xiongnu empire.

Despite the alliance between the Eastern Xiongnu and the Han in the middle decades of the first century B.C.E., with Huhanye's death in 31 B.C.E. the still-nomadic Xiongnu resumed their military struggle against Han rule, finally defeating them in 18 B.C.E. This newly revitalized Eastern Xiongnu empire, however, was unable to sustain its territorial acquisitions and itself broke into northern and southern sections in 48 C.E., in the face of Xianbei and Han incursions earlier in the century. The southern section soon accepted a similar protectorate relationship with the Han, which had protected the Eastern Xiongnu, while the northern section chose to remain independent until falling to the Xianbei in 156 C.E. The southern section itself was finally conquered by the Han in 216.

Although all traces of Xiongnu empires disappeared early in the third century, the Xiongnu people themselves continued to live their largely nomadic lives throughout the steppes of Central Asia. In the east, small Xiongnu kingdoms emerged in the chaos following the fall of the Han dynasty in 220 C.E. Another large group was made up of the remnants of the Western Xiongnu, many of whom had settled in Turkestan and taken up agriculture. However, in 350 this population began migrating westward toward Europe, where it may have formed the backbone of the European Huns, although this remains merely conjecture at this time.

CULTURE

Much of what we know about Xiongnu culture as well as history comes from Chinese texts since the Xiongnu themselves did not leave any writing. Unfortunately, these texts often contradict the archaeological record. For example, the Chinese wrote that the Xiongnu lived solely on hunting and did not build any towns. However, since the late 19th century archaeologists have found a large number of Xiongnu gravesites, fortresses, and even cities along with evidence of agriculture and a highly developed class of craftsmen who worked in wood, leather, felt, gold, iron, and bronze. The majority of these finds come from the Trans-Baikal region of Russia, northern Mongolia, and northern China and thus represent the heartland of Xiongnu culture rather than the outposts established after the breakup of the empires.

The archaeological record does point to a largely nomadic society based primarily on herding cattle and raising horses, living in felt tents, and using bows and arrows while astride a galloping horse. However, at least as early as the first century B.C.E., some Xiongnu had settled down to raise millet, wheat, and barley, while others became master craftsmen. The primary motif on most of the articles created by these craftsmen is animals, especially birds of prey, which can be seen on belt buckles, plaques, statues, and the handles of weapons. There is also evidence in their art that the Xiongnu may have worshiped the sun, moon, earth, and their ancestors, although their specific beliefs and practices are not yet known. From the gravesites that have been found we also know that chiefs and kings were buried with wives, concubines, and servants who were killed and buried along with the ruler, probably to assist him in the afterlife.

The structure of the Xiongnu empire resembled many others that emerged on the steppes. All authority was held by the members of a single royal family and a limited number of related clans. This led to a great deal of instability as brother competed with brother for the ultimate leadership position, and clan competed with clan for influence and power. The lack of any writing system would also have contributed to the instability of the Xiongnu since all questions of inheritance and succession would have to be spread by word of mouth alone. This would have given strong, clever, or even lucky military men the chance to make leadership claims based on their reputations rather than on the inherited legitimacy of their claims.

FURTHER READING

Adam T. Kessler, *Empires beyond the Great Wall: The Heritage of Genghis Khan,* trans. Bettine Birge (Los Angeles: Natural History Museum of Los Angeles County, 1994).

Xodang   *See* SEDANG.

Yakuts (Jeko, Sakhas, Urungkhay Sakhas, Yako)

YAKUTS

location:
Mostly in Yakutia, north-central Siberia, especially along the Lena, Aldan, and Vilyuy Rivers, with smaller populations residing even further to the northeast

time period:
Probably sixth century to the present

ancestry:
Turkic probably mixed with Evens, Evenkis, and other indigenous Siberians

language:
Yakut or Sakha, a northern Turkic language within the larger Altaic language family

The Yakuts are Turkic-speaking tribes who migrated north from the Lake Baikal region in about the sixth century to their current homeland in Yakutia in central Siberia. The largest numbers of Yakuts reside along the Lena, Aldan, and Vilyuy Rivers, but smaller numbers also live further to the northeast along the Yama and Indigirka Rivers and further west on the coast of the Laptev Sea. This region is dominated by taiga vegetation, with tundra prevailing in the north.

The southern Yakuts differed from most of their Siberian neighbors in focusing much of their economic activity on breeding horses and cattle rather than hunting and fishing, although the northern Yakuts tended to combine reindeer herding with hunting and fishing. Larger animals such as wolverines, bears, musk deer, and reindeer as well as smaller animals such as squirrels, foxes, ferrets, and ermine, in addition to the rivers' and seas' large fish supplies, traditionally provided ample food sources for the region's few inhabitants. Both northern and southern Yakuts were seminomadic, moving seasonally to accommodate the needs of their herds or to locate animals and fish. Generally their winter encampments were very small, just one or two families with a total population of less than 20, while summer camps tended to be quite a bit larger because of the greater food supplies at that time of year. These larger summer camps provided ample opportunities for engaging in clan rituals and finding marriage partners. Both populations also lived in easily transportable square yurts, somewhat different from the round yurts evident today in Mongolia.

The social structure of Yakut society was dominated at the lowest level by nuclear families, which resided in the same yurt and moved together seasonally. These were traditionally monogamous families, but in the early 19th century certain wealthy Yakut men adopted polygyny, the practice of marrying more than one wife. Each wife maintained her own yurt but moved together with the common husband seasonally. The next level of social organization was the patrilineage, groups of families in which the men were all related to one another and to a common male ancestor. Patrilineal groups tended to live together in the larger summer camps. Groups of lineages were also loosely organized into exogamous *aymakhs*, or clans; each clan traced its heritage back to a common male ancestor and required clan members to marry someone from a different *aymakh*. These *aymakhs* were the largest unit for which individual Yakuts would go to war, a common occurrence prior to the encroachment on their territory by the RUSSIANS. The clans were divided into commoner and noble lineages, which owned large herds of animals and employed both foreign slaves and commoners to tend them; the leaders of these noble lineages were also the military leaders who led the *aymakh* during times of war.

As was the case throughout Siberia, Yakut traditional religion combined elements from animism, the belief in spirits, and shamanism. The most important spirit was that of fire, considered sacred and, as might be expected given the cold, dark environment in which they lived, the protector of life and family. Shamans were powerful women or men, who were considered less powerful, who had the ability to communicate with, and even migrate back and forth between this world and the world of the spirits. Shamans communicated with the spirits to find out the causes of illness among both humans and animals and to cure them, to foretell the future, and to give advice. As was true of other Turkic peoples, blacksmiths were also believed to have control over some spirits.

The Yakuts were first reached by Russian traders in the 16th and 17th centuries; they were followed by settlers in the 18th century and Russian penal colonies in the 19th century. The Russians formally annexed Yakutia in the 17th century, and from then on the indigenous population was required to pay tribute to the local Russian leadership in the form of native furs. In 1634 and 1642 the Yakuts rebelled against the adversity caused by this tax, because among the southern Yakut hunting had not previously been a major economic activity, and it took time away from tending their horses and cattle. These early European inroads into Yakut territory also coincided with a push by Orthodox missionaries to Christianize the local shamanistic population, which was largely completed by the 1820s. The discovery of gold in the region and the building of the Trans-Siberian Railway in the late 19th and early 20th centuries were the final pushes by the Russian Empire to open up the lands of the northeast to trade and commerce.

The USSR largely took up the same "civilizing" project that had been begun by the czarist administration in north-central Siberia. In 1919 the Soviets created the Yakut Autonomous Soviet Socialist Republic and attempted to settle the seminomadic peoples of the region. Schools and health centers were also established in so-called cultural centers that aimed to divest the local population of their traditional languages, religions, and ways of life. "Red Tents" were introduced throughout Siberia as education centers for communist history and ideology. In 1928 collectivization came to Siberia, and individual families lost their herds to the large, state-owned pastoral collectives. Even fishing, hunting, and reindeer herding, the main economic activities in the far north, were collectiv-

ized at this time. As occurred throughout the USSR, numerous Yakuts lost their lives in the denunciations, reprisals, and political demagoguery that ruled the Soviet Union for several decades. A true relaxation of the laws against native religious practices, which had existed alongside Christianity since the 19th century, and individual ownership of animals and property did not occur until the 1980s.

In 1991 the Soviet leadership of Yakutia declared their independence from Moscow as part of a burgeoning nationalism on the part of many Yakuts. As a result of generations of European migration, however, Yakutia at that time contained far more Russians than indigenous peoples, and independence was easily blocked by the country's leadership in Moscow. Since that time the Yakuts have continued to push for greater autonomy, ecological responsibility, and cultural integrity in their northern homeland, both inside and outside the structure of RAIPON, the Russian Association of Indigenous Peoples of the North.

See also Russians, Asian.

Further Reading

Waldemar Jochelson. *The Yakut* (Washington, D.C.: American Museum of Natural History, 1933).

Yami (Tao)

The Yami are the smallest of the 13 recognized Aboriginal Taiwanese groups but also the least integrated into wider Taiwanese society, probably because of their isolated location on Lanyu or Orchid Island, about 40 miles southeast of Taiwan itself. There is some uncertainty about Yami origins since their language places them much closer to some Austronesians in the Philippines than to other Taiwanese aboriginal people. One theory states that their ancestors fled the Batan Archipelago in the Philippines and took up residence on Lanyu about 800 years ago; this relies on linguistic data showing Batanese and Yami to be very closely related. There is also material evidence of trade in goats, pigs, millet, beads, gold, and weapons between the two regions for hundreds of years until it ceased about 300 years ago due to warfare. Some scholars claim that evidence of trade supports this origin story, while others say that a more ancient Yami population may merely have adopted the language of a stronger people during the course of trade relations.

The Yami traditional economy was based on fishing and farming, especially millet for

YAMI

location:
Lanyu (also known as Orchid Island, Botel Tobago, Pongso No Tawo, and Irala) off the southeast coast of Taiwan

time period:
Possibly 1200 C.E. to the present

ancestry:
Austronesian

language:
Yami, a Malayo-Polynesian language within the larger Austronesian language family; the only aboriginal Taiwanese language related to languages located outside Taiwan

ritual and exchange purposes, and taro, yams, and sweet potatoes for subsistence. Like millet, goat meat and pork were also available to the Yami but generally were used for exchange purposes and eaten only during rituals that required them. Men were entirely responsible for fishing because their fishing boats, made from a single tree carved into a canoe, were taboo for women. Women took care of household needs, children, and all gardening activities with the possible exception of clearing the land in preparation for planting. In addition to the taboo on women using fishing boats, there were also prohibitions against women eating certain kinds of fish. "Good" fish could be eaten by all Yami, male and female, old and young; "bad" fish could be eaten only by males; and "old man fish" could be eaten only by male elders. As a result of these taboos, all Yami families have two sets of cooking and eating utensils, one to be used for "good fish," and the other for "bad fish" and "old man fish."

Traditional Yami society was organized primarily on the two separate principles of patrilineal kinship and residence. Each individual was a member of a patriline based on the lineage of his or her father, father's father, and so on. However, some matrilateral relatives were also recognized because the most basic unit of kinship that defined each individual Yami was called the *ripus* and was made up of three generations—child, father, and paternal grandfather—plus the children of one's parents' siblings and paternal grandparents' siblings. This confusing pattern has been mistaken for bilateral or cognatic kinship, similar to those in the West, in which both parents' families are considered relatives. This is an error because it is only in this most basic unit that the relatives on one's mother's side are considered part of one's innermost circle. For ritual obligations, ancestor worship, and allocation of land and other resources, it is solely the patrilineal group that matters.

In addition to kinship, Yami villages are also important social units. Generally villages contain several segments of a lineage, but the men and children in the community will all be members of the same patriline; women, who move into their husbands' homes at marriage, come from many other lineages since lineage exogamy is generally followed. Each village contains a headman. In the past, Yami society did not recognize the authority of any position, but older men, religious leaders, war heroes, and other military figures were able to influence others due to their expertise in specific areas. Today the village headman tends to be an individual who also holds one of these positions, which connects the bureaucratic authority of a headman to the traditional power invested in these male positions. Rich men in villages also have a degree of power over others, which has been true for as long as records of the Yami have been kept.

While Yami society tends not to recognize the authority of any individual over others based on position, relative status within society is important and marked in a variety of ways. First, a person's generation in the family is marked through a naming system called teknonymy. This means that when a Yami couple has a child, both the mother and father change their name to something that means mother of that child and father of that child, respectively. Later, when that child has his or her first child, the original couple's names change again to grandmother and grandfather of that child; the process is repeated for great-grandchildren as well. The Yami must recognize the generation of everybody they meet in public as well. Older men and women are referred to as uncle and aunt, respectively, while younger people are referred to as "my child." Even peers who are slightly older and younger are referred to with terms meaning older or younger brother or sister, depending on the relative age and sex of the people speaking. While the terms used in these titles are based on kinship, they do not imply actual relatedness but only the Yami sense of the interconnectedness of all village members.

The Yami traditional religion recognizes a variety of different ghosts or spirits and gods, including a supreme god who sent the original progenitors of the Yami people to earth, a boy made of stone and another made of bamboo. The most important mythological figure is the king of the flying fish who taught the Yami how to catch fish, farm, and all the other skills necessary to survive on earth. The most important Yami festival is dedicated to this folk hero and many taboos surround the catching and eating of this particular fish even though it constitutes the people's largest source of protein. The cosmology associated with this religious worldview recognizes eight different levels; ghosts and ancestors live on the lower level, humans in the middle, and gods in the upper levels. Several scholars of comparative religion have pointed out that this eight-level world is similar to that envisioned by another Austronesian population, the SAMOANS. The important distinction between living humans on the one hand and ghosts and ancestors on the other is evident in the Yami naming system, which uses prefixes to indicate this kind of status. For example, a living man named Konpo is referred to as Si-Konpo; he then becomes Simina-Konpo at his death. The importance of gods in this worldview is not based on the relationship between humans and gods; for example, gods are not believed to answer any direct prayers from human beings. Instead, the value of the gods rests on their ability to bless the Yami with plentiful harvests or good fishing of their own accord. Many Yami themselves remain somewhat unclear about the roles and responsibilities of their various gods, a trend that has increased recently as Christianity has become more widespread on the island. While gods are associated with positive benefits such as harvests and are not open to the prayers of humans, ghosts and spirits are associated with illness, death, or other misfortune and can be appeased with gifts and prayers.

Since 1945, when Lanyu became an official part of Taiwan, the conditions for the Yami have changed considerably. While most people continue to engage in subsistence fishing and farming, about one-quarter of the population has left the island to join the cash economy on Taiwan. Even on Lanyu the cash economy has begun to impose itself on some aspects of people's lives. In addition, Christianity has been incorporated into the traditional belief system, and both public education and medical care have been provided on the island, albeit at a very low level. The island has other infrastructure, such as roads for the few privately owned cars, motorbikes, and bicycles, and the few buses that make up the entire public transport system. Unfortunately, the imposition of the Taiwanese state has also meant that Yami land has been stolen. In the 1950s it was Chinese cattle ranchers who disrupted Yami crops and ways of life; they were followed by 2,500 convicts who were dumped on the island by the government in Taipei in 1958. In 1960 Lanyu's tropical forest was entirely cut down by the government, which had devastating effects on the ecology and the ability of the Yami to subsist. However, the worst modern colonial practice has been the dumping of Taiwan's radioactive waste on the island, a practice that has been going on since 1980. Tens of thousands of barrels of waste have begun leaking into Yami farmlands, fishing grounds, and groundwater. At first the Yami were ignorant of the practice and its effects and trusted the government to warn them of any dangers. Starting in 1988, however, the Yami began protesting against the use of their home as a dumping ground. Much of this protest has been from Yami who are active in a Christian church group, but they have been joined by others from throughout Asia as well.

Yanadi (Yenadi)

The Yanadi are one of India's SCHEDULED TRIBES who live in the state of Andhra Pradesh and a few of its offshore islands, including Sriharikota Island. They speak a dialect of the Telugu language, one of the most important of the Dravidian languages of South India. There are two subdivisions within the larger tribe, Manchi and Challa Yanadi, which generally do not mix with each other. Each of these groups is also subdivided into patrilineal clans or house names, membership in which is determined by one's father, father's father, and so on. Clans are exogamous, meaning that people have to marry someone from another clan or risk both social and supernatural sanctions for having committed incest.

Prior to about 1970 the Yanadi lived largely as seminomadic hunter-gatherers, moving from area to area on the fringes of the state's large forests to hunt for game and fish and to forage for tubers, fruits, herbs, honey, and other forest products. Entire families would undertake these foraging trips together, especially in the case of secret medicinal herbs whose efficacy was believed to dissipate if they became known beyond the specialist and his or her family. However, starting in the 1970s the Indian government began settling Yanadi families and communities in hamlets far from their forest homes. Many adopted a more sedentary diet of rice and other grains; cultivated vegetables; and tended domesticated animals such as pigs, sheep, goats, and chickens. Some families continued to eat rats, which were plentiful in their newly settled communities. By 1995 about two-thirds of the Yanadi had been settled in these hamlets, where poverty due to the lack of jobs for unskilled laborers and alienation from both the dominant and their own cultures have been the norm.

In addition, foraging trips for medicinal herbs have diminished along with those for subsistence, and there has been some concern since the early 1990s that the Yanadi's traditional knowledge is being lost. Initiatives by a number of governmental and nongovernmental organizations, such as the Yanadi Education Society (YES), have emerged to assist in the

YANADI

location:
Andhra Pradesh, including some offshore islands, India

time period:
Unknown to the present

ancestry:
Dravidian

language:
A dialect of Telugu, a major Dravidian language

transition of the Yanadi into modern life without the concomitant loss of traditional knowledge this often entails.

In addition to being well-known in the ethnographic literature as one of India's last seminomadic peoples, the Yanadi are also commonly referred to as a nonviolent people. Scholars who have worked with them note that there are no myths or stories about their having engaged in warfare in the past, and domestic disputes are mediated by a maternal uncle before they become large enough to engender violence. Rather than fight with each other, married couples easily obtain divorces, which, at least in the past, did not bring any stigma upon either partner. Even the settlement pattern of the Yanadi has been pointed to as creating a predominantly peaceful society: Each family lives in a cluster of huts that are separated from other family clusters by fences with entrances that do not face each other. These clusters are built with quite a bit of space between them, which affords privacy for all and prevents envy from building up over seeing the successes of neighbors.

See also DRAVIDIANS; TELUGUS.

Yangshao culture (proto-Chinese culture)

The Yangshao people are considered the ancestors of the modern Chinese people. During the late Neolithic period (ca. 4000 B.C.E.), the upper reaches of the Huang He (Yellow River), including the eastern part of Qinghai, Gansu, Shaanxi, Shanxi and northwestern Henan Provinces, was dominated by the Yangshao culture. Many settlements followed the path of the Wei River and its tributaries, largely to the south of the Wei and north of the Qin Ling Mountains.

Yangshao settlements were variable in size, ranging from less than one acre to more than 200 acres. One excavated settlement, Pan-p'o-ts'un village, southeast of Xi'an, serves as a yardstick of the nature of Yangshao settlements. Pan-p'o-ts'un is roughly 11 acres in size, smaller than the average settlement but still able to hold a population of approximately 500–600 people. Early Yangshao housing was either circular or rectangular; the floors were made of beaten earth to flatten and harden it, and the walls were made of wattle and daub. Later houses had compartments divided by partition walls. During the excavation of Pan-p'o-ts'un, a communal house was unearthed in the center of the village, with smaller houses circling it facing the center; all the houses contained hearths. The pottery-making center was to the east, with at least six pottery kilns; to the north was the cemetery. Excavations have unearthed settlements like Pan-p'o-ts'un in which the architecture, tombs, and kilns are arranged in such a way as to suggest that there was a common pattern of material life, reflecting an economic and social stability across the entire culture area. Pan-p'o-ts'un also had what appeared to be an industry of mostly small bone articles, including knives, diggers, needles, awls, arrowheads, fishing hooks, hoe blades, and chisels. There were also stone implements.

The environment of the Yangshao was somewhat restrictive due to the extreme climate, including little rainfall. One advantage, however, was the loess area the people had settled on, a rich and easily farmed loose soil. In about 5000 B.C.E. or perhaps earlier the Yangshao were settled in the southeastern part of the loess highlands. The people of this period grew mainly millet and hemp as well as mulberry, commonly used to feed silkworms. Secondary to their agricultural concerns, the Yangshao also hunted, fished, gathered, and (toward the end of the period) raised domestic pigs; there is also evidence of domesticated dogs during this period.

Yangshao culture is characterized by distinctive red pottery. The Yangshao have been called the painted-pottery culture because this period is renowned for beautiful pottery. From the later period of the Yangshao culture, excavations have also unearthed pottery *tseng*-steamers with holes in the bottom and *ting* tripod vessels. Yangshao potters used both hard, sharp styluses to decorate their vessels as well as soft, natural fiber paintbrushes made from animal hair. Painted pottery originated in what is called the nuclear area of the Yangshao settlements and spread in a variety of directions throughout China.

Yangshao villages generally maintained cemeteries suggestive of the villages' kinship ties. Babies and small children were buried in pottery jars with a small hole in the top or the middle of the urn; they were buried within the settlement between the houses. Adults were buried in a communal cemetery, generally singly, and in an extended position in graves. There were often five or six pottery vessels placed near the legs and feet; the burial of pottery with the deceased suggests a belief in the afterlife. The mortuary pottery evidenced different, more complex motifs in comparison with the house-

YANGSHAO CULTURE

location:
Northwest China

time period:
Approximately 5000 to 3000 B.C.E.

ancestry:
Sino-Tibetan

language:
Sino-Tibetan (Proto-Chinese)

This piece of Yangshao-era pottery has been dated to between 5,000 and 8,500 years ago; it is distinctive in that the two cups have been joined by a hollow tube, which allows liquids to pass from one into the other. *(Art Resource/HIP)*

hold pottery, which was plainer. Rings and pendants made from turquoise and amazonite and beads of marble were also discovered in excavations,

The Yangshao people were literate to a certain extent. Word-signs or symbols were incised onto their pottery for the numbers one, two, five, seven, and eight, which also implies that there were symbols for all numbers up to nine at the very least. It is difficult to systematically trace the evolution of the Chinese written script before 1300 B.C.E. because of the extreme scarcity of archaeological data. Although writing first appeared during the Yangshao period, not until the late Shang period (ca. 1600–ca. 1046 B.C.E.) is established script verifiable. There is still much debate about the first instance of the written word.

Yao (Byau Min, Iu Mian, Kim Mun, Man, Mian, Mien, Pai Yao, Yao Min)

The Yao are one of China's 55 recognized national minority groups and one of Vietnam's 54 recognized groups; there are also populations of Yao in the highlands of northern Laos and Thailand. Prior to their classification as Yao in 1950, each geographic, linguistic, and cultural subgroup, totaling about 30 different groups, used its own ethnonym. They are in no way related to the Yao of Malawi despite sharing the same name.

GEOGRAPHY

The Yao inhabit the mountainous regions of six southern Chinese provinces: Guangdong,

Guangxi, Guizhu, Hunan, Jiangxi, and Yunnan. Much of this territory is covered by the Yunnan-Guizhou and Kweichow Plateaus, with elevations as high as 13,500 feet on Mount Diancang. The region's elevation helps to maintain a relatively stable temperature range; the Yunnan-Guizhou Plateau is said to be constantly in springtime. Melting snows also provide waters for many of southern China and mainland Southeast Asia's major rivers.

The Yao who inhabit mainland Southeast Asia also live in higher elevations but not the highest, which are generally inhabited by the HMONG and other tribes.

ORIGINS

The historical origins of the Yao have not been fully established, and historians continue to debate whether the mention of the Mo Yao, non-corvee laborers, during the Tang dynasty (618–907) is a reference to an ethnic group or merely a category of highlanders from many backgrounds who were exempt from this form of forced labor. Some historians believe that it was during the Song dynasty (960–1279) that the Yao emerged as a separate group. Their original homeland was probably in the region of Dongting Lake in Hunan Province, from where they migrated southward in subsequent centuries.

Regardless of historical fact, the Yao themselves often refer to a tale documented in the fifth century as their origin myth. The story describes how Emperor Gao Xin (2435–2365 B.C.E.) was saved from an enemy chieftain by his faithful dog, Pan Hu. The dog was subsequently rewarded by being turned into a man and given the emperor's daughter in marriage; he became known as King Pan. The descendants of this royal couple then became the Yao. In Tang times this myth was the basis for their status as Mo Yao and their ability to travel without advance permission.

HISTORY

During the Song and Yuan dynasties (960–1279 and 1279–1368, respectively), the Yao were generally governed under the *tusi* system whereby local chiefs gathered tribute and taxes from their own people, administered justice, and paid all of the region's taxes to the emperor from the amounts the chiefs had gathered. This was a *jimi*, or loose system that allowed for significant autonomy at the local level and for Yao chiefs to accumulate significant power and resources. During the Ming and Qing dynasties

YAO

location:
China, Vietnam, Laos, Myanmar (Burma), and Thailand

time period:
Possibly seventh century to the present

ancestry:
Wuling tribes

language:
Several languages in the Hmong-Mien language family, sometimes written as Miao-Yao. Some subgroups also speak Han or languages in the Zhuang-Dong family.

Yao time line

C.E.

seventh to 10th centuries First mention of the Mo Yao during the Tang dynasty.

960–1368 The Yao are loosely governed by the reigning dynasties and largely left alone to farm, trade, and control internal politics.

11th century Possibly the first century in which numbers of Yao begin migrating out of China and into mainland Southeast Asia.

1368–1911 The Yao are more tightly governed by the Ming and Qing dynasties than in the past, using appointed bureaucrats who take control of Yao trade and tribute.

19th century Large numbers of Yao begin entering Thailand from Laos, continuing through the Vietnam War era.

1949 The Communist Party takes power in China and tries to minimize ethnic and national differences under state socialism.

1979 Deng Xiaoping changes course in China, and maintaining the country's 55 recognized minority groups becomes a high priority. Many Yao intellectuals contribute to the re-creation and reintroduction of supposedly ancient Yao traditions.

that followed (1368–1644 and 1644–1911, respectively) this loose system was replaced with a tighter one; HAN and later Manchu bureaucrats were moved into local regions to gather taxes, accumulate local power, and supplant the previously powerful Yao clans and lineages. This action contributed to several Yao uprisings against imperial power; for example, the Yao were important actors in the Taiping Rebellion (1850–64), which began in Guangxi Province.

Although the exact period of large-scale Yao migration south remains contested, some historians believe it began as early as the 11th century when population and land pressure in southern China forced some adventurous Yao communities from their homes. They had been accustomed to moving occasionally in search of fertile land for swidden, or slash-and-burn, farming techniques and may have begun in this period to move out of China entirely. Certainly by the time of the invasion of the MONGOLS in the early 13th century, many Chinese peoples generally, including the Yao, were fleeing from their homes to escape the ravages of war; in the early Yuan dynasty the first definite reports of Yao in Thailand, Laos, and Vietnam are available. This period of migration also led to the settlement of most Yao in Guangxi Province, where many began to adopt a settled, intensive agricultural way of life. Rather than moving in search of fresh forest land to cut down, burn, and then use for planting crops, they emulated their Han neighbors in using irrigation and fertilizers to reuse farmland for several years.

After Mao Zedong's Communist Party defeated the Chinese nationalists in the civil war in the late 1940s, the Yao were classified as one of China's national minority groups. This assignment, which was far from automatic since many other groups were clumped together despite linguistic and cultural differences, led to the creation of 12 Yao counties and more than 2,000 Yao towns and villages. As part of the ideology of equality, many Yao also benefited from education and the ability to join the Communist Party and thus become part of the regional and even national elite; they were often recruited to train as ethnologists, linguists, and historians who would assist with the recognition of their own and other minority groups within the framework of a large, unified China. In addition, even those Yao inhabiting the dense forests of the southern highlands were convinced to give up slash-and-burn farming techniques for more intensive forms of agriculture.

During the Cultural Revolution (1967–77) the Yao suffered the loss of many of the symbols, rituals, and other material aspects of their unique culture as Mao's government tried to rid the country of its past. In 1979, however, the Chinese government radically changed its policies with regard to its minorities, and the Yao have been encouraged to maintain their language, religion, and other aspects of their way of life but within the framework of greater economic opportunity and development brought by improvements to infrastructure, education, health care, and export opportunities.

CULTURE

Although the vast majority of Yao communities have abandoned swidden farming techniques, agriculture remains at the heart of the Yao economy. Dry rice, which can be grown successfully in higher elevations, is the most important subsistence crop. Corn, indigo, anise, and other spices are important cash crops; eggplant, lettuce, and chilies are also important in some regions. In the past, opium was an important Yao product, but this has largely been eradicated in both China and Southeast Asia. Forestry, logging, hunting, and even forest gathering are important supplementary activities in some regions, and some families even continue to use swidden techniques for their own family garden plots. Traditionally hunting and rice production were both communal activities, though the former is generally now practiced individually and for sport. The most important domestic animal is the pig, and most women are responsible for the care and feeding of at least one animal throughout the year.

Yao kinship structures recognize the primacy of the male line of descent in the creation of patrilineal clans, but matrilateral relatives, those on one's mother's side, are important in the creation of alliances for economic and other activities. Clans, or *pai,* of which there are said to be eight that descend from the original dog–Chinese princess pair, are strictly exogamous, and a woman marrying into her husband's clan generally moves into his family's household in patrilocal residence. The exception to this rule is when the man's family has not yet paid the entire bride price, money and gifts given to the woman's family to recognize their role in raising her and to compensate them for the loss of her labor. When this happens the new couple generally lives with the wife's family for a period of time, and the new son-in-law works for his wife's parents to pay off the remainder of the bride price; children born during this period become members of their mother's lineage and clan rather than their father's. Once the agreed-upon period of labor has been completed, the couple may establish a separate household, move in with the husband's family, or even remain in the wife's if she has no brothers to take care of the parents in their old age and to inherit their house. While this generally occurs only among the poor, among the rich the ability to give multiple bride-wealth payments means that polygyny was allowed until the Chinese state outlawed it in the 1950s.

As these marriage rules indicate, extended families are the norm in rural Yao communities. All people who cook, eat, and farm together are part of the same family, and as with marriage, this pattern differs somewhat among rich and poor. Rich households often include adopted children, cousins, and other extended kinfolk, while poorer households may contain only a married couple, their unmarried children, and their married sons and their children. This pattern also differs for Yao families who have moved into China's large cities; urban families tend to be nuclear rather than extended and, since 1979, to have just one child.

Yao religious beliefs and practices resemble those of the dominant Han population in many ways. Both groups engage in ancestor worship based on patrilineal lineage and clan membership, observe the lunar new year, and recognize a variety of Taoist, local, and familial spirits. The Yao recognize 18 specific gods and goddesses, mostly derived from Chinese deities whose images they paint onto scrolls and then preserve on their home altars. They also recognize the existence of many spirits, demons, ancestor heroes, and others who are thanked and propitiated at ceremonies throughout the year, either at designated times of the agricultural calendar or during times of crisis such as illness or death. Yao shamans or priest-exorcists are important members of their communities for their ability to communicate with the supernatural world through divination. They also have access to spells and incantations used to heal illnesses and other misfortunes, after they have divined their supernatural source through reading chicken bones or bamboo sticks. In Thailand a number of Yao communities have relatively recently given up these traditional beliefs and practices and have converted to Christianity, but even in that country this population makes up a small minority of the total Yao group.

FURTHER READING

Eli Alberts. *A History of Daoism and the Yao People of South China* (Youngstown, N.Y.: Cambria Press, 2007).

Jacques Lemoine with Donald Gibson. *Yao Ceremonial Paintings* (Bangkok: White Lotus Co. Ltd., 1982).

Ralph Litzinger. *Other Chinas: The Yao and the Politics of National Belonging* (Durham, N.C.: Duke University Press, 2000).

Yap (Yapese)

The Yap people come from Yap Proper, known as Waab, within the state of Yap, one of the four states of the Federated States of Micronesia (FSM). The first ancient migrants came to Waab from the Malay Peninsula, the Indonesian Archipelago, New Guinea, and the Solomon Islands. The people of the outer islands of Yap State, however, are descendants of Polynesian settlers and have notable ethnic differences from the people of Yap Proper.

Yap Proper consists of four volcanic islands—Yap, Tomil-Gagil, Map, and Runmung—which are closely linked by a common coral reef and surrounded by an outer barrier reef. The first three islands are connected by bridges, but Runmung is forbidden to outsiders and has no bridges.

The Yap live in one of the most isolated and traditional societies in Micronesia. Chiefs still wield considerable power, and a traditional

YAP

location:
Yap is the westernmost state of the Federated States of Micronesia, 9° north of the equator. It is situated in the western Pacific Ocean, east of the Philippines, north of New Guinea and Melanesia, west of Polynesia, and south of Hawaii.

time period:
Probably around 0 to the present

ancestry:
Austronesian and Melanesian

language:
Micronesian, Central-Eastern-Oceanic language

caste system determines status, though the standard of living is less affected. In the past, the chiefs of Yap controlled a large interisland tribute system, commonly referred to as the Yap empire, in which all 24 islands between Yap and Chuuk had to pay tribute to the chiefs in the Gagil region of Yap. While this tribute system, *sawei* in the local languages, has been eliminated, the political and ritual ties that it engendered, as well as the status it conferred, remain important features of Yap identity even today. In addition, there are strict rules about moving from one village to another, and permission must be sought for most journeys. It is not unusual to see bare-breasted women of all ages going about their daily business and older men in loincloths walking on country roads. Lineage is patrilineal, traced through the father, who is head of the family group, or *tabinaw*, unlike the rest of Micronesia, which is matrilineal. Families—usually consisting of an older couple, their children, and at least the oldest son and his family—live on an estate. Various plots of land are assigned to sons, and even though they may be on different parts of the island they are still considered part of the estate. The sons are obligated to take care of the father, and if they fail in this duty they can be stripped of their land and their place in the family. However, despite the significance of the patrilineal group, a son is also a member of his mother's clan and can rely on it for support if ever he loses favor with his patriline.

Another highly unique cultural feature of the Yap is their use of enormous stone disks, some as large as 4,000 pounds, as a form of indigenous money. The larger disks are displayed in various prominent places including village entrances, and people can be seen carrying smaller ones (about one foot in diameter) for the purposes of trade.

The legend of the stone money states that long ago the villagers of Yap were constantly arguing about the most appropriate method of payment for trade and business. One night while contemplating the issue, a chief looked up at the moon and thought, "We need something like the moon that is large, round, and beautiful. Something that will not wear out, break or get stolen." Others agreed, but the hardest material on Yap was the shale rock used for stone paths, which would not be durable enough.

The time had finally come for the Yap to look beyond their island, something they had not done in the past. Outrigger canoes were built, and food and weapons were prepared for the journey. The explorers sailed southwest for a month before spotting land. Their arrival was not welcome, and they were soon killed by hostile locals. When they did not return to Yap, the chiefs ordered another expedition to find them. Once again they set out to the southwest and a month later landed on the same island. This time they were prepared for danger and won the battle with the locals and gained some land as a result. The island was Palau in Aungur.

This island had large deposits of limestone, which were used to carve the moon-shaped disks. Once completed, the Yap stood back and pronounced, *"Lirarai"* (This is it!). The money became known as *rai,* a term still used today by the Yap for stone money. Because the stone disks were so heavy, a hole was carved in the middle for a tree trunk to be passed through, allowing several men to carry it. Bamboo rafts were made to carry the *rai,* which were towed behind the canoes for the long journey back to Yap.

Because of the trials associated with the acquisition of *rai,* its value was unquestioned. In addition, but to a lesser extent, its worth was determined by the history, size, shape, quality, and color of the stones. Ownership can pass from one person to another without actually moving the *rai,* which might be placed in a village stone money bank, outside homes or businesses, or beside a village men's house. Stone money is still used today to buy land and to pay fines, and as bridal gifts.

Two Yap girls pose in traditional outfits with midsized examples of *rai,* or stone money. *(Getty/Hulton Archive)*

The Yap were also famous for their remarkable navigational skills, relying on their knowledge of stars, waves, wind, birds, and fish to navigate their course to far-off destinations. They covered great distances in Oceania using sailing canoes, relying on the sky and ocean to determine their position, without the assistance of modern technology such as compasses and sextants. This system of indigenous navigational skills, called *etak* or *yetak*, has been kept alive for thousands of years but today is at risk of extinction. For several decades, beginning in the latter part of World War II when the U.S. Navy invaded the islands, the locals were discouraged from taking seafaring journeys because the Coast Guard did not want to be responsible for rescuing canoes and crews hit by storms that took them off their course. Over time only smaller interisland canoes were being built, and the larger ocean-going canoes were neglected. People then began to turn to faster plastic and fibreglass boats, and the value of having a canoe faded away. Today most Yap make a living from the local activities of subsistence farming and fishing, while on the outer islands copra (dried coconut) production is still important.

As for future directions for the Yap, there is currently a debate about leaving the arbitrarily constructed nation of the FSM and joining instead with the Republic of Palau. Geographically and culturally, the Yap have far more in common with PALAUANS than they do with the people of the more distant islands of Chuuk, Kosrae, and Pohnpei, which make up the FSM.

See also FEDERATED STATES OF MICRONESIA: NATIONALITY; MICRONESIANS; PALAUANS: NATIONALITY.

FURTHER READING

David Labby. *The Demystification of Yap: Dialectics of Culture on a Micronesian Island* (Chicago: University of Chicago Press, 1976).

Yellow Uighur   *See* YUGUR.

Yi (Axi, Lolo, Luoluo, Misaba, Misapo, Nosu, Nuosu, Sani)

The Yi are one of China's 55 recognized national minority groups; close linguistic and cultural cousins also reside in Thailand, Myanmar, Laos, and Vietnam. Despite this classification, the Yi are actually made up of many subgroups, both those who speak one of the many dialects of the Yi language and others who were rejected for classification as their own nationality group in the 1950s and elected to join the Yi. In Yunnan alone, 260 groups applied for national recognition in 1954; 90 percent of those were rejected.

GEOGRAPHY

The Yi live in the mountainous region of southwest China, which borders on mainland Southeast Asia. The Greater and Lesser Liangshan Mountains that make up their homeland range from about 6,600 feet to about 11,500 feet above sea level. The region is crossed by the Dadu, Bajiang, and Anning Rivers. The Yi are believed to be the original inhabitants of the region around Shilin (Stone) Forest in Yunnan.

ORIGINS

Yi origins remain uncertain since various cultural traits point in different directions. They believe themselves to be the aboriginal people of central Yunnan Province, especially the Shilin region. Their language, however, points to the northwest, especially Tibet, and their cloth and other technology point even further north, to the MONGOLS. At the same time, use of poisoned arrows in hunting is a tradition that comes from southern China. These contradictory bits of evidence concerning their origins mean that a variety of political agendas can be served by pointing to local, northern, western, or southern origins, depending on the situation.

We do know that Chinese documents mention a degree of tribal consolidation in the region of Yunnan by the time of the Sui and Tang

---

YI

location:
Yunnan, Sichuan, Guizhou, and Guanxi Provinces, China; Thailand; Myanmar; Laos; Vietnam

time period:
Possibly early third century to the present

ancestors:
Possibly the Qiang

language:
Yi, a Tibeto-Burman language in the Lolo-Burmese family with six semi-mutually intelligible dialects

---

Yi time line
C.E.
226 The Yi are defeated by the Shu, the southwest dynasty during the Three Dynasties period.
594 The Yi revolt against Chinese domination, and portions of their homeland remain independent afterward.
712 The region of independence expands, and the Tang dynasty is powerless to stop it.
1727 The Qing dynasty pushes the Yi back into a smaller homeland in the Daliang Mountains, although the Yi begin to expand again soon thereafter.
1920 About 20 years of Yi guerrilla activity begins against the weakened central government.
1949 The Communist revolution succeeds in China.
1954 Hundreds of small ethnic groups in Yunnan Province apply to China's state council on minorities for recognition as separate nationalities. Most are rejected, and they either elect or are placed within the larger Yi ethnic group.

People of Yunnan Province

Ethno-linguistic area

SIMAO   Prefecture

Yi   Peoples

0   100 miles
0   100 km

© Infobase Publishing

dynasties (580–907) and that during the Ming dynasty (1368–1644) many other ethnic groups, including the dominant HAN, moved into the region of the Yi. This caused a number of different subgroups of Yi to see themselves as entirely separate ethnicities. The Qing period (1646–1911) consolidated these ethnic differences into such groups as the Sani, Yiqing, Axi, and others, who after 1954 were reclassified as Yi.

HISTORY

The long history of interactions among the Yi; the many other ethnic groups in Yunnan, Si-

chuan, and surrounding areas; and the Han have led to considerable cultural borrowing. Agriculture was adopted after the early third century, and the languages of all these people share vocabulary, grammar structures, and tones. Nonetheless, Yi history has not been one of peaceful interactions with their neighbors. They were first defeated by a Chinese army in 226 C.E. when the Shu dynasty was consolidating its power over the southwest region in the face of two competing dynasties, the Wei and Wu, which simultaneously took power in the north and southeast, respectively, upon the fall of the Han in 220. The Yi had been loyal to

The 96,000-acre Shilin, or Stone Forest, is a major tourist attraction for domestic and international tourists visiting Kunming, Lunan Yi Nationality Autonomous County, China, and has been since the Ming dynasty (1368–1644). *(Shutterstock/szefei)*

the Shu for the first few years of their reign but in 226 had tried to change their allegiance to Wu. This prompted the Shu emperor to send an army under Zhuge Liang to put down the rebellion and bring the Yi back under Shu control. He conquered territory as far west as the Salween River, including all of Yunnan.

Despite this loss, the Yi did not fully succumb to sinicization and continued to reject Chinese hegemony in the region. They rebelled again in 594 at the start of the Sui dynasty and freed a portion of their territory from Chinese taxation and other administrative restrictions. In 712 more Yi territory was liberated from the control of the powerful Tang dynasty, and the situation remained that way until the Mongols of the Yuan dynasty arrived in the 13th century. By the early 18th century Yi territory had shrunk even more and encompassed just the immediate territory around the Daliang Mountains.

The period of greatest Yi military activity was the 1920s through the 1940s, when Yi guerrillas waged war against the Chinese in Yunnan. They burned down whole villages and urban neighborhoods, kidnapped Nationalist government officials, and tried to remain independent from the increasingly weak central government. Most of the Western commentary on the Yi from this period points to a fierce, hierarchical people who continued to engage in slavery and other aspects of their traditional caste-based society while refusing to surrender to the hierarchy of the Chinese government.

CULTURE

Yi culture has developed from an agricultural economic base that combines crops of buckwheat, corn, potatoes, and oats with animal husbandry, especially goats, sheep, pigs, horses, chickens, and cattle. In the first decades after the communist revolution, the Yi were forced to grow rice and other crops more familiar to the Han, but since the 1980s they have been allowed to focus once again on local favorites, particularly buckwheat. Even into the present period, the Yi diet has incorporated certain wild foods as well, such as acorns, herbs, mushrooms, and wild game and fish. In the mountainous region inhabited by the Yi, slash-and-burn, or swidden, horticulture was more prevalent than the use of more intensive or permanent fields; the typical fallow period was five to seven years before a forest plot could be recut, burned, and planted for a season.

Although Yi society was divided into several caste groups, including nobility, commoners, and slaves, there were no full-time craftsmen or artisans who produced cloth, metalwork, or other objects. Each family tended to create its own objects, including woven and felted cloth, ironwork, masonry, woodwork, and others. Like the Mongols far to the north of the Yi, felt was an important material for making clothing and blankets suitable for their cold, mountainous locale; also like the Mongols, the Yi lacked their own tradition of making pottery or ceramics. These objects, along with copper, iron, silver, and a few others were obtained from the Han or other groups through trade.

Yi society prior to the revolution in 1949 was divided into four ranked classes or castes: Nuohuo, or Black Yi; Qunuo, or White Yi; Ajia; and Xiaxi. The Nuohuo, or Black Yi, was the highest and smallest caste at just about 7 percent of the population; these were the owners of slaves and of between 60 and 70 percent of all agricultural land. They required strict endogamy within their noble ranks, not allowing others to marry into the caste, and lived largely as ruling nobles who avoided most forms of agricultural or other strenuous labor. The Qunuo, or White Yi, was the largest caste group at about 50 percent of the population. These were vassals and servants of the Black Yi but themselves were able to control the labor and produce of their subordinate Ajia and Xiaxi populations and thus were usually not considered slaves. Rather, they were like indentured servants who owed about 10 days of labor to their owner each year. A few were able to accumulate their own land, and most would have owned animals and farm implements, but at the same time all were tied to a certain locality in their subordinate status to the Black Yi. They could not be bought and sold, as was the case with the two lowest castes, but Black Yi masters could give away their White Yi servants as gifts to friends, relatives, or allies.

The two lowest caste groups, Ajia at about 33 percent of the population and Xiaxi at about 10 percent, were both owned by Black and White Yi. The Ajia were slightly higher in status than the Xiaxi in that they resembled the White Yi in owning their own tools and animals. However, while the White Yi owed about 10 workdays to their owners, Ajia owed half of their productive time to their owners; in the other half they could produce crops, tools, or other objects for themselves or for trade. Also, some Ajia had to do their White Yi masters' indentured labor in addition to their own, which ate into their personal productive time. The Xiaxi were the lowest of the low in Yi society and had no rights, freedom, or property. They were entirely at the mercy of their owners, and most lived in deplorable conditions with their owner's livestock, eating scraps and wearing rags. They were often shackled to keep them from escaping and were beaten, sold away from their families, and killed for sport or sacrifice.

Membership in all four groups was inherited through patrilineal descent in which fathers handed down their caste group to their children. This was particularly important among the Black Yi, who were strictest about keeping others out of their caste community. Among the other three castes, some degree of mobility was possible over the course of a generation or two, based on hard work, good luck, the kindness of a master, strategic marriages, and cleverness. Patrilineal clan groups among the Black and White Yi came together several times throughout each year to celebrate a variety of life-cycle, agricultural, and ancestral rituals. These groups were also political units in some regions and performed legislative and judicial tasks in the administration of certain villages and districts. Some lineage groups were so large and powerful that they maintained their own militaries or police forces to maintain order and to expand their territory over weaker lineages and villages. Some of these armed organizations became very active in the 1920s until they were finally conquered in the early 1950s.

Yi religion prior to the ban on religious activity imposed by the Communist Party was a syncretic mix of polytheism, or belief in many gods and spirits; Taoism; and Buddhism. Those who resided higher in the Liangshan Mountains were less influenced by the latter two belief systems and incorporated a wider variety of nature spirits into their religious life. All groups used sacrifices to thank and appease their ancestral spirits, and the sun, moon, stars, mountains, and other natural features appeared prominently in mythology and ritual. Two kinds of religious specialists presided over these events: *bimos,* primarily responsible for sacrifice, and *suyis,* who used magic and sorcery. These specialists were joined by Taoist and Buddhist priests who oversaw most life-cycle rituals, such as marriages and funerals. All four specialists tended to participate in village-wide events honoring the dead or giving thanks for a plentiful harvest.

The most notable religious festival of the Yi is the Torch Festival, a three–day-and-night event that begins on June 24, as reckoned by the lunar calendar rather than the solar calen-

The largest Torch Ceremony takes place each year in Chuxiong, the capital of Yi Autonomous Prefecture. These women are lighting the pine torches that they will use to drive out bad luck. *(OnAsia/Jim Goodman)*

dar in use throughout the West. The event requires Yi families of the Black and White castes to dress in their traditional finery, and all but the lowest slaves are able to enjoy wrestling matches, horse races, bullfights, large bonfires, traditional singing, and dancing, among other events. The reason for the festival goes back to a Yi legend about the defeat of a demon named Shidali, who had sent a plague of insects to destroy the people's crops. The Yi destroyed the insects with fire, and thus fire became one of their most sacred elements; the festival is used to commemorate the event. The main part of the event occurs when villagers walk through their fields with burning pine torches to ritually drive out bad luck.

Further Reading

Alain Y. Dessaint. *Minorities of Southwest China: An Introduction to the Yi (Lolo) and Related Peoples and an Annotated Bibliography* (New Haven, Conn.: HRAF Press, 1980).

Stevan Harrell, ed. *Perspectives on the Yi of Southwest China* (Berkeley and Los Angeles: University of California Press, 2001).

Yuezhi *See* Kushans.

Yugur (Yellow Uighur, Yellow Uygur)

The Yugur make up one of the smallest of China's 55 recognized minority groups at about 12,500 people. This small community is then further subdivided into four different language groups. The largest group is the Western Yugur, the descendants of the small Uighur community who fled to Gansu Province in 840 C.E. upon the defeat of the Uighur khanate. The Western Yugur continue to speak their original Turkic language. The smaller Eastern Yugur community, named for its location within the region, speaks a Mongol language, probably as a result of the region's being conquered by the Mongols in the 13th century. Even smaller numbers of Yugur speak Tibetan, usually those who have married into a Tibetan family, as well as Chinese. The traits that link this linguistically disparate group into one ethnic category are their common adherence to a form of Tibetan Buddhism and a belief that they are the descendants of the Turkic Uighur people.

The founding date of 850 for the Yugur ethnic group may be somewhat misleading because it actually refers to the establishment of the independent Kanchou (Ganzhou) Uighur kingdom, a minor state in China's Gansu Province, by Uighur who fled the destruction of their own state in present-day Mongolia in 840. At that point, these people did not differ from other Uighur; they adopted Buddhism only upon settling in Gansu among other Buddhists and converted to the Yellow Sect much later, in the 15th century. In addition, in 1228 their kingdom disappeared into the larger Chinese state, never to emerge as an independent political entity. Politically, they were recognized in February 1954 when the Chinese government created the Sunan Yugur Autonomous County and again in April of the same year with the creation of the Juiquan Huangnibo Yugur Autonomous Township, both in Gansu Province.

The Yugur both self-identify and are known throughout China as the Yellow Uighur because they are members of a sect of Tibetan Buddhism known as Gelugs, or the Yellow Hat Sect, whose monks wear yellow hats. This sect was formed in 1392 by Tsongkapa, a Tibetan religious reformer who wanted to make the Buddhism of his day (1357–1419) more pure. He had his monks wear yellow hats as a sign of their desire for purity and ethical discipline, yellow being the color an earlier reformer had dyed his own hat upon his return to Tibet from exile. Today

YUGUR

location:
South Yugur Autonomous County and the Jiuquan Huangnibao region of Gansu Province, China

time period:
850 to the present

ancestry:
Uighur

language:
Raohul, which is a Turkic language; Engle, which is a Mongol language; Chinese; Tibetan

it is probably the most famous of the various Tibetan Buddhist traditions because the Dalai Lama is its most important member.

Most Yugur today continue to engage in animal husbandry as their primary economic activity, raising cattle, sheep, pigs, chickens, and camels. They also grow a bit of wheat and rice but are limited in their production and consumption of fruit and vegetables. Dairy products, especially milk tea, are also important sources of protein and calories. In addition to their animals, the Yugur are also known for their weaving skills, especially carpets and bags, and for their unique clothing. Both women and men wear felt robes; men's tend to have a high collar and red and blue waistband, while women's red or blue high-collared robes are decorated with embroidered patterns on the collars and sleeves. Men tend to wear leather riding boots, useful in tending to their herds of animals, while women's boots are made of cloth. Both women and men also wear distinctive hats. Men's hats look like flat-topped cylinders, while women's are more trumpet-shaped; both are made of felt.

See also TIBETANS.

Yukagir

The Yukagir are one of the indigenous peoples of Siberia, among the oldest of these groups, with a culture that has been in existence since the third century B.C.E. They are divided into two regional groups, northern and southern, those on the Alazeya River and those on the upper banks of the Kolyma River, respectively; some sources refer to these separate groups as the Tundra Yukagir and Kolyma Yukagir instead of Northern Yukagir and Southern Yukagir. The primary economic activity in both regions was traditionally subsistence hunting of deer, moose, and sable, and fishing, with a small number of individuals possessing herds of reindeer.

The Yukagir first came into contact with the RUSSIANS in the mid-17th century when fur trappers began infiltrating their lands and hunting grounds and Russian Orthodox missionaries began proselytizing. As occurred with the first interactions between Europeans and indigenous peoples in the Americas and the Pacific, these first interactions were largely negative for the Yukagir. They obtained trade goods that made life somewhat easier, but they also began dying of introduced diseases, alcoholism, and violence. As a result, the already small Yukagir population of about 9,000 people began to decline in that period; by the start of the 21st century that number was down to 1,113.

Further damage was done to Yukagir culture and society starting in 1929 when the Soviet Union began implementing its agricultural collectivization and industrialization schemes in the region. The nomadic Yukagir experienced great pressure to give up their subsistence economy and begin work in Russian industry. This became a reality for most Yukagir during World War II and in the second half of the 20th century when the Soviet state moved much of its industrial production east of the Ural Mountains. Many Yukagir joined the socialist economy as laborers on construction sites and oil wells and in factories.

Despite these economic changes and the adoption of the Russian Orthodox religion, many Yukagir also continue to engage in their traditional shamanist practices and believe in the power of their ancestors and the spirits of fire, sun, the hunt, earth, and water. Perhaps not surprising in the cold, dark region they inhabit, the most important of these spirits is the sun, who serves as judge and jury in Yukagir social disputes. Each clan's shaman is also very important, communing with the spirit world to heal the sick, aid in the hunt, bring misfortune to enemies, and protect the clan.

With the fall of the Soviet Union in 1991, the Yukagir and 40 other indigenous Siberian peoples have joined together to form the Russian Association of Indigenous Peoples of the North, Siberia and Far East (RAIPON). The primary goals of the organization are protecting human rights, defending its members' legal interests, and assisting in finding solutions to the environmental, social, and economic problems that plague the region. Cultural development and education are also part of RAIPON's mission. The organization has much work to do in all these areas and in increasing the health of the indigenous people. The Yukagir are particularly vulnerable, with one of the lowest life expectancies in all of Russia: 45 years for men, 54 for women, and the highest infant mortality rate in the Yakut-Sakha Republic.

See also RUSSIANS: NATIONALITY.

Yupiks (Asiatic Eskimoes, Sedentary Chukchi, Siberian Yupik, Yuhyt, Yuity, Yupiget)

The Siberian Yupiks are the few surviving speakers of the Eskimo-Aleut language who continue to live in 16 settlements on the Chuk-

YUKAGIR

location:
Southeastern Siberia

time period:
Third century B.C.E. to the present

ancestry:
Unknown

language:
Yukagir, a nearly extinct Paleosiberian or Ural-Altaic language; most speak Yakut and Russian today

chi Peninsula in Siberia and a few offshore islands; their closest linguistic relatives reside on St. Lawrence Island, Alaska. Like these Alaskan relatives, the Siberian Yupiks live primarily on fishing and on hunting sea mammals such as seals, walrus, and whales. A few Siberian Yupiks have also adopted the practice of herding reindeer from their Chukchi neighbors. Unlike their North American relatives, the Siberian Yupiks tend to use the term *Eskimo* to refer to themselves despite the formal adoption of *Inuit* by the Inuit Circumpolar Conference (ICC).

Historically, Yupik hunters focused most of their efforts on walruses and seals since one whale provided whole villages with fat, meat, and oil for a year. These sea mammals were hunted from open, flat-bottomed boats or closed kayaks, using harpoons tied to buoys made from sealskin. Sometimes walruses and seals were driven onto the shore using a clapper that simulated the sounds made by killer whales; both mammals were much easier to kill with a club or spear while they were lumbering awkwardly on land. These animals provided most food as well as raw materials for many other things. Sealskin was used for mittens, footwear, and even shields and armor used in warfare. Waterproof coats were made from walrus intestines, and the bones of all animals were carved to make toys, decorative pieces, and amulets. Even their traditional summer residences were tents made from walrus skins sewn together and covering a wooden frame. The igloos for which Eskimos are famous, called *nynglyu* in Siberian Yupik, were used until the mid-19th century during the winter, while today walrus-hide tents akin to those of the Chukchi *yaranga* are used throughout the year. In addition to the meat and fat of sea mammals, the Yupik also ate some kinds of seaweed, fish, and reindeer meat obtained in trade with the Chukchis or the few Yupiks who kept these animals.

The Yupik social structure centered around patrilineages, groups of people related through a common male ancestor, and the groups of lineages that constituted patrilineal clans. Men from the same lineage tended to hunt together in the same boat, though villages of 15–40 tents would be made up of many lineages because of the rule of exogamy, the necessity to marry outside one's own lineage and clan. Clans frequently engaged in warfare with one another over territory or resources, and warfare between Yupiks and Chukchis was extremely common. The greater number of Chukchis created a situation in which the Yupiks were gradually pushed further north and east until they were left with just a few villages on the coastal fringe.

After having been pushed to the edge of the world by their numerically stronger neighbors, from the 19th century onward the Yupiks experienced the deleterious effects of disease, alcoholism, and Russian policy toward ethnic minorities. Following the initial population loss due to disease, the Yupiks then suffered the loss of much of their cultural base when they were forced to live in Chukchi villages and to hunt in seasonal collectives. These hunting collectives took far more walruses and seals than could be sustained in the fragile ecology and left few animals for Yupik subsistence. Further damage was done after World War II when the region experienced a great building boom of military bases and airfields to protect the USSR from the United States. At that time many Yupiks were also treated as spies and moved further west because of their frequent communications with their relatives in Alaska. Conditions for the Yupiks did not improve until the dissolution of the Soviet Union in 1991 and their participation with 25 other northern cultural groups in the Russian Association of Indigenous Peoples of the North, Siberia and Far East (RAIPON) in the fight to maintain their linguistic, cultural, and ecological integrity in the face of increasing industrialization in their region.

See also Russians, Asian; Russians: nationality.

Further Reading

Anna M. Kerttula. *Antler on the Sea: The Yupik and Chukchi of the Russian Far East* (Ithaca, N.Y.: Cornell University Press, 2000).

Yuraks   *See* Nenets.

YUPIKS

location:
Far northeast of Siberia

time period:
Between 1000 B.C.E. and 0 to the present

ancestry:
Proto-Aleut/Yupik

language:
Central Siberian Yupik, a member of the Eskimo-Aleut language group within the larger Paleo-Asiatic family

Z

Zhuang (Buban, Budai, Budong, Bulong, Buman, Bumin, Buna, Bunong, Bupian, Bushuang, Butu, Buyang, Buyue, Buzhuang, Gaolan, Nongan, Nung, Tulao)

The Zhuang are the largest of China's 55 recognized national minority groups. Many scholars of the Tai people more generally also believe that Vietnam's NUNG population may essentially be the same ethnic group, although Nung communities living in China today are called Thai Nung. If the Zhuang and Nung are considered a single people, it makes them the second largest ethnic group in the world without a state of their own; the Kurds are the first.

GEOGRAPHY

The majority of contemporary Zhuang live in the Guangxi Zhuang Autonomous Region, although they constitute only about a third of the population there; smaller communities live in Yunnan, Guizhou, and Guangdong Provinces. This entire region is fairly mountainous and is crossed by a number of rivers and streams utilized by the rice-farming Zhuang for irrigation purposes. The subtropical climate of the region, with winter temperatures rarely dipping below 50°F, and an annual rainfall of about 60 inches allows for significant agricultural output, especially in rice.

ORIGINS

There are three competing theories concerning the origins of the Zhuang people: that they are the indigenous population of the Lingnan region of Guangxi and Yunnan, that they migrated into this region from the north and west in the centuries before the HAN dynasty, and that they are a mixed group created when migrants married the indigenes of the region. Most Zhuang scholars favor the first of these hypotheses, with the BAIYUE being the most commonly cited ancestral group, while many Zhuang peasants and a number of other Chinese historians favor the second. Although this remains contested, evidence for the Zhuang as inhabitants of the region earlier than the Han is available in both the Han and Zhuang languages, which refer to the Han as newcomers and the Zhuang as "original people"; many ancient place names in the region also come from Zhuang.

Chinese archaeologists have found material remains from a civilization on Mount Ganzhuang that most believe belong to the ancestors of today's Zhuang. *Ganzhuang* in the Zhuang language means "cave dwelling," while *zhuang* means "cave," which may have been where these proto-Zhuang resided about 5,000 years ago. Along with material remains, archaeologists have also found art from the period depicting frogs and lightning. According to experts in Zhuang symbols, the lightning represents hunting, gathering, and fishing, while the frogs represent farming; these depictions are believed to represent the replacement of one mode of subsistence with the other.

ZHUANG

location:
Mostly western Guangxi and eastern Yunnan Provinces, often called the Lingnan region, China; several closely related groups also live in Vietnam.

time period:
1052 C.E. to the present

ancestry:
Dai

language:
Two dialects of Zhuang, Northern and Southern, both Tai-Kadai languages closely related to Thai, Lao, and Dai

---

HISTORY

The modern history of the Zhuang is said by many historians to have begun with Nong Zhigao's defeat in 1055 because his people's fate as a minority group was sealed at that time. They believe that if he had won the battle against the Han at Kunlun Pass, his people might have taken his clan name, Nong, and established a lasting state that would have incorporated much of southern China and northern Vietnam. Instead, the Zhuang in China continued to be referred to by the ancient ethnonym assigned to them by the Chinese during the Han dynasty, meaning "cave" in their own language; those who found themselves on the VIETNAMESE side of the national boundary came to be known as Nung. The two groups began to diverge based on the historical, political, economic, and social contexts in which they lived so that today they are usually seen as two separate ethnic groups sharing a very similar Tai-Kadai language.

Today the Zhuang rarely draw the attention of Western scholars because they are seen as a largely sinicized group with few markers from their original culture. While this is not entirely accurate, the image comes from the fact that the Zhuang have been interacting with the Han for at least 2,200 years. During the Han dynasty most Zhuang gave up hunting and gathering and adopted settled agricultural practices, iron plows, triple cropping, and fertilizing techniques from the Han. They tended to live in lower elevations than many other southern minority groups and thus competed more with the intensive-farming Han for resources and land than they did with the shifting, or swidden, farmers of the higher regions. As their direct competitors, the Zhuang were forced or found it practical to adopt many Han cultural practices as well, including dress and housing styles. After 1055 many families and communities even found it prudent to give up their language and Zhuang names and assimilate entirely into the Han majority, which was not possible for groups whose physical traits differed significantly from the majority.

This is not to say that the Zhuang were always willing to accommodate either local or national Han "power brokers" without putting up a fight. After Nong Zhigao's failed state, other Zhuang also resisted these external political structures. The best known of these rebellions was in the mid-19th century when significant numbers of Zhuang participated in the Taiping Rebellion. In 1927 a Zhuang community near

Zhuang time line

B.C.E.

206 Start of the Han dynasty, during which the first mention of the Zhuang people occurs. The Han also nominally conquer the Zhuang region but generally fail to govern in any effective way.

C.E.

220 The Han dynasty falls, and the Zhuang disappear from Chinese chronicles for more than 700 years, though much smaller groups of speakers of this language are known by terms that refer to their geography, clothing, or other local markers.

618 Start of the Tang dynasty, when large numbers of Han people begin to move into the Zhuang region.

960 Start of the Song dynasty, during which the Zhuang people reemerge as a large and distinct group recognized by the imperial state, particularly after Nong Zhigao's uprising.

1041 Nong Zhigao establishes the independent state of Dali Guo in the Longzhou area of Guangxi; it is unrelated to the Dali kingdom in Yunnan.

1048 Dali Guo is defeated by the Vietnamese, and the Song emperor refuses to come to its assistance.

Nong Zhigao moves his capital to An-de Zhou and leads his military against the Chinese.

1052 Nong Zhigao begins his peasant uprising against the Han Chinese; this is usually the date that marks the formal creation of the Zhuang people from their Dai antecedents.

1054–55 Nong Zhigao is finally defeated at the Battle of Kunlun Pass, and the Zhuang become a minority people in both China and Vietnam.

1958 The Chinese government creates the Guangxi Zhuang Autonomous Region as well as smaller autonomous regions in Yunnan and Guangdong.

1985 The Chinese government begins a program to assist the rural poor, which raises the standard of living for many Zhuang considerably.

1993 *The Encyclopedia of the Zhuang* is published in China.

Pai-se established one of the first soviets in China, and the Zhuang actively resisted the Nationalist government from 1911 until the Communist Party victory in 1949. The Zhuang were such active members of the communist resistance that a young Deng Xiaoping was sent to Guangxi in 1929 to assist with the organization of civilians into military units to resist Nationalist rule and later JAPANESE aggression; some of these units rose up against the state in 1929 and then again in 1930.

Perhaps as recompense for their support, the Zhunag were honored by being granted their own autonomous region early on in the creation of a communist state in China. By 1958 this region included all of Guangxi Province, and smaller autonomous regions were also established in Yunnan and Guangdong Provinces. Since 1979 and the change in the Chinese state policy with regard to minorities from assimilationist to recognition of and at least marginal respect for the country's 55 national minorities, greater interest in Zhuang history and origins has meant that numerous studies have been done and books published trying to recreate the traditions and culture of the past. An *Encyclopedia of the Zhuang* was published in 1993 to document this past culture and to educate both the Chinese and external scholarly communities about Zhuang contributions to Chinese culture and society more generally.

CULTURE

While the subsistence base for both Zhuang and Han societies is similar—intensively farmed wet rice using manure and chemical fertilizers, complex irrigation systems, and significant contributions of human labor—many other aspects of the two ethnic groups differ. Indeed, even some aspects of their subsistence are not identical since some Zhuang communities prefer glutinous rice to the less sticky varieties favored by the Han. The Zhuang also differ economically in that both women and men have traditionally participated in market selling and buying. Women make and sell batik, embroidered, and brocaded cloth, for which they have been well known in southern China since before the 11th century, as well as food items, household goods, and many other products that are also sold by men. Men plow the fields, while women plant, transplant rice seedlings, weed, and harvest, leaving much child care to be done by the elderly. Men are also more likely to leave their villages to seek work in other regions or urban areas or to gain an education.

While Zhuang kinship resembles that of the Han in giving primacy to three-generation extended households and larger patrilineal groups that trace their descent through men only, some aspects of the system seem to indicate a former matrilineal principle. For example, maternal uncles or mother's brothers have an important role to play in the lives of their nephews and nieces: They choose their given names, participate in marriage ceremonies, and have a ritualized support role during their parents' funerals. There is also a preference for boys to marry their mother's brother's daughter; in a patrilineal system these first cousins are not considered close relatives because they belong to a different patrilineage and clan. Both of these groups are strictly exogamous and thus require people to marry outside them; villages in the past were also generally exogamous. Requiring people to marry outside their lineage, clan, and village meant creating wider networks and associations that provided better support during times of natural disaster or warfare.

In the past, marriages were generally arranged by the parents when the couple was fairly young and the new bride was usually five or six years older than her husband. However, the new couple did not generally reside together right away. Instead, the bride would visit her new husband and his family for significant events, harvest time, and other social occasions but continue to live and work with her natal family until the birth of her first child. At that time she moved into her husband's home and took up the role of the dutiful daughter-in-law. Those Zhuang who were more sinicized differed somewhat from this norm; they used horoscopes to plan marriages between older men and younger women, required the bride's family to pay a dowry to the man's family; and required patrilocal residence in the husband's household immediately following the ceremony. In both kinds of families, youngest sons generally inherited their parents' houses and thus did not move out eventually as their older brothers and their families generally did.

Zhuang religious beliefs and practices differ from the Han as well. Both groups engage in ancestor worship, or did so prior to the crackdown on religion by the Communist Party in the 1950s, but the Zhuang ancestral group always includes a wide variety of historical figures such as kings, military heroes, and Nong Zhigao, in addition to actual patrilineal ancestors. There are also a number of local gods worshiped by the Zhuang, such as Tudigong and Dragon King, protectors of the village, and the Mountain Spirit, which prevents some mountains from being farmed. A number of Taoist and Buddhist elements have entered Zhuang religious practices, especially funerals, where priests from these traditions often supervise chanting, prayers, and other events. In addition, female diviners provide some spiritual guidance during times of illness or misfortune; by going into trances they are able to communicate with the spirit world to determine the cause of the problem as well as what propitiatory activities are necessary to end it. There are male shamans as well who specialize in reading ancient Zhuang and Chinese characters; leading in songs, myths, and chants; and performing at funerals, festivals, and life-cycle rites. These shamans require animal sacrifice as part of their payment, while the female diviners do not.

FURTHER READING

David Holm. *Killing a Buffalo for the Ancestors: A Zhuang Cosmological Text from Southwest China* (DeKalb: Southeast Asia Publications, Center for Southeast Asian Studies, Northern Illinois University, 2003).

Katherine Palmer Kaup. *Creating the Zhuang: Ethnic Politics in China* (Boulder, Colo.: Lynne Rienner Publishers, 2000).

Zo *See* CHIN.

Zunghars (Dzungars, Zungharians, Zuungars)

The Zunghars were a group of Western MONGOLS or OIRAT who were able to unify the various nomadic peoples of the steppes of northwestern China, Mongolia, and southern Siberia

ZUNGHARS

location:
The steppes of northwestern China, Mongolia, Tibet, Kazakhstan, and southern Siberia

time period:
1634–1760

ancestry:
Western Mongols

language:
Mongolian

Zunghars time line

C.E.

15th century Western Mongols establish themselves as the most powerful of the nomadic peoples of the central steppes.

1634–53 Batur Hongtaiji begins constructing the Zunghar state on the back of the largely nomadic Western Mongol people.

1653 Batur Hongtaiji is succeeded by his son Sengge.

1671 Sengge is murdered by his half brother.

1673 Sengge's brother Galdan returns from Lhasa, Tibet, and gains the support of all Zunghar chiefs. By 1679 he has taken over Eastern Turkestan, Hami, and Turfan and seeks legitimacy from the Chinese (Qing) ruler Kangxi through the title Bushuktu Khan.

1681–84 Galdan's armies overrun the Kazakh Great Horde.

1688 Galdan crushes the 5,000-strong forces of the Eastern Mongols, pushing Kangxi to seek alliance with the Mongol enemies, the Russians.

1689 The Treaty of Nerchinsk between the Russian and Chinese empires establishes formal boundaries between these two realms, effectively making the Zunghars subjects to the power of both countries.

1690 Qing troops defeat Galdan at the Battle of Ulan Butong; Galdan escapes and pledges his allegiance to the Qing.

1690s Kangxi's mistrust of Galdan pushes him to pursue the khan with a force of about 37,000 men at one point. Galdan escapes each time.

1697 Galdan finally dies, perhaps by his own hand rather than at the hands of the Qing leader.

1711–12 The Zunghars are invaded by the Kazakhs, who are seeking revenge for the Zunghar incursion in 1681.

1720 The Zunghars are driven out of Tibet.

1727 The Treaty of Kiakhta continues the trends begun in the Treaty of Nerchinsk, 1689.

1731 Zunghar armies decimate those of the Qing, killing 48,000 out of 50,000 soldiers.

1745 Succession issues lead to internal warfare between two rivals for the Zunghar throne, Dawaci and Amursana.

1753–55 Dawaci drives Amursana out of Zunghar and into the arms of the Qing emperor Qianlong.

1755 An enormous Qing army, with Amursana at its head, captures Dawaci and brings him to Qianlong in Beijing in the first Great Campaign. Amursana soon rebels against Qing rule and is forced to defend his state against the Chinese.

1757 Amursana is defeated and dies on the Russian border during the second Great Campaign.

1757–59 The third Great Campaign of the Qing against the Zunghars ends with the genocide of hundreds of thousands of people; smallpox and starvation soon finish the job and eliminate all trace of the Zunghar people.

into a statelike structure. Unification began in the mid-17th century under Batur Hongtaiji and lasted for about a century, when Qing military campaigns, disease, and starvation eliminated the Zunghar people from the region.

During its entire existence, the Zunghar state posed a challenge to the stronger empires that surrounded it, those of the Russian Romanovs and the Qing in China. The Qing were particularly concerned and used a variety of tactics to limit the power of their Mongol neighbors, including withholding trade privileges, campaigning into their lands, and even aligning themselves with their enemy Russia to limit the ability of the Zunghars to do the same.

Although the Zunghar people were unified by the father of Galdan, Batur Hongtaiji, the most important figure in Zunghar history is probably Galdan, who gave up his position as a Tibetan Buddhist lama in order to avenge the murder of his brother at the hands of their half-brother and then take over their father's realm. Galdan was very successful in military campaigns against the other peoples in his region as well as the Eastern Mongols or Khalkha people, which worried the Qing leaders in Beijing. They went on the offensive against the Zunghars in 1690 and defeated Galdan's troops at Ulan Butong; several more military campaigns in the 1690s resulted in even more Zunghar losses at the hands of the Qing. Galdan's final defeat came in 1696 at the Battle of Zuun Mod; he was driven toward the Russian border and died there, perhaps by suicide or through hypothermia and starvation.

After Galdan's death the Zunghars continued to consolidate their state from their central position in the Ili River valley, trading and drawing on the advice from experts from Russia and even Sweden. A Qing invasion of Tibet in 1720 drove the Zunghars out of that region, but a later Qing defeat in 1731 forced the Chinese to recognize the Zunghar state and its borders. Finally, in the 1750s the Qing decided that allowing the Zunghar state to continue to exist posed a permanent threat to their hegemony in the region, and they implemented what has been called "a final solution." Three separate military campaigns undertaken by the Qianlong emperor of the Qing, combined with a complete cutoff of Chinese trade, finally led to the complete extermination of about 600,000 Zunghar people. Warfare, smallpox and other diseases, starvation, and mass migration combined to eliminate the Zunghar problem completely from China's borders in what is still to this day one of the largest genocidal wars in history.

Zunghar culture had been based largely on the nomadic pastoral economy of the Western Mongol people. While they did build cities and traded extensively with the Russians, Chinese, and others, the Zunghar people continued to live on the resources derived from their herds of animals. The state itself drew much of its resources from taxes on the caravan trade across their region and on tribute taken from their weaker neighbors. During times of economic hardship on the steppes, such as drought or excessive winter weather, this nomadic population invaded the settled communities inside Chinese borders and wreaked havoc on both the land and its people. It was these activities, in addition to the metaphysical challenge to the Chinese of a population that refused to recognize their superior society and culture, that drove two successive Qing emperors to dedicate the resources and troops to the ultimate destruction of the Zunghars.

See also Russians: nationality; Tibetans; Chinese: nationality.

Further Reading

Peter C. Perdue. *China Marches West: The Qing Conquest of Central Eurasia* (Cambridge, Mass.: Belknap Press, 2005).

APPENDIX I
CONTEMPORARY PEOPLES WITH ENTRIES IN THE BOOK, BY COUNTRY

AFGHANISTAN

Afghanistanis: nationality
Afridi
Baluchi
Brahui
Durranis
Farsiwan
Ghilzai
Gujaratis
Hazaras
Kamboja
Kyrgyz
Mongols
Nuristanis
Pamiri
Pashai
Pashtuns
Punjabis
Seraikis
Tajiks
Turkic peoples
Turkmen
Uzbeks

ARMENIA

Armenians
Armenians: nationality
Azeris
Georgians
Turkic peoples

AUSTRALIA

Aboriginal Australians
Aboriginal Tasmanians
Australians: nationality
Mardu
Pitjantjatjara
Tiwi

Torres Strait Islanders
Walpiris

AZERBAIJAN

Armenians
Azerbaijanis: nationality
Azeris
Ossetians
Tats and Mountain Jews
Turkic peoples

BANGLADESH

A'chik
Bangladeshis: nationality
Bengalis
Biharis
Chakma
Gujaratis
Hijras
Hindi
Khasi
Mizo
Mundas
Oraon
Punjabis
Rakhines
Santal

BHUTAN

Bhutanese: nationality
Bhutia
Lepcha
Lhotshampa
Monba
Mundas
Newar
Santal

Sharchops
Sherpas
Tibetans

BRUNEI, SULTANATE OF

Bruneians: nationality
Kadazan Dusun
Iban
Malays
Murut

CAMBODIA

Brao
Cambodians: nationality
Chams
Jarai
Khmers
Khmu
Kui
M'nong
Mon
Phnong
Tampuan

CHINA

Achang
Akha
Bai
Bonan
Bouyei
Buriats
Cantonese
Chinese: nationality
Dai
Daur
De'ang
Derung

Dong
Dongxiang
Durbets
Evenkis
Gelao
Hakka
Han
Hani
Hmong
Hong Kong, people of
Hui
Jino
Kachin
Kazakhs
Khmu
Koreans
Kyrgyz
Lahu
Lhoba
Li
Lisu
Macanese
Manchus
Maonan
Monba
Mongols
Mulam
Nanai
Naxi
Nu
Nung
Oirat
Oroqen
Pamiri
Pumi
Qiang
Russians, Asian
Salar
San Chay
She

Sherpas
Shui
Tajiks
Tatars
Tibetans
Tu
Tujia
Turkic peoples
Uighur
Uzbeks
Va
Vietnamese
Xibe
Yao
Yi
Yugur
Zhuang

EAST TIMOR

East Timorese: nationality
Tetun

FIJI

Fijian, Indigenous
Fijian: nationality
Indo-Fijians
Melanesians
Polynesians
Tamils

GEORGIA

Abkhazians
Armenians
Azeris
Georgians: nationality
Laz
Mingrelians
Ossetians
Svan

HAWAII (STATE OF THE UNITED STATES OF AMERICA)

Hawaiians
Polynesians

INDIA

A'chik
Adi
Bengalis
Bhils
Bhuiya

Bhutia
Biharis
Chakma
Chhatisgarhis
Dravidians
Durranis
Ghilzai
Gond
Gujaratis
Gurkhas
Hijras
Hindi
Hindko
Indians: nationality
Jains
Kacharis
Kachin
Kamboja
Kannadigas
Karbis
Kashmiris
Khasi
Khojas
Kol
Kond
Konyak
Lepcha
Lhoba
Lisu
Malayalis
Mappilas
Mara
Marathi
Mundas
Mizo
Monba
Nagas
Nayakas
Newar
Nicobarese
Oraon
Oriyas
Other Backward Classes
Paharis
Parsees
Pashtuns
Rajasthanis
Rakhines
Santal
Scheduled Castes
Scheduled Tribes
Seraikis
Sherpas
Sikhs
Sikkimese
Sindhis

Tamils
Telegus
Tharu
Tibetans
Toda
Yanadis

INDONESIA

Acehnese
Ambonese
Asmat
Atoni
Bali Aga
Balinese
Bataks
Betawis
Buginese
Dani
Dayaks
Gorontalese
Iban
Indonesians: nationality
Javanese
Lampungese
Madurese
Makassarese
Malays
Minahasans
Minangkabau
Mori
New Guinea Highlanders
Osing
Penan
Peranakans
Sasaks
Sea Gypsies
Sundanese
Tenggerese
Tetun
Toala
Toraja

JAPAN

Ainu
Burakumin
Japanese
Japanese: nationality
Koreans
Okinawans

KAZAKHSTAN

Dungans
Durbets
Hui

Karakalpak
Kazakhs
Kazakhstanis: nationality
Kyrgyz
Mongols
Oirat
Tajiks
Tatars
Turkmen
Uzbeks

KIRIBATI

i-Kiribti
Kiribatese: nationality
Micronesians

KYRGYZSTAN

Dungans
Kyrgyz
Kyrgyzstanis: nationality
Tajiks
Tatars
Turkmen
Uzbeks

LAOS

Akha
Brao
Dai
Hani
Hmong
Khmu
Kui
Lahu
Lao
Laotians: nationality
Sedang
T'in
Yao
Yi

MALAYSIA

Buginese
Dayaks
Kadazan Dusun
Iban
Malays
Malaysian Chinese
Malaysian Indian
Malaysians: nationality
Mara
Melayu Asli
Murut

Orang Asli
Penan
Peranakans
Sea Gypsies
Semang
Senoi
Tamils
Tausug

MALDIVES

Divehi
Maldivians: nationality

MARSHALL ISLANDS

Marshall Islanders:
    nationality
Marshallese
Melanesians
Micronesians

MICRONESIA, FEDERATED STATES OF

Chamorro
Micronesians
Micronesians, Federated
    States of: nationality
Polynesians
Yap

MONGOLIA

Buriat
Dariganga
Durbets
Evenkis
Mongols
Mongolians: nationality
Oirat
Tuvans

MYANMAR

Achang
Akha
Burmans
Chakma
Chin
Dai
De'ang
Hmong
Intha
Kacharis
Kachin
Karen
Konyak

Lahu
Lisu
Mizo
Mon
Myanmarese: nationality
Nagas
Rakhines
Rohingya
Sea Gypsies
Shans
Va
Yao
Yi

NAURU

Nauruans: nationality

NEPAL

Bhutia
Dravidians
Gurkhas
Gurung
Hindi
Lepcha
Limbu
Magars
Nepalese: nationality
Newar
Paharis
Santal
Sherpas
Tamang
Tharu
Tibetans

NEW CALEDONIA (FRENCH OVERSEAS TERRITORY)

Kanak
Melanesians
Polynesians

NEW ZEALAND (AOTEAROA)

Maori
New Zealanders: nationality
Polynesians

NORTH KOREA

Koreans
Manchus
Koreans, North: nationality

PAKISTAN

Afridi
Baluchi
Brahui
Burusho
Dravidians
Durranis
Ghilzai
Gujaratis
Hazaras
Hijras
Hindko
Kalasha
Kashmiris
Khojas
Marwats
Muhajirs
Nuristanis
Pakistanis: nationality
Pamiri
Parsees
Pashtuns
Punjabis
Rajasthanis
Seraikis
Sindhis
Tajiks

PALAU

Micronesians
Palauans
Palauans: nationality

PAPUA NEW GUINEA

Chambri
Enga
Etoro
Iatmul
Melanesians
New Guinea Highlanders
New Guinea Sepik Basin
    People
Papua New Guineans:
    nationality
Polynesians
Tolai
Trobriand Islanders

PHILIPPINES

Aeta
Bicolanos
Bontoc
Cebuanos
Filipino Muslims

Filipinos: nationality
Hanunoo
Hiligaynon
Ibanags
Ifugao
Igorot
Ilocano
Ilongots
Ivatans
Kalingas
Kapampangans
Lumad
Mandayas
Mangyans
Manobos
Maranao
Pangasinans
Samals
Sea Gypsies
Tagalog
Tausug
Tirurays
Visayans

RAPANUI (CHILEAN TERRITORY)

Polynesians
Rapanui

RUSSIA (ONLY ASIAN)

Armenians
Azeris
Buriats
Chukchis
Dungans
Durbets
Evenkis
Evens
Georgians
Karakalpak
Kazakhs
Khant
Koryak
Manchus
Mongols
Nanai
Nenets
Oirat
Oroqen
Ossetians
Russians, Asian
Russians: nationality
Tatars
Tats and Mountain Jews
Turkic peoples

Tuvans
Uzbeks
Yakuts
Yukagirs
Yupiks

SAMOA

Polynesians
Samoans: nationality

SINGAPORE

Malays
Peranakans
Singaporean Chinese
Singaporean Indian
Singaporeans: nationality

SOLOMON ISLANDS

Melanesians
Solomon Islanders
Solomon Islanders:
    nationality

SOUTH KOREA

Koreans
Koreans, South:
    nationality

SRI LANKA

Burghers
Dravidians
Sinhalese
Sri Lankan Moors
Sri Lankans: nationality
Tamils
Wanniyala-Aetto

TAIWAN

Ami
Bunun
Hakka
Han
Hui
Aboriginal Taiwanese
Taiwanese: nationality
Yami

TAJIKISTAN

Kamboja
Kyrgyz
Tatars
Tajikistanis: nationality
Tajiks
Turkic peoples
Turkmen
Uzbeks

THAILAND

Akha
Chams
Dai
De'ang
Hill Tribes of Thailand
Hmong
Karen
Khmers
Kui
Lahu
Lao
Lisu
Malays
Mani
Mon
Sea Gypsies
Semang

Thais
T'in
Va
Yao
Yi

TONGA

Polynesians
Tongans
Tongans: nationality

TURKMENISTAN

Baluchi
Tajiks
Turkic peoples
Turkmen
Turkmenistanis: nationality
Uzbeks

TUVALU

Micronesians
Polynesians
Tuvaluans
Tuvaluans: nationality

UZBEKISTAN

Dungans
Karakalpak
Kazakhs
Tajiks
Tatars
Uzbekistanis: nationality
Uzbeks

VANUATU

Melanesians

ni-Vanuatu
Polynesians
Vanuatuans: nationality

VIETNAM

Akha
Bahnar
Bouyei
Brao
Chams
Dai
Dega
Hani
Hmong
Hoa
Jarai
Khmers
Khmu
Kui
Lahu
Lao
M'nong
Mon
Muong
Nung
Rhade
San Chay
Sea Gypsies
Sedang
Shui
Tay
Vietnamese
Vietnamese: nationality
Yao
Yi

APPENDIX II
HISTORICAL PEOPLES WITH ENTRIES IN THE BOOK AND THEIR DATES

Historical Peoples	Dates
Ahom	1228–1826 C.E.
Austronesians	ca. 5000 B.C.E.
Ba	11th century–316 B.C.E.
Bactrians	probably eighth century B.C.E. to eighth century C.E.
Baiyue	before 510 B.C.E.–220 C.E.
Caucasian Albanians	fourth century B.C.E., more likely first century B.C.E. to 700 C.E.
Chenla	600–800 C.E.
Colchians	15–13th century to 63 B.C.E.
Dangxiang	sometime before 317 C.E. to 1227
Dasa	ca. 1500 B.C.E.
Dawenkou culture	ca. 4300–2500 B.C.E.
Dingling	at least third century B.C.E. to before seventh century C.E.
Dong Son culture	possibly 1000–ca. 1 B.C.E.
Donghu	fifth century B.C.E. to first century C.E.
Funanese	400–500 B.C.E. to ca. 550 C.E.
Gandharan Grave culture	ca. 1500–500 B.C.E.
Gojoseon, people of	possibly 2333–108 B.C.E.
Greeks	329–130 B.C.E.
Harappans	ca. 3000–1500 B.C.E.
Hephthalites	fourth and fifth centuries C.E.
Hoa Binh culture	ca. 16,000–5000 B.C.E.
Hu	fourth century B.C.E. to sixth century C.E.
Indo-Aryans	second millennium to ca. 700 B.C.E.
Jomon	ca. 12,000–300 B.C.E.
Jurchens	at least sixth century C.E. to 1234
Karluks	600–1211 C.E.
Khitans	300s–1218 C.E.
Koban	ca. 1100–400 B.C.E.
Kuru	possibly 1500–500 B.C.E.
Kushans	first millennium B.C.E. to fourth century C.E.
Khwarezmians	1300 B.C.E.–11th century C.E.
Lapita culture	1500 B.C.E.–ca. 0 C.E.
Longshan culture	ca. 3000–1900 B.C.E.
Massagetae	first millennium B.C.E.
Medes	840–549 B.C.E.
Mehrgarh	ca. 7000–2000 B.C.E.
Mohe	fifth century to 10th century
Mumun culture	1500–300 B.C.E.

Naiman	unknown to 1218 C.E.
Parthians	247 B.C.E.–224 C.E.
Peiligang-Cishan culture	7000–5000 B.C.E.
Pengtoushan culture	7500–5500 B.C.E. or possibly 6100 B.C.E.
Persians, Achaemenids	554–329 B.C.E.
Persians, Sassanids	224–642 C.E.
Pyu	possibly 400 B.C.E. to 12th century C.E.
Rroma	unknown–1000 C.E.
Rouran	end of the fourth century to middle of the sixth century C.E.
Scythians	10th century to 12 B.C.E.
Shang	ca. 1750–1040 B.C.E.
Sogdians	sixth century B.C.E. to 13th century C.E.
Ta-p'en-k'eng culture	4500–1500 B.C.E.
Tiele	probably sixth to seventh centuries
Tocharians	possibly 2000 B.C.E.–1000 C.E.
Tuyuhun	fourth century to 950 C.E.
Xianbei	first century C.E.–589
Xiongnu	third century B.C.E. to fourth century C.E.
Yangshao culture	ca. 5000–3000 B.C.E.
Zunghars	1634–1760 C.E..

APPENDIX III
LIST OF INDIVIDUALS FEATURED IN BIOGRAPHICAL SIDEBARS

Ahmad Khan Abdali . . . . Pashtuns

Akbar . . . . Hindi

Bhimrao Ramji Ambedkar . . . . Scheduled Castes

Corazon Aquino . . . . Kapampangans

Aung San . . . . Burmans

Sirimavo Bandaranaike . . . . Sri Lankans: nationality

Benazir Bhutto . . . . Pakistanis: nationality

Empress Dowager Cixi . . . . Manchus

Diodotus II . . . . Greeks

Mohandas Karamchand Gandhi . . . . Indians: nationality

Genghis Khan . . . . Mongols

Sultan Shari ul-Hashim (Sharif Abubakar) . . . . Filipino Muslims

Ho Chi Minh . . . . Vietnamese

Kamla Jaan . . . . Hijras

Jayavarman II . . . . Khmers

Kasym Khan . . . . Kazakhs

General Leon Kilat . . . . Cebuanos

Kuo Hsiu-chu and Kuo Ying-nan . . . . Ami

Queen Lili'uokalani . . . . Hawaiians

Eddie Mabo . . . . Australians: nationality

Mahavira . . . . Jains

Katherine Mansfield . . . . New Zealanders: nationality

Mao Zedong . . . . Chinese: nationality

Emperor Meiji . . . . Japanese

Muhammad Ali Jinnah . . . . Bangladeshis: nationality

Tenzing Norgay . . . . Sherpas

Pol Pot (Soloth Sar) . . . . Cambodians: nationality

APPENDIX IV
RELIGIOUS SYSTEMS

There are many different definitions of religion that scholars use when they write on this subject. The most basic can probably be summed up as beliefs, practices, and attitudes related to a society's ultimate existential concerns. Other definitions point to the existence of supernatural or superhuman powers—that is, powers outside the capability of human beings such as gods, ancestors, witches, demons, devils, and the like. Still others indicate that religions are concerned with rituals and beliefs pertaining to things that are sacred, and that they unite people with these common rituals and beliefs into a community of believers. Some definitions focus primarily on the relationship between human beings, such as ones that emphasize the importance of symbols in creating moods and motivations in humans, while others emphasize the importance of nonhumans such as gods, demons, or ancestors. All of these definitions are useful in some contexts, but in others they can get in the way of really understanding the many complex beliefs and behaviors evident in the world. For example, definitions that focus on belief in god or gods or otherwise highlight the relationship between human beings and a supernatural or superhuman world can be problematic when looking at a variety of East Asian belief systems that are certainly concerned with their society's ultimate existential concern, such as Confucianism. Conversely, definitions that are primarily concerned with the relationships between human beings can miss the centrality in many religious systems, such as Christianity or Hinduism, of gods and other supernatural figures.

Throughout this encyclopedia we have tended to use the most basic definition of religion—beliefs, practices, and attitudes related to a society's ultimate existential concerns—while acknowledging that ultimate existential concerns differ widely from culture to culture. For Christians, Muslims, Buddhists, and Jains this ultimate concern is with salvation, while for Jews, Confucianists, Taoists, and believers in most indigenous religions it is living a good, proper, or appropriate life here on earth. The differences between these two kinds of existential concerns and the religions they have engendered have been described by religious scholar Evan Zuesse as the difference between "religions of salvation" and "religions of structure." The former tend to focus on an escape from this world and much of the regulation of human behavior that

stems from this goal paints this world as sinful. The result is often prohibitions on the pleasures of this world, such as dancing, music, feasting, and sexual activity. In contrast, religions of structure often see the sacred world as being here on earth, with food, music, trance, sex, and other bodily pleasures being a way of connecting to this sacred realm. Prohibitions on human behavior in a religion of structure tend to be about living a good or proper life on earth; pleasing the ancestors, gods, or spirits; or gaining benefits such as good hunting or peaceful social relations, rather than on things that might happen after death. Indeed, religions of structure tend to be relatively unconcerned with the afterlife, which is the opposite of religions of salvation.

A second set of important differences between these two kinds of religious systems is their acceptance of relative values or belief in a set of absolutes. Adherents to religions of salvation tend to be absolutists and thus believe that their religion is the only real religion or only real path to salvation. As a result of this belief, many religions of salvation proselytize or try to win converts among nonbelievers through missionary and other activities. Conversely, adherents to religions of structure tend to be relativists and thus believe that each society should rightfully have its own religion, believe in its own gods and spirits, and have its own way of celebrating these relationships. They tend to be much more comfortable combining elements from different religious traditions into their own, such as the numerous tribal societies in Asia and Oceania in which aspects of Christianity, Buddhism, or Islam have been combined with indigenous beliefs and behaviors. Any notion of proselytizing from these religions would also make no sense since no solitary religion is believed to be appropriate for all human beings.

The last important difference between religions of structure and salvation is the relative complexity of the relationship between the realm of the sacred and that of the profane as understood in each kind of system. In general, religions of structure tend to be much more complex in that the personal, social, and cosmic worlds are all believed to be completely intertwined and interacting with each other on a constant basis. As a result, every activity, even the most mundane such as food gathering or cleaning house, requires individuals to consider the ramifications of their actions on the personal, social, and cosmic worlds.

For example, gathering a certain berry or killing a certain animal without asking permission from the spirit world or sweeping dust into the world without apologizing may bring cosmic retribution on the careless. In contrast, religions of salvation tend to narrow spirituality to specific events and to believe that the earthly and cosmic worlds are separate. This separation means that even actions taken in this world that pertain to the sacred are not done due to the complex interactions between sacred and profane but due to the goal of ultimate escape from the profane world and entrance into that of the sacred.

APPENDIX V
KINSHIP SYSTEMS

Kinship, as discussed throughout this encyclopedia, is defined as a culturally recognized system of relationships among people connected by blood, marriage or alliance, and adoption. It is important to distinguish the centrality of cultural recognition of these relationships to this definition. For example, in many unilineal kinship systems, cultural recognition of blood or consanguineous ties is granted just to relatives from one's mother's or father's side of the family, depending on whether it is a matrilineal or a patrilineal system. The father's family members in a matrilineal system are usually not considered kin; the same is true of the mother's family members in a patrilineal system. The fact that humans are genetically related to their mother's and father's siblings' children equally is irrelevant in these kinds of unilineal systems since it is the cultural recognition of ties that matters for defining these connections, including incest taboos.

The other important feature of this definition of kinship is that it constitutes a system, not just a series of relationships. Kinship in many societies is about far more than acknowledging close and distant relatives and defining possible marriage partners. In most small-scale societies, kinship is the primary organizing principle defining all human interactions, including social, economic, and political ties both among members and between them and outsiders. Even in large state societies, however, kinship is sometimes very important for defining members of the group as well as their rights and responsibilities. In Tonga, for example, only those who are born or adopted into one of the large Tongan patrilineal kinship groups can own land; the same is true on Nauru, but there it is matrilineal ties that provide access to property. Similar rules in Germany mean that migrants with German family backgrounds can attain citizenship

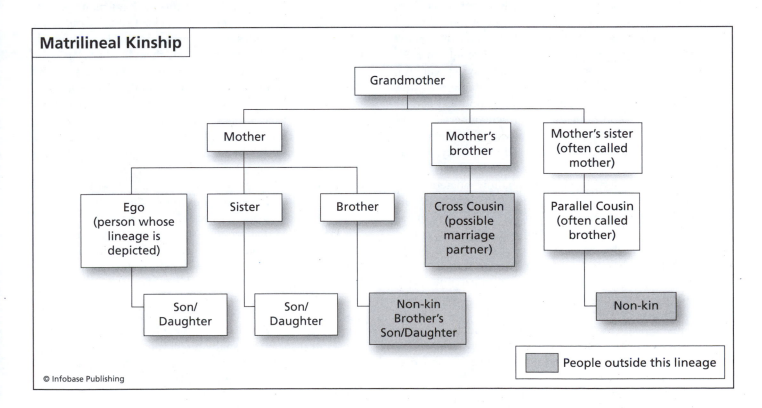

929

Patrilineal Kinship

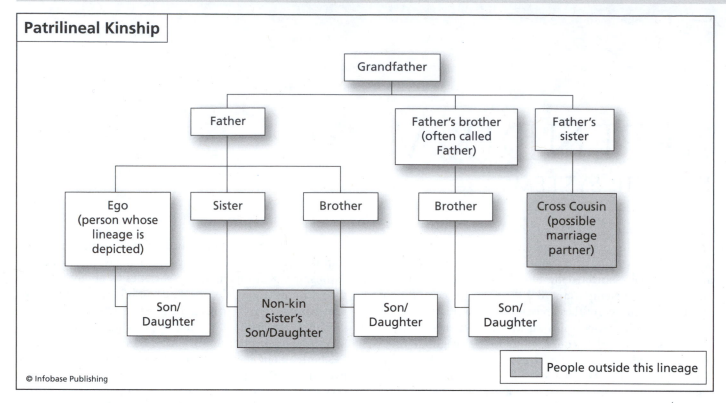

© Infobase Publishing

immediately, while those with no German kinship can live in the country for generations as outsiders.

Although it is a human universal—all societies have kinship systems, which differ immensely in structure and strength of ties—in general there are two broad categories of kinship systems: bilateral and lineal. Bilateral systems are those in which kin groupings recognize both mother's and father's relatives equally; they also tend to be fairly shallow in terms of their recognition of ancestors through time. As is true in the Western world, where bilateral systems are the norm, kinship ties in bilateral societies are often more about personal affinity and choice than social or political obligation, especially beyond immediate family members. However, there are many bilateral societies in which kinship is vital for organizing residence, obligation, and reciprocity, such as among the YUPIKS.

In contrast with the relatively shallow bilateral kinship systems, lineal kinship systems—including matrilineal, patrilineal, double unilineal, and ambilineal organizations—are characterized by large corporate kin groups that extend far back in time to a founding ancestor sometime in the distant past. The most important ties in these systems are those created by descent: through men in patrilineal systems, through women in matrilineal systems, through both in double unilineal systems, and through either in ambilineal systems. Lineal ties are so important in such groups as the patrilineal TURKMEN of Central Asia and matrilineal TIWI of Australia that third, fourth, fifth, and even more distantly related lineal cousins must be treated as brothers and sisters; at the same time, first cousins on the opposite side are

not only suitable marriage partners but often seen as ideal partners.

The third kind of lineal system, double unilineal, dictates that each individual is a member of both his or her matrilineal and patrilineal groups, both of which are exogamous and can delineate its ancestors back for many generations. The TODA, one of the SCHEDULED TRIBES of India, are one of the few societies in the world with this kind of double unilineal kinship structure in which individuals are seen as full-fledged members of both their mother's lineage and their father's; they must marry outside both of these lineages, maintain alliance and ritual ties to both corporate groups, and can trace their ancestry back for 10 or more generations on both sides. While individuals in societies that recognize double unilineal kin groupings are members of both their mother's and father's lineages, those in ambilineal societies, such as the Paiwan, an ABORIGINAL TAIWANESE people, are able to choose membership in one lineage or the other. Once they have made their choice, however, they become full members in that group with all the ritual, social, political, economic, and other rights and responsibilities accorded to lineage members. Having rejected either their mother or father's lineage, they are then able to marry into that group because they are not considered close kin.

While bilateral kinship systems tend not to create large, corporate groupings of related people with mutual obligations, lineal societies usually do. Beyond the level of the lineage, groups of lineages with a common founding ancestor, often a mythological figure, make up matrilineal or patrilineal clans. Clans, just like lineages, are usually exogamous groups that require all individuals to marry someone from another clan. In addition to defining marriage partners, clans also serve as organizing principles for such large events as warfare, political leadership, and some religious rituals. Some societies recognize even larger kinship groupings called moieties, from the French word for half, that organize half the society's clans into one group and half into the other, usually only for the purpose of defining marriage partners. Like clans and lineages, moieties are exogamous and require all members to marry someone from the other group.

APPENDIX VI
SUBSISTENCE SYSTEMS

Subsistence systems are the patterns of activities undertaken by communities in order to provide food and other necessities of life. A subsistence economy is one in which each family or other productive unit takes part almost entirely in self-provisioning rather than in producing food and other items for sale, other profit, or significant trade. However, societies with market or socialist economies also have a predominant subsistence system called intensive agriculture.

In addition to intensive agriculture, anthropologists generally characterize three other primary subsistence systems evident throughout the world: food collecting, which is often called hunting and gathering; horticulture; and pastoralism. During the period of European exploration of the rest of the world and through the European colonial era, often these different systems were ranked hierarchically, with food collecting believed to be associated with "primitive" kinship and religious systems, horticulture and pastoralism with somewhat more advanced kin groupings and religions, and intensive agriculture with the advanced world of Europeans of the 17th–19th centuries. Today we know that much of the Western world actually exhibits one of the globe's least complex kinship systems, bilateral ties, and that the complexity of many small-scale religions as practiced by hunter-gatherer societies can be infinitely greater than the world's primary religions.

What is true, however, is that food collecting, which is often accompanied by fishing and perhaps some control of the environment through burning, digging wells or weirs, and planting of trees, is suitable for the smallest populations and the lowest population densities of the four possible subsistence systems. Hunter-gatherers are usually nomadic or seminomadic, moving seasonally or even more frequently to take advantage of ripening fruits, nuts, or other foods; water supplies; and wild game. Families or larger units, called bands, can also move due to social or political reasons, the avoidance of conflict, or bad luck experienced in a certain locale. Their nomadism requires people in these societies to limit their material possessions to a few necessary objects that can be carried with them on their regular journeys; usually these objects are limited to weapons, carrying bags, and a few ritual objects. Housing, clothing, and all other items are made anew in each new territory. In addition to having few material possessions, individuals in hunter-gatherer societies also have no differences in wealth, no full-time craft specialties, and no ability to inhabit a formal position of authority over other people. Generally, the only socially recognized differences in these societies are those of age, with older people generally garnering more respect and leadership than younger ones, and gender, with men generally in higher positions than women.

Although limited today to just a few small tribal communities living in the most marginal lands on earth, such as the frozen tundra of Siberia; high elevation jungles of the Philippines, India, and Indonesia; and deserts of Australia, hunting and gathering has actually been the most viable subsistence system developed over the course of all of human history. For nearly 2 million years, all human beings lived in hunter-gatherer societies, taking advantage of the richest and most productive lands available. Their lives were not usually characterized as "solitary, poor, nasty, brutish, and short," as described by Thomas Hobbes in his 17th-century description of human beings' "natural state," but rather marked by long periods of rest and inactivity. Even once they had been pushed into the marginal deserts, forests, and tundra, most hunter-gatherers needed to work only about four hours per day to create and find all the resources they needed to survive; most certainly this figure would have been much lower when hunter-gatherers inhabited the best territories available. Compared to the almost constant paid labor and household work engaged in by most contemporary Americans, four hours of work per day in total sounds like a dream!

In addition, hunter-gatherers are also less likely to experience food shortages or malnutrition than their farming counterparts. This may seem unlikely to westerners who can get a large range of foods in their local grocery store, but the history of farming has shown us that this plenty is a very new development and even today is experienced by a relatively small number of the world's 6.2 billion people. Due to their ability to move when provisions are limited and to the very large range of edible foods available in the natural environment, food collectors do not experience the famines that have killed billions of people throughout the world since the development of agriculture about 10,000 years ago. They also tend to have a more varied diet and thus get a much wider range of nutrients than most farming communities, whose primary caloric intake generally comes from a single cereal crop such as corn, rice, or wheat. Traditional food collectors' teeth are generally healthier than even most contemporary Americans, and they do not suffer from heart disease, diabetes, or most cancers. Even life expectancy is estimated to have decreased by many years with the development of agriculture, only rising again in parts of the world with the development of modern medicine in the 20th century.

The one area in which hunting and gathering is clearly deficient in relation to some other forms of subsistence is in the ability to support large, settled populations. The development of agriculture starting about 10,000 years ago in Mesopotamia and China, and somewhat later in the Americas and New Guinea, meant the ability to support more people, at least until famine killed many of them, and to allow some people to specialize in other activities while smaller and smaller numbers of people dedicated themselves to food production. This allowed for the development of class and caste-based societies, increasing division of labor, and complex political structures such as chiefdoms and states. As a result, intensive agriculture, despite its significant drawbacks, has become the dominant subsistence system throughout the world, and practitioners of the other three systems have been integrated into the world economy at its lowest level or pushed onto the world's most difficult terrain.

The simplest subsistence system based on food production instead of collection is often called horticulture, hoe agriculture, or extensive agriculture. Rather than mechanized plowing, irrigation, and artificial fertilizers, horticulture relies entirely on human labor, usually with a digging stick or hoe, rainfall, and natural fertilizers. Often this form of agriculture is accompanied by slash-and-burn preparation of fields, also called swidden, when primary vegetation is cut, allowed to dry, and then burned to provide fertilizer for a year or two of crops. Like hunter-gatherers, horticulturalists usually have to shift their residence occasionally, perhaps every few years, to take advantage of new territories, allowing old fields to remain fallow for up to 20 years or more. This requirement for extensive amounts of land for small numbers of people means low population densities; it is also the source of the term *extensive agriculture.*

While a society will be classified as horticultural if the majority of its inhabitants' calories come from gardened foods, most people in these societies also continue to hunt, gather, and fish to provide protein and a wider array of food items than it is possible to grow; they may also keep a few domesticated animals such as dogs, goats, chickens, or pigs. They tend to accumulate more material possessions than hunter-gatherers and to develop at least a few part-time political and religious officials; however, like hunter-gatherers they experience few food shortages and may engage in only

minimal trade relations. Rather than growing just a single crop or two, horticulturalists tend to plant a wide array of fruit and vegetables together in a small patch, mitigating the deleterious effects of pests or diseases through variation. Today, however, horticulturalists, like hunter-gatherers, have been pushed onto more marginal lands by the military and political strength of intensive agriculturalists and tend to have more difficult lives than they would have had in the past, prior to the powerful competition for land and resources of the present.

The development of intensive agriculture was achieved through improvements in technology and seed stock and may have been driven by population increases; conversely, population increases may have occurred as a result of the development of intensive agriculture. This technological change included the ability to harness animals to use for plowing; the development of iron plows to break through difficult soils; irrigation technology; and the use of artificial fertilizers, whether animal, human, or chemical, to allow each field to be used again and again. While the 1970s Green Revolution is often cited as a period of great innovation in seed stock, leading to greater outputs of rice in developing countries like India and Indonesia, the first green revolution would have occurred thousands of years ago as the first incipient farmers changed the genetic profile of commonly occurring wild plants to produce larger, more plentiful, or more easily harvested seeds.

Throughout history, societies that have developed intensive agriculture or adopted it from others have always been divided by class or considerable differences in wealth as well as by occupation, with the development of full-time political officials and a significant division of labor. These societies, while at risk of famine and malnutrition, have also been able to raise large armies at certain times and thus conquer the much smaller populations of hunter-gatherers and horticulturalists. Today most of the world is dominated by this form of subsistence, which has seen the world's population rise exponentially in the 20th and 21st centuries and the near-elimination of these much more sustainable systems. However, the problems created by this form of subsistence and the societies they have engendered—famine; malnutrition; disparities in wealth; diseases such as diabetes, obesity, and influenza—have yet to be eradicated. It remains to be seen whether this "new" subsistence experiment—far less than 1 percent of human existence has been marked by intensive agriculture—can survive in the coming centuries.

The domestication of plants and especially animals about 10,000 years ago also led to the development of a fourth subsistence system, which continues to be practiced in a few regions of the world: pastoralism. Pastoralists live almost entirely on the meat and milk products supplied by their herds of animals, whether cattle, yaks, sheep, goats, camels, or horses. They may also plant a few trees or other crops that can be visited off and on throughout the year and engage in trade with hunter-gatherers, horticulturalists, or agriculturalists. While most pastoralists move as needed with their herds to take advantage of grass and water, trans-humance pastoralists move seasonally, often into protected valleys in winter and up into cooler mountain climates in summer. Like horticulturalists, pastoralists have few craft specialists and only part-time political officials, but they also resemble intensive agriculturalists in suffering frequent food shortages and relying heavily on trade; they also resemble hunter-gatherers in being able to support only very small populations and population densities.

APPENDIX VII
CHRONOLOGY OF ASIAN AND OCEANIAN HISTORY

The abbreviation B.P., meaning "before present," is often used by archaeologists to describe events that happened in prehistory where exact dating is extremely difficult, if not impossible. B.C.E., before the common era, and C.E., common era, or current era, refer to dates in the Christian calendar before and after the birth of Christ, respectively. For example, the approximate date for the first human inhabitation of the region around Beijing, 40,000 B.P., could be written 38,000 B.C.E. by simply subtracting the 2,000 years of current history calculated in the 40,000 B.P. dating system.

Many of the following dates, those inscribed both as B.P. and as B.C.E., are approximations; a few dates from the common era are likewise approximations based on the best sources possible. Events closer to the present period are much more likely to be exact.

500,000–20,000 B.P.

Acheulian and Soan Valley cultures in India and Pakistan are characterized by stone tools; stone axes may be missing from the Soan Valley culture. Acheulian remains have been found throughout peninsular India, as well as Africa and Europe. This is believed to be the first wave of modern humans who left Africa to colonize the rest of the world.

70,000–58,000 B.P.

Contested dating of some archaeological sites in Arnhem Land showing that Aboriginal Australians and probably New Guinea Highlanders established settlements in the giant Sahul landmass.

This period also saw the colonization by the first humans of the Andaman Islands, off the coast of India.

48,000 B.P.

Asian Neanderthals become extinct as *Homo sapiens* communities expand throughout Asia.

45,000 B.P.

Date used by more conservative archaeologists to mark the establishment of Aboriginal culture in Australia/Sahul.

40,000 B.P.

Evidence of the first humans living in the region of Beijing are dated to this period.

32,000 B.P.

Probable era of Melanesian settlement in the Bismarck Archipelago and Solomon Islands.

30,000–20,000 B.P.

Ice Age hunters move into the territory east of Lake Baikal.

The Aeta peoples settle the Philippines, probably migrating from Borneo across a land bridge.

The first evidence of inhabitation on Hokkaido, Japan, comes from this period.

22,000 B.P.

The aboriginal population has established itself throughout the entire area of today's mainland Australia and Tasmania, and population growth expands at a much faster rate than previously. This is also the date of the Last Glacial Maximal.

The Ryukyu Islands are cut off from both Japan and southern Asia by rising sea levels.

18,000 B.P.

Migrations into far Northeast Asia begin; about 3,000 years later, migrations across the Bering Strait into North America begin.

Start of the Hoa Binh culture in Southeast Asia, especially territory that is today Vietnam and Thailand.

14,000 B.P.

The start of the Jomon period in Japanese history.

14,000–4200 B.P.

The Neolithic period in China is marked by the spread of agricultural communities and increased reliance on agriculture, although hunting and gathering are still practiced. Silk production and pottery have already been developed, the two main types of pottery being black and painted. Clothing is made from hemp; pigs and dogs have been domesticated.

13,000 B.P.

Some highly contested evidence of rice being cultivated in Korea.

Rising sea levels separate the aboriginal population of Tasmania from the mainland.

12,700 B.P.

The invention of pottery in Japan, the first in the world, by the Jomon people.

12,000 B.P.

Australia and New Guinea are separated by rising sea levels, creating the Torres Strait Islands. Japan is separated from the rest of Asia at the same time.

9800–9200 B.P.

Peiligang-Cishan culture in China domesticates millet.

9000 B.P.

Pengtoushan culture, a Neolithic society of the central Yangtze River area of China, domesticates rice.

The people of the Bac Son culture establish themselves in northeast Vietnam.

9000–7000 B.P.

Independent development of agriculture in the New Guinea Highlands.

Aceramic Neolithic period of civilization at Mehrgarh, Pakistan, known as Period I. Early stages of agricultural development, basket making, stone and bone tools.

8000 B.P.

The first signs of crude terra-cotta pottery and figurines begin to appear at Mehrgarh.

7000–6500 B.P.

Most likely dates for the first exodus of Austronesian peoples from southern China to Taiwan.

Probable period for the disintegration of Hoa Binh culture.

6500–6000 B.P.

The horse is domesticated on the Eurasian steppes.

6500–3500 B.P.

Ta-p'en-k'eng culture is established on Taiwan by the earliest Austronesians to have arrived on the island following their departure from southern China; the name comes from an archaeological site in northern Taiwan near the mouth of the Tanshui River.

6300–4500 B.P.

Dawenkou culture is one of many Neolithic societies in territory that is China today; it is primarily located on the lower Huang (Yellow) River in what is present-day Shandong Province.

5000–3900 B.P.

Longshan culture dominates much of the Huang (Yellow) River valley of China.

5000 B.P.

Most likely date of a second exodus of Austronesian peoples from southern China to Taiwan and then the Philippines, Indonesia,

and eventually Rapanui, Madagascar, Hawaii, and the rest of Polynesia and Micronesia.

Urban civilization begins in the area of present-day Afghanistan.

4600–4000 B.P.

At some point during this 600-year period, the people at Mehrgarh, Pakistan, move on, perhaps into true cities at Harappa and Mohenjo-Daro.

4500–4000 B.P.

Afanasievo culture in southern Siberia, an Eneolithic culture (period between the Neolithic and Bronze Ages) notable for copper tools, hunting and pastoralism, a small degree of agriculture.

4500–3500 B.P.

Period of migration when Mon-Khmer peoples move south from the Mongolian plateau to mainland Southeast Asia.

4333 B.P.

Probably mythological founding date of the Gojoseon Kingdom in Korea.

4300–3900 B.P.

The height of Harappan civilization in the Indus Valley.

4200–3750 B.P.

The Xia dynasty in China, which marks the transition between the Neolithic and Bronze Ages.

4000 B.P.

The first definitive evidence of agriculture in Java comes from this era.

The Svan break away from the other Kartvelian language speakers: Georgians, Mingrelians, and Laz.

4000–2000 B.P.

Andronovo culture, a Late Bronze Age culture of sedentary pastoralists, exists in the steppes and southern Siberia.

3800–3500 B.P.

Probable period in which the Indo-Aryans moved into South Asia.

3750–3040 B.P.

China's Shang dynasty; the population becomes more urbanized, and cities become the center of intellectual life, especially the Shang capitals and the king's court. The first evidence of Chinese writing is produced during the Shang dynasty.

3500 B.P.

The Rig Veda, the religious text of the Hindus, is probably composed in this period.

Period when the Gandharan Grave culture begins; it lasts until about 2500 B.P.

Start of the Mumun culture on the Korean Peninsula, named for its unmarked pottery; intensive agriculture arrives on the Korean Peninsula in this period as well.

The earliest period in which we can speak of the Malay people.

3500–2000 B.P.

Era in which most Lapita style pottery was made and left behind in New Guinea, New Caledonia, the Solomon Islands, Vanuatu, Fiji, Samoa, and Tonga.

The Chamorro settle the Micronesian islands of Guam, Saipan, Tinian, Rota, Maug, and Pagan.

3400–3300 B.P.

Perhaps the century in which Zarathustra, founder of Zoroastrianism, is born, legend has it, in the Bactrian capital of Bactra. Years circa 3100 B.P. and 2700 B.P. have also been posited as dates for Zarathustra's life.

Probable era for the founding of the Colchian community on the Black Sea, according to Greek tales describing events in this era.

Sri Lanka begins exporting cinnamon to Egypt.

3200 B.P.

Probable date of Austronesian expansion to Samoa, Tonga, Fiji, and New Caledonia.

3100–2400 B.P.

Koban culture is a late Bronze Age society in the northern and central Caucasus.

3000 B.P. or 1000 B.C.E.

The Bronze Age Dong Son culture probably emerges in Southeast Asia at this time; they are best known for their large bronze drums.

The Li people begin migrating from mainland China to Hainan Island.

Approximate period in which the Mangyans of Mindoro, the Philippines, adopt and adapt a script from India for writing their own poetry.

Desertification and other aspects of climate change result in the development of nomadism in the Eurasian steppes as a strategy for survival in the cold, dry climate.

ca. 840 B.C.E.

First mention of the Mada people, who occupy the area of present-day northwestern Iran, in an Assyrian text of King Shalmaneser III, who claims to have received tribute from them.

834 B.C.E.

An Assyrian text mentions the rebellious people of Parsuash in Iran, the first written record of the Persians.

ca. 800 B.C.E.

Hesiod writes of the Scythians as mare-milking nomads; Homer writes of mare-milkers in the Iliad, dated between 1000 and 800 B.C.E.

739 B.C.E.

One estimated date for the initial migration of the Karen from northern to Southeast Asia.

700 B.C.E.

Time of Achaemenes, the possibly legendary leader of one of the Persian tribes and founder of the royal clan of Cyrus the Great. This tribe rules in southern Iran.

The Sinhalese probably begin migrating to Sri Lanka from India in this and the following century.

600 B.C.E.

The period of classical Sanskrit and the end of the Indo-Aryan phase in India. Some sources date the end of the classical period as late as 250 B.C.E. or 2250 B.P.

599 B.C.E.

Mahavira, Jainism's final Jina, similar to a prophet, is born.

563 B.C.E.

Gautama Siddharta Buddha, the founder of Buddhism, is born.

551–479 B.C.E.

Lifetime of Confucius, founder of Confucianism.

550 B.C.E.

Cyrus the Great vanquishes the Median king Astyages (his own grandfather), becomes king of kings in Persia and Media, and begins the period of expansion of the Persian Achaemenid Empire.

520 B.C.E.

Darius the Great, king of the Persian Achaemenid Empire, has the Behistun Inscription carved to document how his god, Ahuramazda, chose him to lead his people, plus the lands he inherited, the battles he won in his first few years as ruler, and other information about the empire.

486 B.C.E.

Height of the Persian Achaemenid Empire, the largest empire ever known up until that time; it stretches from Macedonia to India. In the same year, the Persian king Darius the Great dies.

400 B.C.E.

The Jomon culture begins disappearing with the migration of farmers from mainland Asia, usually called Yayoi.

Greek historian Xenophon provides the first-known written account of Armenians.

First mention of Colchis, in Aeschylus's tragedy *Promethus Bound*.

331–330 B.C.E.

Alexander the Great conquers the Persian Empire in the Caucasus and Central Asia; the Battle of Gaugamela is the greatest of these battles, when Alexander defeats the forces of Darius III. Alexander dies in Babylon seven years later.

320–180 B.C.E.

The Mauryan empire is spread over most of present-day India, Pakistan, and Bangladesh.

300 B.C.E.

The Rig Veda is probably written down for the first time in this period.

The Chinese begin the Great Wall against various nomadic peoples' incursions into their settled territories.

The Parni tribe moves south from the lower reaches of the Oxus River into the Persian region of Parthava, in today's northeastern Iran.

The Turkic language divides into two branches, the Eastern Oguz and Western Ogur, or Kipchak.

Greek, Iranian, and Chinese sources place the Uighur north of China as early as this period.

Third century B.C.E.

Buddhism arrives in Sri Lanka, perhaps with a monk named Arihath Mahinda Thero.

284–219 B.C.E.

Reign of King Parnavaz I of Iberia (Kartli) when the Kartvelian peoples unite to form the Iberian federation in what is today eastern Georgia.

273–232 B.C.E.

Asoka, grandson of Chandragupta Maurya and the greatest of the Mauryan kings, rules in India and institutes a series of Buddhist edicts designed to bring about moral reform.

258 B.C.E.

The kingdom of Au Lac is formed by combining various smaller kingdoms in northern Vietnam.

235 B.C.E.

A Greco-Bactrian kingdom is established in Transoxiana by the descendants of Alexander the Great's soldiers.

230 B.C.E.

Kannada splits off from the other Dravidian languages, such as Tamil, Telugu, and Malayalam in this period.

221–206 B.C.E.

China's Qin dynasty. Writing systems are first standardized, and China is unified.

End second century B.C.E.

Estimated period of unification of the Caucasian Albanian tribes under one ruler.

209–175 B.C.E.

Maodun expands the Xiongnu empire to its greatest extent.

206 B.C.E.

Start of the Han dynasty in China.

At this time the Xiongnu begin their expansion in the region of contemporary Mongolia, conquering the Donghu among other nomadic peoples.

This is also the possible period in which the proto-Mon-Khmer people migrate into Southeast Asia from China.

200 B.C.E.

Estimated start of the Sangam period of classical Tamil culture.

160 B.C.E.

Beginning of the decline of the Xiongnu empire with the death of Laoshang.

141 B.C.E.

The Parthian king Mithradates I gains access to the Seleucids' capital, Seleucia, and is crowned king, thus replacing the Greek empire with an Iranian one.

130 B.C.E.

Heliocles I, the last Greek king of western Bactria, falls to nomadic invaders.

127 B.C.E.

Possibly the founding date of the Yarlung or Tubo kingdom, which eventually unites Tibet under a single ruler.

First century B.C.E.

The first Pyu city-state, Beikthano, is established in the central plains of Myanmar.

The Parthian king Mithridates II finally defeats the Scythians in Central Asia.

111 B.C.E.

The Han Chinese colonize Vietnam, which they hold for about 1,000 years.

95–66 B.C.E.

The Armenian kingdom reaches its pinnacle under Tigranes (II) the Great.

57 B.C.E.

The founding of the state of Shilla, sometimes called Silla, on the Korean Peninsula.

47–42 B.C.E.

First female ruler of any Asian nation, Queen Anula of Sri Lanka.

1 B.C.E.

Earliest records of Dai peoples, then named Dianyue or Shan, in the historical books of the Han.

FIRST CENTURY

Early first century

Probably the era in which the Xianbei first migrate south from their original homeland in Inner Mongolia. This marks the transition from Donghu to Xianbei and Wuhuan peoples.

Period when the spectacular Ifugao rice terraces are begun on Luzon, the Philippines.

A large number of Hindu kingdoms emerge on Kalimantan (Borneo), Java, Bali, Sulawesi, and Sumatra, many lasting until the 12th century.

Buddhism travels from India to Mongolia along the Silk Road; this continues throughout the following centuries.

The Ossetians believe their ancestors migrated into the southern Caucasus at this time; Georgians believe this event began much later.

2

A Chinese government census finds that more than 59 million people live in the Han empire.

21

Gondophares establishes the Parthian kingdom in the former territories of the Scythian tribes in parts of Afghanistan, Pakistan, and India.

30

Kajula Kadphises unites all the tribes of the Yuezhi and becomes the first of the Kushan emperors.

37

The Three Kingdoms era begins in Korea: Koguryo, Paekche, and Shilla; this period ends in 668.

40

The Trung sisters successfully repel the Chinese ruler To Dinh from the prefecture of Giao Chi (Chinese-dominated northern Vietnam); three years later the sisters are defeated and commit suicide.

SECOND CENTURY

The first Christian Armenian Church is founded by Bartholomew and Thaddaeus.

First reference to Maldives by Greek geographer Ptolemy, who states that "1,378 little islands" lie west of Taprobane (Sri Lanka).

100

The Georgian kingdom of Iberia obtains independence from Rome and reclaims territories formerly lost to Armenia.

Indian chronicles mention the existence of a Hindu kingdom, Jawa Dwipa, on Java.

125

First textual reference to Hephthalites; a Chinese source mentions them as living in Dzungaria.

192

Founding date of the kingdom of Champa by Cri Mara, according to Chinese sources.

THIRD CENTURY

Estimated end of the Sangam period of classical Tamil culture.

Possible date of the initiation of the Kalanay pottery complex on Masbate and other Visayan islands, the Philippines, which displays similarities to Dong Son culture in Vietnam and other groups in Laos.

200

The Kingdom of Funan expands during the rule of Fan Shih-Man, extending from contemporary Malaysia to Burma.

216

Manes, the father of Manichaeanism (a dualistic Persian religion stressing asceticism to release the soul from the body), is born.

220

Fall of the China's Han dynasty.

224

Ardashir I overthrows the Parthian king, Artabanus V, and establishes his empire, named for his distant ancestor, Sasan, a descendant of the Achaemenids.

229–232

The Avesta, the holiest Zoroastrian book, is compiled from earlier sources.

248

Trieu Au leads a Vietnamese rebellion against both Chinese rule and customs, which limit the lives of women much more severely than do traditional Vietnamese customs.

258

The first Xianbei federation is formed from the various Xianbei clans.

FOURTH CENTURY

Yayoi culture has fully established itself on all of Japan's southern islands; Hokkaido is too cold for Yayoi irrigated rice agriculture and remains in the hands of the Jomon-era peoples.

The first wave of Hakka migration begins in the fourth century; they travel from Henan, Shanxi, and Anhui Provinces and make it as far south as Hubei, southern Henan, and central Jiangxi Provinces.

The Ancient Sogdian Letters, a series of letters in this language discovered in western Gansu Province 1907 by archaeologist Aurel Stein and probably written in the early fourth century C.E., point to a string of Sogdian colonies on the Silk Road, including in China.

301–330

National Armenian conversion to Christianity under King Trdat III after his meeting with Saint Gregory the Illuminator; this is possibly the first national conversion to Christianity in the world.

337

Mirian III establishes Christianity as the state religion of Iberia, making Georgia one of the oldest Christian states in the world.

Mid-fourth century

A stone inscription, written half in Cham and half in Sanskrit, found in Trakieu, is the first recording of any Austronesian language.

360

The last Kushan emperor, Varahran II, is defeated by the Kidarites in Pakistan.

372

Koguryo in Korea adopts Buddhism as the state religion, followed by Paekche 12 years later.

FIFTH CENTURY

Start of about 200 years when Javanese travelers begin to transform Balinese society by means of their Hindu religion and *devaraja* social order.

Probable century in which Polynesians settle the Hawaiian Islands.

402

Yujiulu Shelun is the first chief to unite the Rouran into a single people and to adopt the title of *qagan* (khagan, or khan). He also subjugates the Gaoche and Xiongnu tribes.

433

Shilla and Paekche form a military alliance against Koguryo in the north of the Korean Peninsula and against other outside invasions.

478–514

Funan is at its geographic, political, and economic zenith under the reign of King Jayavarman.

SIXTH CENTURY

500

Funan collapses and is replaced by the Chenla kingdom, which also encompasses large parts of modern-day Laos and Vietnam.

522

The height of Hephthalite power after having conquered the Persian Sassanid Empire, Sogdiana, and the Indian Guptas.

Mid-sixth century

Abkhazians, along with other Caucasians, adopt Christianity while ruled by the Byzantine Empire.

552

Western Turkic people known as Gokturks establish the first Turkic state in Central Asia.

The Rouran are defeated by the Gokturk *qagan,* Tumen II. This defeat scatters the surviving Rouran people, and within three years this ethnic group disappears.

565

Almost complete disappearance of Hephthalites in the face of the emergence of the Gokturks.

573

Hongsavatoi (Pegu) is said to be founded by two Mon princes, Samala and Wimala, in what is today Myanmar (Burma).

573–576

The first inscriptions proving the existence of Telugu speakers appear; they are created under the patronage of Chola kings.

582

The Gokturk empire is split into two khanates, Eastern and Western, after a civil war.

Late sixth century

The Mappilas become the first indigenous Muslim population in India; they occupy the Malabar coast and Lakshadweep Islands.

SEVENTH CENTURY

Hinduism begins to replace Buddhism as the major state religion in the kingdoms of Bengal.

The imperial state of Sri Vijaya encompasses Peninsular Malaysia, Sumatra, western Java, and western Borneo, lasting until the 14th century.

601

Erkin Tegin, leader of the Uighur tribe, signs an alliance with the Chinese in which the Uighur are described as living in the Tola Valley (Hindu Kush Mountains of Afghanistan) in 10,000 yurts; within two years they expand to 30,000 yurts.

605

Approximate year of the first written record of Okinawan people, from a Chinese source.

618

Start of China's Tang dynasty. In southern China, rice becomes more easily produced as new technologies are introduced in rice cultivation and population centers begin to shift from the wheat-growing north.

627

Srong-brtsan-sgam-po, 33rd Yarlung king, ascends to the throne in Tibet and over 22 years expands the empire into China, Nepal, and India. His period is often considered the start of historical Tibet.

641

Buddhism comes to Tibet, an act often attributed to the Nepali and Chinese wives of Srong-brtsan-sgam-po.

644

Theravada Buddhism arrives in the region of Thailand.

646

Tumitu Il Teber declares the first Uighur state at Otuken.

651

The last Persian Sassanid emperor, Yazdegerd III, is killed outside the Central Asian city of Merv, contemporary Mary, Turkmenistan.

652–709

The Arab empire annexes and then conquers the region of present-day Afghanistan, converting most of the area to Islam.

690–705

Emperor Tse-t'ien or Empress Wu, China's only female emperor, calls her period the Zhou dynasty. At her death the Tang dynasty retakes China.

EIGHTH CENTURY

The Ahom people, a Tai-speaking population, migrate from southern China to the region of present-day Assam, India.

The first stone temples dedicated to the Hindu god Siva are built in Java.

The Gokturks create the Orkhon inscriptions in their runic script, describing some of the peoples over whom they rule.

703

Arabs conquer the region of Caucasian Albania and convert many to Islam. Despite the survival of an Albanian church as a diocese within the greater Armenian Church, the Caucasian Albanian people cease to exist as a separate ethnic group.

711–715

Muhammad Ibn Qasim conquers Sindh and brings Islam to this region of India.

712

Publication of the first Japanese chronicle, which marks for many the transition from proto-Japanese to Old Japanese history, language, and culture.

713

Founding of the state of Parhae in Manchuria and northern Korea.

716

Probable date for the Parsees's entrance into India after having fled Persia in 651 when Yazdagird III, the last Zoroastrian king, was overthrown by the Muslim Arabs.

729

The Nanzhao kingdom is formed in Yunnan Province, southern China.

751

Battle of Talas between the Chinese and Arabs over control of Central Asia; the Chinese are defeated when the Karluks change sides mid-battle.

775–785

The Oghuz Turkic tribes migrate from the Altai Mountain area to Central Asia, first to the steppes in western Kazakhstan and Kyrgyzstan and by the end of the eighth century spreading through Turkmenistan and Central Asia.

NINTH CENTURY

Unification of the Eastern and Western Christian churches in Georgia.

800

Jayarvarman II, a Khmer prince, declares himself ruler of the Kingdom of Kambuja by founding a cult honoring the Hindu god Siva and linking himself with the divine by declaring himself a *devaraja,* or god-king.

804

Perlak, the region's first Islamic kingdom, is established in Aceh (Indonesia).

832

The final Pyu city-state, Sri Ksetra, falls to the Nanzhao kingdom of China.

840

The Kyrgyz defeat the Uighur khanate in the Orkhon Valley region of central Mongolia.

TENTH CENTURY

Bhil chieftains rule much of central India.

Formation of the earliest Gond kingdoms that constituted Gondwana, India.

The earliest Chinese immigrants to settle in the Malay Archipelago arrive from Guangdong and Fujian Provinces.

The Tamils' Chola kingdom of southern India invades northern Sri Lanka over the course of about two centuries.

The period in which the original Tausug migrants arrive on the island of Jolo from their home on Mindanao, the Philippines.

907

Fall of China's Tang dynasty and start of the Five Dynasties period. The actual dynasties are five officially recognized dynasties of the north, while the south is divided into 10 kingdoms.

920

The Gokturks disappear from history until their script is deciphered more than 900 years later.

933

Shravakachar, a Jain religious text written in Hindi, is considered the first text produced in this language.

934

Many Karakhanid Uighur convert to Islam during the reign of Satuk Bughra Khan, the first Turkic khan in Central Asia to convert.

939

The Vietnamese under Ngo Quyen finally succeed in expelling the Chinese from their territory.

982

First reference to Afghans, in the *Hudud-al-Alam* (The regions of the world), a Persian geographical text.

ELEVENTH CENTURY

The building frenzy of *moai* and *ahu* (giant stone statues and their stone platforms) on Rapanui; lack of resources ends the period of building in about 1600.

Some Turkmen tribes migrate into Mesopotamia, Asia Minor, and Caucasus, where they eventually establish the Kara Koyunlu and Ak Koyunlu states. Others remain in Transoxiana as the ancestors of the contemporary Turkmen people.

1000

Period of Maori settlement on Aotearoa (New Zealand).

1010

Bagrat unifies all of Georgia, except Tbilisi, which has been held by the Arabs since 645.

1037

Toghril Beg I, founder of the Seljuk empire, is born.

1044

Founding of the Kingdom of Pagan, the first Burman state in the region of contemporary Myanmar (Burma); Buddhism is introduced 12 years later.

1052

Nong Zhigao begins his peasant uprising against the Han Chinese in southern China; this is usually the date that marks the formal creation of the Zhuang people from their Dai antecedents. Upon the uprising's defeat at the Battle of Kunlun Pass, the Zhuang become a large minority group in both China and Vietnam. If the uprising had succeeded, many historians believe the country established by the Zhuang would now incorporate much of southern China and northern Vietnam.

1072

Malikshah succeeds Alp Arslan as the sultan of the Seljuks, and it is under his rule that the empire is at its strongest and culturally most influential. Malikshah comes to be known as "The Sultan of East and West," to indicate his vast realm.

TWELFTH CENTURY

1112–50

Suryvarman II begins building the great temple complex of Angkor Wat in what is today Cambodia.

1115

The Jurchen tribes establish the Jin dynasty, which falls to the Yuan dynasty just over a century later.

1157

Collapse of the Seljuk empire.

1162 or 67

Temujin, the future Genghis Khan, is born; he is the grandson of Kabul Khan, the first person to unify some Mongol tribes.

1184–1213

Apex of Georgian power under Queen Tamara.

1181–1219

Khmer king Jayavarman VII converts to Theravada Buddhism, bringing great change to the Khmer cosmology. By the late 13th century most Khmers had likewise converted from Hinduism to Buddhism.

1191

Zen Buddhism arrives in Japan from Korea and China.

THIRTEENTH CENTURY

Arab traders and sultans establish contact with Sulu and most of the rest of the Mindanao region. This marks the period of first conversion to Islam in the Philippines Archipelago.

The Sumatran Sri Vijaya empire, encompassing much of modern-day Malaysia and Indonesia, founds an outpost port on the island of Temasek (Singapore).

1202

Turkic Muslims invade and conquer Bengal and the Islamization of the area begins.

1206

The Delhi Sultanate is established.

Genghis Khan unifies the various Mongol tribes and begins his campaign to conquer the world.

1223

The Mongols overrun most of the southern Caucasus region of Georgia, Armenia, and Azerbaijan.

1227

Genghis Khan dies in China's Gansu Province.

1238

Accepted date for the formation of the first Thai kingdom at Sukhothai from what had formerly been Khmer territory.

ca. 1240

The Secret History of the Mongols is published, documenting Genghis Khan's exploits.

1260–94

Reign of Kublai Khan, first as khan of the Mongol Empire and from 1271 onward as the emperor of the Yuan dynasty of China. The

Yuan dynasty represents the first of two times in Chinese history that non-Chinese rule the entire area of China.

1279

The Tamil Chola dynasty comes to an end due to weak leadership and perhaps overextension of the empire.

1283

The Thai writing system is invented by King Ramkhamhaeng.

FOURTEENTH CENTURY

1300

A group of Maori depart New Zealand to colonize the Chathams and become the Moriori people.

1336

Timur Leng (Timur the Lame, or Tamerlane) is born near Samarkand.

1350–1

A Thai kingdom, whose court is modeled on Angkor, is founded at Ayutthaya (Ayudhya, or Siam), near modern-day Bangkok.

1353

Fa Ngum founds the first Lao kingdom, Lan Xang.

1368

Fall of the Yuan dynasty in China and start of the Ming dynasty.

1369

The first of three Dai attacks on Angkor, which eventually lead to the abandonment of the Khmer capital.

1380

Arab and Malay traders reinforce the introduction of Islam to the Philippine islands through Borneo, later followed by Muslim missionaries who proselytize and convert Filipinos in the southern islands.

Russian forces defeat the Mongol army at Kulikovo, but the Mongols remain in control of much of Russian territory and continue to demand tribute.

1392

Fall of the Koryo dynasty and start of the Choson dynasty in Korea.

FIFTEENTH CENTURY

1400

Several smaller Makassarese kingdoms come together to form the Gowa kingdom, ruled on the same Hindu principles as the main kingdoms of Java and Bali at the time.

1405

The first sultan, Muhammad Shah, ascends the throne and introduces Islam to Brunei.

1446

The first Hangul, or Korean, alphabet document is disseminated throughout the kingdom.

Middle 15th century

The Uzbeks begin to split from other Turkic speakers under Abul Khayr.

1470

Defeat of Champa by the Vietnamese, though remnants of the kingdom survive for about 350 years.

The Kazakhs begin to split from the Uzbeks to establish their own ethnic group.

1475

The Muslim sultanate of Maguindanao is established on Mindanao, promoting the spread of Islam throughout the Philippine Islands.

1499

Guru Nanak achieves enlightenment and begins to accumulate followers in the new Sikh religion.

SIXTEENTH CENTURY

Establishment of the khanates of Bukhara, Khiva, and Kokand by Uzbek emirs and khans fleeing the disintegrating Uzbek khanate. All three khanates are swallowed up by Russia in the 19th century.

1500

Majapahit, the last Hindu kingdom on Java, falls to the Muslim sultanate of Demak, and many of Java's Hindu nobles relocate to Bali.

1511

The Portuguese land at Malacca and establish the first European colonial presence in what is now Indonesia.

1511–23

Khan Kasym unites the Kazakh tribes for the first time, and the Kazakhs are recognized as a separate ethnic group. They are militarily dominant in the steppes.

1513

The colonial era on Macau begins when Portuguese sailors from their colonies in Goa and Malacca land on Lintin Island and claim the territory for the Portuguese king.

1515

Portuguese explorers reach the coast of Timor on what is now the enclave of Oecussi. They export sandalwood and make large profits until the tree becomes nearly extinct.

ca. 1525

Sheikh Mali writes the first Pashto text, *Daftar-e-Shaikh Mali,* which explains the division of land in Swat.

1526

Spanish explorer Toribio Alonso de Salazar discovers the Caroline Islands, naming them the Carolinas after Carlos (Charles) I, king of Spain (Holy Roman Emperor Charles V).

A supposed descendant of two previous conquerors, Timur Leng (Tamerlane) and Genghis Khan, Babur establishes the largely Indian Mughal Empire.

The Delhi Sultanate is absorbed by the expanding Mughal Empire.

Portuguese explorer Jorge de Meneses visits one of New Guinea's largest islands and names it Ilhas dos Papuas, "land of fuzzy-haired people"; 20 years later Spanish sailor Inigo Ortiz de Retes names the other main island New Guinea because the people remind him of the population of African Guinea.

1530

Babur, founder of the Mughal Empire, dies; his grandson Akbar begins to extend the empire as far south as the Krishna River.

1533

The Mon kingdoms fall to the Burman king Thabinshwehti, who takes over the city of Pegu as his capital.

1544

Portuguese explorers discover Taiwan and call it Ilha Formosa, meaning "Beautiful Island."

Mid-16th century

Russia begins to move into the Caucasus region, which had previously been dominated by the standoff between the Persian and Ottoman Empires.

1552

Russia's Ivan IV (the Terrible) defeats the Kazan Khanate on the middle Volga River and later the Astrakhan Khanate where the Volga River meets the Caspian Sea; this expansion gives Russia access to all of the Volga River and the Caspian Sea, as well as a route to Central Asia.

1565

The Spanish begin the process of colonizing the entire Filipino archipelago when Don Miguel López de Legazpi and Fray Andrés de Urdaneta are successful in their Christianization project in the Visayas. They also build Fort San Pedro, the oldest Spanish fort in the Philippines archipelago.

1574

After failing to take Manila from the Spanish, who established this city as their colonial capital in 1571, Chinese pirate Limahong tries to conquer Lingayen. He is driven out after six months but leaves behind the Limahong Channel, a human-made waterway that facilitates his escape.

1575

Twenty-four Spanish missionaries arrive on the Philippine Archipelago and convert much of the lowland population to Catholicism, making the Philippines the only Catholic nation in Asia.

1576

Dhaka is conquered by Mughal emperor Akbar the Great (1556–1605), and Bengal becomes a Mughal province.

1578

The abbot of the Drepung Monastery is named the third Dalai Lama by the head of the Mongol Empire; the first two are named posthumously at this time as well.

1592

Japan invades Korea and instigates more than 400 years of hatred and mistrust of the island nation on the part of many Koreans.

SEVENTEENTH CENTURY

The British East India Company establishes itself as the largest and most important European organization on the Indian subcontinent.

The Dutch East Indies Company begins the process of colonizing the entire Indonesian archipelago, aside from the eastern half of New Guinea.

The Mongol people generally convert to Tibetan Buddhism.

Russians start to migrate into Siberia and Asian Russia.

1600

Start of the Tokugawa era in Japan, when the capital is moved to Edo (Tokyo), and Japan tries to remain isolated from increasing Western pressure in the region.

1609

The Shimazu family leads the Japanese colonial assault on Okinawa.

1616

Ngawang Namgyal, a Drukpa monk, flees religious persecution in Tibet at the hands of the Gelugpas and settles in the eastern Himalayas, where he unites the people into the first incarnation of the Bhutanese state.

1627

Shivaji Bhonsle, often known as the father of the Maratha nation, is born.

1634–53

Batur Hongtaiji begins constructing the Zunghar state on the back of the largely nomadic western Mongol people.

1642

Lobsang Gyatso, fifth Dalai Lama, is made the ruler of Tibet by the ruling Mongol khan, Gushri.

1644

Fall of the Ming dynasty in China and start of the Qing, founded by Manchu invaders, the second group of foreigners to rule all of China.

1662

After 38 years of administration, the Dutch are driven out of Taiwan. Cheng Cheng-kung introduces Chinese ways of life to the island and constructs a Confucian temple.

1689

After a brief skirmish with the Chinese, Russia signs the Treaty of Nerchinsk, relinquishing control of the Amur River valley but establishing Russian control of the area east of Lake Baikal and a trade route to Beijing.

1699

The British East India Company lands on what is now Hong Kong and begins the trading activities for which the region is still famous.

EIGHTEENTH CENTURY

Introduction of the sweet potato to the New Guinea Highlands, which transforms Highlands life.

1711

Many western Mongols flee Russia and return to the Xinjiang area in northwest China, where they are known as Oirats.

1744–1829

Spurred by a priest's refusal to give his brother a Christian burial, Francisco Dagohoy initiates one of the longest and most successful revolts in Philippine history, that outlasts several Spanish governor generals.

1747

Durrani Pashtuns consolidate the Afghan state under what is sometimes called the Durrani empire when Ahmad Khan Abdali is elected as king of all the Pashtun people; kings from the same tribal group continue to rule Afghanistan until 1973.

1749

Timor is split between the Dutch and Portuguese, with the Portuguese taking the eastern half.

1757–59

The third Great Campaign of the Qing against the Zunghars ends with the genocide of hundreds of thousands of people; smallpox and starvation soon finish the job and eliminate all trace of the Zunghar people.

1762–63

The British occupy the city of Manila, and the husband-and-wife team of Diego and Gabriela Silang stage the most famous of the many Ilocano revolts against colonialism.

1767

The Burmans sack the Thai kingdom of Ayutthaya, and in reaction the Thai king moves his capital to Bangkok.

1768

Prithvi Narayan Shah unifies the Nepali kingdom after conquering two rival kings in the region.

1769

The British East India Company first takes control of all European trade in India.

1771–1802

The Tay-Son Uprising in Vietnam overthrows the power of the Nguyen, Trinh, and Le families.

1774

The Ossetians voluntarily become subjects of the Russian czar.

1782

The current Chakri dynasty comes to power in Thailand (Siam) under Rama I; the capital is moved to Bangkok.

1784

The final Rakhine or Arakanese dynasty, Mrauk-U, falls to the Burmese king Boe daw Maung Wyne.

1786

Britain establishes its first colony in the Malay Peninsula on the island of Penang.

1788

Captain Arthur Phillip arrives in Australia with the First Fleet, made up of 11 ships and around 780 convicts, and establishes a settlement at Port Jackson in the new Crown colony of New South Wales. Within months, epidemics of influenza, measles, typhus, and other European diseases kill thousands of Aboriginal Australians.

1790s

Many Hmong begin to leave China and set up communities throughout Southeast Asia due to persecution at home. These migrations continue for about 150 years.

1796

The British take over Ceylon (Sri Lanka) from the Dutch and Portuguese.

1799

Ranjit Singh conquers Lahore and begins his 40-year rule over a unified Sikh kingdom in India's Punjab region.

NINETEENTH CENTURY

The various Hill Tribes of Thailand migrate into their highland Southeast Asian homes from China and Burma.

1801

Georgia is incorporated into the Russian czar's empire.

1802

The French colonial period in Vietnam and throughout Southeast Asia begins.

1807

Northern Maori tribes obtain muskets from European explorers and use them against enemy tribes who are powerless to resist them; the period is known as the Musket Wars.

1819

The first large-scale migration of Indians to Singapore begins with the founding of the British colony on the island in this year.

1820

The Gilbert Islands group (Kiribati) is named after British sea captain Thomas Gilbert, who had landed on them in 1788 on his run between Sydney and China.

1824–85

Three Anglo-Burmese wars see the final defeat of the Burmans and the annexation of all their territory along with that of their neighboring minority groups, including the Kachin, Karen, Chin, and Shan; all these territories are ruled as part of British India.

1828

Russia replaces Persia as the dominant force in Eastern Armenia and makes it a province.

1831

A Frenchman, Jules Dumont d'Urville, coins the terms *Micronesia,* or small islands, and *Melanesia,* or black islands; he also transforms an earlier usage of the term *Polynesia* to refer only to those peoples residing on Polynesian islands.

1835–51

The British send 10 different military expeditions into Nagaland in India's Brahmaputra valley to try to pacify and settle the region. The last rebellion is in 1878.

1840

Maori sign the Treaty of Waitangi with Britain, granting that country authority over the islands and their people; this formally establishes the colony of New Zealand.

1842

The Qing dynasty loses the first of the Opium Wars to the British and sign a treaty transferring control over Hong Kong to the victors.

1845

Tonga is united into a Polynesian kingdom by Tu'i Kanokupolu, later baptized as King George.

1845–72

The New Zealand Land Wars arise from the violent retaliation by the Maori against European settlers attempting to seize Maori land.

1853

U.S. commodore Matthew C. Perry lands in Naha in his effort to open Japan to international trade.

1854

The Eureka Stockade miners' rebellion against British taxation and mistreatment in Australia occurs in Ballarat, Victoria. This event is sometimes referred to as the birth of Australian democracy.

1855–57

The Santal Hul, or Freedom, movement is one of the largest uprisings in India against the British, similar to the Sepoy Mutiny of the same period.

1857

Fall of the Mughal Empire in India.

1858

The British East India Company is dissolved, and the British assume direct control of India; the ensuing colonial period is known as the Raj.

1860

Russia colonizes the northern portion of Tajikistan; the south is retained by the Uzbek khanate of Bukhara.

1865

Fiji's first constitution is drawn up and signed by seven independent chiefs. Ratu Seru Cakobau, the first chief to have accepted Christianity 11 years earlier, is elected president.

1870s

Blackbirding begins in the Pacific, taking about 30,000 Solomon Islanders and others as forced laborers to Fiji, Australia, and elsewhere in the Pacific over the next 40 years.

1879

The *Leonidas* arrives on Fiji, bringing the first group of indentured laborers from India. By 1916, more than 60,000 Indians will be brought to Fiji.

1880s

The Yap begin quarrying stone money on Palau.

1884

Official abolition of slavery in Malaya, although it is known to have continued into the 20th century.

Papua New Guinea is divided, and Britain establishes control over the southeast, Germany annexes the northeast part of New Guinea; the Dutch control the western half of the island.

1887

Britain and France agree to a joint naval commission of the New Hebrides (Vanuatu); this dual colonial system later comes to be called the Condominium.

1890

Robert Louis Stevenson, author of *Treasure Island* and *The Strange Case of Dr. Jekyll and Mr. Hyde,* moves his family to Samoa and is given the name Tusitala, meaning "Teller of Tales." His death in 1894 is acknowledged with the ceremonial burial given to royalty.

1892

The British Protectorate of the Gilbert and Ellice Islands is established; it becomes a colony in 1915.

1893

New Zealand becomes the first nation in the world to grant women the right to vote.

The Durand Line, drawn by Sir Mortimer Durand, marks the almost 750-mile boundary between British India and the Kingdom of Afghanistan, which was held informally by the British. The line is never formally ratified by Afghanistan.

1894–95

The Japanese defeat China in the Sino-Japanese War and receive Taiwan as one of the spoils of war.

1897

Hawaii is annexed by the United States.

1899

The Spanish cede the Philippines and Guam to the United States, and a local war of independence breaks out in the Philippines. Spain sells many of its other Spanish East Indies colonies to Germany.

TWENTIETH CENTURY

1900

Phosphate is discovered on Nauru, and mining begins six years later.

1900–01

Filipino war of independence against the colonizing United States; it fails and the Philippines remain in the American sphere for nearly half a century.

1901

The six Australian colonies federate to become the Commonwealth of Australia.

1904–05

Russia and Japan fight a war over control of Manchuria, Korea, and several islands in the area. The conflict leads to the defeat of the Russian navy and the loss of these territories to the Japanese, including Russia's only Pacific warm-water port.

1906

The All-India Muslim League, led by Mohammed Ali Jinnah, is formed in Dhaka and pushes for separate Hindu and Muslim states for postcolonial India.

1907

Unification of the kingdom of Bhutan and establishment of the current Wangchuk dynasty.

1910

The Japanese annex Korea and bring an end to the 518-year-old Choson dynasty.

China invades Lhasa, Tibet, and the 13th Dalai Lama flees to India.

1911

Fall of China's last dynasty, the Qing, and start of the turbulent Republican era.

1914

The Japanese military secretly takes control of Micronesia from their large base in Truk Lagoon. Their headquarters are in Dublon Town on the island of Tonoas, Chuuk.

Australia occupies German New Guinea during World War I.

1915

Young Turks massacre an estimated 600,000–2 million Armenians living in Turkey. This has been referred to as the first genocide of the 20th century.

1916

The Turkmen, under Dzhunaid Khan, defeat the Russians at Khiva and set up a national government that holds until 1918.

1917

The Bolshevik revolution overthrows czarist rule in Russia and establishes the Soviet state.

1921

The Red Army conquers Georgia, Armenia, and Azerbaijan, which become Soviet republics within the Union of Soviet Socialist Republics (USSR).

1924

The Mongolian People's Republic is declared by the ruling Mongolian People's Revolutionary Party (MPRP).

1929

The USSR begins to collectivize herding and hunting activities among the Chukchis and other indigenous peoples of the north.

1930

The Communist Party of Indochina is established by Ho Chi Minh.

1932

The absolute rule of the Thai kings is ended by a coup in June.

1933

The name *Pakistan,* meaning "Pure Nation" in Urdu, is invented by Choudhary Rahmat Ali.

Gold prospectors enter the New Guinea Highlands and find more than a million people living in areas that had been considered devoid of significant human population.

1935

The infant who becomes the 14th (current) Dalai Lama is born; he is installed as Dalai Lama five years later.

1936

The John Frum millenarian movement begins on the island of Tanna in Vanuatu; the cargo cult–like movement continues to attract followers today.

1937

Tagalog becomes the national language in the Philippines even though Cebuano is spoken by more people.

1939

Siam is renamed Thailand.

1941

The Japanese air force attacks the U.S. naval base at Pearl Harbor, Hawaii, pulling the United States into World War II. Over the course of the following year, Japan occupies Indonesia, the Philippines, and much of Southeast Asia.

1942

The United States defeats Japan in the Battle of Midway, often considered the turning point in the Pacific war.

The Indian National Congress leads a civil disobedience movement demanding that the British leave India (also called the Quit India Movement). This act of civil disobedience is subsequently followed by rioting in Calcutta.

1944

The Marching Law movement, an anticolonial millenarian movement in the Solomon Islands, begins, lasting for about nine years.

1945

The United States drops two atomic bombs on the Japanese cities of Hiroshima and Nagasaki, which brings the complete capitulation of the Japanese emperor, ending World War II.

The Japanese defeat results in the divided rule of the Korean Peninsula along the 38th parallel: the USSR occupies the northern half and the United States occupies the southern half. An independent country is established in each zone by 1948, the Republic of Korea (ROK) in the south and the Democratic People's Republic of Korea (DPRK) in the north.

The Philippines attains independence from the United States.

1946

Operation Crossroads, the code name given to one of a series of U.S. nuclear tests on the Marshall Islands, selects the Bikini Atoll as the site for extensive nuclear testing.

1947

Indian and Pakistani independence, followed by the first of three wars between the two countries; millions of Hindus and Muslims migrate at this time.

Aung San is assassinated, and the hopes for a multiethnic leadership in an independent Burma are extinguished.

1948

Mohandas (Mahatma) Gandhi is assassinated by Hindu radicals Nathuram Godse and Narayan Apte, who blame him for weakening India.

Ceylon (Sri Lanka) achieves full independence from the British.

1948–60

The Malayan Emergency, when rebels under the leadership of the Communist Party launch guerrilla operations designed to force the British out of Malaya.

1949

Indonesian independence from the Dutch following a war against the returning colonizers, who had been pushed from the islands by the Japanese during World War II.

Mao Zedong's Red Army defeats the Nationalists in the Chinese civil war and begins the Communist era.

1950–53

The Korean War rages between the North and South, triggered by an unexpected attack by North Korea against South Korea in June 1950. Troops from the United States and United Nations fight with ROK troops to defend South Korea from DPRK attacks, which are supported by the communist countries of China and the Soviet Union.

1952

The U.S. occupation of Japan comes to an end, except in the Ryukyu Islands. Over the next 40 years Japan's economy explodes to become the second largest in the world after that of the United States.

1953

Tenzing Norgay and Edmund Hillary are the first climbers to reach the top of Mount Everest, the highest mountain in the world.

1954

Vietnamese communist forces called the Viet Minh defeat the French at Dien Bien Phu, ending about 150 years of colonialism in the region.

1958–69

China's Great Leap Forward, in which millions lose their lives to famine.

1960

The general election in Sri Lanka is won by Sirimavo Bandaranaike, the first female prime minister in the world.

1962

A military coup puts Ne Win in control of Burma and ends the short period of democracy in that country; the military remains in control in 2008.

Western Samoa is the first Pacific island to gain independence, from New Zealand, which took over from Germany at the end of World War I; it is recognized by the United Nations as Samoa in 1976 and officially changes the name to Samoa in 1997.

1963

Pol Pot becomes the Cambodian Communist Party's general secretary after his predecessor, Tou Samouth, mysteriously disappears.

The name *Malaysia* is adopted when Singapore, Sabah, and Sarawak form a 14-state federation with Peninsular Malaysia; Singapore leaves Malaysia two years later to become an independent country.

1964

The onset of the Indochina War that eventually envelopes Vietnam, Cambodia, and Laos and includes troops from the United States, Australia, and elsewhere in an attempt to contain communism.

1965

The second war between India and Pakistan over the fate of Kashmir.

Maldives gains independence from Britain.

1965–86

Ferdinand Marcos's autocratic reign in the Philippines.

1966

France begins nuclear testing on the French Polynesian atoll of Moruroa, continuing through 1996.

1966–76

China's Great Cultural Revolution, when the Communist Party tries to eliminate religion and many other traditional cultural practices from China.

1967

Commonwealth referendum, passed by more than 90 percent of voting Australians, makes Aboriginal Australians citizens of the country for the first time since its inception in 1901.

1968

The Aral Sea between Uzbekistan and Kazakhstan begins shrinking when Soviet engineers introduce irrigation that diverts water from two feeder rivers; it splits into two separate seas in 1990.

Nauru attains independence from its position as a trustee of Australia, New Zealand, and the United Kingdom. Its population enjoys the second highest per capita income in the world due to phosphate mining.

1969

The New People's Army is formed as the military arm of the Communist Party of the Philippines.

1970

Tongan independence from Britain.

Sinhalese is declared the only national language in Sri Lanka, causing discontent among the Tamil population that leads eventually to civil war.

The RCA Corporation opens Taiwan's first semiconductor factory.

1971

Bangladesh, formerly East Pakistan, achieves independence from Pakistan in a war that kills at least 1 million and sees about 10 million Hindus flee from the newly independent Bangladesh, a primarily Muslim state. This event sparks the third war between India and Pakistan since independence in 1947.

The United Nations officially recognizes the People's Republic of China as China, replacing the seat held by the Republic of China (Taiwan).

1973

The eastern half of New Guinea achieves self-government as Papua New Guinea; complete independence from Australia comes two years later.

The final Durrani king, Zahir Shah, is overthrown, and Afghanistan is made a republic under the leadership of General Mohammed Daoud.

1974

India tests its first nuclear weapon, hastening Pakistan's efforts to build their own bomb.

The inhabitants of the Ellice Islands vote overwhelmingly to secede from the Gilbert Islands; eventually the two island groups become the independent countries of Tuvalu and Kiribati, respectively.

1975

Portugal abruptly leaves East Timor. Few countries recognize the newly independent nation and nine days later Indonesian troops invade. Falintil (Armed Forces of National Liberation of East Timor) violently opposes the Indonesian occupation; at least 200,000 people die over the next two decades. East Timor becomes Indonesia's 27th province.

The first Hmong refugees arrive in the United States due to persecution in Laos and Vietnam, the result of the significant assistance many Hmong provided to the United States in its failed effort to contain communism in those two countries.

Pol Pot's communist Khmer Rouge overthrow the republic and begin four years of terror. About 2 million Khmer people lose their lives; hundreds of thousands of people from other ethnic groups also perish during the time of the "killing fields."

The United States pulls out of South Vietnam, signaling its loss of the Vietnam War; Saigon falls to the National Liberation Front and North Vietnamese troops.

1976

North and South Vietnam are reunified under a communist government.

1978

The Solomon Islands and Tuvalu gain independence from Britain.

Vietnamese troops invade Cambodia and overthrow Pol Pot, ending the Khmer Rouge genocide. Vietnam eventually leaves the Cambodian administration to the United Nations.

1979

To support the vulnerable Afghan communist government, the Soviet Union invades, assassinating the prime minister, replacing him, and causing widespread violence as the Red Army tries to gain control for its imposed government. More than 5 million Afghanistanis flee to refugee camps in Pakistan and Iran.

Kiribati, the former Gilbert Islands, achieves independence from Britain.

Deng Xiaoping changes course in China; making money is now said to be each Chinese person's most important goal.

1980

Papua New Guinea sends peacekeeping forces to Espiritu Santo, Vanuatu's largest island, to quell a revolt by Jimmy Stevens's Nagriamel movement.

Vanuatu gains its independence from Britain and France.

1983

A civil war erupts between Tamil separatists and Sinhalese nationalists in Sri Lanka.

1984

On January 1, Brunei gains full independence from Great Britain.

1986

The Federated States of Micronesia attains independence from the United States.

1987

The prodemocracy movement in South Korea leads to the restoration of a multiparty political system and the adoption of a new constitution after decades of military rule. The first direct presidential election is held in December, with Roh Tae-Woo becoming the seventh president. The first civilian president is elected four years later.

Martial law is lifted on Taiwan after 37 years, and Aboriginal Taiwanese identity becomes an important tool to differentiate Taiwan from mainland China.

1988

Benazir Bhutto's Pakistan People's Party (PPP) emerges as the largest party in the general elections, and she is sworn in as prime minister; she is dismissed on corruption charges two years later and then reelected three years after that.

1989

Burmese democracy activities Aung San Suu Kyi, daughter of slain Burmese democrat Aung San, is put under house arrest for the first time; she wins the Nobel Peace Prize two years later but is unable to travel to Stockholm to receive her prize.

1990

Hindi becomes the second most widely spoken language in the world after Mandarin Chinese.

1991

The Soviet Union disintegrates, and the constituent Caucasian and Central Asian republics of Armenia, Azerbaijan, Georgia, Kazakhstan, Kyrgyzstan, Tajikistan, Turkmenistan, and Uzbekistan attain independence.

Mount Pinatubo in the Philippines erupts, disrupting the lives of many thousands of indigenous peoples and forcing the United States to abandon Clark Air Base.

Both North and South Korea become members of the United Nations.

1991–96

Civil war in Tajikistan immediately following the country's independence from the disintegrating USSR.

1992

Tajik military leader Ahmed Shah Massoud leads the first mujahideen forces into Kabul to defeat the Afghan Communists and is rewarded with the presidency of Afghanistan.

1993

Ong Teng Cheong becomes the first directly elected president of Singapore.

1994

Palau (Belau) attains independence from the United States.

1996

The Taliban take Kabul, Afghanistan, garnering major international attention for the first time.

Several leftist political organizations begin a "'People's War'" to liberate Nepal from the royalists.

1997

Britain returns Hong Kong to Chinese sovereignty.

The Asian financial crisis hits and severely affects the economies of most of the region's countries.

1999

Portugal returns Macau to Chinese sovereignty.

TWENTY-FIRST CENTURY

2000

Nationalist gunmen storm the Fijian parliament, taking Mahenda Chaudhry, the first Indian prime minister, hostage. The military takes control, imposes martial law, and installs Laisenia Qarase, an indigenous Fijian, as prime minister. The political situation in Fiji remains uncertain in 2008.

The U.S. Supreme Court fails to agree that the indigenous Hawaiians constitute a tribal group with the same rights as mainland Native Americans.

Caroline Island in Kiribati is renamed Millennium Island because it is the first place to usher in the new millennium on New Year's Day.

The first summit takes place in June between South Korea's president, Kim Dae-jung, and North Korea's leader, Kim Jong Il.

Easy-to-reach phosphate reserves on the island of Nauru are exhausted, leaving the small population impoverished and having to import most subsistence resources.

2001

Solomon Islands prime minister Sir Allan Kemakeza requests outside assistance as violence disrupts his country; his call results in the Regional Assistance Mission for the Solomon Islands (RAMSI), an Australian-led security initiative that brings more than 2,000 police and military personnel from more than 20 countries to establish law and order.

A U.S.-led coalition invades Afghanistan in retaliation for its support of al-Qaeda following the attacks in the United States on September 11. The Taliban fall almost immediately but the violence continues into 2008.

The Indian state of Jharkhand, a largely tribal polity, is carved from southern Bihar.

2002

Xanana Gusmão becomes the first elected president of newly independent East Timor.

2003

China's economy outstrips Japan's to become the second largest in the world, after the United States.

The SARS (severe acute respiratory syndrome) epidemic claims 812 lives throughout Asia; Taiwan struggles more than any other country to control the disease and reports 483 probable cases for the year.

2004

A tsunami with its epicenter off the coast of Sumatra kills hundreds of thousands of people across a dozen countries, including Sri Lanka, Maldives, Indonesia, and India.

2005

Azad Kashmir is the epicenter of a massive earthquake that kills more than 70,000 people in Pakistan and several thousand more on India's side of the border.

Palau has the highest standard of living in the Pacific region, due in part to the $12.8 million issued by the United States this year under the Compact of Free Association.

One hundred people from a village on the island of Tegua, Vanuatu, must be evacuated as a result of rising sea levels. Some scientists point to this incident as the first evacuation to result from global warming.

2006

The World Bank announces that Georgia experienced a larger reduction in corruption than any other Eastern European or former Soviet country between 2002 and 2005.

Nepal's 10-year civil war comes to an end when Prime Minister Koirala and the head of the Maoist Communist Party sign the Comprehensive Peace Agreement.

North Korea tests its first nuclear weapon.

A military coup deposes Thailand's prime minister, Thaksin Shinawatr, and suspends the constitution; an interim prime minister, cabinet, and national assembly are appointed.

2008

Indonesia's former president Suharto dies.

Benazir Bhutto is assassinated after having returned to Pakistan in late 2007 to reenter politics. Her husband, Asif Ali Zardari, is elected president.

The Australian federal parliament apologizes to the Aboriginal Australians for the Stolen Generations, which saw tens of thousands of Aboriginal Australians removed from their parents and sent to institutions to be raised as Christians and unskilled laborers; some were also placed into the homes of nonaboriginal peoples as foster children.

East Timor's president, José Ramos-Horta, is injured in an attack of gunfire on his home.

Heavy fighting throughout the previous year pushes the Sri Lankan government to withdraw from a 2002 cease-fire agreement with the Tamil Tigers.

Burmese democracy still suffers from the continued house-arrest of its leader, Aung San Suu Kyi.

Russia invades Georgia in response to an escalation of the Georgian–South Ossetian conflict.

BIBLIOGRAPHY

Abbott, Gerry, ed. *Inroads into Burma: A Travellers' Anthology* (New York: Oxford University Press, 1997).

Abella, Domingo. *Bikol Annals: A Collection of Vignettes of Philippine History,* vol. 1 (Manila: See of Nueva Caceres, 1954).

Abrahamian, Levon, Nancy Sweezy, and Sam Sweezy. *Armenian Folk Arts, Culture, and Identity* (Bloomington: Indiana University Press, 2001).

Abramovich-Gomon, Alla. *The Nenets' Song: A Microcosm of a Vanishing Culture* (Brookfield, Vt.: Ashgate, 1999).

Adams, Douglas Q. *Tocharian Historical Phonology and Morphology* (New Haven, Conn.: American Oriental Society, 1988).

Agoncillo, T. A. *Nationalism in the Philippines* (Kuala Lumpur: Dept. of History, University of Malaya, 1968).

Ahmed, Akbar S. *Pukhtun Economy and Society: Traditional Structure and Economic Development in a Tribal Society* (Boston: Routledge & Kegan Paul, 1980).

Aini, Sadriddin et al. *At the Foot of Blue Mountains: Stories by Tajik Authors* trans. Shavkat Niyazi (Moscow: Raduga Publishers, 1984).

Aiyangar, M. Srinivasa. *Tamil Studies: Essays on the History of the Tamil People, Language, Religion, and Literature.* (New Delhi: Asian Educational Services, 1982).

Alberts, Eli. *A History of Daoism and the Yao People of South China.* (Youngstown, N.Y.: Cambria Press, 2007).

Aldredge, Bob, and Ched Meyers. *Resisting the Serpent: Palau's Struggle for Self-Determination* (Baltimore: Fortkamp Publishing Company, 1990).

Alexander, Paul, ed. *Creating Indonesian Cultures* (Sydney: Oceania Publ., 1989).

Alkire, William. *An Introduction to the Peoples and Cultures of Micronesia,* 2nd ed. (Menlo Park, Calif.: Cummings Publishing, 1977).

Allaby, Michael. *India* (New York: Facts On File, 2005).

Allen, Benedict. *Edge of Blue Heaven: A Journey through Mongolia* (Parkwest, N.Y.: BBC/Parkwest Publications, 1998).

Allen, Michael, ed. *Vanuatu: Politics, Economics, and Ritual in Island Melanesia* (Sydney: Academic Press, 1981).

Allsen, Thomas T. *Culture and Conquest in Mongol Eurasia* (New York: Cambridge University Press, 2001).

Allworth, Edward A. *The Modern Uzbeks: From the 14th Century to the Present: A Cultural History* (Palo Alto, Calif.: Hoover Institution Press, 1990).

Alvarez, Santiago V. *The Katipunan and the Revolution: Memoirs of a General, with the Original Tagalog Text,* trans. Paula Caroline J. Malay (Manila: Ateneo de Manila University Press, 1992).

Amalrik, Guzel. *Memories of a Tatar Childhood,* trans. Marc E. Heine (London: Hutchinson, 1979).

Amin, Mohamed, Duncan Willetts, and Peter Marshall. *Journey through Maldives* (Nairobi: Camerapix Publishers International, 1992).

Anand, V. K. *Nagaland in Transition* (New Delhi: Associated Publishing House, 1969).

Anderson, David G. *Identity and Ecology in Arctic Siberia: The Number One Reindeer Brigade* (New York: Oxford University Press, 2000).

Anderson, Jennifer L. *An Introduction to Japanese Tea Ritual.* (Albany: State University of New York Press, 1991).

Anderson, John. *Kyrgyzstan: Central Asia's Island of Democracy?* (Amsterdam: Routledge, 1999).

Antipina, Claudia, and Temirbek Musakeev. *Kyrgyzstan* (Milan: Skira, 2007).

Apcar, Diana Agabeg. *From the Book of 1000 Tales: Stories of Armenia and Its People, 1892–1922* (Bloomington, Ind.: AuthorHouse, 2004).

Archer, W. G. *Tribal Law and Justice: A Report on the Santal* (New Delhi: Concept Publishing Company, 1984).

Arens, Richard. *Folk Practices and Beliefs of Leyte and Samar* (Tacloban, Philippines: Divine Word University, 1971).

Aris, Michael. *Bhutan: The Early History of a Himalayan Kingdom* (Warminster, U.K.: Aris & Phillips, 1979).

Arno, Andrew. *The World of Talk on a Fijian Island: An Ethnography of Law and Communicative Causation* (Norwood, N.J.: Ablex Pub. Corp., 1993).

Ashwill, Mark A. and Thai Ngoc Diep. *Vietnam Today: A Guide to a Nation at a Crossroads* (Yarmouth, Maine: Intercultural Press, Inc., 2005).

Asian Development Bank. *Federated States of Micronesia: Towards a Self–Sustainable Economy: 2005 Economic Report* (Manila, Philippines: Asian Development Bank, 2006).

Atkin, Muriel. *The Subtlest Battle: Islam in Soviet Tajikistan* (Philadelphia: Foreign Policy Research Institute, 1989).

Azarpay, Guitty. *Sogdian Painting: The Pictorial Epic in Oriental Art* (Berkeley and Los Angeles: University of California Press, 1981).

Aziz, Barbara. *Tibetan Frontier Families* (Durham, N.C.: Carolina Academic Press, 1978).

Babb, Lawrence A. *Absent Lord: Ascetics and Kings in a Jain Ritual Culture* (Berkeley and Los Angeles: University of California Press, 1995).

Babur, Zahir al-Din. *Baburnama: Memoirs of Babur,* ed. and trans. Wheeler M. Thackston (New York: Oxford University Press, 1996).

Baddeley, John F. *The Russian Conquest of the Caucasus* (Richmond, U.K.: Curzon Press, 1999).

Baglin, Douglass. *The Jimi River Expedition, 1950: Exploration in the New Guinea Highlands* (New York: Oxford University Press, 1988).

Baker, Chris, and Pasuk Phongpaichit. *A History of Thailand* (London: Cambridge University Press, 2005).

Baker, Sophie. *Caste: At Home in Hindu India* (London: J. Cape, 1990).

Baker, Victoria J. *A Sinhalese Village in Sri Lanka: Coping with Uncertainty* (Fort Worth, Tex.: Harcourt Brace College Publishers, 1998).

Ball, Desmond, and Hamish McDonald, eds. *Masters of Terror: Indonesia's Military and Violence in East Timor in 1999* (Canberra: Australian National University Strategic & Defence Studies, 2002).

Balzer, Marjorie Mandelstam. *The Tenacity of Ethnicity: A Siberian Saga in Global Perspective* (Princeton, N.J.: Princeton University Press, 1999).

Balzer, Marjorie Mandelstam, ed. *Russian Traditional Culture: Religion, Gender, and Customary Law* (Armonk, N.Y.: M. E. Sharpe, 1992).

Bank of Hawaii. *Republic of Palau Economic Report* (Honolulu: Bank of Hawaii, 2000).

Barbour, Nancy. *Palau*, 2nd ed. (San Francisco: Full Court Press, 1995).

Barme, Geremie R. *In the Red: On Contemporary Chinese Culture* (New York: Columbia University Press, 1999).

Barmé, Scot. *Luang Wichit Wathakan and the Creation of a Thai Identity* (Singapore: Institute of Southeast Asian Studies, 1993).

Barnard, Timothy P., ed. *Contesting Malayness: Malay Identity across Boundaries* (Singapore: Singapore University Press, 2004).

Barrett, Tony, and Rick Tanaka. *Okinawa Dreams OK* (Berlin: Die-Gestalten-Verlag, 1997).

Barrington, Nicholas, Joseph T. Kendrick, Reinhard Schlagintweit, and Sandy Gall. *A Passage to Nuristan: Exploring the Mysterious Afghan Hinterland* (London: I. B. Tauris, 2006).

Barth, Fredrik. *Features of Person and Society in Swat: Collected Essays on Pathans* (Boston: Routledge & K. Paul, 1981).

———. *Political Leadership among Swat Pathans* (New York: Humanities Press, 1965).

Batalden, Stephen K., ed. *Seeking God: The Recovery of Religious Identity in Orthodox Russia, Ukraine, and Georgia* (DeKalb: Northern Illinois University Press, 1993).

Bataua, Batiri T., et al. *Kiribati: A Changing Atoll Culture* (Suva, Fiji: Institute for Pacific Studies, 1985).

Batbayar, Tsedendambyn. *Modern Mongolia: A Concise History* (Ulaanbaatar: Offset Printing, Mongolian Center for Scientific and Technological Information, 1996).

Bauer, Armin, David Green, and Kathleen Kuehnast. *Women and Gender Relations: The Kyrgyz Republic in Transition* (Manila, Philippines: Asian Development Bank, 1997).

Becker, Anne E. *Body, Self, and Society: The View from Fiji* (Philadelphia: University of Pennsylvania Press, 1995).

Becker, Elizabeth. *When the War Was Over: Cambodia and the Khmer Rouge Revolution* (New York: Public Affairs, 1986).

Befu, Harumi. *Hegemony of Homogeneity: An Anthropological Analysis of Nihonjinron* (Rosanna, Australia: Trans Pacific Press, 2001).

Bell, Diane. *Daughters of the Dreaming* (Minneapolis: University of Minnesota Press, 1993).

Bennett, Tony, Michael Emmison, and John Frow. *Accounting for Tastes: Australian Everyday Cultures* (New York: Cambridge University Press, 1999).

Beny, Roloff and John Lindsay Opie. *Island: Ceylon* (Toronto: McLelland & Stewart Ltd., 1971).

Berreman, Gerald D. *Hindus of the Himalayas: Ethnography and Change*, 2nd ed. (New York: Oxford University Press, 1997).

Bestor, Theodore C., Patricia G. Steinhoff, and Victoria Lyon Bestor, eds. *Doing Fieldwork in Japan* (Honolulu: University of Hawaii Press, 2003).

Bhasin, Veena. *Transhumants of Himalayas: Changspas of Ladakh, Gaddis of Himachal Pradesh, and Bhutias of Sikkim* (Delhi: Kamla-Raj Enterprises, 1996).

Billington, James H. *The Face of Russia: Anguish, Aspiration, and Achievement in Russian Culture* (New York: TV Books, 1999).

Biran, Michal. *The Empire of the Qara Khitai in Eurasian History: Between China and the Islamic World* (New York: Cambridge University Press, 2005).

Birdwood, Lord. *India and Pakistan: A Continent Decides* (New York: Frederick A. Praeger, 1954).

Bissell, Tom. *Chasing the Sea: Being a Narrative of a Journey through Uzbekistan, Including Descriptions of Life Therein, Culminating with an Arrival at the Aral Sea, the World's Worst Man-Made Ecological Catastrophe, in One Volume* (New York: Pantheon Books, 2003).

Biswal, Ashok. *Mystic Monpas of Tawang Himalaya* (New Delhi: Indus Pub. Co., 2006).

Blackwell, Carole. *Tradition and Society in Turkmenistan: Gender, Oral Culture, and Song* (Baltimore: Curzon Press, 2001).

Bliss, Frank. *Social and Economic Change in the Pamirs: Gorno-Badakhshan, Tajikistan*, trans. Nicola Pacult and Sonia Guss (New York: Routledge, 2005).

Blundell, David, ed. *Austronesian Taiwan: Linguistics, History, Ethnology, Prehistory* (Taipei: SMC Publishing, 2000).

Bonnemaison, Joel, and Kirk Huffman, eds. *Arts of Vanuatu* (Honolulu: University of Hawaii Press, 1996).

Bornes, Robert Harrison. *Sea Hunters of Indonesia: Fishers and Weavers of Lamalera* (Oxford: Oxford University Press, 1996).

Braund, David. *Georgia in Antiquity: A History of Colchis and Transcaucasian Iberia, 550 BC–AD 562* (New York: Oxford University Press, 1994).

Breen, Michael. *Kim Jong-Il: North Korea's Dear Leader* (Singapore: John Wiley, 2004).

Briggs, Lawrence Palmer. *The Ancient Khmer Empire* (Philadelphia: American Philosophical Society, 1951).

Brookes, Stephen. *Through the Jungle of Death: A Boy's Escape from Wartime Burma* (London: John Murray, 2000).

Brow, James. *Vedda Villages of Anuradhapura: The Historical Anthropology of a Community in Sri Lanka* (Seattle: University of Washington Press, 1978).

Brown, Melissa. *Is Taiwan Chinese?: The Impact of Culture, Power, and Migration on Changing Identities* (Berkeley and Los Angeles: University of California Press, 2004).

Bryant, Edwin F., and Laurie L. Patton, eds. *The Indo-Aryan Controversy: Evidence and Inference in Indian History* (New York: Routledge, 2005).

Bulag, Uradyn E. *Nationalism and Hybridity in Mongolia* (New York: Oxford University Press, 1998).

Cable, Michael, and Rodney Tyler. *Brunei Darussalam: The Country, the Sultan, the People* (London: AMD Brand Evolution, 2000).

Cagatay, Ergun, and Dogan Kuban, eds. *The Turkic Speaking Peoples: 1,500 Years of Art and Culture from Inner Asia to the Balkans* (New York: Prestel Publishing, 2006).

Cameron, Mary M. *On the Edge of the Auspicious: Gender and Caste in Nepal* (Urbana: University of Illinois Press, 1998).

Canfield, Robert L. *Turko-Persia in Historical Perspective* (Cambridge: Cambridge University Press, 1991).

Cannell, Fenella. *Power and Intimacy in the Christian Philippines* (New York: Cambridge University Press, 1999).

Caprio, Mark, and Matsuda Koichiro, eds. *Japan and the Pacific, 1540–1920* (Burlington, Vt.: Ashgate/Variorum, 2006).

Carey, Iskandar. *Orang Asli: The Aboriginal Tribes of Peninsular Malaysia* (New York: Oxford University Press, 1977).

Carey, Peter, ed. *Burma: The Challenge of Change in a Divided Society.* Forward by Aung San Suu Kyi (New York: St. Martin's Press, 1997).

Caroe, Olaf. *The Pathans, 550 BC–AD 1957* (New York: Oxford University Press, 1976).

Carpenter, Russ and Blyth. *The Blessings of Bhutan* (Honolulu: University of Hawaii Press, 2002).

Carpenter, Ted Galen. *America's Coming War with China: A Collision Course Over Taiwan* (New York: Palgrave Macmillan, 2005).

Carter, Anthony. *Elite Politics in Rural India: Political Stratification and Alliances in Western Maharashtra* (Cambridge: Cambridge University Press, 1974).

Carucci, Laurence Marshall. *Nuclear Nativity: Rituals of Renewal and Empowerment in the Marshall Islands* (DeKalb: Northern Illinois University Press, 1997).

Cauquelin, Josiane. *Aborigines of Taiwan: The Puyuma: From Headhunting to the Modern World.* Translated by Caroline Charras-Wheeler (London: RoutledgeCurzon, 2004).

Chahin, Mack. *The Kingdom of Armenia.* (New York: RoutledgeCurzon, 2001).

Chalfont, A. G. J. *By God's Will: A Portrait of the Sultan of Brunei* (New Delhi: Penguin Books, 1989).

Chambers, Keith and Anne Chambers. *Unity of Heart: Culture and Change in a Polynesian Atoll Society* (Prospect Heights, Ill.: Waveland Press, 2001).

Chandler, David P. *History of Cambodia* (Boulder, Colo.: Westview Press, 2000).

Chang, Kwang-chih. *Fengpitou, Tapenking, and the Prehistory of Taiwan,* Yale University Publications in Anthropology, no. 73 (New Haven, Conn.: Yale University, Department of Anthropology, 1969).

Chatterjee, Suchandana. *Politics and Society in Tajikistan: In the Aftermath of the Civil War* (Gurgaon, Haryana: Maulana Abul Kalam Azad Institute of Asian Studies, Kolkata [by] Hope India Publications/Greenwich Millennium, 2002).

Chau-Pech Ollier, Leakthina, and Tim Winter, eds. *Expressions of Cambodia: The Politics of Tradition, Identity, and Change* (New York: Routledge, 2006).

Childress, David Hatcher. *Ancient Tonga and the Lost City of Mu'a: Including Samoa, Fiji, and Rarotonga* (Kempton, Ill.: Adventures Unlimited Press, 1996).

Chit, Khin Myo. *A Wonderland of Burmese Legends* (Bangkok: Tamarind Press, 1984).

Chou, Cynthia. *Indonesian Sea Nomads: Money, Magic, and Fear of the Orang Suku Laut* (London: RoutledgeCurzon, 2003).

Clark, Donald N. *Culture and Customs of Korea* (Westport, Conn.: Greenwood Press, 2000).

Coates, Karen J. *Cambodia Now: Life in the Wake of War* (Jefferson, N.C.: McFarland & Company, Inc. Publishers, 1971).

Cohen, Jonathan, ed. *A Question of Sovereignty: The Georgia-Abkhazia Peace Process* (London: Accord, 1997).

Cohen, Stephen Philip. *The Idea of Pakistan* (Washington, D.C.: Brookings Institution Press, 2004).

Col, Steve. *Ghost Wars: The Secret History of the CIA, Afghanistan, and Bin Laden, from the Soviet Invasion to September 10, 2001* (New York: Penguin Press, 2004.)

Collcutt, Martin, Marius Jansen, and Isao Kumakura. *Cultural Atlas of Japan* (Oxford: Phaidon Press, 1988).

Colledge, Malcolm A. R. *Parthian Art* (Ithaca, N.Y.: Cornell University Press, 1977).

Collins, Robert. *Medes and Persians: Conquerors and Diplomats* (New York: McGraw Hill, 1972).

Conklin, Harold C. *Hanunóo Agriculture; A Report on an Integral System of Shifting Cultivation in the Philippines* (Rome: Food and Agriculture Organization of the United Nations, 1957).

Constable, Nicole, ed. *Guest People: Studies of Hakka Chinese Identity* (Berkeley and Los Angeles: University of California Press, 1994).

Cooper, Randolf G. S. *The Anglo-Maratha Campaigns and the Contest for India: The Struggle for Control of the South Asian Military Economy* (New York: Cambridge University Press, 2003).

Coppieters, Bruno, Ghia Nodia, and Yuri Anchabadze, eds. *Georgians and Abkhazians: The Search for a Peace Settlement* (Cologne, Ger.: Bundesinstitut für Ostwissenschaftliche und Internationale Studien, 1998).

Cordell, Helen. *Laos* (Santa Barbara, Calif.: Clio, 1991).

Cortes, Rosario Mendoza. *Pangasinan, 1572–1800* (Quezon City: University of the Philippines Press, 1974).

———. *Pangasinan, 1801–1900: The Beginnings of Modernization* (Detroit: The Cellar Bookshop, 1991).

———. *Pangasinan, 1901–1986: A Political, Socioeconomic, and Cultural History* (Detroit: The Cellar Bookshop, 1991).

Coulter, John Wesley. *The Drama of Fiji: A Contemporary History* (Melbourne, Austral.: P. Flesch, 1967).

Covell, Jon Carter. *Korea's Cultural Roots* (Elizabeth, N.J.: Hollym International Corp., 1983).

Cowan, James G. *The Elements of the Aborigine Tradition* (Rockport, Mass.: Element, 1992).

Craig, Robert W. *Storm and Sorrow in the High Pamirs* (New York: Simon and Schuster, 1980).

Crossette, Barbara. *So Close to Heaven: The Vanishing Buddhist Kingdoms of the Himalayas* (New York: A. A. Knopf, 1995).

Crossley, Pamela K. *Orphan Warriors: Three Manchu Generations and the End of the Qing World* (Princeton, N.J.: Princeton University Press, 1990).

———. *A Translucent Mirror: History and Identity in Qing Imperial Ideology* (Berkeley and Los Angeles: University of California Press, 1999).

Cumings, Bruce. *North Korea: Another Country* (New York: New Press, 2004).

Cumming, Sir Duncan. *The Country of the Turkomans: An Anthology of Exploration from the Royal Geographical Society* (London: Oguz Press, 1977).

Curtis, Vesta Sarkhosh, Robert Hillenbrand, and J. M. Rogers, eds. *The Art and Archaeology of Ancient Persia: New Light on the Parthian and Sasanian Empires* (London: I. B. Tauris, in association with the British Institute of Persian Studies, 1998).

Dainian, Zhang. *Key Concepts in Chinese Philosophy,* trans. and ed. by Edmund Ryden (New Haven: Yale University Press, 2002).

Dale, Stephen Frederic. *Islamic Society on the South Asian Frontier: The Mappilas of Malabar, 1498–1922* (New York: Oxford University Press, 1980).

Dandamaev, Muhammad A., and Vladimir G. Lukonin. *The Culture and Social Institutions of Ancient Iran* (New York: Cambridge University Press, 1989).

Daniel, E. Valentine. *Charred Lullabies: Chapters in an Anthropography of Violence* (Princeton, N.J.: Princeton University Press, 1996).

———. *Fluid Signs: Being a Person the Tamil Way* (Berkeley and Los Angeles: University of California Press, 1987).

Darmaputera, Eka. *Pancasila and the Search for Identity and Modernity in Indonesian Society: A Cultural and Ethical Analysis* (New York: E. J. Brill, 1988).

Daryn, Gil. *Encompassing a Fractal World: The Energetic Female Core in Myth and Everyday Life—A Few Lessons Drawn from the Nepalese Himalaya* (Lanham, Md.: Lexington Books, 2006).

Das Gupta, Pranab Kumar. *Life and Culture of Matrilineal Tribe of Meghalaya* (New Delhi: Inter-India Publications, 1984).

Dash, Chittaranjan. *Social Ecology and Demographic Structure of Bhotias: Narratives & Discourses* (New Delhi: Concept Publishing Co., 2006).

Dasxuranci, Movses. *The History of the Caucasian Albanians,* trans. C. J. F. Dowsett (London: Oxford University Press, 1961).

Davidson, Basil. *Turkestan Alive* (London: Cape, 1957).

Davis, Edward L. *Encyclopedia of Contemporary Chinese Culture* (New York: Routledge, 2005).

Davis, Marvin. *Rank and Rivalry: The Politics of Inequality in Rural West Bengal* (Cambridge: Cambridge University Press, 1983).

Davis, Sarah Leila Margaret. *Song and Silence: Ethnic Revival on China's Southern Borders* (New York: Columbia University Press, 2005).

Davis, Stephen. *Above Capricorn: Aboriginal Biographies from Northern Australia* (Sydney, New South Wales: Angus & Robertson, 1994).

Davis, Wade, Ian MacKenzie, and Shane Kennedy. *Nomads of the Dawn: The Penan of the Borneo Rain Forest* (Beverly Hills, Calif.: Pomegranate Press, 1995).

Delmendo, Sharon. *The Star-Entangled Banner: One Hundred Years of America in the Philippines* (New Brunswick, N.J.: Rutgers University Press, 2004).

Denoon, Donald, et al., eds. *The Cambridge History of the Pacific Islanders* (London: Cambridge University Press, 2004).

Derevianko, A. P., et al. *Istoriia Respubliki Altai* (History of the Altai Republic) (Gorno-Altaisk: In-t altaiskiki im. S. S. Surazokova: 2002).

Dessaint, Alain Y. *Minorities of Southwest China: An Introduction to the Yi (Lolo) and Related Peoples and an Annotated Bibliography* (New Haven, Conn.: HRAF Press, 1980).

Deuchler, Martina. *The Confucian Transformation of Korea: A Study of Society and Ideology* (Cambridge, Mass.: Harvard University Press, 1992).

Dewey, Alice G. *Peasant Marketing in Java* (New York: Free Press of Glencoe, 1962).

Dharmadasa, K. N. O. *Language, Religion, and Ethnic Assertiveness: The Growth of Sinhalese Nationalism in Sri Lanka* (Ann Arbor: University of Michigan Press, 1992).

Diamond, Jared. *Guns, Germs, and Steel* (New York: W. W.Norton & Co., 1999).

Dizon, Lino L. *A Survey of Kapampangan Folklore* (Tarlac, Philippines: Tarlac State University, 1993).

Djalili, Mohammad-Reza, Frederic Grare, and Shirin Akiner, eds. *Tajikistan: The Trials of Independence* (Richmond, U.K.: Curzon, 1998).

Doi, Mary Masayo. *Gesture, Gender, Nation: Dance and Social Change in Uzbekistan* (Westport, Conn.: Greenwood Press, 2002).

Doi, Takeo. *The Anatomy of Dependence: The Key Analysis of Japanese Behavior* 2nd ed., trans. John Bestor (Tokyo: Kodansha International, 1981).

Dommen, Arthur J. *Laos: Keystone of Indochina.* (Boulder, Colo.: Westview Press, 1985).

Donald, Stephen L. *In Some Sense the Work of an Individual: Alfred Willis and the Tongan Anglican Mission, 1902–1920* (Red Beach, N.Z.: ColCom Press, 1994).

Dowling, Theodore Edward. *Sketches of Georgian Church History* (Boston: Adamant Media Corporation, 2005).

Duff, J. G. *History of the Mahrattas* (London: Longman, Rees, Orme, Brown, and Green, 1826).

Dumarçay, Jacques. *The Site of Angkor,* trans. and ed. Michael Smithies (New York: Oxford University Press, 1998).

Dumont, Jean-Paul. *Visayan Vignettes: Ethnographic Traces of a Philippine Island* (Chicago: University of Chicago Press, 1992).

Dundas, Paul. *The Jains* (New York. Routledge, 1992).

Dutton, George. *The Tay Son Uprising, Society, and Rebellion in Eighteenth-Century Vietnam* (Honolulu: University of Hawaii Press, 2006).

Early, J. D., and T. N. Headland. *Population Dynamics of a Philippine Rain Forest People: The San Ildefonso Agta* (Gainesville: University Press of Florida, 1998).

Eastep, Wayne, Alma Kunanbay, Gareth L. Steen, and William McCaffery. *The Soul of Kazakhstan* (Norwalk, Conn.: Eastern Press, 2001).

Ebihara, May. *Svay: A Khmer Village in Cambodia* (Ann Arbor, Mich: University Microfilms, 1968).

Ebrey, Patricia Buckley. *Chinese Civilization and Society: A Sourcebook* (New York: Free Press, 1981).

Eckert, Carter, and Ki-Baik Lee, et al. *Korea Old and New: A History.* (Cambridge, Mass.: Harvard Korea Institute, 1991).

Edelberg, Lennart, and Schuyler Jones. *Nuristan* (Graz, Austria: Akademische Druck-und Verlagsanstalt, 1979).

Edgar, Adrienne Lynn. *Tribal Nation: The Making of Soviet Turkmenistan* (Princeton, N.J.: Princeton University Press, 2004).

Edmondson, Linda, ed. *Gender in Russian History and Culture* (Houndsmill, N.Y.: Palgrave, 2001).

Eglar, Zekiye. *A Punjabi Village in Pakistan* (New York: Columbia University Press, 1960).

Eldridge, Robert. *The Origins of the Bilateral Okinawa Problem: Okinawa in Postwar US–Japan Relations, 1945–1952* (New York: Routledge, 2001).

Elliot, Mark C. *The Manchu Way: The Eight Banners and Ethnic Identity in Late Imperial China* (Stanford, Calif.: Stanford University Press, 2001).

Ellis, Jean A. *Aboriginal Australia: The Dreaming, Traditional Lifestyle, Traditional Art, Language Groups* (Penrith, New South Wales: Kaliarna Productions, 2001).

Ellison, Joseph W. *Tusitala of the South Seas: The Story of Robert Louis Stevenson's Life in the South Pacific.* (New York: Hastings House, 1953).

Elwin, Verrier. *Leaves from the Jungle; Life in a Gond Village,* 2nd ed. (New York: Oxford University Press, 1958).

Elwin, Verrier, ed. *The Nagas in the Nineteenth Century* (New York: Oxford University Press, 1969).

Emadi, Hafizulla. *Culture and Customs of Afghanistan* (Westport, Conn.: Greenwood Press, 2005).

Enoch, Reuven. *Two Mirrors: Georgian Events of 1988–89, as Reflected in the Georgian and Central Soviet Mass Media* (Jerusalem: Harry S. Truman Research Institute for the Advancement of Peace, Hebrew University, 1998).

Epstein, A. L. *Matupit: Land, Politics, and Chang among the Tolai of New Britain* (Berkeley and Los Angeles: University of California Press, 1970).

Erdosy, George, ed. *The Indo-Aryans of Ancient South Asia: Language, Material Culture, and Ethnicity* (New York: Walter de Gruyter, 1995).

Esherick, Joseph W., Wen-hsin Yeh, and Madeleine Zelin. *Empire, Nation, and Beyond: Chinese History in Late Imperial and Modern*

Times: A Festschrift in Honor of Frederic Wakeman (Berkeley, Calif.: Institute of East Asian Studies, 2006).

Evans, Grant. *Lao Peasants under Socialism* (New Haven: Yale University Press, 1990).

———. *A Short History of Laos: The Land in Between* (Crows Nest, New South Wales: Allen & Unwin, 2002).

Evans, Grant, ed. *Laos: Culture and Society* (Singapore: Institute of Southeast Asian Studies, 2000).

Fairbairn-Dunlop, Peggy. *Tamaitai Samoa: Their Stories* (Suva, Fiji: Institute of Pacific Studies, 1996).

Falkingham, Jane. *Women and Gender Relations in Tajikistan* (Manila: Asian Development Bank, 2000).

Falla, Jonathan. *True Love and Bartholomew: Rebels on the Burmese Border* (Cambridge: Cambridge University Press, 1991).

Farwell, Byron. *The Gurkhas* (London: A. Lane, 1984).

Faure, David, ed. *In Search of the Hunters and Their Tribes: Studies in the History and Culture of the Taiwan Indigenous People* (Taipei: SMC Publishing, 2002).

Fêng, Han-yi. *The Chinese Kinship System* (Cambridge, Mass.: Harvard University Press, 1967).

Fernandes, Leela. *India's New Middle Class: Democratic Politics in an Era of Economic Reform* (Minneapolis: University of Minnesota Press, 2006).

Ferrell, Raleigh. *Taiwan Aboriginal Groups: Problems in Cultural and Linguistic Classification* (Taipei: Academia Sinica, 1969).

Findley, Carter Vaughn. *The Turks in World History* (New York: Oxford University Press, 2005).

Firth, Raymond. *Malay Fishermen: Their Peasant Economy* (New York: W. Norton & Co., 1975).

———. *We, the Tikopia* (Stanford, Calif.: Stanford University Press, 1983).

Fisher, Frederick. *Mongolia* (Milwaukee: Gareth Stevens Pub., 1999).

Fisher, James F. *Sherpas: Reflections on Change in Himalayan Nepal* (Berkeley and Los Angeles: University of California Press, 1990).

Fitzgerald, C. P. *The Tower of Five Glories: A Study of the Min Chia of Ta Li, Yunnan* (London: Cresset Press, 1941).

Fitzgerald, Frances. *Fire in the Lake: The Vietnamese and the Americans in Vietnam.* (Boston: Little, Brown and Co., 1972).

Fitzhugh, William W., and Chisato O. Dubreuil. *Ainu: Spirit of a Northern People* (Seattle: University of Washington Press, 2000).

Fleras, Augie, and Paul Spoonley. *Recalling Aotearoa: Indigenous Politics and Ethnic Relations in New Zealand* (Auckland: Oxford University Press, 1999).

Fondahl, Gail A. *Gaining Ground? Evenkis, Land, and Reform in Southeastern Siberia* (Boston: Allyn and Bacon, 1998).

Forsyth, James. *A History of the Peoples of Siberia: Russia's North Asian Colony, 1581–1990* (New York: Cambridge University Press, 1992).

Foster, Brian L. *Commerce and Ethnic Differences: The Case of the Mons in Thailand* (Athens: Ohio University Center for International Studies, 1982).

Foster, Robert J. *Materializing the Nation: Commodities, Consumption, and Media in Papua New Guinea* (Bloomington: Indiana University Press, 2002).

Fredholm, Michael. *Burma: Ethnicity and Insurgency* (Westport, Conn.: Praeger, 1993).

Freeman, Derek. *The Fateful Hoaxing of Margaret Mead: A Historical Analysis of Her Samoan Research* (Boulder, Colo.: Westview Press, 1999).

French, Paul. *North Korea: The Paranoid Peninsula* (New York: Zed Books, 2004).

Fuchs, Stephen. *The Gond and Bhumia of Eastern Mandla,* 2nd ed. (Bombay: Asia Publishing House, 1968).

Furgus, Michael, and Janar Jandosova. *Kazakhstan: Coming of Age* (London: Stacey International Publishers, 2004).

Gachechiladze, R. G. *The New Georgia: Space, Society, Politics* (College Station: Texas A&M University Press, 1995).

Gailey, Christine Ward. *Kinship to Kingship: Gender Hierarchy and State Formation in the Tongan Islands* (Austin: University of Texas Press, 1987).

Gandhi, M. K. *Non-Violent Resistance (Satyagraha)* (New York: Schocken Books, 1964).

Ganguli, Milada. *A Pilgrimage to the Nagas* (New Delhi: Oxford and IBH Publishing Co., 1984).

Geddes, W. H. *Atoll Economy: Social Change in Kiribati and Tuvalu: Tabiteuea North* (Canberra: ANU Press, 1983).

Geertz, Clifford. *Negara: The Theatre State in Nineteenth Century Bali* (Princeton, N.J.: Princeton University Press, 1980).

———. *The Religion of Java.* (New York: Free Press of Glencoe, 1964).

Geertz, Clifford, and Hildred Geertz. *Kinship in Bali* (Chicago: University of Chicago Press, 1975).

Geertz, Hildred. *The Javanese Family: A Study of Kinship and Socialization* (New York: Free Press of Glencoe, 1961).

Gellner, David N., and Declan Quigley, eds. *Contested Hierarchies: A Collaborative Ethnography of Caste among the Newars of the Kathmandu Valle* (New York: Oxford University Press, 1995).

Gershevitch, Ilya, ed. *The Cambridge History of Iran, Vol. 2: The Median and Achaemenian Periods* (Cambridge: Cambridge University Press, 1985).

Gewertz, Deborah B., and Frederick K. Errington. *Twisted Histories, Altered Contexts: Representing the Chambri in a World System* (New York: Cambridge University Press, 1991).

Ghosh, Abhik. *History and Culture of the Oraon Tribe: Some Aspects of Their Social Life* (New Delhi: Mohit Pub., 2003).

Ghosh, Anandamayee. *The Bhotias in Indian Himalayas: A Socio-linguistic Approach* (Delhi: B. R. Publishing Corporation, 2007).

Ghurye, G. S. *The Scheduled Tribes,* 3d ed. (Bombay: Popular Prakashan, 1963).

Giersch, C. Patterson. *Asian Borderlands: The Transformation of Qing China's Yunnan Frontier* (Boston: Harvard University Press, 2006).

Ginsburg, Mirra. *Little Rystu: Adapted from an Altai Folktale* (New York: Greenwillow Books, 1978).

Giquel, Prosper. *A Journal of the Chinese Civil War, 1864,* trans. Steven A. Leibo and Debbie Weston (Honolulu: University of Hawaii Press, 1985).

Giteau, Madeleine. *The Civilization of Angkor,* trans. Katherine Watson (New York: Rizzoli, 1976).

Goel, N. P. *Hindi Speaking Population in India* (New Delhi: Radha Publications, 1990).

Golden, Peter. *An Introduction to the History of the Turkic Peoples: Ethnogenesis and State Formation in Medieval and Early Modern Eurasia and the Middle East* (Wiesbaden, Ger.: Otto Harrassowitz).

Golovnev, Andrei V., and Gail Osherenko. *Siberian Survival: The Nenets and Their Story* (Ithaca, N.Y.: Cornell University Press, 1999).

Gombrich, Richard F. *Precept and Practice: Traditional Buddhism in the Highlands of Ceylon* (Oxford, U.K.: Clarendon Press, 1971).

Gomez, Edmund Terence, ed. *Politics in Malaysia: The Malay Dimension* (New York: Routledge, 2007).

Goodenough, Ward H. *Property, Kin, and Community on Truk* (Hamden, Conn: Archon Books, 1978).

Goodson, Larry P. *Afghanistan's Endless War: State Failure, Regional Politics, and the Rise of the Taliban* (Seattle: University of Washington Press, 2001.)

Gopal, Ram, and K. V. Paliwal. *Hindu Renaissance: Ways and Means.* (New Delhi: Hindu Writers Forum, 2005).

Gordon, Donald Craigie. *The Australian Frontier in New Guinea, 1870–1885* (New York: Columbia University Press, 1951).

Gottlieb, Nanette. *Language and Society in Japan* (New York: Cambridge University Press, 2005).

Gouda, Frances. *Dutch Culture Overseas: Colonial Practice in the Netherlands Indies, 1900–1942* (Amsterdam: Amsterdam University Press, 1995).

Goulden, Joseph C. *Korea: The Untold Story of the War* (New York: McGraw-Hill Book Company, 1982).

Greenleaf, Monika. *Russian Subjects: Empire, Nation, and the Culture of the Golden Age* (Evanston, Ill.: Northwestern University Press, 1998).

Graham, David. *The Customs and Religion of the Ch'iang* (Washington, D.C.: Smithsonian Miscellaneous Collections, 1957).

Gray, John. *Domestic Mandala: Architecture of Lifeworlds in Nepal* (Burlington, Vt.: Ashgate, 2006).

Grayson, James Huntley. *Korea: A Religious History* (New York: Oxford University Press, 1989).

Griffin, P. Bion, and Agnes Estioko-Griffin, eds. *The Agta of Northeastern Luzon: Recent Studies* (Cebu City, Philippines: San Carlos Publications, 1985).

Griffiths, John C. *Afghanistan: A History of Conflict* (London: Andre Deutsch Ltd., 2002.)

Griffiths, Walter G. *The Kol Tribe of Central India* (New York: AMS Press, 1979).

Grijp, Paul van der. *Identity and Development: Tongan Culture, Agriculture, and the Perenniality of the Gift* (Leiden, Netherlands: KITLV Press, 2004).

———. *Islanders of the South: Production, Kinship, and Ideology in the Polynesian Kingdom of Tonga,* trans. Peter Mason (Leiden, Netherlands: KITLV Press, 1993).

Guillon, Emmanuel. *Cham Art* (London: Thames and Hudson, 2001).

Gunasekera, Tamara. *Hierarchy and Egalitarianism: Caste, Class, and Power in Sinhalese Peasant Society* (Atlantic Highlands, N.J.: Athlone Press, 1994).

Gunn, Geoffrey C. *Rebellion in Laos: Peasant and Politics in a Colonial Backwater* (Boulder, Colo.: Westview Press, 1990).

Gupta, S. K. *The Scheduled Castes in Modern Indian Politics: Their Emergence as a Political Power* (New Delhi: Munshiram Manoharlal Publishers, 1985).

Gupte, Pranay. *India: The Challenge of Change* (London: Methuen/Mandarin, 1989).

Ha, Tae-Hung. *Guide to Korean Culture* (Seoul: Yonsei University Press, 1978).

Habel, Norman C. *Reconciliation: Searching for Australia's Soul* (North Blackburn, Victoria: Harper Collins, 1999).

Habu, Junko. *Ancient Jomon of Japan* (New York: Cambridge University Press, 2004).

Hall, John, and Toyoda Takeshi, eds. *Japan in the Muromachi Age* (Berkeley and Los Angeles: University of California Press: 1977).

Hall, William C. *Aspects of Western Subanon Formal Speech* (Arlington: University of Texas at Arlington, 1987).

Halperin, Charles J. *The Tatar Yoke* (Columbus, Ohio: Slavica Publishers, 1986).

Hamilton, James W. *Pwo Karen: At the Edge of Mountain and Plain* (St. Paul, Minn.: West Publishing, 1976).

Hanks, Lucien M., Jane R. Hanks, and Lauriston Sharp, eds. *Ethnographic Notes on Northern Thailand* (Ithaca, N.Y.: Southeast Asia Program, Dept. of Asian Studies, Cornell University, 1965).

Hanlon, David. *Remaking Micronesia: Discourses over Development in a Pacific Territory, 1944–1982* (Honolulu: University of Hawaii Press, 1998).

Hardy, Grant, and Anne Behnke Kinney. *The Establishment of the Han Empire and Imperial China* (Westport, Conn.: Greenwood Press, 2005).

Harmon, Daniel E. *The Growth and Influence of Islam in the Nations of Asia and Central Asia: Kyrgyzstan* (Broomall, Pa.: Mason Crest Publishers, 2005).

Harrell, Stevan, ed. *Perspectives on the Yi of Southwest China* (Berkeley and Los Angeles: University of California Press, 2001).

Harris, Colette. *Control and Subversion: Gender Relations in Tajikistan* (Sterling, Va.: Pluto Press, 2004).

Harris, Ian. *Cambodian Buddhism: History and Practice* (Honolulu: University of Hawaii Press, 2005).

Harrold, Michael. *Comrades and Strangers: Behind the Closed Doors of North Korea* (Chichester, U.K.: Wiley, 2004).

Hart, C. W. M., Arnold R. Pilling, and Jane C. Goodale. *The Tiwi of North Australia,* 3rd ed. (New York: Holt, Rinehart & Winston, 1988).

Hartmann, Betsy, and James Boyce. *A Quiet Violence: View from a Bangladesh Village* (London: Zed Press, 1983).

Harvey, Robert. *The Undefeated: The Rise, Fall and Rise of Greater Japan* (London: Macmillan, 1994).

Hassan, Mohammad Usman. *Mehergarh, The Oldest Civilization in South Asia* (Rawalpindi: Pap-Board Printers, 1992).

Hauner, Milan. *What Is Asia to Us? Russia's Asian Heartland Yesterday and Today* (Boston: Unwin Hyman, 1990).

Hautzig, Esther. *The Endless Steppe; Growing Up in Siberia* (New York: T. Y. Crowell Co., 1968).

Heimann, Judith M. *The Airmen and the Headhunters: A True Story of Lost Soldiers, Heroic Tribesmen, and the Unlikeliest Rescue of World War II* (Orlando, Fla.: Harcourt, 2007).

Herschensohn, Bruce. *Taiwan: The Threatened Democracy* (Los Angeles: World Ahead Publishing, 2006).

Hershman, Paul. *Punjabi Kinship and Marriage* (Delhi: Hindustan Pub. Corp., 1981).

Heyat, Farideh. *Azeri Women in Transition: Women in Soviet and Post-Soviet Azerbaijan* (New York: Routledge Curzon, 2002).

Hezel, Francis X. *The First Taint of Civilization: A History of the Caroline and Marshall Islands in Pre-Colonial Days, 1521–1885* (Honolulu: University of Hawaii Press, 1983).

Hickey, Gerald Cannon. *Kingdom in the Morning Mist: Mayréna in the Highlands of Vietnam* (Philadelphia: University of Pennsylvania Press, 1988).

———. *Sons of the Mountains: Ethnohistory of the Vietnamese Central Highlands to 1954* (New Haven, Conn.: Yale University Press, 1982).

———. *Village in Vietnam* (New Haven, Conn.: Yale University Press, 1964).

Higler, Mary Inez. *Together with the Ainu* (Norman: University of Oklahoma Press, 1971).

Hill, Hal, and João M. Saldanha, eds. *East Timor: Development Challenges for the World's Newest Nation* (Canberra: Australian National University, 2001).

Hill, Michael, and Lian Kwen Fee. *The Politics of Nation Building and Citizenship in Singapore* (London: Routledge, 1995).

Hinnells, John R. *The Zoroastrian Diaspora: Religion and Migration* (New York: Oxford University Press, 2005).

Hinsch, Bret. *Women in Early Imperial China* (Lanham, Md.: Rowman & Littlefield, 2002).

Hitchcock, R. H. *Peasant Revolt in Malabar: A History of the Malabar Rebellion, 1921* (New Delhi: Usha, 1983).

Holm, David. *Killing a Buffalo for the Ancestors: A Zhuang Cosmological Text from Southwest China* (DeKalb: Southeast Asia Publications, Northern Illinois University, 2003).

Holmes, Lowell D. *Quest for the Real Samoa: the Mead/Freeman Controversy and Beyond* (South Hadley, Mass: Bergin and Garvey Publishers, Inc., 1987).

Holmgren, Jennifer. *Annals of Tai: Early T'o-pa History According to the First Chapter of the Wei-shu* (Canberra: Faculty of Asian Studies in association with Australian National University Press, 1982).

Holt, Frank L. *Alexander the Great and Bactria* (New York: E. J. Brill, 1989).

——. *Into the Land of Bones: Alexander the Great in Afghanistan* (Berkeley and Los Angeles: University of California Press, 2005).

——. *Thundering Zeus: The Making of Hellenistic Bactria* (Berkeley and Los Angeles: University of California Press, 1999).

Hook, Brian, ed. *Guangdong: China's Promised Land* (New York: Oxford University Press, 1996).

Hoon, Vineeta. *Living on the Move: Bhotiyas of the Kumaon Himalaya* (Thousand Oaks, Calif.: Sage Publications, 1996).

Hooper, Antony, and Judith Huntsman. *Transformations of Polynesian Culture* (Auckland, N.Z.: Polynesian Society, 1985).

Horam, M. *Social and Cultural Life of Nagas* (New Delhi: B. R. Publishing Corp., 1977).

Howe, K. R., Robert Kiste, and Brij V. Lal, eds. *Tides of History: The Pacific Islands in the Twentieth Century* (Honolulu: University of Hawaii Press, 1994).

Hsiau, A-chin. *Contemporary Taiwanese Cultural Nationalism* (London: Routledge, 2000).

Hsieh, Jolan. *Collective Rights of Indigenous Peoples: Identity-Based Movement of Plain Indigenous in Taiwan* (New York: Routledge, 2006).

Hsieh, Shih-chung. "On the Dynamics of the Tai/Dai-Lue Ethnicity," in *Cultural Encounters on China's Ethnic Frontiers*, ed. Stevan Harrell (Seattle: University of Washington Press, 1995).

Hsu, Mutsu. *Culture, Self, and Adaptation: The Psychological Anthropology of Two Malayo-Polynesian Groups in Taiwan* (Taipei: Institute of Ethnology, Academia Sinica, 1991).

Hu, Zhen, hua, and Guy Imart. *A Kirghiz Reader* (Bloomington: Indiana University, Research Institute for Inner Asian Studies, 1989).

Hua, Cai. *A Society without Fathers or Husbands: The Na of China*, trans. Asti Hustvedt (New York: Zone Books, 2000).

Hubert, Jean-François. *The Art of Champa* (London: Parkstone Press, 2005).

Hudson, Mark J. *Ruins of Identity: Ethnogenesis in the Japanese Islands* (Honolulu: University of Hawaii Press, 1999).

Husain, I. *Pakistan* (Karachi: Oxford University Press, 1997).

Huters, Theodore, R. Bin Wong, and Pauline Yu. *Culture & State in Chinese History: Conventions, Accommodations, and Critiques* (Stanford, Calif.: Stanford Unversity Press, 1997).

Hyde, Sandra. *Eating Spring Rice: The Cultural Politics of AIDS in Southwest China* (Berkeley and Los Angeles: University of California Press, 2006).

Ibrahim, Zawawi. *The Malay Labourer: By the Window of Capitalism* (Singapore: Institute of Southeast Asian Studies, 1998).

Ihimaera, Witi. *The Whale Rider* (Auckland, N.Z.: Reed Publishing, 1987).

Imamura, Keiji. *Prehistoric Japan: New Perspectives on Insular East Asia* (Honolulu: University of Hawaii Press, 1996).

Inden, Ronald B., and Ralph W. Nicholas. *Kinship in Bengali Culture* (Chicago: University of Chicago Press, 1977).

Ireson, Carol J. *Field, Forest, and Family: Women's Work and Power in Rural Laos* (Boulder, Colo.: Westview Press, 1996).

Ishige, Naomichi. *The History and Culture of Japanese Food* (London: Kegan Paul, 2001).

Islam, A. K. M. Aminul. *A Bangladesh Village: Political Conflict and Cohesion* (Prospect Heights, Ill.: Waveland Press, 1990).

Ivy, Marilyn. *Discourses of the Vanishing: Modernity, Phantasm, Japan* (Chicago: University of Chicago Press, 1995).

Izhboldin, Boris S. *Essays on Tatar History* (New Delhi: New Book Society of India, 1963).

Jacchid, Sechin, and Paul Hyer. *Mongolia's Culture and Society* (Boulder, Colo.: Westview Press, 1979).

Jacobs, Julian, with Alan Macfarlane, Sarah Harrison, and Anita Herle. *The Nagas: Hill Peoples of Northeast India, Society, Culture, and the Colonial Encounter* (New York: Thames and Hudson, 1990).

Jagchid, Sechin, and Van Jay Symons. *Peace, War, and Trade along the Great Wall: Nomadic-Chinese Interaction through Two Millennia* (Bloomington: Indiana University Press, 1989).

Jaini, P. S. *Gender and Salvation: Jaina Debates on the Spiritual Liberation of Women* (Berkeley and Los Angeles: University of California Press, 1991).

Jamieson, Neil L. *Understanding Vietnam* (Berkeley and Los Angeles: University of California Press, 1995).

Janhunen, Juha. *Material on Manchurian Khamnigan Evenki* (Helsinki: Finno-Ugrian Society, 1991).

Jay, Robert. *Javanese Villagers: Social Relations in Rural Modjokuto* (Cambridge, Mass.: MIT Press, 1969).

Jenks, Robert D. *Insurgency and Social Disorder in Guizhou: The "Miao" Rebellion, 1854–1873* (Honolulu: University of Hawaii Press, 1994).

Jettmar, Karl. *Art of the Steppes* (New York: Crown, 1964).

——. *The Religions of the Hindukush: The Religion of the Kafirs: The Pre-Islamic Heritage of Afghan Nuristan* (Oxford, U.K.: Aris & Phillips, 1986).

Jocano, F. Landa. *The Ilocanos: An Ethnography of Family and Community in the Ilocos Region* (Quezon City: Asian Center, University of Philippines, 1982).

Jochelson, Waldemar. *The Yakut* (Washington, D.C.: American Museum of Natural History, 1933).

Johannes. R. E. *Words of the Lagoon: Fishing and Marine Lore in the Palau District of Micronesia* (Berkeley and Los Angeles: University of California Press, 1981).

John, Clement, ed. *East Timor: Prospects for Peace* (Geneva, Switz.: Unit on Justice, Peace, and Creation, World Council of Churches, 1995).

Johns, Brenda, and David Strecker, eds. *The Hmong World* (New Haven, Conn.: Yale University Press, 1986).

Johnson, Charles, ed. *Dab Neeg Hmoob: Myths, Legends, and Folktales from the Hmong of Laos* (St. Paul, Minn.: Macalester College, 1985).

Jolliffe, Jill. *East Timor: Nationalism and Colonialism* (St. Lucia, Queensland: University of Queensland Press, 1978).

Joseph, Joe. *The Japanese: Strange but Not Strangers* (London: Viking, 1993).

Josselin de Jong, P. E. de. *Minangkabau and Negri Sembilan: Socio-Political Structure in Indonesia* (New York: AMS Press, 1980).

Josselin de Jong, P. E. de, ed. *Unity in Diversity: Indonesia as a Field of Anthropological Study* (Dordrecht, Netherlands: Foris Publications, 1984).

Jumper, Roy Davis Linville. *Power and Politics: The Story of Malaysia's Orang Asli* (Lanham, Md.: University Press of America, 1997).

Jupp, James, ed. *The Australian People* (Melbourne, Austral.: Cambridge University Press, 2001).

Kahn, Joel S. *Minangkabau Social Formations: Indonesian Peasants and the World Economy* (New York: Cambridge University Press, 1980).

———. *Other Malays: Nationalism and Cosmopolitanism in the Modern Malay World* (Singapore: Asian Studies Association of Australia in association with Singapore University Press, 2006).

Kakuchi, Yasushi. *Mindoro Highlanders: The Life of the Swidden Agriculturalist* (Quezon City, Philippines: New Day Publishers, 1984).

Kalter, Johannes, and Margareta Pavaloi, eds. *Uzbekistan: Heirs to the Silk Road* (New York: Thames and Hudson, 1997).

Kamm, Henry. *Cambodia: Reports from a Stricken Land* (New York: Arcade Publishing, 1999).

Kapferer, Judith. *Being All Equal: Identity, Difference, and Australian Cultural Practice* (Washington, D.C.: Berg, 1996).

Kappeler, Andreas, *The Russian Empire: A Multiethnic History,* trans. Alfred Clayton (Harlow, U.K.: Longman, 2001).

Karimov, Islam. *Uzbekistan on the Threshold of the Twenty-First Century: Challenges to Stability and Progress* (New York: St. Martin's Press, 1998).

Karnow, Stanley. *Vietnam: A History* (New York: Penguin Books, 1984).

Kaup, Katherine Palmer. *Creating the Zhuang: Ethnic Politics in China* (Boulder, Colo.: Lynne Rienner Publishers, 2000).

Kaushik, Surendra Nath. *Contesting Identities in Pakistan: Region, Religion, and the Nation State* (Jaipur: Pointer, 2006).

Kayano, Shigeru. *Our Land Was a Forest: An Ainu Memoir,* trans. Kyoko Selden and Lili Selden (Boulder, Colo.: Westview Press, 1994).

Keate, George, Karen L. Nero, and Nicholas Thomas. *An Account of the Pelew Islands* (Leicester, U.K.: Leicester University Press, 2001).

Kelly, John D., and Martha Kaplan. *Represented Communities: Fiji and World Decolonization* (Chicago: University of Chicago Press, 2001).

Kelly, Raymond C. *Constructing Inequality: The Fabrication of a Hierarchy of Virtue among the Etoro* (Ann Arbor: University of Michigan Press, 1993).

Kendall, Laurel. *Getting Married in Korea: Of Gender, Morality, and Modernity* (Berkeley and Los Angeles: University of California Press, 1996).

Kenoyer, Jonathan Mark. *Ancient Cities of the Indus Valley Civilization* (Oxford: Oxford University Press, 1998).

Kern, Adam L. *Manga from the Floating World: Comicbook Culture and the Kibyoshi of Edo Japan* (Cambridge, Mass.: Harvard University Press, 2006).

Kerr, George. *Okinawa: The History of an Island People* (Rutland, Vt.: Charles Tuttle Company, 1952).

Kerttula, Anna M. *Antler on the Sea: The Yupik and Chukchi of the Russian Far East* (Ithaca, N.Y.: Cornell University Press, 2000).

Kessinger, Tom G. *Vilayatpur, 1848–1968: Social and Economic Change in a North Indian Village* (Berkeley and Los Angeles: University of California Press, 1974).

Kessler, Adam T. *Empires beyond the Great Wall: The Heritage of Genghis Khan,* trans. Bettine Birge (Los Angeles: Natural History Museum of Los Angeles County, 1994).

Keyes, Charles F. *Thailand, Buddhist Kingdom as Modern Nation-State* (Boulder, Colo.: Westview Press, 1987.

Keyes, Charles F., ed. *Ethnic Adaptation and Identity: The Karen on the Thai Frontier with Burma* (Philadelphia: Institute for the Study of Human Issues, 1979).

Khaidarov, Gafur, and M. Inomov. *Tajikistan, Tragedy and Anguish of a Nation* (Saint Petersburg, Russia: Linko, 1993).

Khan, Akbar Ali. *Discovery of Bangladesh: Explorations into Dynamics of a Hidden Nation* (Dhaka, Bangladesh: University Press, 1996).

Khoo, James C. M., ed. *Art and Archaeology of Fu Nan: Pre-Khmer Kingdom of the Lower Mekong Valley* (Bangkok: Orchid Press, 2003).

Kidder, J. Edward. *Early Buddhist Japan* (London: Thames and Hudson, 1972).

Kiernan, Ben. *The Pol Pot Regime: Race, Power, and Genocide in Cambodia under the Khmer Rouge, 1975–79* (New Haven, Conn.: Yale University Press, 2002).

Kim, Chongho. *Korean Shamanism: The Cultural Paradox* (Burlington, Vt.: Ashgate, 2003).

Kim, Choong Soon. *One Anthropologist, Two Worlds: Three Decades of Reflexive Fieldwork in North America and Asia* (Knoxville: University of Tennessee Press, 2002).

———. *The Culture of Korean Industry: An Ethnography of Poongsan Corporation* (Tucson: University of Arizona Press, 1992).

Kim, Djun Kil. *The History of Korea* (Westport, Conn: Greenwood Press, 2005).

Kim, Hodong. *Holy War in China: The Muslim Rebellion and State in Chinese Central Asia, 1864–1877* (Palo Alto, Calif.: Stanford University Press, 2004).

King, David C. *Cultures of the World: Kyrgyzstan* (Salt Lake City: Benchmark Books, 2006).

Kingsbury, Damien, ed. *Guns and Ballot Boxes: East Timor's Vote for Independence* (Melbourne, Austral.: Monash Asia Institute, 2000).

Kirch, Patrick Vinton, and Marshall Sahlins. *Anahulu: The Anthropology of History in the Kingdom of Hawaii, Volumes 1–2.* (Chicago: University of Chicago Press, 1992).

Kislenko, Arne. *Culture and Customs of Thailand* (Westport, Conn.: Greenwood Press, 2004).

Knapman, Bruce. *Fiji's Economic History, 1874–1939: Studies of Capitalist Colonial Development* (Canberra: Australian National University, 1987).

Knudsen, Eva Rask. *The Circle and the Spiral: A Study of Australian Aboriginal and New Zealand Maori Literature* (New York: Rodopi, 2004).

Koch, Gerd. *Material Culture of Kiribati* (Suva, Fiji: Institute for Pacific Studies, 1986).

Kolas, Ashild, and Monika P. Thowsen. *On the Margins of Tibet: Cultural Survival on the Sino-Tibetan Frontier* (Seattle: University of Washington Press, 2005).

Kotkin, Stephen, and David Wolff. *Rediscovering Russia in Asia: Siberia and the Russian Far East* (Armonk, N.Y.: M. E. Sharpe, 1995).

Krader, Lawrence. *Social Organization of the Mongol-Turkic Pastoral Nomads* (New York: RoutledgeCurzon, 1997).

Kremmer, Christopher. *Stalking the Elephant Kings: In Search of Laos* (Chicago: Independent Publishers Group for Allen and Unwin, 1997).

Krohn, William O. *In Borneo Jungles: Among the Dyak Headhunters* (New York: Oxford University Press, 1991).

Krueger, John R. *The Turkic Peoples* (Bloomington: University of Indiana Press, 1963).

Kuehnast, Kathleen, and Nora Dudwick. *Better a Hundred Friends than a Hundred Rubles? Social Networks in Transition—The Kyrgyz Republic* (Washington, D.C.: World Bank, 2004).

Kuiper, F. B. J. *The Aryans in the Rigveda* (Leiden, Netherlands: Editions Rodopi, 1991).

Kulick, Elliott, and Dick Wilson. *Thailand's Turn: Profile of a New Dragon* (New York: St. Martin's Press, 1992).

Kulke, Hermann. I. W. Mabbett trans. *The Devarāja Cult*, (Ithaca, N.Y.: Southeast Asia Program, Dept. of Asian Studies, Cornell University, 1978).

Kwa'ioloa, Michael. *Living Tradition: A Changing Life in Solomon Islands* (Honolulu: University of Hawaii Press, 1997).

Kyong-hee, Lee. *Korean Culture, Legacies, and Lore* (Seoul: Korea Herald, 1993).

Labby, David. *The Demystification of Yap: Dialectics of Culture on a Micronesian Island* (Chicago: University of Chicago Press, 1976).

Lai Ah Eng, *Meaning of Multiethnicity: A Case-Study of Ethnicity and Ethnic Relations in Singapore* (New York: Oxford University Press, 1995).

Lama, Dalai. *My Land and My People* (New York: Potala Corporation, 1962).

Lamb, David. *Vietnam, Now: A Reporter Returns* (New York: Public Affairs, 2002).

Lande, Carl H. *Southern Tagalog Voting, 1946–1963: Political Behavior in a Philippine Region* (Dekalb: Northern Illinois University Center for Southeast Asian Studies, 1973).

Lang, David Marshall. *Armenia: Cradle of Civilization* (Boston: Allen & Unwin, 1980).

———. *The Georgians* (London: Thames & Hudson, 1966).

———. *A Modern History of Georgia* (Oxford: RoutledgeCurzon, 2007).

Laracy, Hugh, ed. *Tuvalu: A History* (Suva, Fiji: University of the South Pacific and Government of Tuvalu, 1983).

Larkin, John A. *The Pampangans: Colonial Society in a Philippine Province* (Berkeley and Los Angeles: University of California Press, 1972).

Lasaqa, I. Q. *Melanesians' Choice: Tadhimboko Participation in the Solomon Islands Cash Economy* (Portland, Oreg.: International Scholarly Book Services, 1972).

Lauridsen, Suzanne, and Sally Heinrich. *Malay Muslim Festivals* (Singapore: Educational Pub. House, 2001).

Lawrance, Alan. *China since 1919: Revolution and Reform: A Sourcebook* (New York: Routledge, 2003).

Lawrence, Peter, and Mervyn John Meggitt, eds. *Gods, Ghosts, and Men in Melanesia: Some Religions of Australian New Guinea and the New Hebrid* (Oxford: Oxford University Press, 1965).

Lay, Graeme. *Pacific New Zealand* (Auckland: David Ling Pub., 1996).

Leach, Edmund. *Political Systems of Highland Burma* (Cambridge, Mass.: Harvard University Press, 1954).

Leaf, Murray J. *Song of Hope: The Green Revolution in a Panjab Village* (New Brunswick, N.J.: Rutgers University Press, 1984).

Leary, John D. *Violence and the Dream People: The Orang Asli in the Malaysia Emergency 1948–1960* (Athens: Ohio University Center for International Studies, 1995).

Leeuw, Charles van der. *Azerbaijan: A Quest for Identity: A Short History* (New York: St. Martin's Press, 2000).

Lehman, F. K. *The Structure of Chin Society* (Urbana: University of Illinois Press, 1963).

Lemoine, Jacques, with Donald Gibson. *Yao Ceremonial Paintings* (Bangkok: White Lotus Co., 1982).

Leonowens, Anna Harriette. *The English Governess at the Siamese Court: Recollections of Six Years in the Royal Palace at Bangkok* (London: Folio Society, 1980).

Levenson, Joseph R. *Confucian China and Its Modern Fate: The Problem of Intellectual Continuity* (Berkeley and Los Angeles: University of California Press, 1958).

Lewis, James, and Amadu Sesay. *Korea and Globalisation* (New York: Routledge Curzon, 2002).

Lewis, Paul W. *Akha Oral Literature* (Bangkok: White Lotus, 2002).

Liamputtong Rice, Pranee. *Hmong Women and Reproduction* (Westport, Conn.: Greenwood Press, 2000).

Liangwen, Zhu. *The Dai or the Tai and Their Architecture and Customs in South China* (Bangkok: D D Books, 1992).

Lieban, Richard W. *Cebuano Sorcery: Malign Magic in the Philippines* (Berkeley and Los Angeles: University of California Press, 1967).

Lindell, Kristina, Jan-Ojvind Swahn, and Damron Tayanin. *Folk Tales from Kammu III: Pearls of Kammu Literature* (London: Curzon Press, 1983).

———. *A Kammu Story-listener's Tales* (London: Curzon Press, 1977).

Lindell, Kristina, et al. *The Kammu Year: Its Lore and Music* (London: Curzon Press, 1982).

Linn, Brian McAllister. *The Philippine War, 1899–1902 (Modern War Studies)* (Lawrence: University Press of Kansas, 2002).

Lintner, Bertil. *Great Leader, Dear Leader: Demystifying North Korea under the Kim Clan* (Chiang Mai, Thailand: Silkworm Books, 2005).

Litzinger, Ralph. *Other Chinas: The Yao and the Politics of National Belonging* (Durham, N.C.: Duke University Press, 2000).

Lo, Kwai-Cheung. *Chinese Face/Off: The Transnational Popular Culture of Hong Kong* (Chicago: University of Illinois Press, 2005).

Lopez-Gonzaga, Violeta. *Peasants in the Hills: A Study of the Dynamics of Social Change among the Buhid Swidden Cultivators in the Philippines* (Quezon City: New Day Publishers, 1984).

Lordkipanidze, Otar. *Phasis: The River and City in Colchis* (Stuttgart, Ger.: Steiner, 2000).

Luangpraseut, Khamchong. *Laos and the Laotians* (S. El Monte, Calif.: Pacific Asia Press, 1995).

Luna, Severino N. *Born Primitive in the Philippines* (Carbondale: Southern Illinois University, 1975).

Lutkehaus, Nancy, Christian Kaufmann, et al., eds. *Sepik Heritage: Tradition and Change in Papua New Guinea* (Durham: Carolina Academic Press, 1990).

Mabbett, Ian, and David Chandler. *The Khmers* (Cambridge, Mass: Blackwell, 1995).

Mackerras, Colin. *The Uighur Empire (744–840); According to the T'ang Dynastic Histories* (Canberra: Australian National University, 1968).

Maier, Henk. *We Are Playing Relatives: A Survey of Malay Writing* (Singapore: Institute of Southeast Asian Studies, 2004).

Majumdar, R. C. *Champa: History and Culture of an Indian Colonial Kingdom in the Far East, 2nd Century A.D.* (Columbia, Mo.: South Asia Books, 1985).

Malik, Iftikhar H. *Culture and Customs of Pakistan* (Westport, Conn.: Greenwood Press, 2006).

Malik, Jamal. *Colonialization of Islam: Dissolution of Traditional Institutions in Pakistan* (New Delhi: Manohar, 1996).

Malinowski, Bronislaw. *Argonauts of the Western Pacific* (Prospect Heights, Ill.: Waveland Press, 1984).

———. *Coral Gardens and Their Magic*, vols. 1–2 (Bloomington: University of Indiana Press, 1965).

Mallari, Francisco A., and S. J. Ibalon. *Vignettes of Bicol History* (Quezon City, Philippines: New Day Publishers, 1999).

Mallory, J. P., and Victor H. Mair. *The Tarim Mummies* (London: Thames & Hudson, 2000).

Maloney, Clarence. *People of the Maldives Islands* (Mumbai, India: Orient Longman, 1980).

Otto Mänchen-Helfen, *Journey to Tuva,* trans. Alah Leighton (Los Angeles: Ethnographics Press, University of Southern California, 1992).

Mansfield, Katherine. *Prelude* (London: Hesperus Press, 2005).

Manthorpe, Jonathan. *Forbidden Nation: A History of Taiwan* (New York: Palgrave Macmillan, 2005).

Maranci, C. *The Architect Trdat: Building Practices and Cross-Cultural Exchange in Byzantium and Armenia* (New York: Routledge, 2003).

Marat, Erica. *The Tulip Revolution: Kyrgyzstan One Year After* (Washington, D.C.: Jamestown Foundation, 2006).

Marks, Steven G. *Road to Power: The Trans-Siberian Railroad and the Colonization of Asian Russia, 1850–1917* (Ithaca, N.Y.: Cornell University Press, 1991).

Marriott, McKim, ed. *India through Hindu Categories* (Newbury Park, Calif.: Sage Publications, 1990).

Marsden, Philip. *The Crossing Place: A Journey among the Armenians* (London: Flamingo, 1994).

Marshak, Boris. *Legends, Tales, and Fables in the Art of Sogdiana* (New York: Bibliotheca Persica Press, 2002).

Marston, John, and Elizabeth Guthrie, eds. *History, Buddhism, and New Religious Movements in Cambodia* (Honolulu: University of Hawaii Press, 2004).

Martell, Hazel Mary. *The Ancient Chinese* (New York: New Discovery Books, 1993).

Martinkus, John. *A Dirty Little War* (New York: Random House, 2001).

May, R. J. *The Changing Role of the Military in Papua New Guinea* (Canberra: Australian National University, 1993).

McCargo, Duncan, ed. *Rethinking Vietnam* (New York: RoutledgeCurzon, 2004).

McDaniel, Carl N., and John M. Gowdy. *Paradise for Sale: A Parable of Nature* (Berkeley and Los Angeles: University of California Press, 2000).

McGregor, Katharine E. *History in Uniform: Military Ideology and the Construction of Indonesia's Past* (Singapore: NUS Press, 2007).

McHale, Shawn Frederick. *Print and Power: Confucianism, Communism, and Buddhism in the Making of Modern Vietnam* (Honolulu: University of Hawaii Press, 2003).

McKenna, Thomas. *Muslim Rulers and Rebels: Everyday Politics and Armed Separation in the Southern Philippines* (Berkeley and Los Angeles: University of California Press, 1998).

McLeod, Mark W., and Nguyen Thi Dieu. *Culture and Customs of Vietnam* (Westport, Conn.: Greenwood Press, 2001).

McPherson, Naomi M., ed. *In Colonial New Guinea: Anthropological Perspectives* (Pittsburgh: University of Pittsburgh Press, 2001).

McQuarrie, Peter. *Conflict in Kiribati* (Christchurch, N.Z.: University of Canterbury, 2000).

Mead, Margaret. *Coming of Age in Samoa: A Psychological Study of Primitive Youth for Western Civilization* (New York: Harper Perennial Modern Classics, 2001).

———. *Sex and Temperament in Three Primitive Societies* (New York: William Morrow and Company,.1935).

Meadow, Richard H., ed. *Harappa Excavations, 1986–1990: A Multidisciplinary Approach to Third Millenium Urbanism* (Madison, Wisc.: Prehistory Press, 1991).

Meggitt, Mervyn. *Blood Is Their Argument: Warfare among the Mae Enga Tribesmen of the New Guinea Highlands* (Palo Alto, Calif.: Mayfield Publishing, 1977).

———. *Desert People: A Study of the Walbiri Aborigines of Central Australia* (Sydney, Austral.: Angus and Robertson, 1962).

Mehrotra, Raja Ram. *Sociolinguistics in Hindi Contexts* (New York: Mouton de Gruyter, 1985).

Melvin, Neil. *Uzbekistan: Transition to Authoritarianism on the Silk Road* (Amsterdam: Harwood Academic Publishers, 2000).

Menski, Werner, ed. *Coping with 1997: The Reaction of the Hong Kong People to the Transfer of Power* (Stoke-on-Trent, U.K.: Trentham Books, 1995).

Michaud, Roland and Sabrina. *Caravans to Tartary* (New York: Thames and Hudson, 1985).

Miles, William F. S. *Bridging Mental Boundaries in a Postcolonial Microcosm: Identity and Development in Vanuatu* (Honolulu: University of Hawaii Press, 1998).

Mohan Ram. *Sri Lanka: The Fractured Island* (New Delhi: Penguin Books 1989).

Monsutti, Alessandro. *War and Migration: Social Networks and Economic Strategies of the Hazaras of Afghanistan* (New York: Routledge, 2005).

Montgomery, Robert W. *Late Tsarist and Early Soviet Nationality and Cultural Policy: The Buryats and Their Language* (Lewiston, N.Y.: Edwin Mellen Press, 2005).

Montgomery-McGovern, Janet B. *Among the Head-Hunters of Formosa* (Boston: Small Maynard and Co., 1922).

Mookerji, Radhakumud. *The Fundamental Unity of India* (New York: Longmans, Green & Co., 1914).

Moore, Frank J. *Thailand: Its People, Its Society, Its Culture* (New Haven, Conn.: HRAF Press, 1974).

Morris, C. J. *The Gurkhas, An Ethnology* (Delhi: B. R. Pub. Corp., 1985).

Morris-Suzuki, Tessa. *Re-inventing Japan: Time, Space, Nation* (Armonk, N.Y.: M. E. Sharpe, 1998).

Moseley, George. *A Sino-Soviet Cultural Frontier: The Ili Kazakh Autonomous Chou* (Cambridge, Mass.: Harvard University Press, 1966).

Mousavi, Sayed Askar. *The Hazaras of Afghanistan: An Historical, Cultural, Economic, and Political Study* (Richmond, U.K.: Curzon Press, 1998).

Mulder, Niels. *Inside Thai Society* (Chiang Mai, Thailand: Silkworm Books, 2000).

Munis, Shir Muhammad Mirab, and Muhammad Riza Mirab Agahi. *Firdaws al-Iqbāl: History of Khorezm,* trans. and anno. Yuri Bregel (Boston: Brill, 1999).

Munro, Neil Gordon. *Ainu Creed and Cult* (New York: Columbia University Press, 1963).

Murphy, George G. S. *Soviet Mongolia: A Study of the Oldest Political Satellite* (Berkeley and Los Angeles: University of California Press, 1966).

Nabokov, Isabelle. *Religion against the Self: An Ethnography of Tamil Rituals* (New York: Oxford University Press, 2000).

Nanda, Serena. *Neither Man nor Woman: The Hijras of India* (Belmont, Calif.: Wadworth Publishing, 1990).

Narogin, Mudrooro. *Aboriginal Mythology: An A–Z Spanning the History of the Australian Aboriginal People from the Earliest Legends to the Present Day* (London: Aquarian, 1994).

Narula, S. S. *Hindi Language: A Scientific History* (Delhi: Oriental Publishers & Distributors, 1976).

Nash, Manning. *The Golden Road to Modernity: Village Life in Contemporary Burma* (Chicago: University of Chicago Press, 1973).

Nasmyth, Peter. *Georgia: In the Mountains of Poetry* (New York: St. Martin's Press, 1998).

————. *Walking in the Caucasus: Georgia* (New York: Mta publications, 2006).

Nazarov, Bakhtiyar A., and Denis Sinor, eds. *Essays on Uzbek History, Culture, and Language* (Bloomington: Indiana University, Research Institute for Inner Asian Studies, 1993).

Neill, J. S. *Ten Years in Tonga* (London: Hutchinson, 1955).

Nekitel, Otto I. M. S. *Voices of Yesterday, Today, & Tomorrow: Language, Culture, and Identity* (New Delhi: UBS Publishers' Distributors Ltd., 1998).

Neumann, Klaus. *Not the Way It Really Was: Constructing the Tolai Past* (Honolulu: Honolulu University Press, 1992).

Neupert, Ricardo, and Sidney Goldstein. *Urbanization and Population Redistribution in Mongolia* (Honolulu: East-West Center, 1994).

Neville, Adrian. *Dhivehi Raajji: A Portrait of Maldives* (Seoul: Samhwa Printers Ltd., 2003).

Ngor, Haing, and Roger Warner. *Survival in the Killing Fields* (New York: Carroll and Graf Publishers, 1987).

Nguyen Hoai Nhan. *The Early Civilizations of Vietnam and Southeast Asia* (Sarthe, France: Nguyen Hoai Nhan, 1976).

Nguyen Khac Vien. *Vietnam: A Long History* (Hanoi: The Gioi Publishers, 1999).

Nicolle, David. *The Mongol Warlords: Genghis Khan, Kublai Khan, Hülegü, Tamerlane* (New York: Sterling Pub. Co., 1990).

Nimmo, A. H. Arlo. *The Sea People of Sulu: A Study of Social Change in the Philippines* (London: Chandler Pub. Co, 1972).

Niyazov, Saparmurat. *Independence, Democracy, Prosperity* (New York: Noy Publications, 1994).

Norbu, Thubten Jigme, and Colin M. Turnbull. *Tibet, Its History, Religion, and People* (Harmondsworth, U.K.: Penguin, 1972).

Novak, James J. *Bangladesh: Reflection on the Water* (Bloomington: Indiana University Press, 1993).

Novello, Adriano Alpago. *The Armenians*, trans. Bryan Fleming (New York: Rizzoli, 1986).

Nussbaum, Martha C. *The Clash within: Democracy, Religious Violence, and India's Future* (Cambridge, Mass.: Belknap Press of Harvard University Press, 2007).

Oberdorfer, Don. *The Two Koreas: A Contemporary History* (Reading, Mass.: Addison-Wesley, 1997).

————. *The Two Koreas: A Contemporary History* (New York: Basic Books, 2002).

Obeyesekere, Gananath. *Medusa's Hair: An Essay on Personal Symbols and Religious Experience* (Chicago: University of Chicago Press, 1984).

O'Brien, James J., ed. *The Historical and Cultural Heritage of the Bicol People* 2nd ed. (Naga, Philippines: Ateneo de Naga, 1968).

Oblas, Peter B. *Perspectives on Race and Culture in Japanese Society: The Mass Media and Ethnicity* (Lewiston, N.Y.: E. Mellen Press, 1995).

Ohnuki-Tierney, Emiko. *The Ainu of the Northwest Coast of Southern Sakhalin* (Prospect Heights, Ill.: Waveland Press, 1984).

Olcott, Martha Brill. *The Kazakhs*, 2nd ed. (Palo Alto, Calif.: Hoover Institution Press, 1995).

————. *Kazakhstan: Unfulfilled Promise* (Washington, D.C.: Carnegie Endowment for International Peace, 2002).

Orans, Martin. *The Santal: A Tribe in Search of a Great Tradition* (Detroit: Wayne State University, 1965).

Organizing Committee of the 29th International Geographical Congress. *Korea: The Land and People* (Seoul: Kyohaksa, 2000).

Ortner, Sherry B. *High Religion: A Cultural and Political History of Sherpa Buddhism* (Princeton, N.J.: Princeton University Press, 1989).

————. *The Sherpas through Their Rituals* (New York: Cambridge University Press, 1978).

Osborne, Milton E. *The French Presence in Cochinchina and Cambodia; Rule and Response (1859–1905)* (Bangkok: White Lotus Press, 1997).

Ostheimer, John M., ed. *The Politics of the Western Indian Ocean Islands* (New York: Praeger, 1975).

Östör, Ákos. *The Play of the Gods: Locality, Ideology, Structure, and Time in the Festivals of a Bengali Town* (Chicago: University of Chicago Press, 1980).

Owen, Norman G. *The Bikol Blend: Bikolanos and Their History* (Quezon City, Philippines: New Day Publishers, 1999).

Palmier, Leslie, ed. *Understanding Indonesia* (Brookfield, Vt.: Gower, 1985).

Palsetia, Jesse S. *The Parsis of India: Preservation of Identity in Bombay City* (Boston: Brill Academic Publishers, 2001).

Pandey, B. N. *A Book of India* (Delhi: Eastern Book Corporation, 2000).

Panikkar, K. N. *Against Lord and State: Religion and Peasant Uprisings in Malabar, 1836–1921* (New York: Oxford University Press, 1989).

Panossian, Razmik. *The Armenians: From Kings and Priests to Merchants and Commissars* (London: Hurst & Co., 2006).

Park, Alexander G. *Bolshevism in Turkestan* (New York: Columbia University Press, 1957).

Park, Han S. *North Korea: The Politics of Unconventional Wisdom* (Boulder, Colo.: Lynne Rienner Publishers, 2002).

Parnwell, Michael J. G., and Raymond C. Bryant, eds. *Environmental Change in South-East Asia: People, Politics, and Sustainable Development* (New York: Routledge, 1996).

Parpoloa, Asko. *Deciphering the Indus Script* (New York: Cambridge University Press, 1994).

Patnaik, Ajay. *Ethnicity and State-Building in Tajikistan* (Calcutta: Maulana Abul Kalam Azad Institute of Asian Studies, 2000).

Peacock, James L. *Indonesia: An Anthropological Perspective* (Pacific Palisades, Calif.: Goodyear Pub. Co., 1973).

Pelras, Christian. *The Bugis* (Cambridge, Mass.: Blackwell Publishers, 1996).

Peoples, James G. *Island in Trust: Culture Change and Dependence in a Micronesian Economy* (Boulder, Colo.: Westview Press, 1985).

Perdue, Peter C. *China Marches West: The Qing Conquest of Central Eurasia* (Cambridge, Mass.: Belknap Press, 2005).

Peterson, William. *Theater and the Politics of Culture in Contemporary Singapore* (Middletown, Conn.: Wesleyan University Press, 2001).

Petit-Skinner, Solange. *The Nauruans: Nature and Supernature in an Island of the Central Pacific*, 2nd ed., rev. (San Francisco: MacDuff Press, 1995).

Philippi, Donald L. *Songs of Gods, Songs of Humans: The Epic Tradition of the Ainu* (Princeton, N.J.: Princeton University Press, 1979).

Pholsena, Vatthana. *Post-war Laos: The Politics of Culture, History, and Identity* (Ithaca, N.Y.: Cornell University Press, 2006).

Pillay, K. K. *A Social History of the Tamils* (Madras, India: University of Madras, 1975).

Pomus, V. I. *Buriat Mongolia, A Brief Survey of Political, Economic, and Social Progress*, trans. Rose Maurer and Olga Lang (New York: International Secretariat, Institute of Pacific Relations, 1943).

Pope, Hugh. *Sons of the Conquerors: The Rise of the Turkic World* (New York: Overlook Press, 2005).

Possehl, Gregory L. *Indus Age: The Beginnings* (Philadelphia: University of Pennsylvania Press, 1999).

Potapov, L. P. *Ocherk Istorii Oirotii* (A Study of the History of Oirotia). (Novosibirsk, Rus.: OGIZ 1933).

Potier, Tim. *Conflict in Nagorno-Karabakh, Abkhazia, and South Ossetia: A Legal Appraisal* (New York: Springer, 2000).

Prasad, Kameshwar. *Cities, Crafts, and Commerce under the Kusānas* (Delhi: Agam, 1984).

Prasad, R. R. *Bhotia Tribals of India: Dynamics of Economic Transform[a]tion* (New Delhi: Gian Publishing House, 1989).

Pringle, Robert. *A Short History of Bali: Indonesia's Hindu Realm* (New York: Allen and Unwin, 2004).

Quibuyen, Floro C. *A Nation Aborted: Rizal, American Hegemony, and Philippine Nationalism* (Quezon City, Philippines: Ateneo de Manila University Press, 1999).

Rachewiltz, Igor de, trans. *The Secret History of the Mongols: A Mongolian Epic Chronicle of the Thirteenth Century* (Boston: Brill, 2006).

Radcliffe-Brown, A. R. *The Andaman Islanders* (New York: Cambridge University Press, 1933).

Rafael, Vicente L. *Contracting Colonialism: Translation and Christian Conversion in Tagalog Society under Early Spanish Rule* (Ithaca, N.Y.: Cornell University Press, 1988).

Rahman, Aminur. *Women and Microcredit in Rural Bangladesh: An Anthropological Study of Grameen Bank Lending* (Boulder, Colo.: Westview Press, 1999).

Rai, Navin K. *Living in a Lean-to: Philippine Negrito Foragers in Transition* (Ann Arbor: Museum of Anthropology, University of Michigan, 1990).

Ramakant, A., K. Upadhyaya, and S. Upadhyaya. *Contemporary Pakistan: Trends and Issues*, 2 vols. (Delhi: Kalinga, 2001).

Ramsland, John, and Christopher Mooney. *Remembering Aboriginal Heroes: Struggle, Identity and the Media* (Melbourne, Victoria: Brolga Publishing, 2006).

Ranade, Mahadav Govind. *Rise of the Maratha Power* (Bombay: University of Bombay, 1962).

Rao, P. Kodanda. *Language Issue in the Indian Constituent Assembly, 1946–1950: Rational Support for English and Non-Rational Support for Hindi* (Bombay: Distributors, International Book House, 1969).

Rashid, Ahmed. *Taliban: Militant Islam, Oil, and Fundamentalism in Central Asia* (New Haven, Conn.: Yale University Press, 2000.)

Rasul, Amina, ed. *The Road to Peace and Reconciliation: Muslim Perspective on the Mindanao Conflict* (Makati City, Philippines: Asian Institute of Management, 2003).

Raychaudhuri, Tarak C., and Bikash Raychaudhuri. *The Brahmins of Bengal*. (Calcutta: Anthropological Survey of India, 1981).

Rayfield, Donald. *The Literature of Georgia: A History* (Surrey, U.K.: Curzon Press, 2000).

Read, Peter. *Belonging: Australians, Place, and Aboriginal Ownership* (New York: Cambridge University Press, 2000).

Realubit, Maria Lilia F. *Bikols of the Philippines* (Naga City, Philippines: AMS Press, 1983).

Redgate, A. E. *The Armenians* (Ames, Iowa: Blackwell Publishing Professional, 2000).

Reddy, Gayatri. *With Respect to Sex: Negotiating Hijra Identity in South India* (Chicago: University of Chicago Press, 2005).

Reischauer, Edwin O., and Marius B. Jansen. *The Japanese Today: Change and Continuity* (Cambridge, Mass.: Belknap Press of Harvard University Press, 1995).

Reyes, Lynda Angelica N. *The Textiles of Southern Philippines: The Textile Traditions of the Bagobo, Mandaya and Bilaan from Their Beginnings to the 1900s* (Quezon City: University of the Philippines Press, 1992).

Rice, Tamara Talbot. *The Scythians* (New York: F. A. Praeger, 1957).

Riesenberg, Saul H. *The Native Polity of Ponape* (Washington, D.C.: Smithsonian Institution Press, 1968).

Risseeuw, Carla. *Gender Transformation, Power, and Resistance among Women in Sri Lanka: The Fish Don't Talk about the Water* (New Delhi: Manohar Publications, 1991).

Robb, Peter, ed. *Dalit Movements and the Meanings of Labour in India* (Delhi: Oxford University Press, 1993).

Roberts, Michael. *Caste Conflict and Elite Formation: The Rise of a Karava Elite in Sri Lanka, 1500–1931* (New York: Cambridge University Press, 1982).

Rock, Joseph Franz. *The Life and Culture of the Na-khi Tribe of the China-Tibet Borderland* (Wiesbaden, Ger.: F. Steiner, 1963).

Rodman, Margaret C. *Masters of Tradition: Consequences of Customary Land Tenure in Longana, Vanuatu* (Vancouver: University of British Columbia Press, 1987).

Rolle, Renate. *Die Welt der Skythen. The World of the Scythians*, trans. Gayna Walls (London: B. T. Batsford, 1989).

Root, Margaret Cool. *The King and Kingship in Achaemenid Art* (Leiden, Netherlands: E. J. Brill, 1979).

Rose, Leo E., and John T. Scholz. *Nepal: Profile of a Himalayan Kingdom* (Boulder, Colo.: Westview Press, 1980).

Rosenfield, John M. *The Dynastic Arts of the Kushans* (Berkeley and Los Angeles: University of California Press, 1967).

Rossabi, Morris. *Khubilai Khan: His Life and Times* (Berkeley and Los Angeles: University of California Press, 1988).

Rost, Yuri. *Armenian Tragedy: An Eye Witness Account of Human Conflict and Natural Disaster in Armenia and Azerbaijan* (London: Weidenfeld and Nicolson, 1990).

Rosten, Keith. *Once in Kazakhstan: The Snow Leopard Emerges* (Lincoln, Nebr.: iUniverse, Inc., 2005).

Roy, Denny. *Taiwan: A Political History* (New York: Cornell University Press, 2003).

Roy, Manisha. *Bengali Women* (Chicago: University of Chicago Press, 1972).

Roy, Sarat Chandra. *The Mundas and Their Country* (New York: Asia Pub. House, 1970).

Rozwadowski, Andrzej, with Maria M. Kośko. *Spirits and Stones: Shamanism and Rock Art in Central Asia and Siberia* (Poznań, Poland: Instytut Wschodni UAM, 2002).

Rustomji, Nari. *Bhutan: The Dragon Kingdom in Crisis* (New York: Oxford University Press, 1978).

Rydstrøm, Helle. *Embodying Morality: Growing Up in Rural Northern Vietnam* (Honolulu: University of Hawaii Press, 2003).

Sabatier, Ernest. *Astride the Equator: An Account of the Gilbert Islands,* trans. Ursula Nixon (New York: Oxford University Press, 1978).

Sahlins, Marshall David. *Social Stratification in Polynesia* (Seattle: University of Washington Press, 1958).

Saray, Mehmet. *The Turkmens in the Age of Imperialism: A Study of the Turkmen People and Their Incorporation into the Russian Empire* (Ankara: Turkish Historical Society Printing House, 1989).

Sardesai, Rao Bahadur Govind Sakharam. *New History of the Marathas,* 3 vols. (Berkeley and Los Angeles: University of California Press, 1957).

SarDesai, D. R. *Vietnam: The Struggle for National Identity,* 2nd ed. (Boulder, Colo.: Westview, 1992).

Saunders, Graham. *A History of Brunei* (New York: Routledge Curzon, 2002).

Sautman, Barry, and June Teufel Dreyer, eds. *Contemporary Tibet: Politics, Development, and Society in a Disputed Region* (Armonk, N.Y.: M. E. Sharpe, Inc., 2006).

Schatz, Edward. *Modern Clan Politics: The Power of "Blood" in Kazakhstan and Beyond* (Seattle: University of Washington Press, 2004).

Schiller, Jim, and Barbara Martin-Schiller, eds. *Imagining Indonesia: Cultural Politics and Political Culture* (Athens: Ohio University Center for International Studies, 1997).

Schirmer, Daniel B., and Stephen R. Shalom. *The Philippines Reader: A History of Colonialism, Neocolonialism, Dictatorship, and Resistance* (Boston: South End Press, 1987).

Schoppa, R. Keith. *Revolution and Its Past: Identities and Change in Modern Chinese History* (Upper Saddle River, N.J.: Pearson Prentice Hall, 2006).

Scott, William Henry. *The Discovery of the Igorots: Spanish Contacts with the Pagans of Northern Luzon* (Quezon City, Philippines: New Day Publishers, 1974).

Seabrook, Jeremy. *Freedom Unfinished: Fundamentalism and Popular Resistance in Bangladesh Today* (London: Zed Books, 2001).

Sengupta, Nitish. *History of the Bengali-Speaking People* (New Delhi: UBS, 2001).

Seruvakula, Semi B. *Bula Vakavanua* (Suva, Fiji: Institute of Pacific Studies, University of the South Pacific, 2000).

Service, Robert. *A History of Twentieth Century Russia* (Cambridge, Mass.: Harvard University Press, 1998).

Shahrani, M. Nazif Mohib. *The Kirghiz and Wakhi of Afghanistan: Adaptation to Closed Frontiers* (Seattle: University of Washington Press, 1979).

Sharnoff, Lora. *Grand Sumo: The Living Sport and Tradition* (New York: Weatherhill, 1993).

Sharp, Andrew. *Ancient Voyagers in Polynesia* (Berkeley and Los Angeles: University of California Press, 1964).

Sharp, Lauriston, and Lucien M. Hanks. *Bang Chan: Social History of a Rural Community in Thailand* (Ithaca, N.Y.: Cornell University Press, 1978).

Shu-min, Huang. *The Spiral Road: Changes in a Chinese Village through the Eyes of a Communist Party Leader* (Boulder, Colo.: Westview Press, 1989).

Sibeth, Achim. *The Batak: Peoples of the Island of Sumatra: Living with Ancestors* (New York: Thames and Hudson, 1991).

Sillitoe, Paul. *A Place against Time: Land and Environment in the Papua New Guinea Highlands* (New York: Routledge, 1996).

Sims, Holly. *Political Regimes, Public Policy, and Economic Development: Agricultural Performance and Rural Change in the Two Punjabs* (New Delhi: Sage Publications, 1988).

Sims-Williams, Nicolas, ed. *Indo-Iranian Languages and Peoples* (London: British Academy, 2003).

Singh, Gurharpal. *Ethnic Conflict in India: A Case-Study of Punjab* (Basingstoke, U.K.: Macmillan, 2000).

Sinolingua. *The Ins and Outs of Chinese Culture* (Beijing: Sinolingua, 1993).

Skidmore, Monique, ed. *Burma at the Turn of the Twenty-First Century* (Honolulu: University of Hawaii Press, 2005).

Sloane, Patricia. *Islam, Modernity, and Entrepreneurship among the Malays* (New York: St. Martin's Press, 1999).

Smith, Allan. *Ryukyuan Culture and Society: A Survey* (Honolulu: University of Hawaii Press, 1964).

Smith, Martin. *Burma: Insurgency and the Politics of Ethnicity* (London: Zed Books, 1999).

Smith, Phillipa Mein. *A Concise History of New Zealand* (Melbourne, Austral.: Cambridge University Press, 2005).

Smithies, Michael. *The Mons* (Bangkok: Siam Society, 1986).

Snellgrove, David, and Hugh Richardson. *A Cultural History of Tibet* (Boulder, Colo.: Prahna Press, 1980).

Söderberg, Marie, and Ian Reader, eds. *Japanese Influences and Presences in Asia* (Richmond, U.K..: Curzon Press, 2000).

Sogivalu, A. Pulekai. *A Brief History of Niutao* (Suva: Institute of Pacific Studies, 1992).

Sopher, David E. *The Sea Nomads* (Singapore: Singapore National Museum, 1965).

Soucek, Svat. *A History of Inner Asia* (New York: Cambridge University Press, 2000).

South, Ashley. *Mon Nationalism and Civil War in Burma: The Golden Sheldrake* (New York: Routledge Curzon, 2003).

Spector, Ivar. *An Introduction to Russian History and Culture* (Princeton, N.J.: Van Nostrand, 1961).

Speiser, Felix. *Ethnology of Vanuatu: An Early Twentieth Century Study*, trans. D. Q. Stephenson (Honolulu: University of Hawaii Press, 1996).

Spence, Jonathan D. *The Search for Modern China* (New York: W. W. Norton, 1990).

Spiro, Melford E. *Buddhism and Society: A Great Tradition and Its Burmese Vicissitudes* (New York: Harper & Row, 1970).

Spoehr, Alexander. *Majuro, A Village in the Marshall Islands* (Chicago: Chicago Natural History Museum, 1949).

Spriggs, Matthew. *The Island Melanesians* (Boston: Blackwell, 1997).

Stargardt, Janice. *The Ancient Pyu of Burma* (Cambridge, U.K.: Pacsea, 1990).

Starrs, Roy, ed. *Japanese Cultural Nationalism: At Home and in the Asia Pacific* (Folkestone, U.K.: Kent Global Oriental, 2004).

Steinberg, David Joel. *The Philippines, a Singular and a Plural Place* (Boulder, Colo.: Westview Press, 1982).

Stevenson, Michael. *Wokmani: Work, Money, and Discontent in Melanesia* (Sydney, Austral.: Oceania Publications, 1986).

Stewart, Rowan, and Susie Weldon. *Kyrgyz Republic* (Sheung Wan, Hong Kong: Odyssey Publications, 2004).

Stoberg, Eva-Maria. *The Siberian Saga: A History of Russia's Wild East* (New York: P. Lang, 2005).

Stockard, Janice E. *Daughters of the Canton Delta: Marriage Patterns and Economic Strategies in South China, 1860–1930* (Stanford, Calif.: Stanford University Press, 1989).

Strathern, Andrew. *Inequality in New Guinea Highlands Societies* (New York: Cambridge University Press, 1982).

Strathern, Andrew, and Pamela J. Stewart. *Arrow Talk: Transaction, Transition, and Contradiction in New Guinea Highlands History* (Kent, Ohio: Kent State University Press, 2000).

Strathern, Andrew, and Pamela J. Stewart, eds. *Kuk Heritage: Issues and Debates in Papua New Guinea* (Townsville, Austral.: James Cook University, 1998).

Stuart-Fox, Martin. *A History of Laos* (London: Cambridge University Press, 1999).

Sullivan, James. *National Geographic Traveler: Vietnam* (Washington, D.C.: National Geographic, 2006).

Sully, François, ed. *We the Vietnamese; Voices from Vietnam* (New York: Praeger, 1971).

Suny, Ronald Grigor, ed. *Transcaucasia, Nationalism, and Social Change: Essays in the History of Armenia, Azerbaijan, and Georgia* (Ann Arbor: University of Michigan Press, 1996).

Swellengrebel, J. L., et al. *Bali: Further Studies in Life, Thought, and Ritual* (The Hague: W. van Hoeve, 1969).

Swietochowski, Tadeusz. *Russian Azerbaijan, 1905–1920: The Shaping of National Identity in a Muslim Community* (New York: Cambridge University Press, 1985).

Swietochowksi, Tadeusz, and Brian C. Collins. *Historical Dictionary of Azerbaijan* (Lanham, Md.: Scarecrow Press, 1999).

Takeda, Kiyoko. *The Dual-Image of the Japanese Emperor* (Basingstoke, U.K.: Macmillan Education, 1988).

Talu, Sister Alaima. *Kiribati: Aspects of History* (Suva, Fiji: Institute of Pacific Studies, 1979).

Tambiah, Stanley J. *Buddhism and the Spirit Cults in North-East Thailand* (London: Cambridge University Press, 1970).

Tayanin, Damrong. *Being Kammu: My Village, My Life* (Ithaca, N.Y.: Cornell University, 1994).

Tayanin, Damrong, and Kristina Lindell. *Hunting and Fishing in a Kammu Village* (London: Curzon Press, 1991).

Taylor, Keith Weller. *The Birth of Vietnam* (Berkeley and Los Angeles: University of California Press, 1983).

Taylor, Philip, ed. *Social Inequality in Vietnam and the Challenges to Reform* (Singapore: Institute of Southeast Asian Studies, 2004).

Teiwaki, Roniti. *Management of Marine Resources in Kiribati* (Suva, Fiji: Institute of Pacific Studies, 1988).

Templer, Robert. *Shadows and Wind: A View of Modern Vietnam* (New York: Penguin Books, 1999).

Teng, Emma Jinhua. *Taiwan's Imagined Geography: Chinese Colonial Travel Writing and Pictures, 1683–1895* (Cambridge, Mass.: Harvard University Asia Center, 2004).

Tenzing, Tashi and Judy. *Tenzing Norgay and the Sherpas of Everest* (New York: Ragged Mountain Press, 2003).

Thompson, Elaine. *Fair Enough: Egalitarianism in Australia* (Sydney: University of New South Wales Press, 1994).

Thompson, Laura. *The Native Culture of the Marianas Islands* (New York: Kraus, 1971).

Thomson, R. W., trans. and comm. "Agathangelos," in *History of the Armenians* (Albany: State University of New York Press, 1976).

Thöni, Julien. *The Tajik Conflict: The Dialectic between Internal Fragmentation and External Vulnerability, 1991–1994* (Geneva, Switz.: Programme for Strategic and International Security Studies, 1994).

Thurgood, Graham. *From Ancient Cham to Modern Dialectics: Two Thousand Years of Language Contact and Change* (Honolulu: University of Hawaii Press, 1999).

Tillman, Hoyt Cleveland, and Stephen H. West, eds. *China under Jurchen Rule: Essays on Chin Intellectual and Cultural History* (Albany, N.Y.: SUNY Press, 1995).

Tkacik, John J., Jr. *Reshaping the Taiwan Strait* (Westminster, U.K.: Heritage Books, 2007).

Tonkinson, Robert. *The Mardu Aborigines: Living the Dream in Australia's Desert,* 2nd ed. (Forth Worth: Holt, Rinehart and Winston, 1991).

Trautmann, Thomas R. *Dravidian Kinship* (Cambridge: Cambridge University Press, 1981).

Trawick, Margaret. *Notes on Love in a Tamil Family* (Berkeley and Los Angeles: University of California Press, 1990).

Trezise, Percy. *Dream Road: A Journey of Discovery* (St. Leonards, New South Wales: Allen & Unwin, 1997).

Tully, John. *France on the Mekong: A History of the Protectorate in Cambodia, 1863–1953* (Lanham, Md.: University Press of America, 2003).

Turner, George. *Samoa: A Hundred Years Ago and Long Before* (Boston: Adamant Media Corporation, 2005).

Turton, Andrew. *Civility and Savagery: Social Identity in Tai States* (New York: Routledge, 2000).

Tyler, Christian. *Wild West China: The Taming of Xinjiang* (New Brunswick, N.J.: Rutgers University Press, 2004).

Ung, Loung. *First They Killed My Father: A Daughter of Cambodia Remembers* (New York: HarperCollins Publishers, 2000).

Uriam, Kambati K. *In Their Own Words: History and Society in Gilbertese Oral Tradition* (Canberra: Australian National University, 1995).

Utegenov, Quatbay. *Karakalpak Folk Tales* (Oxford, U.K.: Trafford Publishing, 2005).

Van Deusen, Kira. *Singing Story, Healing Drum: Shamans and Storytellers of Turkic Siberia* (Seattle: University of Washington Press, 2004).

Van Esterik, Penny. *Materializing Thailand* (Oxford, U.K.: Berg, 2000).

Varley, Paul. *Japanese Culture: A Short History,* 3rd ed. (Oxford: Premier Book Marketing, Ltd., 1984).

Varma, Pavan K. *Being Indian: Inside the Real India* (Portsmouth, N.H.: Heinemann, 2005).

Vella, Walter F. *Chaiyo! King Vajiravudh and the Development of Thai Nationalism* (Honolulu: University Press of Hawaii, 1978).

Verkaaik, Oskar. *Migrants and Militants: Fun and Urban Violence in Pakistan* (Princeton, N.J.: Princeton University Press, 2004).

Vilgon, Lars. *Maldive Odd History: The Maldive Archipelago,* vols. 1–4 (Stockholm: published privately by Lars Vilgon, 1992–93).

Vitug, Marites Dañguilan, and Glenda M. Gloria. *Under the Crescent Moon: Rebellion in Mindanao* (Quezon City, Philippines: Institute for Popular Democracy, 2000).

Viviani, Nancy. *Nauru, Phosphate, and Political Progress* (Canberra: Australian National University Press, 1970).

Vogelsang, Willem. *The Afghans* (Oxford: Blackwell Publishers, 2002.)

Voyce, Arthur. *Moscow and the Roots of Russian Culture* (Norman: University of Oklahoma Press, 1964).

Waal, Thomas de. *Black Garden: Armenia and Azerbaijan through Peace and War* (New York: New York University Press, 2003).

Wadley, Susan, ed. *The Powers of Tamil Women* (Syracuse, N.Y.: Syracuse University, 1980).

Wallace, Ben J. *The Changing Village Environment in Southeast Asia: Applied Anthropology and Environmental Reclamation in the Northern Philippines* (New York: Routledge, 2006).

Watanabe, Hitoshi. *The Ainu Ecosystem* (Seattle: University of Washington Press, 1973).

Watkins, Joanne C. *Spirited Women: Gender, Religion, and Cultural Identity in the Nepal Himalaya* (New York: Columbia University Press, 1996).

Weatherford, Jack. *Genghis Khan and the Making of the Modern World* (New York: Crown, 2004).

Weatherley, Robert. *Politics in China since 1949: Legitimizing Authoritarian Rule* (New York: Routledge, 2006).

Webb, Paul A. *Maldives, People & Environment* (Bangkok: Media Transasia, 1988).

Wei, Cuiyi, and Karl W. Luckert. *Uighur Stories from along the Silk Road* (Lanham, Md.: University Press of America, 1998).

Weiner, Annette. *Women of Value, Men of Renown: New Perspectives in Trobriand Exchange* (Austen: University of Texas Press, 1983).

Weller, R. Charles. *Rethinking Kazakh and Central Asian Nationhood: A Challenge to Prevailing Western Views* (Los Angeles: Asia Research Associates, 2006).

Wendt, Albert. *Leaves of the Banyan Tree* (Honolulu: University of Hawaii Press, 1994).

Wheatley, Jonathan. *Georgia from National Awakening to Rose Revolution: Delayed Transition in the Former Soviet Union* (Burlington, Vt.: Ashgate Publishing Company, 2005).

White, Geoffrey M., David Gegeo, Karen Ann Watson-Gegeo, and David Akin, eds. *Bikfala Faet: Olketa Solomon Aelanda Rimembarem Wol Wo Tu* (The Big Death: Solomon Islanders Remember World War II) (Suva, Fiji: Institute of Pacific Studies, 1988).

White, Walter Grainge. *The Sea Gypsies of Malaya* (Philadelphia: J. B. Lippincott Co., 1922).

Wiessner, Polly, and Akii Tumu. *Historical Vines: Enga Networks of Exchange, Ritual, and Warfare in Papua New Guinea* (Washington, D.C.: Smithsonian, 1998).

Wiget, Andrew, and Natalia Musina, eds. *Manas: The Great Campaign: Kirghiz Heroic Epos,* trans. Walter May (Bishkek, Kyrgyzstan: Kyrgyz Branch of the International Centre "Traditional Cultures and Environments," 1999).

Williams, Linda B. *Development, Demography, and Family Decision Making: The Status of Women in Rural Java* (Boulder, Colo.: Westview Press, 1990).

Wilson, H. E. *Social Engineering in Singapore: Educational Policies and Social Change, 1819–1972* (Athens: Ohio University Press, 1979).

Winner, Thomas G. *The Oral Art and Literature of the Kazakhs of Russian Central Asia* (Durham, N.C.: Duke University Press, 1958).

Wood, Alan. *The History of Siberia: From Russian Conquest to Revolution* (New York: Routledge, 1991).

Worsley, Peter. *The Trumpet Shall Sound: A Study Of "Cargo" Cults in Melanesia* (London: MacGibbon & Kee, 1957).

Wyatt, David K. *Thailand: A Short History* (Chiang Mai, Thailand: Silkworm Books, 1984).

Yadappanavar, A. V. *Tribal Education in India* (New Delhi: Discovery Publishing House, 2003).

Yalman, Nur. *Under the Bo Tree: Studies in Caste, Kinship, and Marriage in the Interior of Ceylon* (Berkeley and Los Angeles: University of California Press, 1967).

Yamada, Haru. *Different Games Different Rules: Why Americans and Japanese Misunderstand Each Other* (New York: Oxford University Press, 2002).

Yamada, Ryuji. *Cultural Formation of the Mundas* (Tokyo: Tokai University Press, 1970).

Young, Gordon. *Tracks of an Intruder* (New York: Winchester Press. 1970).

Young, Marilyn. *Vietnam Wars, 1945–1990* (New York: HarperCollins, 1991).

Yunusov, Arif. *Islam in Azerbaijan,* trans. Zhala Mammadova and Murad Gassanty (Baku, Azerbaijan: Zaman, 2004).

Zeppa, Jamie. *Beyond the Sky and the Earth: A Journey into Bhutan* (London: Macmillan, 1999).

Zeynaloglu, Jahangir. *A Concise History of Azerbaijan* (Winthrop, Mass.: F. P. Abasov, 1997).

Zhang, Wei-Bin. *Hong Kong: The Pearl Made of British Mastery and Chinese Docile-Diligence* (New York: Nova Science Publishers, 2006).

Zhongshu, Wang. *Han Civilization,* trans. K. C. Chang and collaborators (New Haven, Conn.: Yale University Press, 1982).

Ziran, Bai, ed. *A Happy People: The Miaos* (Beijing: Foreign Languages Press, 1988).

Zongzhen, Luo. *Nationalities in Division and Merger: The Wei and Jin Period as Well as the Northern and Southern Dynasties* (Hong Kong: The Commercial Press Limited, 2001).

Zuesse, Evan M. *Ritual Cosmos: The Sanctification of Life in African Religions* (Athens: Ohio University Press, 1979).

INDEX

Locators in **boldface** indicate main entries. Locators in *italic* indicate illustrations. Locators followed by *m* indicate maps. Locators followed by *g* indicate glossary entries. Locators followed by *c* indicate chronology entries.

A

Abbas I (king of Persia) 832
Abbasid dynasty 746*c*, 747, 839*c*
Abbasid-Seljuk empire 382*c*
ABCFM. *See* American Board of Commissioners for Foreign Missions
Abdali, Ahmad Khan (Durrani) 945*c*
  Afghanistanis: nationality 26, 28*c*, 30
  Aimaq 32
  Durranis 195–196
  Marathi 509*c*
  Pashtuns 648, 649
Abdul Hamid II (Ottoman sultan) 48*c*, 53, 54*c*
Abdul Khayr 943*c*
Abdullah Ahamd Badawi 489*c*
Abdullah Khan 856, 858*c*, 859
Abdul Mumin 856, 859
Abdul Razak, Tunku 489*c*
Abdur Rahman (king of Afghanistan) 28*c*, 207, 272*c*, 273, 604, 860
Abkhazians 1–4, 537
Ablai Khan 375*c*, 377
Aboriginal and Torres Strait Islander Commission (ATSIC) 890
Aboriginal Atayls 767*c*
Aboriginal Australian language 4, 811
Aboriginal Australians xvi, **4–11**, *8, 10,* 935*c*, 949*c*, 951*c*
  Aboriginal Tasmanians **17–18**
  Ami 43
  Australians: nationality 59, 59*c*, 62
  Mardu 511–512

Melanesians 523
New Guinea Highlanders 588
New Guinea Sepik Basin people 592
Pitjantjatjara **666**
Warlpiri **889–890**
Aboriginal Land Rights Act (Australia) 890
Aboriginal Peoples' Ordinance (1954) 611*c*, 612
Aboriginal Taiwanese **12–17,** 13*m*, 950*c*
  Ami **42–44**
  Bicolanos 114
  Bunun **128–129**
  Cebuanos 150
  Igorot 299
  Ilocanos 303
  Javanese 343
  Kapampangans 362
  kinship systems 930
  Lumad 469
  Malays 479
  Mangyans 500
  Pangasinans 637
  Polynesians 670
  Tagalog 762
  Taiwanese: nationality 765, 766*c*, 770
  Visayans 885
  Yami **899–901**
Aboriginal Tasmanians **17–18,** 523
Abramoff, Jack 528*c*
Abu Al Barakaath 492, 494
Abul Khayr 375, 377, 854, 858*c*, 859
Abu Muslim 839*c*
Abung 448
Abu Sayyaf 214*c*, 216
Aceh 315*c*, 316*c*, 941*c*
Aceh Merdeka (Free Aceh) 19
Acehnese **18–20,** 316*c*, 318, 535
Aceh wars 19, 317
Aceramic Neolithic period 936*c*
Achaemenes 658*c*, 937*c*
Achaemenid Empire. *See* Persians, Achaemenids
Achang **20–21**
Acheulian culture 935*c*

A'chik **21–22**
Adi **22–23**
Aeschylus 171, 171*c*, 937*c*
Aeta **23–26,** *25,* 935*c*
  Bicolanos 114–115
  Filipinos: nationality 217*c*
  Hiligaynon 278
  Igorot 299
  Ilocanos 303
  Kapampangans 362, 363
  Mangyans 500
  Pangasinans 637
  Tagalog 763
  Visayans 886
Afanasievo culture 936*c*
Affandi, Yassin 124*c*, 125
Afghanistan **27***m*, 936*c*, 940*c*, 941*c*, 945*c*, 947*c*, 949*c*–951*c*
  Afghanistanis: nationality **26–31**
  Afridi 31
  Aimaq **32–33**
  Bactrians **74–76**
  Baluchi **88–89**
  Bengalis 99
  Brahui **121–122**
  Durranis **195–196**
  Farsiwan **207–208**
  Ghilzai **239–240**
  Hazaras **272–274**
  Kamboja **359–360**
  Kushans **434–436**
  Marathi 509*c*
  Marwats 516
  Nuristanis **604–605**
  Pakistanis: nationality 625*c*, 628
  Pamiri **634–635**
  Parthians 643, 643*c*
  Pashai **646**
  Pashtuns **646–654**
  Russians, Asian 691*c*
  Russians: nationality 697*c*
  Tajiks 774*c*, 775–776
  Uzbekistanis: nationality 855*c*
  Uzbeks 858*c*, 859–860
Afghanistan, Kingdom of 649
Afghanistanis: nationality **26–31**, *30*
Afghanistan Museum in Exile 29*c*
Afghans 942*c*

AFPFL (Anti-Fascist People's Freedom League) 369
Africa 5, 935*c*
Afridi **31**
Afridi, Shahid 31
Afrigids 403*c*, 404
Aga Khanis. *See* Khojas
Agent Orange 876
Agha Mohammad Khan (king of Persia) 832
Aglipay, Father Gregorio 303*c*, 304
Agmashenebeli, David. *See* David the Builder
Aguinaldo, Emilio 219*c*, 220, 636*c*, 637, 762*c*, 763
Agung (sultan of Mataram) 617
Ahmad Khan Abdali. *See* Abdali, Ahmad Khan
Ahom **31–32**, 354, 366, 574, 575*c*, 941*c*
Ahriman 660
Ahura Mazda 937*c*
  Bactrians 76
  Kamboja 359
  Parsees 642
  Persians, Achaemenids 660, 661
  Persians, Sassanids 664, 665
Ai Khanoum 74*c*
Aimaq **32–33**
Ainu **33–37**, 323, 350
Airlangga 84, 84*c*
Aisin Gioro of the Prime Yellow Banner 496–497
Ajanas 300*c*
Ajia 910
Akaev, Askar 437*c*, 442, 444, 444*c*, 445*c*
Akbar the Great (Mughal prince) 90*c*, 282–283, 309*c*, 944*c*
Akha **37–38**, *38,* 265
Akhundazade, Mirza Fath Ali 66*c*, 70*c*
Ak Koyunlu 942*c*
Alamgir I (Mughal ruler) 309*c*, 509
Alans 618, 619*c*
Alaungpaya (king of Burma) 134*c*, 136, 570*c*, 794*c*